THE DIRECT MARKETING HANDBOOK

THE DIRECT MARKETING HANDBOOK

Edward L. Nash

Editor in Chief

McGraw-Hill Book Company

New York St. Louis San Francisco Auckland Bogotá Hamburg Johannesburg London Madrid Mexico Montreal New Delhi Panama Paris São Paulo Singapore Sydney Tokyo Toronto

Library of Congress Cataloging in Publication Data
Main entry under title:

The Direct marketing handbook.

Includes index.
1. Direct selling. 2. Marketing. I. Nash, Edward L.
HF5438.25.D555 1984 658.8'4 83-9871
ISBN 0-07-046017-5

ISBN 0-07-046017-5

234567890DOCDOC898765

The editors for this book were William Sabin and Diane Krumrey. The designer was Jules Perlmutter, and the production supervisor was Thomas G. Kowalczyk. It was set in Zapf Book by Santype-Byrd.

Printed and bound by R. R. Donnelley and Sons Co.

CONTENTS

4. PRODUCTION

5. APPLICATIONS

PREFACE

Direct marketing is a Cinderella story in American business. From a position of relative obscurity on the fringes of general marketing and advertising, direct marketing has blossomed in recent years, achieving continuous substantial growth, introducing exciting new technology, and offering unusual personal opportunities for knowledgeable professionals who understand how to use it effectively.

Direct marketing traces its origins to direct mail and mail order, time-tested ways to sell a wide variety of products and services which had been applied particularly in such fields as catalogs, magazine circulation, and book and record clubs. The emergence of the direct marketing field really began when computers and data processing made it possible to refine the identification and selection of prospects on mailing lists. At about the same time, the introduction of credit and bank cards provided a significant new payment method that also stimulated growth.

About a decade ago, the concepts and techniques of direct mail began to be applied extensively and effectively to other media including print (newspaper and magazine advertising with response coupons), broadcast (television and radio, often with a toll-free telephone response), and outgoing telephone. More recently, new media such as cable television, teletext, and videotex have provided other exciting new applications for direct marketing.

Direct marketing has broadened from the traditional product and service areas and now is being applied for marketing purposes by nearly every type of firm selling to consumer or business customers. In addition, direct marketing has found substantial applications in fund raising, the political process, the arts, education, and organizations advocating social change.

The unique characteristics of direct marketing make it ideally suited for the contemporary needs of individuals and organizations. Individuals are turning to direct marketing because it offers convenience, wider choice of products and services, and in many situations, economy. It is an enjoyable way to shop, with particular attractions for working women, older people, and others who seek a time-saving, energy-saving source of products and services. For organizations, direct marketing offers audience selectivity and, most important, accountability. Organizations can pick the people they most want to reach and then tell how they have responded. Thus, it is particularly attractive to organizations that seek greater efficiency and profitability in their operations.

Exciting new technology also is creating new potential for direct marketing. Sophisticated computerization and data base applications have added precision to audience analysis and selection; electronic printing is providing new opportunities for personalization and customizing, and developments in telephone, cable television and the emerging teletext and videotex systems are offering new media and transaction potential for direct marketing.

Looking to the future, the outlook for direct marketing seems very promising. All of the positive growth factors cited earlier—suitability to contemporary lifestyles, adaptability to present and emerging media, broadening base of applications, and ability to benefit from exciting new technologies—seem likely to continue and to accelerate in the next 5 to 10 years.

The "demassified" society predicted by *Third Wave* author Alvin Toffler and other futurists will, they say, find markets geared to individual needs and expectations rather than to mass output.

Direct marketing is well suited to serve such a social environment. In fact, its traditional method of tailoring its approaches to individuals may turn out to be the forerunner of the "demassified" concept of future marketing.

In such a large, growing, and diverse field, where so much valuable knowledge has been accumulated and where new experience is constantly developing, it is important for the newcomer and the seasoned practitioner to have a practical source of current information. *The Direct Marketing Handbook* is just such a source. It gathers in a single volume the combined wisdom of over sixty well-regarded professionals. They provide both a solid foundation of direct marketing theory and a thorough guide to its practical application in hundreds of areas. Ed Nash, a thoughtful theorist and creative practitioner, has provided a most useful direct marketing text for beginners or experienced professionals.

ROBERT F. DELAY
President
Direct Marketing Association, Inc.

Editor in Chief

Edward L. Nash is president and CEO of BBDO Direct, Inc., the direct marketing subsidiary of one of the largest advertising agencies in the world. BBDO Direct includes among its clients the American Management Association, Chase Manhattan Bank, L'eggs Hosiery and ITT Longer Distance, and has affiliates throughout the United States and the world. Ed Nash has been in the industry for twenty years, starting as a copywriter for Schwab & Beatty and serving as vice president of marketing for LaSalle Extension University, president of Capitol Record Club, and executive vice president of Doyle Dane Bernbach's direct marketing agency. Mr. Nash has been called the "master strategist" of direct marketing, in recognition of his theoretical work and his contributions as chairman of the DMA Awards Committee and the DMA Marketing Council. He has addressed direct marketing groups in Boston, Dallas, Detroit, Minneapolis, New York, and Philadelphia, and has lectured on direct marketing at New York University and Fordham University. He is also a featured speaker at the International Direct Marketing Symposium in Switzerland and the Pan-Pacific Direct Marketing Symposium in Australia. (*Chapter 1*)

Preface by

Robert F. DeLay joined the Direct Marketing Association, New York City, in 1959 as president. Under his dynamic and innovative leadership, the Association has grown in prominence and in size from a membership of 1900 to its present 4906 individual members, representing 2903 member companies. Mr. DeLay established a DMA Washington office in 1963 and a European office in Paris in 1979.

The programs he initiated for DMA include the self-regulation program Mail Preference Service and a consumer service program, Mail Order Action Line, now regarded as indispensable by Action Line Reporters and Better Business Bureaus across the United States. Mr. DeLay created and established the Direct Mail Marketing Educational Foundation, which is devoted to increasing the teaching of direct marketing at the college and graduate level, with Edward N. Mayer, Jr. and Lewis Kleid. He received the prestigious Miles Kimball Award of the Mail Advertising Service Association in 1978.

CONTRIBUTORS

Asher B. Abelow is president of Abelow Response, Inc., a direct marketing list insert manager-broker organization with offices at 430 W. Merrick Road, Valley Stream, New York and in Belvedere, California.

Prior to establishing his own company in 1977, Mr. Abelow was a senior circulation executive with McGraw-Hill, *Newsweek*, and the *New York Daily News* and vice president of a list brokerage firm.

Mr. Abelow is a member of DMA and the Direct Marketing Club of New York Million Club, and was the 1982–1983 president of the Long Island Direct Marketing Association. (*Chapter 26*)

Herbert G. Ahrend has received forty-six national awards for direct marketing results, among them the DMA's Mail Order Plaque for the Outstanding Mail Order Campaign of the Year. President of Ahrend Associates, Inc., New York, he has created advertising for or served as consultant to RCA, NCR, Litton, Xerox, *Business Week*, Montgomery Ward, *Life*, Basic Books, J.C. Penney, etc. He has written *Creating Industrial Direct Mail Advertising*, and many articles in *Direct Marketing, Zip, Folio*, and *Industrial Marketing*. (*Chapter 53*)

James G. Aldige III is executive vice president of The Viguerie Company, the largest conservative direct mail advertising agency in America.

From 1965 to 1968 he was employed as an account representative with Luce Press Clippings, Inc. Then, in 1969 he joined The Viguerie Company as an account executive. In 1974 he was promoted to vice president and in 1979 to his present position as executive vice president of the Viguerie enterprises with full supervisory responsibilities in the fields of advertising, fund raising, mail production, and data processing. (*Chapter 50*)

William C. Allen is the senior vice president and creative director of The DR Group Inc. Mr. Allen is a graduate of Harvard and the Harvard Graduate School of Education. He worked as assistant advertising production manager at Jordan Marsh Company in Boston and as assistant advertising manager at Radio Shack Corporation before joining Dickie-Raymond, Inc. (predecessor of The DR Group) in 1953 as a copywriter. He has written for various trade publications and is currently a member of the Direct Marketing Association and the New England Direct Marketing Association. (*Chapter 33*)

Ira Belth is a veteran of more than 30 years in direct marketing. For more than 10 of these years he has been a list marketing specialist, having first founded Compilers, which later became Compilers Plus, and was acquired by National Business Lists. In 1978, Ira and Stephen Belth (father and son) founded Belth Associates. Ira Belth previously was a cofounder of Computer Profile Marketing, now known as Direct Marketing Agency. He has written numerous articles for *ZIP, Industrial Marketing*, and other publications. He has spoken frequently for AMA, DMA, B/PAA and different direct marketing clubs around the country. Mr. Belth also holds a CBC (certified business communicator) honorarium from B/PAA. He is a key executive in the Business Industrial Council of DMA and currently a major contributor and editorial coordinator for the Monograph on Business/Industrial marketing. (*Chapter 17*)

Allan D. Bilofsky is the mailing list sales manager of Spencer Gifts, Inc., a mail-order gift catalog and retail store subsidiary of MCA. Mr. Bilofsky has been an active member of the List Council Operating Committee of the Direct Marketing Association for many years, and was chairman of the council for 1981–1983. He is also a member of the Direct Marketing Idea Exchange and is a frequent speaker at industry functions. He is a graduate of Temple University with a degree in business administration. (*Chapter 6*)

Arthur Blumenfield is president of Blumenfield Marketing Inc. of Stamford, Connecticut and has been involved in the computer field since 1954. He began his career at the Standard Oil Company (now Exxon) and since then has worked or consulted for many of the leading companies in the United States.

His expertise is the creative use of computers to effectively solve business problems. He is regarded as an authority in the use of computers within the direct marketing industry where he has implemented many innovative and effective solutions.

Mr. Blumenfield is a frequent speaker at industry meetings in both the United States and Europe. He is a director of Direct Marketing Day in New York, Inc. and a consultant to the Direct Marketing Association (DMA) as well as author of *Standards for Computerized Mailing Lists*. (*Chapter 18*)

John W. Booth is a principal and senior vice president in charge of the Financial Services Division of The Direct Marketing Group, Inc., a full-service direct response marketing agency. Mr. Booth is a former marketing director for Lincoln First Bank, NBW division in White Plains, New York; Boatmen's National Bank, St. Louis, Missouri; and Western Pennsylvania National Bank, Pittsburg, Pennsylvania. He began his direct marketing career with Hodes-Daniel Company, now a part of Ogilvy & Mather Direct. The Financial Services Division of The Direct Marketing Group is responsible for developing and implementing direct response marketing programs for commercial banks, mutual savings banks, savings and loan associations, brokerage firms, insurance companies, mutual funds, and finance companies. Mr. Booth is an active member of the national Bank Marketing Association, and currently chairman of the Financial Services Council of the Direct Marketing Association. (*Chapter 51*)

Thomas B. Brady, senior vice president of Kobs & Brady Advertising, Inc., has spent 22 successful years in the direct marketing field—including 12 years as vice president and creative director of Marshall John & Associates, an agency specializing in direct response advertising. He has created numerous award-winning advertisements, and has been responsible for the creation of mailings totalling over 650 million letters, as well as newspapers and magazine advertisements totalling over 7 billion impressions. He is a member of the DMA Echo Awards Committee, and of the board of directors of the Chicago Association of Direct Marketing. (*Chapter 29*)

Robert W. Buckingham joined Krupp-Taylor in 1969 as an account executive, was promoted to sales manager and then to general manager, and became president in May 1970. From 1960 to 1964 he served as production manager for Saul Bass and Associates, considered one of the world's foremost design firms.

Mr. Buckingham is a member of Direct Marketing Association, Associated Third Class Mailers' Union, and the Los Angeles Postal Council (he served as vice chairman for 2 years). He is a graduate of the University of Colorado with bachelor degrees in journalism and fine arts. (*Chapter 40*).

Ed Burnett has helped mailers select well over one billion names during the course of his 26-year career in the direct mail business. As the president of Ed Burnett Consultants, Inc.—a firm specializing in direct mail consultation, compilation and management—he counsels such Fortune 500 clients as Xerox, AT&T, and IBM, and is widely recognized as the pioneer of many of the list marketing concepts and techniques utilized today throughout the industry. Long a popular keynote speaker at industry functions, Ed Burnett also conducts direct mail seminars and on-site training programs for major corporations and universities across the country. In 1983, the DMA named Ed Burnett "List Leader of the Year." (*Chapter 15*)

Steve Burnett grew up in Des Moines, Iowa, and stayed in the midwest to attend the Kansas City Art Institute. After a year of study in the Orient, he came to New York to attend the graduate program in design at Pratt University. He currently runs Steve Burnett, Inc., a full-service design and marketing agency. His clientele includes *Businessweek*, Marsh and McLennan, The New York Mercantile Exchange, McGraw-Hill, The Bibb Company, and Peat, Marwick, Mitchell & Co. (*Chapter 32*)

Allan Caplan was president of Team Telephone, Inc., an Omaha-based telephone direct marketing affiliate of American Express. Purchasing a floundering firm operating under a different name in 1979, Mr. Caplan built Team from just three small accounts serviced by twenty employees to billings totaling millions of dollars a year with a payroll covering more than 600 people. Team is today the second largest response telephone marketing organization in the country. Team has recently been purchased by American Express. The name has been changed to WATS Marketing of America and Mr. Caplan is Senior Vice President of this company.

Mr. Caplan majored in advertising at Youngstown State University. He spent years in sales and direct marketing with Dow-Jones and with *Success Unlimited* magazine, and other telemarketing firms. Mr. Caplan is frequently called upon to conduct marketing techniques seminars both nationally and internationally. He is a regular contributor to DMA publications and a member of DMA's Catalog Council and Telephone Marketing Council. (*Chapter 28*)

Joseph Castelli is vice president and director of research at Ogilvy & Mather Direct. Joseph Castelli began his advertising career at Ogilvy & Mather in 1960. An active member of the Advertising Research Foundation, he has served on the executive committee of its Business Advertising Research Council and has been chairman of the council's direct marketing committee. He has been a featured speaker at the DMA Annual Conference, and has contributed to the DMA *Fact Book*. He is a member of the Marketing Council of the DMA, and has served on the DMA Research Task Force. (*Chapter 7*)

Jean Cohen begin her advertising career in June 1970; 8 1/2 years have been spent in direct response. She is a proponent of the Space Sharing Philosphy (as indicated in her interview with Phil Dougherty of *The New York Times*, published in May 1982). Ms. Cohen's expertise is in all media, including lists. Ms. Cohen has been media director of O&M Direct since May 1980. Prior to that her experience included work for Compton Direct as a media director, for Rapp & Collins (where she began her direct-response career) and as a copywriter for a radio station in Connecticut. (*Chapter 20*)

Sandy Davis is president of Davis-Lee Direct Marketing, a full-service direct response advertising agency. Through her outstanding efforts as a media buyer and planner, she rose to a key executive position in American Consumer of Westport, Connecticut. This subsidiary of Film Corporation of America was formed to capitalize on the tremendous house list which had been developed as well as to sell merchandise to outside lists and media. With Sandy Davis playing a significant role, American Consumer built up to $12 million in annual sales (in television) in just 3 years.

Ms. Davis started her career working in television media at Doyle Dane Bernbach in December 1963. After 3 years in general advertising she turned to direct response. As a pioneer in this field, Sandy set the patterns for direct response negotiations and communications systems. Her overall achievements cover the entire spectrum of direct response television. (*Chapter 23*)

Shan Ellentuck and James R. Springer are the cofounders of Ellentuck & Springer, Inc., an agency that specializes in direct response marketing through the electronic media. Shan Ellentuck and Jim Springer draw on over 25 years of general advertising and direct marketing experience. They are frequent speakers before industry and educational groups on television, radio, and the new electronic media and have written extensively on these subjects. Shan and Jim serve as a totally integrated team in planning, producing, and managing direct response programs for such major clients as *TV Guide*, *U.S. News & World Report, Inc.*, *Cricket* magazine and The Dreyfus Corporation. (*Chapter 25*)

Lee Epstein is president of Mailmen Inc., a volume mailing service located in Long Island, New York. He is a past chairman of Third Class Mail Association and former president of Mail Advertising Service Association (MASA) International.

He is president of Direct Marketing Club of New York, a member of the DMA Government Affairs Committee, and a frequent speaker on postal affairs around the country. He has served as industry chairman of the Postmaster General's Mailers Technical Advisory Committee and is a recipient of numerous service awards from the Postal Service and the industry. Mr. Epstein has represented the industry before Congress and the Postal Rate Commission on postal matters. (*Chapter 43*)

Tony Esposito has an acknowledged reputation in the graphic arts industry as a creative typographer. He is currently director of typography at Cardinal Type Service, Inc., New York City. For 15 years he was director of typography and print art director for the Ogilvy & Mather advertising agency. Mr. Esposito's work has won awards from the Art Directors Club, the Type Directors Club, Art Direction Magazine, Printing Industries of Metropolitan New York, and the National Composition Association. He is coauthor of the award winning volume, *The Designer's Guide to Text Type*. (*Chapter 39*)

Jeffrey Feinman is president of Ventura Associates, Inc. an independent judging organization and sales promotion agency. The firm works for a host of aggressive marketers including General Foods, American Express, *New York* magazine, Revlon, American Family Publishing, and dozens of others. Mr. Feinman teaches at The New School for Social Research. Also a writer, he is the author of six books. (*Chapter 12*)

Joel Feldman is director of marketing and circulation for Consumers Union of United States, publisher of *Consumer Reports* Magazine. He previously worked at Wunderman, Ricotta and Kline advertising agency. Mr. Feldman is a member of the Direct Marketing Club of New York and the DMA Echo Awards Committee. He has spoken at the DMA Annual Conference, DMA Fund Raising Fair, Long Island Direct Marketing Club, New York Direct Marketing Day, and the Direct Mail List Council. In 1982, he spoke at the International Direct Marketing Symposium in Montreaux, Switzerland. (*Chapter 21*)

Stanley J. Fenvessy is an attorney and certified management consultant. He is chairman of Fenvessy & Schwab, Inc., a consulting firm that has served over 100 publishers and direct marketing companies.

He is author of the widely used text, *Keep Your Customers and Keep Them Happy: How To Turn Complaints into Compliments*. His column, "Mail Order Fulfillment Answers," appears every month in the trade newspaper, *Direct Marketing News*. Mr. Fenvessy has conducted seminars on fulfillment—from computers to warehouses—both in this country and abroad, and has served as an expert witness on fulfillment at hearings of the Federal Trade Commission, the U.S. Postal Service, and the U.S. Government Printing Office. (*Chapter 44*)

Larry Fishbein is presently circulation manager for *Country Journal* magazine. Although originally trained as a journalist, he has been involved in the magazine circulation business for the past 10 years. His position and experience (including circulation director for an outdoor publication) have resulted in his expertise in direct mail, including computer modeling, single copy sales, and circulation marketing. (*Chapter 59*)

Ronald Gerwin is a vice president of merchandise sales for the Communications Division of American Express Company in New York City. In that position he both selects and develops new products for direct marketing to American Express cardmembers and public markets. He is a member of the operating committee of the Marketing Council of the Direct Marketing Association. (*Chapter 8*)

Freeman F. Gosden, Jr., is the president of Smith-Hemmings-Gosden, the west's largest direct mail advertising agency. The agency has over 100 clients and employs 100 people. Following early agency experience at Young & Rubicam and BBDO, he served as head of advertising and public relations for Dart Industries, a billion-dollar corporation promoting products for Tupperware, Rexall, and West Bend. He later became the marketing vice president for the Bonus Gifts Continuity Food Products Program as well as president of Dart's Market Compilation and Research Bureau, a compiler of mailing lists. Mr. Gosden developed the concept of personalized computerized children's books, and sold over 2 million by mail order. He is a past member of the board of directors of DMA and past president of the Direct Marketing Club of Southern California. He is the direct mail and mail order columnist for *AdWeek*, a major industry trade magazine. (*Chapter 48*)

Lucille M. Guardala, associate creative director at BBDO Direct, has a wide-ranging background in direct response, having created advertising for major accounts in all disciplines: broadcast, radio, print, and mail.

She came to BBDO Direct from Lane Bryant's Mail Order Division where she was an associate sales promotion manager, conceiving, directing, and managing the advertising for four major efforts. Prior to that, Ms. Guardala was at Foote, Cone & Belding where, among the many client relationships she handled, she created award winning print and radio ads for Emmigrant Savings Bank.

She has also been with Leavitt Advertising, one of the nation's leading mail order firms, Campbell Advertising, and *National Review* magazine. (*Chapter 35*)

Leon Henry, Jr., of Scarsdale, New York, advertising space broker, practically invented the package insert business. In his past 27 years of selling unique advertising media, his approach has been to "find a given marketing situation and see if there is an opportunity for another marketer to tag along for mutual profit."

Since receiving his master's degree from Columbia School of Business, and an undergraduate degree from the Wharton School, Leon has pursued the entrepreneur's dream. Beginning by placing ads on supermarket-distributed grocery bags, he expanded to placing inserts in the bags, and now places direct mail inserts into anything he and his eighteen-person staff can obtain.

Leon's firm now represents over 1500 programs, along with over 400 leading retail stores and banks which accept inserts in their circulars, customer statements, and Mastercard/Visa statements. Leon is the author of *The Home Office Guide* and *How to Earn Twice as Much in Half the Time*. (*Chapter 19*)

Robert H. Jurick is president of FALA Direct Marketing, Inc., and has been with the organization since 1954. Active in many areas in the direct mail industry, he is a former vice president of the Mail Advertising Service Association (MASA) International; a past president of the New York chapter of MASA; a member of the Direct Marketing Association (DMA), Marketing Communications Executives International (MCEI); and the Pharmaceutical Advertising Council (PAC). He was elected to membership in the Young Presidents' Organization (YPO) in 1966. He received his bachelor's degree in 1949 from Syracuse University.

Mr. Jurick has worked at New York University as part of the Management Game Program for masters degrees and has been a frequent guest lecturer at the Syracuse University Newhouse School of Communications. In addition, he instructs a course on Direct Mail Marketing at Hofstra University. (*Chapter 42*)

David L. Kerstein is a vice president of Citicorp, the largest bank holding company in the United States and parent of New York's Citibank, Diners Club, and other subsidiaries. For the past 6 years he has been associated with Citicorp's retail consumer financial center activities, which now operate in 28 states. He has served in various product-marketing capacities, including management of one of the largest national direct-response programs, new product development, and new market licensing. He currently manages the line distribution system for one of his divisions' major markets.

Mr. Kerstein received his master of arts in government and his master of business administration in marketing. He has taught consumer marketing at the college level, lectured on strategy planning and has been active in professional marketing organizations. (*Chapter 9*)

James B. Kobak is president of the consulting firm James B. Kobak Company of Darien, Connecticut. Clients, which are worldwide, are primarily in magazines, books, and other forms of communications; direct marketing; advertising agencies; and associated industries. They include the Magazine Publishers Association, American Business Press, Direct Marketing Association, and the Association of American Publishers.

Prior to starting his consulting firm in 1971, Mr. Kobak, a certified public accountant in New York, Louisiana, and the Union of South Africa, was the head of Lasser, Harwood-Banner & Dunwoody, a public accounting firm with offices in 39 countries. He was one of the founders of Kobak Business Models, which provides computer models and systems for the magazine and direct marketing fields. (*Chapter 11*)

Marge Landrau, manager of Citicorp Diners Club's Direct Marketing Operations, is involved with the merchandise program offered to Citicorp Diners Club/Carte Blanche members. The marketing efforts include list segmentation, list rentals, remittance, envelope advertising, catalogs, solo mailings, the monthly statement insert program, and order processing.

In her years with Citicorp Diners Club she has worked extensively with vendors, syndicators, manufacturers, advertising agencies, service bureaus, list users, and brokers. Ms. Landrau is a member of many professional associations, including the Direct Marketing Association (she is a member of the operating committee of DMA's Marketing Council); Direct Marketing Idea Exchange; DMA List and Marketing Councils, and Who's Who of American Women. She is currently a member of the board of directors of the Direct Marketing Club of New York and Direct Marketing Minority Opportunities. (*Chapter 10*)

Tony Leonardi has held graphic positions at such companies as American Book—Stratford Press, Scholastic Magazines, and Grolier Enterprises. His current position is Director of Advertising and Production for L'eggs Brands, Inc., the direct marketing arm of L'eggs Products.

Mr. Leonardi attended the School of Art and Design, majored in Graphic Arts at New York City Community College, and earned a bachelor of science degree in printing management at Western Michigan University. (*Chapter 38*)

Sy Levy is president of Rosenfeld, Sirowitz & Lawson Direct, the direct marketing subsidiary of Rosenfeld, Sirowitz & Lawson. He was formerly chairman of McCann-Erickson March, one of the Interpublic Group of Companies. He is currently chairman of the Marketing Council of the Direct Marketing Association and a frequent contributor, both as speaker and author, to direct marketing symposiums and publications. (*Chapter 31*)

Alan E. Lewis is the president and chief operating officer of Trans National, Inc. Mr. Lewis is a cofounder and director of this multiservice organization. Trans National currently markets wholesale travel packages, health and group insurance, and other financial services primarily through the direct mail marketing media. Sales volume for 1982 was $50 million and is projected to exceed $60 million in 1983.

When Mr. Lewis was named president and chief operating officer of Trans National, Inc. in 1980, his primary function was to establish the firm as a major direct marketing organization. Since 1980, profits have increased over 300 percent. His more than 10 years of experience in the direct mail market have brought him into contact with nearly every major professional and fraternal organization in the country, resulting in dramatic increase of sales in the travel market as well as expansion into insurance and other markets. (*Chapter 52*)

Charles F. McCarty has been writing copy for the Viguerie Company and its affiliated corporations since 1972, initially as an account supervisor and currently as a contract consultant. A resident of Arlington, Virginia, Charles McCarty has a master's degree in International Relations from George Washington University and a bachelor's degree from West Point. Mr. McCarty has done extensive research and writing on classified subjects for the U.S. government. He has worked with the United Nations forces in Korea and the North Atlantic Treaty Organization in Europe. He served with the U.S. Army for 4 years in southeast Asia in the rank of Colonel. (*Chapter 50*)

Joseph C. McGlone is vice president and creative director of Ayer Direct. Previously, he was copy chief of Wunderman, Ricotta & Klein. From 1969 to 1976, he was the president and creative director of his own agency, Nakono, McGlone, Nightingale.

Mr. McGlone's direct marketing background includes two years at Dennison Manufacturing Company, where he created direct mail packages to draw information inquiries and sales call requests. Mr. McGlone has won virtually every award for TV, from Clios to Cannes to Caples. But, he says, the best recognition of his work occurs when he sees the orders come in. (*Chapter 37*)

Walter S. McKenzie is a partner, media director, and account supervisor at Tatham-Laird & Kudner Direct Marketing.

He came to TLK from the Denney-Rayburn Company where he was advertising and sales promotion director. He was also Media Director of Union Fidelity Insurance Company and involved in account management at Rapp & Collins.

Mr. McKenzie began his advertising career with N.W. Ayer. During his 15 years there in media and client contact positions, he was responsible for a diversified list of general consumer, industrial, and direct marketing accounts. (*Chapter 22*)

Ed McLean is the editor-publisher of *Direct Marketing Copy*, the how-to newsletter for managers, entrepreneurs, and copywriters. He was the founder and first president of the National Association of Direct Mail Writers. Ed has written *The Basics of Copy* and six other direct marketing books and courses and he gives annual copy seminars in thirty-seven cities in six continents. Ed taught the first college course in the United States to be devoted exclusively to direct marketing copy (New York University, 1967). Ed received the DMA's Gold Mailbox award for a five-page letter that rang up $6.5 million in sales of Mercedes-Benz autos, plus six other top awards for copy excellence in direct mail ads. (*Chapter 34*)

Raymond J. Markman is president of R. J. Markman and Co., Inc., marketing consultants. Previously executive vice president of marketing for Encyclopaedia Britannica, U.S.A., Mr. Markman held full responsibility for a number of divisions, including mail order, lead generation, and Britcom (Telemarketing). Prior to this, Mr. Markman was vice president, director of marketing for United Equitable Corporation, an insurance company, and GRI Corp., a mail order marketing company. As vice president and management supervisor of McCann-Erickson advertising agency, Mr. Markman was chiefly responsible for initiating the McCann-Erickson Direct Response Group, a successful direct response subsidiary, and one of the first of its kind.

Mr. Markman is a founder of F.A.C.T., an organization devoted to economic consumer education; director of Seago, a land development company; cofounder of Mayflower Life Insurance Co.; and a director of Chicago City Bank. A member of many professional associations, he is also a speaker for DMA, lecturer at NYU on marketing, coauthor of two books on marketing and the chairman, of DMA's Echo Award advisory committee. (*Chapter 24*)

Edward D. Olsen is the senior vice president of LCS Industries, Inc. in Clifton, New Jersey. LCS is a computer service bureau which has been servicing the direct marketing industry since 1970. They are the leader in the area of lead fulfillment, and have pioneered many of the innovative techniques presently used in inquiry processing. Mr. Olsen has served as president of the company's lead fulfillment division, and presently is national sales manager for LCS. He has spent 20 years in the direct marketing industry and has been a featured speaker for the DMA on numerous occasions. Mr. Olsen is a graduate of Villanova University in Pennsylvania. (*Chapter 45*)

Chuck Orlowski has spent 14 years in direct marketing and has encountered a wide range of experiences. After many years in the advertising and marketing arena, Chuck recently entered the list brokerage business as vice president of marketing, for A Z Lists, Inc. in Greenwich, Connecticut.

Prior to that, Chuck served as director of direct response marketing for the video division of Fotomat Corporation. Prior to Fotomat, Chuck spent almost 8 years as vice president–account supervisor at three major direct marketing agencies: Ogilvy and Mather Direct Response, Inc.; Wunderman Ricotta and Klein; and Rapp and Collins, Inc.

Chuck has had extensive direct marketing experience in servicing accounts such as American Express, Diners Club, Citibank, Time-Life Books and Records, International Correspondence Schools, and Conde Nast Publications. He is currently a member of the operating committee of the Marketing Council for DMA. (*Chapter 16*)

George G. Orme is executive vice president of Client Services of BBDO Direct. He has more than 10 years of experience in direct marketing on both the client and agency sides. Mr. Orme has also worked in both sales and marketing management with CBS (both international and educational publishing) and built a venture business for National Liberty Marketing in Valley Forge, Pennsylvania.

Prior to joining BBDO Direct, he was in charge of the Direct Marketing Division of Lewis & Gilman Advertising in Philadelphia. He has been responsible for a number of direct marketing programs at AT&T, ITT, Sun Oil, Hamilton Mint, Bachman Foods, RJ Reynolds, L'eggs Showcase of Savings, and the Cigna Corporation. Mr. Orme is a past board member of the Philadelphia Marketing Association, and a member of the Direct Marketing Association. (*Chapter 58*)

Pierre A. Passavant has been conducting a worldwide seminar and consulting business, specializing in direct marketing, since 1977. Among his sponsors and clients are the U.S. Direct Marketing Association, Dun & Bradstreet, IBM and several European and Pacific direct marketing trade organizations.

Previously, Mr. Passavant was catalog circulation manager at J.C. Penney, marketing vice president at Gerber Life Insurance and vice president and director of promotion at Xerox Education Publications. He has bachelor of arts and master of business administration degrees from New York University and is a member of the Phi Beta Kappa honor society. (*Chapter 2*)

Dr. Stanley C. Plog has directed his own marketing research company in the Los Angeles area since 1963. It is a full-service organization providing services to a large number of Fortune 500 companies in the United States and Canada, and in various parts of the world. Clients include airlines, automobile companies, retailers, advertising agencies, video game manufacturers, computer companies, TV and print media, beverage companies, banks and financial institutions, telephone companies, and various governmental agencies. Dr. Plog has written four professional books and numerous articles in journals, and has delivered speeches to conferences throughout the world, including different meetings of DMA. He has conducted research on direct marketing campaigns for various companies and uses direct mail to market Showcase Rental Cars, a recent venture of the staff of Plog Research. (*Chapter 30*)

Robert J. Posch, Jr., Esq. has the ideal credentials to write about the growing channel which will dominate marketing in this decade. He is associate counsel of Doubleday & Company, Inc., where his duties include monitoring several aspects of compliance with government regulation. He received his J.D. and later M.B.A. from Hofstra University and was elected to the National Honor Societies in Business and Marketing. He is the author of *The Direct Marketer's Legal Advisor* (McGraw-Hill) and *What Every Manager Needs to Know About Marketing and the Law* (McGraw-Hill). Other writing credits include the monthly column "Legal Outlook" in *Direct Marketing* magazine, as well as articles published in the *Journal of Marketing* and *Fund Raising Management*. (*Chapter 13*)

Eugene R. Raitt has been involved in direct marketing since 1971, and has devoted most of his time to direct insurance marketing. Gene is uniquely qualified in his field, having held virtually every position in the industry, from sales agent through executive vice president, including a vice presidency with National Liberty. A frequent guest speaker at local and national association meetings, Gene's client roster reads like a Who's Who of the insurance industry. Mr. Raitt graduated from the University of Maryland, and Columbia University Graduate School of Business, where he received a certificate in marketing management. (*Chapter 57*)

Eller D. Rama is the marketing director of Rodale Books, a division of Rodale Press. He has written articles on sampling and testing for the DMA Marketing Council of which he is a member. He is also a member of the Executive Council of Direct Marketing—Book Club Division of the Association of American Publishers, Inc. He received his master of business administration degree in marketing and finance from Rutgers University. (*Chapter 47*)

Murray Raphel says, "First of all, I'm a retailer." He developed Gordon's Alley, a multi-million-dollar center city pedestrian mall in the heart of Atlantic City, New Jersey, when the experts said it couldn't be done. For this, he received the Albert Gallatin award as one of the three outstanding executives in the United States.

He consults on marketing and advertising to the banking and retail food industries in the United States, and he is an international speaker. He coauthored *The Great Brain Robbery*, an idea book on promotions and recently published *But Would Saks Fifth Avenue Do It?*, a collection of his columns from *Direct Marketing* magazine. (*Chapter 54*)

David E. Rifkin is general manager of advertising and promotion for Nynex Mobile Communications Company, a provider of cellular mobile telephone service. He served for several years as national advertising director for Barbizon International, a chain of more than 100 modeling schools. Prior to Barbizon, David held the position of direct marketing manager at International Correspondence Schools. In 1982, he joined The Western Union Telegraph Co. as product promotion specialist, working on both the Telex Communications Service and Business Education Service product lines. David is both a marketer and consumer of education; he is currently an M.B.A. candidate at New York University. (*Chapter 55*)

Ernan Roman, president of the New York–based Ernan Roman Direct Marketing Corporation, is an internationally known consultant, author, and lecturer in the field of direct marketing. He has been responsible for structuring innovative marketing programs for a wide range of companies including N.Y. Telephone, IBM, Avis, Johnson & Johnson, Citibank, Pfizer, American Express, and Time.

Mr. Roman is a frequent lecturer at direct marketing seminars including the International Direct Marketing Conference (Paris), British Direct Marketing Day, Pan Pacific Marketing Symposium (Sydney), IBM's Marketing Workshop, The American Management Association's Seminars (seminar leader and speaker), and DMA Annual and Spring Conferences.

Mr. Roman served as chairman of The DMA Telephone Marketing Council in 1979 and 1980 and has been an active member of several special DMA task force groups. His articles on direct marketing have appeared in numerous publications. He is the author of the introduction to *Telemarketing Campaigns That Work!* (McGraw-Hill), and author of the Telephone Marketing section of the DMA *Direct Marketing Manual*. (*Chapter 27*)

David G. Rosenthal has been involved in the production and sale of direct mail, commercial, and packaging printing since 1959. Serving as vice president—sales, national account manager, Mr. Rosenthal has been with Webcraft since 1973. His career started as a hobby when he was 13. He graduated from the Rochester Institute of Technology with associate of applied science and bachelor of science degrees in graphic arts management. Mr. Rosenthal addresses direct mail marketing organizations, including the Direct Marketing Association at Direct Mail Day in New York. He is also active in various civic organizations. (*Chapter 41*).

Peter J. Rosenwald is president of his own firm, Peter J. Rosenwald & International Associates. He was senior vice president of Reeves Communications Corporation and president of Wunderman International, the international group of specialist direct marketing agencies which he founded with Lester Wunderman. It is the largest international direct marketing agency in the world. Mr. Rosenwald is chairman of the Executive Committee of the International Direct Marketing Symposium.

In addition to his direct marketing activities, Mr. Rosenwald is dance critic and a music critic for *The Wall Street Journal* and writes regularly on the arts for other publications. (*Chapter 60*).

C. James Schaefer is the president of The DR Group Inc., a direct-response agency in New York, Boston, and London. Mr. Schaefer is a trustee of the Direct Marketing Educational Foundation, a member of the DMA Committee on Ethical Practices, past chairman of the DMA Hall of Fame Committee and past chairman of the DMA Awards Committee. He is also the current president of the Association of Direct Marketing Agencies. Mr. Schaefer is a graduate of Dartmouth and its Amos Tuck School of Business Administration. He cofounded The DR Group in 1969. (*Chapter 33*).

Richard W. Shaver is internationally known for his profit-producing direct marketing programs. In 1981 he established Response Imperatives, Ltd., his own agency which specializes in strategic planning, creative planning for all major response media, and consulting for special situations.

He has been a full-time practitioner of direct marketing for nine years. Starting in field sales in 1964, he received five promotions in 8 years, which made him the youngest vice president in McGraw-Hill history. As head of marketing for the Sweet's division of McGraw-

Hill, he was responsible for developing marketing plans for all division products in six major markets.

In 1975, Mr. Shaver became the General Manager of Agawam Associates, where he quickly established Strategic Planning Coregroups, and was promoted to executive vice president in 1978. In 1979, he was the driving force in DMA's conversion from the Gold Mailbox to the Echo, and in 1980, he served as chairman of DMA's Marketing Council. (*Chapter 3*)

David D. Shepard is president of David Shepard Associates, Inc., a management consulting firm serving the mail order and cable TV industries. Prior to forming his own company in 1976, Mr. Shepard held vice presidential positions at Doubleday & Co., The Maxwell Sroge Company, and Throckmorton Satin Associates. Mr. Shepard is a graduate of the Columbia Graduate School of Business, and the City College of New York. (*Chapter 4*)

David H. Soskin is president and founder of Soskin/Thompson Associates, the direct marketing division of J. Walter Thompson U.S.A. and a senior vice president of J. Walter Thompson Company. Soskin/Thompson Associates is headquartered in New York City and has offices in Chicago, San Francisco, Los Angeles, and Toronto. From 1971–1978, he was corporate vice president, marketing and advertising, Book-of-the-Month Club, Inc., a subsidiary of Time, Inc. (*Chapter 49*)

Peter Spaulder is vice president of Valley Forge Associates, the in-house agency of National Liberty Marketing. In his years at National Liberty, he also served as Director of Marketing. Previous positions include vice president–account supervisor for Rapp, Collins, Stone & Adler; director of sales for The Franklin Mint; and vice president–advertising for the correspondence school of the Macmillan Company.

Mr. Spaulder is presently teaching a course in direct marketing at Temple University, Center City, now in its sixth year. He has been a frequent speaker at DMA conventions on both the national and local level. He is currently on the board of directors for the Philadelphia Direct Marketing Association having served as both chairman of the board and president.

Mr. Spaulder authored the article "Magazine Advertising Principles for the Direct Marketer" in the DMA Manual. He is a graduate of Columbia College and holds a master's degree from the Columbia University Graduate School of Business. (*Chapter 14*)

Bob Stimolo A specialist in direct marketing to schools, Bob Stimolo has developed and implemented major promotion campaigns for such clients as Encyclopedia Britannica, U.S. Games Inc., Sundance Paperbacks, J. L. Hammett Company, and Ambit Publications. Mr. Stimolo is publisher of *Direct Response Marketing to Schools Newsletter*, a how-to monthly publication for school marketers. Formerly a senior marketing manager for Xerox Education Publications, Bob has mailed many campaigns and conducted hundreds of tests in the school market. (*Chapter 56*)

Jo-Von Tucker is president and CEO of Jo-Von Tucker & Associates, Catalog Consultants, in Dallas, Texas. She has 20 years' experience in producing upscale catalogs for firms like The Horchow Collection, American Express, Sakowitz, Gucci, Williams-Sonoma, Bachrach's, C & P Telephone, *Bon Appetit*, G. Willikers, Neiman-Marcus, Fingerhut Corporation, and I. Magnin. She serves as consultant to firms in the United States, in Europe, and in Asia. She has won over 200 national and international awards for design, including the Silver Echo Award for Catalogs in 1982.

Ms. Tucker is a member of the board of directors and the executive committee of the Direct Marketing Association. She is a sponsor and visiting executive for the Direct Marketing Educational Foundation, and was the recipient in 1978 of the Matrix Award for Advertising Woman of the Year, presented by Women in Communications. She has conducted seminars and given talks on catalog marketing all over the world. (*Chapter 46*)

Brian Christian Turley is a freelance direct-response copywriter living and working in Melrose, Massachusetts, just north of Boston. He is a specialist in subscription promotion and business-to-business mailings and was formerly senior vice president and creative director of The DR Group, Boston and New York. Past president of The New England Direct Marketing Association, Mr. Turley was named Direct Marketer of the Year in 1981. He is a graduate of Harvard College. (*Chapter 36*)

Caroline A. Zimmermann is president of Zimmermann Marketing, Inc., a New York–based direct response advertising agency. Founded more than a decade ago, her firm works for American Express, Home Box Office, Metropolitan Life, Scholastic, and others. She is a well-known speaker at industry functions around the country and is active in a number of professional organizations. In addition, Ms. Zimmermann has achieved recognition as a photographer and author. Her recent books include *How to Break into the Media Professions*, and *Fun with Photography*. (*Chapter 5*)

part 1

PLANNING

chapter 1

INTRODUCTION

Edward L. Nash

President and CEO
BBDO Direct
New York, N.Y.

Welcome to *The Direct Marketing Handbook*. As you are about to discover, it is not just another book. It is, in fact, a monumental project involving seventy-five very busy, very knowledgeable people who together put in $1 million worth of time and experience.

HOW THIS BOOK CAME ABOUT

It took over 2 years from the time this project was conceived by Bill Newton, then a senior editor with McGraw-Hill, to the day when Bill Sabin, manager of McGraw-Hill's business and professional publishing editorial operation, handed me the first copy. In between, a great many people got involved.

Four hundred leaders of the direct marketing industry were asked to nominate the most knowledgeable people in each facet of direct marketing. Virtually all these leaders replied, suggesting people or volunteering themselves. Eventually, sixty people—heads of business, advertising agency executives, lecturers, consultants, marketing directors, and others—found the time in the midst of their other responsibilities to research and write the material you hold in your hands.

Others on my staff and at McGraw-Hill checked the manuscripts, transferred the editing and corrections, sent for permission and releases, and followed up on the critical deadlines for outlines, manuscripts, editorial reviews, illustrations, and proofreading. I am particularly indebted to Caroline Cohen, the editorial coordinator, and Sharon Ross, who served as assistant editor.

THE "WHY" OF THIS HANDBOOK

Why did all these people put in such a major effort? It wasn't for money. All the contributors are doing quite well in their careers. None received any royalty or other compensation for their efforts.

It wasn't for publicity. Virtually all the contributors were well known in their own right before this book was conceived. Many have lectured to direct marketing clubs and at Direct Marketing Association (DMA) conventions. Others write for industry publications, and some have written or are writing books of their own, spelling out in entire volumes what they can only introduce in the chapters they have contributed here.

The reason lies in the nature of the direct marketing field and its recent origins. For the most part, we have been an "oppressed minority" within the larger world of advertising and marketing. For many years we were the stepchild of the advertising world, the "black sheep" of the world of marketing, the "hucksters" who groped for coupons and phone calls in a crass struggle for immediate sales while others dealt with imagery and impressions on a far larger and higher scale.

Like any oppressed minority, we learned to stick together. The handful of direct marketing agencies always referred business we couldn't handle ourselves to our friendly competitors. The marketing executives of competing companies attended each others' lectures, discussed new methods, and congratulated each other on breakthroughs in technology or creativity. The DMA is a model of an industry working together for self-advancement and mutual self-education.

It is in this spirit that these writers share their experiences, theories, facts, and wishes for success with every entrant to this exciting field.

Direct marketing is a much larger field today, and we are no longer oppressed or a minority. In fact, we have become not only respectable but downright fashionable on Madison and Michigan Avenues. Yet the tradition persists. By helping each other, we help direct marketing. By helping our industry, we create new and better opportunities for all marketers.

WHAT IS A "HANDBOOK"?

First of all, the name is a contradiction in terms. It seems a good handbook is one that can't possibly fit in your hand, one whose bulk is so great that it must rest on a desk when being read. Better terms might be "encyclopedia" or "desk reference," but those terms are confining in other ways. This handbook combines all three concepts. In other words, this handbook is a one-volume encyclopedic desk reference.

The Direct Marketing Handbook is a reference work that belongs wherever direct marketing is dealt with: in companies, in agencies, at printers and list brokers, and probably most important, in advertising agencies and departments which are beginning to be exposed to direct marketing but don't really have a full working knowledge of it.

Everyone has experienced the phenomenon of reading a chapter or attending a lecture prematurely, listening to information that has no relevance to one's life or work, and therefore not comprehending it. Later, the need for the knowledge occurs, and we wish that we had paid attention to the earlier input or that the knowledge was available right there, when and where we needed it.

A handbook composed of sixty chapters is too much to comprehend at one sitting. However, it is comforting to know that like an instant memory, it is at your fingertips any time the need for more information in a given area comes up. Each chapter stands alone, and each is designed to be read when and if the need arises or when and if you wish to browse through the world of direct marketing and discover new facets of its interlocking expertise.

It is not a primer on direct marketing. For that purpose I recommend my own *Direct Marketing: Strategy/Planning/Execution,* also published by McGraw-Hill. That book was written to be a "how-to" book; this one has been edited to be a reference work. Their purposes and thus their content are very different.

If you are thinking of starting your own mail-order business, first read Julian Simon's classic *How to Start and Operate a Mail Order Business,* also from McGraw-Hill.

If you want to be a copywriter, by all means read the chapter on writing copy in my *Direct Marketing*. Read John Caples's *Tested Advertising Methods* (Prentice-Hall), and read Victor Schwab's *How to Write a Good Advertisement* (Harper & Row).

If you wish to learn more about the entire business of direct marketing, Bob Stone's *Successful Direct Marketing Methods* (Crain Books) will be helpful. Also, Cecil Hoge's *Mail Order Know-How* (Ten Speed Press) is a fascinating guide to the lore and lessons of the business.

To keep up with it all, don't overlook *Direct Marketing* magazine, *DM News, Zip, Friday Report,* and the continuously updated manual published for members of the DMA.

THE GROWTH OF DIRECT MARKETING

According to the DMA *Fact Book,* 45 percent of all U.S. adults order some item by mail in any 12-month period. Almost $20 billion is spent on direct marketing in the United States, producing $110 billion in sales. Around the world, other countries have similarly impressive marketing expenditures and sales figures.

More significant is the range of companies that are numbered among direct marketing practitioners. Currently, about half the corporations on the Fortune 500 list are engaged in some type of direct marketing activity, either by acquisition of a company that distributes primarily in this manner or by applying direct marketing techniques to the selling of products or services previously promoted only through general advertising methods.

My company, BBDO Direct, has been engaged in applications of direct marketing for companies one would never imagine to be users of this discipline, such as General Electric, ITT, Campbell Soups, and R. J. Reynolds. This is in addition to the expected applications in fields such as banking, insurance, fund raising, and catalog marketing.

Today more than ever, the copywriter's "instinct" and the marketer's "intuition" are not adequate. Practitioners in this field may find themselves working for or competing with highly sophisticated, well-financed companies that are combining a variety of general advertising methods with those of direct marketing and that require a logical, strategy-based plan to justify every action and every investment. This requirement has forced our industry to get its act together. We have learned to use research in ways never before imagined. We have applied computer technology and mathematics to find new ways to plan, project, and analyze every step of the direct marketing process from selecting lists and publications (and segmenting them in new and daring ways) to evaluating the dollars-and-cents effectiveness of alternative creative positioning.

THE NEW INTERDYNAMIC APPROACH

The expanding world of direct marketing has never stopped changing. It is just entering what is probably its most profound period of change: a growing integration with the sophisticated technology of the world of general advertising.

The acquisition or startup of direct marketing agencies by general agencies has led to a growing exchange of information and a deepening reservoir of shared experiences on behalf of shared clients.

Research is no longer a discipline given lip service by direct marketers. It is a practical, powerful preamble to the development of concepts and the testing of alternate approaches by conventional "split run" and other methods.

Marketing planning is no longer a quickie proposal for a mailing, some ads, or a direct-response television test. It involves a methodically developed strategic plan that takes into account every aspect of the product, medium, offer, and creative alternatives.

Product benefits today are perceived not only on the superficial level of product benefits but with a deep insight into the emotional needs and desires that relate to a product and its attributes. "User self-image" is a new term that frequently is brought into play when positioning a product in the marketplace, as important a concept in the world of direct marketing as it has been in that of general advertising.

We are more and more concerned with what I call the awareness by-product of our advertising, recognizing that each advertisement does not necessarily stand alone but is perceived in the context of its media environment and other consumer impressions. More important, each communication benefits by and contributes to the consumer's impression of the product, the company, and direct marketing overall.

This book has been written at a time when these disciplines and their interaction are just beginning to be utilized. The initiate to the world of direct marketing should use this reference work and other books to understand the principles of direct marketing as they have evolved and as they have been applied traditionally. However, to get to and stay in this field, one must search for connections with other disciplines.

This handbook isn't enough, nor is a whole shelf of direct marketing books. The direct marketer today must understand and use the essentials of strategic planning, scientific decision making, interpersonal relations, computer sciences, statistical analysis, and qualitative and quantitative research. More and more, the field of psychology is being brought to bear on both the research and creative disciplines in direct marketing.

The direct marketer today must know more and work harder than in the recent past. On the other hand, the direct marketer has more varied and powerful tools available to meet the challenges of the marketing arena. In direct marketing today, nothing is easy. Yet as a result, nothing is impossible.

If this handbook makes your job a little easier and makes your business a little more successful, it will have accomplished its purpose and repaid your investment. We have tried to make it that kind of book. Please let us know if we have succeeded.

chapter 2

DIRECT MARKETING STRATEGY

Pierre A. Passavant

Owner
Passavant Seminars and Consulting
Middletown, Conn.

Direct marketing is a form of marketing in which an organization seeks to generate a direct and measurable response to advertising which offers goods or services or information about them.

Direct marketing includes not only the creation and distribution of advertising but also all the other activities involved in receiving, processing, recording, analyzing, and following up on the responses to advertising. The advertising may be communicated by mail (including catalogs), broadcast, telephone, or print or may involve combinations of these media. The response may be an order, inquiry, or contribution and may be transmitted by mail, phone, or other electronic means.

Special Characteristics

There are special characteristics that differentiate direct marketing from other methods of marketing, advertising, and promotion.

A Response Directly to the Advertising. Unlike the package goods advertiser or the institutional advertiser, direct marketers try to do more than create awareness of and recognition for a company, product, or brand. The objective of the direct marketer is to get a response, which may be in the form of an inquiry or an order. It may come in by mail, telephone, or other electronic means, but it occurs in direct response to the promotional message.

This does not mean that creating awareness and recognition is unimportant. Even direct marketers benefit from the buildup of marketplace awareness that occurs when many promotions have been sent out over a period of time. The emphasis on getting a response simply means that the advertising must be of a special type. It must contain enough information, must be sufficiently persuasive, and must make the type of offer that will motivate readers to inquire for further information or actually place an order. The chapters in this book that deal with the proposition and with copy and art fully explain the special advertising and promotion techniques used by direct marketers.

The psychology of direct marketing is somewhat special. It tends to blend aspects of personal selling with elements of advertising. The seller actually takes the initiative in presenting specially selected goods directly to the prospect and urges an immediate response. This is quite different from the more passive display of retail merchandise in stores, in which the customer must decide to go shopping before response can occur.

A Data Base of Information about the Respondents. When a response comes in, the direct marketer must fill the order or send out the requested literature. But that is only the beginning of the total marketing process.

Direct marketers make special efforts to capture information about respondents and about the order, contribution, or inquiry received. Identification information about the respondent (name, title, company, address, telephone, etc.) captured in a data base permits the direct marketer to contact the respondent again with additional offers.

In addition, information about the response (purchase versus inquiry, product category, dollar level, method of payment, etc.) permits the direct marketer to make the most appropriate new offers to past respondents. By also capturing the dates of past activity, the direct marketer can classify previous respondents in the data base according to the recency and frequency of prior activity. Since recent and frequent respondents tend to reply to additional offers at a higher rate than other names in the data base, the direct marketers can improve overall response and profitability by selecting only the best candidates for future offers.

Implicit in the concept of building a data base of information is the related direct marketing principle of segmentation. Segmentation refers to the ability to break down a customer file or somebody else's mailing list into segments according to demographic characteristics, psychographic characteristics, or previous response characteristics. The ability to segment gives the direct marketer the option to promote to certain customer classifications and not to others or to promote more frequently to some classifications and less frequently to others. The end purpose of the data base is to permit very selective marketing which results in higher response rates and higher profitability.

Tested and Measurable Advertising. In many cases, the direct marketer can measure the actual response to individual cells of promotion by putting a unique code number on the response piece in a direct mail package, putting a coupon in a magazine ad, etc. As keyed responses come in, the direct marketer can measure the response in magazine A versus magazine B, the response in January versus February, the response to list A versus list B, etc. This means that over the long run, the direct marketer can develop some reasonably scientific information about which media, offers, ads, seasons, and parts of the customer file pull the better rates of response and which pull the less good rates.

Over a period of time, the direct marketer is able to plan future promotions on the basis of past history, not simply on the basis of personal opinion, individual preferences, or general attitudes regarding promotion.

In addition to reading the results of overall promotions, the direct marketer also can fashion some very precise split tests. A-B split tests can be done within mailing lists or periodicals to determine how the marketplace actually reacts to different offers, formats, prices, etc. This kind of testing is much more precise and factual than opinion research that only elicits the attitudes of people regarding different advertising approaches.

The direct marketer's general objective is to test advertising in small quantities first in order to determine what works best and to use the results of those tests as a basis for investing larger amounts of promotion dollars as profitably as possible later. Performing live market tests and measuring results are a way of life for the professional direct marketer.

Promotion Economics. The direct marketer allocates a far larger proportion of the sales dollar to promotion than manufacturers or most sellers of packaged goods. The term "promotion" here refers to the total cost of creating, producing, and distributing advertising which will generate responses. It is not unusual for a direct marketer to spend 15 to 25 percent or more of net sales on promotion. While this may seem like an extraordinary amount, remember that the direct marketer usually does not pay commissions to sales people or give discounts to retailers. Not surprisingly, the direct marketer focuses a lot of attention on the promotion expense line in the profit and loss statement. Not only is it large, it directly reflects the level of response rates achieved and the resulting profitability of individual campaigns.

There are a wide variety of direct marketing methods, and there are many different applications in both the consumer sector and in the business-to-business sector. But whether the direct marketer is concerned with book clubs, insurance, sales leads, or selling copiers, the special characteristics of professional direct marketing that have been outlined here will be equally applicable.

Strategic Considerations

The major strategic factors that affect the nature of a direct marketing promotion are selecting the product, establishing the promotion objective, choosing media, determining which selling system to use, deciding on the level of promotion intensity, and arranging for a fulfillment system.

Product Selection. It is becoming increasingly the case that direct marketing methods can be used to sell, or at least assist in the sale of, all kinds of goods and services. Price level once was considered a barrier, but today $9500 necklaces are sold by mail, $50,000 investment-grade diamonds are sold through newsletters, and used computers are sold over the telephone. A price barrier may be at the low end because in a low-priced item (say, under $10), there may not be sufficient margin to allow for normal levels of promotion and fulfillment expense.

It also used to be said that a successful direct marketing item had to be unique or at least unusual and preferably not available at retail. Yet within the past year, over 500,000 American families have purchased a collection of 2101 simple hardware store items (screws, bolts, washers, cotter pins, etc.) assembled in a cabinet containing twenty-five plastic drawers for $21.95. The packaging is unusual, but the items themselves are anything but.

It also has been said that it is better if the item is discretionary in nature and that basic commodities cannot be sold through mail order. While it is true that it would be almost impossible to sell milk by mail, business-to-business marketers have been highly successful selling ruled pads, pencils, copier paper, doormats, etc., through catalogs and by telephone marketing. Again, the old "rules" seem less applicable than they may have been in the past.

But a few of the old rules still apply today. First, if an item is going to be sold through direct marketing means, it must be something that can be described in words and pictures. There must be enough gross margin (what's left over after product cost is subtracted from selling price) to pay for the typical cost of doing business through a direct marketing channel (see Chapter 4).

Remember, however, that it is not essential that the final sale be completed exclusively through direct marketing methods. Direct marketing can be used simply to generate inquiries which may be followed up by personal selling efforts. This widens the scope of possible products and services even further.

In the final analysis, a product or group of products must be of interest to a definable group of people who can be reached efficiently through an established direct marketing medium. The medium is the market, and the product is the fulfillment of a need or want.

Promotion Objective. Before commencing the development of a campaign, the direct marketer must decide whether the objective is to generate orders or to generate, qualify, and convert leads. There is a major difference between these two direct marketing approaches (as described in the section about the selling system) which will have a great effect on the nature and format of the promotion.

Direct marketing methods (especially direct mail and telephone) also can be used simply to maintain communications with a target audience. A typical example of this would be keeping in contact with customers between sales calls. That type of communications contact is not considered as a primary promotion objective in the context of this chapter.

Media Selection. The media that are available to the direct marketer are

Mail (solo packages, co-ops, and catalogs)
Print (magazines and newspapers plus inserts)
Telephone (outgoing and incoming)
Broadcast (radio and TV, including cable)

The selection of media appropriate for an offer depends on a number of different factors including the degree of audience selectivity required, the amount of space (or time) needed to present the offer, the need to "show" the product, and how high a promotion cost per thousand the marketer can afford in relation to probable response rates.

The Selling System. There are six major methods of selling by direct marketing. The conditions under which each method is most frequently used are described below.

One-Shot. This is an offer to sell an item in a single transaction. When the prospect buys and shipment is made, the transaction is complete, though there may be extended payments. This method of selling generally is used for items that are relatively easy to understand or services that do not require demonstration or personal sales efforts. It is possible to sell low- to high-ticket items in this manner.

Two-Step. First, there is an offer to supply additional information about a product or service, such as literature, a catalog, or a personal visit. Then efforts are made to qualify the inquiries and convert them to sales. This method of selling frequently involves combinations of print, mail, telephone, and personal sales calls. It is used most frequently in connection with complex and high-ticket items which require extended consideration, personalized information, or a demonstration. This method may also be used simply to build a mailing list of names to whom a catalog may be sent.

Catalog. This is an offer of an assortment of merchandise from which the prospect may select one or more items. The catalog may remain in force for months and sometimes for more than a year. The customer frequently keeps a copy for future use. This method of selling is applicable when there is a relatively broad assortment of items to be offered to a target audience. In the consumer sector such items are frequently of a discretionary nature, while in the industrial sector such items often represent recurring supply needs within a particular product area. A catalog is most analogous in concept to a retail store which displays a variety of merchandise and invites customers to make selections.

Subscription. This is an offer of ongoing service, usually for a specified period; it generally is paid for in advance. It is used most frequently in magazine selling.

Club. This is an offer of ongoing product shipments under an automatic shipment plan or a negative option plan. Payment is made on receipt of merchandise, and the customer may have to complete a minimum commitment before canceling. While this selling system most frequently applies to books and records, offers of services such as insurance and special telephone features are conceptually similar to club operations.

Continuity. This is an offer of a specified series of items to be shipped at regular intervals over a period of time. Usually the customer may cancel at any point, and payment is made in installments. Again, the most common application of this method is found in the publishing business.

The selection of the appropriate selling system depends on the nature of the product, the amount of product items available, the selling price of the item, and the complexity of the information that must be presented before a purchase decision can be made. Another important factor is the psychological question of human inertia. Subscription, club, and continuity plans rely to a certain degree on the fact that some customers will continue to accept shipments for some time after they have ceased to be truly interested in the product or service they are receiving.

It sometimes may require an extensive period of testing to determine whether a company can more profitably sell a product through one-shot or two-step marketing. Within that area of testing, it may take quite a few subtests to determine how to convert the maximum percentage of leads.

Promotion Intensity. The direct marketer thinks not only of the product that is being presented to the target audience but also of the total offer or proposition that is being made. The offer or proposition consists of

- The product or service
- The price (regular or in some way special)
- The payment terms (cash, credit, installments, etc.)
- Commitment (what the respondent is making a commitment to)
- The guarantee
- Promotional enhancements (special deals, a free trial, gifts, sweepstakes, etc.)

The type of offer that is made will have a large effect on the response rate. The Xerox Corporation, for example, got an 80 percent higher response when it offered a reconditioned copier with a 15-day free trial offer than when it offered a purchase-with-guarantee offer.

The professional direct marketer typically spends a significant portion of the test budget trying to find an offer that produces the best combination of response and profitability. It is usually one of the objectives of the direct marketer to make extraordinary and exciting offers, especially when the product is not unusual or exceptional. That is why one sees offers such as "4 for $1" and the many variations on it. An extraordinary offer frequently permits the direct marketer to sell an ordinary product or service directly through advertising.

It is not unusual for companies first entering the world of direct marketing to struggle with the question of promotion intensity, because they may be faced with a new tone and style of advertising. Companies that are accustomed to merchandise awards or contests for their sales people sometimes shy away from even the thought of a sweepstakes addressed directly to their customers.

Usually the concern expressed relates to questions of company image. Obviously, every company can choose to have whatever marketing image it feels is best. Some companies, however, may find that the image that they created before direct marketing somewhat impedes the development of truly exciting direct marketing offers and promotions.

Like most other things in direct marketing, the question of image and its effect on response rates can be subjected to extensive testing. Test results then can be used to define the value of different levels of promotion intensity and the impact of predetermined company image on response rates. The final decision regarding the type of promotion most suitable for the company then can be made on the basis of factual test information.

Fulfillment System. As indicated in the definition at the beginning of this chapter, direct marketing includes not only the generation of responses but also the fulfillment of orders, inquiries, etc. The fulfillment system, which includes order processing, inventory control, customer service, etc., is as important a marketing consideration as the offer and the advertising package. This is so because the customer's satisfaction will be a direct result of how the order is handled.

The finest products and the greatest advertising will be of no value in the long run if the customers whose names appear in the data base have had their orders mishandled or delayed. Unhappy customers will not want to respond to the next promotion. Before any direct marketing promotion is started, the company should be sure that it is prepared to

- Respond promptly to requests for information
- Fill orders promptly
- Make adjustments and corrections courteously when problems occur
- Handle routine billing and customer service efficiently and courteously

If the company is unable to handle this back-end part of its business, it should delay the implementation of any front-end promotions.

Not all firms using direct marketing today are 100 percent mail order. Increasingly, companies are entering the field from other areas of marketing: retailing, direct selling, or manufacturing. For these companies, adapting the traditional approaches of the total direct marketer may be particularly difficult. Such a company already has another established way of doing business. It looks at advertising and promotion differently from the direct marketer. Its profit and loss statements distribute expenses in a different way. It is unaccustomed to the continuous ritual of testing and measuring.

As frustrating as the learning period may be for nontraditional direct marketers, it is essential that they approach direct marketing in the professional, disciplined manner that others have found effective and worthwhile. This is not to suggest that old-time direct marketers cannot learn from companies entering the field. But it is an urgent warning to these new companies not to initially ignore or reject what has been learned over many decades of extensive testing.

Direct marketing is a special marketing method. The chapters in this handbook will show you how to begin to implement it successfully and with the least amount of risk.

chapter 3

THE PLANNING PROCESS

Richard W. Shaver

President
Response Imperatives, Ltd
Plum Island, Mass.

By definition, strategic planning is the managerial process by which a company manages change and develops the most profitable fit between its direct marketing operations and its changing marketing opportunities. Since the degree of change during the 1980s and 1990s will dwarf that of the 1970s, strategic planning and those direct marketers who master it will dominate the near-term future as well as generate the customer bases and needed skills for continued real growth beyond the year 2000.

Properly understood and employed, strategic planning is a discovery and control tool that can be applied to two essential endeavors: long-range planning (LRP) and next year's marketing operations (SMP, or strategic marketing planning). While this essay is concerned with using strategic planning to optimize next year's growth, it is important to understand the similarities and differences between SMP and LRP. LRP steers your entire business toward growth opportunities beyond next year's operations. While LRP had some impact on growth in the 1970s, most direct marketing organizations had not truly mastered this discipline. As they approach the mature and aging stages of their base businesses in the 1980s and 1990s, a command of LRP will be imperative.

THE DIFFERENCE BETWEEN LRP AND SMP

On hearing the term "strategic planning," most people tend to think of LRP and simultaneously position next year's operational planning as tactical. This confusion can be extremely costly in that next year's opportunities then are approached tactically, piece by piece, rather than strategically as a whole. Surprisingly to some, LRP and SMP are more alike than different. All the things a strategic planning group must have a command of—the process itself, the phases and sequence involved, the steps to be taken, the tools that can be used, and the skills required—are exactly the same. What differs is the people involved, their subject matter, the resulting document, and the kinds of work generated by the decisions made during the processes.

In the LRP process, presidents and senior executives (probably staff) analyze issues in the light of corporate strengths and weaknesses to develop a mission statement. Then macrogoals are set, and strategies are developed to achieve them. This process results in business plans which call for things such as research projects, acquisitions, new corporate structures, changed personnel requirements, and capital needs for the base business and new businesses over the next 2 to 5 (and sometimes 10) years.

While SMP takes its cue from the goals established during the LRP process, it usually involves line managers who make target market selections, establish next year's objectives, develop strategies, and then correlate tactical plans and a budget that will direct and control next year's marketing activities.

Since nearly all direct marketing companies, other than the most entrepreneurial firms in their startup years, attempt to plan operations 6 to 9 months in advance (simply because direct-response creative development and production require such lead times) there are two fundamental reasons why such planning should be strategic in nature. First, the operational planning must be done anyway. Second, operational plans that are rooted in effective strategic thinking not only catapult profit levels but also point out otherwise unseen disaster areas. It does not matter what size a direct marketer is. SMP is an imperative for realizing the profit potentials that are inherent in the degree of change expected for the remainder of the 1980s and the 1990s—a degree of change that Alvin Toffler calls "the third wave"—which will make that of the 1970s seem small in retrospect.

THE DIRECT MARKETING PLAN: WHAT IT IS AND IS NOT

Before addressing how you should structure and manage the planning process itself, let's examine what a strategic marketing plan is and is not. It is not summary notes from a series of meetings, a proposal, a set of recommendations, an agency program, or a project outline. It is not a suggested course of action, a list of creative ideas or tactics, media or lists to be tested, or projects that may prove interesting to do.

Your direct-response marketing plan should be the written, comprehensive product of direct marketing professionals, resulting from their creative analysis and problem solving, decision making, and specification of all the direct-response operations that will be implemented in the next marketing year. It includes what will be done, who will do each project, when the projects will be started and completed, how they will be done, what they will cost, and the priority of each project. It also states clearly how each project relates to all others and how much revenue and profit, both acquisition year and life cycle, is expected from them.

It spells out the underlying strategies selected to overcome each obstacle identified as having the power to block the specifically stated objectives of the plan. Finally, it provides the essential substructure for everything that follows, the underlying strength for attaining objectives, and the key to maximum profit and growth.

OPERATIONAL BENEFITS OF STRATEGIC PLANNING

Once you have created a plan like the one described above, it has significant and various uses. Top management can use it to gain a more thorough understanding of why requested funding should be approved and how next year's operations relate to their long-range planning, and they can assess line performance more accurately. Line managers, departmental personnel, and vendors can use it to develop superior tactical work as well as to control implementation of project timing and costs and improve quality.

In sum, SMP delivers nine major benefits to a company, because it

1. Forces three-dimensional thinking
2. Allows specialists to perceive interfunction relationships otherwise missed
3. Generates an extraordinary enthusiasm that improves tactical creativity
4. Allocates resources to have an impact on the most profitable potentials
5. Creates benchmarks in advance for future decisions
6. Improves staff quality control and deadline performance
7. Elicits improved vendor performance
8. Enables faster rollouts of successful programs and faster shutoff of failures
9. Saves substantial top and middle management time and stress during the implementation stages

HOW TO STRUCTURE AND MANAGE THE STRATEGIC PLANNING PROCESS

Traditionally, many strategic marketing plans have been produced by a planning department staffed with specialists trained to work with senior and line management inside the traditional corporate structure. Usually these staff personnel begin as honeybees gathering input from line managers and then massage the data into hypothetical possibilities that are presented to and discussed with management. The advantages of this approach are twofold. There is a constant overview perspective that sees the whole and relates each part to bottom-line impact, and the planners are experienced in using the tools available for incisive strategic decision making.

The major disadvantage is that too often the planners, even though intelligent, dedicated to success, and thoroughly professional, are so far removed from the real world that the sometimes illogical but crucial human factors that can determine success or failure are lost in a quagmire of percentages, statistics, and scientific probabilities. Thinking tends to be linear and mathematical to the detriment of innovation and substance. While the planning specialist approach clearly has been effective in many instances, particularly in LRP, over the past 15 years I have found it deficient when applied to creating strategy and marketing plans for next year's direct-response operations.

What is really needed and wanted is a marriage of logical and quantitative factors with psychological and qualitative thinking that is three-dimensional as well as linear: perception that goes outside the lines without violating the principles of geometry. Just as art does not contradict science, marketing strategy need not violate the fundamental principles that govern direct marketing success.

> "Genius, in truth, means little more than the faculty of perceiving in an unhabitual way."
>
> *William James*

> "Creative thinkers continually waver between unimaginable fantasies and systematic attack."
>
> *Harry Hepner*

> "Originality is simply a fresh pair of eyes."
>
> *Woodrow Wilson*

> "When I examined myself, and my methods of thought, I came to the conclusion that the gift of fantasy has meant more to me than my talent for absorbing positive knowledge."
>
> *Albert Einstein*

These four quotations, all taken from 1979–1980 Chevron exhibit, Creativity: The Human Resource, apply to marketing just as much as they do to science, literature, or government. In analyzing 100 years of American creativity in all fields of endeavor, Chevron made an attempt to discover what truly creative people have in common with one another. They concluded that creative people from Socrates through Einstein shared seven basic characteristics. They

Construct networks by forming associations between people for the exchange of ideas, perceptions, and encouragement

Challenge assumptions and question what most automatically accept as true

Use chance to take advantage of the unexpected and are ready at all times to recognize accidents

See in new ways by transforming the familiar into the strange and seeing the commonplace with new perceptions

Recognize patterns by focusing on significant samenesses or differences in physical phenomena, events, or ideas

Make connections and bring together seemingly unrelated events, objects, or ideas

Take risks by daring to try new ways with no guarantee of the outcome

If you set up a strategic planning coregroup in such a way that it effectively forms a network capable of challenging assumptions and using chance, you will find individual members seeing in new ways, recognizing patterns, and making connections that enable the group as a whole to generate innovative and powerful strategic decisions.

As a first step, select your coregroup members from those line personnel who currently are producing your direct-response programs. They can be in house, from your agency, freelancers, or consultants. Make sure that each function needed to engage in direct marketing is represented: marketing, creative media, financial production, data processing, manufacturing or merchandising, and fulfillment (including customer service). If you're a smaller company in which single individuals wear many hats, that is fine. A coregroup can function with as few as three members as long as the various essential perspectives are represented.

Properly directed and interactive, the "composite eyes" of this group of direct marketing specialists can bring obstacles to the surface and create strategies that the best of planning experts by themselves generally could not. Here is what to look for when selecting each coregroup member who will become part of your creative network.

- The plan manager should be a direct marketing generalist who knows how to listen and has superior oral and written communications skills. Experience in planning techniques and strategic development is quite helpful but not absolutely necessary. The plan manager will function as the group's job captain, responsible for scheduling meetings, start and stop tracking during meetings, recording and distributing coregroup decisions, and assigning between-meeting work projects to individual coregroup specialists.
- The marketing member should be a direct-response generalist with the deepest possible background in customer acquisition and life cycle marketing, a creative strategist rather than a tactical specialist.
- The creative director should provide imaginative idea sparks, in contrast to the dimension of logical analysis provided by other group members. Experience in telephone and broadcast as well as direct mail and print space is desirable.
- The media specialist cannot be wedded to lists or publications only but also must bring an informed perspective on the relative strengths and weaknesses of all major response media: mail, magazine, newspaper, telephone, TV, radio, co-ops, syndication, and multimedia.
- The production manager must be conversant with all forms of direct-response production and costs, a tactical generalist whose major contribution will be to keep you in the world of the possible using state-of-the-art technology.
- The data processing specialist is needed for two primary reasons: realistic knowledge of what your marketing data base can process and track, and the

source of information regarding what can and cannot be done in the expanding world of word processing.
- Manufacturing or merchandising and fulfillment members are needed to ensure that your response programs do not outrun or short-circuit your fulfillment and customer service resources. This all too common eventuality will destroy the future profits from customers converted in next year's operations unless expert and well-informed representation expresses itself during strategic planning meetings.

If you do not have sufficient know-how on research, testing, yield analysis, or specialized industry knowledge as a part of your coregroup members' experience and skills, these resources should be brought in on an ad hoc basis.

Whoever said that the whole is greater than the sum of its parts was right, and your coregroup may well prove that observation. However, there is a danger in this kind of group approach. You must ensure that the coregroup will develop and maintain the overview that is absolutely necessary for successful strategic planning and that the group will not get bogged down in detail by addressing pieces of your overall opportunity that are in actuality low-priority items in terms of bottom-line impact and significant growth.

These pitfalls can be avoided if you use proven planning techniques and tools that eliminate tunnel vision and vested interests. You also must make certain that each coregroup member understands the basic planning ground rules and how the tools are supposed to be used, and you must allocate sufficient time for individuals in the planning network to accomplish their normal line functions while participating fully in the strategic planning process. The basic coregroup operating ground rules are simple to state but require a greater than average effort to make them work because they contradict much of what we have been taught as well as the conventional wisdom.

1. **Hierarchy.** During coregroup meetings, there is no pecking order whatsoever. Normal lines of authority and reportability do not obtain, and no individual has the authority to overrule any group decision.
2. **Perspective.** The predominant perspective is that of the group as a whole. While each member can and should contribute from his or her area of expertise or specialization, each must strive to approach decisions and value judgments from the standpoint of a direct marketing generalist assessing the relationship of any part to the whole.
3. **Subject matter.** While all subjects are to be addressed and stressed on an informal, free-form basis, the phases of the planning process cannot be taken out of sequence. Tactics cannot be worked on until all strategy has been fully developed, objectives must be established before obstacles and advantages develop, and objectives cannot be created till all background material has been dissected and organized for the strategic planning process to begin.
4. **Decision making.** Decision making is on a consensus basis only. Ideas, observations, opinions, and individual judgments should flow freely, with dissent encouraged. However, all coregroup members must realize that their ideas must be presented in such a way as to obtain agreement of all other members before positions can be adopted and decisions can be considered

to be made. Given the divergent perspective of each coregroup member, a great deal of heat will be generated on occasion (if not, you probably are not doing it right). That is fine as long as the heat is transmuted into light by the group as a whole.

TOOLS THAT ENERGIZE STRATEGIC PLANNING

I have found four tools to be particularly effective for developing direct-response strategy and plans. Two of these—the task method and fast-tracking—help maintain the needed overview. The other two—adversary analysis and brainstorming—help members of your network use chance, recognize patterns, and make connections.

The task method is in essence zero-base marketing. It requires that each individual block out preconceptions about what is "always best" or what "cannot be done." After relevant marketing information has been isolated from all the data assembled, coregroup members mentally block out all constraints and start to develop objectives, move on to identify and prioritize all obstacles and advantages, create strategy, and only then analyze available resources (total direct marketing resources: people skills, time, and money) to apply constraints to the task decisions that have been made. After modifications or an approved increase in resources that can be made available, tactics are developed, and then the entire plan is subjected to risk-gain analysis.

Fast-tracking is an ideal process for strategic market planning in that it is complementary to the task method, forces overview thinking and decision making, and speeds up the entire planning process by a substantial margin. Developed in the construction industry during the 1960s in order to reduce design and building cost and lapse times, the technique was radical. But it was a successful departure from the traditional step-by-step architectural design process. Instead of architects working virtually alone to interpret the building owner's needs from initial concept to finished specifications, coordinating at various stages with the engineering firms involved, and finally turning completed plans and final specifications over to the general contractor, who then would develop bids from many subcontractor specialists, all major disciplines worked together from the beginning of the design process. Architect, engineers (mechanical, electrical, and sanitary), contractor, and key subcontractors were directed by a construction manager charged with keeping this interdisciplinary group on track. Ideas, observations, and judgments flowed freely, with disagreement encouraged in order to apply maximum feasibility stress to any proposition under evaluation. No detail was allowed because major decisions were made in needed sequence (overall building performance requirements, site location, building size and shape, major systems, basic materials, etc.). Parameter specifications were created and then checked for viability between meetings. They were reviewed at the next group meeting and then modified or finalized before the next set of needed decisions was addressed. Final details were implemented just before actual project work commenced.

The results were significant and a bit startling. Costs were reduced substantially, building performance improved, and costly re-dos were eliminated.

The same process can be used to improve the design and reduce the costs of direct-response marketing programs. The basic criteria governing the process are exactly the same:

1. All major disciplines are involved throughout.
2. Discussions are informal and intensely interactive.
3. Major decisions only; no detail is allowed.
4. Fatigue-stress all proposals surfaced.
5. Develop parameter specifications that allow final detail to be created later.
6. No skipping ahead; subject matter is addressed in rigid sequence.

The adversary system is essentially a series of freewheeling rap sessions rooted in conversational debate by the members of the planning network. Unlike brainstorming, in which negatives are not allowed as ideas surface, all ideas are attacked in the open as they evolve. While coregroup specialists should speak from the standpoint of personal expertise, ideas can and should come from anywhere on any topic. (One of the best creative approaches I've witnessed over the past 6 years came from a dialog between a plan manager and a media supervisor.)

Spontaneity and "top of the mind" reactions are essential, and network members must have the courage and maturity to see some of their ideas dismantled by the group as a whole. All decisions must be reached by a consensus of the entire group, and so it is necessary that votes for and against be taken on the basis of each member's overview rather than that member's specialty. While this ground rule may seem time-consuming on occasion, its importance cannot be overemphasized.

Brainstorming is a creative technique that is useful when a network gets blocked or when an impasse in conversational debate is reached. This fantasy approach is simple, and the ground rules are few; it does not require extensive training or experience with the process to make it work.

First, you select one coregroup member as your brainstorming leader, who will be the only one in the group to maintain contact with reality. All others think outside the lines and free-associate within the following guidelines.

No critical judgments on any ideas are expressed.

Group members let go and simply react to ideas as they evolve (except the leader).

The leader simplifies the meaning of each idea as it comes.

Each idea is developed till the leader stops discussion.

The more free-form and fun, the better.

This kind of brainstorming is a three-step process: preparation, brainstorming, and analysis. Define the problems to be addressed in writing at the outset. Set quotas for the number of ideas to be developed and then set a time limit. Since you will not be analyzing the ideas as they evolve, you will find that you are able to bring many to the surface in a relatively short time period. Make certain that each participant understands the ground rules before you begin. As soon as all are prepared, have at it. After the brainstorming session, use the adversary system to place a comparative value on each idea in terms of logic, reality, and usable resources.

PHASE 1: TURNING DATA INTO DIRECT-RESPONSE MARKETING INFORMATION

Once you have chosen your method of planning and have assigned responsibility for strategic development, you are ready to begin work on the first of six phases that constitute the total planning process. In the first phase, coregroup members will turn raw data about potential markets into information that enables them to identify target markets on a qualitative and then a quantitative basis as well as evaluate the resources available to reach those markets.

If the data available are not reduced to direct marketing essentials, coregroup members will be swamped by unrelated facts and almost certainly will miss relationships that are crucial for strategic decision making.

It is not an exaggeration to state that as much direct-response profit is lost in phase 1 as in any other phase of your work or for any other reason: mispositioned creative strategy, weak media analysis, anemic strategy development, inferior tactical development, deficient capabilities for response tracking, etc.

Recognize the difference between data and information. At the end of each trading day, stock exchange floors are strewn with pieces of paper recording the day's transactions. Imagine the most skilled investment analyst trying to make decisions based on the information buried in all those data. It would be impossible.

But the next morning, when the transaction data have been converted to information in newspaper financial sections, judgment can be applied toward making informed decisions. Turning marketing data into marketing information for your strategic planning coregroup's use is just as critical a process. Too often the assumption that everyone comprehends "enough" leads to too little time and thought being dedicated to organizing and boiling down data so that residual information can be seen in its true significance.

The first step is for the plan manager to gather and format all relevant information. Two resources must be made available for the plan manager to accomplish this: in-depth knowledge of direct marketing principles and librarian skills. If the manager has only the organizing component, the significant will not be separated from the incidental; if he or she has only the direct marketing insight, information will be assembled in formats that confuse rather than enlighten. Available data must be turned into relevant information in each of the following areas:

- Preliminary situation statement
- Industry maturity and business phase
- Competition
- Direct marketing margins

- Product features
- Needs and wants
- Benefits
- Customer profiles
- The buying process
- Perception of need
- Profile summaries
- Market segments
- Current resource levels

Each area should be addressed individually and in this order.

The Preliminary Situation Statement

This should be written before any major effort is devoted to converting data into information. The purpose is to tell you and each coregroup member what you do not know as well as what you do know and what you think you know. The statement addresses each subject listed above in order and is comprehensive but not deep in detail; it is a précis rather than a fully documented narrative. Once completed, the written statement is distributed to each coregroup member as well as any other personnel who might be a source of marketing input. Each recipient should study this opening statement from two standpoints: to suggest any important ingredients that have not been included, and to determine what each recipient can input for amplification.

The following checklist is helpful as a stimulator for coregroup members and as a control reference for the plan manager to ensure that all potential sources of critical information have been probed.

- Your house list (recency, frequency, monetary, and variety)
- Right-hand drawers of company veterans
- Previous research and analytical reports
- Competitive data
- Complementary product info
- Customers
- Ex-customers
- Previous inquirers
- List brokers
- Media vendors
- Production vendors
- Award case histories
- Government reports (federal, state, and municipal)
- Foundation research
- Association reports and statistics
- Industry consultants
- Media libraries

As you all do your homework and scan your memories, contacts, and references, you often will be astonished at how much significant information surfaces from the most mundane and unlikely places.

Once relevant data have been collected by the plan manager, the data must be boiled down and organized into essential facts and relationships. Summary statements should be developed in each subject area in a sequence of most important to least important, and documentation should be included in the background appendix, classified and indexed for ready access. Insofar as possible, express all statistical data incrementally and comparatively as well as absolutely.

Do not spend undue time at this stage initiating research or indulging in work projects to extend the information in hand. When key elements are missing, simply note them as critical yet "missing." You will address them in depth when you reach the phases dealing with objectives and obstacles. When this in-depth revision of the original preliminary situation statement is completed, it should be distributed to each coregroup member for study before the first network session. If the documentation is too bulky for distribution, simply include the classification and index for the supporting materials and distribute them to individual members on request. All documentation should be available, however, at all coregroup meetings.

Finally, do not be surprised if this phase of your work consumes as much as 50 percent of the time needed for the whole process. Louis Nizer, the attorney, attributed his consistent courtroom brilliance to his three P's and commented that 95 percent of his success was due to preparation and perspiration and 5 percent to performance.

At the first meeting, the coregroup members should move on an adversary and evaluation basis through each of the background areas to satisfy themselves that the information at hand has been developed as much as possible before beginning the remaining phases of the planning process.

Do not short-circuit this effort in your anxiety to move on to the next phase. Key elements that are overlooked or not perceived here will have a disproportionately negative impact on strategic development and profits.

Where Are You Starting From? Industry Maturity and Business Phase

The second part of your background organization identifies whether the industry in which you are going to compete is embryonic, growing, mature, or aging. Where your industry is will have a great deal to do with the kinds of objectives you develop and the types of obstacles and advantages you have. Table 3-1 will help you assess this, but you also should define your industry in terms of total dollar sales per year and number of units sold and then in terms of competition by annual sales dollar volume, size of customer base, and market share. Do not at this stage spend much time on in-depth analysis of each competitor and be careful not to include sales figures that include products or services that are not competitive with you.

It is equally important to know the stage your business is in, as shown in Figure 3-1, as well as your own sales statistics in terms of customer base growth, attrition, average dollar sales per year per customer, cost per inquiry, cost per order, etc.

TABLE 3-1 Industry Maturity Guide

	Development Stage			
Descriptors	Embryonic	Growth	Mature	Aging
Growth rate	Accelerating; meaningful rate cannot be calculated because the base is too small	Faster than GNP but constant or decelerating	Equal to or slower than GNP; cyclical	Industry volume cycles but declines over long term
Industry potential	Usually difficult to determine	Substantially exceeds the industry volume but is subject to unforeseen developments	Well known; primary markets approach saturation industry volume	Saturation is reached; no potential remains
Product lines	Basic product line established	Rapid proliferation as product lines are extended	Product turnover but little or no change in breadth	Shrinking
Number of participants	Increasing rapidly	Increasing to peak; followed by shakeout and consolidation	Stable	Declines, but business may break up into many small regional suppliers
Share distribution	Volatile	A few firms have major shares; rankings can change, but those with minor shares are unlikely to gain major shares	Firms with major shares are entrenched	Concentration increases as marginal firms drop out; or shares are dispersed among small local firms
Customer loyalty	Little or none	Some; buyers are aggressive	Suppliers are well known; buying patterns are established	Strong; number of alternatives decreases
Entry	Usually easy, but opportunity may not be apparent	Usually easy; the presence of competitors is offset by vigorous growth	Difficult; competitors are entrenched, and growth is slowing	Difficult; little incentive
Technology	Concept development and product engineering	Product line refinement and extension	Process and materials refinement; new product line development to renew growth	Role is minimal

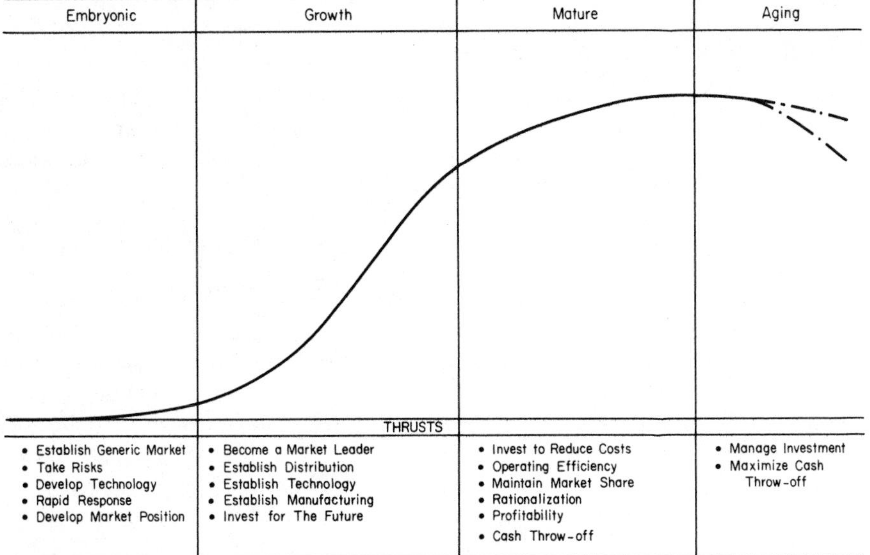

Figure 3-1 Stages in the business life cycle.

Competition: Curse or Cornucopia?

Usually only one business is "firstest with the mostest" in any given marketplace. If you are not that business, view your competitors as a strategic source of crucial information not otherwise available to you and then leverage that information to the maximum.

As competitors communicate in direct-response form, they are telling you continually what is and what is not working in your marketplace. Accurately analyzed, their offers, creative platforms, and media selections can focus customer profiles, needs, and wants related to benefits, price points, and size of markets. But you must work at organizing the signals they are sending you. Determine their media usage in terms of frequency and total expenditures, identifying primary and secondary media. Assemble complete "swipe files" that display their controls, tests, and rollout solicitations: mailing packages, magazine and newspaper ads, TV and radio spots, and telephone work. Watch for test efforts that are not repeated. Knowing what did not work can be as valuable as knowing what did.

Once you have each competitor's solicitation activity in focus and prioritized, write summaries of their relative strengths and weaknesses. Then, when your coregroup members reach this part of their meeting, evaluate all the competitors qualitatively, defining the strategies that have provided them with whatever dominance in the marketplace they currently enjoy.

Direct Marketing Margins: Are They Worth the Effort?

Before you go any further, stop to calculate and reexamine the mathematics direct marketers live by: customer acquisition cost and breakeven, attrition curves, and life cycle sales and profit potentials.

This is particularly important if you are entering a new market or marketing new products. However, it also should be done for your base business in order to precisely track cost and price point trends that may be affecting your traditional markets and products.

For new products or new markets, be certain to apply all manufacturing or merchandise supplier costs and all fulfillment costs (including conservatively estimated sales costs if your program is lead-getting or traffic-building) to establish marketing margin ranges. Then use general media costs per thousand, as shown in the following table.

Media	Average CPM, $
Telephone (outgoing)	1,800
Direct mail	300
Newspaper inserts	27
Magazines	15
Newspaper ROP	9
Television	3

In addition to CPM, you must use conservatively estimated response rates based on your own previous experience (if applicable) or general industry response ranges. (You will be surprised how much response information in terms of ranges is available if you work at: award case histories, companies with similar but noncompetitive products, consultants, etc.). Now allocate overhead costs, and your coregroup members will have a working measurement of allowable cost per order (CPO), cost per inquiry (CPI), and range of contribution to promotion and profit (CPP).

Be certain that these parameter statistics include life cycle values for each customer acquired unless there is absolutely no potential for back-end sales and profits. To sum up, there are five steps involved in preplanning mathematics:

1. Identify conservatively estimated response rates.
2. Compute CPP.
3. Develop pro forma profit and loss statements (P&Ls).
4. Factor customer life cycle values into your analysis.
5. Make a halt decision if your numbers don't make direct marketing sense in terms of risk-gain potential.

Your Product: Features and Descriptions

Here you simply want to define what each product is and what it does. Written descriptions by each coregroup member should be lean and skeletal yet comprehensive. No special effort should be made at this stage to translate product features into customer benefits, although any natural "top of the mind" benefits statements need not be removed. Costs of manufacturing and fulfillment as well as the percentage of overhead to be applied should be included in the written descriptions. There should be no attempt at creative copy since the thrust now is toward clarity, brevity, and inclusiveness.

Needs and Wants: The First Step in Isolating Markets

Although the phrase "Needs and Wants analysis" sounds dull, it often induces dynamic coregroup sessions and is the springboard to benefits evaluation, customer profile identification, market segmentation, and strong creative platforms.

No matter how self-evident needs or wants seem to be, the strategic planning coregroup should put them under a marketing microscope for closer inspection. They should be analyzed at two different stages in phase 1: from the standpoint of common sense, logic, and general knowledge, and again after each potential customer profile's perception of need has been established.

In consumer programs, it is useful for coregroup members to individually apply the basic 8 before discussing needs and wants. These are:

1. Making money
2. Saving money
3. Winning praise
4. Self-improvement
5. Saving time or effort
6. Impressing others
7. Helping children and family
8. Having fun

Then distinguish between a need and a want and decide which your product or service will be satisfying. The owner of an outdoor swimming pool may want a solar sun blanket to keep her pool water warm at less cost, but she needs a basic pool covering for winterizing if she lives in the snowbelt. Similar real distinctions exist in business and industrial markets. When the EPA mandated a large leap in minimum gas mileage per gallon, Detroit needed to find a way to lighten their product by nearly 1000 pounds per car. Before that, product designers and management might have wanted to lighten cars by using lighter metals, but they did not need to.

As the coregroup raps about needs versus wants and the type of satisfaction delivered, inevitably customer characteristics will be mentioned: age, income, sex, education, occupation, and marital status. Lifestyle characteristics such as athletics, politics, intellectual, and hobbies also will be discussed. Capture these demographic and psychographic data as they evolve but do not at this point try to develop complete pictures of various customer potentials. Instead, coregroup members should start to be more specific in their descriptions of the kinds of needs or wants satisfied. How will the customer make more money? Or save it? Or impress others?

As you refine the satisfactions, more profile characteristics will emerge. Capture these and start connecting the characteristics. When you've connected as many as possible, prioritize the satisfactions you've identified from most important to least important by coregroup vote. Stay at it till the network reaches consensus. Then apply the six basic drives to your priority list:

1. Self-preservation
2. Love
3. Gain
4. Duty
5. Pride
6. Self-indulgence

After you have done this, repeat the whole process. Once this is completed, you will have a clear picture of which needs and wants can be satisfied by your products or services and some idea about the types of customers you should seek. These same criteria apply in business and industrial markets, but there you must overlay one pervasive motivation: recognition by business peers and management.

Focusing Benefits

Benefits are what prospects think about and evaluate before buying and what suspects give little or no serious consideration. Consequently, your product's benefits not only govern creative strategy and tactics but also are a prime tool in determining who the best potential customers actually are. Benefits prioritization is often a critical tool in certain marketing situations, and it is always an important one.

Here the coregroup starts by listing every possible benefit anyone can think of. Translate all the product features described in step 2 into clear, tight benefits statements. Take each need and want satisfaction developed in the previous session and state them in terms of benefits. Review the benefits statements in your competitors' solicitations.

Now have the coregroup vote on the most important benefit and rap till consensus is reached. Do the same until all benefits have been prioritized. Do you have a unique selling proposition, the USP all direct marketers covet? Be brutally honest with yourselves about this, for the marketplace will be. If you truly have the competitive advantage of a USP, your ultimate strategy will be vastly different.

As you are ranking benefits in terms of their sales-closing power, more customer characteristics will be mentioned and discussed. Add these to the profile pictures that emerged during the needs and wants session. If the coregroup cannot reach consensus after sufficient interaction and analysis, write tight descriptions of the disagreements and the reasons why agreement cannot be reached. These will be of key importance when you reach the objectives and obstacles phases of the planning process.

Customer Profiles

Customer profile analysis is crucial in direct-response marketing. A direct marketer's most important resource is not the order but the orderer, not the response but the responder. Discovery, accumulation, retention, maintenance, and retrievability of profiles and response history are the cornerstone of profit in direct marketing. Maximum profit is generated by defining customer profiles accurately, searching out segments of the total potential customer base with similar characteristics, and then soliciting and resoliciting them effectively to maximize sales during responder life cycles. When only a one-time sale is possible, identifying customer profiles in terms of best CPO through to breakeven profiles enables you to spend your direct-response dollars most cost-effectively.

In short, the more precisely you define and rank your profiles, the less you will spend to obtain initial orders and the higher will be your response rates, average order dollars, and dollars per customer per year. Direct mail, the parent of direct-response marketing, has proved this time and again. This is why your best ZIP codes will pull 300 percent better than your worst: there are more similar profiles within the best ZIPs. (As soon as census tract geocoding becomes more widespread, even greater response swings will be obtained because census tracts have been constructed on the basis of cluster homogeneity, while ZIPs have been constructed primarily for the convenience of the branch post office, therefore capturing only some of the clustering effect.) Profile similarity makes it possible for the various forms of regression analysis to identify markets on the basis of profitability.

Consequently, the strategic planning coregroup should spend whatever time and effort are necessary at this stage to categorize and rank profiles as precisely and accurately as possible.

Five major tools can be used to isolate the profiles you must find: response graphics, demographics, psychographics, geographics, and special graphics. While sufficient information from only one of these can be enough for profitable direct marketing, the more relevant information you have from each area, the sooner you will reach maximum profits, both acquisition and life cycle. Therefore, each source must be examined in depth.

Response graphics are simply the historical actions taken by customers in response to specific types of products. The basic formula employed by the mail-order industry since the 1930s has been recency, frequency, and monetary value (RFM), but it is helpful to isolate variety (V) also. Run this analysis against your house file first if applicable. It is axiomatic in direct-response marketing that previous responders will respond better than nonresponders. Most research supports the contention that roughly one-third of wage-earning Americans are not responders yet and may never be but that the remaining two-thirds are responders, with half of them responding on a regular basis and half on a sporadic basis. Some posit that 50 percent of adults in the United States are mail-order buyers and that the remainder are "see, touch, and feel" buyers at retail. Whatever the actual split, the difference between the two is critical in your profile analysis.

However, keep in mind that large numbers of previous nonresponders have been converted to responders over the past 10 years and that magazine subscription responders are not mail-order buyers until proved otherwise. (TV and some telephone responders are not yet proven mail-order buyers in the traditional sense. Initial findings indicate that they respond to repeated solicitations at lower rates than mail- or print-generated responders.)

When you are entering a new market or selling a new product unlike those you have marketed before, your house file response information will not help much. Always test the house file, but explore to identify responder lists and publications for similar or complementary products, preferably products with comparable price points.

Demographics refers to the factors of age, sex, marital and family status, education, income, occupation, and shelter. At a minimum, accurately identifying demographic customer characteristics enables you to zero in on publications and specify microsegments of lists for mail and telephone efforts; sometimes this is a key analytical factor in determining your best broadcast markets for television response. These customer indicators can be computer-combined with responder files through list-grafting techniques or can be positively merge-purged against master computer data bases (census track-based, usually) to identify where the best customers are.

In business and industrial markets, demographics relates to business entities rather than individual consumers but is no less useful or important. SICs (Standard Industrial Classifications) isolate businesses by industry and type of business within an industry, and various list compilers further segment by annual dollar volume, number of employees, etc.

Psychographics isolates potential customers in terms of their Lifestyle characteristics. Everything from antique collecting, avid book reading, camping, fishing, and flying through political activism, stamp collecting, investing, tennis, and wine drinking is grist for the marketing analyst. By 1982, one fast-growing computer data base had 6 million consumers identified by any of 54 lifestyle characteristics crossed with age, sex, marital and family status, occupation, and type of shelter.

Geographics tells one where the current customers reside and in certain instances where the best prospects are likely to be. For example, salt-polluted areas adjacent to the U.S. coastline are clearly targets for the sale of home water distillers, whereas municipal wells invaded by toxic chemicals are not necessarily adjacent to bodies of salt water. In the United States, isolation of target markets by geographic location is nearly unlimited in flexibility and reach.

Country	1
Census regions	9
States	52
ADIs	200
SMAs	265
Sectional centers	870
Counties	3,150
School districts	12,500
Census tracts	34,600
ZIPs	36,000
Census blocks	287,000

Special graphics are any characteristics not included among the four first sources. For example, pool ownership could conceivably indicate a lifestyle characteristic, but it does not necessarily do so. Individuals with high blood pressure, who are prime targets for the sale of a water distiller, do not necessarily have any demographic, psychographic, geographic, or responder characteristics in common.

Once the coregroup has gathered, organized, and preliminarily combined characteristics into discrete profiles, here is a process that can be used to further verify or refine customer profiles.

1. Coregroup members study individually each profile established thus far.
2. Each member jots down "top of mind" characteristics that relate to specific product purchase potentials.
3. Each member then compares the prime benefit with each profile. Is it the same? If not, match benefits to appropriate profiles or describe a profile that would relate to the prime benefit.
4. Do the same for each benefit on the benefits list.
5. Coregroup adversary analyzes each member's benefits and profiles list, raps, and ranks agreed on profile and benefit combinations from best to least.
6. Depending on the consensus and confidence level of the coregroup as a whole, profiles then are identified as viable or as needing further verification in the objectives, obstacles, or strategy phases of the planning process.

Diagraming the Buying Process

No matter what your market—consumer, business, or industrial—there are always steps before the buy-no buy decision is made. There are always buying actions and sometimes buying influences.

There are five steps, or buying actions:

1. Recognition of need (or want)
2. Evaluation of solutions
3. Recommendation of product types
4. Selection of brand
5. Approval of purchase decision

In consumer markets, very often one individual takes all the actions, sometimes in a matter of minutes in a very informal way. He or she recognizes the need (stimulated by the seller or self-recognized), mentally or actually compares and evaluates types of products that could satisfy the need, makes a mental recommendation about brand, and then mentally approves the expenditures needed to acquire the product.

In other instances, usually with more expensive products or products that will be used by more than the individual in question, there can be buying influences who can have an impact on the buying decision. The sale of water distillers is a case in point. Any family member may recognize the need for pure drinking water, but the mother of the house probably will want to compare makes, features, and benefits of various types of this kitchen appliance, and the father will have a voice in an expenditure of $250.

However, this type of multi-influence buying process is a prime characteristic of business and industrial markets, in which many individuals, often specialists, control the buying actions before a purchase decision can evolve. Professional analysis, specifications and requisitions, budgets, and approvals are par for the course. Be aware that the buying process is a gauntlet and that any one of the buying influences has the power to negate the sale.

Consequently, your creative strategy, the amount of versioning you do, the number of solicitations you make, and your entire marketing strategy may well depend on exactly what the buying process is: how many influences there are and the steps each influence must take in the process itself.

Once you have discovered the process as it relates to your products, revisit your list of profiles and link any buying influences that exist to the related profile. Assess whether any identified buying influence may be strong enough to constitute a discrete profile.

Perception of Need: Creative Quicksilver or Gold?

Never assume that actual needs are perceived needs. Often they are not the same, and your response will misfire to whatever degree your assumed perception of need was off target. Examples abound, but one of the best is Monex International's direct marketing program to sell Krugerrands shortly after Americans once again could buy and own gold. It was 1979, and Monex assumed that investors knew why they should invest in gold and understood the mechanics of making the purchase. They headlined their response ads in the financial press "Get 20 for the money and one for the show" and concentrated on convincing potential investors that gold coins were the best way to invest in gold as compared with bullion or gold stocks. The program was not a bomb, but someone challenged the assumption that most investors knew much about gold at all, since 40 years had passed since Americans could legally own it. After research, their new ad approach was headlined

GOLD—how to buy it, where to buy it . . .
and why you should.

The ad went on to give the history of gold's reemergence into America's financial investment opportunities and how simple it was to buy and sell gold. The results? The cost for an inquiry was reduced by an increment of 56 percent, and the average order size grew by an increment of 20 percent. The reason for this was a more accurate assessment of perception of need combined with creative execution as professional as on the first attempt.

Take our home water distilling appliance. In areas where municipal aquifers have been salt-polluted, perception of need is acute, as evidenced by the fact that these areas consume 56 percent of all bottled water in the United States, and in 1979 bottled water sales exceeded $550 million. Yet the actual need of residents in those areas was comparatively lower than that of residents in areas where the municipal wells had been invaded by toxic chemicals carried by groundwater movement. Until local people became seriously ill and water supplies were checked, perception of need never would have helped you market a water distiller.

Your coregroup now should evaluate each customer profile identified in terms of perception of need and then rerank profile priorities according to the perception factor.

Building Profiles into Direct-Response Market Segments

While it is true in one sense that the medium is the market in direct response, do not limit your strategic analysis of target markets in terms of the existing media reach. Instead, start by identifying the quantity of customer potentials that exist within each one of the profile segments your coregroup has isolated and then start to work on where they are located and how to reach them cost-effectively. Do not start with any specific medium and explore laterally.

Here is a sequence of steps that can be used to examine the total U.S. marketplace to ferret out those market segments which represent profitable marketing potentials for direct-response operations. Not all the steps apply to each product or marketing situation. Your coregroup members may find themselves moving through any given step simply by deciding that it is not applicable to this specific situation.

1. Start with your number one profile, complete your analysis of it, and then move on to the next profile until you have analyzed each profile on your potential customer list.
2. Define each profile segment geographically on the basis of any relevant distribution limits.
   a. For retail traffic building, apply store location parameters.
   b. For lead-getting programs for localized sales people, apply sales office parameters. Keep in mind that all consumer segments are reachable by mail.
3. Reduce any geographic "wholes" by special graphics that are applicable: snow belt for pool covers, salt-polluted areas for water distillers, entire country for new mothers, etc.
4. When your profiles contain key demographic characteristics, quantify each by applying national census summary statistics.
5. Overlay national superlist files to determine the geographic locations of your profile, identifying any clustering effect within census tracts, ZIPs, SMAs (Standard Metropolitan Statistical Areas), ADIs (Areas of Dominant Influence), states, or regions. Some examples of the differing kinds of demographic selections explorable are:

   Donnelly National Household Database (55 million households)

   Demographic Systems, Inc (47 million households; 127 million individuals)

   Executive Services Birthday File (55 million households; 80 million individuals)

   MDC Families with Children (25 million households)

   MetroMail Telephone File (60 million households)

   R. L. Polk Households by Occupation (25 million households)

6. Merge-purge your own customer file segments against the quantities determined in step 5 and determine if geocoded census tract back-scanning can isolate and identify similar-profile tracts throughout the country. If not, cluster by ZIP code counts.
7. For each profile segment, apply maximum media reach quantities to your total universe in terms of each medium in the following order of priority:

   Responder lists

   Mail-order publications

   Listed telephone numbers

   Compiled lists and general publications

   TV, newspaper, and regional and local magazines against high-priority clusters
8. Explore all list-grafting potentials.
9. Evaluate each medium in terms of response potential versus cost efficiency. Keep in mind that at this point, your coregroup is not specifying precise media to be employed (that will come later, in the strategy or tactics phases) but rather applying the relative strengths and weaknesses of each major response medium to the market segments you have isolated and ranked in order of response profitability potential.

Now that the coregroup has determined target markets by size and by the types of customers within them as well as product benefits and media available to reach each segment, you are ready to analyze the resources you have at your disposal to address these market opportunities.

Resource Analysis: Key to Future Profit

If the strategies and plans you create produce sales that outrun your organization's fulfillment capabilities, consider your program a failure rather than a success. One of the fundamental differences between selling and marketing is that the prime function of selling is to create an order, whereas the prime function of marketing is to create the most profitable customer. By definition, marketing must go beyond selling to produce satisfied, enthusiastic customers who will want to buy again and recommend your products and company to others.

This principle of marketing applies to all businesses but especially to mail-order and direct-response marketing because there is no person-to-person contact between buyer and seller. Consequently, the strategic planning coregroup must be as diligent and creative in providing for your order fulfillment and customer service performance as they are in providing for customer solicitation and order generation. A few years ago, an industry veteran claimed that "If we could deliver the product in 3 days, we'd own the world," and there is reason to believe he was right. Research clearly shows that repeat purchase and the lifetime value of a customer are directly related to the speed and accuracy with which initial orders are handled.

L. L. Bean, a mail-order company that experienced geometric sales and profit growth between 1975 and 1981 (from $30 million to $181 million), ships 75 percent

TABLE 3-2 Capabilities of Major Direct-Response Media

Medium	Advantages	Disadvantages
Direct mail	Reaches all households Selectivity & personalization Most suitable for testing Most flexible Maximizes customer list dollars Second highest response rates Contains all action elements	Second most expensive Long startup time Profile analysis Potential limited
Telephone	Powerful "one-on-one" capability Fastest response time Selectivity Flexibility Excellent for research and profile analysis Can increase average order size substantially Highest response rates Powerful cross- and upgrade-sell	Dangerous with prospects No visual appeal Most expensive CPM 55% household reachability
Magazines	Reach mass or class Good color reproduction Long ad life Low CPM Test inexpensively Moderate lead time	Less space to tell story Less personal Slower response Less selectivity than mail or phone
Newspapers	Shortest startup time Fast response Wide variety of formats Broad local coverage Inexpensive to test	Poor color Poor ROP production Poor selectivity No personalization Rates vary Sometimes affected by local conditions
Television	Powerful demonstration capability Fast response Wide choice of time buys Can reach all U.S. households Strong support medium Watch for strong selectivity as cable grows	Limited copy time No permanent response device Difficult to split test Network time scarce Limited time available in second and fourth quarters
Radio	High-frequency, inexpensive Many profiles can be isolated by choice of show and time Short startup times Powerful support medium	No response device Limited copy time No visual appeal

of its 3 million annual orders within 24 hours of order receipt. Conversely, during 1981, six mail-order companies went out of business because of difficulties with fulfillment operations.

As an integral part of the planning process, the following ten capabilities must be assessed in terms of handling current order levels and any growth that the strategic plan may call for:

1. Ordering forms and instructions
2. Receiving mail and telephone calls
3. Checking credit
4. Processing orders
5. Addressing and list maintenance
6. Controlling inventory
7. Billing
8. Reporting and controlling
9. Order filling and shipping
10. Handling complaints and adjustments

You cannot achieve 100 percent effectiveness in any of the ten areas because of three factors that are not under your complete control: customers, vendors, and carriers. But it is critical that you identify deficiencies in all operations that are under your complete control. Any that are discovered not to be controllable should be precisely identified for consideration in the objectives phase.

While all these areas are important, reporting and controlling bears further investigation, for it is this "feed" to your marketing data base that enables you to track response, sales, and profits in terms of customer profiles (market segments). Any deficiency in this area of tracking and measuring response should be considered a major obstacle that must be corrected in the strategic planning process and the allocation of resources that the plan will call for.

The strength, weakness, and extent of your front-end resources also must be determined accurately in the planning process. Be as brutally honest with yourselves on this point as you were in assessing your USP. Do you really have state-of-the-art knowledge and hands-on skills in all the recently developed areas of direct-response marketing? If your creative people are great in print, are they as effective in telephone, film, or multimedia? Are your list personnel skilled in the other response media that have emerged or are emerging rapidly?

Of course, you must consider the financial resources available for use. This does not preclude the task method approach. It merely lets the coregroup know when additional financial resources must be requested if they are justified by risk-gain analysis in phase 6.

Comprehensive Situation Statement

After each of the foregoing areas has been addressed and evaluated by the coregroup, the plan manager is ready to put together the final preplanning situation statement, which should be written in the same sequence in which subjects were addressed during the background analysis process. Now all relevant information in order of importance under each information category will definitively identify what is known and that which is not yet known or in hand.

The completed document should be distributed to all coregroup members for in-depth study before the first coregroup meeting to establish objectives. Each coregroup member should bring his or her situation document to each meeting, and the plan manager is responsible for having all documentation available at each meeting.

PHASE 2: STRATEGIC OBJECTIVES: PRIORITIZING THE TARGETS

Developing objectives that permit effective strategic decision making is as much an art as a science, but it is not magic. Your planning group's command of this skill will determine whether you aim the organization's time, money, and talent at operations that in reality have a low priority or steer your direct-response horsepower into channels of substantial growth that are somewhat self-renewing. Objectives that are conceived or expressed too broadly spread your resources across too great a number of targets, many of which are incidental rather than essential. Objectives that are conceived too narrowly apply an enormously wasteful amount of direct marketing activity to profit potentials that represent only a small portion of the growth that is realizable.

Recognize that objectives are rudders that pull your direct-response strategies toward the most important marketing opportunities. Realize that a 10 degree error here can turn into a 1000-mile "miss" of the major ports you are headed for, leaving you at sea rather than unloading cargo. Here is a step-by-step method that can help you create objectives that are reachable and worth reaching.

1. Have your coregroup free-associate a list of possible objectives for next year's operations, never losing sight of lifecycle implications.
2. Adversary analyze each potential objective on the list in terms of the following criteria:
   a. Does it *focus on results*?
   b. Is it *measurable*? *If yes, how?*
      Rate of return
      Ratio to sales
      Percentage of market
      Number of units
      Dollars to accomplish
      Time to accomplish
      Other
   c. Does it contain a *single theme*?
   d. Is it *challenging*? A strategic objective should stretch your existing capabilities but not break any corporate bones. Setting comfortable objectives is as damaging to profit production as tilting at windmills is to morale.
   e. Is it *realistic*? Do you have, or can you obtain, the resources needed in time?
   f. Does it contribute to *higher goals*, such as long-range goals, department-to-division goals, division-to-corporate goals, or corporate-to-parent goals?

   If any objective evaluated cannot be developed to the point where it satisfies the first five criteria of adversary analysis (coregroup consensus), remove it from your list of possible objectives. Only without meeting objective f can you proceed without damage to your strategic plan. As a matter of business courtesy and practical judgment, it is best when ranking objectives to state why any objective has the priority assigned it even though it does not contribute to a higher goal.

3. Place any objectives that are totally financial in nature in a category separate from those which are not totally financial in nature. (Remember that many will contain some financial criteria since all must be measurable in some way.)
4. Rank the financial objectives and then the other objectives on the basis of two factors only: next year's bottom line and life cycle contribution. Consider your numbers from two standpoints in each case: marketing margin and contribution to overhead and profit (CTOP).
5. Examine the kinds of objectives you have developed and prioritized in the light of the industry's phase and the phase your own business is in.

   Objectives will and should vary depending on the condition of your markets (emerging, growing, mature, or aging) and the stage your company is in (entry level, rollout and second-stage testing, growing, mature, or saturated). If either your company or your markets are moving from one stage to another and your objectives remain the same, something is wrong; you should review the objectives in depth.
6. Bring in a fresh set of eyes, either a direct marketing generalist or a group that has not been part of the planning process thus far. This devil's advocate can be from within your company or the outside. Background should be provided prior to the attempt to find any weakness or omissions in your statement of objectives. Finalization of the objectives phase occurs only after your coregroup has analyzed objectives in light of the devil's advocate's input.

PHASE 3: OBSTACLES AND ADVANTAGES: THE BRIDGES FROM OBJECTIVES TO STRATEGY

Most treatments of strategic planning move directly from developing objectives to the creation of strategy. While that sequence obviously has produced a great deal of profitable strategy, the introduction of a step between objectives and strategy can yield uncommon results. It is a step that illuminates the mind and vitalizes the judgment. It simply involves addressing, evaluating, and "connecting" obstacles and advantages to the objectives you just completed working on. Of the two, obstacles are the most misunderstood and underutilized.

Obstacles that are clearly seen and assessed can lead to profits. When discovered, evaluated accurately, and linked to objectives, they can galvanize the coregroup's innovative insights unlike any other tool available. Considered from another angle, if only one major obstacle is overlooked or badly underestimated during the planning process, it can turn a profitable marketing program into a total loser.

Two examples will clarify this point. For our manufacturer of pool covers, product quality was as good as but no better than that of two larger competitors, price was the same, and delivery was comparable. There was no realistic way to change those three factors. There was no competitive advantage. Clearly, a powerful strategy would have to be discovered and implemented if any significant gains were to be realized. For our manufacturer of water distillers, residents were drinking toxic chemicals in their tap water but had no knowledge of the danger, in contrast to residents in salt-polluted areas. This was a major obstacle that steered the strategy for marketing to them.

Turning obstacles into profits during the planning process can be managed in much the same way that objectives were addressed, using the same basic planning tools.

1. Free-associate any and all obstacles of whatever type that come to mind. (Remember that obstacles can be internal as well as external and that a production problem can be as important as a marketing problem.)
2. Link each obstacle that surfaces to the specific objectives it impacts. Do not be concerned if a single obstacle blocks multiple objectives. List it under each one that is relevant, since it is likely that a different strategy may be needed to overcome it.
3. Rank the obstacles to each objective on the basis of the resources needed (time, money, people skills) to overcome each one. (The overall priority of any given obstacle is established by the objective to which it is related.)

Throughout this process, significant clues as to how to allocate resources and also some hints as to "right-on" strategies will evolve. Do not pursue strategy development at this point. Simply capture the ideas and bring them up for work in phase 4.

Once you have developed and assessed the obstacles to next year's direct marketing efforts, you are ready to work on competitive advantages. Use the same process and the same tools to discover, evaluate, and link your advantages to your objectives.

PHASE 4: STRATEGY: FINDING THE LEVERAGE

Trying to answer the question "How do you actually develop strategy?" is like trying to answer the question "How do you actually get an idea?" While both questions are rooted in logic and understanding, both go beyond mere logical analysis and linear thinking. Effective strategies, like creative ideas, emerge from "outside-the-lines" thinking that does not violate fundamental principles.

"Eureka" moments—those moments of illumination and insight when you *know* you have it—cannot be produced on demand or in a production-line atmosphere. Harry Hepner's comment, quoted earlier in the chapter, "Creative thinkers continually waver between unimaginable fantasies and systematic attack" is relevant here. So it is of the utmost importance to establish an atmosphere in which the free play of the mind, and the free interplay of minds, can readily occur. (While much strategic planning takes place away from the office, this is not essentially a corporate reward of nontaxable income. The changed environment and the intangible perception that this whole process is unusual and fun are important to the success of the process itself.)

Let's define strategy before going any further. It is an elusive concept and too often is confused with tactics. There is good reason for this confusion, as can be seen when one consults the dictionary for clarification. The standard dictionary defines strategy and tactics as follows:

Strategy: the art of devising a plan toward a goal
Tactics: a device for accomplishing an end

Since these definitions do not shed much light on the distinction, our working definitions will be as follows:

Strategy is the advantageous employment of various resources as an integrated whole to cause a planned effect.
Tactics involves actions of lesser magnitude than strategy and are carried out with a limited end in view.

With that distinction in mind, here are some guidelines for your strategy-creating sessions.

1. Work on the strategy to achieve one objective at a time.
2. Review each objective and its associated obstacles and advantages before development activity begins.
3. Maximize the interaction between coregroup members during the strategy sessions.
4. Start with your highest-priority objective and work your way through to the last.
5. Assess the viability of your strategies between working sessions.
6. Prioritize the strategies agreed on within each objective the strategies impact.
7. Give your devil's advocate maximum latitude when he or she attempts to destroy the rationale for your strategies.

Keep in mind throughout the process that strategy can and does obtain in any activity related to direct-response marketing: production and fulfillment as well as creative and media, research and testing as well as financial and customer service, morale and administration as well as marketing and sales.

For the swimming-pool cover manufacturer with no unique selling proposition for its dealers in snow-belt areas, three strategies were developed, and they resulted in an increase in sales volume of over 40 percent with no decrease in profit level on sales. They were:

1. **A dealer push-pull program** A customer information booklet comes from Century Products and the dealer who stocks Century pool covers. Pool owners will be offered the booklet "free from their dealer" through an ad in *Pool News*, which has a biennial circulation to 700,000 pool owners. Dealers are preinformed of this offer to their potential customers (see Figure 3-2). Those who stock Century covers receive an inventory of the booklets free of charge.

Figure 3-2 The dealer push-pull strategy: A full-page advertiesment in *Pool News,* a trade magazine.

Figure 3-3 The offer strategy: A full-page advertisement in *Poolife*, a consumer magazine. While this format is not typical of a direct-response ad, it *is* response advertising in that it contains the two essentials which distinguish direct marketing from general advertising: a specific-benefits offer and a call to action.

The marketing plan covered eight areas: Background; Objectives; Obstacles; Strategy; Tactics; Implementation Schedules; Sales and Profit Projections; and Program Charges.

What Media and or Lists Were Used?

Direct mail was sent to a house list composed of Dealer/Distributor customers and prospects. Advertisements appeared in POOL NEWS, a trade magazine, and POOLIFE, a consumer publication.

What were the demographics and/or psychographics of your market?

Many of the pool product dealers are not in the pool business on a year-round basis.

What were dates of mailings, print ads, broadcast, etc.? Indicate quantities mailed, frequency of ads, estimated and/or actual audience reached.

Direct Mail, Print Ads, and Trade Show Handouts	Dates	Quantities Mailed or Handed Out	Frequency	Reach
1. Dealer/Distributor mailing prior to trade show	Oct.16,1978	3042	-	-
2. Full page ad in POOL NEWS prior to trade show	Nov.6, 1978	-	1	10,217
3. Trade show handouts	Nov.15-18,1978	3600	-	-
4. Follow-up telegraf to Dealer/Distributors	Dec. 1978	3042	-	-
5. Direct Mail Package	March 1979	3042	-	-
6. Direct Mail Package	April 1979	3042	-	-
7. Last chance telegraf mailing	June 1979	3042	-	-
8. Full page ad in POOLIFE	June 1979	-	1	700,000
9. Ad mats to Dealers/ Distributors	July 1979	240	-	-

Figure 3-4 The multimedia blitz strategy.

2. **An offer that adds a customer information value to the basic commodity being sold** The dealers said that it takes pool owners 3 days to winterize the pool properly and that they often make mistakes that cause their pools to deteriorate, or cost them money for repair. So the cornerstone of the October to April direct-response program is a small booklet entitled *How to Winterize Your Pool* (see Figure 3-3). It gives complete and truly useful step-by-step information to pool owners.
3. **Use of integrated multimedia to dramatize the first two items** Direct mail, print ads, and trade shows (see Figure 3-4).

PHASE 5: TACTICS: DESIGNING THE LEVERS

Tactics are as natural and integral to a marketing plan as children are to a family. No strategic marketing plan can be considered complete without them since no true assessment of the resources called for by the plan can be made without them.

Plan tactics are the written parameter specifications that define the work projects needed to implement strategic plans and guide the people who actually will do the tactics during the upcoming marketing year. It is important that these parameter specifications control the work to be done without restricting the creativity of those who actually will perform the work.

	Plan Tactics	Operational Tactics
Timing	During planning process	During marketing year
What is Produced	Written document specifying project parameters	The "actual" direct mail package, ad, telephone call, TV spot, focus group research, computer software, etc.
Results	Line projects	Orders, dollars, and customers

This part of your written plan spells out exactly what projects will be worked on in the coming year, when they will start and finish, who will do each, approximately what they will cost, and how each project relates to all others called for by the plan. Tactics include but are not necessarily limited to the following:

Solicitation packaging for all media: Direct mail, magazine and newspaper ROP and insert ads, telephone scripts, TV and radio ads, collateral, and multimedia combination

- Concept and themes
- Copy platforms or story boards
- Graphic approach
- Component specifications

Table 3-3 shows how specific this effort can be.

Media selections for all programs, both test and controls, in all media to be utilized

- Lists and specifications
- Magazines and newspapers
- Telephone, incoming and outgoing
- TV and radio
- Collateral outlets
- Support media such as co-ops, stuffers, and syndication

Research projects and test structures

- Focus group
- Intercept personal
- Direct mail and telephone
- Test cell specifications
- Timing and rollout parameters

Fulfillment, customer service, and response tracking specifications

Schedules, quality control procedures, and costs for all projects

Remember, the planning process must go far enough into detail that there is absolutely no doubt in the minds of those who will implement the projects as to what is to be done and what results are expected from their efforts.

TABLE 3-3 Tactics: Parameter Specifications for Direct Mail Series Traffic Building

Category Number	Category	Basic Appeal Category	Mailing 1			Mailing 2			
			Format	Copy Approach	Pieces Included	Format	Copy Approach	Pieces Included	Timing
1	Homeowners in right geographic area, segmented by income; Estimated recipients—3000	Have advantage of city life and easy-care apartment while staying in the North Shore area where your friends and ties are	Superelegant invitation, engraved, sealing was commemorative stamp, etc.	1. Elegance of building 2. Location of building in their preferred area	1. Envelope 2. 1-page letter 3. Invitation 4. RSVP card 5. RSVP envelope 6. Comm. stamp (2) 7. Sealing wax	Testimonial from present resident of building	"These are the reasons I like living at Ferncroft Tower"	1. Envelope 2. Brief small note from Ferncroft manager 3. Letter from resident 4. Reply card 5. BRE 6. Comm. stamp (2)	2 weeks after mailing 1 to this category
2	Country club members in right area; Estimated recipients—1000	A golf course right at your door plus all the appeals for category 1	Same as category 1	1 and 2; Same for category 1 plus 3; golf course at your door	Same as for category 1 but with different letter	Same as for category 1	Same as for category 1	Same as for category 1	Same as for category 1
3	Residents of expensive Boston apartments or condominiums; Estimated recipients—5000	Fears about city living versus security of Ferncroft Tower	Very nice; high quality, but not as elegant and formal as for categories 1 and 2	1. Play on fears of city living 2. Ferncroft security 3. Proximity to city with advantages of country 4. Lower car insurance 5. Desirability of building itself	1. Envelope 2. 3-page letter 3. Appointment reservation card 4. Small card with map and directions 5. BRE 6. Comm. stamp (2)	Very nice, high-quality, similar to first mailing to this category	Position Ferncroft geographically, not so far from city, near to beaches, resort areas, etc.; use time frame comparisons	1. Envelope 2. 2-page letter 3. Small flyer with driving times and map and direction 4. Appointment reservation card 5. BRE 6. Comm. stamp (2)	2 weeks after mailing 1 to this category

PHASE 6: FREEZING THE DESIGN

Now that you have completed the tactical elements of the marketing plan, six more steps are required before you "freeze" the plan for presentation to management for approval and funding:

1. Predictive yield analysis
2. Writing the plan
3. Devil's advocacy
4. Final coregroup consensus
5. Implementation criteria
6. Formatting the presentation

Predictive Yield Analysis

This is the moment of truth in the planning process, the point at which you pull together all your cost factors, compare them with reasonable forecasts of response, and then relate those to your calculations on Breakeven, CTOP, and life cycle value. Use your own previous response rates, recision data, and attrition curves if they are applicable. If they are not, search out industry statistics and apply them conservatively.

It is possible these calculations will send you back to the drawing board if the coregroup judges the amount of resources called for to be prohibitive in terms of risk-gain probabilities. As agonizing as this is when it occurs, it is less agonizing than failure after implementation, and much less costly.

Two examples of predictive yield analysis follow. Table 3-4 details acquisition year exposure and gain levels, and Table 3-5 displays life cycle gain potentials.

Writing the Plan

The entire plan, including documentation, must be committed to written form. The sequence of information is exactly the sequence in which the planning process took place:

Background summary
Objectives
Obstacles and advantages
Strategy
Tactics
Yield analysis
Implementation criteria

While each coregroup specialist should provide factual and rationale input at the plan manager's request, they also may be asked to contribute copy. If so, it is still the plan manager's responsibility for final editing that ensures that the written plan will reflect the decisions made by the coregroup consensus during the plan development process.

TABLE 3-4 Dealer/Distributor Prospect Breakeven and Acquisition Year Profit Potentials*

	Response Rate			
	0.5%	1%	1.5%	2.0%
Number of new customers	21	41	62	82
Gross dollars	$136,500	$266,500	$403,000	$533,000
25% margin	$34,125	$66,625	$100,750	$133,250
Promotion cost	$47,932	$47,932	$47,932	$47,932
Booklet cost	$1,386	$2,706	$4,092	$5,412
Net profit	$15,193	$15,987	$48,726	$79,906

Assumptions

Cost of solicitation	$11.69
Average annual order	$6500.00
Margin per customer	$1625.00
Cost of winterizing booklets per prospect buyer (500 per buyer at 13¢ per booklet)	$66.00
Net profit	$1559.00
Breakeven response rate	0.74%
Number of customers acquired based on universe of 4100 prospects	30

* At four different rates of response.

TABLE 3-5 Potential Sales Dollars To Be Generated from New Customers* over 6 Years

	Year 1	Year 2	Year 3	Year 4	Year 5	Year 6	Six-Year Total
Percentage of new customers retained	100%	75%	67.5%	61%	55%	50%	
Number of new customers retained	41	31	28	25	23	21	
Average annual gross revenue for customer	$10,000	$10,000	$10,000	$10,000	$10,000	$10,000	
Gross sales dollars	$410,000	$310,000	$280,000	$250,000	$230,000	$210,000	*$1,690,000*
Gross contribution	$102,500	$77,500	$70,000	$62,500	$57,500	$52,500	*$422,500*

Assumptions

1. New customer quantity based on a 1-percent response rate at a $10,000 annual revenue level from prospect program
2. Annual revenue for customer life cycle set at $10,000, with no upgrading considered
3. 25/10 attrition curve applied
4. Six-year life cycle (per client input)
5. Cost of additional solicitations not included
6. Gross profit based on prototype 25-percent gross margin

* Acquired from prospect program.

Devil's Advocacy

When the written plan is distributed to coregroup members before the final adversary review meeting, give it also to a devil's advocate who previously has not been part of the planning process in any way and include that person or group in the final coregroup review meeting.

Final Coregroup Consensus

The ground rules for adversary analysis and consensus approval also apply to this last meeting before presentation to management. The "we already decided that" mentality must not be allowed to govern this session, and so it is important that the devil's advocate participate as a forceful critic.

Implementation Criteria

Clearly, the line personnel who actually will implement the plan's projects must have some flexibility when addressing real-world problems that cannot be foreseen in any planning process. However, the plan's essential specifications cannot be changed arbitrarily without sacrificing the value and probably the intended performance of the projects undertaken. I recommend that you use the adversary system throughout implementation during your operational year. Any line personnel who interpret plan specifications differently—creative, graphics, and data processing, for example—must attempt to reach consensus on the best way to proceed. If they cannot reach consensus after a reasonable amount of time has been spent in discussion, the matter is taken to the next logical superior with oversight responsibility. All sides of the question at hand are presented with pros and cons, and then a decision is made. If the manager hearing the case is unable to decide, it goes up the line; in certain instances, the coregroup itself may have to be reconvened. Generally speaking,

Essential changes such as offer, creative platform, media, price, product, etc., require coregroup analysis and approval.

Important changes such as list substitutes, test structures, etc., require marketing director approval.

Incidental changes such as paper stock, copywriter switches, etc., require only appropriate department head approval.

The criteria and guidelines you use should be spelled out in writing as part of the written plan itself, because after the plan has been approved, all departments will use their copy of the plan's rationale and specifications in much the same way that a building contractor uses architectural plans and specifications to erect a building.

Formatting the Presentation

The plan in final written form should be distributed to top managers for review and study at least 1 week before the formal presentation for approval. However, the sequence of the plan summary presented at that meeting should be different from the sequence in which the plan was written.

Financial analysis summary
Objectives
Obstacles and advantages
Strategy
Summary of tactics

As these summary areas are presented and discussed, the coregroup's knowledge, and the written plan itself (plus all documentation which should be available at the approval meeting sessions) can and should be used to respond to specific questions that arise, clarify positions taken, and explain decisions.

STRATEGIC MANAGEMENT: AN ESSENTIAL

There are, after all is said and done, only three types of direct marketing companies: those which really don't plan at all, those which plan and don't act, and those which plan and then turn the plan into action. You can tell which is which after observing any company for a few days. The first type is always wondering what happened, the second watches what is happening, and the third is making things happen.

Working with the third kind of company is electrifying. The shared belief that the company can largely create its own future is almost tangible. In fact, that attitude is one of the four characteristics this type of direct marketing enterprise almost always exhibits. Employees from top to bottom exude an entrepreneurial drive which does make things happen. Communications between peers is open at all times (there is no closet mentality), and the recognition of the value of teamwork as the major force in successfully completing preplanned tasks predominates.

How does this kind of direct marketing company come into being? Not surprisingly, it must start at the top with the chief executive officer (CEO) and the layer of management reporting directly to the CEO. They set the tone and then involve operating management in the strategic decision-making process. This in turn increases middle management's understanding and enthusiasm, which in turn transmits itself to those working for the middle managers. When people realize why they are doing what they are doing, the "what" begins to gain substantial ground. Soon business touchdowns occur, and the satisfaction of knowing that you have helped achieve the score develops a life of its own within the organization. Recognition of "planning the game and playing the plan" takes hold quickly, and the momentum soon becomes beautiful to behold. In companies in which incentive compensation and additional responsibility are linked to plan performance, strategic management becomes the norm rather than the exception. And with strategic management comes stable yet extraordinary growth.

chapter 4

ECONOMICS OF DIRECT MARKETING

David D. Shepard

President
David Shepard Associates, Inc.
Dix Hills, N.Y.

This chapter will develop the economic framework within which direct marketing businesses operate. Seven important examples of major direct marketing businesses will be examined. The initial presentation will be qualitative, focusing on the economic trade-offs that characterize the decision-making process within each type of business. The latter part of the chapter will be devoted to a quantitative analysis of the economic issues that are at the center of all direct marketing decisions.

Solo Promotions

The simplest form of direct marketing is the solo, or single-shot, promotion. In this situation, the marketer must design, produce, and mail promotion pieces to enough potential buyers to generate a response that will cover the cost of the promotion and yield an acceptable level of profit.

Single-shot promotions are relatively simple, but the seller must answer many questions in the course of the promotion process. Should the promotion piece be a traditional direct-response "full mailing package" including an outer envelope, letter, brochure, business reply card, and return envelope? Or should the seller use a less expensive mailing piece? If the traditional full mailing package is used, should the letter be two pages or four pages, and should the flier be black and white or in full color? Should the seller offer credit or require cash with the order? Should credit cards be used? Should the seller offer an inexpensive premium to hype sales or as a reward for cash with order? Should the mailing use third class postage or would the extra costs of first class postage somehow result in extra sales and thereby pay for itself? Should the outer envelope contain copy and an illustration of the product or just inviting copy or no copy at all?

The list of legitimate questions that can be raised about even the simplest form of direct marketing is extensive, and answers to these questions will affect the economics of the promotion. Essentially, all of these questions have to do with economic trade-offs. Does it pay to spend more on the promotion piece, to offer a premium, to offer credit, to mail first class, etc.? The questions apply to all types of direct-response businesses and will be raised again and again throughout this chapter.

Multistep Promotions Leading to a Direct Sale

Frequently it is possible to identify the potential market for a product in terms of the circulation of one or more magazines while at the same time it is not profitable to sell the product "off the page" in those magazines regardless of the unit of space employed. In these situations, the price of the product is usually high, and closing the sale requires the power of a more expensive direct mail package with full-color illustrations and sufficient copy to define all the features and benefits of the product. In these instances, magazine space often is used to generate leads or inquiries, which are followed up by one or a series of direct mail pieces. In some cases, the initial leads are followed up by phone. Products sold in this fashion include encyclopedias, expensive exercise equipment, financial services, and many business-to-business services. The "bingo cards" found in trade magazines and airline magazines are prime examples of this kind of direct-response marketing.

The economics of this kind of multistep marketing differs from the economics of single-shot promotions in that the total costs of both the initial effort and the costs of all of the follow-up efforts must be tracked carefully and balanced against the sales and gross margin resulting from the total effort.

Catalog Sales. A catalog may be thought of as a very expensive solo mailing selling anywhere from a few dozen to hundreds or even thousands of products. It is also possible, as in the case of the solo mailing, to compare the total gross margin resulting from a catalog mailing with the total costs of the mailing, but the analogy between a catalog business and a business based on solo mailings can not be taken much further.

The success of a catalog business is related directly to a catalog manager's ability to efficiently develop and manage a company's past-buyers list, or "house list" as it is referred to in the industry. Catalogs are generally too expensive to be mailed exclusively to outside rented lists. In very general terms, the response of an outside rented list to a catalog mailing may range anywhere from 0.5 percent to 2 or 3 percent, depending on the quality of the rented names and their predisposition to the products being offered in the catalog. By way of comparison, the response of past buyers to another catalog offering may range from 5 to 20 percent or even higher.

Naturally, a new catalog company cannot open its doors with a list of past buyers. However, catalog operators have developed a number of techniques for developing house lists. One technique is to develop a relatively inexpensive "prospecting" catalog that can be mailed to names that have been rented from "outside" list owners. Respondents to these prospect mailings then are entered on the catalog company's prospect list. Of course, it is possible to mail a company's complete catalog to an outside rented list, and the limiting or deciding factor in this decision often is the catalog company's willingness and ability to sustain a large negative cash position while building its house file. Large companies wishing to enter the direct marketing business often are in a position to finance this development period, provided that they are convinced the eventual returns will justify the initial cash investment.

Smaller entrepreneurs generally attempt to exhaust all the other more conservative ways of building prospecting lists that can be converted eventually into buyers' lists. Other techniques for building house lists include advertising the catalog free or for a token price in targeted-space media, using the same space to sell the most popular items in the catalog, and sending out solo mailings of individual popular products to names on rented lists. In general, regardless of the techniques used, it is common for a catalog operation to be in a net loss position with regard to new names added to the house list. As the mix between new names that result from cold prospect mailings and space advertising and catalog buyer names changes in favor of the buyers, the profitability of the catalog operation will increase.

Not only must the catalog manager worry about adding new names to the house list, equal concern must be given to the problem of removing names from the file of past buyers who are no longer buying and therefore should not be mailed additional catalogs. Of course, it is not possible to be absolutely sure who will or will not respond to future mailings. Therefore, catalog managers must use statistical probability techniques based primarily on data from past performance to determine which buyers should be mailed to again, how often they should be mailed to, and when they should be dropped from the active mailing list. The ability of a catalog manager to perform this task is related directly to the information retained on the customer file with regard to past buying habits and the ability of the catalog company to manipulate this information so that the necessary statistical analyses can be performed.

While it is certainly true that acquiring a unique product and making effective presentations are of paramount concern to the health of a catalog operation, equal attention must be given to the management of the buyers' list.

Finally, no discussion of the catalog business would be complete without mention of the extraordinary problems of inventory control and fulfillment that are inherent in the catalog business. Success in mail order requires almost immediate fulfillment of orders as they are received, and with high interest rates, the costs of carrying excess inventory can be as disastrous as the cost of being out of stock. Again, the ability of the catalog manager to perform advanced statistical analyses comes into play. Not only must catalog managers be able to forecast the expected level of overall response to a catalog mailing, they must be able to forecast the mix of products purchased so as to be in a position to manage inventories correctly.

Continuity Programs. Continuity programs represent an important segment of the direct marketing business. The Time-Life book series, the Betty Crocker

Cooking Card program, and the books and collectibles sold by the Franklin Mint are prime examples of products that are marketed this way.

The management of a continuity operation is in many ways much less complicated than the management of a catalog operation. Given the product, such as a series of books, cards, or coins or any other item that fits neatly into the continuity formula of periodic delivery of a product or service against periodic payments from the customer, the marketing problem is relatively straightforward.

New members or subscribers are acquired through the traditional direct marketing channels: direct mail, magazine advertisements, newspaper preprints, broadcast (generally spot TV), and package inserts. In most cases, the first item in the continuity program is offered free or at a substantial discount. The subscriber then receives periodic shipments of the remaining items in the program until all the items have been shipped or until the subscriber notifies the seller to stop shipping the product.

From the subscriber's point of view, continuity programs are simple and easy to understand. From the seller's viewpoint, a number of key questions must be answered before the program can become operational. How should the items in the series be priced? Should the items be priced relatively high and therefore targeted against the upper end of the potential market, or should a lower-price–higher-volume strategy be attempted? How generous should the initial offer be? Should the first item in the series be given away free or for $1 or at no discount at all? Should the interval between shipments be 4 weeks, 6 weeks, or 8 weeks? How much open credit should be granted? Does it make sense to ship the third item in a series if payment has not been received for the first item? How does the credit decision depend on the interval between shipments? Should the program be open-ended with no limit on the number of items in the series, or should the series be limited to a fixed number of items, and if so, what is that number?

Clearly, the answers to these questions will have an important impact on the economics of the continuity program. Again we are faced with a question of trade-offs. The more generous the offer and credit policy, the larger the program in terms of subscribers and sales volume. But what will the effect on returns, bad debts, and profits be?

Finally, let us briefly discuss the concept of a continuity load-up. The continuity programs we have described rely on periodic shipment of a product until cancellation or completion of the program. In continuity load-ups, the subscriber is informed that after he or she receives three or four single shipments, the balance of the items in the program will be shipped in a single load-up shipment.

The load-up plan is an effective device for increasing the total number of items shipped to the average subscriber, but again there are economic trade-offs to consider. Federal trade regulations require that the load-up provision be defined clearly in all promotional messages, and this can reduce the total number of respondents to any given promotion. Second, most load-up programs follow a policy of reminding subscribers that the load-up shipment is about to be mailed unless the subscriber notifies the company not to proceed with the shipment and to cancel membership in the program. This reminder will cause some subscribers to cancel their membership faster than they might have done in an open-ended continuity program. Finally, there is the problem of collections. A load-up program is based on the assumption that after the subscriber receives the full load-up shipment, he or she will pay for the shipment on a monthly or bimonthly basis. Of course, some percentage of the load-up shipment will not be paid for and eventually will have to be written off as a bad debt.

On balance, only testing the load-up concept against the open-ended, or "till forbid," continuity plan will determine which plan is best for any given product.

Negative Option Clubs. Negative option clubs are efficient vehicles for the distribution of books and records. The Book-of-the-Month Club and the Columbia Record Club are well-known examples of this type of direct marketing business. There are some similarities between continuity operations and negative option clubs. Both vehicles often are used as a means of distributing books, and both use the same media and direct marketing techniques for acquiring new members. But after the new member is acquired, the similarity from an operations or fulfillment point of view ends.

Negative option clubs constantly must ask their subscribers whether they wish to receive the coming selection, receive an alternative selection, or receive no product at all from the current catalog offering. If the member fails to respond, the "shipment of the month" is sent automatically. The fulfillment systems needed to handle a negative option club are much more complicated than those needed for a continuity program. In addition, the Federal Trade Commission has placed stringent restrictions on negative option clubs to ensure that members have sufficient time to return the negative option card should they wish not to receive the automatic shipment of the month.

Despite the differences in operating characteristics between negative option clubs and continuity programs, the economics of both types of businesses are remarkably similar. In both operations, new members are always acquired at a loss. The $1.00 or even the $4.95 that often is charged for the introductory shipment (the first book in a continuity series or the four books chosen from a book club's lead list) is never enough to cover the costs of promotion plus the cost of the introductory shipment. Therefore, continuity programs and negative option clubs are always in an investment position. The return on investment stems from future sales to the continuity subscriber or club member. In the case of continuity programs, future sales are simply a function of the price of the items in the program and the number of periods a subscriber chooses to stay in the program. In a negative option club, the member need not buy from every catalog offering, and sales therefore are more dependent on the quality of the merchandise offered and the effectiveness of the ongoing marketing effort. In both continuity and negative option, the final measure of profitability is the relationship between the cost of acquiring new members and the sales and payments those members yield over their economic life in the club or program. Much of the remainder of this chapter will be devoted to the techniques used to forecast and measure these statistics.

Newsletters. Newsletters can be very profitable vehicles for distributing information to highly targeted markets. The most profitable newsletters often are aimed at small professional or business markets. Newsletters that are editorially able to provide critically needed information to a business audience that has both the need to know and the ability to pay (often referred to as "company money") have the greatest chance for success. This does not mean that more broadly based, lower-priced mass-market newsletters can't be profitable, as witnessed by the continuing success of the *Kiplinger Washington Newsletter*.

The economics of newsletters centers on four key variables: pricing, new order acquisition, conversion or pay rates, and renewal rates. Pricing is the most controllable of all the variables and perhaps the most important. Newsletters targeted at business markets can be priced anywhere from $9.95 to $495.00. Generally, it is not difficult to determine whether the value of the information is worth closer to $10 than to $500, but it is often next to impossible to tell without testing whether a given newsletter should be priced at $37, $49, or even $97.

Clearly, pricing can make an enormous difference in profitability. Price testing is therefore almost always a necessity when one starts out in the newsletter business, particularly if the newsletter has little or no perceived competition.

Newsletters are almost always marketed solely by direct mail; therefore, it is critical that before starting out in the newsletter business, the publisher be assured of continued access to the target market. If access to the market depends on the cooperation of a trade association, provisions should be made with the association to guarantee a continuous supply of names.

Properly priced newsletters can be successful with a relatively small response to initial new subscriber promotions. Profits can be achieved with initial response rates as low as five to ten orders per thousand names mailed, because production costs are usually low in relation to price and because renewal rates are usually high.

However, before a newsletter can be considered a proven success, it must demonstrate the merits of the editorial material. The first test of the quality of the editorial material is the "pay rate" on new orders. Most newsletter promotions allow for payment (and cancellation) after one or more issues have been sampled by the reader. A high pay rate (over 70 percent) will be indicative of a high future renewal rate. Products which demonstrate a high cancellation rate should not count on a high renewal rate to ensure the profits of the newsletter venture.

Magazines. Magazines are, of course, much like newsletters in that they depend on direct mail for much of their new subscriber marketing and are highly sensitive to fluctuations in pay rates and renewal rates. The obvious differences between newsletters and magazines are that magazines are much more costly to produce and have two additional revenue streams: newsstand sales and advertising revenues. But even in the subscription circulation area, where one finds the greatest similarity to newsletters, there are important differences.

Magazine subscriptions are sold in many more ways than newsletter subscriptions. There are door-to-door sales, telephone sales, and sweepstakes-sold subscriptions from companies such as Publishers Clearing House. In addition, a magazine company's direct mail efforts may be dependent on preview offers or premium offers to an extent not often found in newsletter circulation. Each of these promotional channels and devices runs the risk of producing subscriptions with relatively low pay and renewal rates. Therefore, the evaluation and management of a magazine's circulation list is considerably more complicated and subject to greater risk than the evaluation and management of a newsletter.

FRONT-END PERFORMANCE

"Front-end performance" and "front-end analysis" are terms used by direct marketers to describe the process of measuring the initial costs of and response to a direct marketing promotion. The economic analysis of the process that takes place after an initial response is received is referred to as back-end analysis or back-end performance.

Measuring Direct Marketing Promotion Expense

The first step in the process of measuring front-end performance is the measurement of the total expense attributable to a promotion. The only difficulty associated with this task is deciding which expenses will be included in the analysis and which expenses, if any, will be excluded.

Later we shall see how direct marketers generally approach this problem, but for now let's assume we agree that it costs exactly $16,250 to mail 50,000 pieces of direct mail. The first statistic to be calculated is cost per thousand pieces mailed, more simply referred to as cost per thousand (CPM).

$$\text{CPM} = \frac{\text{total promotion expense}}{\text{number of pieces mailed}} \times 1000$$

In our example

$$\text{CPM} = \frac{\$16{,}250}{50{,}000} \times 1000$$

$$\text{CPM} = \$325$$

The CPM concept applies to space advertising as well as to direct mail. In space advertising, CPM is calculated by dividing total media costs plus the costs of printing any special insert material by the circulation of the magazine.

$$\text{Space CPM} = \frac{\text{media costs} + \text{insert costs}}{\text{circulation}} \times 1000$$

In both direct mail and space advertising, the question always arises whether the fixed creative fees paid to an agency or a freelancer and the fixed mechanical preparation and art expenses should be included in the calculation of CPM. Opinion is divided on this subject. Some direct-response marketers insist on including all costs in the calculation of CPM to ensure that their profitability analyses will include consideration of all costs associated with the promotion. Other direct marketers argue that creative material and mechanicals are intended for use in multiple promotions. These marketers either allocate a portion of the fixed creative expenses to each use of the material or maintain separate budgets and controls for creative expenses; they do not include consideration of fixed nonrecurring costs in the analysis of promotion results. This latter approach, which is more oriented to decision making, is favored by most large mailers who are concerned more with the decision to remail a promotion or repeat a space insertion than with the recording of historical costs. For decision-making purposes, the direct marketer wants to know the incremental costs of repeating a promotion that has been used in the past, regardless of such costs.

Calculating CPM for Different Direct-Response Media

Direct Mail. There are three major types of direct mail promotion pieces, excluding catalogs, that are used by direct marketers to generate new orders or new leads: the full-package solo mailing, the less expensive self-mailer, and the insert piece.

Table 4-1 shows the components of a standard direct mail package, including a four-page letter and color brochure. The CPM of the full package is shown at two mailing quantities: 50,000 and 250,000. Printing costs per thousand are shown to vary with the quantity printed as the fixed printing preparation expenses (which must be incurred at each print run) are amortized over the number of pieces to be mailed. These fixed printing preparation expenses should not be confused with creative fees and mechanical costs, which are truly one-time costs and do not vary with the quantity mailed or the number of print runs.

The example shown in Table 4-1 is typical of a consumer mailing of the kind used by book and record clubs, continuity programs, and magazines. In these situations, a color brochure generally is required to display the product fully, and third class postage almost always is employed.

On the other end of the direct-response spectrum, a high-priced newsletter aimed at top corporate management may not use a full color brochure but may be mailed first class to create a more businesslike impression in order to get past the secretary. In this case, the cost of the promotion will be reduced because the flier has been removed but increased because of the use of first class postage.

Therefore, there is no hard and fast rule to determine the correct cost of a direct mail promotion. Costs are a function of the components of the mailing

TABLE 4-1 Calculating CPM for a Typical Direct Mail Promotion at Two Mailing Quantities

	50,000	250,000
Outer envelope	$28	$20
Four-page letter	36	26
Four color brochure	84	52
Reply card	21	14
Return envelope	21	16
Total printing cost	190	128
Outside list rental	45	45
Letter shop	23	20
Merge-purge	6	6
Postage	109	109
Total CPM	$373	$308

Source: Direct Mail Marketing Association, October 1982, *1983 Fact Book*.

package. Direct mail package costs can vary from $200 to $500 per thousand. The real question is what mailing package will be most profitable for the product or service being offered.

Self-Mailers. One sure way to reduce mailing costs is to use a self-mailer, which is a promotion piece that does not contain multiple loose components. The most common format is the two- or three-panel 8½ by 11 card stock format. A self-mailer eliminates the need for an outer envelope, reduces letter shop expense, and combines the selling message of the letter and the brochure in one format. There is also no need for a separate business reply card and business reply envelope. A portion of the self-mailer is a perforated business reply card, and the respondent is instructed to tear off this card and return it to the mailer. With the use of a self-mailer, promotion costs can be reduced significantly, but again the question arises as to what will happen to response. Will the self-mailer turn out to be more or less profitable than a full mailing package? As usual in direct response, only testing can provide the answer.

Inserts or Enclosures. Another very inexpensive but cost-effective mailing format is the insert piece or enclosure promotion. An insert or enclosure is any promotion piece that is mailed at no additional postage expense inside an invoice, statement, merchandise shipment, or other primary mailing piece. Insert pieces that are mailed along with first class mailings such as bills or statements must be small so that they do not increase postage expense. Enclosures in third class mailings and merchandise shipments are not weight-restricted.

In general, insert pieces pull a much lower response than direct mail packages or self-mailers. But because of the lower cost, which can be as low as $20 per thousand, response does not have to be very great in order to generate a profit.

Space Advertising. The cost per thousand for space advertising is considerably lower than the CPM for direct mail. A typical magazine page may cost from $5 to $75 per thousand circulation, as compared with direct mail, which ranges between $200 and $500 per thousand pieces mailed. Of course, the response to a space advertisement will be less than the response to a direct mail promotion.

In direct mail, a 3 percent response to a promotion costing $300 per thousand will result in a cost per response of $10 and is not atypical. In space advertising, a $10 cost per response is likely to be the result of a response rate of 0.1 percent in a medium with a CPM of $10.

As small as these numbers seem, they nevertheless result in very significant absolute numbers. For example, consider a mass-market magazine with a circulation of 3 million. The cost of a single black and white page is likely to be around $18,000, for a CPM of $6. If an ad in that magazine pulls at a rate of just 0.05 percent, or a rate of 0.5 orders per thousand circulation, the ad will generate 1500 responses at an average cost of $12 per response. See Table 4-2.

The actual CPM for an ad in any magazine will vary greatly, depending on a number of factors. For example, cover positions cost more than inside-the-book positions, color costs more than black and white, advertising in the direct mail section frequently costs less than advertising in the general editorial section, and discounts are available for multiple usage. Regional editions may be purchased, generally increasing the CPM but lowering the total dollar expenditure, and so

TABLE 4-2 Calculating Front-End Space Results

Total circulation	3,000,000
Cost per single black and white page	$18,000
Total response	1,500
CPM = (18,000/3000)	$6
Percent response:	
(1500/3 million) × 100	0.05%
Orders per thousand circulation (OPM):	
(1500/3000)	0.5
Cost per response (CPR):	
CPM/OPM = $6.00/0.50	$12

on. The point is that buying space advertising is not simply a matter of placing an ad in a magazine. As always, the key decision is whether the more expensive ad format will result in a significantly greater response and increased profitability or, conversely, whether the less expensive format will result in fewer responses and lower profits.

Broadcast. Broadcast is becoming an increasingly important direct-response vehicle, and the emergence of cable TV with its highly targeted audiences will increase the significance of this medium.

TV broadcast advertising generally is purchased in one of two ways. In the first instance, an advertiser will purchase a certain amount of time from a local station or national network at an agreed on price. The exact times the commercial is to be aired and the number of spots or showings are agreed to in advance. This procedure is similar to placing an ad in a magazine. Before the running of the ad or the showing of the commercial, the total investment in the medium is known. The cost per response will depend on the number of responses in the form of telephone calls to the local station or to an 800 number or on the number of responses received in the mail.

The second method of purchase is per inquiry (PI). Very often a broadcast station will agree with an advertiser to run a given commercial at times chosen by the station. In exchange for this air time, the advertiser will pay the station a fixed amount based on the number of responses received. This method of payment also is referred to as PO (per order). In these situations, the initial response usually is directed to the local station and sent from there to the advertiser. PI or PO arrangements also are frequently available in space advertising.

Telephone. The telephone is a very important direct-response device, particularly for magazine solicitations offering a one-issue trial examination offer. The phone also is used with great success in business-to-business direct response, in which the goal is to generate a lead or qualify a lead generated from a space ad or a direct mail offer.

Independent telephone operations currently sell their services at rates of approximately $25 to $35 per hour. Within this time period, a qualified phone operator can make between six and twenty contacts. The contact rate will vary depending on the time of day, the day of the week, and whether the call is to a consumer at home or to a business executive or professional at the place of work. Because of its ability to generate low-cost trial subscriptions or leads, the telephone must be used with care.

A low conversion rate can transform a very low cost per lead into a very high cost per order.

Measuring Response

One-Step Promotions. The response to a direct mail promotion is expressed as a percentage of the quantity mailed or stated in terms of the number of responses per thousand pieces mailed (RPM). If the response is an order, the term "orders per thousand" (OPM) is used.

$$\text{Percentage response} = \frac{\text{total responses} \times 100}{\text{quantity mailed}}$$

$$\text{RPM} = \frac{\text{total responses}}{\text{quantity mailed/1000}}$$

$$\text{OPM} = \frac{\text{total orders}}{\text{quantity mailed/1000}}$$

Because the response to a direct mail promotion often is less than 1 percent, many direct marketers prefer to use the RPM or OPM terminology rather than express results in terms of a fraction of a percent. This is particularly true with regard to space advertising, in which a response of one order per thousand or even less is not uncommon.

Two-Step Promotions. Not all direct-response promotions are one-step promotions. Often the initial response to a direct-response promotion is only the first step in a two-step or even a multistep promotion process. A magazine promoted by direct mail, using an offer that allows the potential subscriber to cancel after previewing one issue, is an example of a two-step promotion.

Consider a direct mail promotion of a magazine through a preview offer. Assume that 500,000 pieces are mailed and that 12,500 responses are received. The initial RPM is equal to

$$\text{RPM} = \frac{12{,}500}{500{,}000/1{,}000}$$

$$\text{RPM} = 25$$

If only 40 percent of the respondents to the preview offer convert to paid subscriptions, the final paid orders per thousand pieces mailed will be equal to

$$\text{OPM} = 25 \text{ RPM} \times 40\%$$
$$\text{OPM} = 10$$

Calculating Cost per Response

One-Step Promotions. In a one-step promotion, the cost per response can be calculated by dividing the total number of responses into the total cost of the promotion. A quicker way that is preferred by many direct marketers is to divide the cost per thousand of the promotion by the number of responses per thousand to arrive at the cost per response (CPR):

$$\text{CPR} = \frac{\text{CPM}}{\text{OPM}}$$

Referring back to our magazine example, assume that the cost of the mailing was \$300 per thousand. The initial cost per response would be

$$\text{CPR} = \frac{\$300}{25} = \$12$$

Two-Step Promotions. In two-step promotions, the final cost per order is equal to at least the initial cost per response divided by the conversion rate. In our magazine example, the cost per response was \$12 and the conversion rate was 40 percent. Therefore, the minimum cost per order is equal to

$$\text{Final CPO} = \frac{\text{initial CPR}}{\text{conversion rate}}$$

$$\text{CPO} = \frac{\$12}{0.40} = \$30$$

However, dividing the initial cost per response by the conversion rate understates the total cost of acquiring a new magazine subscriber.

Assume that in the process of converting preview subscribers into paid subscribers, those potential subscribers who eventually will cancel will receive three issues of the magazine and five invoices. Let's also assume that those who decide to subscribe will receive an average of three invoices before paying. The costs of this conversion process can be added legitimately to the cost of acquiring the average paid subscription.

The calculations would be as follows. If the cost of one issue of the magazine on an incremental basis is \$0.60 and the cost of one invoice including first class postage, computer expense, and printing is \$0.50, the amount spent on each eventual nonsubscriber or "cancel" is equal to

3 issues × \$0.60 per issue	= \$1.80
+ 5 invoices × \$0.50 per invoice	= \$2.50
Total cost per cancel	= \$4.30

Since only 40 percent of the initial respondents will subscribe, the cost of attempting to convert the eventual cancels or nonsubscribers must be allocated over those who do subscribe. The equation for this calculation is as follows:

$$\text{Conversion expense per subscriber because of cancellations} = \frac{\text{cost per cancel} \times (1 - \text{pay rate})}{\text{pay rate}}$$

$$\text{Conversion expense per subscriber} = \frac{\$4.30 \times (1 - 0.40)}{0.40}$$

$$\text{Conversion expense per subscriber} = \$6.45$$

In addition, the cost of billing the respondents who eventually will pay will be equal to 3 × \$0.50, or \$1.50. Therefore, the total conversion expense is equal to \$6.45 plus \$1.50, or \$7.95 per paid order.

The total cost per new subscriber including both promotion expense and conversion expense is equal to the total new subscriber acquisition expense:

Promotion expense	+	conversion expense	=	total acquisition expense
\$30.00	+	\$7.95	=	\$37.95

The lesson to be remembered from this example is that the initial CPR may be only a small part of the total cost per final order in a multistep promotion. The costs of converting initial responses or leads can be particularly expensive when the conversion process requires expensive sales literature or requires a sales call.

TRACKING BACK-END PERFORMANCE

In the last section, we discussed the techniques used to measure the costs of acquiring groups of leads, buyers, or subscribers. In each case, costs were expressed not in terms of the total dollars spent but rather in terms of the amount spent to acquire the average customer from a particular media investment. By defining costs in terms of the average cost per customer, it is possible for us to compare alternative media without regard to their size.

This same approach will be followed in the discussion of back-end performance. In general, back-end performance refers to the purchase behavior of a group of respondents from the time their names are entered on the customer file. More specifically, we shall define back-end performance as the sales, contribution, and profits resulting from a group of respondents acquired from a particular advertising medium.

In order to measure, or "track," back-end performance, it is necessary to maintain a system in which each individual customer is identified as coming from a specific advertising medium: a list, a space insertion, or a broadcast flight. When this is done, it is possible to accumulate the behavior of all customers from the same initial source medium and calculate average sales, contribution, or profits.

For this reason, direct marketing advertisers include a "key code" on every coupon in every space ad and print a key code on the return card or label of every direct mail promotion. The key code identifies the advertising medium and becomes a permanent part of the responding customer's record, along with name, address, and purchase history.

Direct marketers have proved over and over that for a given order, back-end performance will vary significantly from one advertising medium to another. In general, direct marketers have discovered that buyers acquired from direct mail behave better than buyers acquired from space or magazine advertisements and that buyers acquired from direct mail or space will perform better than buyers acquired from broadcast promotions. However, there are wide variations in performance within the same media category. The best customers acquired from space media will perform better than the worst customers acquired from direct mail, and so on.

The critical concept to remember is that back-end performance will vary from medium to medium and that the only way to operate a profitable direct-response business is to be able to track the performance of your customers in terms of their original source group so that the decision to reinvest promotion dollars can be made on the basis of proven performance.

Measuring Back-End Performance for a Single-Shot Mailing

The measurement of back-end performance for a solo, or single-shot, mailing is simply the statement of profit or loss for the promotion. Table 4-3 lists the assumptions that would be typical of a solo mailing of a product with a sales price of $60. The profit and loss statement that follows (Table 4-4) is based on the assumptions defined in Table 4-3.

Clubs and Continuity Programs

In clubs and continuity programs, the statistic that measures back-end performance is the contribution to promotion, overhead, and profit. If this contribution for a group of new orders or starters is greater than the cost of acquiring the starting group, the investment in the starting group can be considered to be at least marginally profitable.

TABLE 4-3 Assumptions for a Single-Shot Promotion

Selling price	$60.00
Shipping and handling charge	$2.50
Return rate (percent of gross sales)	12%
Percentage of returns reusable	75%
Cost of product per unit	$15.00
Order processing:	
Reply postage per gross response	0.20
Order processing and setup per gross response	$1.75
Percentage of gross orders using:	
credit cards	60%
checks	40%
Credit card expense	4%
Percentage of charge orders with bad checks	3%
Shipping and handling per gross response	$2.50
Return processing:	
Return postage per gross response	$1.50
Handling per gross response	$0.50
Refurbishing costs per usable return	$2.00
Premium expense per gross response	$5.00
Promotion CPM	$300
Quantity mailed	100,000
Percentage response of quantity mailed	2%
Overhead factor of net sales	10%

TABLE 4-4 Profit and Loss Statement for a Single-Shot Promotion

	Units	Dollars	Percent
Gross sales	2000	$120,000	
Shipping and handling	2000	5,000	
Total revenue	2000	125,000	113.64
Returns	240	15,000	13.64
Net sales	1760	110,000	100.000
Cost of sales:			
Product			
Net shipments	1760	26,400	24.00
Nonreusable units	60	900	0.82
Order processing			
Reply postage	2000	400	0.36
Setup costs	2000	3,500	3.18
Credit card costs	1200	3,000	2.73
Bad check expense	24	1,500	1.36
Shipping and handling	2000	5,000	4.55
Return processing			
Postage	240	360	0.33
Handling	240	120	0.11
Refurbishing	180	360	0.33
Premium	2000	10,000	9.09
Total cost of sales		51,540	46.85
Operating gross margin		58,460	53.15
Promotion expense		30,000	27.27
Contribution to overhead and profit		28,460	25.87
Overhead allocation		11,000	10.00
Profit		$17,460	15.87

This contribution statistic sometimes is referred to as the order margin, the allowable, or the breakeven. Each term implies a comparison to the cost per order expended to bring the starters into the business.

The contribution statistic excludes consideration of all fixed costs and overhead. Contribution is calculated by subtracting all direct expenses from the net sales of a group of starters and then dividing the result by the number of starters in the group.

In a club or continuity program, sales accumulate over the economic life of the starting group, and that life often can extend over a number of years. Therefore, in clubs or programs with an exceptionally long member life, the contribution from each monthly cycle should be discounted by some amount, generally the seller's cost of capital or opportunity cost, to take the time value of money into consideration.

The ability to forecast final sales and payments from individual starting groups on the basis of early performance data is critical in clubs and continuity programs. In these businesses, as in most direct-response businesses, the key marketing decision is the decision to reinvest in media that already have been tested. Because of the long economic life of a club or continuity member, the decision to reinvest must be made on the basis of forecasted behavior. For example, if a new list is mailed in the winter and pulls as well as most other lists used by the club, the marketer may wish to remail the same names or test a larger segment of the list universe in the summer or fall campaign. However, by that time only a few cycles of actual data will be available for analysis. The decision therefore must be made on the basis of expected final contribution per starter. The forecast itself is based on the actual data accumulated to date.

In both clubs and continuity programs, the most important forecast variable is the attrition rate. This is the term used to measure the rate at which members in a club or program either cancel their memberships or are canceled because of failure to pay for previously shipped items.

In negative option clubs, the attrition pattern measures the percentage of original starters eligible to receive the periodic advance announcements which advertise the negative option selection of the cycle and the alternative selections. In addition to having to be able to forecast the attrition pattern, it is also necessary to be able to forecast the acceptance rate of the featured negative option selection and the acceptance of the alternative selections as well as the average price of each category of sale.

Table 4-5 shows a simplified negative option club model which forecasts and accumulates average gross sales per starting member. As was mentioned before, in an actual club operation, the forecast would include separate estimates for the negative option selection and the alternative selections.

According to the model shown in Table 4-5, the average sale per starter will be $48.19. Assuming that direct costs, excluding all promotion and premium costs, are equal to 35 percent of gross sales, the contribution to promotion, overhead, and profit from this group of starters would be $31.32. It is this number minus premium costs which would be compared with promotion costs to determine the profitability of the starting group.

In continuity programs, there are two attrition patterns to be concerned with. The first pattern measures the percentage of starters who initially receive each shipment level at the earliest possible date. This attrition pattern reflects the payment behavior of starters who pay for each shipment on time and continue in the program. The second pattern represents the percentage of original starters who eventually receive each shipment level by the end of the economic life of the starting group. The difference in the two patterns is due to starters who fall behind in their payments and are suspended temporarily from receiving further shipments. As these starters eventually pay, the percentage of starters receiving each shipment level gradually increases.

In order to forecast sales properly it is necessary to be able to forecast both attrition patterns. A forecast using only the first attrition pattern will understate eventual sales. A forecast using just the second pattern will forecast final sales correctly but will not be able to forecast when those sales will occur. Table 4-6 provides an example of a continuity attrition and the growth of the average number of units shipped over time to a group of starters in a continuity program in which one item is shipped per month.

TABLE 4-5 Average Sales Accumulated over Time in a Negative Option Club

	Percent			Sales per Starting Member	
Cycle	Still Active	Buying Product	Average Price	Incre-mental	Cumu-lative
			Actual Data		
1	97	51	10.00	4.95	4.95
2	94	47	10.00	4.42	9.37
3	80	42	10.00	3.36	12.73
4	70	38	10.00	2.66	15.39
5	65	33	10.00	2.15	17.53
			Forecast Data		
6	60	32	10.00	1.92	19.45
7	57	31	10.00	1.77	21.22
8	53	31	10.00	1.64	22.86
9	47	30	10.00	1.41	24.27
10	43	30	10.00	1.29	25.56
11	41	30	10.00	1.23	26.79
12	39	30	10.00	1.17	27.96
13	37	30	10.00	1.11	29.07
14	35	30	10.00	1.06	30.13
15	33	30	10.00	1.00	31.13
16	32	30	10.00	0.95	32.08
17	30	30	10.00	0.91	32.99
18	29	30	10.00	0.86	33.85
19	27	30	10.00	0.82	34.67
20	26	30	10.00	0.78	35.44
21	25	30	10.00	0.74	36.18
22	23	30	10.00	0.70	36.88
23	22	30	10.00	0.67	37.55
24	21	30	10.00	0.63	38.18
25	20	30	10.00	0.60	38.78
26	19	30	10.00	0.57	39.35
27	18	30	10.00	0.54	39.89
28	17	30	10.00	0.51	40.41
29	16	30	10.00	0.49	40.90
30	15	30	10.00	0.46	41.36
31	15	30	10.00	0.44	41.80
32	14	30	10.00	0.42	42.22
33	13	30	10.00	0.40	42.62
34	13	30	10.00	0.38	43.00
35	12	30	10.00	0.36	43.36
36	11	30	10.00	0.34	43.70
37	11	30	10.00	0.32	44.02
38	10	30	10.00	0.31	44.33
39	10	30	10.00	0.29	44.62
40	9	30	10.00	0.28	44.90
41–70					48.19

TABLE 4-6 Attrition Patterns in a Continuity Program

Shipment Number	Attrition Pattern Start	Attrition Pattern End	By End of Week	Average Units Shipped	By End of Week	Average Units Shipped
1	1.00	1.00	1	1.00	33	4.56
2	0.90	0.90	2	1.00	34	4.59
3	0.65	0.77	3	1.00	35	4.61
4	0.45	0.55	4	1.00	36	4.63
5	0.30	0.40	5	1.90	37	4.80
6	0.25	0.35	6	1.90	38	4.82
7	0.20	0.30	7	1.90	39	4.84
8	0.18	0.28	8	1.90	40	4.86
9	0.17	0.25	9	2.55	41	5.03
10	0.15	0.23	10	2.57	42	5.05
11	0.14	0.21	11	2.59	43	5.07
12	0.13	0.20	12	2.60	44	5.09
13	0.12	0.19	13	3.07	45	5.25
14	0.11	0.18	14	3.09	46	5.27
15	0.10	0.17	15	3.10	47	5.29
Total		5.98	16	3.11	48	5.30
			17	3.43	49	5.45
			18	3.45	50	5.47
			19	3.46	51	5.49
			20	3.48	52	5.51
			21	3.75	53	5.64
			22	3.77	54	5.66
			23	3.79	55	5.68
			24	3.81	56	5.70
			25	4.04	57	5.83
			26	4.06	58	5.84
			27	4.08	59	5.86
			28	4.10	60	5.88
			29	4.30	61	5.93
			30	4.32	62	5.95
			31	4.56	63	5.96
			32	4.59	64	5.98

Newsletters and Magazines

The key economic variables which determine the profitability of a newsletter are (1) price, (2) the initial pay or conversion rate, (3) renewal rates, and (4) the response rate to direct mail promotions at different levels of promotion expense.

As was mentioned earlier in this chapter, many newsletters and magazines are successful in attracting trial subscribers through the use of preview offers which allow the potential subscriber to cancel without paying after examining one or a few sample issues. In these situations, the initial pay rate or conversion rate is the single most important variable affecting the ultimate success of the venture. However, even a relatively high initial pay rate can be offset by a poor renewal rate. Only after both conversion rates and renewal rates have been tested can one be sure of the potential profits of a newsletter. Table 4-7 shows the range of profits

TABLE 4-7 The Economics of Newsletter Direct Mail Marketing

	Initial Pay or Conversion Rate				
	30%	40%	50%	60%	70%
	First-Year Results*				
Subscribers	75	100	125	150	175
Revenues	$2025	$2700	$3375	$4050	$4725
Fulfillment and renewal costs	946	1058	1169	1280	1391
Promotion costs	3000	3000	3000	3000	3000
First-year profits	−$1921	−$1358	−$ 794	−$ 230	−$ 334
	Second-Year Profits†				
If renewal rates are:					
40%	$ 493	$ 657	$ 821	$ 986	$1150
50%	662	883	1103	1324	1544
60%	831	1108	1385	1662	1939
70%	1000	1334	1667	2000	2334
	Cumulative Second-Year Profits				
If renewal rates are:					
40%	−$1429	−$ 701	28	756	1484
50%	−1259	−474	309	1094	1878
60%	−1090	−250	591	1432	2273
70%	−921	−24	873	1770	2667

Assumptions	
1. The price of the newsletter	$27.00
2. The cost of fulfilling a paying subscriber	$5.85
3. The cost of fulfilling a canceling subscriber	$2.45
4. The cost of renewing a subscriber per starting subscriber	$1.05
5. The cost of fulfilling a subscriber who fails to renew	$2.25
6. Range of possible conversion rates from trial to paid subscriber	30%
	40%
	50%
	60%
	70%
7. Range of possible first renewal rates	40%
	50%
	60%
	70%
8. Mailing quantity	10,000
9. Mailing costs	$3,000
10. Percent response	2.5

Results	
Number of gross orders (2.5% × 10,000)	250

* Based on range of possible conversions.

† Sample calculation of second-year profits at 70% renewal rate: (175 × .70 × 27.00 − [175 × .70 × (5.85 + 1.05)] − (175 × .30 × 2.45) = 2334.

after 2 years from a direct mail investment of $3000 which resulted in 250 responses. In this situation, the $3000 investment is recovered in the first year if the conversion rate is 70 percent or greater. The investment is profitable within 2 years if the initial conversion rate is 50 percent or more and the first renewal rate is 40 percent or better.

The profits that can be generated from a newsletter are related directly to the price charged for the newsletter, since editorial costs and printing costs are not affected by the price of the service. Thus, it is very important that price testing be employed at the outset to determine the best and most profitable price for the service. Tables 4-8 and 4-9 show the effect of a $10 increase or decrease in price on the newsletter described in Table 4-7.

The economics of magazines is similar to the economics of newsletters but with a number of critical differences. First, magazines rely heavily on newsstand sales and advertising to supplement the revenue stream provided by subscription income. Second, because of competition and because magazines are targeted to reach circulation levels measured in the hundreds of thousands rather than the thousands, as is the case with most newsletters, there is much less price-setting flexibility. However, just as in newsletters, the response rate to direct mail, the conversion rate, and the renewal rates are the key economic variables which eventually will determine the success or lack of success of the magazine venture.

Catalogs

The term "back-end analysis" in a catalog operation can have two meanings. Individual customer groups defined by a common key code are analyzed for their profitability in much the same way as they are in a club environment. The key question again is, Is the average contribution from a group of starters greater than the cost of acquiring the average starter, and if so, by how much? In a catalog operation, however, a starter is much more likely to be dropped for failure to purchase than in a club operation in which there is an obligation on the part of the club to continue sending advance announcements for at least a year or two depending on the commitment made by the customer on joining the club.

A person becomes a name on a catalog company's house file because he or she has purchased from a prospecting catalog or has asked for a catalog either free or for a token price. There is no obligation on anyone's part to buy or send additional catalogs. Therefore, the economics of catalogs dictates that potential browsers be eliminated as quickly as possible and that potential heavy buyers be

TABLE 4-8 Cumulative Second-Year Profits if Price is Reduced to $17

Renewal Rates, %	Conversion Rates, % 30	40	50	60	70
40%	−2479	−2101	−1723	−1345	−967
50%	−2384	−1975	−1566	−1156	−747
60%	−2290	−1850	−1409	−968	−527
70%	−2196	−1724	−1252	−780	−308

TABLE 4-9 Cumulative Second-Year Profits if Price is Increased to $37

Renewal Rates, %	Conversion Rates, %				
	30	40	50	60	70
40	−379	700	1778	2856	3934
50	−134	1025	2184	3344	4503
60	110	1351	2591	3832	5073
70	354	1676	2998	4320	5642

mailed to as often as possible. In catalogs there is no sitting back and waiting to see what a group of customers will do. Names should be marketed and sold to aggressively or dropped from the house file.

In addition to measuring the back-end performance of customer groups and managing the house list, back-end analysis can refer to the analysis of the individual products sold in the catalog. Each product as well as each page of products is analyzed to determine whether the gross margin from the product or group of products exceeds the cost of space allocated to the product or grouping. In general, products or groupings with a better than average contribution will be repeated and given equal space if not more space in the next catalog. By the same token, products that fail to cover their allocated costs will be removed from the next catalog or given less space.

MEASURING PROFITABILITY: COMBINING FRONT-END AND BACK-END STATISTICS

In the previous section on clubs and continuities, it was stated that if the contribution to promotion, overhead, and profit for a given media investment was greater than the cost per order, the investment could be considered to be at least marginally profitable. In this section, we shall continue to develop the relationship between front-end and back-end statistics.

Many direct marketers, particularly those engaged in club and continuity programs, prefer to use the concept of return on promotion to measure the relationship between front-end and back-end performance. Return on promotion (ROP) is defined as the ratio of the contribution to promotion, overhead, and profit minus the cost per order divided by the cost per order.

$$\text{ROP \%} = \left[\frac{\text{contribution} - \text{cost per order}}{\text{cost per order}}\right] \times 100$$

Conceptually, the ROP approach treats the decision to run a space ad or mail a list as an investment against which some financial return is expected. The return is measured by the difference between the contribution that results from all the purchases that occur after the order enters the house and the cost of acquiring the order.

For example, in the section on clubs and continuities, we showed how a group of starters with average sales of $48.19 might generate a contribution per starter of $31.12. Let's assume that the cost of acquiring this group of starters was $20 per starter. In this case the ROP would be

$$\text{ROP} = \left[\frac{\$31.12 - \$20.00}{\$20.00}\right] \times 100 = 55.6\%$$

The ROP statistic can be used in a variety of ways by direct marketers. One important use of this statistic is to evaluate alternative offers. The decision rule to be followed is that if the media investment required to implement both offers is the same, the offer with the highest ROP is the best offer.

Consider the example described in Table 4-10. In this example, the decision concerns whether to use a premium costing $5 per starter or a premium costing $8 per starter. The assumption is made that the average sales resulting from the use of either premium offer will be the same and will be equal to $65 per starter.

Naturally, increasing premium expense will reduce profits unless the premium offer results in an increased response. Thus, the question is, What increase in response is necessary to justify the use of a $8 premium? One way to answer this question is to assume a response rate to the $5 premium offer and then search by trial and error for a response rate to the $8 offer that would result in the same profit and loss as the profit and loss resulting from the $5 offer.

Under the Results column (Case 1) in Table 4-10, we see the profit and loss resulting from the $5 premium if a response rate of 20 OPM is assumed. At a response rate of 25 OPM, which is assumed to result from the use of the $8 premium, contribution to overhead and profit would be increased by a total of $3750. The ROP for each case is shown at the bottom of Table 4-10. The ROP for Case 2 is 93 percent, which is greater than the ROP of 73 percent for Case 1. As long as the media investment is the same—in this case, the $17,500 required to

TABLE 4-10 Using ROP to Evaluate New Offers

Assumptions			Results			Increment Results
	Case 1	Case 2		Case 1	Case 2	
Quantity mailed	50,000	50,000				
Orders per thousand	20	25				
Average revenue			Orders	1,000	1,250	250
per starter	65.00	65.00	Sales	65,000	81,250	16,250
Direct costs excluding premium expense	30.00	30.00	Costs	30,000	37,500	7,500
Contribution	35.00	35.00	Contribution	35,000	43,750	8,750
Advertising CPM	350	350				
Advertising expense	17,500	17,500	Advertising	17,500	17,500	0
Advertising CPO	17.50	14.00				
Premium expense	5.00	8.00	Premium	5,000	10,000	5,000
	Total contribution to overhead and profit			12,500	16,250	3,750
			per starter	12.50	13.00	0.50
			ROP	0.71	0.93	

mail 50,000 pieces at a CPM of $350—the alternative with the higher ROP will be the most profitable.

Therefore, it is possible to use the ROP equation directly to determine the response rate that would cause the ROP on the $8 premium offer to equal the ROP on the $5 premium offer:

$$\text{ROP} = \frac{\text{contribution} - \text{premium} - \text{CPO}}{\text{CPO}}$$

$$\text{Old ROP} = .71 = \frac{\$35.00 - \$5.00 - \$17.50}{\$17.50}$$

$$\text{New ROP} = .71 = \frac{\$35.00 - \$8.00 - \text{new CPO}}{\text{new CPO}}$$

$$\text{New CPO} = \$15.75$$

$$\text{New OPM} = \frac{\text{CPM}}{\text{new CPO}} = \frac{\$350.00}{\$15.75} = 22.222$$

This calculation is shown above. The required new response rate is 22.22 orders per thousand.

When the initial media investment is not the same, the ROP analysis must be applied to the incremental investment in order to result in the correct decision. In these situations, if the incremental ROP is greater than zero, there will be an increase in the contribution to overhead and profit.

Refer to Table 4-11. In this example, the decision is whether to increase the quality of the mailing package in order to increase response. Costs are expected

TABLE 4-11 Using Incremental ROP to Evaluate New Offers

Assumptions			Results			Incremental Results
	Case 1	Case 2		Case 1	Case 2	
Quantity mailed	50,000	50,000				
Orders per thousand	20	22				
Average revenue			Orders	1,000	1,100	100
per starter	$ 65.00	$ 65.00	Sales	65,000	71,500	6,500
Direct costs excluding premium expense	$ 30.00	$ 30.00	Costs	30,000	33,000	3,000
Contribution	$ 35.00	$ 35.00	Contributions	35,000	38,500	3,500
Advertising CPM	$350.00	$400.00				
Advertising expense	17,500	20,000	Advertising	17,500	20,000	2,500
Advertising CPO	17.50	18.46				
Premium expense	$ 5.00	$ 5.00	Gift	5,000	5.500	500
	Total contribution to overhead and profit			$12,500	$13,000	$500
			per starter	$ 12.50	$ 11.82	
			ROP	0.71	0.65	
			Incremental ROP			0.20

TABLE 4-12 Using Incremental ROP to Evaluate New Offers

Assumptions			Results			Incremental Results
	Case 1	Case 2		Case 1	Case 2	
Quantity mailed	50,000	50,000				
Orders per thousand	20	21				
Average revenue			Orders	1,000	1,050	50
per starter	$ 65.00	$ 65.00	Sales	65,000	68,250	3.250
Direct costs excluding premium expense	$ 30.00	$ 30.00	Costs	$30,000	$31,500	$1,500
Contribution	$ 35.00	$ 35.00	Contributions	$35,000	36,750	$1,750
Advertising CPM	$350.00	$400.00				
Advertising expense	$17,500	$20,000	Advertising	$17,500	$20,000	$2,500
Advertising CPO	$ 17.50	$ 19.05				
Premium expense	$ 5.00	$ 5.00	Gift	$ 5,000	$ 5.250	$ 250
	Total contribution to overhead and profit			$12,500	$11,500	− $1,000
			per starter	$ 12.50	$ 10.95	
			ROP	0.71	0.58	
			Incremental ROP			−0.40

to increase from $350 per thousand to $400 per thousand, and the response rate is expected to increase from 20 OPM to 22 OPM. In Table 4-11, we see that if the more expensive mailing package was chosen, the average ROP would decline from 71 percent to 65 percent, but the incremental ROP would be 20 percent and total dollar contribution would increase by $500.

However, if the response rate increased to only 21 OPM, as shown in Table 4-12, the incremental ROP would be negative, and contribution would decline.

The decision to invest funds up to the point at which the incremental ROP is zero is a management decision. Generally, the cutoff rate is substantially higher, around 30 percent, to reflect other factors such as risk, the company's cost of capital, and opportunity costs resulting from competing uses of funds from other investments.

Another important use of the return on promotion statistic is to rank alternative investment opportunities for budget allocations. We have seen already that if the size of the investment is held constant, the investment alternative with the highest ROP is the most profitable.

In planning annual media budgets, a good first step is to begin by calculating the expected ROP for each independent media opportunity and then rank all such opportunities in terms of descending order of ROP. Conceptually, as the size of the media budget increases, the average ROP generated by the budget decreases, but for any given budget total, a media budget constructed in such a fashion always will yield the highest possible ROP.

Of course, there are numerous practical problems with this approach. For example, if a book club were to advertise in *Cosmopolitan* magazine twelve times a year rather than three times a year, the average ROP on the twelve times a year plan would be less than the average ROP on the three times a year plan, but the twelve times a year plan might be the best profit plan for the club. Therefore, considerable judgment and care must be used in putting together a media plan based on ROP allocations. But such difficulties aside, an annual media plan developed with the aid of ROP calculations for each investment opportunity will result in a plan which tends to maximize the financial return on the funds invested in the acquisition of new customers.

Finally, one last caution in the use of ROP in budget planning. The ROP statistic is an economic measure and does not take fiscal year P&L considerations into account. An investment with a 50 percent ROP and a first of the year expense date is considered to be the same in an ROP ranking scheme as an investment with a 50 percent ROP with an end of the fiscal year expense date.

From a financial accounting point of view, the investment made on the first of the year will result in sales from new members in that same fiscal year. The investment made at the end of the fiscal year will result in only expense; the corresponding sales will come in the next fiscal year.

This problem is alleviated to some extent by accounting procedures which allow new member acquisition expense to be amortized over the economic life of the acquired new members or subscribers. For example, assuming an economic life of twelve months, only one-twelfth of the expense of a promotion that was released in the last fiscal month would be charged to the current fiscal year.

chapter 5

THE PROPOSITION

Caroline Zimmermann

Zimmermann Marketing, Inc.
New York, N.Y.

The purpose of all direct marketing efforts is to have the maximum number of qualified prospects accept a company's offers and accept them as often as possible. Thus, it stands to reason that all the aspects of the offer, i.e., the complete selling proposition, constitute the most important element of any direct marketing promotion. The proposition can make a promotion a dismal failure or a resounding success. The product or service, which is the main part of the offer, is of great importance, but so is every aspect of the proposition: the price, the premium, the guarantees, etc.

THE IMPORTANCE OF THE PROPOSITION

How do you get quality prospects to say yes? Once they are customers, how do you get them to say yes more often?

You do this with your proposition. You make the offer so good that the prospects and customers simply can't resist. Except for changes in the product itself, the single variable in a print ad, commercial, direct mail package, or other promotion which probably can affect the sale of a product most is the proposition.

This is so important that direct marketers sometimes actually tailor-make the product or service to the proposition. For example, a direct marketer determines that a lengthy guarantee gives him a competitive lead. He therefore adapts the product for longer life and adds a 10-year guarantee.

Sometimes the product or service will determine the proposition to a large degree. Depending on its cost, the price will be higher or lower. Depending on the margin of profit, the marketer may be able to offer premiums, add-ons, credit, and other advantages. Depending on the product and the environment in which you sell, you can offer stronger or less strong guarantees.

In fact, you may want to tailor-make your proposition to the particular problems of your business, such as special offers during the summer season to stimulate a slow period, special inducements for cash in advance if cash is short or you can't afford to give long credit terms, special offers to move sluggish inventory, etc. But whatever the reason for making the proposition, it deserves the most careful and detailed attention.

THE PROPOSITION: A DEFINITION

There are many definitions of what a sales proposition is, but for the purposes of this chapter, we shall consider the proposition to be the statement of the offer, including price and payment terms, return privileges, premiums, guarantees, and all other inducements as well as all obligations on the part of the buyer. Propositions are used to help overcome human inertia (a natural resistance on the part of the reader to become involved) and to make the buyer aware of all the terms of the sale.

If any terms are left out, your proposition is not completely revealed, and this is likely to affect sales adversely.

INVOLVING THE PROSPECT

Commonly referred to as the offer, the proposition is a way to involve the reader and make him or her aware of the terms and also to get the prospect to say yes by dramatizing the advantages of the product or service. For example, a highly successful publisher recently tested a new direct mail package against the old one. Using a money-back cash refund for the unused portion any time during the life of the subscription plus a free, specialized premium, she was able to increase response 45 percent over the control.

With the new offer the publisher made the proposition more attractive and gave her prospects a sense of freedom by not committing them to a lengthy subscription. Instead, she offered them an open-ended subscription which they could cancel at any time. She overcame additional sales resistance by offering a specialized and exclusive premium for fast action.

An insurance company offered the first month of insurance free while the prospects examined the information package which they were encouraged to request. In effect, the insurance company was giving away a month of coverage as a free premium in order to get requests for information.

The proposition was so attractive that the response was increased by over 100 percent. The quality of the people responding improved, and conversions increased as well. Because the prospective customers found themselves in the position of terminating after 30 days of coverage, it was easier to let the coverage continue.

A manufacturer decided to charge $0.10 for a packet of information that previously had been given away free. Response jumped by 25 percent. Charging a token fee for the information, the manufacturer increased the perceived value of what he was giving away.

How did these marketers, all with very different objectives, achieve such success? They found ways to use the proposition to increase response.

Guarantees, merchandise tokens, and information packets are propositions that can go into making up the offer. You can use them and build on them in a multitude of ways to get your prospects and customers to take action on your sales offer.

THE ELEMENTS OF A PROPOSITION

Your offer is so essential to the success of your advertising that it is not at all unusual to see differences of 20, 40, or even 100 percent and more with the right propositions. The challenge, of course, is to build the kind of proposition that makes sense for your product or service and your objectives.

Your proposition can be based on price, convenience of subscription, freedom of return, easy credit terms, various guarantees, or any number of other elements. These variables, however, have the potential to dramatically affect for better or worse the response rate, the bad debts, the rate of return, cancellations, and future relations with your customers.

The following elements may enter into your proposition. This list is by no means exclusive; many other elements can be found and added by an ingenious marketer.

1. **Your product or service.** This is the central focus of the proposition. If you are advertising in order to obtain inquiries, you are "selling" a package of information.
2. **The price.** All elements of the price should be disclosed clearly, including shipping, handling, and other charges.
3. **The payment terms.** You can offer cash in advance, cash on delivery, credit terms, installment terms, or any combination.
4. **Time of delivery.** Alert the prospective customer of anticipated lapse time. "We will rush you the information you requested." "Allow 3 weeks for processing." "Books will be shipped to you at approximately 3-week intervals."
5. **Guarantees of various kinds.** Provide clear information on return privileges, guarantees of cancellation, unlimited quality guarantees, no cheaper price available elsewhere, etc.
6. **Premiums.** Notify the prospects whether the premium is shipped with the merchandise and whether it is a premium for loyalty, for quantity, for payment or even prepayment, or for quick acceptance (5-day response), etc.
7. **Self-liquidating premiums.** For example, a book club offers a $40 encyclopedic dictionary for only $5 as an inducement to join. The $5 actually covers the cost of printing and binding the dictionary and shipping and handling. It is self-liquidating.
8. **Service commitments.** For example, "If at any time during the next 5 years your merchandise needs servicing, you need only call this 800 number." Or

"Buyers of our encyclopedia may send in 100 questions which will be answered promptly within the limits of our service capabilities."

9. **Certificates of completion.** For example, "People who complete their collection of the complete Dickens set will be given a framed certificate stating their interest in the English language and the beauty of literature."
10. **Multiple offers.** For example, "Buy one, the second only 1 cent"; "Buy the camera and get film at 50 percent off for 1 year"; "If you buy this record, you can purchase the $100 cassette attachment for only $25 extra"; "Buy this cookware and get all accessories at half price"; "If you buy accidental death insurance for yourself, you can cover your spouse and minor children for only $1 extra per month."
11. **Obligations on the part of the customer.** For example, "Your only obligation is to buy six books each year from the hundreds offered to you"; "You can cancel any time by giving us 30 days written notice"; "Bills must be paid within 5 days"; "The first book free, just pay shipping and handling"; "To get your coffee maker serviced, all you need do is send it postage-paid to one of our convenient service centers"; "Failure to pay any installment when due will make the total outstanding amount due."

Any of these elements of the proposition can be combined to fulfill your short-term and long-term objectives.

RELATING THE PROPOSITION TO SHORT-TERM AND LONG-TERM OBJECTIVES

One of the most common mistakes marketers make is to design a proposition without clearly relating the elements to the short-term and long-term objectives of management.

It's often tempting to increase up-front response by increasing premiums or special introductory offers. But care must be taken that the advantages gained by such a proposition will not be offset by getting a lower-quality customer with the resulting higher bad debts, returns, cancellations, etc. The astute marketer must carefully track not only the front-end response but the customers' behavior pattern for each proposition.

It is essential to determine the optimum balance between quantity of orders and quality of orders. This balance can be achieved by creating a proposition which will maximize immediate response without attracting an undue amount of nonpayers, returners, or premium chasers—in short, the deadbeats.

For example, a business specialty advertiser offered a mini-portable radio as a free gift just for sending for the catalog of merchandise. The response was overwhelming; they never had so many requests. But when the advertiser tracked the orders from the special promotion with this wonderful free gift as part of the proposition, she found that the conversion from request to actual order was very low. To make matters worse, the amount of the average order was well below the norm.

The objectives (both short-term and long-term) were to boost requests for the catalog and to convert requests to sales, with an average order of $100 or more. The free mini-portable radio certainly boosted requests and met the firm's short-term objectives, but in the long term it did not meet another corporate sales objective: build a list of buyers who spend at least $100 per order with the company.

USING PROPOSITIONS TO MEET YOUR OBJECTIVES

The proposition may have to be tailor-made to the media or mailing list to which it is offered as a means of meeting your objectives. You obviously can offer more generous credit terms to a list of your own customers who have proved their creditworthiness than to a list of people with whom you have never done business before. Similar considerations even may induce you to have several different propositions under which the product or service is sold, depending on where, when, and in which media or lists your offer is included. However, it is important to check with your legal counsel before you do anything of this nature to make sure that your different propositions are within the parameters of the law.

As a policy, you should think out your short-term and long-term objectives carefully and then build a proposition to create an offer that meets those objectives. Rules are made to be broken, and with that in mind, the following example demonstrates how and why a publisher chose to be concerned only with short-term objectives.

The advertising department of a national women's magazine guarantees a certain rate base to its advertisers. If the circulation falls below that rate base, a rebate must be issued to all advertisers. The problem the magazine faced was a dropping rate base. Subscribers were not renewing in great enough numbers, and the response rate was off with new subscribers.

The magazine was willing to take a limited loss on subscriber income if it could obtain enough new subscribers to maintain its guaranteed rate base. The objective in building the proposition was to put the accent on the front-end response, even though bad debts and renewals might suffer. Consequently, the cost of acquiring these new subscriptions would not be offset entirely by the subscription income from the subscribers.

In spite of the fact that long-term objectives included building a circulation base with quality subscribers, it was decided to create and implement a promotion that would provide good front-end response even though the publisher knew that their back end would be sacrificed to some extent. Quite simply, they were buying lots of subscribers (big numbers) whose long-term performance would not pay out totally.

With these clear objectives and sacrifices defined, the control package was changed to include a "free issue" when the reader subscribed. If the subscriber was not happy with the magazine, she could write "cancel" on the invoice, with no further obligation. Traditionally, this offer is a great way to build numbers rapidly. However, most publishers have found that such an offer also costs a great deal of extra money because of fulfillment costs, cancellations, bad debts, etc.

Although this magazine had to contend with the same problems, the mailing saved the day by boosting the rate base back up to safe levels.

It is essential to be aware continuously of your objectives and how they change if you want to market a product or service successfully.

Some magazine publishers make it a policy to test the acceptance of a new magazine by offering the first issue free, as was described in the previous example. Even though they know that this offer may not pay out for them and know that they may launch the publication under a different proposition, they have an important objective. The purpose is to find out whether there is any interest at all in the new magazine, with the theory being that if people are not interested in the magazine, they will not ask for it even for "free." Such tests must be approached with a great deal of caution. Obviously, if people don't want a product, even a free one, it's very likely that they will not accept it if they have to pay for it.

This concept of "for free" carries across most product and service lines. When using a proposition that is especially attractive (such as "free"), it is essential to remember, that this process should be a screening method to eliminate products which are totally unacceptable or for testing the acceptability of one product against another by comparing the response to the free offer. This is not to say that you shouldn't use a "free" proposition. It is still one of the most attractive and effective techniques. But when the technique is tested, you must track it carefully to make sure that it pays out for you not only on the front end but in all aspects of your marketing.

RELATING PROPOSITIONS TO YOUR PRODUCT

The basic question you must be concerned with is how the proposition supports your objectives. This is so important to the successful growth of your business that I suggest you include the written answer to this question as part of your marketing strategy.

There are literally hundreds of ways to build a proposition, not to mention those unique ones which can be built around a specific product or service. The trick is to relate those propositions so that they support the selling process.

By clearly defining your objectives, as was suggested previously, you can ask yourself another key question: How will the proposition affect the objectives?

As you think about the proposition you will make to your prospects and customers, you must always be concerned with the effect it will have on your objectives and the support it will lend.

THE IMPORTANCE OF PRICING

Perhaps the simplest yet most important proposition is the price and the price change. The price customers pay can literally make or break a business.

In retailing, it is common to have what is called a "keystone" markup, that is, a markup to double the wholesale cost. In marketing directly to the consumer, it often is not possible to support this kind of markup.

High-end merchandise ($50 to $75 and up) can support a 2- to 4-time markup, but generally, merchandise below that level requires a 5- to 7-time markup. You should bear in mind that the lower the final cost to the consumer, the higher your markup is likely to have to be. A 7-time markup is considered the norm in our business.

I mention this because one sees all too many marketers making the mistake of using a "keystone" markup as the norm for obtaining a final price for their customers, regardless of the retail cost.

Often it is necessary to restructure the pricing in order to bring profits more in line. Sometimes this can be achieved simply by raising the price (although you must always test this first). But more often than not, it will be necessary to find other means to increase the profit spread. For example, you might consider cheaper materials, look for suppliers that can give you better prices, or use a combination of devices.

One of our clients was selling a product directly to the consumer for $28.95 with a product cost of $8. This was not enough of a profit spread, and so in order to raise the price, we "blinded" the product by adding an exclusive premium without a perceivable price value. The premiums cost $0.55 in the mail, but testing at different price levels finally showed that we were able to raise the total selling cost to $34.95, a $6 increase in selling price for an expenditure of $0.55.

OVERCOMING HUMAN INERTIA

Direct marketers have an axiom that goes something like this: When selling to a prospect or customer, you have approximately 10 seconds to reach that person and involve him or her with your promotion.

Human inertia, or the natural resistance to becoming involved, is probably the biggest killer of advertising sales. An offer that gets a whopping 10 percent response still leaves 90 percent of the audience unsold. Those people took no action; this demonstrates human inertia.

As part of the selling process, you must include a strategy to get your prospects' and customers' attention and get them over the first hump: the tendency not to read your message.

Your goal is to involve them immediately with the sales offer. Finally, you must overcome the natural instinct of almost every person to postpone a decision. The ideal proposition will take all these factors into consideration. The competent advertiser then will present the various elements of the proposition graphically and in words which will overcome all these obstacles so that the proposition as a whole is accepted.

Throughout this book, there will be solid advice given on how to present the proposition, how involvement devices can dramatize it, how copy and graphics can draw the reader in, and how other means can put the proposition at its best advantage and increase the chances of its being accepted by the prospect.

MAKING BASIC PROPOSITIONS MORE ATTRACTIVE

A proposition does not have to be new or unique in order to draw in the reader. Many old propositions can be made to sound new or more attractive by rewording or graphic presentation.

For example, a publisher had been enrolling subscribers successfully in her book club with an offer of "the first book free" sent along with the second book at full price. She found that she increased response by restating the proposition and making the following offer: "two books for the price of one."

It's important to remember that you often can give old propositions which have had too much exposure new life simply by restating them.

Earlier in this chapter, I discussed the sales value of putting together a number of elements in your proposition. There is another very sound reason to include a number of elements: The more elements you can include (after carefully testing their viability, of course), the stronger your proposition usually will be and the more likely you will be to overcome human inertia.

One successful continuity publisher includes many elements as a means of building an "irresistible" proposition. His mailing includes the following:

1. **Free samples.** This is a classic involvement device that allows prospects to see the product before purchase. The proposition should start on the envelope with an offer of "free samples right inside."
2. **Sweepstakes.** More than 50,000 prizes may be given away with no obligation to buy a thing. Traditionally, a sweeps appeals to the ability to fulfill a dream. The proposition would offer "free sweepstakes participation."
3. **Early bird incentive.** Tied into the sweepstakes, this is an extra prize that gets people to take action within a limited time frame. Including an early bird gift as part of the proposition helps overcome the tendency to postpone a decision.
4. **Rub-off spot.** This is an extra involvement device within the early bird incentive. The prospect rubs the spot for a lucky number. While this is not part of the proposition as such, it dramatizes the proposition to attract more attention to it.
5. **Guarantee.** The guarantee assures the prospect of the ability to be secure in his or her decision by making the decision reversible. The decision becomes a matter of examining the product rather than purchasing it.
6. **Discount on the first book.** Offering a great money-saving deal is another classic way to involve the prospect.
7. **Extra free gift.** This is an extra incentive to get the prospect to take action.
8. **Till forbid shipment.** Literally, this term means "until you forbid us to send any more." The seller sends a product on a monthly basis until the customer tells the seller to stop. Each month, the customer is billed the small price of a single book. The sales resistance that has to be overcome at any one time is only for that one small amount, even though the publisher

knows in this case that the average subscriber will stay for almost 2 years and will purchase over $100 worth of books.

9. **Credit approval.** The prospect can take advantage of the offer without sending money in advance.
10. **Free examination of each monthly shipment.** This is another assurance of not getting a book that will disappoint the subscriber. The customer can return any book that does not please him or her.
11. **Monthly billing.** As another part of the financial terms, the prospect has to pay for each shipment only after he or she has received and examined it. The customer is not put in a position in which he or she must trust the publisher. The publisher shows confidence in the product by asking for payment only after the customer is satisfied.
12. **Easy cancellation privileges.** The customer can stop shipment at any time simply by writing "please cancel" on the invoice of the last book received; no further books will be shipped. Here again, the customer is encouraged to accept all the advantages of subscribing because the publisher has built the proposition so that there is an easy way out of all purchase commitments.

This proposition obviously was not improvised. Each aspect of it was tested carefully both for its effect on the front end and the quality of the subscribers enrolled.

The publisher has linked twelve different elements into a highly successful proposition. However, it is important to remember that this proposition was not built in a day. In fact, the original offer included only the free sample, the guarantee, the till forbid, the credit approval, the monthly billing, and the cancellation. The other elements of the proposition were added gradually to increase the pulling power of the mailing and to decrease cancellations.

IMPROVING THE PROPOSITION

The astute marketer will analyze the effect of a change in the proposition not only as a one-time phenomenon but in order to detect trends on which one can cash in. If, for instance, adding a "speed" premium of a jade elephant for people who answer an offer for a book series within 5 days of receipt increases the pull by 5 percent, the marketer not only will try out different premiums to see whether they will increase the pull even further but also may change the proposition to give a choice of premiums.

If you find that a premium works, it may be worthwhile to test the idea of dramatizing the premium part of the proposition by adding an extra "buckslip" or flier to merchandise the desirability of the premium.

A marketer who has found that giving the option to pay in three installments increases the profitability of the proposition may want to try four installments or even five to increase profitability even further.

Again, a marketer who finds that a premium increases profitability and in another test finds that credit also improves profitability may test whether adding the two elements (premium plus credit) will have a cumulative effect. If adding a premium increases the pull by 5 percent and the profitability by 10 percent, and if adding credit increases the profitability by 10 percent, it stands to reason that the two elements together may improve the profitability by 21 percent (since the two increases are cumulative).

By changing your proposition in this way, you may come up with ever increasing profitability, provided that each change is tested carefully and the total effect on profitability is calculated.

PROPOSITIONS FOR REPEAT BUSINESS

It was mentioned earlier that proven credit customers can be given advantages that may not pay off in the case of strangers.

Here are some specific propositions that may increase repeat business.

1. Premiums for repeat orders.
2. Ever increasing premiums (as the frequency of orders is increased).
3. Special advance announcements.
4. Discount offers.
5. Introductory prices on new products.
6. More advantageous credit terms.
7. A holding premium, in which the customer is given a booklet with a number of spaces for pasting value stamps in order to redeem a gift.
8. Member-get-a-member (also known as friend-get-a-friend), in which old members or customers get a gift if they introduce a new customer to the company.
9. Free participation in a sweepstakes every month as long as the account is active. This has to be set up carefully with an experienced sweepstakes administrator since a sweeps can't be tied to a purchase.
10. Negative option is the familiar plan of most book and record clubs. Subscribers undertake to accept and pay for a book or record periodically unless they return a rejection card which the club provides in announcing the next selection.
11. Till forbid is a plan in which the customer accepts periodic shipments until the customer cancels. These plans have been applied successfully not only to book and record series but to card series, insurance, collectibles, etc.

SUBSCRIPTIONS, CONTINUITY, CLUB PROGRAMS, AND NEGATIVE AND POSITIVE OPTIONS

Like retail outlets, most direct marketing businesses are built on the basis of repeat sales. After all, a satisfied customer will *want* to buy again.

Operating a business so that you build a list of satisfied customers (no matter by what means they purchase) is a basic tenet of direct marketing. However, in addition to repeat sales, there are several other methods available to sophisticated marketers that should not be overlooked as viable and highly profitable ways to build a business and build additional sales that otherwise might be lost.

These methods are subscription, continuity, and club plans. Depending on the other propositions you use, they can provide either negative or positive buying options for the customer.

What makes these propositions advantageous to the marketer is that each provides a means to an ongoing buying relationship with the customer. The customer has made a commitment at the onset of the purchasing decision to buy more over a period of time. If one of these propositions can be incorporated successfully into your product sell, this can add real profits to your bottom line.

Often direct marketers look to develop specific subscription, club, and continuity programs. However, this doesn't mean that a marketer must be limited to this approach. Sometimes a marketer can examine the product and find new ways to add to or segment it so that an ongoing, continuous buying relationship can develop. We know from past experience that the dollar amount expended by the customer will be much greater in this type of program than in a single sale.

Let's talk about each of the available methods.

Subscription

This is probably the oldest proposition of this type, and most people are familiar with it through the purchase of magazines.

In essence, the publisher sends the subscriber copies of the magazine over a period of time (weekly, biweekly, monthly, quarterly, etc.). The subscriber makes a commitment to have the magazine sent for a specific period of time. The most common time period is 1 year, but commits range from a 3-month trial to many years.

We know from experience that subscribers often will renew their subscriptions at a rate of 50 to 60 percent after 1 year; after that, the renewal rate becomes much higher. With this kind of performance, it's easy to see why subscription selling is profitable.

However, magazines are not the only products which can be sold through a subscription type of effort.

Continuity

A similar method of selling is called continuity. Instead of selling a fixed amount at a fixed price, paid for in advance (which is then delivered in installments), as is done in subscription selling, a series of individual sales are made at a fixed price. The subscriber buys each product on an individual or "pay as you go" basis. However, the original sell to the subscriber stated that there would be a series of offerings on a continuing basis.

It is usual with any kind of continuity plan to have automatic shipment of the product as part of the program. This means that the item will be shipped to the customer at regular intervals. By law, the customer must have this shipping information divulged to him or her as part of the selling proposition.

Time-Life Books, Grolier, Margrace, Franklin Mint, and Fruit-of-the-Month are classic marketers that use this proposition as part of their business.

Advertising specialties (calendars, diaries, and organizers), encyclopedias, gourmet foods, beauty aids, and vitamin and other daily health pills are classic examples of products that use the continuity proposition.

Clubs

This proposition is a variation on the others. It is found most commonly in the book and record industries. The difference is that the member is given choices in addition to the commitment.

The Book-of-the-Month Club, now owned by Time-Life, was the originator of this proposition. In its most simple form, the member, who must commit to a certain number of selections before fulfilling the obligation to the club, generally is offered a number of books or records at an extremely discounted price in return for joining. Within a certain time period, that member must buy an agreed on number of products. Unlike most continuity plans, the member is sent information about a variety of offerings from which to choose. The member then can either buy or not buy from that offering as long as the overall commitment is kept.

Negative Option

This proposition often is combined with the continuity or club sell.

In essence, the customer is told at the onset that the product will be shipped automatically unless notification is sent back by the buyer instructing the advertiser not to ship.

There are several variations within the negative option plan.

1. No—ship nothing during this time interval.
2. No—ship no more product (cancellation).

The buyer is given a certain time period in which to respond.

Negative options generally are used with most continuity and club plans because they represent an ideal way to overcome human inertia. With the negative option, the buyer simply does nothing.

However, when the negative option is used, it is imperative to make it clear exactly how the option will work. Otherwise, your back-end performance and bad debt probably will suffer.

Positive Option

This proposition is the opposite of the negative option. Like the negative option, it is combined with the continuity or club sell. However, it is not as popular as negative option because it requires that the buyer take action.

Before the product is shipped, the buyer receives notification that it is ready. If the buyer wants to receive the product, he or she must notify the advertiser to ship within a certain time frame.

Response is never as good with the positive option since the buyer must take action in order to receive the product.

TWO-STEP MARKETING

Sometimes, for any number of reasons, it simply is not possible to sell a product or service directly to the buyer. When two-step marketing is used, you don't ask for the order but ask instead for an inquiry. Once the inquiry is received, more detailed selling information is sent that "asks for the order."

Two-step marketing is different from two-step selling, in which an inquiry is obtained which is followed up by a sales person either in person or by phone.

Two-step marketing generally is used when it is prohibitively expensive to send selling information to prospects or when the market is so narrow that the waste involved is too great to make direct solicitation affordable.

Financial institutions such as Scudder, Stevens, & Clark, Dreyfus, and Fidelity are marketers that use the two-step approach. The law requires that a prospectus accompany the first solicitation on any of their products. To mail to prospects without knowing whether they have any real interest in a financial investment has proved to be inordinately expensive, except with the most highly qualified lists.

Marketers seeking very segmented audiences also use this technique. For example, an antique music box dealer used an inquiry ad in a variety of publications to find prospects who were interested in obtaining a free copy of his catalog.

TRADE-UPS

This underutilized but highly profitable proposition is a great way to ring up more sales. It's used so commonly in retailing that I often wonder why more marketers don't look for ways to incorporate it into their selling.

Quite simply, it is an "add-on" to your sell. When you go into a retail outlet, the sales clerk may show you a wonderful belt to complement a new dress or a tie that is especially nice with a particular shirt.

Direct marketers also can do this by offering buyers a deluxe version of a book or an extra year's subscription to a magazine at a substantial discount or a free gift when one buys two of a particular product.

Unlike the continuity or club propositions, almost every single marketer can employ a trade-up as part of the selling. You need only remember to include it. However, as in every aspect of marketing, the marketer should test it first.

LEGALITY

When you present the proposition to a prospective customer, it is essential that it be clearly and completely spelled out in a manner that is not misleading to the unwary reader.

If the proposition includes automatic shipments, it is illegal and bad business not to spell it out clearly that these shipments will be forthcoming. A number of mail-order stamp dealers and some book promoters have gotten into trouble by not stating clearly that by accepting the attractive up-front premium offer, the customer later will receive additional merchandise for which the customer will be billed and dunned unless the merchandise is returned promptly.

The astute mail-order marketer knows that the more clearly the proposition is spelled out, the less likely it is that excessive correspondence, returns, and bad debts will be encountered. In this manner, the marketer can avoid breaching legal requirements.

There are stringent laws against shipping and asking for payment for unordered merchandise. Law enforcers repeatedly have held that unless the proposition is stated clearly, merchandise can be considered unordered even though the proposition was stated in its entirety somewhere in small type. These agencies have held that the test is whether an unwary reader is misled by the proposition as it is stated in the promotion.

In this respect, advertising propositions aimed at children are especially sensitive and must be stated clearly. In many instances, the marketer must go so far as to require the signature of a parent or guardian before accepting orders which the marketer has reason to believe have been placed by children.

In structuring your proposition, it is important that the legality of every aspect of it be checked. There may be laws governing the amount of interest and handling charges that can be charged and how they must be revealed to the prospect.

Sweepstakes are highly regulated, and an expert should be consulted when your proposition includes them. Some regulatory agencies may forbid them in particular states, and so you must adhere to legal counsel.

You also may find that it is forbidden to sell the same product at different prices. Also, the legality of having more or less in the advertising proposition, especially if you are addressing different ethnic groups, must be checked carefully.

This chapter can't attempt even to start giving advice on the law. It can only caution you to check the legality of your proposition and every element of it with competent counsel before making the offer.

CALIBRATING THE PROFITABILITY EFFECT OF CHANGES IN PROPOSITIONS

Changing the proposition can affect the calculation of the profitability of your promotion. Adding a premium will increase the cost of the order by the cost of the premium. Giving longer credit terms will increase the cost by the higher interest and carrying expenses. Allowing more generous return privileges may increase the cost because of merchandise returns.

Inversely, a reduction in any of these advantages of your proposition may save you in cost per order. The essential task, therefore, is to carefully track and calculate how much your increase in pull on a promotion has to be, that is, how many orders per $1000 spent in advertising you have to receive in order to make up for the increased costs of the proposition. If the proposition actually saves you in dollars expended per order, how many fewer orders can you afford to receive in order to come out even with the previous proposition?

Before testing a new proposition, the marketer should estimate the effect that it will have on the advertising cost per order, the back-end response, and all other factors. As a marketer, you should budget carefully for the advantages you expect to obtain by making these changes in the proposition. Too often, one hears the command "Let's try a new offer" or "Let's try giving a premium." With that, a test is made without the marketer ever estimating or even guessing how much more adding the premium to the proposition will have to increase the effectiveness of the promotion before there is any advantage obtained through this change.

Just measuring the percentage of increase or decrease in the pull of an ad or the increase or decrease in the number of orders received from any one ad can be very misleading, as can the cost per order if one looks only at that.

The real question is the effect on profits that changes in the proposition will produce. A hypothetical example may illustrate this point.

> A mailer is selling alarm clocks for $100 each. Her cost of the clocks, including direct handling and overhead expenses, is $60. She sells the clock on strict cash with order terms and has experienced negligible returns. In her last advertising campaign, she sold 50 clocks for every $1000 in advertising spent. Her advertising cost was $20 per order.

The mailer decided to try to boost her profitability by offering a free barometer with every clock in the next campaign. The barometers cost $5 each. On the next test, she found that for every $1000 in advertising she now spent, she received 60 orders. The advertising cost per order was reduced to $16.66. But to this cost she had to add the $5 premium cost, bringing the total cost per order to $21.66.

A quick comparison will reveal that the total promotion cost per order was increased from $5 to $6.66 by adding the premium. The inexperienced marketer might conclude that adding the premium is a less advantageous promotion for the marketer than remaining with the old proposition. That person would be wrong.

If we look at the profitability of the two propositions, the conclusion will be quite different. In the old proposition, the calculation of profits for every $1000 spent in advertising was computed in the following way:

Sales: 50 clocks at $100 each	$5000
Less: Cost of clocks (50 × $60)	− 3000
Gross profit	$2000
Less: Advertising costs	− 1000
Net profit	$1000

On the other hand, the calculation for the new proposition would be as follows:

Sales: 60 clocks at $100 each	$6000
Less: Cost of clocks (60 × $60)	− 3600
	$2400
Less: 60 premiums at 5% each	− 300
Gross profit	$2100
Less: Advertising costs	− 1000
Net profit	$1100

As you can see, the new proposition is 10 percent more profitable than the old one.

Another example may illustrate the importance of thorough net profit calculations to determine a budget of profitability on a new proposition as well as to analyze the results.

Again, let us take the example of the clock marketer. She now has determined that adding a premium to the proposition has increased the pull. But she wants to go one step further by offering credit. The proposition is now $100 cash plus the free barometer. Or if the customer prefers, payment can be made in four installments of $25 each plus $6 carrying charges plus the free barometer. The test results showed that the mailer received thirty orders with cash in advance and forty orders on credit terms. The immediate reaction on the part of the mailer was to increase the pull from sixty to seventy orders per $1000 spent in advertising, and the cost per order went from $16.66 to $14.28.

Careful tracking of orders showed that bad debts overall amount to 10 percent or $10 per order on the $100 sales price. The interest expenses for the four monthly installments plus dunning and bookkeeping charges cost as much as the $6 carrying charge that she was adding to the credit orders. A careful analysis showed the following calculation on the new proposition. (For simplicity's sake, we have assumed that the return rate on the credit proposition remained the same, which in reality probably would not be the case.)

Sales: 30 cash orders at $100 each	$3000
40 credit orders at $106 each	4240
Total sales	$7240
Less: 10% bad debts (on credit orders)	− 424
Total paid sales	$6816
Less: Cost of clocks (70 × $60)	− 4200
	$2616
Less: 70 premiums at $5 each	− 350
	$2266
Less: Carrying costs (40 × $6)	− 240
Gross profit	$2026
Less: Advertising costs	− 1000
Net profit	$1026

Although adding a credit option increased sales and reduced advertising costs per order, the net result was a reduction of profit primarily resulting from the high bad debt experience.

The next step for the mailer might be to reduce bad debts by offering the credit option to credit-proven lists, to discourage freeloaders by changing the proposition to ask for a small down payment on credit orders, or to undertake any of the other methods used in the industry to control bad debts.

In each case, the proposition must be tested for profitability. It cannot be stressed too much that testing for pull or sales volume alone can be misleading. I have seen experienced mail-order people fall into the trap of comparing the cost per order rather than profitability per $1000 of advertising expended.

CONCLUSION

The right proposition presented badly does not have a chance of succeeding. A bad proposition that is presented well also will not work. The proposition is probably the most important part of your advertising. That's why it pays to invest your effort and testing budget to come up with propositions that appeal to your customers and give optimal results for your company.

chapter 6

LISTS AS AN ASSET

Allan D. Bilofsky

Mailing List Sales Manager
Spencer Gifts, Inc.
Pleasantville, N.J.

A mailing list as a profit-producing asset is almost too good to be true. Income can be earned from an asset that is not depleted (the names are rented, not sold, so that ownership of the list is maintained), and the asset is virtually cost-free, making the "sales" price almost the same as the profit. The mailing list can be considered virtually cost-free; all the costs attributable to the development of the list exist anyway because the list was developed originally for in-house utilization. The only costs directly attributable to the rental of a mailing list are the list manager's time in developing the order and the computer time needed to run the list order, along with a small accounting cost for invoicing and collecting rental fees. These costs are minute in comparison to the costs of acquiring names for the mailing list in the first place.

BUILDING THE HOUSE FILE

In most cases, the mailing list is developed through outside sources, for example, mailing an offer to another concern's mailing list or placing an advertisement in a newspaper or magazine. There are two exceptions. The first occurs when a company with a retail outlet accumulates a mailing list of customers who purchase at the retail store. The second exception would be a magazine that advertises for subscribers within its covers in order to solicit names from among newsstand purchases.

Today, the most common method of building a house file of customers is by renting a mailing list of people (or companies if the mailing is an industrial offer) with a history that would indicate a possible interest in the product or service being offered.

Two major groups of lists are available for rental. The first is the direct mail list, which is a list of customers who have responded to a direct mail offer. The offer could have been business or consumer, a catalog, a flier, a television ad, or any form of advertising that requires a direct mail response. The other type of list is one that has been compiled from among people or companies with a specific affinity. This affinity can be anything from an airplane pilot's license to a degree in zoology. Many compiled lists are in the public domain, such as state automobile registrations. Another source of compiled names is the rosters of attendees at trade shows and industrial conferences. Compiled lists work best for very narrowly targeted offers such as advertising for attendance at a seminar or a specific business topic. In contrast, direct mail lists respond better to more generalized offers for which the fact that these people have shown an inclination to purchase through the mail is important.

Although mailing an offer to a rented list is the most common method of developing a house file of buyers, it is not the only method. The other methods can be utilized with lower cost than a mailing to a rented list, but this is offset by smaller response rates. These other methods are excellent for smaller companies that are testing the feasibility of a direct-response approach. They also are used successfully by many mailers as supplementary direct marketing approaches.

The largest of these approaches are space advertisements, in which an offer is placed on the pages of a periodical. Others are television advertisements, package inserts (placing an advertising piece into the outgoing packages of another direct marketing company), statement stuffers (which are similar to package inserts), and co-ops. A co-op exists when several companies combine to do a single mailing, with each placing its offer into the mailing piece.

STRUCTURING THE FILE

Years ago, building a house file meant storing file cards with customers' names and purchases in a shoe box. Next came the permanent addressing machine and finally the computer. With the advent of computerized mailing lists, historical information became highly accessible. It was therefore important to capture as much information about a purchaser as possible. The three most significant factors in customer information were the first to be computerized: recency, frequency, and monetary value (RFM). Of these, the recency factor is the single most important element both for in-house utilization of the file and for rental purposes. It is imperative to update a file frequently to keep this factor as current as possible. Many companies update customer data on a monthly basis, while others update quarterly. The number of times that a customer purchases is the frequency in the RFM matrix. Obviously, for in-house purposes, the more frequently a customer purchases, the more loyal the customer. For rental purposes, most mailers refer to a customer who has purchased more than once as a "multibuyer." The monetary value (the amount spent by a customer) is kept in one or both of two ways. The most common is based on the amount spent on that customer's latest order. The other method is to accumulate the amount spent during the lifetime of the customer's relationship. When a list is offered for rental by monetary value, it should be stated clearly which method is involved.

Besides the RFM factors, any additional information that can be captured about the customer can be used to enhance list rentals. Much information about the customer is readily available but not always apparent.

Product selection, or at least product categories, gives a prospective list renter a more finely tuned universe from which to choose a list. The sex of the purchaser is also important. Many offers work only when mailed to a male-only or a female-only list. Most computerized lists are kept in ZIP code sequence so that mailers that require a list from specific geographic areas can target their mailings properly.

Other selection criteria also can enhance list rentals. Such criteria include age, title (Miss, Ms. Mrs., President, Doctor, etc.), indications of a change of address, and business versus home address. Some additional information can be made available by overlaying, or matching, outside information with a house file. This would include such things as geographic overlays, which are important in determining the psychographics (lifestyles) of the customer, and religion or ethnic origin overlays, which are matched against both the names and the locations of the customers.

WHO MARKETS THE LIST

The Owner

This is the most obvious choice. The list belongs to the owner, and no one can be more familiar with its makeup and how it performs. Since the list owner ultimately has to decide whether a prospective renter is acceptable, an intermediate step (the list management firm), as well as time, is eliminated by the owner marketing the list. Also, having a proprietary interest in the mailing list, the owner can control the content and quantity of information disseminated about the company. This information is beneficial to prospective renters in determining the viability of the list for their needs.

In order to market the list, the owner would need a staff whose job ideally would consist of full-time work on list rentals. Small companies combine the duties of an in-house list manager with other responsibilities such as obtaining outside lists for the companies' own mailings. Besides marketing the list, the in-house list manager's duties include coordinating list rental orders with the company's computer department or service bureau and assisting in developing additional methods of segmenting the file to present to list renters.

Financially, the in-house management is successful when a list owner can command a very large list rental income. The list owner receives all the revenue from a list rental except for the list broker's commission. When the list is managed in-house, the cost of the in-house management (salaries, benefits, travel expenses, and list promotion costs) must be weighed against the fee charged by a list management firm.

Outside List Management

Utilizing the services of a professional list management firm is the more logical choice for most small and medium-size lists. List managers are experienced in promoting the mailing lists in their control. Most management firms are skilled at computerizing lists, segmenting, applying overlays, invoicing, and collecting for list rentals. Most important, however, is the network of contacts at the list brokerage houses and at many list user companies, which take years to develop. These contacts give them immediate access to a large market for almost any new list that would be assigned to them. Through a concentration of their efforts, list management firms (as opposed to list owners) are able to build a staff of knowledgeable list sales personnel as well as list-oriented computer and advertising professionals. When contracting with a list management firm, list owners are freed from most concerns involved with developing rental income from their mailing lists.

As with any such situation, there are trade-offs. The list owner of necessity must relinquish some control over the mailing list, the information disseminated about the list, and the companies to which the list is rented. The owner does regulate this to some extent by assigning parameters within which the list manager must operate. However, unless the owner is willing to be contacted constantly for approval of exceptions, the parameters should give the managers enough latitude that their marketing efforts are not hindered.

Financially, the owner receives less gross income from list rentals when using a list management concern. Most management firms charge a percentage of the list rental as their fee. This fee, usually 10 percent of the rental, covers their sales efforts, promotion costs, reporting costs, and credit and collection efforts. If the list is highly successful as a rental property, there will come a time when this 10 percent charge will become greater than the cost of in-house management. At that point, the owner must decide whether to maintain the relationship with the management firm or bring the list into the house.

The List Broker

The list broker is the keystone in most list rental transactions. The list broker's primary function is to recommend mailing lists and segments within mailing lists to list users. In the simplest terms, the list manager has the list, and the list broker has the client. Although the list owner or manager can contact the list users directly, it is inconceivable that the users could sift through thousands of ideas, meet with hundreds of list owners, and still meet mailing deadlines. This is the raison d'être of the list broker. The staff of the list brokerage firm can screen thousands of list possibilities and recommend only those which appear to have the best chance of working for the client (having already been made privy to the lists and segments that previously have performed successfully).

There is also a benefit to the list manager in this arrangement. When the list manager makes a presentation to describe the mailing list, the broker's staff listening to the manager represents many prospective users. Several list orders can be generated from one meeting. It is imperative that the manager bring as much information as possible to these presentations, since each broker will have questions brought to mind by his or her client's needs. In effect, the manager's presentation is being screened by as many as 100 or more prospective list renters at any one presentation.

This convenience does not come free. The broker's charges come in the form of a commission charged to the list owner, currently 20 percent of the list price. For this commission, the brokers place orders for the list and collect the funds in payment for the lists. The brokers collect the full amount of the list rental fees, deduct their commissions where applicable, and remit the balance to the list owners or managers. However, not all charges on a list rental are subject to a broker's commission. Many list owners do not allow commissions on selection charges such as frequency, sex, or product categories.

Also, after a mailer has used a rented list for some time, the mailer's house file will include many names that still are being supplied by the list owner. To compensate for this, it is customary for list owners to allow a reasonable number of names to be deducted from payment for continuation list orders; this is referred to as a net name arrangement. It is done in the form of a percentage of the list rental for which the mailer guarantees payment (traditionally 85 percent). The balance, should it represent names already on the mailer's file, will be paid only at a rate set to cover the owner's cost and the cost for running the names. This is referred to as a running charge and is usually $3 to $4 per thousand names. Most owners will allow this type of arrangement on orders with a minimum of 25,000 or 50,000 names. Of course, if a mailer gives an 85 percent guarantee and finds that only 10 percent of the names are on the house file, the owner is paid for the other 90 percent of unduplicated names. The run charges are applied against the other 10 percent. Run charges are not commissionable to list brokers.

MARKETING THE MAILING LIST

Data Cards

The data card is the primary source of information on any given list. They are usually printed on 51/2- by 81/2-inch card stock so that they can be filed for easy reference by list brokers and mailers. They should have as much information as possible. Data cards should be dated with the most current counts available and should carry a description of the makeup of the list, the price, the methods of addressing that are available, the availability of any segmentation on the list, and whether the list has been matched against the Mail Preference Service (MPS) of the Direct Marketing Association (DMA). This MPS is a list of people who have notified the DMA that they do not wish to be on any mailing list. If people feel this way, it is safe to say that they would not be good prospects for most direct mail offers, and it would therefore be beneficial to remove them from all mailing lists.

A separate data card should be produced for each major segment of the file. The entire set of data cards should be updated at least twice a year and mailed to all brokers and as many list mailers as is appropriate. The purpose of the data cards is to inform clients, prospective clients, and brokers about updated counts on the mailing list. The other purpose is to explain available selections to potential users. A typical data card is shown in Figure 6-1.

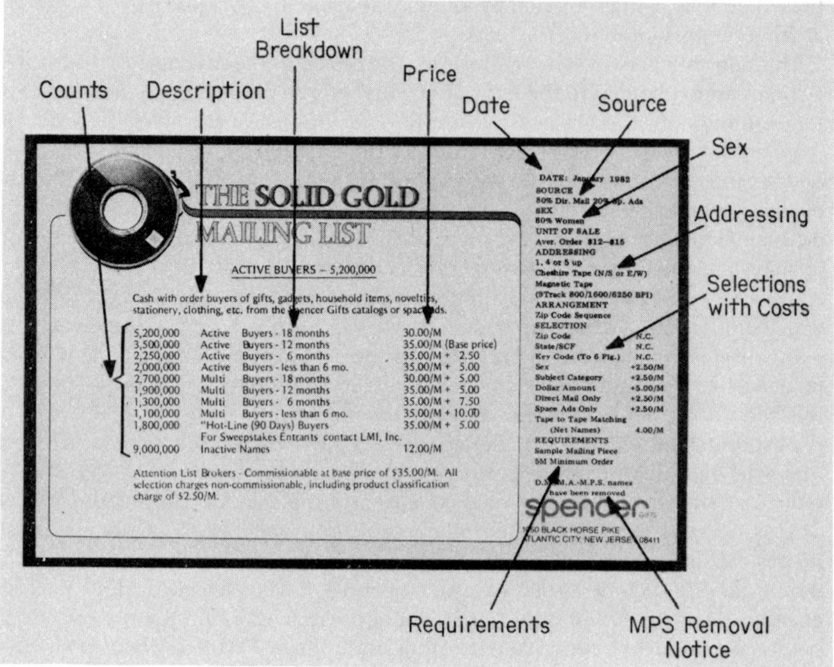

Figure 6-1 Mailing list data card.

List Bulletins

Bulletins are special notices mailed to brokers, clients, and prospective clients whenever something significant occurs between updates of the data cards. Bulletins may be used to advise mailers of new selections, overlays, or any other changes in the makeup of the list. They can be used to remind brokers to recommend a list or to advise brokers and clients about new and successful uses of the list.

Advertisements

The obvious purpose of advertising is to attract new clients and list brokers. A more subtle purpose is to keep the visibility of the list high. The more successful a list appears, the more it will be considered for testing. The higher the visibility, the more clients will be aware of a list when a broker recommends it.

The advertisements should give an indication of the type of list, the quantities that are available, the appeal that the list has, and the types of offers that have been successful with the list.

The advertisements should appear wherever they are likely to be read by list renters. Trade journals and list directories are the two most important media for list advertising. Most people in direct marketing read the trade journals, and all list brokers use the list directories. Other sources of advertising space are direct marketing trade show directories, convention rosters, and the newsletters of the many direct marketing clubs throughout the country. Some major list managers use direct marketing trade shows to advertise in a different way. Most direct marketing conferences include a trade show in which booths may be rented. These booths are used to disseminate information about the mailing list to passersby as well as to discuss suggestions for efficient use of various segments of the file with specific clients.

FINDING LIST RENTERS

Current List Users

Clients who are using a mailing list successfully represent the first place to develop additional list revenue. This can be accomplished through several methods. The first method of increasing utilization by a specific client involves recommending additional segments of the file that can be tested. For example, if a male selection criterion was successful and all the men on a particular list were ordered, a further recommendation would be to test the women on the list who are designated as "Mrs." with the assumption that for the most part, women who are referred to as "Mrs." have a husband who might be interested in a direct marketing offer. This recommendation could not be presumed to work as well as a male select, but with testing, it could yield a sufficient number of responses to warrant further use.

Another approach of particular interest when a client already is using all or a major portion of an active file is to recommend using the same list for a second mailing. The list manager can make the offer more attractive by offering a discount for a reuse. This is justified by the fact that the manager does not need to do any additional work on a second usage order, since the list is already in the possession of the list user. The discount could be sufficient to offset the presumably lower response rate of the second mailing. Some companies allow this reuse discount no matter what the second offer is, while others permit the discount only if the offer is the same in both mailings.

A third method for increasing list usage is to offer a third-party endorsement. It is assumed that a person who purchases goods or services from a particular company develops an identification with that company. Therefore, that person would be more apt to purchase something with the company's name on it rather than a name that held no particular significance. A third-party endorsement would involve the rental of a company's list plus the use of its name for a mailing by another company.

This type of arrangement can be used to enhance the response rate of marginally successful lists. The third-party endorsement should increase the list usage and increase the rental profits by the amount of the premium paid (anywhere from $5 to $25 per thousand names) for the use of the list owner's endorsement. This arrangement can be used only for offers in which the list owner has complete confidence, since the offer will be associated with the list owner.

Developing New Clients

Although increasing list rental usage by current clients will increase list revenue, a significant opportunity for increased income occurs when one expands the number of clients who can use a list successfully. The first step is to examine the composition of the current list users and then solicit orders from companies that are in the same businesses as the current clients. The rationale behind this idea is not ironclad. There are other variables at work besides the mailing list. Even so, this is still the prime source for additional list clients.

Another area of list leads to be considered would be the house mailings of the company itself. Besides the house file, a mailer also rents outside lists. The owners of lists that are working successfully for the company are possible users of the company's list as well. The fact that their lists are working indicates a similarity of lifestyles among the people on the two files so that an exchange of files could be beneficial to both firms.

The word "exchange" also can mean a free exchange of names, or a "swap." In this case, neither company generates list rental income, nor do the companies incur a list rental expense in an effort to generate new customers for their house files.

Other sources of new list clients include broker contacts in which the brokers make recommendations of new files to their clients. Sending a representative to industry functions at which list users are apt to be present is essential in soliciting new clients. The most significant of these functions are DMA conferences and trade shows, major direct marketing club conferences, and List Day, an annual meeting of companies involved in mailing lists that also is sponsored by the DMA.

Cold canvassing usually is not cost-efficient. However, this too can be a source of list revenue if done properly. A good way to increase cost-efficiency is to include a business reply card (BRC) with list advertising, as was discussed already. Companies that reply for more information, although a product of a cold canvassing, already show an interest in the list, making the possibility of developing them into list users that much greater.

INCOME

List rentals that are worked on diligently can be a significant profit center. The following is a conservative example of the amount of income that can be earned from releasing a mailing list for rental. We assume that we have a mailing list of 250,000 active names, with an annual turnover rate (the number of times the entire 250,000 are rented) of 10 times renting at $40 per thousand. We will be using a list broker charging 20 percent, a list manager charging 10 percent, an additional 10 percent charge to cover the cost of the service bureau plus all other overhead, and an additional 10 percent deduction to allow for some net name rental guarantees. The breakdown is as follows:

	250,000	names
×	10	turnover
	2,500,000	annual quantity rented
×	$40.00	per thousand rental price
	$100,000	gross rental
−	$20,000	minus broker commission (20%)
	$80,000	
	$80,000	
−	10,000	minus managers fee (10%)
	$70,000	
−	10,000	minus service bureau and overhead
	$60,000	
−	10,000	minus net name guarantee (10%)
	$50,000	net income

This example is extremely conservative. Many mailing lists have a turnover rate of 20 to 30 times. Also, the service bureau and overhead charges vary from company to company. In this case, the company with a base of 250,000 active customer names can generate an additional $50,000 of net income a year with relatively little effort and no depletion in the "inventory" of names. In fact, many mailers report that exposing their customers to other direct mail offers sharpens the customers' awareness of direct marketing and enhances the companies' response rates.

Mailers are always looking for new lists. The market for mailing lists grows every year. Mailing lists represent a low-cost, high-profit marketing tool with a ready market.

chapter 7

RESEARCH METHODS

Joseph Castelli

Vice President,
Director of Research
Ogilvy & Mather
Direct
New York, N.Y.

INTRODUCTION

This chapter will tell you how to use research to improve the effectiveness of a direct-response campaign. While some basic research terminology and concepts will be discussed so that you will have a better understanding of research, the goal is not to turn you into a professional researcher. The objective is to provide some insight into the variety of ways in which research can help the direct marketer.

RESEARCH VERSUS TESTING

Most people in direct marketing are familiar with the concept of testing. Direct marketers test several mailing packages before deciding which one to use. We test a variety of mailing lists to see how well each list does before we rent entire lists. We test different offers and premiums to determine which ones generate the greatest response.

Research involves surveys that are conducted among consumers. Much of this research is conducted before the testing phase that often occurs in direct marketing. The question you may ask is, "Why do we need research when we can test in the mail?" The answer would be that research can help answer some critical marketing and advertising questions that cannot be answered as easily, if at all, by testing.

However, research should not replace testing. Instead, research and testing should be used in tandem to produce more effective direct-response campaigns.

QUALITATIVE RESEARCH AND QUANTITATIVE RESEARCH

Qualitative research has the following characteristics:

- It is often the first stage of a research program.
- It is exploratory in nature. For example, it may be used to explore the reasons why people buy a product, how they use it, and what they like and dislike about it.
- It generally is conducted among a relatively small number of people, very often fewer than twenty-five.
- It often is conducted through group sessions, although it also may be conducted with in-depth interviews.
- It is used primarily to generate ideas or develop hypotheses.

Quantitative research has the following characteristics:

- It generally follows the qualitative stage of research.
- It generally is fairly well structured. For example, respondents may be asked to rate a product according to a series of specific product attributes such as easy to use, saves time, and good value for the money. The list of attributes may in fact have been developed on the basis of qualitative research.
- It is conducted among a relatively large number of respondents. The sample size for a quantitative study can run anywhere from 100 respondents to well over 1000.
- It is conducted through individual interviews.
- It is used to determine the extent to which the behavior and attitudes uncovered in qualitative research are shared by others.

Qualitative Research

As was mentioned earlier, there are two basic forms of qualitative research: group sessions and in-depth interviews. Since group sessions are used more frequently, let us discuss them first.

Group Sessions. Basically, a group session consists of eight to ten people. Usually a series of two to four sessions is conducted in a given study. Each session runs about 2 hours. If possible, these sessions should be conducted in several geographically dispersed areas rather than in a single area.

Participants should be recruited either by telephone or in shopping malls and prescreened to determine that they are qualified respondents, i.e., members of the target market. Those who qualify are invited to attend a group session. They are told that the session is being conducted for research and that they will be asked to discuss a given topic with others. They also are told that they will receive a monetary gift in appreciation for their help.

The sessions usually are held at a research facility. Many of these facilities are equipped with a one-way mirror so that the client and the agency can observe the sessions from an adjoining room. The main reason for using a one-way mirror is to avoid distracting the participants. The sessions are taped to free the moderator from the responsibility of taking notes. However, respondents are told that the sessions will be taped and that they will be observed.

These sessions should be conducted by a professional group session moderator. A professional moderator should:

- Be sensitive to the critical issues
- Put participants at ease
- Be a good listener
- Encourage participants to interact with one another
- Keep the conversation lively
- Avoid revealing personal views regarding the product
- Be sure the participants stay focused on the subject

Let's consider some of the ways in which group sessions can be of help in developing an advertising strategy.

1. They can help us understand consumer language. This helps to ensure that we know how to talk to the consumer. For example, we can determine what terms and expressions the consumer uses to describe our product and therefore is likely to understand in our advertising.
2. They can help us uncover attitudes and motivations relevant to our product. This is done by exploring the needs, desires, and problems of consumers.
3. They may uncover new ways in which the product can be used.
4. They can provide insight into the decision-making process. They can give us clues about who is involved in deciding whether to buy a given product and about the basis upon which the decision to buy that product is made.
5. Respondents are likely to be more spontaneous than they would be in other interviewing situations. They are more likely to reveal their inner feelings when they believe that others in the room are doing so.
6. Finally, they are a good first step in the research process. They can provide a great deal of insight in a relatively short period of time and at a reasonable cost.

In-Depth Interviews. In-depth interviews are more appropriate than group sessions when:

- The people you want to talk to are geographically dispersed and it would be difficult to get a sufficient number of them together for a group session
- The respondents have little in common with one another and it would be difficult to develop group interaction
- The discussion is likely to be very technical and complex
- The experiences of each respondent are likely to be very different

Question Areas. Whether group sessions or in-depth interviews are conducted, the discussion should go from the general to the specific. The moderator or in-depth interviewer may begin with a general discussion of the product category, such as who uses it, when they use it, and why they use it. Participants then may be asked to compare the various brands in the category. Finally, they may be asked to discuss a specific brand in greater detail.

Before the session is conducted, the moderator develops a discussion guide. This discussion guide is used to ensure that all the topics that are of interest are covered before the session is over. The discussion guide is not a questionnaire to be adhered to very strictly. There are times when the conversation will move into areas that do not appear until later in the guide. If there is no danger of bias arising from covering the subject earlier, the moderator may pursue the topic when it arises. But it takes a professional researcher to know when this can be done.

As was mentioned earlier, qualitative research is used to generate ideas or develop hypotheses. The next logical step is to test the hypotheses in a quantitative study.

Quantitative Research

Quantitative research can be done in one of three ways:

- Personal interviews
- Telephone survey
- Mail survey

There are advantages and limitations with each technique. You should be aware of what they are before deciding which method to use for a particular study.

Personal Interviewing. Personal interviewing can be conducted through door-to-door interviews. However, this approach is less popular these days because it's often the most expensive way of conducting a study and because it's more time-consuming than a telephone survey.

Still, there are two major advantages to conducting a study through personal interviews. You can use a fairly long and complex questionnaire, and you can present the respondent with a series of concept statements, photographs of the product, or the product itself. Also, you can demonstrate how a product should be used or have respondents try the product.

One approach that offers many of the advantages of door-to-door interviewing and eliminates the disadvantages is personal interviewing on an intercept basis. In this case, interviews generally are conducted in shopping malls. Respondents are stopped and screened to ensure that they are qualified. Those who qualify are interviewed in a facility at the shopping mall.

This form of interviewing is less expensive than door-to-door interviewing. It usually can be done in less time as well since respondents often can be screened visually. For example, if the study is to be conducted among women 18 to 35 years of age, interviewers can screen visually for women who are likely to qualify.

One disadvantage of this approach is that it is relatively expensive and time-consuming when the incidence of qualified respondents in the population is very low. For example, if you had to conduct a study among architectural engineers or dental technicians, it would not be feasible to conduct the study in this manner.

Telephone Survey. One of the most popular ways of conducting research these days is by telephone. It offers several advantages over personal interviewing, including the following:

- Wide area telephone service (WATS) lines have made it possible to conduct a telephone survey across the United States from one location.
- The interviews can be supervised closely as they take place.
- Callbacks can be made to those who were not reached on the initial call. This approach helps provide a more representative sample.

- It is a particularly effective way of conducting a study among a select group of individuals such as garden club members or farm tractor dealers when a list of these individuals is available.
- While the cost of conducting telephone surveys has risen in recent years, it is still a fairly economical technique. Although a telephone survey costs more than a mail survey, it often is less expensive than a study conducted through personal interviews.
- It can be conducted quickly.

On the other hand, telephone surveys have one disadvantage. It becomes difficult and expensive to present concept statements or products to respondents. While these can be mailed to respondents before the interview, a device such as a metal box with a combination lock should be used to ensure that respondents are not exposed to the test materials before the interview. (The respondent is allowed to keep the metal storage box and the lock as a gift.) Because of the additional expense involved, this device generally is used on a selective basis.

Mail Survey. There are certain advantages to conducting a survey by mail.

- It's often less expensive to conduct a survey by mail than by personal or telephone interviews. This cost difference becomes more apparent in studies that involve a large sample.
- It's possible in a mail survey to expose respondents to new product concepts and product samples.

However, mail surveys have a number of disadvantages.

- One of the main concerns is the relatively low response rate one is likely to have with a mail survey. While the use of an incentive—e.g., sending the respondent a gift with the questionnaire—is likely to increase the response rate, a mail survey is still likely to yield a lower completion rate than one would have with personal or telephone interviews. One may ask, "Why not simply mail out more questionnaires?" The answer is that the sample size is only one issue.
- The other issue related to the low response rate is the representativeness of the sample. For example, suppose we mail a questionnaire to 1000 people and only 200 respond. We don't know how the 200 people who responded differ in attitude from the 800 who did not. It may be that only those who are the most enthusiastic about the product have responded. Or perhaps only those who are dissatisfied with the product have responded.
- We don't really know who completed the questionnaire. Those who receive a questionnaire in the mail may complete it themselves, have someone else complete it for them, or simply throw it away.
- If the mailing list has not been updated, it will add to the problem of obtaining a satisfactory response rate.
- There are limitations in terms of what questions can be asked. For example, you should not ask a question such as, "When I mention television sets, what brands come to mind?" if you provide a list of these brands somewhere else in the questionnaire. Obviously, a respondent may report in one part of the questionnaire something that he or she has learned from another part. There is no way to prevent a respondent from reading ahead in a mail survey.

- The questionnaire must be relatively short. As the questionnaire increases in size, the response rate is likely to decrease.
- The questionnaire has to be fairly easy to complete. You cannot ask complicated questions in a mail survey, nor can you expect respondents to write lengthy responses to open-ended questions.
- A mail survey generally takes longer to complete than one done by telephone or in person. In addition, a low response rate may necessitate a follow-up mailing to nonresponders. This in turn will increase the time it takes to complete the study.

So far we have discussed the two basic kinds of research: qualitative and quantitative. We also have discussed the alternative methods of conducting each of these forms of research and the pros and cons of each. We are now ready to consider the key applications of research to direct-response marketing.

RESEARCH APPLICATIONS

There are four main areas in which research can contribute to the success of a direct-response program:

- Identifying the target market
- Determining what to say in the advertising
- Determining the corporate image
- Developing new products

Identifying the Target Market

You are more likely to reach your marketing goals if you determine which consumers represent your best opportunity. Therefore, one of the most important things research can do is provide a clear picture of the target market.

One way to identify the target market is by examining your current customers. For example, you can determine their demographic characteristics. It might be helpful to know whether your current customers are primarily:

- Men or women
- Young adults or older people
- College-educated or not
- Professionals or blue-collar workers
- Single or married
- City folk or rural dwellers

Beyond this, you also should learn something about their behavior and attitudes. For example, you should try to determine:

- What products they currently buy
- How often they buy the products
- How frequently they use the products
- On what occasions they use them
- What they like about the products
- What they dislike about them
- What needs, if any, are not being satisfied by the products currently on the market

You should learn about their lifestyles. For example, it might be helpful to know whether your customers are more likely to:

- Spend money or save money
- Go to parties or stay home
- Prefer gourmet cooking or meat and potatoes
- Have a broad or a limited range of interests
- Attend rock concerts or PTA meetings

Once you determine who your target is, selecting the right mailing lists and print media becomes much easier. You also will be more certain that the tone of your advertising is correct.

Here are some suggestions for conducting such a study.

- Ideally, the study should be conducted by telephone rather than by mail.
- The sample should be drawn from a list of current customers. You should interview at least 200 respondents. However, you may wish to segment the sample. For example, you may wish to see how the heavy buyers differ from the light buyers. In this case, each of these groups should be represented by at least 100 respondents.
- To avoid any bias in response, respondents should not be told for whom the study is being conducted.
- The questionnaire should consist primarily of structured questions.

Determining What to Say in the Advertising

Once you know your target market, the next thing to determine is what to say in the advertising. For this, we recommend a two-phase research program.

The first phase consists of qualitative research. In most cases, this would consist of a series of group sessions. Group sessions can be helpful in several ways.

- As was mentioned earlier, they can help one develop an understanding of consumer language. Therefore, they can help ensure that one knows how to talk to the consumer.
- They can help one identify the reasons why people buy a given product.

On the basis of these group sessions and creative judgment, a series of copy promises or product benefit statements are developed. We are now ready for the quantitative phase of the research program, in which the relative importance of each of these product benefits is determined. This is done with a technique called the copy promise test.

We begin by developing a series of copy promises or product benefit statements. These statements should be in the form of single sentences. Here are some examples of copy promises that might be tested for a new series of books on photography to be offered on a continuity basis.

This series of books:

- Is a handsome collection of volumes on your favorite subject
- Can help you become a better photographer
- Contains the latest information on photography

- Can show you how to improve your photographic skills
- Allows you to learn photography at your own pace at home
- Helps you develop a personal photographic style
- Is a comprehensive course in creative photography

While this list includes only seven promises, a copy promise test could evaluate as many as twenty-five promises at one time.

After the promises are developed, each is typed on a 3 by 5 card. The cards then are incorporated into a deck.

The copy promise test then can be conducted either on an intercept basis in shopping malls or by telephone. The decision about which method to use should take into account the difficulty one would encounter in locating members of the target market in a shopping mall. For example, if your target market consists of women 18 to 35 years of age, it may be relatively easy to locate a sufficient number of them in shopping malls. On the other hand, it would be very difficult to find a sufficient number of antique dealers this way. Given the fact that many direct-response campaigns are directed at fairly narrow target markets, you probably will find that a telephone survey is the most practical way of conducting a copy promise test.

A typical copy promise test is conducted among 150 respondents. Whether the survey is done in person or by telephone, respondents first are screened to ensure that they are in the target market. For example, if one conducted a study for a new series of books on photography, respondents might be screened to ensure that they own a camera, use at least six rolls of film per year, and regularly read at least one of the major photography magazines.

Before the promises are presented or read to these respondents, there is a brief introduction. For example, in the case of the photography series, respondents would be told that a leading publisher is planning to introduce a new series of books on photography and that this series may offer its readers a variety of benefits. They then would be told that we would like to read some of the benefits that such a series might offer photographers and ask them to tell us how important each benefit is to them. They would be asked to use a 10-point scale. Therefore, if they perceived the benefit to be very important, they would give it a rating of 10. If they perceived it to be not at all important, they would give it a rating of 1. They would be told that they could give each benefit any rating from 1 to 10 depending on how important they perceived the benefit to be.

When all the promises have been rated, the respondents are asked to rate each promise in terms of its perceived uniqueness. That is, they are asked to indicate whether they believe that each benefit is available in all, most, some, few, or none of the photography books currently available on the market.

Ideally, a few promises are regarded to be both important and unique. We would consider these to be the most effective promises.

At this point, it should be mentioned that you should not accept the results of a copy promise test with blind faith. You should verify the results with an in-mail test. Select the three or four winning promises and test them in the mail. In one such test, the winning promise won by a significant degree in the mail. The response rate was 25 percent higher than that of the next best test mailing.

Here are some things to keep in mind in regard to promise testing.

1. The key to the success of promise testing is to start with a good set of promises. This means that the top creative people on the account should be involved in the development of the copy promises.
2. Each promise should be in the form of a simple sentence.
3. Each promise should contain only one benefit. Otherwise, it will be difficult to interpret the results.
4. Be sure that the promises to be tested can in fact be used in advertising. The promises should be discussed with your legal department before the promise test is conducted.

Determining the Corporate Image

It is important for a firm to know what image it has in the minds of the target market. Obviously, if your company is not well known or is perceived to be selling inferior merchandise or to be slow in fulfilling orders, your business will be affected adversely. Therefore, it is important to know how your firm is viewed by the prospective customers. To determine this, a corporate image study can be conducted among the members of the target market.

Corporate image studies can be conducted through personal interviews, a telephone survey, or a mail survey. For the reasons stated earlier, a telephone survey is often the preferred method.

The sample should consist of members of the target market. However, you should also include in the study a sample of current customers.

The study should be designed to obtain the following information:

- Top-of-mind awareness of companies in your industry. For example, you might ask, "When I mention sporting goods manufacturers, what companies come to mind?"
- Awareness of these companies on an aided basis. For example, you might say, "I'm going to read to you the names of some companies that manufacture sporting goods. As I read each name to you, please tell me whether you have heard of that company." Of the two measures of awareness, more confidence should be placed in top-of-mind awareness. However, if consumers do not recognize the name of your firm even on an aided basis, this would suggest that some effort should be made to increase their awareness of your firm.
- Perception of your firm and its competitors on a series of key attributes. You can begin by asking respondents to rate a series of attributes in terms of how important they are in the selection of a firm from which to buy sporting goods. The list of attributes might include:

    1. Is a leader in the industry
    2. Offers quality merchandise
    3. Offers a wide selection of merchandise
    4. Provides speedy delivery
    5. Guarantees the products it sells

Once they have rated these attributes in terms of importance, you should ask them to rate your firm and its competitors on the basis of these same attributes. You then will know which attributes are the most critical and how well your firm stacks up against the competition in terms of these critical attributes. This information can be used to help identify potential problem areas or provide assurance that no outstanding problems exist in the awareness or perception of your firm.

Developing New Products

Another key area in which research can be helpful is new product development. A new product development program generally involves two stages of research.

The first stage is the idea generation stage. One way to develop new product ideas is through the use of qualitative research. For example, several group session or a series of in-depth interviews can be conducted with consumers. However, these should not be regarded as brainstorming sessions. That is, these consumers are not asked to provide ideas for new products. Instead, they are asked to discuss a range of topics such as

- The products they use
- How often they purchase them
- How frequently they use them
- In what ways they use them
- What they like about them
- What they dislike about them
- What needs are not being satisfied by these products

On the basis of this qualitative research, a series of new product concepts are developed. These concepts may be ideas for entirely new products or ideas for improving existing products. After these concepts are developed, they should be discussed with the product development staff to be sure that the new products actually can be made. If any cannot be made, the concepts should be revised or dropped from the next stage of research.

We are now ready for the concept testing stage. The objective of this stage of research is to determine the relative interest in each new product idea on the basis of the concept alone.

This research generally is conducted among a sample of 150 members of the target market. While the ideal way to conduct such a study is through personal interviews, the cost of doing the study by telephone is considerably lower. The interview is similar to the one used in the copy promise test that was discussed earlier. After respondents are screened to make sure they are members of the target market, they are told that a leading company is planning to introduce a series of new products on the market and that we would like their reaction to these new products.

Respondents then are exposed to one concept at a time. After each concept is read, the respondents are asked to indicate their interest in buying the product. A scale is used to measure buying interest. For example, this scale might consist of the following five points:

- Definitely will buy
- Probably will buy
- May or may not buy
- Probably will not buy
- Definitely will not buy

In addition, reasons for interest or lack of interest usually are obtained. Respondents then may be asked to rate the product according to a series of product attributes. For example, if you were testing concepts for new office equipment, you might ask respondents to indicate how they perceive the product in terms of the following attributes:

- Easy to use
- Saves time
- Saves work
- Good value for the money
- Attractive appearance
- Reduces error
- Fewer repair bills

After the respondents evaluate the first concept, the next concept is presented, and the same procedure is followed. To avoid any bias arising from the order in which the concepts are presented, the order should be rotated. In other words, the first respondent would see concept A, then concept B, and finally concept C. The second respondent would begin with concept B, then evaluate concept C, and finally rate concept A.

In evaluating the results, one should keep in mind that this type of research, like much of the research we have discussed, is designed to provide a relative rather than an absolute measure. That is, the test will measure interest relative to the other concepts being tested. Therefore, it may be safe to assume that respondents prefer concept A to either concept B or concept C if that is what the results show. However, it would not be safe to assume that you could project the buying interest levels to the marketplace. For example, if 20 percent of those interviewed say they definitely will buy the product, that does not mean that 20 percent of the target market actually will do so. For many reasons, the level of interest you obtain in the research is likely to be higher than the one you will achieve in the marketplace.

Obviously, we have oversimplified the procedure. Beyond the research already discussed, there may be a need for product testing to determine whether the product lives up to consumer expectations. There also may be a need for name testing and research to determine product positioning.

THE NEED FOR PROFESSIONALISM

The previous section of this chapter listed four key areas in which research can be useful. While it was shown how these studies should be conducted, I did not wish to imply that I recommend that the direct marketer should take it upon himself or herself to conduct research.

It was said at the start of this chapter that the objective is not to turn you into a professional researcher. Research should be conducted by professionals, and therefore, you should use the services of a professional research firm. Here are some guidelines to help you select a research firm. Select a firm that

- Has a broad range of experience and a proven track record of helping other companies.
- Is problem-oriented rather than technique-oriented. Good researchers make sure they understand the problem before offering a solution. They have no vested interest in using a particular research technique.
- Has a staff that can communicate well both verbally and in writing. The most brilliant research study will be of little value unless the results and implications are communicated clearly to those who have to act on the results.
- Is concerned with quality control. Choose a firm that pretests the questionnaire as a standard practice and provides a series of controls in the interviewing and tabulation stages of the research process.
- Is marketing-oriented. Their conclusions and recommendations should be specific and practical.

Here are some hints on how to get research firms to do their best for you.

- Confide in them. Tell them what your problems are. Give them all the background they need to understand the situation fully.
- Trust them. Rely on them to determine whether research can be helpful, and if so, how the research should be done. Don't tell them that you want to do some group sessions or a telephone survey. Tell them what you want to learn and how you plan to use the information. Let them decide how research can best solve your problem.
- Don't be penny-wise and dollar-foolish. If they recommend research that you regard as too expensive, consider the value of the information you will receive. It may well be worth the cost.

To summarize, I would like to make two recommendations. The first is that you use research to improve the effectiveness of your direct marketing campaigns. The second is that you have the research designed, conducted, and analyzed by a professional.

chapter 8

PRODUCT DEVELOPMENT

Ronald Gerwin

*Vice President—
Merchandising Sales
American Express
Company
New York, N.Y.*

The most effective weapon in the battle of the marketplace is a dynamic product line that is thoughtfully conceived, carefully developed, skillfully positioned, and fired directly at the market targets. I'm talking about starting with ideas and going through the systematic process of evaluation, rejection, adoption, development, testing (and sometimes retesting), and then rolling out.

MERCHANDISE

I'm not knocking the traditional method of finding products: evaluating and selecting merchandise from syndicators or with-it little shops and trade shows here and abroad. This is a source of many ideas for mail-order people, and it's also one of the steps in prospecting for products to develop yourself. Many marketers successfully shop that way and let it go at that.

For these marketers who advertise existing products instead of developing their own, one of the best guides was developed by Len Carlson at Sunset House. His personal guidelines, which are listed in Figure 8-1, are timeless for merchandisers and integral to proprietary product development people as well. The difference comes in applying the principles to marketing your own product rather than selling the finished products of others.

1. Is there a perceived need for the product?
2. Is it practical?
3. Is it unique?
4. Is the price right?
5. Is it good value?
6. Is the markup sufficient?
7. Does it have broad appeal?
8. Or are there specific smaller segments of my list that have a strong desire for the product?
9. Is it new? Or, will my customers perceive it to be new?
10. Will it photograph or illustrate interestingly?
11. Are there sufficient unusual selling features to make the copy exciting?
12. Is it economical to ship? Too fragile? Odd-shaped? Too heavy? Too big?
13. Can it be personalized?
14. Are there any legal problems to overcome?
15. Is it safe to use?
16. Is the supplier reputable?
17. Will backup merchandise be available for fast shipment on reorders?
18. Does my mother (wife, brother, husband) like it? (If so, it probably should be discarded!)
19. Might returns be too huge?
20. Will refurbishing of returned merchandise be practical?
21. Is it, or can it be, packaged attractively?
22. Are usage instructions clear?
23. How does it compare to competitive products?
24. Will it have exclusivity?
25. Will it lend itself to repeat business?
26. Is it consumable (for repeat orders)?
27. Is it faddy? Too short-lived?
28. Is it seasonal for mail-order selling?
29. Can an add-on to the product make it more distinctive and saleable?
30. Will the number of stockkeeping units (sizes and colors) create inventory problems?
31. Does it lend itself to multiple pricing?
32. Is it too readily available in stores?
33. Is it like an old, hot item that guarantees its success?
34. Or is it doomed because similar items failed before?

Figure 8-1 Factors to consider when selecting direct-response merchandise. They are also integral to developing your own proprietary products from scratch.

PRODUCT DEVELOPMENT

Even though merchandising of products is a vital part of direct marketing, it is being preempted by a growing number in the business who are discovering the advantages of being more active very early in the game, putting their hands on product development, and getting the job done their way for the benefit of their customers and their future. This extra measure of control can pay off handsomely on the bottom line.

The Assets Are Permanent

American Express, Time-Life Books, L. L. Bean, the Horchow Collection, Franklin Mint, and Fingerhut are just a few of the major names that bank on exclusive products to ensure a franchise in the marketplace. They trade off a temporary advantage of breaking first with somebody else's product or service for the more permanent asset of testing and rolling distinctive products of their own with far greater potential for building loyal customers. Or they may do both.

You Have More Control

Making your own products puts you in charge. You are less dependent on outside sources for the lifeblood of your business. Your products can be truly proprietary, belonging to you alone, not you this month and your competitor next month.

Your Customers Will Notice

Given a disciplined conceptualizing technique and strong follow-through, products you develop for yourself should be far more innovative and distinctive in the eyes of your customers and prospects. Customers soon will realize that your advertisements carry a far more meaningful message than those of the competition. You will be perceived as being more genuinely alert to serving your customers.

You Can Go Direct

Ultimately the payoff comes at the bottom line of your profit and loss (P&L) statement. By dealing directly with primary sources of manufactured items, you have control and can see exactly what the costs are at every step from idea to customer. You can "eliminate the middleman," enjoy wider margins, or set prices lower, as Figure 8-2 suggests.

EVERYTHING STARTS WITH AN IDEA

Essentially, we're talking about new combinations of existing concepts or applications, everything from a better mousetrap to Rubik's Cube. In the old days, a table-thumping boss often was the idea source. Today, things have evolved into more systematic procedures conducted by committees, departments, or even semiautonomous venture teams. Whatever the system, the basic road map is similar.

Where Do Ideas Come From?

They come from all over, but a lot of them should come from you, of course. Read everything you can that ties in with the life and times of your customers.

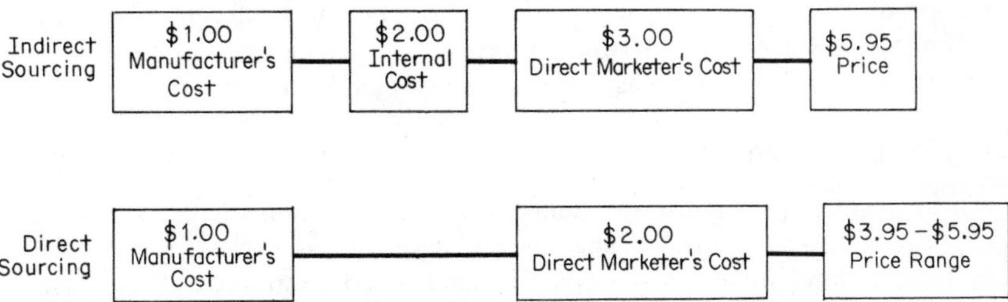

Figure 8-2 The potential advantages of direct sourcing of proprietary products for direct marketers: lower selling price or wider margins.

Concentrate on general-interest and general-business media. Pay particular attention to articles about consumer confidence, housing starts, new car sales, real estate turnover, cost of living, savings deposits, and the Dow-Jones Index. They are traditionally and constantly predictors of tomorrow's buying behavior. Use them to help guide your thinking about products, price points, and timing. Pay attention to your own sales pattern, too. If your customers are buying goodly amounts of Whammies, think about serving up Whammy II or a spinoff, say, Bammy I.

You probably won't find much to spark the product juices in trade publications. They're important for technical news, current events, and public relations more than for creativity.

Your advertising agency should be included in the idea process, too. They can provide strong inputs and be a key part of the team. They see your business and its position from a less subjective, more market-tuned viewpoint than many insiders. Besides that, they instinctively think in terms of media and lists—the potential selling universe.

Customers Tell You a Lot

Talk to them and listen to them continually. Don't get out of touch. Use nonscientific as well as scientific means. At trade shows, be sure you mingle in the crowds. Visit the stores at which articles similar to yours are sold, exchanging thoughts with clerks and customers. If your industry conducts shows which customers are close enough to attend, sponsor a reception for them. It can yield rewarding customer service, market input, and product feedback. Read customer correspondence regularly. Over time, you'll find valuable critiques and germs of ideas. An occasional customer service phone call about a product problem can be enlightening.

Direct Customer Surveys

Attitude questionnaires that are professionally prepared for mail or phone delivery can give new directions to your thinking. How do new customers compare with established ones in terms of age, income, sex, and other key demographic variables? How do they feel about key products and prices? Are they interested in related products you may not sell now but are thinking about? Are they positive or negative about buying in the next 6 months? Have their purchases been consistent with their statements? Do they sound like bargain hunters or status seekers? Do they respond positively to questions about continuity purchases? Are one-time purchases more in favor? Annual or semiannual surveys costing as little as $5000 each can help build your idea bank.

Listen to the Office

You can receive a lot of useful intelligence from people in the office. It's done every day in large and small companies, and it's remarkably useful as an informal way to check your subjective notions against an inside sounding board. You can't make a commitment to a major product budget on the word of peers, pals, and passersby, but you can get frank and candid replies about price points, style, color, and design and packaging. As with scientific questionnaire research, the answers you get from one-on-one exchanges can be more direct and "projectable" than remarks from group discussions.

Competitors Often Tell You a Lot

Actions speak louder than words, of course, and this is especially true in our business. While you'll never be in on proprietary plans, competitors always fall into specific action categories that can tell you a lot. There usually are one or two leaders who set a pace that is followed by imitators and others who seem to be along for the ride. Then there are the strategic entrepreneurs who study the field, know their own strengths and weaknesses, and identify what the competition is not doing that they can do.

If you're the leader, you've got most of the ideas before everybody else. If company B or company C breaks with a new product, you surely are in a position to outgun them and keep the lead before the upstart can cut in very far. Customer loyalty will protect you while you rev up.

If you're one of the imitators, you'll spot a good idea in a flash, follow it for future rollouts, and then do a very nifty knockoff at a cheaper price. That will keep your customers happy and may expand your market share as well.

Those who serve the late adopters in the marketplace, the customers who don't respond until it's safe or until it can't get any cheaper, always will have a steady flow of ideas too, and they'll always be last.

The people who keep things interesting in any business, however, are the ones who live with an "up or around" strategy. They don't exactly copy or knock off or sell cheaper, but they always avoid head-on collisions. Mostly they survive and prosper by finding the holes the other companies leave open. They are like direct marketing guerrillas, but they don't just hit and run. They build niches. Interestingly, they share many characteristics with the leaders in a field, but they seldom are the single largest factor.

Also, keep elaborate clipping and note files and refer to them periodically. Organize them by theme, subject, and date. All ideas have their time.

Get Smart at Conferences and Trade Shows

Stay away from these affairs unless you're determined to leave with at least one useful product idea. Actually, you have two opportunities. One is the formal agenda of speakers and programs; the other is the casual talk you take part in and overhear.

Look Beyond Your Borders

It's axiomatic that the major innovations that benefit most industries are thought of by entrepreneurs outside those industries. We can all help ourselves and our industry by raising our eyes and minds to the horizon.

For example, an industry valued in 1981 at more than $750 million annually was spawned less than 20 years ago by the Franklin Mint: the planned limited-edition collectible. The occasions were the removal of silver from U.S. coinage and the death of General Douglas MacArthur. They exploded in the minds of some Philadelphia entrepreneurs, and the commemorative medal—forerunner to a $400 million multinational corporation—was born.

Another example of an idea whose time had come is the Bradford Exchange. They took porcelain plate collecting out of the closet and put it onto the walls and mantles and into the parlors of middle America. Franklin Porcelain and Danbury Mint did the same for the upscale plate market.

Many other businesses were launched by other one-time upstarts: Montgomery Ward, the Book-of-the-Month Club, Time-Life Books, the old Kenton Collection, Brookstone, L. L. Bean, the Columbia Record Club, and Frederick's of Hollywood.

Somewhere today, in the minds of entrepreneurs, the next frontier is about to be crossed. They are looking beyond today's products and trends. In their inventive minds, the everyday data available to all of us are being analyzed and synthesized into new combinations that will send us into the next generation of product marketing.

Ideas in Your Inventory?

The products you are marketing already can give off sparks. Hot ones, of course, need little identification and encouragement. When they start to cool, however, and you start to worry, the next step should be restaging, repositioning, or recycling, as it is called in various parts of the industry.

Every successful product or product classification has a life cycle: an introduction stage and then a growth stage followed by maturity and decline, as shown in Figure 8-3. The trick is to extend the growth and maturity phases and avoid decline as long as possible.

To halt declines and pump new vigor into products, a growing number of direct marketers are adopting the tactics of package goods companies. This often means changing customers' perception of the product rather than chang-

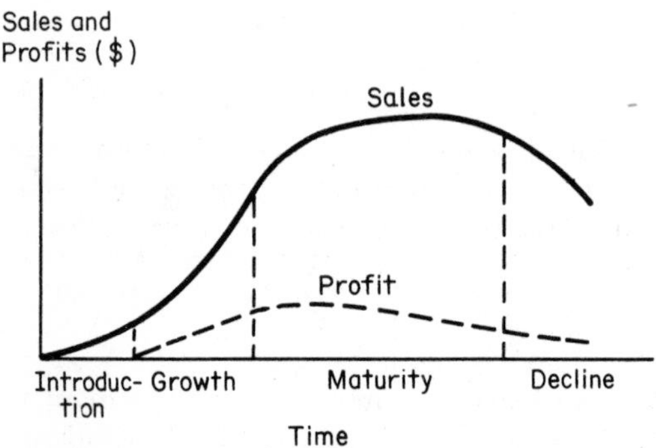

Figure 8-3 Sales and profit life cycles. (*Philip Kotler, Marketing Management: Analysis, Planning, and Control, Prentice-Hall, Inc., Englewood Cliffs, N. J., 1976.*)

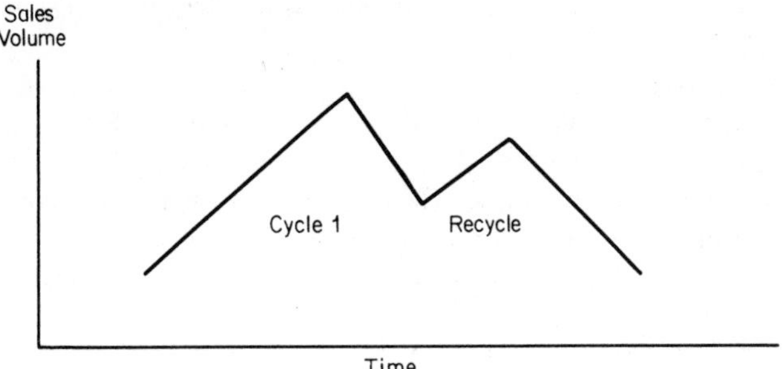

Figure 8-4 How a product might perform if a cycle-recycle strategy were used.

ing the product. Perception is in the mind, of course, and so you set out to paint a different picture of the product by repositioning against competition ("better value"), attracting a new market segment ("Attention, apartment dwellers!"), or identifying another attribute and then testing it for results.

On the other hand, something new might be added to the old standby to stave off decline. Consider adding value by reformulating ingredients, restyling, repackaging, or repricing. Figure 8-4 shows what can happen when a product is recycled.

How Do You Get Ideas?

The discussion wouldn't be complete without a description of how people who make a living by being creative do it. Over the years, more than a few have been influenced by the writings of James Webb Young, who contributed so much to creativity at J. Walter Thompson Co.

Young spelled out a Technique for Producing Ideas for the advertising world, but it grew into other areas too, such as product development. His five-step discipline for the mind "must be taken in strict order, with each step completely finished before going to the next one":

1. Gather raw material about the problem at hand: specific materials relating to the product and market and general materials on a wide range of subjects assimilated on a continuing basis.
2. Mentally digest the information. Look at it from all sides and angles. Look for relationships between the particles. Synthesize. Do it over until the whole mixture seems to lose its form.
3. Then drop the whole subject and put it out of mind. Let the subconscious take over while you do something else such as listening to music or taking a walk.
4. The idea will appear when you don't expect it but only after you stop straining and relax.
5. The final shaping and development of the idea is crucial too. Expose it to

criticism. Good ideas get stronger with examination and grow with thought and challenging.[1]

If you would like specialized help, consider retaining a consultant in your area of direct marketing. The Direct Marketing Association (DMA) membership roster lists many successful consultants and product sources. Your local or regional DMA group or major manufacturers and syndicators also can help. And don't forget the with-it boutiques and trade shows.

GETTING THINGS ORGANIZED

Before you start to sift through product ideas, be sure you have a carefully constructed product strategy. Without such a commitment about what your product or service is and how it should be perceived by the people in the marketplace, you cannot develop successful programs.

The strategy must be customer-oriented and concerned with satisfying needs and wants rather than simply supplying more products. It's your strategy, so be sure to make it specific to the experience, resources, and personality of your business, not a competitor's. You're in business to build a unique character and loyal customers, so I'm ruling out emulation or imitation as part of strategy building.

A solid strategy which is thoughtfully written and rewritten and consistently referred to for general direction becomes a strong guide in evaluating new product ideas. It helps you recognize attributes which can become reasons for customers to buy your product instead of a rationale for trying to sell it to them.

For example, the Alpha Company might generate a strategy statement that provides for "the development of collectible miniature objects, beginning with pewter soldiers, that are durable and of authentic design, appealing to customers with traditional values and strong price-value appreciation but with sufficient discretionary income to rationalize purchase for cultural or lifestyle enhancement." That should keep Alpha from drifting off into mail-order vitamins but not too far from miniature furniture craft kits if economic and social factors turn on the lights.

Strategy can direct your creative juices in productive ways, and you'll be lost without it. But how do you go about shaping your strategy into specific projects, products, and profits?

You Need Help to Make It Happen

Depending on your situation, help can range from several hours a week of your own time to working with a consultant, an assistant, a staff, or some combination of these elements.

[1] Reprinted with permission from James Webb Young, *A Technique for Producing Ideas*, Crain Books, Chicago, 1975.

Someone has to be responsible. Ultimately, of course, that someone is you. Responsibility can't be delegated, although some may try, but authority and accountability can be. Get the job done through a consultant, manager, director, vice president, or combination of talents if your needs are diverse. Typical product development functions are shown in Figure 8-5.

The importance of clear accountability in product development has been underscored by *Wharton* magazine, published by the Wharton School of the University of Pennsylvania. Citing the results of a study of fifty successful and fifty failed new product projects by members of the Industrial Research Institute, it was shown that one ingredient was crucial to success: Most of the successful projects had one individual who entrepreneured the job.

These key people need a clear license to carry out the entrepreneurial function, and this usually is granted when they are designated project manager or project director.

Moreover, while peer respect, charisma, and negotiating power are important, one-person shows are seldom effective. Project managers or entrepreneurs need someone higher in the organization to sponsor and champion their cause. Of course, their licenses must be adaptable to changing times.

Along with organizational discipline, you need a grip on your enthusiasm. While a sense of urgency is vital to product development, never rush concept evaluation or development. Be especially on guard against the seductive sure winner or the equally compelling sure loser. There just aren't any products that fit neatly into either category. Don't fall in or out of love with ideas too quickly or

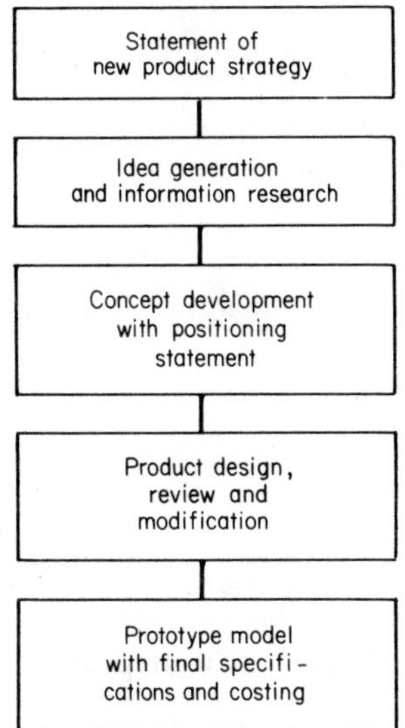

Figure 8-5 Typical product development functions.

easily, especially your own. Be sure every product suggestion is screened and evaluated on the merits it has or might have with a little more work. And be sure to look at these suggestions through the eyes of a customer.

How to Prepare an Idea for Evaluation

Start by thinking it through. Position it even before you decide on the size, parts, and colors. When you position a product, you are calculating where you want it to fit in the minds of your customers and in the market. Never put it next to or below the competition but always separate and distinct, above or beyond. You also may think of this as moving the competition. Once you find the right place, you may say, "It was so obvious."

But if it was so obvious, why did it take so much work to find it? Why didn't someone else think of it? Sometimes the obvious can be obscure.

Examples of product positioning, or mind bending, in direct marketing are the upscale private libraries of booksellers such as Franklin Library (Franklin Mint) and Easton Press (MBI-Danbury Mint) as opposed to the more traditional Time-Life Books and Book-of-the-Month Club and Hanover House's positioning of products vis-à-vis its many in-house "competitors" such as Adam York and Pennsylvania Station. Or consider how Lands End and American Express contemporary products look compared with the traditional catalogs of L. L. Bean and Eddie Bauer. These distinctions are the result of deliberate development of creative insight and devoted application of positioning strategy.

For detailed dissertations by masters, look into *Direct Marketing: Strategy/Planning/Execution* by Ed Nash and *Positioning: The Battle for Your Mind* by Al Ries and Jack Trout. Both books will help you identify and understand the strategies of others for your own benefit.

The positioning objective has to be put into words as part of the total product offer and then reviewed for strength of concept. A typical concept review summary includes the following:

- The working title or name of the product
- The form or type of product accompanied by a preliminary drawing or drawings
- Its theme: utilitarian? exotic? Americana? import?
- How it will be positioned against the competition
- The major supporting product appeals
- Promotional enhancement
- Possible production source or sources with rating
- Whether the product is a single item, a set, or a continuity series
- In a series, how frequently each item will be issued to buyers
- Target cost and selling price of each unit packaged and ready to ship, along with the overall budget figure
- Postage and handling (included in selling price or separate charge?)
- Target profitability utilizing P&L criteria
- Target date for test marketing (make it realistic)

- Whether the product will be tested to the house list, outside media, or both
- Overall evaluation rating (usually from accepted down to rejected)

The Extra Step to Take

An additional component of the review process can be market research. Because of the volatile and climbing costs of product development, more direct marketers are researching their ideas by scientific techniques to help spot the losers.

Techniques are available for concept testing, product design, and line expansion. Concept testing often relies on a product questionnaire which evaluates new ideas against an established product or "control." Product design testing often utilizes dummy designs in a roundtable discussion, while buyer interest surveys conducted by mail can tap hidden product interests in your house list.

Be Realistic

Since most new products can require 12 to 18 months or more to grow from an idea to a production model, you'll want to prepare a complete schedule of key development points and their target completion dates so that you can manage things. Start with the date you have targeted for test marketing and work back to the present, including everything and allowing time for reviews and Murphy's law, as in Figure 8-6. Right at the outset, it's wise to recognize reality. Can you do the job in the time available and within the budget? The answer, of course, must be yes, but make it the real answer. If it's not, recalculate your timetable and push back the test date if necessary.

Top management approval must be obtained, of course, but this needn't be a traumatic experience. If you run the right kind of review system in the development cycle, topside involvement will be implicit from the outset since input from top management will be a factor throughout. Avoid precarious final approvals and their inevitable consequences by keeping the boss(es) on the team.

MAKING IDEAS COME TRUE

Taking a concept to the prototype stage is a human and emotional process somewhat analogous to gestation. But real mothers often have an easier time of it today, and it may not take them as long.

Get the Most Out of Your Design(er)

Before you make the new product, be sure it's designed for efficiency as well as effectiveness. If you don't have staff designers, be sure to work with a designer who understands the product and its manufacturing process. Large manufacturers in every field have staff designers who may assist customers, and in many cases the result can be excellent. It's your responsibility to get the best for your customers, and so you must be the judge.

Key Date Development Schedule	
Date: 11/11/80 ☐ Preliminary ☐ Revised ☐ Final	Project No. A112
Title: Four Seasons Vases	Home Receipt : 11/29/82
1/12/81 Concept Review with Full Summary Notes: Reposition as Oriental Four Seasons Vases in miniature format.	10/1/81 Vendor(s) Selected Notes: Vases – Okura Ltd. Decals – Hong Kong Arts
1/30/81 Information Research Complete Notes: Additional background on "seasons" needed .	4/29/82 First Prototype Review Notes: Lower firing temperatures. Artists signature lost.
2/2/81 Designer Selected Notes: Agreement to be ready for signature 2/16/82.	9/29/82 Final Prototype Review Notes: OK for promotion photography.
8/3/81 Preliminary Design Review Notes: Spring, Winter – OK. Revise Summer, Autumn by 9/1.	11/29/82 Production Sample Review Notes: All four OK as is
9/1/81 Final Design Review with Collateral Components and Packaging Notes: Revise design of reference folders and certificate per vase floral motif.	1/31/83 First Shipment to Warehouse. Spring – Quantity 25,000

Figure 8-6 Typical key date development schedule for organizing major components in new product development cycle.

Particularly important new products may require a competitive process between two designers or between two manufacturers with design services. This can provide a more balanced view of qualifications and results. Whichever route you go, always negotiate all costs, expenses, and timing up front. Avoid verbal agreements and be sure you retain rights to the preliminary sketches and final drawings—and get them back.

The Paths Are Parallel

Simultaneously with designing, think of manufacturing. If you are working with a producer's design service, manufacturing obviously will be thought of. Otherwise, you should include prospective makers in a design review after they sign a confidentiality agreement.

The project manager brings together the various participants and is generally responsible for getting the job done right, on time, and within budget with top management support and approval. Depending on the policies and confidence of management, the project manager may have varying degrees of authority, but this person is always the one charged with "doing the job." It's neither simple nor easy work.

The Factory Connection

From all qualified manufacturers, select two for negotiation about a new product in a new category. For a new product in an existing category or a revamped product, you can go sole source if cost, value, and timing are right. Avoid inertia in this area, however. Value and appeal are forged by the direct marketer in the factory, not in the copywriter's typewriter.

The successful bidder then becomes your unofficial partner in getting the prototype made on time and within the total budget. Set a subschedule that fits your key data development schedule, being realistic about each step. The number of intermediate reviews of progress, complete with actual versus estimated costs and time, depends on the product. But since few new products go together perfectly the first time, avoid oversimplification and undue optimism. Count on periodic reviews and constant communication back and forth between the players. Cost overruns are not strictly an affliction of government contractors. Keep the reins tight.

Corollary concerns involve quality control and legal advice and counsel. Specifications sometimes are misunderstood or not defined as completely and clearly as intended. This can result in unintentional deviations or shortcomings. An internal or independent testing lab should be retained to run checks at key steps in the prototype process. Of course, the rare unscrupulous act will be uncovered as well.

Legal counsel is also necessary in product development to protect clients or the company in matters of copyright, proprietary rights, product liability, and intellectual property. Not all lawyers are deal killers. They can provide valuable services and are increasingly involved in product development as companies seek to prevent piracy and protect their marketing assets.

But Will It Fly?

After the preliminary, or sequential, reviews of work in progress that follow final design approval, you're ready for the dress rehearsal, the final product review before the full tribunal. If you have a competent project manager with defined responsibilities and full support, the final product review should be quite positive and possibly even a warmup for the promotion development phase as ideas gel to help match the product to the marketplace.

To be systematic and thorough, the concept review summary and its revisions and accompanying meeting notes should be a ready reference at each intermediate review. At the final review, it's a good idea for the project manager to update the summary for final signoff.

With the project manager as chairperson, the product is checked point by point against the blueprint as if it were a supersonic jet or the *Columbia*. This is the spot where you should see satisfying results for the months of devoted effort you have invested in your customers' satisfaction.

The advertising specialists will be looking for camera angles, imagining the new product in a promotion design, and getting ideas for photography props that will merchandise the product through environmental setting or by showing its size relationship to other objects. They will be running through copy and headline drills, probably aloud.

The project manager and, in diversified companies, the marketing director sharpen target costs, selling prices, and the total product offer. Revised financial projections may be issued as part of the final package.

The detail machine also spins on at this point, with the myriad of corollary work and materials getting final definition, including things such as primary packaging, what the product comes in (maybe a gift box), and secondary packaging, or the protective outer box or envelope that must be light enough to conserve postage or shipping charges yet tough enough to stand up to a potentially hazardous journey with large temperature extremes. Arrangements have to be made for sample drop testing, and a decision must be made on shipping method (U.S. Postal Service, United Parcel Service, single or bulk).

Collateral packaging and promotion materials which may be pertinent to completing the product offer include well-written and well-produced reference material that enhances satisfaction and knowledge such as booklets, reference cards, certificates, care and handling information, or even a letter with the boss's signature.

If your product ties in neatly with an add-on item, this is the last chance to include it in the product offer. It's already too late, of course, if extensive development is required, so let's say we only have to be sure to plan the promotion flier.

The Back End Belongs at the Front End

Implicit in the entire product development process is face-to-face involvement with operations management to ensure effective coordination and communication at key points. The ultimate payoff is timely fulfillment, or getting the product into the hands of the customer as quickly as possible. It's axiomatic in direct marketing that from the moment the customer places the order, every day without the product increases the probability of its being returned when it finally arrives. This is not something that has to be tested.

Smart product developers include key operations personnel in the early stages. This not only enlists support and cooperation, it helps ensure that the product offer will fit into the computer system or allow sufficient time to program software for the system.

Tight product definition in the early development of the concept helps produce tight operational definitions later on, of course. Every key product parameter translates into some kind of operational requirement at some point in the process. Keep operations management on the team and see how smoothly your order entry, invoicing and shipping label cycles, stockkeeping unit system, and even inventory control will run. This advice is sound for those who work with outside fulfillment services as well as internal ones.

WHO NEEDS IT?

The acid test for your new product comes when you break with your first advertisement or mailing. Very few products fail to attract any orders, and so that particular anxiety is not worth your time. On the other hand, there aren't many tidal waves, either. The majority of products probably will be either healthy infants or incubator babies, and you have to be ready for either outcome. That means knowing your business and being in control of the production situation.

How Many Should We Order?

With inventory carrying costs eating up balance sheets, this question takes on a lot of weight in regard to new products. The answer actually may be different for different companies with varying lines and financial requirements. Let's assume for simplicity that the product is totally new, never before offered by the firm, and that you want to be as free of risk as possible.

If the product is a one-shot or a catalog item, you'll want to order some percentage of forecast on the basis of the manufacturer's turnaround capability and related logistical considerations, be they domestic or foreign. Then fill in as results come in. The product is exclusive to you, and so there are no return privileges.

If the product is a series continuity (customers subscribe to the whole offer and receive one shipment per month), you'll want to order enough for the first two shipments, perhaps three if the manufacturer is foreign. Be sure to factor in returns, attrition, and up-front dropoff, which accounts for the people who send in an order form when no payment is required and then change their minds when the invoice arrives.

Maybe We Shouldn't Order Yet

If the product requires heavy up-front capital investment or if you have more than one version, model, or color to test, you may want to plan a dry test. That means you don't buy the product until you understand exactly what your advertising test has told you. It also means adjusting the product offer.

This is not the place for a lengthy discussion of dry test regulations. Just be sure you neither take payment nor process charges without a product to ship and that you position the offer as a preview or advance announcement. On the other hand, if you are testing a product about which you have knowledge and experience, you probably will be less cautious but still conservative in times of economic uncertainty.

Simultaneous tests to the house list, rental lists, and public media carry with them accompanying requirements for product availability based on timing of mail drops and on-sale dates of magazines. Staggered testing of various media, of course, also staggers your product logistics and may be inadvisable.

Whatever you do, try to keep the finished cost of product—that's ex-factory before packaging, freight, and related costs—at 20 to 25 percent of the selling price. There will be exceptions, of course, in order to make price points, but the 5:1 or 4:1 ratio of raw cost to selling price is a rule of thumb that the big guns in the business use.

In the beginning, there was merchandise, then merchandising, and now product development. But it's not for everybody. A disciplined approach to merchandise selection may be enough.

Remember that everything starts with an idea and that ideas are essentially new combinations of existing concepts or applications.

Getting things organized will help you separate the wheat from the chaff. It's one of the most important disciplines in the product development process. Be sure to make one person accountable for the entire job and give that person all the support necessary to do the job.

Position your new product in the market or in the minds of your customers by moving the competition mentally if you have to. Evaluate your product ideas rigorously, avoiding the untenable love trap or hate thing and seeking the input of as many contributors as the situation will allow. Then make a time schedule and a budget, resisting all human temptations and those of Murphy's law to thwart it.

Making your ideas come true requires a dedicated mind and the deft intertwining of creative, manufacturing, and financial disciplines. Recognize the valuable realities of these areas but don't be swayed easily.

The acid test of sending your product out into the real world is the most dynamic and courageous act of all. Enjoy it.

chapter **9**

PRODUCT MANAGEMENT

David L. Kerstein

Area Vice President
Citicorp
Minneapolis, Minn.

This chapter is about marketing management. More specifically, it's about adapting the marketing management process usually associated with packaged goods firms like Procter & Gamble and General Foods to the specialized needs of direct-response marketers.

The organizational structure called product management will be the focal point of this chapter. In the traditional sense, product management refers to a specific type of organization which is best suited for specific marketing situations. But product management has taken on a broader meaning (especially outside the packaged goods fraternity) which refers to something more than organization structure alone. It is a style of management and a process of making consumer marketing decisions.

The purpose of this chapter is to help you answer key questions about product management and its effectiveness for your company.

- What is product management?
- When is this type of organization most effective?
- How has this process worked in direct-response organizations?
- How can I implement a product management organization? What practical problems will I face?

OBJECTIVES, OBSTACLES, AND SOLUTIONS

Product management is one of the most successful and durable forms of marketing organization. Introduced over 50 years ago, it came into general use among consumer packaged goods companies in the 1950s; today, over 85 percent of packaged goods marketers use it. But product management isn't restricted to Procter & Gamble or General Foods. The type of organization, marketing philosophy, and management style that built some of the top packaged goods marketing companies is sweeping through American business. Companies which once were considered to have unique and specialized needs—such as industrial, financial, or direct-response firms—now are adopting product management expertise.

- A large financial institution was concerned that in an increasingly competitive environment in which business expansion was becoming a function of product proliferation and market segmentation, no one was focusing specifically on managing its most important products. Its business managers were absorbed in running the branch distribution system, while its marketing department consisted of technical specialists. Its answer was to reorganize the marketing department into product groups.
- A major department store wanted to expand its catalog sales. Instead of continuing to coordinate the catalog with in-store promotions, it established a product manager for nonstore sales and developed an entirely separate profit center.
- A well-known direct-response marketer's product line had expanded over the years, and the marketer was uncertain whether to continue managing its advertising as a unified effort. Ultimately, it decided to segment its marketing with product managers decked against key markets. Their function was to serve as advocates for the marketing needs of specialized consumer groups and thus to expand business opportunities.

All these companies shared a belief that product managers would serve them better than the existing form of organization. But what exactly did they mean by product management? The common thread is, of course, a belief that corporate success, and therefore the best allocation of resources, is linked directly to the effective management and development of individual products.

Beyond this, definitions vary substantially. For some the key is a packaged goods marketing philosophy which places the strategic focus on the consumer (versus the perceived requirements of the manufacturing or distribution system) and develops advertising which emphasizes a product's benefits, tangible or intangible, as opposed to its features. For others it is the management style of aggressive, highly educated product managers trained in companies in which they perceived themselves as small-scale chief executive officers for their products. Finally, the very fact that product management results in decentralization of certain key marketing decisions is seen by many companies as a means of furthering the entrepreneurial thrust.

Product management isn't right for every company. Even within companies in which it has been established, it almost never has been introduced at the outset.

The first step is usually a functional form of organization with an advertising or marketing specialist supporting the business manager. In very small firms, the marketing function may be performed by the advertising agency.

Marketing Organization

These definitions represent insight into the fact that product management is a process of managing a marketing organization. It is a process that varies according to each company's needs, and it cannot be defined merely by describing organizational charts or the experience of certain well-known consumer marketers. For the purpose of this discussion, these are all appropriate definitions.

By Function. A functional organization is appropriate for companies with a very narrow product line serving limited and well-defined markets. In this case, all effort is focused on supporting the company's single product or closely related group of products, and the marketing function (often called marketing services) serves as the specialist in advertising, promotion, research, and public relations. Because this organization already is focused on key products, it is usually not efficient to introduce a product manager as a new layer of management between the business manager and the marketing specialists. In fact, it may be counterproductive since many companies at this stage of their development need to direct their attention to rationalizing their manufacturing or distribution processes rather than refining their market segmentation.

By Product. As products and markets proliferate, most companies find that a functional organization fails to provide the focus needed to achieve maximum profitability. The recognition that success results from the performance of individual products and that control over the fundamentals of the product is basic to fulfilling corporate strategy generally leads to implementation of a product management organization.

Historically, product managers have been most successful in companies in which multiple products flow into a single market or a single distribution channel. That is why consumer packaged goods companies with multiple products sold almost exclusively through supermarket chains have found

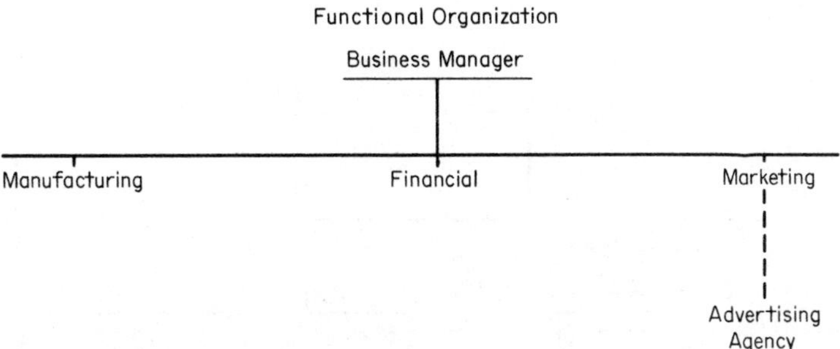

Figure 9-1 The functional organization is most appropriate for companies with a single product or product group.

marketing organizations with managers dedicated to specific products to be successful.

By Market. The difference between a product manager and a market manager is subtle. In many companies, the title of product manager is bestowed on all professional marketing personnel even though the term "market manager" might be a technically more appropriate description of the job.

While product management is most effective in companies in which different products generally are sold through limited distribution channels, market managers have proved optimal when limited products are distributed through multiple channels. For example, an insurance company may sell the same set of products on a wholesale basis to other companies (reinsurance), on a retail basis through licensed agents, and through direct response directly to consumers. In this case, the products don't vary but the markets do.

In these situations, a marketing management approach is more appropriate. Market managers who will identify the particular needs of each key market and seek modifications of existing products to meet these needs are preferable to product managers whose efforts cut across markets by focusing on maintaining product-line integrity.

Hybrid Organizations. As marketing programs get more complex and both products and markets proliferate, some companies have gone one step further by combining product managers and market managers within the same organization. This would seem to provide the best of both worlds, but it raises personnel cost significantly and increases the need for coordination between two groups of managers, both of which make demands on manufacturing, the advertising agency, and various corporate services. But when both products and markets crisscross, combined product manager and market manager organizations make sense.

Roles and Functions

We have discussed the role of product managers in a conceptual way. More specifically, product managers have two primary functions: as advocates for their products and as coordinators of product support.

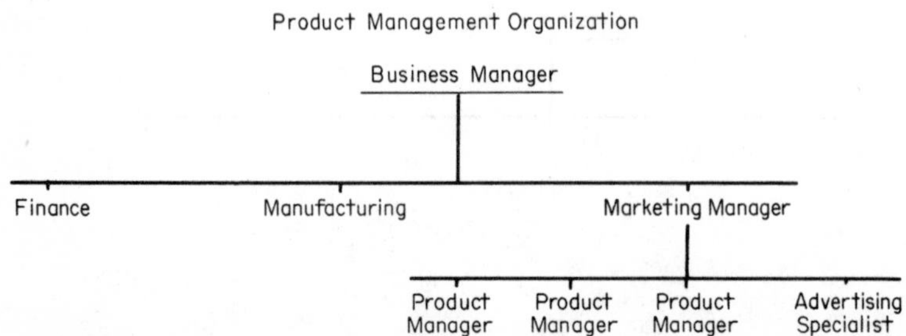

Figure 9-2 Product managers are called for when products proliferate but markets or distribution channels are few; market managers are the answer when limited products flow into multiple markets or distribution channels.

Brand Champion. Product managers often have been likened to business managers in that they are responsible for managing the business objectives of their products. This conception of the product manager as a "little president" is in theory supposed to generate an aggressive, entrepreneurial spirit which will drive forward the goals of the corporation by putting greater focus on the goals of its individual products. The concept of a product manager as a general manager is an important one because many product managers perceive themselves as line managers, even though they may not have line management responsibility. My personal experience has been that this often represents a self-image of business school-trained marketing professionals rather than the reality of the day-to-day job. Product managers are general managers in the sense that they establish objectives and strategies for their products and thus provide direction for the entire corporate effort. But that is often not their key role.

Brand Coordinator. If you were to survey product managers to determine the types of marketing decisions they make, you most likely would find that they function primarily as coordinators of various corporate efforts relating to their products. They are responsible for ensuring that their product or product group receives the type of support required to obtain its objectives. In many organizations, this may be the only truly matrixed function since product managers who may not manage any personnel resources directly are nevertheless responsible for accomplishing business objectives which can be achieved only through the efforts of a variety of production, line, and staff departments. This puts the manager in a liaison position with internal and external resources such as resource and development (R&D), sales, manufacturing, the advertising agency, and trade channels. Typically, a product manager will provide market information or a recommendation and business plan to management. After obtaining their approval, the manager will communicate the plans to internal and external resources and will coordinate their efforts.

In most companies, product managers do not have direct responsibility for the resources they require in order to perform their function, yet they are responsible for the ultimate accomplishment of their objectives. This would appear to violate a basic rule of organization which dictates that responsibility and authority cannot be separated. In terms of managerial style it requires people who have the self-direction to function in an environment in which reporting relationships are not always direct line, who have the interpersonal skills to work with a variety of support groups that may have somewhat different objectives, and who have the leadership skills to make the product's objectives those of the entire organization. As a result, the product manager must have greater managerial skills than a marketing support specialist, e.g., a media planner or advertising manager. Thus, there is a greater need for coordination on an organizational level to ensure that the proper environment is created so that product managers can meet their objectives. Without that support, and because product managers do not have direct authority over their resources, it is unlikely that they can accomplish their goals.

Success Stories

It is hard to implement a new organizational structure, but the rewards for doing so often far outweigh the disruption caused by organizational change. The success of the three companies described below dramatically demonstrates the successes which can be achieved from a product management system in a direct marketing environment.

New Strategic Direction. In the mid-1970s, a large financial institution acquired a smaller consumer financial services subsidiary. As part of an overall evaluation of that division's management needs, it began to review its marketing organization. The marketing department at that time was organized functionally. That is, it consisted of specific support functions such as advertising and public relations. When line business managers wanted marketing support, they would go to the marketing department, which would create plans for them. For example, a sales manager responsible for geographic territory would determine that a direct mail program was needed to help support the area's business objectives. The manager would go to the marketing department, which would develop the program and coordinate the execution of the advertising. This is not to say that marketing personnel were never pro-active. However, their general approach to developing new programs was to say, "You have identified your needs. Here are the ways we can execute the program," rather than, "I have evaluated our customers' needs and have developed this specific program which will further the company's business objectives."

Initially, no basic changes were made in this organization as the company focused on rationalizing its distribution and sales network. After that was accomplished, management began to focus on strategic plans for increasing market share. That effort brought to a head the realization that a product strategy versus a defined target market was critical to meeting that objective and that a functionally organized marketing services department could not support the strategic planning effort adequately.

Two product managers were hired to develop a product marketing department. After initial evaluation of corporate needs, they recommended that the company shift some of its marketing effort from overall corporate positioning and awareness-building to direct-response marketing of specific products. The rationale was simple. With loan products, the target audience is well defined as a result of both product use and credit criteria. Therefore, it seemed to make sense to focus only on that target. But establishing an effective direct-response program is easier said than done. Objective customer data which can be used for media targeting are often hard to obtain, and product profitability is hard to measure for many financial products. This leads to problems in selecting promotional targets. In addition, lead conversion often is complicated by the credit procedure. These issues all work to inhibit the product management ethic and reinforce a marketing services orientation dominated by a manufacturing mentality.

One of the first tasks of the product management team was to develop a management information system (MIS) for product tracking. Customer demographics was surveyed and compared with research data on potential target audiences. Product profitability was modeled to assist in making pricing tradeoffs. Most important, line managers were trained to think like marketers, that is, to identify and sell benefits sought by target markets rather than make credit (manufacturing) decisions.

Establishing a new marketing orientation, as was done by this company, is very difficult because it gets at the heart of the firm's definition of itself. It also results in a great deal of organizational turmoil. But 5 years after the first introduction of product management, the company no longer had a marketing services unit. The primary function of marketing became the development, distribution, and promotion of specific products. Organizationally, this process did not always go smoothly, but the strategy was sound. The key to success in a highly regulated, undifferentiated marketplace was targeting benefits (products) to audiences with identifiable needs. As long as success is dependent on a product marketing strategy, the corporate organization should mirror that need. The result of this focus has been growth of over 20 percent compounded annually.

New Distribution Channel. A major department store was seeking to expand its catalog sales but felt that its advertising department lacked the expertise to handle the strategic decisions involved in developing what was essentially a new business venture. Typically, an advertising department for a department store serves as a link between the buyers who make promotional decisions and the promotional media. But what happens when merchandise decisions have to be made which cut across the traditional buyer process?

In order to make the catalog successful, the major department store had to resolve several issues. First, merchandise decisions had to be consistent with the needs of the recipients of the catalog, which was not necessarily the same as the retail trade in its branch stores. Second, the store had limited catalog fulfillment capability. Merchandise typically passed through the warehouse on the way to the designated store, and there was a limited ability to stock merchandise centrally to fill orders. Finally, although some success had been obtained in mailings to store charge account customers, the catalog customer might not be the same. How could the target audience and the potential for nonstore distribution be assessed?

Because the appropriate expertise did not exist in the store's advertising department, a new manager was hired to develop a catalog sales department. The product manager for catalog sales set about establishing a marketing plan for nonstore sales. The steps this individual took were as follows.

- The mailing list for the store's highly successful Christmas catalog was analyzed to determine prospects for other catalogs. Compared with the store's charge customer base, the people on the catalog mailing list were more likely to have a higher income, live outside the trading area, and make only limited use of store charge accounts. This revealed a potential target audience which was distinctly different from the normal in-store customer.
- The catalog customer also had different purchasing habits, which led to the conclusion that a unique positioning for the catalog was possible. While catalog customers tended to purchase unusual and unique items, in-store trade was oriented toward high-turn items.
- Finally, the distribution needs were different. Catalog fulfillment required the use of outside vendors and drop-ship facilities. This permitted the store to fulfill orders while limiting incremental warehousing and distribution expense.

Unlike the large financial institution, whose problem was one of corporate marketing focus, the major department store had to establish a new marketing channel which cut across traditional organizational lines. The solution, however, was the same: a specific individual who would be responsible for managing product integrity, delivery, and profitability.

Reorganizing for Growth. Many companies reach a point in their growth at which their product array has become so broad that a decision has to be made whether to continue to expand, and if so, in what manner. A catalog marketer had to face this issue when its product array expanded to the point at which inventory control was getting difficult and, it believed, it was in danger of saturating the target market with promotional material.

The company undertook a detailed analysis of its market, products, and advertising. Surprisingly, the analysis indicated that the company had three product groups, each of which had the potential for additional growth. The problem was the lack of clarity and focus caused by integrating them.

As a result of the analysis, the company reorganized its marketing effort into a target market strategy. This allowed the marketing managers—retitled product managers—to focus on the needs of its target markets and to focus product decisions on those needs.

When the company started its analysis, it believed that it needed to reduce the number of products and catalogs it was offering. Instead, it decided to expand its offerings, although targeted differently, and it leveraged a classic mature product line into a period of new growth.

IMPLEMENTING PRODUCT MANAGEMENT: KEYS TO SUCCESS

If you're considering implementing product management within your organization, the first thing to do is to establish a clear need. The concept must be weighed against alternative organizational scenarios to make sure it is really needed and not being implemented only because it is fashionable. Is it right for your company? What exactly do you expect your product managers to do? Product management, with its broad responsibilities and limited line authority, is not the easiest form of organization to use effectively. If it is really what your company needs, there are four elements to success.

- **People.** The product manager concept is not an easy one under any circumstances, and it will never work unless you have qualified people in place. It is especially important that your managers be able to develop concrete programs for establishing product objectives and measuring results. In contrast to other advertising, in which the objective is to build awareness or create more favorable attitudes but tangible sales results are less measurable, the essence of direct-response marketing is that it demands action by the target audience. It is vital that the product manager understand and manage this process. And they should be the right people for your organization. The characteristics of a successful manager at Procter & Gamble may be very different from the dimensions needed by your company. Taking the approach "off the shelf" in terms of organizational structure or personnel requirements brings a high risk of failure.

- **Support.** Your product managers need support in two ways. First, they need to learn the business. Obviously, bringing in generalists who understand the process of managing a product won't bear fruit until they understand the important and unique aspects of your specific industry. Second, they need organizational protection. They will be asked to cut across the organization without line authority. They need a protector, supporter, and coordinator to ensure that they can do the job.
- **Information.** Since product management is the nerve center of the organization, its contribution is proportional to the effectiveness of the MIS. Within packaged goods companies, sales reports are combined with competitive volume, consumer research, and feedback from the sales force. This national network of data forms the basis against which both product potential and performance are dimensioned.
- **Time.** The processes and attitudes of organizations don't change overnight. The transition from a distribution-based management to a product management system may take several years to accomplish effectively. While immediate results should be expected in certain areas, exaggerated expectations drastically reduce chances for success.

These ground rules are the first steps toward making the product manager concept work. Direct-response marketers face the same challenges as other consumer and industrial marketers, and so there is no reason why product management cannot be equally effective within our industry. Following these guidelines can contribute to successful and effective implementation within your firm.

chapter **10**

THIRD-PARTY ENDORSEMENTS

Marge Landrau

Manager, Direct Marketing
Citicorp Diners Club
New York, N.Y.

Third-party endorsements have been around for decades. Sometimes they are called syndications, other times endorsements.

Third-party endorsements combine elements of convenience and necessity. They are direct-response campaigns combining all the strategies of direct marketing; in the background there usually is a party known as a merchandise syndicator, manufacturer's representative, or broker.

In third-party endorsements, most of the risk is taken by the syndicator, who assumes the risk of maintaining the merchandise inventory. The manufacturer provides the merchandise. Another party to this type of endorsement is an endorser who owns a list and can extend credit to its customers, usually as part of its primary business.

Third-party endorsements originated shortly after World War II with retail credit jewelers and credit furniture stores. They took off early in the 1960s when a major oil company decided to enhance the value of its credit card by allowing its use for the purchase of nonrelated merchandise. Since then, third-party endorsements have been growing at a rapid pace.

Currently, they are offered to customers of large book publishers of encyclopedias and card holders of oil companies, banks, and airlines as well as travel and entertainment credit card holders. Our credit-oriented society has enabled this business to continue its growth at a rapid pace.

Third-party endorsements started as billing inserts and expanded into catalogs and solo direct mail pieces. Package inserts and bouncebacks also are being used. The newest medium, cable television, is experimenting with a type of endorsement. Third-party endorsements will continue to grow, especially if electronic funds transfers become a national or worldwide reality. Wherever there is credit available, there will be third-party endorsements.

THIRD-PARTY ENDORSEMENTS

The most common type of third-party endorsement involves a manufacturer, a merchandise syndicator, and the endorser who has a customer list. Each of these parties brings assets and liabilities into the marriage. For reasons which will be covered later, neither can or wants to promote products and services via direct-response vehicles without the other two parties.

Manufacturer

1. A manufacturer is usually only in the business of manufacturing.
2. It can develop products for mass marketing and can wholesale them to retailers and others.
3. Its resources are concentrated in the manufacturing and product development processes.
4. Its mass-media advertising is geared toward overall customer acceptance and the selling of its products to wholesalers and retailers.
5. It is not economically feasible for a large manufacturer to spend advertising dollars in selling directly to the consumer.
6. Its primary asset is the product.
7. Its primary liability is the lack of direct response know-how and the economics of drop-shipping individual pieces of merchandise.

Merchandise Syndicator

1. A syndicator is like a jobber, buying in bulk and reselling in units. It arranges to buy the merchandise in bulk from the manufacturer.
2. It warehouses the merchandise and in some instances repacks it into individual shippable units.
3. A syndicator is also very knowledgeable in the direct marketing field. It can put a complete direct marketing package together, drop-ship merchandise, bill the endorser's customer, and handle customer returns as well as most customer service inquiries and problems relating to its merchandise.
4. Its expertise in the field and the ability to do mass distribution of its mailing piece or campaign are its primary assets.
5. Its primary liability is the need for constant financing because it pays in advance not only for the merchandise but also for the development, printing, and mailing of the advertising campaign as well as the warehousing of its merchandise inventory.

Endorser

1. The endorser is the third party to the arrangement.
2. The endorser is usually in a different (nondirect marketing) business, such as a bank whose primary business is banking services like checking accounts, loans, etc.
3. The endorser does direct mail because it is a profitable business to be in.
4. It does not want to take title to the merchandise. It may be prevented by law or management policy.
5. Endorsers do not warehouse or handle drop-shipments of merchandise.
6. There are retailers that do such endorsements without warehousing and treat them as they would concessions within a store and share in the profits.
7. The endorser's primary assets are its customers' files and credit facility (prescreened credit customers).
8. Its liability has to do with lack of knowledge in the product purchase, pricing, warehousing, and drop-shipment, mainly because as a result of being in a different primary business, it does not want to get involved.
9. The endorser's name is also an asset because the customers trust it and will continue to buy from it.
10. It may be capable of preparing the campaign or may require a special direct mail campaign developed to maintain the image it would like to project.

As a result of the unwillingness of the manufacturer to sell directly to the consumer and the endorser's inability to do so, the syndicator came into being. There was a need for someone to put all the pieces together to promote the products of major manufacturers successfully.

Subsequently, syndicators also got into the import business to further increase their margins and expose the public to products which many Americans couldn't get unless they did extensive traveling overseas. Major syndicators are now also able to get products developed for a specific audience. This is possible because of the substantial involvement with the manufacturer, who is willing to give the syndicator a direct mail exclusive.

TYPES OF THIRD-PARTY ENDORSEMENTS

Syndications

Syndicated endorsements are the most common of the third-party endorsements and the most advantageous to the endorser.

1. The syndicator makes an agreement with a manufacturer to become the exclusive direct mail representative of the manufacturer. The syndicator has very good credit terms with the manufacturer, who may go to the extent of carrying "paper," or the cost of money.

2. The syndicator selects merchandise with mass appeal that can be taken to many different types of endorsers (credit card companies, oil companies, airline catalogs, retailers, etc.). Currently, mass-appeal merchandise is found primarily in the electronics area, with products such as calculators, stereo systems, and video cassette recorders. This category, however, traditionally has poor profit margins. Therefore, a syndicator must be able to sell in thousands of units in order to make a profit.
3. The syndicator develops an insert or other direct mail piece with general appeal. Usually, with just a plate change, it can print the same piece for several endorsers, thereby reducing its cost over a much larger print run than would be possible if it had to print for just one company.

Wholesaling

Wholesaling works almost like syndication and is very advantageous to the syndicator. The differences are as follows.

1. The endorser shares in the cost of developing the direct mail campaign but restricts the use of the campaign to its own audience.
2. The endorser pays the syndicator net 30 days and carries the receivables. Therefore, there is no cost of money on the part of the syndicator.
3. The remuneration to the endorser is a much larger percentage of the sale, allowing the endorser to cover the cost of money and also make a substantial profit. The percentage is usually double the amount of the syndication remuneration.

In this situation, the endorser assumes the risks, but the syndicator still warehouses and drop-ships the merchandise.

HOW THIRD-PARTY ENDORSEMENTS WORK

To illustrate how third-party endorsements work, here is a hypothetical case.

1. The XYZ Company is a very big manufacturer of stereo components. It advertises heavily on television, and it is well known. XYZ has up to now sold stereos to jobbers and retailers at 55 percent off the suggested list price, minus 10 percent, net 30 days. The basic units are shipped in lots of twenty, and speakers in lots of forty. The jobbers usually break down the shipments into more manageable lots and individual sets into four cartons. XYZ's latest stereo is the state of the art. The company has put together a specially matched component system which will not be available at retail as a package. XYZ is approached by ML Company, a merchandise syndicator interested in an exclusive arrangement to sell the product through direct-response advertising.
2. ML Company makes a contractual agreement with the manufacturer. The system will retail for a minimum of $1000. ML agrees to warehouse, and the

manufacturer will pack the system in four individual cartons. ML's cost is based on the same jobber terms (55 percent/10 percent, net 30). ML gives XYZ a letter of credit and asks XYZ to ship 5 units immediately (4 to ML's warehouse and 1 unit to SOL Company). ML has been in business for 10 years and has complete warehousing, drop-shipping, and customer service capabilities. It services ten major clients including SOL Company (a third-party endorser).

3. ML meets with the direct marketing people of SOL. ML tells SOL that it believes SOL's customers would be receptive to a unique stereo system. SOL's customers are in the upper-income brackets; 90 percent own homes with an average market value of $74,500. They are college-educated, busy executives who do not have time to shop. They are also used to reasonable credit terms and are allowed to take up to 10 months to pay for any merchandise that sells for at least $250.
4. The stereo system is the best money can buy. It has been packaged in such a manner that it would take months of shopping to be able to put it together at its special price. The stereo will be shipped by truck after the trucking firm makes an appointment with the customer. Returns will be handled in the same manner; the trucker will pick up the system from the customer. This process will give the customer confidence since there will be no hassles should the customer decide to return the stereo.
5. SOL agrees to promote the stereo system. For its participation, it will get a commission equal to 20 percent of the gross amount of the sale. However, it may retain 12 percent of the sale as a reserve against future credits for returned merchandise. The participation includes the endorsement, carrying the receivables on installments, and guaranteeing the sale to ML. SOL gives ML a few pointers on the way it sees the promotional piece developed to fit its image with its customers. It asks ML to develop a basic composition of the mailing piece and advertising copy. It gives ML a contract to sign which is subject to approval of the advertising material and an independent testing laboratory's confirmation of all the claims made in the advertising.
6. ML asks its advertising agency to develop the basic layout, theme, and copy. It takes it to SOL, which will ask for changes until it is satisfied with the presentation. SOL works very closely with ML in the development of the mailing piece, including the photographs to be used in it.
7. It is decided that they will go with a self-mailer format. The cover will be a very modernistic and futuristic shot of the components floating out of the sky. As you open the self-mailer, the first page will have a letter of endorsement signed by the president of SOL, introducing the stereo system and leading into the basic features and advantages of owning the system. The latter is one of the most important parts of an endorsed promotion. Not only should it be a merchandising letter, it also should bring out the relationship between the customer and the endorser. It should emphasize the convenient monthly terms and the ease of shopping by mail for the merchandise endorsed by the company. The consumer trusts the endorser, and this point must be reinforced constantly so that the customer believes that the endorser is giving its seal of approval. (See Figure 10-1.)

THE SOL COMPANY, Anytown, U.S.A.

Dear Sol Member:

Selecting the right stereo system no longer has to be a time-consuming task. As part of our continuing service to you, we have asked XYZ, one of the most respected names in audio equipment, to create a stereo system exclusively for our members. The result is the XYZ Special Stereo System which is being made available to you through this advanced private invitation.

The XYZ Special Stereo System has all the sophisticated features you need to produce truly outstanding stereo sound. It incorporates the latest technology available with perfectly matched speakers to give you the sound you only heard while seated in the best seats at a concert hall. And the system is ready and waiting for you to try it in your own home with no obligation to buy.

Selecting the proper components is the difficult part of acquiring a truly outstanding stereo system. The selection of the components has been made by XYZ's audio engineers, the best qualified people to make such a selection. Now, all you have to do is listen to this Special Stereo System in the comfort of your home with no obligation to buy. *If you're not completely satisfied with the performance and quality of this stereo system, it will be picked up directly from your home at no cost to you.*

If you decide to keep the XYZ Special Stereo System, you can take up to 12 months to pay. To acquire your exclusive stereo for a 30-day risk-free trial, simply fill out and mail the enclosed postage-paid order form today!

Sincerely,

Marge Landrau
President

ML:cd

P.S. For the details of this exclusive stereo, I suggest you review the enclosed brochure now.

Figure 10-1 Sample of letter of endorsement.

8. The next two spreads of the self-mailer will contain a full-blown shot of the entire system with callouts pointing out the best features. Don't be afraid to get technical when describing a stereo system. Consumers are better educated now. Lack of information about the product may cause you to lose a sale.
9. The last inside panel will be devoted to the order form and the special purchase terms. While there are certain legal requirements on installment sales, don't let the order form become a legalistic document. If there is a warranty, don't just bring out the specific legal requirements but also bring out the uniqueness of the warranty in a positive manner. Let it be the last thing the customer reads on the order form. Sometimes this can clinch the sale.

10. The outside panel will include individual photographs of all the components, with subparagraphs outlining the state of the art of each component.
11. ML is given the go-ahead to print and mail. SOL supplies the mailing list in segments mutually agreed on by the parties, and the test is mailed.
12. The orders in this case will go to ML's address for the sake of expediency in fulfillment. In other instances, the orders would go to the endorser mainly for control purposes. Or if you prefer, have an independent service bureau do the order processing. (The cost should be charged to the syndicator.) You will have better control and better financial reporting.
13. ML obtains credit approval from SOL for every order before shipment of the merchandise. This is a guarantee that ML will be paid for the merchandise whether or not SOL gets paid by its customers. It also gives SOL a chance to double-check its customers' prior payment history.
14. ML computerizes the order and generates shipping labels, which it forwards to its warehouse with a manifest.
15. ML's warehouse arranges with the trucking firm to ship the stereo to SOL's customers and sends the appropriate shipping documents with a copy of the manifest back to ML's headquarters. ML prepares the billing on magnetic tape for SOL to bill its customers and forwards the magnetic tape with its own invoice to SOL.
16. SOL will bill its customers in installments and pay ML according to the terms mutually agreed on. In this case, ML gets 80 percent of the amount billed and charged by SOL's customers. The difference between the 45 percent ML paid the manufacturer (XYZ) and the 80 percent it gets from the third party is its margin. Its 35 percent margin must cover ML's promotional expense, warehousing, drop-shipping and the cost of handling returns, and refurbishing as well as its profit.
17. SOL's 20 percent margin basically covers the cost of billing its customers, the cost of carrying the receivables until it receives payment in full from its customers, and any losses for accounts which may go bad during the length of the installment payment plan. SOL has developed a fairly good credit history file on each of its customers. As a result, less than 0.5 percent of the receivables are never paid for.
18. Merchandise returned for credit or refund is received at ML's warehouse. Depending on the condition of the merchandise, it may be returned to the manufacturer (XYZ), which in turn will refurbish the merchandise. XYZ may charge a refurbishing charge between $30 and $50 per unit to ML. If the merchandise cannot be refurbished, ML may have to sell it at cost to a discounter who may get rid of it through a warehouse sale. ML sometimes also runs its own warehouse sale to sell returned merchandise for slightly above its cost in order to recover the cost as well as make a very small profit. In some instances, the syndicator and the endorser will share refurbishing costs; in other instances, the endorser pays the refurbishing costs and auctions off the returned merchandise.

This hypothetical case applies to almost any medium. The only differences would be in the cost of printing and mailing. In the case of a billing insert (bill stuffer), the endorser pays for the cost of placing the insert into its statement envelope; the syndicator pays for the cost of printing the insert. This also applies to other types of inserts such as package inserts and bouncebacks.

Service-type offers such as insurance policies and credit card registration services are promoted in this manner. However, the traditional syndicator may be replaced by a broker or agent. They also can become two-party endorsements as in the case of some insurance offers in which the marketing arm of the insurance company, which usually is a division of the company, or an underwriter replaces the syndicator. The basic concept remains the same.

Large mail-order catalog firms use endorsed promotions as an additional benefit for their customers. Promotions are usually for services but are also for unique merchandise offers such as a negative option monogrammed glassware offer in which one glass is shipped each month. Merchandise offers are noncompetitive and are used for merchandise which is not economically feasible for the catalog firm to warehouse and drop-ship.

Banks use third-party endorsements because banking laws and regulations prohibit them from being the legal seller of merchandise. The syndicator therefore plays a more important role and is the legal seller of the merchandise. Oil companies also are restricted in the selling of nonrelated merchandise. For these endorsers, the syndicator also assumes the state sales tax liability. The endorser collects the sales taxes, but the syndicator remits them to the appropriate states. In some instances, taxes are collected only in states in which the syndicator has a physical presence; in other instances, the endorser collects taxes in states in which it is liable for sales tax collection, but the syndicator still is responsible for remitting to the states.

BENEFITS

There are benefits to all the parties involved in endorsements.

Manufacturer

1. Manufacturers gain an additional distribution outlet for their products.
2. They can diversify into other products with minimal risk. Tests of new gadgetry can be done at a much lower cost than if the manufacturer had to expose it to the mass market.
3. Manufacturer's representatives can serve syndicators without a need for staff expansion.
4. It can devote time to the primary business: developing and manufacturing products.
5. There is no need to expand and train staff in the direct marketing field.

Syndicator

1. A syndicator can mass-market products at substantially lower cost as a result of being able to develop one direct-response campaign for many endorsers.

2. As a result of getting guaranteed orders from the endorser, the risk of collection and extension of credit is eliminated.
3. Syndicators can become self-employed by subcontracting all the work to established firms.
4. The syndicator does not need to establish itself with customers because the endorser has already done this. Therefore, there is no need to develop a customers' list. It takes a free ride on the endorser's image and the customers' trust.
5. A syndicator can be one person or a very small operation that subcontracts all its administrative needs.

Endorser

1. Endorsers generate profits by using their customers' lists.
2. Endorsers add benefits of a nonrelated nature to their credit facility, therefore making their primary business more attractive to their customers.
3. The endorser saves on payroll because it does not have to have in-house merchandising talent.
4. The endorser turns its major asset (its customers' list) into a major profit center.
5. The endorser does not assume unknown risks such as may occur in the warehousing of merchandise.
6. The endorser has an automatic customer activation program. Card holders who may not use their credit cards frequently for regular purchases will be tempted to use them for the purchase of merchandise on installments. If a card holder is in the middle of an installment payment plan, the card holder is most likely to renew the memberhip in order not to have to pay for the remaining installments all at once.

Third-party endorsements are easy to implement. All you have to do is find a reputable syndicator who will work with you. However, third-party endorsements are not for everyone. If your list size is under 200,000, most syndicators will not want to work with you unless you can give them an exclusive contract which includes not only all your billing inserts but also all your direct mail campaigns for at least 1 year. You could, however, offer other services such as insurance and credit card registry without the need of a syndicator. When in doubt, ask the experts for advice. They will help you protect one of your most valuable assets: your customers' list.

chapter 11

ACCOUNTING CONSIDERATIONS

James B. Kobak

James B. Kobak &
Company
Darien, Conn.

PURPOSES OF ACCOUNTING

There are two ways of attacking the subject of accounting in relation to direct marketing or any other business. One can either take the "bean counter" approach of many accountants or assume the broader, more creative, and more useful attitude that accounting and accountants were put on earth to help run businesses and therefore should be expected to provide all the data, analyses, and future projections which can be useful.

Because I take the latter approach, this chapter may disappoint some of the purists in the profession who would like to see detailed conversation about the mumbo-jumbo of accounting principles which are not very useful in making more money. Whenever I have my way, the accounting department is intimately involved in planning, in projections of the future, and in other creative thinking as well as in controlling what goes on. This, of course, requires accountants who are capable of the right kind of open-minded thinking.

There are two other major purposes of accounting which should not, however, be overlooked. A good accounting system must be designed to safeguard the funds of the business: controlling spending and making sure that collections are made, discounts are taken, bills are reviewed and paid only if proper, and the like.

The accounting system also must provide the necessary data to meet various governmental requirements such as income, sales, and other taxes.

BASIC PRINCIPLES OF ACCOUNTING

Accountants, like all professionals, have their own jargon, which probably was developed to create a mystique that prevents others from knowing what the accountants are doing. Everything is done in accordance with "generally accepted accounting principles" (GAAP). Many of these principles can become terribly technical at times and make you feel that you are arguing about how many angels can stand on the head of a pin.

For our major purpose of using accounting to help run the business, only a handful of basics are important.

The Accounting System

The accounting system must be set up to follow the way the business is organized and operated, not for the convenience of the accountants. In the magazine business, for instance, there generally are several sources of income: subscription, single copy, advertising, and other (list rental, etc.). There are five major departments which operate a magazine: production (including paper, printing, and postage), editorial, advertising sales, circulation sales and fulfillment, and administrative. The accounting system for a magazine should be organized in the same way. A brief operating statement would look like this:

	Income	
Subscription		$1,406,000
Single copy		395,000
Advertising		2,224,000
Other		63,000
		$4,088,000
	Expenses	
Production		$1,690,000
Editorial		436,000
Advertising		478,000
Circulation		812,000
Administrative		436,000
		3,852,000
Income (loss)		$236,000

It doesn't have to be that way, however. If you have a marketing department which sells both advertising and circulation, your statements will be changed to reflect that.

You also will note that the statement for a magazine does not contain two items which are on the operating statement of most other businesses: costs of goods sold and gross profit. If the figures were shown that way, interpretation would be difficult because a magazine is unusual; it is one product with several interdependent revenue streams. The advertising rate, for instance, depends on the amount of circulation. But the profit depends not only on the advertising rate but also on the cost of obtaining circulation and the price you can get for it. Thus, you cannot consider them separately.

In most direct marketing businesses, the cost of sales and gross profit approach is used because you are selling a series of products which are not interdependent.

Accrual versus Cash Basis

There are two basic methods of doing accounting: accrual and cash. Cash is just what it says. You record transactions as the money changes hands, i.e., when you receive dollars from a customer or when you actually pay a bill.

With the accrual method, you record transactions when they take place, for example, when you ship an order to a customer or when you incur an expense, even though you may not pay for it right away.

Most people keep personal records on a cash basis. In running a business, however, it is vital to record things as they happen, not at the time the money changes hands; otherwise, you will not know what is going on. Thus, the accrual basis is applied universally. This does not mean, however, that the cash flow aspects can be ignored.

Match Income with Applicable Expenses

In order to get an accurate picture of what is going on in a business, it is essential to measure things at the same time. In a magazine, for instance, advertising income is recorded at the time the issue is published. At the same time, you must record the cost of paper, printing, and postage as well as the sales-people's commissions and other expenses which apply to that issue.

Allocations of Expenses

In every company, there are people who do jobs which overlap into two or more areas. For instance, you may have an advertising promotion director who works for two magazines. When this happens, in order to get the most accurate picture of the expenses applicable to each of the magazines, an allocation of the promotion director's salary and other applicable costs is made between the two magazines as accurately as the situation warrants.

Allocations of other costs also are often made: telephone, rent, overhead, and any other items for which an allocation would be meaningful.

Practicality

The tendency of many accounting types is to try to do everything in as detailed and precise a way as possible. Very often the cost and trouble are not worth the reward. An element of practicality is needed. In the allocation of the promotion director's salary, for instance, an estimate of the time he or she spends on each magazine is sufficient. Time records are not needed, although they probably are necessary for production workers, in which case you must know the precise cost of each item made.

In the same way, while an editor works on the June issue of a magazine in April—and one of our principles is that we must match income with expense—it is not worth the trouble of accruing the April salary and applying it to June because the editor's salary is the same in both periods.

ACCOUNTING STATEMENTS

There are only four types of accounting statements used in any business, although the subsets and details may be quite extensive.

1. The operating statement tells what has happened during a given period on the accrual basis.
2. Cash flow tells what has happened during a given period on the cash basis.
3. The balance sheet tells the condition of a company at one point in time by showing the assets, liabilities, and owners' equity.
4. The source and application of funds shows what has happened to the assets and liabilities during a given period.

Certain statistics which measure the most important features of the business also are of value. These will, of course, vary from field to field. Such things as the cost to obtain a customer and the renewal rate are of great help in the direct marketing business.

After the form of the accounting statements has been determined, a chart of accounts is developed. This is simply a list of the accounts in the accounting system with a definition of what should be in each so that there is uniformity in handling items. A number code usually is assigned to each account so that bills and other items can be marked easily and applied where they belong.

For the accounting statements to be as useful as possible in helping run the business, it is best to design them so that you can take a three-dimensional view of what is going on.

Figure 11-1 shows a form of operating statement for a book publishing company. This form is similar to those used by some other businesses doing direct marketing. Of course, the company in the exhibit sells books in many ways other than direct marketing.

The various dimensions of viewing operations which are available on this one sheet are as follows.

1. Actual operations for the 7 months through July.
2. Actual operations for July alone.
3. Each item as a percentage of net sales for each of these periods.
4. Comparison of data for this year against the data for the prior year for the same period.
5. Comparison of percentages of net sales for the same periods versus the prior year.
6. Comparison of data for this year against the previously developed budget.

A Book Company
Summary Operating Statement
July, 198X
(In thousands)

Current Month							Seven Months to Date					
Last Year		Budget		This Year			This Year		Budget		Last Year	
$	%	$	%	$	%		$	%	$	%	$	%
						Gross sales	$31,999	109.2%				
						Less: Returns and allowances	2,697	9.2				
	100%		100%		100%	Net sales	29,302	100.0		100%		100%
						Cost of sales						
						Manufacturing	5,963	20.4				
						Royalty	955	3.3				
							6,918	23.7				
						Gross profit	22,384	76.3				
						Subsidiary rights income	256	.9				
							22,640	77.2				
						Operating Expenses						
						Editorial						
						Salaries	1,209	4.1				
						Outside editorial fees	222	.8				
						Other	413	1.4				
							1,844	6.3				
						Selling						
						Salaries and commissions	548	1.9				
						Travel and entertainment	124	.4				
						Other	203	.7				
							875	3.0				
						Promotion						
						Salaries	374	1.3				
						Advertising	2,113	7.2				
						Direct mail, catalogs	8,327	28.4				
						Other	227	.8				
							11,041	37.7				
						Fulfillment						
						Order processing—salaries	1,247	4.3				
						Order processing—other	918	3.1				
						Shipping and warehousing	1,514	5.1				
						Other	2,284	7.8				
							5,963	20.3				
						Administrative						
						Salaries	655	2.2				
						Travel and entertainment	122	.4				
						Employee benefits, taxes	73	.2				
						Occupancy	325	1.1				
						Office costs	474	1.6				
						Taxes	133	.5				
						Professional fees	106	.4				
						Other	145	.5				
							2,033	6.9				
						Total expenses	21,756	74.2				
						Publishing income	884	3.0				
						Less: Cost of money	2,461	8.4				
						Operating income (loss)	$ (1,577)	(5.4)%				

Figure 11-1 Summary operating statement for a book company.

7. Comparison of percentages of net sales for the same periods versus the budget.

Figure 11-2 adds a number of statistical dimensions to the picture. It's probable that further details would be developed to show the results of different marketing methods.

ACCOUNTING FOR DIRECT MARKETING OPERATIONS

We have been talking so far about principles which apply to any business. Let's now get into specifics for direct marketing operations.

We first must recognize that while some companies are completely devoted to

A Book Company
Statistics
July, 198X
(In thousands)

Current Month							Seven Months to Date					
Last Year		Budget		This Year			This Year		Budget		Last Year	
$	%	$	%	$	%		$	%	$	%	$	%
						Sales by type of customer						
						Book stores	$ 2,504	8.5				
						Wholesalers	429	1.5				
						Libraries and institutions	173	.6				
						Mass market outlets	145	.5				
						Direct to customer	25,869	88.3				
						Special sales	182	.6				
	100%		100%		100%		$29,302	100.0%		100%		100%
						Units sold						
						Hard cover	2,224					
						Soft cover	527					
						Net sales per unit						
						Hard cover	$ 11.92					
						Soft cover	5.30					
						Production cost per unit						
						Hard cover	$ 2.37					
						Soft cover	1.31					
						Number of invoices	1,932					
						Average sale per invoice	$ 15.17					
						Fulfillment cost per unit	$ 2.17					
						Inventory turnover	1.8 times					
						Accounts receivable	$ 9,728					
						Percentage of net sales	33.2%					
						Average collection period	101 days					
						Aging of receivables						
						Current	50.4%					
						1 to 30 days overdue	22.7					
						31 to 60	11.2					
						61 and over	15.7					
						Employees	137					
						Employees per $1,000,000 of sales	4.7					

Figure 11-2 Example of a statistics statement for a book company.

direct marketing, for most firms it is just one method of selling products and services. It is not an industry by itself, as steelmaking or real estate is. For that reason, there is no universal method for presenting accounting statements.

We already have seen the approach taken for magazines and book publishers. In each field, the presentation methods used will be those which fit best. Mail-order companies follow retail accounting systems and may use the retail inventory method, fund raisers use fund-raising systems, insurance companies use insurance systems, and so forth.

There are, however, common factors and methods to be considered in accounting for the direct marketing portion even though some aspects may be handled differently.

DIRECT MARKETING IS A STATISTICAL BUSINESS

Probably more than any other business, direct marketing is based on the sophisticated massaging and understanding of numbers. Creativity is required in developing or finding products or services which people want and in developing sales techniques and programs. But just as much creativity is needed to develop, understand, and interpret data after the results are in.

Because of this, whether you like it or not, the development of accurate data, sometimes in excruciating detail, is essential. Also essential, however, is knowing what is most important. Otherwise, you can drown in a sea of figures.

THE BASE: THE PROMOTION EFFORT

In direct marketing, everything starts with the promotion effort. Accounting begins with careful recording of the results of each effort, whether it is directed toward new or old customers and whether it is a test or a rollout. The data to be collected for each direct mail effort, for instance, are as follows:

Number of pieces mailed
Cost per thousand pieces
Gross response
Gross response percentage
Gross income per average order, including shipping and handling charge
Returns
Return percentage
Percentage cash, credit, and credit card
Bad debts
Bad debt percentage
Net response
Net response percentage

Net income per average order

Cost of premium

Average cost of goods sold (manufacturing, royalty, etc.)

Percent cost of sales is of net income

Fulfillment cost

Fulfillment cost per order

Cost of handling returns

These items all apply specifically to the direct income and direct costs of a particular mailing.

With all these data in hand, it is useful also to develop an entire operating statement for each separate promotion effort. Allocations of indirect costs such as editorial, promotion, and administrative should be included so that you reach an operating profit figure.

With operating statements of this kind, comparisons can be made of the relative profitability of different products, prices and offers, mailing pieces, lists, and other variables. Naturally, a budget will have been made previously with which results can be compared.

While these figures are designed for direct mail efforts, similar data should be developed for each other source.

IMPORTANCE OF TYING DATA INTO ACCOUNTING REPORTS

Too often in a marketing business, the marketing people are separate from accounting. The tendency for the marketers is to develop their own forms and methods of tabulating and analyzing results. This seemingly makes sense because they understand their end of the business and know what they are trying to accomplish. On the other hand, it almost invariably leads to erroneous figures because such marketers lack the discipline of having to make everything balance. I have seen many companies which thought they had made good profits based on informal marketing department figures only to find that there were important items missing.

With the ubiquitous computer to handle the storing of information and the calculation of results, there is no reason why the correct basic data cannot be made available for both areas. Accounting statements for the operation as a whole should be developed by adding the data from all the promotion efforts together, using the same basic information. Then there will be no surprises or misconceptions.

HANDLING DIFFERENT DIRECT MARKETING SALES TECHNIQUES

The promotion effort is the base from which all knowledge starts. The information required from its results is pretty much the same regardless of the sales technique. A number of other factors, however, are needed in judging the success of some methods.

The techniques which cover the vast majority of selling efforts are

Sale of single items
Catalog sales
Clubs
Continuity series
Subscriptions

Each has a set of special factors to be weighed in conjunction with the others and with the basics to determine results and, more important, to develop future plans.

Sale of Single Items

The simplest direct marketing method involves selling one item or a set of items to one customer at a time. Prices and costs are relatively uniform. Interpretation is simpler than in some of the other methods. The operating statement and statistics would be very much like those in Figures 11-1 and 11-2.

Catalog Sales

While the operating statement for the operation may not be very different from that of the single-item sale, interpreting results becomes a high art. Statistics are needed on such things as the following:

Which catalog
Number of items purchased
Price of items purchased
Total value of the order
Sales of each item and class of item in the catalog
Returns in the same categories
Pages in the catalog from which the items were purchased
Area of the page showing the purchased items

Clubs

Clubs lose money on each new member they acquire. Profits are achieved only if a member stays long enough and buys enough items. The following factors are vital:

Results of each mailing. In this case, we include each member bulletin which may include thirteen or more cycles per year. This is normally kept by entry class (the time first becoming a member) and by source.

Cost to obtain a member.

Number of selections taken before ceasing to be a member.

Price of items taken, reduced price or full price.

Price per unit.

Cost per unit.

Prime selections versus alternatives.

Percentage of members taking prime selection.

The operating statement for a club reflects the importance of the type of selection taken by members and of the cost of acquiring them. As you can see in Figure 11-3, the cost of acquiring a new member is considered an operating expense because of the very small amount of income normally received. Because it will be some time before a member is profitable, the calculation of the cost of money is particularly important.

Club
Operating Statement

Gross sales: Regular	$2,531,000
Reduced price	91,000
	2,622,000
Less: Returns and allowances	533,000
	2,089,000
Less: Bad debts	154,000
Net Sales	1,935,000
Cost of Sales	
Manufacturing	511,000
Royalties	99,000
	610,000
Gross Profit	1,325,000
Operating expense	
Advertising and promotion	
New member offers	
Cost of books	150,000
Space advertising	127,000
Direct mail	131,000
Other	42,000
	450,000
Less: Income from offers	24,000
	426,000
Promotion to members	143,000
Salaries, other costs	102,000
	671,000
Fulfillment (net of recoveries)	241,000
Administrative	223,000
Total expenses	1,135,000
Marketing income	190,000
Less: Cost of money	203,000
Operating income (loss)	$ (13,000)

Figure 11-3 Example of an operating statement for a club.

Continuity Series

While continuity series operate somewhat differently from clubs, the idea is the same. If a buyer stays with the series long enough, it can be profitable. If not, it can be a disaster.

The items to be measured are the same as with clubs, but the mix which brings profit may be very different. Operating statements usually are very much like those of clubs.

Subscriptions

By their nature, magazine, newsletter, and other subscriptions result in repeat exposure to the product and with it a familiarity which brings higher repeat purchases than other direct marketing methods. Key factors involve renewal rates, which should be kept track of for the first, second, third, etc., renewals, and also the original source of the subscription as well as the renewal effort to which a subscriber responded.

IMPORTANCE OF REPEAT SALES

It is very difficult to make money on one-shots. The whole function of clubs, continuity series, and subscriptions is to develop repeat sales. While sales of single items and catalog sales seemingly are one-time events, the real goal should be to develop loyal customers. For that reason, marketers that sell in these ways should keep records about the behavior of their buyers that are as detailed as those kept by magazine publishers and record clubs. They need lifetime histories of customers, including the following:

When they bought
What they bought
Size of orders
Whether they bought by cash, credit, or credit card
Return and bad debt history

VALUE OF A CUSTOMER

To get the most out of a customer, you must think of the customer buying not just in the way he or she started out but through any other means available. After all, Time-Life and Readers' Digest book and record operations grew from magazine buyers, and oil company mailings arose from gas station buyers.

The most sophisticated direct marketers think far beyond the initial sale. They plan in terms which are very long term. They expect to acquire a customer today and perhaps not make profit for 2 or 3 years. Through careful recordkeeping and analysis they can determine interests and the likelihood of buying again. It becomes a terribly complex calculation, but you can determine the eventual value of a customer and then figure out how much you can pay initially to acquire a new one.

COMBINATION OF SOURCES

We have been talking about keeping track of each individual effort in detail. Let's not forget that a combination of different sources of new orders also can make a project go.

A magazine, for instance, may not be able to develop sufficient circulation through direct mail. But by adding subscriptions obtained through exchange advertising, insert cards, and agent-sold (or other) methods plus single-copy sales, you may be able to develop a winner. In the same way, a book publisher may be able to develop enough volume for a title by selling it as a one-shot, through a book club, and in bookstores to make it profitable, whereas any one of those sources alone would not work.

IMPORTANCE OF CASH FLOW

We concluded earlier that the accrual method of accounting gives more accurate results than the cash method. In planning, however, cash flow is very important, particularly in direct marketing. Many direct marketing efforts call for large up-front payments for promotion and inventory, and customer responses and payments may lag for some time. If you have not planned for the required amount of cash, you may find that you cannot carry out the programs you want.

INVENTORY WRITE-OFFS

Frequently, the cost of sales is determined without taking into account the fact that no matter how well the business is run, a sizable part of the inventory of virtually any item will have to be written off or sold at a depressed price. If allowance is not made for that in the regular cost of sales calculation, you may find that you have a disaster when you thought you were making profits.

COST OF MONEY

I have carefully put in a line at the bottom of each sample operating statement for the cost of money. Too many companies ignore this or think about it only once a year. In all direct marketing operations except magazines, the cost of money comes into play and should be included every time you try to determine what profits might be. Inventories and accounts receivable represent cash which might be used better in other ways. In addition, if you have calculated the value of a customer with profits not coming for a long time, the calculation is incomplete without the cost of carrying the customer during that period.

USE OF COMPUTER MODELS

It was stated earlier that direct marketing is a statistical business, but it must be apparent by now that it is much more complex than that. It is long-term, and you cannot be successful without careful planning.

Some very powerful tools have been developed to assist with the planning process. For example, a magazine publishing model and direct marketing model have been developed by Kobak Business Models to help in the process. They have been used by more than 1000 magazines and other direct marketers in various parts of the world.

These models enable a company to play "what if" games to determine the optimum plans over a period of 5 or more years. They enable you to determine accrual basis and cash basis profits in accordance with various assumptions which you can control as well as to find circulation levels and other statistical information during the period. These are calculations which you theoretically could do by hand but which the models enable you to do much faster and more accurately, as well as giving you the opportunity to examine many variations.

chapter 12

SWEEPSTAKES

Jeffrey Feinman

President
Ventura Associates, Inc.
New York, N.Y.

Sweepstakes have been proved historically to be the most successful method of dramatically increasing response to direct mail offers. They are used for single-product offers, subscription mailings, catalogs of general merchandise, service firms, industrial mailers, and most recently, fund raisers. In fact, there is hardly a mail order seller that has not used the device effectively.

The chance to win a valuable prize entices readers to open and become involved with the product offered. It is not at all unusual to register sales increases of 40 to 100 percent over a control. As the cost is fixed (prizes, sweepstakes brochure, and administration), the incremental cost is minimal. That is, a typical sweepstakes may add less than 1 percent to the mailing cost, with a gain of 100 percent in response.

HISTORY

There are examples of prize promotions as early as 1900 in advertising mail. However, sweepstakes in the form we know them began in the early 1950s. By 1952, the states had liberalized legislation to permit widespread use of chance promotions. The real heyday was in the late 1950s and early 1960s.

By 1960, almost any piece of direct mail could be seen carrying the familiar words "you may have already won." The real difference was that prizes were awarded only to the degree to which they were claimed. That is, only winning prize numbers which actually were returned were given awards. Since mailers seldom would receive a response of over 10 percent, they could be safe in knowing that not more than 10 percent of the "available" prizes would be awarded. A $50,000 sweepstakes seldom cost the advertiser more than $5000.

In April 1966, the Federal Trade Commission began its famed "Investigation of Pre-selected Winner Sweepstakes." There followed congressional hearings with a seemingly endless line of marketers that had awarded few if any of the promised prizes. Most marketers were convinced that sweepstakes were doomed. What emerged instead was an informed public and an industry that was stronger than ever. Through a series of agreements and self-policing, almost every marketer began to make the statement, "All prizes guaranteed to be awarded." This return to sanity and honesty helped create the current billion-dollar prize promotion industry.

Today more firms use sweepstakes than ever before. Currently, they are conducted under safeguards that assure the awarding of all prizes and compliance with a host of regulatory actions.

TYPES OF PRIZE PROMOTIONS

Prize offers frequently are considered under the general heading of sweepstakes. However, there are a number of distinct types.

A lucky number is the most common type of direct mail promotion. A number is preselected, and all returns are compared against this number. It offers the advantage of being able to say, "You may have already won," which is a powerful copy platform. It offers the disadvantage that all returns must be "screened" or checked for winning numbers. Screening is a costly process in large mailings.

With a random draw, all returns (buyers and nonbuyers) participate in a drawing from all returns for prizes.

In a contest of skill, the entrant must take a skill test. Typically, a request is made to complete a twenty-five-word statement. These traditionally have proved unsuccessful in the mail as response is slowed down while consumers work on their entries.

LEGALITY

All fifty states and the federal government have legislation governing prize promotions. Traditionally, this legislation changes to fit the climate of the country and the views of the current governing authorities. During periods of strong consumerism, the number of regulations and their enforcement tend to increase. The independent judging organization that administers a sweepstakes must be familiar with the latest laws. More important than the law is the practical application of this legislation, which is open to considerable interpretation. Currently, sweepstakes are legal in all fifty states.

It is important to understand that lotteries are illegal in all fifty states. A lottery has the elements of prize, chance, and consideration present simultaneously. What transforms a lottery to a sweepstakes is the deletion of one of those elements, usually the element of consideration. That is, consumers are told that they do not have to buy to enter. In a contest of skill, the element of chance is eliminated. Skill rather than chance determines the winner.

Although various other laws are applicable, the lottery law is the most important. Violation carries both criminal and civil penalties. It is a serious matter. Disregard of the law can result in mail not being distributed by the post office or return mail not being delivered.

Consumers are further protected by New York State and Florida regulations that require the posting of a surety bond or an escrow account for each sweepstakes. This law assures residents of those states that should the sponsor fail to have funds to pay for prize awards, the insurance company will meet the obligation.

The overall guideline is simply that rules must clearly, and in detail disclose the mechanics of the offer. Figure 12-1 shows a typical one for *New York* magazine.

OFFICIAL RULES

No purchase necessary

1. To enter, follow the directions published in this offer. Your entry must be received by September 30, 19—, the final closing date of the sweepstakes.

2. Our individual Sweepstakes numbers will be compared against a list of winning numbers selected by computer. In the event all prizes are not claimed via the return of winning numbers, which is likely, random drawings will be held from among all entries received to award unclaimed prizes. A special drawing will be conducted to award the "Special Early Bird Bonus Award" from among all qualified entries received by the Early Bird deadline specified. This Early Bird Bonus will be awarded in addition to any other prize which may be won.

3. Selection of winning numbers and random drawings are under the supervision of VENTURA ASSOCIATES, INC., an independent judging organization whose decisions are final. One prize to a family with the exception of the "Special Early Bird Bonus Award." No substitution will be made for any prize except as offered herein. Certain versions of this sweepstakes may offer alternative prizes. Winners will have the opportunity to choose among alternative prizes in their winning category. Travel prizes are subject to space and departure availability and must be taken by December 31, 1983. The China trip must be booked at least 5 months prior to planned departure date, and is subject to the then existing rules as to passport, visa and travel requirements as specified by The People's Republic of China and the Department of State of the United States of America. Taxes on all prizes are the sole responsibility of the winners. All prizes will be awarded.

Sweepstakes open to residents of the United States. Employees of News Group Publications Inc., its affiliates, agencies and members of their families are not eligible. Sweepstakes is subject to all Federal, State and local laws and regulations and is void in North Carolina and wherever prohibited by law. Odds of winning are determined by the total number of entries received. This sweepstakes may be jointly used by the other titles published by News Group Publications, Incorporated.

4. Winners of major prizes will be obligated to sign and return an Affidavit of Eligibility within 60 days of notification. In the event of non-compliance within this time period, alternative winners will be selected. Any prize returned to the sponsor or to Ventura Associates as undeliverable will be awarded to alternative winners.

For a list of winners, send a separate, stamped, self-addressed envelope to:

Winners List
New York Magazine

Figure 12-1 Sample sweepstakes rules.

PSYCHOLOGY

On one level, it is unimportant why sweepstakes work. The mere fact that they are so successful should be enough. However, the power of the device generates academic interest in the motivational forces.

To understand sweepstakes one need only look to Las Vegas, Atlantic City, or any other casino. Rich and poor alike stream there for the opportunity to win a dream. In many western European countries, e.g., Spain, the lottery has become an institution.

In direct mail, sweepstakes recipients are offered an opportunity to play with no financial risk. In the process, they must at least open the envelope and become involved in the offer. As one widely touted study indicates, upwards of 60 percent of all third class mail is thrown away unopened. Herein may lie one answer. It's hard to toss out an envelope that says, "You may have already won $25,000."

Once inside, the consumer must complete the order form even to reply no. Beyond this hurdle the sale is much easier.

The sweepstakes package itself, with cars and boats and TVs, is often more exciting than the direct mail package with a straight offer.

Finally, there is one school of thought that still believes consumers buy because they believe it increases their chance to win. Smart mailers pander to this psychology by providing the recipient with a package that looks "lucky." Headlines that scream out about big dollar numbers and show customers' names on simulated passbooks, airline tickets, and bank vaults all contribute to the sweepstakes fantasy. Successful sweepstakes packages leave each consumer with a strong sense that he or she could easily be the winner.

"NO-NAMES"

Even nonbuyers must be given a chance to enter. This legal requirement is actually a positive regulation. In fact, even if the law were changed, many would still emblazon their envelopes with the words "no purchase required." The "free" entry gets readers involved with the package. Having filled in the order blank, it's a short step to making a nonbuyer into a buyer.

Furthermore, a "no" name is not without merit. Many mailers remail to all those who reply no. They simply send a repeat of the offer with a cover letter that says, "We've forwarded your entry to the judging organization. However, we did want to give you one last opportunity to take advantage of our special offer."

"No" names are also a good revenue source. List managers will usually put up "no" names on a special list. For some offers, they are better than buyers. What we know about "no" names is that they are interested in something for nothing, read their direct mail, and are willing to spend a 20 cent stamp for a chance to win. The result is an excellent list for certain types of insurance offers, opportunity seeker plans, good luck jewelry, and of course, puzzle and contest clubs. Many mailers earn significant revenue from rental of "no" names.

MYTHS

Probably no part of direct mail has as many myths as the sweepstakes industry. We'll seek to examine some of the frequently made statements and compare them with the facts.

Myth 1. Sweepstakes work only on downscale offers.

Fact 1. Sweepstakes have been successful for such upscale mailers as Home Box Office, American Express, *New York* magazine, and *Newsweek*. There is a psychographic aspect to sweepstakes respondents, not a demographic one. Sweepstakes transcend age, income, height, and other artificial, nonapplicable barriers to their use. The success rate applies equally to Adam & Eve (marital aids), Hanover House (general catalog), *Catholic Digest* (religious magazine), McGraw-Hill (business publications), and hundreds of other aggressive marketers.

Myth 2. Sweepstakes are not good with complicated offers.

Fact 2. Sweepstakes have worked with clubs, continuity plans, and almost every item that has been sold by mail. Vitamins, which require detailed product communication, find sweepstakes a key sales element. Vitamin companies that use sweepstakes include Stur-Dee, BioOrganic, U.S. Health Club, Hudson Vitamin, RVP, and General Nutrition. In fact, it is almost impossible to find an aggressive mailer in this category that does not use sweepstakes.

Myth 3. Bad pays make sweepstakes unaffordable.

Fact 3. Sweepstakes people perform almost identically to nonsweepstakes people. This includes bad pays, bad checks, renewals, and mail list income.

Myth 4. Sweepstakes have worn out.

Fact 4. We've been hearing that for 20 years. This week's results:

Product	Sweeps Pkg., %*	Nonsweeps Pkg., %
X	8.2	5.1
Y	10.1	5.7
Z	4.2	1.9

* For purpose of sweepstakes reporting, we count only those who order, not those who do not buy but want to enter the sweepstakes.

Myth 5. Most of the big prizes go to customers. Alternate myth: They go to noncustomers.

Fact 5. As a practical matter, the marketer shouldn't care who gets the prize. The worth of a sweepstakes is decided long before the prize is awarded. However, in fact, prizes go to both buyers and nonbuyers, and show a fairly accurate ratio of buyer to nonbuyer entrants.

Myth 6. Sweepstakes cannot be done within our image.

Fact 6. Usually sweepstakes require a "look" to be effective. However, they need not always be "bells and whistles."

PRIZES

Consumers enter for the chance to win a dream. To the degree that you can push that "dream button," you'll gain response. Traditionally, the most successful offers have a large first prize and lots of prizes at the bottom. The strong copy lines are "Win $25,000" and "Over 1000 chances to win." Consumers are attracted by big prizes. Pyramid prize structures tend to work best. However, you don't have to spend millions to play in the sweepstakes game. Fully half of all successful sweepstakes have prize budgets under $25,000 in total.

Relating prizes to your audience is important. Trips to play golf in Bermuda will outpull cars for a golfing list. By the same token, be careful that you know enough about your audience to make the offer appealing. Spending a lot of money is seldom enough. An affluent, liberal, upscale audience doesn't want to win mink stoles. Downscale folks in rural Wyoming don't want to win boats or Louis XV furniture. The prize should reflect the audience.

Don't fall into the trap of substituting your personal taste for that of your buyer. For example, as a business person you probably would enjoy a vacation trip to Europe. Yet in a recent sweepstakes offering "twenty-five trips anywhere in the world," more than half chose domestic travel. In fact, several selected a location less than 500 miles from home.

Focus groups and the advice of judging agencies will help provide this answer. At one focus group, we searched for the best way to portray the excitement of winning $100,000. The client's ad agency opted for picturing vacation homes, boats, and gold. Interestingly, this blue-collar audience responded best to an offer of "$100,000 toward starting your own business." The idea came up at a focus group when someone said, "I'd sure like to have my own bait and tackle shop someday."

Equally important to prize selection is prize presentation. The same skill that goes into illustrating products should be used to arouse reader interest in prizes. There are stock photo houses that have shots of the most commonly used photos. The cost is minimal (less than $100 each). Frequently, these transparencies are better in subject matter and reproduction quality than manufacturer photos.

Choices can make a prize structure look bigger. If the grand prize is a car or a truck or $10,000 in cash or $10,000 in gold or a 1-carat diamond or a trip to Europe, you can show many prizes and still award only one prize.

Prizes are the fuel that make the promotion happen. Pay careful attention to their selection and presentation.

SWEEPSTAKES OBJECTIVES

Of course, the main objective served by sweepstakes is simply increasing response to direct mail. However, there are some special objectives that can be served by use of sweepstakes.

Information gathering can be accomplished. A requirement of entry can be the answering of questions. In the early day of Mastercharge, the goal was to obtain completed applications. A requirement of entry in a Mastercharge sweepstakes was to "complete the application." Whereas it was difficult to get people to spend 20 minutes filling out an application, the offer of a compelling prize increased response. A current example is list development projects in which what is wanted is smokers' names and addresses and current brand preference. To obtain the information, the client simply made brand preference a requirement of entry.

Sweepstakes also work as a collection device. A number of mailers have increased the pay-up rate by adding a sweepstakes to their collection series.

Retention can be heightened through prize promotions. At least one book club and one major cable network find that subscribers who are offered monthly sweepstakes tend to stay as members longer. This usually can be accomplished even with a very small prize budget.

Traffic building is dramatically increased through the use of sweepstakes. This includes fast-food traffic, land development site traffic, and most recently, movie traffic.

Finally, sweepstakes can increase total readership of your marketing message. The excitement of sweeps offers gets consumers involved with direct mail offers.

SWEEPSTAKES CREATIVE ELEMENTS

Sweepstakes creative elements are a reponse to the classical marketing task of attracting attention, creating interest, arousing desire, and forcing action. This is done through a series of hard-hitting words and visuals that leave readers with a belief that a dream prize is well within their grasp.

The creative tends to be more formularized, with eagles, fancy borders, special certificates, and a sense of genuine value. Coupled with this are devices to make the simplest prizes exciting and compelling. All the direct mail devices (e.g., tokens, pull tabs, and computer letters) are doubly important as applied to direct mail.

SWEEPSTAKES RESEARCH

Focus groups are very helpful in eliciting consumer opinions about prize promotions. Specifically, ideas as to prizes, graphics, and type of offer frequently can be elicited from a well-run group. However, all the caveats about research are even more prevalent in this area. Even the most avid sweepstakes player usually associates the offer with gambling. The consumers' public image psychology must be regarded. Any researcher will tell you that consumers all say they read *Newsweek* and never the *National Enquirer*. Much of the same protective information exists here. In focus groups compiled from sweepstakes entrants only, the interviewer often is told, "I never enter sweepstakes."

In short, do research but be careful. You may be touted off sweepstakes by potential customers who would say no in a research home but would respond in the privacy of their own homes.

SWEEPSTAKES ECONOMICS

Sweepstakes tend to have a fixed cost. That is, the basic elements are prizes, administration, and creative actions. These costs are essentially the same whether amortized over 200,000 pieces mailed or 20,000,000. The successful approach is to amortize one's sweepstakes over the greatest number of pieces. This can be accomplished by keeping the sweepstakes open 12 months or longer in order to use over several mailings and using it as an overlay to all products mailed.

Here are some sample costs.

TABLE 12-1 Fixed and Variable Costs for a Sample Sweepstakes

Fixed Costs	
Prizes	$30,000
Administration	5,000
Creative, art, copy, mechanicals	15,000
Total fixed cost	$50,000
Variable Costs	
Additional brochure (4C/4C) to promote sweepstakes prizes	$20,000
Additional buckslip	10,000
Total variable cost	$30,000

TABLE 12-2 Economic Comparison of Sweepstakes and Nonsweepstakes Packages

	Sweepstakes		Nonsweepstakes	
Control direct mail package	$300,000	$275,000	$300,000	$275,000
Fixed costs ($50,000)	50,000	5,000	—	—
Variable costs	30,000	30,000	—	—
Package cost	$380,000	$310,000	$300,000	$275,000
Orders per thousand	80	80	50	50
Cost per order	$4.70	$4.00	$6.00	$5.50

CO-OP SWEEPSTAKES

So that a marketer can test the sweepstakes idea, a number of judging agencies have begun offering co-op sweepstakes. Essentially, they put together a number of marketers to share the cost of prizes, creative elements, and administration. Usually the cost is under $10,000 in total. Obviously, the benefit of tailoring an offer to your exact market is lost. Furthermore, the sweepstakes brochure is generic and therefore loses the benefit of developing a piece to your specification.

However, this is a method of testing the waters without making a major commitment of money or labor power.

THE FUTURE OF SWEEPSTAKES

At least one economic authority indicates that gambling (legal and illegal) is a $100 billion industry in the United States. That makes gambling bigger than the auto, steel, and oil industries combined.

The power of something for nothing is a strong motivator. As long as a consumer perceives that throwing away an entry is tantamount to throwing away a chance of a lifetime, sweepstakes will endure. The giant casinos of Atlantic City and Las Vegas provide testimony to the natural human gambling instinct.

All direct mail tests indicate that the chance to win a dream will get envelopes opened and increase response dramatically. There's no evidence to support any decline. As in Las Vegas, it seems that each new sweepstakes purveyor simply broadens the total marketplace.

chapter 13

LEGAL CONSIDERATIONS

Robert J. Posch, Jr.

Associate Counsel
Doubleday & Co., Inc.
Garden City, N.Y.

INTRODUCTION

In light of the foreseen business climate of the 1980s, direct marketing will continue to have a high visibility to government. The successful marketer will therefore be the one who reaches a targeted audience with the least intrusion from governmental regulatory bodies. Merely creating and fulfilling promotions will not suffice if this is done at the cost of excessive fines, legal defense fees, bad publicity, and government-dictated consent agreements affecting future policy. To avoid this pitfall, the marketer cannot dwell in uncertainty concerning the regulatory environment.

This chapter will go far to eliminate such uncertainty for you. It discusses the law and offers feasible solutions to potential problems. It directly addresses the fundamental compliance test issues facing the direct marketer in areas of primary impact. Because of space limitations, we must focus attention on areas of interest to all direct marketers. Therefore, we'll begin with and stress one key channel: the mails. This is important because no matter how rapidly your customer registers the desire to purchase your product or even pays (electronic transfer), you must contend with the delivery constraints of the U.S. Postal Service or some similar private carrier.[1]

One final note. In reviewing these areas here and elsewhere, you'll see frequent reference to FTC "rules and guidelines." These are not interchangeable terms but are legally distinguishable as to their effect on you.

A Trade Regulation Rule specifically defines acts or practices which are unfair or deceptive within the meaning of the FTC's mandate under section 5. They carry the force of substantive law, and literal compliance is required. Examples include the rules for games of chance[2] and mail-order merchandise[3] and the negative option rule.[4]

Industry guides are administrative interpretations of laws issued by the FTC for guidance of the public in conducting its affairs in conformity with legal requirements.[5] These guides do not have the force of substantive law, though failure to comply may result in corrective action by the FTC. Examples include the Guides Concerning Use Of Endorsements and Testimonials in Advertising[6] and the Guide Concerning Use of the Word "Free" and Similar Representations.[7]

CHANNEL COMPLIANCE

Direct marketers have little difficulty determining the length of the product marketing channel necessary to reach their markets. The channel is the U.S. Postal Service or certain specialized mail carriers. Intermediaries are few, though drop-shippers may be used. Formerly, the direct marketer was concerned mainly with postal regulations and costs and with physical distribution management. More recently, four major areas of compliance have arisen: the Thirty Day Rule, the Federal Unordered Merchandise Statute, "dry testing," and merchandise substitution.

With increases in costs for almost all aspects of mail-order selling (e.g., postage, printing, and the goods themselves), most firms have sought to cut back on inventories. As a result, they can't always fill incoming orders promptly. Furthermore, some marginal companies caught in the vise of inflation have sought to obtain interest-free, or "dry," loans, holding their cash flow vis-à-vis fulfillment for as long as possible.

The FTC and many states[8] have enacted Thirty Day rules and laws. The latter must be consulted, especially as to the situs of the corporate domicile. Note 5 of the FTC rule specifically states that the FTC does not wish to preempt consistent but narrower state laws on point. Therefore, certain firms will find that they must comply with a narrower state law. For our purposes, we'll focus on the FTC's rules.[9]

Thirty Day Rule

The FTC's mail order rule was adopted in 1976; it will be enforced literally, and penalties up to $10,000 may be issued for each violation. Since it is only three and a half pages long, it is worth your time to review it. It is written for laypeople, avoids legalese, and boils down to three key areas:

1. Initial solicitation requirements
2. First and subsequent delay notifications
3. Internal procedures

Initial Solicitation

It is an unfair or deceptive act to solicit any order through the mails unless you have a reasonable basis (arrived at in good faith and with objective substantiation) to believe that you can fulfill the order within the time you specify or, if no time is specified, 30 days after the receipt of a properly completed order from the buyer.

What is reasonable is reflected by the variables of your industry, product, and market. This is a factual issue affected by the interplay of many considerations. We all know the value of a dollar in hand and the value of its retention. The FTC understands the "float" value of money too and doesn't want your customers providing you with interest-free loans. Your best protection as to your good-faith, reasonable expectations at the time of solicitation is to maintain an organized system of written internal records which will validate your expectations objectively.

However, bear in mind that you elect to become involved with the 30-day aspect of this rule. You can insulate yourself from problems here if you state at the outset a date you can live with clearly and conspicuously on the promotion piece. You might state, "90 days from receipt" of order. Then there is no first delay problem (see below) until 90 days has elapsed, not 30. The trade-off here could be a loss of "spontaneity," since customers may be discouraged by a long wait. However, the choice is yours.

You also elect to come within the provisions of this rule by accepting cash orders. Bill only by outside credit cards (this may help your bad debt problem too) or by a system of internal credit adjustments or even COD. In none of these cases will you bill before delivery, and therefore, you will not be affected by the Thirty Day Rule.

Finally, there are methods to decrease potential legal problems as well as customer dissatisfaction. Remember, a customer complaint to the FTC, a state attorney general office, or the Better Business Bureau is not helpful even if totally unjustified. Such complaints attract unwanted attention to your firm and may accumulate. Examine the following ways to lessen complaints.

1. Don't wait until checks clear. The 30-day meter is running. Test whether this delay is resulting in 30-day shipment problems. If so, does the trade-off vis-à-vis your bad debt picture justify this practice?
2. Test different post offices or even times of the day when you ship if this option is available. Your legal requirement is to ship, not deliver, within 30 days. Legally, your customer then must contend with the inherent delays in the U.S. Postal Service or some other similar system of distribution. However, your customer knows only that he or she is waiting. Maximizing your deliveries by finding the best post office will enhance goodwill and possibly avoid complaints to the regulatory agencies.
3. The 30-day meter begins only after you receive in house a properly completed order. If you write back to the customer, make sure you keep a record. You'd be wise to retain a copy of the incomplete order as well as refrain from cashing any checks. Customers may forget that the initial delay was not prompted by you but by them. When they complain to you or to an agency, it will be clear that once a properly completed order was returned, you fulfilled it and shipped it within the required time.

First Delay Situations

The reality of any marketplace is that unanticipated delays occur, e.g., a welcome deluge of orders or a simple delay by your supplier. When you are unable to ship the merchandise within the applicable time (the specific time you stated in your promotion or 30 days if no time is specified), you have the option to cancel the agreement and so inform the buyer or attempt to preserve the sale.

To do this, you must send a postage-paid return notice to the buyer, clearly and conspicuously offering the buyer the choice to either cancel the order and receive a full and prompt refund or extend the time for shipment to a specified revised shipping date. Tactically, you have an advantage here since inertia is in your favor. If the buyer does not answer at all, you get the delay. Silence is construed as acceptance.

Don't attempt to improve on the prepaid reply device (postal card or letter). You may feel that an 800 number is more spontaneous and actually of greater benefit in facilitating the customer's response. The FTC won't. Just make sure to use a prepaid response letter. The postage-paid factor is very important since buyers must not have to exercise their rights at the penalty of even a first class stamp.

Multiple Delay Situations

As was discussed, you may obtain as much as 60 days' grace in fulfilling an order unless the buyer specifically returns the postage-paid notice requesting a refund. The buyer's silence is construed as an acceptance of the delay.

If after 60 days there remains some unanticipated delay (e.g., a strike), you still may be able to save the order. The rule will allow further delays in certain circumstances.

You must notify the buyer of the additional delay. You may request the buyer's permission to ship at a certain specified future date or even a vague, indefinite date. The buyer then may cancel or may affirmatively agree to extend the time for delivery. At this time, you must also notify buyers that if they consent to the delay, they still may cancel at any subsequent time by notifying the seller prior to the actual shipment. The buyer then may cancel or affirmatively agree to extend the time for delivery.

This situation is distinguishable from the first delay situation insofar as silence by the buyer cannot be construed as acceptance. If the buyer remains "silent" (fails to return the postage-paid card), you must treat the order as canceled and return a refund promptly to the buyer.

What is a prompt refund? This depends on the payment option elected. If the buyer sent cash or a check, the buyer is entitled to have a refund in full mailed first class within 7 business days. If a credit card or other form of credit adjustment is required, you have a full billing cycle from the date on which the buyer's right to a refund begins. All refunds are to be sent by first class mail and returned in the form received where practical; for example, if cash is received, a return check is permissible and prudent. Under no circumstances are mere credit vouchers or scrip permitted.

Internal Procedures

The Mail Order Rule stresses the need for adequate systems and procedures to create a presumption of a good-faith effort present to satisfy customer inquiries or complaints. These systems and procedures also should be adequate to establish your good-faith basis on which to solicit the initial order or to request a delay or delays.

The rule does not apply to negative option forms of selling or to magazine sales (except for the initial shipment) or COD orders, orders for seeds and growing plants, and credit orders in which the buyer's account is not charged before you ship the merchandise.

Dry Testing

We have stated that the social policy behind the Mail Order Merchandise Rule was to discourage the practice of dry loans. We also stressed that the FTC considers it an unfair or deceptive act to solicit an order through the mails unless you have a reasonable basis to believe you can fulfill the order within a certain time. In light of all this, can you still "dry test," or solicit for, a product before it tangibly exists? Interestingly, the answer is yes in certain circumstances.

There is limited law on point, but you should be aware of FTC Advisory Opinion 753 7003.[10] Specifically:

> the Commission does not object to the use of dry-testing a continuity book series marketed by mail order as long as the following conditions are observed: (1) No representation, express or implied, is made in advertisements, brochures, or other promotional material, which has the tendency or capacity to mislead the public into believing that the books have been or will definitely be published, or that by expressing an interest in receiving the books a prospective purchaser will necessarily receive them. (2) In all solicitations for subscriptions and other promotional material, clear and conspicuous disclosure is made of the terms and conditions of the publication, distribution, and other material aspects of the continuity book series program. Such disclosure must provide adequate notice of the conditional nature of publication of the book series, i.e., the fact that the book series is only planned and may not actually be published. (3) If the decision is reached not to publish the book series, due notice is given to persons who have subscribed, within a reasonable time after the date of first mailing the solicitations for subscriptions. The Commission considers four months or less to be a reasonable time, unless extenuating circumstances exist. If the decision whether or not to publish the book series has not been made within that time period, persons who expressed a desire to subscribe should be notified of the fact that a decision has not yet been reached, and should be given an opportunity to cancel their order. (4) There is no substitution of any books for those ordered.[11]

What Are Your Rights under an Advisory Opinion?

The above discussion suggests a topic one hears about frequently: obtaining an advisory opinion from the FTC.[12] In 1979, the FTC substantially changed its advisory opinion procedures. The FTC will issue formal opinions on written applications by specified parties (unnamed parties may not receive a response) in the following areas:

1. Where the matter involves a substantial or novel question of law and there is no clear precedent
2. Where a proposed merger or acquisition is involved
3. Where the subject matter is of significant public interest

Requests for advice and the commission's response are placed on the public record immediately after the requesting party has received the advisory opinion.

Any advice received does not preclude the commission's later right to reconsider, rescind, or revoke. However, the original requesting party will be notified.

If you are concerned whether an advisory opinion is still valid, call the commission at (202) 523-3598.

Unordered Merchandise

We've reviewed the situation in which there are delays in getting your customer a desired product. Now let's review what happens when the recipient receives something unordered.[13]

The law[14] (Mailing of Unordered Merchandise) on point is short and should be read by all direct mail marketing managers. This law forbids not just blatant sending of unordered merchandise but also sending of merchandise "on approval" without your "customer's" prior permission. The FTC specifically warned the mail-order stamp industry of this in 1979.[15]

Only two kinds of merchandise may be sent through the mails without prior consent:

1. Free samples, which must be marked as such
2. Merchandise mailed by charitable organizations

However, merchandise mailed by charitable organizations is sent "on approval" and need not be paid for. The customer may return it or keep it but need not pay for it.

Your best strategy is that when in doubt, don't dun. If an innocent error is made (e.g., computer mislabeling), write off the order. The customer won't complain unless an effort is made to compel payment. Your dunning for unordered merchandise can be the trigger for unwanted involvement with the Federal Trade Commission or a state attorney general or simply bad customer relations. Dunning accomplishes this in two ways.

1. Billing or dunning for unordered merchandise is itself an unfair practice.
2. Many customers do not complain to a regulatory body until dunning begins, because they were not aware of the problem or violation.

What is the rule concerning the mailing of unordered merchandise, and how can you avoid problems with it? We shall review it paragraph by paragraph and then discuss its exceptions.

Mailing Of Unordered Merchandise

> (a) Except for (1) free samples clearly and conspicuously marked as such, and (2) merchandise mailed by a charitable organization soliciting contributions, the mailing of unordered merchandise or of communications prohibited by subsection (c) of this section constitutes an unfair method of competition and an unfair trade practice in violation of section 45(a)(1) of title 15 (15 USCS § 45(a)(1).

This paragraph clearly makes it a per se violation of the law to ship unordered merchandise, which is defined as "merchandise mailed without the prior expressed request or consent of the recipient."[16] The only ambiguity here is the reference to "mailed."

Because the original pronouncement referred to the Postal Reorganization Act, some thought that enforcement would be limited to marketers using the U.S. Postal Service. The FTC clarified its position in 1978 by stating that all unordered merchandise was included whether shipped by mail, United Parcel, other private alternate delivery, or any other carrier.

> (b) Any merchandise mailed in violation of subsection (a) of this section, or within the exceptions contained there, may be treated as a gift by the recipient, who shall have the right to retain, use, discard, or dispose of it in any manner he sees fit without any obligation whatsoever to the sender. All such merchandise shall have attached to it a clear and conspicuous statement informing the recipient that he may treat the merchandise as a gift to him and has the right to retain, use, discard, or dispose of it in any manner he sees fit without any obligation to the sender.

It should be noted that it is a separate violation (apart from the initial sending itself) for anyone to mail unordered merchandise without attaching a clear and conspicuous statement informing the recipient that it may be treated as a gift.

> (c) No mailer of any merchandise mailed in violation of subsection (a) of this section, or within the exceptions contained therein, shall mail to any recipient of such merchandise a bill for such merchandise or any dunning communications.

It also is a violation of this statute for any sender of unordered merchandise (including correctly marked free samples and merchandise sent by charitable organizations) to send the recipient any bill or dunning communication or suggestion of the same in connection with such unordered merchandise.

Again, your best strategy may well be, "When in doubt, don't dun." A customer's complaint to a regulatory body or private action rarely will occur unless an effort is made to compel payment.

Now that we've reviewed the text of the law, a number of questions remain.

What Are the Penalties? The penalties for both firms and individuals are up to $10,000 per violation. State laws may carry varied penalties and also may be drawn more narrowly. You should review the law for each state in which you're doing business and monitor legislation and regulations in each state.

Must the Consumer Obtain a Remedy by Complaint to an Agency? No. It was Congress's intent to permit consumers to protect themselves under the terms of the Federal Unordered Merchandise Statute.

What If the Customer Denies the Existence of an Agreement? You are in a strong position if you have a signed order that unequivocally states the contractual relationship to which the individual is subscribing. If the signature was a forgery or was contested by the recipient in good faith, you should request that the customer return the item at your expense (postage).

Prior course of dealings, such as a call with follow-up shipment, is not a valid argument when dealing with a consumer on a one-shot basis. Under the Uniform Commercial Code (UCC), two merchants can develop such prior course of dealings. However, the UCC is not applicable to consumers. The fact that you have shipped before and the customer has paid for similar items by check or otherwise proves nothing in this instance.

If you dun, expect problems if the recipient complains to a public body. Your common-law implied contract probably will not be compelling to the FTC or a state regulatory body, though by all means argue it in order to establish good faith.

The weakest position of all is that of the telephone marketer making "cold call ordering."[17] In this case, without a prior business relationship, the seller ships on order with no confirming documents. There is little possibility of enforcing such a call against a complaint filed under the Federal Unordered Merchandise Statute. You have no acceptable proof at all of an order. Some ways you might consider to protect yourself include the following.

1. Send all orders COD so that unordered merchandise may be rejected up-front.
2. Send a postage-paid envelope with the order so that recipients of unordered merchandise may be encouraged to return such goods immediately, at no cost to themselves, thereby saving the merchandise itself.
3. Comply with the cooling off provisions as worded or provide your customer with a follow-up written confirmation which can be responded to in a positive or negative option manner (the former response probably will negate any problems as to cold calls).
4. Follow up all orders with a subsequent phone call confirming the original order. This provides still weaker protection (because it is oral) than the first two methods, but it is a procedure which may prove to an agency that you employ bona fide methods to avoid unordered merchandise problems.

No matter what safeguards you employ, an oral order is not a provable order, and this must be considered at all stages, especially before you dun.

How Does This Statute Affect Negative Option Plans? During the commitment period and at all subsequent times, there is an ongoing business relationship subject to the FTC's rule on point.

Furthermore, the rule[18] permits the sender to ask for its return (but not bill) this one time. Any subsequent shipments after this one constitute unordered merchandise.

What about a Continuity Plan? Your rights are less clear because there is no rule on point. You could use a similar approach as to the one isolated shipment after cancellation, but I wouldn't dun.

What about Substituted Merchandise? The entire area is fraught with peril, even if the substitution is of equivalent or superior quality.[19] Artistic property by its very nature is too unique to be substituted for. If a seasonal surge or other unanticipated ordering deluge is overwhelming your inventory reserve, get expressed consent in writing before you substitute.

This will save your sale as well as satisfy customers who prefer the substitution to nothing when they need the item by a given date. Substitution without the prior expressed consent or request of the recipient falls within the literal terms of the statute and will be considered an unfair trade practice.

Finally, when a valid substitution is offered, the customer must be afforded the opportunity to return the item without a postage penalty.

Conclusion

The above is a brief review of the Federal Unordered Merchandise Statute. The law is written in uncomplicated language and has been reproduced here in its entirety. Most states have similar laws on their books, and some state laws are drawn more narrowly.

Whenever possible, coupons or order forms authorizing the shipment of merchandise to a consumer should be signed and laid out clearly in separate and distinct paragraphs. All wording should be in lay English, and the merchandise or purchase plan should be described in detail.

When a serious doubt arises as to the validity of your efforts to recover payment, don't dun.

THREE COPY HEADLINERS

You design your promotion piece to catch the viewer's eye both aesthetically and in terms of simple dollars and cents.

The former is primarily the work of the creative team, though they must be careful that all visual depictions convey a correct impression of the size and identity of the product. Deceptive mock-ups or those having a "tendency to deceive" are counterproductive. However, the major compliance issues arise when certain wording is used to capture the reader's interest. A thorough knowledge of the subtleties of "sale," "new," "free," and words of similar impact will assist your goal of maximizing reader interest while minimizing negative involvement as a result of deceptive wording.

Sale

From time to time, you'll wish to offer your customers special offers. The ad copy may at times signify the promotion as a "sale,"[20] "savings," or price "reduction." The most commonly asked questions are these:

1. What is a sale?
2. What discount reduction from our former prices is sufficient to constitute a sale?
3. Does every item featured in the promotion piece have to be on sale?

What Is a Sale? This involves offering a reduction from the advertiser's former price for an article. If the former price is the actual, bona fide price at which the article was offered and sold to the public on a regular basis for a reasonably substantial period of time, it provides a legitimate basis of price comparison.

The objectively proved "sales test" is a necessary hurdle. Significant previous sales must be demonstrated in the same product and geographic marketplace to discourage the entry of an overpriced article (for which few if any sales are made) being "reduced" to its realistic market price and then being offered as a "sale."

What Discount Should Be Offered? You must take care that the amount of reduction is not so insignificant as to be meaningless. The reduction should be sufficiently large that consumers, if they knew what it was, would believe that a genuine bargain or saving was being offered. A nominal reduction, e.g., less than 5 percent, is unacceptable. Depending on the market, the ticket price, and trade practices, 10 percent or more would be a safe starting point. The alert customer may well be suspicious of a promotion claiming a large reduction or discount but not stating the actual amount of the reduction or discount.

Must Every Item in a Sale Promotion Be Reduced to Satisfy Compliance? Every item so designated in a "sale promotion" should represent a reduction from a former price that was openly and actively offered for a reasonable period of time in the regular course of business.

An item not reduced from a former price at which the same (not a similar) product was openly and actively offered for sale, for a reasonably substantial period of time, in the recent regular course of business, honestly and in good faith, has no business being offered in a sales promotion. Furthermore, you should not use language such as "formerly sold at *X* dollars" unless substantial sales at that price actually were made.

Therefore, the use of expressions such as "annual sale," "fall sale," etc., in catalogs, advertising, or other promotional pieces containing nonsale items without revealing in immediate conjunction with such representations that nonsale items were contained therein and without distinctively identifying such nonsale items is prohibited.

To Conclude A sale price must be a reasonable and honest statement of a valid former market price which is now reduced.

All items advertised as being on "sale" in a sales promotion should represent an honest bona fide reduction from a previous benchmark price.

You should be prepared to substantiate your claim that every item in a "sale" was sold in the marketplace (and was not just "offered") previously.

Items not on sale in a sales promotion must be identified and distinguished distinctively.

If quantities are limited, you must disclose any limitation up front.

New

This is a relatively straightforward term. Merchandise may not be offered as new if it has been used or refurbished. This means that you may not clean or "improve" your returned merchandise in any way and then return it to your inventory. Unless you state otherwise, merchandise offered for sale must be new and may not have been used during a "trial period" or otherwise.

The word "new" also is used to promote a product which has not been introduced into the marketplace yet or has been "improved," enabling you to advertise the item as "new and improved." There is no particular usage period for an offer, but FTC Advisory Opinion 120[21] has indicated 6 months as a tentative outer limit. This suggestion is subject to certain variables. A new product should constitute the latest model in a particular product line and certainly not have been marketed widely elsewhere. However, in a bona fide test marketing of a new product which does not cover more than 15 percent of the population and does not exceed 6 months in duration, the 6-months rule does not apply until the test period has terminated. Certain states have very exact disclosure requirements; therefore, make sure you ask counsel to review all state laws that have an impact on your operations and to monitor the legislatures. As always, you must consult state law and not be content with merely understanding the FTC's position.

Free

One word which any marketer knows will always prompt a second glance is "free." Because of its ability to highlight and enhance the promotion piece, it is a highly regulated term of art as to both definition and disclosure. The following discussion will guide you through the regulatory thicket.

What Is a Free Item? The word "free" indicates that a person is paying nothing for an article and no more than the regular price for the other article. Thus, a purchaser has a right to believe that the seller will not directly and immediately recover, in whole or in part, the cost of the free merchandise by marking up the price of the article which must be purchased, or by the substitution of inferior merchandise.[22] Finally, shipping and handling charges cannot be built into or added to a free item. For example, if a free offer is sent as part of a total package for examination or trial, a prepaid mailing label must be included in the package to cover the cost of returning the item. If a return postage charge might burden the recipient, the item is not free.

Words of similar connotation (e.g., "gift," "given without charge," "no cost or obligation," "bonus," etc.) "which tend to convey the impression to the consuming public that an article of merchandise is 'Free' "[23] are held to the same standard.

What Conditions Must Be Disclosed? All the terms, conditions, and obligations (e.g., any credit limitations or qualifications, prepayment requirements, etc.) should appear in close conjunction (i.e., physically adjacent so that the elements are naturally read together) with the offer of the "free" merchandise. If there are conditions, the following rules obtain.

1. The type size in which any limitations are printed must be at least half as large as the largest type size in the introductory offer copy, exclusive of numerals.
2. I'd recommend a minimum type size of 6 to 8 points.

3. The qualification terms must be stated together in the same location in the ad, not separated by copy or graphics.
4. Disclosure of the terms of the offer set forth in a footnote of an advertisement to which reference is made by an asterisk or similar symbol does not constitute disclosure at the outset and will constitute noncompliance.

In summary, you may use the word "free" if your product is an unconditional gift or when a purchase is required. All the conditions, obligations, or other prerequisites to the receipt and retention of the free product offered must be set forth clearly and conspicuously in immediate conjunction with the first use of the word "free," leaving no reasonable probability that the terms of the offer will be misunderstood. No "hidden" requirements are permitted. Ambiguity is no asset. Language which may be construed in favor of a free ad will be so construed against the creator of the ad.

SOME PRACTICAL MARKETING HINTS WHICH WILL SAVE YOU DOLLARS IN COPY DRAFTING

To avoid copy clutter and redundancy, you should regard each promotion piece as constituting one component offer. To meet the "clearly and conspicuously" test, the qualifications merely need to be stated at the outset after the first use of the word "free." Thereafter, the term "free" may be used as often per offer as you believe advisable regardless of how many items are being offered for sale.

USE OF CURRENCY AND FLAGS

Showing certain highlights of a free offer may be prohibited. For example, you cannot advertise a free $10 value by showing a $10 bill. Printed illustrations of paper money, checks, negotiable instruments, and other obligations and securities of the United States are not permitted for advertising purposes.[24] The reproduction of coins is allowed; e.g., reproduction of a penny could be used to highlight a 1 cent sale. Finally, all states as well as the District of Columbia have statutes prohibiting the use in advertising of their own flags as well as the U.S. flag.

CONCLUSION

In this brief review of only a few salient areas of law affecting the direct marketer, we have not focused on horror stories. However, they abound, and a brief comment is warranted here.

When it comes to government regulations, following a policy of noncompliance either deliberately or through lack of knowledge is like playing Russian roulette. If you lose, the penalty can harm your firm and your career growth. But if you know the rules of the game, the decision about whether to abide by those rules is yours. However, sometimes after receiving advice of counsel, a marketer elects to make a "business decision" to violate the law. There is nothing in the law which insulates such a "business decision" from legal sanction. You may subject both your firm and yourself to criminal as well as civil sanctions. Before electing to make a business decision which violates a law, you should consult counsel as to the law and the penalties imposed as a result of such violation. The penalties or fines generally are based on a number of factors such as number of infractions involved, previous warnings, size and financial status of the company, and public deception (even if not intentional in many instances).

The fines and other legal sanctions don't tell the whole story. The greater hardship may involve not the fine but the counsel fees, adverse publicity and loss of goodwill, and special measures which may have to be taken to counteract the "harm" which results from the violation. It is a sad reality that the cost in terms of both time and money of having to discontinue an ad or promotion which is not in compliance with federal or state regulations even when no fine per se is involved can be monumental. It's essential, therefore, not to dismiss the myriad laws and regulations which affect your profession.

It is my hope that this chapter will prove to be a useful tool for direct marketers who wish to protect their firms from adverse visibility to government as well as to give their buyers a fair shake.

Best of luck in your future career endeavors.

NOTES

[1] Robert Posch, "Legal Outlook—The U.S. Postal Service: Dinosaur or Dynamic Carrier," *Direct Marketing,* March 1982, pp. 128–131.

[2] 16 C.F.R. § 419.

[3] 16 C.F.R. § 435.

[4] 16 C.F.R. § 425.

[5] 16 C.F.R. § 1.5.

[6] 16 C.F.R. § 255.

[7] 16 C.F.R. § 251.

[8] For example, review NYS General Business Law 396(m).

[9] See also Robert Posch, "Legal Outlook—The 30 Day Mail Order Rule: Satisfying FTC, Customers," *Direct Marketing,* December 1981, pp. 84–87.

[10] "Dry Testing" and "Bulk Loading," a Continuity Book Series By Mail Order. 85 F.T.C. 1192–1197 (1975).

[11] Ibid, pp. 1193–1194.

[12] 16 C.F.R. 1-1-1.4.

[13] See also Robert Posch, "Legal Outlook—Avoiding The Pitfalls of Unordered Merchandise," *Direct Marketing,* January 1982, pp. 98–101.

[14] 39 U.S.C.S. 3009. New York direct marketers might wish to review General Obligations Law, article 5-332.

[15] FTC press release, May 24, 1979.

[16] 39 U.S.C.S. 3009(d).

[17] Such marketers should note that more than ten states have incorporated such calls into their respective home solicitation laws requiring a 3-day cooling-off period.

[18] 16 C.F.R. 425.1(b)(1)(iii).

[19] For example, see NYS General Obligations Law 396-m(3)(z)(i) and (ii).

[20] 16 C.F.R. 233.

[21] See also Advisory Opinions 120, 246, and 325.

[22] 16 C.F.R. 251, 251.1.

[23] Ibid, 251.1(2)(j).

[24] As this book goes to press, however, the matter is in the courts; the rule may soon be altered.

part 2

MEDIA

chapter **14**

BASICS OF MEDIA PLANNING

Peter Spaulder

Vice President
Valley Forge
Associates
National Liberty
Marketing, Inc.
Valley Forge, Pa.

THE MEDIA PLAN

Media "carry" the advertising message to the prospect. The media plan is the part of a total marketing plan which explains how the media will reach the prospects for the product or service being sold.

The plan consists of a statement of the following elements:

1. **Objective:** the measurable result to be achieved from the advertising.
2. **Target audience:** who the customer is expressed in terms of the customer's vital statistics (demographics) or behavior and lifestyle (psychographics).
3. **Geography:** where the advertiser is aiming the advertising messages to reach the target audience.
4. **Medium:** how the marketer will attempt to reach and influence the consumer and by what type of advertising.
5. **Cost:** how much the marketer will spend to reach the consumer. Costs are expressed in terms of cost per thousand readers or viewers and the total dollar investment necessary to use the medium to deliver the advertising message to the target audience.
6. **Timing:** when the advertising will take place and the timing for the preparatory work necessary in advance of the advertising appearing.

7. **Competition:** a statement of anticipated activity illustrating the competitive environment.
8. **Testing:** the planned exploration of other media opportunities to build a foundation for the future growth and expansion of the business.
9. **Schedule:** a statement of the actual media selected, the target dates, and costs exhibited in a condensed summary form.

This chapter will deal in detail with each of these nine elements.

Media Objectives

The objective of the media plan is a clearly defined statement of the anticipated result of the advertising expenditure. The objective should be specific not only in terms of the expenditures but also in terms of the results expected from those expenditures. For example, the well-stated objective of a plan would be "to spend $10,000 to produce 1000 orders for a specific product at an average cost of $10." ($10,000 divided by 1000 equals $10.00). Alternatively, the statement of a lead procurement media plan might be "to spend $10,000 to produce 10,000 prospect inquiries at $1 each. These 10,000 inquiries will be convertible at 10 percent and produce a total of 1000 orders."

A key element of the objective is the statement of the anticipated measurable result. Only through the development and statement of such a numerical relationship can the results of the effort be evaluated after the advertising is completed.

Target Audience

Who the customer is, is defined in terms of the customer's vital statistics, called demographics, and the customer's behavioral characteristics or lifestyle, called psychographics.

Demographics is a primary means of defining the prospect for the product or service to be sold. Defining the prospect in terms of demographics permits the marketer to evaluate media alternatives as the media report the demographic profile of their audience. Key vital population statistics which are most frequently used when applicable are

1. Age, or more frequently, the age range of the prospect expressed in terms of actual years of age, i.e., "between 18 and 34," or a range of "young," "middle," and "older."
2. Sex of the prospect: male or female.
3. Marital status, expressed as single or married or, depending on the product, divorced or widowed.
4. The absence or presence of children in a household and the number of children present. Occasionally, this also includes the ages of children, e.g., parents of children 6 to 8 years of age.
5. Income, expressed in dollars or in a range which gives an indication as to whether the customer is high-, middle-, or low-income.
6. Educational attainment. Did the prospect enter high school, graduate high school, enter college, graduate college, etc.?

7. Occupation expressed in terms of specific job category (teacher, truck driver, accountant) or in a more broad grouping (blue-collar, white-collar, professional, etc.).
8. Type of dwelling. Relates to either a multiple-family dwelling unit (apartment house) or a single-family unit (house).
9. Dwelling ownership. Reveals whether the prospects own or rent. Dwelling ownership or rental frequently can help further define either the lifestyle or the person within the dwelling.

Psychographics talks about the lifestyle or behavioral characteristics of the potential customer. Lifestyles take into consideration the unique buying needs of various population groups such as working women, young marrieds, parents of young children, senior citizens, etc.

Other ways of defining the behavioral characteristics of the potential consumer involve behavioral patterns which have an impact on the customers' likelihood of buying a product by mail or other form of direct response. The key elements are

1. Previous purchase of products or services by mail
2. The recency of that purchase or when a purchase was made
3. Frequency of the purchase, or how often the prospect bought by mail
4. The amount of purchase, usually expressed in terms of a dollar range, i.e., under $10, $10 to $14, $15 to $24, etc.
5. Method of payment: cash, credit card, or COD

Such behavioral characteristics are important to the direct marketer because once a consumer has taken action in the past, this action may indicate the likelihood of taking similar action in the future. A person who has bought by mail in the past is more likely to buy by mail in the future than someone who has not. A person who has bought more often is more likely to buy than someone who has not bought as often.

Geography

"Where" the prospect is or where the advertiser elects to aim the advertising has an important impact on media selection. While geography is actually a population statistic and hence a demographic factor, it is mentioned separately because of its great importance in defining where the advertising effort will be placed.

Most often, a direct marketer has the advantage of being able to advertise across a wide geographic area, even nationally if the marketer so decides. As stated earlier in this handbook, one of the advantages of direct marketing is that an advertiser need not have a retail outlet in a specific geographic location. When the advertiser does not wish to advertise nationally, media selection can be adjusted accordingly. Media may be targeted by region (north, east, south, west), by state, or by metropolitan area or city.

As we shall see later in this chapter, the use of direct mail permits the marketer to zero in the advertising efforts on sectional centers (the first three digits of the ZIP code) or even the ZIP code itself. Selection can even be made on a smaller geographic area—the carrier route—which is defined by the post office as all the people receiving their mail from a single postal delivery worker during the worker's "rounds" within the ZIP code. This selection has important considerations other than geographic, because by clustering mail on a carrier route basis, the mailer can reduce postage expense significantly.

Media

The medium is the vehicle by which the advertising message will be carried to the consumer. Each medium has specific advantages and disadvantages which have an impact on the manner in which the advertising takes place. This section will highlight the key differences between the types of media (direct mail, magazines, newspapers, and radio and television) and discuss the differences in how they can segment the target markets as well as point out their creative and cost differences and other pertinent considerations.

Direct Mail. This offers the direct marketer the greatest flexibility in reaching the target audience since a decision can be made about whether to mail to individual names. Direct mail actually is sent to the prospects "one at a time." This differs dramatically from other print and broadcast media, in which all the people in the audience for a medium must be reached by an identical message at the same time.

Direct mail selectivity provides the marketer with total control as to whom within the market they desire to reach. For example, one mailing can be sent to one group of prospects on a list of names while a different mailing is sent to a different group of individuals. At the same time, selected individuals can be omitted from the mailing altogether.

Creatively, direct mail has great flexibility. The mailing piece can vary considerably in size and hence in the amount of copy or advertising that can be contained in it. It also can vary in its physical dimensions. While there are postal restrictions regarding how small a mailing piece can be and cost considerations which serve as practical limitations on how large, the advertiser has the widest possible flexibility concerning the format, content, and layout.

Direct mail also offers the possibility of personalization of the advertising copy. Through the use of computers, we can vary the advertising message or specific information given to each prospect within the target audience. The copy can be personalized through effective use of this "one on one" characteristic of the medium. The marketer has the opportunity to speak with all the prospects in the target audience on a much more personal and direct basis than is possible with the broad-scale approaches used in print and broadcast media.

It must be noted that direct mail is more complex operationally than its media counterparts. In addition to selecting lists (the advertising medium), the direct marketer must arrange for the creation, printing, and delivery of advertising materials to a mailing house. The list of names and addresses must be affixed to the mailing pieces through the use of labels or printed in computer letters. Then the various elements must be collated, inserted, and mailed. This activity is far more complex and requires more control than sending a print ad to an advertising medium or a broadcast commercial to a station.

Overall, direct mail produces the highest level of response (the most orders per quantity mailed) of any of the advertising media because of its selectivity in reaching the target audience and its creative flexibility combined with the use of personalization.

An overview of direct mail media opportunities would be incomplete without the mention of two other special direct mail media used effectively by direct marketers.

The cooperative mailing is a mailing effort in which two or more mailers "cooperate" and share the costs of a mailing. The mailing package contains multiple advertising messages within the same outside envelope. Its significance is that it offers the direct marketer a means of using the mails at a far lower cost, frequently as low as $30 to $50 per thousand, compared with a noncooperative direct mail effort, which might cost 5 to 10 times the price of the cooperative mailing.

The package insert is an advertising message carried in the shipment of a product to a customer. By placing an advertising message and order form in materials just received by the customer, the advertiser enjoys the benefit of a low-cost distribution system while reaching the customer at a potentially high point of consumer satisfaction, i.e., when the customer has received the requested merchandise.

Creatively, the package insert is limited in size and is carried in the same envelope with many other advertising messages. However, the positive aspect—the sharp reduction of costs—makes this a useful alternative or additive for many advertisers.

Here too there are creative limitations on the piece which can be inserted in the package insert. However, reaching the product at the moment of high interest and satisfaction combined with the low cost provides a useful advertising medium for many direct marketers.

Magazines. Magazines are categorized in two groups: mass publications, or "horizontal" books, and special-interest publications, or "vertical" publications.

Magazine audiences are large, generally larger than the number of names on a direct mail list. There are dozens of magazines with a circulation in excess of 10 million readers. These publications provide the direct marketer with large numbers of people who can be reached on a repetitive basis, mostly monthly but occasionally weekly.

"Vertical" publications reach people because of their similar interest. These vertical publications are heavily targeted at consumers' behavioral or lifestyle interests. Publications such as sports magazines and home decorating magazines provide the advertiser with an opportunity to place an advertisement within a publication aimed editorially at people with an interest similar to that of the target audience.

Because people generally purchase magazines to "read" them, there is increased likelihood that the consumer will see, read, and respond to an advertising message in a magazine. Additionally, magazines generally last weeks or even months in a consumer household, increasing the number of times the advertising message may come to the attention of the consumer.

Magazines offer high-quality reproduction in black and white but especially in four colors. Food advertising and home decorating provide good examples of the high quality of reproduction.

Creatively, reproduction quality is high, but there is generally less space available for copy and less flexibility in the use of that copy. Sometimes a page or even two pages will not be enough to tell the advertiser's story in sufficient detail to move the consumer to action. There is a great deal of advertising in space units smaller than a page, such as a half page or column. Added to the limitations of space, there is the limitation in format, little possibility for the use of devices and special effects, and none of the personalization used in direct mail.

Advertising in magazines is less complex than putting out a direct mail piece because the advertiser need only produce the advertising material and supply it to the magazine, which in turn prints the advertisement. The closing date of monthly publications, or the date in advance of publication by which the advertising must be at the printer, is frequently 60 to 90 days before publication. This time is necessary so that the publisher can print the magazine. This puts the planning of a magazine advertising campaign on a much longer time cycle than in other media.

Magazines have long "life," which refers to the period of time over which they may be read, and this causes response to come over an extended period. The slower response period combined with the long closing date provides the direct marketer with a slower pattern of response and ultimate cash flow.

Advertising space occasionally is limited as to availability or the availability of a particular position (the page within the magazine) desired by the advertiser. This space limitation can restrict or inhibit the marketer from obtaining the space desired or the optimum position on a specific date to produce good results.

Finally, while magazines generally are purchased in order to be read, there is a great deal of competition for the reader's attention within a magazine. First there is competition with the editorial content, and second there is the direct competition of other advertising for similar products or services or just for the consumer's dollars.

While most magazines are national, many larger magazines, those with a circulation over 100,000, offer some geographic selectivity. The large ones, those with a circulation over 1 million, offer geographic selectivity through the availability of local editions on a market or regional basis.

Newspapers. Newspapers reach over 60 million households on a daily basis through the use of on-page (run of press) advertising in an individual paper, preprinted inserts or free-falls, or one of the four-color rotogravure newspaper supplements.

Owing to the large audiences they reach, newspapers provide extremely broad coverage of a marketplace at efficient cost. In most markets in the United States, newspapers reach between 40 and 60 percent of households on a given day of the week or on the weekend.

By selecting a specific newspaper, the advertiser can control the geographic area in which the advertising will appear. By selecting from a variety of different sections within a newspaper (news, business, food, sports, etc.), the marketer has an opportunity to tailor the advertising message to the specific interests of readers.

On-page advertising in newspapers offers the advertiser a wide variety in advertising sizes, giving the advertiser flexibility in the length of the advertising message. Because the cost of the advertising message is related directly to the size of the ad, flexibility in ad sizes also gives the advertiser great flexibility in the cost of the advertising.

Because of the nature of newspaper publishing itself, closing dates are extremely short, usually a day or two. Because of the rapid distribution of newspapers to the consumer and the virtually "instantaneous" 1-day readership, response to a newspaper advertising message is faster than it is with other print media and direct mail. Newspapers virtually guarantee delivery to the consumer on a given day. With the increase in problems of delivery and uncertainty in the mail, this has become an important advantage in comparison to the use of the mails.

Newspaper reproduction is generally poor compared with other forms of advertising. The use of color is severely limited. In the past, the lack of standardization between newspapers caused increased production costs. However, recent efforts by the newspaper industry to create standard advertising units have made it far easier for an advertiser to run ads in many newspapers simultaneously without having to prepare an ad in similar but slightly different sizes.

Consumer interest is immediate and lasts only a day or so following publication. The advertising messages do not last long, and occasionally the news or other contents of the paper can have the effect of drawing the reader's attention away from the advertising messages.

Newspaper inserts, also called free-falls or stuffers, offer the advertiser several improvements in the newspaper advertising effort. The insert is a preprinted piece delivered to the newspaper for insertion. Because an insert can be printed on many different kinds of paper, there is greater flexibility in size, format, color, and quality of reproduction than there is in on-page advertising.

Retailer stores and other advertisers use inserts to deliver catalogs to the consumer at a lower distribution cost than through the postal system, gaining the advantage of virtually guaranteed delivery on a specific day of the week.

Newspaper supplements are technically inserts, but they contain editorial content as well as advertising. The three major newspaper supplements (*Parade*, *Family Weekly*, and *Sunday Metro*) provide the advertiser with the means of reaching over 60 million households in a single weekend by advertising in only three publications. The large circulation, along with high-quality reproduction and low costs, provides some advertisers with an important advertising opportunity.

Not only do newspaper supplements offer the advertiser low cost per thousand (generally under $10), their use of standard sizes provides the advertiser with an opportunity to reach large numbers of prospects with a minimum of production. Supplements are produced by a rotogravure process, assuring high quality. Because supplements first must be printed and then shipped to the newspapers before distribution, they have 5- or 6-week closing dates.

Newspaper inserts and supplements provide the advertiser with a high degree of geographic flexibility, and both may be selected or omitted from an advertising plan in the same way that newspapers themselves can be used.

Television. Television offers the advertiser an opportunity to reach large numbers of consumers with great geographic flexibility and at low cost. As in the case of newspapers, markets can be included or excluded in virtually any combination geographically. The medium offers an opportunity for unexcelled product demonstration and the use of the emotional impact of the advertising.

While most direct marketers use 2-minute commercials, copy time in a television commercial is still very limited. This makes it extremely difficult to communicate a complex message. The TV advertising message has an extremely short life because of the shortness of the message and the consumers' inability to "reread" it. Additionally, television does not provide a direct-response device. The telephone and the telephone used in connection with the credit card are becoming important parts of the response mechanism.

This advertising medium offers a great deal of geographic flexibility through the selection of stations, days of the week, and the time of the day in which the advertising can appear.

The length of the advertising campaign is flexible. Television provides unusual opportunities for staying on the air when the program is successful or getting off the air when the resulting response is not cost-efficient or when product availability requires an immediate cessation of advertising. Television advertising, especially with the use of a toll-free in-WATS telephone number and credit cards, results in the receipt of orders within minutes of the appearance of the commercial. Hence, the flow of inquiries and orders is fast. Products or product information can be shipped immediately, and the resulting cash flow follows close behind.

Television advertising is broadcast advertising at its finest. However, it is broadcast with little demographic selectivity. Additionally, the positioning of 2-minute direct-response commercials within the advertising schedules of a station is restricted by limited availability, and the advertiser cannot target the advertising message to specific audiences.

Television direct-response advertising tends to be highly seasonal because of competition from other advertisers for air time. This results in heavy expenditures concentrated in the first and third quarters of the year.

Air time is perishable and represents a loss to the station if it is unsold. Thus, rates are negotiable. In return for the negotiable rate, the station has the right to preempt, or not run, the commercial in return for having granted the lower rates. While this lowers the rates paid, it also removes the assurance that a commercial will run on a given day or at a specific time.

Radio. Radio advertising is one of the least frequently used direct-response media. However, this medium offers the advantage of having time readily available and being easy to schedule. Because a script can be provided to a station and no production is necessary, advertising can be placed on a station within days.

Radio generally is considered to be a "frequency" medium in which messages can be repeated as often as fifteen to thirty times a week on a given station. As with other broadcast and print media, great geographic flexibility is available. Radio does offer some degree of demographic selectivity since the various stations appeal to different audiences. The programming on most stations is targeted to a particular broad audience.

Creatively, there are limitations in the use of the medium because it is not visual. But radio is occasionally referred to as the "theater of the mind," providing the consumer's imagination with the opportunity for greatly enhancing or envisioning a message.

Radio's heavy listening during "drive time" frequently places listeners in a position where they are unable to respond to the advertising. The commercial message is short, generally only 30 seconds, and radio even more than television suffers from commercial clutter. Radio also is used often in the home as "background sound."

Media Costs

Costs of advertising media vary greatly. Direct mail lists range in cost from $35 to $50 per thousand. The marketer would pay additional amounts ranging from $2.50 to $10 per thousand for additional selection of demographic (sex, age, geography, etc.), or psychographic (recency of purchase, direct mail purchase, etc.) characteristics. These additional "selection charges" are worth the investment because they permit marketers to target the advertising message more closely to the consumers they are trying to reach. However, the list cost is only part of the total cost of the mailing, which includes the costs of printing, inserting, labeling, postage, and mailing. Total cost of the mailing "in the mail" can range from as low as $200 to $300 per thousand to as much as $1000 per thousand ($1 per mail piece).

Contributing to this high cost are the postage rates. First class postage currently is $200 per thousand, and third class is $104 per thousand. Unfortunately, the rates are destined to continue to increase with little likelihood of increasing the efficiency of mail delivery.

Very small direct mail efforts may include 10 to 25,000 pieces for a total cost ranging from $2500 to $10,000. The quantities of larger mailings can run into millions, with some reduction in costs because of greater efficiency which results in the reduction of printing and mailing costs.

Magazines are inexpensive when compared with direct mail. Costs run under $10 per thousand for a four-color page in a national magazine. Using regional issues of magazines can raise the price to the $10 to $15 per thousand range. Because the amount of space used impacts almost directly on the cost of the ad, the use of the smaller space will result in lower costs per thousand, occasionally as low as $2 or $3 per thousand.

The circulation of a smaller magazine can be as low as 100,000 or less. Thus, small space advertising in smaller magazines can cost only a few hundred dollars. Even full-page advertising can be purchased in smaller magazines for $5000 to $10,000. Needless to say, the use of large-circulation publications can cost several hundred thousand dollars.

Newspaper advertising is even less expensive. A quarter page in a newspaper, which is about the size of a magazine page, generally costs between $4 and $5 per thousand. A full page in a standard-size newspaper can be purchased for $15 to $20 per thousand. As with magazines, the smaller the size of the ad, the lower the cost, so that units smaller than a quarter page can be purchased for only a few dollars per thousand.

As many newspapers have a circulation between 100,000 and 500,000, it is readily apparent that advertising campaigns can be run in newspapers for as little as a few thousand dollars. Small space advertising can be used for under $1000.

Newspaper inserts are the most expensive form of all print advertising. Current rates for space in a newspaper run between $25 and $45 per thousand. Added to this is the cost of printing, which can bring the cost of the total advertising to between $40 and $75 per thousand. However, in order to print inserts for $10 to $20 per thousand, large quantities, possibly even into the millions, must be purchased to gain printing efficiency.

Newspaper supplements can be an efficient purchase, with the costs of inserts running between $7 and $10 per thousand for a four-color ad. Smaller units are less expensive, and the quantities purchased and the resulting total costs can vary.

Broadcast media, both radio and television, are the most efficient on a cost per thousand basis—well below $1 per thousand. This explains the tremendous use of television by all advertisers. While television advertising can be extremely expensive for a national advertiser, at over $50,000 per spot, the actual cost per thousand viewers is less than $1.

The direct marketer has the opportunity to use both these advertising media, purchasing spots at many times on many stations at a cost between $100 and $500 per spot. Therefore, an advertising schedule on a particular station frequently can be bought for under $1500, and the resulting testing of the advertising medium can cost as little as $10,000 to $15,000.

While the cost per thousand of advertising is extremely high in direct mail and very low in broadcast, the cost of the advertising medium is not indicative of the resulting cost of acquiring an order. The acquisition cost of an inquiry or an order (the cost of the advertising divided by the number of orders received) tends to produce a much narrower variation between media.

While direct mail is the most expensive advertising medium, it is also the most responsive because of its selectivity and the use of personalization. Hence, in spite of its very high costs, the resulting costs per order can fall well within the objectives of the direct marketer.

At the other end of the spectrum, the relatively low cost of print media and the extremely low cost of broadcast media are to some degree offset by the relatively low response rates.

While media schedules must be evaluated in terms of the total dollars to be invested, individual media types should not be evaluated merely in terms of cost. Mail will always have the highest cost and broadcast the lowest, but their relative measures of effectiveness may not be in that proportion.

Timing

In planning the implementation of an advertising program, the marketer must recognize the time differences involved in the use of various advertising media.

Direct mail lists generally take between 2 and 4 weeks for delivery following the order plus another week or two for labeling, insertion, and mailing. Since most marketers use third class mail, another few weeks goes by before receipt by the consumer. Hence, the total planning cycle for a direct mail program can be as much as 8 to 12 weeks.

Magazine advertising can be spread over a more extended period of time because of the 60- to 90-day closing dates. While weekly publications have a faster close, a 3- to 5-week cycle is not unusual for this medium.

Newspaper advertising placement is extremely quick, and an ad can be prepared and inserted in less than 1 week, occasionally in a few days.

Because of the printing necessary in newspaper inserts and newspaper supplements, the cycles for the use of these insertions are frequently a month or two, with even longer periods being necessary because of the time involved in preprinting larger quantities of inserts.

Both television and radio are extremely quick, although earlier purchasing is desirable. A week or two is possible, but a month is more likely.

These timings are ranges and will vary greatly with the amount of advertising to be run, especially in media which must be printed, such as direct mail and newspapers. There is an added time delay involved in production as a result of the use of color and the readership or viewer pattern of the consumer.

Competition

As mentioned throughout this handbook, all forms of direct marketing are measurable. Therefore, every direct marketer has the opportunity to repeat that which is successful and eliminate that which is either unsuccessful or less successful than something else. This principle carries over to media. By observing the media used in direct mail, print, or broadcast, you can get an indication of which media are working for your competitors. At any particular point in time, a competitor may be doing something that ultimately will be less successful than something else. Therefore, it is advisable to study what your competitors are doing over time and see whether they are repeating something that they have done before. If they are, the chances are that it is successful and may be worth examining more carefully.

Think in terms of locating a retail store. Two options exist. One is to locate the store in the middle of a shopping center in which there is a high degree of competitive traffic. On the other hand, you can situate your store in a completely new neighborhood in which there is no competition. While a degree of exclusivity is desirable, there may be no traffic. Therefore, in the same way a retailer puts a store where competitor stores are, you may wish to consider placing your advertising where your competition is and has been successful.

In researching appropriate direct mail lists, don't look only for lists which seem to reach the right market audiences both demographically and psychographically but also determine which lists are being used repetitively by people offering directly competitive or similar products. It is generally better to mail to the same list that your competitor uses than to use other lists which possibly are not working as well or which have been tested and found to be unsuccessful. Of course, this may not be true for new media which have not been used by competitors yet.

Investigating where a competitor ran print advertising is not difficult. You can ask the sales representative of the newspapers or magazines which competitors are using and even acquire copies of the advertising that is running. A trip to the library will provide you with examples of competitive advertising as you examine back issues of publications. Another way to do this would be through subscription to a service such as the Publishers Information Bureau (PIB), which tracks competitive advertising by product group, indicating the frequency with which advertising appears in major magazines and the costs of those insertions.

Television and radio are so widely broadcast that you can see these efforts by merely watching TV or listening to the radio. Broadcast Advertisers Reports

(BARs) carry summaries of activity in both television and radio. Because selected stations are responsive for many products, one tends to see much direct marketing advertising on some stations and little or none on others.

Remember that direct marketers measure the results of their activities and tend to repeat what they have found to work effectively and minimize or eliminate what they find does not work. Observing your competitors or other major advertisers in the industry can give you important leads about media or other approaches you might test.

While a knowledge of what your competitor is doing is important, don't follow it blindly. It is important to see for yourself whether advertising where competitors do is effective for you. Two companies may be similar in their marketing approaches, but their economic needs, breakeven levels, profit ratios, etc., may be different, causing what one company does to be less than totally applicable to another firm.

Testing

While testing is covered in more depth elsewhere in this handbook, a discussion of media planning would be incomplete without some mention of media testing considerations.

Before identifying the unique testing capabilities of the various types of media, this section will highlight several overall considerations vital to testing in any medium.

1. Testing is the byword of the direct marketer. Regardless of the size of the organization or the available budget, a testing program is essential to the growth and success of any business. In the initial marketing effort, all media used may be considered as tests. But as subsequent marketing efforts take place, it is good practice to allocate no less than 10 to 15 percent of the dollars to testing new media opportunities.
2. Testing should be representative. The names in the test effort or the media selected in the test effort should be representative of the target audience that the advertising and marketing plans are endeavoring to reach. If this is not followed, the creative element being used will not impact appropriately on the target audience, and the conclusions that will be drawn from the advertising efforts will not be representative of their continuation.
3. While testing should be "representative," the experience of many marketers suggests the advisability of segmenting media to avail the direct marketer of the best opportunity for success. For example, in direct mail, select the most recent "hotline" names which will have the greatest opportunity for working. In the selection of newspaper and broadcast, advertisers pick geographic areas in which the company has been most successful on those in which previous results have indicated the likelihood of success.

   Lest this approach seem somewhat at variance with being representative, it must be remembered that testing is expensive and that a direct marketer must take the opportunity for limiting risk and being successful.

   When results are evaluated after having biased the test in this manner, future projections should be adjusted accordingly. However, these adjustments can be made and are more than worth the offset in terms of the profitability of the test efforts.

4. Testing must be done on a large enough scale that the resulting information is statistically reliable and therefore actionable. Chapter 16 deals with sample sizes. However, it is important to point out here that it is better to reduce the number of media (lists, magazines, and broadcast stations) being tested than to reduce the size of the media in the test. In this manner, you can be assured that the results of the test will be meaningful and actionable.
5. Successful media testing should be expanded as soon as possible because media are dynamic and changing. The longer the period of time that occurs between the initial test and the subsequent retest or expansion, the greater the likelihood that results may be different.

   For this reason, it is occasionally practical for the marketer to plan on expanding a successful test at the earliest possible moment at which reliable information may be received. This may be as short as a few days or weeks within the rapidly moving environment of broadcast or as long as several months or even half a year with a medium like magazine in which the response is slow and a resulting time lag of placing additional advertising exists.
6. Seasonality should be considered at all times. While it is important to continue to expand on tests as rapidly as possible, as outlined above, the direct marketer must recognize that there are meaningful fluctuations in the seasonality of response. For products which are not seasonal in nature, e.g., business gifts, swim wear, etc., there is a definite seasonal pattern. The winter months, particularly late December and January, provide the best response of the year. The fall, particularly August and September, is second best, with the spring months of March and April coming in third. The summer is traditionally poor, as is the end of the year just before the holidays.

   Therefore, while the direct marketer is considering the need to expand on successful testing rapidly, the marketer must also consider the effect, positive or negative, that advertising in a particular season of the year may have.

   Occasionally, the direct marketer will wait for the next "season." Testing will be done in the fall but not expanded until January, or it will be done in January but not expanded until fall. This can be done to gain the added cost efficiency of the higher-response periods of time.

Direct mail offers the greatest testing flexibility in terms of the ability to split, or divide up, the names for creative testing in any way desired or to vary the size of the effort.

The most recent names should be selected for initial list testing as they invariably will produce the best results. Between the time of the test effort and continuation, there will be additional "most recent" names so that this does not bias the test.

Magazine advertising can be purchased on a regional basis. This permits the advertiser to limit the expenditure, with the marketer picking the best regions or several best regions in which to do the initial test advertising.

Magazines generally are printed several copies at a time. This facilitates a two-way, or A-B, split for copy testing, price testing, etc.

Newspapers also offer the A-B split capabilities of magazines. While newspapers cover specific markets, it is possible to limit advertising to specific geographic areas within the target market. Additionally, inserts can be limited to even smaller areas such as newspaper "truck routes."

Broadcast testing is more difficult to do than print or direct mail advertising because of the inherent problems in duplicating an advertising schedule on different stations in different parts of the country at the same time. However, the broadcast medium does provide great flexibility in terms of the length of the purchase. The direct marketer with a new product can go on the air for extremely short periods of time (as little as 2 weeks) and determine the results before continuing. By limiting the schedule in this manner and limiting the number of markets used in the test, the advertiser can limit the advertising effort and hence the risk.

Be sure to read the sections on testing throughout this handbook before planning a direct marketing campaign.

The Schedule

The media schedule is a concise yet detailed listing of the pertinent specifics concerning medium, critical dates, and costs. Because schedules vary slightly according to the type of media used, specifics will be given according to type.

Direct mail media schedules include

1. The name of the list
2. The specific segments of the list being ordered
3. The quantity to be mailed
4. The delivery date when the list is expected
5. The mail date
6. The cost of the list, usually expressed in terms of cost per thousand

Magazine schedules include

1. The name of the magazine
2. The issue of the magazine to be used
3. The (desired) position of the advertisement
4. The size of the advertisement
5. The closing date of publication
6. The desired issue of the magazine
7. The cost per thousand
8. The total cost of the insertion

Newspaper advertisers schedules include

1. The name of the publication
2. The size of the ad
3. The (desired) position or an indication it is an insert
4. The closing date
5. The publication date

6. The cost per thousand
7. The total cost of the advertisement

Broadcast schedules for both radio and television include

1. The name of the station (call letters)
2. The desired program, period of time, and day during which the commercials will run
3. The length of the commercial
4. The starting date of the schedule
5. The termination date of the schedule
6. The cost of the spot
7. The total cost of the schedule

Additionally, included in all of the schedules is usually the designation of the key number or code which will be used in the measurement of results by the direct marketer.

The more care and attention given toward defining objectives and developing the plan, the more successful the actual program will be. The chapters which follow provide an in-depth look at each of these advertising media.

chapter 15

INTRODUCTION TO MAILING LISTS

Ed Burnett

Ed Burnett Consultants, Inc. New York, N.Y.

SIZE AND SCOPE

There are some problems with the U.S. Postal Service, but size is certainly not one of them. The mail handled by the New York post office is greater than the total volume of mail in Germany; the mail handled by the Chicago post office is greater than the total volume in Japan. With over 600,000 employees and 35,000 local offices, the U.S. Postal Service handles over half the world's total mail flow.

Two Universes

All mail is delivered to some 94 million delivery points, consisting of 87 million households and just over 7 million nonhouseholds.

Nonhouseholds include the entire range of business establishments as well as 1 million institutions and over 900,000 offices of professionals. Major groups of businesses include establishments in mining, construction, metalworking, manufacturing, wholesaling, transportation, communication, finance, insurance, real estate, and business services. Some 80 percent of nonhouseholds have fewer than ten employees.

A growing gray area in the nonhousehold category covers businesses being operated out of households by individuals either "moonlighting" in businesses of their own or working full time out of their homes. Over 7 million Americans pay taxes on such operations.

Size of the Mailing List Business

The total number of prospect names rented by nonhouseholds for prospect mailings is 17 billion. For these names, the mailers of America pay approximately $300 million.

These rental lists, by quantity and dollars, are divided roughly as follows:

Business-compiled names	1,500,000,000 names at $30 per thousand =	$45,000,000
Consumer-compiled names	5,000,000,000 names at $17 per thousand =	$85,000,000
Response names	5,000,000,000 names at $30 per thousand =	$150,000,000
Occupant names	6,000,000,000 names at $ 5 per thousand =	$30,000,000
	17,500,000,000 names	$310,000,000

Of the response names, approximately one-seventh, or 700 million, are estimated to be business response names, including business magazine and service recipients and mail-order buyers of business-related items. On this basis, nonhousehold names make up about one-seventh of all prospecting names rented in the United States, while household names account for the remainder.

However, direct mail is not the major medium used for direct-response prospecting among "cold prospects." Matchbook covers top direct mail by many billions, and the ubiquitous self-standing stuffers which drop out of Sunday editions of daily newspapers reach twice as many prospects per year as all direct mail, both household and nonhousehold combined.

Other Uses for Mailing List Data

While mailing lists are obviously a media source for promotion, there are a number of major uses for mailing lists which are ancillary to the primary use. Current files of householders and of businesses can be used to refurbish aging lists. In such a utilization, only those records on the old file which match a current file are maintained. Lists of new householders and new businesses can be used to correct and augment current customers and prospect files. Lists, almost by definition, can become printed directories; such directories, even of households, can be regional, state, or local. Major newspapers with home delivery customers can match their customer base against an occupant or name list to identify households in a given trading area that are not on the customer file. This facilitates complete saturation coverage by permitting them to reach those households with the same piece delivered as a self-standing insert in the newspaper. Of course, lists provide the necessary data for teleprospecting and telemarketing as well as for all levels of market research by mail.

Advertising Mail

Advertising matter is included in 27 percent of all mail generated by nonhouseholds, or a total of 25 billion pieces. Since a very large majority of all prospect mailings carry advertising, some 17 billion of this 25 billion are for prospecting, leaving 8 billion pieces with advertising to customer files. (Such files include donors of fund-raising organizations; subscribers and recipients of magazines, newsletters, and services; and customers of mail order and catalog operators.)

How Advertising Is Distributed

Eighty percent of advertising literature sent by mail is included in third class mail. Ninety-nine percent of third class for profit mail with advertising is mailed at the third class bulk rate. Thus, third class bulk is a solid indicator of advertising volume.

While nonprofit bulk mail has increased every year since 1965, there was no growth in third class bulk for profit mail in the 7 years from 1969 through 1975, a period in which rates increased from 2.875 cents to 6.3 cents per piece. Measured against the number of pieces of mail per family, or per $1 million of gross national product, third class bulk for profit mail actually declined. In fact, between 1973 and 1975, actual volume declined about 5 percent each year.

In the years since 1975, third class bulk for profit mail has increased each year through 1980. In this period, volume increased from 15.7 billion to 22 billion, or 40 percent. In these same 5 years, third class bulk for profit postage increased from 6.3 cents to 8.4 cents, or 33 percent. Thus the mail flow increased by 40 percent despite a rate increase of one-third.

In 1982, the third class bulk for profit rate increased to 10.9 cents, an increase over 1981 of an additional 30 percent. Total volume in early 1982 increased modestly despite the rate increase.

But there was an abrupt rise in volume from 1978 to 1981. All of this is due to a new class called carrier route presort (6.4 cents on profit mail until 1982 against 8.4 cents; in 1982, 7.9 cents against 10.9 cents). Volume in this class totalled 2.9 billion in postal fiscal year 1979, 7 billion in 1980, and 11 billion in 1981. Significantly, this huge increase is greater than the entire increase in third class volume beyond the 15.7 billion pieces logged in 1975. Thus, there has been no increase in third class bulk for profit mailings (other than presort) since 1975.

Since carrier route presort requires a qualifying density of ten per carrier route (not just per post office), it rarely is used for business-to-business mailings. Thus, it is clear that the total of third class mailings for profit sent from business to business has not increased over the past 10 or 12 years.

The nonprofit increase from 7.9 billion to 8.2 billion (about a 4 percent increase) is the smallest percentage increase logged since 1965. The January 1982 rate increase from 3.5 cents to 5.9 cents per piece is almost certain to bring about the first decline in this form of mail in over 15 years.

State of the Art

A. Mobility

1. Consumer (Households) The total number of American households is about 87 million, including one-person households. Over the course of a year, 18 to 20 percent of these are newly established or move. In some communities, the turnover rate is 100 percent within 1 year.
2. Business (Nonhouseholds) There are approximately 7,100,000 Ameri-

can business establishments, of which 15 percent go bankrupt, change name, move, or are absorbed each year. Fifteen percent each year are new starts, though only one in five survives for 5 years. Thus, 70 percent of the file stays untouched, while 15 percent more addresses are added and 15 percent deleted, with the total number remaining about the same.

B. Updating: Current files are compiled from telephone books a few months after publication. All but a small percentage of the directories are updated once during the course of a year. (The gap is due to missing directories and directories published less often than annually.) But the average is about 7 months from the date of acquisition (one-twelfth today, one-twelfth next month, etc.). To this must be added the time to acquire the books, or about 2 months, plus the time needed in compiling and printing the books after establishing a cutoff date for listings. This averages about 4 months. Thus, even the most accurate compilations include an average time lag of over 1 year. Since phone books are about 2 percent wrong when they are published, commercially available name and address compilations from telephone books (both consumer and nonconsumer) are wrong by a minimum of 10 percent as they are updated. Since phone numbers prove worse when published than address data, the average "good" list of phone numbers from commercially viable lists is wrong by 15 percent or more. It should be noted that a major city or an area not updated on a file for 12 to 14 months—which happens all the time—will have a nondeliverable rate of over 20 percent.

"Current" Changes

At the present time, "new" data from telephone books (from one year to the next, and thus well out of date so far as currency is concerned) produce a file of some 11 million consumer records and a file of approximately 900,000 business records. These are sold as "current" records by the expedient of publishing or offering them monthly or bimonthly as the data are developed.

To fill the gap, a number of services have sprung up, some in the list field but most in the "information retrieval" field in which data can be priced at $0.15 to $0.25 per unit rather than the $0.02 to $0.04 per unit charged for conventional compiled names and addresses.

A number of lists used as suppression files to eliminate address data no longer deliverable are being created from "address change" data developed by major magazines. A few of the major suppliers of compiled names offer a service to update files from such records, even to the point of removing the old address and inserting the new. Costs for this service, which are intended to save not just the postage but the entire cost of the mailing package, tend to be rather high. But no supplier has a complete or reasonably complete list of current data to work with.

CODING

Consumer Files

Major files are all coded for carrier route, county code, metro area code, and subblock within a census tract. All are coded for a five-digit ZIP; the nine-digit ZIP is not used. No major consumer list compiler has embraced the nine-digit ZIP, since its only purpose is to reach what could be a seven-digit carrier route.

Business Files

- All files are coded for five-digit ZIP and for counties and metro areas. Two lists are carrier route-coded. Such coding does not have high impact, as only saturation coverage of all establishments in major markets has any chance to qualify for the discount offered. The same is true of most business mailings for third class presort, where the requirement of fifty pieces per ZIP code is not often met.
- None are coded for a nine-digit ZIP.

NEAR-TERM PROJECTIONS

1. Postage has been increasing at 9 percent per year, compounded, for over 20 years. There is nothing to indicate that this will not continue. First class and third class bulk (the major form of mail containing advertising) have now arrived at about a 2 to 1 price relationship (20 cents versus 10.9 cents). This relationship is likely to continue with rates at 25 cents and 12.5 cents, respectively, by 1985. Costs of all other advertising will in all probability increase as fast (and perhaps faster), and the cost of making an individual sales call will increase likewise. Mail will not suffer appreciably by comparison.
2. The present $300 per thousand direct mail package (printing, envelopes, mailing list, postage, and fulfillment) probably will cost close to $400 per thousand in 1985.
3. The volume of direct mail is not likely to increase or decrease appreciably in the next five years.
4. Business-to-business prospect mail, which has been on somewhat of a plateau for the last 10 years, is likely to increase modestly over the next few years.
5. Business-to-consumer prospect mail is likely to increase, but very modestly, over the 1981 high. The huge increase over the past few years has been in mail sorted by carrier route. The new rate initiated at the end of 1981 increased the rate by $15 per thousand or 23 percent, enough to slow down the increase in volume appreciably.

THE GROWTH OF CATALOGS

The total number of catalogs mailed in 1979 was 2717 million, or 3.3 percent of all nonhousehold created-mail. Of this quantity, 2224 million went to households (or thirty catalogs per household), and 493 million went to nonhouseholds (or seventy catalogs per establishment, with about one-fifth from or for manufacturers directly).

Receipt of catalogs by class of nonhousehold was as follows.

Business	310,500,000
Government	12,800,000
Schools	169,400,000
Nonprofits	2,300,000
Hospitals and medical services	5,700,000
Foreign governments	2,500,000

Some idea of the value of the school market in America is indicated by the vast number of catalogs they receive: over 1000 per year per school and per school district. Hospitals and medical services receive over 100 catalogs per year. Business establishments as a whole, including offices of professionals, receive some fifty catalogs per year.

It is estimated that some 80,000 of 5,200,000 business establishments (1.5 percent) use catalogs in their promotional efforts. The figures for originators of catalogs by major classification are as follows.

	Catalog Operators	Universe of Firms
Mail-order companies	11,500	13,500
Department stores	10,500	58,000
Home delivery sales operations	15,000	59,000
Manufacturers other than printers and publishers	15,000	300,000
Publishers	15,000	30,000
Mail service companies	6,000	7,000
Printers	5,000	46,000
Other businesses	3,500	4,700,000

A few predictions seem reasonably safe in this turbulent field.

1. Catalog volume will increase. One major study predicts that the volume printed in 1990 will double the 1979 total of 2700 million.
2. Specialty catalogs will grow in number, but the number of operators will be reduced by combination, attrition, and acquisition.
3. Retail catalogs will continue their strong growth.
4. Catalog showrooms, which became prominent in the 1970s, will grow in the 1980s, but at a much lower rate.
5. Catalogs produced by big business will increase in number as well as volume. The larger the firm, the larger the number of mailings and the greater the volume.

It is a bit difficult to recognize that one-tenth of all the catalogs produced in America are for just one firm: Sears Roebuck.

SEARS, ROEBUCK AND CO.

One-fifth of Sears's huge volume comes from catalog sales (over 90 percent of which are phoned in, which boggles the mind of most mail-minded merchandisers). Catalogs display and sell merchandise. The phone is the personal link in the sales chain.

The Sears catalog operation employs 350 people, with a budget of over $250 million. Each year, 9500 new catalog pages are produced (most are now for specialized segmented catalogs). Over 155,000 tons of paper are consumed yearly. Split-run ad tests run into hundreds per year.

Single-item testing is done by using selected cells (based on recency, frequency, dollars, item source, and method of payment in the credit buyers file of some 25 million names).

Sears operates 850 retail stores, 375 of which are full-line and 475 condensed or incomplete, with a restricted number of departments. Of forty-nine separate selling divisions in Sears, the catalog sales division is the largest.

Sears does a huge business in specialty catalogs, offering a much broader assortment than any general-merchandise store could possibly handle. Among these specialty catalogs (seventeen in all) are

40-page western-style clothing
80-page big and tall men
44-page floor covering
144-page power and hand tools

Sears publishes more specialized catalogs today than copies of the general book, but not more total pages as yet.

J. B. Kelley, formerly vice president of catalog sales and the man in charge of a program that produces 300 million catalogs a year (over 1 million every day) recently summarized the philosophy of Sears in six points. For his first point, orientation, he utilizes a comment by the marketing specialist, Bob Stone:

> It is not the awesome size of Sears' catalog operation that makes it unique, but the emphasis on catalogs as a marketing force instead of an advertising or promotional effort. Each of Sears' seventeen specialty catalogs support the retailer's philosophy that catalog circulation and retail stores should support one another.

Kelley goes on to make these other points:

- Catalog sales set the pattern for the geographic location of new stores, both full-line and restricted. The best customers of a new retail store are catalog customers. Stores tend to be located where catalog sales indicate sufficient penetration.
- The catalogs supplement the assortment of merchandise which can be carried economically within the walls of a retail store.
- A family that receives a Sears catalog is twice as likely to shop in a Sears retail store as a family that has not qualified to receive one, and such a family will spend twice as much at Sears.
- Catalogs help develop more credit customers for Sears. Credit enhances customer use of Sears, and the convenience of personal shopping or ordering by phone and paying later picks up extra business. One-third of the households in America have a Sears credit card.
- Catalogs are the forerunners of merchandise directions. Millions of dollars of business is transacted through the catalog in the very items and lines which Sears is offering on a test basis.

It is no accident that Sears is opening business machine stores in five test markets (self-standing, or not associated with main stores and not in shopping centers). These stores will stock and sell small business computers (including the new IBM home computers), software, copying machines, calculators, typewriters, word processors, and dictation equipment. Hundreds of Sears stores are projected.

It would be surprising if Sears did not have on the drawing board two catalogs in this field, one for electronic gadgets for the home and a second for office and business equipment. The pattern for the latter may have been set by the gourmet food catalog now mailed for gift purposes to 350,000 businesses.

Sears, perhaps better than any other retailer in America, is aware of the great recent changes in society, including the following:

1. The rise in the cost of energy.
2. The changing attitude about women's place in the work force. (Sears stores are now open 80 hours a week to serve the needs this creates.)
3. Shifts in population and the mobility of the American people.
4. The shift away from shopping as a pleasant leisure-time family activity and the gravitation of business toward marketers that make shopping increasingly convenient.

It should be no surprise to find that Sears is experimenting with electronic catalogs. The initial experiment utilizes the Pioneer system laser disc, which is not compatible with the RCA discs which Sears sells. The complete catalog on discs with stop action, played through a home TV, is serving 1000 test customers near six selected stores.

DIRECT MAIL TESTING

No construction of a modern building is possible until a few test core samples of the underlying soil have been analyzed. No chemical company would build a new plant for a chemical process until that process had been proved in a test mode. And no marketer worthy of the name launches a new product full blast before sampling reception in a few "test" markets.

In the field of direct mail, there are two primary reasons for adequate test procedures: to save you from disaster by providing a measure of viability for a given offer at a minimum expenditure, to improve your average response rate and thus maximize your net dollar returns.

There are just five factors that affect response, and they are the same whether you wish to acquire a buyer, an inquirer, a donor, or a subscriber.

Copy the words you use to create your appeal

Package the "attire" your appeal wears

Offer your appeal (in fund raising, your offer satisfies someone else's need)

Timing when your appeal arrives

List to whom your appeal is directed

After you have a reasonably adequate mailing, these factors can be improved through careful testing, as follows:

Copy	about 20 percent
Package	from 15 to 30 percent
Offer	from 50 to 200 percent
Timing	about 20 percent except at Christmas
List	from 300 to 1000 percent

This indicates that testing will be most productive when offers and lists are varied. And if all other factors must be held for budgetary reasons, whatever testing is done should include various list segments. There are a number of rules for proper testing. Here are the first five.

Rule 1. Do not be guilty of the "continuous series of one experiment" syndrome. In this system, one offer in one package is sent to one list, and the "results" are recorded. At the very least, test four or five separate list concepts or segments.

Rule 2. Once established, a "control" package (your standard offer) should never be retired until you have created a new "control" which outpulls the old.

Rule 3. Never test two new packages against each other to determine which is better. Unless you include your control, you will not know if either of the two new offers is better than the control you are arbitrarily retiring.

Rule 4. Confirm any successful list test with a "continuation" consisting of some modest multiple of the test. If a test of 5000 from a list of several hundred thousand looks promising, test five more cross-sectional lots of 5000, not one lot of 25,000. You are looking here for confirmation of results. The smaller the variance from the mean (the average of all 25,000 in this case), the greater your confidence can be that a large continuation, say 50,000 or 100,000, will work as well.

Rule 5. Recognize that the size of the list has nothing to do with the size of the sample you select. Virtually every user of direct mail follows the conventional wisdom of increasing the size of the sample as list size increases. But the conventional wisdom is wrong. The size of the list has nothing to do with the size of the sample.

There are just two factors which determine the number of names you will wish to draw from any list.

- You must obtain the response rate or the contribution rate (or both) that you have determined is your breakeven for testing. (What this says is that if a list does not return a given response, no matter what its size, you are not going to continue. If the results are pathetically negative, you aren't even going to retest.) Not so incidentally, this breakeven percentage can be and most often is at a modest loss. (What this means is that you usually "pay" for a new customer, a new subscriber, or a new donor rather than make money from mailings to even well-qualified prospects.)
- You must receive enough responses for statistical stability. (This says that you have confidence that on continuations, the list will tend to do about as well.)

Thus, it is not the size of the list which dictates the size of the sample; it is the size of the response.

Statistically, you can select the size of sample for the level of confidence you wish. Doubling the size of the sample size, however, does not double the confidence level; rather, it increases that level by some 50 percent. And since most tests are "blind" in that you do not know whether your particular sample is truly representative of the universe it comes from, such charts should be used as guides, not as gospel. What the charts indicate is the confidence factor that continuations to the same list will do about as well. (Why not exactly as well? Because of a fixed statistical concept called the null hypothesis which says that responses to samples in general tend to vary; they do not come out exactly the same way each time.)

What this all boils down to is that it is the number of responses that is important, not the size of the sample from which the responses came. We can grasp this a bit more firmly with the following illustration.

Let us assume that we have made 100 tests of 1000 each of a list consisting of 100,000 names. This means that we have 100 keys of 1000 each. Let us further assume that the average response to the particular offer we have made is 2 percent. This means that on the complete 100,000 names mailed, we have received twenty responses per thousand, or a total of 100 × 20 = 2000. The question now is, Did each of the 100 tests come in at 2 percent?

As you visualize this, your mind may balk at the idea that every one of the 100 tests came in exactly at 2 percent. It may be assumed that some came in at under 2 percent, some came in at more than 2 percent, and some came in at just 2 percent. That, of course, is what happens.

The distribution, irrespective of the list that's used, the offer that's made, or the package put into the mail, will show that some come in below average and some come in above average. What this looks like is a standard distribution curve.

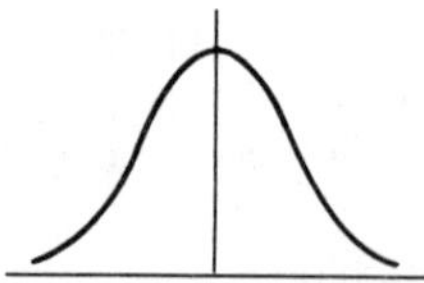

In the particular case we are discussing, it is likely that one of those test 1000s came in as low as 0.5 or 0.3 and that one of them or maybe a couple came in as high as 3.0 or 4.0, but most of them probably came in between 1.5 and 2.5. In fact, statisticians can tell you that approximately two-thirds of the responses will come within the basic shoulders of this particular curve. You can handicap any test by checking it against the general expectancy which this chart describes.

One of the first things the chart indicates is that a response of 1.5, 1.7, 2.0, 2.1, 2.3, or 2.5 is valid. This will explain why, when you make a test the first time and get, say, 1.8 and then make a continuation, the continuation comes in at 1.6 or 2.0, which does not sound like the first sample. Obviously, all these answers are within the realm of statistical probability.

In other words, your first test at 1.8 only said that you are likely to come in between 1.4 and about 2.2, and therefore, any continuation which falls within that range is to be expected. Thus, we can see that it is possible to get a highly skewed or erratic answer from a small sample of a whole. For example, it would be possible to get an answer as low as 0.3, even though the average for 100 tests came out at 2.0. This testing says that you need to obtain enough responses to have statistical validity.

Let us look at a series of responses:

0.7% (7 responses per thousand)
0.75% (7.5 responses per thousand)
0.8% (8 responses per thousand)
0.85% (8.5 responses per thousand)
1.0% (10 responses per thousand)

One might pounce on the last response and say, "That is the winner," but which is the winner in this case if these are the results of five tests of the same list, using the same mailing package at the same time? All that these various responses indicate is the null hypothesis, which says that the responses to a group of tests of the same variable also will vary.

The minimum number of responses required to evaluate a list test or a test of any other factor in the mailing field is between thirty and forty. Let's look at this number. What we are saying is that if you have an offer which can be expected to produce 1 percent or 10 per 1000, you need to test 3000 to 4000 pieces for an adequate test of that particular offer on that particular list.

If you were dealing with a refrigerator to be sold by mail at $99.95, where the breakeven point was at or near 0.4 percent, it is obvious that the number of responses required—thirty to forty—could be obtained only if each list test had some 10,000 to 12,000 in it. On the other hand, if you have a product which can produce 2 percent returns, or 20 per 1000, a list test of 2000 names may be adequate.

How do you know what response is going to be generated? You don't. You have experience, a "feeling" for the offer, and some idea of how given lists have worked on given offers. You also have one landmark: the responses you need to break even on your particular mailing.

At this point we are able to answer the question, How does one select how many names to test from a given list? The answer is, Enough names to break even and enough names to give a sufficient response to provide thirty or forty sales, inquiries, leads, or answers.

It is clear that if you need a 1 percent response, or 10 per 1000, to break even and a list produces 5 per 1000 on a test, you are not going to continue. One of the things to look at first is, What kind of response must you have to justify continuation? If a list is not going to pay off, it is a list you are not going to continue. This by itself should limit the size of the list test you have to make.

If you need 1 percent and a test comes in at 0.7 or 0.8 percent or some other marginal figure, you really have an indication that within the list there must be some 1.5 money or maybe some 2.0 money, but at the present moment you are only getting out part of it. This kind of marginal result can lead to one of several decisions on your part.

If you have enough successful tests, you will, of course, continue with the successes and hold off on the marginal lists.

If there is some way of increasing your batting average by changing the selection or mix of the list in which you have a marginal result, you may decide to make further tests along that route. For example, you may have tested inquirers and decided that perhaps the buyers will do somewhat better, or you may have chosen a list of 1982 buyers and found that you now have access to 1983 buyers, or you may have selected a list which is strong in the south and decided now to test the same list in the north and the midwest.

You may decide, having performed too many marginal tests and achieving too few successes, that you have to change your offer or your package or perhaps your timing to get a better result. In this case, you can go back to segments of the same list to see if you can improve your chances.

You may decide that for this product, on this offer, marginal lists are just not worth continuing at this time.

After proper sample size is determined, there are still more rules for testing.

Rule 6. Do not test for inconsequential changes such as the color of paper, underlining significant text, or signature by A instead of B. The only factors worth testing for are the big five noted earlier: copy, package, offer (appeal), timing, and lists. One major mailer tested red dots before the first three paragraphs, and the response increased 7 percent; an underline was tested for the PS., which increased response 4.5 percent. Light blue paper increased response 3 percent. The three factors were combined, and there was no net effect. What these minor changes were measuring was the Null effect. It is obviously necessary, except on huge continuations, to have a noticeably "significant difference" in order to be certain that one change outpulls another.

Rule 7. Don't be concerned about doing too much testing. For every campaign that gets "tested to death," there are 100 in which tests, particularly of appeal and lists, will improve results remarkably.

Incidentally, there is no end to testing. Every time you are out in the marketplace, you are testing, and so you must key every offer and every mailing and record every envelope, letter, card, and check you receive. Did you mail list A 6 months ago? Then you are testing to see if that list can be used twice a year instead of once. If you uncover a list that works at Christmas and you mail a new segment of that list at Easter, you are testing whether you can extend the range of your seasonal mailings.

For this purpose, set up a large notebook marked plainly, "Office Copy—No Item Is to Be Removed by Anybody." In this you keep a copy of each mailing and every fact about that mailing: quantity, cost, variable if any is being tested, list, and response. If you do not provide such an inviolate historical record, you probably are dooming yourself to repeat mailing mistakes (and costs) over and over again that can be prevented.

As you study such results, patterns will develop. Certain list concepts, for example, "work." Others never do. This helps you make better decisions on new lists as you become aware of them.

What other rules for testing should you know?

Rule 8. Never fail to attempt to improve results from a successful offer. (Every offer eventually begins to lose its appeal.)

Rule 9. Never fail to attempt to lower the cost of the effort.

Rule 10. Never vary more than one element (copy, package, offer, timing, or market) at a time unless grid testing techniques are utilized.

Rule 11. Do not attempt to decide, either by predilection or through "market research" inside or outside the company, which offer, price, or premium is best. What people say they will do can have very little relation to the action they take with a specific offer in hand.

Costs to plan, create, write, lay out, type spec, and provide photos, drawings, and artwork as well as set type have nothing to do with continuation costs. If they are included in the test mode, they may well change a winning piece into an apparent loser. Costs of preparation are the research and development costs of direct mail prospecting. Work so done may never be used. Thus, evaluation of results for purposes of continuing a given promotion depend exclusively on costs to buy the space or produce and mail the piece.

To sum up this advice, in direct response, every mailing and every phone campaign can be and should be made part of a learning curve. This means that "testing" must be a continuous process, not something hidden beneath another guise. If testing is not made a part of the program, you will be consigned to throw away much more than the cost of testing in misdirected or inadequate mailings.

chapter 16

MAIL-ORDER LISTS

Chuck Orlowski

Vice President,
Marketing
AZ Lists, Inc.
Greenwich, Conn.

Mailing lists of all sorts have proved to be an important marketing tool for a wide range of businesses: banks, insurance companies, merchandisers, fund raisers, and the like. Tens of thousands of businesses, from small privately owned companies to large Fortune 500 companies, rent billions of names a year in order to market their products and services.

Over the years, direct mail has become a highly persuasive medium and a key element in many marketing and advertising budgets. Whether it stands alone or works to support other advertising, direct mail still remains the most accurate means of reaching an individual on a personal level with a minimum of waste.

The growth in the use of lists is largely due to the advancement of computer technologies that enable mailers to be highly selective in targeting a potential market. The end result is greater efficiency: better response rates, better customer performance, and most important in this time of growing inflation, the ability to mail more with greater cost efficiency.

More and more mailers today realize the importance of fine-tuning their own house lists. It can cost as little as $0.30 or as much as $75 to generate a lead. That's an investment one makes in the direct marketing business. While the primary purpose is to generate sales from these names, an important factor is the list rental income that can be generated from marketing these names on the open market. It is a means of recouping the investment one has made to acquire the name initially.

Every list has a profile. The more you know about the individuals on a list, the better your ability to market to them.

LIST SOURCES

If you're new to planning a direct mail campaign, the first question that probably comes to mind is, "Where do I find lists to mail to?"

List brokers, managers, and compilers are an integral part of the direct marketing industry. Whether you work with one or several, they should be considered part of your marketing team. The more information you can supply them about your business or product and the type of individual you're trying to reach, the better they can help you plan your mailing campaign.

List Broker

Very simply, a list broker is an individual who will research and recommend lists that are best suited for your mailing program. The broker will make all necessary arrangements for ordering your list and seeing that it arrives at the specified letter shop or mail house on a timely basis. Brokers have their fingers on the pulse of what's happening in the marketplace and generally know what lists or segments work best for specific promotions. In some instances a broker also will help you evaluate your mailing promotion.

List Manager

This is an individual or a firm serving the list owner. A list manager's basic responsibility is making available a company's list for use by others. The list manager promotes to brokers and other list users. In addition, the manager generally maintains or advises on the maintenance of the list, secures list clearance, and is responsible for all record keeping, billing, and accounting for the use of the list by others.

List Compiler

A compiler develops lists of names and addresses from newspapers, directories, public records, questionnaire mailings, etc., of individuals or companies having something in common. The compiler has full responsibility for the maintenance and promotion of a specific list.

In some instances, a single outfit will serve all three capacities. The most important thing to keep in mind is that these individuals are always eager to work with you. However, the quality of the recommendation given is a reflection of the "tools" you provide them to work with. Know your customer better than you know yourself. Who is buying your product or service? What key characteristics about these customers can you readily identify that would enable you to locate more customers just like them? The more you know about your own list, the easier it will be to structure promotion plans for your product or service.

Brokers, managers, and compilers know which lists have worked best for their clients. While it is common industry practice not to divulge privileged information regarding a specific client, the wealth of information gleaned over years of service to the direct marketing industry provides these individuals with the most comprehensive, up-to-date data bank available. Keep the lines of communication open between you and your broker. You'll find the broker invaluable in researching, planning, evaluating, and finding new markets for your product or service.

The DMA, 6 East 43 Street, New York, NY 10017, (212) 689-4977, can provide you with a members roster which lists brokers, managers, and compilers. In addition, a comprehensive source of information on mailing lists can be obtained from

Direct Mail Lists Rates & Data,
Standard Rate and Data Service, Inc.,
5201 Old Orchard Road,
Skokie, IL 60077

HOW TO SHOP FOR A LIST

The best advice given to anyone about to select lists for a mailing program is to know the customer. The more you know about that individual, the more selective you can be in choosing lists for your mailing program. Once you've established a clearly defined profile, selection of lists for future promotion is simple. Direct-response lists develop profiles as a result of the type of promotion directed toward those individuals. As an example, subscribers to *Bon Appetit* magazine obviously would have an interest in knowing more about the preparation and consumption of fine foods. Those individuals would be likely prospects to mail to for gourmet cookware, gourmet foods and cheeses, mail-order fruit or meat, cookbook promotions, etc. As you begin to review list data cards, you'll clearly see a variety of profiles emerging from each list. Careful scrutiny of the information provided will aid you in selecting the lists or segments of a list that most closely match your customer profile.

LIST CATEGORIES

Lists generally are broken down into categories. These categories serve to quickly define types of lists and briefly define one or more characteristics about the individuals on them. Here are some of the more commonly used categories.

Actives Individuals within a list who have more recently (usually within the last 12 months) demonstrated some form of action, i.e., purchase, rent, subscribe to a service, etc.

Buyers People who have made a purchase.

Multibuyer An individual who has made more than one purchase. Multibuyers, if available on a list, are most often a better selection to make when renting a list.

Former buyer One who has purchased but has not done so within the last 12 months. Be careful here. These names age; unless the list has been cleaned recently, you may incur many bad addresses.

Cash versus credit card buyers This simply denotes an individual's method of payment.

Contributor or donor lists Names and addresses of individuals who have contributed to one or more fund-raising efforts.

Gift buyer An individual who has purchased a product or service for someone else.

Hotline list The most recent names added to a list. These names are usually no older than 3 months and may be broken down even further into weekly or monthly names. If this selection is available on a list you are testing (usually at an additional charge), it is wise to consider testing it since these individuals are in a "buying mode," having recently demonstrated some action.

House list A list maintained by a specific company of its customers, subscribers, inquiries, etc.

Inquiry The name and address of an individual who has inquired about a product or service but has not taken any action to purchase.

Premium buyer One who has purchased a product or service in an effort to get another product or service (usually free or discounted) as part of the same offer.

Catalog buyers, space buyers, and television buyers This category simply defines the source of the critical purchase, e.g., catalogs distributed or mailed into the home, ads in magazines and newspapers, or television-mail order buyers.

Within this general range of categories, as you begin to examine list information cards, you will find more information as it applies to the specific list. These valuable data will aid you in targeting specific individuals as efficiently and economically as possible.

TARGETING YOUR MARKET

The Advent of Computer Technology

The computer has given marketers instant access to a wide range of information and represents one of the greatest advances in the direct marketing industry in many years. Not only does the computer contain names, addresses, and ZIP codes by the thousands, it also provides other vital information. List owners today know which parts of their lists are productive and which parts contain customers who are potentially bad credit risks. The computer also can indicate the incidence of name duplication within a list, individuals who purchase certain types of products, the frequent purchaser versus the one-time buyer, and cash purchasers versus credit card purchasers.

Mailing lists have become a highly sophisticated business. List renting has grown by leaps and bounds over the last 10 to 15 years. But list owners are finding that the days of renting a list of 250,000 names to one mailer are fast disappearing. Instead, target marketing, or the selection of smaller segments of a list with similar characteristics, is found to be more productive.

Hotline selection gives you recency. Multibuyers give you frequency, and to that can be added selectivity by dollar value unit of sale. These are the three key factors in successfully selecting a list for testing: recency, frequency, and unit of sale. One can become even more sophisticated by taking advantage of other available selections: sex, age, income, geographic, original source of acquisition, married or single, incidence of children within a household, etc. Don't overindulge. Demographics has given way to psychographics. It's a matter of reaching people by the demographics of where they live so much as by the psychographics of how they live.

Psychographics has become a buzz word in the industry. Lifestyles are changing, and people with like interests do tend to cluster. Purchase decisions often are influenced by a desire to maintain the same lifestyle as a friend or neighbor. Psychographic considerations often provide far more dramatic results. Such considerations give you the opportunity to communicate on a higher level, directing your product or service to exactly the right audience in a tone and manner that motivate an individual to take action.

List Aging

Like everything else, lists age. As was mentioned earlier, the more current the names, the better your response is likely to be. Recency is the key. The longer the time span between a customer's purchases, the less responsive that individual is likely to be.

Lists age rapidly. We live in a very mobile society. Chances are that if you mail a list of names older than a year and it has not been cleaned and updated, you'll find a high percentage of "nixies," or bad addresses. When you take into consideration the cost of mailing today—a 20 to 30 percent nixie rate is not out of line—this can cost you a pretty penny.

Mail the most recent names first. As the supply of fresh names dwindles test the older names. You can expect to find a 20 to 30 percent drop-off in response when you mail to names a year older than the current year and as much as a 40 to 50 percent drop-off on names 2 years old or more.

List Testing

Work closely with your list broker in putting together the most logical list test program possible. If you're testing a product or service for the first time, sort your lists into groups or categories based on a single common factor within each one.

Test several of these categories, as you may find that one or more may not work. Thus, you can eliminate the possibility of expanding into that category on your next go-round and instead expand mailing quantities on those lists which did work well for you while testing additional new lists and new list categories.

Keep track of what you test-mail. Remember, if you plan on turning around quickly on a remailing, you don't want to remail to those same names.

Alert your list broker when you are ordering that you have a second mailing planned for a specific date. Ask the broker to be sure to advise the list owner that you may be coming back to rent another portion or the balance of the list so that you can avoid mailing to names a second time.

Many people have found that a timely remailing to names previously mailed to who did not respond to the initial offer will generate an additional positive response. A client of mine once remailed to a list of individuals who had responded with a "no, not interested" to the initial offer. Surprisingly, this client found that almost 20 percent changed their minds and took advantage of the offer, and with no additional incentive to do so. Timing is key to the success of such a mailing. Allowing for mail delivery and return response, 6 to 8 weeks after the initial mailing you probably will find that the consumer will recall receiving the first mailing.

Check all the selectivities available on a specific list and make sure you've chosen those which will improve your response level.

Be sure to ask for a representative cross-sample of the entire list. "*N*th name sample" is a term commonly used when selecting names for testing. If you are planning on testing 10,000 names from a list of 100,000 names, every tenth name on file should be selected, giving you a 10,000 sample in ZIP sequence, east coast to west coast.

A common question that arises is, "How many names should I test?" Most list owners today require a minimum test of 5000 names. Usually, 5000 to 10,000 names constitutes an ample test. What you're ultimately looking for is a sufficient quantity of responses to allow you to evaluate the quality of a list adequately. Chances are that if you ask six different people about their methodology for list testing, you'll get six different answers.

There is no rule of thumb. Testing is often in line with the scope and cost of the marketing program. More sophisticated mailers rely on probability tables when planning a test. Common sense will tell you that the smaller the test quantity, the smaller the statistical base for evaluation and probably the greater the chance for error.

There are several factors to consider.

1. What is the cost to the consumer of the product you're selling? The response level will be lower on a $300 product than on a $3 product.
2. What is a reasonable response rate to expect? If you have past mailing history to draw on, use it. If not, calculate the response rate necessary to achieve breakeven: a 10 to 20 percent profit. That rate then can be used to determine the size of your list test.
3. If you are doing a mailing for which a second criterion of evaluation is necessary—e.g., a credit card solicitation mailing in which credit approval is key to the issuance of the card—you may find that testing a larger quantity of

names is necessary. The quality of lists varies. In this instance, one list may be approved at 70 percent rate while another may be approved at only a 15 to 20 percent rate.

Don't test small lists of 10,000 and 20,000 quantity. If successful, you have nothing to rollout to on your next mailing. Save those small lists for a major mailing when you can test at least 50 percent or all of the list and not suffer dramatically if the list fails. Ask yourself when testing a list, "If the list works, what have I got to go back to?" Your total anticipated rollout quantity will govern the growth of your future mailing plans. If the lists you're testing are relatively small, your growth will be gradual. If you're testing lists with significant universes, you can be more aggressive in your mailing plans.

If within your mailing program you have multiple test cells for various offers or creative approaches, be doubly sure that you have the same list sampling for each test cell; otherwise, your test is invalid. Communication is the key here. What might appear to be the simplest of tests can be botched up if you fail to assure proper list selection, key coding, delivery to a letter shop, and addressing of the proper mailing packages. A list broker can be very helpful here in assuring that everything runs smoothly.

While it is often necessary to test several elements at one time—e.g., lists, creative packages, price, offer, etc.—too many elements can cause misinterpretation.

Be especially sure that within the constraints of the test the lists used have an obvious relation to the product being offered. Look at the list's history. Was it used for similar offers? Is the list large enough to give you sufficient quantities on each test cell? Be sure to select an *N*th name sampling of each list for the test and within the test matrix break that sampling down, again on an *N*th name basis for each of your test cells. Table 16-1 shows how to break down three lists for a testing program.

Within lists A, B, and C in Table 16-1, there are five equal cells of 10,000 names, each a representative sampling of the entire list. Within each test cell, there is a minimum of three lists on which to read response. If one list fails, you have at least two others to evaluate. All tests are read against the control package as a whole and on a list-by-list basis.

TABLE 16-1 Breakdown for a Testing Program

	Number of Names		
	List A	List B	List C
Control			
basic package	10,000	10,000	10,000
Test 1:			
creative package A	10,000	10,000	10,000
Test 2:			
creative package B	10,000	10,000	10,000
Test 3:			
price test	10,000	10,000	10,000
Test 4:			
control with premium	10,000	10,000	10,000

Many factors influence response levels: when you mail, where you mail, what you mail, how you structure your offer, pricing, etc. Correct analysis of your mailing program is key to the success and growth of your business.

ANALYZING RESPONSE

Of course, front-end response is only the beginning of your evaluation. Keep in mind other considerations that should be noted.

1. Timing. There are definite seasonal trends in direct marketing.
2. Be sure that your entire test program was mailed on the same day. Salt your mailing with names and addresses of individuals who can report back to you about when they received the promotion in the mail.
3. Bad weather, a poor economy, a national tragedy, or a holiday can all affect the mood of the buyer. Keep this in mind.

Since we're dealing only with lists in this chapter, let us examine what to look for in evaluating a list's performance. But keep in mind the other factors that must be taken into consideration in the overall evaluation of your entire mailing program.

What's a good response level—1 percent, 2 percent, 4 percent? That depends. As mentioned before, front-end response is only the beginning. The next step is to evaluate the quality of the customer brought in from a specific list. The criteria you yourself establish for that evaluation largely depend on the nature of your business. If you're in the continuity book business, you want someone who will complete the series and perhaps subscribe to a second. If it's the catalog or merchandising business, you want repeat buyers. If it's magazine circulation, you want people who will renew their subscriptions. If it's the credit card business, you want high-volume charge customers who pay their bills on time. I have seen lists pull as much as 14 percent on a credit card solicitation mailing and only approve at 23 percent. The annual revenue contribution from individuals on that list is as little as $18 to $20. At the same time, I have seen lists pull 1.0 to 1.5 percent and approve at 75 to 80 percent, with a revenue contribution per customer of $60 to $70. As you can see, one cannot say that a list that pulls only 1.0 to 1.5 percent is not a good list.

The important thing is to track lists continually on an ongoing basis. A single list's performance is not constant. List owners change and supplement their sources of name acquisition as their marketing efforts grow and as they set new goals for themselves. It is not unlikely to see a list perform extremely well one year and then poorly the next. A distinct combination of both front-end response and back-end performance is the determining factor for a successful list.

Step-Testing and Rollout

You've tested 10,000 names out of a universe of 300,000. The list pulled well, and your next mail date is 2 months away. You'd like to reuse the list. What next? You've hardly had time to track the list's performance. Many marketers who mail frequently often are faced with this problem coupled with the desire to capitalize on the apparent success of a list. If you've not had time to analyze a list adequately, step-test on the next mailing. Step-testing involves mailing another small portion of the list (unduplicated names). This is usually 3 to 5 times your original test quantity, assuming you make the same selection (e.g., sex, geographic skew, creative, offer, etc.) previously made. Remember, the slightest deviation from the criteria previously selected and mailed to throws another variable into the picture. You cannot expect to achieve the same response level if you introduce other variables into the second mail program.

As mentioned before, sophisticated mailers use probability tables into which confidence levels have been built for varying response levels and margins of error. The best advice one can give is to proceed with caution, a reasonable bit of risk, and lots of common sense.

Keep in mind that the data furnished on a list card represent the average of the entire list. There are high and low units of sale. There probably are geographic skews that have distinct purchase patterns. There may be a heavier concentration of low-ticket buyers in a given geographic area or a large incidence of people within a list who initially subscribed to a "low-ticket come-on offer" and did not repurchase. Careful scrutiny of list data cards often will provide interesting insight into a list's makeup.

Don't be afraid to ask questions of your list broker. If that individual can't answer your question, he or she can inquire directly of the list owner to obtain the information you need.

Ordering the List

Selecting the right mailing lists is certainly critical to the ultimate success of your mailing, but ordering them correctly is just as important.

Most often, lists are ordered directly through a list broker. A few individuals order directly from the list owner when such a relationship is established. No matter how you go about it, detail is an important aspect. Work closely with your list broker. Consider that individual part of your marketing team. Often a broker's experience with a mailing list will provide additional insight into possible ways for you to use the list most advantageously.

When ordering, be specific about the selection criteria you want to make: buyers by year, inquiries, geographic selection, unit of sale, hotline names, etc.

Select a test quantity you feel will provide you with a sufficient response for evaluation. Most list owners require a minimum test of 5000 names, but on a large list you may want to test 10,000 names. Discuss this with your broker. Remember, mailing costs add up quickly. One of your key objectives should be to test as broad a range of lists as possible. If you have a fixed budget, large list test quantities limit the number of lists you can test.

Selectivity is important. If you are not limiting your mailing to specific geographic areas or specific ZIP codes and want a typical cross section of a list for test purposes, ask for an *N*th name sample of the entire list. Very simply, if a list contains 100,000 names and a test of 10,000 names is desired, every tenth name should be selected.

Be sure to specify the format in which you want the names furnished—computer tape, cheshire labels, peel-off labels—and whether you want the list key coded when run for you. If you are breaking down a single list into smaller test segments, be sure to assign a separate key code for each segment. Some mailers also code the various components of their mailing packages when printing them to assure proper controls at the letter shop. This helps to assure that all the right components are inserted into the right envelope and that all the right lists are addressed on the right order card.

Key codes can vary from two to several digits, all alpha, all numeric, or a combination of both. Size or length of a key code usually depends on the capacity of the computer field to accept a specific number of digits.

Specify your mail date, and if you eventually find that there may be a problem in meeting it, be sure to advise your list broker. Usually, when placing your initial order, a list owner will guarantee you protection a week before and a week after your mail date from other competitors using the same list. Be sure to indicate also the date by which you would like all lists to arrive at the letter shop or by which all computer tapes should arrive for processing. Peak mailing periods produce tremendous workloads for many mailing houses. Often a longer lead time is necessary to prepare your material for mailing. This all can be worked out with your mailing house before placing your list orders.

It is extremely important to outline specifically the complexity of your mailing program for both your list broker and your letter shop. This can help assure that the proper list with the proper key code will be labeled correctly. Eliminate all guesswork. A simple written document outlining the mail date, the test matrix, the mailing package components, and the lists and their respective key codes and the mailing package to which they are assigned makes things easy for everyone involved.

Even the most complex tests can run smoothly if all the people involved are in communication with one another. Communication is a key word in this business.

Mail-order lists are easily the most refined method of reaching the best possible customer you can hope for. It's a complex but pliable medium, workable and refinable but one of the most important marketing tools you have in today's changing consumer marketplace.

chapter 17

BUSINESS LISTS

Ira Belth

President
Belth Associates, Inc.
East Meadow, N.Y.

INTRODUCTION

Numerically, business lists outnumber consumer lists by almost 4 to 1. According to Standard Rate and Data Service, there are about 40,000 business lists compared with about 10,000 consumer lists. In those 40,000 business listings, there is a considerable degree of duplication of the same source lists itemized more than once. Suffice it to say, however, that there are clearly many more business lists than consumer lists. Also, there are more than twice as many list classifications for business lists as there are for consumer lists.

Naturally, the total consumer market is many times greater than the business market. When you talk about consumers, you're talking about upwards of 70 million households and the lion's share of the population of our country. Talk business, and you're talking about something in the neighborhood of 10 million companies, of which more than 85 percent are considered small companies with under twenty employees. Talk about the business executive marketplace, and you're talking about a universe of something like 20 million individuals.

In terms of business consumption, the comparison with consumer consumption becomes significant because you're involved with an abundance of the big-ticket item. Accordingly, a thorough understanding of the more concentrated business market is of great importance to the business-to-business marketer.

When it comes to direct mail marketing and mailing lists, the first thing to appreciate is that a mailing list is not a mailing list. It's an alignment of carefully selected people to whom you want to sell something. To achieve a high effectiveness quotient, your campaign has to be directed to the individual buyers, specifiers, and influencers. If in fact you're dealing with mailing lists, your energy and investment are being misdirected.

Market identification is the product of internal experience and research, although several service organizations are doing an outstanding job of market identification through model building and input-output data bases. The companion to the marketer's ability to identify the marketplace is the assembly of buying individuals from both internal and external sources.

A first step in determining how to position direct mail and list marketing in your sales strategy is to analyze the size and dimension of your market. If your market is very tight and limited, a direct-response advertising program isn't called for. Some industrial marketers may have a potential market of a dozen companies appropriately reached with other approaches.

Yet numerous case histories of prize-winning direct marketing programs include expensive $25 per unit or more creations directed at a target market of, say, 800 potential clients. If it is so specialized, intensive internal research (including information gathered by the sales force) can identify markets more than an outside list marketing professional can do. But if the market is broad, and if there are aspects the marketer hasn't realized, the joint effort of marketer and objective consultant can uncover paydirt.

Standard Rate and Data Service briefly divided its editions of *Direct Mail List Rates and Data* into separate business and consumer editions, but reverted to the seemingly clumsy single business-consumer edition in the spring of 1983. The business section describes tens of thousands of different mailing lists, and there may be something like an additional 4000 to 5000 that are not officially on the market but may be available under acceptable circumstances.

The point is that there's an incredible reservoir of source material out there. It calls for experienced and intelligent handling to avoid serious errors of commission or omission.

THE USES OF BUSINESS LISTS

Business lists are one of the core ingredients in the total elements of direct marketing as an instrument of greater effectiveness in business and industrial selling. They may be used in a variety of situations.

1. A sales support complex, helping to develop sales effectiveness by providing a source for lead generation, with the ability to establish a considerable degree of prequalification based on known characteristics contained in the list information records.
2. For use in supplemental sales of products and services that don't justify the price of a costly industrial sales call. If the cost of a sales call approaches the $200 per call average, there are many valuable auxiliary services that must be sold in an alternative, cost-efficient manner.
3. Direct sales of universal, broad-scale products and services. The proliferation of office equipment, electronic instruments, calculators, communications equipment, etc., can be consummated without the requirement of sales follow-up by direct marketing to the right target market.

4. A low-cost, direct sales effort or lead generation for the small business person who can't afford a sales force. This could be particularly applicable to marketing with regional boundaries, local rather than national or even covering a wide geographic area.
5. Business-to-business mail order and catalog sales. Over the past decade or so, a breed of successful marketers has emerged who account for a substantial volume of sales activity solely through catalog sales and mail order. This ranges from desk items, stationery, and forms to office furniture and equipment, factory warehouse storage and machinery, and a multitude of other products and services that help a company operate.
6. A clear recognition of the business executive and the professional as an important element in the consumer market. Whether at home or in the office, they are candidates for personal products, seminars, publications, and other services or products that are geared to their own advancement or self-improvement.

In all these instances and for an infinity of job assignments that don't necessarily fit into any of these categories, there are profile characteristics of business lists that coincide with the marketer's objectives.

Understanding the qualities of business lists that most suitably meet the marketer's objectives involves a combination of (1) knowledge of the sources and quality of individual lists or clusters of lists, (2) experience, or a genuine track record that provides clear understanding of what will work effectively and what won't work, and (3) common sense and imagination, which encourage the testing of new ideas, new avenues of investigation, and experimentation to unlock new potential markets.

Detailed evaluations can, of course, go much further. It depends on whether the marketer's objective is to sell an item, generate a lead, or develop an awareness of the company or product. The sales department can expect a better chance for a sale when it follows up a response generated from a highly targeted list.

The clarification of objectives simply means that there may be more list types with different characteristics that may fit the marketer's needs precisely. For instance, for catalog sales, there's a vast reservoir of business mail-order buyers. They read mail, and they buy things: forms, printing, and advertising; furniture and office items; factory products; educational materials, etc. Depending on purpose, there are governing factors that will determine the best kinds of lists.

LIST LEVELS

Establishing a priority sequence of importance for the different levels of the business lists available to the marketer, also known as "seeding," requires appropriate levels of attention, refinement, and cultivation. These basic levels include the following:

1. Top priority: active customer files
2. Middle priority: qualified prospects

3. Lower priority: additional coverage of "suspects" who then can be turned into customers

The different levels of importance denote the fact that a "stand still" attitude always means that there will be erosion at the top level that must be compensated by upgrading of the second level. There will be erosion at the middle level, which must be upgraded from the lower level. There always has to be the ingestion of new blood to maintain the quality of balance and improve the sales position of the company.

Maintaining the level of an internal house list invariably derives from names coming from customarily available sources, such as a combination of these:

- **Customers:** people who currently are buying from you.
- **Former customers:** people who once were active customers and who still may be potential customers.
- **Prospects:** people whom you suspect should become customers.
- **Warranties:** people who have signed warranty cards and returned them as instructed.
- **Advertising inquirers:** respondents to your advertising.
- **Sales force recommendations:** your sales force can secure names from within your assigned territory, using call report systems or direct assignment.
- **Sales records:** these will supply names of companies, addresses, people, titles, and other valuable information.
- **Distributors, jobbers, and wholesalers:** these companies maintain mailing lists of their own and may be persuaded to share these names with you.
- **Technical service people:** their activities may contribute names.
- **Company correspondence:** an active publicity campaign can generate names of people interested in your products.
- **Stockholders:** if you're a publicly held company, stockholder lists may prove valuable.

A key consideration in the structure of the "house" file is that it can be done most comprehensively and accurately at the firm's headquarters. Data accumulated by people in the field can provide you with first hand knowledge. But bring the data in to the central data base so that you can add additional profile information and impose important disciplines and controls that can enhance the file as an effective working tool. You can structure it for effective retrieval and usage that can't be achieved at the local level. Local input is important, but a sharply honed file that captures the total potential market should be achieved centrally, under a clearly defined marketing structure.

TYPES OF LISTS AVAILABLE FOR RENTAL OR PURCHASE FOR UNRESTRICTED USAGE

In terms of the fundamentals of lists, here are several categories. Compiled lists are the product of a group of "data manufacturing" specialists. They may range from the Dun & Bradstreet compilation of "all" American businesses by Standard Industrial Classification or company size, directed to the individual head of the company, to the National Business Lists or Market Data Retrieval compilations of American businesses from the Yellow Page phone books, with their additional input. Also, special compilations from published directories offer widely diverse information.

Publication lists are a by-product of the readership of trade publications. These lists are either paid or controlled circulation and are provided by major publishers such as McGraw-Hill, Penton/IPC, Cahners, Technical, and Chilton or by many other multimagazine or individual magazine publishers.

For most industrial marketing situations, lists from publishers provide the most productive approach. It's fairly obvious. Magazine lists are designed to achieve in-depth coverage of your potentially biggest accounts, and the subscriber profile information is also the most complete relative to other list sources. In order to establish appropriate controlled-circulation acceptability under Business Publications Audit standards, the depth of information logged makes the comprehension and accuracy of the individual's job function and responsibilities the best target market both for the industrial space advertiser and direct mail marketer.

Responder lists consist of mail-order buyers from such as Daytimers, Drawing Board, Eimicke, Fidelity File, National Pen, National Cash Register, and many others or inquiry and reader services from publishers and many others. A company's own inquiry lists can be rich with potential.

Miscellaneous lists are the "everything else" that doesn't fit the standard categories. This could include association membership rosters, custom compilation, or data derived from special sources.

It's all a vast, diversified body of information. It's the world of the compiled lists: Dun & Bradstreet and Standard & Poors; National Business Lists; Hugo Dunhill; Market Development, Market Compilation, and Market Data Retrieval; Ed Burnett and Zeller and Letica; and the other compilers.

It's the world of the trade publishers: McGraw-Hill, *Wall Street Journal*, *Time* and *Newsweek*, Cahners, Penton/IPC, Chilton, Technical, Hitchcock and Hayden, and many other business publications.

It's the world of the associations: American Medical Association, American Dental Association, National Association of Pharmacies, American Bar Association, American Association of Certified Public Accountants, and scores of others.

It's the world of the business mail-order marketers: U.S. Pencil, Revere Chemical, Drawing Board, Daytimers, Eimicke, Grayarc, Fidelity File, and dozens of others.

Even more, it's the world of special lists and special markets, the world of information that defies classification. It's also the world of lists not officially on the market, often available for special programs and special (exchange) arrangements.

PROFILE CHARACTERISTICS OF THE DIFFERENT LIST CATEGORIES

Like consumer lists, business lists can be defined by the qualities of demographics (statistical facts about status of the individual) and psychographics (special insights into the lifestyle interests of the individual). But there is another factor in the profile of the business executive: "ergraphics," which refers to the definition of the executive's job function and importance as a decision maker, influencer, or purchaser based on who he or she is within the company.

The combination of these descriptive qualities can therefore be itemized as follows:

1. Job function, company size, and purchasing interest, particularly as a by-product of trade magazine information
2. Selective coverage of special categories, which is frequently a product of special-interest directory compilation
3. The buying interest and mail responsiveness, especially determinable by mail-order buyer lists
4. Income ranges based on job levels and surveys performed by magazines and their publishers

There's an even greater ability to pinpoint your marketing pitch in the business and industrial lists market as compared with the consumer market. There's more measurable information available.

What are the standards you should apply? What is that cluster of factors that will give you the best chance to win the attention of and motivate the audience that is most likely to buy? There are many factors.

Start with the Standard Industrial Classification (SIC). Depending on how sharply you want to define the industries that are your marketing targets, you can reach companies by two-digit, three-digit, four-digit, or even five-digit SICs. This is simply a matter of taking an industrial classification and giving it a more finite definition.

For all practical purposes relating to company identification, the government has gotten up to four digits. Industrial marketers have gone to five in many cases, giving more precise definition and greater segmentation of four-digit SIC categories. One impetus here is that classifications found in Yellow Page directories are more fully defined than a four-digit SIC.

A good basic guide in helping to define and reach your market is often the size of the target company. A considerable universal in company size determination is number of employees; in most business and industrial lists of quality, this is readily available. A number of lists will provide annual sales volume in dollars. Others will give you a fix on net worth. Oddly, there is no absolute relationship between these factors. A company with a high net worth can achieve this on a relatively small sales volume, and a company with fifteen employees can enjoy $23 million in annual sales. But by and large, you can be much more precise in your market definition by using any or all of these company size criteria.

A valuable factor, though less easy to arrive at when you're dealing with lists coming out of computers, is the kind of markets or activity in which the company is engaged. You've got the SIC and know the company size, but when you've asked for companies engaged in consumer products versus products for industry or when you've asked for products for factories versus products for offices, you've got to dig more deeply and make selections from a variety of sources not readily coded into the record.

Is your offer most suitable to the company headquarters? The factory? A division or subsidiary? If your market is the big company, your message may be wasted at the headquarters office if it really pertains to the functions in the shop in another city which has its own decision-making options. On the other hand, if your prospect is a one-location operation, your mail stands a much better chance of being read and acted on. Thus, it is important to consider both the physical structure and the location of the company you're prospecting.

The key, of course, is job function, or reaching the right person by name or at least by title. But it is the individual rather than the company who is going to buy your product.

Job function and job title aren't simple factors. As a company's position in society and the economy becomes more complex, the functions in the company become much more varied. Nor are function and title the same thing. There are many companies in which the president is also the advertising manager, and the chairperson also may be the chief financial officer. Then you have the vast and undigested job title mass classed as vice president. In many cases, we readily identify what a person is vice president of: marketing, sales, finance, production, international trade, etc. In many cases, we can't. When this occurs, what do we do with those vice presidents who are just coded as vice presidents? To throw them away is wasteful. To identify them more completely requires a lot more science.

Let's look at a couple of magazine lists. Their "bible" is the Business Publications Audit of Circulation (BPA) Buyers Guide.

Material Handling Engineering magazine (Penton/IPC) has a "controlled circulation" of 85,000. It "serves the field of management, engineering and supervision of material handling and packaging including both manufacturing and non-manufacturing industries and businesses using material handling, packaging and shipping equipment and those utilizing warehousing and storage. . . . Qualified recipients are corporate management, engineering, plant and production, purchasing and sales personnel whose responsibilities include material handling and/or industrial packaging machinery and material."

The circulation statement goes on to break down the readership by four-digit SIC, by the size of the company with which the individual is affiliated, and by geography. In terms of the job functional factors, the 85,000 breaks down this way:

- Company management (corporate officials, vice presidents, general managers, owners, and partners): 15,000 = 17.6 percent
- Plant management (plant managers, superintendents, materials, supervisors, general line supervisors, and production managers): 24,000 = 29.4 percent
- Engineering (materials handling engineers, industrial engineers, chief engineers, plant engineers, methods engineers, and packaging engineers): 25,000 = 29.4 percent
- Purchasing (purchasing directors, purchasing agents, and buyers): 6500 = 7.6 percent
- Storage, warehousing, and distribution (physical distribution managers, traffic managers, warehouse managers, storekeepers, and inventory managers): 6000 = 7 percent
- Company copies, sales marketing, and other titled and nontitled personnel: 6000 = 7 percent

Industrial Research magazine (Dun-Donnelley), with a circulation of 95,000, reaches

- 8.3 percent corporate officers
- 8.6 percent of research and development executives
- 48.3 percent of project managers
- 34.2 percent of professional staff members without managerial or supervisory authority
- A few technical purchasing agents and libraries

Plastics Machinery and Equipment (Industry Media) has a circulation of $25,000, consisting of

- 25.3 percent of general and corporate management
- 40.6 percent of production and manufacturing engineers (including management)
- 11 percent of research and development engineers
- 12 percent of designers and design engineers
- 5.5 percent of purchasers
- 3.1 percent of sales and marketing personnel
- 2.3 percent of other qualified personnel

The price goes up dramatically, but several trade publications offer the possibility of purchasing influence by specific product or plant function. Cleworth Publishing (*Transmission and Distribution* magazine), for example, offers product specification for "substations, overhead transmission, overhead distribution, underground distribution, system protection, communication and control, transportation, mechanized construction, etc."

In addition to BPA guides, most publishers produce media comparability reports "to assist advertisers and agencies in their media analysis of business and professional magazines by helping publishers to present pertinent information in a concise and orderly manner." This net effect is to provide details of some twenty-eight categories of support data, including "passalong" studies and other available services, such as list rental, card-pack mailings, etc.

THE BUSINESS LIST SERVICE STRUCTURE

The mailing list industry consists of compilers, managers, and brokers. It also includes list owners—publishers or marketers—who manage and merchandise their own properties.

In trade definitions each specialty is clearly recognizable, but in reality there is frequent spillover among specialties. Compilers broker, brokers manage, and managers compile, and certain degrees of competence and experience give some practitioners an edge over others.

By and large, list brokers tend to have greater objectivity because they are less product-oriented. Dealing with them tends to have additional value for a client because like an agency or media rep in other areas, brokers are paid by the list owner rather than by the client. Thus, the price to the customer remains the same whether the customer buys or rents from the owner directly or through a broker.

There is, however, another qualifier to this declaration of objectivity. By and large, leading brokers have to deal with large quantities to make the assignment worth their while. If you're marketing an office copier or an engineering desk calculator to a wide-ranging audience, the broker will be eager to handle this for you. If, however, you're dealing with a highly selective target market that involves a lot of research and time but small numbers, for most brokers it just doesn't pay.

Up to this point we've presented a description of the three basic categories of business lists: compiled lists, publication lists, and mail-order buyer lists. In terms of use, there are no easy answers as to how and when to employ a particular list or a particular combination of lists. The list marketing function for the business and industrial marketer cautions you never to take anything for granted or oversimplify. If you're selling pecans in the consumer markets, try to get approvals from pecan buyers or epicurean food buyers. Don't go too far away from that, because almost invariably the slightly remote lists will produce substandard results.

But when you're dealing with a business and industrial lead generation factor, you need special insights. You need an understanding of complex marketing factors, and you need an open-mindedness that doesn't insist that you try only compiled lists versus mail-order buyer lists. The demographics, psychographics, and ergraphics have to mesh with your marketing requirements.

In terms of service, the answer isn't necessarily the descriptive category of the supplier. The supplier could be a consultant, an advertising agency, a compiler, a broker, or a combination of these, but he or she must be able to provide superior service based on interest, experience, and knowledge.

SOURCE MATERIAL

Plying one's trade in the area of business lists involves collecting and having available a wide diversity of source material. Even so, one invariably has to cope with the haunting thought that it's never enough, that it's difficult to keep it under such control that it's properly accessible, and that new technology, information retrieval, and information data banks are developing that will streamline the entire craft.

Basic source material consists of most of the following elements:

1. Acquisition, perusal, and retention of books, directories, and publications that are pertinent to the world of business lists and will expand the practitioner's knowledge of the business
2. Standard Rate and Data editions, especially in the area of direct marketing and business publications
3. Bureau of Publication Audits information on the world of trade publications including media comparability reports for additional insights into individual publication information
4. Mailing list standard information: data cards, catalogs, mailing list circulars

and descriptions, trade magazine advertising, and all conceivable information from list owners and managers

5. Directories (from Gale's or B. Klein), attendee records (from trade shows and seminars), trade association rosters, phone books, government records, and clipping services
6. Marketing reports and information: Dun & Bradstreet business studies; government reports such as Country Business Patterns; Sales and Marketing Management Annual Industry Surveys; Direct Marketing Association publications and meetings, especially from its Business-to-Business Council; and trade publications and professional marketing books from the American Management Association and other business and industrial publishers.

If it sounds as if we've gone far beyond the source material needed for business lists marketing, we're simply trying to emphasize that the people on the lists to whom you are trying to market require a background knowledge of circumstances and conditions that transcend the name itself.

Simply to reemphasize the sources for list building and list development, here are a few points that were contained in Ed Mayer's *The Handbook of Industrial Direct Mail Advertising*.

BUILDING THE MAILING LIST: WHERE TO START

When you're ready to build your mailing lists, you will have these alternatives:

1. You may compile your own list from internal company records or from external printed sources.
2. You may seek outside supplier sources to compile to your specifications from internal company records or from external printed sources.
3. You may search for a supplier who already has compiled a mailing list approximating your specifications and who has placed it in inventory, anticipating requests either for rental or for outright purchase.

Should you develop or maintain your own mailing list, or should you buy or rent from outside supplier sources? There is no ready answer. Individual circumstances will dictate your direction. It is, however, important to note that outside lists are available from a variety of supplier companies and that there will be occasions when you will find it more efficient to rent or buy than to compile.

Generally available external printed sources include the following:

- **Directories:** Directories in general distribution usually include company names, addresses, and often personnel. They are reported by industry, market, state, or community, and they are classified by size of company or by products sold.
- **Trade show registrants:** By exhibiting at trade shows, you can compile a list of names of people who approached your exhibit.
- **Attendance rosters:** These rosters contain the names of persons attending a convention, meeting, or show within your market.

- **Telephone directories:** Telephone directories are available for any city, and they identify companies by class of products made and/or sold.
- **Credit rating books:** Such rating books identify companies by types of products sold.
- **Clipping services:** Magazine and newspaper clipping services will supply a steady flow of names in almost any category.
- **Government reports:** Government departments print and distribute directories, as do city and local governments. Often original data can be compiled from the existing government records for activities requiring licensing, registration, or permits.

JUDGMENT CRITERIA FOR BUSINESS LISTS

The bottom line is an overworked cliche. Its survival, however, is guaranteed because it's almost impossible to find a more pertinent expression. In regard to business lists, the bottom line is how well they work: the response generated, the quality of the leads generated, and the conversion factor of turning the responses into customers.

The final consideration invariably has to be how the list use and direct marketing effort have helped improve the sales picture.

Direct-response list use should follow the logical sequence of sales effectiveness. A direct sales call is best, a telephone call comes second, a personalized letter comes next, and a nonpersonal direct mail piece comes last. An individual name, accordingly, has greater attention-getting and response-evoking possibilities than a title only. But you'll no doubt find exceptions to the rule.

Proper attention to direct mail as part of your media mix and building a data base for your total market can surely be a "best bet" in your sales effort.

1. It helps you reach all companies in your target market, going beyond the normal scope of the trade publication.
2. It takes you into the offices of all your key individuals: the buyers, influencers, and decision makers of the companies that are responsible for the bulk of productivity in your market.
3. It gives you the ability to segment by company size, type of products produced, job functions, and responsibilities of individuals.
4. You have the opportunity to adjust your offer and copy approach to fit each market segment, and you can strike a particularly responsive chord by introducing personalization that can be directed to the individual characteristics of the individual prospect.
5. It offers you the options of combining direct mail with telephone marketing and of enriching your file with customer and prospect information that is fed back into it by the sales department.
6. It gives you the ability to "dealerize" your file and direct marketing efforts, providing a planned program that is tuned into the region, district, or individual sales representative. And it makes it possible to produce "availability" information to the sales organization.

Sales people, distributors, and dealers are in an ideal position to do a complete checking job for you. But the field representative will not voluntarily send you changes. The representative is not in the list-checking business, and it takes more than an occasional note from the home office to make the representative aware of its importance.

One large industrial advertiser uses a series of monthly bulletins, suitably illustrated in cartoon style. It explains to the person on the firing line the importance of accurate lists. These bulletins are prepared to show how much the salesperson loses if names are inaccurate. They tell of sales that were lost because a prospect didn't receive a catalog and of catalogs that were addressed inappropriately.

Another company runs semiannual contests, giving prizes to field representatives for the most accurate and the largest number of new names added to the territory list. Here too, the light touch is evident in the material used. But the copy is hard-hitting and pounds home the value to the salesperson of keeping his or her part of the list up to date.

Several industrial advertisers have found that they can build an excellent list and keep it up to date by paying sales people as much as $0.25 for each new name added to their lists. In addition to payment for new names, there are a few instances in which (as in the contest idea outlined above) a cash payment is made to each salesperson based on the annual overall accuracy of his or her particular group of names.

All the bulletins, light or heavy, all the contests, and even the payment plan will be almost completely valueless unless you give your representatives a simple form to use for mailing list changes. Make it as simple as possible, small enough to fit in a pocket yet containing all pertinent information. See Figure 17-1 for a sample of one you may use or adapt.

The judgment factor can't be oversimplified. Responses are important, but a good quantitative response doesn't tell the story. The responses may have a low percentage of qualification and a poor conversion factor. There have been numerous instances in which responses hit four times the anticipated volume. But the leads were almost entirely worthless; they were responses from the wrong people.

Thus, judgment is a matter of the bottom-line conversion of responses to sales. And sales is a matter of front-end–back-end consideration. How much did it cost to close a sale, and of what volume? More important, what is the anticipated value of the new customer in terms of customer life cycle?

In dealing with consumer mailing lists, you can test numerous lists. Those which bring a satisfactory response can be rolled out. Those which don't can be dropped. When it comes to business lists, the story is different when you know you have a particular market to penetrate (SICs or other market characteristics) and particular people to reach. If one effort fails and you know that your market is there anyway, you have to keep up the effort until you hit the "hot button."

In terms of judgment, you know that your customer and "inside" prospect lists have particular value. But you can't stop until you've covered your total potential market from compiled lists, publication lists, and mail-order buyer lists. You have to set up controls and make determinations about the scoring from each possible

Sales Report Mailing List Changes

Customer ☐ Company ID No. ______
Prospect ☐ (If Known)

Company ____________________

Street ____________________

City ____________ State ______ Zip ______

Add: Name ____________ Title ____________

Add: Name ____________ Title ____________

Remove: Name ____________ Title ____________

Remove: Name ____________ Title ____________

Change ____________ To ____________
Name Title Name Title

Change ____________ To ____________
Name Title Name Title

Source: Sales Representative's Name Territorial Code Date of Information

Figure 17-1 An example of a simple form which can be used to record mailing list changes.

market segment. All of it requires a heavy dose of ingenuity, meeting challenges that can be much more complex and sophisticated than the consumer marketing bottom line.

NEW DEVELOPMENTS: THE MASTER FILE

Without getting hung up on semantics, the most complete development area in business lists has involved the arrival of the science of the data base, or master file. Probably "master file" is a more accurate description, because "data base" means an on-line system that provides immediate access and has the means of adding, changing, or withdrawing information on a daily or continuous basis. "Master file" means a combining and refining of different list ingredients into a new composite.

One major virtue of master file is that it eliminates the necessity of unduplicating different files every time they're used. Also, by combining elements from different sources, the master file offers ingredients, segments, and selections that aren't possible from a single file only. A master file is symbiotic. It puts different factors together and adds an overriding new dimension because the various elements create a new chemistry.

A significant master file development over the past decade has been the master files from most of the major trade magazine publishers. McGraw-Hill created the Business Leaders master file. It embodies most of their publications, including *Business Week*, and McGraw-Hill offers in-depth selections of executives At Office and At Home. Penton/IPC has its Management Millions master file. This captures the input from every one of the Penton/IPC publications and penetrates very deeply into the manufacturing industries. Master files also have emerged from Cahners, Hitchcock, Technical, Chilton, Thomas, and Hayden.

This trend of developing the master file also has extended into the area of building customized master files for individual client use. One pioneering example is that of American Management Associations (AMA). Some years ago, AMA realized that their 100 million annual mailing rate was steeped in outmoded technology. They would order labels from a diversity of lists and handle these clusters of labels for each individual seminar program. The duplication factor was enormous.

Finally, AMA marketing executives realized that they could accomplish great economy and efficiency as well as prompt delivery if they made arrangements with all list owners who supplied them with lists to commit these lists into the AMA master file. Payment is made on the basis of use, duplication is vastly reduced, and all the other improved procedures are achieved. Accordingly, the customized data base for a major mailer shows significant value. Following the AMA example, Penton Learning Systems built its own customized data base. Merrill Lynch periodically updates and operates with its own customized data base.

In the area of the master file for business mail-order buyers, a useful development has come from Direct Media, a service organization that has become dominant in this specialized area. By merging several dozen lists from catalog and mail-order merchandisers, Direct Media conceived the idea of adding additional source coding to each of the lists, showing the multiple factors for each individual buyer. When one mailer rents the names from a series of other mailers with proper approval and the runs are made, duplications are eliminated automatically because of the multicoding system, and the "net-name" principle is readily attained. Although the Direct Media mail-order buyer file is not strictly a data base or master file, it employs this concept to achieve greater efficiency.

Further into the master file development, during the past year or two, a new concept has begun to appear in regard to "general" master files. Direct Media started a broad-range executive name data base, but this is generally confined to use by the participants. Recently, Mal Dunn Associates has begun a business executive data base that aims at including approximately 11 million executives, using an overlay of the compiled business files of Market Data Retrieval and National Business Lists. Another Executive master file in development is that of Market Data Retrieval, the American Executives Registry. Another master file has been developed by two former AMA executives under the trade style List Technology.

While the general master file has a long way to go and a lot of technology to conquer, this general trend will have considerable value, especially for the marketer who wants to penetrate regional markets in depth. Previously, quantities in limited markets were too small to justify economic use of executive name files. Master files will improve this situation. And for larger mailers, the ability to select by SIC, job function, management level, and other selection characteristics will offer many additional advantages.

MISCELLANY: A DIVERSITY OF QUESTIONS AND ANSWERS

The technology in business-to-business marketing and business and industrial lists has made enormous strides over the past decade. Yet new developments are available to meet new challenges. All of this is reflective of the new dynamics of doing business.

Keeping Up with Job Functions

The modern corporate complex has assumed responsibilities that call for many more job functions than ever before: safety, security, environmental affairs, community relations, personnel administration, training, human resources, pension fund management, product management, transportation, traffic, special procurement programs, information management, communications, and efficiency. And that isn't all: legal, real estate affairs, compensation, research and development, data processing and management information system (MIS), distribution, energy management, waste and pollution, etc.

Compilers are able to supply entry to many of these specialties from special trade association and job function association directories. Publications increasingly develop controlled-circulation information based on horizontal publications in particular. Magazines such as *Industrial Marketing, Datamation, Purchasing, Modern Material Handling, Occupational Hazards, Administrative Management, Security Management*, and many others cut across broad SIC lines to reach the interest specialist. In almost all cases, these special interests can be reached at the corporate management level, the specialist management level, and the specialist staff level.

Name versus Title

People never tire of asking the question, What's better, a name or a title? Mailing lists will never be perfect. Job mobility being what it is, there is always a percentage of error even with the most actively updated lists. Compilers who don't have access to the individual by name will proclaim that the use of the title only works better, and some have done surveys to prove the point. Users of publication lists that are aimed at the particular functionary by name can prove that they are right. In the final analysis, common sense will give you the right answer. If you can reach the person in the particular job you want to reach by the individual name and that person is still on the job, you can't beat that. If you don't have a name, use a title; it certainly stands a chance. If there is a certain amount of error in terms of the name, the successor could still receive the piece of mail and could respond.

The Business Executive and Professional as Consumer

Add up the number of business executives and professionals in the marketplace, and you have a very large, very upscale consumer market. List owners reap sizable benefits from this fact. If you want to reach the businessperson or professional at home, that will generally work better for the consumer product. But even so, personal mail at the office may produce satisfactory results.

Major publishers reach the business and professional markets at the home address, primarily because subscribers prefer to get the magazine at home. McGraw-Hill's business leaders list has a strong element of executives at home, and this derives principally from *Business Week* readers. Hayden Publishing recently logged in a master file of its computer executives at home. Other general business publications supply this information (usually readership at home is 70 percent or more). These include *Wall Street Journal, U.S. News, Forbes, Dun's Business Month, Fortune, Industry Week, Nation's Business*, and *Venture*.

On a somewhat random basis, certain compilers are able to produce lists of professionals at home: doctors, dentists, lawyers, architects, engineers, accountants, and others. For certain promotions of a consumer nature, "at home" lists will outperform "at office" lists, even though the coverage may be somewhat randomized.

A High Score: The Personalized Letter

One traditional fact of life that hasn't changed very much over the years is the "personalized" letter as an effective means of communication from one business executive to another. The more the letter looks as if it were dictated by the sender to a secretary and then typed by the secretary and addressed in typical letter fashion to an individual name, title, name of company, street address, city, state, ZIP, and proper salutation, the better chance your direct marketing effort has of being received and read. A business letter with all those ingredients is the primary way of communicating with your prospective business customer.

Naturally, there are problems. Many compiled lists contain no individual names, Others are undisciplined to the requirements of proper form. For example, Harold L. Eskenazi Company may appear as Eskenazi, Harold L. Company. But another company whose name is Eskenazi, Faulhaber Company will appear as the Faulhaber, Eskenazi Company. But the greatest area of confusion comes from trade publications lists in which the name of the executive and an abbreviated and undecipherable title appear in the same "field" in the computer record. These records, after all, are simply for the purpose of generating a label that gets affixed to the magazine. As long as it makes the magazine deliverable, it's all right. But that same record will not provide the input for a good individualized letter, and this is the area in which new technology and new disciplines are needed to keep up with the best way to market your idea.

In many cases, the best business lists are by-products of other primary functions. From magazines, the primary business is the magazine and the advertising in the magazine. In the case of Dun's Marketing, the list is a by-product of the credit service. In the case of Yellow Pages compilation, the compilers have to reformat to meet the requirements of direct mail needs. But here there's a lot missing, and the same is true of trade directory and association roster compilation.

Keeping Lists Up to Date

An up-to-date list can figure significantly in the mathematics of direct mail results. Basic business lists are updated daily as new Yellow Pages appear. This in effect means that the update is annual; that is, each individual record is updated once a year. Basically, such lists will produce a 95 percent rate of deliverability. Directory compilations are updated on the basis of the publication schedule of the directory, usually on an annual basis but sometimes every 2 or even 3 years. In all cases, accuracy also depends on the accuracy of the source information. When a phone directory appears in print, there's already a percentage of inaccuracy. This factor is even higher in a trade or association directory.

Mail-order buyer lists have a high degree of accuracy because part of normal business is maintaining accurate information about the customers. In the case of less active or inactive customers, the nondeliverability percentage mounts, which is why it's important to deal with hotlines and recent "actives."

Publication lists resurvey their readership periodically in order to qualify and update their BPA and ABP reports. Individual name updating is done daily, when change information is supplied. There is always some degree of inaccuracy when Jones takes over Smith's job and is too lazy to send in a change for his receipt of a business magazine which is still addressed to Smith (who's no longer there) but is delivered to Jones. Publication lists, however, justifiably declare a high degree of deliverability.

The "inside" house list, of course, requires a great deal of nutrition. There are several things that must be done to keep your list up to date. The most vital is that you check and clean it constantly. Every one of the suggestions that follows is worthwhile, but unless you work on your list literally all the time, you'll never reach anything like a state of reasonable accuracy.

It's important that one person in your organization be made responsible for the upkeep of the list because no successful list can exist that isn't checked and cleaned at least twice a year. Pick an intelligent member of your organization who is particularly good on small details to take care of this for you. Then, before making a single move, be sure to set aside sufficient money to check the list twice a year and make the corrections you're lucky enough to find.

Keep in mind that outside organizations (list houses or letter shops) provide an excellent list correction service. You may save money by working with such a company in your locality.

When you add new names or correct old ones, be sure to put the date on your list card. You'll have to decide how long a name should be kept on the list, and without an original date to guide you, you'll be completely in the dark.

Many successful industrial direct mailers believe a name should be discarded if there's been no response after 2 years; others recommend 3 to 5 years. However, all agree that names should be dropped after some specific period and added again only if they appear in some new and dependable list source.

The post office offers two services for list owners that are both underused and overrated.

Return Requested Service. One economical way of cleaning your list is to print "return postage guaranteed" below your name and address in the upper left-hand corner of the face of the envelope. In this way, all undeliverable third or fourth class mail will be returned to you marked "undeliverable as addressed." Mail so returned will be charged for at the regular third or fourth class rate, whichever is applicable. However, the reason why the piece is undeliverable as addressed will not be shown on the piece, which also will not show the address.

Address Correction Service. The second service offered by the post office enables the mailer to obtain the addressee's new address or the reason why the mailing piece is undeliverable. Printing the inscription "address correction requested" on the mail will constitute a guarantee on your part to pay the charge of notice or return postage due in the event it is necessary to return the mail as undeliverable. Mail matter so returned will be charged for at the regular third or fourth class rate, whichever is applicable.

The post office then will pass along the knowledge they have about the name. If an individual has left the company's employ, generally the company itself will give the carrier any further information it possesses to send along to you.

But remember, you can get only what the carrier has or can gather gratuitously. Correct titles and spelling are usually out the question, and you're probably not going to get more than the right company and the right address.

However, it will be well worth your while to check with your postmaster for complete information and instructions about the address correction service. The service you will get won't be perfect, but it certainly is worth using for the small sum it costs.

The Importance of Touching All the Bases

Why use direct mail when you can reach the same audience at a lower cost through publications? One reason is that a multimedia approach to generating leads is better than a single-medium approach. Also, you can attain greater selectivity by mailing to portions of publishers' lists. "Purchasing" and "plant operation" may be where your action is, while "administration and management" is secondary. Third, the one-on-one effectiveness of direct mail may be particularly effective for generating leads for sales follow-up.

But the virtues of publication lists do not knock compiled or response lists out of consideration. Smaller customers reached poorly or not at all by publications may account for a significant portion of your potential business.

Sometimes the only way to reach an industry across the board or to uncover a special market is to work out a balanced list marketing pattern using a variety of sources.

MAILING LISTS AND DIRECT MAIL AS PART OF THE TOTAL SALES ACTIVITY

Mention direct mail to an industrial marketer, and the likely comment is, "Huh?" Talk to that marketer about information to improve sales, and the marketer's interest will be aroused.

In industrial marketing, language is important. It has to be understood and positioned correctly in terms of the marketer's ultimate objectives. If you try to mix direct mail apples with industrial marketing pears, you'll get nowhere. If it's in context and holistic, it's meaningful.

Let's look at some words.

- **Dealerization:** a combination of information and prospect names related to the sales organizational cell, be that a dealer, an internal sales territory or region, the geography covered by a manufacturers' representative, or any sales element.
- **Mailing list:** a prospect and customer list that can provide sales information for the "dealer" cell; incidentally, a mailing list to generate leads.
- **Direct mail:** a medium for generating sales leads, preferably prequalified ones. It's a door opener, not a sales closer. And in terms of lead quality, it may or may not outperform trade magazine coupons, bind-in cards, card-pack mailings, white mail, or telephone response.

Let's take a look at dealerization in depth. Structured and executed correctly, it can be a core element in any company's successful sales program. It's certainly an integral element in a total marketing plan.

The information system starts with the use of baseline experience which defines the location and characteristics of the market. This can mean an understanding of your present customers, additional market research that defines your actual or potential market, or even "gut feel" which is the product of your own experience.

Using this information by translating it into such definable criteria as type of business (SIC), size of company, and job function of the buying influence makes it possible for you to extend your knowledge of your market from the known to the unknown, from the customer base to the targeted prospect market.

Dealerization is not an abstraction. Most business-to-business marketers with a sales force use it to achieve cost efficiency and maximum results in their sales efforts. NCR has several hundred offices and an elaborate dealerization program that is aimed at particular industries and individual geographic territories. Reports and cards are provided to managers and sales reps. Their elaborate direct mail program, in support of other media, generates leads which are fed into the sales organization with discipline and control.

Companies in all industries can tell dealerization stories. In banking, Long Island Trust generates a business marketing program for each of its branch managers, providing them with detailed information about the businesses located in their particular market. Many other banks do the same. Chase Manhattan won a DMA Gold Medal for its branch "dealer" program.

Federal Express tags its customer file with all the available profile information (SIC, annual sales dollars, number of employees, etc.). This information is captured in a report, and the profile information is extended from customers to prospects who have similar characteristics.

Internally generated information regarding your customers is most important. This can come from your sales force, from telephone or mail surveys, or from other data generated by your sales activities. For greater uniformity in those typical definitions of the market (SIC, company size, etc.) and for an analysis of your market penetration, this should be supplemented by a matching computer run from one or another of the basic business files. These include the compilations available from

- Dun's Marketing Services' DMI file
- National Business Lists' compiled business file
- Market Data Retrieval

These files give you a means of matching your customers to a body of "profile" information. This includes these basic characteristics of a business (to varying degrees): SIC, employee counts, annual sales, net worth, headquarters or branch, and telephone number. There are qualifers, of course. The match run's success depends on the discipline of your records versus the structure of the file record in the compiled file. Thus, you may attain only a percentage of match. The amount of information in the compiled file may vary by category.

There is a significant cost differential between the different systems. Specifically, Dun & Bradstreet (D&B) has a greater depth of information about individual companies, at a much higher cost. The NBL and MDR information is not as complete, but the cost is less, and these two also capture more companies, especially in retail and service SICs, than does D&B.

Once you've enriched your file with the basic qualifiers, you're ready for several important steps that can move you into an advanced stage of marketing dynamics.

By programming Census Bureau and Survey of Industrial Purchasing Power information into the computer, you can establish statistically what your share of market is by SIC and within each geographic unit of your sales organization.

For a highly sophisticated service in this critical marketing area, an organization called Information Management Group (IMG) has a remarkable data base of information and an unusual capability to develop this information. Economic Information Systems (EIS) is another research group specializing in market identification. EIS statistics reflecting the 223,000 large companies in its data base show that the largest 200 companies account for 34 percent of accumulated sales volume, the largest 2000 account for 61 percent, and the largest 50,000 account for 87 percent.

You then can generate statistical "availability" reports to conform with the exact geographic structure of your sales organization. This availability information will tell you what the untapped market consists of by territory. It will enable you to make adjustments in your sales coverage.

The availability reports then can lead to the ordering of prospect names to be used for direct mail promotion, direct sales calls, or a combination of sales effort factors.

This prospect potential can be enriched by ordering and merging additional lists that will supplement your basic files. This will provide a broader base of information and an enhanced mix of names that can magnify the quality and responsiveness of your sales support and selling effort significantly.

An effective dealerization program can improve your marketing effort and give better direction to your sales energy. It will make you smarter than your competition, improve the quality of each sales call, and fine-tune the direction and precision of your direct mail. It will even help you make better media judgments for your journal advertising by providing you with better intelligence on the precise location of your markets.

Of course, that's a mouthful of claims. But it's based on logic, since more and better marketing information, marshaled more professionally, has to generate more productive sales. It's based on the fact that many sophisticated marketers have been using dealerization programs extensively for years. I've mentioned a few, but there are many more: Bell Telephone, Armco Steel, A. B. Dick, Connecticut Mutual Life, Ennis Business Forms, IBM, Honeywell, GE, Pepsi Cola, etc.

It is significant that Dun's Marketing Services and National Business Lists both attest to the fact that their revenue derives almost as much from generating marketing information—dealerization data—as it does from generating names for direct mail programs.

What provides new horizons is something comparatively few marketers have cashed in on: the mix, or the blending of base files with the more responsive individual names from magazine subscriber lists. A comprehensive merged file in a classic mold can tell you how to reach the precise buying individual and then add to your reach with that segment of the market covered sparsely or not at all by the trade magazines. It fills the gaps, giving you total market coverage.

Industrial marketers must comprehend that a sales information system linked to the strategic support of a direct marketing program will always improve sales performance. Mailing lists are basically information that can help you reach your marketing objectives.

chapter 18

LIST PROCESSING

Arthur Blumenfield

President
Blumenfield Marketing Inc.
Stamford, Conn.

In the early days of direct marketing, a "mailing list" was precisely that—a group of names and addresses, usually in sequence by city name within state, kept on Addressograph® plates, Scriptomatic® stencils, or "33-up labels" which could be used only to send out additional mailings on a nonselective basis to the individuals or organizations it contained.

The computer has changed all that. We no longer speak of mailing lists. Instead, this information is now referred to as a data base. This change in terminology reflects the enormous difference that the computer has made in the ways in which such information can be used. However, in order to get the maximum value out of a list, attention must be paid to the data that are captured, the way the data are maintained, and the way they are used.

As computers and their storage media have become less expensive, many things which were uneconomical in the past are now practical. Specifically, the costs of maintaining large amounts of data about each entry on a list are not as prohibitive as they once were. Nevertheless, one still should evaluate the amount of storage required to keep each piece of information with respect to its potential value.

As computers and their software have matured, the applications available to direct marketers have expanded. Therefore, when defining the way in which a list will be built and maintained, one should consider not only the immediate applications that it will support but also those for which it may be used in the future.

TAPE VERSUS DISK

Currently, the most practical way to transfer all or parts of a list to another computer is to output it on magnetic tape. While it is technically possible to transfer the data from machine to machine over the phone, the costs of such transfers generally make this economically unfeasible.

The choice of whether to maintain your list on disk rather than on magnetic tape depends on the type and size of computer equipment being used and the frequency of use of the data.

Maintaining a list on magnetic tape is referred to as off-line storage. The data are not available to the computer except when the tape is mounted on the machine. This is the least costly method of data storage, and it minimizes the amount of disk storage space that the computer system must have.

If your operations are such that you enter the data once and then use the data infrequently (perhaps no more than a few times each week), keeping the file off-line is practical. In such cases, updating of the file is accomplished by accumulating a "batch" of input data (additions, deletions, and changes) and periodically applying these to the file. The computer "reads" the old file and the batch of input data simultaneously, combines them, and writes out a new, updated file.

It should be noted that this updating process requires that the entire file be copied no matter how many or how few additions or changes are made. Generally, most organizations perform such file updates monthly or quarterly.

Assuming that sufficient computer hardware is available, a list can also be maintained on disk storage units which are left attached to the machine. This is referred to as on-line storage.

Having the data available to the machine at all times permits you to do a number of things that off-line storage does not. For example, new entries can be looked up to see whether they already exist on the file; if so, the existing records can be updated to reflect the additional data that a new entry represents. This same look-up capability can be used to display or print out the details contained in a customer's records, providing a means for supporting customer service activities.

The list is updated instantly with the entry of data. As a result, any new records are in the file as soon as they are input; deletions are removed promptly, and changes of address are put into effect when they are received. In addition, the system can inform the operators if they have not properly identified a record to be deleted or changed instantly. In the case of off-line operations, such mismatches are printed out as "exception reports" which then must be investigated, fixed, and reprocessed.

Records kept on a magnetic tape can be read only serially (from start to finish), whereas those kept on disk can be accessed randomly. Therefore, if a small number of records must be retrieved, as would be the case if a selection from the file was being made, it is usually unnecessary to read the entire file; the desired records often can be accessed and copied out directly. This can reduce processing time considerably.

DATA ENTRY

When you are entering name and address data, certain steps should be taken to minimize error and maximize deliverability. Of these data, the single most important piece is the ZIP code. Typos or other small mistakes in most other parts of a name or address rarely will affect the deliverability of a piece. However, an error in the ZIP code usually will result in a nondeliverable piece.

Depending on the volume of data to be entered, the size of the computer being used, etc., a number of different ZIP verification techniques can be used. The least costly in terms of computer overhead is one which simply verifies that the ZIP falls within the range of ZIPs for the given state. This technique requires that the standard USPS state abbreviation be used.

If the system can support it, a table can be generated and maintained containing the city, state, and ZIP name for each ZIP code entered. The operators would not enter the city or state, just the ZIP. The computer then would look up the ZIP in the table and display the city and state name for the operator to verify. If the data displayed were wrong, the operator would change it, thereby updating the table at the same time. If there was no entry for that ZIP code in the table, the operator would enter the city and state, which then would update the table. This technique provides extremely accurate results and also reduces data entry time by 10 to 15 percent by eliminating the keying of city and state.

The next critical piece of data in a name and address is the address line. Unfortunately, because of the free-form nature of these data, no effective editing techniques other than visual verification are available. However, to facilitate numerous other tasks for which the data will be used, a series of editing standards should be applied to these data as well as to the remaining parts of the name and address. The Direct Marketing Association (DMA) has a publication titled *Standards for Computerized Mailing Lists* which outlines many of these editing guidelines.

When entering the names of individuals, it is most practical to capture separately the prefix (Mr., Mrs., Ms., Miss, etc.), the first name or initials, the last name, and the suffix (Jr., II, MD, CLU, etc.). This will facilitate the creation of the salutation line on letters and will avoid sending out letters addressed to "Dear A. Jones" or "Dear Mr. Jones, Jr."

A factor that should be considered is whether to enter and maintain the data in all upper case or upper and lower case form. There are computer techniques which permit the conversion of name and address data from all upper case to upper and lower, but these are not 100 percent accurate. In the case of company names, they make a lot of mistakes. For example, TWA comes out Twa, IBM becomes Ibm, etc. If you have to do such a conversion, one common technique is to avoid converting the company name line. The resulting address has the name, street address, city, state, and ZIP lines in upper and lower case and the company name in all caps.

The advantage of entering the data in upper and lower case is that the resulting address is portrayed accurately and requires no further conversion. When printed on envelopes or labels, the address looks more "personal" since it more closely resembles a hand-typed document. When printed as a salutation on letters, anything other than upper and lower case generally brands the letter as machine-generated and may affect its performance.

The disadvantage of entering data in upper and lower case is that it is somewhat slower than entering all upper case, thereby increasing data entry costs.

It is generally advantageous to capture a number of additional pieces of information at data entry time in order to provide for the selective reuse of the data. Among the other pieces of information which are most commonly utilized are the following:

Date entered
Source code
Amount of sale
Merchandise ordered (either by category or by item)
Standard Industrial Classification (SIC) in the case of an organization

On subsequent orders from the same individual, these data can be used to update various data fields in the record in order to provide the following information:

Date of first order
Original source code
Date of most recent order
Amount of most recent order
Date of largest order
Amount of largest order
Number of orders to date
Total purchases amount to date

SELECTIONS

The most fundamental use for a list is to serve as a source of names and addresses for future mailings. However, if you take advantage of the information that is contained in the list, it is both possible and practical to do such mailings selectively.

For years, the standard selection criteria used by direct marketers were recency, frequency, and dollars. These still apply.

If you select the date of last purchase or the date when the record was added to the file, a list can be broken down into several different segments. For example, different key codes can be assigned to individuals who have not purchased within 6 months, 12 months, 18 months, etc. By analyzing the response rates to these different key codes, you can tell when to stop mailing to an individual.

Frequency (the number of purchases or responses to date or the average number of purchases or responses per year) can be used similarly to break down a list. When you determine which segments respond sufficiently, those segments of a list which would not yield a profitable response can be eliminated from a mailing.

The total dollars figure or the average dollars per order or per year can enter into the selection process as well. Special mailings can be directed to individuals who your testing indicates are worthwhile to mail to. When combined with recency and frequency, this selection process can be extremely efficient in targeting your most profitable customers and as a result can give you a small but highly responsive core to whom you can profitably mail very frequently.

In addition to these standard selection criteria, a computerized data base can provide you with the ability to select customers who have responded to a specific promotion or through a specific medium (direct mail, ads in certain magazines, freestanding stuffers, package inserts, etc.).

Selections also can be made on the basis of the specific item or items purchased or the type (category) of merchandise purchased. This permits you to offer adjunct products or parts, service, etc., to purchasers of certain items or to identify individuals who have indicated specific interests for special mailings of catalogs or promotions containing items related to those previously purchased.

If applicable, the method of payment utilized by the purchaser (check, credit card, COD, etc.) also can be used for selection purposes, and special promotions which are aimed at the specific type of purchaser can be directed to the appropriate audience.

Selections need not be limited to only one of these criteria but can be made on the basis of several of them in concert. As a result, your ability to segment your list increases significantly with each additional piece of data that is added to the data base.

All these criteria apply equally to list rental, another use which the data base can support.

List owners should be concerned with ensuring that organizations renting their lists have the best chance to get a good response since that is the criterion which will determine whether additional list rentals will result from the tests.

By being able to select segments which appear to offer the greatest potential for high response or eliminate segments which seem to have the lowest potential, list owners can significantly improve their list's chances of being successful for the list renter and therefore their own chances of getting additional list rentals.

MERGE AND PURGE

If your list is to be used in conjunction with other lists, it probably will make sense to have it processed through a merge and purge system. This process will identify and remove the duplications that are found within and between the various lists.

While the computer services that provide merge and purge have become quite adept at handling complicated list formats, it pays to keep a list in a format that facilitates such handling. This will reduce the amount of time needed to convert the file, thereby reducing the lead time necessary to get into a merge and purge program. Furthermore, the results obtained will be enhanced if the list is kept in an easily handled form.

Virtually all the merge and purge techniques used by different service bureaus use the same information: ZIP code, name (broken down into given name and surname fields), and street address. As a result, keeping these pieces of data in separate fields is generally a good idea. It also will be of value in the production of computer personalized letters since it simplifies the process of isolating the part of the name field that goes on the salutation line.

The first step involves getting all the various names and addresses standardized into a common format and into some specific sequence. This conversion process is the most difficult step in the procedure. It is not uncommon for the various lists included in the program to have widely varying characteristics. For example, they may have been produced on different computers and as a result have different technical specifications such as the number of "tracks" (seven or nine), the recording density (800, 1600, or 6450 bits per inch), whether it is written in ASCII or EBCDIC coding, etc.

In addition, the way in which the data are recorded on the file (the format) usually varies from file to file. As a result, fairly sophisticated programming often is needed to permit the location and extraction of the various elements required by the matching process.

To give you some idea of the magnitude of the problem, consider the task involved in telling a computer how to find the last name and street name in an address like this one:

Mr. A. John Van Sickel, VP Finance
A. Wattenstein and Assoc. Inc.
117–119 Avenue A West, Suite 27
Los Angeles, CA 90765

The computer should be able to identify "Van Sickel" as the surname, "A" as the street name, and "117" as the house number.

The conversion program also must standardize many variable words which appear in the address line, such as Box, PO Box, PO Drawer, Post Office Box, Drawer, Bx, etc. In addition, it must recognize the standard abbreviations and "spelled out" numerics so that it can equate MT with Mount, ST with Saint, ONE with 1, etc.

At the same time it is standardizing the files, the conversion program usually extracts and builds up a terse code for each record. In the simpler system, these codes (referred to as match codes) are built by taking specific characters from the standardized name and address, for example, the ZIP code; the first, third, and fourth characters of the surname; the house number; and the first three characters of the street name.

In more sophisticated systems, the characters to be used are chosen by various schemes. These schemes are proprietary to the organizations that developed them so that the companies can minimize the number of erroneous duplications identified by these processes while maximizing their ability to locate the actual duplicates that exist. One of the simpler schemes is a program which can extract the first letter of the surname and then the three following letters, skipping the vowels and bypassing the second occurrence in the case of double letters. This relatively simple modification to the match code will improve its ability to identify numerous actual duplicates which, because they are misspelled slightly, would be missed by the basic technique described above. However, the real key to the success rate of any merge and purge program lies in the thoroughness of the conversion process, not in the trickiness of the matching algorithm.

LABELS

The data in your file can be printed out in several different forms. The most common forms are labels, personalized forms, and letters.

Labels generally are printed either 1-up or 4-up (four labels across the page). For large-volume mailings, it is customary to have the labels affixed by a labeling machine into which are fed the unburst computer printouts containing the labels. This machine cuts the labels and glues them to the envelope or mailing piece.

The labels can be printed either on plain computer paper or on pressure-sensitive "peel-off" labels. If printed on pressure-sensitive forms, they can be affixed by hand (for small-volume mailings) or by machine, in which case the resulting label can then be peeled off by the recipient and pasted onto an order form, reply card, etc. The Internal Revenue Service uses this type of label on the tax forms they send out each year.

The most common size labels are approximately 3.2 inches wide by 1 inch high. As a result, the amount of data which can be printed on them varies depending on the technical characteristics of the computer printer.

Most computer printers print ten characters to the inch horizontally and six lines per inch vertically. Thus, a label could contain five lines of thirty characters each. If the printer can be adjusted to print at eight lines per inch, this will allow up to seven lines of data to be printed on the label. A number of printers are now available which can print more than ten characters per inch (horizontally), in which case longer lines can be printed on each label.

To facilitate the batching of the mailing according to U.S. Postal Service specifications, it is extremely helpful if the labels at the end of each ZIP code or sectional center are identified. The most common coding is a single asterisk to identify the end of a ZIP code and a double asterisk to identify the end of a sectional center.

PERSONALIZED FORMS

The name and address data plus other pieces of information contained in the data base can be printed directly onto continuous forms rather than onto labels which then would be affixed. This type of operation sometimes is used to produce personalized reply cards, partially filled out "applications," and other direct mail formats. The forms should be designed by a computer forms specialist. Forms manufacturer's sales people often will do this for their customers.

This is very important since the presses on which computer forms are produced have various limitations and because the computer printers also have special requirements. Despite these limitations, you will find that you have amazing flexibility in the design and will be able to do almost anything you desire.

It should be kept in mind that the printing time required on the computer will be affected by the design of the form. For example, if you have a computer printer that prints at 300 lines per minute, you can get approximately 12,000 labels per hour. If you print the same data onto forms (1-up) which are 4 inches high and contain 6 lines of computer-printed data, your output may drop to under 2000 per hour. The actual speeds depend on the technical specifications of the printer, the spacing between the print lines, etc.

COMPUTER PERSONALIZED LETTERS

One of the newer output forms is computer personalized letters, in which the name, address, and salutation of the recipient are printed onto the letter in a form simulating that of a personally typed letter. In addition, certain information can be inserted into the text of the letter itself, offering considerable flexibility to the copywriter.

Personally typed letters are almost always typed in upper and lower case type as well as in a "typewriter" font. As a result, it is usually desirable to print the name and address information in upper and lower case. If the name has been entered and maintained in this form, this is a simple process. However, many computer systems have been designed to enter and maintain name and address data in all upper case. As a result, the names must be printed this way or converted. Conversion is not as simple as it may appear since one must properly handle such sources of inconsistency as McAdams, Mac Intyre, Van Courtlandt, O Hara, D Angelo, etc.

As is the case with computer personalized forms, the time required to print letters is considerably longer than that required to print labels. To minimize this time, preprinted forms can be used. These are forms onto which the manufacturer has preprinted those portions of the letter which are "standard," or nonpersonalized. The type style and ink color are matched to those of the printer to be used for the personalization by printing the standard copy on that printer and then sending a proof copy to the print shop for use in producing the printing plates used for the forms.

This type of letter is called a "fill-in" letter. It is significantly faster to print than fully printed letters and, when properly done and carefully controlled (by having an alert operator adjust the printer correctly, change ribbons frequently, etc.), yields excellent results.

CUSTOMER SERVICE

It is often advantageous to utilize the data stored in the computer for customer service purposes. This generally requires that the system be capable of quickly retrieving and displaying, or printing out, specific information about an order.

Often this must be done in response to a telephone inquiry. The system should be able to find an order on the basis of the information that a customer will give. Usually customers do not know their account numbers or your order or invoice number. Therefore, if possible, the system should be built to permit retrieval of orders by the customer's purchase order number or by customer name.

It should be kept in mind that different customers may use the same purchase order numbers, and so your system should be designed to display as many orders as there are with the given purchase order number and permit you to select the desired one.

For customer service purposes, therefore, consider capturing the following additional data:

Customer's purchase order number

Your order and invoice numbers

Order status
Shipping date
Method of shipping
Payments and credits to date
Balance due

If practical, the details of the order (items, quantities, prices, etc.) also can be included.

This information need be kept on-line only for the length of time during which customer inquiries are likely to occur. In most cases, detail data can be purged safely 3 months after an order has been paid for in full since few inquiries come in after that period has elapsed. Obviously, this can vary depending on the type of merchandise involved.

Your own experience with inquiries should be used to determine how long to maintain detail order data on-line.

LIST RENTALS

If you are planning to rent your list or exchange it with other list owners, a number of other considerations become important.

The more ways a list can be selected, the easier it is to rent. Therefore, the value of the data elements listed above is increased since they will enable you to supply your list rental customers with that segment of your list which will fit their requirements best. In addition, you must be able to select names from your list based on ZIP codes, sectional centers, and states as well as draw off statistically reliable segments by means of *N*th name selection. This is done by dividing the total number of names on the list by the number of names you wish to select. The resulting number (dropping any remainders) is *N*. By reading the file and selecting every *N*th name, you will wind up with the desired number of records. For example, if your list contains 275,530 records and you wish to select 5000 records, divide 275,530 by 5000, yielding 55.106. Drop the 0.106 and then choose every fifty-fifth record. This will give you 5009 records.

Continuations also must be provided for when doing list rentals. This comes about when a renter rents a portion of your list (often for a test mailing) and then comes back to get more of the names. Often they will indicate that they do not want you to supply them with any names which were included in the previously supplied segment.

It is as important to you to suppress these names as it is for renters not to receive them since you want to do everything you can to ensure the highest level of response for your renter. After all, if your list works well for them, they will continue to rent it, thereby providing you with list rental income.

Obviously, if you are to be able to provide continuations, you must have a means of identifying the names that were supplied to a list renter on a previous order. This can be accomplished in a number of ways. Generally, every record on a file will have a unique identification (ID) code. If you record the ID numbers which were included in a particular list rental and retain that list in machine-readable form, you can suppress those records from future rentals.

Another method of generating continuations is to divide the file into a number of subfiles by sequentially assigning records a subfile code as they are added to the file. For example, if the list is about 300,000 records long and is divided up into fifty segments, each segment will contain about 6000 records. As each record is added to the file, it is assigned a number from 01 to 50 (in sequence). A list rental then can be drawn from one or more specific segments, and the segment codes can be recorded. If a continuation is requested, these segments can be skipped, thereby assuring that no previously supplied records are included. In the event that a renter wants all the names on your list not previously supplied, you can select these since the records added to the previously used segments after the date of the original order now can be extracted.

It is common practice in the list industry to provide for continuations for a period of up to 6 months after a rental, assuming that the renter has requested that you do so at the time of placing the original order. As a result, the retention of information about previously supplied lists has a defined life span, and the data can be destroyed after this period has elapsed.

ZIP CODE ANALYSIS

When the post office first indicated that ZIP codes were going to be mandatory, direct mailers were very upset. They complained about the costs that they would have to bear in conversion, the equipment in which they had invested which would now be obsolete, and similar problems. As it has turned out, the ZIP code has been a great boon to mailers.

Among its features is the ability to analyze a customer base by geographic breakdown and the inclusion or exclusion of specific areas based on this analysis. However, you must be cautious about how this analysis is done or you may find that you are drawing conclusions that are not based on solid statistical evidence.

If you currently have a file of significant size, it may seem practical for you to analyze where your current customers are and then advertise primarily in those areas. This type of analysis is often not valid because the location of your current customers is based on where you advertised before and how much advertising you did in each area. For example, if you never mailed any promotions into Utah, it is likely that you will not have any customers on your file from Utah. This does not mean that Utah is a bad area for you. By the same token, if there are two areas which have roughly the same populations, demographics, etc., and you find that you have twice as many customers from one of these areas as from the other, you cannot conclude that that area is a better prospect for you.

The missing element is the number of pieces that you sent into each area. If you find that you sent five times as much mail into the area which is only yielding twice as many customers, the conclusion is that the first area is better, not the second. Therefore, when you do a ZIP analysis of your file, the data that must be measured are the response rates that previous mailings have generated.

From a purely mathematical standpoint, the smaller the number of records you are measuring, the less reliable your predictions will be. Since there are over 35,000 active ZIP codes in the United States, it is likely that the number of records on your file from a single ZIP code will be relatively small. (Usually, we try to use test segments of about 5000 records in order to get a reasonably reliable test base.)

If your file is small but concentrated in a small geographic area as opposed to being "national," you may find that there are sufficient quantities in individual ZIP codes to study. However, in most cases, the sizes of lists are such that individual ZIP code analysis cannot be reliably done. In these cases, analysis sometimes can be done by measuring response by sectional center (the first three digits of the ZIP code).

Another factor to keep in mind when doing such analysis is that you can reach different audiences in the same areas if you use different advertising media. Therefore, if you have been using space advertising, you cannot assume that a "good" area will continue to respond well if you now are doing a direct mail promotion.

MULTIPLE REGRESSION ANALYSIS

Ed Mayer used to tell his students that "the direct marketing business is a business of 'whats,' not a business of 'whys.'" He implied that we could very accurately measure what people were doing but could not as accurately determine why they were doing it.

Multiple regression analysis is not aimed at determining why people acted in a particular way but is used to try to see whether there are common patterns which we can detect which then can be used in an attempt to improve the response rate. Bear in mind that it is as valuable to determine patterns within nonrespondents (which then can be eliminated in future promotions) as it is to find them in respondents.

Basically, a multiple regression analysis analyzes as much descriptive information as is available about both respondents and nonrespondents to see if there are any statistically significant patterns in either. It then reports these findings so that they can be reviewed and, if found to be reasonable, used in an attempt to improve future promotions. Obviously, the more accurate descriptive data there are about the various records to be analyzed, the better the chance of finding something significant.

Earlier in this chapter, we indicated some of the data which might be captured in the building of a data base. In some cases, additional data can be obtained. For example, if data are being picked up from warranty cards, other demographic information can be obtained. This can include the age and sex of the individual, marital status, type of home, income range, etc. When this type of information is available, multiple regression analysis sometimes can suggest a particular profile that is either positive or negative for future promotions. These data then can be used in selecting specific advertising media and lists and in the creation of copy.

Keep in mind that the data provided by such analysis are statistical and treat the individuals on the file as numbers, not as persons. People, on the other hand, do not always operate logically. Therefore, review any such results carefully and interpret them in conjunction with your own insights before taking actions based on them.

DATA BANKS

Data banks are groups of mailing lists of similar types which have been put together in order to permit a potential renter who needs a certain type of list to get a large number of unduplicated names without having to make arrangements with many different list owners. These list owners have combined their lists into one large list from which a renter can draw names. Each owner whose names are in the "bank" then is paid for the rental in proportion to the relative sizes of his or her list.

Data banks are particularly successful in situations in which the number of names on any individual list is small. In addition, they offer the renter the advantage of not having to handle many different lists. If the names are being supplied in label form, the renters can get one ZIP sequence, thereby enabling them to take advantage of postal presort discounts. If the list is being supplied on magnetic tape, there is only one file format to be handled. The most common data banks today are in the business list area.

NIXIES AND CHANGES OF ADDRESS

It appears that approximately 20 percent of the population moves each year. This means that any file of names and addresses is going to contain a large number of wrong addresses as time goes on. If you or the mailers who rent your list use third class postage, there is no forwarding on these pieces. Accordingly, such pieces are theoretically undeliverable.

The economics of keeping an address file current vary from organization to organization. At current postal rates, it costs $0.25 to get back a notification of change of address. These CHAD (changes of address) then must be entered into the system to update the file.

If the piece comes from your own list and if you will be mailing to that name several more times, it may pay to take advantage of this feature. On the other hand, if you are using a rented list, unless you can get the list owner to pay for the change of address fee, it does not pay to request one.

Nondeliverable pieces are referred to as nixies. Generally, unless special conditions prevail, you can assume that a list will contain from 6 to 10 percent nixies. There are services available which can identify and eliminate large numbers of nixies from a potential mailing. They do this by building up lists of changed addresses which are compiled from various sources, the most common being the telephone directories. You send your file or files to the company providing this service, and they will pass it against their file of nixie names and address, identifying your bad addresses. Some of them can supply you with correct new addresses as well.

Another address change which takes place is the changed ZIP code. The U.S. Postal Service makes many ZIP code changes each year. Therefore, any of the addresses which you have on your list that fall into one of these changed ZIP codes can wind up undeliverable even though the person did not move. Once again, there are services available that can identify and correct these changed ZIP codes for you.

LIST SECURITY

The entire concept of list rentals rests on the assumption that records supplied by a list owner will be used only one time and in accordance with the specifications agreed on. Therefore, certain precautions must be taken to ensure that this understanding is complied with as well as to deter misuse of a list to the largest degree practical.

The most effective way to do this is by inserting uniquely identifiable records into each list rental or exchange that is created. This procedure is known as "seeding" or "salting" a list.

The inclusion of these unique but deliverable records provides the following benefits to the list supplier:

- Samples of the actual mailing will be received, providing a means of assuring that the mailing is in accordance with the specifications of the order in terms of content and mailing time.
- Misuse of the list (mailing a different offer, multiple mailings, or mailing at a different time) will be detected.
- Theft of a list is deterred since misuse is likely to be detected.
- The actual date on which mailed pieces arrive is determined and can be used in measuring response activity as well as post office efficiency.

Many list suppliers paste a label on each reel of tape they send out or on each label printout, indicating that "This file contains seeded names to prevent unauthorized misuse." This is done primarily to inform people who, because of a lack of experience in direct marketing, may not be aware of the rules of the game.

There are many different ways to create these "salt" names. One method is to have a list of specific addresses which are modified and inserted into every list rental. The form of modification used can vary. To give you an idea of how it can be done, suppose you have a real address such as the following:

Arthur Blumenfield
300 Broad Street
Stamford, CT 06901

The last name can be modified so that it is identifiable as the "salt" record. For example, it might be changed to "Bluminfelt." Then, instead of using "Arthur," each list rental order would use two letters as if they were initials. The first order would be to "A A Bluminfelt," the next order to "A B Bluminfelt," etc. Each of the "salt" names on the order would get the same two initials. Therefore, when a mailing piece is received, it can be identified as a "salt" by the "Bluminfelt," and the specific renter can be identified by the first initials.

Misuse of a list is documented by being able to show several different "salts," all of which were included only in the specific list delivered to a renter.

MAIL PREFERENCE SERVICE

As a mailer, you have a vested interest in the continued availability of mailing lists as well as in seeing to it that few if any restrictions are imposed on your right to mail. Therefore, it is important to recognize that some people (thankfully not too many) do not wish to receive advertising mail and are quite vociferous about it.

Your system should provide a means whereby you can code such individuals' records to suppress mailing to them or exclude their names on any list rentals or exchanges which you create.

In addition, you should participate in the DMA's Mail Preference Service (MPS). This is a program in which the DMA provides those individuals who do not wish to receive such mail with a means of diminishing the amount of mail they receive. Their names are put onto a special list which is made available to direct marketers. These names then can be suppressed from any mailings.

If you rent lists from other list suppliers, it is good practice to request that they suppress any names which appear on this MPS list. If you supply names, you should automatically suppress any such names as well as the names of any individuals on your list who have requested that you not send them additional mailings.

Experience has shown that if they are given that option, a very small percentage of individuals will request that their names not be rented or reused. As a result, it is highly recommended that mailers follow such a procedure as well as other practices which from time to time may be recommended by the List Council of the DMA. Doing so will help all of us to continue to operate in an atmosphere as free of crippling regulations and restrictions as possible.

chapter **19**

CO-OPS AND INSERTS

Leon Henry, Jr.

Chairman of the Board
Leon Henry, Inc.
Scarsdale, N. Y.

The direct mail industry has always looked for and found alternative media to use. As postal rates have climbed, so has the number of alternative media. Two which have had a greater than expected impact on the industry are co-ops and package inserts.

Package inserts should be considered the more viable medium because the availabilities are greater. Co-ops, which once were in the same class of expansion as package inserts, have demonstrated a number of inhibiting factors so that their growth beyond the current level is somewhat in doubt.

Package inserts came about in a casual way approximately 20 years ago when the few advertisers who were placing their advertisements in mail-order packages on a direct basis were approached by an entrepreneur to use the entrepreneur's expertise to make the appropriate connections, do the paperwork, and see the jobs through to completion. The original advertisers were some of the bigger names in the direct mail field: RCA Record Club, Nashua Photo (then called Best Photo), GRI World of Beauty, etc. The distributors of the inserts, which were not then called inserts, were often the same companies. They were in effect trading among themselves through several "brokers." The list brokerage fraternity was not involved then. Pricing was in the $15 per thousand range. The number of participants was limited, as was the number of inserts placed. There were several entrepreneurs taking various other avenues of activity. One was in the retailer statement area, another in supermarkets, and another in toys and games.

Competition brought greater recognition to the emerging medium. Several additional developments resulted in the next level of activity. The medium worked well enough for repeat use. The repeaters were more conspicuous, drawing in more users. Some of the users were very heavily involved in the new medium and needed more outlets than were in existence. The new outlets needed more than one or two insert users and put pressure on the fledgling insert brokers to come up with even more users. Finally, the first in the series of postal rate increases made the medium more viable for all concerned.

The co-op market went through a similar evolution. The low price of third class postage made this medium more viable in the beginning and less so as time passed. The costs of most co-ops were too high to allow the requisite profit to the entrepreneurs involved so that the co-op market has evolved to be a ride-along situation. That is, the mailer accepts others in the mailing to amortize the costs. This is what the market looks like now, with the exception of the Carol Wright Co-op.

WHAT IS A PACKAGE INSERT?

As the name implies, these are inserts from the company selling the product or from outsiders that are placed in packages being delivered to customers. Depending on the way in which the purchase was made, the packages and the advertising inserts are delivered to mail-order or retail buyers. The packages naturally vary in size, weight, and method of delivery: post office, United Parcel Service (UPS), retail, or taken. The packages are from well-known company names such as Drawing Board and Spencer Gifts or exotic ones such as Le Jardin du Gourmet (shallots), Atlas Pen (pencils), and Wecolite (kitchen gadgets).

The number of inserts varies from four to eight, with the most common number being six. They are loose or contained within a folder, catalog, or envelope. There probably will be house inserts if the package is from a mail-order company.

The conventionally packed and mailed package allows for variations in the number of items ordered; therefore, the space is usually available for inserts. The packing of the insert usually takes place after the merchandise has been packed. This provides the insert with extra exposure and the opportunity to attract the customer's attention. Of course, the excitement of opening the purchase can negate some of the effect of the package inserts. Large furniture items, for example, need packing material to protect them during shipment. Inserts can be lost in this type of package.

The mailer has to be alert to the variations of packaging and at the same time should provide only one insert format for the entire variety of package insert situations. Otherwise, the cost will be too high, and the added expense will reduce the probability of success.

By asking the insert broker to check with the distributing program, the advertiser can find out how the inserts are packed. The problem is that at any given time, the number of inserts and the participants will vary. Therefore, an advertiser has to expect some variations in response to the offer depending to some extent on the number of other inserts and the relative strength of their offers compared with his or her offer.

Since the one unwritten rule of the insert business is that there must be no advertiser duplications, the advertiser who gains the position within the package can stay as long as it is economically feasible. You can be sure that there are advertisers which occupy categories longer than it is economically viable to do so simply to preserve their position in the package insert program.

Retail distributed packages, which are a growing force in the package insert industry, have their own peculiarities, which can best be described as the problems inherent in the retail distribution cycle of the particular product involved. For example, a manufacturer of diapers who offers a package insert program has to have the inserts collated in an outside mailing house and then moved to the packing line where they are inserted. This is only the beginning of the cycle of distribution. After the inserts are in the package, there is a minimum period of storage in the plant before the goods are moved to the various retailers. If the goods go to a wholesaler as an interim step, the time that it takes for the inserts to reach the consumer will be that much longer. If the inserts go directly from the plant to a high-volume retailer with rapid turnover, the inserts will be distributed more quickly. The advertiser dealing with the retail distribution of inserts must be prepared for the time that distribution of the goods takes.

TV-generated merchandise has its own peculiarities. Since this merchandise is predominately for mail order against COD delivery, there is the problem of unsold merchandise. An understanding of the nature of the distribution function will preclude the problem of undelivered merchandise and consequently undelivered inserts. Be sure to find out what happens to the undelivered inserts.

Another problem with TV- or radio-sold merchandise is the life span of the merchandise. These products often have a short life cycle. The advertiser has to be alert to the timing of the product. Too many inserts are delivered to a product with a short life cycle, producing an overage of inserts coupled with an invalid reading on the keying of the inserts.

WHAT IS A CO-OP?

By definition, a noncompetitive group of advertisers mailing together to reduce costs and reach the same prospective customers constitutes a co-op mailing. If the co-op mailing is run by a company whose primary purpose is to mail a catalog or announcement and it carries outside inserts, it should be called a ride-along.

Co-ops have had a spotty history. The major reason for the lack of continuity of a given co-op seems to lie in the increasing costs for the organization sponsoring the co-op. This reason also seems to be at the heart of the increase in ride-alongs.

Pricing for ride-alongs seem to be lower than for co-ops because any contribution by the participating advertisers lowers the expense of the sponsor, whereas with a co-op all costs have to be covered before the first dollar of profit is earned. Since the results will be diluted by the increase in the number of participants, you have a circular situation, currently leading to a decrease in the number of co-ops.

One method of offsetting the increased number of mail-order participants is to substitute non-mail-order advertisers such as couponers or local advertisers. The problems here are that major couponers need very large distributions for their coupons and that the number of co-ops that fit this need is very low and may include only the Carol Wright Co-op. A non-mail-order industry which has some history of insert production, such as the travel industry, cannot seem to understand the potential in the co-op field; hence, the lack of non-mail-order inserts within co-ops.

Ride-alongs are more assured now than co-ops because the sponsor of the ride-along must have the catalog or mailing out on a specified date. It doesn't make sense to have a mailing for Christmas greeting cards except in August or September. Therefore, a ride-along with a company offering this product is sure to be delivered as contracted for. A problem of co-ops has been postponement of the delivery date while waiting for the sale and arrival of the inserts. Some advertiser is always ready to come in for a lower price at the last minute; this is advantageous to that advertiser, and it provides a problem for the sponsor.

A ride-along with a membership bulletin or announcement such as the RCA Record Club or the Columbia Record Club ride-along has all the benefits that the insert advertiser seeks: reliability of delivery, volume of recipients, reasonable cost, and readership. The major problem for an advertiser who has not used these vehicles is the heavy prior commitment made by participants who have had successful experiences and therefore occupy the category which the new advertiser is seeking. An excellent example is the mail-order photo-finisher category, which is next to impossible to obtain in either of these ride-alongs.

WHAT TYPES OF ADVERTISERS USE PACKAGE INSERTS AND CO-OPS?

At this point in the development of this phase of the medium, there are several major categories of advertisers:

Book and record club application forms
Mail-order photo finishers
Clothing offers
Catalog inquiries
Magazine subscription offers
Jewelry and various merchandise offers
Insurance applications
Collectibles

Historically, the medium has been dominated by the photo finishers, magazines, clubs, and jewelry groups. There have been very heavy users of the medium. A heavy user can be defined as an advertiser which takes all the insert space available in the programs appropriate for its offer. A photo finisher would want to be in all the consumer-directed package insert and co-op programs, especially those which target the young homeowner. A magazine reaching an older audience would be interested in insert programs directed to buyers of vitamins and similar merchandise ordered by older persons.

Advertisers whose products are limited to a specific audience must inquire whether there are enough package insert programs to consider participating. There are still many categories of programs that are not extensive enough to produce an insert. For example, there is only one scientific program: Edmund Scientific. An advertiser looking for the young boy who buys by mail or for his parents will find very few insert programs, but there are enough to build a media schedule.

Efforts to enlarge the industry have been undertaken by the major brokers, but such efforts seem to occur in those categories of programs which offer the most participation by advertisers. The industry is heavily weighted toward the woman mail-order buyer. Efforts on the part of the active brokers are therefore in this direction.

Advertisers have come into the medium in an increasing number, as would be expected from the publicity generated in the last 5 years as well as the increase in postage rates. The newer entrants are finding some problems, including a lack of understanding of the direct mail industry. Since the principles of the industry dictate the success of the insert segment, it is necessary to know what to expect in general before using a specific medium.

Too rapid results and success on every effort seem to be common expectations of the newer advertisers. Unwillingness to understand the testing procedure and lack of knowledge of the mathematics of direct mail are additional hurdles to be overcome by the newer entrants.

Many of the newer advertisers have financing problems as well. The low cost of entry is enticing as well as the ability to conceal the effort from potential competitors. However, the undercapitalized entrant is requested to pay up front for participation in most programs.

WHAT ARE THE FORMATS FOR INSERTS?

The basic industry format is a 5 ½- by 8 ½-inch, one- or two-panel, four-color advertisement. The second basic format is one which fits a statement. These are generally 3 ½ by 6 inches. The two common ways of accommodating this situation are to create an insert for each size only or to fold the larger insert to fit the smaller situation. There are some sound reasons for the second approach. First, there are many fewer small distributions. Second, there are extensive examples of the folded insert being used which cover all situations. Perhaps the best known is the Western Publishing Company's insert for the Betty Crocker recipe offer. Only one insert was prepared. The only variations were in the fold, and later in the cycle a sample was affixed to the card. This raised the weight so that in some distributions these inserts required additional payment for the additional weight.

The insert must be prepared so that it is machine-insertable. The printer must pack the insert material in a way which leaves the material readily usable by the inserting vehicle. Since most inserting is done on a Phillipsburg or a Bell & Howell, the material is banded in uniform amounts of approximately 200 pieces; when it is stored in the cartons, care should be exercised that material does not slip in the cartons.

Each carton should be marked with the amount contained and the key code on the inserts. There should be notification on each carton of the total number of cartons included in the shipment. Shippers should obtain signed receipts from the receivers.

There are two basic ways of inserting: by machine and by hand. All preparations should be made for machine insertion.

The use of a return vehicle is taken for granted in the insert medium. How it is used depends on the offer, of course. The two standard ways use a business reply card (BRC) as part of the format. In some cases, the BRC is interleaved with the insert. The price of inserting is always quoted on a per thousand basis and so it is important to have only one insert provided to the inserting house. With two separate pieces, there may be an increase in price, and the insert may be lost or not distributed.

The other return vehicle that is used frequently is the envelope. With the development of the Webcraft envelope, cash-with-order offers can be accommodated in the insert medium. Previously, the mailer would have to provide an additional envelope in order to receive cash or checks.

Lately there have been several new format developments to consider. One is the extremely lightweight or smaller insert. The second is the heavier or bulky insert. In each case, creative mailers are looking at the distribution problem and seeing whether they can bend the rather simple pricing structure to their own ends. The lightweight insert offers the broker some reason for negotiating lower prices. There are some justifiable situations for the smaller insert, one of which is for inquiries or for very low priced products or very simple offers. The combination of lower printing costs and lower insert costs gives this approach a viability that some other methods do not have.

The heavier or bulkier insert can be used only in packages that are large enough to accept them and when the packing is done by hand. The advantage to the mailer is the considerable additional copy that is distributed for the same or proportionately lower price. Even if the program charges more than the normal pricing, the heavier insert puts the mailer ahead of the game.

The weight of inserts is considered to be a quarter ounce or less. Some programs have begun to price their programs on a one-tenth-ounce basis.

Statement situations are those which have the closest weight tolerances because of the first class nature of the distributions.

Oversize or nonfolded inserts create a problem in that the majority of insert situations accept the 5½- by 8½-inch format. When dealing with a 6- by 9-inch envelope, the mailer who provides a small insert loses visibility within the program. The outsized insert is not always acceptable, thereby reducing the number of insert programs available to the mailer.

WHAT ARE THE COSTS OF PARTICIPATING?

The medium has two costs: distribution and printing. Printing prices are determined by the format used and the quantity of inserts ordered, the keying, and the delivery charges. The cost of inserts has risen along with everything else. You can use $20 per thousand for a rough estimate in computing the cost of printing.

The price which is set by the program providing the distribution facilities varies widely. The determining factors are the popularity of the program, the number of inserts per package, the number of packages or mailings per year, the competitive situation, and the availability at any given time. Just as yesterday's empty airline seat has no value, a package that goes out without the requisite number of inserts is not producing the anticipated income that the owner intended to receive for providing the service.

The average cost of package inserts is between $35 and $40 per thousand. The average cost of co-op and ride-along mailings is edging above the $30 per thousand mark. The overriding concern to the mailer is the number of orders or inquiries and the translation of these into cost per order or cost per inquiry, depending on the measurement of success for the mailer's participation. Naturally, rising prices do not portend improved results.

During testing, which is the first step any direct mailer takes, the cost of printing will be higher than it is for rollouts. Be sure to evaluate results by determining the cost of the printing on a rollout basis, and not on the basis of the test quantities. The same situation will occur with distribution prices. When the mailer negotiates through a broker for rollouts, many prices are reduced somewhat. The profit and loss determination for each distributing program will be influenced by the lower prices obtained.

WHAT ARE THE RESPONSE RATES?

This is the most common question posed to any package insert broker, and it is the most difficult question to answer. First, most mailers consider the package insert medium to be a small part of the marketing program. Its costs are lower than those of mailing, and the attendent risks are less. Thus, most brokers are given less information than they would receive in a list selection, with its higher costs and risks. Second, most brokers do not work exclusively with the mailer. The state of the industry is such that most mailers use more than one broker and presumably keep privileged information to themselves for this reason among others.

In any event, the real question does not concern the response rates but rather the cost per order or inquiry. If the responses divided into the costs are such that they are viable, the response rate is only part of the equation. Let's look at an example.

Cost of inserts	$20 per thousand
Cost of distribution	$40 per thousand
Total costs	$60 per thousand
Needed cost per order	$10

A response rate of six orders per thousand is acceptable. Below that the cost per order is too high, and above there is an increasing profit to the mailer.

Each distribution has to be analyzed in a profit and loss statement (P&L) just as each mailing has to be gone over. In a two-step situation, the mailer has to know the allowable back end as well.

In the above example, if after some testing the mailer receives only four to five responses per thousand, one or both costs will have to be reduced. Let's examine a second example:

	A	*B*
Cost of inserts	$15 per thousand	$20 per thousand
Cost of distribution	$40 per thousand	$35 per thousand
Total costs	$60 per thousand	$50 per thousand
Response rate	4	4
Cost per order	$15.00	$12.00
Response rate	5	5
Cost per order	$12.00	$10.00

Therefore, at a lower response rate, the costs of either the insert or the distribution will have to be lowered by $10 per thousand to make an average and successful use of the particular package insert or co-op program.

WHAT ARE THE ADVANTAGES OF USING PACKAGE INSERTS?

The most obvious advantage is the low initial cost relative to the benefits to be obtained. For under $5000, the average mailer can have a well-diversified and correctly constructed test of the package insert and co-op medium. This would include five to ten tests of 10,000 each for package inserts and two tests of 25,000 each for the co-ops.

There are more advantages. Multiple copy approaches can be tested once a successful format is in place. With several programs that are producing the desired results, the adventurous mailer can refine his or her strategy by testing various copy formats within the successful programs. Under no circumstances should the format be tested before the medium is tested. Among the tests that can be run are copy, format, and offer.

The exposure to competitors is minimal with this medium. You have to receive a package to see the insert of your competitor. The brokerage fraternity is reasonably good about keeping secrets, and so the exposure remains reasonably minimal.

A business can be built around the insert medium. While this is not the usual case, it has been done. As in any marketing effort, more than one medium should be used. Each should be used for its particular benefits.

Lists can be tested through the use of inserts. In doubt over the use of a particular list? Try the insert route. If you have developed correlations among your list and package insert results, you can interpolate the list results from the package insert use. Obviously, you are reaching a hotline buyer when you use package inserts. You also can consider giving up some of the list expense and substituting lower-cost package inserts.

Package insert users preempt their competition. Since one insert or product per package is the normal rule, you are in the package until you decide to leave if you are the first one in.

Supplement your advertising campaign. The insert medium can be localized so that the insert advertising supplements the general proposition.

Determine whether you want to sell your product through catalog houses by using inserts. There's nothing to prevent the mailer from broadening a line to include direct sales through the very catalog houses inserting the insert.

Test a new product or publication inexpensively. Test a new market. If you feel that your offer will work in other markets than the staple ones, here is a low-cost medium to provide the answer.

Create a larger market for your product. A good package insert broker will continue to try to develop more programs. If your offer is general in nature, you can expect to have more places to put your insert. It pays to have extra keys available for tests.

Revive a product. If your product is on the downslope through your conventional media approach, the low-cost insert route may breathe life into it for some additional time.

Test a publication without advertising in it. Many publications offer insert space in their statements. You can get a feel for the publication through the responses received from inserts.

Expand your cash flow. Since most inserts are billed at the completion of the job, you can receive orders before you pay for them.

WHAT ARE THE DISADVANTAGES OF THE INSERT MEDIUM?

Every advertising medium provides reason for not using it. The insert medium had as its major problem the unreliability of the distribution program. Today this situation is relatively rare. Most responsible package insert brokers employ checkers who monitor the flow of inserts and invoice accordingly. Most disadvantages come from not understanding the insert process or expecting more of what was purchased than can be delivered.

Keying correctly lies at the heart of both successful uses of and unsuccessful experiences with inserts. Most printers suggest key blocks that are too large to be useful. Even with retests and continuations, the alert user will have subkeys within the master block. Programs tend to have fluctuations in the number of products sold at any given time. Correct keying will let you analyze the number of inserts going out. The same thing is true of co-op distributions. A co-op mailing 500,000 should have several keys within to be sure that all keys were used. The temptation is not the problem, but the temptation is removed.

Any time you forget to key, you risk the chance of error. It is important that every insert used have one key or more and that the broker insist that the program provide a sample of the insert received prior to inserting.

Package insert programs have different lives at different times. Before Christmas is the most active time for many products, and so the insert users receive heavy distributions. The same program can be nonexistent in January. A question to the broker will bring monthly or weekly counts to preclude this problem.

Media use by programs can change without warning. What did well for you in the test can be disastrous in the retest or continuation if the program's advertising changes radically. The same situation can be observed when the distribution goes to a different geographic area or to a different type of buyer.

You are to some extent the partner of the other insertees. If your offer is not strong enough, you can be "knocked off" by another insert. It rarely is the number of inserts in a package that reduces the response; it is more likely to be one or more of the variations mentioned above.

If your insert is not visible, you can suffer lack of response. Since you are paying the same as the other inserts, why not get as much visibility as possible for your money?

A lack of correlation between advertiser and program can be devastatingly unprofitable. It pays to test with a pretested and successful insert. Be prepared for some surprises.

SUCCESS FACTORS: WHAT ARE THEY?

There seem to be two stages to reaching success in this medium. The first is the test phase, and the second is the rollout phase. Without a successful test, there can be no rollout.

Most new insert users have to create an insert. As simple as this seems, it is where the success or failure will start. The new insert has to be pretested to avoid the problem of determining the cause of failure. In other words, if the tests are not successful, is it the medium or the message? The best way to overcome this problem is to have enough tests so that a range of results will be available for analysis. As previously described, we feel that a minimum of ten tests is necessary in this initial stage.

The successful insert user analyzes the responses in the same fashion that would be undertaken with direct mail or space campaigns. That is, a P&L is done to determine the cost per order or inquiry of each program used. The analysis determines the ability to move forward or the adjustments to be made before more funds are committed to the medium.

As each distributing category is costed out, the user should expand in two directions. The first is within the individual program; this is called a retest or confirmation. The increase can safely be between 2 ½ and 5 times the initial test. If the initial test was statistically reliable, the rollout should reconfirm the test results. This will lead to the continuation phase.

The other possibility is to use additional distribution programs similar to each successful test program. For example, if yours is a consumer product aimed at mothers and you've tested a co-op mailing to recent mothers, you should have your broker look for additional co-op mailings to recent mothers. At the same time, you should consider additional programs such as those to be found by exploring age, geographic, and media selections that reach mothers.

In the insert field, success in the rollout phase is tricky, but with moderation it can be profitable. Here are what the really successful users seem to be doing.

1. Keying in such a way that they can read results quickly. This ensures the ability to reorder new programs and therefore reserve their category. It also enables them to see if the program is holding up. Under disadvantages, we discussed the many ways programs can deteriorate. Small key blocks, while more expensive, keep all parties alert.
2. Testing for copy and format adjustments only within successful programs.

Too much testing can be self-defeating and expensive in any phase of direct mail, including the insert medium. Finding ways to cut costs and improve response should be done only within the confines of programs that have proved themselves.

3. Taking advantage of what's new is important when you have decided on a format that works. Since this is an emerging medium, the advertiser will have a considerable number of selections brought in by alert brokers. Knowing that your insert works gives you confidence to use the programs that come along. There are two stages in new programs: test and rollout.
4. Negotiating for price. Fewer prices are negotiable than before. The prices are rising so that rollouts represent a way to leverage the price in your favor.
5. Act where you think you are right. The really good programs fill up. However, lately there has been a trend toward booking and not fulfilling the contract. Naturally, something has to be done.
6. Look beyond the obvious. Once your testing is done, move into collateral areas of distribution. The opening of the business mailers' packages to female offers is an excellent example of using a program category that on the surface did not seem to be viable until tested. Some alert book clubs and inquiry seekers are finding that nearly every program available works for their offers.
7. Have your broker see whether the program has additional areas of distribution available, for example, inserts in the catalog of a successfully used program if there is one or inserts in the bills if they are sent.
8. Pay promptly. The industry is suffering from too many slow pays. There will be a place made for the known prompt payer. See to it that your broker remits your money promptly.
9. Decoy your insert. If you can afford to, buy a package from every product distributing your inserts. One advertiser who does this uses the purchases as gifts at Christmas. In the meantime, he knows who is in the package with his insert. Be sure your broker decoys the co-ops. There is no way you can be sure of the other participants in the package insert program without purchasing products.
10. See that your insert dominates the others. Good graphics can be better. Good copy can be better. Size can be increased within limits.
11. Monitor the flow of inserts. It changes depending on the season, the advertising done by the package insert distributor, and various other factors.
12. Look at other successes. There is much to be said for copying, but it can get you in trouble if it is not done with flair.

WHAT'S NEW NOW AND IN THE FUTURE?

The co-op end of the insert medium seems to be headed toward ride-alongs for the economic reasons discussed previously. There would seem to be an increase in the number of mailings which accept outside inserts, but at an increased price. For example, in the mail-order photo-finishing industry, nearly all major finishers have accepted inserts in their mailings.

The package insert end will see an increase or perhaps even an explosion caused in part by the aggressive brokerage fraternity and the obvious need for reduction in costs. The retail end of the package insert field is barely touched. There are more categories of insert distribution available than are being used.

Some of the reasons for the slowness of the increase in the numbers of insert programs available have to do with the relatively low postage rate. Each increase has brought in more package insert programs. The me-tooism within industry groups tends to create more insert programs.

There will be an effort to increase the number of inserts within the more popular insert programs. One of the ways this will be done will be by using envelopes directed to interest groups within the packages. For example, in the business mailer category, it seems possible to have an envelope with inserts addressed to the boss or the office manager.

Small packages have obvious difficulty accepting inserts. Someone who is creative will develop an insert to take advantage of this area of the medium.

Multiple offers from different advertisers in an "all on one" format will be developed. There have been several attempts, but none seems to have been completely successful. One called Priority Post has been in a preprinted format with a number of advertisers sharing the cost of the production and distribution. Another effort has involved providing collated inserts within one envelope to take advantage of the per thousand distribution rate.

chapter **20**

NEWSPAPER ADVERTISING

Jean Cohen

Media Director
Ogilvy & Mather
Direct
New York, N.Y.

According to the Newspaper Advertising Bureau, there are more than 1750 daily newspapers in the United States, reaching seven out of ten adults. This represents a great potential audience for direct-response advertisers.

WHY NEWSPAPERS?

What unique combination of benefits can newspapers offer that magazines, lists, television, and radio can't? There are many benefits to newspapers:

1. Low cost
2. Audience targeting
3. Short closing dates
4. More variation in ad size
5. Daily or weekly publishing frequency
6. Three different ways to advertise: ROP, Sunday magazines, and inserts
7. Enormous circulation potential

Let's start with the attribute that you are probably most interested in: low cost. The cost per thousand (CPM) of newspaper advertising is a small fraction of that for direct mail.

"Low cost" is a relative term. To some advertisers, it means low dollar outlay. To others, it means low CPM. To the smartest advertisers, it means both. In the case of newspapers, both forms of low cost are available. Of course, this will vary depending on the size of the ad you run. Circulation is a factor too. The rule of thumb is, the higher the circulation, the higher the dollar outlay, the lower the CPM. Lower-circulation newspapers usually cost more per thousand.

Cost per Thousand

CPM is a very important figure. The higher the CPM, the harder your ad will have to work to produce a successful result. Always be aware of your CPM figures and compare them. You may find that you can afford to pay only up to a certain CPM, say, $12, and that any insertion in a newspaper that costs more per thousand, say, $15.50, will not work. Use the CPM figures as a guideline when selecting newspapers to carry your ad. Your budget limitations usually will dictate guidelines for your dollar outlay. Always try to get the biggest bang for the buck.

For the smaller direct-response advertiser or the more cautious one, there is a company that can give you especially low rates for newspaper space: Top Value Media, owned primarily by David Geller. Top Value Media has standby pages from over fifty newspapers. Standby means that the page may or may not be run in the newspaper on that particular day. For advertisers who are willing to take that risk, newspapers make a special rate available through Top Value Media. These standby pages are all mail-order and are run as mail-order shopping pages. You can get a good buy on this space, either small units or large, if you're willing to live with an uncertain insertion date. Most of the time, your ad will run as scheduled. The staff at Top Value is very diligent about getting these ads in and conscientious with follow-up to keep you abreast of the status of your advertising.

Special Sections

We know that we can reach millions of people through newspapers. What do we do about selecting just a few who would be interested in a specialized product? The simple answer is to run in a special section. Newspapers of larger circulation, mainly in and around major cities, have special pages editorially tailored to the special interests of their readers. Some of these special pages or sections are

- Gardening
- Financial and business
- Women's and society
- Stamp columns
- Coin columns
- Travel
- Restaurant guides
- Mail-order pages
- Movie and theater listings
- Home improvement column
- Book page
- Real estate
- TV and radio listings

Only the largest and most sophisticated newspapers, such as *The New York Times* and *The Chicago Tribune* offer such a wide range of special interest editorial content. Even then, most of this is offered only on Sunday. But the smaller newspapers do offer some special-interest editorial space. Most newspapers are cooperative about placing your advertising adjacent to the stamp column, for example, if you so request.

This special targeting by section is used by many large and small advertisers, from individuals who sell stamps from their homes to financial investment companies to large gardening and seed companies. Usually there is no premium, or extra charge, for placing an ad in these special sections. Sometimes the newspaper will have special rates for these sections which may be even lower than those for the main news section.

Positioning should make an important difference in your response. A gardening offer in the garden section will pull much better than it will anywhere else in the newspaper. If you need a list of newspapers that have a particular section or column, you can call the Newspaper Advertising Bureau (NAB) or the newspaper sales representatives and get a list of newspapers to fit your needs at no charge. This process of targeting your audience by using special sections can be a less expensive method than using magazines. The cheapest method of reaching all upscale gardeners in the New York area is to use *The New York Times* garden page on Sunday. However, this special targeting applies only to on-page advertising space. Newspapers cannot guarantee that a preprinted insert will be inserted adjacent to a special section. Usually all the freestanding inserts are inserted in one place only.

Timing

The fact that newspapers are published so often can work for or against your ad. This frequency of issue means that you can get your ad in at practically a moment's notice. If you decide on Monday that you want to run an ad in the Sunday paper, you can make the closing date, provided that your materials are ready. This is true of every newspaper in the United States. You may run up some heavy air freight charges getting your materials to the newspapers, but you can make the closings. This is not true of direct mail or magazines.

Daily newspapers close 2 to 4 days before publication; Sunday newspapers close from 3 to 5 days before publication. There are a few exceptions, but for the most part this is true. This means that you can wait for the last-minute results before repeating an ad and still have a quick turnaround. Magazine closing dates vary from 4 to 10 weeks before the date of issue. That can be a long time to wait if you have a "hot" product.

Fast Response

Another benefit of daily or weekly newspapers is that your results come in quickly. Because of the short life of the newspaper, your initial response should be 95 percent complete within the first 3 weeks after the ad appears. This frequency of issue means that you can run several insertions in a single year or test and rollout to other markets quickly.

The Drawback

It is true that the newspaper you appear in is here today and gone tomorrow. Nobody would buy yesterday's newspaper, even at half price. ROP sections of the newspaper do not hang around the house for long as monthly magazines do. Your prospect will not have a long time to consider purchasing your product before another newspaper with new ads has arrived. If ever there was a medium in which a strong creative "call to action" is needed, it would be newspapers. But even with this short life, newspapers do carry ROP mail-order advertising. It must be working for these companies, since they continue to use it, short life or not.

Size

What size ad do you run in a newspaper? There is no definite answer. The unit size is probably the trickiest decision to make. At Ogilvy & Mather Direct, this decision is either made or confirmed in the media department. But I always go for help to the creative department. I get upset if I recommend a horizontal unit and later find out that we only have vertical artwork. Besides, the creative team can help with this tough decision by suggesting how much space they need to work with to sell the product. There are some guidelines, though, and they are based on your strategy.

Before discussing these strategies individually, let's talk about the revolution in newspaper unit sizes. There finally has been standardization in newspaper unit sizes. For years, large schedules of fractional space ads in newspapers had production departments leaping from windows. All those different size mechanicals were difficult to work with and expensive. If you didn't make mechanicals in several different sizes, you "floated" the ad, with white space appearing around it. Several mechanicals became expensive, and floating looked dreadful. Neither was a great solution, and so newspapers created a standard advertising unit (SAU) that would fit all newspapers. This took effect about a year ago, catapulting newspapers into the twentieth century. These SAUs come in many sizes. Newspapers offer one rate for each unit, and this eliminates the need to multiply all those numbers of lines by line rates. It means that you can get away with much less in the line of production materials.

STRATEGIES

What are you trying to accomplish? Must you sell the product directly off the page or are you interested only in generating leads that will be followed up with a fulfillment package? Are you promoting a catalog and using newspapers to get inquiries? Is your product high-priced (over $100), medium-priced ($40 to $99), or low-priced (under $40)? Are you selling a loss leader or self-liquidator, hoping to gather names that will be promoted for other products at a later date? Are you announcing a new product? Are you announcing a change in a tried and true product? Each of these questions relates to a separate strategy.

Selling Off the Page

Some people believe that small space for a high-priced item is all that's necessary. But how can you sell a high-priced item without enough space to give your prospects plenty of information so that they can consider parting with a large sum of money? The higher the price on the item, the less you have to sell to break even. You should use enough space to do the product justice. Larger space is needed to reassure your prospect about shipping and delivery and to include a coupon with credit card options for this big purchase. Larger space will grab more attention. It just doesn't appear worth it to try to sell a $300 item in small space and receive one or two orders. Larger space may generate many more orders while creating awareness of your product. If your budget can handle it, a unit 10 (approximately 8 by 10) would be a good size to test.

The strategy for selling medium- and low-priced items directly off the page is similar to that for high-priced items. But here it would be wise to use larger space because the price points are more attractive. This would vary by type of product. If I were selling a kitchen gadget that has universal appeal, I would use larger space. Since this product doesn't have a narrowly targeted section to run in but only the women's pages, larger space would be necessary to attract attention and generate orders in volume. Stay away from food pages, especially on "best food days," as they are loaded with grocery store bargains and cents-off coupons that readers tear out of the newspaper. Part of the ad could end up on the cutting room floor, leaving the ad with no resemblance to its original beauty. At best, it would be ignored in favor of saving $0.10 on dog food or cat litter.

If the product is as specialized as stamps, you can have more confidence in smaller space appearing adjacent to the stamp column. Real stamp collectors have very sharp eyes for new stamp deals, or they have magnifying glasses. A sharp stamp collector will not miss your ad, even if it is only 2 inches by 5 inches, and probably will read every word. Smaller space should be all that is necessary to sell your product. But as always in direct response, testing is the only way to be sure.

Generating Leads

Generating inquiries for a high-priced item and then using a fulfillment package to close the sale is a fairly standard practice. The strategy for generating leads is somewhat different from the strategy for selling directly off the page. You don't have to sell the item so heavily. You need to pique the interest of your prospect. You need less detailed copy. Credit card options are unnecessary. Shipping and delivery assurances will appear in the follow-up package. But you need plenty of hard-sell copy. For this strategy, you probably could use smaller space. In fact, you don't want to generate many unqualified leads from a large-size ad. It can be very costly to send fulfillment packages to curiosity seekers. The rule of thumb here is that the bigger the ad, the more response it will generate unless you charge for the follow-up package. This response is not necessarily qualified response. Perhaps you should test a unit 14 (6 inches by 5 inches approximately) if you are giving the follow-up package away. Again, the key word is "test." Until you have the right unit, based on solid information, you should always be testing.

Catalog Promotion

This is similar to the lead-generation strategy that was just discussed, but a catalog is usually more expensive than a fulfillment package, and you don't want to send it to people who will use it for lining the parakeet's cage. If you watch experienced companies such as L. L. Bean, you can see that the more well known the name is, the smaller the unit sizes one needs to use in newspapers or magazines. L. L. Bean uses much smaller space in magazines because people know the quality of its merchandise, shipping, and return policy. But a new catalog such as Land's End buys full-page ads in magazines to generate awareness and establish its name. These are important considerations when you're deciding on unit sizes.

There is a rule of thumb for catalogs: The more general in nature your merchandise is and the less well known your name, use larger space such as unit 13 (6 inches by 10 inches). Repeat the ad as often as you can without losing money. When residual awareness has built up and your name is known, you can comfortably reduce your units to small space while still generating income. But it is your money. Test your way through this on a scale that is in tune with your budgetary limitations.

For very specific merchandise such as a coin catalog, use smaller space adjacent to the coin column. Unit 20 (4 inches by 3 inches) or unit 14 (6 inches by 5 inches) would be sufficient. You could also test a smaller unit such as unit 22A (2 inches by 5 inches) to see how small an ad you can run and still make money.

ANNOUNCING A NEW PRODUCT OR A CHANGE IN A KNOWN PRODUCT

A new product launch campaign should be done the same way you launch a new ship—with plenty of champagne and cheering crowds. Start off with the largest space you can afford and run it in as many places as you can as many times as possible. This awareness is invaluable, and future campaigns will benefit from it. You are launching something, and this is no time to be timid. The same is true for a relaunch or for announcing an "improvement" in a well-known product. Start big.

Behind all these strategies and various unit sizes there is one constant: testing. The cost of testing unit sizes can be inconsequential compared with the cost of fulfilling thousands of unqualified leads. I have seen newspapers being thrown off schedule and being accused of not working because the unit sizes tried were too small to generate any volume or maybe even enough orders to break even.

Many newspapers can perform A-B splits with ROP space advertising. You can ask the newspaper to find you a partner and arrange a special split test to try two different unit sizes at the same time, with another advertiser filling the gap. Keep your eyes open to see what the competition is up to. Compare the unit sizes that are working for you in magazines. Make projections based on breakeven and beyond. If you have to sell eight $300 items in *The Hartford Courant* as opposed to generating thirty inquiries at 10 percent conversion to break even on your $300 item, perhaps the smaller space for the inquiry generation would have a better chance for success. Make your own projections and decide whether it is possible to achieve them. Consult your creative staff as to their needs to sell the product. Talk to your friends in the business, and *test*.

Let's recap ROP space briefly. You would use on-page ROP space to save money and target in on a special audience such as gardeners. ROP on-page space affords you the luxury of more different unit sizes to test than are available in a Sunday magazine or in preprinted inserts. But ROP space has a shorter "life," or pulling time for response, than a Sunday magazine or preprinted insert.

NEWSPAPER-DISTRIBUTED MAGAZINES

Newspapers carry and distribute several different types of magazines tucked inside the Sunday edition, including the following:

Family Weekly
Parade
Sunday Magazine
Independent supplements

Sunday supplements carry a lot of mail-order advertising from both big and small companies. That is because they work. These supplements are hybrids, half newspaper and half magazine. Many direct-response marketers think of Sunday supplements as the best of newspapers and magazines without the worst. Sunday supplements have a longer life than newspapers and a lower CPM than magazines. Closing dates are usually 7 weeks for reservations and 6 weeks for materials. Let's look at *Family Weekly* first.

Family Weekly

Family Weekly is the fourth largest circulation magazine in the United States. Total circulation is almost 13 million. It is distributed mostly in "C" and "D" counties, or rural America, and not so much in big cities. Of the circulation, 3,500,000 is west of the Mississippi; the other 9,500,000 is east. It is printed on good quality newsprint and can reproduce four-color ads surprisingly well.

The smart mail-order advertiser buys "remnant" space in *Family Weekly*. Remnant space is leftover space. When a general or national advertiser buys a few test markets, *Family Weekly* has to sell the rest of the circulation of the magazine around those few markets. They call it remnant, or distress, space and discount the selling price. When someone buys the western portion of *Family Weekly*, the magazine is stuck with the east to sell, and you, the advertiser, can cash in. The discount is 30 percent and up depending on the unit size and color you choose.

How often are these remnants available? I usually give the publication a choice of three consecutive Sundays that would be suitable for my client, and I have never missed an insertion. The sales staff at *Family Weekly* has been very accommodating. Remnant space is available only in full-page, junior-page (7 inches by 10 inches), and vertical half-page sizes. Rates are figured on the basis of the amount of circulation you receive. Since production costs are enormous on a state-by-state basis, it usually is best to buy either the whole east or the whole west portion. The remnant CPM is figured against the circulation I am buying to come up with the total cost. The remnant CPMs vary by unit size and color of the ad.

There are some special features about *Family Weekly* that make it attractive. The premium, or extra cost, you pay to run four-color over black-and-white is nominal. But the cost of producing four-color roto materials is high. The cost for split testing is also nominal. This is a great advantage. Whenever we launch a new product or a new client and we don't have a proven ad handy, I recommend split testing in *Family Weekly* before any other media testing. This way I can test media with a winning creative approach. The short close and quick results reading (95 percent of the returns are received in 3 weeks) and the large circulation are ideal for creative and offer testing before risking a big space budget. Of course, it eliminates the option of blaming subsequent media failures on creative elements.

Family Weekly offers a tip-on card on the back cover. I have seen direct-response advertisers buy this unit of back page plus tip-on card and pay the full rate (as you cannot get remnant on the back cover) and pay out. But don't try this unit until you have tested *Family Weekly*.

Although you wouldn't classify *Family Weekly* as a "quality" magazine editorially, the quality of the customer has been very good. With a solid offer, *Family Weekly* will produce a solid customer on the back end: a good credit risk who sticks with your program and makes additional purchases.

I would recommend *Family Weekly* as a good test vehicle and a good vehicle for maintaining a business. The low cost, test capabilities, weekly frequency, and good back-end history make it an excellent addition to a business-building schedule. But as always, test first.

Parade

Parade's circulation is in excess of 21 million. Its circulation does not overlap with that of *Family Weekly*. Most of *Parade*'s circulation is in "B" and "C" counties, which include some rural and some suburban locations.

Parade also offers remnant space, but it works a little differently from *Family Weekly*. With *Parade*, you can buy as much or as little circulation as you need. *Parade* sells by market, not by region. You will have a harder time getting the dates you want with *Parade*. Usually I give *Parade* three Sundays on which I am willing to run the ad. They call at closing with a list of markets and circulation, and I can say yes or no. If I say no, they will call me the next week with another list of markets. It isn't as complicated as it sounds. I have more market control with *Parade* than with *Family Weekly*. It is worth it to have to wait a little longer to get the ad in to gain the market selectivity available in *Parade*.

Remnants are available only on full-page and half-page units in *Parade*. The cost is figured the same way as in *Family Weekly*: CPM times the circulation basis. The reps from *Parade* are very helpful and eager to please. They do everything they can to get your ad in when you want it and where you want it to appear. After all, they want your repeat business.

Parade offers the same split test opportunity that *Family Weekly* does, also for a nominal cost, but there is an added benefit. With *Parade*, you can buy several remnants consisting of smaller circulation and split each one. But don't try to split a test with small circulation. You should have at least 500,000 circulation to read the results accurately. Let's look at this split test business a little more closely. If you have one control ad and two test ads, you can buy two remnants of 1 million or more circulation and do an A-B split on the same date. This will allow you to run both tests at the same time in different markets. This is a definite added benefit, as weather or seasonality cannot skew your test.

The "answercard" or tip-on card on the back cover is a very expensive unit and is available full run, full rate only. But it pulls well. Once you have a history of response with *Parade*, you might consider trying it if you have the budget. The back end of *Parade*, or the good-credit, multibuying habits of *Parade* readers, is the same as for *Family Weekly*. I would recommend testing *Parade* remnant space for its split run capabilities, low cost, and good all-around performance.

Sunday Magazine

Sunday Magazine is similar to *Parade* and *Family Weekly*, but it appears primarily in "A" counties, or major metropolitan areas. There are some other benefits too.

You can obtain a mail-order discount if you buy *Sunday Magazine* through Top Value Media. This mail-order discount offers a slice off the rate that is comparable to the remnant rates we looked at before. There is an added benefit. With the mail-order discount, you are not on a standby basis. When you run in the *Sunday Magazine*, you run in the *Sunday Magazine*. You pick the date and place the space as you would with any magazine, and you get the mail-order discount. Sometimes having the assurance of knowing when your ad will appear is preferable to having the remnant rate.

One drawback is that split runs are rare in *Sunday Magazine*. You'll just have to run your winners only.

You can buy *Sunday Magazine* by actual newspaper rather than by region or by market. This will permit you to have tighter control and a more cohesive marketing strategy. My recommendation is that you test them all to determine which supplement will produce the best results for your product. If all goes well, it will be a three-way tie.

Independent Supplements

There are three major independent Sunday magazines available: *The New York Times Magazine*, *The Chicago Tribune Magazine*, and *The Los Angeles Times Magazine*.

The New York Times Magazine is one of the hottest media available today. This magazine has pulled response for offers that didn't work anywhere else. The mail-order section keeps growing, with a wide range of products being sold.

I haven't had the same results with *The Chicago Tribune* or *The Los Angeles Times*, but that is more a function of not pursuing the markets rather than of the papers. Both *The Chicago Tribune Magazine* and *The Los Angeles Times Magazine* carry a lot of mail-order advertising, which is always proof of a successful medium.

chapter **21**

NEWSPAPER PREPRINTS

Joel Feldman

Director of Marketing and Circulation Consumers Union of U.S., Inc. Mt. Vernon, N.Y.

Preprints are exactly what the name suggests: advertising materials which are printed in advance (preprinted) by the advertiser and then delivered to the newspaper for insertion in a specific edition. This advertising device also is known as a free-fall, a newspaper insert, or a freestanding stuffer. Its popularity as an effective, profitable direct-response vehicle has increased dramatically over the past several years. In fact, many direct marketers find that preprints are second only to direct mail as a source of profitable orders. There are also companies, particularly mail-order insurance companies, that use preprints as their prime source of order generation, especially when coupled with a television-supported ad campaign.

Orders generated through preprints can be measured quickly since they are used in newspapers, which have a short "shelf life." Therefore, the prospects react quickly to your offer, and response flow is speedy and occurs within a contracted period of time. This allows the marketer to obtain a quick reading of results; if the results are favorable, the marketer can turn around with inserts for fast generation of additional orders. Preprints offer the direct marketer's message high visibility, which, of course, is the first goal in the marketing of any product.

This high visibility is due to two major factors. First, there is an almost limitless variety of formats available to marketers which allow unique and unusual copy, art, and layout treatments. Second, a newspaper preprint acts like a blow-in card in a magazine. It is inserted loosely in the newspaper and therefore falls in the lap of the prospective purchaser. Also, because it is not bound in, it can be retained in the home when the newspaper is discarded.

Many direct mailers use newspaper preprints successfully three or more times a year. Preprints are also an excellent testing vehicle for creative approaches and product offers. Results of these tests can be used to rollout to larger quantities of preprints and often can be used directly or adapted for use in other media. Another major advantage of newspaper preprints is that no newspaper charges a premium for color, and some newspapers don't charge a premium even for multipage inserts. The benefits of these policies are obvious. With most other forms of advertising, it costs more to print additional pages and to use more color, and you also pay additional media costs. With newspaper preprints, your incremental costs for paper and color are limited to printing expenses, not to media.

Historically speaking, newspaper preprints have been a viable advertising medium for many decades. The earliest uses were on a local level. Although data and statistics were not kept until recently, it is thought that the significant use of preprints on a national basis began shortly after World War II. At that time, the major users were probably general advertisers and couponers. It is not known when direct marketers began using this vehicle for order generation.

According to the Newspaper Advertising Bureau, Inc., between 1970 and 1980, the number of newspaper inserts increased 400 percent, from 7.057 billion to 27.33 billion. It is obvious that this incredible growth was due in no small part to the increased use of this advertising medium by direct marketers. The direct marketers that use newspaper preprints are as varied as the products they offer. Some of the most common products advertised are magazine subscriptions, book clubs, record clubs, clothing, and insurance.

THE MEDIUM

Before you proceed to expend a large amount of your company's resources on a large preprint campaign, you first must test to see whether it has the potential of becoming a profitable source of new business.

When sitting down to plan a preprint test, you begin by establishing your criteria for newspaper selection. The first step in this process is to choose newspapers whose readership matches your customer profile demographically and psychographically. Demographic information is the easiest to ascertain. Figures concerning household income, educational levels, male:female ratios, and age levels are available from newspapers. Psychographic information, which refers to how people live their lives, their beliefs, and what motivates them, are more difficult to obtain. Some newspapers may be able to provide this information, but in most cases you will have to make this determination by careful review of the geographic area in which the newspaper is distributed. This should provide a good indication of readers' lifestyle and habits.

The second step is to review your competitors' use of newspaper preprints completely. Which newspapers have they used previously, which ones are they currently using, and how often? Competition should be considered on two levels: both head-to-head product competition and general competition for the mail-order dollar. Repeat preprint advertisements within the same newspaper by the same company are a sure-fire indication that the newspaper is a good preprint vehicle. It was a good newspaper for your competition, and it might possibly, although not necessarily, be a good newspaper for your product. It is a good indicator that the people who read that particular newspaper are receptive to direct-response offers.

The third step is ascertaining newspapers that historically have been known to be good direct-response vehicles irrespective of the product advertised. Newspapers that fit this criterion are generally known to direct-response ad agencies and media buying services.

The fourth and fifth steps involve establishing criteria for size of circulation and cost per thousand (CPM). The circulation of newspapers for your test should be of a size sufficient to produce large enough numbers of orders which are projectable to a larger universe. When making your newspaper selections, do not be overly concerned with cost per thousand or overemphasize its importance. Alone, CPM is no criterion for success in a preprint campaign. I have seen newspaper preprints priced at a low CPM fail miserably and others priced at a very high CPM produce huge successes. Use CPM as a guideline along with all the other criteria used in making your newspaper selections but do not be fearful of newspapers with a high CPM. However, the cost of acquisition is always important, so be careful not to stack your schedule with newspapers that all have a high CPM. There should be a mix of low, medium, and high CPMs if these newspapers meet the other selection criteria.

Testing the Medium

As with other forms of direct-response marketing, the purpose of testing for a new source of orders is to develop a medium which will produce long-range profitability. It is poor business judgment to expend energy, time, real costs, and opportunity costs to develop and implement a newspaper preprint test without prior indication that there is a profitable future for this vehicle. Therefore, when planning to test preprints, look first at where you want to end and then work backward to where you will begin.

This process involves three steps. First, choose the total possible universe of newspapers you will use in a full-scale ongoing preprint campaign. This selection process involves using the criteria outlined above and any others that are specific to your business. Since this list of newspapers will be large, most of them probably will meet only two or three of your criteria. Once this full list of newspapers is developed, choose from it a secondary core of papers. The criteria for selecting these newspapers will be more stringent and will lead to the group of newspapers to which you rollout with additional preprints once your initial tests have proved successful.

From this secondary core, you will choose the primary test list of newspapers. This group of newspapers used for the first test will be the cream of the crop. Your criteria for selecting these newspapers will be the most stringent of all. You must be as sure as anyone can be in this business that if preprints are to be successful for your product, they will be in this group of newspapers.

Exclude from this primary list any newspapers that give you even the slightest doubt that they will succeed. This is critical. You must "test down" from the strongest newspapers to the weakest. If you do not follow this procedure and begin to test marginal newspapers during the first step, and if the test is not successful, you will never know whether the reason for failure was weak newspapers or a lack of product acceptance in the medium. It also will be almost impossible to convince yourself and your management that you should do further testing. But if you begin with solid newspapers and the test fails, you can be sure (consistent with good creative elements) that preprints will not work for you. Your investment and losses will be minimal and limited. If the test is successful, you will have a clear indication of the total potential universe from which you can produce more profitable orders.

As stated before, if the initial test is a success, you will proceed to a rollout test to the secondary core of newspapers. If the results of this secondary test remain positive, you are ready to expand your preprint program to the total universe of newspapers. Of course, in the best of all worlds, each successive test produces positive results. Practically speaking, though, this is an unrealistic expectation. However, positive results for the bulk of newspapers in the first two stages should indicate a large enough universe for an ongoing profitable preprint program. Remember that the original three-step testing schedule you design is not written in stone. The results of each test level will suggest changes that should be made in the plan. The likelihood is great that the differences between your original plan and the final revised plan will be substantial.

Testing Repeat Insertions

As was mentioned previously, many advertisers use newspaper preprints successfully three or more times annually. Therefore, once you have established the optimum number of newspapers that can be used profitably, you then should begin to test repeat insertions in some of these newspapers. Again, begin with your highest yielding newspapers and build on them. Measuring the profitability of repeat insertions is much like measuring additional insert cards in a magazine. You continue running preprints in the newspaper until you find that incremental insertion which no longer produces profitable orders. Obviously, the profitability criterion is one which you and your company establish, and it should be viewed in relation to other income streams.

The Cost

The cost of preprint space in a newspaper varies widely, depending on market, circulation size, and the newspaper's ability to generate a high volume of proven direct-response orders. Similarly, there is a wide range of circulation levels, from a low of 5000 to a high of 1,400,000. Unless you have hard facts that indicate that your product will receive a more favorable response at a given circulation level, any test and rollout should contain an even mix of small-, medium-, and large-circulation newspapers. This mix should be maintained through all three levels of the program. If during the program you can make a correlation between profitable preprint orders and the level of circulation, you then can revise the remainder of your plan accordingly.

Printing costs also vary widely, depending on the format, size, number of colors, and number of pages of the preprint. Perhaps the biggest factor in terms of costs is the number of preprints to be produced. The more preprints produced, the cheaper the cost of each preprint. You will, however, eventually reach a level of production at which there is no reduction in the cost per piece. Fortunately, the level of production at which you will reach flat pricing is very high. When your preprint has been designed, request that the printer provide you with prices at various levels of production. Specifically request prices at those levels for which there are significant reductions in costs (price break levels). This information is invaluable when you formulate your media plan. You may discover that it is worthwhile to increase the media schedule so that you can cross over a price break level. The printing savings enjoyed can allow you the luxury of optimizing the exposure of your preprint at an incrementally efficient cost level.

Market Segmentation

One of the benefits of newspaper preprints is that they allow you the flexibility of segmenting your market into a wide range of geographic possibilities. You can segment within broad areas of the country, within clearly and narrowly defined markets, or within various sections of an individual newspaper's distribution area such as rural, suburban, or urban. The segments you choose will depend on the nature of your product and offer, but be aware that newspapers usually charge a premium for splitting circulation. You should carefully research whether it is cost-efficient to run your preprint in partial segments of a newspaper's circulation. With some newspapers, it may make better business sense to pay for the marginal circulation even though it is less productive than your prime segment.

Co-op Inserts

Another type of newspaper preprint advertising is known as co-op insert programs. This form of preprint program involves a third-party company. Such companies package various inserts from different advertisers in an envelope or as part of a multipage preprint and arrange for insertion in Sunday editions of newspapers. Insertion dates and frequencies depend on the fixed schedules of the individual co-op companies. These schedules are published just like newspaper and magazine rate cards.

Because advertising space is shared by many advertisers in a co-op program, the cost for newspaper preprint space is available to individual participants at a rate that is significantly lower than it would be if the participants purchased separately. Additionally, preprints are limited by the specifications of the co-op company in regard to size and format. Therefore, co-op inserts are likely to be less costly to produce. It is relatively inexpensive to be a participant; this is the greatest benefit of participating in co-op newspaper programs.

Paradoxically, the very attribute that makes co-op advertising attractive also gives cause for concern. Because you are sharing the same package with many other advertisers, you are also in immediate, direct competition for the direct mail buyer's money. Therefore, co-op preprint programs tend to produce fewer gross responses than you would get running your own preprint. This is not necessarily a negative. If the income lost from reduced orders is less than the cost savings realized for media and printing, co-ops will be more profitable than inserting your own preprint.

Although some latitude is given to advertisers with respect to the specifications of inserts in co-op programs, the parameters are defined narrowly. These restrictions in format and size may seriously limit your ability to tell your product's story adequately. This will, of course, translate into reducing your potential response rate. This problem is particularly acute for products and offers which require a significant amount of copy, such as a new product introduction or a product that is technical in nature and requires a great deal of explanation. Space limitations also become a problem in advertising products which are colorful and aesthetically appealing. Room for four-color graphics becomes critical for such a product. Not having the necessary space for pictorial representation can hamper the product's sell severely.

All things considered, it is not a good idea to test a newspaper co-op preprint before testing your own individual preprint. Instead, you should test a co-op preprint in the secondary core of tests or during the full rollout. The exact timing will depend on your budget and the number of newspapers in each of the stages of testing. The greater the number of newspapers, the less likely you are to affect the bottom line severely if the co-op test is unsuccessful. However, if your budget is so limited as to preclude testing your own preprint, try testing a co-op preprint. If the results are disappointing, do not consider preprints a failure, because the results of co-op preprints are not projectable to individually supplied preprints. Of course, your product may be perfectly suited to co-op programs, and such programs may be very successful for your product. By and large, though, this type of preprint advertising works best as a complement to a regular preprint program.

If you are conducting a dual program (regular inserts and co-op), it is important to remember that in order to save printing costs, the preprint should be designed so that it can be used for both individual and co-op insertion.

Discounts

When purchasing space for your own preprint program, it is possible although difficult to effect savings through media discounts. The standard discount available, as in other space advertising, is frequency discounts. Such a discount usually is based on lineage, with a minimum of three insertions per year required. Since it is unusual to have three or more annual insertions for one product, this discount more likely will be available on a corporate basis. Therefore, if your company sells more than one product through newspaper preprints, it will be able to realize media discounts. These savings can be apportioned among each product group in the same ratio as the actual use of the space by each product category. But realizing these savings will involve coordination within your organization and with each product group.

Although rare, remnant buys are also available for newspaper preprints. The advantage of these buys is obvious, since you may effect a media cost which is reduced between 30 and 40 percent from the card rate. Although these savings are quite attractive, remnant buys for newspaper preprints are dangerous. In order to take advantage of remnants, the advertiser has to produce and deliver preprints to the newspapers for insertion on an "as available" basis. Obviously, this is a gamble, since remnant space may never become available and you may incur the cost of printing and shipping the preprints without realizing any returns.

Even if the problem is not as drastic as the ones mentioned above, without a specific insertion date, your preprint may be inserted so late that it will be useless. This problem is even more acute for advertisers whose offers are time-sensitive or whose copy contains dated information. Avoid remnant buys unless you can obtain assurances from the newspapers that your preprint will run within a specific time period.

CREATIVE

The overwhelming majority of preprints are inserted in Sunday or weekend issues of newspapers in order to give the advertising material as long a shelf life as possible. Sunday newspapers stay in the home longer than daily newspapers. However, even a Sunday insertion allows the prospect a relatively short period of time in which to read and react to the offer. The maximum exposure that can be realistically expected is 1 week. Therefore, this copy should have very strong headlines and subheads. Your creative approach with preprints must grab the prospects' attention immediately so that they can react the first time, and possibly the last time, they see the preprint.

To the extent possible, the headlines and subheads should inform potential customers as to the nature of your product, its price, and your offer without their having to read the copy.

The piece you have designed should contain many visuals (halftones or line art) for strong, immediate impact. The emphasis should be on the offer and premium. Because preprints fall freely from the newspaper, it is impossible to know which side of the preprint the prospect will see first. Therefore, the main thrust of your sell should appear on both the front and the back of the preprint. It is not necessary that the position or presentation of this information be identical on both sides, but the message should be.

Color

You should give careful consideration to whether your preprints will be in four colors, two colors, or black and white. It is not necessarily a benefit to have your piece printed in four colors. Since newspapers rarely contain color, a black-and-white or two-color preprint will not be lost within the newspaper and probably will be as cost-effective as a four-color one. The use of four-color inserts depends on the nature of your product and whether its presentation will be enhanced greatly. After you've developed a preprint and have an ongoing newspaper campaign, you should test color variations. If your existing piece is in four colors, test two colors to measure whether you can realize cost savings without diminishing orders. Conversely, if you have a two-color preprint, test a four-color one to see whether you can produce a lift in orders which will provide enough incremental income to at least equal the increased printing cost.

Testing

When you begin to test a preprint program or if you are actively involved in an ongoing program, you should test a number of creative approaches. As long as the formats of each preprint are identical, this is an easy process to undertake. The process and problems of testing different formats will be discussed later in this chapter. Copy approach, offer treatment, and graphic presentation can be tested within each newspaper. However, be aware that the newspapers will be able to provide only 50-50 testing, in which half of the circulation receives one preprint and half receives the other. A perfect A-B split, in which every other newspaper receives a different preprint, must be arranged with the printer. The printer will be able to set up the press sheets so that the preprints are produced and delivered, with every other preprint being a different version. This procedure also applies to a campaign which includes several tests. As was mentioned earlier, newspaper preprints offer a wide opportunity for geographic segmentation. Therefore, you also might want to test different creative approaches targeted to different geographic segments.

The medium of newspaper preprints offers a wide variety of format possibilities because most newspapers do not charge a premium for size, color, or number of pages. This offers you the ability to test a wide variety of formats relatively inexpensively. The possibilities for formats are almost limitless.

Formats

One of the most popular sizes is identical to a *TV Guide* two-page insert. This preprint measures approximately 10 by 7 ⅜ inches and folds to a width of 5 inches. The drawback with this format is that its small size may cause it to go unnoticed in the newspaper, buried among larger inserts. However, many advertisers have had success with this unit. This format will be of particular interest if you also are involved with *TV Guide* inserts. If this is the case, you can overprint a *TV Guide* run and enjoy substantial printing savings.

Possibly the most common newspaper preprint is a single sheet of paper which is printed front and back. Sizes vary considerably, but the standard is 8 ½ by 11 inches. The advantage of this piece is that its substantial size gives it high visibility. It is also fairly inexpensive to print. The gatefold preprint is another widely used format. This piece contains a flap which folds out from the preprint itself in much the same way some magazines do when displaying pictorials. The advantage of this technique is that you will get heavy impact for your message whether you want to highlight your product, offer, or premium. With this technique you also can make the fold-out portion of the preprint a perforated envelope. Depending on the number of pages in the insert, envelopes also can be bound into the center of the preprint.

Multipage units are also available with preprints. These formats are particularly useful for catalog and book club offers which require substantial product presentation. You also can tip on a reply card to your preprint. This format involves a two-step printing process. The card and preprint are printed separately, and the card is affixed to the preprint. The complete unit then is delivered to the newspaper for inserting. This device produces high visibility for the reply card and provides an easy and clearly visible method for detaching it.

Involvement Devices

There are also preprints that employ involvement devices. The most common of these uses a die-cut token. A portion of the preprint is perforated and may or may not contain glue on the back. This detachable portion usually highlights a premium or offer. This device enjoys a great deal of success in direct mail and some success in preprints.

Plastic or cardboard cards can be affixed to preprints. This technique is excellent for membership offers. Pop-ups are also available with preprints. When the piece is opened, a portion of the preprint is projected upward. This portion is obviously the most visible part of the preprint; therefore, the most important part of the message is displayed there. Preprints also can be used to distribute samples of your product. Many forms of samples can be attached to the piece itself as a free giveaway. This technique is used extensively by general advertisers and merchandisers.

Newspaper preprints can be produced on a wide variety of paper stock and weights. The two broad categories of paper are offset and coated. Coated paper, also known as letterpress paper, is used primarily with four-color reproduction. Offset paper, while less expensive, does not do justice to four-color reproduction because of its porosity. The choice of paper stock is obviously yours. Be aware that if your preprint contains a business reply card, postal regulations require that the paper bulk to a weight of 7 points. If this is not met, it is likely that the order card will be rejected by the post office or that a surcharge for special handling will be added to your business reply postage.

Format Testing

Unfortunately, it is not possible to effect a test of different formats within the same newspaper. This restriction is due to the limitations of newspapers' inserting machines. The machinery cannot handle different sizes and formats of preprints concurrently. Therefore, the best method of testing formats is to use matched markets. With this method, newspapers are chosen for testing on the basis of the homogeneity of readership demographics. Therefore, to the extent possible, all test newspapers should have a readership profile with relatively the same income, education, and age levels.

Aside from the above demographic considerations, it is critical to make sure that psychographic profiles also are closely matched. That is, lifestyles and buying habits of readership in matched markets also should be identical. Your test probably will be invalid if your markets are matched demographically but some of the newspapers cover rural areas and some cover urban areas. These two segments of the population probably will react differently to your offer.

When you test, be sure that your sample sizes (circulation) are large enough to produce projectable results. It may be helpful to employ prescreening techniques in order to establish your test markets. Before choosing newspapers for a format test, review your experience in these markets from other promotional campaigns. This probably will give you a strong indication of sales potential, irrespective of the style of format. In this way, you will limit your variables to only one.

Printing

An important part of the creative process for preprints is the actual printing of the piece. As with other areas of promotion, the most creative piece containing the most expensive artwork can be rendered useless if it is produced poorly. Your creative people should work closely with the printer as early in the process as possible.

Good, competent printers can be creative and innovative in their own right. They may be able to devise special preprint formats tailored exactly to your product. It is critical to choose a printer who has the equipment and expertise to produce newspaper preprints. It is important to work closely with the printer. Such a close alliance can save you time, money, and aggravation. A printer who is well versed in newspaper preprints and deals heavily with this type of printing may be able to arrange to gang-print your piece with those of other advertisers. This can produce substantial savings on your printing bill. Of course, you will have to overcome obstacles if you choose this method of printing. You will have to meet with other advertisers to devise a common format and a similar color scheme. This will be difficult, but if you can effect these compromises, your savings can be significant. A printer who is well versed in the logistics of newspaper preprints also can effect significant savings on freight charges. Such a printer will be able to devise intelligent delivery routes so that trucks are fully loaded and transportation routes logical.

Newspapers have extremely stringent requirements concerning the packing and palleting of preprints. If these requirements are not met, your preprints could be rejected or a surcharge could be levied to cover the costs of repacking. Most newspapers publish a booklet outlining their shipping requirements. Good printers have all this information on file and will keep it current. If they do not, make sure they get it.

TV SUPPORT

Within this section, I will give a brief overview of TV support: its structure and its desired effect. A more detailed discussion of this subject is presented in another chapter.

A TV support commercial does not attempt to garner orders by itself. Its sole purpose is to create awareness of and direct attention to another advertising vehicle. In this case, the vehicle is newspaper preprints. By creating awareness and prerecognition, TV support is designed to increase order generation within the allowable cost per order (CPO) allocated for preprints. Penetration of preprint markets must be substantial for TV support to be effective. It cannot be stressed enough that TV support was never designed to reduce the allowable CPO of the primary medium. Its sole purpose is to increase order generation within the allowable CPO.

Generally speaking, a successful TV support campaign is one which produces an increase in order generation that is equal to or greater than the percentage increase in costs incurred from the TV campaign. Since TV support is designed to create prerecognition and an awareness of the primary medium, it is critical that the message related in the commercial be fresh in prospects' minds when they sit down with the Sunday newspaper. If it is not, the whole purpose of the commercial is defeated. Therefore, the commercial should start airing no sooner than 3 days before the insertion of the preprint. The frequency of airings also should increase each successive day as the insertion day approaches.

Always remember that in a TV support commercial, you are not selling your product but rather your preprint. The preprint will sell the product. Therefore, the commercial must display the preprint frequently and stress both the newspapers in which it will run and the date on which it will appear.

Another element that must be emphasized and reemphasized in a TV support commercial is the transfer device, or what may be called the "additional key number." The transfer device is usually a picture of the product or premium, and it is positioned within the order card. In the commercial, this device is heavily emphasized. Viewers are instructed to be sure to mark the transfer device so that they can take advantage of the special TV offer. The benefit is usually an additional premium. There is a dual purpose in using a transfer device. It induces the prospective customer to seek out the preprint in the newspaper, and it is used as an additional key to measure the incremental orders generated by the commercial. It is indeed the only method by which you will be able to measure the effectiveness of your TV support campaign. The one negative aspect of the transfer device is that it biases your results because it is coupled with a premium. However, if it produces a significant lift in orders, one can live with this bias.

Testing TV Support

The method for testing TV support is identical to that for testing preprint formats. One must use matched markets. Once TV support has been proved successful, you can test various creative or offer approaches. As was stated earlier, measuring the success of TV support is based on an allowable CPO level. To see whether you are within this level, add all TV and preprint costs and divide by the total number of orders received.

As was discussed previously, tabulating the number of marked transfer devices on the order cards will tell you the number of people who reacted to the TV support commercial. However, you still do not really know the effect of the commercial on order generation because you don't know the number of TV respondents who would have ordered through the preprint even without the benefit of the commercial. The corollary is also true. There will be orders generated through the support commercial which you will never know about because the transfer device was not marked.

In order to get a better measure of the overall effectiveness of TV support, you must use a common denominator: orders per thousand (OPM). For the control preprints and the supported preprints, divide the number of orders received for each group by the total circulation of each group of newspapers. The difference between these two numbers represents the number of orders attributable to the commercial.

I strongly recommend that you test TV support only after you have proved conclusively that preprints are a viable source of profitable orders by themselves. As was noted earlier, a TV support commercial will not reduce your CPO. Before you venture into TV support, you must be sure that preprints alone will generate orders at an allowable CPO. Preprint promotions are expensive, and the addition of TV will increase costs substantially. You do not want to be exposed to an additional large financial liability before you are positive that preprints are profitable. When you eventually have a successful preprint campaign supported by TV, do not become complacent. Back-test periodically to assure that support continues to produce the desired results. To back-test TV support results, designate a small portion of a preprint campaign which will not be supported (test) and an equal portion that will be supported (control). The results of this back test will tell you whether your TV support continues to be cost-efficient.

Other Support Vehicles

TV is overwhelmingly the most widely used and most successful support vehicle, but it is not the only one. Radio also can be used for support. Radio enjoys the advantage of being far less expensive than TV in terms of production and air time. Unfortunately, radio cannot provide one of the key elements necessary for a successful support vehicle: visualization of the preprint and transfer device. Because of this deficiency, it is difficult for radio to be a successful support medium. Once you have an ongoing successful preprint program, you may want to venture into a small test.

Another form of support which is used infrequently is an on-page ad within the same newspaper and issue in which your preprint is appearing. These ads can run the gamut of sizes. The creative approach would be the same as in broadcast support. The ad should depict the preprint, highlight the benefits of the transfer device, and create awareness of the preprint's presence within the newspaper. These ads are relatively inexpensive and are certainly worth testing once you have an established preprint campaign. However, it is an experimental technique, and no results are available to attest to its likelihood of success or failure.

PROBLEMS AND PITFALLS

As with other forms of promotion, you should be wary of complacency following success. Assuming that you have followed the procedure detailed in this chapter and have progressed from the testing stages to a successful rollout preprint program with or without TV support, do not rest on your laurels.

Many advertisers have found that the profitability of newspaper preprints is cyclical. For some unexplained reason, this direct marketing vehicle enjoys periods of success followed by periods of failure. Perhaps this has to do with an oversaturation of the market. Unfortunately, no correlation seems evident to explain these cycles, and no one can predict when the profitability of preprints will peak or fall. Therefore, keep close watch on your results and be cautious about oversaturating your market. Once you are involved in an ongoing program, it will become evident which newspapers can sustain profitable results with multi-insertions during a year. Those which do not enjoy this advantage should be rested periodically.

Another potential problem with preprints is that they are highly susceptible to sudden changes in the marketplace. They are very sensitive to negative news, fluctuations in the economy, and adverse weather conditions. This sensitivity is due to the short life of the preprint in the hands of the prospect. The maximum household exposure for your preprint is 1 week, and that time frame is generous. This will become evident when you chart your results and see how quickly after your insertion your returns peak and how quickly and precipitately they fall off.

You also should be aware that unlike other print media, the closing dates for delivery of newspaper preprints are extremely stringent. By and large, a list of newspaper preprint closing dates will reveal this fact. Quite literally, the material cannot be delivered early, nor can it be delivered late. Compounding the problem is the fact that many newspapers also specify a particular range of hours on a given day for delivery of the material. If you do not meet these stringent due dates and times, there is a strong likelihood that you will miss your insertion date.

There is a very practical reason for these stringent closing dates. The physical capacity of newspaper plants is limited. These plants can accommodate only so many inserts at one time and do not have the available space to store a backlog of preprints weeks in advance of insertion. Because of limited capacity, closing dates are very near to the insertion date. Therefore, the possibility of obtaining extensions is almost nonexistent. Where they do exist, they are only for 1 to 3 days.

Obviously, a missed insertion date can spell disaster for your preprint program. Even if you are able to arrange a makeup insertion, it may be so late that you will miss the prime advertising season, and if your preprint is supported by TV, missing an insertion will be disastrous. You will be airing a commercial and incurring costs to support a preprint that will not appear.

When planning a preprint schedule, you naturally will gather the circulation and print order figures for each newspaper in order to receive printing prices and formulate a budget. At the time you request this information, the newspapers will give you their best estimate of total quantities. It is important, however, that you remember that these figures are estimates. Several months will pass between the time when you receive the estimate and the time when the preprints are actually delivered to the newspaper. During this period, the dynamics of each newspaper's own business will change, changing the estimated print order figures. Therefore, it is important that the print orders be verified just before the inserts are printed. If you don't do this, you may well print more inserts than needed and incur a greater cost than necessary, reducing the efficiency of your preprint program. Perhaps a more dangerous consequence of not checking print orders is underprinting. In this case, some portion of the newspapers will be distributed without your preprint, resulting in a loss of potential orders.

Several years ago, advertisers were required to include a masthead on all newspaper preprints. The masthead simply listed the newspapers in which the preprint was being inserted. This requirement still exists today, but you have some flexibility in applying it. You are permitted to reproduce the newspaper's name in a type face of your choice, or you can obtain and reproduce each newspaper's logo. You also may have a common masthead which lists all the newspapers in which the preprint is to appear or segment this list regionally or individually.

The choice of presentation is entirely up to the advertiser, but producing individual mastheads is costly. Printers charge extra for each plate change, and if you have an extensive schedule, your printing expense will be substantially higher than you planned. The choice of presentation is usually a creative one. A solid block of type listing hundreds of newspapers, while less expensive, is aesthetically unappealing. Also, you may not be able to find the space within your preprint to accommodate such an imposing block of nonsell copy.

With many preprint formats, you will realize a very low percentage of cash with orders. One way of mitigating this is to offer a credit card option. This should be tested first as there are data to indicate that this option can depress overall response. Once tested, a simple profit and loss analysis will determine which approach produces the best bottom line. Another method of increasing cash orders is to test the inclusion of an envelope within the preprint. However, the addition of an envelope usually increases the cost of the preprint, sometimes substantially. Therefore, you will have to measure the positive aspect of cash increase versus the negative aspect of cost increase.

Many advertisers experience high bad debts with newspaper preprints. A way of diminishing this negative effect may be to withhold the premium until receipt of payment. Of course, this may produce the undesired effect of reducing your gross response severely. This should be watched carefully. Another caveat is to be careful with the wording of your copy. It is best to receive legal advice concerning the language of this offer to be sure that you do not violate state and federal rulings concerning "free" offers.

SUMMARY

Preprints have enjoyed a great deal of success in direct marketing but they have pitfalls and problems, and they are costly. Watch your expenses carefully and work on increasing cash with order and decreasing bad pay.

When planning your program, look toward the long term and proceed slowly and cautiously. Begin by testing the format and offer within a small core of newspapers. Be sure that you test a large enough circulation so that your results are reliable and projectable. Based on the success of the first stage, rollout to your second-stage test, which will include a larger universe of newspapers. During this stage, overlay a TV support test. After enjoying successful returns with the first two steps and having your results checked and validated, rollout to a full-scale preprint program.

Do not become complacent and be sure to periodically rest those newspapers which you have used frequently. Above all, back-test regularly to retest the validity of your preprint and TV support results.

chapter 22

MAGAZINE ADVERTISING

Walter S. McKenzie

Media Director,
Account Supervisor,
and Partner
TLK Direct Marketing
New York, N. Y.

DEFINE YOUR MARKET

Before you can select magazines or any other medium intelligently, you must define the market to be reached. Marketers of established products can survey existing customers, while new marketers, without customers to survey, must create a demographic picture of the buyer. This picture would include information or estimates on age, income, sex, geographic location, and possibly other factors such as type of employment, presence of children, product seasonality, and personal interests or hobbies.

After you define the market, this information can be compared with the audience characteristics of likely magazine candidates for your advertising schedule. Magazines with audiences that closely match your target market are logical choices for your initial magazine tests.

Magazine Audience Research

Most magazines can supply demographic and psychographic data on their audiences. In highly competitive fields, readership preference studies sometimes are available that illustrate the relative importance of major magazines in the field.

Research sponsored by an individual publication can be helpful to your understanding of the magazine and its field, but publishers are usually sensible individuals who are favorably disposed to research findings that illustrate the positive attributes of their books. Publishers are good salespeople who naturally stress the positive over the negative. Publication research can help your understanding, but do not consider it the last word in the selection of your media schedule.

Independent research organizations such as Simmons Market Research Bureau, Inc. provide objective, comparative magazine audience data on everything from reader demographics to product use. This research can be vitally important in helping you understand your media options. But keep in mind that such studies measure total audience. This is considerably different from the publication's basic circulation.

Basic circulation consists of subscribers and single-copy buyers. They generally are considered to be the most responsive readers because they have proved their interest in the publication by paying for it. Many direct marketers believe that newsstand buyers are the most valuable because they have demonstrated their interest in the magazine by paying a comparatively high single-copy price. Direct marketers theorize that some magazine subscribers, especially multiple-year subscribers, may lose interest in the magazine or its editorial content with the passage of time.

Total audience consists of:

- Basic circulation, i.e., single-copy buyers, subscribers, and members of the buyers' and subscribers' households
- Passalong readers, i.e., friends, neighbors, etc.
- Those who read the publication in public places such as barbershops, doctors' waiting rooms, airplanes, etc.

While most advertisers have always known that the people who make up basic circulations are the most valuable part of the media buy, the total audience concept was introduced to compete with early television's popularity and ability to reach massive audiences. The battle for big numbers was lost long ago to television, but the total audience concept has remained like a relic of bygone days. Indeed, in recent years, publishers have shown creativity and imagination by developing magazines that appeal to small special-interest groups. Even cable TV, which has taken unending pride in that overused word "narrowcasting," often refers to its efforts as the magazine concept of TV programming.

All properly developed audience research can be a useful tool in helping you reach good media decisions, but other factors also contribute to the decision-making process.

Editorial Analysis

Editorial analysis is usually the most important part of the media selection process. Take the time to review at least half a dozen issues of each publication under consideration. These can be obtained from each magazine's advertising sales department. Ask each magazine for a statement of its editorial philosophy. Ask yourself whether your typical buyer might be interested in each editorial product. The closer the relationship between your product and the publication's editorial content, the better your sales should be. For example, companies selling photography equipment would expect to do well in photography magazines.

In general magazines, be alert for special issues or major articles that relate to your product and consider running your advertising there. Such editorial content attracts readers who may be more inclined to buy.

Obviously, a magazine does not need a close editorial relationship with your product to be successful for you, but in today's highly segmented media environment, it makes sense to look there first. However, general magazines also should be considered, as a major segment of their readership may be in your market.

Advertising Analysis

Most companies have competitors, and it's a good idea to find out which magazines they use. Repeated insertions in a publication are generally an indication of success.

If it is available, check Publishers Information Bureau (PIB), published by Leading National Advertisers (LNA). This reference lists magazine advertising schedules by publication, issue date, size of insertion, use of color, and estimated expenditure for most major advertisers. If PIB is not available, ask your magazine sales reps for information and tearsheets of competitive advertising carried in the past year.

When scheduling your advertising, try to avoid running in the same issue with a competitor. In most cases, both advertisers split the available respondents and therefore experience unprofitable insertions. Since the publication has an interest in your success, the sales rep usually will tell you when a competitor is scheduled for "your" issue and give you the chance to stay or move to another issue. Unless being a "spoiler" is more important than profit, it is usually better to move if the competitor won't. If a magazine refuses to tell you that a competitor is scheduled for your issue, include instructions in your insertion order that your ad is not to run if a competitor is scheduled for the same issue. Such a clause will relieve you of the responsibility of paying for the publication of an unprofitable insertion as a result of one or more competitors appearing in the same issue.

There are always exceptions to general rules, and it's important to find out what they are. Readers often expect to find a specific type of advertising in a publication and are drawn to it. Like shopping malls that contain several competitive stores, the variety of choice helps create a profitable market for all.

Perhaps the most obvious examples of this are newspaper classified advertising sections that contain highly competitive advertising for employment, automobiles, and real estate. The variety of restaurant ads in metropolitan magazines provides another example.

Today's highly segmented media makes it harder to avoid competitors. For example, personal computer magazines are loaded with competitive ads that seem to work for all. This is often true for mechanics books, business and financial publications, crafts and hobbies, automotive, and others.

You will learn from personal experience and the experience of others how competitive advertising affects your response. Not all publications are good response media, and it's important to know the good from the bad. The easiest way is to have a knowledgeable direct marketer tell you, but you can figure it out for yourself.

At the same time that you make your editorial analysis, do an advertising analysis as well. Like the editorial content, the advertising creates an environment that either does or doesn't encourage the reader to respond. If the publication carries a lot of response advertising in issue after issue, it's a safe bet that the audience is responsive. Conversely, if little or no response advertising is found, proceed with caution.

REGIONAL AND DEMOGRAPHIC EDITIONS

Regional and demographic editions enable the advertiser to select a desirable portion of a magazine's total circulation. Most major magazines offer regionals. Demographic editions are still relatively few.

Regional editions are offered in a variety of ways. For example, *Newsweek* offers the following choices:

- 41 major metropolitan editions
- 16 regional editions
- A state marketing plan that enables an advertiser to buy any of the fifty states individually or in combination
- The top ten Area of Dominant Influence (ADI) markets

Newsweek also offers three demographic editions defined as follows:

1. **Newsweek Executive.** Questionnaire-qualified subscribers; 100 percent are professional or managerial by title, having a minimum annual income of $25,000. Average personal income is $54,800.
2. **Newsweek Executive Plus.** This is a larger group of questionnaire-qualified subscribers; 100 percent are professional or managerial by title. Average personal income is $44,100.
3. **Newsweek Women.** A select circulation of a half million upscale, mostly working women.

Time offers similar regional and demographic editions plus others, such as a Student/Educator Edition, an Ex-Urban Edition, and *Time* Z that circulates to subscribers in 1414 top income quintile ZIPs located in 158 metro markets in 43 states and the District of Columbia.

The advantages of demographic editions are obvious. If the demographic offered matches your market closely, it can be a highly profitable medium.

Advantages

There are several advantages to regional editions:

1. You can copy test several different ads in one issue. Magazines such as *TV Guide* offer A-B splits in each of their regional editions at nominal cost. This capability enables you to learn which ad is most productive as well as the relative response levels for the areas of the country tested. Inserts as well as page or fractional space can be tested regionally.

2. You can test the medium without paying the national price. A regional will give you an indication of the publication's value, particularly if you have a good idea of the relative merits of various sections of the country or metropolitan areas against which to compare the response of the regional buy.
3. You can use regionals for added advertising exposure in the best reponse areas for your particular offer.
4. You can use regionals to support other promotional activity. For example, regional space and TV can be used to support an intensive direct mail drop into an area.

Disadvantages

There are two disadvantages to regionals and demographic editions. First, you rarely can obtain superior position, and this can affect your level of response. Second, you pay a space premium for using less than national circulation. If you are testing a new magazine with a regional and hope to use it nationally, be sure to take the extra cost and poor position into account when evaluating results.

MAIL-ORDER AND SHOPPING SECTIONS

Mail-order and shopping sections can be a bonanza of marketing information as well as profits to a new direct marketer.

Mail-order and shopping sections usually offer space at lower rates than the rates for equivalent space in the rest of the magazine. Small space ads are the rule, and readers are comfortable with the format. These sections provide an economical way to test magazines and magazine categories.

In addition, many shopping sections are offered regionally, cutting your costs even further. After successfully testing small space in these sections, some advertisers move on to larger units in the main body of the book. Others are content to stay in the shopping section with similar or larger units of space. Intelligent testing of these options will demonstrate which course of action is best for you.

Evaluate shopping sections the same way you analyze the advertising environment of any magazine. After studying the general editorial and audience characteristics of the publication and reviewing the list of current advertisers, decide whether the shopping section will provide an atmosphere that is compatible with your proposition.

Experiment with advertising unit size. If your current small space ad is working well, think about testing a larger ad.

The book *Direct Marketing: Strategy/Planning/Execution* describes the universe-constellation concept, which is a way of sorting publications into categories and subcategories by subject matter. This concept is used in planning your first test insertions, and it will enable you to evaluate one magazine and also point the way to other publications that logically follow from your first successes. Structure your tests to maximize the amount learned.

NEGOTIATING POSITION

Where your ad is positioned can have a dramatic effect on response. The closer your ad is positioned to the front of the book, the better response will be. A right-hand page is better than a left-hand page. Publishers usually reserve right-hand pages for full-page advertisers. If you are using smaller units, accept the left-hand page but stay in the front of the book unless you want the mail-order section, which is usually in the back.

Obtaining front of book position is no easy matter. Almost every insertion order requests a right-hand page and a front of book position, and the publisher has only a few available to offer.

Many publishers offer readership studies that show fairly even readership throughout the book. They argue that position is not important since readership is roughly the same regardless of position. Believe such arguments at your peril. Readership is very different from response. A well-known direct marketer used the same ad for 15 years. It was his most productive ad for generating inquiries, but it always scored very low on readership studies. We concluded that it was read primarily by people who were interested in the service being offered while the uninterested readers passed it by. The result was low readership and high productivity.

A comparison of different positions in descending order follows, with the two best positions indexed at 100.

TABLE 22-1

Position Preference Sequence	Position	Index
1	First right-hand page and back cover	100
		Approximate Response Reduction from First Choices Above, %
2	Second right-hand page	−5
3	Third right-hand page and inside third cover	−10
4	Fourth right-hand page and page opposite third cover	−15
5	Midbook (preceding editorial matter)	−30
6	Back of book (following main editorial section)	−50

Some publishers attempt to reduce demand for the front of the book by requesting a position premium. Smart direct marketers rarely pay position premiums. Such premiums only cut into profit, and a magazine that wants the advertiser's business should cooperate in making the insertion as successful as possible.

Insert cards are also subject to the effects of position and proximity to the front of the book. Relative pulling power is as follows:

TABLE 22-2

Insert Position Preference Sequence	Insert Position	Index
1	First insert card position	100 Approximate Response Reduction from First Choice Above, %
2	Second insert card position	−5
3	Third insert card position and card opposite third cover	−15
4	Fourth insert card position (after main editorial)	−25
5	Fifth insert card position (after main editorial)	−30

Because position is so important, it should not be left to chance. Reach an understanding with the publication before you make a commitment for the space.

NEGOTIATING RATES

Most major magazines offer lower mail-order rates because they realize that many direct marketers can't make a profit if they are required to buy at the higher general advertising rates.

The continued use of special mail-order rates is a testimony to their practicality. There are occasions when you may need more of a rate concession to make a magazine work profitably. For example, when tests show a magazine to be a winner or a loser, your next actions are obvious. You continue to use the magazine or you don't. The hard decisions come when magazines fall into the gray area of being almost profitable. Since it isn't profitable or is only marginally so, you could just drop the book and never think about it again, or you could tell the magazine what's needed to make it acceptable. Give the publisher the chance to say yes or no. The publisher may agree to a special rate in return for a minimum number of insertions during the year or for some other requirement that's important to the publisher and acceptable to you.

Ask about the availability of a special remnant rate. Remnants are pieces of leftover circulation after a regional advertiser has placed an order. This leftover circulation is usually available at a substantial discount, generally about 30 to 35 percent below the card rates.

Remnant space usually is offered to advertisers at the issue's closing date, and so it is necessary to have your advertising reproduction material available to send to the publication on short notice.

SPACE UNITS

Ad size is determined by two factors:

1. The amount of space needed to present the proposition adequately
2. The size that maximizes response at the most efficient rate

Most new marketers start small and test their way into larger units. If you build to an ad covering one-third of a page and have an acceptable cost per response, there is a good possibility that you can make the transition to a full page in that publication with little or no increase in cost per response. If your proposition is seasonal, attempt the move upward in your good season.

If a full page works for you, give careful thought to running a page and an insert card. Generally, if you are looking for inquiries, the cost per inquiry will fall significantly, but so too will your sales conversion. You also will have higher inquiry fulfillment costs.

Despite these negative aspects, many advertisers are able to use page and postal card units successfully. Careful testing will determine whether you are one of them.

Full-page inserts also can hype response. The same words of caution about the page and postal cards apply to the full-page insert. Test it regionally, or if *TV Guide* is one of your productive publications, take advantage of their ability to insert full-page or larger inserts in individual editions.

By keeping the number of editions used to a relative few, you can keep space and printing costs low and still obtain a valid reading of the inserts' profitability.

When structuring your test, use enough editions so that the response will be indicative of national pull. Select and separately key editions in the major geographic sections of the country.

Color

Black and white continues to be the most popular and efficient choice for most direct-response advertising. Generally, adding color only increases your advertising cost and is not rewarded with increased response.

A four-color ad often is cost-efficient if there is a relationship with the product or offer, but use of color only to be colorful tends to be nonproductive.

Frequency

After your first test of a publication has proved to be successful, your next step is to determine how many insertions (and what size) can be run profitably. A seasonal advertiser may have the option of testing only a few issues. The nonseasonal advertiser may first test those months which are usually the most responsive and then ease into the poorer months to determine how long profitability can be maintained.

Some advertisers may be able to run only once a year in a publication. Others will be able to run every month with multipage insertions. Finding out what you can do profitably should be an adventure.

Split Runs

There are three kinds of split runs available:

A-B splits
50-50 splits
Geographic splits

A-B Splits. A-B splits offer even distribution of two or more ads throughout the magazine coverage area. This type of split is used to determine the relative pulling power of various copy approaches or offers.

If you ran an A-B split in a given issue and found a large stack of that issue at your newsstand, the first copy would contain ad A, the second would contain ad B, the third would contain ad A, and so on. The even distribution provides representative coverage of the audience, and this makes the response results comparable. Magazines usually offer A-B splits at a small extra charge. If a publication asks an exorbitant premium, run your tests elsewhere.

50-50 Splits. Sometimes a publication is unable to offer an A-B split but can deliver a 50-50 split in which half the circulation will get ad A and half ad B.

Beware the 50-50 split. You have no guarantee that each ad will be shown to representative samples of the audience or that it will be distributed evenly throughout the coverage area.

The 50-50 split should be considered only as a last resort, and then its results shouldn't be trusted. They should be subjected to intensive reconfirmation tests.

Geographic Splits. Most major publications offer geographic splits or regional editions, enabling you to limit advertising coverage to a particular area or to test copy appeals or offers against a regional segment of the population.

Geographic splits should not be used to test comparative ad response because different sections of the country may have different response patterns. A geographic test would be unfair to an ad that appeared in a poor-response area and would hype the response of an ad that went to a high-response area.

chapter **23**

TELEVISION DIRECT RESPONSE

Sandy Davis

President
Davis-Lee Direct Marketing
Midland Park, N. J.

The most extraordinary thing about the history of direct-response television is its tremendous growth; no other industry can boast such rapid expansion and development. As a marketing tool, direct-response television became invaluable as the number of television households grew and as an increasing number of advertisers entered the direct marketing field.

Television became the most highly competitive advertising medium. Direct-response advertising was the child of what is called general or retail advertising. Direct-response television's defining characteristic came to be a lengthy advertising message that told viewers to send a check or money order to an address to get what they wanted through the mail.

"Not sold in stores" was a key promotional factor. The commercials were not 30-second (:30) or 1-minute (:60) spots but 15-minute programs. The ability to expand in length would be restricted, since there was just so much that could be said about the music on a record or the features of a product. But a concept was developed: mail-order marketing through television. The record industry was the first major direct-response advertiser, promoting "specialty" records or collections of records. Gradually, the length of the commercials shrank from 15-minute programs to 120-second (:120) spots.

Although the record advertisers dominated direct-response television in the mid-1960s, they were soon to be joined by various gadgets and household appliances. For the next 10 years, direct-response TV would perpetuate a poor image and carry the label of "schlock" as viewed by the television stations selling the time. But it was nevertheless profitable and increased revenues of both stations and advertisers.

The 1960s gave the television industry its revolution. Stations had an abundance of television time to sell, and competition among advertisers was minimal. Direct-response advertising touched on a virgin marketplace. To invest in this "risky unknown" medium could cost as little as $2000 for a commercial (nonunion talent, studio, etc.) plus a limited test buy of one to two stations for a few hundred dollars. The :120 spots were not even published as part of the station's rate card. (Indeed, they remain unpublished.) It is important to understand that at that time the general advertising industry was not a major consumer of television "spot" time, and this allowed for the development of direct-response television advertising. Time was cheap, and there was plenty to go around.

The financial success of direct-response advertising was recognized immediately. A spot would air, and 2 days later orders would be retrieved from a post office box or sent directly to the advertiser's office. They would continue to arrive for days: checks, money orders, and cash. Product costs and advertising costs were offset by sales revenue within 48 hours of the first spot airing.

The length of the :120 spot was needed to permit repetition of the mailing address. The number of spots bought were at high-frequency levels, which added to the viewer's awareness of the item being sold and gave the viewer time to find a pencil and paper to copy the mailing address. Specific programming could be selected that was suited to the product being advertised.

Today this could be likened to cable narrowcasting, or reaching a specific type of audience for a specific advertising message. The cost of direct-response advertising was highly negotiated. The main factor considered in the negotiations was the station's availabilities of time (which were great). Direct-response advertising became a strong source of revenue for stations in off-seasons, when general advertisers were not airing heavy schedules.

The first quarter (which starts on the first Monday following the final Sunday in December, for a 13-week period) and the third quarter of the broadcast calendar year (starting on the Monday following the final Sunday of June) were the off-seasons for general advertisers and became the seasons which direct-response advertisers plan campaigns around and base their business on.

With the increase of television households, the area of programming expanded rapidly. The networks, of course, were the major contributors of new programs; independent stations were limited in their ability to develop new programs because of the high cost. The area of "barter" television became a spinoff for direct-response advertisers; programs were created inexpensively or old film "packages" were revitalized and offered to stations in exchange for television spot time. The "banking," or collecting, of these spots later created another business in itself. If the bartered time was in excess of what actually was going to be used by an advertiser, the excess time was sold to another advertiser at a cost far lower than the stations' published advertising rates. This marketing vehicle was used exclusively by the direct-response industry and did not achieve until later years the success it currently enjoys in the general advertising category.

The idea of spots being bartered was not limited to programming as the barter source; stations' needs also were met by exchanging "giveaway" trips as incentives to station personnel and advertisers, products, holiday tributes, and hotel scrip. In the mid-1960s, a small midwestern television station even tried bartering its spots for a new television tower since the old tower had been lost in a storm.

To increase the volume of orders being generated by television advertising, advertisers began including telephone numbers for COD orders, laying the foundation for yet another industry: the 800 number in-WATS service. These 800 number services would become the lifeline of direct response advertisers.

The volume of orders increased with every spot aired. Previously local private answering services were used. These services were used basically by doctors and small local businesses. For the advertiser it was a full-time job to find the services and set them up in every market in which a station was bought.

Calls to the answering services had to be placed daily at the beginning of runs (and then semiweekly as the scheduling weeks progressed) to find out the "counts" that were generated by the previous day's aired spots. The service's job was simply to capture the caller's name and address. When airing on two stations in a market, the operator had to ask on which station the caller saw the commercial and give "credit" to the station from which the order was generated. It was preferable to use separate services with different phone numbers, but two services large enough to handle the volume were not always available in smaller markets.

This was the era of direct-response television advertising that laid the cornerstone for multiple industries established to mine the rewards of a thriving marketing vehicle. It was to include the record industry, physical fitness and diet aids, and kitchen gadgets and countless inexpensive utensils. The field would later be enlarged as it became more sophisticated to include magazines and book clubs and insurance and fund-raising organizations.

PER INQUIRY ADVERTISING

The transition period that direct-response television went through was both swift and innovative. Today, many people confuse the term "per inquiry" (PI) with direct response. Direct response is the type of advertising. PI is merely a method of securing television time in which a television station will air spots for an advertiser at no charge to the advertiser for the spots themselves. Instead, payment to the station is based on the number of inquiries, leads, or orders generated by the spots aired. Prior to airing, a fixed cost per response is negotiated, based on what the advertiser can afford.

Stations are paid on a monthly basis for the inquiries generated. This method of television advertising still is conducted, but it is not as prevalent today. Stations accepting this method of advertising are generally found in smaller markets or are stations in larger markets that are not as advanced or competitive as others in the marketplace.

Generally, PI stations turn unsold time into revenue. The nature of this method of advertising does not lend itself to preciseness because spots are aired totally at the station's discretion. Projection of orders cannot be accomplished, nor can dollar expenditures be allocated. Depending entirely on their availability, an advertiser can see five spots or fifty spots aired within a given week. It is because of this wide variation that costs and responses cannot be projected but are just added and accumulated each month.

PI arrangements with spot TV stations require lots of time to establish both goodwill and a reporting system; each station has its own method to which advertisers must adjust.

PI advertising is no longer a major factor in generating orders. The orders generated are at a fixed cost which, since it is known in advance, eliminates all risk. Consequently, PIs can help offset spot TV buys that may not have been profitable. If a PI station is generating sufficient volume, it usually will attempt to air more spots in better time periods to increase the income; if a schedule is not doing well, the station simply will pull the schedule off the air and replace it with another advertiser whose product might generate a higher income for the station.

It is important to note that unless an advertiser is spending significant dollars for a paid spot campaign, it is generally not worth the time or effort to set up PI arrangements. The use of PI-generated orders should be viewed as an "add-on," not as a primary source of leads or orders.

PIs are currently the main source of income for major cable networks that are trying to establish themselves in the industry.

800 NUMBER TOLL-FREE SYSTEMS

With the increased competition among direct-response advertisers and the resulting market expansion and multiple station buys within a market, the industry faced an enormous problem: the lack of capable local answering services to capture the calls. Initially, in-bound 800 number services were limited to those involved in retail dealer referral; capturing calls and sourcing by media still were being done by hand, although some companies transferred the data to microfilm.

The manual 800 number system simply gave advertisers the advantage of having many lines and operators available to take calls in one central location. However, it did not eliminate the problem of sourcing by media or that of converting the hard copy orders to computer format for fulfillment and order processing. These needs had to be satisfied if the direct-response industry was to grow.

Eventually, national 800 number answering service companies sprang up around the country, all vying for the opportunity to become involved in this lucrative business. Public awareness of the "toll-free" system was swift as a result of the barrage of 800 numbers on millions of television screens, each reminding the viewer that the call was free.

In selecting answering services to capture the orders generated by direct-response television, three factors should be considered: (1) the advertiser's needs, (2) the ability of the service to fulfill these needs, and (3) the track record of the 800 number service for other advertisers.

It is also recommended that more than one service be used when running a large campaign. The reason is the "Don't put all your eggs in one basket" rule. If for some reason, technical or other, a service is out of order for any length of time, responses from the spots aired will be lost unless another service can be substituted. If two services are used from the beginning, it is a simple matter to switch the commercial and use the second 800 number and service. If only one service is used, and it goes "down," valuable time will be lost searching for a replacement. In addition, when you are running on multiple stations in a market, the use of more than one service will enable the sourcing to be exact, leaving no room for error.

When individual services are used for each different station in a market, they can source for specific stations without having to ask the caller for the last four digits dialed or the station call letters. More and more 800 number services currently are making available banks of different 800 numbers that in essence accomplish this, enabling an advertiser to give them all their business, even in a multiple-station market.

In addition to keeping track of different stations, the advertiser also must resolve geographic overlap situations. An example of this would be an advertiser airing spots in Washington, D.C., and Baltimore, Maryland. The overlap of station signals could interfere with an operator properly sourcing the origin of the call. By using separate services or different banks of numbers within a service, this problem is eliminated, as the Washington, D.C., phone number would be different from Baltimore, and responses would be totally separate.

With 800 number services improving their systems for capturing and sourcing responses and computerizing data for fulfillment purposes, direct-response advertisers are able to ship more quickly and efficiently to their customers. This fact alone has contributed to lowering the "refusal" or "rejection" rate and increasing profitability.

The refusal factor is aggravated by the impulse buyer using the telephone as an ordering device. Viewers ordering a product may change their minds if orders are delayed in shipment.

The refusal rate also varies from one product to another and must be calculated in the financial or business plan—specifically the allowable order margin—to determine the point at which it no longer becomes profitable when compared with advertising costs.

Each advertiser will have its own specifications that the services must meet. A record marketer would require that a service be able to record multiple orders versus single orders. Publications might require an "up-sell" of an order from a 1-year subscription to a 2-year subscription. The number of people who order a 1-year subscription versus a 2-year subscription then must be reported.

In choosing a service or services, first consider the advertiser's needs and then determine which service can best fulfill them. To further aid the services in capturing responses properly, the projected volume of calls should be computed. This will allow the service to gear up for calls by putting in additional lines and operators if needed. As stations are added and deleted from campaigns, the services must be advised of start and termination dates. The services should be given as much advance notice as possible so that they can modify the information in their computer systems and adjust their staffing and the number of lines ordered from the telephone company.

The final consideration in selecting an 800 number service is the daily procedure for conveying counts to the agency or advertiser. Facsimile transmission machines and TWX machines have aided tremendously in recording daily counts of responses. Equipment used by service and agency or advertiser must be compatible. Flexibility is needed here as well as additional equipment; if your telecopier machine is being used heavily, a TWX would be helpful as a backup. Since it is preferable to get these counts as early in the morning as possible, using several machines avoids delays in getting daily counts. This will give you the advantage of posting the counts against specific stations daily, allowing for daily analysis.

In addition to establishing this procedure for getting the numbers, the printout or hard copy computer sheets may be part of your client's need. The daily transmission of counts to the agency basically lists the stations and responses. They also may give multiple orders by stations or up-sells by station. These figures are broken down only by station. Most services also will supply an hour-by-hour breakdown by station (a very necessary piece of data that is used for quick analysis).

This report is generated by the hard copy containing the specifics of the individual call. As most fulfillment centers are computerized to varying degrees, these data are needed quickly for mailing. Client needs again must be determined in terms of how they want these data received. If computer capabilities are compatible, the use of an on-line computer service may become a factor in selecting an 800 number company. This aspect would certainly be an advantage in expediting shipping.

Whether or not hard copy is to be mailed directly or magnetic tape sent or an on-line computer used is determined by the client and the fulfillment centers. Such capabilities have to be recognized as part of service selection. The 800 number systems available to direct-response advertisers are the lifeline of this aspect of the industry. Some services may be good for one client and not another.

STATION AND STATION REPRESENTATION

The choice of dealing directly with the stations' management and sales personnel or with the stations' representatives when buying direct-response TV time is a decision that is made by individual TV time buyers. Since dollar levels have increased to what now can represent excellent commissions for the stations' representatives, dealing with a local source instead of the "home" office is frequently advantageous.

The rep handling direct-response accounts is more knowledgeable about the specialized direct-response television medium and aware of special techniques for planning television time buys. This enables advertisers to deal with one person who also may represent a number of other stations that will be bought in the same campaign.

Time is always of the essence in making decisions; going through one person who can reach numerous stations obviously will save time and expedite orders and order changes.

Sales commissions to the stations' representatives now must be paid whether the order was placed through the station or through the rep firm. When dealing with a rep who is "on top" of the station and the rep's accounts, where the communication with the station is precise and the rep's information is up to date, the rep can be as valuable as negotiating directly with the station.

Station representative firms' basic revenues are derived from selling time to "general" or retail advertisers; these advertisers need extensive programming, audience viewership, and station data. Direct-response advertisers do not require such data as they are irrelevant. The test of direct-response advertisers is not cost per thousand (CPM) but cost per order (CPO). An adage in the industry is that if the cost is low enough, it will pay out. The rep firm can increase its sales revenues without providing the type of detailed and time-consuming research that cuts into profits. This factor accounts in part for the highly discounted rates offered to direct-response advertisers.

With the influx of direct-response advertisers vying for TV spots, buying time basically comes down to determining from whom you can secure the best deal. The decision to deal with the station directly or with its representative is based purely on the people aspect of this business.

STATION SELECTION OF ADVERTISERS

The length of the :120 spot commercial presents limitations on spot availabilities. The general use of :30 spots within station programming means that four :30 spots or two :60 spots make up for one :120 commercial. Since direct-response television time is sold at substantial discount off the card rate, stations would, of course, prefer to sell four :30 spots at the full rate rather than one :120 spot at a discounted rate.

It comes down to supply and demand. On the agency level, the strength is dollar volume. With many general advertising agencies having direct-response divisions, payment no longer represents a risk to the station. Television stations require payment 30 days after receipt of the previous month's final Sunday billing. In dealing with direct-response advertisers, some stations demand payment in 10 to 15 days. This is not unreasonable in light of the low rate that is being offered.

The station will establish its own criteria for favoring direct-response advertising agencies. Prompt payment of bills will always remain on top of the list in designating the preferable agencies or advertisers. For a new advertiser or agency, stations may request a "cash up front" payment basis until credit is established.

The quality of direct-response commercials has become another factor in favoring certain advertisers. As more prestigious general advertising agencies add direct-response divisions, commercial standards have become higher. Stations will in general weigh the "image" being portrayed to their audience as a factor in the selection and elimination of advertisers.

There are exceptions to this rule, of course, and some stations forgo commercial quality and image in lieu of revenue. But basically, claims, statements, and order fulfillment time must meet specifications instituted by the networks.

A contributing factor to station selection of agencies and advertisers is customer service. People calling to order a product expect a response within a reasonable period of time. Complaints for unfilled orders often are received by the station on which the caller saw the spot. The more complaints a station receives about an advertiser, the less chance that client has for future acceptance by the station.

CREDIT CHECKS

When a direct-response agency is a division of a recognized general advertising agency, credit checks by stations are not necessary. For an "in-house" or newly formed agency, credit information will be requested by the station. This information will include names of banks, officers of the corporation, and credit references. The information should be made available in written form to any station or station representative firm requesting it, along with a financial statement if one is available.

CALLING FOR STATION SPOT AVAILABILITIES

Until a station-by-station track record can be established by an advertiser or agency, all stations in a market should be contacted when you are planning to buy time.

Contacting each station in a market will provide an up-to-the minute picture of the availability of spot time and a comparison of rates in the market. This comparison then can be weighed to determine which station is offering the best deal, the most scheduling flexibility, and the most cost-efficient buy. Each buying quarter will present its own set of stipulations and criteria based on station availability of spots and supply and demand conditions.

In direct-response time buying, it isn't necessary to look at Nielsen or Arbitron ratings but is merely a matter of analyzing daily responses to determine where your audience is. In evaluating station rates, the cost of individual "dayparts" is a major factor.

Direct-response television is bought in "broad dayparts." They vary per station, depending on programming and whether a station is an independent or a network affiliate. Independent stations always will have more :120 availabilities than a network owned and operated (O&O) station or a network affiliate that picks up the majority of a network feed for its "local" programming.

This, of course, accounts for independent stations originating direct-response advertising availabilities. Not only do they have more spots available to direct-response advertisers, they also are less costly from a starting negotiation point than spots sold by networks and network affiliates.

Independent stations have fulfilled the needs of direct-response advertisers and have become the cornerstone of many television advertising campaigns. Although the audience reach is not as extensive as in networks buys, the availability of frequency and the lower costs put the independent stations in a favored position for direct-response advertisers. If the network O&Os and affiliates can be negotiated at cost-efficient levels, they too can become strong contributing factors to efficient advertising schedules, even with lower frequency levels. The O&Os and affiliates certainly are able to reach a larger audience, but at higher cost to the advertiser.

Many stations are putting together specified "packages" to be offered to direct-response advertisers, and broad dayparts are the basis of these packages. A station's dayparts may be broken down as follows: 6A-10A, 10A-3P, 3P-6P, 6P-8P, 8P-11:30P, and 11:30P-conclusion (signoff).

A specific number of spots may be assigned to each daypart by the station. These assignments of the number of spots to be aired in each daypart usually are based on station availability of :120 spots. In addition to assigning specific costs and a specific number of spots to dayparts, stations also will sell packages at a fixed "direct-response rate" for the entire package.

They will designate how many spots will air in each daypart, but all spots will cost the same. What does this mean to the advertiser? Basically, it means that the spot run at 9 A.M. is going to cost the same as the spot aired at 7 P.M. A balance must, of course, be created in establishing how much additional weight or how many responses the 7 P.M. spot must carry to compensate for the advertiser's overpayment for the 9 A.M. spot aired.

Though both are at great cost reductions compared with what the general advertiser would pay, the response level of each daypart still must be reconciled as to cost per order. Package plans cannot be renegotiated. If the stronger areas cannot pull their own weight (plus the weight of those areas in which you are "overpaying"), the end result will be cancellation.

This cancellation does not necessarily mean loss of revenue to a station. On their "waiting lists" of advertisers trying to buy direct-response time is someone else whose product, item , or service will pay out.

Another method of securing television time on a direct-response basis is the run of station (ROS) plan. This plan involves scheduling a specific number of spots to air at the station's discretion and availabilities. ROS is basically the same as signon to signoff (SO/SO), another term used frequently in direct-response television.

An ROS schedule is the least expensive way to advertise. Airing on an ROS basis is very similar to airing on a PI basis. The spot placement is left entirely to the station's discretion. Although a number of spots are scheduled, you do not know ahead of time where they actually will air. This type of scheduling should carry a low rate per spot, but because of the supply and demand situation, it doesn't. You are basically left at the mercy of the station.

Contrary to a PI arrangement, this method of buying television time is not on a guaranteed, or fixed cost per order, basis. Until a track record is established for every individual station airing your schedules on an ROS basis, you will not be able to determine which of these stations gives a "fair rotation." (By a fair rotation, I mean a decent rotation among all dayparts.)

Stations need to earn the reputation of being "good" ROS stations. A typical example of a station airing a poor ROS schedule would be one in which the spots were aired generally 6A-8A and in the wee hours of the morning only. This particular scheduling would not enable the advertiser to reach the bulk of the stations' audience but simply offer the advertiser the stations' unsold time at a special rate with the hope of "falling" into better dayparts by chance.

The ROS buy does not allow the buyer the advantage of rearranging schedules for spots to air in more productive dayparts. Unless a station has the reputation of fair rotation, this method of scheduling should be avoided. Because of the competitive nature of the direct-response industry today, specific station representative firms have aided in the development of ROS scheduling. Instead of recognizing the advertisers' needs, these representatives have been influential in dictating a vague ROS schedule technique to the stations they represent.

Although it may seem that the station and rep firm profit, in the long run they do not. Schedules are canceled, the station gains a bad reputation, and the station representative firm soon is discarded. If you're "burned" by a poor rotation schedule, you don't go back for a second burning by either the station or the rep who sold you the schedule.

A tremendous "edge," recognized by stations and station representatives as the most predictable and dependable, is based on the "13-week commitment." The commitment to stations when scheduling time for a 13-week quarter means nothing unless you don't cancel. All direct-response television time is bought on the basis of 48- to 72-hour cancellation policies. This specifically means that if you buy a 2-week schedule of a 13-week schedule, it can be canceled at any point on 48 to 72 hours' notice. This is not something that will come as a shock to stations. It is a practice with all direct-response advertisers, and in general it has been accepted by all television stations that have direct-response advertising schedules.

A daily evaluation can determine whether a station should continue to air your schedule. A profit or loss situation can be determined within 48 to 72 hours after airing or sooner because the responses are in your hands to evaluate.

A recap of the considerations for reviewing when "calling for availabilities" would read like this.

1. Contact with all stations in a market
2. Comparative rate structure
3. Daypart rate comparisons
4. Allowable frequency
5. Packages
6. ROS schedules
7. Flexibility

These seven points must be considered before you actually place a buy with your contact.

An advantage to agencies in establishing a relationship as a 13-week advertiser is that it enables the station to project its quarterly income. If there is a "shortfall" of local or general advertising business, this can be made up by direct-response advertisers. This factor could put the agency on a "preferred" list as being less apt to cancel schedules. Agencies have the advantage of rotating various clients within the same 13-week schedule. This gives clients a fair rotation and enables the agency to hold on to its secured spots. The established 13-week schedule that is not canceled before the last telecast date (LTC) also may result in lower rates to the advertiser as a negotiated bonus for consistency.

At the time of "buy placements," certain considerations should be extended to the advertiser or agency. We forgo the marketing specifications used by general advertisers, but the direct-response advertiser has other specifications which are needed to determine the success or failure of the spots aired.

The 48- to 72-hour cancellation clause is a necessity for advertisers. These cancellation clauses must be established and accepted at the time when buys are placed.

Another requirement of direct-response advertisers is to establish up front whether "exact times" will be made available. As a general rule, stations can give their information during the week after a schedule has aired. "Exact times" means just what it says: You can get verbal confirmation of exactly where and when your scheduled spots aired, and you can find out what was missing. This will determine immediately whether the schedule was profitable and what areas were productive. If a station will not release this information, estimates based on track records of stations have to be taken into consideration. These estimates of projected dollars spent on a station have to reflect the maximum dollar expenditure on that station for that week.

If the allowable limit is not based on maximum estimated dollars spent, this can lead to a cancellation. This has proved to be an extreme step, but the loss of clients' dollars would be worse. Although it is obvious to the advertiser, the advantage of giving exact times by the stations is not always viewed as important to the station. Although the work involved on the stations' end is minimal to obtain these data, some consider it a "bother." But to the direct-response advertiser this information is as much a necessity as the general advertiser establishing ratings and reach and frequency data. This requirement should be firmly established with each station at the time the buy is made.

If a station cannot supply you with exact times, it should at least be able to advise you of the spots that have been missed (preemptions); this will enable you to compare the actual expenditure with the orders received.

After a buy is placed verbally, written documentation should be sent either to your rep or to the station. It is generally preferable to send it to the station since it also will serve the purpose of traffic instruction. Other copies of the broadcast order may go to the client, accounting department, account management group, etc., if you are an advertising agency.

Shortly after a buy is placed verbally, the station or the station's representative will send a written confirmation of the schedule. It is important that these confirmations be checked against the broadcast order. Any variations should be noted and resolved immediately.

Often, when this information is not checked, you can find yourself on the air with a schedule different from the one you thought you bought. Verbal contact with stations or reps regarding changes should be noted as to date, time, and to whom you spoke. It is also a good practice to TWX the stations directly, specifically the traffic department, if a schedule is canceled before a scheduled date. This serves as a backup confirmation of cancellation.

The traffic department at the stations and the advertising agency are the hearts of the functioning process of direct-response television advertising. In addition to the traffic function of assigning the right 800 numbers for every station, the responsibility of sending the tapes to the stations is critical. Each station has its own requirements with regard to air tapes. As a general rule, tapes should be at the station at least 48 hours before airing. It is safer to allow for more time, for if a tape is damaged or found not to be airworthy, you will need extra time to ship out another tape.

The end tag information at the end of the commercial must, of course, comply with FTC regulations. In addition, networks and independent stations also may have their own policy requirements which will have to be adhered to. It is the responsibility of the traffic department to see that in the process of dubbing, specific station requirements are met. The broadcast order that was sent to the station is in essence the traffic instruction. If this was not sent, notification must be issued when the tape is mailed as to when the schedule is to start, client, agency, and agency contact.

ANALYSIS OF BUYS

For daily and weekly analysis of schedules, it is necessary to get "exact times" either through your rep or from the station directly. When you first schedule a buy, arrangements are made. Particulars such as by what day you will need the exact times, person to contact, etc., then are resolved.

Knowing when the spots aired and using the hour-by-hour report from the 800 services along with the daily counts are the tools necessary to evaluate a schedule. These tools help tell you what areas are better than others, whether the schedule can be improved on, and whether cancellation is required. By canceling a schedule on Thursday at the latest, you can avoid going on the air for the following week and thus avoid losing additional dollars in an unprofitable situation.

If a schedule was placed for a limited time, Thursday would be the latest time for reordering if you're planning on the schedule to air without a "hiatus." A hiatus simply refers to a break in the scheduling weeks of a flight. A schedule can be put on hiatus as a practice in evaluating the buys. This usually occurs when exact times are not given by the station or cannot be obtained until the following week.

Putting a schedule on hiatus will afford the buyer more time to determine whether a schedule was profitable. Premature cancellations can result in the permanent loss of a schedule since your spots can be resold easily in the competitive direct-response marketplace. This situation must be avoided, and a hiatus can achieve this. Although a hiatus of a schedule is standard practice, it should not be abused. It should be used only for evaluation purposes for stations that represent a sizable budget expenditure.

When spots are missed during a schedule, the normal procedure for general advertisers is to accept "make goods" or spot replacements in comparable areas. In buying direct-response television time, although you want to maintain the frequency level of spots bought, this is not usually possible primarily because of the limitation on :120 availabilities. Your spot probably was missed as a result of a lack of availabilities, and additional availabilities are few and far between. The paperwork involved in rescheduling spots and the time spent in communicating this information are not profitable to the station or its representatives. The low cost you're paying for spots dictates this.

In the attempt to circumvent the problem of spot preemption, "overbuying" of schedules can help. The loss of frequency will directly deter the "build factor" of awareness levels that must be reached. This point also must be part of evaluating a station's responsiveness.

Premature cancellations should also be recognized as a contributing factor to poor results as a result of the lack of repetition of the commercial message.

Although there are general guidelines for analyzing the schedules aired, each station must be viewed individually. Judgment comes only with experience in evaluating buys. A complete understanding of objectives for each client will establish the procedures needed to best serve the advertiser's needs.

TESTING

Testing methods vary depending on what the test is to achieve. When you are testing a new commercial against a proven one, objectives must be established to determine what the test results will signify. If the new spot is meant to replace, the test results will have to reflect the strength of the new spot. If testing is being conducted to establish "another" strong spot that can be used in rotation with an existing commercial, response levels generally would have to be the same when testing. The optimum test occurs when you're trying to find a new creative strategy that will surpass the control in lead generation by at least 35 percent.

By achieving this, you appeal to more of the audience with your commercial message. Testing should be conducted in off-campaign periods that will allow a time for the decision-making process and evaluation. The result of testing will determine your plans for the next campaign or rollout.

The following method of testing generally is used for direct-response television testing. Although each agency uses different methods, they are basically variations of this procedure. An important point to note here is that variables should be kept to a minimum. Know exactly what you're trying to achieve with a test; adding other factors to tests at the same time can dilute results, making them unreadable.

An average test base would involve the use of ten stations, with a mix of independent and network affiliates. If you already have a track record for stations, it is best to choose stations that are "proven" for your offer. This eliminates another variable. Specifically, if the station ended up producing poorly, was it the station or the commercial? Controlled creative tests can air for as little as 2 weeks or as long as 4. Whether you are testing for a 2-week or a 4-week period, the method is the same. If you are using ten stations, you can split up the ten markets and have five start with the control and the other five start with the test commercial.

This method seems to be the preference of many agencies. After airing for a week or two, the stations showing the test spot then will switch to the control, and the stations airing the control will switch to the test commercial. In using this method of testing, you can properly read the results station by station. You are not judging one station against another but testing the results applicable to a particular station.

In testing length of spots, a similar method is used. An example of this occurs when the control is a :120 spot. The stations that are airing the :120 are the same stations that in 1 or 2 weeks' time will switch to another length spot, say, a :60. Although the pursuit of shorter length spots continues to be an ongoing struggle, results in this area have been far from successful. It would certainly be to a client's advantage to have a working :60 spot, but the industry at this point is staying with the :120 spot as the key to promotions. Because of the influx of direct marketing advertisers and the limited number of :120 spots available, the use of :60s would allow tremendous flexibility.

The :60 spot is at a further discounted rate. The objective in testing :60s is not to save money but to get more spots and maintain frequency levels for comparable budgets. The objective should be to keep the station dollar expenditures the same, increase the frequency, and generate equal responses.

In evaluating test results, another area to watch is the actual cost per order. In addition to measuring actual CPOs of a control commercial versus the test commercial, another question must be raised: did the stronger spot still meet the allowable or order margin level? You can have a breakthrough spot that still failed to generate enough orders to make it profitable though it generated more than the spot it was being tested against. Too many people say that they are not testing CPOs but response levels. This is a dangerous practice.

ROLLOUT

With your test results in hand, the campaign must be planned, researched, and executed carefully. A client's past performance records are your major tools. Campaigns are broken up into four categories.

Proven Markets and Stations

The bulk of the dollars budgeted are placed in this area because there is a limited risk involved. The same stations bought previously for a campaign are to be bought again. This, of course, is applicable only if the station did well in the same quarter that is being planned now. The fact that a station did well in a first-quarter run does not mean you can project it to do well in a third-quarter run. It can, however, be projected to air satisfactorily in a future first-quarter run. Through experience and testing you will discover that some stations do better in the third quarter than in any other time. As a general rule, though, the first quarter is still the most viable time of the year for direct-response advertisers.

Testing "new" or untried stations for a particular client should be done during the first quarter if possible. Again, this is flexible and depends on the type of client and offer. Putting the bulk of your budget allotment into the proven stations will balance the potential losses from untested areas.

Proven Market Expansion

The secondary budget allotment should be placed in this category, as the risks are considered minimal. Proven market expansion means advertising "deeper" in a market that has shown itself to be profitable. If one or two stations were bought and were profitable, additional stations in the market should be tested. This, of course, is going on the assumption that the market has accepted your offer. There is still a risk involved in testing a new station in a proven market which could be reflective of the stations' programming, cost, rotation patterns, etc. Nevertheless, it is a calculated risk and one worth taking.

Retest Markets

Retesting stations that previously were bought and did not do well or were marginal is another standard practice. Bear in mind that the dollar allocation in this area should be minimal to avoid a potential loss. The objective is to determine whether it is the client's offer that lacks appeal or simply a station variable such as the season when aired, competition in the market, etc. One-time airing can give you a "handle" on a station; airing two times will give you conclusive data to determine a station's potential for a particular client.

Test Markets and Stations

This list of new markets for testing is valuable in that they can become the proven expansion market for future campaigns. Depending on the exposure your clients wish and their objectives, the number of new test markets will vary. When testing new markets, a good practice is to buy time on a station in the market that has a proven track record for other clients. This procedure will reduce risk. By selecting a known station, you're giving your client the best possible shot for success if the client's product is to make it in that particular market.

Included in the area of new spot TV test markets would be any other area related to television. The primary "other areas" specifically would include network cable. A client's success in a "rollout" situation is going to reflect the marketing research, track record, and dollar allocations for each part of your strategy. The units must be weighed in accordance with potential and with "risk dollars" being limited. Here again, using PI stations as part of your campaign will aid in keeping the risk in line by offsetting some of the losing situations.

CABLE TV: "THE PRESENT FUTURE"

What started out as a means for getting better reception in urban areas has had an astounding impact on the television industry. The original cable "superstations" were actually spot TV stations: WOR in New York and WGN in Chicago. At the present time, neither station promotes itself as a "cable station" but rather as a major spot "independent" TV station in their markets.

The largest cable "superstation" and one that has had tremendous impact on the industry is WTBS, which originates from Atlanta, Georgia. The number of potential TV households receiving this station currently approaches 32 million. Although cable networks generally do "narrowcasting," WTBS appeals to the general mass audience, making it the largest independent station in the television industry. The narrowcasting element of cable TV is perceived as a valuable factor by advertisers.

TV narrowcasting can be compared to special-interest magazines. While spot

TV reaches the general mass audience, narrowcasting allows an advertiser to reach a specific type of audience. If buying time on a cable network appears to be costly, factors to consider are the quality of viewership, increase in up-sells, better backend, higher renewal rates, etc. If you are looking at the bottom line CPO and basing it against your allowable, the risks are there and must be watched closely.

The ability to be received in millions of cable households does not necessarily mean that you will reach these millions of viewers at any given point. The nature of cable, with repetition of programming on a rotation basis, gives you a better chance of reaching an unduplicated audience within any daypart. For example, if a cable network ran a program at 9 a.m. and repeated it at 4 p.m., you would not duplicate your audience with spots airing at each time but theoretically would reach two different audiences.

This theory applies to any cable network repeating programming. In line with this thought, the frequency of spots aired becomes a critical factor. Because of the unduplicated audience viewership, it becomes necessary to increase the number of spots bought on cables to reach many dayparts. On a cash buy basis, this can be a costly venture. When airing on a PI basis, an average weekly schedule would consist of approximately twenty spots per week. This can represent an increase of 25 to 50 percent of the amount of spots that generally would be bought on regular spot TV stations. This is an advantage if you are airing on a PI basis, but it is costly on a cash buy basis.

The main point is the need for frequency to reach potential viewers. You won't realize your potential unless it is tried, and this is a learning process that should be taken one way or the other: riskless PI or risky paid.

An offshoot of the cable network industry is interactive cable. This type of operation can best be compared to the direct-response industry itself. Direct-response advertising is interactive. Your commercial message requests an immediate response. The viewer uses the telephone as the tool or mechanism of response, and the answering service is the receiver of that response. The interaction from commercial to operator capturing the viewer's response is the basis for interactive cable.

The concept is not new, but it has been refined. The computer takes the place of the 800 number services. The computer is the agent that will transmit the fulfillment data for processing to the various clients involved.

In reality, interactive television is a marketer's dream come true. When a marketer subscribes to such an operation, demographic profiles are determined via questionnaires. Through "shopping at home" shows, buying habits can be attributed directly to audiences because data have been loaded into the computer already. The data can enable an advertiser to select, qualify, and expand in particular demographic groups. Marketing refinement of this nature takes the guessing out of guesswork.

All variables are eliminated, and the use of rating services becomes inconsequential. The very nature of interactive cable lends itself to a particular type of narrowcasting.

The use of interactive cable is a luxury. This is not a profound statement but a fact: luxury in the form of convenience. Our lifestyle seems to give credibility to this dimension of advertising. At the present time, the "testing" of such cable networks is limited to less populated areas. The result, which is due to the low volume of subscribers and undeveloped program concepts, has not yet been conclusive. We can view interactive cable at being at the stage where direct-response television advertising was 20 years ago. But it will not take another 20 years for it to develop.

A concern in this area, contrary to the marketer's dream, is invasion of privacy. The computer that is the storehouse of all responses is not owned by an advertiser but by the cable network. The information being compiled is vast. The cable network now has access not only to the buying habits or trends of its viewers but also to the individual habits of the particular cable subscribers involved. The relating of this information or its use by the cable networks has not been determined but obviously can serve many a marketer in establishing in-depth information about customers. In this situation, the viewer must be protected.

This "protection" is presently in the Senate as a bill which could limit the use of data obtained by the cable networks.

The Cable "Ripoff"

The sales appeal to general advertisers lies in the bulk number of cable households reached (or more accurately, the potential of reaching them), and costs are based on these numbers. A direct-response advertiser looking at the bottom line of CPO instead of CPM will see the inefficiency of inflated rates against projected audience levels sooner than the general advertiser.

In effect, the cable network stations, as with many spot TV stations, probably will price themselves out of the marketplace. In reality, they will "bite the hand that feeds them." Unfair perhaps, but this seems to be the trend, and it will continue. The gold mine is available on a limited basis only.

The subject of cable being monitored remains just that: a subject for discussion. Cable networks claiming under 10 million cable home memberships don't qualify for the major rating services. Over that figure, when they have the option, in most cases it appears as a negative option. This would establish more accurate numbers for audience levels, not potential audience levels, and thereby result in spot pricings more favorable to the advertisers than to the station.

The near future will see more cable networks being monitored, as advertisers must have a tool to weigh the effectiveness of these networks.

A direct-response advertiser using cable has a unique problem in terms of sourcing calls. It is advantageous to assign a separate phone number for each individual network which is not to be used by any other network or spot TV station. As calls are received from all over the country in response to a commercial, it would be impossible to trace their origin and source them to a particular cable network if the same numbers were being shared. You should not rely on viewers to tell the operators what station they were watching. A separate number allocation allows for immediate and accurate sourcing. The same applies to local cable operations. They should be treated as another station within a marketplace, a separate entity.

Local Cable Operations

Local cable operations are composed of network cable feeds in addition to locally produced shows. This further spreads out audience viewership since the choices are extensive as to what channel will be watched at any given time in addition to the spot networks, network affiliates, and independent spot TV stations in a market. If a market has a low penetration of cable subscribers, a direct-response advertiser probably will not achieve an affordable CPO because the cost of advertising on these stations is not commensurate with the potential viewership. In high cable penetration, the same is applicable, only it is more costly.

Local cable advertising seems to serve the local retail advertiser, not the national advertiser. In addition these stations have limited :120 spots available as the cable networks allot them only a specific number per hour or per program segment to sell on their own. Local cable-originated programming usually does not carry :120 breaks, which means your spots will be falling on the cable network feeds. It therefore would be more cost-efficient to buy the cable network and reach a higher audience level at a potentially lower CPM than to buy the same cable network through local sources and pay a premium for less viewership. Again, this theory is applicable to the national advertiser, not the local retail advertiser who is not interested in reaching a mass market but rather the local community.

CONCLUSION

The tremendous growth of the television medium has literally changed lifestyles. Commercial messages are viewed by the masses and are acted upon. It remains the quickest and most cost-efficient medium for selling products and creating awareness. The approaches to this medium are just as varied. In addition to the general advertiser and the direct-response advertiser, the medium is used as TV support to bring attention to other advertising media. It is used to create awareness of direct mail, and it is used frequently by local advertisers promoting specials and sales in newspapers.

Its overwhelming success has in turn generated new programming to appeal to a more affluent, sophisticated audience. "Specials," extended news programs, movies created for television, and variety shows have found their way into our homes. With networks vying for the numbers and independents increasing their program budgets, the industry has become one of the most competitive advertising sources. Through their narrowcasting features, the cable TV networks add to the competition by audience selection.

With television's advancement, it is inevitable that the direct-response advertiser will move ahead in this same sphere of sophistication. Although flexibility in buying direct-response TV time becomes more and more limited, analysis of these buys becomes vital to the advertiser. It either works or doesn't, and the sooner you know this, the lower your dollar loss will be.

The growing use of computers will aid in this area. By tracking program dayparts by station and by product over a period of time, it also can limit advertising losses by letting you know when and when not to go on the air on a specific station at a particular time. Computers also will serve as a factor in the postanalyses of campaigns, which are always tremendously time-consuming. In general, the use of computers can aid the direct-response agency and its clients.

In direct-response TV, buyers remain the key element, the human element in this specialized medium. The logic attained through experience cannot be replaced by a computer; it simply becomes an aid to the computer. Negotiations are part of the "people" aspect of the business. At times it is not who you know but how well you know them. A good direct-response media person knows to cultivate these relationships and thus benefit clients and agencies over a course of time.

It is necessary to direct a point of importance to the advertiser. The opportunities that arise within the course of a campaign must be acted on. Although it is not always possible to bypass corporate structure, clients and agencies alike must be made aware of the "quick decision" needs. Client flexibility also must be dealt with. Establish broad guidelines and criteria to avoid losing out on an opportunity. Although client requirements are the most important aspect of a campaign, clients must be taught to understand the nature of direct response. Their requests may not always be reasonable in relation to direct-response TV time buying, and therefore an "education" of limitations must be acknowledged and expressed. Limitations should be acknowledged, and those areas of flexibility should be worked on.

The appeal of direct-response advertising relates directly to an advertiser knowing immediately whether its commercial message is a potential success or failure. The excitement that this knowledge creates is unsurpassed. The immediate success stirs the motivation to continue and expand on the commercial success. The ability to react immediately with schedule changes and adjustments is available only with this specialized medium. The buyer, usually under qualified supervision, has been taught this. It is the nature of the business and is learned through training and experience.

As the TV industry continues to grow and expand into our lives and as more direct-response advertisers realize the value of this type of advertising, innovations and adjustments will occur to better serve the client, agency, and community. To be ready and able to accept the changes and "ride the wave" of television direct response can assure you a place in the future of direct-response advertising.

chapter 24

TELEVISION SUPPORT

Raymond J. Markman

President
R. J. Markman and Co., Inc.
Marketing Consultants
Chicago, Ill.

To some direct marketers, television support promises a quantum leap forward in obtaining leads or inquiries. I prefer to look at television support as another marketing tool to increase efficiency in obtaining direct responses.

What is TV support? Basically, it involves using television commercials to generate additional leads and orders from another medium: print advertising, direct mail programs, or preprints. The TV support is designed to evoke extra interest and curiosity about your program and push viewers to look for and read it. TV support is like the marching band before the circus arrives. Think of the advertising you're supporting as the primary medium and the TV support as the secondary.

CAN YOU USE IT?

The standard advertising prescription to put your money where your sales are is also true in television support. If your current magazine, newspaper, or direct mail advertising is not successful, i.e., does not come within 50 percent of the desired cost per inquiry, your television support also probably will not succeed. If, however, your current advertising is generating marginal cost per lead or good leads, television support can be extremely helpful in expanding your lead generation. That solves the first problem: whether you should use television support.

The second question is, Which markets? Again, we go back to an axiom: "Put your money where your sales are." Break down your primary media by markets. Would it pay to put television in Buffalo or New Orleans or Providence, Rhode Island?

The first thing to check is whether your primary medium will be in a sufficient number of homes to afford television support. Many marketers use the rule that if they are not going to be in at least 25 percent of the homes in the market with the primary medium, they should not use television support.

The second thing to check is whether your primary medium has worked successfully in the market before. If you are at least better than 50 percent of the desired cost per lead in your primary medium, it probably would pay to use television support, in some cases pay handsomely.

What do you do? First, find a primary ad or program that is a marginal success or a winner and support it. Second, support it only in the markets in which you have a chance of success.

One of the gravest mistakes in analyzing TV support is to total all cities with television support versus all cities with nontelevision support and decide that television support does or doesn't work. It's probably not a good comparison because the very unsuccessful markets will dilute the effectiveness of television support. Television support is not very different from print A-B splits. It's a matter of different terminology. The same logic used in print splits can be applied to television.

HOW MANY DOLLARS FOR TV SUPPORT?

Over the past few years, different formulas have been tested for determining how much money should be put into television to support other media. See Table 24-1.

Percentage of Dollars Expended

One method is to determine how many dollars you currently are spending in a market for all the costs of your primary advertising program and then take a percentage of that expenditure and put it into your TV support medium. If you are spending $20,000 in Des Moines and want to spend 50 percent in TV support, your budget obviously is $10,000. This is a questionable approach because the efficiency of your current TV costs may be quite different in Des Moines from what it is in Salt Lake City. But if you bottom-line a large number of markets in the country, you may arrive at a formula which will show successful patterns. However, there is a distinct element of chance according to the markets in the test. The best approach is to spend in each market the media dollars required to do a satisfactory job in TV support.

Gross Rating Point Levels

Another formula is to use various gross rating point (GRP) levels in your TV support markets. You decide the number of GRPs you need to support your current primary medium. One gross rating point represents 1 percent of the total homes in the area that are watching television at any one time. Thus, if you generate 100 GRPs on one broadcast of your commercial, it would indicate that every home in the market has the potential to see your commercial.

In the case of the *Encyclopaedia Britannica*, we usually support our print ads with 200 GRPs in each market. We run 100 GRPs in 30-second "look for my ad"

TABLE 24-1 Paired Test Markets: TV versus Non-TV Markets for Print Support (60-second announcements for *TV Guide*, 1979)

Selected Paired Markets	DMA* Rank	TV Households, thousands	U.S., %	PFUS, %†	*TV Guide* Circulation, thousands	*TV Guide* Coverage, %	$9 CPM Circulation	Estimated TV Expenditure, $	Target GRPs
Raleigh/Durham	52	419	0.58	0.53	99.9	25.2	899.10	2,000.00	100
Orlando	42	469	0.65	0.59	105.3	24.7	947.70	—	—
Greenville, SC	37	511	0.71	0.59	121.7	23.7	1,095.30	2,500.00	200
Des Moines	69	342	0.47	0.44	94.2	29.2	847.80	—	—
Chicago	3	2,904	4.01	4.34	518.7	22.1	5,235.30	6,000.00	100
San Francisco	5	1,807	2.50	2.68	713.6	42.4	6,422.40	—	—
Phoenix	32	555	0.77	0.75	293.9	36.6	2,645.10	1,500.00	100
San Diego	28	616	0.85	0.77	265.5	47.2	2,389.50	—	—
Seattle	16	901	1.24	1.19	271.3	32.9	2,441.70	4,000.00	200
Portland	22	682	0.94	0.85	241.3	37.8	2,171.70	—	—
Salt Lake City	47	448	0.62	0.56	120.9	31.6	1,169.10	2,500.00	200
Denver	21	682	0.94	0.92	186.0	25.5	1,674.00	—	—
Milwaukee	27	658	0.91	0.91	115.9	19.0	1,043.10	3,200.00	200
Minneapolis	14	968	1.34	1.31	183.9	19.6	1,655.10	—	—

* Dominant market area

† Percentage of U.S. family units

TABLE 24-2 Results: Change in Cost per Inquiry: TV Support versus Non-TV Support

Selected Paired Markets	Circulation	Inquiries	Pull, %	Promotional Cost	GRPs	CPI Support	CPI Non-support	Results
Raleigh/Durham	106,448	1,516	1.4	2,968	200	1.96	—	33% cut in CPI
Orlando	105,333	321	.3	933	—	—	2.91	
Greenville	122,061	1,690	1.4	3,681	200	2.18	—	76% cut in CPI
Des Moines	94,751	92	.1	839	—	—	9.13	
Chicago	581,703	3,009	.5	9,814	100	3.26	—	29% cut in CPI
San Francisco	711,155	1,379	.2	6,301	—	—	4.57	
Phoenix	284,000	1,955	.7	4,976	100	2.56	—	18% cut in CPI
San Diego	251,000	710	.3	2,224	—	—	3.13	
Seattle	274,000	2,911	1.1	7,073	200	2.43	—	42% cut in CPI
Portland	238,000	500	.2	2,109	—	—	4.22	
Salt Lake City	122,000	1,393	1.1	4,061	200	2.92	—	72% cut in CPI
Denver	181,000	153	.1	1,604	—	—	10.48	
Milwaukee	115,935	978	.8	4,107	100	4.20	—	56% cut in CPI
Minneapolis	182,802	168	.1	1,620	—	—	9.64	
100 GRPs								
Support		4,964		14,789		3.00	—	26% cut in CPI
Nonsupport		2,089		8,523		—	4.08	
200 GRPs								
Support		8,488		21,888		2.58	—	55% cut in CPI
Nonsupport		1,234		7,102		—	5.76	

commercials and another 100 GRPs in our regular 1- and 2-minute lead-generating commercials with no reference to the print ad that is running.

Another product using television support tested 200 GRPs versus 100 GRPs. The criterion of success was the reduction in lead cost in paired support versus nonsupport markets.

The 200-GRP markets reduced the cost per lead (CPL) by 55 percent versus the nonsupport markets. The 100-GRP markets reduced the CPL by 26 percent. See Table 24-2.

WHEN TO BROADCAST?

You must coordinate the length of time your primary ad program will be available in the home with the time your commercials are on the air. Obviously, it doesn't help to advertise on Tuesday for a Sunday supplement that has been discarded already. Likewise, if you are in *National Geographic*, it will be around the home considerably longer, and so you can extend your schedule over several weeks.

If it is a *TV Guide* ad, we will run the advertising on Thursday to Monday, using the 200 GRPs over this period. If it is a Sunday supplement, we break the advertising on Friday afternoon and stop it on Sunday afternoon.

If you are supporting a direct mail campaign that should arrive at the home on Monday, start on the preceding Friday and run daily through the following Thursday.

Advertisers have experimented with 100 GRPs, 200 GRPs, and as high as 400 GRPs in a week. The 200-GRP level appears to be the most efficient. However, both the 100-GRP and 200-GRP levels in most television markets were more efficient than the nontelevision support markets.

FREQUENCY VERSUS REACH

Another question to consider when you are running TV support is, Do you buy a few highly rated prime-time spots (8 P.M. to 11 P.M.) to achieve your GRP level and strive to reach as many different people as possible or go for greater frequency by buying a greater number of lower rated spots in nonprime time? Most advertisers using TV support go for the frequency of the lower rated spots. These usually are purchased at a lower cost per thousand (CPM) than prime-time spots, reducing your overall dollar expenditure in the marketplace to reach your GRP level. This has a second advantage of making a greater impact on people who see your commercial more than once. I have noticed that the schedules with more frequency usually generate a greater number of leads per dollar expenditure.

If you are using 30-second commercials that basically say, "Look for my ad in this week's *TV Guide*," you can afford to use some expensive prime-time reach commercials. Definitely, if you are in any longer length than 30 seconds, efficiency demands that you purchase non-prime-time television and use the less expensive, lower rated time periods.

TYPES OF COMMERCIALS

Look for My Ad

This type of commercial is usually 30 seconds long and features something about the product being advertised for 25 seconds, with the last 5 seconds directing the viewer to "look for my ad in *TV Guide* (or another publication)." You can include more than one publication in the "look for" tag. Try to include an audio announcement as well as the video display of the publications to which you are directing the viewers' attention. It is a good idea to use the logo of the publication wherever possible to aid the viewer's quick identification. Five seconds goes by very rapidly. Do not overload the tag with too many publications. It is better to rotate different publications on different commercials. Do not put more than four publications in one "look for my ad."

Another playoff of this type of ad is the direction to "look in your mailbox for this special green envelope." Obviously, this is supporting direct mail, and the important thing to do is to make the envelope unique in color or design.

The Transfer Device

"Circle the star in the coupon and receive a free gift." This type of commercial is usually 1 minute long. It contains a message about the product being advertised and shows the coupon in the publication that contains some device by which the viewer can receive a free gift for performing the requested action. It can involve circling the star, putting an additional record number in a box, putting an arrow through the heart, and so forth. Obviously, the action has two purposes: (1) to spark the curiosity of the viewer so that he or she will look for the coupon and (2) to increase response by giving the viewer a free gift. Many companies give the free gift whether the requested action has been followed or not. The transfer device also can be used to measure the additional orders generated by TV support. As with the "look for my ad" type of commercial, this carries an audiovisual statement of the publication the ad is in.

A Standard 1-Minute or 2-Minute Lead Commercial

It has been found that regular lead commercials which say "call this 800 number" also work extremely well as print support even with no reference to a publication. You produce a lead commercial, and when it has been tested and has proved itself successful, you then can run it on the same days of the week on which you would run a 30- or 60-second print support commercial. Obviously, your lead commercial is making viewers aware of the product that they will be encountering in your print medium.

Case History of a New Breakthrough Strategy

Traditionally, the basic TV unit used by direct-response marketers to support other media has been the 30-second commercial. *Britannica* was no exception, and we used this same length to back up our print.

We had established specific benchmarks for pull in our most important print media, both nationally and by specific markets, using very sophisticated statistical techniques. We thus were able to measure the increased pull of our television support markets versus nontelevision markets in terms of certain criteria. The rationale for the increased pull resulting from the addition of television is the increased awareness it generates and the message, "See my ad."

Thirty-second commercials are the basic unit used in television advertising. This length "fits" in all time periods and is especially valuable in getting prime-time slots, thus generating the rating point goals.

The disadvantage of the 30-second commercial is its inability to pull reponses, since there is no time for the 20-second "tag" which contains vital response information such as the phone number or mailing address repeated two or more times and appearing on both audio and video at the same time.

The 1-minute and especially the 2-minute commercial provide sufficient time for presenting the offer and the response-producing tag. They have the disadvantage of not having as many placement opportunities as 30-second commercials, particularly in time periods with high ratings. Thus, they have not been used traditionally as support but only to generate immediate response.

We developed a new television strategy using both 1- and 2-minute commercials to generate leads and serve the support function at the same time. The objective of the strategy was to produce more total leads—both generating direct leads off the air and increasing the pull of the print media.

The rationale behind the strategy was that the longer commercial provided the time to tell a complete although capsulated story of *Britannica 3* and that this dimension would make up for any rating point advantage of the 30-second spot. They also had to overcome another disadvantage. We were not going to refer to the print ads since this would detract from the single-minded objective of pulling a lead off the air.

We developed a three-way split test to determine the viability of the strategy. All markets in each split received 200 GRPs. In one group of markets, we ran all 30-second commercials containing the direction to "see my ad" at 100 GRPs. In a second group of markets, we used a configuration of :30s at 100 GRPs and :60s and :120s at 100 GRPs. In a third group of markets, we ran all :60s and :120s at 200 GRPs.

The measure of success was a direct comparison among commercials of the reduction of only the print cost per lead in TV-supported markets versus nonsupported markets. No allowances were made for the direct leads off the air. These were a bonus, even though significant.

Decrease in CPL Support versus Nonsupport

:60s and :120s	Only :30s	Combination :30s and :60s plus :120s
18%	15%	19%

As you can see, the results were very close. We adopted the strategy of using the combination of :30s and :60s plus :120s. We did this because we are able to place :30s into broadcast hours that aren't available to the direct-response 1- and

2-minute ads. We not only receive a good CPL from the direct-response television commercials, we also derive a considerable incremental increase in our print response.

In addition, we are able to utilize the lower-cost direct-response rates. In essence, in this way we make our television direct-response dollars work twice. More recently, we adopted the strategy of utilizing only the 200 GRPs in :60s and :120s in order to produce more direct leads as well as support print. We thus have prioritized our measurement differently, giving primary importance to direct leads off the air and secondary importance to the incremental leads resulting from increased pull in print.

READING THE RESULTS

Like all testing, you must begin with matched pairs. You can't get A-B splits in TV, but you can try to match markets as closely as possible. You match them according to market size, regionality, current economic conditions, and whether the prime medium is equally efficient. We usually try to pair a minimum of three sets of markets for any test. We then take the cost of the primary medium being tested in each paired market and try for a balance there. See Table 24-3.

The dollars of the prime medium being tested are used in the nonsupport market, while the support TV dollars and the prime medium dollars are totaled for the TV support market. Then it is handled in a traditional CPO or CPL manner, dividing the leads into the media to determine which market had the lowest CPO.

TABLE 24-3 TV Support versus TV Nonsupport

	Market A: Nonsupport, $	Market B: TV Support, $
Prime medium	20,000	20,000
TV support	—	18,000
Total budget	20,000	38,000
Total leads	2,000	4,300
CPL	10	8.34

If you are using a transfer device, you can separate the print leads from those inspired by the TV support. This will give you another index.

As was stated before, you use TV support only with an ad or program that has shown a degree of success. The TV commercial is obviously another variable, and because of this, you must continue to retest your TV support efficiency in other markets. Of course, you don't retest with the same commercials if you are looking at an unsuccessful support program.

SUMMARY

TV support can work effectively if you test carefully. Use the following guidelines:

1. Test only primary media that have at least reached 50 percent of your desired CPO or better.

2. Use TV support only in markets in which your primary medium has reached 50 percent or more of the desired CPO and reaches at least 25 percent of the homes.
3. When testing, match your primary support levels as closely as you can in the nonsupport and support markets.
4. Test various GRP levels to determine which one is most successful for you.
5. Use CPO or CPL as the guiding criteria. If you are using a transfer device, use it as a supplementary index of failure or success.
6. Continue to retest your TV support commercial. Remember that every ad needs new testing before you project.

chapter 25

RADIO ADVERTISING: WHAT RADIO OFFERS TO DIRECT MARKETERS

Shan Ellentuck and James R. Springer

Ellentuck & Springer, Inc.
Princeton, N.J.

Long before cable TV began to woo advertisers with the promise of "narrowcasting," an electronic medium existed that already had done about everything cable TV said it was going to do: It had saturated and segmented the entire country. An advertiser who wanted to sell soap to homemakers, for instance, could find hundreds of audience units consisting almost entirely of homemakers and could consistently, conveniently, and cost-efficiently present a sales message to all of them or to any combination of them that suited his or her needs.

Similarly, an interested advertiser could "buy" farmers, executives, teenyboppers, or senior citizens and, thanks to programs aimed specifically at Madison Avenue, could even buy other interested advertisers.

The medium, of course, is radio. Although few companies have chosen radio as their only sales channel, broadcast has been an effective direct-response medium since its earliest days, when listeners were exhorted to "Send one dollar—just *one* dollar—to B-I-B-L-E" at a post office box in Texas.

RADIO BLANKETS AMERICA

At last count, according to the Radio Advertising Bureau, there were roughly two radios for every man, woman, and child in the country, or some 470 million sets. More than 80 percent of all Americans over the age of 12 listen to radio every day.

Radio is so pervasive that it is an essential element in our civil defense network;

it is the only medium that can be used in case of national emergency to reach virtually all the people in the country at the same time.

Yet broadcast is not monolithic. Because radio stations design their programming to appeal to groups of listeners with similar interests—such as country music, religion, news, or Spanish-language features—this vast, seemingly uniform audience is in fact made up of hundreds or even thousands of individual audience units, each a separate market segment.

If you think of these audience units in traditional direct marketing terms, they are much like direct mail lists. As with lists, they can be identified by their geographic, demographic, and psychographic characteristics, and one then can select them to match the profile of existing customers or to search out new and potentially wider markets.

Today, radio offers great opportunities for direct marketers, particularly in light of escalating print and mail costs. Used as a primary medium to produce orders or leads, radio can meet or beat other media in terms of cost efficiency and volume; as a support medium, it has proved that it can increase the overall efficiency of direct mail and print.

WHAT RADIO OFFERS THE DIRECT MARKETER

Our agency, with over 98 percent of its billings in the electronic media, uses broadcast television predominantly. However, all our clients use radio either as a quick, inexpensive broadcast test medium or as an efficient, productive source in its own right.

In addition to its enormous reach and its ability to break the total audience into small, discrete segments, radio offers these following advantages as a direct marketing medium.

Radio can be tested at low cost and low risk.

- Production costs are minimal.
- Air time can be bought in inexpensive units.
- Results are known quickly.

Radio is flexible.

- Air time usually can be bought, canceled, or changed on relatively short notice.
- Copy can be changed within a few days or even hours.
- Programs can be fine-tuned while they are being conducted.

Radio can be extremely cost-efficient.

- The cost of acquiring a customer or a lead, as well as pay-up, upgrade, conversion, renewal, etc., should be as good as with other sources if not better.
- There is little waste. The ability to get response fast and react fast cuts losses from unprofitable activities.
- Radio can reach first-time buyers and other prospects who are not easily available through lists.
- The cost of air time usually can be negotiated.
- The up-front cash outlay is negligible.

Clearly, many of these characteristics of radio are advantages only in the hands of a direct marketer who is actively turning them to his or her advantage. It takes the same planning and attention to detail to be a success in radio as it does to be successful in direct mail or print.

IS RADIO RIGHT FOR YOU?

Neither radio nor any other medium will be successful for a product that has been introduced to the public too early or too late or that is positioned improperly or priced poorly. Only if the right product has been matched with the right offer and presented to the right market at the right time will profitable, productive programs result.

Assume that you are thinking of broadcast for a product or service that has met these criteria and already has a history of profitable sales. How do you decide whether to use radio and how to use radio? How do you go about planning, executing, and analyzing a direct-response radio campaign? First, ask yourself these three questions.

Can You Identify Broadcast Audience Units That Have the "Right" Characteristics?

In other words, can you find radio programs or stations with listening audiences largely made up of people whose interests, attitudes, needs, and desires are similar to those of your own customer base or other sources such as direct mail lists that have worked for you in the past?

Your product does not necessarily have to have a national market or mass appeal to use radio successfully. If you were selling shares in a mutual fund, for instance, and you got good results by mailing to subscribers of the *Wall Street Journal, Business Week,* and *U.S. News & World Report,* you would try to identify the kind of radio programming that attracts mature, serious-minded, successful business people. Business news and general news bulletins and features would be strong possibilities, as would be classical music, sports programs, and male-oriented talk shows.

Can You Explain Your Product or Service and Its Benefits in 100 Words or Less?

On radio, your chances for success are greatest if your product, offer, and response device are easy to explain. A 1-minute commercial contains only about 200 words, and one-third to one-half of those words must be devoted to a clear statement of such essential details as what to send for, how much it costs, what the address or phone number is, and so on. That leaves only about 100 to 130 words in which to catch the attention of potential customers and present a sales message so convincing that they are propelled to take immediate action.

Do you feel that you cannot make your sale in so short a time? Consider using radio for two-step promotions, i.e., getting well-qualified leads that can be followed up by direct mail, telephone, or a sales visit. Two-step advertising may be called for if the following conditions exist.

- Your product requires lengthy explanation or demonstration.
- You need information from the customer in order to make the sale.
- The government requires that you give customers a prospectus or that you spell out obligations, terms of sale, disclaimers, etc., before closing the sale.
- Many options are offered to the customer.
- The price is high or the payment terms are complex.

Among the products and services that have been sold successfully with two-step radio promotion are encyclopedias, insurance policies, office equipment, home alarm systems, mutual funds, and exercise equipment.

Will Advertising on Radio Help You Tap Hard to Reach Market Segments?

Radio can deliver prospects for your product or services whom you would find difficult and very expensive to reach through more tightly targeted sources.

RADIO CAN HELP YOUR PROSPECTS FIND YOU

For example, for *Cricket*, a children's magazine, our agency has used radio extensively to reach a very desirable market: third-party donors. These are grandparents, friends of a child's family, next-door neighbors, doting aunts and uncles, and various other people who have nothing in common except the need or desire to buy a gift for a child. While they are an excellent subscriber group, paying and renewing much better than the average, it's unlikely that their names would show up on an appropriate direct mail list because they have never before qualified as likely buyers of a product for 7- to 10-year-olds. Radio gives them an opportunity to qualify themselves.

In many cases it's surprisingly difficult or at least very inconvenient for a potential customer to order or get information about products and services that are widely known. What would you do to get a prospectus from Dreyfus Liquid Assets, for instance? How can you contact a company that saves you money on long-distance calls? Radio advertising has worked well for organizations such as publishing companies, financial services, and the like simply by providing a means of getting in touch.

On the other hand, you need not be selling something unique or inaccessible to find radio a profitable sales medium. While it is undoubtedly easier to market a product that everybody wants and that only you can provide, marketers have used various direct-response media time and again to sell kitchen gadgets, tools, magazines, and all sorts of other items that are readily available through normal retail outlets.

In radio advertising, the factor of convenience is enormously important, particularly if the response device is the telephone. Your prospects need not open an envelope, turn a page, or open an eye to receive your sales message. To respond, all they need do is call in an order or a request for information. This is a spur to impulse buyers and a practical advantage for people who are house-bound or too busy to shop or who live far from stores.

RADIO CAN BOOST RESPONSE FROM OTHER MEDIA

As well as being a direct selling communications channel, radio can be effective as a support medium for direct mail, print, or TV campaigns that promote direct-response products that are too complex to explain quickly or products such as insurance that require a signature to close the sale. In these instances, the radio commercial doesn't try to give all the details of an offer, nor does it provide a toll-free number or mailing address. It's used simply to draw attention to the primary medium as well as to reinforce the sales message.

By using radio, you can encourage listeners to respond to a special offer soon to arrive in the mail. You can alert people to look for a freestanding insert in the following Sunday's paper. You can extend the reach and frequency of a TV direct-response spot, draw attention to on-page newspaper or magazine advertising, and even remind people after the ad has run or the mail has arrived that they should take advantage of a promotional offer while there is still time.

Planning a Support Program

Developing an efficient, productive support program requires careful, detailed planning, but the use of radio in conjunction with other media can boost overall response substantially without boosting the cost per response (CPR).

In order to have an effective campaign, it's important that the coverage area of both primary media (such as direct mail) and secondary media (radio) be a good match. Otherwise, you will be wasting a substantial part of your advertising dollar. Unfortunately, even in the best of circumstances there is bound to be some waste.

If you are saturating a market with direct mail, for instance, you may want to eliminate low-demographic ZIP code areas, but you can't eliminate radio listeners in those ZIPs. Alternatively, you often will find that a good-sized radio station covers hundreds of thousands of households outside the area where a newspaper carrying your advertising is on sale.

An Important Factor: Timing

It isn't difficult to plan a radio support program for a Sunday newspaper insert, because you know specifically when the newspaper—your primary medium—will hit. For maximum impact at minimum cost, you probably will air your commercials on the target Sunday as well as a day or two before.

Magazine ads require a longer or more widely spaced series of commercials on radio since the on-sale date of the magazine and its arrival at the homes of subscribers may span 3 or 4 days or more. Because of the problem of projecting postal service delivery accurately, supporting a direct mail campaign may require you to bracket your anticipated delivery dates and advertise for an entire week.

Determining the cost efficiency of radio support is simple. It comes down to this: Does the combined cost of your primary medium plus the cost of radio support yield an increased number of responses at an acceptable CPR?

COLLATERAL BENEFITS

Evaluation of radio direct marketing programs tends to concentrate on clearly measurable aspects. Programs must meet goals that have been set for return on investment, volume of response, and quality of respondents (as measured by pay-up, conversion, dollar volume, renewal or reorder, etc.) or they are considered worthless and are scrapped. Yet general advertisers use radio extensively and pay top dollar for it without demanding or expecting this sort of immediate payoff. They value radio for its effectiveness in building brand awareness, positioning products competitively, and in turning prospects into customers over a period of time.

Direct marketers get the same promotional impact as general advertisers as a spin-off of self-supporting direct-response programs. In many cases, therefore, it may be worth keeping your commercials on the air even if they are not immediately profitable. If the program is at or close to the breakeven point, it can be a remarkably inexpensive way to support direct mail, print, or even retail sales. And it eventually may overcome the inertia of borderline prospects and convert them to active respondents.

WHAT DOES IT COST TO USE RADIO?

In the long run, the most important yardstick for judging the cost of radio advertising is the cost per retained customer. This is a figure you can arrive at for your own product or service only by using the medium and then tracking your respondents' behavior over a period of time.

Experimenting with radio does not require an enormous cash outlay. Air time is available in units that are relatively inexpensive. The cost of producing a radio commercial can be kept low. If you test carefully before mounting full-scale campaigns, the risk can be minimized even further.

During the initial testing period, however, a simple, practical cost-efficiency guide is the acquisition cost per response, frequently referred to as the cost per order (CPO). This is arrived at by dividing the total cost of air time by the number of leads or orders generated and adding answering service charges.

As an example, $1000 worth of radio air time which generated 200 responses would give you a per response media cost of $5. If you used an answering service that charged $1.10 for each call taken, you would add that to your media cost to arrive at an acquisition cost of $6.10.

Expenses associated with creating and producing commercials, follow-up, and fulfillment are not part of this basic figure, although obviously they will have a bearing on the bottom-line results.

THE ECONOMICS OF DIRECT-RESPONSE RADIO

As a very general rule of thumb, the average cost of radio-generated responses should be about the same as the average cost of responses from all other outside sources (i.e., sources other than house lists, bind-in cards, etc.). If you are used to paying $10 to get a qualified lead from print and direct mail, be prepared to pay the same for a radio lead. With a known CPR as your target, the complexities of time buying for direct-response radio activities are considerably simplified, at least in theory.

Seasonality can be an important cost factor in your use of radio. Broadcast time is most expensive and most difficult to buy in the months before Christmas and in April, May, and June. If you must promote heavily during these periods, you will find it harder to make radio work for you as economically as it does for a marketer who can take advantage of more favorable conditions.

Evaluating a potential broadcast media buy tends to come down to simple, pragmatic questions like the following.

- If 1 minute of air time costs $200 and the target CPR is $2, is it reasonable to expect 100 responses from that station at that time of day?

  Many factors enter into such a decision, including the coverage area of the station, the size of its primary market area, its share of that market, the time periods and program adjacencies available, competitive programming, and even the weather. Only experience can provide guidance. Because there are so many variables in broadcast, every new media buy becomes a new test.
- If ten $200 spots can be bought for a bargain price of $1200, if the station has the option of running them any time of the day or night it sees fit, is it reasonable to expect an average of 60 responses per spot (600 total) during that schedule?

  A novice in broadcast tends to think that each spot aired should represent a perfect match between product and program (i.e., newsweekly and newsbreak) and that each spot must pay out on its own.

  Actually, getting a perfect match may cost much more than you can afford to pay. If you must lock up time adjacent to the hourly newsbreak, you probably will have to pay the full rate card rates. On the other hand, if you give the station the flexibility of running your spot on a standby basis whenever it has a time slot available, you usually can negotiate discounts of 60 percent or more. This may mean that during any single week only half your spots will be aired and that many spots won't generate the number of orders you hoped for. If the total number of responses is satisfactory, however, and the CPR meets or betters your target, the schedule has been a success.
- If it's possible to buy a network spot capable of generating 1000 responses, is it possible for your answering service to handle all those calls at one time? If the service "busies out" and loses half of them, will the spot still be cost-efficient?

  Nine out of ten responses you get from a broadcast spot probably will come in the first 5 minutes. Very few answering services can handle 900 calls in 5 minutes from a single "hit," and they will tell you so. Under these circumstances, a media buy that looks like a terrific bargain may end up costing you money.

BUYING AIR TIME

While the principles for planning, developing, and creating direct-response campaigns for radio are remarkably similar to those for direct mail, there is a vast difference in the buying process.

The price of a direct mail list is relatively stable and predictable, but the cost of radio time can fluctuate widely from market to market or even from day to day according to supply and demand.

If there is a high demand for a station's time, every announcement will command a top price. However, broadcast time is a perishable commodity; if the demand is low, the station frequently will reduce prices on its unsold inventory. For this reason, direct-response marketers who use broadcast regularly must evaluate and reevaluate the cost of radio time continually as they prepare budgets and project their results.

Where Radio Rates Are Published

Standard Rate and Data Service, Inc. (SRDS), of Skokie, Illinois, publishes a number of directories available by subscription and in many libraries which list rates for spot and network radio. In addition, individual radio stations publish rate cards that generally are intended for local advertisers.

Published rates reflect an estimate (based on research) of the expected audience size and a projection (guided by past experience) of the overall demand by advertisers to reach that audience as well as the length of the commercial.

The length of a commercial also is reflected in the rate structure. Air time is widely available in 10-, 20-, 30-, and 60-second units, and some stations sell units of 90 and 120 seconds. Shorter commercials cost less than longer ones, but the price difference is not proportional; some stations charge 50 percent or more of the 1-minute rate for a 10-second announcement.

Premium Time Commands Premium Prices

General advertisers use rating points which reflect the percentage of people in a market exposed to a commercial as a guideline for buying broadcast time. By and large, the more rating points and the more advertiser demand there is for a time period, the higher the rate for the time. Yet as direct-response broadcast users know, audience size and ratings based on size frequently are irrelevant. There are, after all, many stations with high ratings and high rates that program nothing but "elevator music," i.e., continuous background music with low-keyed news and commercial breaks. Thousands of people have the radio tuned to these stations, but only a small percentage listen intently. On the other hand, the tiny audience giving rapt attention to a 5 A.M. bulletin on farm prices may be very responsive to your commercial and much less expensive to reach.

It almost always pays to search out programs that have high listener involvement, but you must use common sense. A major league ball game may be so involving that you can't get potential customers unglued from their radios long enough to call and order your product. You also may find that "drive time," i.e., the early morning and late afternoon hours when people are driving to and from work, is not as productive as you think it should be. Although an attentive audience may be there in substantial numbers, the tools for response are not; there are no phones, no pencils, and no paper.

If you want to reach working people, test drive time by all means, but don't be mystified if the response does not live up to the promise of the audience "numbers."

Network versus Spot Buying

As far as a direct marketer is concerned, there is nothing inherently better about spot buying (i.e., on a market-by-market basis from individual stations) versus buying network radio.

Making a network buy can be extremely efficient because you can air your commercial on hundreds of stations around the country with one sales contact, minimum outlay for audio tapes and shipping, and minimum paperwork, at a cost that is considerably lower than what you would have to pay if you were negotiating rates station by station.

The advantages to spot buying are that you can target your sales message much more accurately, skipping markets or even entire sections of the country which are not of interest to you. You choose which station to use in a market, and you can custom fit your media buy to local conditions. The higher cost per station is no disadvantage if you actually get better cost efficiency by "cherry picking" your spot buys.

If you buy network time, you have to be able to establish a good system for capturing responses across the country. A commercial aired in 200 markets at the same time can generate hundreds or even thousands of phone calls in a few minutes. If you don't have adequate phone lines set up to take the calls, you'll lose the responses and the cost efficiency of your program.

Negotiating Rates and Schedules

Realistically, the cost of radio time almost always is negotiable. In addition to straightforward discounts from published rates, there are a number of "special" arrangements that are traditional in the industry, including per inquiry, run of station schedules, response guarantees, and barter.

Per Inquiry (PI). This is perhaps the most familiar of the off-rate card arrangements. In a PI, the station agrees to run your commercial whenever it has available time; you agree to pay for all orders or leads generated at a prearranged price. If there are no responses, you pay nothing.

This can be a very satisfactory arrangement if you know exactly how much you can afford to pay for a response and can deal with fluctuating and uncertain order volume. Be fair in setting a PI rate. It's important that the deal be a money maker for the station as well as for you; otherwise, it will not succeed.

Response Guarantees. These sometimes can be arranged with stations that will not accept an advertiser at less than the card rates. In effect, the station is making a bet with you. It is wagering that you can reach an agreed-on number of responses from its audience by running a schedule at regular rates. If you can't, the station will run your spots free until you reach the target.

Cash in Advance. This is a sweetener that can help considerably in negotiating favorable rates. Even a station with a limited amount of unsold time and a cool view of off-card deals may be willing to make special arrangements or go for a guaranteed response schedule if air time is paid for up front.

Barter Arrangements. These usually are handled through organizations that specialize in this trading process. The concept is simple: In exchange for each dollar's worth of a client's products or services, the barter organization will provide a dollar's worth of air time on radio or TV stations, usually at the published rate card value.

In evaluating a barter arrangement, keep in mind that the rate card value may bear little relationship to the cost of comparable time purchased directly from the station. Try to get an idea of the true street value of the time that is being offered; it will put you in a better negotiating position. Also keep in mind that stations view barter time as their lowest scheduling priority and will preempt it for any paid advertising. As with PI deals, this may be a problem if you require a specific number of leads or orders to meet a target.

Finally, be sure the barter organization spells out the guidelines for running the schedule (markets, stations, time periods, etc.) so that you can evaluate the response you're getting in terms of what you expected to get.

Run of Station (ROS) Arrangements. In this case you are buying a weekly "package" of spots. ROS rates are the lowest published rates available for air time; they are priced to be a bargain. But an ROS spot always can be bumped off the air by any advertiser willing to pay a higher rate. In addition, because this is a type of standby arrangement, stations reserve the right to place ROS spots wherever it is convenient for them. This can mean that all your commercials will be aired between midnight and dawn. Before agreeing to an ROS schedule, therefore, try to negotiate with the station sales rep to get good rotation through all dayparts or through specific dayparts that work well for your offer. If you are successful, you may not get a lower rate per spot, but you may get a lower CPO.

As a general principle, always negotiate for good positioning as well as good rates. Radio never should be bought solely on the basis of cost. Bargain spots are no bargain if they do not deliver the responses you need.

How to Set Up a Schedule

If you are ready to buy air time, here are some general guidelines.

1. If at all possible, use an advertising agency or time-buying service that is experienced in planning and buying for direct marketers. Media commissions paid by the stations to recognized agencies will offset most or all of the cost of their services in your behalf.
2. If you are talking to station or network representatives yourself, try to deal with someone who understands direct-response broadcast. Give the rep a good idea of what your target audience is. Let the rep make suggestions about programming that will reach your market. Remember at all times that high ratings do not automatically translate into high response.

3. Talk to more than one rep and one station. Ask reps whom else you should talk to in their market and which stations they would buy in addition to their own. Published data may be out of date, but the reps know what is happening among their competitors.
4. Get information on local market conditions. High unemployment levels, for instance, can affect response or pay rates.
5. Don't commit yourself to an extensive schedule until you've tested the station and the market. A week or two on the air should be enough to get an idea of the response. If you want to buy a longer schedule, be sure you can cancel after the first week if the results are poor.

As a final consideration, remember that if the cost of air time is out of line in a given market, you can ignore the market completely and put your dollars where they will get a higher return. Incidentally, let the reps you have been dealing with know what you are doing. The best negotiating tactic for tomorrow's rates may be to pick up your marbles and go away today.

CREATIVE COPY IS COPY THAT SELLS

Like a good direct mail package or print ad, a good radio commercial may last indefinitely. Its effectiveness can always be measured directly in terms of sales or customer leads. We have had one commercial running continually for close to 8 years. Although we test new copy against it periodically, no other copy has beaten our control, and the control keeps pulling.

Do Your Homework Before You Write

To write effective copy, you don't have to be a great writer, but you do have to be a good salesperson. You must be thoroughly familiar with your product and market. You should know precisely what you can do for a potential customer and why you can do it better than your competition. But most important, you must be able to develop copy that answers the prospect's unspoken question, "What's in it for me?"

Experience is the best teacher. If you have promoted your product or service through other media, look carefully at creative appeals, product positioning, benefits, and offer statements that have worked before. You may find that the headline of a print ad or the lead line of a successful direct mail package will translate superbly into the lead sentence of a winning radio spot.

Make It Short and Make It Sweet

Creative radio copy that works distills the essence of the sales message in words, images, and a flow of ideas that are compact, clear, and compelling.

A one-minute, copy-packed commercial spot is only about 200 words long. When the spot is a vehicle for direct-response sales, fully one-third of those words must be given over to offer statements and response instructions. For these reasons, your copy must be telegraphic; every word has to do double duty, telling and selling at the same time. Yet it must sound conversational or you will lose the immediacy and intimacy that are one of radio's advantages as a one-to-one sales medium.

While every word in your copy should contribute to making the sale, it's important that you do the following.

1. Find opening statements that select and qualify prospective respondents efficiently. The first few words of your commercial are like teaser copy on a direct mail envelope; they induce the prospect to get involved with the message. In radio, they may be required to find the prospect as well.
2. Discover the clearest, most irresistible offer statement you can make. Your copy may influence a prospect to think favorably about your product, but if your offer and response statements aren't clear and compelling, you won't complete the sale.

Clarity is essential in radio. Remember that listeners have no written record to refer to later other than a phone number or box number jotted down on a scrap of paper. It is essential that you give them a full and honest description of your product or service, a precise statement of its cost, clear explanations of any obligations or limitations, and easy-to-understand instructions for responding to your offer. Otherwise, they are likely to be misled, disappointed, and confused, and you will have to deal with refusal of shipments, poor conversion, bad pay, and other avoidable back-end problems.

When you're writing or evaluating radio scripts, make sure you do the following.

- Use vocabulary everyone in your target audience will understand.
- Stick to simple, short words and phrases.
- Repeat vital information; it's particularly difficult to grasp numbers unless they are repeated.

USING RADIO AS A TEST MEDIUM

Our first recommendation to clients who are interested in broadcast for a direct marketing campaign is to conduct a battery of radio tests before committing themselves to an expanded radio campaign or to television.

Radio is a close to ideal testing medium because it's flexible and relatively inexpensive. The cost of producing a quality radio commercial is low, especially in comparison with TV production costs. And the results of a radio test are reliable enough to project not only to a larger radio schedule but to television as well.

The tests we run on radio are very similar to the pyramid tests one conducts in direct mail. That is, they start out on a very limited basis and build up to an increasingly larger broadcast schedule only as indicated by positive responses.

For projectable, reliable information, we usually need to see somewhere between 1000 and 2000 orders in order to get a good profile of the people who are responding, where they are responding from, what copy appeal they are responding to, and very importantly, how they pay, convert, renew, etc.

Then, if it is called for, we conduct additional testing on important elements such as prices, terms, premiums, or other offer variations and methods of response, being careful to test only one element at a time. If more than one element is tested, there's no way to know which change is causing a difference in response rates.

Structuring the Test

Experience suggests that you not try to learn everything at once in a radio test. In the initial stage, concentrate on identifying the most productive creative approaches.

Frequently we begin with as many as six different commercials running on only a few stations or in only a few markets until we find the one bit of information we're looking for: the relative difference in pull between various copy approaches.

If you have a product or service that appeals to a very large audience, you may want to explore every type of programming available throughout the country. However, if your product has a more restricted appeal, look to your previous direct mail and print experience as you decide where to start testing.

An example that was used earlier was a mutual fund with a customer base heavily skewed to business men and women. Since close to 50 percent of the fund's shareholders are in California or the northeast, a logical starting point would be stations in those two geographical areas.

Logical programming formats to start the test with would be newsbreaks and news business features because they attract business executives and because people who tune in to "talk radio" are likely to listen actively.

Generally it's sensible to buy time on two or three stations in a market during a test so that you can get a feel for the entire market's response. To reduce the number of test variables, it may be helpful to restrict your schedule to specific time spans, known as dayparts. The agency for the mutual fund magazine might recommend buying late afternoon (the daypart called "p.m. drivetime") and early evening in New York, Boston, Philadelphia, Los Angeles, and San Francisco, on news and talk shows.

If results are good in this stage of the test, the agency may recommend dropping the least productive copy, stations, and dayparts and trying new markets such as Atlanta, Chicago, Dallas, or Washington. Alternatively, the recommendation may be to move into other stations in the original test markets and into other dayparts. In any event, tests would pyramid until the agency could plan national schedules, confident that it knew where to find potential readers of the magazine, when to reach them, and how to get them to subscribe.

Using the Results of a Radio Test

Information gained from broadcast can be used for planning an ongoing campaign that fits the marketing strategies and sales objectives of the client.

In addition to using radio as an inexpensive, convenient medium for gathering information for an order-generating campaign, it can be used to acquire other information, such as the anticipated falloff in response from a price increase, which you normally would seek only from A-B splits in print or from direct mail tests.

At the end of a comprehensive radio test, you should have gathered enough information to project a full year's volume of responses in order to get an idea of what should be budgeted for and what schedules you should make a commitment to.

However, a word of caution: Broadcast testing can give you a very reliable indication of what will happen, it cannot pin down results with the fraction of a percentage point precision of direct mail.

Analyzing radio test results requires a great deal more than just looking at numbers. Factors beyond your control must be taken into consideration, such as unusual weather, big news events, strikes, or anything that might change or influence the listening habits of a market in a particular time period. For instance, you can be misled seriously by unusually good results from a Kansas station that has been airing your test spots during the height of the tornado season, when everyone stays tuned for weather updates.

Testing Your Backup Systems

It's important not only to set up an efficient system to capture your orders or leads but also to test its performance along with your fulfillment system during your initial on-air testing phase.

If you are using a toll-free number, recognize the critical importance of a good telephone answering service. Your service must have considerable experience in taking broadcast responses, and it must have enough telephone lines, staffed with trained operators, to handle your calls 24 hours a day. Before you make a final decision on which answering service to use, investigate a number of them and talk to other marketers who use broadcast extensively. Your toll-free service can make or break your program.

An order-handling performance test would include the following elements:

1. Making arrangements with telephone answering services
2. Making all U.S. Postal Service or private delivery and COD arrangements
3. Making all credit card arrangements
4. Renting a post office box with an easily remembered number
5. Checking out your mail pickup system
6. Gearing your fulfillment or lead follow-up procedures to the highest efficiency
7. Structuring your information systems for gathering and analyzing respondents' behavior (i.e., pay-up, conversion, order size, renewal, etc.)

During the media test phase, you have an opportunity to test your back-end systems, improving and refining them and then retesting them until you are sure everything is running smoothly. If order-capturing and fulfillment procedures aren't working well, don't proceed with a full-scale program until the problems are ironed out completely. Delays in follow-up, poor fulfillment, and inadequate information about respondents' performance can wreak havoc with an otherwise outstandingly successful program.

Most people who respond to broadcast promotions are acting on impulse and may lose their enthusiasm quickly. Try to get back to them fast with a sales call, with information, with the product they've ordered, and with an invoice or whatever else is required.

Broadcast respondents have nothing in writing, nothing to hold on to that clarifies or reinforces the details of your offer. If you have a complex offer such as a multipayment plan, send along some kind of restatement of their rights, options, and obligations. Finally, make sure you are tracking all the facts about respondent behavior that you may need in the future. If everything you test on radio works and if everybody who responds pays, converts, etc., you may not need to know where the best and worst responses are coming from. But until you are sure that this is the case, collect the information meticulously. The chances are that you will need it.

MEASURING AND ANALYZING RESPONSE

Recordkeeping, tracking, and analysis are as important for radio as for direct mail. The more information you have, the better your chance of maximizing the program's productivity and efficiency. Get as much information as you can as quickly as possible and then use it and share it; station reps are at least as receptive to guidance as list brokers.

There are six steps to this process.

1. Keep records on a station-by-station, day-by-day or even hour-by-hour basis.
2. Review response records daily to fine-tune the program while it is in operation; that is, cancel schedules that are not working, adjust marginal ones, and most important, zero in on the most productive stations so that their schedules can be increased.
3. Calculate your projected order volume for each station by dividing the cost of a week's air time on that station by your target CPO for the entire program. For example, $1000 worth of air time divided by a target CPO of $10 equals a projected volume of 100 orders. This gives you a helpful benchmark when you review station performance.
4. Track broadcast results through their back-end performance, or how they pay, convert, etc. Not all broadcast orders are equal; audience units vary in demographic, psychographic, and geographic characteristics just as lists do. You may find a large number of good customers in one market, one time period, or one kind of program but have poor experience with customers from other audiences.
5. Note your customers' mode of response at entry: mail or phone. When it's time to reapproach them for renewals or reorders, give them the same response option.
6. Try to determine what collateral benefits resulted from your radio program, such as increased response from your direct mail or retail sales. Unless you keep an eye on collateral benefits, you may not know how significant a contribution radio has made to your overall marketing efforts until you cut back on it.

SUMMARY

With each new medium of communication that is developed, with each new technological advance, there are predictions that the old media will wither away and disappear; our grandchildren won't know what a newspaper looks like, futurists say. For radio, however, new electronic technology has meant change, but it has also meant growth. For instance, radio has been "adopted" by the cable systems to provide the sound track for video text.

For the direct marketer, learning to exploit radio as a direct-response medium will be well worth the effort. Radio reaches and influences more people than ever. As the population grows, radio grows. It is a powerful, effective medium. If narrowcasting on video is the wave of the future, radio is the place to practice it today.

chapter **26**

CREATIVE MEDIA

Asher B. Abelow

President
Abelow Response, Inc.
Valley Stream, N.Y.

As the various creative elements necessary for a successful direct marketing effort are developed, it falls to the media department in an agency or to the marketer's own staff to analyze, select, and schedule the specific media that can be expected to produce the best projected dollar volume results at an acceptable cost. It is an axiom of direct marketing that measurability of all advertising efforts controls every media decision.

While the traditional media—direct mail, newspapers, magazines, radio, television, and more recently cable TV—have been the basic sources of direct-response revenue, rapidly rising postage, space, and time rates have spawned a new and growing range of "creative media." In this chapter, we will identify and cover methods direct marketers are using to go beyond the traditional media in an effort to reach and penetrate smaller but nonetheless significant segments of the consumer and business markets that will respond at cost-effective rates.

Before getting into the specifics of creative media, it is important to analyze and examine the reasons (beyond cost considerations) why advertisers have taken so strongly to these devices. Credit and attention must be given to a device born in the post-World War II era and blessed by hundreds of brand name manufacturers: the coupon. Originally developed to introduce new products and stimulate or revitalize old ones, the coupon became an integral part of many advertising campaigns. In 1971, coupon distribution was only 20 billion; in 1976, just under 46 billion. In 1981, distribution of cents-off coupons reached 102.4 billion. Of this number, 27.3 percent were daily newspaper ROP solo offers; 17.7 percent were found in co-op offers in daily newspapers; and 26.2 percent appeared in freestanding inserts. Sunday newspapers got 7.3 percent, magazines 11.8 percent, direct mail 3.3 percent, and in-pack or on-pack coupons 6.4 percent.

Clearly, the American public had taken coupons to its economic heart. As the evidence of coupon redemption power mounted, direct marketers, always on the alert for devices that would increase response rates, began to adopt the national advertisers' coupon format to their own needs. Highly creative art directors began by addressing the objective of making it as easy as possible for the reader to respond. They simply took the coupon, provided space for the reader to fill in his or her name and address or have it pretyped or labeled, and stated the offer in visual and written terms so concise that it would take but a few moments to complete the required transaction.

Gradually, a format evolved that is now commonly known as an insert, a self-contained two-, four-, six-, or even eight-page booklet folded as necessary to a 5½- by 8½-inch or 5- by 7-inch (or smaller) size, usually printed on 60- or 70-pound plain or coated stock. It contains a built-in, perforated reply card that can be removed easily from the insert, filled out, and dropped into the mail. The 70-pound paper referred to is necessary to meet minimum postal requirements for business reply cards. If the stock is lighter than required, some insert formats can be folded over and have a patch of glue along several key edges that then create a reply envelope that meets the requirement.

Once the physical aspects of the insert were mastered, inserts appeared in the pages of a variety of magazines in a folded format or as a single page the size of the magazine but printed on high-bulk stock with the perforated order form usually found in the lower right-hand side of the facing page. This became known as a bind-in insert. Advertisers most successful in the early stages of this type of bind-in ads were basically in a single category: continuity clubs. Thus, book, record, and various kinds of crafts, hobbies, publishers, and manufacturers such as food, needlework, handicraft, sewing, etc., turned to this new advertising technique with reassuring success. It was so successful that magazines had to develop special rate structures and production techniques to accommodate the new method. One variation of this technique became familiar as a bind-in insert card which was placed adjacent to a full-page ad usually run by a magazine for subscription sales or by a book club for new members. Despite the appearance of an order form on the page ad and the additional cost of the adjacent bind-in card, this consistently produced cost-effective orders for the advertiser. In more recent years, magazines also have resorted to the blow-in technique to self-promote their own publications. This device permits low-cost loose insertion of a postal card-size reply form, again printed on the minimum .007 card stock. Many major magazines still use this technique with great effectiveness.

As the insert started to prove itself cost-effective for pioneer advertisers who first experimented with it, the law of media supply and demand began to take effect. The balance of this chapter will concentrate on those creative media devices which have been developed over the past 20 years to meet the demands of advertisers for better, more cost-effective ways of reaching specific targets of direct marketing opportunity.

FORMS OF CREATIVE MEDIA

Take-Ones

We have seen how advertisers used the insert as a bind-in in a magazine. With all the creative, mechanical, art, and production costs already in place, advertisers began seeking additional ways to distribute this material with only the actual printing cost to be added to the media rate.

Although take-one material had been around at airport and bus terminals for many years, it was not considered a productive area for most major direct-response advertisers and remained largely a device for car rental agencies, hotels, and general tourist and entertainment facilities to promote their services; only occasionally would such an advertiser use a direct-response technique in a brochure to test its effectiveness.

Several take-one devices are currently in use by specific kinds of advertisers. They can be found in buses and subways in large urban areas such as New York City. They are usually part of a card format to which is affixed a packet of reply cards that can be torn off one at a time and returned postage-paid to the advertiser.

Because of the lower demographic profiles generally found in the large urban subway and bus riding public, there are several predominantly successful advertising categories: secretarial and trade schools, educational services, and offers for lower-cost reference encyclopedias. Bus take-ones frequently are available on a route basis, and sometimes a higher demographic audience can be reached effectively with an appropriate offer such as banking or investment services.

Several years ago, the author helped develop a take-one insert program for taxi riders in New York City, primarily in the borough of Manhattan. The system consisted of an attractive white plastic rack that was affixed behind the front seat, facing the passenger. It contained room for six different advertisers' inserts with each pocket holding up to 500 inserts, depending on their thickness. A fleet of 300 taxis was contracted to install, service, and maintain the racks.

After several months of testing, five advertisers reported excellent results and made substantial commitments to the program. These advertisers included a photo finisher, several major news magazines, two credit card services, and a money-fund investment firm.

College Market. Take-one direct-response advertising on campuses plays a major role for certain categories that have a natural stake in the youth market, including record clubs, magazines, and photo finishers. Several direct marketing companies offer complete distribution services to cover the college market and employ students who install the various support materials that are placed on bulletin boards in campus buildings and student dormitories.

Supermarkets. Supermarkets have become an important location for the distribution of direct-response offers. By creating a display rack with a community bulletin board, one firm has developed a service with over 5000 locations in hundreds of supermarket chains with a total annual take-one count of over 500 million printed inserts. The advertiser supplies the material and pays a fixed fee per insert per location. Since the inserts are taken only by someone who is sufficiently interested in the offer as it is exposed on the rack, the waste factor is low and is reflected in the subsequent low cost per order or inquiry.

Among the hundreds of successful and consistent users of supermarket take-ones are magazines; book and record clubs; insurance; local, state, and federal government pamphlet offers; some merchandise and high-ticket items; credit card plans; photo finishing, etc. Recently, several consumer catalog companies have been distributing a minicatalog through this system.

Postal Card Advertising

A more recent technique, postal card direct-response advertising, was introduced by magazine publishers who developed it as an alternative method for advertisers to reach their subscribers. As its success grew, new companies created magazine-format bound editions that carried three or four postal card-size ads per page, often printed in four colors and always on card stock. By selecting specific areas of interest—doctors, lawyers, accountants, business executives, engineers, scientists, investors, gardeners, etc.—an advertiser can select a precise market with the sure knowledge that the message will be read by a legitimate prospect for his or her offer. Rates are very attractive, and the publisher prints all the cards from the advertiser's artwork.

There has been a lot of controversy about which format is more effective, the bound magazine or the "loose deck," in which fifty or more individual cards are collated and mailed in an envelope or a shrink-wrap package. Both formats can be effective, and there is no hard evidence that one will outpull the other. Study the lists that are being used, for this is most often the key to successful results. Postal card advertising has been proved to be highly cost-effective and should be included in every advertising budget if the right program is available.

Catalog Advertising

This is a creative medium with a very mixed and inconclusive performance record. In theory, it should work for any advertiser who is not directly competitive with the catalog owner and whose advertising is therefore acceptable and whose offer is sufficiently compatible to be of interest to the catalog reader.

In tests conducted by Montgomery Ward in 1975 and 1976, a group of major advertisers ran full-page four-color ads, each of which had a proven performance record in national magazines. Of the five advertisers, not a single one was able to report success results based on the projected cost per thousand (CPM) for each ad.

Other national catalog producers have had similar poor results from companies that ran on-page ads. While no precise studies have been made of reader attitudes toward such advertising, it is felt that extraneous offers in the page environment of a catalog tend to distract the reader from the subject matter of the catalog.

Nevertheless, there have been some successful techniques involving the use of mail-order catalogs as an advertising medium. These include the use of solo or co-op bind-in postal cards or solo blow-in postal cards. Many shelter-type magazines have been successful with this technique, particularly gardening and nursery catalogs.

Rates for this type of advertising are usually negotiable and vary from one cataloger to another. Frequently, a cataloger willing to accept a card will overprice the service, making it impossible for the advertiser to achieve results at a cost-effective rate. Large quantity commitments also are generally required, and planning and contracting must be done well in advance of the catalog distribution schedule, frequently a year ahead.

Retail-Distributed Inserts

The distribution of direct-response inserts through products sold at the retail level is a relatively recent development. Except for a very few categories, it cannot be called a phenomenon. There are at present two methods of reaching the average retail consumer purchaser with a direct-response offer.

In-Packs. In-packs involve actual placement of the insert into the retail package which is placed on the shelf for sale to the consumer.

Egg cartons constitute the major category of retail-distributed inserts. The insert is placed mechanically into the carton on top of the eggs and is printed on lightweight stock in large volume by high-speed offset web presses. The key to success here is the low cost, extremely high-volume reach (500 million per year), and fast product turnover. Offers of low-ticket merchandise and broad-interest consumer magazines have been the major advertisers in the medium.

Several large-volume, nationally distributed product manufacturers in such categories as kitchen utensils, drugs, toys, and housewares have opened their packages to direct-response inserts with mixed results.

This type of advertising has to be approached with caution, for the pitfalls are many. The product line may be too slow moving and thereby drag out too long for the advertisers to measure the results accurately. The merchandise may be diverted from its original destinations as a result of closeouts, bankruptcies, or other losses and never reach its intended customers. If pricing is sensitive and subject to frequent changes, this type of program can be disastrous.

Here too, CPM is important. Retail-distributed inserts simply do not produce as effectively as mail-order package inserts and must be priced accordingly if the advertiser is to succeed.

On-Packs. The second method for retail-distributed direct-response offers involves the use of on-pack advertising by the manufacturer, who offers a premium or a related product, usually as a stimulant to repeat sales. This offer can be printed on the side of the package or carton or on a separate form that is glue-affixed to the package or is visible beneath a plastic or shrink-wrap cover. In both cases, the offer is termed direct-response-generated because it requires the respondent to mail in the form with whatever charges are requested. It is not designed for redemption at the retail location.

Newspaper Inserts

Despite their general negative attitude toward direct marketing (a posture born of competition of the advertising dollar), newspapers have been accepting powerful freestanding devices that are worthy of examination here as prime examples of creative media.

Solo Freestanding Inserts. First used as a corporate public relations technique, the solo insert has proved highly cost effective for such direct-response advertisers as insurance companies, book clubs, real estate firms, high-ticket collectibles, etc.

In most cases, the advertiser supplies the insert and is charged a fixed rate per thousand to have the insert included with the newspaper's Sunday edition in preselected areas. Based on the size specifications, the advertiser has great creative flexibility and can develop as strong a format as the creative and printing budget will permit.

Co-op Multiadvertiser Inserts. This is a more recent technique and currently is being offered by at least four companies that bring together a grouping of national coupon and direct-response advertisers in a magazine-size, twelve- or sixteen-page format colorfully printed on coated stock.

Because of the co-op nature of this format and because it doesn't go through the mail, rates are very attractive for both national brand coupons and direct-response firms. It is also possible to make geographic or demographic selections of this format.

Co-op Newspaper-Distributed Envelopes. The success of the direct mail co-op, where advertisers are grouped into an envelope in order to save on postage and production costs, has generated yet another idea: the newspaper-distributed co-op envelope.

At least two formats are now available. The first, called *Your Sunday Extra*, covers Sunday newspapers in "B," "C," and "D" counties and usually is distributed three times a year via a different group of newspapers in cities throughout the country. Rates are low, and a broad range of offers have been consistently successful: magazines, film processing, insurance, record clubs, and medium-ticket merchandise and services. Selections can be made by city or state. The advertiser supplies the insert for placement into a 6- by 9-inch outer envelope which also frequently carries a direct-response offer on the back.

Another more recent newspaper co-op is that offered by *The New York Times*. After some testing, *The New York Times* is now regularly offering its *Easy Shopper* co-op to advertisers who can reach all *Sunday Times* readers both in and outside the metropolitan New York City distribution area. Successful advertisers have included a photo finisher, a book club, several magazines, and merchandise categories.

The key to success in both the formats described here is the low rate per thousand, generally $10 or less in large quantities. These low rates are attainable mainly because there are none of the postage or sorting and handling charges that normally are applicable to co-ops sent through the mail. Also, the audiences reached are not mail-order-defined, and a low rate is needed to enable the advertiser to be successful.

Statement and Invoice Stuffers and Order Acknowledgments

In the search for additional ways to reach up and tap already "vulnerable" direct marketing-responsive audiences, many publishers, banks, department stores, oil companies, and mail-order firms have turned to their own files to bring news of additional products or services or to carry (for a fee on a syndicated basis) inserts supplied by unrelated though compatible noncompetitive firms. Thus, a magazine like *McCalls* will accept an insert into its invoices for new subscriptions that will be compatible, e.g., an offer from a cosmetics company. Business product firms such as Grayarc, U.S. Pencil, and Eimicke accept offers from business magazines or financially oriented investment firms. Almost everyone has received a monthly oil company invoice loaded with merchandise offers. These usually are supplied by syndication companies.

Several large consumer mail-order firms also accept outside offers into their order acknowledgment envelopes. As with most invoices and statements, these are mailed first class and have almost a 100 percent deliverability factor.

Before making large quantity commitments, it is wise to test your insert in as many statement programs as are available that meet your criteria. Rates for these programs are generally the same as for package insert and co-op programs: $30 to $50 per thousand.

Matchbooks

This category of direct-response media has had a long and productive history for a very few types of direct-response advertisers: insurance, self-improvement (correspondence schools), and some hobby offers, especially stamps.

For mass coverage at a low CPM, this device is hard to beat. But it is difficult to control on a geographic or a rate of distribution basis. Test this medium only if your offer can be described adequately and quickly in the small space available and you can wait long periods of time for responses to come back. Don't use matchbooks if the price of your offer or the offer itself may change within a 6-month period.

Cable TV

Cable TV is the newest arena for direct-response advertisers, many of whom are already hard at work with experimental thrusts in several different directions.

Unlike commercial television, which relies on vast numbers of viewers who are measured by research methodology (Nielsen or Arbitron), cable TV has the unique initial advantage of measurement in terms of actual numbers of subscribers who are paying a cable TV company a fixed monthly rate for either basic service or a combination of basic and extra programming called pay TV. These fees vary from about $6 up to $35 or $40 per month. With a projected 1982 nationwide cable TV subscriber audience of 25 million, half of whom will be paying for programming beyond the basic service, the figure of 12.5 million subscribers begins to become significant to an advertiser, provided that these subscribers can be reached effectively and economically.

Several current developments in cable TV direct-response advertising are of prime interest.

On-Cable Advertising. The most successful record is being produced by Turner Broadcasting, which currently operates three cable networks: WTBS, CNN, and CNN2. These stations, powered by satellite, operate 24 hours daily, 7 days a week. They can carry a direct-response commercial into over 10 million cable subscribers' homes.

Advertisers whose commercials have successfully run on regular TV can participate in this program on a per inquiry (PI) basis, paying only for orders that are received, processed, and paid for at Turner's Atlanta headquarters. This new direct-response advertising medium is producing over 150,000 orders monthly from a variety of offers, including records, tapes and cassettes, insurance, housewares and automotive products, clothing and luggage, books and magazines, and health and beauty products.

Cable TV Invoice Inserts. Since all cable systems maintain files of their subscribers and mail them an invoice on a monthly or bimonthly basis, some have accepted carefully screened outside solo offers to ride with these invoices.

There has been a mixed reaction to this new concept by the cable systems, although the advertisers seem to be quite willing to explore the idea. Some systems express concern over the use by outside companies of their subscriber base, and considerable education is needed to convince cable companies that such an effort rarely disturbs company-subscriber relations and in fact can help improve them. Another obvious advantage is the additional income this type of program brings to offset the cable system's monthly postage and computer processing costs. Current rates average $45 per thousand.

While it is still experimental, more direct-response companies are turning to this method of reaching the cable TV subscriber. Types of firms that have tested include records, collectibles, magazines, jewelry, video clubs, cosmetics, credit cards, gourmet products, and health clubs.

One new format involves a booklet of discount coupons from national consumer goods manufacturers that is inserted along with the cable subscriber's invoice. This device called *Cable Cash*, also carries several direct-response offers. No results are available as of April 1982.

Infomercials. Partly as a result of the availability of larger blocks of time on cable TV, several creative media firms have developed a new technique called infomercials. An infomercial usually features a live demonstration of the product (this can take from 1 to 5 or more minutes per product over a half-hour showtime slot) and a closing reference to ordering information through the use of a merchandise catalog that has been mailed to the cable subscriber.

This is not truly a direct-response effort, since the buyer is requested to go to the advertiser's nearest warehouse or fulfillment location to pick up the selected item. It is still largely in the experimental stage, with mixed results reported by current advertisers.

Infomercials are but a forerunner of the ultimate cable TV direct-response technique: a mass utilization of the two-way Qube system that currently is being offered by Warner Amex in limited markets. What could be simpler than watching an infomercial, pushing a button to order the desired product or service, and then having it delivered to your home within a week or 10 days, accompanied by an invoice payable by check or already charged to your favorite credit card?

As America moves towards the twenty-first century, direct-response advertisers are keeping pace with the vast potentials being opened by high-tech communications facilities. This is a particularly compatible industry for these new methods for consumer-supplier relationships.

New Direct-Response Media

Here are some of the newer creative media that are just beginning to make their impact felt on direct-response advertisers.

Airline Ticket Holders. An enterprising new firm recently found a way to reach air travelers with direct-response-oriented offers along with conventional ads in the form of multiple inserts built into the pockets of the ticket holders supplied to the traveler when he or she purchases a ticket. While no figures are available (the idea was launched in early 1982), it has almost every element of success for direct marketers: large captive audience (although not sufficiently segmentable), low CPO, repeat factor based on publishers' frequency print runs for each airline, and a national scope with regional selectivity based on an airline's franchise.

Attached Mail. On December 6, 1981, the U.S. Postal Service authorized the use of a physical attachment by means of a paper or plastic envelope, a tip-on card, or a wraparound on the cover of a magazine, book, or record package at second, third, or fourth class rates. For the first time, first class mail can be attached and charged for at the lower total rate of the host piece based on the total combined weight.

Without delving into the myriad production and mechanical problems that this extraordinary rate change implies, the impact of this new breakthrough will be considerable on the publishing segment of the direct marketing industry. New opportunities for renewal efforts by the circulation department will open up, at savings estimated to be $0.70 to $0.90 per subscriber per year. The advertising department can look to this change as an added revenue factor by accepting advertising on the wraparound or on a solo postal card that can be tipped onto the magazine cover. The book or record club can carry extraneous inserts in the envelope that contains the invoice, thus reducing the costs.

GENERAL RULES FOR ADVERTISER PARTICIPATION IN CREATIVE MEDIA PROGRAMS

Most of the media discussed in this chapter carry some basic rules for effective participation. The use of inserts particularly requires close supervision through every phase from creative to delivery. Here is a step-by-step approach that will assure maximum efficiency and help avoid many problems.

Specifications

If you are becoming involved for the first time in insert media and have not yet created your material, study the available data from your insert broker or the supplier and predetermine the most common size and weight that will fit the several programs you wish to test.

One of the most common and adaptable sizes today is a format that folds to 3½ by 6½ inches and weighs no more than one-fifth of an ounce. A three- or four-panel piece printed on number 70 coated stock and folded to this size will meet this standard. It can even have strips of gum affixed to create an acceptable business reply envelope when folded properly by the customer.

Scheduling and Delivery

Once you have your insert or a photocopy of it prior to actual printing, you will have to submit it to the program owner through your broker for approval of the offer, size, and weight. If you submit a copy, be sure to specify the kind of paper it is being printed on; this can save anxious moments when the actual insert is delivered to the program owner and the owner decides that it is too heavy and cannot be inserted without a high surcharge that may make the entire effort uneconomical.

All shipments must be made to the owner or the owner's fulfillment house on a prepaid basis. All rates quoted are on the basis of the advertiser prepaying the freight charges to the destination. When shipping, instruct your printer to mark each carton with the exact quantity and the key identification.

Obligation of Program Owner to Advertiser

When the program owner approves your insert and you ship on a previously agreed on schedule, it is the owner's obligation to fulfill this order as specified. When invoice or statement inserts are involved, this usually is done on a regularly maintained schedule (monthly, bimonthly, etc.); assuming that your material arrives in time, it will be properly processed. But there are problems that arise in the direct marketing business, and they must be taken into account if they are beyond the normal control of the owner. Problems that do arise are usually rectified by the owner, often with the assistance of the middleman in the transaction, the broker.

When invoicing, the owner is requested to state the starting and completion dates when the inserts were mailed; this enables you to start the tracking of the responses that will be a measure of the success or failure of the program.

The decision to use creative media in the total direct marketing mix is dependent on the advertiser's own spirit of creativity. One can stick to the tried and true media—direct mail, space, and TV—for the basic results required to meet the program's goals or broaden the entire range of potential business through careful and selective testing of some of the creative media discussed in this chapter.

How do you broaden your "spirit of creativity"? By exposing yourself to everything this dynamic industry has to offer: membership in national and local direct marketing clubs, regular reading of the industry's trade journals and newsletters, and probably most important, working with specialists in the industry who, through their exposure to a variety of clients with different products and services, can spark creative ideas for your projects that will pay off on the bottom line. These specialists include package insert brokers and managers, syndicators, specialty envelope manufacturers, direct marketing advertising agencies, and magazine and newspaper publishers with direct marketing involvement. Attendance at some of the key industry national or regional conventions is also an important source of new information and ideas.

Of the many disciplines that make up the field of direct marketing, there is no greater opportunity than to test a new media concept that has the potential to generate major new sources of revenue for your product or service. That is what creative media are really all about.

chapter 27

TELEMARKETING: OUTBOUND

Ernan Roman

President
Ernan Roman
Direct Marketing
Corporation
New York, N.Y.

INTRODUCTION

This chapter will provide information about the marketing strategies, presentation approaches, and operational requirements essential for successful telephone marketing. These ideas can stimulate your thinking and help you take advantage of the contributions telephone marketing can make to a company's overall marketing efforts. The chapter is divided into six sections that bring together lessons learned over the course of many years of working with both large and small companies.

This chapter will give you a sense of the excitement of telephone as a marketing medium. Telephone marketing offers immediate results in the form of quick and definitive feedback on what you're doing right or wrong. It involves teamwork and personal interaction both within your organization and with the people you're calling. There is lots of room for new concepts and ideas. It is a challenging and rewarding field.

THE SCOPE OF TELEPHONE MARKETING

Over a century ago, in 1876, Bell invented the telephone. Folklore tells us how Mr. Watson was urgently summoned with the famous words, "Watson, come here, I want you," after the inventor spilled battery acid on his trousers.

Despite this auspicious beginning, telephone marketing has been a late bloomer. The first telephone mass-marketing campaign did not take place until 1962, when 20 million calls were made for the Ford Motor Company to generate leads for its car dealer sales force. The program generated two leads per day for each of the 23,000 Ford sales people.

In 1968, an event of technological and economic significance took place: the introduction of wide area telephone service (WATS). WATS provided flat monthly rates for fixed numbers of hours, with the rates governed by geographic coverage. This included the introduction of the ubiquitous 800 number. The fixed rate structure offered tremendous advantages for high-volume outgoing and 800 number telephone marketers by sharply decreasing the cost for long-distance calling.

However, the telephone was not recognized as a true direct marketing medium until the mid-1970s. By the early 1980s, telephone marketing was skyrocketing. Estimated expenditures for telephone marketing in 1975 were $8 billion; in 1981, they leaped to $20 billion. These figures include expenditures for equipment, marketing, and labor.

Why did this dramatic change occur? The primary reason was economic. The shock waves from the Arab oil fields after 1973 rocked every business either directly or indirectly. Traditional marketing methods quickly proved inadequate or cost-prohibitive. Between 1976 and 1981, the cost of a salesperson's visit increased 75 to 80 percent, first class mail jumped 55 percent, and bulk mail rates increased 70 percent. WATS rates, which had been relatively stable through 1981, increased 25 percent because of the June 1, 1981, rate changes. These factors, combined with intensifying domestic and international competition, forced businesses to explore new marketing methods. Today, not surprisingly, the telephone has become a major channel of distribution for many companies.

- A major pharmaceutical company markets many of its products to tens of thousands of drugstores by phone instead of using a costly detail force.
- A leading bank introduces a new product by mail and phone and within 2 years generates 200,000 customers.
- A national publisher renews over 200,000 lapsed subscribers per year by phone.

The entry of Fortune 500 firms into telephone marketing has provided tremendous impetus to the growth and prestige of the industry. Such companies include IBM, Xerox, Citycorp, Pfizer, Polaroid, Montgomery Ward, Avis, Time Inc., ITT, AT & T, Johnson & Johnson, and Procter & Gamble. This, however, does not mean that smaller companies have not profited from telephone marketing. In fact, small companies, because of their size and limited resources, have felt the greatest impact in terms of increased cost efficiencies and profitability. These companies include Foley Manufacturing, Scholastic, D.C.A. Educational, Modern Farm, and Baldwin-Cooke.

STRATEGIC PLANNING

> Strategy and timing are the Himalayas.
> Everything else is the Catskills.
>
> *Jack Trout and Al Ries*

Telephone marketing is no longer a peripheral element in the media mix. It has become an integral factor in the distribution process, and it requires careful strategic planning which includes three interdependent elements: market segmentation, the media mix, and the creative strategy.

Planning Requirements

Every channel of distribution is used in accordance with a strategic plan. This precept also applies to telephone marketing. Although this may seem obvious, a formal strategic plan for telephone marketing is the exception rather than the rule. Conceivably, this is caused by the easy access to the telephone by every businessperson. The ever-present desk telephone is used constantly to market products and services. Therefore, some marketers have failed to comprehend the value of this medium as a vehicle for mass distribution. However, once marketers conceive of the telephone as a channel of distribution, they recognize that the medium requires a strategic framework. The criteria and components of any strategic plan apply here as well. For example, the following elements should be included:

- Situation analysis
- Objectives
- Goals
- Strategy
- Tactics
- Resource requirements
- Budget
- Measurement and analysis

These principles are universal. However, their careful use will guarantee the greatest returns from the telephone marketing investment.

Market Segmentation

Accurate market definition is critical for all direct marketing media. Approximately 60 to 70 percent of the success potential of a telephone marketing effort is dependent on pinpoint market segmentation. There are two reasons for this, one consumerist and the other economic.

Consumerist. Today's decision maker, business or consumer, demands personalized attention. In fact, for many industries where the line differentiating one company from another begins to blur, the customer service and consumerist orientation of the telephone contact may make the major difference in stimulating the prospect to do business with one firm versus another. Therefore, the call must have relevance to the needs of that individual. Nonselective, random calls do not fit this requirement and are perceived not as welcome customer service contacts but as annoying intrusions.

Economic. While the "cost per image" for telephone marketing is not increasing as rapidly as in other media, the telephone is not inexpensive. Calls to lists which have not been properly qualified will produce poor results and wipe out profits from a given effort.

TABLE 27-1 Weighting for House List Variables

Recency	55%
Frequency	35%
Dollar amount	10%

Here are some important guidelines for successful list segmentation:

House List Is Best. This is an elementary principle which also applies to the telephone. It stands to reason that a previous buyer is a stronger prospect than a nonbuyer. The preexisting relationship with the customer justifies the telephone call and enables the consumer to respond to the communicator as one who is initiating a customer service call.

We have found that the house list segmentation guidelines quoted by Bob Stone for direct mail pertain equally to the telephone. See Table 27-1.

Another important factor in house list segmentation which applies to outside lists as well is source coding. For example, previous telephone buyers are the best prospects for future telephone offers; 800 number buyers or out-WATS buyers within each of the recency, frequency, and dollar amount categories are your best prospects. As another example, previous mail-order buyers are better telephone prospects than people who have never bought by mail.

Outside Lists. Nowadays it is possible to rent any one of 200,000 lists, most of which are available to telephone marketers. These lists can be segmented easily into various subclusters, for example, ZIP code clustering by demographic criteria such as income, type of dwelling, and lifestyle. Services such as Claritas, Metromail, Polk, and Urban Data are good sources. With this capability, one can profile the lifestyle characteristics of a house list against the demographic factors of a prospect universe, thereby clustering prospects into high probability pockets. If the target market is large, this process can be critical in maximizing returns from mail and telephone efforts and can pay for itself by eliminating non-prospects.

Media Mix

The combination of telephone with other elements in the media mix generates incremental and synergistic results. Telephone follow-up to a direct mailing will generate an incremental response 2½ to 10 times the response achieved by mail.

Direct mail response	2%
Incremental telephone response	5 to 20%
Total mail and phone responses	7 to 22%

This lift in response must be incremental; it must not be the result of cannibalized responses that would have come in by mail anyway. To determine true incremental response we recommend the following.

A-B Tests. When testing, structure two cells which are based on an Nth name selection.

- Group A: direct mail only (control group)
- Group B: direct mail with telephone follow-up

This will provide you with an absolute measurement regarding the magnitude of the incremental telephone response.

Creaming the Response via Mail. Another strategy is to "cream" the mail response first and then follow up with the telephone call. This strategy, however, depends on the level of mail response.

- If mail response is less than 10 percent, do not wait to cream the response before starting telephone calls. In this instance, it is not cost-effective to let the mail message get "cold" for 90 percent of your universe before starting follow-up calls.
- If mail response exceeds 10 percent (this usually occurs in subscription renewal, insurance, or continuity mail cycles) it is generally more cost-effective to position telephone after mail has creamed the initial response. As was mentioned earlier, the best method of quantifying mail versus phone response rates is through repeated A-B testing.

Some marketers have found that phone also lifts mail response after the call. Of the universe contacted by phone who said they were not interested in the offer at the time of the call, a meaningful percentage subsequently order by mail. This is a direct result of the customer service thrust of the call and the detailed product information which creates a positive impression with the prospects even though they elected not to place an order when they originally were called. The ability to measure this is dependent on two variables.

- Source code all names to be used in a telephone test. This is necessary for general back-end tracking of performance as well as for measuring subsequent mail conversion from the group which did not order by phone.
- It is essential to recognize the need for adequate computer capabilities. It is surprising how many major marketers are severely restricted in their ability to perform nonroutine response measurements over time, for example, tracking mail response activity from people who were not interested in purchasing at the time of the call. This is changing slowly, a process which should be helped by the proliferation and increasing sophistication of minicomputers.

In summary, telephone generates a quantifiable 2½- to 10-time incremental response rate when positioned as a follow-up to a direct mailing. Telephone also improves the response rate from subsequent mailings sent to prospects who were not interested during the initial call.

More Is Better

As marketers begin to use telephone marketing, some have eliminated direct mailings because of the large responses that phone is able to generate by itself. Generally, this is a mistake. Mail is an effective door opener and an influential vehicle for educating the decision maker and securing confidence. Simultaneously, it generates orders relatively inexpensively. Cutting back on mail because you now have the telephone as part of the mix would be similar to dispensing with space advertising because the sales force is performing well.

Creative Strategy

Positioning the Call. Telephone marketing provides the most vital quality of the personal sales call: two human beings in a one-to-one dialog. The medium is truly interactive. To maximize the value of this characteristic, the positioning of every contact with a decision maker must be directed toward establishing a dialog, not a one-way broadcast.

Today's consumer wants to speak out, demands to be recognized as an individual. Encourage consumers to speak out. Their responsiveness to your offer will increase dramatically once they feel that the caller is genuinely attentive to what they have to say.

This distinction between a call with a customer service orientation and a self-serving sales effort by a hard-hitting salesperson unfortunately escapes some marketers. That's the main reason we hear complaints about telephone marketing from time to time and occasionally even calls for a ban on phone solicitation from overzealous legislators. However, a properly handled telephone contact has value to both prospect and marketer. In many cases, the prospects thank the marketers for calling as quickly as the marketers thank them for listening. This is the kind of telephone marketing that succeeds, as it generates both goodwill and financial rewards.

Scripting. A critical factor in establishing a low-key, customer service-oriented dialog is the script. Telephone communicators should follow carefully prepared scripted presentations. Scripts should include pretested answers to questions and objections that may arise. These scripts are written by management and tested by supervisors. Only after thorough testing by supervisors during which revisions and rewrites take place should communicators begin using the script.

There are two compelling reasons to use a scripted presentation.

- **Quality control.** Successful marketers have developed a corporate image of quality and integrity. These are valuable assets and provide an important competitive edge. Management must have assurances that the consumer who receives the call is treated in a manner consistent with the company's own high standards. Careful scripting and continuous call monitoring ensure quality presentations.
- **Projectability.** A scripted presentation is essential to ensure that the results of a particular test effort are projectable to a volume universe. Once the testing process is completed, one can project the response rate for the next 10,000 or 100,000 calls.

Telephone's interactive quality requires that the copy

- Avoid vague claims, half-truths, and hard-sell tactics
- Anticipate questions or objections that require additional data
- Elicit and encourage response from the prospect

Here are six steps for preparing an effective script.

1. Set a limit to length. This should be governed by the type of decision maker you are contacting and the dollar value of the item you are selling.
2. Ask for the prospect by name and verify that the person is actually on the telephone.
3. The communicator must identify himself or herself, the company, and the purpose of the call as soon as contact is made with the targeted decision maker.
4. Highlight key benefits of the offer to the customer in a concise, clear manner.
5. Include in the script answers to questions, objections, and problems.
6. Where possible, present the offer as an either-or choice.

You can test the effectiveness of your script within panels of 500 to 1000 calls. To make corrections in the script, you must control the quality of your communicators' messages by live monitoring of their calls. This way, modifications of questions and answers, style, and tone can be made as the calls progress. The immediacy of the telephone allows for fast testing and retesting. By keeping accurate records and taping calls with an FCC-approved beeper, you can begin to analyze and evaluate results within a few hours.

Constant analysis of questions, objections, and very importantly, the reasons why people are not interested in the offer will enable you to react with an ongoing script and offer modifications until you reach maximum productivity.

The script development process also should include testing of multiple product offerings. For example, banks and merchandisers successfully package their services or products for the telephone into multiple service and product offers, thereby increasing the revenue per order. Effective multiple product offers have included "add-on" or "step-down" offers as well as "packaged" selling in which a family of products is packaged into one offer.

Here are some dos and don'ts for structuring the telephone offer.

- *Do* sell items by phone which can be described simply and quickly. If your product or service is too complex to be described to the prospect in 30 to 60 seconds, try including all the details in a mailing piece and then follow the mailing with a phone call once your prospects have familiarized themselves with the specifics.
- *Do* test prices, product combinations, and even product features. The phone is a fantastic medium for product testing. You get results immediately, you can change your promotional copy on short notice, and it doesn't take very many calls to determine the most effective creative approach or offer.
- *Do* offer credit terms whenever possible. If the names you are calling are not already customers who have established credit with your firm, screen the prospect list for creditworthiness before calling. Furthermore, when calling consumers, offer to accept bank credit cards if at all possible. Many marketers have found that offering credit and time payment plans boosts response dramatically.
- *Don't* offer too many options to the decision maker. A successful telephone offer is clear and comprehensible. If respondents get too bogged down in details and choices, they will not make a purchase decision.
- *Do* cross-sell customers on items related to the initial purchase. If someone purchased a pool, for example, call to offer a new model of filter or chemicals or

sale-priced accessories. Be sure to keep seasonal needs in mind; offer a new pool patio as a summer approach or a cover for the pool as winter nears.

- *Don't* offer merchandise which is not high quality and reliable. No one can satisfy all customers all the time, but it is particularly important for telephone marketers to try their hardest to do just that. A smart marketer works at developing a group of satisfied customers who will become repeat buyers. Endeavor to establish an ongoing telephone relationship with your customers based on quality products.
- *Don't* forget the critical importance of offering appropriate guarantees and assurance of quality. Knowing that you will make good if the product you deliver is not satisfactory goes a long way toward overcoming the initial skepticism that too often is associated with telephone sales. After all, telephone buyers are essentially buying an unknown. They can't see, feel, touch, or taste the merchandise firsthand. Anything you can do to assure them that you will live up to your promises is well worth doing.

When making an offer, keep in mind the four C's. Your offer, indeed the entire presentation, must be clear, concise, conversational, and convincing. Of course, all offers are not accepted immediately, regardless of how well worded they are or how convincing the benefits. Generally, objections fall into four categories.

1. **No money.** This means that the customer can't afford it or that you haven't justified the price.
2. **Not now.** This means that the customer doesn't feel a sense of immediacy to order.
3. **No interest.** This means that the customer doesn't see the benefit or lacks confidence in the company or caller.
4. **No need.** This means that the customer doesn't know what to do with it.

Objections require preplanned and tested answers. Prepared answers should respond with a commonsense approach, not a high-pressure one. Although each objection needs closely related reponses, taking the opposite stand must be avoided in order to prevent a confrontation. Facts and benefits must be repeated continually. Above all, reasons are necessary to satisfy objections.

Take advantage of the market research bonus of the phone contact. When you make an offer by telephone, respondents not only will tell you whether they want to buy, they generally will offer a reason why they choose not to buy. Don't ignore those comments. Write them down, study them, learn from them, and make changes based on them if necessary. Sometimes the negative responses can be more valuable than the positive ones if they provide you with data for worthwhile product improvements or motivate the adoption of a new marketing strategy.

OPERATIONAL PARAMETERS

You've got to get everybody going in the same direction.

Jack Trout and Al Ries

This section will address the operational requirements for telephone marketing: the role of management, list management, communicator hiring and training, measurement and accountability, fulfillment systems, and costing guidelines.

The Role of Management

Management must be involved in all phases of the telephone marketing process—from planning to monitoring calls to analyzing results.

The organizational structure of the telephone marketing facility should be determined by the objectives, strategies, and scope of the operation. Although you may be organizing a telephone marketing program to achieve sales, you should not put a crack salesperson in charge. Management skills are far more important for phone center supervisors than sales skills or product knowledge. Select and train supervisors to coach, motivate, provide feedback, teach, and appraise; reward them for managing successfully.

List Management

Names are a scarce and valuable resource. Telephone marketing demands a discipline of list management that is not required for other media. Each step in the calling process results in fewer usable names. For instance, if we start with a random selection of 1000 consumer names without telephone numbers, we will end up with 552 names spoken with. See Table 27-2.

Therefore, after a 65 percent phone number look-up rate and an 85 percent completion rate, we net down to 552 completed names (names actually spoken with). These are averages that apply to consumer lists that require telephone number look-up, and they have to be taken into account when you project the total number of orders that will be generated from a given gross universe of names.

We can quickly recognize two important list management areas.

- Laborious manual telephone look-up procedures which necessitate hunting through a directory or calling information assistance tend to be most practical and expedient for low volumes of names. Average costs are $0.18 per name attempted or $0.25 per number found (again, because of the 65 percent look-up rate).
- Another method of securing phone numbers is to use computers to match the calling list against a central list of households with telephone numbers. Costs average $0.03 per name attempted and $0.06 per number found. Yet since the computer look-up rate is approximately 50 percent, manual look-up procedures to the balance of the 50 percent without numbers should be made to generate the additional 15 percent. This way, we raise the total callable universe to the 65 percent level. The only current limitations of the computer look-up process are the volume requirements and the delay factor associated

TABLE 27-2

Consumer Universe	Number	Percentage
Total names	1000	100
Universe of callable names after telephone number look-up	650	65
Number of names spoken with (completed) after multiple attempts (assuming an 85% completion rate)	552	55

with low volume. This requires a waiting period for a sufficient number of names to be batched by the service bureau to allow a cost-effective volume run.

Communicator Hiring and Training

You need communicators with an outgoing personality, native intelligence, good reading skills, objectivity, and responsibility. They must have the ability to listen and be flexible within the structure of a program script. Of course, a voice that reflects sincerity, maturity, and knowledge is indispensable.

Remember that an entirely different set of skills is required for telephone selling than for person-to-person sales. This is based on the inability of the prospect to see the product or the communicator. There is no value to a pretty face and no opportunity for a convincing demonstration.

Before inviting potential communicators in for an interview, screen them by telephone. After all, your primary hiring consideration is the impression they project over the phone. Include a phone-in number in your help wanted ad and evaluate the respondent's phone personality during a telephone conversation. Don't hesitate to inquire about previous experience, ability to work the days and hours required, knowledge of your industry, etc., and judge the quality of the response then and there.

It is a mandate that once you hire, you have to train. The primary purpose of training is to develop a staff that performs more productively. However, the nature, time span, and degree of intensity of training depends on many factors, including the relative complexity of the offer, the parameters of the objectives, the level of the target audience, and the desired results. Nevertheless, the training procedures must encompass theoretical instruction and simulated practice sessions. Groups of trainees should be small for maximum individual attention. They should be instructed by trainers who themselves have been adequately trained to do their job.

A well-structured training course should include the following elements:

1. Adequate input so that trainees understand your operation
2. Consistent and repetitive questioning
3. Sufficient opportunity for responses to questions
4. Reinforcement through examples and experience
5. Constant repetition of all major points
6. Simulation techniques to familiarize trainees with equipment and procedures
7. Adequate motivation for maximum performance
8. Performance objectives so that each trainee knows what is expected

If you're hiring a group of communicators, try to put together a compatible team of individuals. This consideration is especially important in a small startup operation where a few people will be working very closely together and learning from one another's experiences. Establishing a team spirit to help achieve your goals is crucial to success.

There should be constant testing at all stages. This enables the trainer and trainee to gauge the progress. Through practical demonstration procedures, trainees can master key areas of telephone selling such as reaching decision makers after dealing with a secretarial screen, handling objections, detailing product benefits, and proposing package offers.

After the initial training, the job is far from over. Training and retraining are continuous processes. Monitoring of actual calls has been found to be the most effective tool for both training and evaluation of telephone communicators. However, management is not alone in benefiting from this procedure. Try giving your telephone communicators a tape recorder and let them review their own calls. You'll be surprised at the level of their self-criticism. (Whenever taping actual calls, remember to use an FCC-approved beeper and check state laws as well.)

Measurement and Accountability

The telephone is the most immediately accountable medium. Thus, results of tests are highly projectable. However, none of this is possible without detailed control systems to ensure the consistency, quality, and standardization necessary for optimum results. These systems establish checks and balances that permit accurate testing and retesting. Most important, control systems deliver reliable feedback about your campaign, product or service, and prospects for measuring and evaluating results. While the physical design of control forms varies, there are common basic elements in all three fundamental forms.

Production Call Card. Used by communicators directly after completion of each call, the production call card does the following:

- Details results of each dialing
- Enables coding for future measurement
- Controls work flow pattern and speed (best time of day to call)
- Permits correct follow-up procedures
- Establishes a basis for interpretation and analysis

Production Tally Sheet. This provides a quick but complete record of the work of each communicator on an hourly or daily basis. It also shows kinds and numbers of responses and is valuable for comparisons between communicators.

Program Master Log Sheet. This is produced from the individual production call cards turned in daily by each communicator. It affords a consistent, current, cumulative overview of the program's progress. Also, it helps spot strengths and shortcomings that may require day-to-day correction or modification. Naturally, it is used in preparing a daily results curve chart for overseeing progress and drawing comparisons.

For your program to work efficiently, you will have to establish paperwork systems which handle data smoothly, both going to the telephones and coming from them. Here are some pointers.

- Be sure to provide adequate clerical support for your telephone sales staff. Do not waste precious communicator time by having them write out order forms, file, send samples or literature, etc.
- Set up a filing system which allows you to call numbers which did not respond at different times of the day. Someone who did not pick up the phone at 10 A.M. on two attempts should not be called at 10 A.M. again; 3 P.M. or even 8 P.M. for consumer calling may yield better results.
- Design call-record forms which require a minimum amount of handwriting. Check-off boxes in multiple-choice forms with space designed for further comments if needed make the communicator's job easier and help organize the data for easy retrieval by anyone using the forms.

The use of structured control systems, properly trained communicators, and well-tested scripts and offers will enable you to generate profitable and cost-accountable results from the telephone marketing process.

Fulfillment Systems

Common sense and legal requirements dictate adequate inventory levels and efficient systems for order fulfillment. However, more than one high-volume marketer has been caught short in terms of the inventory levels required to support a rollout telephone program. Proper planning and projections for inventory are essential before you expand into a volume calling effort. For example, a leading marketer generates approximately 15,000 telephone orders per month through out-WATS calling programs. Special inventory and fulfillment systems had to be developed to expedite the accelerated fulfillment that is essential for telephone-generated orders.

Rapid fulfillment is desirable for all media. However, given the immediacy and personal nature of the telephone order, prompt fulfillment is critical in terms of both the pay factor for the current transaction and the customer's future purchasing potential.

Costing Guidelines

In evaluating the profitability of your telephone marketing efforts, you need to establish certain standard measurement tools. The communicator-hour is one way to gauge costs versus income. Add up all the costs of your program—communicator wages, supervisory costs, clerical operations, list costs, general administration, and overhead—and divide the total by the number of hours spent on the phones. This will give you the cost of operations per communicator-hour, a figure which can be employed in determining profitability and required performance standards.

For example, in a well-managed, volume calling telephone operation, a communicator speaks with 3.5 to 7 business decision makers per hour. This translates to an approximate cost per completed call of $6 to $10. For consumer market calls, a communicator speaks with seven to twelve decision makers per hour at an approximate cost of $3 to $5 per completed call.

These costs should be taken as general guidelines, with the understanding that they will vary as a function of the complexity of product or offer and the difficulty of reaching a particular type of decision maker.

Decision Maker	Conversations per Hour
Physicians	3.5
Middle managers	5.0
CEO or president	3.5
Small retail store managers	7.0
School principals	3.5

LEGAL ASPECTS

You can always tell when a competitor is panic stricken. They sue.

Jack Trout and Al Ries

Telephone marketing has become a burgeoning phenomenon drawing substantial attention within the industry. However, this has occurred concomitantly with an increased level of scrutiny from governmental sources, both state and federal. They have been focusing on establishing guidelines for conducting telephone marketing.

Formerly, the telephone had never been caught in the glare of the legislative spotlight. This changed because of the media publicity given to automatic dialing equipment. In 1977, automatic dialing and recorded message players (ADRMPs), which had been in existence for over a decade but had not been accepted by marketers because of their dismal results, suddenly aroused the wrath of the media. Distorted reports of their potential to invade privacy galvanized the interest of legislators and regulators. In 1978, the FCC issued a notice of inquiry into telephone marketing. The response culminated in the introduction of bills in Congress that would have hampered telephone marketing.

There was a clamor by businesses such as Hertz, Avis, Citicorp, and Olan Mills and by industry associations including the Direct Marketing Association (DMA), which all filed briefs with the FCC. This spurred the FCC to conduct an independent study. Finally, in 1980, the FCC published a decision concluding that no federal regulations were needed.

The current status of telephone legislation can be found in the DMA's *The Law and Direct Marketing*, which describes state and local laws involving telephone marketing. In summary, several states have passed bills restricting the use of ADRMPs. Other states have enlarged the provisions of their home solicitation acts to include telephone marketing, and a few communities have passed ordinances restricting or prohibiting telephone marketing. Nevertheless, the fundamental constitutional and jurisdictional issues that apply to interstate and intercommunity calls have yet to be settled.

The most effective method employed by professional telephone marketers has been self-regulation. Voluntary enforcement of ethical and consumerist standards is the best way to ensure self-regulation as opposed to government-imposed regulation.

The DMA's guidelines for ethical business practices offer practical and useful standards for telephone marketers. The DMA *Fact Book* (1981) states the following.

1. Advertisers and marketers selling products or services or raising funds for nonprofit organizations should make their telephone presentations clear and honest. There should be no attempt to mislead, exaggerate, or use partial truths. Telephone marketers should not make calls in the guise of research or a survey when the real intent is to sell.
2. Telephone contacts should be made within the framework of federal, state, and local laws. Taping of telephone conversations is illegal without a beeping device.
3. Telephone contacts to consumers should be made during reasonable hours.
4. Telephone orders should not be accepted from minors without adult approval. The legal definition of a minor may vary from state to state.
5. Telephone marketers should not use what is commonly referred to as high-pressure tactics. They should observe the normal rules of telephone courtesy.
6. Telephone marketers should make conscientious efforts to remove names from their contact lists when requested to do so.
7. Telephone marketers should not call unlisted or unpublished telephone numbers unless a current telephone relationship exists.

LANDMARK TELEMARKETING CAMPAIGNS

This section outlines several case histories which illustrate how creative marketers are coping with the challenges posed by the fluctuating economy and the fluid marketplace.

Business-to-Business Marketing

The cost for a salesperson's visit in 1972 was $32. In 1983, the figure has risen to over $200. Given these costs, it has become essential for businesses to maximize sales force productivity through territory management programs. These programs generally include telephone screening and qualifying of prospects or inquiries for sales force follow-up.

- Telephone communicators can screen prospects and identify those who need or want a personal sales call. They can screen, qualify, and prioritize the companies or individuals to determine whether their interest is immediate enough to justify the expense of a sales visit and whether the product or service offered will truly suit their needs.
- Information gathered by phone increases the productivity and effectiveness of sales force presentations. With the benefit of detailed information regarding the prospect's needs, budget limitations, and the immediacy of a "buy" decision, the salesperson can arrive for a meeting fully prepared, with a presentation designed to highlight the expressed needs of the company he or she is calling on. This eliminates the needs for the traditional initial sales visit to identify potential, the follow-up with literature or samples, etc. The sales rep can make the right offer the first time after screening by phone.

- Make the most of the salesperson's time by having someone else do the initial calling. A trained telephone communicator can open the door for the salesperson, leaving the salesperson free to make a greater number of productive sales presentations. The telephone communicator can make actual appointments over the phone. If that is not advisable, have the communicator provide the salesperson with the data sheet on the qualified lead. The rep then can call to set the time for an appointment. This eliminates scheduling conflicts and avoids the feeling on the part of the sales force that they have lost control of their workload.
- The in-house telephone sales staff and the field sales staff should work as a team. It is essential to establish a rapport between these two segments of the sales force so that the program will run more smoothly and yield greater profits. Let the telephone people know what becomes of the leads they generate; encourage interaction between the field force and the telephone communicators.

However, when the costs of face-to-face selling become prohibitive, the marketer is left with two choices in servicing relatively small accounts: give up the customer or begin a telephone marketing program to provide personalized, regular attention without the overhead of a salesperson's time and travel.

Key elements to consider in structuring a telephone program to service marginal accounts include the following.

- **Continuity of contact.** Regularly scheduled calls which are tied to fit the needs of the given universe are the most productive.
- **Direct mail and collateral materials.** Catalogs and newsletters supporting the special telephone service program provide continuity between calls.
- **Professionalism of the caller.** The telephone communicator must be courteous and knowledgeable about product specifications. That communicator represents the image of your company to the prospects.

How effective is this type of program? A telephone program to service marginal accounts for a business equipment and supplies company produced orders from 10 percent of the customers contacted by phone the first time around. Another 60 percent agreed to conduct all future business by phone. What's more, the telephone contact produced "hot leads" for highly profitable major equipment purchases.

Another example of how innovative marketers are increasing the productivity of their field sales force is provided by the case history of one of the world's leaders in manufacturing business machines.

Business Equipment Marketing

Background. This company achieved a leadership position in the "high-end" marketplace and determined that it needed a marketing program to penetrate the "low-end" market. However, the existing field sales force was not to be included in this new marketing thrust because the high cost per sales visit could not be justified for a "low-end" product priced at approximately $1000.

Telephone Objectives. The objective was to generate direct telephone sales of business equipment priced at approximately $1000.

Strategies. A direct marketing campaign including trade journal advertising, direct mail, and telephone was developed. Space advertising was used to soften the market and create awareness. Direct mail followed to present the product benefits and ask for the order.

Telephone calls were timed within 1 to 2 weeks after receipt of direct mail. Communicators worked from totally structured, management-pretested scripts. Because of the complexity of the product offering, the testing process took over 4 months as scripts were refined to the point of maximum productivity.

Results. The results of this program exceeded the firm's expectations. Large numbers of machines were placed in the hands of qualified buyers without any sales force involvement.

An important incremental benefit from this program was that calls also uncovered prospects who did require a personal sales visit. This information was transmitted to regional representatives for immediate follow-up.

Financial Marketing

Background. In the short span of 5 years, the banking industry has undergone dramatic changes. Soaring interest rates charged by the Federal Reserve have forced banks to develop new sources of capital. This has resulted in greater dependence on consumer banking, which in turn has led banks to offer expanded consumer services to attract depositors.

Recently, a leading New York bank introduced an investment vehicle requiring a minimum investment of $3000. The goal was to market this product by direct response to prospects who lived outside of New York.

Telephone Objectives. The objective was to generate direct telephone sales of the certificate of deposit (CD).

Strategies. A multimedia program was developed which included space advertising, direct mail to select compiled lists, and incoming and outbound telephone.

The mailing explained the investment vehicle and offered additional information either by response coupon or 800 number. When prospects called the 800 number, they received additional information and were asked what was the best time for a bank representative to call.

Communicators then called with the objective of closing the sale. They presented the product benefits and used current interest figures to tell the prospects exactly what to expect on the basis of the amount they would be willing to invest. Since interest rates were changing weekly, the scripts were revised constantly to reflect current rates. Communicator scripts also included answers to over thirty commonly raised questions.

Results. The investment commitment was taken directly by phone. The communicators issued a certificate number on the phone which reserved the certificate in the customer's name. The customer wrote this number on his or her check and on the registration forms received by mail.

The cost per CD sold was substantially lower than the cost for those sold at the bank's branches in New York. What is equally significant about this program is the enormous potential for marketing bank products to prospects thousands of miles from the bank's charter area.

Nonstore Marketing

Background. Today consumers have more money, yet they spend less time shopping. Factors such as the "leisure-time" ethic and the increasing number of women in the work force are responsible for this.

Nonstore marketers are taking advantage of this by marketing their products and services directly to the consumer, without reliance on the retail store. For example, the first marketing division of a major retailer introduced an automobile club targeted to holders of the retail charge card. The goal was to market this product by direct response and to build the club into a major force within a short period of time.

Objectives. The objective was to generate direct telephone enrollments for the club.

Strategies. Direct mailings, billing inserts, and telephone calls were targeted to list segments which had been identified as productive in previous mail programs.

Initial telephone results, though promising, required significant improvements. To achieve this, more refined segmentation was required. High-potential telephone responders in the approximately 15 million-name file were identified through multivariate linear regression analysis.

Results. As the selection criteria for building the telephone list were refined, telephone results rose dramatically.

The telephone program has been in place, with ongoing list refinements, for over 6 years. In 1981 alone, over 150,000 memberships were generated by telephone.

THE FUTURE OF OUTBOUND TELEPHONE MARKETING

The future of outbound telephone marketing will be determined by three factors: economics, technology, and the consumer.

The primary factor having an impact on the future of telephone marketing is economics. If the cost of doing business continues to escalate at rates resembling those of the 1970s, companies will be forced to develop and refine alternative, more efficient channels of distribution. Telephone marketing thus will become an increasingly important factor in the sales and marketing efforts of all companies. Thanks to the technological revolution in telecommunications, the cost of marketing by telephone will not increase at the same rates as mail, sales force, or any of the other labor-intensive distribution systems.

The second factor driving the future of marketing by phone is technology. This will be most evident in the area of interactive marketing, i.e., the electronic in-home and in-office shopping capability resulting from the marriage of data banks, telephone lines, cable TV, and either a TV screen or a cathode-ray tube (CRT). Using these systems, consumers will have immediate access to tax, budget, and financial services that will enable them to pay bills, balance checkbooks, and review computer analyses of investments on a home television screen. "Living room" shopping will become a reality, with merchandise orders processed through TV or telephone.

Currently, nearly all industrialized nations are conducting experiments with their own variations of this technology. However, the current consumer users are limited to small test groups and generally are not paying for the service. According to some experts, interactive systems will not become a significant factor until the mid-1990s. Until then however, plain old telephone systems (POTSs) will be the order of the day. Telephone marketing is already benefiting from the economies available through technologies such as WATS and the many specialized carriers which provide inexpensive microwave transmission.

In addition to these telecommunications enhancements, the most important current technological factor is the computer. A wide range of tasks have already benefited from the aid of EDP.

- Computerized telephone number look-up has helped automate what until very recently was a time-consuming process requiring phone books or information assistance calls.
- Immediate access to a customer's files to determine previous purchasing history is of tremendous value in cross-selling, upgrading, or customer service.
- Immediate order entry and order processing have compressed the time required for fulfillment of telephone orders.

The last factor influencing the future growth and shape of telephone marketing is the consumer. As free time available for shopping decreases, the need for fast, convenient, and reliable methods of satisfying these shopping needs will increase. Direct marketing and certainly the telephone fit this requirement.

In summary, it is exciting to visualize the melding of consumer needs, technological capabilities, and economic requirements. These all have congruent goals. The convergence of these three factors will create a distribution process which satisfies the needs of individual consumers through targeted, cost-effective marketing systems. These systems will be the result of technology which facilitates the pinpoint market segmentation that will make it all come together.

chapter 28

TELEMARKETING —INBOUND

Allan Caplan

Senior Vice President
WATS Marketing of America
Omaha, Neb.

The American society is a telephone society. The fact that the telephone provides nearly universal market coverage has catapulted the U.S. direct marketer in the forward position in the worldwide race to achieve marketplace "interactivity." The telephone is present in over 98 percent of all U.S. households to the ring of 134 million phones, and it is also present in 14.5 million American business establishments wired to 48 million phones. If an American business or private consumer wishes to make a purchase or obtain information, it is not far from second nature to pick up the phone and complete some part of the order sequence. This is a truly interactive phenomenon.

The emergence of the 800 number has fueled this consumer-telephone familiarity and has established 800 number dialing as a viable way to obtain goods and services that suit an increasingly demographically and psychographically segmented population. To harness and manage the power of a marketing technique with such vast implications for society in order to achieve corporate profit is both complex and a competitive necessity.

TELEPHONE MARKETING DEFINED

Telephone as a marketing medium derives its power from its transactional nature—one human being in a controlled dialog with another. What began as "ordering by telephone" soon evolved into "telemarketing," a concept defined by AT&T as the "marriage of telecommunications technology and direct marketing techniques." Telemarketing enables companies to offer their customers the speed and convenience required in selling to a more demanding and faster-paced society. One of the key operational components of a telemarketing system is the toll-free 800, or in-WATS, number.

There are two types of telephone WATS (wide area telephone service) lines: in-WATS, also known as the 800 number service, and out-WATS, which is used to place calls to carefully selected contacts based on characteristics which indicate a close affinity with products and services and therefore a likely buyer.

This chapter will concentrate on in-WATS, or 800, numbers exclusively. An incoming WATS telephonic system establishes on a nationwide or regional basis a method by which potential customers may respond to national media advertising by long-distance telephone, using a publicized number. The service is provided using the market's phone lines without the customer incurring any long-distance charges and thus invites consumer response regarding offered products.[1]

In 1980 alone, in-WATS and out-WATS telephone expenditures by direct marketers represented a whopping $9.845 billion, or 43 percent of total direct marketing media expenditures. However, each of the transactions effected through WATS contact was a personal dialog between an operator or communicator representing a company's "personality" and a valued direct marketing customer.

This contact can be orchestrated in several aspects, from the insertion of motivation buttons that will stimulate the 800 customer to respond to a carefully written order script dialog that combines the order-taking function and customer relations practices for maximum efficiency and customer development effects.

THE 800 NUMBER: AN INTEGRAL FACTOR IN TELEPHONE MARKETING

The 800 number in-WATS service, now commonly referred to as the 800 service, has been in existence approximately 15 years. At first, WATS was viewed by industry as a means of placing and receiving large numbers of long-distance calls for a fixed, predetermined fee. Then the travel industry discovered that WATS could provide a means for marketing reservations to the public (hotel reservations, car rentals, etc.). A rapid expansion of industry groups offering a central, toll-free reservation service resulted. At the same time, independent entrepreneurial companies sprang up and began offering WATS service for such varied applications as credit card authorization and the matching of missing interline freight shipments with overages. Finally, a dealer-locator service was established which advised callers, based on their ZIP codes, of the location of the nearest sales outlet for a specifically advertised product or service. This dealer locator application still exists.[2] A wide use of 800 numbers for consumer product ordering has been building steadily; the number of companies using 800 numbers has gone from zero to 55,000. In September 1973, Joe Sugarman of JS&A was the first to use the 800 number for direct marketing merchandise-ordering purposes.

Direct marketers who employ 800 numbers use them commonly in space ads, broadcast advertising (both radio and TV), direct mail, catalogs, and cable TV. In addition, 800 numbers are being used on everything from packaged goods (cereal boxes) to outdoor advertising billboards.

Today's buyers are action-oriented, especially those who respond to catalog or broadcast direct marketing through the 800 number. They want action now, and telemarketing, with its rapid order capability, gives it to them. Instant communications have become a solid part of the American lifestyle and will continue to be.

Societal changes have provided catalytic effects that promote telephone order placement. Most notable are changes in lifestyle, the widespread availability of credit, and the unprecedented number of working women seeking convenience and a simplified approach to tasks involving the daily maintenance of a household or the pleasure of personal shopping. For increasingly large segments of the American population time is a more precious commodity than money.

Americans' love affair with the credit card also adds a major convenience factor to 800 number shopping. In many interviews conducted for the purpose of this roundup, direct marketers who employ the 800 number in their ordering operations invariably pointed out that the credit card and 800 number combination spells huge profitability, in many instances representing sales of 35 to 50 percent of the total volume. A recent study conducted jointly by New York University (NYU) Graduate School of Business Administration and the Direct Marketing Association (DMA), *The Effectiveness of 800 Numbers in Direct Mail Catalogs* confirms these comments or rules of thumb. The study is referred to throughout the following pages.

WHY USE AN 800 NUMBER?

The basic reason is simple: to solicit incremental orders that would not have been generated without this marketing motivator. The 800 number has been used consistently to increase space ads' pulling power. Many direct-response ads with an 800 number are commonly found in the *Wall Street Journal* and men's how-to magazines, among hundreds of other magazines. In some instances, the number can generate as much as 85 percent of the order volume.

In catalogs, the incorporation of an 800 number as a response vehicle can net incremental orders totaling 18 to 23 percent. In addition, the 800 number can deliver orders with an increased dollar value per order of 20 to 40 percent.

In TV direct response, depending on the demographics of the viewing audience and the nature of the offer, the 800 number can deliver between 50 and 90 percent of orders. In fact, in most instances, TV direct response as a successful selling medium is directly indebted to the toll-free number which channels the "immediate desire to order the product" that has been created by the message.

Besides the convenience of 800 number order capability, telephone access lends credibility to your entire operation. Customers are more confident when they can talk with a "real person" representing your firm. Your telephone number continually assures your catalog or other direct media shoppers that they are dealing with real people.

Of course, in order to obtain optimum results, the 800 number must be displayed and promoted correctly. For each medium in which the 800 number is used, special graphic and copy tactics can yield greater consumer attention and subsequent orders.

Once you have decided to use an 800 number, you have two choices: to do it yourself or to use a service bureau. Both routes have benefits, and the cost-effectiveness of both routes must be evaluated on a regular basis. This discussion is presented to give you guidance either way you go and to provide you with the 800 number experiences of many companies whose customers choose to "order now."[3]

800 NUMBERS IN PRINT MEDIA: CATALOG AND 800 NUMBER ORDER MAGIC

Four or 5 years ago, the aggressive cataloger who used the 800 number benefited by incorporating this "order trigger." Now it is not a matter of benefit; the use of the 800 number has become a catalog marketplace necessity.

Approximately 80 percent of all major consumer catalog operations have a toll-free 800 number service. This number plays an integral role in these companies' sales goals. Telemarketing's impact on catalog sales in particular can be seen in the percentage of sales that the telephone directly accounts for: 20 to 50 percent of total sales. In addition, there is a net incremental increase of orders received by a company in the range of 18 to 23 percent. The NYU/DMA study found that incremental sales experience for catalogers using the 800 number was 21.07 percent.

PRIMARY RESEARCH STUDY: THE EFFECTIVENESS OF 800 NUMBERS IN DIRECT MAIL CATALOGS

The benefits of toll-free ordering in catalog sales have received widespread acclaim. However, there have been relatively few significant data supporting those claims, aside from platform exchanges and industry "network" discussions. The purpose of the NYU/DMA study, authored by Esther Lazaros, was to determine whether sales generated by toll-free ordering profitably compensated for the operational expenses of the system.[4] The study results are based on the quantifiable assessments made by 191 catalog companies who completed and returned a four-page questionnaire consisting of fifty-three questions. This represents a 44.4 percent response since 434 companies were mailed a copy of the questionnaire. Each catalog company responding marketed merchandise to the consumer across a wide product variety that ranged from soft goods and gifts to sporting gear and housewares. Most respondents (63 percent) reported $1 to $15 million in annual sales. Seventy-five percent of the respondents had an in-house 800 service; 25 percent used a service bureau.

Selected Findings

1. Fifty-nine percent of the respondents have been offering 800 service ordering for at least 3 years.
2. Over 75 percent of the respondents use the 800 number for media other than catalog advertising.
3. Almost 66 percent not only take orders but check inventory and offer substitutions, point out specials or sales, and upgrade sell.
4. Fifty-six percent of all respondents' telephone orders require credit card payments.
5. Only 27 percent are open 24 hours a day, 7 days a week, and 61 percent of the respondents make no provision for after-hours calls. Yet it is widely recognized by telemarketing experts that after-hours calls are integral to the success of the mail-order catalog operation. Part of catalog shopping's appeal is the convenience for working women who may order while at work, but also may choose to call after the work day.
6. More than 90 percent of the respondents were satisfied with the results of the 800 number based on their initial expectations.
7. Clearly, over half the respondents experienced an increase in the value of a phone order over a mail order. The mean response to this question indicated an increase of 23.7 percent of the value of the average phone order over a mail order.
8. Fifty-one percent of the respondents receive 36 to 100 percent of their orders via the 800 line.
9. In the first 6 months during which the 800 number was printed in the catalog, over 90 percent of the respondents reported an increase in the number of orders; for 53 percent of these, the increase was significant. More than 66 percent of the respondents attributed the increase to the 800 number, with only 10 percent not giving credit to the 800 number at all.
10. Approximately 33 percent of the respondents received a 10 percent increase in sales volume, 37 percent experienced an 11 to 25 percent increase in business, and 25 percent enjoyed an increase of 26 to over 100 percent in business. The average increase was 21.07 percent.
11. Over 97 percent of the respondents felt that they would lose business if they did not provide an 800 number; over 33 percent thought the loss would be significant.

12. More than half the respondents provide toll-free communication for customer service.

Comments

Two significant issues relative to the use of the 800 number for catalog order operations are the effect of 800 numbers on high-ticket items and the stipulation that credit card payment must be used with 800 orders. Catalogs in which the average price of product is relatively low receive a significantly lower increase in the number of orders as a result of the 800 line than catalogs in which the average price of a product is relatively high.

Toll-free ordering therefore should be encouraged, particularly in catalogs in which the average price of a product exceeds $50. It is important to stipulate credit card payment with telephone ordering because these orders appear to be of far greater average value than mail orders and telephone orders paid for by other means.

Promoting Your 800 Number Service for Maximum Profit in Catalogs

In order to motivate your catalog customers to pick up the phone on impulse or at their convenience and place their orders, your 800 number should be presented exclusively throughout your catalog, no less frequently than every four to six pages.

It is important to place this 800 number information in a very clean, consistent, and professional manner throughout the book as well. The customers may read the copy on it only once, but every time they see it, it will be a reminder for them to move to action or to do it now. They'll be reminded, "Yes, this is the place, and I know they're open 24 hours a day, and I can call my order in now and get it over with." That's when the impulse buyer responds.

The 800 number is an extremely profitable marketing tool that every cataloger should take advantage of. Promote it extensively and correctly.

Catalogers' Comments on 800 Number Use

In a sampling of interviews with catalogers in which candid comments regarding their experiences with the 800 number were sought, one very clear concensus arose: The 800 number generated a substantial amount of incremental business. A second point that emerged was that there must be a phone offering proposition, since consumers and customers seek it, but increasing costs are a factor in 800 order generation as with every other aspect of doing business. The order of the day seems to indicate undeniable advantages coupled with financial considerations that must be monitored carefully.

Merle Schirado, vice president of Career Guild, a division of Aparacor, Inc., reports that Career Guild, a women's apparel catalog, has employed the 800 number as an order mechanism for 5 years. The 800 number is used not only in their catalog but also in print space and promotional mailings which stand alone selling merchandise. Mr. Schirado reports that 20 to 25 percent of Career Guild's total orders are generated through the 800 number. Fifty percent of the company's total credit card orders are received via the 800 number, and these orders are approximately $16 higher than the average order value. The 800 number is also used to an extent for customer servicing. It is the inevitable complement of customers who call the number for order status, inquiries, and complaints. However, the company policy is to try to deflect these calls to the regular customer service numbers while providing a courteous exchange and the most satisfaction possible. In Schirado's opinion, the greatest aspect of the 800 number is the fact that 99.9 percent of women customers have the opportunity to do something transactional about registering their purchasing desires immediately. The 800 number is an extremely valuable tool in the immediate completion of the order loop for Career Guild. In comment sheets which are shipped routinely with every order, Career Guild customers are asked to indicate the "level of satisfaction they received by placing their order by telephone." The overwhelming indication is that customers have a high degree of satisfaction with the 800 system in terms of the major consideration of saving time.

Erv Magram, vice president of Lew Magram, Ltd., a catalog specializing in high-fashion men's merchandise, indicates that in the 5 years that their catalog has used the 800 order device, telephone orders have accounted for 42 percent of total orders. In addition, the telephone order has a higher order value than the average order ticket of $80. Owing to the fact that all phone orders are credit card orders, Mr. Magram believes that the 800 factor in and of itself does not raise the phone order value. Rather, it is the credit card order size stimulus that is at work. In their sixty-four-page catalog, the 800 number is displayed on every seven to eight pages and on the order form. Magram feels that the 800 number is a good service to offer the customer and that the majority of their customers who are men might be less likely to fill out an order form. The convenience provided by the 800 number is therefore the company's major motivation for 800 number maintenance.

Sy Zuckerman, general manager of the French Boot Shop, a catalog specializing in high-fashion women's clothing, also has been using the 800 number order vehicle for about 5 years. Approximately 35 percent of all FBS orders come in through an 800 number. There has been a very noticeable increase in sales volume since the introduction of the 800 number. The dollar value of the orders also has increased, but so have the prices of goods, and so the company was reluctant to indicate absolute percentages in each category of growth activity. The 800 number is also used in print space: off-page advertising for order placement.

Doreen McCurley, former vice president of direct-response marketing for Bloomingdale's, revealed that in the 3 years that Bloomingdale's used the 800 number for its catalog operations, a net increase of 25 percent additional orders were received. The incremental dollar value of the 800 orders was approximately 15 percent higher than the mail-order value. Approximately 45 percent of total sales were transacted through 800 numbers. McCurley indicated that Bloomingdale's integrated the 800 number into approximately every four pages of their catalog, being very careful not to overpower the design of the high-fashion book with 800 number overkill. McCurley feels that if a company is serious about entering the direct marketing business, it is impossible to conceive of a direct marketing operation without an 800 number. It is as important an ordering tool as the order blank.

Catalog consultant Herb Krug of Herbert Krug & Associates, Inc., cautions that companies who have always taken it for granted that their 800 number operations were cost-effective must carefully evaluate whether this truth is constant. At a time when the cost of an 800 number order taken through a service bureau can approach $3, consideration must be given to whether the use of service bureau 800 number representation is cost-effective when measured against the company's ability to operate an in-house staff and an 800 center. The question is not whether to have an 800 number; the 800 number certainly has proved its value. Rather, the question has become whether a company can take an operation in-house and be more cost-effective than it would if it remained with the service bureau. A full discussion of the advantages and drawbacks of both in-house and service bureau 800 services is presented later in this chapter.

THE USE OF 800 NUMBERS IN PRINT SPACE DIRECT-RESPONSE ADVERTISING

As marketers began gradually to realize that 800 numbers in print ads could increase response by as much as 45 percent and could produce upscale credit card buyers, 800 number print ads became more sophisticated as well as more numerous. A survey by the Advertising Information Service of recent issues of twenty-one major daily newspapers revealed that over 5 percent of the national ads they carried displayed 800 numbers. Approximately 15 percent of the ads in *Time* and *Newsweek* carry 800 numbers, while the figure is over 20 percent for *Fortune* and *Business Week*.[5]

800 Number Action Motivator

At the March 1982 annual conference of the Advertising Research Foundation, David P. Forsyth, vice president of research for McGraw-Hill Publications, presented the results of a multiyear study of which factors in a business-to-business print space advertisement motivate readers to purchasing action among other desirable and measurable customer attitude data.[6] One of the most interesting findings was that the presence of the 800 number ordering option provided optimum success for an ad with the objective of "causing action."

The umbrella data base which recorded and analyzed the data of this particular ongoing study is called Ad Sell. In total, approximately 3597 advertisements appearing in twenty-six specialized business publications were studied and analyzed by physical characteristics (size, color, etc.) and content (headline content, copy length, coupon use, and the use of the 800 WATS number). This information was measured against respondent data with the ultimate objective of providing decision criteria by which advertisers could select the most powerful individual characteristics and combinations of characteristics.

The aggregate findings about the major question of what elements contributed to action confirmed several direct marketing rules of thumb and most importantly revealed the following.

Here are the individual variables which were meaningful to those advertisements which caused the reader to take or plan action.

Extremely significant	Product ad (as opposed to a corporate or service ad)
	Product by itself (as opposed to multiple product offer)
Highly significant	Use of the 800 in-WATS number
	Tables, Charts
	Three to five illustrations
	More than 300 words of copy
	Four or more copy blocks
Fairly significant	Color with diagram
	Product in actual setting
	Use of "new" in headline
	Color with headline

Print Space 800 Numbers in Action

As was mentioned earlier, print space is often either an adjunct medium in gathering catalog prospects or a separate media program to sell merchandise off-page. Very frequently, both functions are served by print space catalog company ads which bear the 800 number. As with all direct marketing media, the functions of single-item direct merchandise sales, two-step lead-generation programs, fund-raising programs, etc., are accomplished through the powerful combination of print and 800 numbers for many marketers.

For Joe Sugarman, president of JS&A, a major electronics direct marketing firm with both catalog objectives and a strong single-item print space program, the 800 number's importance is legendary. Sugarman was the first to use the 800 number for direct merchandise order. Sugarman reveals that one of the most beneficial aspects of the 800 number was its "early indicator" power, or the ability to determine in a matter of hours whether a product or ad is successful and if any revision in inventory projection or ad insertion schedule may be desirable. Before the advent of its 800 program, it may have taken 2 to 3 days to determine break-even indicators; on that very first day, JS&A had the answer by noon.

At this point, JS&A receives 80 percent of its orders through an 800 number. The average order is approximately $140. The telephone order is slightly lower in dollar value because it is usually a one product order generated from print space. All 800 orders are credit card orders. According to Sugarman, the 800 number is an extremely important part of this business.

According to the NYU/DMA study of 800 numbers and catalog operations, most catalogers use the 800 number when advertising in additional media outside the primary medium vehicle of the catalog. Of the 191 catalogs profiled in that study, 76 percent included the 800 number in other media; 59 percent of these catalogs used the 800 number when advertising for catalog requests and for the sale of catalog products off-page through print space.

Peter Spaulder, media director of National Liberty Marketing, Inc., a prominent direct marketing insurance company, indicates that the 800 number is used extensively in two-step consumer lead-generation print space campaigns for their health and life insurance products. The leads generated through 800 numbers convert to buyers at a very acceptable rate.

Clem Sevde, subscription circulation manager for Meredith Corporation, reports that Meredith's major use of the 800 number is in "gift donor programs." Bind-in cards are inserted in subscriber copies of their major publications, *Better Homes & Gardens*, *Metropolitan Home*, and *Successful Farming*. These cards provide an 800 number ordering option and have proved successful over the course of well-structured tests. One particularly innovative Meredith application of the 800 order option was in *Successful Farming*'s bind-in bingo card. Instead of having the reader circle the advertiser's product number for which more information was desired, the interested reader was instructed to call the 800 number indicated to register interest in more information. This 800 number application lifted response significantly for advertisers.

One major consumer publisher with a well-known sweepstakes identity in consumers' minds indicated similar success with 800 number gift donor programs but also indicated selective success with other 800 order option programs. The circulation director considers this limited range to be a by-product of a strong mail response identity which is promoted extensively and may be synonymous with the product.

Special Space Ad 800 Display Tips

Most successful magazine and newspaper space advertising layouts which incorporate the 800 number have displayed the 800 number as boldly as possible without detracting from the ad itself. According to the way the reader's eye usually travels, the best space ad position for the number is approximately in the lower right-hand corner, in the place where you traditionally would place the coupon. Many consumer electronic product advertisers have chosen to run the ad with only the 800 number ordering vehicle. In the body copy of the ad, they may indicate a mail-order address for check orders. This presentation has delivered 75 to 80 percent of the orders by phone.

However, there are several factors that would enter into a decision to present only an 800 number ordering option. In the special case of the electronic product direct marketer, this technique presents a very clean, high-tech image for the product. There have been several tests with space advertisements, comparing just the 800 number versus the 800 number with a coupon. Some of the tests for the higher-priced products in the $70 and up range pulled better with just the straight phone number than with the mailing address in a paragraph without the formal coupon. Others have tested it in products from the $39 and under range and have found that the addition of the coupon with the toll-free number has not had any gross impact on sales. At that point, they're generating approximately 65 percent by phone and 35 percent by mail-in. In that price range, including a coupon would save some money on the toll-free calls. The idea may be worth testing on your own.

Print Copywriting That Incorporates 800 Number Power

Successful 800 number print ads have a few things in common with all successful ads. In Aldyn McKean's roundup for print and 800 number action copy, the direct marketing basics are restated well.[7] First of all, the headline and artwork must attract the reader's attention. The best ad copy for the world's greatest product will never be read if the headline and art in the ad do not attract attention. If the product being advertised is not well known, solid product information should be provided. The chief benefits to the user of the product should be stressed, either implied by the artwork or stated explicitly in the copy.

In addition to these tenets which all print ad designers should observe, there are other factors which 800 number ad writers must take into account. For an 800 number print ad to be successful, the reader must be encouraged to take prompt action by putting down the periodical and picking up the telephone. Remember that a prospective customer who does not call before throwing away the magazine which contains the ad is a lost customer. Quick action can be encouraged by offering a premium to the first specified number of callers. Or the ad can read "limited time offer," "while supplies last," or some other phrase which will indicate that the reader may lose out if a call is not made soon. If these approaches are deemed too hard-sell, the reader can be encouraged to "call now" or "call today."

It also will increase the response to your ad if you mention a specific benefit which the reader can realize by dialing the 800 number. The most obvious benefit from ordering by phone is promptness of delivery. For example, the Buckingham Corporation's ad for Wines-by-Wire tells prospective customers that their "gift of Mouton-Cadet can be delivered overnight."

Companies which offer toll-free customer service can increase the response to their ads by emphasizing this fact. Whirlpool and more recently General Motors have been effective in doing this.

In addition, let the reader know that you're "open 24 hours a day, 7 days a week." If you run your ad in a Sunday supplement, don't hesitate to include the redundant "Open 24 hours a day, 7 days a week . . . *including Sunday*." On A-B split tests in Sunday publications, the ad with the "including Sunday" tag increased the response by a clear one-third on the telephone over the ad which just stated, "available 24 hours a day, 7 days a week."

800 DISPLAY AND COPY RULES COMMON TO BOTH SPACE ADS AND CATALOGS

1. The 800 number itself should always be displayed correctly, e.g., 800-228-2258. Many direct marketers mistakenly put parentheses or quotation marks around the 800 number. This is a signal to the reader that this is the area code. An area code signals to the reader that it is a long-distance call, *not* toll-free, and that the caller will be charged for the call. The seemingly helpful parentheses, emphatic quotation marks, or innocuous slash marks are confusing and detrimental to your purpose.

Over the years, Ma Bell has spent tens of millions of dollars promoting the fact that it is properly, universally recognized as call TOLL-FREE 800-228-2258. Capitalize on this advance PR. In addition, never print the 800 number on a separate line from the exchange number or make it larger or bolder than the number itself.

2. Should the number 1 be placed in front of the 800 number? In many places, your customer must dial a number 1. It is used as a prefix for any number out of the local area. The phone company has promoted the 1 as a dialing instruction. It's not part of your intra- or interstate 800 number, and when placed in front of the 800, it does nothing but confuse the infrequent or first-time toll-free 800 dialer. Again, it is simply a dialing instruction; people in those areas know they must dial a 1 to get out of the area.

3. Make sure your 800 number lets the customers know the area it covers. For example, if you have a toll-free number for the nation and a separate 800 number for New York State (you're located there), let them know that. Include this intrastate 800 alternative number in or by the phone logo. Most states have a specific intrastate 800 number.

   If you don't have a separate 800 number for the state, provide a local number. Let prospects know if you accept collect calls.

   However, when displaying an intrastate number (800 or local) in a national print promotion or catalog, don't give this second number equal prominence. Frankly, the broad population base doesn't warrant it. Display your main national number big and bold; then place the second number underneath it.

4. Let them know the hours. When you are promoting a number, and if you have a service bureau, let your customers know that you are available 24 hours a day, 7 days a week. This is a tremendous benefit. If you have an in-house operation and are open 9 to 5 or 8 to 6, let your customers know that, too, and be sure to let them know what time zone you are in.

   Avoid frustrating your callers and deterring them from ordering because you are not there when they have decided to order.

   As a point of information, clearly some 48 percent of our toll-free catalog orders come in after 5 o'clock Central Standard Time, when 24-hour-a-day service is offered.

   Do not have your copywriters or graphics people try to get cute and use the word "anytime." It doesn't work. The public doesn't know when "anytime" is, nor do they believe the term. They may think that you have nothing more than an answering machine on the other end, and they're not calling an 800 number to talk to an answering machine.

800 NUMBERS IN DIRECT MAIL CAMPAIGNS

Although a number of companies use 800 numbers in their solo direct mail packages as an ordering tool alongside the order form or coupon, the majority of direct mailers choose not to use 800 numbers on a wide basis. In direct mail related to catalogs, however, the 800 number works "magic." For solo direct mail packages sent to customer lists, the 800 number order option, if it is used at all, is often an extension of the more common "customer service or convenience" role that 800 numbers play for direct mailers. For these mailers, if a prior established relationship exists with a customer, any communication that person wishes to make with the company, whether it is an order or a service request, will be transacted via an 800 number courtesy. Extending this same option to prospects, however, is not usually done.

Circulation consultant Betty Ann Noakes feels that when a prospect is presented with a direct mail offer, the very action of completing the order form indicates a total commitment to the order decision, a commitment that the direct mail buyer needs to make. According to Marilyn Crouchelli, director of telemarketing for Listmark Computer Systems, Inc., a major fulfillment and data processing firm with numerous direct mail clients, experience has indicated that the direct mail purchase is a "considered purchase" as compared with the "impulse purchase" which the 800 number serves so well. Often the direct mail buyer mulls over the purchase decision several times before filling out and mailing in the order form with the rest of the monthly bills. Direct mail response caters to a purchase cycle different from the emotional and convenience factors which cater to the 800 number buyer. The theorem that a direct mail buyer responds to direct mail offers via a mail completion of the order loop is simplistic yet apparently true.

For fund raisers, for example, the direct mail medium is the message and the response vehicle. A positive answer to a direct mail solicitation will take the form of a return envelope bearing a check. The positive agreement by the donor with the terms and needs stated by the fund raiser must be a written monetary transaction, at least until home banking or credit card uses extend universally.

Exceptions abound, and every direct marketer must test a primary or adjunct medium's compatibility with his or her product. As a general observation, the 800 number order option seems to be a more conducive order stimulator for media other than solo direct mail packages.

TELEVISION AND TELEPHONE

Known throughout the direct marketing industry as TNT, the 800 number in combination with a professional direct marketing commercial and a carefully structured media schedule can deliver highly profitable sales or targeted qualified leads. An estimated $253 million was invested by direct marketers in placing direct marketing commercials on the broadcast air waves in 1980. It is difficult to gauge the extensive expansion since 1980 of direct marketing schedules on broadcast TV in addition to the significant plunge direct marketing advertisers have taken into cable TV schedules. But direct-response TV has come of age and will continue to service the shopping needs of many categories of buyers with products ranging from insurance to charitable contributions and from fine recordings and publications to hobby items.

One of the most important factors in assuring the success of a TV offer is undeniably the 800 number—the order catalyst. There are several critical elements that will determine the profitability of the commercial: the right product, the price, correct positioning, the right schedule, the offer terms, the appropriate spokesperson, and production quality. All these elements combine to create a positive purchase decision to bring the customer to the TV storefront, the 800 center. The manner in which that call is handled, however, or even whether that call can get through to the 800 center determines all. The 800 number is the critical end factor in the TV order development sequence.

Jim Springer of Ellentuck & Springer, a leading direct-response broadcast and cable TV agency, states that the 800 number is a very convenient street address for the TV merchant. The customer can find you simply by walking to the phone. It is as imperative in the TV-800 number media combination as with other 800-media combos that the telephone personnel, whether in-house or service bureau, be professionally scripted, cordially disposed, and time-efficient. The key difference seems to be, however, that 70 to 80 percent of the TV telephone responses take place right after the commercial has run and that 30 percent of the calls take place during the day. This burst requires flexible 800 management experience. On the average the consumer will call approximately 3½ times, accept a blocked 800 signal, and still maintain a positive purchase intent. After that point, and quite often before that point for half the callers, the sale is lost.

There are several key questions direct marketers ask in order to be sure that they are presenting the 800 number in its most effective manner for a TV offer. Accordingly, there are answers to these questions or at least rules of thumb.

Length of 800 Number TV Display

Successful practitioners and their agencies consistently report that the 800 number tag must be left on screen for at least 20 seconds whether the commercial is 120 or 90 seconds long. There are advocates of displaying the number for a shorter period of time, but this advice is erroneous. The number should be repeated in the audio tag at least two to three times along with the mail address and the offer terms. If the commercial is 60 seconds, 15 seconds will suffice. In the production of the 2-minute spot, the actual production visual display is 1 minute and 40 seconds in length. Twenty seconds must be left blank for every station to insert the tag tape and slide of the 800 number assigned to it. In most major markets, sending the tag slide with a script for a station announcer overdub is no longer accepted; a separate audiotape of the 20 seconds of order information copy must accompany the commercial tape and an end tag visual slide.

For two reasons, the 800 number should not be built into the commercial's body copy in the majority of instances. First, a station receives its own 800 number because this number is essential to building in the direct-response tracking or sourcing controls. A firm in New York City, for example, will receive an 800 number with the last four digits 1234. Callers are asked to repeat these digits and identify the station they were viewing.

Many major accounts use twenty to twenty-five different 800 numbers. In fact, an increasingly significant factor in the success of an 800 number TV campaign is whether the 800 center has sufficient answering capacity. All numbers should have the same answering strength, and 30 to 50 lines are often needed for a major account. A center may use 80 numbers that can be answered on 30 to 120 lines, but each one of those numbers should be able to be picked up on multiple lines. The experienced management of these lines is critical to the advertiser.

A second reason why copy giving the exact 800 number to call should not be included in the body of the commercial is that the actors' unions SAG and AFTRA consider a single core commercial spliced with individualized 800 number copy tailored to individual markets to be separate commercials if this number is edited into the body of the commercial. Royalties must be paid on a multiple commercial basis rather than as the commercial was intended, as one spot inserted in different markets. However, the spot definitely should contain wording that extols the benefit of using the toll-free number, for example, "Call now, operators are on duty to receive your order" or "To start receiving your issues of *XYZ* magazine sooner, call us toll free."

The TV Bad Debt Factor?

In discussions with Jim Springer, Carol Krajewski, account supervisor for A. Eicoff & Co., and Harold Bolling, director of broadcast for TLK, whose companies together are responsible for the generation of millions of TV orders, three points for consideration emerged. There always will be a TV bad debt factor, there are techniques to decrease this factor, and the 800 number in this context is no more a bad debt stimulant than any other element of a campaign. In general, you might expect a 5 to 20 percent drop-off in payment performances with even the bill-me-later TV 800 number customer from what you might expect from other media. All these factors must be taken into account when you determine your allowable cost per order.

There are two elements which figure prominently in the bad debt discussion: COD orders and inappropriate or high-risk media schedules.

COD orders account for the lion's share of TV-generated orders. In a recent WTBS run of a needlepunch product, 75 percent of the orders received were COD and 5 percent were credit card, with 20 percent mail-in prepaid making up the balance. Since in many instances 80 to 100 percent of the orders are generated through the 800 number, COD orders will be a major operational and financial factor in the back-end analysis. It seems to be an accepted fact of life in the industry that products with a heavy ethnic or urban delivery rate can have a COD nixie (undeliverable) rate of 50 percent, and even a product with appeal to an older, more mature audience still may generate 20 to 25 percent nixies. It is also a given that the TV direct-response product must have a four- to five-time mark up to counterbalance these facts. There are several marketing methods for reducing the nixie rate.

1. Strict attention must be paid to the media schedule. For example, with a record package offer, children may call in a COD order. If the time buy includes run-of-station (ROS) scheduling, your spot can end up running in a *Popeye* or *Gilligan's Island* program. The 800 number record offer should be placed in a specific daytime or late night schedule; the 4 p.m. to 6 p.m. early access hours have a high risk for bad debt in this instance.
2. Many companies are trying to reduce the number of COD orders by offering a premium for every prepaid order, whether 800 number credit card order or mail-in charge or check. For example, *Newsweek* and *Time* and other mass

distribution publishers have offered such premiums as a pocket calculator, radio, thesaurus, dictionary, etc., with prepayment of the order.

3. COD charges are very expensive. A $19 item can end up costing $26 or $27 when delivered COD. If the consumer does not expect this handling expense, the shipment may be rejected. Many companies are highlighting the fact that these charges are unnecessary: "Save COD charges by dialing toll-free . . ." Many advertisers are testing eliminating the COD option altogether. A larger prepaid cash flow may be desirable along with the major reduction in product rejections.
4. If the fulfillment time on the order is condensed to shipment received within two weeks rather than the four weeks allowed, the buyer still may be high on the purchase decision. An aging unfulfilled order has a tendency to lose its appeal and is riper for COD rejection.
5. Many TV media buyers study ZIP code analysis charts with census demographic information overlays in order to select markets with an acceptable household income range and other data flags. If a COD order has been received from a high rejection area, a card is sent asking for prepayment or a phone call can confirm the order payment prospects.

Two-Step: Inquiry Generation TV Success

It is well known that direct merchandise sales can be attained very successfully via the 800 number and TV TNT. In one week alone, the Needlepunch craft kit mentioned earlier generated 30,000 orders running on WTBS alone. What is less frequently known is that the 800 number TV spot can deliver huge quantities of leads at a very acceptable cost per inquiry that convert to sales at a highly profitable rate.

An example of an appropriate product for which this approach has worked well is a "Total Gym" spot with an $800 ticket which has delivered several thousand inquiries per TV schedule. Vitamix, the $450 wonder product, states its case simply and successfully: "We don't have the time on TV to show you all the marvelous things this machine can do. To receive a free brochure with no obligation, simply call this number." In a California 800 number TV spot, a $60,000 boat was described and detailed information was offered. The stations for which inquiries were converted to sales received a commission. In one campaign, four boats were sold. The Dreyfus Liquid Assets two-step campaign has been successful in generating qualified leads which convert very well along with many other financial products, most notably insurance information inquiries. In all these instances, a successful closure or conversion factor of 0.1 to 2 percent of the leads can be extraordinarily profitable.

Fund Raising via 800 Number and TV

Increasingly, fund raisers are turning to the power of 800 numbers in combination with a TV message to deliver donors. One specific example was a campaign put together by the Animal Protection Institute in which a 2-minute spot featuring actress Jessica Walters as spokesperson appealed to viewers for assistance in influencing "the battered seals' plight." A $15 membership fee was offered which would not only further the cause but allow the new member to receive a newsletter and bumper sticker and be put on an action cause mailing list. The 800 number was stressed and delivered three-fourths of the members. The campaign was hugely successful signing up members in the "tens of thousands." Specifically, for the 75 percent call-ins, an additional benefit was realized by the fund raiser in that a significant number of donors' contributions were upgraded on the spot. Credit card pledges also were offered via the 800 number along with a bill-me option. The fund raiser also realized a 60 percent pledge fulfillment rate of the 800 call-ins, which is considered excellent.

800 Number Marketing and the Cable TV Connection

With the limited number of 120-second commercial spots available on national spot TV stations, the introduction of cable TV enabled direct-response advertisers to expand their marketing media, achieve budget allocation profitability, and focus and balance their audience objectives.[8]

The many positive factors that attracted direct-response advertisers could have been turned into negatives if not for the equal advancements of 800 number toll-free operations. As with broadcast television, capturing and sourcing calls is the lifeline of cable direct marketers.

The 800 number services also play a key role in the market development of cable advertising. The responses generated through cable can be attributed to distinct demographic groups within a DMA area. In designating where the bulk of responses was generated, you can establish a market expansion by the use of spot TV and other advertising media. You can determine the particular markets that have responded favorably to your advertising, which therefore can be viewed as a potential area for additional responses through other sources of advertising. Test markets can be established, lowering the risk element of uncharted areas. This, of course, is accomplished by daily results reported by 800 number centers through national exposure provided by airing on cable TV.

Audience profiles, of course, can be established by having the 800 operators ask additional demographic questions of the caller, i.e., school years completed, etc. There are cost factors attendant with the additonal WATS time needed, however.

A factor of critical importance exists relative to the cable viewer. The cable audience seems to fit the profile by which cable viewers differentiate themselves from spot TV viewers. The narrowcasting element that is portrayed by an upscale audience profile viewership has become an item of interest to potential cable advertisers. Through the 800 number, information obtained from the caller can qualify this point. As a basic example, two publishers who recently ventured into cable experienced an increase of "up-sells" for cable viewers ordering subscriptions for their magazines. This profitable and demonstrable increase in 2-year subscribers over 1-year subscribers compared with a spot TV experience can be attributed to the narrowcasting element and the upgrade or upscale audience.

EFFICIENT PRINT AND BROADCAST 800 NUMBER ORDER SCRIPTING

In developing a procedure for taking orders by telephone, the basic steps are the same for both direct dial (where the customer pays for the call) and toll-free 800 number service calls.

Three basic factors are essential to successful telemarketing order taking: speed, accuracy, and courtesy. Accuracy and courtesy are essential for obvious reasons, but speed warrants further explanation. The caller has only a certain attention span, patience, and time. Cost is also a motivating speed factor, either the cost on the part of your caller or your toll-free number costs. Speed is readily achieved by the use of organized procedures which will drive the call to a complete and professionally carried through conclusion.

With proper planning plus operator training and order flow scripting, you can prepare any operator to take an order for any advertising product or service.

The Opening

The opening for all calls should be brief and friendly. This can be accomplished by stating, "This is Dianne. May I help you?" The personalization sets the mood for the call and helps put the caller at ease.

Media Identification: Source of Orders

The initial fact that must be obtained by the operator involves determining which medium originated the call. There are two basic advertising categories for telemarketing order purposes: print and broadcast. Print calls include catalogs, space ads, fliers, and direct mail. Broadcast-originated calls include radio and television. Once this source is identified, the operator can follow one of two order-taking procedures.

Telephone Order Scripting: Print Advertising

The major steps in print order taking are

1. Opening
2. Where advertised, if necessary (type of medium)
3. Credit card information
4. Billing information
5. Source code
6. Merchandise
7. Up-sell, if there is one
8. Closing

From this point, the very nature of the advertising that prompted the call will determine the specific information necessary to ensure the accurate completion of the order. Therefore, the first question asked by the operator after the opening should be, "Where did you see this advertised?"

Next, nearly 90 percent of all print-generated calls require the caller to use a credit card when ordering by phone. This is the next step in the order process. Specifically ask which credit card the customer will be using, what the numbers are, the expiration date, and in some cases determined by your bank, the Mastercard Interbank number.

Trained operators know what digit each credit card begins with and how many numbers constitute an account number. Immediately after the caller has given the card number, the operator should state, "Could you please repeat the number for verification?" This enables the operator to double-check the accuracy of the number. It is highly recommended that the caller, not the operator, repeat the number because if it has been recorded inaccurately in the first place, valuable phone time is wasted.

Logically, the next step is identifying the name of the caller as it appears on the charge card, billing address, city, state, ZIP code, and daytime phone number, area code first. If the caller mentions a "ship-to" address, obtain it after the billing information.

At this point, it is important to note that most phone credit card fraud involves ship-to addresses. Many marketers run these orders against a "fraud address" file; if the order dollar value is high, they call the telephone information operator for the telephone number at the billing address. If these two phone numbers are different, red flags should go up. Even if the number checks out but the order is being sent into what you consider a less than desirable geographic area, you may want to call and verify the order.

The source code is vitally important to analyzing response. Operators who are knowledgeable in advance about where an advertiser's codes are located are able to direct the caller quickly and clearly to that position in the advertising. As a point of reference, obtaining the code is the most difficult and costly (phone time) information item to retrieve from the consumer. It is also a valuable bit of information that will contribute to future market success.

At this point, it cannot be overemphasized that your code should be consistently simple and consistently placed or positioned in all your advertising. The average phone time to retrieve an accurate source number or digit code is 30 seconds. For the most part, the callers have a degree of difficulty in locating them and a feeling of insecurity in relaying them. Make it as simple and painless for the customer as possible.

The locations that seem to be the most effective for acquiring accurately relayed codes are as follows:

For catalogs and direct mail Be careful to position the source code on the mailing label so that it will not conflict with match code numbers or carrier route numbers. It is a good idea to use as few digits as possible, but do not use four digits; this will avoid misinterpretation with carrier route numbers. If you use an alpha letter in your source codes, do not use the letter c to start the code since this will result in a large number of calls giving you the carrier route "CR88" number.

For space ads Use a department number in the address that is printed in the ad. This will save time and confusion, and you will achieve the highest percentage of correct key code information. We find that simply getting the name of the publication is a very poor way of getting the proper source code because often magazines are mistaken for one another in the caller's recollection.

Scripting (operator's instructions) the question of "finding the code" should be specified right on the order blank. This procedure will result in retrieving a greater number of codes than you would get if you left the question an option in the operator's memory.

Tight operator and management control of the call is essential throughout the order transaction, especially when the merchandise information is obtained. Rather than asking a general question about what the caller wants to order, an operator handling catalog orders should clearly state, "Catalog number of your first item? Name of the item? Quantity? Price?" In this way the operator is leading the call throughout the order, enabling the operator to maintain control of the call.

It has been demonstrated in hundreds of order calls that giving the delivery date prompts unnecessary talk time. With this in mind, a pleasant, conclusive "Thank you for calling" can terminate the call effectively. If the caller inquires about delivery, it can be discussed, but analysis indicates that the caller seldom asks.

Telephone Order Scripting: Broadcast Orders

Broadcast calls can be taken in an average of 1 minute or less if you follow these steps:

1. Opening
2. Name of product and specifics
3. Last four numbers dialed or channel identity
4. Billing information
5. Closing

The difference in broadcast and print telephone order taking stems from two factors: the method of payment and the source code. Just as print is almost always a charge order, broadcast is almost always COD. If a caller is entitled to use a charge card on a broadcast item, proceed to take the information as in print. The source code needed in broadcast is the station where the ad was seen or heard. This is obtained by the operator asking for the last four numbers of the toll-free number dialed by the caller or the channel identity if multiple numbers are not available.

In print calls, obtaining the name of the advertiser precedes the progression of the order, whereas in broadcast, the name of the product, quantity, and item description, if necessary, are obtained first. Next, since the caller has just dialed, the operator should ask, "What were the last four numbers you just dialed to reach me?" Then the operator only needs to ask for the name, billing address, city, state, and ZIP code. Customer phone numbers in broadcast are necessary only if the promotion indicates this requirement. The operator should conclude the call by saying, "Thank you for calling." The same rules applies in broadcast as in print in regard to delivery dates. The date should be given only on direct request.

To sum up, proper planning, operator training, and order flow scripting can produce the speed, accuracy, and courtesy necessary for telephone marketing success.

THE POWER OF THE 800 NUMBER UP-SELL

Whether the 800 number is combined with TV or print media, the "up-sell" concept works phenomenally well when the 800 center personnel are provided with the proper scripting and incentive to upgrade the sale. The person who is on your 800 line is your most qualified customer; he or she is in the purchase sequence and is obviously interested in your product. It is a relatively simple task to convert a book order into a deluxe edition order or a 1-year subscription into a 2-year subscription. By many accounts, an up-sell can be accomplished on 25 to 30 percent of the 800 orders.

The up-sell offer must be simple and clear so that the caller can visualize and understand the offer immediately. Experience has shown that the up-sell should never be larger than 25 percent of the value of your average order for merchandise orders. Subscription up-selling, however, can be double the subscription order and in some circumstances triple it.

An extension of the up-sell concept is carried on through lead-generation programs that involve "friend get a friend." A good up-sell merchandise or offer yardstick should be merchandise up sell, 15 to 25 percent; subscription up-sell, 25 to 30 percent.

We conducted an up-sell campaign for the *Wall Street Journal* in which we converted 22 percent of the calls for short-term subscriptions to full-year subscriptions. *Playboy*'s Christmas gift subscriptions up-sell effort resulted in an approximate 30 percent up-sell. In another campaign we handled for a cosmetic company's low-ticket product line, we were able to up-sell on 40 percent of the calls.

800 NUMBER FAST ACTION CUSTOMER SERVICE

One very definite inevitability that accompanies the use of the 800 number order option is customer appropriation of the 800 number as a customer service option as well. Be ready for the customer service calls because they will come. In the NYU/DMA catalog and 800 number operation study cited earlier, 25 percent of the catalog respondents indicated that customers used the 800 number service to express problems, call for the status of orders, or ask questions not related to orders. However, these communications are legitimate customer concerns, and an increasing number of 800 number marketers are using the immediate action nature of the 800 number customer service contact to cement long-term customer goodwill.

Some direct marketers have turned a "problem" into impressive systems that are much more efficient than prior manual customer service operations.

Time Inc. is one of the pioneers in this 800 number application. In the early 1970s, Time Inc. initiated a subscriber relations 800 number service which was charged primarily with handling change of address requests for the millions of subscribers to Time Inc. publications, which now include *Time, Money, People, Sports Illustrated, Discover*, and others. Eventually, with the expansion of 800 number TV promotions and an increasing use of the 800 number in all forms of promotion, the department's function grew to order taking, as well. In 1981, the volume of activity for these functions warranted the establishment of a separate 800 number customer service center.

At this time, the customer service center, which services only Time Inc. magazines and is located in Chicago, is open 7 A.M. to 7 P.M., which effectively provides 8 A.M. to 4 P.M. service across the country. According to Jackie Mutnansky, operations manager for the Chicago response center, the customer service 800 number is not promoted separately. Rather, it is a referred second 800 number to the nonorder customers who call the TV-advertised 800 order number. Nineteen operators, or customer service "adjusters," handle any customer service request ranging from change of address, billing problems, and late copies to missed copies, credit for missed copies, and the extension of subscriptions—in effect, any adjustment possibility. On a slow day 1200 calls for adjustments come through the 800 lines, and on a heavy day as many as 3000 adjustments are handled. A key factor, of course, is the fact that all adjusters are on-line, and any query or adjustment goes straight to the source, the customer's record.

Charter Data Services, Inc., is a contract subscription fulfillment company with a powerful difference: an 800 number center which handles the customer service relations for over 100 magazine clients in addition to their monthly fulfillment mailings. Consumer publications from Hearst, ABC Leisure, and many other publishers have their customer subscription records on-line at Charter. Any subscriber problem is resolved on the spot, from change of address, which accounts for 60 percent of the volume of calls, to renewals. The 800 number is promoted on the masthead or information page of every participating publication. The service, which has been offered to Charter clients and their subscribers, has been in operation for 2 years. The overwhelming satisfaction claimed by clients, states Roger Stover, vice president and director of marketing for Charter, is the major customer goodwill factor and the publisher's convenience.

Whenever a customer (catalog, TV, or subscriber) contacts the 800 center with a customer service request, it is extremely important that the complaint be handled to the customer's satisfaction in order to keep the customer. The 800 number may not be staffed by a customer service adjuster who represents your company alone; very often it is staffed by a service bureau communicator. However, the quality of the response must reflect your company's customer service policies and must be planned and scripted accordingly.

Facilitating the customer's resolution of any problem through an 800 number contact can be one of your company's soundest fiscal and operational policies. In many instances, receiving and processing a written customer complaint can be more expensive than adjusting the problem through an 800 number contact, although 800 number time is money. Many marketers turn a customer problem call into an extended order term or an additional catalog request. Long-term investment returns surely accrue from enhanced customer satisfaction, loyalty, and the convenience provided by this service option to your most valued of company assets, established buyers.

At the very least, the 800 number customer service contact should be anticipated and channeled to a mutually advantageous conclusion. This is an inevitable and achievable scenario.

ESTABLISHING THE 800 NUMBER PROGRAM

In-House versus Service Bureau Handling

If you have made the decision to incorporate the 800 number order or customer service options into your direct marketing operations, deciding how to implement this center is a major consideration. The choice between using a service bureau 800 facility and establishing a separate in-house facility determines many operational and control requirements as well as bottom-line measurability. There are merits in taking both routes.

An 800 number service bureau is a company specializing in order taking and upgrade selling for a number of direct marketing firms that are advertising in any of the direct marketing media of catalog, print space, direct mail, radio, or television. The 800 numbers are shared among client companies. This arrangement will cost the marketer less than the cost of dedicated in-house number maintenance, although this is not always the case. Calls are charged on a fee basis, with the price ranging from $1.85 to $3.00 per call and up depending on the extent of the information which must be recorded, whether there is an up-sell involved, etc. Additional services that may be performed include credit checking, generation of shipping labels, maintenance of data through the client's own computer system, issuance of operations reports on a daily, weekly, or monthly basis, etc.

Service bureaus are staffed with experienced telephone communicators who most often work with cathode ray tube (CRT) screens which display client specifics for a given offer or catalog. Information for orders usually is sent to the direct marketing firms on a daily basis in a printout or tape format.

Each operation mentioned can be performed within the in-house 800 number center, in addition to an extensive customer service program. It is also only with an in-house operation that a company has the full opportunity to derive the benefits of an on-line computerized management information system which may include information on inventory status of each stock-keeping unit, back-order status, substitution items, customer order history, and many other order and customer service enhancement facts.

The following are three quick checklists for a comparative merit examination of in-house versus service bureau operations attributes and one very important factoring exercise that should be made before you select a service bureau to handle your operation.

Positive Aspects of an In-House 800 Number Facility

1. If you will be generating a very small volume of calls, this is best handled in house.
2. If your product or service is highly technical, it lends itself to in-house handling.
3. You will have a better control of information flowing to your own operators.
4. Your own operators will have a higher degree of product knowledge generated through a repetition cycle of very similar calls for your products.
5. If you have an on-line computer, inventory information and customer order history information are available to the operator during the call sequence.
6. You can offer better customer service. This does have a price tag, but it is valuable.

Positive Aspects of an Out-of-House 800 Number Service Bureau

1. The cost savings for this operation can be as high as 30 percent. You can avoid the downside risks of under or overstaffing as well as having too few or too many phone lines available.
2. OPE (other people's experience). A good service bureau can provide you with very helpful information based on the promotion experience of direct marketers in similar situations. This information can include expectation of call volumes and up-sell experience.
3. Extended hours of operation. Most teleresponse centers work around the clock 365 days a year. Many orders come in after 5 P.M. CST and on the weekends. Some media, for example the *Wall Street Journal*, may generate a very high percentage of orders after 5 P.M. The broadcast media advertisement, owing to the station prerogative of choosing the time when some spots will run, can generate orders unpredictably and deliver a volume burst of calls. These two factors in combination can be very hard to handle in-house.
4. Your startup time for 800 number service implementation is short in comparison to in-house startup. Also, the operators who will handle your calls are already professionally trained.

How to Select an Outside 800 Number Service

If you decide to use an outside 800 service, there is a checklist of factors to be considered before you make your choice.

1. Pull a Dun & Bradstreet report. Ask for bank references and customer references.
2. Check their client references. Ask for five references and then five more.
3. Determine what their experience level has been in the medium generating your calls. If you are using TV, go with a bureau that knows TV. Each medium or program has unique requirements. "We do everything" must be validated.
4. Compare costs. In today's phone environment, most services are similar in price. Watch out for the low ball; there are no free lunches.
5. What kind of support does the service get from its local Bell operating company? Verify the information with that Bell company. You may need to upgrade your phone power on an immediate basis in the middle of a rollout.
6. Place test calls to the facility. Evaluate the way your call is handled. Do it several times during the course of a few weeks.
7. Visit the facility. You will learn a great deal about the people who are representing you. I can't overemphasize the importance of visiting two or three service centers. You will be able to get a reading on the management control as well. Scout their daily reporting system and billing system in advance.
8. Can the service offer up-selling? More important, how cost-efficiently do they do it? Time is your money. An up-sell should be scripted clearly and concisely for the operators to read back. Be cautious of commissions paid to operators for up-selling. This may affect your back-end conversions.
9. Specialized services may not be warranted in your case, but what backup services can they offer? Do they authorize credit cards, provide mailing labels, or do fulfillment, or can they handle a lengthy, sophisticated up-sell where warranted?
10. Are you compatible? Will your fulfillment and operations management staff be compatible with the service management?

NOTES

[1] Murray Roman, *Telephone Marketing: How to Build Your Business by Telephone*, McGraw-Hill, New York, 1976, p. 93.

[2] Errol Davis, "Synopsis of the Origin of Telephone Marketing," *Telephone Marketing*, Monograph Series, vol. 3, Direct Marketing Association, New York, 1981, p. 1.

[3] Allan Caplan, "The 800 Number—An Integral Factor in Telephone Marketing," *Telephone Marketing*—Monograph Series, vol. 3, Direct Marketing Association, New York, 1981, pp. 43–55. The author holds joint copyright with the DMA for the contents of two chapters

in this work. Throughout this article, several discussion points draw on the author's prior writings.

[4] Esther Lazaros, "The Effectiveness of 800 Numbers in Direct Mail Catalogs," MBA thesis, New York University Graduate School of Business Administration, May 1982. Ms. Lazaros was sponsored by the DMA research department in developing this primary research study. The work presented represents the joint effort, but the authorship is entirely that of Ms. Lazaros. A full copy of the thesis and an abridged findings version are available through the DMA research department.

[5] Aldyn McKean, "Print Ads Can Make Phones Ring," *AIS Handbook of Toll Free 800 Telephone Marketing*, Advertising Information Service, New York, 1981, p. 57.

[6] David P. Forsyth, "Strategic Positioning through a New Business-to-Business Advertising Data Base." From a speech delivered to the Advertising Research Foundation annual conference, March 2, 1982. New York, Advertising Research Foundation, 1982.

[7] McKean, op. cit., p. 58.

[8] Sandy Davis, "Telephone Marketing and the Cable TV Connection," *Cable/Videotex: A Compendium for Direct Marketers,* Monograph Series, vol. 6, Direct Marketing Association, New York, 1982, pp. 117–120 (abstracted).

part 3

CREATIVE

chapter **29**

CREATIVE CONCEPTS

Thomas B. Brady

Senior Vice President
Kobs & Brady
Advertising, Inc.
Chicago, Ill.

Direct marketing has been called "an art and a science," and this is especially true of the creative part of the business.

Faced with the job of creating a newspaper or magazine advertisement, a television commercial, or a direct mail package, the direct-response copywriter can and should separate the task into two distinct parts: the scientific part and the artistic part.

The art of effective copywriting is a complex subject and will be covered elsewhere in this handbook. Suffice it to say here that as in all other forms of artistry, the ability to write a truly brilliant piece of direct-response advertising copy is probably an innate talent given to relatively few people. Still, with study and practice, most writers can become very effective direct marketing "craftspersons."

This chapter will deal primarily with the scientific aspect of direct marketing copywriting.

Since the whole purpose of advertising is to persuade someone to do something—buy a certain product, vote for a certain candidate, contribute to a certain charity—the creativity of an advertisement or direct mail package ought to be measured by how successful it is in accomplishing its goals.

However, many people judge the creativeness of an advertisement on the basis of how different or flashy or clever or new it was. This is especially true in general advertising, in which the goal usually is to build a favorable awareness of a product or service and which makes no special or at least precise effort to determine exactly how many sales were made as a direct result of any one specific advertisement.

For this reason, within certain obvious limits of good taste, legal considerations, etc., general advertisers are free to be as creative as they wish.

Direct-response copywriters, however, do not have the same degree of creative latitude. Their own experience, plus their awareness of a vast body of data built up by others over decades of precisely measured tests of every single element that goes into a direct marketing ad or direct mail package—offers, headlines, body copy, order forms, etc.—tells knowledgeable direct-response copywriters that their creative freedom is almost always limited by certain dos and don'ts. If these rules are not observed, this is very likely to have an adverse effect on the results.

To newcomers to the direct marketing field—be they individuals or corporations—the idea that they cannot be really creative but instead must do everything according to certain rules and formulas can seem very restrictive.

Actually, the opposite is true. The mere fact of knowing that there are rules and formulas to consider opens up to the alert direct-response copywriter a vast array of opportunities to modify, combine, expand, or in special cases even ignore these rules and formulas in new and creative ways. At the same time, the rules eliminate the need for the copywriter to consider and worry about using those creative approaches which long experience has shown simply do not work in direct marketing—such as humor, or ads that contain large illustrations but only a handful of words.

Thus, a copywriter who thoroughly knows and carefully applies the appropriate rules and the formulas will—if all other factors are equal, such as having a viable product at a reasonable price targeted to the right audience—almost always produce a successful promotion or at least one that comes close to success.

There are, of course, an extensive number of these rules and formulas. Since entire books and articles have been written about them, this chapter will give only a very broad overview of how the direct marketing copywriter can apply the "scientific" aspects of direct marketing to the job at hand.

THE AIDA FORMULA

Broadly speaking, experienced direct-response creative people almost always develop their advertising approach—be it for a direct mail package, a TV commercial, a package insert, or a magazine or newspaper ad—according to the well-known AIDA formula or sequence: attention, interest, desire, action.

First, you must gain the prospect's attention. If you don't, the rest of your sales message will not be read. Next, you must arouse the prospect's interest in what you are selling. If you fail to do this quickly, the prospect will just as quickly stop reading the rest of your message. Then, you must create a desire on the part of the prospect to buy your product or service. Finally, you must convince the prospect to take the necessary action to obtain it.

THE SEVEN KEY CREATIVE STRATEGY AREAS

Obviously, the AIDA formula describes only the general sequence of most direct marketing advertising efforts. Before they even put pencil to paper, direct marketing copywriters must give serious creative thought to seven basic questions.

1. How do we get our target audience to stop and read our message?
2. How do we best position our product or service to this audience?
3. How do we get the reader involved in what we're offering?
4. What format and style should we use?
5. How do we make our product and offer believable?
6. How do we get prospects to respond now?
7. How do we make it easy for prospects to respond?

Not included in this list but of critical importance to the success of any direct marketing promotion is the offer, or the "terms" under which prospects can buy the product, get more information, or use the service. The offer usually will include such factors as price, time, incentives, and payment terms. The wise direct marketer will pay the greatest possible attention to constructing the offer to make it as attractive as possible.

As Ed Nash, president and chief executive officer of BBDO Direct, points out in his book *Direct Marketing*, even so straightforward a part of the offer as the price usually can be expressed in many different ways that can influence response materially. For example, a magazine offer of twelve issues for $6 a year (normally $12 a year) can be stated in at least six different ways:

- One year for only $6 (basic price statement)
- 50¢ per copy (basic price expressed by unit)
- Half price (price expressed in fractions)
- Six issues free (savings dramatized by units)
- Save $6 (savings expressed numerically)
- Save 50 percent (savings expressed in percentages)

Unless each of these seven questions is explored carefully and thoroughly and answered before the actual copywriting is begun—preferably in the form of a written plan or creative strategy outline or statement—the chances of creating an advertisement or direct mail package that will produce maximum results are diminished greatly.

How Do We Get Our Target Audience to Stop and Read Our Message?

Assuming that your media or direct mail lists have been selected carefully to reach your target audience as efficiently as possible, what can you do to get your audience to at least stop and notice your message (the attention part of the AIDA formula)?

Your advertisement or direct mail package will always get far better readership and openership if the headline or envelope copy is written so that it has a direct appeal to the specific audience you're trying to reach.

There are numerous ways to do this, and much, of course, depends on the kind of product or service you're promoting as well as the nature of your audience.

Audience Identification. Obviously, a simple and effective way to develop your ad or direct mail package so that it will attract the attention of the target audience is to identify the audience itself, by occupation or avocation, in the headline or on the direct mail envelope. Nothing attracts people's attention more forcefully than their own occupations or names, which is why personalizing a direct mail letter or order form via computers, lasers, or ink jet imaging is usually so effective.

For example, if you're selling a service to owners of businesses, your headline could read something like, "Seven Reasons Why Business Owners Can Profit from a Unique New Service." A money-saving product for homemakers could be announced as, "How Homemakers Can Save an Extra $10 a Week on Food Bills." Business people and homemakers will be much more interested in reading the rest of your message because you've told them that they specifically can benefit by doing so.

It's not always necessary or even possible to use specific titles like "business owners" or "homemakers" to identify your message as being of special interest to a certain audience. For example, a direct mail package for life insurance can have an envelope that says, "Now! An important bonus for people who haven't smoked in 5 years!" Nonsmokers will, of course, be very much inclined to open the envelope to see what this bonus is.

A headline for an advertisement for a book club for young children might proclaim, "Give your child a big head start in life!" Almost every parent will stop to read the rest of that message.

Often, even very short headlines will be extremely effective at getting your target audience to stop and read.

"Good News If You're Over 65!"

"Overweight?"

"Breakthrough for Denture Wearers"

"Reduce Employee Theft"

"Hawaii for Only $495!"

Appeal to Need. Many products or services have "mass" appeal; that is, they can be used by doctors or car owners or homemakers, etc. Thus, you must get your audience to stop and read by appealing to one or more needs.

It's virtually impossible to sell something to someone who doesn't need it. "Need" should not, of course, be interpreted to mean only the absolute necessities of life such as food, clothing, and shelter. The term also includes the satisfaction of a wide range of powerful human emotions and drives: happiness, love, health, envy, status, job and personal success, fun, sex, fear, security, companionship, comfort, self-improvement, peace of mind, pride or self-image, home and family, adventure, money, concern for others, and so on.

Most products or services will fulfill more than one of these needs, even though that fact may not be obvious at first glance. For example, a catalog offering office supplies would seem to appeal only to the office manager's businesslike desire to buy a good product at a decent price. But what about the office manager's desire to get a raise or promotion (money and ambition) from the boss by being a smart buyer, protect his or her job (personal security), or make the office or the company stationery look better (pride)? These secondary needs often are overlooked, yet they can be a powerful stimulus to added sales.

Thus, you should make a careful, written list of all possible needs—physical and emotional—which your product or service might fill. Armed with such a list, you will be much better equipped to develop copy appeals that will attract the attention of the widest possible audience because they touch on more than a single need.

One of the most famous and most successful headlines and book titles of all times, Dale Carnegie's "How to Win Friends and Influence People," had a powerful double appeal. It is a rare person who doesn't feel the need to have more friends. But the added appeal of also being able to influence people conjures up all kinds of significant benefits—money, power, love, status—which few readers can resist, regardless of what kind of people they are, what professions they're in, or what emotional needs they have.

A headline that says, "Lose Dangerous Fat and Start Enjoying Life," is literally loaded with powerful appeals: to better health, to love and romance, to a good self-image, etc.

Appeal to Curiosity. Human beings are intensely curious. They can be attracted by headlines or envelope copy that piques their curiosity. Some of the greatest advertisements of all time took advantage of that fact.

- "Do You Make These Mistakes in English?" This great Sherwin Cody ad, written by Maxwell Sackheim, produced profitable results for 40 years. Because people were fearful of making grammatical mistakes that would hurt them in their jobs or personal lives, they had to read the rest of the ad to find out what those mistakes might be.
- John Caple's famous headline, "They Laughed When I Sat Down at the Piano." What reader could possibly resist reading further to find out exactly why people laughed at such a commonplace action?

Using a quiz can be a very effective way to attract more readers. People are curious about their own level of knowledge or intelligence, and a quiz promises to help them find out how smart they really are:

"Take this 60-Second Quiz about Vitamins."

"Can You Answer these Five Vital Questions about Life Insurance?"

"Nine Out of Ten People Fail This Home Energy Quiz! Will You?"

In a somewhat similar vein, many direct marketers prefer to use "teaser" copy, especially on the outer envelopes of direct mail packages, in order to make it impossible for the prospect to make a quick decision not to read further. Good teaser copy literally forces most prospects to read the rest of the advertisement or open the envelope to see what's inside.

One piece of teaser copy that has been used with great success by a life insurance company for nearly 10 years asks the question, "What will *you* do with your $700,000?" The reader has to read on to find out what is meant by "your $700,000." (It's the amount of money the average person will earn in a lifetime.)

Appeal to Greed. Some products are so well known or so "generic" that the best course of action is simply to come right out and offer prospects a good reason to buy them, such as attractive savings or a special deal.

"Now! 16 Issues of *Famous* Magazine for Only $5.95"

"Join the Go-Go Motor Club for One Month *Free*!"

"Get a $500 Rebate on the Impresso Office Copier"

"15 Hit Records for 10¢"

Headlines like this not only attract readers who are directly interested in the specific product but also have a powerful appeal to an even wider audience of the many people who find it virtually impossible to turn their backs on the opportunity to get "something for (next to) nothing."

That's why the word "free" continues to be one of the most powerful words you can use not only to attract maximum attention to your ad or direct mail package but also to overcome buyer resistance.

In summary, a really powerful and effective headline or direct mail envelope makes your target audience stop and say, "Hey, they're talking about me," makes people literally itch to read the rest of your sales story, or offers a benefit or "deal" too good to ignore.

How Do We Best Position the Product or Service to Our Target Audience?

Positioning essentially refers to how you choose to define or portray your product or service in relation to other products or services. For example, is the product "completely new and different" or is it "time-tested for over 50 years"? Is it the "best bargain" of its type or is it the "finest that money can buy"? Is it "simple to use" or is it "loaded with extras"? Does it offer the "ultimate in luxury" or is it "for the practical-minded"? Does it promise "enjoyable reading" or "profitable reading"? Will your political candidate "throw the rascals out" or "preserve the Constitution"? Will your product or service "cut business expenses" or "increase business profits"?

Almost any product or service can be positioned in many different ways in terms of both physical properties (including cost) and the needs it may fulfill. It will be very much worth your while to make a detailed written list of all possible ways your product or service could be positioned and then carefully test or use other methods of research to find out which of the various positionings has the strongest appeal. Never assume, for example, that because you feel that the best feature of your product is its quality construction and low cost, the public will think so too. Prospects may be much more turned on by your product's convenience, by the fact that owning it will give them a feeling of being superior to everyone else, or by that extra feature or "gizmo" that no other similar product has.

An example of the power of proper positioning can be found in the health insurance field, where for years the usual and logical approach was to "back the ambulance up to the door" and try to frighten people into buying the product by threatening them with the specter of big medical bills. But when this essentially negative approach was downplayed in favor of highlighting the positive values of health insurance—financial security, peace of mind, cash to get the best treatment possible, etc.—response increased dramatically.

In addition to positioning by product features or benefits, you can gain important positioning advantages in other ways. For example, consider the size of your advertisement or direct mail package. A full-page newspaper ad, a two-page magazine spread, or a 9- by 12-inch direct mail package will by their very size suggest to your audience that your message is important, that your product is a popular one, and that you are a big and dependable company.

The graphic treatment of your ad or direct mail package can position your product or service as being low in cost, high in quality, for women only, new and exciting, for top-level business people, and so on. Many products are sold by direct mail packages or catalogs that are deliberately designed to look inexpensive because this strongly suggests to the reader that the products are inexpensive too.

Proper positioning can increase response by 50 to 100 percent or more, and so you cannot give too much attention or thought to this aspect of the creative planning process.

How Do We Get the Reader Involved in What We're Offering?

When prospects stop to read your ad headline or open your direct mail envelope, they become intellectually and perhaps emotionally involved in your sales story. The degree of this involvement depends, of course, on the product and the offer and especially on the "artistic" skill of the copywriter in weaving a sales story that the reader cannot turn away from easily.

However, there's another powerful way to get the prospect more fully "into" your message, and that's through the use of involvement devices.

An involvement device is anything that asks the reader to take some physical action in addition to simply reading the message and sending in the order form or picking up the telephone to place an order. For obvious reasons, they are used mainly in direct mail, but they also can be used in magazine inserts, newspaper inserts, package inserts, and the like.

If they are done well and intelligently used, involvement devices almost always will increase response, sometimes by as much as 30 or 40 percent or more, though the normal or average increase is probably in the 10 to 25 percent range. However, they do add to the cost of the promotion, and this added cost can offset much or even all of the increase in response.

Involvement devices can be used to promote almost any product or service to any audience, though the more upscale the audience, the greater the need to design and use them with discretion.

The reason why involvement devices work is suggested by the name itself. Once you are able to get your prospect physically involved in your sales story, you change the prospect's basic attitude to your message from one of more or less passive interest to one of active, physical participation. This produces far greater attention to and interest in what you're saying. Once you get the reader to take one physical step, it's that much easier to get the reader to take the next physical step, that of sending you the order. There are many different kinds of involvement devices, including the following.

Stamps and Tokens. Here the usual procedure is to ask the reader to take a stamp or a token that's been placed somewhere else in the direct mail package—at the top of the letter or on a "stub" portion of the order form—and put it in a slot or paste it on the order form itself to signify that the reader is accepting the offer. Usually, the stamp or token will picture this product or capsulize the offer with words like "free trial stamp" or "$40 savings token." You should try to make the stamp or token look important and valuable so that the prospect will feel a certain reluctance to throw away such an impressive-looking item.

Quizzes. We've already seen how the use of a quiz can attract the reader's attention to your message. If the reader then can be persuaded to get a pen or pencil and answer the quiz, the desired physical involvement will have taken place. Better yet, the prospect will have a pen or pencil already in hand to fill out the order form.

Checks and Coupons. Simulated or even real checks and coupons which are redeemable for something of value if returned with the order form—a free bonus gift, a 10 percent discount, a free trial, a $25 reduction in the price, etc.—almost always provide a powerful stimulus to getting the order. Once people actually hold checks or coupons in their hands, they are naturally reluctant to throw them away unused. Again, checks and coupons should be designed to look official, valuable, and important.

Sweepstakes. Offering people the opportunity to win something of great value—a huge amount of cash, a luxury car, a trip to Tahiti, a year's supply of groceries—materially increases the readership of and interest in any advertisement or direct mail package.

Naturally, most people who enter a sweepstakes do not buy the product. But sweepstakes do help motivate many other people to make an immediate decision to buy—people who otherwise might have procrastinated and then failed to order for one reason or another. For this reason, sweepstakes can increase sales 25 or 50 percent or more.

There are many ways to structure a sweepstakes. Generally speaking, you should try to offer attractive top prizes (cash, automobiles, and vacations are very popular), offer a large number of "secondary" prizes so that people will feel they have a better chance of winning at least *something*, give one or more bonus prizes if the person enters the sweepstakes promptly (usually called "early bird" prizes), and include involvement devices such as stamps or tokens or numbers to match against a "winner's list," etc. Especially if your sweepstakes is going to a small audience such as a select group of business people, people in a small geographic area, or present and former customers, it may be possible to award an inexpensive prize to everyone who enters. This permits you to tell prospects that "you have already won a prize in our XYZ sweepstakes," an obvious additional incentive for people to respond.

Setting up a sweepstakes and awarding prizes is a tricky business from a legal standpoint. For example, by law you cannot require that people buy your product in order to enter the sweepstakes. You would be wise to seek professional help from companies which specialize in handling such promotions, such as D. L. Blair Co. or Ventura Associates, both of New York. The subject of sweepstakes is covered more thoroughly in Chapter 12.

Rub-Offs or Lifts. Rub-offs or "lifts" are involvement devices that require the prospect to physically rub off an opaque covering or lift a stamp or seal in order to be able to read something that's been printed underneath. That "something" can be the announcement of a free gift which the prospect gets by ordering, the answer to a certain question, a "lucky number," a special introductory price, and so on. Rub-offs and lifts appeal strongly to people's curiosity and thus are almost impossible to ignore.

Choice and Yes-No Devices. Good "live" sales people always try to give prospects a choice between two or more products, offers, or desired courses of action rather than just the choice of buying or not buying. Thus, the direct marketer should examine the product or service to see whether it can be offered to prospects on a "which do you want" basis.

"Take 10 issues of *Super* magazine for $9.95 or 20 issues for only $15."

"Free bonus! Your choice of the desk-top dictionary or the pocket calculator."

"$20 deluxe edition—or save $5 with the regular edition."

While you can tell the prospect to make such choices simply by checking a box on the order form, providing suitably worded stamps, tokens, or coupons will call greater attention to the choices and, of course, achieve a desirable degree of involvement.

"Yes-no" options do let you give the prospects a clear choice between buying or not buying, usually by using a stamp or token to tell you their decision. They are no longer used as much as they used to be, probably because the high cost of paying the return postage for large numbers of people to tell you that they are not buying outweighs the increase in sales that this device can produce. Still, it can be worth testing on a small scale because of the great reluctance some people have of coming right out and saying no, especially if the answer is worded with a strong negative such as, "No, I don't want to have an extra $400 a month income when I retire." The prospect has to be pretty tough-minded to say no to something like that.

A useful variation of the yes-no device is to permit the prospect to say yes at the same time he or she is saying no; for example, "No, I don't want the forty-five piece deluxe set, but do send me the ten-piece starter set."

Other Involvement Devices. Because of cost factors, most involvement devices are simply printed pieces of paper. However, if you are selling a high-ticket item or are advertising to a limited audience or want to make a special impact, you might consider such ideas as including a pen or pencil in your direct mail package which the prospect is to use to fill out the order. You also might offer real coins ("Use this dime to phone right now"), real trading stamps ("Start saving these Gold Border stamps now. We'll send you more with each future order"), and so on.

Many other kinds of items can be added to a direct mail package to attract attention, such as sample swatches of clothing material, wallet calendars, identification cards, first-aid charts, etc. While these are not technically involvement devices since the prospect seldom is asked to use them as part of the ordering process, they can hype response by giving the prospect a feel of the product (as in the case of material swatches), by getting the prospect to pay closer attention to your sales story, or by making the prospect feel a bit more obligated to respond in appreciation for having received a free item, however inexpensive.

What Format and Style Should We Use?

As was indicated earlier, size and format can have a powerful effect on how prospects perceive your product and company. As a general rule, the bigger your space advertisement or the more lavish your direct mail package, the greater your response will be, although there are numerous exceptions. It's also important to realize that the added increase in response may not be enough to pay for the added cost. All other things being equal, when you are advertising a new product or service, it's best to go with the "biggest and the best" you can afford because at this stage you're more interested in finding out if you have a salable item than in realizing the greatest possible profits. If that works, then test smaller ads or cheaper direct mail packages to see whether you still can produce acceptable results with a smaller investment.

It would be impossible to list the almost infinite number of ways in which a direct marketer can design an advertisement or direct mail package. The type of product, the offer, and the target audience all play an important role in how the ad or direct mail package should be designed. Type sizes and faces, color, illustrations, paper stock, etc., can impart feelings of low cost, important news, super quality, urgency, drama, or exclusivity.

In space advertising, many direct marketers have found that using an editorial format, which refers to an ad that looks like a newspaper story or a magazine article, can be an effective way to get prospects to start reading the sales message before they realize it's actually an advertisement.

In direct mail, there are several basic formats which have proved themselves over and over in the marketplace and which—perhaps modified to suit the product, the offer, or the audience—offer the direct marketer a reasonably good chance of success.

The Telegram Format. Here the outer envelope simulates a telegram, usually using a yellow paper stock. The telegram format suggests "news" and "urgency," and so the envelope usually will get a better than average degree of openership.

The Invitation Format. Here the visual effect is that of a formal invitation, such as a wedding invitation or a "white tie" party invitation, and this visual effect usually is carried through to most of the other components in the direct mail package. This format usually is used when you want to impart a feeling of dignity or class to your product or offer and also to suggest to your prospects that they are special enough to merit this kind of exclusive treatment.

The Business Letter Format. Here the visual effect is that of a genuine, no-nonsense business letter, usually with no envelope copy other than the company address or copy that's short, tailored, and subdued. This is often the preferred format for business-to-business mailings or for direct marketers who feel they'll get better envelope openership if the package doesn't look like junk mail.

The Check Format. Here the visual effect is to suggest that there's a check inside the envelope; indeed, the envelope copy often will say that there's a check inside. It can produce a high degree of envelope openership for obvious reasons.

How Do We Make Our Product and Our Offer Believable?

Today's direct marketing copywriter faces audiences that are better educated and more skeptical and distrustful of advertising and business than ever before. Thus, it's highly important that you seek out and use every means you can to overcome this skepticism and distrust.

Basic to this is the use of such obvious things as offering free trials, money-back guarantees, product warranties, offers to buy back the product at the same price any time within a year, and so on, to reassure prospects that they risk little or nothing by responding. But there are other things you can do to allay the fears and suspicions of your prospects.

Testimonials and Endorsements. Glowing statements by satisfied customers help reassure prospects that your product is a good one and that your company can be trusted. If you don't have any testimonials, solicit them by making a mailing to some of your customers. Most customers will be glad to give you a good testimonial, often better than you would dare write yourself. Be sure to get a signed release if you plan to use actual names or photographs.

Mentioning the number of people who have bought your product or used your service constitutes a good indirect endorsement and promotes a desirable bandwagon effect. Most people prefer to do business with big and leading companies.

Endorsements by famous persons or recognized authorities or organizations also can be extremely effective. You'll have to pay for the privilege, but it can be well worth it.

Outside Guarantors. These are extra touches that you can add to your promotion to give readers a greater feeling of security in dealing with you. For example, get a notary public to verify that your offer or guarantee is exactly as advertised. Mention that you bank at this or that well-known bank or that you're a member of this association or that chamber of commerce. If you can get clearance, mention that your customers include specific well-known companies or reputable executives. Mention that your product is "UL-approved" or that some ingredient in your product has been approved by a government agency such as the FDA. Naturally, all such claims and endorsements must be true, and you should take whatever legal precautions the particular situation calls for.

Be Specific. People place more belief and trust in statements that are specific rather than general. Thus, "15 million people" is more believable than "millions of people," and "Department of Labor figures show" is more believable than just "Figures show." Instead of saying, "Our sales manager has authorized me . . ." say, "Bob McBride, our sales manager, has authorized me . . ."

Use Competitive Comparisons. Don't just say that your product or service is better. If at all possible, develop a "comparison chart" that shows point by point how your product or service compares with others.

Newspaper Stories. If the need for your product or service has been written up in newspapers or magazines, include a reproduction of the article, since people place much more trust in an "outside," authoritative source than in your own unsupported statements. For example, if you're selling home fire alarms, find and reproduce a news story that says something like, "Home fires claimed 15,000 lives last year."

How Do We Get Prospects to Respond Now?

Most people tend to procrastinate, or put things off, even though they may actually have some interest in getting your product or service. Thus, overcoming human inertia is central to achieving maximum results.

In addition to generalized verbal appeals for prompt action such as, "Do it today, while everything is close at hand," "Every day you wait costs you money," or "Order today so you'll be sure to have it in time for Christmas," there are specific things you can do to inspire prospects to take immediate action.

Time-Limited Bonus Offers. Offer a bonus gift if the prospect orders promptly or by a certain date. The bonus can be a separate item or more of the product itself: "Subscribe today, and we'll send you *Super* magazine for an additional month at no extra cost."

Time-Limited Price Discounts or Offers. Offer a discount if the prospect orders promptly or by a certain date. A reverse twist is to urge the prospect to order now because the price may or will increase soon. Or say that the "offer ends on March 15."

Often response can be increased simply by showing a specific date: "Please reply before April 17" or "We cannot guarantee this price beyond August 2." The date may be totally meaningless, but it will get more people to respond.

Limited Supplies. Many people can be moved to take immediate action for fear of missing out on a good deal because somebody else got an order in ahead of them.

> "Only 10,000 of these sets will be manufactured."
>
> "Mystery gift for the first 1000 folks who order."
>
> "Only 715 machines available at this low price."

Certain graphics treatments also contribute to getting more prospects to take prompt action, such as using a red, white, and blue business reply envelope that looks like the old "air mail" service, handwriting the postscript of the letter to look like a last-minute "call to action," using simulated rubber stamps that urge immediate action, and so on.

How Do We Make It Easy for Prospects to Respond?

Untold millions of direct marketing sales have been lost simply because of a failure to make it as easy as possible for the prospect to respond. Even highly interested prospects may decide to forget the whole thing at the last minute if they're confused about the offer, if the order form looks too complicated or hard to use, or if they have to stop and figure out what it's going to cost them or what they're going to get.

The greatest possible attention should be paid to the way your order form or coupon is designed and worded, since that's what your prospect looks at most carefully before deciding to order or not order. It's often the very first thing many prospects look at when they read your ad or open your envelope, because they know that it will give them a quick summary of your proposition.

It is so important that the order form be done exactly right that many direct marketing creative experts say that it's the very first part of the ad or direct mail package that should be created. Unfortunately, it's almost always the last item that's created, and it usually suffers badly as a result.

Your offer should be stated clearly on the order form in the most attractive and positive terms possible. If space permits, you should highlight or recap the main benefits of your product or service and mention special guarantees, free trials, free gift offers, reply-by dates, and so on. Graphically, the order form should give a feeling of importance and value—too valuable to throw away.

If prospects are to fill in their names and addresses as on a newspaper or magazine coupon, you should provide all the room possible for them to do this. A tiny, cramped coupon can reduce your response 50 percent or more.

It's wise to provide a business reply envelope or card so that the prospect doesn't have to hunt for an envelope or a stamp, although some direct marketers today find that response is not significantly hurt if the prospect is asked to pay the postage. This, of course, saves today's high cost of return postage.

Toll-free telephone numbers make it especially easy for people to respond immediately and should be included wherever possible.

When prospects have to pay something as opposed to just sending for more facts, offering them the option of charging the purchase price to a credit card usually will increase response significantly. A "bill me later" option also will increase response, but it can be used only with certain types of audiences and products to avoid getting too many "deadbeats."

When a payment is involved, avoid forcing prospects to stop and figure what it's going to cost them. For example, say, "The Fly Right is only $9.95, plus $0.75 shipping—total, $10.70" or "The Fly Right is only $10.70, which includes all shipping" instead of forcing prospects to add $9.95 plus $0.75 in their heads.

If you're looking for orders of more than one item, it's even more important to do as much of the math as possible for your prospects.

TESTING OF CREATIVE CONCEPTS

One of the most attractive aspects of the direct marketing business is that you do not have to rely on anyone's opinion or guess as to whether offer A is better than offer B, whether it's better to use a two-page letter or a four-page letter, or whether it's better to position your product as being "fun" or "educational." You can let the public tell you which is better by testing these alternatives head to head in the marketplace.

Curiously, even some people who have been in the direct marketing field for years fail to fully appreciate the importance and value of a continual program of creative testing. They argue that testing costs too much or that most of the tests they made in the past did not work.

As a result, they miss out on the opportunity not only to get what could be a healthy or even spectacular increase in the response to a current promotion but also to gain information that can be of critical value in developing future promotions.

Of course, testing costs money. But if you think of it as comparable to the research and development department of a business, the expense of testing can be viewed not as a cost but as an investment in present and future profits.

A test doesn't have to "work" in order to tell you something of importance. Most direct marketing creative experts agree that they often learn as much from their failures as from their successes.

Two basic methods can be used to test creative concepts. (There are also many important noncreative things that can and should be tested: mailing lists, print and broadcast media, seasonality, and the like.)

One method is to test only single elements. That is, only one thing in the control ad or direct mail package is changed: the price, the offer, the headline, the free gift, the length or basic thrust of the letter copy, or some other key element. The changed version then is split tested directly against the unchanged control.

The special value of element testing is that it gives you a precise comparison between the pulling power of different offers, gifts, headlines, or whatever element is being tested. The information gained can be used to increase response to your future promotions, and more element tests can be made against the new control. This way, over a period of time your overall response may be increased by 50 or 100 percent even though no one element test produced over, say, a 15 percent increase in response. In order to be able to read the test results accurately and with confidence, it's vital that only one element be tested in any one ad or direct mail package.

The danger of element testing is that you can get carried away and start testing things that have little or no chance of improving your response or profits to any significant degree, such as the color of your reply envelope or whether underscores in your letter should be in color or black.

The other method of creative testing is called breakthrough testing. Here the idea is to try a more or less completely new creative approach—a completely new graphics treatment, a totally different positioning of the product or service, a whole new offer, and so on—in hopes of finding a major new winner.

The special value of breakthrough testing is that it lets you strike out in new creative directions that can quickly result in major improvements in response compared with the usually slower and more modest improvements to be gained by element testing. However, your chances of success may not be all that good. In fact, you may produce a real loser since you're in effect starting from scratch. And you may learn little of value to use in future promotions.

The wise direct marketer will set up a testing program that combines both element and breakthrough tests: the element tests to virtually guarantee a steady increase in results, and the breakthrough tests to keep searching for the dynamite new approach that can pile up much bigger profits immediately.

As Jim Kobs, president of Kobs & Brady Advertising, points out in his book *Profitable Direct Marketing*, testing different offers—price, payment options, premiums, etc.—generally will give you the best chance of scoring a major increase in response. Tests that position the product or service in different ways also can result in dramatic improvements in response.

Your chances of increasing response by sizable amounts through format tests or copy tests are not as great as in testing offers or positionings. But it is not uncommon to achieve a 25 percent or greater increase in response by using a different format or even by changing just the headline of your ad or letter or the copy on your outer envelope or by adding an involvement device.

Since it is all too easy to be tempted, often on the spur of the moment, into testing things that have little or no hope of producing any meaningful increase in results, you should develop a written plan for an ongoing testing program that shows exactly what you plan to test, why you plan to test it, and what you expect to learn from the test.

The budget permitting, your plan also should provide for tests within all four major opportunity areas: (1) offer, (2) positioning, (3) format, and (4) copy. If your test budget is limited, concentrate on testing offers and positioning since they offer the greatest opportunities for gaining significant improvements.

In summary, the creation of profitable direct marketing ads and direct mail packages can and should be started well before the actual writing of the words is begun. The truly effective direct-response copywriter is both a "scientist" who knows and applies, in the earliest planning stages, those creative concepts and strategies which have proved themselves over and over in the marketplace and an "artist" who then writes the copy that makes the product and the offer come alive in the mind of the prospect.

chapter 30

PSYCHOLOGY OF DIRECT MARKETING

Stanley C. Plog, Ph.D.

President
Plog Research, Inc.
Reseda, Calif.

Kings and queens, truck drivers and plumbers—all agree that it's nice to receive mail from someone you care about. Who can forget the anxious hours of waiting for the mail to arrive to see if there is a letter from someone you love or to see if a package you ordered has been delivered? Who can describe the excitement when it comes and you find out that your loved one loves you or the dejection that is felt when it turns out to be a "Dear John" or "Dear Jane" letter? Poets, music lyricists, and novelists have used their talents to describe those moments of ecstasy and depression associated with the daily event known as the mail call.

It may be a high form of bliss to open your mailbox and find a letter from someone who is important in your life, but what about mail that you do not expect to receive, mail that is unsolicited and covers topics you did not know you are supposed to be interested in? Is this mail desired or does it constitute an interference in the daily lives of its recipients? Is it likely to be read and viewed favorably or will it be thrown away or read with a negative bias?

This chapter presents information on the psychology of the direct marketing situation. What are the positive or negative factors that are present in a typical reader's mind when solicitations are made through the mail, and what are some of the more important factors to consider in order to make appeals more effective? We shall examine the psychology and personal needs of consumers. Most of the chapter will be devoted to mail appeals because of their dominance in direct marketing and because many of the concepts of selling by mail are applicable to other direct selling situations, including the use of television.

The majority of the statistics presented here are derived from a nationwide study conducted by Plog Research, Inc., which compared attitudes and behaviors of current buyers of direct mail solicitations (people who have bought one or more products from a specific direct mail company within the past 2 years), former buyers (people who previously bought one or more items from that same company, but not within the past 2 years), and nonbuyers (people who have not purchased items within this period of time). The study consisted of nine focus groups (ten to twelve people prescreened to represent direct mail buyers, former buyers, and nonbuyers) and 450 in-depth interviews (requiring 45 minutes to 1 hour each) among these same types of persons. All interviews were in person, based on telephone appointments (names obtained from a computerized list) and conducted in small to large cities in the United States.

The chapter begins with information about the psychology of buyers and nonbuyers and concludes with suggestions on how to make solicitations more effective.

GOOD FEELINGS ABOUT MAIL

With a considerable amount of discussion in the press about junk mail and the various well-publicized congressional hearings in which junk mail has come under close scrutiny (for postal rate increases), direct marketing solicitations often are portrayed as both unwanted and a burdensome expense to taxpayers. The term "junk mail" is pejorative, and it covers a plethora of types of mail: department store catalogs, finance company solicitations, insurance offers, gift-a-month plans, etc.

With a prevalence of negative opinion rampant in the press, is mail that is not from a known friend or business associate desired or is it considered an interference in one's daily life? The surprising answer is that most people like to receive mail even when it is unsolicited. And people like it when their mailboxes are filled to overflowing. Thus, most junk mail gets read by its target audience.

In general, most of the mail that ends up in the hands of recipients around the country is well received, including the great volumes of unsolicited mail and fliers which are distributed by local companies. The roots of this positive perception stem from childhood, a time when mail is a source of surprise and gratification. The arrival of a small toy ordered from a cereal box top, an invitation to a playmate's birthday party, and one's first personal letter all were important. The message carried by each of these stated that "I am important" or that "Somebody loves me" because someone bothered to write or send a gift. This positive image of mail is pervasive and tends to cover any kind of mail received during the childhood years. It means that one's sense of self-worth and importance has been enhanced because a person or company wants to communicate with that individual and perhaps sell him or her a product or service (a further reinforcement of the sense of power that one feels from receiving mail early in life).

These attitudes and feelings which are fixed early in life carry over and become influential in the adult years. None of the mail was considered junk at an earlier time, and this implies that the definition of what is undesirable is vague and seldom is examined critically during the adult years.

In the large research study referred to earlier, which was based on a nationwide sample, seven out of ten people consistently said that they look forward to receiving all sorts of mail. This figure varies little between active buyers of direct mail products and services and nonbuyers. Only 7 to 10 percent of the population stated that they do not look forward to receiving mail, while the remainder expressed no feelings either way.

Interestingly, in the majority of households (over 60 percent), mail is opened by the addressee even when it obviously has been sent from a mail-order house or another direct mail solicitor. The assumption of most household members is that the mail either has some personal meaning to the addressee or is of little interest to anyone other than that individual.

DEFINITIONS OF BAD MAIL

Obviously, not all mail can be received favorably, and that which is not liked tends to be classified as junk mail. What, then, is junk mail, and what can be done to avoid the appearance of junk? The recipients of specific types of mail tell us this in fairly clear terms.

Table 30-1 summarizes the reactions of the nationwide sample to different types of solicitations.

As can be seen, solicitations to buy recreational land, invest money, or buy insurance receive strong disapproval and are classified by buyers and nonbuyers alike as junk mail. There is a strong feeling that most of these organizations tend to be disreputable and will fleece anyone who is foolish enough to answer their solicitations. According to our respondents, these companies see mail recipients as suckers who may bite at the dumbest kind of offer.

Letters addressed to "occupant" or "resident" are extremely high on the list because they run counter to the basic psychology of what mail means to its recipient. Early in life, a letter or package means that someone cares. To send something that is addressed to an occupant of a street number suggests that someone does not care, bringing up the potential feeling of rejection. "Occupant" or "resident" solicitations suggest that a large mail-order house is trying to manipulate people throughout the country for its own economic purposes.

Similarly, when a name is inserted by computer, the technique arouses

TABLE 30-1 Percentage of Respondents Viewing Solicitations and Other Types of Mailings as Junk Mail

	Current Buyers, %	Former Buyers, %	Non-buyers, %
Solicitations to buy recreational land	82	90	84
Letters addressed to occupant or resident	82	85	84
Solicitations to invest money	80	81	82
Solicitations to buy insurance	79	84	84
Chance to win money, prizes, or sweepstakes	77	84	84
Letters with name inserted by computer	58	65	74
Solicitations from charities	44	45	49
Free sample offers	19	16	18
Merchandise offers from credit card companies	16	18	24
Catalogs from major department stores	6	5	9

relatively uniform feelings. "Someone is trying to make me feel like they are concerned about me, but they really are not" was how one study participant described the situation.

The tendency to classify solicitations from charities as junk mail originates from a feeling that there are too many of them and that it has become big business. The attempt to play on the guilt of readers has become tiresome and suggests that these charities are more interested in self-perpetuation than in helping others.

THE PSYCHOLOGY OF BUYERS AND NONBUYERS

The simple statement that some buyers respond to mail solicitations and some do not leads to the obvious thought that there must be psychological differences between these two types of people. The answer is that there are, but these differences are not as great as might be assumed.

In general, buyers and nonbuyers are similar in terms of most demographic dimensions, including income, marital status, average family size, age, sex, and educational level. They differ only slightly on occupation in that nonbuyers tend to be more heavily represented in the more senior professional and executive-level positions.

Buyers and nonbuyers are also similar in terms of a number of psychographic dimensions related to conservatism, impulsiveness, venturesomeness, need for change from routine in daily life, style consciousness, and personal happiness. The only areas in which these two groups tend to differ consistently relates specifically to attitudes about solicitations coming through the mail. For example, answers to specific questions about direct mail buying are contained in Table 30-2.

Differences between buyers and nonbuyers tend to be greatest in areas which strike at the most central points of what direct mail represents.

- There is a 27 percentage point differential in agreement levels between the two groups on whether products offered by mail "are usually of very high quality." Nonbuyers obviously are much less inclined to believe this.
- There is a similar spread in believing that it is an advantage to be able to "spread your payments over time instead of paying all at once" when using direct mail. Nonbuyers agree less.
- Nonbuyers are also not as interested in looking forward to something after they have ordered it. This is a 17 point spread.
- Nonbuyers also do not agree that a product offered often "happens to meet a person's needs at the moment." This is an 18 point spread.
- There is also a difference in opinion as to whether "products offered are priced about the same or even lower than in stores." This is a 17 point spread.
- However busy the lives of nonbuyers may be, they agree less frequently with the statement that they "often have trouble getting to a store, so buying by mail is a help." This is a 17 point spread.

TABLE 30-2 Proportion of Respondents Agreeing at Least Somewhat with Various Positive Statements about Mail-Order Buying

Statement	Buyers, %	Nonbuyers, %
To avoid interest charges on merchandise you order, you can simply make one payment for the total amount.	89	81
There is no pressure from a salesperson when you order through the mail.	80	69
It's a pleasant surprise when the package containing your order arrives.	71	61
Often a product offered just happens to meet a person's needs at the moment.	77	62
These mail solicitations often have good ideas for gifts.	76	64
One good thing about this kind of mail-order buying is that you can spread your payments over time instead of paying all at once.	63	46
After you order something, it's fun looking forward to when it will arrive.	71	54
I wouldn't order something through the mail unless there was a free home trial period.	60	56
Buying through the mail is an easy way of sending a gift to someone.	62	53
Buying through the mail saves all the trouble of having to go shopping.	61	46
One advantage of buying by mail this way is that you always get a free home trial.	58	46
The products offered are usually of a very high quality.	57	30
Often the products offered are priced about the same as or even lower than in stores.	54	39
Buying through the mail is a good way to get new and unique products.	49	33
It is more uncomfortable to have to return something in person at a store than just to send it back by mail.	30	23
I often have trouble getting to a store, so buying by mail is a help.	32	15

SATISFACTION WITH PRODUCTS PURCHASED

A critical question for anyone involved in direct mail and marketing approaches is the level of satisfaction with products sent, since the likelihood for future purchases should be dependent on how satisfied the buyer is with previously purchased products.

Levels of satisfaction obviously vary with the type of goods sold, the purchase price paid for them, the reputation of the company offering the items, the length of time until delivery, and a host of related factors. However, the study referred to above shows that the vast majority of people (usually 60 percent or more) typically are "very satisfied" with the products they receive by direct mail, and most of the remainder (an additional 25 to 30 percent) are "somewhat satisfied."

TABLE 30-3 Percentage of Current and Former Buyers Expressing Differing Levels of Satisfaction with Prior Purchases and Indicating Various Degrees of Interest in Future Purchases

	Very Satisfied, %	At Least Somewhat Satisfied, %	At Least Somewhat Dissatis-fied, %	Very Dissatis-fied, %
At least somewhat likely	76	73	59	34
At least somewhat unlikely	24	27	41	66
Total	100	100	100	100

Thus, 85 percent or more of the people who order by mail usually are relatively happy with the products they have received. Only 5 or 6 percent are very unhappy with their products. The primary reason for unhappiness cited by nearly four out of five buyers is product failure; i.e., it doesn't work. The second most important reason among this small group of unhappy purchasers is that the items do not live up to the advertising copy. In other words, the glorious, one-of-a-kind product which is offered for a limited time only just isn't so hot once you have it in your hands.

A central question arising out of these findings concerns what influence prior levels of satisfaction have on future purchase intentions. Table 30-3 summarizes these differences, indicating that three out of four of those who are "very satisfied" or "somewhat satisfied" are likely to purchase a product by mail again from the same company in the future. More surprising is the fact that six out of ten (59 percent) of those who are at least "somewhat dissatisfied" also plan to buy something from the same company in the future. Slightly over one-third (34 percent) of mail buyers who were "very dissatisfied" indicate they too will buy in the future.

A clear message grows out of these research findings. Once a customer has been hooked, that customer has a strong potential for future sales, even when there has been some dissatisfaction with the product.

Related to this topic is the case of returned items and whether these people plan to buy in the future. The results are similar to the results presented in the previous paragraph. See Table 30-4.

TABLE 30-4 Percentage of Respondents Who Have and Have Not Returned Items and Willingness to Buy by Mail in the Future

Likelihood of Future Purchases	Have Returned, %	Have Not Returned, %
At least somewhat likely	68	71
At least somewhat unlikely	32	29

Other question items in this study point out that "no-risk" and "trial-free" offers are very important in overcoming potential buyer resistance. The uncertainty and anxiety that many people feel about buying a product sight unseen often are allayed by telling the prospect forcefully and clearly that the payment will be returned promptly and cheerfully if the product does not live up to its expectations.

WHY PRODUCTS ARE BOUGHT BY MAIL

There are multiple reasons why people buy products on the basis of direct marketing approaches. Some have been discussed already, but it is useful to present them in a more clearly defined manner.

- The interest and surprise at receiving a package in the mail are fundamental and relate to psychological needs originating in childhood. Thus, it seems imperative for companies which want to do business on a continuing basis with a customer list to develop more "giftlike" packages for their products. The product should be wrapped attractively, not just thrown into a mailer packet or cardboard box.
- A product often happens to meet the presumed needs of a person for that moment. Thus, the most clever direct marketers discover unique products and get out the announcements to the right target audiences. Solicitations also often present good ideas for gifts for others.
- Buying by mail saves the trouble of having to shop in person. This statement is used by many direct marketers as a sales approach, and it has a considerable degree of validity.
- Products offered by mail frequently are priced lower than similar products in stores. The number of people who agree with this statement has declined over the years, since many are finding that there is no price advantage to shopping by mail. Other reasons for purchasing by mail have to be presented if the product is not lower priced than similar store items, for example, "superior quality in all products," "widest selection available anywhere," "fast, prompt delivery," etc.
- Finally, among major purchase motivations is the belief that buying through the mail is a good way to get new and unique products. Many individuals peruse mailers and catalogs to find items that are not available through more typical retail channels. Phrases such as "not available elsewhere," "just arrived," and "latest technology" are keys to convincing prospects of the uniqueness of the items.

WAITING FOR DELIVERY

One of the problems of direct marketing approaches is that the product is not immediately available to take home after purchase. The lack of immediate gratification at the time of purchase has the unfortunate consequence that many

TABLE 30-5 How Long Respondents Will Wait for Delivery Before Becoming Impatient

Time Lag	Current Buyers, %	Former Buyers, %	Nonbuyers, %
Up to 2 weeks	76	75	68
Up to 3 weeks	52	47	38

people do not follow through on their inclinations to buy an item they like. The ability to delay gratification is a mature personality characteristic, and as we have seen, some of the basic motives that relate to interest in mail purchases are relatively immature in character. The question is, How long will the average user of direct mail be willing to wait for products that have been ordered?

Table 30-5 shows that most people are relatively impatient; the number of people who will wait 3 weeks rather than 2 drops off dramatically among all types of buyers. These data point out that it is important to let prospective buyers know that their orders will be processed very quickly and that delivery times will not be long. Suggestions to allow 4 to 6 weeks for delivery are necessary to remove the frustration of people who expect delivery to occur much sooner. But when that amount of time is required, the warning on the order form is likely to alienate many potential prospects.

THE PHYSICAL CHARACTERISTICS OF GOOD SOLICITATIONS

Solicitations by mail which have the highest returns have certain characteristics in common.

1. The entire presentation is of high quality, including design and layout, graphics, grade of paper, and copy. The representation of the quality of the product is implied through the quality of the direct mail piece.
2. Color photography is used throughout rather than black-and-white illustrations. Color photographs give a better sense of what the merchandise is like and support the believability and credibility of the copy.
3. There is an ordered and logical sequence to the presentation of information.
4. The accompanying letter and ideas in the text are presented as briefly as possible. Long, tedious explanations are, to use the words of some respondents, "hated with a passion and ignored." Some direct mail pieces which have long letters are successful, but these are the exceptions to the rule.
5. Whenever possible, leaflets and brochures should unfold to reveal larger illustrations, adding a sense of excitement, anticipation, and drama as larger pictures of the product are revealed.
6. Cheerful statements about fast refunds on returned merchandise should be displayed prominently because of their importance in overcoming buyer resistance.
7. Mystery gifts and other offers which have a ring of being hokey should be avoided because of sensitivities about excess hype from these types of offers.

These offers may catch the more naïve first-time direct mail user but are a turnoff to sophisticated and frequent users of direct mail.

8. Toll-free numbers are important and must be displayed prominently since this provides an opportunity for a buyer not only to place an order but to ask questions and clear up doubts, confusions, and anxieties.
9. Involvement devices such as tokens to insert in a card or peel-off stickers are effective since they allow the prospect to take small action steps before reaching the ultimate act of dropping the reply card in the mail.

SUMMARY

Good direct mail and marketing approaches are dependent on a host of interrelated and important variables. Understanding the psychology of the intended audience and knowing more about what types of appeals are likely to fit this psychology are two fundamentals that cannot be ignored.

In the final analysis, there is no substitute for the concerted effort it takes to define who the audience is, what their special psychology is, how the products offered meet the needs of the audience, how the direct mail materials will support the presentation of this psychology, and how that audience can best be reached from the thousands of lists that are available for sale. Nothing can substitute for good creative writing—writing in which the writer has a specific individual in mind as a representative of the target audience when the words are placed on paper. All in all, hard work may not guarantee success, but it certainly can make up for a lot of mistakes.

chapter **31**

WRITING HEADLINES

Sy Levy

President
Rosenfeld,
Sirowitz &
Lawson
Direct
New York,
N.Y.

Imagine an angler standing at the tip of a jetty casting lures into the churning sea. Then think of the angler as an advertising writer and the lures as headlines and you will understand the problem—and the opportunity. The writer must come up with a headline that, in a sea of advertising clutter, will hook the prospect into reading the ad. This crucial function makes the headline the most important part of the ad. But today's readers have become increasingly sophisticated and more difficult to catch. To add to the problem, many major companies have gone into direct marketing. They have great resources and highly developed marketing skills, and they want to catch that elusive reader before you do. To achieve success in the frenzied competition of the marketplace, advertising writers must define their objectives. To write better headlines, advertising writers must have a clear idea of who they want to catch and how they plan to do it.

SETTING OBJECTIVES

Objectives come from three major sources. First, objectives come from management as corporate goals to be achieved. For example, management may want to introduce a completely new product, get a larger share of the market for an existing product, open new markets for that product, or generate a greater number of leads for the sales force. Second, objectives come from market conditions as problems to be solved. One competitor launches a new product, another lowers the price of an old one, and a third adds improvements to a current model. Meanwhile, consumer attitudes toward your product have changed. Third, objectives come from research and testing which tell us about buying patterns and what the public thinks about product or service benefits and advantages, price points, and offers.

Why Set Objectives?

Whatever their source—management, the marketplace, or research and testing—objectives define what the advertiser wants the audience to do or not do, think or not think, and feel or not feel.

Objectives provide a framework for advertising. They help discipline, organize, and direct the thinking and efforts of everyone involved in the advertising process, and they provide a gauge to measure the effectiveness of those efforts after the advertising has run. While response remains a major criterion, many of today's direct marketing advertisers also feel a deep concern about the effect that direct marketing advertising has on the corporate image, an image their companies already may have invested many years and millions of dollars to build.

Putting Objectives to Work to Develop Winning Headlines

With the objectives clearly in mind, the advertising writer can begin to marshal the arguments and appeals that will support them. The creation of such a copy platform ranks as the first major step in the actual creative process. The copy platform establishes the major selling points in order of importance, and it serves as an indispensable guide to the creation of an irresistible headline consonant with your marketing strategy.

THE IDEAL HEADLINE

What would make a headline irresistible to both advertiser and audience? It would have to meet many of the following specifications:

- Supports the advertising objectives
- Conforms with the copy platform
- Offers a benefit to the reader
- Addresses audience interests
- Makes a concise, pertinent point
- Sounds interesting and informative
- Offers a solution to a problem
- Uses fresh, provocative language

Although some advertising authorities may disagree, these criteria apply to both general and direct-response advertising headlines.

THE PSYCHOLOGY OF A DIRECT-RESPONSE HEADLINE

A good headline motivates prospects to continue reading the ad, starting the process of persuasion that leads to a direct response by appealing to the most important needs and desires of the target audience. The most powerful headlines promise a benefit or reward in terms so forceful that they compel individual readers to identify themselves immediately as members of the target audience. But even the most powerful headlines have limitations. People who do not have active or even latent interest in your product or service will forever remain unreached, unconvinced, and unsold by your advertising.

POSITIVE AND NEGATIVE WAYS OF WRITING HEADLINES

Some advertising authorities feel very negative about negative headlines. They maintain that negatives discourage readership and response. When they find themselves confronted with negative headlines, they tend to "think small," though obviously, Doyle Dane Bernbach, Volkswagen, and several million Volkswagen owners think otherwise.

What positive things can you say in negative headlines? You can tell the reader how to survive a depression or how to avoid ill health, unemployment, marital discord, emotional distress, unprofitable investments, nagging backaches, and the heartbreak of psoriasis. Good negative headlines can have great value despite the fact that they don't come easy, but then, neither do good positive headlines.

POSITIVE THINKING

Both neophyte and veteran advertising writers usually find it far easier to write successful positive headlines. How can anybody go wrong telling readers how to save money, get free premiums, and enjoy life, success, happiness, financial security, good health, and sex appeal, not to mention how to grow giant zinnias and zucchini in their gardens *this very summer*.

Positive or negative headlines that produce results almost always use simple language and familiar word combinations and sentence structure. In other words, those headlines talk the way people really talk to other people. To write a winning headline, it often helps to visualize the prospect and write directly to that person. Imagine yourself in the same room, face to face with the person you want to buy your product or service. This approach helps avoid stilted language, overclever phraseology, and vague generalities.

DIFFERENT TYPES OF HEADLINES

In *Hamlet*, Polonius attempted to name all the different kinds of classical plays. He listed "tragedy, comedy, history, pastoral, pastoral-comical, historical-pastoral, tragical-historical, tragical-comical-historical-pastoral, scene individable, or poem unlimited."

It would not take a Polonius to come up with an even longer, and more complicated list of headline types. In addition to the tragical-comical-historical-pastoral headline, you can consider the following eight categories as a basic guide to the creation of powerful, exciting, involving, response-producing headlines.

The Offer Headline

What do readers get for their time, money, or effort in responding to your proposition? The offer stands as the single most important element in direct-response advertising and the simplest, most direct way to elicit or increase response. "Four books for $1" is a good offer, but if you want to increase response even more dramatically, try "Four books for $1 plus a tote bag free." Direct-response experts have compiled lists of dozens of effective offers, including "free gift," "free trial," "free information," "free catalog," "two for the price of one," and "special benefits with charter membership" plus all kinds of "no purchase required" offers for entries in sweepstakes and giveaways.

The News Headline

Everybody knows that the word "new" adds an almost magical pulling power to almost any headline, and genuine news adds even more power. Examples would include "New space-age alarm protects your home 24 hours a day," "At last! A home computer every family can afford," and "Tea lovers—send for new catalog of rare and exclusive blends!"

The How-To Headline

This must rank as one of the earliest and most successful direct-response headline techniques. You can almost imagine a Neanderthal scratching "How to catch a sabre-tooth tiger" on the walls of a cave. Almost everyone wants to find out "how to" do something. You're reading this chapter because you want to know how to write great headlines. Other people want to know "how to win friends and influence people," "how to read three times as fast in just 1 week," or "how to invest successfully in the stock market."

Flashy headlines? No. But invariably powerful, involving, and appealing strongly to the self-interest of the reader. A "how to" headline also lends itself to rational, descriptive body copy.

The Numerical Headline

This approach enumerates the ways the reader can become wealthier, healthier, wiser, richer, or smarter or the many ways in which a product can perform better, do more, save more, etc.

Often, the more reasons you can list, the more interesting and powerful your advertising will prove, because the reader feels reasonably certain of finding one or more rewarding items on your list. The more the reader finds, the more likely he or she is to take the action you want.

Examples include "ten ways to improve your appearance," "seven simple steps to better health," "twelve rewarding reasons why you should invest in real estate," and "the eight most important ways to get ahead in business." Usually an explanation of each item listed constitutes the body copy of the ad. The more compelling each reason, the more effective the ad.

The Competitive Comparison

Does your product or service offer features, benefits, and advantages that your competitors can't match? Then your headlines should tell the good news to the world. You can do this by direct comparison which names the competition or through a sweeping statement of superiority such as, "Learn French with the fastest, easiest home instruction course ever offered."

Other examples of competitive comparisons include "Check the performance, check the price, then send for this remarkable $29.95 stereo tape recorder," "Subscribe to the newsmagazine that has won more journalism awards than any other," and "Their price: $89. Our price: $59. For the exact same quality!"

The Command Headline

"Read this!" Most people find it difficult to ignore a direct command. Even if their instinctive response to your command lasts only a few seconds, you've managed to arrest their attention, and that gives you a better chance to lead them into the body copy where you do your selling.

Command headlines can take many forms: "Act now and save 50 percent," "Clip this coupon," "Order by March 15, and save 10 percent," and "Prove it to yourself; 30-day free trial." A book club once ran a very effective headline which said, "Read it slowly!" The headline referred to an introductory offer of a single-volume anthology of science fiction. This command seemed to pique the curiosity of readers. Did the command refer to the book or to the ad itself? Nobody knows how readers interpreted the command, but the ad remained an unbeatable control for several years.

The Story Headline

Almost everyone wants to know what happened "once upon a time," and direct-response advertising writers can take advantage of this willingness to hear a good story. Toss in the chance of tangible gain or the opportunity to learn something important or valuable and you will capture the attention of your audience.

John Caples wrote the classic example of the nearly irresistible story headline: "They laughed when I sat down at the piano, but then I started to play!"

Story headlines lend themselves to editorial formats that are perfect for the communication of important sales points in a powerful, convincing way. Examples include "How I turned a $1000 investment into a sizable fortune," "How a simple device helped save my life," "The business secret my boss never let me forget," and "I used to be lonely and overweight, but now . . ."

The Question Headline

Does it really work? You bet it does. Questions attract attention, and provocative questions generate interest and involvement. Curiosity ranks high on the list of human traits, and well-phrased question headlines can pull a reader right into your copy.

Sherman Cody gets credit for perhaps the most famous question headline ever: "Do you make these mistakes in English?" Other examples include "With the same income, how does my neighbor live so much better than I do?" "Why is this the best rug hooking catalog?" "How much money have you wasted today?" and "Why do other people always seem happier?"

THE COMPARATIVE ADVANTAGE OF RUNNING VERY LONG HEADLINES VERSUS SHORT ONES

Dozens if not hundreds of books and articles have discussed the questions of headline length, position, and size. Research and experience seem to indicate that shorter headlines do better than longer ones because they are easier to read and understand. Certainly advertising writers would find it hard to beat such famous headlines as "Lemon" and "Think small" for brevity. Yet an equally famous automotive headline runs much longer: "At 40 miles an hour, the loudest noise you hear is the ticking of the clock." However, most direct-response professionals take the pragmatic view that a headline should contain as many or as few words as needed to do the job.

HEADLINE RESEARCH

Several companies have come up with different "reading machines" that help determine the eyeball movements and reading patterns of people studying different ads. One company uses an unusual technique to determine the optimum length of headlines in their ads. They pin layouts on the wall, step back about 10 feet, and "squint" at the headlines in question. Headlines that remain legible under these conditions survive for further consideration; the others get discarded. Research and the sales charts seem to indicate that the reading audience of this particular company responds better to headlines that can pass this "eyeball" test.

Other, more orthodox research techniques exist to guide the advertising writer. They include focus groups, one-on-one interviews, and other forms of scientific copy testing.

HEADLINE RULES BY GREAT HEADLINE WRITERS

A number of highly respected advertising writers have agreed to set down the rules they follow instinctively or deliberately in writing the headlines that have put them at the top of their profession. Their comments reflect years of experience and enormous expertise.

TOM COLLINS, RAPP & COLLINS, INC.

I can put everything I know about headlines in either 1000 words or in one sentence, but nothing in between. Here is my one sentence:

Writing a good direct marketing headline involves determining and visualizing the most likely prospect and then attracting that prospect with a credible and compelling product advantage or customer benefit in a way that encourages readership of the copy.

ARTHUR CERF MAYER, JUST CREATIVE, INC.

Use the power of negative thinking. For example, try a headline with the words "don't" or "no" or "never" or "warning" or "danger" or something like that because some of the most important statements in human history have been stated in the negative.

The Creator, in developing the famous ten-point Mt. Sinai program, couched all but one of the famous commandments in the negative. Today, when we want people to avoid killing one another at crossroads, we put up just one negative word: "Stop." Some of the most memorable headlines in advertising have been couched in the negative:

They laughed when I sat down at the piano.

Think small.

Lemon.

Don't be half-safe.

WILLIAM NORTH JAYME, JAYME, RATALAHTI, INC.

Two favorite headlines I've written:

Do you close the bathroom door even when you're the only one home? (for *Psychology Today* magazine)

How much extra should you tip when you're planning to pocket the ashtray? (for a new travel magazine from *Bon Appetit*)

Basic advice on writing headlines: Cut.

HENRY (HANK) BURNETT

I have just one rule for headlines: A headline must catch the reader's attention, engage the reader, and lure him or her into the body copy. Any way this can be accomplished is fine—surprise, shock, intrigue, cognitive dissonance, provocation, outrage, mystery, innuendo, or double entendre. And there are many others. I like to include figures in a headline when feasible. I like to use the tried-and-true buzz words such as "free," "now," "introducing," "new," etc., and when it makes sense to do so, I like to include a word or a name that may be unfamiliar to a large portion of the audience. I like to use "you," but that's not imperative. The most successful headlines are ones that succeed in the objectives I've outlined above and still tie into the body of the ad itself. But my rule is a sine qua non. If a headline doesn't catch the reader's attention, engaging the reader and luring him or her into the ad, it really doesn't matter much whether it ties in logically with the copy.

Very much the same rules apply, incidentally, to the teaser copy on the outer envelope of a direct mail package.

CHRIS STAGG

I always write headlines last. That's about the only personal rule I always observe.

The function of a headline is twofold. First, it should stop casual readers in their tracks. Second, it should seduce the still inattentive reader into moving on to the beginning of the advertising which follows.

The reason I write the headline after I have written and polished the advertisement is that only then do I know precisely which benefit among many is the strongest. That benefit then becomes the heart of the headline. It fits as naturally as a worn cap on the head.

LINDA WELLS

Here are the rules I *try* to follow.

The headline should sell the bottom line. It should not only promote the product or service but also increase the chances of good pay, encourage further purchases, and enhance the corporate image. Those among the following words that can be used honestly and believably should be used: new, first, exclusive, inside, charter, free, sweeps, bonus, bargain, money-saving, money-making, profitable, time-saving, easy, quick, fast, fun, fashionable, and healthy. Whatever the words, the headline should relate more to the purchaser than to the product; it should stress benefits, not just product specs. It should tell the benefit story clearly, concisely, and colorfully in language the consumer wishes he or she had thought of. It should have the kind of rhythm that makes it easy to remember and repeat. It should be in perfect sync with the illustration. In a perfect world, the headline should be written by a writer and art director team working together from the start.

In a less than perfect world, here are the rules I follow:

1. Pretend you are Dorothy Parker faced with a headline deadline you've got to meet or miss a Round Table lunch.
2. Pretend your copy chief is John Caples.
3. Pretend the agency boss is David Ogilvy.
4. Pretend the marketing consultant is Richard V. Benson.
5. Pretend the client is the Marquis de Sade.
6. Write before you die of fright.

ARTHUR BLACK

How to write a good headline like this one.

1. Don't confuse the copy platform with a headline, but don't ignore the copy platform either. (If you don't have a copy platform, write one.)
2. No puns or plays on words unless you can write out of them.
3. Try to present the experience. Tell the reader what you want him or her to know and do.
4. Avoid passive words. That goes for copy too.
5. Emphasize benefits. Explain product features in terms of benefits.
6. Write as many headlines as you can think of. Then write twenty more. Then write twenty more than that. Then pick out the best of the bunch and try to improve them.
7. Try to answer the unspoken question in every reader's or viewer's mind: "What's in it for me?"
8. Don't try to get a long, complicated story into one long, complicated headline. Better a good provocative short headline supported by a well-thought-out and hard-selling subhead.
9. Listen to what clients say. Don't automatically reject their suggestions.
10. Listen to what clients say. Don't automatically accept their suggestions.
11. Listen to what people complain about. You will learn about the things in their lives which they want improved. Perhaps your product or service can help them.
12. Listen to what people praise. Perhaps your product or service has it.
13. Fight for the headlines you believe in.
14. Put your headlines to the supreme test. If *you* had to pay for the ad to run, would you put the headline on it?
15. If you can't think of a good headline, write the body copy first. Sometimes the headline will come from the text.
16. Edit headlines as well as copy. Cut all unnecessary words.
17. Prepare to abandon all belief systems.
18. Avoid starchy foods.

HEADLINES: THE BOTTOM LINE

These are seven of the best headline writers in the business. Their methods may differ, but they have certain ideas in common. They agree that good headline writing requires total familiarity with the product or service involved. They put great stress on benefits. In their own ways, they all attempt to get "under the skin" or "inside the head" of a prospect. And they all seem prepared to discard the rules when necessary. And that, after all, may be the first rule for writing good headlines.

WHAT DO YOU DO AFTER YOU WRITE THE HEADLINE?

That question has a very simple answer: You start working on the subhead. Each ad has two versions: the one the writer writes and the one the reader reads. The writer pays attention to every single word in the ad, but the reader doesn't. Instead, the reader tends to skim the ad, reading only those elements which catch the eye.

Research seems to support this view. Most readership studies show that the great majority of casual ad readers tend to read only the headline, the subhead or subheads, the picture captions, and the advertiser's company name or slogan. A relatively small percentage of readers, if sufficiently interested and motivated, will go back to the headline and read the entire ad. This means more often than not that the advertising writer must somehow pack the entire story of the ad into just a small fraction of all the words that actually appear in the ad. Thus, the realities of advertising make the subhead a vitally important element in meeting the objectives of the ad. The best advertising writers consider picture captions as another form of subhead, and they put as much care and attention into writing captions as they invest in creating other important elements of an ad.

What Subheads Do

Advertising writers use subheads for a number of different purposes. Subheads can "call out" the benefits and advantages of a product or service. They can highlight a special offer. They can serve as transitions from one copy point to another. If nothing else, they can break long stretches of copy into shorter, more readable chunks.

Should Every Ad Have a Subhead?

For all their virtues and benefits, subheads are not indispensable. Some great advertisements have no subheads because the headlines say it all. Rules serve as guidelines, not rigid doctrine. You have to trust your own talent and judgment.

A Practical Exercise for All Writers of Headlines and Subheads

One of the advertising writers I respect most told me of a helpful exercise he uses to keep his considerable writing skills at their sharpest. He writes "make believe" billboards. As he explains it, "The best billboards use only very short headlines—a few well-chosen words that must work along with a very strong graphic idea." When he finds himself confronted with a complicated copy problem, he tries to isolate the major points and condense them into one good workable billboard headline. He admits that he doesn't always succeed in writing an outstanding billboard line, but he often comes up with some excellent advertising headlines and subheads.

Other Ways to Attract Attention

Print advertising allows for the use of many other devices for attracting attention, telling the story, or selling the product or service. These include eyebrows (lead-in lines over the headline), bursts, and bold paragraph leads. Each serves a legitimate purpose. But we must always remember that sometimes "less is more." One should use these devices with discretion, always keeping in mind the major marketing objectives that govern the advertising effort. A barrage of starbursts and exclamatory statements tends to give an ad the look of a somewhat frenzied "retail clearance sale" announcement. If the strategy calls for that, feel free to indulge in starbursts. But if the client wishes to create an image of elegance and exclusivity, a constellation of starbursts may prove inappropriate.

Writing Headlines for Radio, Television, and Direct Mail

When you stop to think about it, a headline amounts to nothing more than a major idea encapsulated in relatively few words. And the disciplines of good print headline writing translate easily into other media as well. Effective advertising in all media, including TV, almost always begins with "word ideas" that express a solid selling proposition in a novel, original, forceful way.

Where to Put the Headline

At the top, the bottom, or the middle of the ad? Over the illustration or under it? The rule to follow is: Don't follow any rules. Headline placement is a matter of judgment between you and your art director. As long as the copy and the graphics work together to achieve clarity, excitement, and a quick visual grasp of the central idea, the headline can go anywhere.

chapter **32**

ADVERTISING DESIGN AND LAYOUT

Steve Burnett

President
Steve Burnett, Inc.
New York, N. Y.

A good ad sells. It effectively motivates a specific audience to buy a product or service. For an advertising agency, developing an ad or direct mail package is a complex process that requires a well-coordinated group effort. The account group, marketing research team, production and traffic specialists, media planners, copywriters, and art directors all contribute to producing an ad that works for the client.

This chapter will discuss the role of the art director in creating a direct-response ad, a powerful visual communication that persuades an audience to take direct action: to call for a demonstration, to write for further information, or to send in a check. While our examples deal with print ads, the principles apply just as much to direct mail design, with the added dimension of format variations (discussed in another chapter).

In developing a direct-response ad, 90 percent of the art director's task is devoted to reaching a practical solution to a specific creative challenge. The remaining 10 percent involves the technical skill necessary to execute a final mechanical for the camera. Our purpose here is to concentrate on the thought process used by the art director to approach and solve an advertising problem.

This process will be examined in three stages. First, we'll discuss what the art director needs to know in order to begin creating an ad. We'll call this the background. Next, we'll look at many of the strategies and techniques the art director uses in constructing an ad once the background has been established. These will be referred to as building blocks. Finally, we'll examine how the building blocks of a direct-response ad come together to produce a dynamic, compelling sales message which places the audience in a receptive frame of mind from the beginning of the ad to the end. This is known as the buying commitment.

THE BACKGROUND

What the Art Director Needs to Know

The first step in producing an ad is to evaluate all the information necessary to develop an effective selling vehicle.

Figure 32-1 illustrates a series of questions an art director might have about any ad in the beginning of the creative process. At this stage, an ad is little more than a blank sheet of paper. However, once the art director has the answers to these questions, the ad will begin to take shape.

The Product: What Are We Selling? Like any good salesperson, the AD needs accurate product knowledge to sell effectively. The AD relies primarily on the account group for learning exactly what product or service is being offered. Direct client contact also can be extremely helpful in familiarizing the AD with the product.

The USP: Does the Product or Service Have a USP? The ideal characteristic of something being advertised is a unique selling proposition (USP). This simply means that nothing else like the product exists in the marketplace and that it fills a definite consumer need. To advertise effectively in such a case, the art director would do little more than let people know that such a remarkable product is available for immediate purchase. In today's world, however, most products and services have many competitive counterparts. Thus, the USP must be replaced by one or more special advantages which the client feels make the product worth marketing. The art director learns what these special selling points are through the account group or directly from the client.

The Audience: To Whom Are We Talking? To create an effective communication, the art director has to know exactly who the audience is. An ad talks to people. In order to speak their language through copy and the right visual images, it is necessary to have a well-researched demographic profile of who they are and what kind of advertising they are likely to receive favorably. This information generally comes from the agency's research department.

The Print Ad: Why Has a Print Ad Been Selected as the Right Advertising Vehicle to Reach Our Audience? It is important for the AD to know why print has been selected for the ad rather than TV, radio, direct mail, or some other selling medium. For example, if the ad is part of a larger campaign involving a multimedia approach, the AD must relate it to the overall campaign. On the other hand, if print is the only medium of advertising being used, it must be designed to achieve a somewhat different impact. The media selection is the responsibility of the agency's media services group.

1. THE PRODUCT:
What are we selling?
2. THE USP:
Does the product contain a Unique Selling Proposition?
3. THE AUDIENCE:
To whom are we talking?
4. THE PRINT AD:
Why has print been selected as the right advertising vehicle to teach our audience?
5. THE PUBLICATIONS:
In what editorial context will we reach our audience?
6. THE RESPONSE:
What do we want our audience to do?
7. THE CALL:
How will we motivate our audience to respond?
8. THE BUDGET:
How much can we spend on production?
9. THE TECHNIQUES:
What will the ad look like, and how will we achieve this?
10. THE TIMING:
How much time do we have to create the ad?

Figure 32-1 This is what an ad might look like to the art director in the beginning of the creative process. At this stage, the ad is a blank sheet of paper surrounded by a number of important questions which must be answered in order to move the process along.

The Publications: In What Editorial Context Will We Reach Our Audience? If we know our audience, we also know what they read. In fact, media planners today can pinpoint accurately the publications that are best suited to almost any kind of print advertising. They also can determine when that audience will be most receptive to an ad for a specific product or service, e.g., during business hours, during leisure time, etc. The choice of publications then will coincide with this assessment. When the art director knows where an ad will be placed and for what reasons, the ad can be tailored to the context in which it will appear, thus taking full advantage of its surroundings.

The Response: What Action Do We Want Our Audience to Take? A direct-response ad is first and foremost a call to action. The audience generally is asked to call a telephone number, send in a coupon for purchase or for additional information, or request an actual sales visit. The art director must know which of these actions is desired in order to create an ad that leads inevitably to this action as a natural response.

The Call: How Will We Motivate Our Audience to Respond? Once we have defined what product or service is being sold and what response we want to elicit from the audience, these product data are translated into a positive selling strategy by the account group or marketing department. Then it becomes the task of the creative team (art director and copywriter) to mold this strategy into an effective selling communication. At this point, the copywriter often takes the lead and produces a first draft which forms the basis for a preliminary layout of the ad.

The Budget: How Much Money Can We Spend? A creative budget must be defined clearly before the art director's work can begin. Once costs are established firmly, creative concepts can be recommended within the limitations of the budget.

The Techniques: What Will the Ad Look Like, and How Will We Achieve This? Once the budget is fixed, the art director can begin to make preliminary choices of technique. This usually means deciding on a four-color, two-color, or black-and-white ad. It also involves the selection of a visual approach, i.e., the choice of photography, illustration, line drawing, or other graphic elements. Finally, various typefaces may be considered in terms of how they will enhance the overall look of the ad. Such choices may be guided in part by existing ads or current client image. At this stage, of course, no final decisions are made. However, the art director develops an overview of technical limitations or specific client preferences during these initial discussions.

The Timing: How Much Time Do We Have to Create the Ad? Sometimes almost everything hinges on timing. If an ad absolutely must be ready within a week or less to meet a competitive emergency, a seasonal sales cycle, or some other deadline, all other considerations may become secondary. The choice of techniques—in fact, the entire creative process—often depends on how much time is available in which to produce the ad. It is extremely important, therefore, for the art director to know exactly when the ad has to be ready for insertion.

Answering the questions above provides a strong framework for beginning to build an ad. Let's discuss what the individual building blocks of a good ad are, showing how each depends on the answers to these questions for its form and content.

THE BUILDING BLOCKS

A Direct-Response Ad Calls for a Specific Strategy

A direct-response ad is unique in that it contains a direct link between the company running the ad and the audience, accompanied by a definite call to immediate action. With other forms of advertising, the reader may be asked to buy a product or service at some undefined time in the future, usually at an unspecified retail outlet. Some ads may not even require the reader to take any action but simply to remember the company being advertised as a leader in its field.

The direct-response ad, however, attempts to create an actual, immediate selling situation. This may involve the following elements:

1. Asking for the order in the form of a check or a "bill me later" commitment.
2. Soliciting a request for further information.

Either response may be generated through a coupon, a telephone call, or another means of direct contact.

Constructing a Direct-Response Ad

The elements most often found in a direct-response ad are a headline, a visual element, body copy, a concluding statement, and an audience response mechanism. For a direct-response ad to be effective, these elements must work together to generate the appropriate audience response.

The Visual Element. Assuming that an ad has a specific visual element, this is the first thing a reader generally sees. Some ads create visual impact through type only and thus don't require an additional graphic element. Usually there is a visual element: a picture in the form of a photograph, an illustration, or some other graphic element. The primary purpose of the visual is to arrest the reader's attention immediately and create the desire for a more detailed examination of the ad. The visual element appeals to the audience's intuitive or emotional senses. Thus, impact should be the primary focus of the visual.

In developing the visual, the art director must take into consideration not only the "message" which is to be communicated visually but the limitations of the client's budget and the timing.

The Headline. The first verbal communication with the reader occurs through the boldface words of the headline. The purpose of the headline is to create intellectual rather than intuitive or emotional impact. There are certain words which elicit a definite emotional response, e.g., "free," "new," and "exciting." Most readers perceive and react to these words in the same way they would react to a visual designed to achieve the same effect. This is because the words have taken on symbolic, nonverbal overtones. They literally have become pictures.

Most words, however, do not evoke this spontaneous emotional reaction. Rather, they produce an intellectual response which may take a moment or two longer to achieve. For this reason, short, simple headlines generally are regarded as more effective than those which are longer and more complex.

The headline is generally a reflection of the product's USP if it has one or of how the consumer will derive substantial benefit from using the product. The headline even may serve as the call to action. Taken together, the visual element and the headline should lead the audience into reading the rest of the ad.

The headline is not, of course, the responsibility of the art director. However, a good art director should be able to tell a well-written headline from a poor one and be able to give constructive criticism when necessary.

The Body Copy. Like the headline, the copy is not the specific responsibility of the art director, but knowing good copy from bad can help an art director consistently produce the best ads possible. The standards for well-written copy are virtually the same as those for a well-designed ad.

1. Get to the point as quickly as possible.
2. Talk to the assumed audience, using language and tone which are designed to appeal specifically to them.
3. Be sure the line of thought leads directly and persuasively to the call to action.

In judging the merits of copy, the art director can bring to bear all knowledge about the product or service which has been obtained during client or internal staff meetings. Playing the role of the reader, the art director can decide whether the copy seems to create a climate in which to act. This subjective test is often the most accurate in assessing whether the copy works.

The Concluding Statement. This may be the final sentence or paragraph of the body copy. It also may be one or two well-chosen words in boldface type at the bottom of the page. No matter what form it takes, however, the concluding statement—sometimes called the tag or tag line—is one of the unique characteristics of direct-response ads. The concluding statement leaves no doubt in the consumer's mind about what to do after reading the ad: Take positive action. "Buy now," "Call today," and "Write for our free brochure" are good examples.

The concluding statement is a definite call to action designed to spur the consumer into buying or at least finding out more. In fact there is often a three-way link among the visual element of an ad, the headline, and the tag line in which the three taken together are designed to motivate the appropriate audience response even if the body copy isn't read.

The Response Mechanism. In a direct-response ad, the call to action asks the audience to use a response mechanism immediately. Most often they are asked to complete a coupon and send it in or to call a toll-free telephone number. Taking either of these actions will get them an actual product or service, a brochure or other form of further information, or a direct contact from a salesperson.

Many experts believe the coupon to be the most important element of a direct-response ad and pay a great deal of attention to its design. The theory behind this is quite sound. You not only want your audience to respond to your ad, you also must make it as easy and convenient for them to respond as possible.

Ads That Flow Freely Pull Plenty

A good direct-response ad is more than the sum of its parts. While each element must be developed carefully, it is the whole ad that ultimately generates the desired response. A well-designed direct-response ad produces a dynamic movement of positive energy from the beginning of the ad to the end. This is the concept of flow. Flow sometimes is defined as the synergistic interaction of the elements of an ad to produce the desired effect. It is a continuous action which starts when the consumer first sees an ad and experiences a positive reaction.

The flow continues from the visual and headline of the ad directly into the consumer's decision to read the body copy. Within the body copy are many small decision points which bring the reader effortlessly to the concluding statement or call to action and then ask for the order. If the flow has been established effectively in the consumer's mind and there is enough interest in the product or service being offered, the final decision will be to respond positively to the ad: to buy the product, to call for a demonstration, or to request further information.

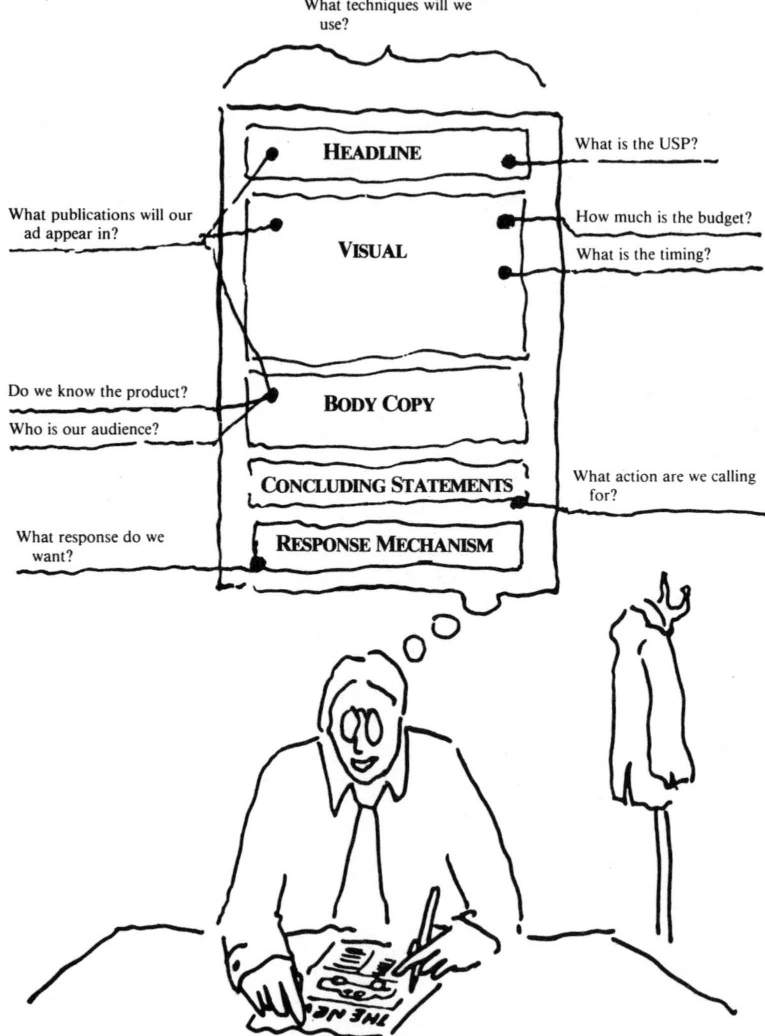

Figure 32-2 In this diagram the elements contained in most direct-response ads are shown as they relate to the preliminary question that was asked in the beginning of this chapter.

THE BUYING COMMITMENT

Now that we've discussed the various elements of a direct-response ad, let's look at how an art director actually uses these building blocks in creating a strong commitment on the reader's part to buy the product or service being offered. See Figure 32-2.

Bringing the Elements of the Ad Together

As was discussed in the previous section, most direct-response ads contain a headline, a visual, body copy, a concluding statement or tag line, and a response mechanism. Once the copy has been written, a preliminary layout can be made which will provide a general idea of how the art director feels the ad should look.

In creating the layout, one of the first decisions the art director makes is whether the product visual should be a photograph or an illustration. Many studies have shown that photographs attract attention far more effectively than illustrations. There may, of course, be specific circumstances where a photograph does not serve the needs of an ad adequately. The creation of a sense of fantasy, a special mood, a period of history, or some other subject difficult to capture photographically may be better achieved through illustration. However, for the most part, well-planned photos are more effective in communicating visual messages.

Once the visual has been selected, the next step is to develop a comprehensive, or comp. The comp should look as much like the actual ad as possible. If timing is crucial, this step sometimes is eliminated and a mechanical is made directly from the preliminary layout.

However, it is almost always in the client's interest to see a comp first. No one really knows what an ad will look like from a layout. From a comp, however, it's easy to imagine the final results. It is in the development of the comp that the art director makes most of the creative decisions that determine the success of the ad as a visual selling vehicle. With a comp, the client can make any desired changes before the final type and art are in place. This is far more economical and efficient than resetting type, reshooting a photo, or redrawing an illustration.

A Dynamic Ad Generates a Dynamic Response

The purpose of an ad is to create a lasting effect, generate excitement, and move the audience to action. If the art director's job were merely to place the elements of an ad in some logical order on the page, the ad might look like the one shown in Figure 32-3.

For Direct Response, Two Dimensions Are Not Enough

In Figure 32-3, the elements are all present, but they're flat and lifeless. The reader probably will glance at the ad, turn the page, and forget that the ad ever existed, even if it's for a product or service he or she would like to have. One reason for

Figure 32-3 Placed in logical order only, the elements of a direct-response ad have a flat, two-dimensional appearance.

this is that such an ad has only two dimensions. What is really needed here is for the ad to jump right off the page and then lead the reader deeper into itself until the only way to respond properly is to fill in the coupon or call the telephone number. To achieve this, we have to create two additional dimensions to the ad: the third dimension of depth and the fourth dimension of flow.

Creating the Third Dimension: Depth

To give an ad the effect of jumping off the page, the art director first should make the most important, exciting, or unique elements in the ad the primary visual focus. The headline should stand out strongly. The photograph should be shot for maximum dimensionality, creating the illusion that the product can almost be touched. Finally the tag line and telephone number should read almost as a part of the headline. These three elements should be immediately accessible to the audience at a glance. They are the foreground, or the primary layer, of the ad.

If the reader's decision at this point is to be drawn into the ad, a definite secondary layer, or middle ground, also must be created. This may consist first of a secondary headline specifically designed to draw the reader into this next layer. Then individual subheads may be used to serve as shorthand introductions to what is contained in the body copy. The coupon also exists in this second layer.

Once the audience has scanned the foreground and has examined the middle ground, in which the coupon has become an enticement, the decision may be made to act.

But before the response is assured, the reader may need to be led even deeper into the ad. For this, the third layer is provided in the form of body copy ready to spell out all details, answer any questions or objections, and redirect the reader's attention to the tag line: the call to action.

Creating the Fourth Dimension: Flow

By creating the multilayered third dimension of depth, the art director is activating in the reader's mind the fourth dimension: flow. Flow can be thought of as the time spent by the audience in reading an ad as determined by how dynamically one element of the ad flows into another. To ensure this dynamic flow, each individual element in the ad must exist only as a part of the whole. Type must be chosen for effortless readability and for maintaining the mood and style of the ad. White space or negative space must serve as a precise grid which holds the entire ad together. Too much white space can cause an otherwise well-designed ad to fall completely apart by confusing the flow.

Finally, the response must be effortless to act on. The coupon must be easy to complete, easy to cut out from the ad, and easy to mail. In fact, the coupon should be designed as a self-contained ad for the product, restating the selling message and the call to action. Ample space must be provided for filling in the necessary information, and all audience options must be clear and attractive.

Once these goals have been achieved by the art director, the ad will have both the dimension of depth and the dimension of flow, as illustrated in Figure 32-4.

Special Format Considerations

Each advertising format presents its own special challenges. Newspapers, for example, generally limit the choice of color to one or at most two, and newspaper size is usually quite large. Thus, an art director must evaluate how the elements of an ad can be made to work together effectively in this area.

It may be decided that a separate insert is best suited to the needs of a particular campaign. In such a case, the art director can create an ad, a booklet, a mailer, or any other format which is desirable within timing and budget limitations. No matter which format is chosen, however, the principles of creating depth and flow may be applied to help create in the reader's mind a climate for responding positively and immediately to the product or service offered.

Clear Thinking: The Key to Designing an Effective Ad

The process of creating an ad often is seen as ephemeral or mysterious. To the professional art director, however, it is a precise craft which combines creative intuition with clear thinking.

As has been discussed, the art director first defines the creative problem by analyzing the background. Once this is accomplished, the art director constructs the building blocks of the individual selling vehicle. Finally, these building blocks are synthesized into a multidimensional, dynamic ad whose sole purpose is to generate a buying commitment from the target audience.

Every good art director uses an approach similar to this every time an ad or mailing piece is created. Since products, services, ad agencies, clients, and selling

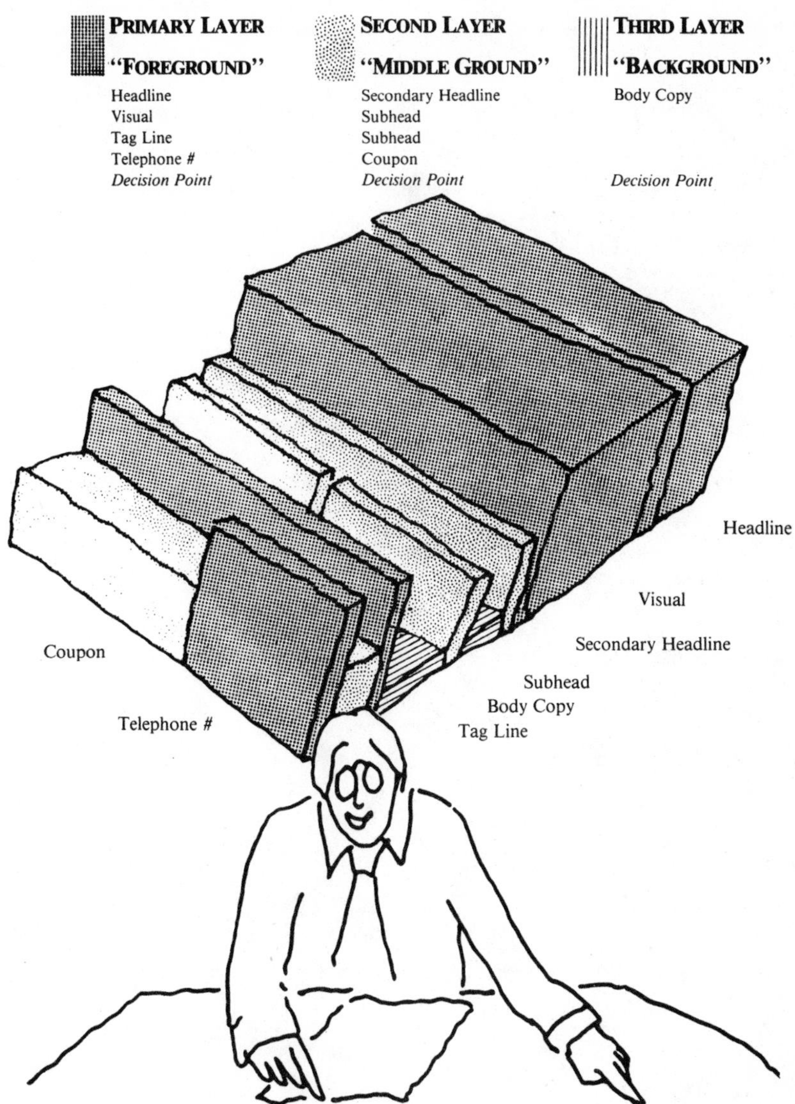

Figure 32-4 A well-designed direct-response ad consists of three distinct layers of perception of depth and a fourth dimension of dynamic flow. Each layer becomes a decision point for the reader to probe deeper. The decision to take action can occur at each layer.

messages are unique, the individual elements vary with each situation. But the clear, step-by-step thought process remains essentially the same. Clear, well-defined thinking results in clear, well-designed communications. It is this ability to think clearly and intuitively that ultimately distinguishes a fine art director from all the rest.

chapter 33

RESPONSE DEVICE VARIATIONS

C. James Schaefer

President
The DR Group Inc.
New York, N. Y.

William C. Allen

Senior Vice President
and Creative Director
The DR Group Inc.
Boston, Mass.

FROM MATCHBOOKS TO NIEMAN-MARCUS, FROM TAKE-ONES TO TIME-LIFE

Almost every day, every literate person is exposed to one or possibly several direct marketing messages, each complete with a response device. You pick up a matchbook and see a black-and-white line cut of a pretty girl. "Copy me," reads the copy, "and we'll see if you're talented enough to make it at our art school. Just copy the sketch, fill in your name and address below, and return this cover."

You've just enjoyed a fine dinner at a good restaurant, and at the checkout counter there's a little box full of folders. "Take one," says the headline. American Express, with subtle timing, is telling you that you could have charged your dinner. Here's an application for an Amex Card.

If you travel home by bus or subway, you may be exposed to another take-one: a card box full of folders offering information about the opportunities in computer programming or nursing or welding.

You reach home and start to read your mail. Nieman-Marcus is beguiling you with a handsome Christmas gift catalog complete with bound-in order form to make ordering easy. Then there's Time-Life Books with another colorful mailing. After you have a chance to read all about it, you put the reply card aside in case you want to order later.

Importance of the Reply Device: You're Asking for the Order

Basic to the concept of most direct marketing is the reply device, which is something to make the prospect take the action you want: answer a survey, send a contribution, take out a membership, request a booklet, or place an order. Making an advertising mailing without a response device, unless it's pure advertising to a select list, would be like employing a salesperson who never asks for the order.

Today, for many mail marketers, the response device has become virtually a highly sophisticated art form. It wasn't always like this, however.

In the beginning was the reply card, a functional, no-nonsense piece of card stock printed in one color, or, in the case of a space ad, a tiny coupon. If you wanted to order the corset or consumption cure or subscribe to the magazine, you weren't pampered with free postage. You had to find and lick and stick a stamp. If you clipped a coupon from a space ad, you also had to find an envelope. A pencil or pen also had to be located for writing in your home address.

In those unsophisticated days, when mail marketing was a novelty rather than an industry, the office clerk could be assigned the task of creating the reply device. There wasn't the competition for the prospect's dollar that exists today. When retailers were few and far between, to be invited to order by mail was almost flattering and certainly a real and appreciated convenience.

Response Devices Can Be Creative Too

Competition was inevitable, though, and gradually the mailing "package," including the response device, improved. The government cooperated by offering the business reply card and envelope. In fact, without this "postage-will-be-paid-by" concept, it's difficult to believe that mail marketing ever could have come so far, so fast.

When imaginations went to work on reply devices specifically, in addition to creating the basic package, some wonderful innovative ideas emerged. A few were so creative and original that they were granted patents or copyrights.

One example is the Reply-O-Letter and others of similar design. A filled-in business reply card slides out of a built-in sleeve on the letter, which is cut out to show the filled-in name and address. To respond to the offer, the prospect simply pulls out the card from the sleeve and drops it in the mail. Over the years, millions of such letters have been mailed, and a multitude of tests have been made to determine their effectiveness versus other reply techniques. The bottom line, of course, is cost per reply and, if applicable, cost per order (CPO). But beyond that, these pull-out reply ideas presented a welcome creative change of pace.

At first, self-mailers (mailings without envelopes) often came with tear-off business reply cards. Since there was no reply envelope, this limited their usefulness to non-mail-order situations, such as requests for booklets or samples or more information, except for pure credit card or "bill me" applications.

Later, self-mailers appeared with business reply envelopes inside, stuck on with an adhesive wafer; this was a hand operation which of course added to the cost. Now, with more sophisticated printing and folding techniques, business reply envelopes can be manufactured into the self-mailer at the time it is printed, gumming and all. Replyvelope is one name for them.

It's a Jungle Out There Now

These days, it's not at all unusual for mail-responsive individuals (people who are on a number of lists because of their past record of responding to mail) to receive several direct mail packages in a single day.

Obviously, it's not possible to subscribe to every publication being promoted, order every item so enticingly described, respond to every charity appeal, or even send for every free booklet or catalog. For the prospect, there's a veritable embarrassment of riches. But for the mail marketer, it's a jungle.

To get attention and action for your product or proposition, you have to be increasingly imaginative and innovative. That includes not only the basic mailing package but all the components, right down to the all-important reply device.

A POTPOURRI OF RESPONSE TECHNIQUES AND TIPS

Despite all the colorful and imaginative response formats emerging in recent years, the simple reply card or reply envelope still is fundamental and probably the most appropriate for the vast majority of goods and services marketed by mail. Even so, often there are opportunities to dress up the reply card or envelope to make it more effective when it's appropriate to do so. Be alert for these opportunities. The key word is "appropriate."

For example, a publisher offering a new cookbook by mail might use a reply card or envelope with printing superimposed on a background of a lightly tinted tablecloth. Another publisher offering a new secretary's handbook might use a card or envelope with ruled lines suggesting a stenographer's notebook. An investment advisory service might have a reply card with a toned-down background of stock market quotations.

Any one of these graphic ideas can be appropriate and relevant for a particular situation. It's a matter of association. However, it may not be in character for the *Wall Street Journal* to send out a lavish color brochure soliciting subscriptions or even to use a colorful reply card in a letter mailing. After all, there's no color in the *Journal* except in the writing. There aren't even any black-and-white photos.

Even with such restraining conditions, it's still possible to put imagination to work on the graphics to get the reply device noticed, the objective being, of course, to increase response and lower the cost per order or inquiry by giving the reply device "implied value."

Although we've referred to relevance in reply card design and graphics, relevance isn't always essential. Sometimes a "universal" idea comes along, something attention-getting which can be adapted to many different situations. For example, facsimile IBM-type cards have been used effectively by a number of mailers even when the perforations had no useful function, perhaps because they somehow made the card look official. Round punch holes, also with no real function, have been used to dress up a reply card, with interesting results. Stock certificate borders, check paper, notary-type seals, facsimile checks, and even real checks (for a nominal sum) also have been used to make a response device appear to be valuable.

The Mailing Label Technique

For an interesting change of pace, consider using a mailing label instead of a reply card. It's certainly relevant, provided that the offered product or literature can be sent for with the label. In lead-getting promotion, there's a psychological factor working in your favor because the label itself dramatizes the fact that no salesperson will call. In situations where you want as many booklet requests as possible, this technique can be especially effective.

Several options are available when it comes to the mailing label format. The label can be loose in the offering letter, along with a business reply envelope for sending it back, in which case the prospect has to fill in his or her name and address. It probably is better to use a filled-in label with a tear-off stub attached, with name and address showing through the outgoing window envelope or die cut in the catalog. Or the label (filled-in) can be built into the top or bottom of a letter, with perforations to make removal easy.

It's not necessary to gum the back of the label since most readers won't even notice. Nor is it necessary actually to use the label when it's returned. Some firms prefer to affix their own. But the label format has served a useful function.

Stamps Are Still Here

Without the "postage-will-be-paid-by" concept, direct mail marketing probably would not have become the big business it is today. However, adhesive postage stamps are still with us and under the right conditions still can play a useful part in response getting.

You may have opened a letter, say, from *Time* magazine, and found in the middle of the page a stuck-on first class stamp. Instead of sending your subscription renewal card back with a check in a business reply envelope, you were asked to remove the stamp from the letter and apply it to the plain self-addressed envelope. This is a real attention getter.

Other mailers have picked up the stamp-stuck-to-letter technique, not necessarily just for subscription renewals and often with interesting results. Sometimes a current commemorative stamp is used instead of the common variety for added attention and impact.

Given today's postage rates, this idea costs a lot more than it used to, but there are occasions when it should be considered. For example, if you're making an important survey to a rather limited group and it's important that you get back as many responses as possible, a first class stamp affixed to a self-addressed envelope (or a premetered envelope) will show the recipient that you really care.

The Token Technique: Fun and Games

Some years ago, some genius came up with the concept that an individual responding to a mailing should really participate, taking some action beyond merely checking the correctness of name and address on a reply before sending it back. The theory was that more time would be spent with the reply card in hand, and response therefore would increase.

Accordingly, a reply card was provided with a stub on which was a perforated token. To respond to the offer, the reader was asked to punch out the token and place it in the slot provided on the reply card before tearing off the card and dropping it in the mail.

Some skeptics derided the idea, calling it a flash in the pan that might work once. As it turned out, those who came to scoff remained to play, for the participation concept proved highly effective and still is used widely.

Some thought the idea might work on unsophisticated consumers but not on business executives. They were wrong. Over the years, hundreds of thousands of business types, some accustomed to making million-dollar decisions, have made the decision to move a little token or adhesive sticker from here to there.

Less dramatic perhaps than tokens but still in the realm of involvement devices is the address label, with the reader being asked to peel it from the envelope or letter and affix it to a business reply card.

Tokens Can Be Beautiful Too

The first tokens and stickers were rather plain. Perhaps they contained words such as "money-saving offer," but the graphics weren't particularly colorful or relevant to the offer. Then imaginations went to work. Money-oriented mailers, appropriately enough, used a token in the form of a cardboard silver dollar. Publications and subscription services have reproduced in miniature a full-color cover of the first issue to be removed and inserted in the usual slot provided.

In a variation of the token technique, book and record clubs have reproduced full-color record covers or book jackets in miniature in perforated sheet form. To order, the reader-prospect is asked to tear off and return the desired books or records represented by the miniatures. Sometimes, instead of the miniatures being reproduced on card stock, a sheet of perforated gummed stickers is used.

It appears that tokens and their spinoffs have come of age. In the right situation with the right "product," they can be highly effective as reply devices, enough to more than justify their extra cost.

RETURNING TO BASICS

Although it's easy to get carried away by the excitement of colorful and original response devices, they're not always necessary or even appropriate. Moreover, people can get surfeited with color. Sometimes a Spartan-looking reply card in an otherwise unexciting-looking mailing can provide a welcome and effective change, provided, of course, that the offer is a good one.

A major publishing house backed off in a recent mail promotion; in fact, they reversed direction and sent out an envelope-enclosed mailing with no letter at all, just a gift/savings voucher. But most mailed reply devices need a transmittal letter in order to generate a satisfactory response.

Sweepstakes Promotions: Yes or No?

There's at least a latent gambling instinct in most people. When it doesn't cost anything to enter a sweepstakes with the possibility of winning $50,000 or a trip around the world, it's pretty hard to resist. Thus, it's not surprising that sweepstakes promotions have become popular in direct marketing.

Aside from the prize money, these promotions can be expensive when it comes to production, especially if business reply envelopes are enclosed. They're usually not because of today's postage rates. Instead, the reader is asked to return the numbered sweepstakes entry bearing name and address in one of two envelopes supplied. These are plain envelopes, and the reader has to put on a first class stamp.

To enter the sweepstakes and order the magazine, book, or records, the tickets sometimes are returned in an envelope plainly marked "yes." If the individual wants to enter the sweepstakes without subscribing or ordering, the tickets are returned in the envelope marked "no." That way, of course, the sponsors can process new subscriptions or new orders quickly and avoid paying for any response.

Sometimes the yes or no technique is useful in promotions other than sweepstakes in which there are no numbered tickets to be returned, perhaps just a yes or no card. In this case, the cards can be ordinary reply cards. If there's some good reason for returning one card or the other in an envelope, it can be a window envelope, cut out so that the word "yes" or the word "no" shows through.

Negative Options

Occasionally there's a situation where it's desirable to ask the reader to return a reply card only if the item being offered isn't wanted. This is tricky, though, and can cause problems. For example, if many people on the list claim they were out of town and didn't get the notice, they will refuse to pay for the item which was sent automatically and will return it at the company's expense. Become familiar with negative option selling, including its legal ramifications, before using it for mail-order applications. Proceed with caution.

The Temporary Membership Card

For service organizations such as automobile clubs soliciting memberships or insurance companies offering health or accident insurance by mail, one useful and often highly effective device is the temporary membership card. The copy suggests that this temporary card is good until a certain date and will give the reader all the privileges of membership "until we are able to process your application."

Obviously, this technique has a sound psychological basis. In effect, you're already a member or you have insurance protection as soon as you send in your check.

Frequently the temporary membership card is on a stub attached to the filled-in reply card or application. A more dramatic if more expensive way is to use an embossed plastic card affixed to the application.

Dial 800

Devices such as temporary membership cards tend to appeal to the nonprocrastinators, or those who like instant action and gratification, the same people who prefer to call an 800 number rather than fill out an order form. They think they're getting faster action, and ordinarily they are. Many direct marketing firms arrange for a toll-free 800 number and feature it prominently not only in their print ads, TV and radio commercials, and descriptive folders but also on the order coupon or other reply device. Sometimes the combination of an 800 number with reply mail will increase response substantially over the response pulled by either technique used alone.

Operators working on 800 numbers obviously must be thoroughly familiar with the product or service being offered, able to answer questions with real conviction. But more than that, they must be capable "closers," able to come up with the right buzz words that lead to the order. In the case of circulation promotion, they must be able to get a certain percentage of prospects to "trade up."

Because the operation is so highly specialized, firms have been set up to handle 800 number inquiries exclusively. The operators, who are pros to begin with, are made familiar with the service or product. A number of telemarketing firms have found such an arrangement with an outside company to be more satisfactory than handling the 800 number operation internally.

Provided that you're willing to hire and train individuals with the proper potential and qualifications, it's possible to handle the dial 800 number setup within your own organization. This has one advantage. During intervals when the operators aren't handling 800 number inquiries, they can be calling nonrespondents, or individuals who haven't sent back a reply device or made an 800 number call. Telemarketing has become such a specialized form of direct marketing that it sometimes is considered a new advertising medium. The telephone company can help you when you're in need of professional advice.

THE RIGHT WORDS CAN WORK WONDERS ON RESPONSE DEVICES

Perhaps more than other advertising writers, those who work in direct marketing have a special reason for agonizing as they search for the elusive right words. They know that their work is going to be judged on the basis of results, not on how many awards are received but on how many reply devices, including checks and "bill-me's," show up in the morning mail.

The wording on the reply card or coupon needs as much care and attention as the copy for other parts of the mailings or print advertisements.

Which sounds better on a response device, "Enclosed is my check for $35 covering membership in ________" or "I accept your invitation to join the ________ Society"? The second example suggests that you're special and have been singled out and invited to join. In the first example, the first few words are all about money; you're reminded of what it's going to cost you. If you write the offer like the second example, you'll help your bottom line.

Another example of reply device creativity was occasioned by the resentment most publishers feel about the impact of postage rates on subscription costs. Although it's been common practice for many years for mail-order firms to add a charge for postage and handling, magazine publishers generally haven't done so. However, following one recent boost in postage rates, *Reader's Digest* decided to act. Determined apparently to make their basic subscription rate seem as low as possible, they pointed a finger at the post office. Their reply cards began to read something like this: "Please renew my subscription for $9.97 plus $0.96 postage."

Some mail marketers have used reply cards gimmicked up with overprinted facsimile hand stamps reading "credit OK," "confirmed by," etc., all with facsimile initials. How effective such additions are is hard to say. In most cases, they probably do no harm. But for maximum effectiveness, be sure it's truthful before you write it.

Trade-Up Techniques

Suppose you've just opened a mailing from a magazine offering a year's subscription for $11.95. The promotional letter was persuasive. It sold you on subscribing, and now the reply card is right in front of you, ready to mail. But at the bottom of the card you see the words, "If you prefer a 2-year subscription for $19.95, please check here." You ponder just long enough for the 2-year saving to register. Then you check the box. The reply device with proper wording has scored again. Without a penny of extra cost, it's brought in a 2-year subscription instead of a 1-year subscription.

Look for these opportunities to trade up. Even when the option isn't mentioned elsewhere in the mailing, make a trade-up offer on the reply device. For example, the deluxe edition of a book, with special binding and perhaps with the name stamped in gold on the cover, may cost $5 more than the regular trade edition.

Sometimes the major emphasis on the reply device, just as in the sales letter, is on the basic offer, as with the 1-year subscription. The longer-term mention is almost an afterthought. However, after many tests, some mailers have discovered that equal emphasis on the reply device, with side-by-side check boxes for 1-year and 2-year subscriptions, has brought more 2-year subscribers than are gained when the long-term option is subordinated.

Another option for reply card wording is the "trade-down." For example, if the basic subscription offer is 1-year for $20.95, this is featured. But below, in smaller type, the prospect also is offered a 6-month trial subscription at a somewhat higher pro rata cost. This can be especially useful for new publications with no track record.

Using the Reply Device for Mission Control

Getting leads for sales people certainly is one important mission for direct marketing. A popular and effective method for doing this is by offering a booklet in a space ad or a direct mailing. But the type of booklet being offered and the words on the reply device are important in controlling the quality and quantity of leads.

Sometimes quality of leads is more important than quantity, and sometimes the reverse is true. In any case, the response device, whether it's a coupon in a space ad or a reply card in a mailing piece, can be used to control and qualify response. It's a matter of careful wording.

For example, a manufacturer of security equipment with a large and capable sales force may want as many leads as possible. The reply device might say, "Please send me your helpful booklet '16 Danger Spots to Check Before Your Building Can Be Secure.' " There is no mention of equipment. The prospect who replies will indeed be getting some helpful hints, followed up at the back of the booklet with a pitch for the product.

On the other hand, if only a relatively few well-qualified leads are wanted, the offer on the reply device could read, "Please send me your helpful booklet along with full information and prices on your Model 417 Frammis."

Perhaps the ultimate in lead qualification would be a coupon or other reply device not mentioning a helpful booklet at all and reading something like this: "I want to order the Model 417 Frammis at $1175. Please have a representative confirm my order right away."

Testing

The need for constant testing is inherent in the entire process of direct marketing, including the testing of response devices.

Over the years, thousands of tests have been conducted dealing with reply techniques alone. Few firm conclusions have endured consistently. In fact, the great truth of today can be the big question mark of tomorrow.

But in most cases, is it more effective to provide a business reply envelope for returning the reply card than simply to furnish a business reply card alone? Most tests indicate that except in special cases, the extra cost of providing an envelope isn't justified. Obviously, an envelope must be included in any mail-order situation or when the reader is asked to provide confidential information.

Speaking of envelope tests, is one color better than another? Some mailers operate on the theory that recommends using any color except white.

Does an envelope printed in two colors bring back more requests or orders than a one-color printing? Ordinarily, the extra cost isn't justified unless the second color is used with imagination to create, say, a certain pattern effect relating to the proposition.

Almost every variation of response device technique warrants testing to determine what works best in your marketplace. About the only thing you can take at face value without a test is that you do need a response device if you expect a satisfactory response, whether it be sales leads, payments, or customer orders.

A Checklist of Tested Response Device Variations

1. Self-mailer with tear-off reply card
2. Self-mailer with plain reply card and business reply envelope
3. Pull-out card
3. Business reply card showing through window in envelope-enclosed letter mailing
5. Return-the-letter technique (fill-in on letter) with business reply envelope enclosed
6. Letter fill-in at bottom (tear off perforated bottom and return in business reply envelope)
7. Return the filled-in mailing label
8. Token technique (with sticker variations)
9. Sweepstakes technique
10. 800 number
11. Return card only if you don't want the item being promoted (negative option)
12. Premetered envelope or first class postage stamp for returning envelope, either stuck to letter, ready to remove and affix or already affixed to reply envelope.
13. Pressure-sensitive address label to be peeled off and applied to reply card

chapter **34**

DIRECT MAIL ENVELOPES

Ed McLean

Direct Marketing Copy
Ghent, N. Y.

USES OF DIRECT MAIL

To create more effective direct mail envelopes, it is necessary to understand the various uses of direct mail. The majority of those who use direct mail use it for indirect response: unkeyed advertising or sales promotion.

Manufacturers and distributors employ direct mail to promote new lines or deals. With mailings of advertising reprints and specification sheets, they seek to impress and influence dealers or decision makers in business, engineering, and other professions.

Service firms use direct mail to inform prospects and remind clients about their services. Many of these firms get good results with quarterly newsletters, publicity sheets, and success story brochures mailed with a covering note.

The largest category of mailers—retailers—use direct mail to promote sales and item "specials" to their trading areas. Newsprint shoppers, broadsides, and self-mailers often are favored by these retailers over the traditional direct mail package. Their goal is to motivate as many "occupants" and "box holders" as possible to visit their stores or showrooms.

If a reply form or coupon is used in these indirect-response mailings, it rarely is keyed. Even when it is, the number of forms or coupons mailed back is considered secondary to the larger purpose of advertising and sales promotion.

Note: All the illustrations in this chapter were supplied by Ed McLean, editor and publisher of *Direct Marketing Copy*.

When put to work in this way, the direct mail package has two major elements:

The outer envelope or, in the case of a self-mailer, the outer panels
The message

In advertising and sales promotion direct mail, the message is simple and usually brief. When copy is used on the outer envelope or on the outer panels of a self-mailer, it generally announces.

For many mailers, however, an announcement is not enough. They require a direct response from their mailings. Thus, they add a third major element to their direct mail packages and self-mailers:

The method of reply

When a mailer's main goal is to pull as many replies as possible at a reasonable cost per reply, the message cannot be quite as simple as in advertising and sales promotion direct mail. And it often must be lengthy, for the message now has to perform two tasks.

Task 1

The message must express in words and pictures (and sometimes in sound) the potential benefits the reader can reap by

- Purchasing the product or service offered
- Contributing to a certain cause
- Accepting membership in a club or association
- Completing a mail questionnaire
- Enrolling in a course
- Attending a seminar or other meeting

These benefits may be tangible, involving good quality, advantageous price, multiple uses, increased earnings, or greater productivity. Or they may be intangible, providing convenience, peace of mind, knowledge, personal satisfaction, or a sense of accomplishment.

Task 2

The message also must express the offer the mailer makes to the reader. The offer is a carefully structured stimulus or set of stimuli that encourages the reader to respond favorably immediately or to make a firm decision to do so at a more convenient time. One stimulus may consist of a deadline (offer expiration date) or a premium for prompt response. Another may be a special deal: "two for the price of one," "your first 30 days of membership free," or "three cassettes free when you join and agree to purchase three more at club members' prices in your first year of membership." Still another stimulus may be created by expressing the mailer's confidence with a money-back guarantee that is also a sporting proposition: "If after 1 year of receiving your monthly issues of *Direct Marketing Copy*, your own direct marketing copy is not pulling at least 25 percent better than before, send me a written statement to that effect and I will refund your entire 1-year subscription payment in full, promptly and without question."

The message is contained in the letter and in one, several, or all of the following enclosures:

Reply form
Brochure, flier, or prospectus
Catalog or fact sheet
Buckslip
Lift letter
Pop-up or gimmick
Sample or swatch
Plastic sound sheet
Article reprint

The message should be summarized in the letter and on the reply form. In some mailings, there may be no reply coupon or form, "yes-no" tokens, or money-back guarantee stub. Instead, the mailer may offer only instructions to initial and return the sales letter or to order by telephone. Whatever the method of reply may be, it should be considered carefully and tested to see whether it is the best one for the market and the message.

Each of the three major elements plays a key role in the success of a direct-response mailing. Their relationship to one another may be expressed in a simple pyramid.

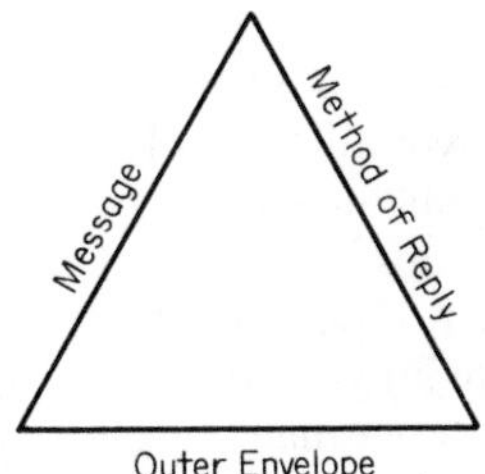

The supporting base of the pyramid and of every mailing is the outer envelope. If it is not effective, even the most persuasive message and method of reply will fail.

The outer envelope is the first thing a direct mail recipient sees. In many cases, it is the only part of the package that is seen. Why? Because a certain percentage of direct mail packages are tossed away unopened by busy or distracted customers and prospects or by intermediaries such as receptionists and mail clerks.

There are no recent studies of how high this "toss-out percentage" is in the United States and Canada. Research for the British Post Office (BPO) shows that 3 percent of people in the United Kingdom who receive direct mail at work say they don't open it. In the same study, 90 percent of those questioned said they like getting direct mail so long as it is relevant to their own interests.

It is probable that a larger number of Britons than 3 out of 100 do not open every piece of direct mail they receive, especially if the immediate perception they have of an outer envelope is that it doesn't contain something that is relevant to their own interests.

Even assuming that the BPO figures hold true for the United States and Canada (it is possible that the toss-out percentage here is greater), there can be no doubt that the written or unwritten statement an outer envelope makes to the reader plays a significant role in whether it is opened.

The direct mail outer envelope is equivalent in impact and importance to the headline and overall look of an advertisement. Both try to communicate quickly to the reader that "there's something here for you."

Within 5 or at the most 10 seconds, the reader scans an advertisement headline and illustration or guesses at the importance of what may be inside a direct mail outer envelope. Then the reader makes a judgment to learn more about the offer by reading the rest of the ad or (in the case of direct mail) by opening and reading at least part of the contents and skimming the rest. The reader can, of course, reject the message unread simply by turning the page or tossing away the mailing.

How can you use the outer envelope to convince the reader that the message inside is relevant to his or her interests and that the envelope should be opened?

First, you must forget about the 3 percent cited by the BPO as that percentage of the population who do not open the direct mail they receive. You must not be concerned about the one out of five individuals on any mailing list compiled from directories who according to an old A. C. Nielsen survey never order or inquire by mail. You also must ignore the reality that even when you are mailing to your own active customer list, some customers will not read your mailing for any of a variety of reasons including relocation, retirement, and death.

If you mail to a rented list, you must overlook the fact that even fewer of those on the rented list than on your own active customer list will open and read at least part of the contents of your mailing package.

You cannot allow the negative possibilities of delivery or acceptance to color your thinking on what to say on your outer envelope or in the message inside. You can hope to have your direct mail package read only by those on your list who currently are interested in what you have to say or to sell. All others will toss it out no matter what you do.

This is not meant to imply that a direct mail package can take only an order that is waiting to be taken. Every direct mail user knows of mailings that successfully introduced an entirely new concept or rekindled a latent demand for a product and sold it by mail.

Identifying a Want

We don't need books or life insurance policies or collectibles. Most people can survive without them. But marketing serves both needs and wants. Direct mail—a method of marketing—is an especially powerful tool for those who sell any of the products or services that we can do without but that some of us want.

If the active demand for needed essentials—food, clothing, and shelter—is satisfied by local merchants and agents, the latent demand for things people would like to have or want is being served more and more by firms using direct marketing methods, including direct mail.

The direct mail outer envelope must start the process of identifying a want that can be described by the message and satisfied by means of the method of reply. This process is important no matter what your mailing goal may be. It includes the following steps:

1. Soliciting an inquiry from a prospect or active customer
2. Following up on an inquiry and converting it to a sale
3. Selling to a prospect
4. Selling to an active customer
5. Selling a publication or membership renewal

There are other goals for direct mail, of course, but space limitations prohibit an extended discussion here. Let us examine in detail the five major mailing goals and explore some ways to create outer envelopes that will get opened and start the process of identifying a want that can be described by the message and satisfied by the method of reply.

SOLICITING AN INQUIRY FROM A PROSPECT OR ACTIVE CUSTOMER

Although costs have risen, direct mail is still an economical method of soliciting inquiries from prospects on a carefully selected mailing list. When it is used with a telephone follow-up, there is no better low-cost means of soliciting new inquiries from active customers.

Some mailers have found that an outer envelope without copy or art and often without a corner card (name of mailer and return address) is more likely to be opened out of curiosity than one that "gives away" the message inside. If you care more about results than about receiving nixies (undeliverable mail), a completely blank outer envelope may be worth testing even if the postal delivery worker has no way of returning to you those with inadequate addresses.

The fact that blank outer envelopes have been tested widely and have not been successful for a majority of mailers—particularly to their own customer lists—should not keep you from testing a split of copy and corner card versus no copy and no corner card. You may be lucky and discover that the blank outer envelope works well for you.

While you are testing these two approaches, it may be worthwhile to increase the size of your test by one-third and try an outer envelope with copy and no corner card.

What kind of copy should you use? If you are trying for an inquiry, there is almost no middle ground, especially if you intend to go back to the list again with the same offer. Use no copy or make a full disclosure of what the message inside is all about.

Figure 34-1 shows a "full disclosure" approach that was used successfully to get inquiries from prospects and active (book buyer) customers. It uses the outer envelope as an "instant" reply form.

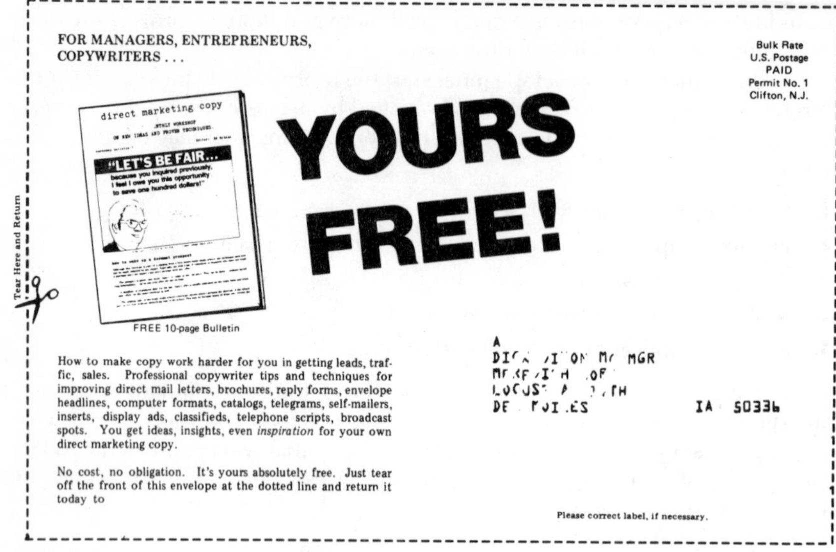

Figure 34-1 Direct mail envelope.

Although this is an inexpensive, one-color envelope, note how the "YOURS FREE!" and the newsletter illustration lead the reader's eye away from the bulk rate indicia. Figure 34-2 shows how the same envelope would appear if it were sent out as a "blank."

Obviously, one of the drawbacks of mailing a blank or nearly blank outer envelope is that it tends to focus attention on the bulk rate indicia.

Research conducted 3 years ago demonstrated conclusively that many consumers and business people view the indicia as evidence that the mail has less importance than mail bearing a metered frank or a live stamp. One respondent said: "That little bulk rate gizmo is the kiss of death as far as I'm concerned. It means *unimportant*."

If you have a relatively small universe or active customer list and you must mail to the same names several times a year, it is worth testing as many different outer envelope approaches as you can afford to test, including the blank or almost blank envelope.

One little-known advantage of the blank or almost blank envelope is the new lease on life a direct mail letter can have if it proves successful initially with an outer envelope that is blank or almost blank. When the package no longer pulls as well as it did in its first months or years, it is worth testing some element from the once-successful letter as a teaser line on the outer envelope.

The enormously successful *Newsweek* "Sincere" letter was originally mailed in a plain white Monarch envelope (3⅞ by 7 inches) with only the *Newsweek* name and return address in the upper left-hand corner.

When, after many years, this "classic" letter's pulling power waned, a test package was developed using the same letter but a radically different envelope.

Figure 34-2 Plain envelope

The stock was changed from number 20 white-wove to number 24 golden kraft. The size of the outer envelope went from Monarch to 4⅝ by 11⅞ inches. The opening phrase of the letter was featured on the new envelope. See Figure 34-3.

The new version of the "Sincere" letter outpulled the old version, and the highly effective copy approach was given extra years to produce trial subscriptions at a low cost per order.

If blank or almost blank outer envelopes turn you off and you don't test them, you may be 100 percent right for your offer or market. Or you may be missing out on an exciting new breakthrough on your cost per inquiry sheet. You can't be sure if you don't test.

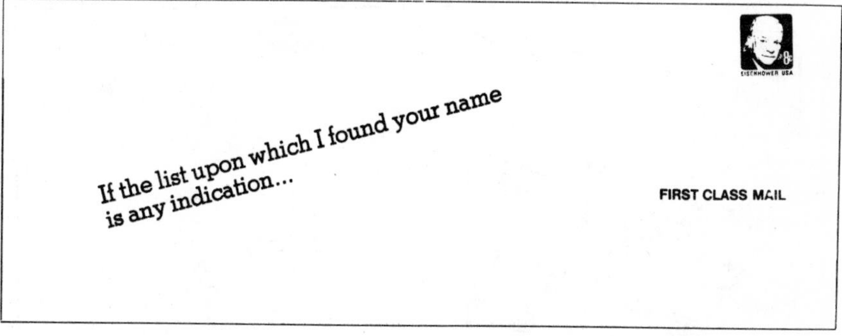

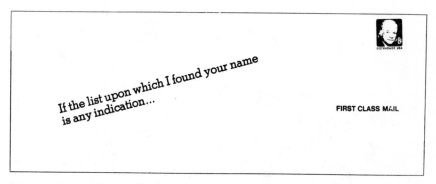

Figure 34-3 Envelope with opening phrase on cover.

FOLLOWING UP ON AN INQUIRY AND CONVERTING IT TO A SALE

The outer envelope for the first follow-up message almost always should acknowledge the fact that it contains something or some information that the reader has requested, whether that request comes by direct mail, ad coupon, bingo card, or telephone. Figure 34-4 shows how a coupon book printer follows up on information requests received through classified ads. The envelope is a white number 10 printed in one color.

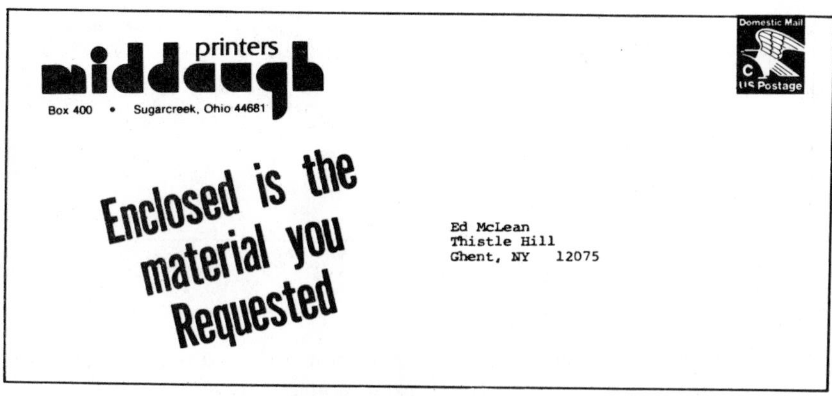

Figure 34-4 Envelope to follow up classified ads.

Later follow-up mailings can use other copy approaches such as the question approach used by a home study school shown in Figure 34-5.

The letter inside uses a miniature set of pliers as an attention getter and a puzzle as a means of involving the mechanically inclined reader. See Figure 34-6.

Even blank envelopes may have a "change-of-pace" niche in a long series of follow-ups. But the first follow-up should be safeguarded against being tossed out

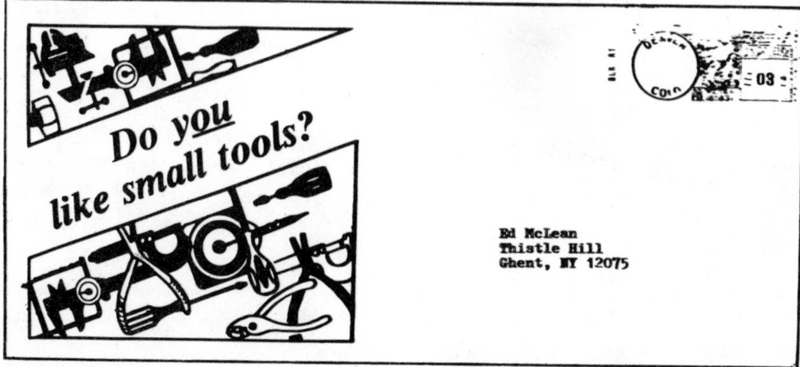

Figure 34-5 Envelope with question approach.

Technical Training Division 2000 West Union Avenue Englewood, Colorado 80110

MEMO FROM : R. E. Ellerbusch

These tiny pliers actually work! Try them

These clever pliers were made in one automatic operation, without an assembly step; diecast of tough zinc alloy in a process devised by an American diecasting firm specializing in small, precision work.

Know how it was done? Most people are pretty well stumped on this puzzle -- but you may have it solved. Drop me a note with your explanation and I'll tell you all about it.

And while you're writing that note, take an extra minute to let me know about your plans for the future. A few months ago you requested some information on National Camera training, but something kept you from deciding to enroll at that time. Perhaps you had other priorities that have now been taken care of and you'd like to reconsider the opportunities available to you in camera repair.

If so, we want to send you all the current information you need. Just let us know - we'll appreciate hearing from you.

Rod Ellerbusch

MEMO

TO: R. E. Ellerbusch

FROM: DATE:

Here's my explanation of the little pliers puzzle. Send me your answer and another pair of pliers. ______________________________

____

Use reverse side if you need more room.

Important: Attach the address label on the envelope you received this in, or enter your name and address here.

____

____

____

Check one

☐ Yes, I'm ready to think about learning camera repair. Send me a current school catalog and complete information.

☐ I have some questions. Call me at (give your phone number and best time of day and day of week to reach you) ______________

☐ I'm not interested in camera repair - please take me off your mailing list.

REE/dz

Figure 34-6 Letter inside envelope with question approach.

by a forgetful inquirer or an intermediary. Use some variation of "here is the information you requested."

SELLING TO A PROSPECT

This is the greatest test of the outer envelope: to seize the attention, to get opened, and to start the process that leads to the sale.

Unlike the follow-up, the "cold sale" package mailed to a prospect comes unsolicited and unannounced. You have a choice. You can try to make the outer envelope look as unobtrusive as possible, as IBM did with the 6⅜- by 9¾-inch outer envelope, shown in Figure 34-7. Or you can make a bold bid for the reader's attention and involvement. This is the approach often favored by Jayme/Ratalahti, a writer-designer team in San Francisco with an impressive track record of successful mailings, such as the 6- by 9-inch outer envelope with two colors on coated stock shown in Figure 34-8.

Still another "involvement" approach is reflected in the more traditional combination of art and copy employed by veteran copywriter Richard D. Jordan on the two-color 6 by 9 shown in Figure 34-9.

A number 10 outer envelope on a mailing for another law enforcement publication used a narrative opening which was continued on the top of the four-page folder letter inside. See Figure 34-10.

In selling to prospects, your outer envelope has to get attention and involve the reader. As you can see, there is no only way or winning formula for achieving this. You can use a completely blank envelope, one bearing only your return address, a poly envelope that shows its contents, an envelope with a pull tab or "zipper,"

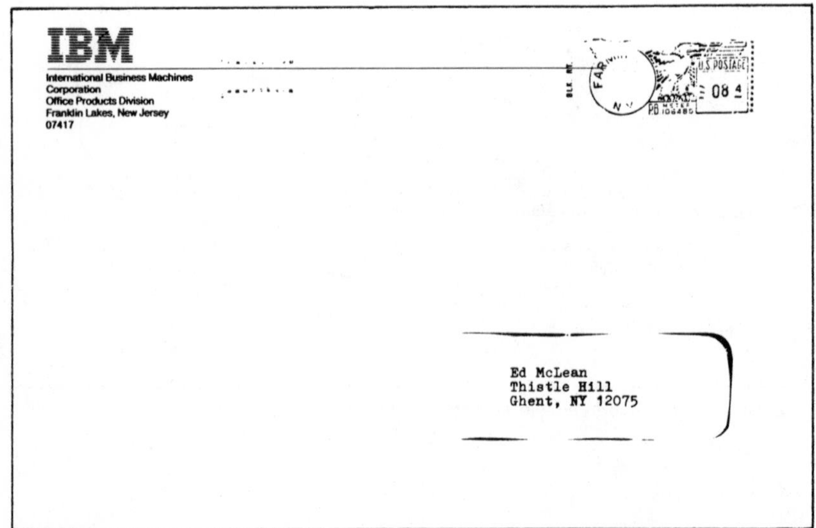

Figure 34-7 Envelope selling to a prospect—unobtrusive.

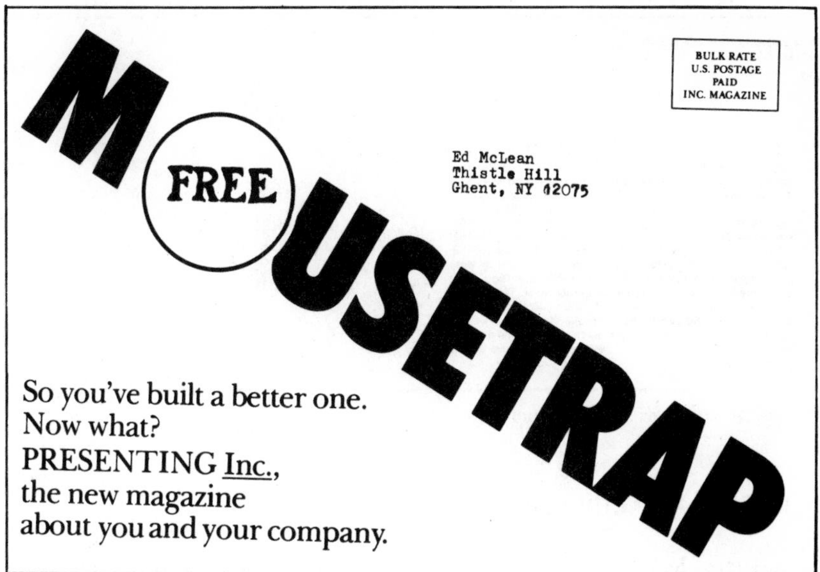

Figure 34-8 Envelope selling to a prospect—bold.

one showing a big "yes" token, a quiz envelope, or one telling a story that leads the reader inside.

If your outer envelopes this year look the same as those you used last year to sell to prospects, it is probably time to test some new approaches.

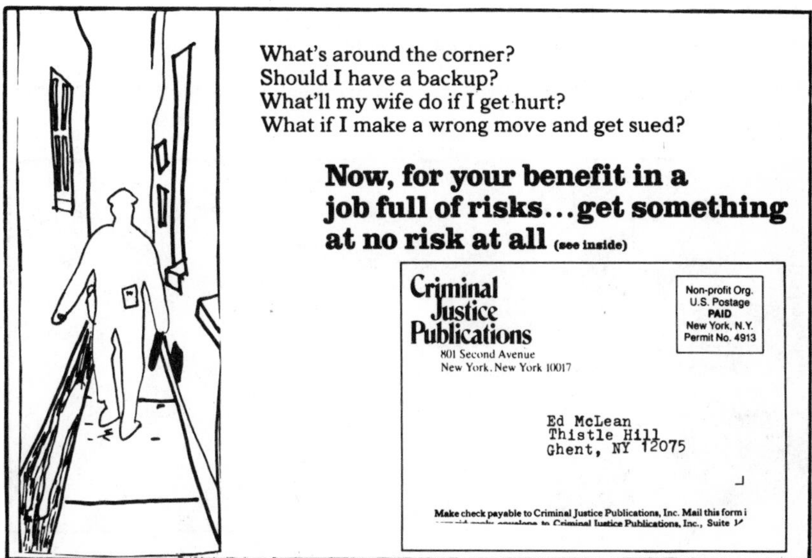

Figure 34-9 Envelope using art and copy.

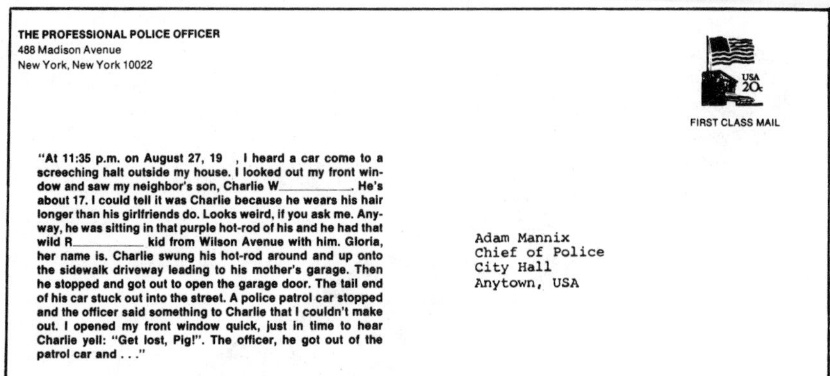

Figure 34-10 Envelope with narrative opening.

SELLING TO AN ACTIVE CUSTOMER

Do you get at least 60 percent of your revenue from repeat sales? If you don't, you should consider new approaches as well as new products or services to sell.

The outer envelope in mailings to the active customer list should "carry the news" about the following items:

New products or services

New auxiliary services such as trade-ins, training, etc.

New price or premium

Mainstream user success stories plus unusual applications

New facilities or capabilities that can benefit the active customer

Figure 34-11 shows how a merchandise syndicator identifies the customer

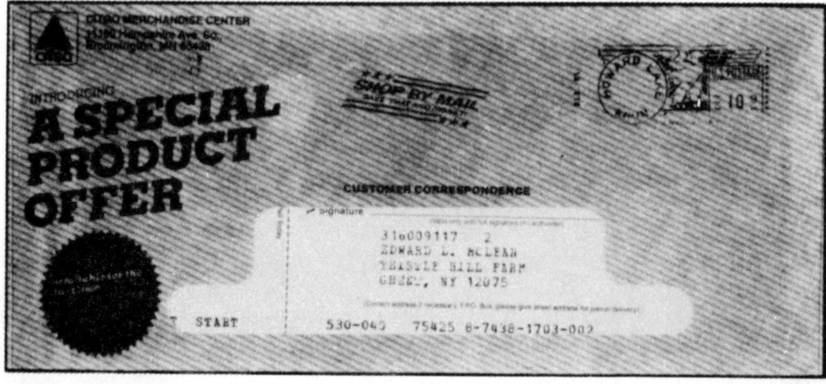

Figure 34-11 Envelope selling to active customer using "customer correspondence" tag.

relationship on an outer envelope containing an offer to credit charge card customers of an oil company. Note the "customer correspondence" tag above the address label area on this number 10 envelope.

A Washington, D.C., department store used an unusual 5½- by 5½-inch yellow and green outer envelope simulating a box of school crayons to get attention for an announcement for a back-to-school sale for its charge customer list. See Figure 34-12.

Since news is such a powerful envelope opener with active customers, it is wise to use new "news" for each mailing. Thus, it is rarely wise to order stock envelopes in large quantities for mailings to your active customer list.

One final point. If your outer envelope "news" copy is on target, it will interest your active customers and bore everyone else.

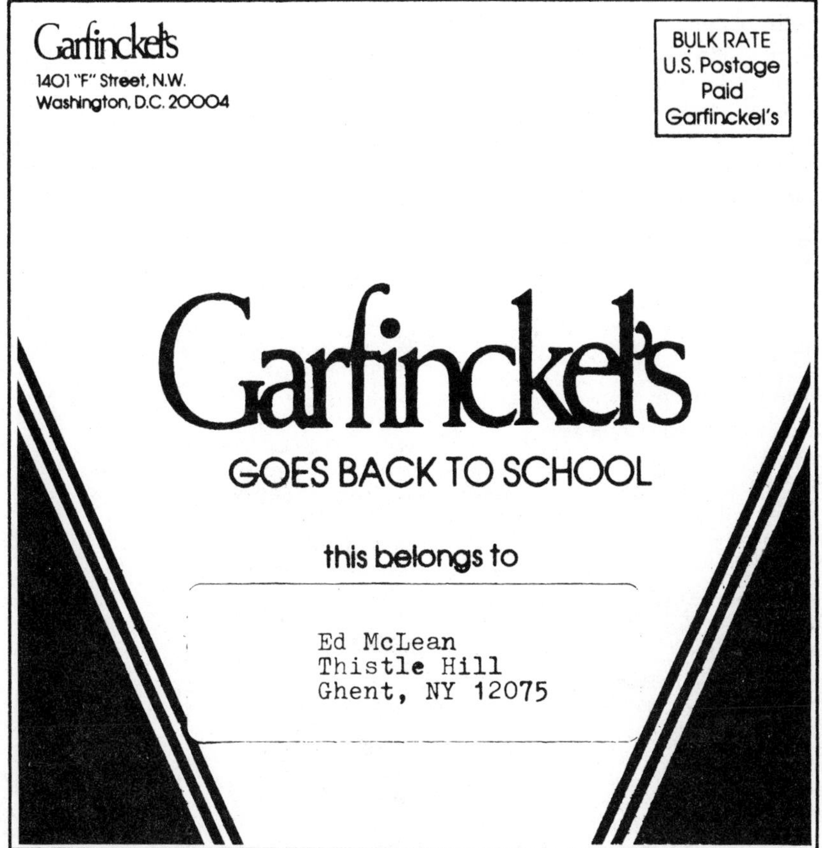

Figure 34-12 Envelope selling to active customer for "back-to-school" customer list.

SELLING A PUBLICATION OR MEMBERSHIP RENEWAL

Naturally, your choice of outer envelope copy will depend on whether the renewal package comes early or late in the series.

Each outer envelope in a renewal series should be different in general appearance, size, color, copy, and art from the outer envelopes used in the series. Try not to let the dictates of a "canned" computer renewal form program lock you into a "lookalike" series that gives your subscriber or member a sense of déjà vu!

There are an incredible number and variety of envelope formats and designs from which to choose. There are envelopes that are opened by pulling a tab, a piece of string, or a built-in "zipper." There are paper envelopes with display windows that show off your color brochure or yes token inside and others made of polyethylene that can truly dramatize your offer. There are Jumbo (9- by 12-inch) envelopes, Monarch (3⅞- by 7½-inch) envelopes, and a whole lot of useful and interesting sizes in between.

With this remarkable range from which to choose, it is unfortunate that some mailers choose not to stray from the ordinary, selecting one of the two most commonly used direct mail outer envelope sizes: the "legal-sized" number 10 (4⅛- by 9½-inch) or that tired old warhorse, the 6 by 9.

Before you turn the page, make a decision to call or write to a direct mail envelope company today. Send along a sample of your most recent mailing and ask for envelope suggestions. You have nothing to lose, and quite a bit to gain if even one of the suggestions pays off. A number of these companies are listed below.

Atlantic Envelope Company
P. O. Box 1267
Atlanta, GA 30301

Automated Packaging Systems, Inc.
8400 Darrow Road
Twinsburg, OH 44087

The B & W Press, Inc.
100 Lynn Street
Peabody, MA 01960

Berlin & Jones Envelope Co., Inc.
2 E. Union Street
East Rutherford, NJ 07070

Boise Cascade Envelopes
72 Cascade Drive
Rochester, NY 14614

Design Distributors, Inc.
45 E. Industry Ct.
Deer Park, NY 11729

Double Envelope Corporation
7702 Plantation Rd., N.W.
Roanoke, VA 24019

Federal Envelope Company
660 Forbes Blvd.
S. San Francisco, CA 94080

Golden State Envelopes
1601 Gower Street
Los Angeles, CA 90028

Gotham Envelope Corp.
100 Avenue of the Americas
New York, NY 10013

Heco Envelope
5445 N. Elston Avenue
Chicago, IL 60630

Karolton Envelope
209 E. 56 Street
New York, NY 10022

Mail-Well Envelope Company
P.O. Box 765
Houston, TX 77001

Specialty Envelope Company
4890 Spring Grove Avenue
Cincinnati, OH 45232

Tension Envelope Corp.
19th & Campbell Streets
Kansas City, MO 64108

Transo Envelope Company
3542 N. Kimball Avenue
Chicago, IL 60618

U.S. Envelope
P.O. Box 3300
Springfield, MA 01101

chapter **35**

DIRECT MAIL PERSONALIZATION

Lucille M. Guardala

Vice President and Creative Director
BBDO Direct
New York, N.Y.

Personalization is a creative cornerstone of direct marketing. It is not a technique exclusive to direct mail, nor can we lay claim to its invention. But no other form of advertising communication is so pertinent.

Personalization is the ultimate form of person-to-person communication in print. We can take a product or service and zero in on the people who need it, why they want it, and where they'll use it right down to the street number and the industry or special-interest group whose needs will be served.

Personalization is the stuff to sell scores by. No headline, product attitude, photo, or illustration, no matter how powerful or brilliant, affects the prospect so powerfully as seeing his or her name, address, or occupation as an integral part of the creative message. For all the information, chapters, case histories, and printing company handouts disseminated in the last several years about the theory and technique of direct mail personalization, the art can be distilled into a simple, direct statement: It's the ultimate "you" benefit.

BACKGROUND

Like direct-response advertising in general, personalization is part art, part science, and part psychology, plus that extra invisible ingredient: creativity. This chapter will be concerned with how, when, where, and why this technique will add response and potency to advertising efforts, not with the technology of the microchips that make a personalized letter or envelope emerge from a precision piece of modern printing equipment.

Targeting

The personalized direct mail piece has something that no other advertising medium can offer: the prospect's name as an integral part of the selling message. When understood and used properly, it is a powerful selling tool that doesn't depend on huge media outlays and four-color space for success. This is something to keep in mind the next time you get a new product assignment that doesn't include TV, exotic preprints, or the other accoutrements of a large budget.

Impossible to Ignore

Chase Manhattan Bank spends hundreds of thousands of dollars weekly to get New Yorkers' banking business. Currently, "the Chase is on" TV, newspapers, bus shelters, brochures, and handouts. Yet when Chase Commercial Corporation wanted to sell executives on its Export Credit Services, it chose a simple personalized business letter on Chase stationery to generate leads rather than a more elaborately constructed mailing piece.

The reason is simple. While four-color brochures are powerful and can spell out in a graphically arresting format the benefits inherent in Chase's service, nothing is better suited to the needs of today's busy executives than a straightforward business letter with the executive's name on it. Nothing gets by a secretary easier than a typed number 10 business envelope with a bank corner card. Such a mailing isn't expensive, just effective.

The Creative Consideration

Personalization is not necessarily the writer's province. Later we'll look at elaborate visual presentations—lavish multipiece mailings in which personalization is an essential part of the layout itself. But for starters, ask yourself a question: Given the choice, would you rather respond to words that said ABC Car Rental saved New Yorkers money on trips to Washington or words that said ABC Car Rental could save "Jon Oak" $50 if the car was picked up locally in "Floral Park" and driven 562 miles to Washington? Obviously, you'd choose the "Jon Oak" letter. So did Avis, to the tune of $4 million.

A Case for Personalization

Before we get into the mechanics of deciding when or whether to personalize, let's look briefly at some cases where the personal touch has proved successful.

Success Stories

Avis Rent-a-Car. The corporate rental market is lucrative, and though Avis was penetrating it with a fair degree of success through its sales force, it couldn't reach many smaller companies successfully because of the high cost of sales calls. To achieve higher penetration, Avis decided on a highly targeted business-to-business direct mail program in which a deeply personalized letter replaced the in-person sales call.

The List. The Dun & Bradstreet list was used because it provided the name of the president or chief executive officer (CEO) of a prospect company plus other significant data for personalized appeals: sales volume and ZIP codes which made selection by industry possible and other information, including the length of time a business has been operating.

Benefit Strategy. Appeals were tailored to the needs of the president of a smaller business: personal prestige and saving money. The president was offered membership in the Avis President's Club; this gave the prospect prestige plus special, members-only service and discounts. The company also would receive a discount for signing up a corporate customer and issuing Avis charge cards to all employees who traveled regularly. This appeal put the president of any small company in the presence of his or her Fortune 500 counterparts when it came to perceived perks. The mailing program made this appeal personal, pertinent, and believable.

Creative Direct Mail Strategy. A four-step, highly personalized mailing series was designed to reach the decision maker. The style was highly businesslike to get past the secretarial barrier. A "teaser" computer letter was sent first, but it had the appearance of being individually typed. Then followed the "confidential proposal," which included a four-page personalized section in a blue window cover, an application, and a personalized four-color brochure. All the benefits of the program were spelled out in this piece. The brochure, for example, had all the earmarks of a private report prepared especially for the prospect, mentioning annual sales volume and the year the company was founded.

Should anyone find it possible to ignore such compellingly presented data married to benefit, Avis followed up several weeks later with a personalized computer letter and finally with a last contact package designed to look like a mailgram. Not many executives needed the extra prodding, however.

The Result. The first test to target companies fielded a 7 percent response. Rollout to a larger segment of the product universe yielded 8 percent. Against an investment of $300,000, the Avis Corporate Program generated $4 million in sales.

American Management Association. Most people who hold some type of supervisory position could always look forward to a monthly or even weekly flier from AMA announcing yet another course offering to improve or sharpen their professional skills. The trouble was that not enough would-be course takers noticed.

Traditionally, AMA's literature was personalized no further than a mailing label, and each piece was an element unto itself. There was no "campaign" or "corporate" look to the graphics. Since it didn't look like important business mail, it often wouldn't make it past the secretary.

A Personal Approach. AMA's educational activities had such wide scope that a highly personalized creative approach coupled with a clutter-eliminating strategy was constructed. Earlier thrusts appealed to reason alone: "Improve this skill," etc. The strategy developed by BBDO Direct presented a more emotional appeal instead of a situation: "Look good to your boss" and "Manage your career."

A two-step process was used. Leads were generated from print ads and personalized direct mail. One piece used a closed-face personal envelope with a discrete corner card. Another was personalized by name and address on the outer envelope, calling the prospect's attention to a 3-day period when the course would be available in that city. Both were fulfilled with a management information kit which contained a personalized letter and made a "tentative" course reservation for the prospect.

The Result. This testing program achieved a 17 percent lift over previous efforts.

The Personal Type

There are types of direct mail in which the technique of personalization gives the package a distinct advantage no matter how powerful the creative thrust. All creatives sweating out an imminent bake-off or testing situation should weigh very seriously the added value that personalization can give their efforts. Some of the following categories seem like naturals; the answer for others lies below the surface. There are other "special project" types that don't fit neatly into compartments; they're your judgment call. The following are prime, popular targets for personalization.

Sweepstakes. You'd be suspicious if someone paid you with a check with no name, nor would anyone take seriously the chance of winning half a million dollars without receiving a personalized eligibility certificate. There is no sense being subtle in a sweeps, and so the big companies personalize multiple certificates, even the instructions: "Jon Oak, choose the prize you prefer."

The involvement generated by a personalized, multilevel sweeps is precisely what's required to get action and generate the order. In list building, even the negative responses become valuable.

How sweepstakes personalization is done to the optimum is easily answered by referring to the latest Publisher's Clearing House or *Reader's Digest* mailing. These are state-of-the-art and "how-to" texts for techniques. *Reader's Digest* even goes so far as to announce an upcoming sweeps with a personalized postal card.

Businesses. Anything delivered to a business address should be personalized or it will never reach the hands of the desired prospect.

Sending direct mail to business prospects without personalization is like a salesperson never calling on a major account. The seller is soon out of business. The reason why is obvious: Secretaries and assistants screen mail. If it looks like junk mail, it gets treated like junk mail.

By business personalization, we don't mean just a label through a window. The best response rates in business direct mail are generated by packages that look like business mail: a standard number 10 envelope with a typed closed-face envelope. No wonder the Letterlope and similar formats are popular.

Business also offers the most creative uses for this technique. Available lists give you the capability of targeting appeals by name and city, title, industry, or even sales volume. If sweepstakes are the junk food of personalization, business personalization is the seven-course gourmet repast, at least from a creative standpoint.

Financial. The impact of getting a personalized mailing from a bank or credit card company is exactly like that of receiving a letter from the IRS: You open it. This is exactly why personalization is used almost to the exclusion of all other techniques by banks, credit card companies, stockbrokers, and other financial services.

One of the most compelling uses of this technique is for credit cards. The recipient receives a package with a "preapproved" credit limit. The application already has been filled out partially; almost the only thing required is the prospect's signature. The need for the prospects to complete it is almost as overwhelming as their desire to add another $2000 to their credit lines. The more value prospects receive in a selling message regarding their own finances, the more you increase the likelihood of a positive response.

Insurance. Since this is a serious business, much of what applies to business and financial mail is applicable here, except that in insurance, techniques tend to be more elaborate. Obviously, the prospect of protecting one's family to the tune of $50,000 takes on heightened pertinence when the surname is boldly emblazoned beside the payoff. A typical package often includes a personalized plastic card with prospect name and "policy number," a personalized "guaranteed eligibility" certificate, a personalized application, a personalized letter and brochure, and often even a "policy" facsimile. Since many insurance companies that sell by mail often market by special affinity groups or trusts, the pieces also are "personalized" by appealing to the "veteran" or "over 50" category. Life insurance also uses the "birth certificate" technique since birthdate information is available from some list sources.

Circulation Promotion. For special-interest magazines, the obvious path is to personalize a hobby: "How to be a better cook than you already are, Ms. Layton." Or a nationality may be personalized: "As an Italian, Ms. Gucci, I know you'll enjoy exploring your rich heritage each month." Since the ethnic selling message is already pertinent, personalization makes it much more engaging. Nor is personalization ignored by the mass-market publications. *Time* and *Sports Illustrated* make use of laser personalization techniques to help their packages break through the clutter exploding through everyone's mail slot every day.

Political. People often tend to think of political mailings only around election time, but political fund raising has become a year-round campaign. When an issue can be made to appeal to or affect an individual through a cleverly designed personalized package, the contributions roll in. There is personalization not only by name but by issue or by the "moral" personalization achieved through sophisticated mailing list selection.

Much political, issue-oriented mail is conservative in nature and comes from Richard Viguerie's organization outside Washington. The theme of the package is patriotic: "Help the President fight the recession." Or it may stress preparedness: "Are our defenses down?" The packages often include a confidential report or dossier. It's one thing when crime concerns a nation; when a personalized letter can put the issue on someone's own street, that person will react and respond.

Catalog. It's called "the wrap," and it has to work. Why else cover a catalog cover? Large catalog companies have good buyers on their list plus those whose purchases are sporadic at best. The problem of how to make the good buyers better and also encourage nonbuyers is solved by companies such as Lane Bryant through catalog wrap letters. For example, better customers are sent a previous catalog, promoted by a computer-personalized wrap letter that promises deferred billing if they order from the special catalog before the cutoff date. These customers later receive the regular catalog from which they'll also buy. Personalization makes the prospects feel privileged and special. This technique helps Lane Bryant get more purchases per catalog life from a customer and helps buyers forecast the best items before the main catalog mailing. For less active customers, Lane Bryant uses "reactivation" personalized wraps instructing the customer that no more catalogs will come to his or her residence unless a purchase is made from the current book. Other catalog houses such as Hanover House use personalized wraps with a sweeps to stimulate consumer interest and response.

These are seven basic areas where personalization is the popular technique. There also are other applications and other products where the personal touch is called for. But how do you decide it's the right creative approach for the assignment you're working on now? Ask yourself these eight basic questions. If you can say yes to the majority of them, use the technique.

1. **Budget.** While personalization is an expressive technique, it can be expensive. Anything you do beyond applying a label in the production process adds extra dollars to the cost. Will the extra response outweigh the added cost? If you can't answer this question yourself, find an account executive or production expert who can. Many out-pulling packages have become losers in the final cost analysis.
2. **Product.** Does the product or service fall into one of the categories, such as "insurance," mentioned above? Does the product lend itself to the personalized technique? For instance, will personalizing a piece about a wood-burning stove really add creative and sales value to a higher degree than praising the stove's construction and durability powerfully? Is it worth the expense?
3. **Audience.** Are the prospects upscale, downscale, or middlescale? Will they feel silly about half-inch laser lettering that adds their names to the rolls of the Smithsonian? While people love looking at their names in print and are instantly drawn to personalized pieces, they can be distracted quickly if it's off target. Apply the same aesthetic standards as you would to a page of copy or a layout. The Franklin Mint has built a huge direct mail business without personalization.
4. **Strategy.** As illustrated by the Avis and AMA case histories, the strategy called for a highly targeted, highly personalized technique to achieve its objectives. If the technique fits in as well with your strategy, use it.
5. **Lists.** While the creative possibilities are limitless, the list buy often isn't. If lists cannot provide information such as industry and sales volume breakdown that you thought could be worked magnificently into the personalization creative, find out before you've sold the client on the idea.
6. **Category history.** If the product is insurance or sweepstakes or if there is a long and extant history that argues for the personal touch, don't feel

compelled to reinvent the wheel. A key rule of thumb is to go through your swipe files and your mental files. If you've never seen a mailing of that type go out without personalization, use this technique.

7. **Universe.** Where can this technique take you? If the maximum limit of known lists for the technique you want is 50,000 and the client wants a rollout of 1 million, switch to a simpler technique.
8. **Timing.** Personalization requires more production. Does the mailing date give you enough time? Most clients don't include overtime when they define time.

TECHNIQUES

What does the technique of personalization achieve on the part of the prospect? An irresistible urge to take notice. Of all forms of communication creative workers can put on paper, nothing captivates the reader more than the sight of his or her own name. Thus, the more places where a name can appear in a mail package, the more chance you get to draw the reader in. No other technique besides personalization gives you this edge. It is direct mail's unique capability.

How to Create the Personal Touch

We've seen what an effective use of data meant in terms of response for the Avis and AMA mail campaigns. The creative workers involved not only used the technique, they used it well. Since prospects are irresistibly drawn to the sight of their own names, addresses, interests, etc., make certain these elements appear in a way they'll smile at, agree with, and enjoy—not get mad at. Too often the technique is selected because "it works" without an understanding of why it works. Before you've taken pen or marker to paper, use this three-step process to guide your flow.

A Creative Checklist

Let Product Define Technique. Is the product exciting, impressive, or just expensive? On mass-market items such as magazine subscriptions, sweepstakes, or insurance, it's fine to use large laser lettering for names, addresses, etc., but this strategy is totally wrong if your creative thrust is a "confidential report to key executives." The more expensive and exclusive the product, the more quietly you should tread.

Let Audience Define Technique. Much of what applies for the previous category applies here but with certain exceptions. Where will the package be received? If the destination is a business address, make it look businesslike. If the mail is received at the home, homey personal appeals are fine. It's never a good idea to mix styles. Potential book club joiners see themselves in a different light than potential seed catalog buyers, though they may be the same people.

Make It Real. There is so much personalized mail out there that falls flat. Read it. The bad stuff merely scatters personal data throughout a letter without achieving a true person-to-person touch. Always make the available information relate to the individual as well as the product.

DON'T Mr. Matthew Smith will find thirty recipes each month in *Gourmet*.

DO Mr. Smith, the next four-star dining experience people will talk about in Boston could very well be at 42 Southlake Dr. The talk might well center around *your* truffled chicken, one of the 60-minute recipes you'll find in our free bonus issue of *Gourmet*.

DON'T I'd like to send these slacks to 121 South River Dr. for a 15-day free trial, Mrs. Smith.

DO What's the advantage of our 15-day free trial offer, Mrs. Smith? Something no store in Dallas will let you do. When the slacks arrive at 121 South River Dr., wash them, wear them. If you think there's a better value in Dallas ...

DON'T The next twenty-six issues of *Time* are yours for 53 cents each, Ms. Jones.

DO Sitting in a chair at 95 Raff Avenue, you can take the pulse of world capitals in 60 minutes. That's how long it takes to keep up with the world in *Time* each week, Ms. Jones. All it costs, Damascus to Dayton, is 53 cents.

The beauty of this technique is that it's so personal. Relate the data to a person's life, occupation, fears and hopes, and you've made the message more relevant than $30 million in ad campaigns can.

Lists: A Creative Person's Guide to Computers

The mailing list is where to zero in on the audience. Creative personnel who are weak in math absolutely panic at the thought of computer lists. Let how the machines store, sort, and deliver information remain a mystery. Instead, concentrate on what lists can and cannot do.

Lists and their proper use are often the key to response. They represent the people to whom the personal appeal is delivered. The state of technology today is such that you can reach people not only by where they live but by how they live. For example, education is demographic, but what people do with that schooling, the magazines they read, and the interests they have are psychographic data. Many lists have those data available.

It is cast in bronze that a good list can be profitable and that a good mailing sent to a bad list won't work. The lists of lists are the province of the list buyer and broker. The information available is astonishing, but too often a lack of knowledge limits creative possibilities.

There are mailing lists available from A to Z, from art buyers to affluent ZIPs. A list can tell us about a person's lifestyle. For example, an automotive list provides the make, model, and age of a car; a record club list, the kind of music the prospects like and even the equipment they play it on.

Ask the Right Questions. Let's discuss a business list. Your assignment is to sell office equipment such as desktop copiers, etc. Talk to the person buying the lists; this can affect your creative approach dramatically. There are many segmental factors that can have a bearing on your approach, and they are all available.

- Age of business: how long the company has been in business
- Size: sales volume and number of employees
- Headquarters
- Credit, including the Dun & Bradstreet rating of this particular concern and even the general trend of the business

Avis used much of this information in its successful rental car mailing to smaller business. Imagine how such data can dramatize the product's attributes in a way that clearly makes it relevant to the prospect's needs.

The Broker. Who has all this information? Where does it come from? The broker is the key and can provide much useful information for creative workers. A simple conference call between list broker, creative worker, and list buyer can unlock vast storehouses of stimulating data for the creative department. You may think your mailing is going out to homeowners. The broker may know the list consists of single-family residences with incomes of $30,000 plus, all with more than one child. There are a lot more specific creative appeals in those data than just the "homeowners" thrust.

A good list broker will be happy to share the data with you. It's what your agency is paying for. Finding a good list broker is like having a good client-agency relationship; it's creative and involves the mutual sharing of data for the collective good.

There are over a billion names you can mail to. What you say to them and how you say it are determined by the list they appear on. The raw data are out there, but it's your imaginative use of the data that makes the people on the list come alive. Relate the data to them; they'll respond. What they've bought is just as important as where they live. Understand the psychology and you've unlocked the list mystery.

Formats for Personal Success

The personalization format is totally tied to technology. As with so many other technologically related items, it changes faster than it takes to write a headline. Someone is always coming up with a new format. But mail order isn't medicine. It's not necessary to take the pulse of constant change to do effective personalized pieces. Leave that for the truly unique project, for when you invent your own format. But for now, there are several proven, effective formats that have worked or are still working and can work for you.

As important as personalization technique is to direct mail is the marriage of computer data to high-speed printing technology. Together they combine to create the following formats, from the simple to the space-age.

Message Personalization. This is not a name personalization at all but a personalization by desired action or information. For example, it can be a cheese club's buckslip to good customers offering an "ignore these prices" special discount. Or as ITT recently did, it can include a "waiver of registration fee" slip to selected names as an offer test. Another way to employ this technique is to change the letter. In circulation promotion, one letter would be send to prospects, and another letter would urge ex-subscribers to reactivate.

Name Personalization. This is the "true" personalization as most people perceive it. It is the standard, often a computer fill-in letter with name and address and often with fill-ins within the body of the letter and on the reply card which shows through the window as well. But don't let the personalization become window dressing. Make it live and use it to relate to the prospect. The worst thing to do is let a personal letter sound impersonal.

There is another type of fill-in often used for business, a patented process from the Kurt Volk company called the Letterlope. It uses a standard businesslike closed envelope with computer-printed name and address. Letter and response devices are personalized in the same businesslike fashion.

Technically, this look is achieved because the computer portions are preprinted on a continuous form right down to the envelope so that all the elements in the package are essentially formed by one piece. To the recipient, the completed package presents itself as buttoned up and professional. The Letterlope or one of its variations thus is the format of choice for most business mailings.

Multipiece Personalization. Want to really make the offer's presence felt? Have all the personalized pieces (such as letter, lift note, etc.) printed on the same form as the personalized response device. Such high saturation is surprisingly affordable. The key to cost efficiency is to avoid wasting paper.

You take the ordinary size of the computer form and then design letter and response device to fit within that area. A 22- by 18½-inch maximum letter size (a standard format maximum) can become a 6- by 8-inch letter and 3- by 6-inch reply form. These can be printed 6-up on each sheet, and they are very cost-effective. There are very complex variations available. From a single computer form, it is possible to extract letter, certificate, lift letter, and response device. But the more you do, the more it costs. Thus, it is vital to be sure that the extra personalized "lift" letter you want gives the mailing package a lift that's worth the extra cost.

Laser Printing. If it is a given that the prospect is irresistibly drawn to the sight of his or her name on the address label, imagine how the effect multiplies when the name is almost an inch high. Laser printing is the Hollywood of direct mail personalization, a marquee on which the prospects themselves play a major role in the creative platform.

Creatives tend to call many electronic processes by the generic term "laser," including ink jet and other electrographic processes. While the mechanics differ, all these lettering techniques are tied into computers which allow higher-speed printing than ever before. The bottom line is enormous creative flexibility and economy.

Now new formats are dashed off at a dazzling rate: unique folds that compel involvement, color lettering, sideways lettering. Many companies can even print, personalize, or fold on press, permitting an economic application of even a complex design idea.

Suppose you've chosen one of the formats just mentioned. What are your costs in terms of time and money? Don't make the costly error many creative workers commit by failing to talk to the production department.

Working with Production

All too often, in the headlong rush to meet schedules and squeeze that last minute of creative time into the presentation piece, production is the last to know of your wonderful idea. All too often the idea isn't practical either in format or cost, and the result is a compromise no one wants to live with, including the client. Of course, there also will be a compromise in terms of response.

Bring production into your complex personalization format discussions early; it's worth the time. Even if the production department thinks the ideas can't be done, they have the time to call in big-gun suppliers like Webcraft and Response Graphics who may know of a solution. You'd be surprised how often the impossible becomes possible when there's enough time.

It's part of production's job to keep up on the state of the art. Often they can suggest a new format or a better, more involving fold. They've been to conventions and trade shows and have walked the displays. A brief meeting with production can be a real money saver, not to mention a face saver.

Art Directors

Let form follow function. An art director working on a direct mail piece gives you advantages no other form of advertising can. You are not restricted by time or size. The graphics don't have to fit into 60 seconds or a 7- by 10-inch space. The possibilities are limited only by imagination. There are letters to be designed in a new and intriguing way, brochures with a myriad of folding possibilities, additional pieces to dream up from certificates to cards, and envelopes calling for lush color photography.

Doing a business-to-business mailing? Use a Letterlope format to make it businesslike. Planning the world's biggest and best sweepstakes ever? Electronically letter the entry form and design twelve other prize certificates, all imprinted with the entrant's name. There is so much technology extant for fold, use of color, or personalized message that it's sometimes easy to be overwhelmed by it.

As a rule of thumb, let form follow function. Business mailings must look professional. Sweepstakes can be playful, with involvement tokens and personalized entry forms. Insurance mailings must look official, with a personalized guarantee of eligibility. Use the same criterion you'd use when choosing a color or typeface: your good taste.

CONCLUSIONS

We've established what personalization is, what it can mean to a mailing, how it's done, and when it's been successful. But here are two other things to consider: creative elements and cost.

Creative Cautions

First artist and writer must work together. Review the rules for the use of personalization. Is it right for the package? If so, both must be aware of the fact that personalization is the technique so that the prospect will feel the unity of thought behind the creative package. Even in concert, involve production. How big can the name be on the enrollment certificate? What are the limitations on the fill-in letter? Know before you've sold the client on your wonderful idea; check it out thoroughly with production before presentation.

Cost Cautions

This caveat flows out of the creative caution. Some personalization methods are expensive. For instance, if the mailing quantity is small, there may not be enough additional response to justify using personalization. This question also should be addressed at the production "checkout."

CAN YOU BEAT IT?

Is there a better creative solution? Does the cost justify the use of personalization? By the time the comps and rough headlines are finished for your piece, someone already may have invented a new personalization technique. Your package could be a world beater because of it.

Change is a constant in direct response. We've seen our discipline go from stamps to satellites in a few years. But through it all, direct response is still the province of people-to-people communication. Personalization proves this over and over again.

chapter 36

DIRECT MAIL INSERTS

Brian Turley

President
Brian Turley & Company
Melrose, Mass.

WHAT IS A DIRECT MAIL INSERT?

In the broadest sense, it's anything that goes into an outgoing envelope beyond what's considered basic to a direct mail package. It is something "extra," something in addition to a letter and response vehicle.

Very simply, it's an enclosure. It can be a flier, coupon, discount slip, stuffer, brochure, or broadside. It can be anything one wants to make it, provided, of course, that it fits into the outgoing envelope and is, in the case of large volume mailings, machine-insertable.

Insertability is a serious concern when you're thinking in terms of an unusual insert format: a die-cut shape, an accordion-folded piece, a multipage booklet, and the like. In general, an insert must have a hard, straight edge so that it can be handled at high speeds. Some equipment grips inserts and pulls them into envelopes; other machines work on a pushing principle by which envelopes are opened slightly by suction and inserts are pushed inside by metal arms.

It's important in designing an insert to check it out with an experienced letter shop professional before going ahead with anything "different." (A printer, who may know the craft, will not be conversant with the intricacies of letter shop operation.) Or refer to Chapter 42 in this handbook. Otherwise, you may create a handsome, eye-catching insert but one that has to be stuffed laboriously and at great expense by hand.

WHY HAVE INSERTS AT ALL?

Direct mail critics say mailers cram as much as they can into an envelope in an attempt to overwhelm the audience. Not true, of course, but not entirely false.

Inserts are designed to reinforce the primary selling message; to make additional sales points, to hype, to emphasize, to urge, and to present the wisdom of the proposition from a different angle.

This has been called the additive approach, meaning simply that something is added to increase the efficiency of a mailing package at no significant increase in cost. Therein may lie the key to the whole subject of inserts.

Although it may seem obvious, even the shrewdest direct mailers often fail to get the most for their postal dollar. First class mail entitles the user to mail a full ounce for the price of a stamp, but mailers rarely take full advantage of the weight provision. Third class bulk, the most common direct mail vehicle, entitles the user to nearly 4 ounces; again, this often is underutilized.

Their strategy aspects aside, inserts are the most effective means of getting full mileage out of what you pay the post office. Inserts in effect get a free ride, and you get the opportunity to say more, sell harder, or approach your reader from a different tack.

Types of Inserts

This chapter began by pointing out that an insert or enclosure can be virtually anything; it is not limited to "paper" items. Very successful mailings have included coins, packets of sand, tiny pencils, and cloth swatches.

Thus, it's difficult to categorize inserts or lay down hard and fast rules about what they should say and how or what size they should be. But there are some rules of thumb.

The insert should be distinctive in color and size, very obviously something "separate" from a letter, for example. If it's a discount coupon, make it dollar bill or check size, on green or checklike stock. Color is important in making your insert stand out from the primary selling vehicle. Color is subject to debate, although it's hardly arguable that any tone comes close to orange Day-Glo for getting attention. Psychologists say that purple, blue, and green are "quiet." Red, orange, and yellow incite action, and browns spell stability. Yellow is safest as an all-around attention getter, and red should be avoided in matters financial. Color is a reasonably arbitrary decision. What's important is to make the insert somehow stand out.

The insert should be distinctive in tone and message. Copy techniques and strategies are discussed in detail elsewhere in this handbook, but for inserts the rule is a simple one: Say something different or say it a different way. In other words, the insert should not be simply an echo of the primary selling piece. Indeed, no two sentences or selling points should be the same.

For example, should the primary element of the mailing package—usually a letter—talk about the benefits of a product (speed, convenience, money savings), the insert should complement and support those points, but not in the same language. Indeed, the insert can address a "sidebar" or secondary benefits, attempt to sweeten the offer, or merely catch the eye of the casual reader. But the language should be different and the proposition distinct and separate. By no means should copy simply be lifted from one element of a mailing and reconfigured in an insert just for the sake of "saying it one more time."

An insert should be supportive, an additive, a complement to the primary message and its action device. Thus, an insert should in no way "fight" the primary response mechanism.

An example would be an insert describing options to the primary "deal" under discussion. While direct mailers have had success with inserts making secondary offers ("You're probably most interested in our console machine, but we make an inexpensive table model, too"), a cardinal direct mail rule is to limit choices, keeping options to a minimum to avoid confusion in the reader's mind.

Certainly, in subscription promotion and in mail order, inserts routinely offer "upgrade" deals and "bonus bargains" and often a choice of payment plans and terms. The caution here is to regard an insert as an enhancement rather than a device which forces the reader to make a choice—the wastebasket, in most cases.

The Letter. Should a letter be considered an insert? Earlier in this chapter, it was suggested that a letter not be viewed as an add-on or enclosure but rather as the primary element in a mailing package.

Some direct mailers question the value and importance of a letter. Others insist that every direct mail package contain a letter, that a package without a letter is simply "advertising in the mail." For purposes of this discussion, a letter will be classified as an insert despite strong feeling that it is the essence of a mailing package, the most critical element.

Creating the letter is a craft in itself. It is not easily accomplished, especially considering that its mission most often is to elicit a check, a coupon, a card, or another form of response through the mail.

Experienced direct mail copywriters will tell you that how the words appear on a page is often as important as what they say. In other words, in letter writing, copy arrangement goes hand in hand with content.

It is basic direct mail knowledge that a letter should look like a letter. It should be a personal, one-on-one communication arriving in the privacy of an envelope, from one individual to another, inviting and easy to read.

Of course, this rule was made to be broken. These days, direct mailers successfully use any number of letter variants: tip-ons, illustrations, die cuts, computer-generated fill-ins in 48-point type, stickers, peel-offs, highlighting, callouts, and countless other devices. These are found most often in mail directed toward "consumer" audiences as opposed to business-to-business mailings. In the case of business-to-business mailings, the "classic" rules still have applicability. Use typewriter type, not "printing" or set type. Keep paragraphs short, no more than five or six lines. Sign the letter in a different color ink, preferably blue. Indent paragraphs for emphasis. Underscore where necessary but avoid visual tricks such as marginal notes or words and phrases in a second color which only detract from the personal look of the letter. Make liberal use of dashes and ellipses (. . .) as well as connectives to help the reader keep moving along.

Arrange the letter on the page with wide margins and plenty of room for the signature. In general, try to give it an airy look so that it invites readership rather than signaling with dense paragraphs and tight margins that there's a reading chore ahead. In short, the letter should be familiar physically to the reader. It should simulate correspondence of the type an executive is used to seeing.

The number of pages you choose depends on what you have to say and how skillfully you can involve the reader. In most instances, when you're asking for money or an order back in the mail, long letters pull best. Two-page letters to executive audiences outpull one-pagers. The question then becomes, Two separate sheets of paper or one sheet printed on both sides? The answer is two sheets to executive audiences, and one sheet printed on both sides to householders and consumers.

Letters are intended to convey benefits to your audience. Although it's in the realm of copywriting, this edict is worthy of mention here. Letters should be directed to, and concerned with, the reader's wants, needs, and desires. They should be benefit-oriented exclusively, telling the reader "what's in it" for him or her. Features such as the size of a product or how it works, colors, horsepower, capacity, how large your organization is and how long you've been in business—all these things belong somewhere apart from the letter as a general rule.

In sum, benefits, motivations, rationales, and urges to action all contribute to making a letter work hard. Features—product descriptions, specifications, and "hardware"—are best put somewhere else, not in the letter, but in an insert of a different sort.

Broadsides. Because of the multitude of variations possible, there is no way to give a precise definition of a broadside. Perhaps it's best described as any "oversized" enclosure, usually 17 by 22 inches or larger and most often designed as an insert for booklet envelope-size mailing packages: 6 by 9 inches or 9 by 12 inches.

A broadside, especially in full color, has impact because of its size and the expanse of space available in which to tell a full product story. Similar to a poster, it offers the opportunity to show products or at least components of them life size, fixing in the mind of the reader a fair picture of what he or she is being asked to consider. It's always a good idea to show people in a broadside to give a representation of the relative size of what's being sold and to convey the usefulness of the product by showing people enjoying it, using it productively, and benefiting from it.

A broadside rather than a letter is the place to ennumerate product features: colors, weight, capacity, number of pages, richness of the binding, and quality of the printing.

"Hardware" is the prime concern of a broadside, shown through the liberal use of photographs and illustrations. Copy should be factual and explanatory rather than motivational. One way to think of a broadside is as a visual aid a salesperson might use, a device to illustrate product features and show specific details. The sales pitch, reasons why, rationales, and benefit story are reserved for letter copy.

Broadsides often are filed away for future reference. If the mission of the mailing is to obtain a direct order, it's wise to design the broadside to incorporate a built-in order form, that is, a form in addition to the one which is primary in the mailing package. This does not imply that a broadside can be sent alone in an envelope. It should always travel with a letter and a separate response device.

Self-Mailers. They're not direct mail inserts, of course, but they combine into one format the jobs which a letter package with inserts does. A self-mailer is essentially a self-contained piece with either a single sheet folded a number of times or several pages bound into a booklet format. There is no outgoing envelope or separate letter.

Widely used, mostly for reasons of economy, self-mailers will not perform as well as traditional letter, folder, or reply form formats. For one thing, they "flag" advertising, with little or no opportunity for a personal look.

In instances where a personal look and image are of no real concern, self-mailers are perfectly appropriate to reach large audiences at low cost (seminar promotion is the best example). They garner wide passalong readership. They frequently are posted on bulletin boards or automatically put into an office routing stream so that exposure per impression ratios are high.

An effective self-mailer should attempt to combine all the elements of a classic mailing package: one panel to do the job of a letter, another to hit hard at features, another for testimonials and the like, and another for a detachable order form. These days, there are hundreds of standard "shell" formats available, many with built-in preformed envelopes for retrieving cash with order. If the objective is simply to get a card back in the mail, it's wise to die-cut a window in the outgoing face of the self-mailer with the address showing through the window so that that same address will show on the response card which comes back.

Because self-mailers are in many ways "ads in the mail," they must fight for readership and acceptance. A strong benefit headline is critical, along with tight copy and dramatic illustrations. Self-mailers don't have much room for "romance" or philosophizing. Perhaps more than any other direct mail vehicle, they should be approached with a conscious tone of "Dear Reader: Here's what's in it for *you*."

The Lift Letter. Relatively new to the direct mail scene, lift letters were first developed by publishers in an attempt to "take one more shot" at potential subscribers. Now called by various names and with various intents (publisher's letter, hype note, lift letter), these seek to approach customers or prospects in an oblique way as a "last gasp" to incite interest or elicit response. The theme of "To those who have decided not to respond to this offer" is a common tactic used to build responses by as much as 25 percent according to some reports.

A lift of that magnitude is likely to be rare, but because a lift letter will help to some degree for very little extra expense, it's really too good to pass up.

Formats vary, but in general they're "undersized," or smaller than the primary letter, frequently folded once down to approximately 5 by 7 inches. A simulated script or "handwritten" headline is most popular, and a "From the Desk of" legend is seen commonly.

The efficacy of lift letters is dependent largely on their "third-party" or "straight-from-the-shoulder" approach. They should be signed by an individual other than the signatory of the primary letter. Their tone should be "From where I sit, I see things a little differently. I can tell you in a no-nonsense way that this is a good deal."

The offer should be restated very clearly in the lift letter. But again, straight from the shoulder and from a different perspective, explained by an individual who seems somehow "apart."

As usually is the case with direct mail, the subject can be handled in a variety of ways. The essence of lift letters remains, however, an honest third-party endorsement. In effect, it says, "Hey, I wouldn't kid you, would I?"

Combination Mailings. The ideal or "classic" mailing package is still a letter and brochure with a response device. Self-mailers combine these elements into an economical self-containment. Somewhere in between are "combo" packages: a letter tipped on to a brochure, the reply form as part of the letter, a brochure with a built-in envelope device, etc. These differ from self-mailers in that they are envelope-enclosed. A letter in some form is the primary element.

These formats are popular, particularly in bookselling and subscription promotion, because they combine the best features of personal direct mail with those of consumer-type advertising. New, high-speed laser printing techniques allow a variety of fill-ins and personalization with no sacrifice of vivid graphics, tokens, tip-ons, stamps, and stickers.

The place for combination mailings seems to lie among mass consumer audiences. Such mailings combine the personal aspects of direct mail with the attention and awareness qualities of pure advertising. A good example is the approach being taken by more and more catalog mailers. Knowing full well the value of a letter yet appreciating at the same time the importance of an exciting visual presentation, they combine the two: a catalog with a wraparound letter as a "second cover."

As a general rule, combination mailings are not appropriate for executive audiences or in lead-generation efforts. Indeed, list size may preclude their use since these vehicles are cost-efficient only in the largest rollout quantities.

Circulars, Folders, and Product Sheets. These are distinct from broadsides only by virtue of their size. They generally measure only 8½ by 11 inches or 11 by 17 inches and frequently appear in two colors. What is a circular to one person—even the most experienced direct mail professional—is a folder to another. Whatever the case, they warrant careful creative consideration, mostly involving the presentation of the complete product story: nuts and bolts, colors, specifications, typical applications, the guarantee, and a listing of satisfied users. The story should be presented like a symphony. Minor sales points are presented first, building to the biggest selling ideas.

Liberal use of bullets, check marks, or similar devices helps get ideas across quickly, as does an almost exaggerated use of subheads. Keep in mind that the readers may not get involved with a folder to the degree they may with a letter. There's very little room for "mood" copy, and so the reader must be kept moving along with staccato phrases and capsulized sales points. The real "benefit thrust" belongs in a letter, but a folder should stand fairly well on its own. A good test is to see whether a folder anticipates questions and then answers them quickly. "Any special power source needed? What's the daily capacity? Is there a choice of colors? How often does the unit need servicing?"

When they are working on typical folder or circular copy, many copywriters try to put themselves in the role of a salesperson answering rapid-fire questions on the fly. Or they subscribe to the "yup, nope" school: Does the product do such and such? "Yup." Will I have to worry about so and so? "Nope."

In many instances, both sides of one page just won't do the job. Two pages printed on both sides would be overkill, subject to puffery and "filling." The best idea is to compromise by designing a folder which is in effect a page and a half, measuring 11 by 12¾ inches flat. One vertical fold takes care of the extra 4¼-inch "flap"; two horizontal folds configure the piece to fit a standard business envelope nicely. The extra flap is a perfect surface for "teasing" headlines to entice the reader into the main selling surface inside.

It should be understood that folders, brochures, or circulars are designed to "help go for the order." Put another way, they are not appropriate as a general rule in lead-getting or inquiry-pulling situations. Where "tell me more" is the name of the game, including a folder "tells too much," taking the mystery and intrigue out of responding for more details.

Gift Slips and Discount Slips. These commonly used devices are a simple and economic "hype" to response in themselves, although mailers must budget for the value these inserts represent. Because they generally are printed in one or two colors on a single small sheet, slips of this kind are ideally "testable" when added to a mailing to see how they affect performance. Of course, their success will impact significantly on "the back end."

Slips of this kind—whether offering a discount, a free gift for fast action, a premium, or an extended term—are "bonus" benefits to your proposition. Therefore, they should be distinctive; that is, they should stand alone, separately. Bright colors, borders, and their relatively smaller size should make them stand out. However it's done, their job is to shout, "I represent something extra and worthwhile." Building a gift slip into your folder or circular will not achieve the desired result.

Offering a discount or price break presents no real problem in terms of appropriateness. "Dollars off" or "save 20 percent" is compelling and inherently attractive. The difficulty often comes with offering a tangible gift item—a premium—which is inappropriate to the marketplace.

Whatever's being offered should have relevancy and be reflective of your product, service, or selling proposition: a pocket calculator in return for prompt response to an accounting magazine effort, a tape dispenser in return for an art supplies order, or a travel tote in response to a 14-day island cruise offer. Without question, selecting the proper gift or premium is a science in itself, but relevancy rather than "I'd like to have one of those myself" is what brings in worthwhile responses. How often have advertisers been heard to say, with remarkable hindsight, "The orders came rolling in. But nobody paid. No one renewed. All they wanted was the gift." This is avoidable to a large degree if the premium is relevant and somewhat "self-qualifying."

Multiple Inserts. Among the most frequently asked questions at direct mail seminars is, "Will too many enclosures kill my mailing?" Certainly there is little danger of too many inserts because postal rate restrictions dictate the volume "affordable" in a single envelope. The appropriate number in most cases should be determined by synergism. Do the inserts work together or are they fighting one another? Does one insert complement, enhance, and round out the theme of its companion? Is the reader able to deal with several themes without a feeling of being overwhelmed and assaulted by too much, too fast?

Good judgment and instinct are the best measure of what's too much, of course. A rule that continues to hold up, however, is that the reader should not be offered too many options or forced to make too many choices. Err on the side of keeping things simple, although it's perfectly permissible to say things twice, on two different pieces of paper.

Sound ambiguous? It is, because of the wide variety of circumstances encountered. If there has to be a rule, it's that multiple inserts will boost response incrementally. Should you add an extra? Probably.

Unique Formats

A call to the letter shop can get you a quick answer about what will run on machines and what must be handled manually. Often a minor adjustment to a fold or the addition of a flap to form a "carrier" can help even the most unusual shapes run smoothly. Vinyl phonograph records, for example, are a popular item, along with a variety of plastic cards, foils, vellums, and the like. Many enclosures in unusual shapes incorporate some sort of involvement device; this is an age-old direct mail trick which gets the reader "involved" by punching out a token, peeling off a sticker, or repositioning a stamp. No one really knows why involvement works; it's probably a compulsion to "fiddle" and do something that prompts the reader into action.

Action, though, is the key, meaning that an involvement device has little or no value unless it relates directly to the response vehicle. The "yes" or "no" token, the stamp, or the peel-off must relate clearly to what comes back. Taking action with the involvement device is actually a three-step process: "Take it from here, put it there, and then mail the card."

When the involvement device is part of a separate enclosure, it's vital that it relate unquestionably to the response mechanism. Label it. Make the graphics relate. Spell out instructions in copy on both pieces: "Remove token from here and reposition it in the gold color 'yes' slot on the request form." On the form state, "Remove token from separate card and place here in this gold slot to indicate your 'yes.' "

Business Reply Envelopes

A business reply envelope (BRE) is essential if you are looking for cash with an order. But it's a good idea to use BREs even in "bill me later" and "charge it" situations. Where it is affordable, many major mailers, especially in the publications field, include both a business reply card and a business reply envelope. The card can be returned by itself or tucked into the envelope and returned with a check. That way, readers have a convenient way of completing the transaction should they want to send payment right away rather than go through a billing process. As a general rule, including a BRE will generate more cash with orders, but it does add an extra expense to the overall cost of the mailing.

Of course, any mailing of a confidential or private nature always should include a business reply envelope. Insurance or health-oriented mailings or those which ask specific questions about the reader's financial situation are examples.

Should the return envelope or card be postage-paid? The rule has always been yes, as a means of increasing response significantly. Recently, however, some major mailers have been trying response vehicles without prepaying postage, and the results seem to be good. The jury is still out; paid versus nonpaid is very likely an ideal element to test in your own specific situation. The caution is to test actively and not be swayed by the isolated experiences of others. Fund raisers, for example, have been using nonpaid response vehicles for years. But they have a very strong rationale going for them: "Your stamp here will help."

For some reason, light blue business reply envelopes seem to work best.

Besides light blue, BREs with some color are more productive. Again, it's something to test in your own situation, with the reservation, of course, that it be far down the ladder of your testing priorities. It is something to think about once the "big" testing concepts have been resolved.

Insert Economies

If an insert is to be regarded as an enclosure, an add-on, or an "extra," it need not fall within the same quality parameters as the primary elements of your mailing. In other words, the stock, printing, and artwork (except in cases of a major broadside or basic selling brochure) need not be "special." Indeed, some inserts are improved by the nature of their immediacy, with a stop-press or bulletin look which is inherent in an urgent message. Simulated "grams" of all types are an example.

Keep postal weight restrictions in mind. A simple enclosure slip may not seem significant, but it does weigh something, maybe just enough to jump your mailing over the weight limit line. When in doubt, make up a complete dummy of your mailing package, using stocks you intend to print on and making allowances for glue, staples, and the weight of printing ink.

In regard to production costs, consider that inserts very often can "come out of something else." In other words, a brochure or circular may be designed to fit a particular press size with some waste or trim involved. What might normally be thrown away may be perfect for your insert. By planning carefully and working out the right kinds of impositions with your printer, you can save on printing and stock costs, creating a separate insert for the price of a trim.

Checklist for Inserts

While an insert can be any number of things, some basic principles apply, highlighted by the following questions.

1. Is your insert supportive of your letter?
2. Does your insert contain mostly features rather than benefits?
3. Does it reinforce the primary selling message visually?
4. Is it easily "insertable?"
5. Does it have a language of its own as distinct from pickup of copy from other elements?
6. Is your insert obviously separate, approaching the proposition from another tack?
7. Is it compatible with other elements, supportive of them rather than fighting them or offering the reader too many choices?
8. Does it show your product in use?
9. Does it contain a response form built in for those who may file it away for later reference?
10. Does it have telegraphic language such as bullets, subheads, and visual devices to keep the reader moving along?

11. Is it more than an echo of companion pieces?
12. Is it distinctive in color and size?
13. Can it be regarded as a visual aid, something a salesperson might use to sell from?
14. Is it light enough to keep the mailing package within postal weight limits?
15. Does it relate to the response mechanism in both copy and graphics?

chapter **37**

BROADCAST CREATIVE

Joseph McGlone

Creative Director
Aver Direct
New York, N. Y.

A LINEAR PROCESS

You are reading a printed page. One word comes after the next. The sentences follow each other. You are using one sense—sight—to communicate the word pictures to your brain. Your experience with the information on this page is linear, involving one piece of information after another.

Print direct marketing—whether direct mail, printed inserts, magazine ads, or newspaper ads—assumes that communication is a linear process. The traditional formula is attention, interest, desire, action (AIDA). First you get attention, and then you arouse interest. It is a linear formula.

When direct marketers moved into television, they assumed that communication would be linear, as it had been in print. They constructed their selling arguments as though the television screen were a page that happened to move. The next time you see a knife sharpener commercial on television, listen to it carefully. The sequence of the argument is exactly as it might have been written for the printed page, with the exception of cutting demonstrations which physically move rather than being static photographs on a printed page.

NONLINEAR COMMUNICATION

However, television has a character of communication which is quite different from the printed page. On many television shows, there are romantic moments in which little is said, but considerable tender communication is shown. There may be slam-bang action; once again, little is being said, but a great deal of highly involving action is being shown. This is definitely nonlinear communication.

Marshall McLuhan said that the medium is the message. He meant that there is a basic character of communication to each medium, and this determines a great deal of what will be taken away from any attempt at communication on the medium. The awareness of your medium's character of communication will influence your judgment greatly as you ask the question, Is this an effective selling message? The important point is that because of the differences in the character of communication, an effective selling message in television may be quite different from one in print.

TELEVISION AWARENESS

Most television advertising springs from roots vastly different from those of direct marketing. Television advertising began as "radio before cameras," done with live scripts, but it quickly developed its own technology. It became increasingly "awareness" advertising rather than "reason why" advertising. The most widely used commercial lengths shrank from 60 to 30 seconds. Increasingly, the struggle was for "share of mind," and the winners were those whose commercials achieved the greatest awareness.

Television awareness advertisers have developed a high degree of sophistication about their medium. They realize that they are dealing with a multisensual medium which depends on empathetic experience. They use arresting visuals to seize attention and also create a mood which is sympathetic to the product message. They use music adroitly. (The famous Coca-Cola jingle of several years ago, "It's The Real Thing," became one of the top pop hits of the year.) The sophistication of the dance routines on a number of soft drink commercials surpasses anything shown on commercial television. TV awareness advertisers definitely know that the medium is the message and that it would be foolish to put forth sequential selling arguments, plain and unadorned, in 30 seconds of commercial time.

There has been a migration of creative practitioners from the TV awareness world into direct marketing. The former president of the largest direct marketing advertising agency and the creative director of that same agency are both former TV awareness commercial makers. Obviously, commercial makers like these view the question "What makes an effective selling message?" quite differently from direct marketers with more traditional backgrounds. Like traditional direct marketers, they see it as a means of delivering an offer with excitement and advancing the sequential "reason why" arguments that can persuade a viewer to call an 800 number. But they also view it as a vehicle for gaining awareness as well as standing out from the surrounding commercial clutter and communicating as much as possible about experiencing the product.

When soft drink TV commercials show dancing feet and choruses of singers, they are attempting to do more than seize your attention and entertain you. They are trying to communicate the experience of the product: the lift, the refreshment, a sense of well-being. When a well-known light beer shows a 30-second comedy with ex-athletes in a barroom situation, it is attempting to convey in a nonverbal way things about the product's essence: It is "manly" (even though it is a light beer)—it has a real beer taste and it is "OK to order" in a male group.

The new TV direct marketers, many of whom have migrated to direct marketing from awareness advertising, approach commercials in the same way. They try to use dramatic vehicles that will convey the essence of the product itself. In doing so, they use many techniques that usually are thought of as the province of awareness advertising.

For example, Wunderman Ricotta and Klein has done hilarious commercials for Dial-a-Joke. In one of these, under the influence of the full moon, a man begins to turn into a werewolf. He calls Dial-a-Joke. The joke is so funny that his laughter changes him back to human form. It has been said many times that comedy is deadly in direct response and is useful only in awareness advertising. Yet the Dial-a-Joke commercials have been extremely successful because they communicate the reality of the product they are selling.

Direct marketers of insurance on television have long used celebrity presenters. The credibility of the celebrity communicates the credibility of the insurance policies. Chuck Beisch, former creative director of the Ingalls agency of Boston, had the inspiration to use Orson Welles for Preview, a subscription television service. Welles, a legendary film maker (*Citizen Kane*), by his very presence makes an important statement about the quality of the films Preview subscribers will experience.

The techniques of awareness advertising are used well by the new TV direct marketers. The United States Army has integrated music and words brilliantly to create emotional impact. Time-Life Books' World War II Library uses dramatic integration of the preparation for battle of a kamikazi flier with live film footage of planes being shot down to communicate the sense of commitment to win or die that underlay the Japanese war in the Pacific. Another Time-Life Library, the Life Library of Photography, uses surrealistic lighting to convey the ultramodern nature of the photographic techniques presented in the library. Preview has done a commercial using a quick cut technique, with sixty-two cuts within 30 seconds.

The big difference between awareness TV commercial makers and the new direct marketing TV commercial makers is the desired end result. One group wants awareness on the part of TV watchers. The other group, the direct marketers, wants an action to be taken. They want viewers to call an 800 number or reach into their pockets and write out checks. Because of the different end result desired, different emphasis is given to the mechanism to achieve it; the offer.

THE OFFER

In direct marketing, the offer is the centerpiece. Everything contributes to its importance, timeliness, and desirability. It takes more time to describe the many and varied advantages of a great offer than it does to gain attention for a major selling point. Thus, a direct marketing commercial must of necessity take longer than an awareness commercial.

The direct marketer is approached continually about the relative merits of 60-second and 120-second commercials. If you are with an agency, your client will ask for your opinion. If you are selling your own product, your wallet will ask for you. After all, 60-second spots are less expensive. They are more available. There are many reasons to wish you could say, "Yes, do the :60s. They'll pull fewer orders, but because they cost less, dollar for dollar you'll come out about the same."

Don't succumb to temptation. It's simply not true. There are no hard and fast rules, but experience leads one to suspect that :120s are at least twice as efficient dollar for dollar.

Why? Simply because the offer has more time to be repeated, elaborated, and experienced. Also, there is more time for the 800 number or ordering address to be exposed. This may sound like a minor matter, but it is not. An agency once tested the effect on a commercial's "pull" of lengthening the end tag. It was found that by increasing the tag (the section at the end of the commercial given over to ordering information) from 12 seconds to 20 seconds, the "pull" of the spot could be increased 50 percent. That's 50 percent more orders and more checks, with no increase in media costs.

The difference in pull between a 12-second end tag and a 20-second tag should not be surprising. It takes viewers 12 to 15 seconds to write down a company's name and address. We can reasonably make the assumption that people are not sitting there with pencil and paper poised, and they will have to fumble around a bit to get their writing instruments. When you go to a 20-second end tag, it merely means that you are giving people a reasonable chance to finish writing the address or phone number while it still is being shown on the screen. Following this line of logic, results can be improved still more by showing the address or phone number earlier in the commercial as well as at the end. This will warn viewers of the commercial that there is an address coming. They will have time to get their pencils ready before the end tag appears.

Thus, the offer is the main difference between direct-response TV and awareness TV. It is the reason why direct-response commercials should be considerably longer. What else can one do to make direct-response commercials more effective? Obviously one can improve the offer.

Everything that has been said about the effect of the offer on direct mail and mail-order ads is true of direct-response TV. A change in the offer outweighs all other changes to increase pull that might be made in the commercial. Substantial price variations have been tested on libraries with relatively little effect. However, price and premium tests in gift foods and in magazines have resulted in changes of over 200 percent. In general, price point importance is the same as in print and in direct mail. However, in TV, the premium has an even stronger effect than in other media, probably because TV is more visual. The use of a premium with relevance to the product, good perceived value, and strong visual impact seems to have the greatest effect on lift.

FORMAT

How important is format? This is where the great creative difference exists between TV and other direct-response media. In direct mail, for example, you often are told that the envelope "tease," the "Johnson box" or opening paragraph of a personally addressed letter, and the offer represent 90 percent of the pulling power of the piece. But in the case of TV, we are dealing with a nonlinear medium. The character of TV is one of emotional involvement. It has a total impact on viewers which is different from the effect on readers of changes in the format of a direct mail piece. Changes in format of a direct-response TV commercial can influence response rates by as much as 100 percent.

Figure 37-1 Frames from the Harlequin Presents commercial "Journey"

To examine what can occur when changes in TV formats take place and to show the methods used in the development of commercials, let's take a look at a new television commercial which ran for Harlequin early in 1982.

HARLEQUIN ROMANCES

Harlequin is the largest publisher of romantic fiction. This genre, which Harlequin had to itself for a number of years, has become extremely "hot," with a half dozen major publishers competing for the consumer's dollars. One of Harlequin's major lines is Harlequin Romances. These are sweet, gentle, worldly older man–innocent younger woman romances, never more than 195 pages. Another major Harlequin line is Harlequin Presents, consisting of slightly spicier, more conflict-filled romances in exotic locales, about the same length. The standard Harlequin home subscription offer is for a certain number of books free. You see the ad or commercial. You send in your request for, say, four free Harlequin Presents novels. You receive the novels in the mail. Four weeks later, six more books are mailed to you for which you are billed $9. You continue to receive the six-book mailings every month until you cancel. Once you are a paying subscriber, there are many cross-offers to other libraries. The usual entry into the Harlequin subscription list is through either the Harlequin Romances or the Harlequin Presents four-book offer.

Harlequin Presents had been appearing periodically on television for about 5 years. Frames from three of the commercials are shown in Figures 37-1 through 37-3. As you can see, they all use the four-book offer. Commercial 1 employs an appeal of "journey to far off places." Commercial 2 appeals to you to "add romance to your life." Commercial 3 asks you to "take a Harlequin break."

Commercial 1 (Figure 37-1) employs a format of a male presenter showing book covers and describing the action within. Commercial 2 (Figure 37-2), through the

Figure 37-2 Frames from "Add Romance"

Figure 37-3 Frames from the "Harlequin Break" commercial

use of dream sequences, shows a woman, obviously a surrogate for the viewer, involved in the action of the four free books. Commercial 3 presents a woman taking a break from her housework and reading, telling the viewer of the pleasures of a "Harlequin break" (Figure 37-3). None of the commercials take advantage of the involvement character of television. Commercial 2 comes closest to it, but it is still linear in its narrative method and lacks emotional impact.

These three commercials had pulled orders at, say, *X* dollars (that is, a total media cost divided by the number of requests for four free books, which yielded a cost of *X* dollars per four-free-book request). It seemed that *X* dollars per order or its prorated equivalent, since media costs today are obviously higher than they were in 1976, might be a foundation cost below which it was impossible to go. However, we recently had achieved a major cost per order (CPO) breakthrough in direct mail. Fired by that enthusiasm, we determined to achieve the same breakthrough in television.

The AyerPlan

We started our exploratory by constructing the AyerPlan shown in Figure 37-4.

The AyerPlan is simply a formal laying down of the strategy logic which will guide the creation of commercials. Most of the large advertising agencies use something like it. The form may be different, but the purpose is the same: to make the thinking that lies behind the creation of advertising accessible to everybody. That way the copywriter and art director, the creative director, and the client all will know that they are on the same track.

As you can see from the AyerPlan, the key fact is the flooding of the marketplace with competitive romances. The problem to overcome is that all romances are perceived as being alike. The objective is to convince potential readers that Harlequin Presents is a perfect match for the type of romances they desire most. The clients—the merchandising manager, the director of merchandising, and the vice president of direct marketing—agreed with us. We had an agreed on track down which we could proceed.

Two creative teams from AyerDirect went to work on the problem, led by a creative supervisor and her art director creative partner. I was the creative director.

People sometimes think of an art director as an artist. In the days before television, maybe they were, but not now. Some art directors can't draw. What they can do is visualize, especially in the moving medium of television. The work between the copywriter and art director is a continual verbal ping-pong which eventually results in the definition of a selling concept and the visualization of a dramatic vehicle for expressing it.

Here's the kind of dialog that probably went on between Doris (the creative supervisor) and Bob (the art director) during their work on the exploratory:

Doris I just can't stand to have a man telling me about romance. I don't want a male presenter.

Bob (kiddingly) What do we know about romance, anyway? Everyone knows we're just after sex.

Doris Oh, go trim your beard. I know what I'd like for the commercial.

AYERPLAN

APPROVED CREATIVE STRATEGY

CLIENT Harlequin **PRODUCT/SERVICE** Harlequin Romances ~~Harlequin Presents~~ **DATE** Sept. 11 1981

P. Cunningham G. Eversman

ADVERTISING OBJECTIVES

Competition: Other romance fiction. All escapist reading and entertainment.

Prospect: Female. Married. 35+. C and D counties.

Desired Behavior: Respond to offer of 4 free Harlequin Romances, or Harlequin Presents novels.

CREATIVE DIRECTION

Key Fact: Non-heavy romance fiction readers feel romance fiction is too lightweight to interest them.

The Promise: Harlequin romances are totally involving. You will relate to them intensly. They are your kind of reading.

Support: Harlequin is number one in romance fiction the world over. Harlequin romances are particularly involving.

Net Impression: These romances are far more interesting than one realized. So interesting that a phone call to an 800 number offering free books is strongly motivated.

Perceived User Personality: A woman who is a romantic personality and enjoys vicarious romantic relationships.

Figure 37-4 AyerPlan for the Harlequin Romances

Bob Burt Reynolds as the presenter—no, you don't like men presenters—Marilyn Monroe as the presenter. No, she's dead.

Doris The book. The real book.

Bob Which one of the four?

Doris Whichever is the best.

Bob How about this. *No Quarter Asked.* "Cord Harris grasped her by the wrist. 'You owe me, and it's time I collected, by God.' Stacey tried to pull free, but the man was too strong for her.' " That's my kind of romance.

Doris It's too rough. Which one of these four books has the most romantic scenes? I'd like to take that book and show it on screen. Get people involved in it.

Bob Sort of like they're reading it.

Doris That's it. And after they're really into it for 30 or 40 seconds, we come on with the pitch. We tell them if they'd like to read the rest of *No Quarter Asked* or *Devil in a Silver Room* or whatever, they'll have to call this toll-free number.

Bob We'll have to get into the Harlequin Books identification early. Look at this. What if we show the cover of the book and zoom right up through the Harlequin logo on the top of the cover.

Out of this interplay between copywriter and art director (see Figure 37-5), the two teams developed eight ideas. The first of these, which was very close to the idea developed by Doris and Bob in the imaginary interplay, is shown in Figure 37-6.

Storyboards

Let's stop for a moment and take a look at the format in which the "zoom through the cover" idea is shown. It's called a storyboard. It is a cartoon sequence method of presenting moving picture action in still drawings. It is a basic tool of the commercial-making trade.

Storyboards are sheets of cardboard. The front sheet usually has either eight or twelve holes, called "frames." They are shaped roughly like a television screen. Within the cardboard sheets, a sheet of drawing paper is placed. Drawings go on

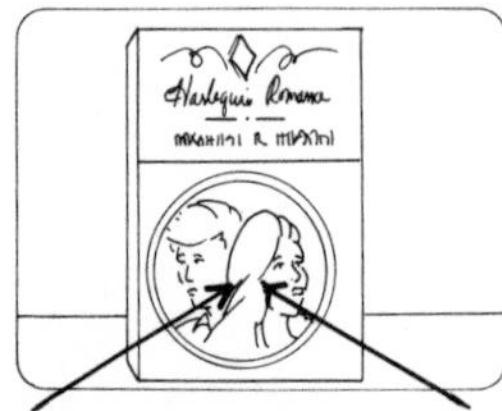

Figure 37-5 The art director's thumbnail sketch of the "zoom through the cover" idea

Figure 37-6 Storyboard of the "zoom through the cover" idea

the drawing paper and show through the cardboard frames. The drawings are usually pen and ink or magic marker, with black and white or color tones. In cases where a more elaborate representation of reality is desired, photographic scrap or even Polaroids can be pasted in place within the frames.

Concept Boards

For purposes of inside-the-agency presentation, I prefer concept boards to full storyboards. The concept board is a one- or two-frame drawing which shows the kind of visual which will be used in the commercial. The script of the commercial should be attached to either the front or the back of the board. See Figure 37-7.

CHOICES

"Zoom through the Cover" was the first of our ideas. Another was "Harlequin Mime." As you can see from the storyboard in Figure 37-8, the concept employed a mime telling the advantages of Harlequin Presents through gestures and mimicry. Harlequin was often a mime figure in the theater. This seemed to be a natural use of the symbol. We regarded this as a "generic" commercial, one which focused on no particular novel to tell the Harlequin Presents story. See Fig. 37-8.

Another generic idea was the "panel discussion." Figure 37-9 shows you that

Figure 37-7 "Zoom through the cover" concept board

Figure 37-8 Storyboard of "Harlequin Mime" idea

this was a panel of four women with a moderator. Each of the women discusses her favorite male lead in one of the four free books. The moderator delivers the pitch. It is a way of presenting the attractive male characters in terms of readers' responses to them and doing it believably.

After the generic, we moved to the specific. We picked *Devil in a Silver Room* as the most romantic of the books. Its hero, Paul Cassalis, seems to be a violent man but turns out to be the man of the heroine's dreams. There is an old castle, a fire, lots of atmosphere and some tender moments between Paul and Margo, the heroine. The creative supervisor and the art director had the idea of using a music box with a Harlequin figure upon it as a romantic way of registering the company's identity and leading into the story. The Harlequin music box could be shot beautifully and would dissolve to a music box in the heroine's room. Then we would widen to an embrace between Paul and Margo. Figure 37-10 shows how the commercial would develop.

Another dramatization of *Devil in a Silver Room* began with a Harlequin figure similar to the symbol on the covers of the books. However, this figure was alive. A mime, dressed in the costume of Harlequin, alights from a cross-bar and gestures, bowing, to one side of the screen. There the words "Harlequin Presents" appear while the announcer says, "Harlequin Presents. Stories of love and romance so real you don't just read them. You live them." The screen then dissolves to a romantic scene from *Devil in a Silver Room* which would be identified by the announcer, who would urge the viewer to "find out what happens next. Send for your four free Harlequin Romances today." This idea, in an expanded form, can be seen in Figure 37-13.

The dramatic action of the "Harlequin Presents" approach to *Devil in a Silver Room* (Figure 37-11) would be reasonably expensive to shoot. There was another method of handling the characters in *Devil in a Silver Room* which could be done without much cost: putting them in still photographs framed and displayed across a long table. Then panning of the table with the camera would reveal the photographs that tell the story, with romantic mood music playing behind the narrator's voice. The integration with Harlequin probably could be accomplished simply by moving in on the Harlequin logo on the cover of a book placed on the table after the last of the photographs.

The last of our exploratory ideas focused not on Harlequin generally and not on an incident from *Devil in a Silver Room* but on the novel's hero, Paul Cassalis. The copywriter had the idea of letting the camera follow Cassalis as he dressed for a confrontation with the heroine and then presenting their romantic conflict from a point of view that featured Cassalis (Figure 37-12).

Figure 37-9 Storyboard for "Panel Discussion"

Figure 37-10 Storyboard of "Music Box"

Now we had seven ideas. Which one should we recommend to our Harlequin client for production? Often, when you arrive at this stage, cost becomes a factor. I prefer to present the work on its own merits. After the clients have responded, giving a reaction to the ideas uninfluenced by financial considerations, there is plenty of time for measurement by budgetary yardsticks.

There was strong advocacy in our agency creative and account group for several ideas. Here are some of the arguments.

Figure 37-11 "Fated Photographs" storyboard

The "Harlequin Mime" idea was very good because it focused so strongly on the Harlequin figure as the storyteller. Differentiating Harlequin from other romances was a major point in the AyerPlan. This commercial would do that well.

The "Harlequin Presents" idea used the Harlequin mime as a master of ceremonies at the opening of the commercial. This was not merely good differentiation of Harlequin, it also dovetailed with the creative approach being used by the retail division to promote Harlequin novels sold on the newsstand. Unlike the "Harlequin Mime" idea, a major part of this commercial would be taken up by a romantic scene, a dramatization of the romantic material to be found within the covers of *Devil in a Silver Room*.

The "music box" idea had strong Harlequin identification because of the use of the figurine of a Harlequin on top of the music box. We liked this concept because

Figure 37-12 "Hero" storyboard

it was extremely romantic, an ideal frame for the romantic scene from *Devil in a Silver Room*.

"Hero" had adherents within our group simply because we liked it. It would make a great commercial. But admittedly, it did not differentiate Harlequin romances from other romances as effectively as the other commercials we were considering seriously.

It should be obvious that the selection of one of these commercials over another involved a series of choices. None of the commercials were without merit. Was identification with Harlequin as a brand the most important consideration or was emphasis on the superior romantic quality of Harlequin romances more important?

We talked through the choices casually and informally over a period of 4 days and then very thoroughly in a long meeting. We decided that the most important objective was to pull inquiries at the lowest possible CPO. The commercial that would do this and at the same time provide the Harlequin identification asked for in the AyerPlan would be our recommendation.

Our recommendation was the "Harlequin Presents" concept. We took the plan to Harlequin's home office in Don Mills, Ontario, and they rejected our recommendation.

"Rejected" is really too strong a word for what happened. Realistically, they made a series of choices. They made a fundamental choice and agreed with us that taking advantage of the involvement character of television was most advantageous, and so they rejected the generic "Harlequin Mime" approach in which the mime acted out the action. They made a second choice and disagreed with us on the relative merits of romantic quality versus Harlequin identification. In other words, they agreed that the music box was the most romantic introduction to the commercial that we could use. But they felt that employing the same Harlequin figure in our commercial that was used in the Harlequin retail spots would result in a cumulative Harlequin awareness on the part of viewers that was very desirable.

They disagreed with us on one other point. Our "Harlequin Presents" commercial showed a scene from *Devil in a Silver Room* and identified it as such. We felt that exposure to the spot would be almost like starting a book, becoming interested in its first chapter, and then having the book taken away from you. Naturally, you would want to continue and find out what happened. This should result in a lot of calls on our 800 line.

Yes, they said, but what would happen then? Would you have as good a back end as you would have had if you had done an involving scene and not identified it with a specific book? This is a question that comes up repeatedly in direct marketing, especially in television, which tends to be a high-volume front-end-pull medium. A good CPO depends on front-end pull. But far more important, when you are selling a "pay and stay" product, a sound profit depends on the back end. We finally decided to make certain changes in our offer which would help the back end and make our scene generic rather than letting it be identified specifically with *Devil in a Silver Room*.

Again, the decisions about which concepts to pursue, which to recommend, and finally, which ones would be chosen were based on a series of choices. When you and your client are operating according to the same yardsticks, your choices are similar. Therefore, your work is accepted and approved for production without too many false starts. When the yardsticks are not the same, the road to approval becomes rockier. The yardsticks must be brought into close approximation or the account eventually will be lost. This is why tools like the AyerPlan are used to bring the bases for choice closer together. Of equal importance to the creative person should be the question, "How do I satisfy myself?" You must know the basis for your own personal series of choices. Otherwise, you will be all over the lot in your decisions and often will be caught in an agony of indecision. Examine your own subjective principles. Where possible, rank them. Until you do this, you will be unable to approach projects with the greatest possible creative efficiency and security.

PRODUCTION

The process of making a storyboard also presents a series of choices. We first did the "Harlequin Presents" spot as a two-frame concept board. We felt that the two most important things to show were the Harlequin figure up front as master of ceremonies and the scene from *Devil in a Silver Room.* A spokesperson would come in later and deliver the pitch. But we felt this was so standard that it could be described rather than shown in the concept board.

When we prepared the storyboard for presentation to Harlequin in Ontario, we did a complete storyboard, as shown in Figure 37-13. We felt that three frames would show the Harlequin figure swinging on a trapeze, dismounting, and gesturing to a "Harlequin Presents" title against black. Five frames would show the romantic drama of the two principals and the "other woman." Five more frames would show the positions of the spokesperson as he sold the "four free books" offer. Two final frames would visualize the zoom-in on the Harlequin logo on a book cover at the end of the commercial.

Once we had approval to proceed with the concept, we did two things. We sent the storyboard out for bids, and we created a production board. The production board was a scene-by-scene presentation of the sequence of shots required to make the commercial (once again, a series of choices) in the judgment of our art direction and television producer. The television producer was an experienced direct-response freelancer I had worked with at a previous agency. If you are going to make a direct-response commercial, use a direct-response TV producer. The price levels are different in direct-response TV from general-advertising TV. You will save money with the direct-response TV producer. If you are careful to choose someone whose creative yardsticks agree with yours, the work you get for your investment will be of better quality.

The producer bid three production houses. The middle bid got the job. It was $2000 higher than the low bid and $5000 below the high bid. I had worked with the director several times before and felt that his presence assured that we would get our money's worth on the job.

Almost every direct marketer wants the lowest possible production cost on jobs where there is no prior "control." (A control is a prior test winner which provides a CPO benchmark.) The reason is simple. A marketer's production money is "pure risk" until the marketer has a track record proving he or she can

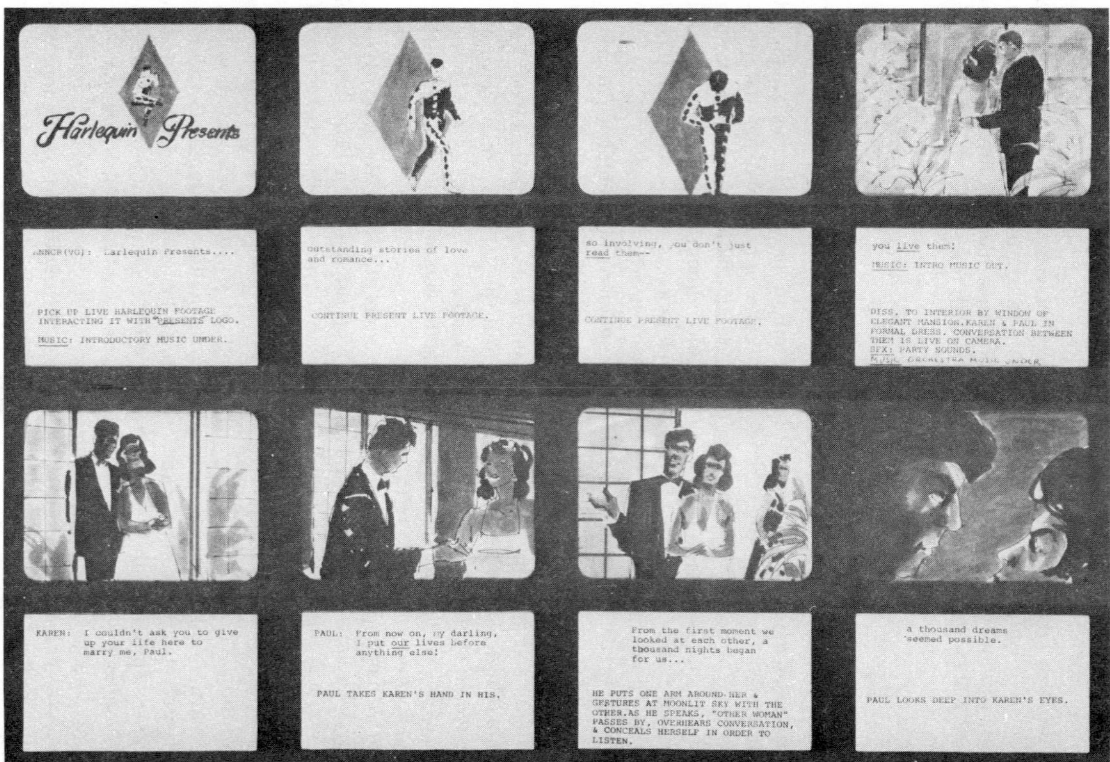

Figure 37-13 Final storyboard for Harlequin Presents, featuring the novel *Devil in a Silver Room*

I never wanted a woman who would melt at my touch...

HE TOUCHES HER FACE TENDERLY.

but one who would take fire!

HE KISSES HER PASSIONATELY.

CU "OTHER WOMAN"'S FACE AS SHE REACTS WITH SHOCK & SURPRISE.

MUSIC: ORCHESTRA MUSIC OUT.

ANNCR(OC): You've just experienced a romantic moment from the world of Harlequin Presents...a world that you are invited to enter with four free romance novels Harlequin will

send you when you call our special number.

ANNCR. COMES ON CAMERA IN SUMPTUOUS SETTING WHICH COULD BE ANOTHER ROOM OF THE MANSION & CONTINUES WITH HIS PRESENTATION THROUGH REMAINDER OF COMM'L.

SUPER: 800-000-0000. Call toll free.

123-4567

These four books are a FREE GIFT from Harlequin to introduce you to Harlequin Presents and the Harlequin home subscription plan. Because we believe that, once you've read one Harlequin romance, you'll want to read many, many more.

If you decide to join our family of Harlequin home subscribers, you'll receive six new Harlequin novels each month--delivered right to your door--for only $1.75 apiece.

These are brand new titles that are mailed to home subscribers as soon as they come off the presses. And, Harlequin pays all shipping and handling charges. You pay nothing extra for the convenience of home delivery.

123-4567

Why wait? Call our special number today for your FOUR FREE introductory romances. There's no obligation.

SUPER: 800-000-0000. Call toll free.

HOLD THROUGH END OF COMM'L.

Figure 37-13 *(Cont'd)*

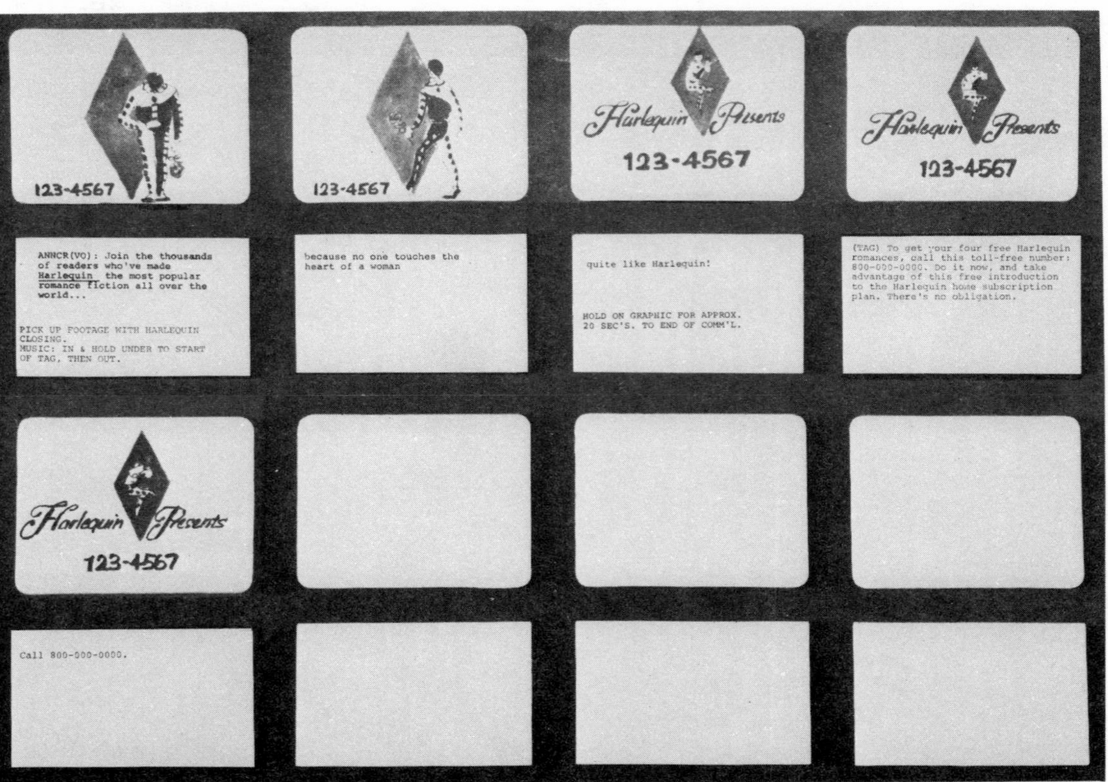

Figure 37-13 *(Cont'd)*

pull at a certain CPO. (Harlequin, having a track record in television on the "four free books" offer, had some history here and was not so cautious. The temptation for the direct-response commercial maker is to get the cheapest job possible. However, there is a rule of thumb. Long after they have forgotten whether you came in with the prices they wanted, they will remember whether you came in with the orders they wanted. Spend enough to do the job right.

We sat down with the production house and went over the production board. Here the production board became a vehicle for communication with the production house. It showed them how we saw the commercial, shot setup by shot setup. The director disagreed on two points on the staging of the dramatic scene. We had viewed it as a move in on two people at an embassy or high society party who were outside on the balcony, the point of view being that of the "other woman." The director felt that being indoors and moving outdoors gave us lighting problems. He preferred to have the couple leaving the room where the party was being held, moving instead to a deserted drawing room. The camera would not show the "other woman's" viewpoint. It would be an objective camera, following the loving couple and discovering the other woman spying on them. We accepted these suggestions. With our first preproduction meeting completed, we at the agency proceeded with casting, while the production company conducted a location search to find the site for our day of shooting.

CASTING

The casting took in the casting department of N W Ayer. It took 2 full days of casting and part of a third day. Casting is the most crucial part of a commercial. Who can bring it off? Who makes it feel "natural"? Who adds the extra bit of business that makes a scene jump out from the surrounding "grayness" on television? We found our female lead almost immediately, but the man was difficult. There was a charming fellow with an Austrian accent who looked great for the part. The director thought he would do well, but our clients at Harlequin were concerned about his accent. What if extra takes were required? How much would that delay the shooting and increase overtime costs? They preferred Jim York, a tall, good-looking, dark-haired man with no diction problems. He became the male lead.

Jim York, by the way, turned out to be absolutely superb for the part. This is an example of the advantage of having clients who work closely with you all the way through production. Some agencies try to "touch base" with clients at key points but generally keep them at arm's length from the production. I prefer the opposite approach. The closer we work, the better. If there are problems, they occur because we do not have our creative yardsticks lined up. We should do that before we get into production.

We shot the commercial in one long day's shooting (12 hours) at a mansion in Riverdale, New York. We shot in 35 mm and transferred the selected takes (the ones that looked like they might be usable in the commercial) to videotape. Videotape editing and color balancing can be accomplished much more quickly than on film. The television producer picked up the film masters of the Harlequin figure from the film editor who had worked on the retail commercials. We transferred them to videotape along with our own film. The director stayed with us all the way through the editing process, and in our editing, we came to an impasse.

We had planned to shoot the commercial following the romantic couple in their departure from the party room, across a marble vestibule, to their embrace before a floor-to-ceiling window, looking out at the moonlight. The other woman would be seen in passing, peeking out at them. They would kiss. The camera would cut to a close-up of her. She would toss her head angrily and leave.

However, the romantic couple were too attractive. They were "electric." You just didn't see anyone in the same scene with them. The establishing shot of the "other woman" was lost.

Here was a point at which another creative choice had to be made. We had an excellent romantic scene. Should we change it to include more of the "other woman"? And if so, how?

The client decided that we should change it. His reasoning was that we wanted our commercial to approximate as closely as possible the feeling of Harlequin romances. Virtually every romance has a romantic triangle with an "other woman." Therefore, the other woman should be strongly present in our commercial. Following a specific suggestion from our client at Harlequin, we changed the visual flow of the commercial and cut first to a close-up of the "other woman" listening while the dialog between the romantic couple, leaving the party, played off camera.

The new Harlequin commercials, :120 and :60 lengths, began running in early 1982. In contrast to earlier Harlequin commercials, which had been linear and discursive, this execution was nonlinear and dramatized the subject matter in a way that took advantage of television's essential character.

The new commercials pulled markedly better than the old. The exact numbers are privileged information at the present time. However, our plan called for us to run through March to achieve our objectives, and we were able to go off the air by the end of February.

Whether an advertising agency is creating the commercial or it is being done in-house or by a consultant or the production company itself, the process remains essentially the same. There are a series of choices to be made. Make them soundly and you will have an effective selling commercial. Make them honestly as far as you are concerned and you will have a commercial you can point to with creative pride.

part 4

PRODUCTION

chapter **38**

WORKING WITH SUPPLIERS

Tony Leonardi

Director of Advertising
L'eggs Brands, Inc.
Winston-Salem, N.C.

The customer-vendor relationship represents a balance of give and take. Although it is true that each party is most interested in how he or she will benefit best from this union, it is of the utmost importance that each realize that a mutual benefit is necessary. Customers who consistently look for a one-sided advantage can cause irreparable damage to the relationship and an eventual loss to the companies both parties represent.

This chapter deals with the "ways and hows" of developing and keeping a relationship intact. It delves into the philosophy and techniques of building team spirit.

The benefits a customer and his or her company receive from such a mutually responsible relationship are far-reaching. There is an almost immediate payback in terms of more flexible and timely schedules, fair pricing for the additional work not covered by previous agreement or contracts, and extra effort.

One basic fact should always remain in one's mind when one is working with suppliers. The production vendor is as much a team member to the company as the company's employees. Without the dedication, concern, and total support of the vendor, the up-front effort that goes into marketing planning, creative development, research, and scheduling can be wasted if the all-important mailing drop date is lost.

THE COMPANY ORGANIZATION AND ITS RELATIONSHIP WITH VENDORS

It is essential that the supplier both know and be aware of the company's organization and its players. For a vendor to be effective and to feel like part of the team, the vendor's knowledge of a company should go beyond the scope of just knowing the department from which he or she receives the purchase order.

Most direct marketing organizations with a purchasing budget of $1 million or more have a professional staff performing the purchasing function. Such a staff normally takes the form of a production department and is typically responsible for the purchasing of type and mechanical production, separations, paper, printing, and letter shop operations.

Vendors normally confine their day-to-day activities to working with the production staff. This is typical and proper, but it should not stop there.

Vendors want to know "who's who" in your company. This attitude should be encouraged. The more your vendors understand your organization and its members, the more likely they will feel like part of the team. Also, the vendors will make more of an effort on your behalf.

It is important to remember that although it's suggested your vendors get to know your organization and its people, it's of equal importance that direction and communication to your vendors come from a single source. This is usually the production team.

Taking this approach will minimize the potential for confusion and misdirection, and your vendors will appreciate knowing who to talk with and be responsible to.

QUALIFYING VENDORS

Cultivating a strong business relationship is a time-consuming effort, requiring an individual to call on all his or her talents.

It becomes very important to properly qualify vendors before precious time and energy are spent. Some cardinal steps to follow in qualifying a salesperson and a company are as follows.

Equipment

Does the candidate company have the proper equipment to do your type of work? Most companies publish an equipment list. They also provide samples of work to demonstrate the versatility of any customization of their equipment. It's important for the production team to understand the potentials and limitations of the equipment available to them. A customer's knowledge of equipment and awareness of the versatility of the vendor's line allow deeper communication between the buyer and vendor.

Capacity

The right equipment is not synonymous with adequate capacity. Make certain that the prospective vendor has the capacity to meet the deadlines and schedules your organization works under. Sometimes preplanning and advance scheduling can allow one to work around a supplier's limited capacity. If this tactic is considered, remember that your vendor is the last one in line who must compensate for schedule collapse. If capacity is limited to one press or minimal inserting machines, there is a potential for missed drop dates. Equipment capacity is limited by "engineered" output measured in thousands per hour. There are only so many productive work hours in a day.

Know-How

Now that you have qualified your candidate's equipment and capacity, the next thing to consider is know-how. Is the candidate up to date with current postal regulations? Does he or she have the internal systems intact to track work in process, raw materials, etc.? Can the candidate track your job through the plant, keeping you posted about the problems and progress of work? The biggest question you need answered is, "Does the candidate understand the mail-order industry?" Understanding the particular problems and requirements of a mail-order company is the single most important item of know-how your vendor can bring into the relationship. Quality of work also falls into this area. More on this subject is presented later in the chapter.

Competitiveness

This is probably the easiest qualifier of all, since it requires only objective analysis. The bottom line is still the bottom line. If good specifications have been provided by you to all competing vendors, it becomes a simple matter of arithmetic to determine how competitive your candidate is. It is important to make certain that you provide the same specifications to all bidding vendors. Items such as paper are a major contributor to the cost of printing. Alterations, substitutions, or ambiguous specifications can give wide fluctuations to the quote price. It becomes very important to the production coordinator to provide clear specifications and ask for specs in all bids submitted by the vendor. This will provide an accurate gauge of the competitiveness of your vendors and avoid misunderstandings.

Financial Solvency

One of the worst things a production manager can get into is a situation where a vendor goes bankrupt while his or her job is running in the plant. Usually all work in process stops dead in the tracks, and extracting film, paper, or work in process is such a lengthy process that making a drop date is impossible. Always check the financial solvency of a potential vendor through Dun & Bradstreet or Standard and Poors as well as bank references. It's a good idea to check their accounts payable schedule. A vendor who pays suppliers in 30 to 60 days is a better risk than one who pays in 90 to 120 days. This is one area where overkill is well worth the trouble.

Intercorporate Personality Mesh

Companies take on personalities and traits similar to the traits of the key executives who run them. If the chief executive officer (CEO) is a service-oriented, sincere individual, that trait will trickle down to the rank and file. It is important that the vendors you deal with have a working philosophy compatible with that of your company. It is just as important to make certain that key people on your vendor's staff can mesh with your own staff. If all other factors work but this, there are options available short of walking away from a business relationship. Sometimes vendors are willing to change customer service operators and even sales personnel. Sometimes customers will change the production coordinator in instances where staffing is adequate to accommodate a shift in personnel. When personalities work well between vendor and customer, problems can be solved more easily.

References

When negotiating with new vendors, always ask for references. It's probably best to ask for a customer list and then determine whom you would like to get a reference from. You would do best choosing a customer in a business similar to your own. References are the last check before work is seriously considered, and they should be sought vigorously. Ask about the vendor's track record in quality control, meeting deadlines, and responsiveness to problems. There isn't a better judge of a vendor than a previous or current customer.

ESTABLISHING STANDARDS

Establishing acceptable quality is important before any job is awarded. The definition of acceptable quality is usually "what is commercially acceptable." By that we mean the quality that usually is turned out on a press running at "rated" speeds (rated by the press manufacturer) using predetermined process inks and densities and running against customer-approved proofs that are pulled on the job stock.

The printer should be aware of specific quality areas the customer feels particularly strong about such as garment color swatches, balanced flesh tones, etc. Both separator and printer, if they are different, want to know what is important to you.

The following functions are the usual areas of importance that need both customer's and vendor's input and attention.

Art Preparation

The best results (and the most cost-effective) are achieved when mechanical preparation is tied into the vendor's stripping system. Many customers have their base boards and acetate punched to the separator's or stripper's hole system. This speeds the stripping process and improves registration.

Proofing and Color Correction Terminology

There is industry terminology and jargon that has developed over the years and has very specific meanings. Unfortunately, misuse of some words has caused miscommunications, resulted in mistakes in corrections, and strained relationships. It is always helpful to agree on terminology and definition. The best way to achieve common agreement on terminology is to correct proofs with the vendor present. Any variance in the understanding in terminology will surface and be cleared.

Communications

The three most important rules of vendor relationships are communications, communications, and communications. Your printer and separator should meet your key people in merchandising, marketing, and creative. These are normally the people who have input into the mailing package, and they should relay their ideas of what the quality level should be.

Separations and Proofing Systems

The single most difficult problem facing creative and production people is achieving and maintaining quality color reproduction, from photography and art through separations and printing. The quality control system begins with the photographer and creative staff and ends with the separators and printers. If you involve all parties in the quality control system, the end result will be a better job printed. The following steps will help.

1. Photography and art should be executed with an eye toward what the printed piece will look like. Contrasts, exposure, densities, and color combinations will help or hurt the print process.
2. Separations should be made only from transparencies of common densities. If the separator and printer are different people, they should communicate with each other on the running densities and ink rotation to be used. If wet proofs are requested, provide the separator with the inks and job stock that will be used. It is important that proofs be executed as closely as possible to the production job. If proofing specifications and parameters are established beforehand, it is easier to get the desired results.

Pressroom Standards

Follow the same rules as prepress. Running densities should be established, and test sheets should be pulled at random and "read" on a densitometer. There are other elements that will affect the color balance in the pressroom, such as the following.

Press Sheet Imposition. The way the art is laid on the plates will affect the color balance. This is especially true for offset and letterpress but is not really a problem for gravure. The reason for this is that ink flows from the fountain onto rollers and finally onto the plate. The amount of ink flowing onto the plate is adjustable. Art requiring heavy ink may be positioned above or below art that requires less ink.

On-Press Approvals. It then becomes a problem of balancing the needs of both. It's good to have a customer representative at press runs to make decisions as to how color is best balanced. If the decision is made by the customer to have a representative at press runs, it's probably best to keep it a contingent of one. When more than one person attends, direction should be given by a single spokesperson. Conflicting directions or numerous directions can result in confusion and crossed signals for the printer.

Letter Shop Standards

The letter shop is the last operation on the totem pole and the last one to correct and make up for the scheduling sins of everyone else. Letter shops also provide the last opportunity for a problem. Establishing the right communications with your letter shop is as important as with other vendors if not more so. Our problems with separators and printers concern themselves with schedules and color balance, and we can always work around schedules and live with compromise in color. The element that can forever foul a mailing is the letter shop. It's almost too simple to leave elements out, insert wrong elements in test packages, apply wrong labels, etc.

Even if you feel that the letter shop instructions are clear, be sure your letter shop supplies you with a hand-inserted sample of each code prior to inserting and mailing. This will help ensure smooth mailing. It is also a good idea to seed your list with names of employees and use a monitoring service to help you monitor the continued correctness of the letter shop function. It also will give you a gauge as to how many days your package is in the mail. This is particularly good in establishing a forecast and curve.

ESTABLISHING SCHEDULES

The marketing group usually establishes and coordinates the general marketing plan. As a rule, they will secure time elements from operations, fulfillment, merchandising, data processing, creative, and production for the necessary working time frame. Most of the more complex types of coordination fall within the production area. The production department not only supervises the activities of external vendors such as separators, printers, letter shops, paper merchants, etc., it also must guarantee that list houses get labels in on time and that postage is at the letter shop on time.

Before any event is implemented, it is good to have a round-table meeting involving the departments that will be involved in the execution of the mailing. If there are problems with the time frame, a general meeting will bring out the concerns and should resolve any potential problem.

The established timetable should be shared with all your vendors so that they can see the whole picture as you do. The more they understand, the better they can serve.

It is also good to have an action plan to handle schedule slippage. This can be as simple as the execution of a series of phone calls to vendors advising them of new dates. It also may take the form of reducing time in review and approvals of proofs. The idea is to keep intact the all-important drop date.

TEAMWORK

As was mentioned earlier, it is important for the good of your company and your vendors' companies that you instill a team spirit. When your vendor misses scheduled dates or quality is below par, look to the reasons rather than just complaining. If the vendor feels part of the team, he or she will want to know why quality and work are not up to snuff.

Before you reprimand a supplier, delve into the reason why there was a failure. Did a separator blow a schedule because mechanicals were confusing or poorly executed? Was quality off because transparencies were bad? Did a printer or letter shop lose a date because people upstream blew theirs?

You are the captain of the team, and it's your job to monitor the schedules and anticipate problems before they happen. A team will respect and react to a good team captain.

Compliment the player when a good job is done. A compliment, like a reprimand, will be remembered.

TYPOGRAPHY

Tony Esposito

Director of Typography
Cardinal Type Service, Inc.
New York, N.Y.

HOW TO ACCOMPLISH YOUR TYPOGRAPHIC OBJECTIVES

> Typography is a servant, the servant of thought and language to which it gives visible existence.
>
> *T. M. Cleland*

The function of typography is not to decorate but to convey meaning. The strongest selling message is wasted if it isn't read. Observing the rules of typography helps ensure that a message will be read.

Advertising typography must work especially hard. One quick glance may be all your advertisement will get. In this brief moment, it must sell.

Effective typography recognizes that the eye is a creature of habit and never risks confusing it and losing its attention. It also recognizes the dangers of monotony. The eye seeks variety and, without it, wanders away.

In every advertisement there should be an order of importance, and that order should be clearly visible. The reluctant eye must be led from headline to subhead and from copy to captions by the easiest route. The reader's eye will not do this voluntarily. It must be compelled and guided. If you want to sell, never expect the buyer to do the work for you.

What is the correct order of importance? The answer comes from knowing the three hurdles every advertisement must clear.

1. It must catch the reader's attention with headline and picture.
2. It must keep the reader's attention with easily readable copy.
3. It must make sure the brand is remembered.

A feature that catches the reader's eye and captures his or her attention is first in order of importance. It may be a striking picture or a headline that makes the reader ask, "What's next?"

The headline should send the reader a telegram. It should seem important and informative. It should be immediately intelligible.

Remember that a headline usually is read at less than arm's length, not as it appears on the wall in a presentation room. To get a precise sense of the visual impact your ad may have, always paste the actual layout in the newspaper or magazine in which the ad will appear to test the proper relationships. Also, never present advertisements in layouts with large white frames.

Headlines should always be broken in a way that makes the statement clear and easily accessible. Additional white space is one device to make them more readable. Large headlines in limited space have impact, but their heavy blackness may smother their sense. Remember that the reader should not be aware of the typography as such, only the meaning it is intended to deliver.

Complicated typefaces tend to distract from and diminish the message. Drama belongs in the illustration and the sense of the message; not in "interesting" typefaces. Indulge your adventurous spirit elsewhere.

To spice up a headline, consider a single word or two in color or in black with a color underscore. A single word in all caps of a contrasting color, with the follow-up headline several sizes smaller and darker, can look good, especially if surrounded by ample white space.

The current vogue is to mass large lines close together, forming blocks. They are either coal-black or hair-fine, a victory of decoration over efficiency. Both retard comprehension. When they are printed in white on black, the strength of the message is reduced further.

A headline should never cover an important part of an illustration. Surprinting requires delicate care if the result is to be pleasing. If embellishment is needed, use it with restraint. If in doubt, avoid it.

Colored type increases interest, but it also may decrease impact. For example, a line printed in green, in the same size and weight as a black line, reduces the impact value 40 percent. Of all colors, red loses the least in impact.

The subhead or bold lead-in should be noticeably smaller than the headline. Minor differences in type size are not apparent to the average reader.

What makes copy "easy to read?" First, short paragraphs. You do not speak to your friends in long, monotonous sentences. You say something and then give them a chance to react.

You can alter your tone of voice with many typographic devices: cross heads, italics, indentions, boxes, thumbnail sketches, and coupons, for instance. Variety keeps readers interested and helps prevent their drifting away, but a balance must be kept. In typography, too many changes can produce confusion and too few can produce monotony.

Is there a right type size? There should always be a close relationship between the type size and the length of the line. As a rule of thumb, 35 to 40 characters to a line is effortless to read.

Narrow measures are also desirable. A newspaper column, for example, is set narrow so that the eye will be guided to the next line without effort, even in a rattling train. The column rules permit very narrow measures, when otherwise the eye would travel right across to another column.

Think before you choose a typeface. What atmosphere are you trying to convey? Should you think bold or gentle, newsy or fashionable? Any product has a personality that you can either enhance or hinder.

Remember that the more unusual the typeface, the more it may detract from your message by distracting the reader's interest.

Is the message to be direct, informative, hard-hitting? The type can reflect this feeling. Are you looking for an air of elegance? Be uncluttered. Leave sufficient air between the elements. A more styled face will create atmosphere if the copy is fairly short.

Know your product and try to create an appropriate atmosphere for it. You wouldn't stock jewelry on shelves like soapboxes, yet many advertisements still do this. It is possible to upgrade a product and even a company in the consumer's mind by giving it an elegant treatment. In this regard, typography is a vital factor.

Careful attention to typographical detail can make the difference between a good advertisement and a great one.

Since the acid test of a good type treatment is whether it is readable, sufficient line lead is a critical detail to watch. The typographic point is one seventy-second of an inch, but it may make the difference between a pleasant, readable page and one that is black and forbidding to read.

Publications understand this rule and do not try to save space at the reader's expense. Publishers are extremely sensitive to readability. This is why they rarely use sans-serif faces.

Strive to add life to the body text. A large initial will lead the eye directly from the headline or subhead to the first text paragraph. So will a boldface first paragraph.

Occasional cutoff rules and boxes add interest and ensure that the elements that need to be separated from the main text are set apart visually. Paragraphs that are indented on the left margin and have sufficient separation above and below also assist in this objective.

Changes of pace should always be made for sense, not simply decoration. Research shows that copy broken up in these ways brings higher readership.

No hard evidence supports the popular myth that a reader is intimidated by long copy. If the copy is informative and interesting, the hazards of imposing length can be reduced significantly by resourceful typographic treatment.

It adds life to long copy, for example, if the illustrations within the columns occasionally are of a different width. A sense of airiness is introduced when illustrations are narrower than the column and the captions are set to the same width as the illustrations.

STAGGERED TYPOGRAPHY

Staggered typography requires special handling. It is loaded with pitfalls for the designer who, in trying to avoid the rigid appearance of the justified setting, treats it casually. Staggered typography calls for common sense and sensitivity to produce a job of readable typesetting. Here are a few tips.

1. **Stagger with restraint.** Avoid violent jumps. Lines should not vary in length by more than 2 or 3 ems. Where the lines vary only slightly in length, the

reader can follow the sense to the end of the sentence more easily. Alternating very short lines with very long lines is confusing to the eye. The ideal is to set lines by phrases or by the unity of word sense.

2. **Avoid paragraph indentions.** Combining staggered type with indented paragraphs tends to give the appearance of staggered right and left. The function of paragraph pause is lost. Flushed paragraphs are a better solution. Where copy is short, running in several paragraphs can be a good solution.
3. **Use paragraph spacing.** Inserting extra space between paragraphs is functional when setting staggered right compositions. Where copy is long, it infuses the text with white space and enables faster reading.
4. **Regard leading as critical.** Staggered type calls for more careful attention to leading than does the justified setting. Depending on the face, of course, the text is generally more readable when more than solid leading is used.
5. **Confine the stagger to one side.** A flush-left arrangement gives the reader a fixed starting point from line to line and conforms best to the reading habits of most people.

It should be remembered that the carefully controlled, random look of staggered typography rarely can be achieved in the first setting. Typographers report that staggered typography almost always requires at least one resetting, and this means higher typesetting charges. Even when the type director carefully casts the copy and renders the type arrangement line for line and word for word, it frequently is necessary to alter the layout and sometimes the copy to achieve the final result. Word breaks should be held to a minimum, especially one above the other. A cooperative copywriter always helps in the staggered setting.

Special emphasis or a change in subject should be indicated by the copywriter. The typographer should take a cue from the copywriter. It is of great help when the copywriter indicates special emphasis with typewritten copy by indention, underscoring, or caps.

Resist the temptation of innovation for its own sake. Most magazines abound in enormous headlines, reversed text, and busy arrangements. An understated advertisement can be a clearing in the jungle. It is likely to be the one that is read and remembered.

Don't be a copycat. The fear of not being up to date frequently results in mindless imitation. Styles come and go. Whenever a style is "in," abandon it.

White space often can be the most valuable ingredient in an advertisement. It should not necessarily be considered as inert, empty space. It can give your message impact and make it stand out on a crowded page.

The atmosphere in an advertisement is created by the illustration, the promise, and the white space. Think of the atmosphere you want to create before you begin a layout.

Tidiness need not mean dullness. It should mean that the reader can absorb your message without conscious effort and remember it.

A coupon always should look like a coupon. The broken-rule box is usually the simplest way to make the coupon irresistible. There is no specific "right" size, but there must be enough space for the reader to fill in the necessary information.

Someone has to sort out all those coupons and address envelopes. Don't make that work unnecessarily difficult by using odd shapes for your coupon.

Brand identification should be clearly visible. If it is not, your competitor will be the only beneficiary of your work.

Most people are not aware of typography, even though they are bombarded with it every day. This is as it should be. If it is properly done, typography is an invisible labor. It is the message that you want to impress upon the reader, not your flair for design.

INTERNAL PROCEDURES TO FOLLOW

Typing Instructions for Print Advertising

Typographical revisions are very expensive. A great many of them can be eliminated if the elements of a print manuscript are labeled properly straight from your typewriter. The rules are simple.

1. **Marginal notations.** The following specific elements in the manuscript should be identified in the left-hand column:

   Headline
   Subhead
   Crosshead
   Picture caption
   Main body text (copy)
   Signature and address or logo
   Indented paragraphs
   Italicized or boldface paragraphs
   Box or coupon copy (if any)

   Regardless of position in layouts, always type box copy at end of main body text. All subsequent pages should have client and product identification. For legal lines (if any), type after box or coupon copy.
2. **Capitals.** Headlines should be typed in all caps. Everywhere else, use caps only when copy must so appear in print.
3. **Crossheads.** Center in column with a continuous underscore.
4. **Emphasized leads.** Opening phrases that you want emphasized should be shown by a continuous underscore under the entire phrase.
5. **Italics or boldface.** When the copywriter shows a word or phrase in the body text underscored, the typesetter will assume that the word is to be italicized. Indicate in the left-hand column any instructions to the contrary.
6. **Corrections.** Make all copy corrections in the right-hand column. The left is to be reserved for instructions to the typographer. No matter how obvious corrections may look to you, when they are mixed with type specifications, they can create confusion.

   Don't send manuscript copy that is overloaded with corrections to the printer. This invites mistakes, and the initial typesetting cost will soar. It is better to have the copy retyped.

7. **Typing quality.** Unless the copy has been multilithed, make it standard practice to reserve the first carbon for the typographer. A typographer's eyesight is no better than yours. A blurry fifth carbon can result in an unexpectedly steep typesetting bill.

COPYFITTING

When working with type, it is absolutely essential that you know how to copyfit in order to establish the amount of space typewritten copy will occupy when set. Only then can you specify the typeface, point size, line spacing, etc.

Typewriters

To understand copyfitting one must start with an understanding of the typewriter. The two typewriters most commonly used are the pica and the elite. The pica typewriter has large characters and types 10 characters to the inch. The elite has smaller characters and types 12 characters to the inch.

Character Counting

To convert typewritten characters into typeset characters, one must determine the total number of typewritten characters in the copy. Counting each character individually is time-consuming and unnecessary. The simplest method is to count the number of characters in an average line and multiply this by the number of lines on each page.

First, establish the kind of typewriter that has been used by counting the number of characters per inch. Next, take an average line and, using a ruler, measure it to the nearest inch. Multiply the line length by the number of characters per inch. For a more accurate count, adjust the total by adding all the characters that extend beyond the average line and subtracting all the characters that fall short of it.

If there is more than one page of copy, multiply the number of characters on an average page by the total number of pages. Where extreme acccuracy is important, you may find it necessary to count each paragraph and page separately.

When working with lengthy manuscripts, check each page for inconsistencies such as a varying number of lines per page, additions and deletions, and change of typewriters. Any of these circumstances will affect your count.

Let's examine how much space the typewritten copy will occupy when converted into type.

First, you must make certain of design decisions such as the choice of typeface and type size you want to use and the amount of space you want the copy to occupy. These choices can be changed or modified if they do not work.

To establish the number of typeset characters that will fit a given measure, refer to a character count table. These tables are found in most type specimen books, and they indicate the number of characters to a given pica measure for each size of type.

Most character count tables are based on normal letter and word spacing. If you want to set type either tight or loose, call your typographer for a more accurate character count.

If a character count table is not available, determine the number of characters per pica and multiply that figure by the pica measure required. The number of characters per pica of a specific typeface varies from system to system. If you do not have a character count table or a set alphabet for the equipment you are using, call the typographer.

Establishing the Depth

Once the number of lines has been determined, the next step is to establish the depth. Use a pica rule, which is calibrated in points and covers the more popular sizes, such as 6, 7, 8, 9, 10, 11, 12, 13, 15, 17, and 19. When measuring type, these increments represent the baselines to baseline measurement, not necessarily the type size; that is, the 10-point increment could represent 10-point type set solid, but it also could represent 7/10, 8/10, or 9/10.

If you find that the type sets too long or too short and you decide to adjust it by changing the typeface, type size, or measure, you must refigure the characters per pica. On the other hand, you can adjust the line spacing without refiguring. Adding or deleting space between lines does not affect the characters per pica or the number of lines; it merely increases or decreases the depth.

Writing to Fit

In most cases, the designer gets the typewritten copy and then designs the piece. There are times, however, when the procedure is reversed; the designer designs the piece first, and then the copy is written to fit the layout. In this case, the designer will have to specify the number of characters or words to be written.

Specifying the number of characters and lines needed is the most accurate guide you can give the copywriter. To do this, the designer first must determine the typeface, type size, measure, and leading. By referring to a character count table, it is possible to establish the number of characters per line. Ask the copywriter to set the typewriter margin at this character count and indicate the number of lines required. This will give the copywriter a very accurate indication of when he or she has accomplished your objectives.

Type Specification Chart

When preparing copy, especially complex copy, it is sometimes handy to have a checklist of the various design decisions that must be made: typeface, type size, measure, word spacing, letter spacing, etc. After the form is filled out, it should be sent to the typographer along with the job. It is also a good idea for the designer to keep a copy in the event that the job has to be matched at some future date or in case patches have to be set.

A sample type specification chart is shown in Figure 39-1. Some of the items shown on the chart may affect the cost of the job: makeup, kerning, hung punctuation, and extra proofs, for instance. You may want to check with the typographer before specifying them.

Date	Job Number	
Typographer	System	
Type (typeface, type size, line spacing, and measure)		
Type arrangement		
Justified		
Unjustified		
Flush left, ragged right	Minimum line	picas
Flush right, ragged left	Minimum line	picas
Centered		
OK to hyphenate		
Letter spacing		
Normal		
Loose		
Tight		
Very tight		
Touching		
Ligatures		
Letter spacing acceptable to justify line	Yes	No
Word spacing		
Normal		
Loose		
Tight		
Very tight		
If justified, set with ______ units minimum and ______ units maximum word spacing		

Figure 39-1 Sample type specification chart

PROOFREADER'S MARKS

Proofreader's marks are a standard set of symbols used to convey instructions to the typesetter. They are clear and brief, and they communicate rapidly and efficiently. For example, a single line under a word means "set in italic," and three lines mean "set in caps." These symbols are used and understood by everyone associated with copy or type: copywriters, editors, designers, typesetters, proofreaders, etc. Although you probably will use only a dozen or so of these marks, it helps if you are familiar with all of them (see Figure 39-2).

EXPLANATION	MARGINAL MARK	ERRORS MARKED
Take out letter, letters, or words indicated.		He opened the windoww.
Insert space.	#	He opened thewindow.
Insert letter.	e	He opned the window.
Set in lowercase.	lc	He Opened the window.
Wrong font.	wf	He opefed the window.
Broken letter. Must replace.	x	He opened the window.
Reset in italic.	ital	He opened the window.
Reset in roman.	rom	He opened *the* window.
Reset in bold face.	bf	He opened the window.
Replace with capital letter.	cap	he opened the window.
Use small capitals instead of type now used.	sc	He opened the window.
Insert period.	⊙	He opened the window
Transpose letters or words as indicated.	tr	He the window opened.
Let it stand as is. Disregard all marks above dots.	stet	He opened the window.
Insert hyphen.	=/	He made the proofmark.
Equalize spacing.	eq #	He opened the window.
Move over to point indicated. [if to the left; if to the right]		[He opened the window.
Insert comma.	^	Yes he opened the window.
Insert apostrophe.	∨	He opened the boys window.
Enclose in quotation marks.	∨ ∨	He opened the window.
Draw the word together.	⁀	He op ened the window.
Insert inferior figure.	^2	Sulphuric Acid is HSO..
Insert superior figure.	∨2	2a + b = c
Used when words left out are to be set from copy.	out, see copy	He window.
Spell out words marked with circle.	spell out	He opened the 2d window.
Start a new paragraph.	¶	door. He opened the
Should not be a paragraph. Run in.	no ¶	door. He opened the window.
Query to author. Encircled.	(was?)	The proof read by.
Out of alignment. Straighten.	=	He opened the window.
1-em dash.	1/m	He opened the window
2-em dash.	2/m	He opened the window
En dash.	1/n	He opened the window
Indent 1 em.	□	] He opened the window.
Indent 2 ems.	□□	] He opened the window.

Figure 39-2 Proofreader's marks

PHOTO DISPLAY: WHY, WHEN, AND HOW TO ORDER IT

Photo display typesetting which refers to photographic composition of headlines and large-size typography, is well known to most designers today. Most of these systems—Photo Typositor, Star-o-mat, Letterphoto, Headliner, Filmotype, etc.—use negative reels or font grids made from actual metal typefaces.

The primary advantage of these systems is the ability to expose one character after another in full view of the operator, permitting flexibility and perfect control at all times for most typographic refinements. Letters can be superimposed or placed inside each other; they can be blurred, overexposed, underexposed, condensed, expanded, italicized, and back-slanted; they even can be made to achieve certain stroboscopic effects.

Spacing is one of the important distinguishing features of photo display typesetters. It is possible to control the spacing between letters to eliminate many unsightly gaps. For very close letter kerning, reduction of punctuation marks, or single characters within a line, these typesetting systems are unequalled.

Some Words of Caution

Headlines are meant to be read quickly and to entice the reader into the text matter. It takes a sensitive and highly trained eye to set display type, someone with the experience and ability to correctly set and interlock characters to create a pleasing graphic form.

It is the responsibility of the designer or type specifier to be aware of poor letter combinations, typeface styles with full serifs or faces which have strong thick and thin contrasts, and typefaces which are extended in design or have large open counters. These styles must be dealt with and spaced with extra care. If a headline is to reverse or surprint, it should not be set as tightly as it would be set for positive use.

If the headline is not absolutely readable, it is defeating its purpose, and the accompanying text matter probably won't be read.

Camera Distortions and Special Typographic Effects

Many type designs do not come in every weight, spread, or outline. The more advanced typographic suppliers have added new equipment which has the ability to expand, condense, oblique, back-slant, curve, inline, outline, contour, shadow, and create halos and circles. With the use of this equipment and special lenses, it is possible to create many typeface variations to achieve special effects from one basic film font.

How to Order Display Typography

1. First specify the typeface desired. Table 39-1 shows three sample sets of type specifications.
2. Specify typefaces in terms of point sizes or inch measurements. In-between sizes also can be obtained when necessary. When specifying in inch measurements, use a lower-case x height as a guide for lower-case settings and a cap H

TABLE 39-1 Examples of Specifications

48-point Helvetica Medium
Upper and lower case
Set tight spacing
Makeup as per layout

News Gothic 1-1/4-inch height on cap letters
Upper and lower case
Set normal spacing
Galley strips only

Times Roman Bold
All caps
Set touching
One line 7 inches wide

for all-cap settings. Either x or H heights can be used for measurements. You also can request that a line be a certain width in inches. Be aware, however, that this always requires a camera shot at additional expense.

3. If a font has alternate characters and you intend to use them, be sure to be specific about the ones you want.
4. Specify the kind of letter spacing you wish: "touching," "tight with discretionary touch," "tight-not-touching," "normal," or "TV" (for television supers). If a condensed, expanded, or oblique letter is required, specify percentages or degrees as you require. Most skilled typositor operators will take into consideration all factors necessary to achieve the best typographic appearance for each style of type. The proper word spacing should follow automatically.
5. Wherever possible, provide a layout of the area to be set in photo display. Rough layouts are acceptable and are always preferable to no layout at all.
6. Indicate whether you wish to receive photo display as galley strips or made up into position per your layout and the number of proofs required. Photo display type is produced on a roll of paper which is 2 inches in width. While it is technically possible to set 100 feet of copy on a single continuous roll of paper, it is not possible to set more than one line vertically at a time. For precise makeup, the display strips are shot onto film and then stripped up to specification. Reproduction proofs of the complete job are supplied.
   When ordering photo display, always specify "galley strips," "galley repros," or "makeup as per layout."
7. If you are in doubt about any job, discuss it with your supplier. A trained representative will be glad to discuss the job with you.

TYPOGRAPHY FOR TV SUPERS

Following are guidelines that should be considered before ordering type for TV supers.

1. Whenever possible, keep the type size the same throughout a commercial. In an already busy 30 seconds, it is important to achieve visual consistency.
2. When the title is unbearably lengthy, consider a full-screen treatment. It may interrupt the photography, but if the words are important enough, it will be worth it.
3. Type should be kept well within the "safety" parameter provided. Keep the title on view at least 1 second for every four words to ensure readability.
4. Classic and simple typefaces have proved the most legible. Even with the worst reception, classic forms still can be recognized.
5. Both sans-serif and serif faces can be used successfully, but special care should be exercised in letter and word spacing. See example below in both serif and sans-serif types.

TELEVISION TELEVISION

6. Thin sans-serif letters as well as serif faces with fine serifs should be avoided. They tend to break up and become illegible.
7. Do not change the typeface style within one commercial without good reason. Type, which may be thought of as "graphic conversation," sometimes can be rude to the viewer when an abrupt change of pace occurs.
8. All caps can be used successfully if the words are few and there is an obvious reason for using them, for example, a short news announcement. But upper- and lower-case letters generally read better because of their more distinctive, more recognizable shapes.
9. Do not scatter capital letters indiscriminately throughout a title.
10. Make a logical, left-to-right reading arrangement.
11. Try to avoid slanted or tilted lines of type. Otherwise, you force viewers to work too hard to understand the words and risk losing them.
12. People peer into a light source when viewing television, and consequently, it is preferable to use white or "reverse" lettering whenever possible. Reverse lettering affords the greatest dropout effect possible, divorcing the reading matter from the various values that are in motion in the background.
13. "Outline" types, which have a tendency to fall apart, should be avoided.
14. It is always useful to show the type director your storyboard. If you advise the type director about the actual film tone that the super will go over, he or she can help select the best typeface for the situation.

TODAY'S TECHNOLOGY

A quiet technological revolution has been taking place within the field of typography during the past 25 years. In this short period of time, three generations of commercial photographic typesetting equipment have been introduced; a fourth generation is already in the research and development stage.

For everyone concerned with the printed message, phototypesetting has opened up new avenues in typography in terms of flexibility, refinement, quality, and speed of production. We have a freedom of shapes and spacing beyond our greatest hopes.

Today, the typographer and the designer have been freed from almost every vestige of inhibiting mechanical restriction. Digital typesetters with sophisticated front-end systems are able to set, kern, and position fractions; create small caps; set underscores and vertical and horizontal rules; set and position superior and inferior characters; and condense, expand, and oblique every type style. These machines can create and store special characters and logotypes. Hundreds of letter combinations can be kerned, ligatures selected, and spacing controlled, all automatically.

Let us now give more thought to the self-imposed restriction of disciplining creativity in the service of taste.

Most typesetters, depending on their knowledge and application of typographic principles, can produce quality typography, but quality has always been in the eye of the beholder. Once you separate type from design and layout, you can rate quality on the basis of the following criteria:

- **Legibility.** Is the type readable and does it communicate the message?
- **Image clarity.** Is the type clear and sharp?
- **Spacing.** Are characters and word spacing consistent?
- **Aesthetics.** Is there kerning where required? Have ligatures been used?
- **Layout.** Is the type laid out for optimum readability, using the best point size and line lengths?
- **Character design.** Is the type style appropriate to the subject?

Typographic excellence is reached when someone operating a typesetting device or supervising its operation exercises typographic knowledge.

TYPOGRAPHY COSTS: TWENTY WAYS TO KEEP THEM DOWN

When proper care is taken, phototypography costs can be kept within predictable limits. Remember that the mechanics of the phototypographic process differ radically from those associated with hot-metal typography. Use the resources of phototypography to their fullest advantage and avoid the problem areas.

Here are a few pointers that can help you save money on your next job.

1. Plan ahead. Make sure that all copy questions are settled in the manuscript stage. Before the job is sent out for typesetting, the copy should be typed accurately and proofread carefully. Furnish your typographer with clean copy, double-spaced and with generous margins.
2. Prepare your copy as meticulously as possible before it is sent out for typesetting. Attention to detail at this stage is absolutely essential.
3. Supply an accurate tissue layout showing the true dimensions of your ad (line area, bleed and trim sizes, etc.).
4. Set a small block of copy for style. Through experimentation, familiarize

yourself with the feel of each particular typeface that you are using. By doing so, you can prevent unhappy surprises.

5. Phototypography has a language of its own. Be sure you are speaking the same language as your typographer. Meanings can vary dramatically, and frequently they differ from one typographer to another.
6. Specify a display typeface that can be keyboarded rather than hand set if this is at all possible. The savings will be significant.
7. If the display face you require is available on the microtypositor system, specify it. There are significant savings to be gained here.
8. Ask for display strips rather than repro proofs. This procedure saves both the supplier and the user time and money.
9. Contours are expensive to set. If you decide to use them, a ragged-left margin or a ragged-right margin may help keep costs down.
10. Avoid using reproduction proofs for proofreading purposes. A less expensive reader's proof, such as a diazo copy, works just as well.
11. Copy and layout changes can be extremely costly. Keep them to a minimum. Sometimes it costs less to rekeyboard the entire job than to set and strip in the changes.
12. It is a good policy not to go to film makeup the first time around. Have the job proofread and approved by the client first. Make any layout or position changes that are necessary and then go to a complete makeup. This is the most economical procedure.
13. Do not order reproduction proofs until your ad is absolutely perfect and ready to be engraved, with no additional changes to be made. Extra proofs cost money and often end up in the wastebasket. Analyze your needs and keep them at a workable minimum.
14. Specify the method of reproduction—offset or letter press—to the type director so that he or she can request the right film for the process.
15. Whenever possible, order only patches rather than complete proofs on revises.
16. Avoid if possible the grim word "rush." It breeds errors, needless expense, and grief. It often has three or four workers jostling one another around the plant to produce in 1 hour what one worker might have accomplished more economically and with more typographic nicety in 2 or 3 hours. The cost of that little four-letter word can be considerable.
17. A savings of between 10 and 15 percent often can be realized if you give your supplier an extra day or two to complete a job. Ask your supplier if he or she has a time allowance program; the savings can be significant.
18. Investigate "in-house" type preparation. Approximately 20 to 30 percent of typesetting costs are for rekeyboarding the manuscript sent to the typographer. Since most larger companies and advertising agencies have word processing centers and because there is a natural link between word processing and typesetting, connecting the two can result in substantial savings.
19. Communicate problems. Most honest suppliers are willing to help educate their clients in the best ways of ordering type—ways which can help save

money, speed delivery, and reduce authors' alterations—without sacrificing quality.

20. Try to set some time aside to visit your suppliers and learn about the nuts and bolts of phototypography. In an hour, you can see for yourself most of the mechanical reasons behind the flexibilities and rigidities inherent in the phototypographic process. It will help you obtain a better-looking and ultimately less expensive product.

CHOOSING AND WORKING WITH YOUR TYPOGRAPHIC SUPPLIER

Before sending a job to a new supplier, ask for a sample of the "house style" for display, text settings (both justified and ragged right), and one reproduction proof. You will see immediately whether your tastes are compatible.

The client who prepares a manuscript as meticulously as possible; furnishes clean, double-spaced copy with generous margins and with specific typographic instructions as to type size, measures, leading, indents, letter and word spacing, weight of rules, etc.; and provides an accurate layout indicating line areas and trim size stands to receive a superior product from the supplier.

The supplier who exhibits expertise in dealing with the specific typographic problems of clients, sets an alternate line or paragraph in galley or an alternate word of typositor to achieve better spacing, corrects a client error, and suggests ways to accomplish something that may look or fit better or reduce costs for the client gains the reputation of being a "creative typographer." This is an enviable position to be in.

Suppliers should make their clients aware of the technological advances being made in the typographic industry and how to use them. They should explain the flexibilities and limitations of their particular equipment and how best to order type using their system.

Another area of responsibility for suppliers is to explain their billing procedures. Do they bill by the area, the inch, the hour? Do they give volume discounts? Do they have a time allowance program in which discounts are given when additional time is allowed to set your type?

Do their bills reflect a full disclosure of services performed, backed by billing proofs, indicating all original composition and client revisions made, and defining:

Typositor
Text composition
Camera shots
Makeup
Proofs
Etc.
Revises

When I bought typography, I insisted that each supplier itemize each function and each product being supplied to me. This was not done to harass the supplier but because after examining bills for a period of time, I could evaluate internal or client problems which were leading to exorbitant revisions on a particular account and try to eliminate that problem.

IN-HOUSE TYPOGRAPHIC INSTALLATIONS

Many users of typography believe that a viable alternative to buying type from a commercial typesetter is establishing an in-house facility. There are pros and cons to each approach, and they all should be considered before you make a final decision.

There is much more involved in an in-house operation than purchasing equipment. Typography is an intangible operation. It requires highly skilled and properly trained people functioning under pressure to make it work. Indeed, the demand for speed, accuracy, and quality is something that only those who are close to the scene can appreciate fully.

Intelligent equipping of a plant presents a difficult problem for even the most experienced typographer. One should not be misled by performance claims for a piece of equipment someone is trying to sell. In the in-house facility just as in the commercial world, machinery and equipment purchases always have to be cost-justified.

The professional knows that there is an array of cost-efficient equipment on the market today that can lead to significant savings. But the professional also knows that cost savings are not automatic but rather are the result of management skills and operating efficiency.

Rapidly changing technology and obsolescence of equipment can take a toll on efficiency. Because photocomposition machinery is sensitive equipment, it quickly loses quality and reliability unless preventive and expert maintenance is performed regularly. Such maintenance can be quite costly.

Volume is the initial consideration in establishing an in-house typesetting capability. The mechanics of scheduling work to avoid peaks and valleys can be a full-time job in and of itself.

Turnaround requirements are a key factor in volume. If the time frame calls for overnight service, only a fully staffed typesetting department can meet such a demand. Even with a well-distributed workload, machine malfunctions and absenteeism will mean missed deadlines.

Assuming that a company has sufficient volume to justify establishing an in-plant facility, here are some of the other areas to consider carefully before making a final decision.

- Initial research
- Initial equipment and its backup
- Leasehold improvements
- Installation of equipment
- Training
- Typography and the computer
- Volume and work flow
- Productivity

- Nonproductive people
- Outside maintenance
- Inside maintenance
- Overtime
- Production norms
- Timekeeping and recordkeeping
- Billing
- Continuing research and development
- Film, paper, or both
- Payroll
- Welfare, benefits, and vacations
- Factory environment
- Intracompany discipline

When a company "deals with itself," it may encounter service problems which would not arise in a normal vendor-customer relationship. One should avoid the attitude that an in-house operation can be used on a trial and error basis with superfluous setting and resetting simply because the operation is conducted in-house.

In a city like New York, company art directors or designers may be dealing with the broadest range of typographic services available in the country. If they are cut off even partially from these services or if they are pressured into using an in-house operation, will the quality level deteriorate? Such possibilities cannot be assigned to a profit and loss statement.

Advertising agencies and others selling creative talents to a client are basically bringing creative concepts to fruition. Toward this end, they order services and products (which they mark up) from outside sources. In doing so, they take advantage of existing competition to get the best price for the services required.

At the point where an agency also becomes a supplier, is it so blurring its function that it will be impossible to treat the in-house product in the same manner as outside sources when "selling" to clients? Is the creative function diluted in the client's mind in order to protect an in-house facility?

Approximately 20 to 30 percent of typesetting costs are for rekeyboarding the manuscript sent to the typographer. Because most larger companies and advertising agencies have word processing centers and because there is a natural link between word processing and typesetting, connecting the two can result in substantial savings. Through the use of proper interface techniques, most typesetters can be driven by the input from a word processing unit.

The principal benefit is the ability to turn the already captured keystrokes into typeset copy with a minimum amount of additional labor and expense. The most obvious benefit, of course, is the elimination of rekeyboarding of material for typesetting. The result is a saving not only in keyboarding but also in time spent on additional proofing and correcting.

The principal methods of hooking up word processing equipment with a typesetter are telecommunication via telephone lines, various interface devices, optical character recognition devices, and direct disc compatibility. Each method has certain advantages and disadvantages, and so an agency should consult with its typographer for the best approach.

Before deciding whether to go to an in-house typesetting facility, talk directly with other agencies and companies who are using one. Manufacturer's representatives can provide you with lists in your area, or you can compile your own. Listen for the pros and cons, responses and reactions. Keep in mind that each agency's needs are different; what may work well for others may not work to your best advantage.

Plan to attend trade shows in your area. There is a wealth of information and knowledge to be had along with opportunities to see the equipment in action and get some hard answers to your questions.

Again, take a careful look at volume, the kind of work involved, the level of quality, and the basic turnaround requirements. These are critical factors in the final decision.

WORD PROCESSING, TELECOMMUNICATION, DATA PROCESSING, AND TYPOGRAPHY

Word processing technology currently is making tremendous inroads into the traditional office environment. The machines of the business office are being linked with the machines of the graphic arts. More typographers and printers are offering word processing connections which can accept the cassettes and floppies and telecommunication data and turn them into type.

This trend, which allows the originators of information to capture it in a form of typesetting, is seen not only in the business office. Book publishers and magazines also are using word processing devices and multiterminal computer systems to prepare copy for typesetting. But they do not do the typesetting. They do the input and editing and then buy the typesetting itself from typographers and printers.

The conversion of word processing data to finished type has many advantages for the typographer's clients. Most obvious is the fact that the typographer no longer does the keyboarding, proofreading, and in many cases, the typesetting commands. The amount of work a client is willing to do will determine the amount of savings.

1. Typesetting allows you to pack more words into less space while improving the appearance and readability of a document and conserving space, paper, and postage.
2. Typeset material is more legible, especially when set single-spaced in a reduced size. The ability to mix different weights and sizes contributes to this improved legibility.
3. Typeset documents look more important and more impressive and command more attention than a typewritten version.
4. There is increased comprehension and retention of content in typeset material.
5. Turnaround time at the typographer should be decreased greatly, avoiding costly rush situations.

Direct Interfaces

Conceptually, the direct interface method is the most simple. It is also perhaps the most limited. This type of interface requires you to physically insert the media that you obtain from the word processor into the interface unit. The unit's software then makes whatever code translations are necessary and either outputs a new medium compatible with the phototypesetter or connects to an output unit. As a practical matter, most word processing material is translated by some type of editing terminal or front-end system so that any necessary coding may be inserted, further translation done, and certain error-checking procedures followed.

Telecommunication Interfaces

A second method of interfacing uses the telecommunication port available with many word processing units. The data from the word processing installation are sent over telephone lines via a modulator-demodulator (modem) to an interface at the receiving end which translates and stores the data in a form understandable by the typesetting hardware. A major advantage of this method is that media compatibility is not required, since the data are translated into a common code structure for data transmission from one type of machine to another.

Modems

In order to telecommunicate, at least two other pieces of hardware are needed: a modem on the sending end and a modem connected to an interface on the receiving end. There are several different types of modems available.

The Word Processing–Data Processing Connection

Today, technology exists to link or even merge word processing and data processing systems. This connection can accomplish such operations as the following.

1. **Sorting.** It can rearrange data in numeric order or alphabetically by cities, last names, etc. It can sort an address list by ZIP code and, within ZIP codes, by name.
2. **Merging.** Two or more sets of records can be merged.
3. **Collating.** This function merges data in a specified order.
4. **Selecting.** Specific records or groups of data can be called up from the electronic file.
5. **Updating.** It is possible to add, delete, or change data or text in the file.
6. **Calculating.** Mathematical functions such as addition, subtraction, multiplication, and division can be performed.
7. **Storing.** It has the capability to store data on magnetic media for future editing or processing.

8. **Reporting.** It can furnish information called up from the file on the CRT display or print out a paper record as well as transmit to a communication system.

The future is now for word processing and telecommunication and data processing technology. Since word processing equipment is taking over most large-volume typing applications, including most manuscript preparation for typesetting, it is only logical to conclude that a greater and greater percentage of typesetting input will be prepared by word processors.

chapter **40**

MECHANICAL PASTE-UP

Robert W. Buckingham

President
Krupp-Taylor
Marina del Rey, Calif.

Almost without exception, printing begins with a piece of art that has been designed and pasted up carefully by an artist for reproduction. Anyone who has used an office copier has seen an original transformed into many duplicates of itself. Since printing is a form of duplication for distribution, the original must be as good as possible. As with the copier, each generation of duplicates is never as precise as the original.

When the original is created by an artist, it is called a mechanical or camera-ready art (CRA). The term "finished art" is also common.

CRA consists of varying components which artists have at their disposal. It is important to be familiar with these components and know some of the terms that are used.

Mechanicals are also called boards and paste-ups. This is a slight misnomer, since the two terms also may apply to artwork in varying stages, whereas "camera-ready" and "mechanical" imply that the art is finished and ready for reproduction. You may hear the phrase "the boards are ready" used within the industry. More often than not, this statement refers to a mechanical.

The objectives of a mechanical are rather simple.

1. The mechanicals should be clean and crisp, with no excess rubber cement or smears.
2. They must be square, with all lines of type running perfectly parallel rather than uphill or downhill and all vertical lines and columns a perfect 90-degree angle to the horizontal.
3. The mechanicals should be properly glued down so that type, photostats, or prints will not move out of square or fall off the board. They should be protected with a cover flap and packaged to prevent damage.

Mechanicals should be packaged and handled with extreme care during shipping so that the illustration board (used generally as a piece to paste on) is not bent, torn, or smeared. It's a good idea to send a photostat of the artboard when shipping is required, although in some cases the mechanicals are so complex that they must be viewed in their original condition.

THE STAGES OF A MECHANICAL

Once a mechanical has been created, it generally moves through a cycle of approval by the agency as well as the client. The client may have several different departments that view the artwork, e.g., marketing, advertising, sales, or legal. Comments and suggestions are made by each viewing department and signed off as approved.

It's common practice for agencies to use a rubber stamp on the corner of each artboard to indicate the approval signature and date that is required for approval before printing. Let's consider some of the things that may take place in the life of a mechanical once the art department has finished it and protected it with a covering flap.

First, the original comprehensive (comp) or rough layout should accompany the mechanical. When the shape of the piece is complex or a number of pages are involved, it can be difficult to look at a mechanical and know exactly how the piece will go together or how it will appear in final form. In addition to the comp, an actual dummy using the specific paper stock, often is sent along so that the feel and texture of the piece also may be assessed.

Folds are extremely important, especially intricate ones. As a piece is being printed and folded, a comp or dummy simplifies the task a great deal for the worker. The position of a window on an envelope has to be measured carefully so that the address piece shows through in proper alignment.

Mechanicals typically become corrected mechanicals, and corrected mechanicals often become corrected-again mechanicals. It's important to provide continuity throughout the process of comments and corrections. For this purpose, a piece of tissue always is fastened by the artist to lay over the mechanical. Then comments, additions, deletions, explanations, and the like can be written on the tissue without defacing the artwork.

One company, when correcting a mechanical, marks on the tissue over each correction with a particular felt tip color and then keys that color to a date. Then the mechanical goes back for approval, during which additional corrections may be made. The company marks through these corrections with another color on the tissue. One can visualize a mechanical with numerous comments on the tissue overlay marked through with transparent purple, green, and orange. Perfect continuity is achieved. One can quickly see the first round of corrections (purple) and the date they were made, the second round (green), and the third (orange). This is particularly important as a control to make sure that all corrections were made while at the same time portraying the sequence of all the corrections made since the mechanical first began its journey for approval.

Obviously, when all the amendments have been completed and all the approvals are obtained, the mechanical is ready for reproduction.

PREPARATION FOR THE RIGHT MEDIA

Mechanicals almost always appear identical: a piece of illustration board generally 20 by 30 but dependent on the scale of the piece. However, depending on the type of reproduction, the actual components can vary considerably. Some printing techniques have finer resolution than others. Some are able to print coarse paper stocks while others are not, and some printing techniques are able to lay down larger areas of solid ink better than their counterparts. These things must be considered when you prepare a mechanical. It's not enough to know where it will be reproduced; you must know how it will be reproduced. Below is a list of the more common printing techniques and a couple of short notes about how the mechanical must be geared.

Flexographic

This involves a rubber printing process that is typically in-line like web offset lithography, except that the rubber is printing directly onto the surface rather than in offset fashion, in which the plate prints onto a rubber blanket and the rubber blanket transfers the image onto the paper. Designed to print extremely coarse and thick materials, this technique is common in the corrugated cardboard industry. Resolution is rather poor, and so fine lines and delicate borders as well as reverses cannot be reproduced successfully.

Letterpress

This is a printing process where the ink is applied from above the surface. In other words, the negative areas are etched away, leaving the printing area in high relief. Owing to the etching property of copper, fine screens are not recommended. Letterpress also is unsuitable for anything other than fairly smooth paper stock.

Gravure

Known as intaglio, this process is perhaps the finest printing technique available. It is a form of engraving where the positive areas are etched into the copper plate and printed from below the surface. Under pressure, the paper is forced into the etched grooves. Extremely fine screens can be used, and the most minute detail can be reproduced beautifully. Gravure is the greatest way to simulate continuous-tone printing (photography).

Newspapers

This is a coarse printing medium because of the newsprint quality. Screens must be no finer than about 65 lines. (This means 65 individual dots to the linear inch.) Some newspapers, on higher-quality newsprint, can take slightly finer line screens. Make sure you consult the newspaper mechanical requirements.

Magazines

Unlike newspapers, magazines appear in all sorts of grades and finishes of paper. From tabloid style (like newsprint) to extremely high grade gloss stock, mechanical requirements vary tremendously. A publisher's mechanical requirements must be reviewed carefully before you create the mechanical.

Inserts and Collateral

Once again, the paper to be used and the equipment of the producer must be considered carefully. Large presses have ink trains capable of laying down large solid areas without streaking, whereas small presses cannot. The resolution of the equipment and the particular paper to be printed must be taken into consideration. The screens, color, and registry capabilities all must be reviewed carefully before the camera-ready art is fabricated.

SELECTING THE PROPER MATERIALS

Making Sure the Mechanical Is "Mechanical"

Earlier I cautioned against creating a mechanical or finished art that is less than perfect. I'd like to stress now the criticality of making sure that all horizontal lines are square and that all vertical lines are perpendicular. Sometimes the eye can be fooled, and there's nothing quite so distressing as finding a headline or piece of copy that runs uphill or downhill after it's printed. Even with attention and care, this can happen. It's especially apt to happen when artboards have had numerous corrections, e.g., lines of type removed or changed and then repasted down. When having your type set, it can be time-saving to order a lot of it composed rather than in "floated" form. When it's floated, the artist has to cut the type and piece it together in sections on the mechanical rather than lay down complete sections or pages at one time. Since typographers and machines deliver type completely square, it's sometimes wise to accomplish the mechanical in as few pieces as possible.

Wax versus Rubber Cement

There are two principal forms of laying down photostats, prints, and type on the illustration board: wax and rubber cement. For many years, rubber cement was the mainstay of the artist. Whether an artist used two coats or one, it was easy to work with and cleaned up rapidly. If changes were required, a rubber cement thinner was applied in order to lift the previously pasted down portion for re-do or adjustment.

Hot wax is a newcomer to the industry; although it is not widely accepted, it is used by many artists. One of the principal attractions is that it is clean and fast, and the backs of large pieces can be coated prior to fastening to the board without drying or losing the adhesive quality. The principal failing is that the wax is not as adhesive as the cement even when carefully used and is affected by heat, especially in a car on a hot day. Both adhesives can be effective; it's a matter of personal preference.

Four-Color Process and Flat Colors

When accomplished in only one color, finished art is rather simple. The involvement of additional colors creates complexity. The four-color process is considered to be the most difficult, but this is not true. Typically, the most complex finished art and stripping jobs involve the laying in of multiple flat colors created by screens. There's much more work required by both the artist and the stripper. (The term "stripper" refers to the person who handles the film and strips it together for a plate.) The four-color process, whether it is a photographic transparency or reflective art (anything that is nontransparent, such as an illustration), is separated by the eye of the camera. The artist may use a keyline technique and provide the four-color material to be used.

In the use of flat colors, the artist frequently has to cut a series of masks in which one color is separated from another. The artist can achieve a multiplicity of colors by using screened percentages of two, three, or four colors, and many elect to do so. Some of these masks are so critical, they are best done by camera, but in almost all cases, the artist provides the opaque masks, placed on overlays. Each overlay relates to a particular color that is requested. When screened to a percentage of color and mixed with other screened colors, it becomes the formula for the exact shade the artist has in mind. For instance, 20 percent blue, 20 percent yellow, and 20 percent black, printed over one another appear much different from 40 percent blue, 40 percent yellow, and 10 percent black. The artist generally stays with the primary colors; if the artist wants to achieve a number of different colors, the primaries may be combined. However, on a simple two-color job using a simple brown or black, a number of other shades also can be created.

Dimensions, Window Position, and Postal Regulations

These may be the most important considerations in a mechanical when you are dealing with a direct mail piece. One day you are likely to create a reply card that doesn't fit in the return envelope, a window piece that shows improperly through a window envelope, or a piece of mail that the post office either rejects or is reluctant to accept.

Recall the earlier mention of actual dummies. If you check the dimensions of the mechanical carefully against the folded dummy, which should accompany the mechanical, it will go a long way toward preventing the first two of these common errors.

Postal regulations should be the responsibility of the artist. When you are in doubt, have your package preapproved by the post office. A comp or dummy is shown to Mailing Regulations, a section of major post offices everywhere, and postal approval (if forthcoming) is granted. This preapproval can be quite comforting in terms of creating a piece of mail which does not conform to a standard appearance.

When you find that a piece doesn't fit, has extraneous print showing through the window improperly, etc., investigation will show that one of the graphic arts stages was missed or ignored. The evolution of a printed piece requires a number of carefully determined steps. All of us tend to ignore the basic steps and create shortcuts. Almost without exception, when backtracking an error, you will find that a final proof wasn't obtained or that a folding dummy wasn't submitted.

Planning For Computerization

It's interesting to think about how many pieces require computerization today. The cheshire label, which was the primary mode of addressing direct mail until the mid-1960s, has given way to direct addressing in the last 15 years. Whether they be envelopes, window envelopes, or self-mailers, some form of direct addressing is common. The standard computer printer has been joined by the ink jet and laser as additional methods of direct imaging.

The artist must understand the process to be used and the mechanical requirements of the particular process. Take, for example, an 8 1/2 by 11 letter, the basic workhorse of direct mail. It can be produced 2-up on an IBM chain printer or 1-up on an ink jet or laser printer. The IBM printer takes a form up to 17 1/2 inches wide, the laser printer takes a form up to 14 7/8 inches wide, and the ink jet, while its limitations vary, takes a form up to 17 3/4 inches wide. The allowance for a punched-pin feed on the side of the form must conform perfectly to the apparatus on which it will be run. For example, if the pin feed margin is stripped away from a 2-up computer form, it reduces the size of the letter from 8 1/2 by 11 to 8 1/4 by 11. In addition to this, there is the added problem of where the direct addressing and computer work will appear. The versatility and capability of printing from the left edge of the paper to the right edge varies considerably. The ink jet, for instance, prints diagonally, vertically, or up and down with no loss of speed, while the standard IBM printer does not. Type size, styles, fonts, and reverses are additional considerations.

While it's nice for printers and computer personnel to study the actual mechanical products before submitting an estimate, it's not always practical.

If all vendors are required to submit an estimate from specifications and then the selection of a producer is made, it can be of help to the artist. By knowing the vendor who has won the job, the artist, before doing the mechanical, can confer with the producer about the kind of equipment and the methods for producing the job. The artist can even receive helpful layouts for the finished art, and this simplifies his or her tasks and provides solid communication. A vendor often has to "undo" parts of a carefully prepared mechanical in order to fit the equipment. To limit communication between the artist and the supplier would be as foolish as constructing a house without the architect and contractor ever meeting.

Duplicating the Mechanical

Certain instances require duplication of a mechanical. It's best done on film. One mechanical is produced, and additional sets of film are made of the original. However, when the artboards must be furnished to more than one geographic location simultaneously, make sure the finest quality line prints are received, not photostats.

Place a high-powered magnifying glass on the type to make sure that the lines are crisp and that letters such as o and a have not started to distort or fill in. It's a good idea to scrutinize all parts of a mechanical under a glass to make sure the original is of the highest fidelity. Negatives and prints are a generation away in reproduction and will always be less than the original. This makes it essential to start with as good an original as possibly can be constructed.

MECHANICAL TECHNIQUES

Tissues

A vellum tissue always must be laid down over the art. It's a protective layer but, more important, a guide to the stripper or printer. The tissue is the place where the artist can indicate each direction to be followed. Things such as color, percentage of screens, strip-ins, duotones, reverses, and the like generally are indicated on the tissue.

On a complex job where there are many different colors and screens to be combined, it's common for the artist actually to color on the tissue certain sections which indicate how it will look on completion. It's not necessary for the artist to color the entire tissue, only a cross section (a vertical or horizontal strip about 2 or 3 inches wide) running across the artboard, which shows the various colors and tones next to one another.

Ink Colors

Each mechanical must be explicit about the colors of ink the artist has selected. It's preferable for the artist to paste down actual ink book sample swatches of the various colors requested. For example, the base of the artboard may have three small squares which show and indicate the colors to be used, e.g., Blue 280, Brown 463, and Yellow 100. Most ink books provide sample color swatches that are perforated for easy removal. One such book is *Pantone*. Once these colors are established, a direction that states 20 percent brown, 20 percent yellow, etc., becomes clear for the stripper.

The four-color process, of course, needs little explanation since the four process colors (magenta, yellow, cyan, and black) are always the same. Rhodamine red can be a substitute for process red if desired by the artist. It provides a slightly cooler look to the finished product.

Overlays

Overlays should be placed carefully over the artboard, with each one indicating whether it's a mask, different copy, or color. They should be carefully registered to the main board as well as each other through small registration marks (sample: ⌖). In many cases, lithographers prefer to strip in their own registration marks, which are more accurate than those of the artist. The overlays should be acetate because acetate doesn't stretch or shrink; they may be clear or frosted. Clear is used when only opaque material is applied for a mask or when new copy is used. Frosted acetate must be used when there is an application of ink by the artist. Never use paper tissue as an overlay, as it is not stable.

When using multiple overlays, hinge each one from a different side of the board. For instance, hinge one on the left so that it opens like a book, hinge one from the top so that it lifts up, hinge one on the right, etc. This will prevent a massive buildup of tape at the top of the board as well as distortion from registering one overlay to another.

Keylines and Strip-Ins

A keyline is a technique which aids the stripper in preparing the negatives. It's an excellent technique and is often essential.

A keyline is simply a thinly ruled ink line on the mechanical which shows the stripper where a photograph or other piece of art should be stripped in. It is as important on single-color jobs as on four-color ones. Perhaps the most common use of strip-ins is seen in halftones. Picture a series of vertical ovals on a finished artboard which will house photographs much like cameo portraits. The artist simply draws the oval outline mechanically or from a template and asks that the vendor strip in the matching photographs which are submitted. The photographs usually are 8 by 10 and may have more area than is required. The photographs also may be of varying sizes. The process also is essential when the photographs cannot be cut up.

The prep department shoots an original halftone from each photograph, reduced to a common size, and strips the halftones inside each oval. The original photographs remain unblemished and can be returned to the owner in their original form. This process, however, requires a number of steps by the printer's prep department.

In the alternative method, the artist creates a board with all the line work (type and borders, etc.). The artist cuts each halftone into an oval and places them down in position on an overlay. If the halftones are not all a common size, the artist has to have a duplicate print made in which each one is reduced to a size which matches the others.

The mechanical is given to the printer, who then has two simple shots to make: a line shot and a halftone shot. If the artist has done a proper job of registering the two together, the printer strips them quickly and is off and running. The artist has undoubtedly created a simpler task for the printer but has also created a piece of art that is very fragile. The halftone edges can be nicked easily, and the nick may not be noticed until the job is printed. It is very difficult to cut a halftone perfectly true to shape.

The advantage of a keyline or strip-in is that the original photograph is shot by the printer, and this keeps the reproduction only one generation away from the original. If the artist makes the reduction in a continuous-tone copy first, the printer's halftone becomes two generations away (this yields less fidelity), and the artist has cut up the original photographs, possibly destroying irreplaceable material if there is no negative.

Veloxes

A velox is a photograph that already has been screened with the appropriate dot pattern required. It is a common and useful tool of camera-ready art. The velox is a way of simplifying the printer's job.

Suppose the camera halftones are going to be reproduced in a newspaper in 65-line screen. This means the screening will be rather coarse and the reproduction less than high quality. The halftones are sent to a photographic shop (stats and prints) for velox prints. The photostat house shoots each photograph through a halftone screen while it is reduced to a common size. These negatives are printed onto photographic paper as velox prints. The artist cuts them into an oval or provides an oval mask and submits it to the printer. Since the halftones are already screened, they can be incorporated on the original artboard (no overlay), and the printer has to make only one line shot before reproduction. In other words, any halftone that is photographically printed with a screen or dot pattern becomes a line shot for a camera. Veloxes effectively combine line and halftone, which otherwise would have to be separated through an overlay process.

Duotones and Tritones

There are many special effects that can be created by the artist or camera operator, and we shall not be able to mention all of them. However, duotones and tritones are common items, and it's important to be familiar with them.

A duotone is a halftone printed in two colors. Blue and black and black and brown are common combinations, but it's not unusual to run duotones in black and black. The gray scale is a shading of tones which run the gamut from solid black to 10 percent gray. This scale is what the camera operator is able to see. Depending on the camera operator, the gray scale can be compressed for more contrast, which will yield a "blacker" black and a "whiter" white. The camera operator also can stretch the gray scale, picking up more subtle changes of gray but yielding a black that's not so black and a white that's not so white.

With a duotone, the camera operator shoots the same halftones, each with a different camera setting: one with a compressed gray scale and one with a stretched gray scale. The camera operator shoots the duotones by using predetermined screen angles so that the dots will not overprint each other but print alongside one another. By making two shots, the camera operator achieves the best of all possible worlds: a dark black, a white, and all the grays in between. The result is a halftone reproduction that looks infinitely more rich than a straight one-shot halftone.

A tritone uses the same process, except that three shots are used instead of two.

Stats, Prints, and Masking

We touched before on the differences between a photostat and a line print. Please be cautious as to the resolution of these two photographic tools. Photostats are fine when working with logos, shapes, borders, etc. They are perfect for comps, roughs, and anything that requires less than perfect fidelity.

A line print should be obtained whenever possible for camera-ready art, but it's still wise to put it under the glass for resolution scrutiny.

Masks must be cut carefully and registered as precisely as possible. Make sure the edges are clean. There are a number of artist-aid materials which are applied on board or acetate and cut away with an Exacto blade. This leaves a photographic mask for color separations or dropouts. Make sure the masking material is specified as a masking material and is therefore opaque to the camera. Certain forms of adhesive papers are for use in comps only; while they appear opaque they are not.

When cutting masks to create the edge of one color meeting another, be certain that a small overlap or "trap" exists on one mask or the other. The darker color should slightly trap the lighter color where the two edges meet. If the mask is a critical one to cut (a complex silhouette shape versus a straight line), a mask can be painted on with a brush, using an opaque ink or paint.

The trap also can be accomplished by the camera operator through the use of a spread negative. The negative is photographed through an extra thickness of clear film which causes an enlargement. This small growth in size is enough to create a trapping effect when the edge of two colors or tones meet one another.

Don't hesitate to ask the prep department of your supplier or printer for advice in preparation of the artboards.

SUBMITTING THE BOARDS

Identification

When the boards are ready to go, each should be identified carefully with the project or job number, the client or agency or both, etc. It's a good practice to have the boards carry the names of all of the people involved in the production process. If there are multiple CRA artboards, they should also be identified as 1 of 5, 2 of 5, etc.

Strip-ins should be carefully keyed as copy A, copy B, etc. For instance, the keylines on a particular artboard which notes "copy A" and a series of supplied halftones are marked with the corresponding "copy A." The stripper then knows the appropriate halftones that are to be placed within the keyline areas.

Checklist

Without question, the ultimate printed direct mail piece can never be better than the original camera-ready art. This is especially true in the use of the four-color process. However, with care, it can be a faithful reproduction. If you examine four-color process printing which delivers less than good reproduction, more often than not you will find inferior transparencies or color separations.

Start with the best, reproduce with high fidelity, and you will have the best final product possible.

1. Make sure the mechanical is in good shape: crisp, clean, and well protected.
2. Make sure all the pieces have been included and are correctly identified 1 of 2, 2 of 2, photos for strip-in, etc.
3. The mechanical should be labeled so that questions can be directed to the correct department. The mechanical also should have all the necessary approvals.
4. A comp or dummy should accompany the art, representing the way the piece will look on completion. It should be folded exactly as the finished product.

5. The tissue overlay should contain all the directions to be followed by the stripping department. Each mask, screen, percentage, trap, dropout, reverse, or strip-in should be understood clearly by the viewer.
6. Colors of ink with or without accompanying swatches should be denoted on each board.
7. A purchase order or copy of a purchase order to be mailed later generally accompanies the mechanical and spells out who receives the proofs and the time schedule under which they should be submitted. It also should spell out the number of proofs requested and whether they should be blueline, color keys, or chromolins. Proofing processes have changed rapidly the last few years; there's even a new system which is able to show the accurate color on the particular stock to be printed. The industry is striving continually to provide a proofing technique which yields a proof as close to the final printed piece as possible.

   The artwork or purchase order also may spell out the publication and its mechanical requirements and indicate whether it is an advertisement or a direct mail piece.
8. Make sure that all directions on the mechanical are understood easily by the viewer so that questions can be answered at the mechanical stage, not at a later stage when the piece is being photographed and stripped. A change of instructions at the mechanical stage is inexpensive compared with making changes after a proof has been prepared incorrectly.

chapter 41

BUYING PRINTING AND PAPER

David G. Rosenthal

Vice President of Sales and National Account Manager
Webcraft
North Brunswick, N.J.

This chapter is about buying printing and paper effectively. The intent is not to make the reader a printing technician but to provide a basic step-by-step understanding of the necessary ingredients for ensuring the successful completion of your printing requirements. This chapter will discuss how the printer can help you avoid some of the pitfalls that occur during the production of a job.

BUYING PRINTING

The most important ingredient when buying printing is understanding what you want to buy and communicating your wants and needs to the printer. You are buying a service that will produce a product that is custom-made to your specifications. Printing is an art form and a science that for the most part is mass-produced on machines operated by people. When the specifications and expectations are mutually understood, the job will be produced to your satisfaction. Dissatisfaction occurs when the buyer expects a certain desired result and the printer produces something else.

Proper channels of communication should begin at the inception of the job. Job specifications should be established first for the end use of the printed piece. Specifications should follow for size and quality levels. From this starting point, job detail specifications such as size, grade of paper, colors, and finishing operations must be established.

When buying printing, it is not essential that the buyer know how to operate a printing press or know much about such things as the tack of ink or how to set dot angles on a scanner. It is important that you communicate to the printer what you want. It is important that you understand some of the limitations of graphic technology. It is also important to understand printing terminology and the basic tools of the trade with which you will be working.

Simply stated, client satisfaction generally results when your job looks good. What does looking good mean? If you are a marketer of fashions, are the garments more important than the flesh tones of the models wearing them or is the background setting most important? How red should the garment be? Don't ask the printer to guess by asking for, say, a 5 percent increase in the magenta. Give the printer a swatch of the fabric and then view the press proof under the proper lighting. And remember to be reasonable. The printer is putting ink in dot form on paper, not the fabrics that your garments are made of.

Prior to color separating, comprehensive communication about what is important to you is essential toward the successful production of your job. The adage "We'll fix the color on the press" does not always work. When possible, correct the film before going to press.

People make mistakes. Proofs can be incorrect. Blueprints, color keys, or any other proof should be proofread carefully before you give an "okay to print." Make sure that copy, size, folds, color break, and anything else you can think of are correct.

Visit the printer at the job startup. Make sure that all the instructions have been understood and produced to your satisfaction. Also, make certain that the copy is correct and that the job will fold, glue, finish, convert, personalize, or bind correctly. Make certain that you have given the printer your most recent quantity requirements and have advised whether you'll require an overrun.

When the lines of communication are open and mutually understood, your job will work better and run more efficiently. Subsequently, you and the printer will establish a rapport that will work toward your mutual satisfaction.

Finding the Right Printer

Finding and using the right printer to satisfy your printing requirements is a key to the success of your business. The job specifications of direct marketers generally exceed the capabilities of the corner storefront printer. Thus, you must plan to do some traveling in your quest to find the right printer.

Today, many printing firms specialize in specific types of work. These companies generally offer expertise in their specialties and efficiency in their production operations.

To find printers that can serve your goals best, ask for suggestions and recommendations from your advertising agency or creative staff. Should you see a printed piece that is unique or has a special treatment, call the print production manager of the advertiser and ask who printed or produced it. Other excellent sources for locating specific printers are other printers, letter shops, and advertising agencies.

Make the Printer Part of Your Team

Your printer is a valuable member of your creative team. The printer should be called in with your creative staff to help develop and implement new concepts. A competent printer can offer new ideas, new products, and better production methods. The printer can help solve a potential problem in printing or a related problem. The printer also may offer additional insight into concepts that your competitor is using successfully or has tested.

Develop Your Package Cost Effectively

As your direct mail package starts to develop and take shape, you should be looking at the cost effectiveness of producing the package. Have your printer supply you with suggested or preferred sizes to best fit the printing press on which the job will run. In many cases, minimal size adjustments can result in thousands of dollars of cost and time savings.

Before preparing any artwork, request an exact size template from the printer. See Figure 41-1. This template will serve as a guide for the artist. It will indicate bleed areas, type safety areas, folds, perforations, die cuts, and any other specifications. Do not prepare final mechanicals without a template.

Figure 41-1 Template for four-page catalog bind-in order form plus envelope. Template illustrates each side of sheet, sizes, folds, print, glue, and trim areas. *Webcraft, patents number 3665817, 3713673, 3743273, and 3784185, 1980.*

Develop Your Package Cautiously and Thoughtfully

Before preparing a template, all the components must be designed to work well together.

If the window of an envelope does not allow the personalized name and address on the enclosed letter to show through, or if the enclosed letter is so large that it does not fit in its envelope at the letter shop, unnecessary aggravation, mailing delays, possible reprints, and extra costs most definitely will occur.

Following through on your package also must include internal use of the printed product. For example, a catalog bind-in order form must complement the look of your book, make for ease of customer ordering, satisfy the trimming specifications of the catalog printer and binder, work well in the mailstream, and work well in your order-processing department. Also, bind-in order forms must be designed to facilitate ease of envelope opening and order entry.

If you are planning to use computer personalization, precise planning is of the utmost importance. You must verify that the form is compatible with the transport system on which it will be used, that the space allowed for fill-ins is accurate, that alignment of copy is precise, and that a fill-in match is attainable. If you are planning to scan computer-printed copy optically, make sure that a scannable typeface is used with scannable inks that are printed to necessary reflectance levels.

When having computer tapes supplied to your ink jet, laser, or line printer facility, make sure that the supplier and the user of the tapes understand the necessary specifications that each will need before any preparation of tapes. A test tape should be run of several hundred names to verify that the program and information on the tapes are correct.

Verify the Package with the U.S. Postal Service

Make sure that your package conforms to U.S. Postal Service regulations. Some of the specifications to verify follow:

1. Size
2. Required copy and clear areas
3. Position and size of copy
4. Recommended ink colors
5. Mail classification
6. Postal sorts

Note that questions can be directed to a customer service representative at your local post office. Mailings to locations outside the United States may require different treatments from those mailed domestically. Verify specifications with the postal service in the country you will be mailing to.

Establish Specifications

Once your concept has been developed, production specifications should be established. The following are necessary specifications to establish a price estimate of printing costs:

1. Size of printed piece
2. Number of pages
3. Number of colors and amount of ink coverage
4. Bleed: none, common, or uncommon
5. Preparatory
   a. Camera
   b. Stripping
   c. Color separations
   d. Press proving
   e. Chromalin
   f. Blueprint
   g. Color key
6. Stock (paper) grade and basis weight
7. Quantity
   a. Desired overrun
   b. Spoilage allowance for additional finishing operations
8. Versions, imprints, and key codes
9. Finishing operations
   a. Folding
   b. Die cutting and embossing
   c. Glue
   d. Perforating and scoring
   e. Bind, stitch, and trim
10. Additional operations
    a. Computerization (personalization)
    b. Burst and fold
    c. Insertion
    d. Affix label and card
11. Sorting and mailing

It is of paramount importance to advise the printer about the quality level desired and the end use of the printed piece.

Quality Levels

We all want the best quality for the lowest price. The importance of having a meeting of the minds on this aspect of your job is that you probably will not require annual report quality for an envelope stuffer. The quality level of materials and workmanship should be appropriate for the nature of the business for the end use of the job. That quality level must be understood by both the direct marketer and the printer.

End Use

Film mailer envelopes that carry film cartridges through the mail may necessitate the use of Kraft-grade paper stocks that are of great strength. Four-color brochures generally are printed on weaker coated stocks. Each is appropriate for its end use, but they should not be substituted for each other. Materials and labor should be used appropriately for the end use of the printed product.

The Bidding Process

The sweetness of a low price is quickly forgotten as the constant reminder of a job gone sour lingers.

The key to effective print buying is careful planning and a strong relationship with your printer. Work with your printer to establish specifications to fit the press; ask the printer if there is a better or more cost-efficient way to produce the job.

Review with the printer your complete package with all details. Advise the printer of all specifications and additional information. Review paper and schedule requirements. Advise of any key codes, copy (version) changes, overall packing, palleting, and shipping requirements.

As you collect the bids, remember that the low bid may not be the lowest price. A slightly higher bid may buy far more value than the low price. The most astute buyer and seller of printing will work toward a continuing team relationship.

Some of the additional mutual benefits of a continuing relationship are as follows:

1. Avoiding the learning curve of a new supplier with each order
2. Experience and knowledge of your business
3. Price consistency
4. Quality consistency
5. Loyalty
6. Dependability

When possible, try to have your job produced with the fewest manufacturing operations. When more operations are accomplished in a single press run, you will benefit in terms of very innovative formats produced faster and more cost efficiently. Also, having fewer finishing operations involved generally promotes faster and more efficient production schedules. When multiple operations are required, always attempt to have them accomplished under a single roof. The levels of control will be far greater, and potential freight or trucking costs will be eliminated.

Scheduling

Your printer wants to satisfy your scheduling requirements. Establish schedules that are reasonable and workable for you and the printer. Allow ample time for preparatory work, color separations, stock availability, or any special materials. If your job is time-sensitive and involves outside media costs, tell the printer. Allow adequate shipping time in your schedule.

Advise the printer about any changes in the schedule as early as possible. Last minute postponements can induce very costly press downtime. Also, your job may be delayed getting back into the press schedule.

Occasionally printers will offer a discount if you schedule a job in a seasonally slow period. Also, some printers may offer some form of discount for a long-term schedule commitment.

Periodic Contracts

As your business develops and you are purchasing the same type of printing on a regular basis, you and the printer may want to consider a contract. Some of the benefits of a contract are that it protects press time and protects paper availability.

WHAT PAPER TO BUY

The appropriate grade of paper involves more than just choosing the medium that molds together your printed image. Paper supplies texture, bulk, and "feel" to printed matter. Along with designer shape and size, it determines the kind of impression this representative of management will have.*

Paper Finishes

Finish is a complex paper properly related to its smoothness. Paper can be used as it comes off the driers of a paper machine, or it can be machine-calendered and then later supercalendered. Uncalendered, machine-calendered, and supercalendered papers vary greatly in smoothness.

The usual finishes of uncoated book papers are in order of increasing smoothness antique, eggshell, vellum, and machine-finish (MF). Additional smoothness is obtained with supercalendering. Coating further improves the finish and smoothness.

Top (Felt) Side and Wire Side

Paper is considered a two-sided material. Each side has different characteristics because of the way paper is made. The side directly in contact with the wire of the paper machine is called the wire side; the other side is the top or felt side. The felt side usually has a closer formation with less grain and better crossing of the fibers. The wire side, however, has fewer lines on the surface and usually gives less trouble in the depositing of loose paper dust, fiber picking, or lint on the blanket of an offset press.

PAPER CHARACTERISTICS

Grain

Grain is an important factor for both printing and binding. It refers to the position of the fibers. During papermaking, most fibers are oriented with their length parallel to that of the paper machine and their width running across the

* Some of the following has been excerpted with permission from *Pocket Pal,* published by International Paper Company. (Twelth Edition, July 1981) I wish to thank International Paper Company for their cooperation and expertise.

machine. In other words, the grain of the sheet is in the machine direction; the other dimension is called the cross direction. See Figure 41-2.

Grain affects paper in several ways, and these facts need to be considered in the proper use of paper.

1. Paper folds smoothly with the grain direction and roughens or cracks when folding cross-grain. This is often important in planning a printed piece.
2. Paper is stiffer in the grain direction.
3. Paper expands or contracts more in the cross direction when exposed to moisture changes.

Basis Weight

With few exceptions, printing papers are manufactured and identified by their basis weight. In the United States, it is the weight in pounds of a ream (500 sheets) in the basic size for that grade. Basis 70 means that 500 sheets 25 by 38 of book paper weigh 70 pounds.

The basic size is not the same for all grades. It is 25 by 38 for book papers (coated, text, offset, opaque, etc.), 17 by 22 for writing papers (bond, ledger, mimeograph, duplicator), 20 by 26 for cover papers (coated and uncoated), 25½ by 30½ for index bristol, 22½ by 28½ or 22½ by 35 for mill bristol and postal card, and 24 by 36 for tag and newsprint.

Paper is referred to in terms of its ream weight: 20-pound bond, 70-pound coated, etc. However, paper usually is listed in sizes and weight tables and price

Tear and Fold Tests

Paper tears straighter with grain.

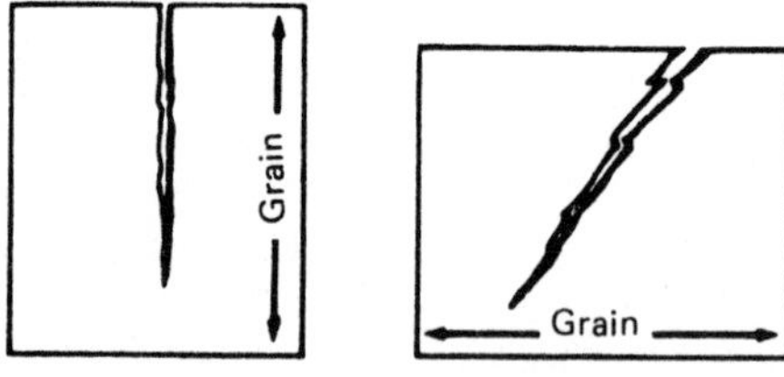

Paper folds more easily with grain.

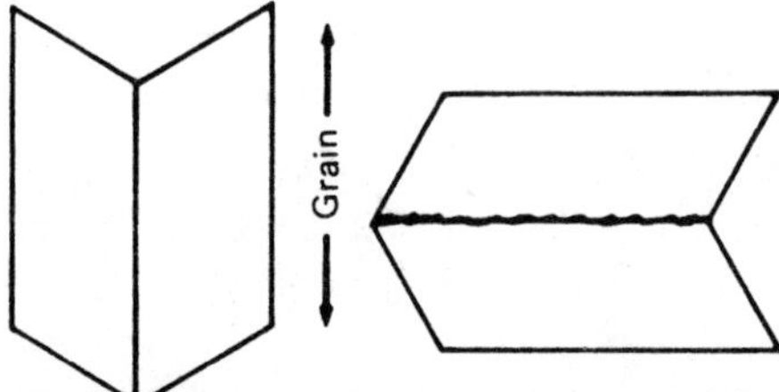

Figure 41-2 Tear and fold tests. *Pocket Pal, International Paper Company, New York, 1981.*

lists on a thousand-sheet basis: 25 by 38—140 per thousand for a 70-pound book paper. The M means that 1000 sheets 25 by 38 weigh 140 pounds.

Each grade is made in many standard sizes other than the basic size and in many weights. For example, book papers are made in weights from 50-pound to 100-pound in 10-pound increments.

Strength

The strength of paper is dependent more on the nature of its fiber than on its thickness. High bursting strength is achieved by closely intermingling long pulp fibers during the forming of the sheet on the paper machine wire.

Runability and Print Quality

Two important factors that affect the printing of papers by any process are runability and print quality. Runability affects the ability to get the paper through the press, and failures in runability can cause expensive downtime. Print quality factors affect the appearance of the printed image on the paper.

Runability. This is more of a problem in offset than in letterpress or gravure because of the overall contact of the paper with the blanket during impression and the use of water and tacky inks. The following paper properties can affect runability.

Flatness. This refers to freedom from buckles, puckers, wave, and curl. This is especially important in offset.

Trimming. Sheets should be square and accurate in size.

Dirt. Loose material from all manufacturing sources, such as slitter and trimmer dust, lint, loose pigments, or loosely bonded fibers on the surface are especially troublesome in offset.

Moisture Content or RH. The paper should be in balance with the pressroom RH (relative humidity). An increase in RH can cause wavy edges and infiltration of foreign matter. Paper rolls should be evenly and tightly wound with smooth even edges and a minimum of splices.

Print Quality

The appearance characteristics of the printed image can be affected by the following paper properties. These are especially important when the same job is being printed in more than one plant or when a job is being reprinted.

Color. Paper color is important because it affects color reproduction, especially for lighter tints. Paper colors vary with advertising fads from cool to warm shades. Type is most easily read against a soft (yellowish) white, while process colors reproduce most accurately on neutral white paper.

Brightness. Brightness affects the contrast, brilliance, snap, or sparkle of the printed subject. Artificial brighteners, like fluorescent additives, can affect color reproduction since most are not neutral in color and have excess blue reflectance.

Opacity. Opacity relates to the "show-through" of the printed image from the opposite side of the sheet of the adjoining sheet. It is affected by the thickness of the sheet and the use of fillers.

Smoothness. Smoothness is a very important property for letterpress and gravure but has little effect on offset. Smooth surfaces have irregularities of the order of 0.005 inch to 0.010 inch apart. They cannot be seen by the naked eye but can be detected by a magnifying glass and low-angle illumination. As smoothness decreases, solids and halftones get sandy and rough in appearance, but type is not affected much.

Gloss. Gloss affects the appearance of the ink film. Coupled with ink absorption, it can be used as a measure of paper surface efficiency (PSE) or the purity of ink reproduction.

Refractiveness. Refractiveness relates to light absorption in the surface of the paper causing halftones to appear darker than they should.

Paper for Web Offset

Paper for web offset naturally has its grain direction paralleling the web. The printer and paper mill must work together on the specifications for each order. Rolls must be properly wound, protected, and stored on end and must have good tensile strength to minimize tearing or breaking of the web on press. Paper should be of uniform caliper (thickness); be free from holes, scum spots, slitter dust, fiber picking, and lint; have a minimum of contraction and expansion; contain a minimum number of splices; and have sound cores for winding and delivery.

Paper Grades

Paper may be defined in terms of its use. Each grade serves a purpose that usually is suggested by its grade name. Some of the most common classifications of printing papers are bond, coated, text, cover, book, offset, index, label, tag, and newsprint. The size shown in parentheses is the basic size for that particular grade. See Figures 41-3 and 41-4.

Basis	50	60	70	80	100	120
8½ × 11	9.8	11.8	13.8	15.7	19.7	23.6
17½ × 22½	41	50	58	66	83	99
19 × 25	50	60	70	80	100	120
23 × 29	70	84	98	112	140	169
23 × 35	85	102	119	136	169	203
24 × 36	90	110	128	146	182	218
25 × 38	100	120	140	160	200	240
35 × 45	166	198	232	266	332	398
36 × 48	182	218	254	292	364	436
38 × 50	200	240	280	320	400	480

Figure 41-3 Comparative weights of book papers per 1000 sheets. *Pocket Pal, International Paper Company, New York, 1981.*

Grade of Paper	Book 25 x 38	Bond 17 x 22	Cover 20 x 26	Bristol 22½ x 28½	Index 25½ x 30½	Tag 24 x 36	Grammage g/m²
Book	**30**	12	16	20	25	27	44
	40	16	22	27	33	36	59
	45	18	25	30	37	41	67
	50	20	27	34	41	45	74
	60	24	33	40	49	55	89
	70	28	38	47	57	64	104
	80	31	44	54	65	73	118
	90	35	49	60	74	82	133
	100	39	55	67	82	91	148
	120	47	66	80	98	109	178
Bond	33	**13**	18	22	27	30	49
	41	**16**	22	27	33	37	61
	51	**20**	28	34	42	46	75
	61	**24**	33	41	50	56	90
	71	**28**	39	48	58	64	105
	81	**32**	45	55	67	74	120
	91	**36**	50	62	75	83	135
	102	**40**	56	69	83	93	151
Cover	91	36	**50**	62	75	82	135
	110	43	**60**	74	90	100	163
	119	47	**65**	80	97	108	176
	146	58	**80**	99	120	134	216
	164	65	**90**	111	135	149	243
	183	72	**100**	124	150	166	271
Bristol	100	39	54	**67**	81	91	148
	120	47	65	**80**	98	109	178
	148	58	81	**100**	121	135	219
	176	70	97	**120**	146	162	261
	207	82	114	**140**	170	189	306
	237	93	130	**160**	194	216	351
Index	110	43	60	74	**90**	100	163
	135	53	74	91	**110**	122	203
	170	67	93	115	**140**	156	252
	208	82	114	140	**170**	189	328
Tag	110	43	60	74	90	**100**	163
	137	54	75	93	113	**125**	203
	165	65	90	111	135	**150**	244
	192	76	105	130	158	**175**	284
	220	87	120	148	180	**200**	326
	275	109	151	186	225	**250**	407

Figure 41-4 Equivalent weights in reams of 500 sheets, with basis weights in bold type. *Pocket Pal, International Paper Company, New York, 1981.*

Bond (17 by 22). Bond papers are used commonly for letters and business forms. They have surfaces which accept ink readily from a pen or typewriter, and they can be erased easily. Most letterheads and business forms are a standard 8 1/2 by 11 size. Four pieces this size can be cut from a 17 by 22 sheet without waste.

Coated (25 by 38). This is base paper which has been given a smooth, glossy coating. Coated papers are used when high printing quality is desired because of their greater surface smoothness and uniform ink receptivity. There are many kinds: cast coated, gloss coated, dull coated, machine coated, coated one and two sides, etc.

Text (25 by 38). These papers are notable for their interesting textures and attractive colors. They enjoy frequent use for announcements, booklets, and brochures. Most text papers are treated with a sizing to make them more resistant to water penetration and easier to print by offset lithography.

Book (25 by 38). These papers are used for trade and textbooks as well as general printing. They are less expensive than text papers and are made in antique or smooth finishes. Book papers have a wider range of weights and bulk than text papers, and so it is possible to secure almost any desired bulking.

Offset (25 by 38). This is similar to the coated and uncoated book paper used for letterpress printing except that sizing is added to resist the slight moisture present in offset printing. Also, the surface is treated to resist picking.

Cover (20 by 26). Quite often, coated and text papers are made in heavier weights and matching colors which are used as covers on booklets, etc. There are also papers made for cover purposes only. Many surface textures are available, with finishes ranging from antique to smooth, including many special finishes. Special characteristics of cover papers include dimensional stability; uniform printing surface; good scoring, folding, embossing, and die-cutting qualities; and durability. It is a useful rule of thumb that cover stock of the same basis weight as text paper has about twice the thickness.

Index (22 1/2 by 35 and 25 1/2 by 30 1/2). Two outstanding characteristics are stiffness and receptivity to writing ink. Index is commonly used whenever an inexpensive stiff paper is required. It is available in both smooth and vellum finish.

Newsprint (24 by 36). This is the kind of paper used in printing newspapers. Furnish is chiefly groundwood pulp with some chemical pulp. It is made in basis weights from 28 to 35 pounds, with 30-pound used most extensively.

Tag (24 by 36). This is a utility sheet ranging in weight from 100 to 250 pounds. It is suitable for the manufacture of tags. It may be made from sulfite, sulfate or mechanical pulp, and various types of waste papers. Tag board sometimes is tinted and colored on one or both sides. Tag stock has good bending or folding qualities, suitable bursting and tensile strength, good tearing and water resistance, and a surface adaptable to printing, stamping, or writing.

HOW TO BUY PAPER

The printer should establish the size and specifications for the paper to be used. The printer will allow for spoilage, trims, bleeds, pickup laps, core size, roll diameter, and other requirements that another person may not consider.

Benefits for Client Purchasing Paper

- Possible price saving
- Establish allotments during possible market shortages

Benefits for Printer Purchasing Paper

- Printers buy more paper more frequently than clients. A printer may buy at a lower price, may get faster delivery, and will handle ordering, follow-up, shipping, and the headaches that occur.
- The printer will warehouse stock and bring paper to press. These costs generally are added as a handling charge to customer-supplied stock.
- The printer may offer a specific grade of stock to the client "at cost" in order to maintain the mill allotment. This practice works well in contractual or repetitive pressruns.
- If a paper-related problem arises, the printer generally will be responsible. The printer will replace the paper, will incur press downtime charges, but most important, is responsible for producing your job on time.
- Each printer may use a different sheet or roll size of stock to best fit the job and the printing press. Allow the printer to determine the most efficient size specifications rather than advising the printer of your stock on hand to be used.
- This relieves client cash flow. Paper usually represents the largest single element of your printing bill. Frequently, paper is ordered and paid for well before your job goes to press. When the printer buys your paper, the printer in a sense is acting as your banker.

Paper Selection

Too extravagant a sheet may destroy a budget; too inferior a sheet may destroy the promotion.

Choose the appropriate weight and grade of paper to do the job adequately. Discuss with your creative staff, your printer, and the paper merchant the design and purpose of the finished product.

The paper merchant will present various grades of paper that will accomplish the proper function of the printed piece at a price that will fit into your budget.

The printer should make known any preferences or specifications that are necessary to ensure quality printing, efficient production, and satisfactory use of the finished product.

If there will be die cuts, perforations, adhesives, or other excessive or stress requirements needed from the paper, relate all these requirements to the printer or paper supplier.

ERRORS CAN BE COSTLY

Never assume anything. Always ask questions and confirm job specifications verbally and in writing. Discuss and review all job details with the printer.

The following is a checklist of points to review before going to press.

1. Copy
2. Size
3. Folds
4. Color
5. Overall workability and compatibility of components
6. Conformity to postal regulations
7. Compatibility to computer operations
8. Insertability and bindability at bindery
9. Packing, labeling, and shipping requirements

The above is also a checklist of points to review at the press.

SOME GENERAL COMMENTS

Be wary of a very low price. Most printers of similar size and equipment all have similar operating costs and are price-competitive. A significantly lower or higher price may indicate that an error has been made in the estimate.

Buy quality, service, dependability, experience, and integrity. These are the elements that are important. Mistakes happen, and when they do, you will want to be working with a supplier who will stand behind his or product and rally to support your requirements.

Allow your printer to make a fair profit. If management is running a sound business, the printer will be reinvesting these profit dollars into some of the many rapidly changing new equipment in the graphic arts. You will benefit in that you will be able to avail yourself of the most modern equipment. The printer may need this equipment to remain price- and quality-competitive in the marketplace. The printer also must pay competitive wage scales to attract and maintain the best, most competent personnel.

People are not sold printing; they buy printing. They buy from companies that best fill a need. That need develops from providing a service, producing a product, or creating a more efficient way to achieve a desired result.

Make your printer part of your team. The printer will be happy to work hand in hand with your creative staff. Visit your printer periodically and become familiar with his or her operations and staff. This will promote a better understanding and relationship for you both.

chapter **42**

LETTERSHOP PROCESSING

Robert H. Jurick

President
FALA Direct
Marketing, Inc.
Melville, N.Y.

In years gone by, the term "lettershop" came about when companies would deliver envelopes and letters to a production organization that had the employees available to address the envelopes, fold and insert the letters, and seal, stamp, and deliver the mail to the post office. At that time, almost all methods for producing lettershop services were hand-operated. Today, modern technology has made lettershops rather diverse organizations. Some operations still need many hands, but planning and technical expertise have changed the industry.

In the past, a well-rounded lettershop had an addressing department, a mimeograph-multigraph printing department, folding departments (both machine and hand), and of course, an inserting department.

Today these departments are still similar, but almost all have been mechanized. Even so, every shop still requires experienced personnel to do hand operations.

SELECTING A LETTERSHOP

There are certain basics to look for in determining whether a particular organization can provide the services you require.

Meeting the people who run the shop is a prime requisite in selecting a lettershop. From the salesperson to management to the production team, the machine and hand operation as well as the receiving and materials handling personnel add up to a team that must have the ability and experience to produce your project.

The sales personnel who work with you in starting a project are the key.

Experienced salespeople who are fortunate enough to have started in the plant have the technical ability to help you organize a mailing project. Their production experience often can make the difference in saving dollars in postage through recommending a minor size or weight change.

Who are the backup people to the sales executive? Are they knowledgeable people, capable of answering your questions when the salesperson is on another call? Can they help make proper production decisions?

The equipment in the lettershop is, of course, the next key area to be checked. If you're producing a mailing of 1 million or more, the equipment required will be more substantial than it would for a mailing of 25,000. The lettershop you are seeking will have the equipment necessary for two or three times the production you require.

What type of equipment does a lettershop require? First, it needs material handling equipment capable of taking your printed materials from a truck and storing them in the facility, whether Hi-Lo, pallet trucks, or dollies. Also look for some kind of storage area that is neat and well marked as to skid or carton position.

Basic equipment for a lettershop would include a burster for separating computerized forms, a burster and folder for separating and folding the forms, and folding machines to fold letters and brochures. Folding machines are important as backup in case an additional fold is required or an element of a mailing was not folded.

A shop's labeling machine must be capable of affixing 1-up, 3-, 4-, or 5-across labels or even cut labels in various sizes. The attachments for this equipment should be examined when you visit the shop.

Inserting machines are a necessity. There are two types: 6 by 9 and 9 by 12. Note the number of stations the machines have. Generally, most lettershops have six-station machines. How many inserts does your mailing have? If six or less, a shop with six-station machines is adequate. Ten or eleven inserts create a difficult problem. If your mailing quantity is under 100,000, a double pass on a 6-station machine is possible. If it is in the millions, the shop should have machines capable of inserting all eleven inserts at one pass.

For estimating purposes, always use 2000 to 2500 inserts per hour for determining the length of production time on a machine.

The minimum equipment a shop should have should be equal to three times the production you require. For example, inserting a 50,000 of four inserts into a 6 by 9 envelope would take 25 hours (2000 an hour × 25 = 50,000 units). If the plant works an 8-hour day, it would take 3 days on one machine.

If you are producing millions of pieces, the same formula will work. However, lettershops that mail millions of pieces generally work a minimum of two shifts (if not three). The minimum number of machines to look for here would be twelve.

When looking at a shop, it is important to know that they have good mechanics (the people who set up the machines) and capable repair people in case there is a breakdown.

Larger shops may have mail sorting departments. Most shops today will sort the mail at the end of the machine cycle. If you're seeking a major mailer, it is important that they have a post office operation in the plant. If small mailings are required, this is not a necessity. It is an asset to you because you know your mail will move more rapidly.

Smaller mailings generally are delivered by your lettershop to the local post office. It is important to know where the post office is and whether your vendor has in-plant loading.

Basically, all this equipment is found in the lettershop of today. Many shops also have data centers, fulfillment centers, and printing plants which augment and round out the lettershop services.

Once you have seen the people and the equipment, how do you select the lettershop for you? To do efficient work, a lettershop must be neat and tidy. An inspection tour will give you this input.

Next, ask for three customer references with work similar to yours. Make the calls and find out how long they've done business, the type of work performed, and the record for on-time service.

After completing your investigation, you'll see how your materials were received and reported. You'll discover how you're posted as far as deliveries and mailings are concerned, and you will see how you're billed for the project at the end, along with reports about the leftover material.

Postage is always required in advance. Whether it is an advance deposit to the permit number at the post office or a check to the mailer, the monies always should be delivered at least 5 to 7 days before the mailing date to allow for clearance of the postage check. An industry rule prevails: "No mailing without postage advance." The lettershop does not earn a profit on postage.

SIZE OF THE MAILING PROJECT

There is no magic number. Through the years, the quantity that has separated the volume mail class of work from the smaller or hand operation has been 25,000. Over this quantity, plan on making use of machines; under 25,000, be prepared to produce by hand. How the smaller quantity finally is produced is not really the question. The planning approach should assume that this project will be done at a much lower rate of production than the higher quantity.

TIMING OF THE VARIED PARTS

Whether you are producing the project in your facility or are using a lettershop, the information that is required will make for an easier production schedule.

When will the material to be used in the mailing be delivered to the lettershop? Most direct mail companies will not schedule the production of the project until all the materials have been received. Planning with your envelope manufacturers, printers, and list houses certainly can make the difference between success and failure. A commitment from a reliable vendor in each of these areas allows the mailer to set the tentative schedule.

Scheduling the Mail Date

After you review the delivery of each of the components, the mail date for the project should be scheduled. The rule of inserting 2000 pieces per hour should be your means of double-checking the scheduling by your lettershop. Most lettershops will give you the number of working days to produce a project from the time all the material has been received. Don't forget that this refers to working days. Do not include holidays, Saturdays, or Sundays. Always add an extra day to any schedule. If that timing does not work out, you know you'll have to spend overtime charges on the printing to get your project to the mailer so that it can drop on the proper mail date.

Typing of Lists

The lettershop must know what they will receive so that they know what equipment they'll need to affix labels (if that is the source). They may have to plan to type addresses.

As soon as you know how the project is to be done, get this information to the lettershop. Make it easy. In your instructions, indicate the following.

1. You will receive labels 1-up, 3-up, 4-up, or 5-up.
2. You will receive a list to be typed onto number 10 envelopes.
3. You will receive a computer letter form 2-up, 17 3/4 by 11, that must burst to 8 3/8 by 11 and two parallel folds, copy out to fit in a number 10 window envelope.

These are only a few of the ways to clarify the input on types of lists to be used for the project.

Number of Enclosures

It is also important to notify the mailer as to the number of inserts or enclosures.

1. We will have four inserts into a number 10 envelope.
2. We will have six inserts into a 6 by 9 booklet envelope.

Where possible, make up a physical dummy using the actual paper if the printed samples are not yet available. This will serve a twofold purpose.

1. It is a double check that the pieces are mechanically insertable.
2. The weight of the unit helps determine postage costs.

Method of Mailing

With the weight and size determined, the class of mail can be determined. If the weight is very close and you're still in the planning stage, you still may be able to trim a unit down in size slightly or change the weight of one of the stocks.

It is important to give a dummy to the lettershop in advance. Their scales generally are attuned to the postal requirements. When in doubt, most shops will walk the dummy package directly to the post office and verify the weights. The shop can give you the weights and tell you the postage costs for both third and first class so that you can make the decision.

KEY ITEMS TO DISCUSS IN PLANNING A MAILING

Envelopes

The envelope is the carrier of the contents of your mailing project. It should be sturdy enough to carry your package through the mails so that it gets there without damage.

Size

Every mailing package may require a different size. Below is a listing of the basic sizes of envelopes. The size is known by most lettershops. Give the dimensions at the same time. Not many people give this information, yet it is of great assistance to the mailer.

BASIC SIZES OF ENVELOPES

Monarch	3⅞ by 7½	6¼ envelope	3½ by 6
Check	3⅝ by 8⅝	6¾ envelope	3⅝ by 6½
Standard number 10	4⅛ by 9½	Number 7	3¾ by 6¾
Number 11	4½ by 10⅜	Number 9	3⅞ by 8⅞

Booklet or Open End

It's very simple to recognize the two basic types of envelopes once you've seen them. A booklet type, with the flap on the top or bottom of the long side, is machine-insertable. The open-ended type, with the flap on the narrow edge, is not machine-insertable.

Even when you plan to hand insert a job, check with the lettershop as to which type, "booklet" or "open end," they would prefer for the project.

Window or Regular Envelope

This is one of the easier pieces of information to determine. Where are you addressing? On the envelope. Then use a regular envelope. On a reply device, a letter, or even on the reply envelope, use a window envelope.

There are basic types of windows: with or without glassine and with or without poly. Some areas for windows can come die cut for position with nothing pasted behind. Again, this is a decision for you to make, but it should be specified to the mailer.

Paper Envelopes

Two basic types of envelope material are used today. Envelopes made of paper, of course, have been the standard for years. However, plastic envelopes have been popular in recent times. Which type you use is important to the lettershop. Not all lettershops have the ability to handle plastic. Let them know early which way you are going.

Type of Inserts

Flat, folded, fan-folded, booklets, single sheets, thick, or thin. It would be terrific for the lettershop if you could give them the proper dummy of the entire project as discussed above, but sometimes this information is not available. You should, however, very explicitly describe the number of pieces in the package and what they are physically: a single sheet (one-page letter), two sheets (four-page letter), and so on. Bulky pieces or unusual folds should be pointed out.

Will the lettershop have to fold one or more elements? What size will they be, and how will they be folded?

Number of Inserts

How many inserts? Very simple. Let the lettershop know the exact number of inserts and the size.

Inserting

What is the order of the pieces as they go into the envelope? List the pieces as you count them, inserted from the flap to the front of the envelope. Be specific. Don't leave anything to chance. Will the package be hand-inserted or machine-inserted?

Self-Mailers

Self-mailers fall into a category of their own. You must do everything to a self-mailer that you do to an envelope package except the inserting.

There are certain things you must tell the lettershop.

1. What is the size of the self-mailer—simple card, folder, brochure, or catalog? Knowing the weight is helpful both for postage and for proper handling.
2. Does the self-mailer have a preprinted indicia? This is advisable, but sometimes it doesn't happen. If there is no indicia, it will be necessary to meter. Is the unit machineable?
3. How many lists are going to be used for the mailing? If third class or catalog rate, are the lists in ZIP sequence?

Weight, size, and number of pages are all key pieces of information for the mailing house. With this information in advance, we can better help to schedule and plan the project and can get the best possible postage rate.

METHODS OF ADDRESSING

Today we use two distinct categories of addressing: noncomputer and computer. Our industry, of course, started without computers. Today we still use many of the older methods, but computer addressing is dominant.

Noncomputer Addressing

We can go from the very basic handwritten means of addressing to one of the mechanical methods of addressing. From the handwritten, we go easily to the typewritten. Type the address directly onto the envelope. Type the name, address, and salutation onto a preprinted letter. Use that unit in a window envelope or type address a matching envelope. If your lettershop is to do the job, they should know exactly what you want to do.

Typewriting led to many mechanical addressing systems: Speedomat, Addressograph, Scriptomatic, Elliot Stencils, etc. Based on quantity and data to be maintained, the system that a mailing list is kept on must be predetermined. However your lettershop is handling your mailing, the form in which the list gets to them is important.

Computer

Generally, lists of 20,000 or more are maintained on computers. That was almost a rule when computers came into being. Today, with all kinds of minicomputers and word processors, lists of all sizes may be maintained on the computer. Regardless of the size of the computer, almost all are capable of producing labels in any number of formats: 1-up, 3-up, 4-up, 5-up, etc.

The computer produces these labels on varied stocks. Cheshire stock is the ordinary computer paper (basic, 50-pound stock): pressure-sensitive, peel-off pressure-sensitive, and gum stock. These labels are produced on continuous forms which are machineable by either the Kirk Rudy or Cheshire labeling machines which most lettershops have.

The computer also produces computer letters, either full or match fill. These too can be used as an addressing vehicle.

Finally, laser printers can produce labels and letters and can even be part of Web printing equipment and address catalogs as they are being printed in multiple colors at high speeds.

How the list comes to the direct mail company, when it arrives, and the format and sequence are of key importance to the lettershop. The more information given to the vendor or to your own production facility, the better chance you have to get the quality and dependability you seek.

IMPORTANCE OF SUPERVISION

Earlier, it was suggested that you check into the supervision of the lettershop. Now that you've selected the shop, the first job you do will tell you a lot about your original decision. It is important to follow through on this job from start to finish.

You've done your job. You gave the lettershop the dates material would be received. It's their turn now to show you that they are the company they've claimed to be.

Material starts to arrive at their door. You should be informed with some type of written receiving report within a day of the receipt of your material. This report should tell you the following:

1. Name of vendor that delivered the material
2. Number of cartons received or skids of material
3. Weight of carton or skid
4. Number of pieces received per shipper's report
5. Estimated quantity based on weight
6. Condition of the material
7. How it compares with the dummy you submitted
8. Samples of the material (a minimum of two)

On receipt of this report, you are completely aware of what has been delivered. This information is important in case you have any kind of problem in the future.

If you receive this report, you can be assured that the same information has been passed on to the production department of the lettershop. This is the point where the team effort pays off. As material comes into the receiving department, the production department should check it out to see if it clearly meets the specifications you discussed in the original planning of the project. This is the time to catch an error.

The production department's efficiency and knowledge will be apparent at this point. When they receive the samples, their promptness in reviewing the sample against the actual piece will be indicated. There is nothing more frustrating than being informed on the day of a mailing that a printed piece that arrived days earlier does not meet your requirements. Situations like this certainly would change your opinion. However, your experience will always tell you how well the supervisory people in the shop are performing.

COMPUTERIZED FORMS

You may be shipping your lettershop fully computerized forms from an EDP company. In almost all cases, computerized forms will be shipped in the same cartons in which the continuous forms printer delivered them. One additional piece of information should be on the cartons: the sequence number of the production of the form (e.g., carton 1 of 40, carton 2 of 40, and so on). Receiving the material with this simple information on it will save many hours of work that would be wasted otherwise. If a program was in ZIP sequence and the cartons were not numbered, it would create a problem in sorting out the cartons.

Samples from a number of different cartons should be pulled. Some of these samples should be shipped to the clients so that they can double-check that all is correct.

Computer Form Mail Production

Your computer forms have been received at the lettershop. You've received samples from the lettershop along with the receiving report.

It is a good idea to have a carefully ruled out form delivered to the lettershop so that they can set up their equipment to burst, trim, or fold the form in question. This rule-out is a key element in the proper handling of any computerized job.

If the form, for example, is a 2-up, one-page letter measuring 17 3/4 inches wide by 11 inches deep, the rule-out pictured in Figure 42-1 will be most helpful and will save time and eliminate any chance for error.

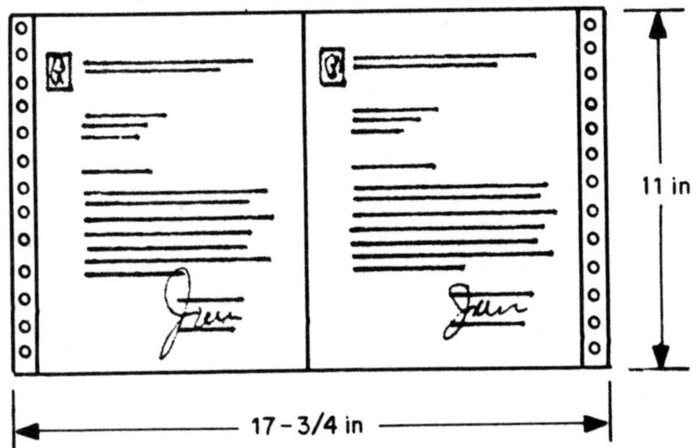

Figure 42-1 Sample ruled-out computer form.

On the 17 3/4 by 11 2-up letter form, the rule-out tells the lettershop to perform the following steps in preparing the project.

1. When the form is burst, take off 1/2 inch of holes on each side.
2. Halfway across the sheet, slit so that the form when cut measures 8 3/8 inches wide.
3. The sheet on the right must interstack behind the sheet on the left.
4. It folds in thirds, copy out, so that the personalization shows through the number 10 window.
5. Make a hand-cut dummy of the cut piece.

These steps will help eliminate any chance for error. In an instance where the computer form may have been produced incorrectly, you would know about the accuracy prior to any work being done. If an error did occur, you would have the opportunity to make minor alterations to salvage the package.

INSERTING

Regardless of whether the machine work is 9 by 12 or 6 by 9, the basic input that should be known is the same. We saw the dummy when we estimated the job. We now must produce the project.

Machine Inserting

Once the components of the project are all in the shop, a good management team will make up two basic dummies: one for you and one for the plant. The two samples are made so that you can check the estimated package and also double-check in the case of machine inserting that all pieces meet the machine requirements.

It is suggested that a six-insert job, for example, have a sample piece hung above each station on the inserting machine that is producing the job. These samples should be numbered and dated along with the time. Management in the lettershop should check these samples and, of course, check all samples every hour from every machine.

In essence, this step gives the lettershop producer the security of knowing that the work is being performed accurately. The chance of any major error is now limited.

On multiple-pass jobs, an envelope should be taken each hour from each facet of the job. These hourly checks protect the lettershop but also show the client that the work was performed accurately. These hourly samples should be retained, although some clients want all the material to be mailed. In that case, on the last day of mailing, all the samples pulled during production also would drop.

Inserting by Hand

There is no difference between the procedures for hand and machine inserting. Each rule followed by the shop for machine inserting should be followed for hand operations.

One of the major differences in the work is, of course, the envelope that you can use for hand inserting. It is not required that you use the booklet-style envelope; the open-ended envelope may be used. In fact, the reason why you are doing the project by hand might be that you had in stock or wanted to use an open-ended envelope.

In most cases, you're doing handwork because the quantities are too small for the machines or because an insert or two is not machine-insertable.

Again, it's most important to mock up the dummy package for the lettershop. Number the pieces from the flap side of the envelope to the face or address side. The hand collation department should also display—near where the work is being done—samples of the inserts in the proper sequence. This eliminates the need for the operator to exercise judgment or interpret specifications. If there are similar pieces in the package, the shop's management should explain the difference to the inserters. Usually the pieces to be inserted have key codes which help identify the pieces. These should be pointed out and written in large letters on the display near the work station.

Another portion of handwork occurs when you've designed personalized packages. For example, the outer envelope has the name and address as follows:

Mr. John Sample
110 Sample Street
Any City, NY 00000

The letter in the package may be personalized as follows:

Mr. John Sample
110 Sample Street
Any City, NY 00000

Dear Mr. Sample:

The response device may be personalized with a list code, mail date using the Julian calendar, the account number, and the name and address, as follows:

AB-001-000000
Mr. John Sample
110 Sample Street
Any City, NY 00000

These other inserts also may be included in the package. If none are related to the personalization, you have two personalized inserts to match with the outer envelope. In a job of this type, it's most important to mark the trays of completed work with the inserter or operator's number or name so that you can check the accuracy of each handworker's performance.

When planning match jobs, it's always good to give thought to how the job will be assembled. Always try to leave the address portion on the side of the piece that is facing out. This will make it easier to check the operators.

When match work is performed, it is suggested that it not carry a preprinted indicia. Instead, use either stamps or a meter imprint. The client is spending added dollars for the hand assembly to get a more personal-looking package, and the postage method should support this image.

In a final review of this work, thought should be given to attempting to make it machine-insertable. Sometimes the letter, the order form, or even the envelope may be addressable by a computer process. This can simplify the whole project. Of course, quantity plays a major role. If possible, review the project with the lettershop sales executive prior to designing the mailing. These sales people can offer good suggestions to save dollars and speed production.

LABELING

When you hear the salesperson ask what type of label it is, understand that he or she is asking this in order to help.

In simple terms, a label is a piece of paper that contains the name and address of the recipient, which then can be applied to a mailing piece or envelope for use as the address vehicle. There are many different kinds of labels.

Cheshire Label

These involve specially prepared paper: rolls, fan-fold or accordian fold, continuous form papers used to reproduce names and addresses to be mechanically affixed one at a time to a mailing piece. These labels generally are available in 1-up, 3-up, 4-up, and 5-up. The stocks that are available are

1. Plain paper, generally 50 pound white offset (called Cheshire stock)
2. Davac gum stock, which is paper that will stick to the piece when moistened

3. Pressure-sensitive stock, which is paper that can be affixed by machine or peeled off by hand and attached to the mail piece.

North-South Labels

These are mailing labels (1-up) that read from top to bottom and can be affixed with label-affixing equipment. This product usually is generated by processes other than computer.

Peel-off Label

This is a self-adhesive label attached to a backing sheet which then is attached to a mailing piece. This label is designed so that it may be removed from the mailing piece and attached to an order blank or card. It is another form of a Cheshire label.

All other labels can be designed to any specifications one desires. For anything other than the labels listed above, always give the size and type of paper it has been produced on.

The next important question to ask is, What order is the list in?

Alphabetical by name

Alphabetical by company

State order

ZIP code order

No order (just names acquired)

The order the list is in has a lot to do with what postage will be spent to produce the job. If it is a national list in ZIP code order, you probably could sort for the cheapest postage, whether first or third class.

The next question to ask is, What size is the piece we're going to label? Again, the size of the piece and the type of the label tell us by what method we can affix the labels—machine or hand.

Of course, one of the remaining questions to be asked is, Is the finished job to be sorted in ZIP sequence? If not, the relative costs of sorting and postage for each class should be determined.

A labeled job does not always have to be mailed. It may be intended for distribution at an office, plant, or school. The job then would be packed and marked by number. A cover sheet would tell the client what alpha is covered in each carton.

First Class Presort. At the date of the publishing of the book, specifications for first class presort call for fifty or more pieces to a ZIP code being kept together in trays, for the special rate of $0.17 each instead of $0.20 each. The minimum quantity allowed for this mailing is 500 pieces. Where there is a great quantity, the postage requires a printout giving exact quantities of all mail by qualified portion and also a report on counts that do not qualify for the reduced rate.

Third Class Bulk Rate. The minimum quantity for this mailing is 200 pieces. Such a mailing must be sorted by ZIP code, and the postage rate is 11 cents each, or $110 per thousand.

Third Class Five-Digit ZIP Sort. The minimum quantity for this mailing is 200 pieces or 50 pounds of mail, presorted to five-digit destinations. Each piece must be part of a package of ten or more pieces to the same five-digit ZIP code, and the postage rate is 9.3 cents each, or $93 per thousand.

Third Class Carrier Route. The minimum quantity for mailing under this regulation is also 200 pieces, but the ruling calls for large mailings broken down by carrier route, rural route, etc., and should bear the imprint or endorsement of "CARRIER ROUTE PRESORT." The postage rate is 7.9 cents, or $79 per thousand.

Nonprofit

All carry the same rulings as the bulk rate. The following are the postage rates for each class.

Regular third class	4.9 cents each, or $49 per thousand
Five-digit presort	4.0 cents each, or $40 per thousand
Carrier route presort	3.0 cents each, or $30 per thousand

WHAT LIABILITIES MUST BE CONSIDERED?

The following are the trade customs that have been in use for over 50 years. They are released by the Mail Advertising Service Association (MASA) International.

TRADE CUSTOMS[1]

The use of Trade Customs is a defensive position that can best be avoided by clear written agreements. In an effort to clarify this naturally complex situation, we have reviewed the Trade Customs previously stated by MASA and those of several other trade associations covering various aspects of work commonly performed by MASA member companies. Because of differences in type of services sold, we have segregated this edition of Trade Customs into three categories: GENERAL, MAILING AND RELATED, and PRINTING. These Trade Customs have been in general use in the mail advertising and printing industries for over 50 years.

To avoid confusion, the term "vendor" is used throughout to refer to the supplier of mailing services, fulfillment, creative services, printing, "lettershop" activities, etc.—any facet of work performed by mailing or printing companies for their customers.

General

Quotations. Quotations are subject to acceptance within 30 days. Quotations are based on the cost of labor and materials on the date of the quote. If changes occur in cost of material, labor or other costs prior to acceptance, the right is

[1] Mail Advertising Service Association International, *Trade Customs*, revised February 1979.

reserved to change the price quoted. Subsequent orders will be subject to price revision if required. Quotations do not include postage, customers' shipping costs or applicable taxes unless specified separately.

Cancellation. After acceptance, order may be cancelled by the customer at any time by notice in writing with the understanding that vendor will be compensated in full for any work or services performed prior to cancellation.

Alterations/Specifications. Prices quoted herein are based upon vendor's understanding of the specifications submitted. If there are changes in specifications or instructions resulting in additional costs, the work performed will be billed at current rates.

Delivery. Unless otherwise specified, the price quoted is for a single delivery FOB the vendor's plant or to the local post office for jobs mailed. All estimates are based on continuous and uninterrupted delivery of complete order, unless specifications distinctly state otherwise.

Shipping charges from client to plant, or from client supplier to plant are not included in any quotations, unless specified.

At buyer's request, special priority pick-up or delivery service by outside services will be provided at prevailing rates.

Material delivered is verified with the receiving ticket as to cartons, packages, or items shown only. The accuracy of units per package quantities indicated on shipping forms cannot be verified and vendor cannot accept liability for shortage based on suppliers' stated quantities.

Acceptance of Order. The customer or purchaser agrees that vendor may refuse at any time to print or mail any copy, photographs or illustrations of any kind that in his sole judgment he believes is an invasion of privacy, is degrading, libelous, unlawful, profane, obscene, pornographic, tends to ridicule or embarrass, or is in bad taste, or which in his sole judgment is an infringement on a trademark, trade name or copyright belonging to others.

The customer also agrees to defend and hold vendor harmless in any suit or court action brought against him for alleged damages, costs and reasonable attorney fees, resulting from his printing or mailing any of customer's material that is deemed legally actionable.

Claims. Work performed shall be deemed to be acceptable to customer unless advised in writing within 10 days of completion of the order. Vendor's liability for error in all cases shall be limited to value of the work performed.

Mailing and Related Services

Postage and Freight Charges. Payment of postage in advance is required on all orders. In special cases, if requested, vendors may agree to advance postage but will add a service fee. Customer freight bills, paid by vendor, will be rebilled and are subject to a service charge.

Materials. Vendor assumes in quotations that all material provided will permit efficient handling on vendor's equipment. Materials furnished to vendor which are not up to standard and result in excessive production time will be subject to pricing at special rates. Customer will be notified when deficiency is discovered and approval obtained for handling at special rates before proceeding with work.

All direct mail handling and processing involves spoilage. Allowances for spoilage should be taken into consideration in ordering necessary material for further handling. Every effort will be made to handle customer's material at minimal expense and to prevent undue spoilage. Vendor does not process material which is running at excessive spoilage rates without notification to the buyer. Nevertheless, vendor cannot accept responsibility for shortages of material as a result of spoilage in processing.

All stock and materials belonging to customer will be held and stored only at customer's risk.

Delivery Schedules. Vendor will make every effort to meet scheduled delivery and mailing dates, but accept no liability for our vendor failure to meet any requested delivery dates. In addition, vendor has no control over U.S. Postal Service delivery schedules and cannot guarantee when mail deposited by vendor will be delivered by the Postal Service. All work orders accepted contingent to fire, accident, act of God, mechanical breakdown or other cause beyond vendor's control. Since the time element is an integral part of vendor's business, quoted prices are based upon a specific set of time schedules for completion. Any requested deviation from the schedules described or agreed by both parties at commencement of order may alter the quoted price.

Mailing Lists. Customer's mailing list(s) in vendor's possession for storage or otherwise is the exclusive property of customer and shall be used only at customer's instructions. Mailing list(s) either compiled or rented and furnished by vendor for customer use are for one time mailing only and are not to be copied, reused or resold by customer unless specific arrangements are made otherwise. Unless stated to the contrary, no guaranty of deliverability or results is given. Vendor does not accept liability or responsibility for compilation of list(s) used nor for any intangible or special value attached thereto.

Printing

Experimental Work. Sketches, drawings, layouts, copywriting, and other experimental work, including presswork and materials supplied by vendor, will be charged for at current rates. Such layouts, sketches, copy and drawing are the property of vendor and no use of them shall be made and no idea obtained therefrom shall be used, except upon vendor's written permission.

Artwork, Negatives, Plates. All art, mechanicals, paste-ups, lithograph negatives and plates supplied by vendor are vendor's property, unless otherwise specified.

Proofs. Proof approval by customer is necessary prior to any processing. Brown prints and press proofs are available on request at established rates for same. At customer's request (and waiver of our liability for error), vendor will proofread any order. Vendor will do this as a convenience for the customer, particularly in connection with order with a tight deadline, but vendor does not guarantee accuracy.

Sketches, Copy, Dummies. All preparatory work created or furnished by vendor shall remain vendor's exclusive property and no use of same shall be made, nor may ideas obtained therefrom be used, except upon compensation to be determined by vendor.

Press Proofs. An extra charge will be made for press proofs, unless the customer is present when the form is made ready on the press, so that no press time is lost. Presses standing awaiting approval of customer will be charged at current rates for the time so consumed.

MAILING SPECIFICATION CHECKLIST

Having been involved in the direct mail business for over 30 years, I've made up a list of basic questions to help my sales executives determine what work has to be done.

1. What is the quantity? Under 25,000 is lettershop; over 25,000 is volume mail.
2. When will material be received and what is the mail date?
3. Envelopes
   - a. Size; booklet or open ended; preprinted indicia?
   - b. Window or closed (if window, open or cello)?
   - c. Paper or plastic (polybag)?
4. Addressing
   - a. If labels, what kind—Cheshire, pressure-sensitive, gummed?
   - b. If labels, what is labeled (envelope, BRC, etc.)?
   - c. If computer forms, do we burst and trim? Size of forms, number up, trim size?
   - d. Type of address? What font? To what piece? What is the source—directory, cards, galleys, handwritten?
5. Mailing
   - a. Is list provided in strict ZIP code sequence?
   - b. How many lists and the sizes from smallest to largest?
   - c. Class of mail (first, third, bulk, etc.)?
   - d. Is indicia preprinted? Do we meter or provide meter strips?
   - e. Do we stamp and what kind—regular, commemorative, bulk rate stamp, United Nations?
6. Self-mailer: same questions as in items 5 and 6
   - a. Size?
   - b. Number of pages or thickness?
7. Bursting and folding
   - a. Size of full finished sheet?
   - b. Number up (1 or 2)?
   - c. Number of folds and type of fold?

8. Shipping
  - **a.** Where?
  - **b.** How (what carrier)?
  - **c.** If packed in cartons, do we supply?
  - **d.** Should shipping be included in price or additional?

9. Incidentals
  - **a.** Tipping, stapling, clipping, etc.?
  - **b.** Keying: separately or while labeling? How many different keys and sizes of each key (approximate)?

chapter 43

POSTAL REGULATIONS

Lee Epstein

President
Mailmen Inc.
New York, N.Y.

This chapter will acquaint you with the U.S. Postal Service rules and regulations in order to make you knowledgeable about the various classes of mail and their specifications. It will enable you to determine the most economical rates for the level of service you require based on the type of material you wish to mail.

A BRIEF HISTORY OF THE U.S. POSTAL SERVICE

In 1789, Congress created a government agency called the Post Office Department. Its purpose was to set up a universal communications and delivery system which would provide for the delivery of mail to all citizens, regardless of location or distance, with the same postage rates for everyone. The private express statutes mandated that this agency would have a monopoly on the delivery of letters. Congress would set postage rates and provide the necessary funding; the postmaster general would be a member of the President's Cabinet. At that time, there were seventy-five post offices.

A postal system was created by the Continental Congress in 1774, with Benjamin Franklin as the postmaster general. In 1847, the first postage stamp was issued. In 1970, Congress discontinued direct control over rates and wages and passed the Postal Reorganization Act, which established the U.S. Postal Service as an independent government operation. This act permitted the service to negotiate directly on wages with its employees and, through the Postal Rate Commission, establish postage rates which eventually would permit the service to break even.

THE CURRENT RATE-MAKING PROCESS

When the U.S. Postal Service feels that it needs more revenue, it makes recommendations for rate increases to the Postal Rate Commission, based on cost studies. The commission then conducts its own studies and hearings on revenue requirements in which not only the service but any association or individual can participate as intervenors. The Postal Rate Commission in turn must recommend to the Board of Governors of the Postal Service its conclusions and recommendations for rates within 10 months. The Board of Governors then can accept, reject, or resubmit its case to the Rate Commission for reconsideration. In the interim, the U.S. Postal Service can put in place temporary rates until the case is resolved. After the third rejection of the Rate Commission recommendations, the Board of Governors can modify these rates as they see fit. Since 1970, rate increases have taken place every 2 or 3 years.

CLASSES OF MAIL

There are four basic classes of mail: first, second, third, and fourth. Each class services a different product line and has different levels of service as well as different mailing requirements. Within each class there are subclasses, such as priority mail for first class, controlled magazines for second class, nonprofit mail for third class, and special fourth and library rate for fourth class.

In discussing each class of mail, I have specifically avoided mentioning rates, since rates are subject to periodic changes. Check with your mailing service or the U.S. Postal Service for the latest information.

First Class Mail

First class mail is a preferred category. It receives expedited handling and transportation. Postage may be paid by meter or by stamp, and any mailable matter up to 12 ounces may be sent. It receives free forwarding and return service and may not be opened for postal inspections. Postal cards, personal correspondence, or typewritten bills and statements of accounts must be mailed first class. Delivery may be expected in 1 to 3 days, depending on the distance.

Priority Mail

First class mail over 12 ounces is called priority mail. Postage is determined by weight and by zone distances. The maximum weight permissible is 70 pounds.

Second Class Mail

This class is used by newspapers and magazines issued at least four times a year. To qualify for a permit, a publication must have request (controlled) or paid subscribers and must not be designed primarily for advertising purposes.

Second class mail generally receives speedy delivery. Daily and weekly publications are entitled to newspaper or "red tag" treatment.

Third Class Mail

Third class mail consists of advertising circulars, brochures, booklets, catalogs, and other printed matter (e.g., letters, order forms, reply envelopes, etc.) weighing less than 1 pound. Small parcels and merchandise under a pound also can be mailed in this class. There are two subclasses.

1. The single-piece rate does not require the ZIP code and needs no mail preparation for acceptance. Delivery is slower than for first class, and it receives no free forwarding or return privileges.
2. Bulk rate is by far the most popular class for solicitation or prospect contact. A permit is required as well as an annual bulk mail fee. A minimum of 200 pieces or 50 pounds is required. All pieces must be ZIP coded. The mail then must be separated by ZIP code and tied and bagged before being presented to the U.S. Postal Service for mailing, along with a statement of mailing. Postage may be paid by preprinted indicia, meter impression, or precanceled stamp. Since this is a deferred category of mail, its delivery can run from 3 to 30 days, depending on its makeup and dispatch.

Fourth Class Mail

Parcels weighing 1 pound or more are mailed as fourth class or parcel post up to a maximum of 70 pounds. Some post offices are restricted to 40-pound packages. Postage is computed by weight and by zone.

Fourth Class, Special

This subclass is used to mail books and records weighing 1 pound or more. It is a subclass with postage computed by weight regardless of zone.

Fourth Class, Library Rate

This subclass is for items weighing 1 pound or more mailed for or to recognized schools, libraries, and nonprofit organizations.

Fourth Class, Bound Printed Matter

This is fourth class matter weighing between 1 and 10 pounds, including advertising, promotional, directory, or editorial matter. It must be bound securely and does not permit loose-leaf binders. There is also a special rate for bulk-bound printed matter when 300 or more identical pieces are mailed.

PRESORT PROGRAM

The U.S. Postal Service has developed lower rates for first, second, third, and fourth class mail when the mailer performs the preparation and sorting functions. These work-sharing programs can result in significantly lower rates when there is sufficient density and volume. There are three tiers to the presort program.

Carrier Presort

To qualify for this rate, the mailing piece must be identified as part of the address, must have at least ten pieces to a carrier route (six for second class), and must be tied and bagged by carrier route and placed in the proper five-digit bag. The U.S. Postal Service will provide a mailer with computerized carrier route tapes which then can be used (with the proper computer software) to identify the carrier route number for your name and address file. Labels or computer letters then are printed with the carrier route number as part of the address.

Five-Digit Presort

For this discount level, you must have at least 50 pieces or 10 pounds of mail for a ZIP code, and each ZIP code must be put in a separate sack. You may combine certain three-digit codes.

Regular Rate

All mail which cannot qualify for the carrier or five-digit rate falls into this category.

Presorted mail may be presented and paid for by preprinted indicia, meter, or precanceled stamps. Minimum quantities are required which differ for each class of mail. It is now possible to commingle first class presorted mail from more than one mailer. There are first class presort services in many cities that will take your daily mail and merge it with other first class mail, thus achieving greater density and greater discounts, resulting in additional savings to the mailer. Your customer service representative can supply you with the names and addresses of firms offering this service.

NONPROFIT RATES

For organizations which qualify as nonprofit, Congress annually provides appropriations to the U.S. Postal Service to permit the service to charge lower rates. The amount of the subsidy Congress appropriates each year determines the rate.

BUSINESS REPLY MAIL

Another service to business enables mailers to include in their solicitation postage-paid reply mail (envelopes or cards) to be used by recipients to send orders and payments back to the mailer. The mailer then pays the U.S. Postal

Service the first class rate and a surcharge for this service. A permit is required for this service, which is permitted only for first class mail. Cards must be at least 0.007 of an inch thick, and specific formats and markings are mandated for the face of reply mail. See Figure 43-1.

RESIDENT OR OCCUPANT MAIL

It is possible to mail without the use of an individual's name, with only the address and a line which says "Occupant" or "Householder." This technique is used primarily for saturation mailings by supermarkets, penny savers, local retailers, and companies wishing to send samples of merchandise.

PERMIT IMPRINTS

For mailers who choose not to meter or use live stamps on their mailings, permit imprints may be used. These are indicia which are preprinted on the mailing piece at the time the envelope, catalog, or self-mailer is being printed. Figure 43-2 illustrates some of the variations in style that are acceptable to the U.S. Postal Service.

ADDRESS CORRECTION AND MAIL FORWARDING

This service is for direct marketers who wish to clean their lists by receiving changes of address. If mail is not deliverable as addressed, they can have the piece forwarded or returned to the sender. Various endorsements can be printed under the corner card (return address) in the upper left-hand corner of the mailing piece. If there is no endorsement on a mailing piece and it cannot be delivered as addressed, third class mail will be deemed "of no obvious value" and will be destroyed.

If you wish to receive additional handling, the following options are available.

Address Correction Service

First class mail bearing the endorsement "address correction requested" will be forwarded to the new address, and a Form 3547 will be sent to the mailer with the new address. For a fee, third class mail will be returned to sender with the new address if it is under 2 ounces. If it is over 2 ounces, the U.S. Postal Service can use Form 3547 or return the piece.

Forwarding and Return

Undeliverable as addressed third class mail bearing the words "forwarding and return postage guaranteed" will be forwarded to the addressee. Postage at the single-piece rate will be collected from the addressee. If the addressee refuses to pay the single-piece rate, the piece will be returned to the sender, who must pay postage for the forwarding and return.

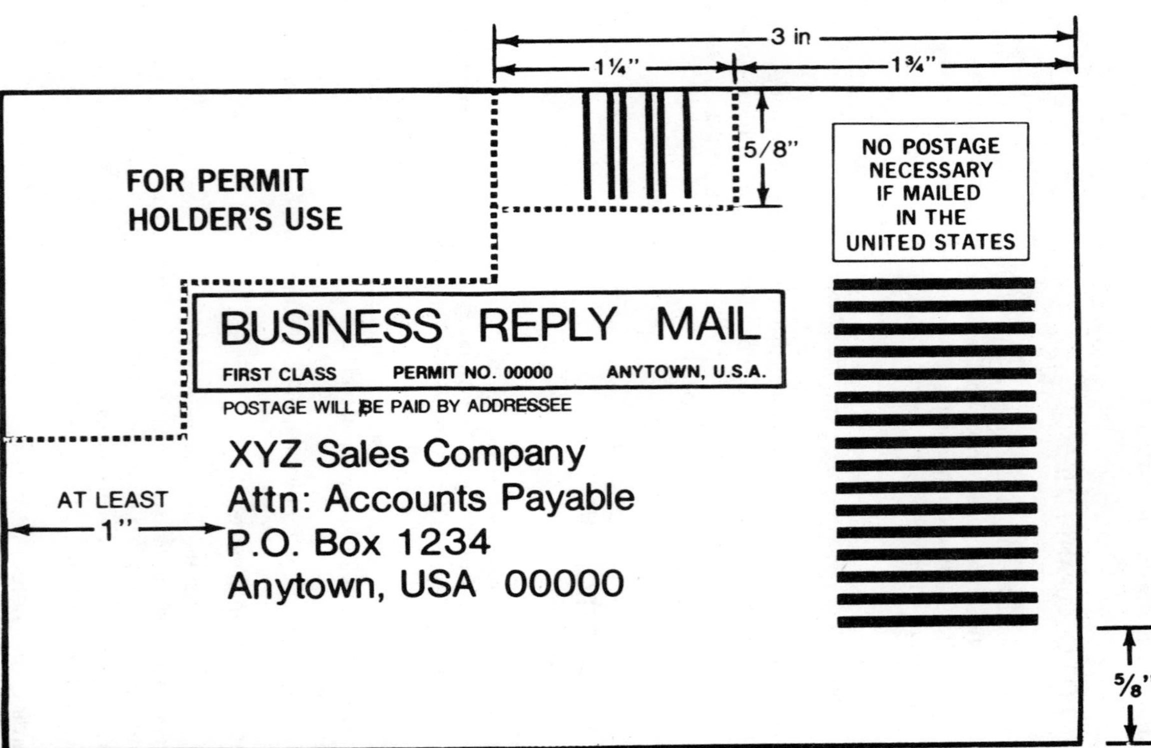

Figure 43-1 Business reply mail (*U.S. Postal Service*)

Return Postage Guaranteed

As used by third class mailers, this will not get you the new address, but you will get your piece back at the single-piece rate.

The endorsement rules vary for each class of mail (see Figure 43-3) and should be checked carefully before you print your envelopes to determine which service you may want or not want. House lists should be cleaned regularly, whereas outside lists (rentals) are usually for one-time use and are not to be cleaned by the list user.

Service Standards

Figure 43-4 can be used as a guide for estimating average delivery time for any class of mail. Note that the U.S. Postal Service does not meet these standards in all cases. When planning for home delivery dates, allow additional time, particularly for third class, which is a deferred category.

NONSTANDARD MAIL

First class mail weighing 1 ounce or less and third class single-piece mail weighing 2 ounces or less are nonstandard if their length exceeds 11 1/2 inches or their height exceeds 6 1/8 inches or their thickness exceeds one-quarter of an inch. A surcharge is levied on each piece of nonstandard mail.

Third class bulk mail does not have maximum size limitations but must be 0.007 of an inch thick. The only exception is carrier-routed mail, which cannot exceed 11 1/2 by 13 1/2 inches and cannot be more than three-quarters of an inch thick.

MINIMUM SIZE STANDARDS

For all classes of mail, any piece under 3 1/2 by 5 inches will be rejected by the post office and returned to the sender. Mail which does not have sufficient postage also will be returned to the sender as short-paid mail.

SPECIAL SERVICES

Express Mail

This is an expedited service for high-priority shipments within the United States and to selected foreign countries. Domestic mail posted by 5 P.M. is guaranteed to be delivered by 3 P.M. the next day or your postage will be refunded.

Mailgram

This is an expedited message service using Western Union for the message transmission. Mailgrams are delivered by a letter carrier the next business day.

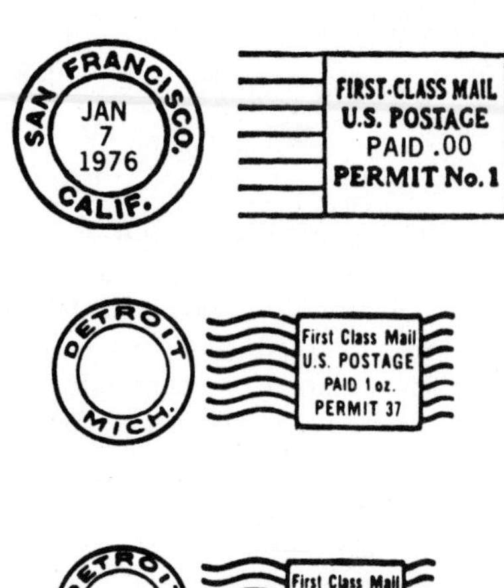

FIRST-CLASS MAIL
U.S. POSTAGE
PAID
New York, N.Y.
Permit No. 1

PRESORTED
FIRST CLASS MAIL
US POSTAGE PAID
NEW YORK, NY
Permit No. 1

First-Class Mail

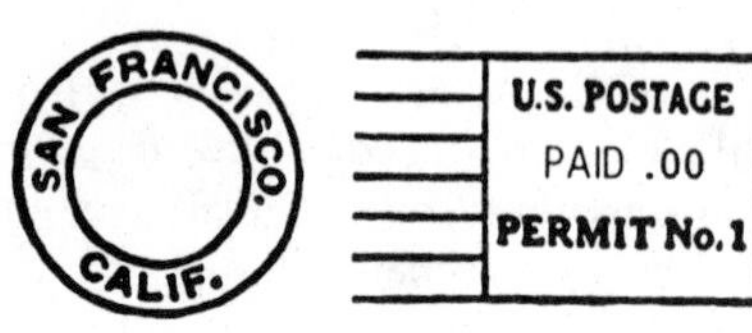

BOUND PRINTED MATTER BLK RT
US POSTAGE
PAID
New York, NY
Permit No. 1

FOURTH-CLASS BULK RATE
U.S. POSTAGE PAID
NEW YORK, NY
Permit No. 1

U.S. POSTAGE
PAID
New York, N.Y.
Permit No. 1
ZIP Code 10001

U.S. POSTAGE
PAID
John Doe Company

PRESORTED
SPECIAL FOURTH-CLASS RATE
US POSTAGE PAID
New York, NY
Permit No. 1

U.S. POSTAGE
PAID
New York, N.Y.
Permit No. 1
ZIP Code 10001

Second-, Third-, and Fourth-Class Mail
(Date and First-Class Mail Omitted)

Figure 43-2 Formats of permit imprints (*U.S. Postal Service*)

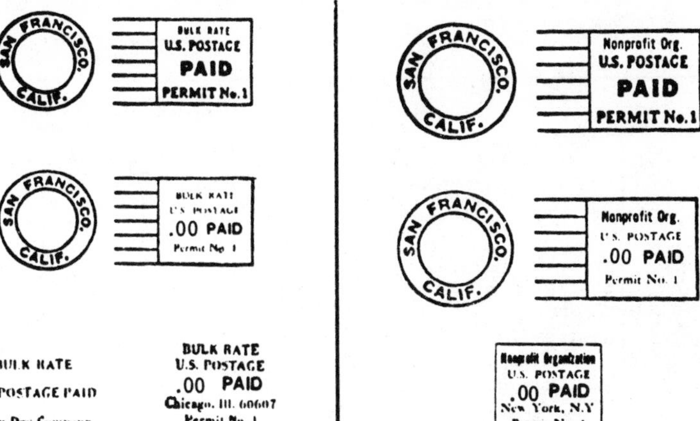

Bulk Third-Class Mail

Special Rates for Authorized Organizations Only

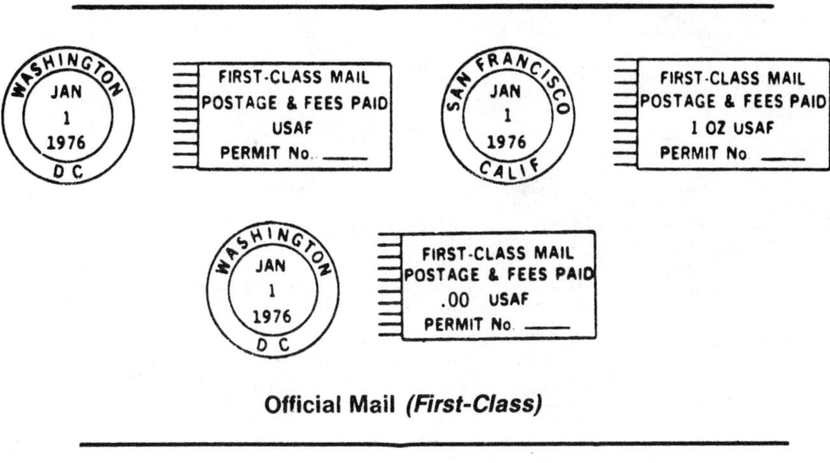

Official Mail *(First-Class)*

WASHINGTON
D C

FOURTH-CLASS MAIL
POSTAGE & FEES PAID
USAF
PERMIT No. ____

Official Mail *(Fourth Class) (Date and First-Class Mail Omitted)*

Figure 43-2 Cont'd.

<table>
<tr><th colspan="6">FORWARDING</th><th rowspan="2">APPLICABLE RATES:
a. First Class Zone Rate between forwarding and destination PO.
b. Transient Rate.
c. 3rd or 4th Rate, as applicable.
d. 3rd single piece.
e. Applicable 4th.
f. Postcard Rate or Service Fee, as indicated.</th><th colspan="7">RETURN</th></tr>
<tr><th>First Class up to 12 ozs. incl Postal and postcards</th><th>First Class Zone Rated (Priority) (1st over 12 ozs.)</th><th>Second Class</th><th></th><th>Third Class</th><th>Fourth Class</th><th>All 1st (including Zone Rated)</th><th>Postal and postcards</th><th>Second Class</th><th></th><th>Third Class up to 2 ozs. incl.</th><th>Third Class over 2 ozs.</th><th>Fourth Class</th></tr>
<tr><td></td><td>a.</td><td>b.</td><td></td><td>d.</td><td>e.</td><td>RATES</td><td></td><td>f.</td><td>b.</td><td></td><td colspan="2">d.</td><td>e.</td></tr>
<tr><td rowspan="3">A</td><td rowspan="3">D</td><td colspan="2">FG</td><td colspan="2" rowspan="2">J</td><td>← NO MARKINGS →</td><td rowspan="3">B</td><td>L</td><td colspan="2">G</td><td colspan="3">O</td></tr>
<tr><td colspan="2" rowspan="4">FH</td><td>RETURN POSTAGE GUARANTEED</td><td rowspan="2">M</td><td colspan="2" rowspan="4">H</td><td colspan="3">M</td></tr>
<tr><td colspan="2">IE</td><td>FORWARDING & RETURN POSTAGE GUARANTEED</td><td colspan="3">ME</td></tr>
<tr><td rowspan="3">AC</td><td rowspan="3">DC</td><td colspan="2">ICE</td><td>ADDRESS CORRECTION REQUESTED FORWARDING & RETURN POSTAGE GUARANTEED</td><td rowspan="3">B & C</td><td rowspan="3">N</td><td rowspan="3">N</td><td colspan="2" rowspan="2">K</td></tr>
<tr><td colspan="2" rowspan="2">JC</td><td>ADDRESS CORRECTION REQUESTED RETURN POSTAGE GUARANTEED</td></tr>
<tr><td colspan="2">FG</td><td>ADDRESS CORRECTION REQUESTED OR OBSOLETE WORDING RETURN REQUESTED</td><td colspan="2">G</td><td colspan="2">P</td></tr>
</table>

KEY
A — Forward free.
B — Return free endorsed with reason for nondelivery.
C — Send address correction to mailer, collect address correction fee.
D — Transfer locally free, forward out of town at rate "A".
E — Sender must pay Forwarding & Return Postage if addressee refuses mail.
F — For 3-month Period: Transfer locally free, and forward out of town postage due if addressee guarantees forwarding postage. Furnish Form 3578 to addressee. After 3 months, or if not forwardable originally, apply G, H, below as appropriate.
G — Send address correction together with old address, collect address Correction fee.
H — Return complete copy with address correction attached. Collect "b" rate plus address correction fee.
I — Transfer locally free, forward out of town at applicable rate.
J — Transfer all fourth-class locally free. Transfer third-class locally free if it has obvious value (159.23), if endorsed *Return Postage Guaranteed* or if addressee has guaranteed forwarding postage. Forward third- and fourth-class out of town only if addressee has guaranteed forwarding postage.
K — Return at applicable rate plus fee for address correction attached.
L — No return-treat as waste.
M—Return at applicable rate, marked NOT DELIVERABLE AS ADDRESSED—UNABLE TO FORWARD only.
N — Return endorsed with reason for nondelivery, collect address correction fee.
O — If of obvious value, return at applicable rate—otherwise treat as waste.
P — If of obvious value, return at applicable rate plus fee for address correction—otherwise send address correction and collect fee.

Figure 43-3 Treatment of undeliverable as addressed mail (*U.S. Postal Service*)

ECOM

This is a new program of electronic mail which transmits your message to a serving post office. Your letter is printed out on a computer, which folds, inserts, and seals it for delivery the next business day.

Attached Mail

A recent change in regulations permits the attachment or enclosure of incidental first class mail with other classes of mail, with postage paid on the combined piece at the applicable rate of the host piece. This applies to second class mail,

UNITED STATES POSTAL SERVICE

Service Standards

(ZIP CODED MAIL ONLY)

EFFECTIVE 10-11-75

	OVERNIGHT	OVERNIGHT REQUIREMENTS	2nd DAY	3rd DAY	4th DAY	5th DAY	6th DAY	7th DAY	8th DAY	9th DAY	10th DAY
FIRST CLASS	LOCALLY DESIGNATED CITIES AND SCF's	UP TO AND INCLUDING 5:00 P.M. COLLECTIONS	LOCALLY DESIGNATED STATES	REMAINING OUTLYING AREAS							
AIR PRIORITY	DESIGNATED CITIES	STATED AT MAILING POST OFFICE	NATIONWIDE								
SURFACE PREF-ERENTIAL	UP TO 150 MILES	5:00 P.M. MAILINGS	300 MILES ZONE 3	600 MILES ZONE 4	1,000 MILES ZONE 5	1,400 MILES ZONE 6	1,800 MILES ZONE 7	OVER 1,800 MILES ZONE 8			
ORDINARY 2nd & 3rd CLASS	AS DEVELOPED LOCALLY	—	INTRA-SCF (FOR 5:00 P.M. CARRIER PRESORTED MAILINGS)	DESIGNATED SCF's AND NON-PRESORTED INTRA-SCF	UP TO 150 MILES ZONE 2	300 MILES ZONE 3	600 MILES ZONE 4	1,000 MILES ZONE 5	1,400 MILES ZONE 6	1,800 MILES ZONE 7	OVER 1,800 MILES ZONE 8
PARCEL POST	SEE SEPARATE STANDARDS ISSUED FOR EACH BULK MAIL CENTER.										
PLANT LOADED	DELIVERY SCHEDULES WORKED OUT BETWEEN USPS AND MAILER.										

NOTE: 2nd TO 10th DAY DELIVERY TARGETS COVER ALL OF A DAY'S MAILINGS, EXCEPT AS NOTED

Figure 43-4 Service standards of the U.S. Postal Service (*U.S. Postal Service*)

third class merchandise including books but excluding merchandise samples, and fourth class mail. In practical terms, this means that an invoice, statement of account, or renewal notice can be included in a mailing without paying first class postage.

ZIP Plus Four (Nine-digit ZIP Code)

The U.S. Postal Service has introduced the expanded ZIP code program to automate the sorting process and eliminate the manual handling of first class mail. The process involves scanning the address and imprinting a bar code on the envelope. Mail which qualifies is processed by bar code readers which sort the mail at high speeds directly to the letter carrier.

WORKING WITH THE POST OFFICE

Every mailer has a customer service representative (CSR). This individual should be consulted on any question you may have concerning rules and regulations, postage rates, and services. The CSR also can be consulted for approval of your direct mail package to make sure that you conform to the standards for acceptable mail.

POSTAL SERVICE PUBLICATIONS

Domestic Mail Manual

This manual includes all postal regulations and information. This book, in loose-leaf form, can be bought for a fee from

The Superintendent of Documents
U.S. Government Printing Office
Washington, D.C. 20402

Revisions are furnished free as published.

Postal Bulletin

This is for mailers who need advance information relating to U.S. Postal Service changes in rules and regulations. Subscriptions are available from the superintendent of documents for an annual fee.

Memo to Mailers

This newsletter is issued by the U.S. Postal Service monthly at no charge. It covers various items of interest to users of the mail. To get on the mailing list, write to

Memo to Mailers
U.S. Postal Service
PO Box 1600
La Plata, Maryland 20646

ZIP Code Directory

A complete listing of all correct and current ZIP codes can be purchased from your local post office.

Mailers' Guide

While not all-inclusive, this does provide in summary form the current postal rules and regulations. It can be obtained from your local post office.

chapter **44**

FULFILLMENT

Stanley J. Fenvessy

Chairman
Fenvessy & Schwab, Inc.
New York, N.Y.

"Wide assortments, fast delivery, and customer service are the basics of a successful catalog business, and we have been successful because we have concentrated on the basics." So stated the chairperson of one of the world's largest mail-order businesses.

Two-thirds of the basics are related to the back-end, or fulfillment, facet of a direct marketing business. This is not surprising if you consider that many consumers are turning to mail order for greater convenience. They are revolting against crowded stores, insufficient parking, poorly informed sales clerks, and long checkout lines.

Service-hungry consumers are staying with direct marketing because of

- Easy at-home ordering, 24 hours a day
- Toll-free telephone service
- Many types of credit cards and payment plans
- Speedy delivery
- Automatic shipping of out-of-stock items when they become available
- Friendly and courteous adjustment service

IMPORTANCE OF SUPERIOR FULFILLMENT

In addition to giving customers all the conveniences they are seeking, superior fulfillment affects the general operation and success of a direct marketing business in three ways.

Superior Fulfillment Improves Marketing Results

Your company image and therefore much of your sales revenue depend on how well you handle the critical back end. Successful direct marketing businesses are built on repeat orders. If the customer promptly receives everything ordered, there is a strong likelihood that the customer will order again. If it takes weeks for merchandise to be received, customers may change their minds or purchase similar items elsewhere and return or refuse your packages.

Efficient Fulfillment Raises Profits

In some businesses, fulfillment costs amount to over 20 percent of net sales. In a direct marketing business, fulfilling the order utilizes more space, people, equipment, and computer time than all the other facets of the business combined. It is therefore essential that fulfillment costs be controlled carefully.

Good Fulfillment Is Necessary to Avoid Consumerism Problems

A majority of the complaints investigated by the Federal Trade Commission, Better Business Bureau, state attorney generals, and action line columnists involve fulfillment. Consistently good fulfillment service will keep these agencies and consumer advocates from your door.

THE FULFILLMENT CYCLE

In the area of mail-order service, there are two aspects of customer satisfaction.

- **Order completion:** how promptly, accurately, and completely an order is filled and the condition in which it arrives
- **Customer service:** how promptly, fairly, and courteously a customer who has a question or a problem or who has been disappointed is handled

There are ten steps in the fulfillment cycle, which is designed both to serve and satisfy the customer and to provide essential management information and control. These steps are illustrated in Figure 44-1. Here is a brief description of each of those steps.

Order Forms and Instructions

The entire chain of events commences with the customer's understanding of the offer and the way the customer completes the order form or places a telephone order.

Order Information and Form. Essential product data such as product number, description, sizes, colors, and prices should be in legible bold type and should be grouped together at the end of the copy. The order form should be easy to complete, and the customer should be provided with clear instructions when special information (such as monograms or measurements) is required.

Getting the customer to provide all the required information correctly will solve many internal problems. In some instances, 15 to 20 percent of all order forms are completed inadequately by customers.

Shipping Charges. Most mail-order companies charge separately for shipping and handling. L. L. Bean, the Maine outdoor sporting specialist, and the cheese and fruit vendors are notable exceptions, shipping almost everything prepaid. There are three principal ways to collect shipping and handling charges.

1. Indicate the shipping weight for every item in the catalog, requiring the customer to total the weights and refer to a table to obtain shipping charges. The big catalog houses such as Sears and Wards use this method.
2. Show in parentheses after the price a separate shipping charge for each item. This method is used by American Express and other high-ticket gift houses.
3. Relate shipping charges to the dollar value of the order and provide a shipping charge table on the order form. This technique is used by gift and novelty concerns such as Lillian Vernon.

Sales Taxes. A mail-order enterprise normally collects sales taxes only for the state in which it is located. However, direct marketing divisions of national corporations are required to collect sales taxes for all fifty states. Customers need an explanation of this situation and clear instructions and rates when they are sending gifts out of state.

Order Receipt

This step involves initial receipt by telephone or mail and subsequent internal clerical and data entry processing.

Telephone Orders. An increasing percentage of orders now are being received by telephone, and the trend is expected to continue. It is reported that 87 percent of Sears' orders are telephone orders. Many direct marketers utilize the toll-free WATS 800 number service; others do not believe that it is cost-effective.

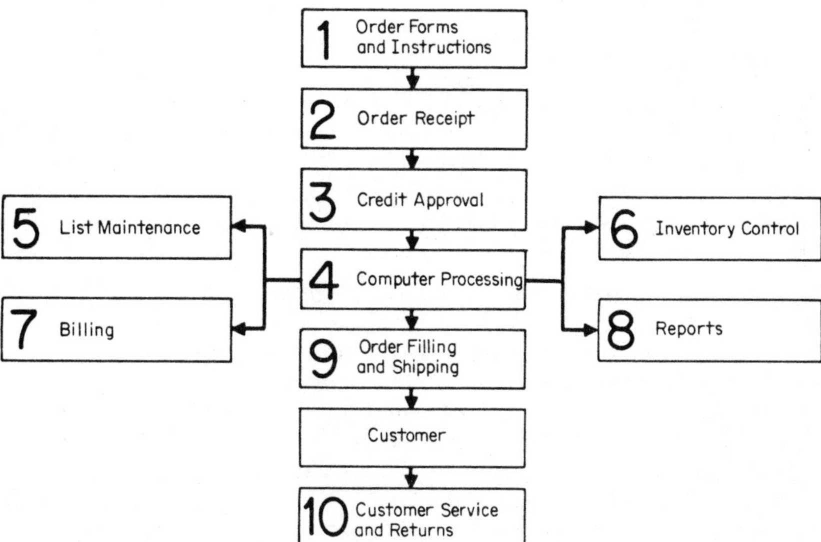

Figure 44-1 The ten steps in the fulfillment cycle

Two telephone order-taking options are available.

1. Use of an outside contractor, which is frequently more economical and relieves the company of the difficult problems of staffing and managing the telephone function
2. Establishing an internal telephone order-taking operation, which usually provides a more personal and responsive service and therefore a better company image

In sophisticated operations, telephone order takers use computer terminals to enter orders directly into the data processing system. This technique enables order clerks to tell customers whether an item is in stock.

Mail Orders. In larger operations, automatic envelope extractors are employed. These machines slice the top of the envelope and, using rubber suction cups, separate the envelope so that the operator can remove the contents easily. The envelope then is "candled" by an electric eye to verify that it is empty before it is deposited in a trash container. In smaller operations, hand-fed electric envelope slitters are used, and then the contents are removed manually.

Orders then are sorted and batched by type: cash or credit. Most direct marketers do not accept COD orders.

Next, the cash orders are "batch balanced." This step involves matching the total cash received with the totals shown on the individual orders in the batch. If a balance is struck, the cash is deposited. The orders then are reviewed for completeness and are entered into the computer for processing. Frequently, larger checks (over $100 to $150) are verified by calling the bank before the order is entered.

Efficient operations complete the mail-opening function by late morning, making it possible for orders to be entered into the computer by the end of the day.

Credit Approval

Credit is a very important part of direct marketing. Credit orders normally are larger than cash orders. High-ticket merchandise must be offered on a credit plan; otherwise, many sales will be lost. Credit is usually one of two types: through charge cards issued by banks and travel and expense cards such as American Express or Diners Club, or through internal company time payment or open account plans.

Bank and T&E Cards. These provide a credit facility without the risk and bother of establishing your own credit department. The cost of the services depends on the volume of charges processed and the average transaction value. It can range from 2 to 5 percent of sales.

Card companies establish a "floor limit," frequently between $50 and $100. Orders over the limit must be authorized by the card issuer before the order can be processed. There are three methods: (1) calling the card company to obtain an authorization number, (2) keying the order into a special authorization terminal, or (3) having your computer verify directly with the credit company's computer. Orders under the floor limit do not require authorization.

Internal Credit. If you are offering large-ticket items or selling to industrial or commercial accounts, you probably will have to extend credit and bill. This may involve using credit-checking services or at least keeping records of nonpaying customers.

Many of the large book and record clubs, which offer free merchandise as an enticement to enroll, maintain extensive lists of consumers who previously have tried to rip them off. All orders are screened through a large "bad consumer" list before they are entered. Each company maintains its own list. There is no exchange of such information among mail-order marketers because of privacy considerations and credit regulations.

Because of the large percentage of direct marketing credit sales (frequently over 50 percent of volume) and the impracticality of having the customer present a plastic credit card (as is required in a store or restaurant), adequate credit screening and collection practices are essential in the mail-order industry.

Computer Processing

The use of the computer in direct marketing is widespread. Only very small or startup businesses employ manual procedures for order processing, inventory control, and list maintenance. Once the direct marketing venture is off and running, it has two principal options. It can employ an outside data processing service contractor or install its own computer system.

Outside Contractors. A number of data processing services are equipped to serve direct marketers in all sections of the country. Many have order processing, continuity, list maintenance, inventory control, and a variety of marketing reporting programs. Using outside service organizations provides four benefits:

1. Low initial investment
2. More powerful equipment than if you rented or owned your own machine
3. Immediate availability of professional data processing assistance that might take months or years to develop
4. No day-to-day annoying problems of computer operation

In-House Installation. The availability of complete computer packages to fulfill most direct marketing requirements has made data processing more accessible, even for smaller ventures. There are computer packages for almost every manufacturer's hardware. Having your own installation should enable you to

1. Achieve dollar savings in payroll, space, and supervision in your office and warehouse
2. Reduce fulfillment processing time
3. Obtain better facts and figures on a more timely basis to help you evaluate marketing results and administer your business

List Maintenance

Before the advent of the computer, customers' names and addresses were maintained on metal plates or ink stencils. This required as much as a square city block of floor space in the major catalog houses. The plates were used to create package labels and address catalog mailings. Today, a mail-order business selects its list maintenace and addressing system on the basis of its individual requirements. This can involve one of many noncomputerized systems or one of several computerized techniques.

Noncomputerized Systems. These include hand-held systems, embossed metal or plastic plates, typewritten stencils and plates, and typewritten chemical transfer cards. Such systems should be considered only when the following conditions are present:

1. Small list size (under 25,000)
2. Low usage
3. Limited selection criteria
4. Small amount of required customer information in addition to name and address
5. No need to eliminate duplications with rented lists
6. Addresses always prepared in the same sequence

Computerized Systems. The increased use of computerized mailing lists can be attributed to cost-effective volume processing, the high degree of speed and flexibility available, and the growth in computer service organizations specializing in list maintenance.

Magnetic tape is the commonly used recording medium for mailing lists because of its low cost for storing large files. Computers can print over 1000 addresses per minute on labels. On the other hand, ink jet printers can produce up to 80,000 lines of information per minute directly on catalogs or magazines.

It is not unusual for a mail-order company that is processing orders and maintaining inventory and accounting records on its own computer to contract out the task of list maintenance. This is done because state-of-the-art hardware and sophisticated list maintenance programs are available at contractors, in-house operations are relieved of processing list rental requests, and equipment and personnel are shared with others, making the cost lower.

Inventory Control

A speedy and economical fulfillment system is worthless if the item to be shipped is out of stock. Therefore, maintaining a balanced inventory position is essential to good fulfillment. If an item must be back-ordered and shipped separately at a later date, it means extra handling and extra shipping costs.

To achieve effective inventory control, there should be accounting for the stock that is supporting the direct marketing program. This is essential when a business is selling similar items through wholesale and retail store distribution channels. Once the separate stock has been identified, inventory records can be maintained manually or on a computer.

Manual Inventory Control. Manual controls are used when the product line is small and when there is a limited number of stockkeeping units (e.g., size and color variations). Receipts, sales, returns, and purchase orders are posted to a visual card or multiring notebook recordkeeping system. Then the sales, stock position, and open order information are used to manually determine the coverage amount of merchandise on hand or on order for each item. Inventory requirements are forecasted on the basis of sales experience and anticipated needs.

With items that are offered for a long period of time, some companies establish minimum stock levels and reorder when the inventory approaches that point. Identifying items that will be big sellers is a key element in reducing back-orders. "Runaway" items usually can be recognized during the first week of order receipts.

Computerized Stock Management. Computerized inventory management systems have saved huge sums for large mail-order companies. The savings have included reduced clerical recordkeeping costs, lower inventory investment, fewer stockouts, and less warehouse storage space.

The computer maintains a perpetual inventory of each stockkeeping unit. As shipping documents are produced, the inventory position is reduced. Inventory status reports are produced at intervals, depending on the sales experience. These reports frequently are supplemented with "exception-type" printouts that highlight products needing immediate review. In the more sophisticated systems, up-to-the-minute inventory status for an item can be displayed on a CRT screen for buyers, inventory control clerks, telephone order takers, or anyone needing the information.

In more sophisticated catalog businesses, statistical forecasting techniques such as exponential smoothing are used to determine inventory requirements and economical order quantities.

Billing

For many years, mail order was conducted on a cash basis, with billing only for insufficient postage or taxes or incorrectly totaled orders. Today, a large percentage of the orders involve some form of credit. In many ways, credit order processing is simpler. There is no cash to handle initially or refunds to prepare for out-of-stock items. The customer is billed for the exact amount owed.

Direct marketers use one of two billing approaches: prebilling or postbilling.

Prebilling. Here the customer's invoice is prepared before the merchandise is shipped. This system assumes that the computer has correct information indicating whether the item is in stock, and it must include a predetermined shipping and handling charge. In this approach, the invoice is enclosed in the package or inserted in an envelope which then is affixed to the outside of the carton. This is the practice of the book and record clubs.

If one of the items is found to be out of stock, the invoice frequently is adjusted manually on the shipping floor.

Postbilling. This system is used when one or more of the following conditions is present.

1. The company is unable to determine accurately whether the product is on hand before picking.

2. The company wishes to bill the customer for exact shipping charges and show the actual shipping date and carrier.
3. The company does not want to create manually adjusted invoices.

In this arrangement, copies of the picking document, which shows the method and cost of shipment, are returned and rekeyed into the computer. A separate invoice is produced and mailed to the customer.

The production of a combination invoice and shipping directive is usually part of the invoice processing step. The document not only serves as a financial reconciliation of the customer's order and payment or charge amount, it also provides shipping labels, packing list, and picking list on which the items are sequenced for efficient picking by item number or warehouse location.

Reports

One of the significant by-products of computer processing is the production of meaningful and timely reports that enable management to make marketing and merchandising decisions and maintain adequate controls. In addition to inventory control reports, there are four other general categories of management reports: marketing, merchandising, financial, and operations.

Marketing. These reports show such information as customer profiles by demographic and physiographic factors, profitability of mailings, test results of list rentals, and market segmentations.

Merchandising. This can include sales and profit results by product categories, price points, country of origin, or catalog placement position.

Financial. In addition to the usual profit statements and accounts receivable agings, this should include evaluations of individual tests, promotions, or media.

Operations. The purpose of these reports should be to control service levels, backlogs, worker productivity, and operating costs by individual processing centers (e.g., mail opening, keying, picking, packing, etc.).

The number and types of reports depend on the size and sophistication of the business. However, one should always remember that, more than in most businesses, direct marketing is a measurable endeavor in all its facets.

Order Filling and Shipping

Physical fulfillment includes receiving, storage, forward line replenishment, picking, packing, scaling, and metering. Together these tasks account for the largest part of the total fulfillment cost. In some catalog businesses, this represents two-thirds of the order-handling expense. The two most labor-intensive elements are order picking and packing and shipping.

Order picking. There are five principal order filling methods.

1. Individual order picking, in which each individual order is picked by a filler going from one stock location to the next
2. Multiple picking, in which a number of orders are picked at the same time by one picker using a truck or cart

3. Sequential zone picking, in which the order moves by truck or conveyor from zone to zone and items are added by a different picker in each zone
4. Order explosion and assembly, in which the order is translated into a separate ticket for each item, items for many orders are picked in bulk, and items are then sorted out for individual orders at specified packing stations
5. Automatic picking, in which computer-controlled equipment retrieves items from specially designed storage units.

Packing and Shipping. Packing requirements are determined by such factors as the nature of the merchandise, the number of items, and the type of packing material required. Methods range from the insertion of a single item into a mailing envelope to the cushioning of fragile items with preformed styrofoam pellets and the use of automatic machinery to seal the carton.

It is reported that over 90 percent of mail-order merchandise is shipped by United Parcel Service. The U.S. Postal Service is principally used where (1) special rate programs provide substantial savings, for example, items under 16 ounces (third class bulk rate) and books, (2) the package is addressed to a post office box, or (3) the item is oversized or too heavy for United Parcel Service.

Most volume shippers employ electronic scales that interface with a postage meter. They can compute several shipping costs automatically; when the operator determines the most appropriate service, the meter instantaneously dispenses a tape for the proper fee. Some units imprint shipping charges on the shipping document and produce daily or weekly summaries of accumulated costs for each department or service.

Customer Service and Returns

A typical direct marketing venture can expect 8 to 20 percent of the shipped packages to be returned because of such factors as customer dissatisfaction, wrong address, or damage in transit. Additionally, the volume of customer requests for information or adjustment can be 4 to 10 percent of the orders shipped. The business must be organized to handle this backlash of the initial shipping function.

Customer Service. A separate customer service telephone number should be publicized, and customers should be encouraged to call rather than write for information or assistance. For this to be effective, highly efficient reearch tools must be available to the telephone clerk so that the customer's problem can be resolved quickly and at a low cost. The three Rs of customer service mail handling—reading, researching, and responding—should be handled by individuals with large measures of patience and understanding.

About 85 percent of customer service inquiries can be answered with a preprinted form. Many companies respond with handwritten fill-in postal cards. They not only speed the response but also save postage and stationery costs. Tests have shown that customers prefer a quick form response to a delayed personalized letter.

Returns. The most frustrating part of a mail-order transaction is the time between a customer's mailing of returned goods and the receipt of an acknowledgment, exchange, or refund. Therefore, keeping current with opening and processing returned packages is an important fulfillment task.

Data should be accumulated on a regular basis, showing the number of returns by reason. These compilations will highlight important information such as product quality problems, poor packaging, inadequate assembly or operating instructions, and order fulfillment shortcomings.

DISAPPOINTMENT FACTORS

The nature of the direct marketing business makes it impossible to achieve 100 percent performance in each of the ten fulfillment steps and to make every customer totally satisfied. Fulfillment service problems that are unrelated to merchandise quality can result from the sheer volume of transactions or from many sources outside of your control, such as the following.

- Your customers make mistakes or don't read the copy or follow instructions.
- Your vendors fail to deliver as promised.
- Your carriers delay, damage, or lose your shipments.

A customer who contacts a direct marketing company by mail or telephone subsequent to placing an order is in some way disappointed with the transaction.

There are four general types of customer contacts that indicate disappointment:

- Inquiries about shipping status or back-orders
- Returns for credit or refund
- Exchanges for the same or another item
- Complaints about the service or product

Direct marketing companies with the lowest customer disappointment ratios are well-managed businesses whose systems are deemed exceptional or highly effective.

FULFILLMENT SERVICE STANDARDS

The standards listed below are achieved by most major direct marketers. The total sales volume of these companies comprises substantially over half the total mail-order business.

Turnaround Time on Orders. The package should be received by the customer within 2 calendar weeks of mailing the order; this should be shorter for telephone orders. It is a proven axiom in mail-order operations that the faster the order is fulfilled, the lower the unit fulfillment cost. Therefore, quick service makes good sense from the standpoint of both customer relations and the botttom line.

Customer Service Response Cycle. An answer should be received by the customer in the calendar week following mailing of the letter. Considering incoming and outgoing mailing time and nonworking weekends, that leaves 2 or 3 working days to read, research, and respond.

In-Stock Condition. Where merchandise is repeated in a following catalog or staple products are involved, less than 5 percent of the orders should be shipped incomplete. In the case of new products or fashion merchandise, not more than 10 percent of the orders should involve a back-order.

Ratio of Customer Service Contacts to Orders. Only 4 to 6 percent of the shipped orders should result in an inquiry or adjustment. In the fashion business, the ratio increases to about 10 percent.

Returns. The number of returns is greatly affected by the clarity of the promotion, the fulfillment cycle, and the extent of merchandise inspection. Returns should be less than 8 percent unless it is a fashion business with size and color offerings. Then returns from 15 to 20 percent can be expected. Approximately one-quarter of the returns probably will involve an exchange and reshipment.

Answering Telephone Calls. Both incoming orders and service calls should be answered 90 percent of the time without a holding delay. Seventy-five percent of customers' inquiries or problems should be resolved while customers are on the line.

Serious Complaints. Less than 2 percent of the complaints should be consumer advocate letters, mail from government agencies, communications addressed to company officers, or letters indicating that the customer has written before and has not received an answer.

Work Backlogs. Orders in process should not exceed 1 day's shipments; in peak period, this can increase to 3 days.

Personnel Turnover. Less than 15 percent of the regular fulfillment employees should have less than 6 months' service.

Housekeeping. The order-handling offices, the data center, and the warehouse should look neat and well organized. There should be a place for everything, and everything should be in its place. If the operation does not look well organized, it probably isn't.

ORGANIZING THE FULFILLMENT FUNCTION

The two most important factors in a superior fulfillment operation are good organization and good people. A company cannot provide a high level of service to its customers without both. Sometimes a direct marketing business can operate efficiently with good people although it is imperfectly organized, or it can be supported by only average people who are well organized, but the key to complete effectiveness is competent personnel properly organized.

Successful direct marketing businesses first develop an ideal long-range plan of organization. Then that plan is modified to meet the peculiarities or shortcomings of the existing staff. As executives are replaced or added to the organization, they are positioned and given responsibilities that conform with the overall organizational strategy.

Organizing by Function

With the exception of large catalog houses which have multiple fulfillment plants and therefore are organized on a regional basis, direct marketing businesses are almost entirely organized according to a functional concept. This means that a company's activities are grouped entirely on the basis of the functions performed.

The three primary functional groupings of a direct marketing business are marketing and merchandising, finance and operations. Generally, the subfunctions within each group are as follows.

Marketing and Merchandising

Product selection	Catalog production
Inventory control	Circulation
Overstock disposal	Advertising
Mailing lists	

Finance

Accounting
Credit
Control

Operations

Order processing	Telephone order
Warehousing	Customer service
Order filling	Data processing
Shipping	Personnel

Support Organizational Concepts

As a direct marketing business expands, an administrative support concept often is employed in order to centralize in a single organizational pyramid many of the functions that are shared by the various facets of the business. Specifically, the two types of support concepts are as follows.

Expanding the Finance Function. In addition to the regular financial activities, the financial group is made responsible for data processing, purchasing of nonresale products, and personnel. Each of these functions serves marketing, merchandising, and operations. See Figure 44-2.

Establishing a Separate Administrative Support Function. In this concept, a fourth organizational pyramid—administration—is established to coordinate all support and related functions such as order processing, data processing, personnel, purchasing (nonresale), telephone order, customer service, and other types of office services. The finance group is dedicated to purely financial matters, and operations is concerned principally with the physical activities of receiving and shipping the product. See Figure 44-3.

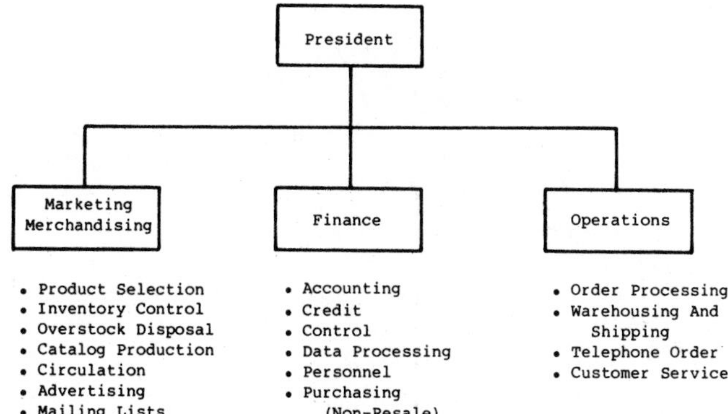

Figure 44-2 Expanding the finance function to provide administrative support

Organizational Alternatives

There are many options as to where certain operating and fulfillment-related functions can be assigned in the organization. The final determination often is based on such factors as the management style of the chief executive officer, the amount of operations control desired, and the degree of marketing emphasis in functions with direct customer contact, such as telephone order taking and customer service. Figure 44-4 shows the options available for certain key fulfillment functions and the reporting relationships used by a majority of direct marketers.

PHYSICAL FACILITIES

A key element in achieving fulfillment efficiency is having sufficient and appropriate space to perform both the office and materials handling tasks. It has been said that space is the least expensive element in the overall fulfillment cost structure.

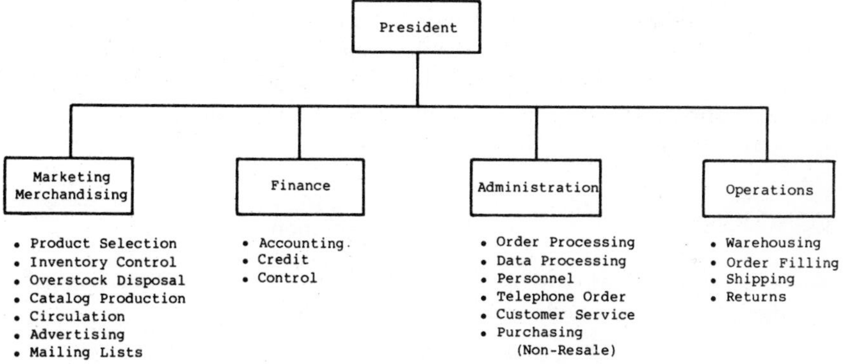

Figure 44-3 Establishing a separate administrative support function

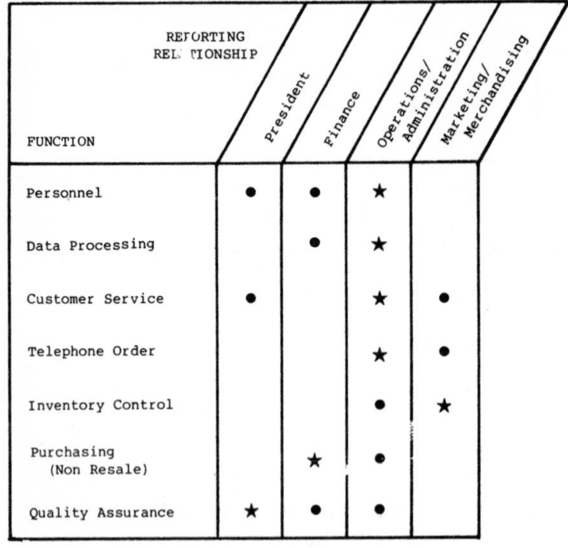

FUNCTION / REPORTING RELATIONSHIP	President	Finance	Operations/ Administration	Marketing/ Merchandising
Personnel	●	●	★	
Data Processing		●	★	
Customer Service	●		★	●
Telephone Order			★	●
Inventory Control			●	★
Purchasing (Non Resale)		★	●	
Quality Assurance	★	●	●	

★ Preferable

Figure 44-4 Organizational alternatives: Selected operating and fulfillment functions

Lack of proper space can affect both service and costs. It can have an impact on the following elements:

1. **Introduction of new equipment.** Frequently, new systems and mechanization must be postponed because of lack of space.
2. **Work flow.** Multiple locations and backtracking of the processing steps are time-consuming and costly.
3. **Supervision.** The ability of the supervisor to observe and get around is important in achieving high worker productivity.
4. **Security and merchandise protection.** Both pilferage and merchandise damage increase in overcrowded conditions.
5. **Employee morale and efficiency.** Today employees expect and can demand reasonably pleasant working conditions. Good work stations, adequate lighting, and access to supplies are major factors affecting efficiency.
6. **Recruiting and training.** You can't obtain or keep a good labor force in a substandard working environment.

CONCLUSION

Providing customers with two of the three basics of a successful direct marketing business—fast delivery and customer service—requires

- Sound organizational structure
- Good people

- Sufficient space
- Appropriate equipment
- Effective processing systems and techniques designed for the direct marketing industry

The fulfillment steps, the possible pitfalls, the operating standards, and the management philosophies outlined in this chapter indicate what is required to support your marketing efforts.

chapter **45**

LEAD PROCESSING

Edward D. Olsen

Senior Vice President of Sales
LCS Industries, Inc.
Clifton, N.J.

This chapter will cover the method by which a company should answer prospects who have responded to an advertising message. The process can be very simple if a company generates only a few leads per year or if it is selling its wares through a small sales force in a localized area. It would be done manually, utilizing the part-time services of a current employee.

Many companies, however, produce thousands of inquiries each year through multimedia advertising campaigns. These responses often cross many product lines, and the resultant inquiries often are distributed to a sales network across the country. This type of company faces a far more complex task.

Studies have shown that a typical sales call can cost upwards of $200. That's not bad if every sales call produces a sale, but only a certain number of every group of inquiries possess real sales potential.

Every successful sales organization knows that the sooner a prospect is contacted, the greater his or her interest will be. The greater the interest, the better the chances of buying. The key is identifying a bona fide prospect, sending the information concerning the company's product or service which was requested, and turning the prospect over to a salesperson.

Computerized lead processing is the most effective method of performing these tasks. In addition, through the use of the computer, reports can be generated which measure the effectiveness of every advertisement from cost through sales dollars produced. Figure 45-1 illustrates the eight steps involved as an inquiry flows through processing in a computerized fulfillment system.

1. The system begins with your ads (magazine, direct mail, radio, or TV). The ads carry a special code number for tracking.
2. The prospects respond to the ad by writing or calling the company. Each day's raw inquiries are logged onto a control sheet and coded in preparation for processing by the computer.

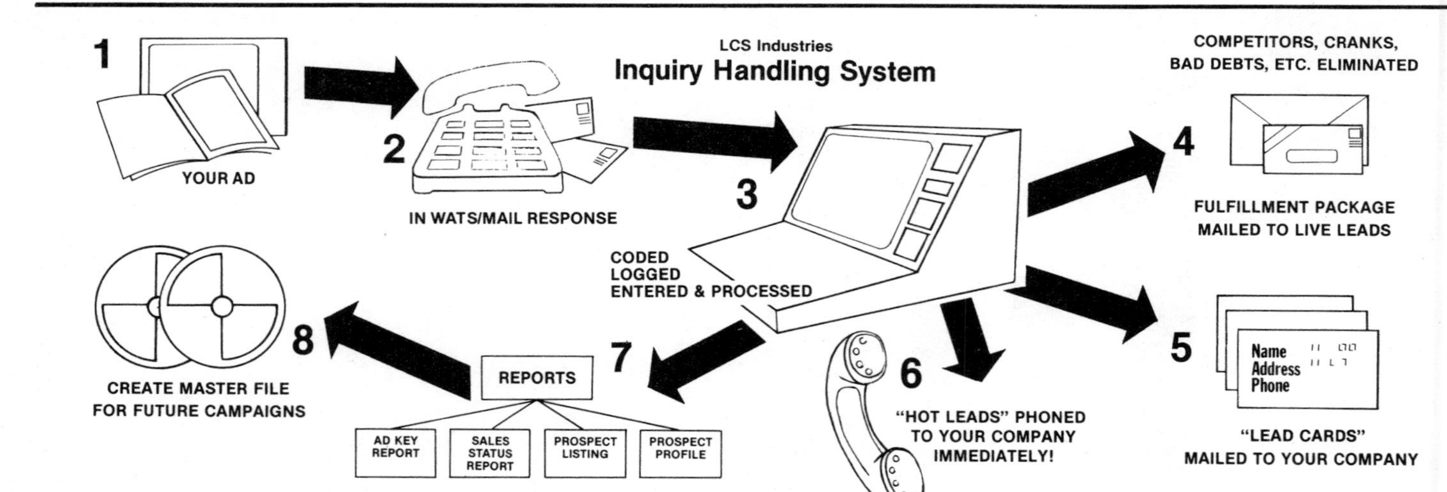
LCS Industries
Inquiry Handling System
1
YOUR AD
2
IN WATS/MAIL RESPONSE
3
CODED
LOGGED
ENTERED & PROCESSED
4
COMPETITORS, CRANKS, BAD DEBTS, ETC. ELIMINATED
FULFILLMENT PACKAGE MAILED TO LIVE LEADS
5
Name
Address
Phone
"LEAD CARDS" MAILED TO YOUR COMPANY
6
"HOT LEADS" PHONED TO YOUR COMPANY IMMEDIATELY!
7
REPORTS
AD KEY REPORT
SALES STATUS REPORT
PROSPECT LISTING
PROSPECT PROFILE
8
CREATE MASTER FILE FOR FUTURE CAMPAIGNS

Figure 45-1 Basic lead fulfillment system

3. Coded and logged inquiries are turned over to the data entry department for keying and conversion onto magnetic tape. The computer begins processing the leads by first editing these leads for validity. Alphabetical and numeric data in the correct field, sectional center and state code validation, and blank fields that must have data are all checked by computer.
4. The computer's suppression file screens the inquiries and immediately eliminates non-productive leads such as competitors, cranks, duplicates, bad debts, or too frequent respondents. Your fulfillment package is mailed to live leads only. With the computer fulfilling requested information, your response time is shortened to 24 to 72 hours. You can further qualify these leads by way of a mailed questionnaire or telephone call.
5. Using the ZIP code data base of your own sales network, the computer sends out lead cards containing all available prospect information including name, address, and phone number. More important, this lead has been validated, prequalified, and turned over to the appropriate sales branch within 24 to 72 hours of receiving the inquiry.
6. A hot lead received by the system is immediately phoned in to the sales person covering that territory.
7. To allow the client to fully utilize the inquiry handling system, the computer generates a full range of reports, allowing the client to check the effectiveness of its ad message as well as the accountability of its sales forces.
8. The system provides not only for the client's needs today but for future sales campaigns. A master file created from the client's current job establishes a bank of qualified prospects. This master file therefore becomes an excellent source in any future sales campaign, allowing better media selection.

Let us analyze in detail how each of these steps is accomplished.

THE BASIC COMPUTERIZED LEAD-PROCESSING SYSTEM

The Customer Service Center

Most sales forces are supported by advertising campaigns that attempt to create awareness of a company's products and services. Once individuals receive the promotion by whatever media the company is employing (magazine, direct mail, radio, TV, or trade shows), they express an interest by writing or calling the company. The company faces the task of receiving the inquiry, fulfilling the individual's request, informing its sales force of the existence and needs of the individual, and accepting data back from the sales force.

In order to fulfill these requirements, it is necessary to establish a customer service center (CSC). The CSC receives the inquiries and performs the clerical processing steps necessary to prepare the leads for computerized processing.

It is important at the outset to ensure that these inquiries are segregated from the other types of mail or phone calls which come into a company's facilities daily. For this reason, a separate post office box or department number should be established to ensure that all leads come to one location. In the case of telephone inquiries, a separate line or extension should be used. If the company has different divisions or wishes to keep leads sorted for other purposes, it can use more than one department number or telephone extension.

The basic premise of a lead-processing system is quick response. Therefore, the CSC should arrange for the pickup or delivery of all response coupons at least daily. If the coupon volume is heavy as a result of a heavy promotion schedule, there should be more than a single delivery daily.

Once the leads have been received at the CSC, they are sorted into categories by interest or product group and logged onto a control sheet before processing begins. The leads then are coded for their particular interest by product, service, information requested, etc. The coded leads are put into batches and made ready for computer processing.

Let us examine some of the elements and steps in the system.

Control Log. This is a clerical log which is kept for the purpose of recording all new input into the system. An entry is made each time new coupons are received. This is the first step in a balancing procedure which ensures that all coupons received eventually will be processed through the system and that the same amount of output will be recorded at the end of the processing cycle. Control logs are extremely important for tracking purposes, especially when certain processing functions take place outside the CSC or off the company premises.

Coding. This is a term used for the processing which takes place in preparing a coupon for computerization. It is the method by which the CSC clerk communicates with the data entry clerk as to what information should be transferred from the original coupon onto magnetic tape. In most instances, the coding procedures are fairly simple. In fact, some operations eliminate this function all together by training the data entry clerk to code the information as it is being transferred to tape. Whether the processing is done by two individual clerks or as a combined effort, it is a necessary step in the lead-processing cycle.

There are two main purposes for coding coupons.

1. To ensure that all the pertinent information on a coupon is highlighted.
2. To minimize the number of keystrokes necessary to make the transfer of information. (This is done for both cost effectiveness and time conservation.)

Batching. This is another control function. The process combines a number of coupons into one group in preparation for their transfer from the coding clerk to the data entry clerk. A typical batch header record is shown in Figure 45-2. It contains all pertinent category information concerning the coupons within the batch. Wherever possible, it is preferable to batch all records of one type together. This makes it easier for the data entry clerk to transfer the information.

One very important function of the batch header is the recording of the date when the coupons were processed. This date, along with an individual sequence number for each coupon, represents the first step in building a unique identification number for each lead entered into the system. This number becomes a permanent part of the prospect's record, and it ensures that no two prospects will have a duplicate identification number. In addition, since a date is contained within the number, full control over the amount of time it takes to process a lead through the system is guaranteed.

Data Entry

This is the process by which the original information contained on a coupon is transferred to magnetic tape. The most common method is keypunching. The data entry clerks receive batches of coded leads. By utilizing a keyboard similar to a typewriter, they type or key all the information which must be transferred from the original coupon. Through the aid of a CRT (a television screen attached to the keyboard), they are able to see that the information they have transferred is correct. Once the accuracy of the record is confirmed, the information is released into a console which stores it and eventually releases it on command. Through the use of computerized programs, this console is able to store information being entered by a number of data entry clerks simultaneously and at the same time release individual batches as directed. The information is released in the form of a magnetic tape.

After the data entry clerks have completed a batch, they sign the batch header record and enter that batch header into their respective data entry logs. At the end of a processing cycle, all batches are cross-checked against this log to ensure that there is total accountability. The batches then are sent along with the magnetic tape to the computer center for processing.

Computer Editing

The dictionary defines the word "edit" as "to correct and prepare for publication." A computer edit does exactly that. It corrects mistakes which have resulted from bad prospect information (e.g., an improper ZIP code) and keypunch errors (e.g., a bad ad key code). This is done through the use of tables which are built into the editing procedure. There can be as many tables in an edit as are necessary to check all the information a company considers pertinent. Some standard tables would include

1. A post office city and ZIP file
2. An advertising key code table
3. A product line table
4. A sequence number check
5. A territory data base

Regardless of the number of tables used, the purpose of the edit remains the same: to highlight any incorrect information which appears in a record and to have that record corrected before it is processed further.

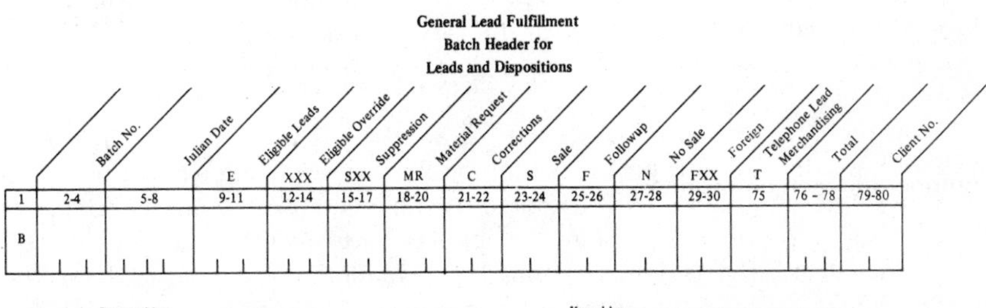

General Lead Fulfillment
Batch Header for
Leads and Dispositions

	Batch No.	Julian Date	Eligible Leads	Eligible Override	Suppression	Material Request	Corrections	Sale	Followup	No Sale	Foreign	Telephone Lead Merchandising	Total	Client No.
			E	XXX	SXX	MR	C	S	F	N	FXX	T		
1	2-4	5-8	9-11	12-14	15-17	18-20	21-22	23-24	25-26	27-28	29-30	75	76 - 78	79-80
B														

Prepared by ____________ Keyed by ____________

Figure 45-2 Batch header record

The Update

Once the records on the magnetic tape have passed all edit checks, the tape is ready for daily processing. This processing is known as the update cycle. It is referred to as an update because this is the first step in the processing cycle, where the information which is being processed for a given day is mixed with information which was processed previously. All the previous information resides on a magnetic tape which is known as the master file. When the new day's information is added to the previous file, this results in an updated master file. In addition, the update does the following.

- Assigns all the leads to their proper territories for sales force distribution.
- Produces the labels or computer letters which will be sent to the prospect along with a company's catalogs, brochures, or other fulfillment materials.
- Produces all the information concerning a lead and arranges it on a lead form which is distributed to the sales force.
- Stores all the statistical advertising and sales information which will be used in producing key management reports.
- Provides control totals which should match the clerical batch control totals. These totals are broken down further to display sales territory assignments and fulfillment records by type (product, service, etc.).

These totals are used in the letter shop processing as a final balancing procedure before the mailing of the fulfillment literature and the lead forms.

LEAD PROCESSING: THE OUTPUT

Fulfillment Materials

There are a number of options a company can take with regard to the materials it sends to individuals who have responded to its advertising. The options which finally are chosen depend on both the company's philosophy and the image it wishes to convey to potential customers. In many cases, decisions may be based on budgetary constraints.

Should Materials Requested Be Mailed or Delivered by the Sales People? If the product or service is highly technical in nature or if a potential customer needs expert help in choosing the right model or mix from a company's list of products, a sales call may be required before a decision can be made. In these cases, it probably would not be worthwhile to send a catalog or brochure through the mail. In this situation, at the very least a letter of acknowledgment should be sent to the prospects, informing them that the company has received their inquiry and is acting on it.

On the other hand, a company's catalog may be so big and contain such a cross section of products that it prohibits sending the entire catalog when a prospect has requested information on only one or two items or even a number of items within a given product line. Many companies have resolved this problem by producing "tear" sheets which contain information on individual items or product lines. While they incur the initial expenses of subdividing the catalog, the expense is often more than offset by the savings in materials and postage.

Prospects have taken the time to write or call after seeing a company's message. They have shown an interest in the offer being advertised. The company must show at least as much interest in them by responding to their requests as quickly as possible. There is a very good possibility that these individuals have requested similar information from the competition. In most instances, the company that responds first will get the order.

How Fast Is It Necessary to Respond? It is extremely important to fulfill the prospect's request as quickly as possible. It generally takes 3 to 5 days for the post office to deliver the initial coupon. The company should process the lead through the system and send out fulfillment literature within 24 to 72 hours from the time it is received. It will take the post office 3 to 5 days to deliver this material. Thus, it will take 7 to 13 days to complete the cycle if this schedule can be maintained.

What Type of Correspondence Should Accompany My Material? The answer to this question depends on the individual needs of a company to convey to its prospects something which is not already included in its standard catalogs or brochures. There are five basic options:

1. No correspondence
2. A preprinted nonpersonalized form letter
3. A preprinted personalized form letter
4. A partially preprinted letter with specific information computer printed
5. A fully computerized personal letter

Both image and budget constraints will affect your decision here. However, as a general rule, unless your catalog or brochure contains a personalized message from a company representative, it is good form to include a covering letter along with the company literature.

Experience has shown that form letters, whether personalized or not, are an acceptable means of communicating with prospects. This is especially true in business-to-business correspondence. When products and services are being offered to consumers, the personal touch usually gets better results.

Nevertheless, there are times when a partially or fully computerized letter is called for. A company may want to respond to a specific question raised by a prospect. It may want to include pricing information in the initial correspondence. It may be running specials periodically which it wants highlighted in these letters. It may want to inform its prospects of the location of the company's nearest dealer or sales office.

Sales Lead Forms

This chapter began by discussing the importance of supplying a company's sales force or dealers with qualified leads. Let us discuss how this information should be transmitted and what information can be expected from the sales people in return.

There are three basic axioms to be remembered when communicating with a field sales force.

1. The faster a company gets the leads into the hands of its sales people, the more likely the company is to meet with prospects before the competition does.

2. The more information a company can give its sales people concerning its prospects, the more likely they are to make a sale.
3. The more information a salesperson transmits to a company after making a sales call, the better prepared the company will be to target its marketplace and produce more qualified leads in future advertising campaigns.

A sales lead can be transmitted to the sales force in a number of ways.

- It can be done telephonically, with no written documentation.
- The original coupon can be handed or mailed to the salesperson.
- The information can be typed on an index card and transmitted.
- A multipart document may be typed, with one copy kept by the sales manager for follow-up.
- A computerized lead form can be produced, with multiple copies distributed to the sales manager and advertising department.

It is possible that both the index card and the typed multipart document could contain enough information to satisfy the second principle of sending complete information.

With the use of a computerized lead form, however, all three principles can be accomplished. Of even more importance, if the form is constructed correctly, it will take little effort on the part of the sales people to complete their portion and return it to the company. Figure 45-3 shows a computerized lead form. This form can be single or multipart. Individual sections have been numbered for easy identification.

Section 1 contains all the information which was contained on the original coupon. In addition, it tells the salesperson from what advertising effort the individual response was generated, the theme of the advertising, the product being advertised, the material mailed to the prospect, and the date it was mailed. In more sophisticated systems, this section also informs the salesperson whether this individual has inquired before, and if so, how many times and concerning what products or services; the date of the last inquiry; and whether a sale resulted.

This very valuable prospect information can be given to the sales people with a minimum of effort when a computerized lead-processing system is used. All the information can reside on the company's prospect and customer master files. It is generated through programs used in the update cycle.

Section 2 is a message center in which a company can communicate current information to its sales people on a daily basis or as often as it wishes. The messages contained in this section can be standard and repetitive, such as, "This is a national sales lead. You must contact the prospect and report the results of your call within 30 days." These messages serve as a reminder to the sales force that they have an obligation to report information to the company regardless of whether a sale has been made.

Another type of message could be an announcement such as, "Remember, this product is included in the sales contest and can earn you extra bonus points." A timely message can generate enthusiasm in the field. It lets your sales people know that you are aware of them and are interested in the results they generate.

Section 3 is used by the sales people to report the results of their calls. At the

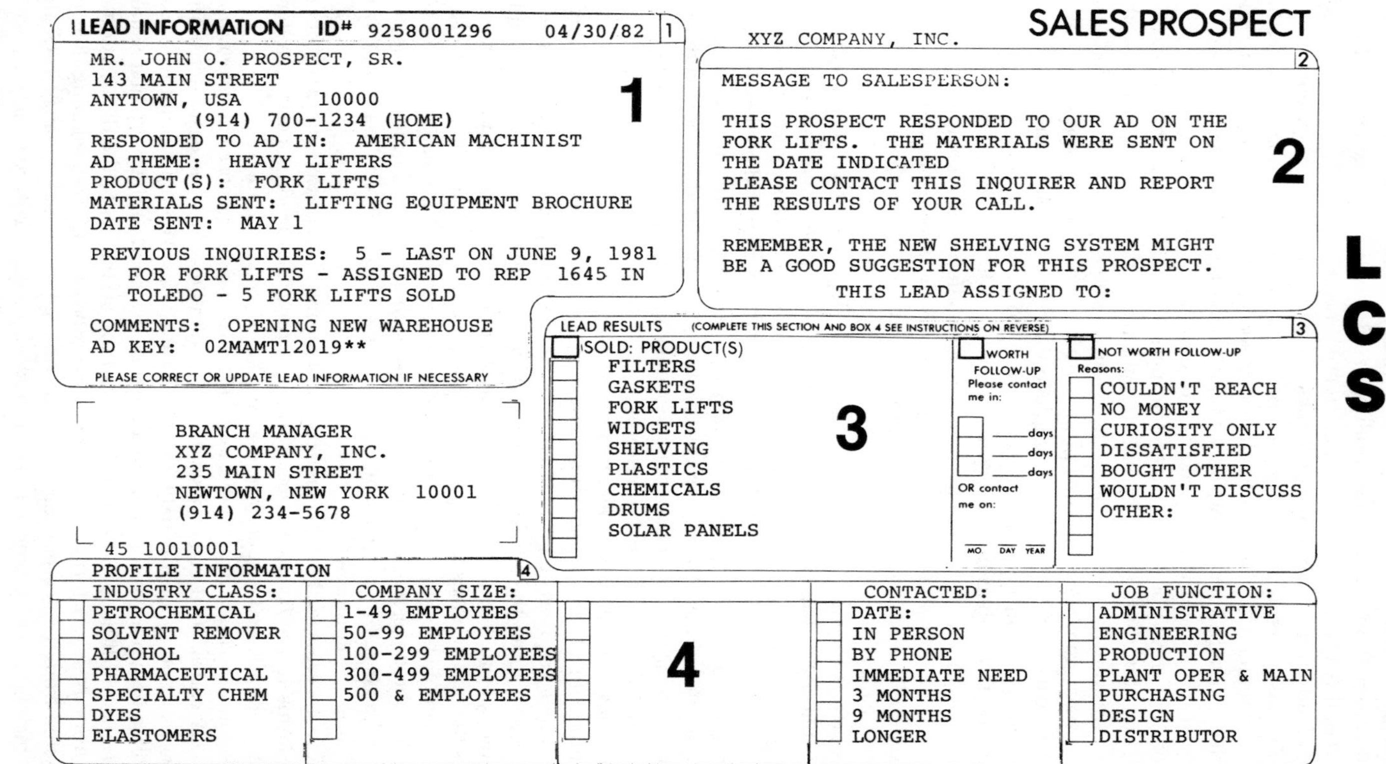

SALES PROSPECT

LCS

XYZ COMPANY, INC.

LEAD INFORMATION ID# 9258001296 04/30/82 [1]

MR. JOHN O. PROSPECT, SR.
143 MAIN STREET
ANYTOWN, USA 10000
(914) 700-1234 (HOME)
RESPONDED TO AD IN: AMERICAN MACHINIST
AD THEME: HEAVY LIFTERS
PRODUCT(S): FORK LIFTS
MATERIALS SENT: LIFTING EQUIPMENT BROCHURE
DATE SENT: MAY 1

PREVIOUS INQUIRIES: 5 - LAST ON JUNE 9, 1981
FOR FORK LIFTS - ASSIGNED TO REP 1645 IN
TOLEDO - 5 FORK LIFTS SOLD

COMMENTS: OPENING NEW WAREHOUSE
AD KEY: 02MAMT12019**

PLEASE CORRECT OR UPDATE LEAD INFORMATION IF NECESSARY

[2]

MESSAGE TO SALESPERSON:

THIS PROSPECT RESPONDED TO OUR AD ON THE
FORK LIFTS. THE MATERIALS WERE SENT ON
THE DATE INDICATED
PLEASE CONTACT THIS INQUIRER AND REPORT
THE RESULTS OF YOUR CALL.

REMEMBER, THE NEW SHELVING SYSTEM MIGHT
BE A GOOD SUGGESTION FOR THIS PROSPECT.

THIS LEAD ASSIGNED TO:

BRANCH MANAGER
XYZ COMPANY, INC.
235 MAIN STREET
NEWTOWN, NEW YORK 10001
(914) 234-5678

45 10010001

LEAD RESULTS (COMPLETE THIS SECTION AND BOX 4 SEE INSTRUCTIONS ON REVERSE) [3]

SOLD: PRODUCT(S)	WORTH FOLLOW-UP	NOT WORTH FOLLOW-UP
FILTERS	Please contact me in:	Reasons:
GASKETS	____ days	COULDN'T REACH
FORK LIFTS	____ days	NO MONEY
WIDGETS	____ days	CURIOSITY ONLY
SHELVING	OR contact me on:	DISSATISFIED
PLASTICS	MO DAY YEAR	BOUGHT OTHER
CHEMICALS		WOULDN'T DISCUSS
DRUMS		OTHER:
SOLAR PANELS		

PROFILE INFORMATION [4]

INDUSTRY CLASS:	COMPANY SIZE:		CONTACTED:	JOB FUNCTION:
PETROCHEMICAL	1-49 EMPLOYEES		DATE:	ADMINISTRATIVE
SOLVENT REMOVER	50-99 EMPLOYEES		IN PERSON	ENGINEERING
ALCOHOL	100-299 EMPLOYEES		BY PHONE	PRODUCTION
PHARMACEUTICAL	300-499 EMPLOYEES		IMMEDIATE NEED	PLANT OPER & MAIN
SPECIALTY CHEM	500 & EMPLOYEES		3 MONTHS	PURCHASING
DYES			9 MONTHS	DESIGN
ELASTOMERS			LONGER	DISTRIBUTOR

LCS INDUSTRIES · LPF · 3 1/81 40M

Figure 45-3 Computerized lead form

very least , it should have an area for reporting sales or the reasons for failure to sell. If information concerning products sold and income generated can be captured, this will enhance the program even more.

Each lead contains information concerning the original advertisement from which it was generated. This information resides on the company's master file. When information is returned by the sales people through the use of this lead form, it eventually finds its way back to the master file and will be analyzed and displayed in the reports produced by the system.

It may not always be possible for a salesperson to make a sale on an initial call. At the same time, it may be determined that a particular prospect is well worth a second or even fifth visit because an eventual sale seems likely. A good lead-processing system allows for this probability and gives the salesperson a way to report such a finding. As with the sample form, the salesperson can request that a reminder lead form be generated in a specified period of time. This puts the burden of remembering when the follow-up call should be made on the computer rather than the salesperson. It also informs the company that the salesperson is working on the lead but as yet has not been able to report a final disposition. There is no guesswork on the company's part about why the lead has not been closed.

Section 4 is very important to the advertising department. While the salesperson is making a call, it may be possible to obtain pertinent marketing data concerning the prospect. Whether a sale is made or not, this information can be vital in analyzing past advertising campaigns and giving direction to future campaigns. The data being collected may change from campaign to campaign or across product lines. These changes can be accommodated by most computer systems. As was true of section 3, all these data become part of the master file and eventually will be presented in reports.

The sales form shown in Figure 45-3 is a very complete one. It was built to accommodate all the information which could be ascertained concerning a prospect. It requires a flow of information to and from the sales force. It completely closes the marketing loop. It enables its user to track the initial advertising from cost per inquiry through cost per sale. If used properly, it even allows the user to measure the sales dollars generated by each advertising effort.

It is a simple form for the sales people to use, requiring no more than a check alongside the boxes which are pertinent to each sales call. In most cases, it is designed as a self-mailer so that the salesperson need only fold and seal it to return it to the company.

Before the sales lead can become useful, a means must be devised to distribute these forms to the field sales force. In a computerized lead-processing system, this is accomplished through the use of a sales territory data base.

The sales territory data base can be constructed on almost any geographic basis: ZIP codes, sectional centers, counties, or states. In some cases, territories can be assigned to a combination of these categories. The main point is that all territories within a given selling area must be assigned. If there are unassigned areas, specific directions must be built into the system as to the distribution of leads from these territories. The directions may be as simple as assigning all leads generated from a sales territory with no coverage to the sales manager. Or the leads may be force assigned to the next closest sales territory which has sales coverage.

Territories do not have to be, and indeed often are not, mutually exclusive. A company may have a national sales force but have only one person covering the states of Utah, Nevada, and New Mexico. At the same time, it may have four people covering New York City. Because of population density, many more leads are generated in the one city than in all three states. How are these leads distributed among the four sales people? This can be done by allocating leads on a percentage basis each time they are distributed. The allocation can be equal, or it can be a fixed rate based on the success of each of the sales people. Another method would be to give the first salesperson a set amount of leads, give an equal amount to the second, and so on. Whatever method is chosen, a computerized lead-processing system can accommodate it.

Many companies have more than one sales force, with overlapping territories. One reason for multiple sales forces could be a diversity in technical product lines. Each sales force would be made up of experts in their particular product areas. Again, because details concerning product information requested are contained within the master file records, leads can be distributed to the correct sales force by product through the update cycle.

Management Reports

To this point we have discussed a working lead-processing system. Inquiries are received daily. Fulfillment materials are sent to prospects. The sales force is receiving leads, working, and returning leads. Valuable information concerning prospects and new customers has been stored. Now we must array this information in order to analyze our advertising and sales efforts.

If a lead-processing system were limited to only two reports, it is probable that every company using that system would choose the same two: the advertising key report and the sales performance report.

The Advertising Key Report. Figure 45-4 is a sample advertising key report. Attention is drawn to the way this report is structured. The major classification is by product advertised. This is necessary only when multiple product lines are being advertised across a number of promotional campaigns.

The next classification is by media and within media by interest. This structure enables the advertising department to measure the productivity of each individual insert. At the same time, it summarizes all inserts by media and all media by medium. Thus, when advertising results are being compared, the productivity of direct mail campaigns can be measured on a dollar for dollar basis against publications, trade shows, etc. Within each medium, one magazine or list can be compared against another to gauge the effectiveness of each. This type of summary information is made possible by the incorporation of a standardized advertising key code into the lead-processing system. An example of this advertising key is shown here.

CBMWSJ41183CY

Product	Medium	Publication	Month	Day	Year	Fulfillment
CB	M	WSJ	4	11	83	CY

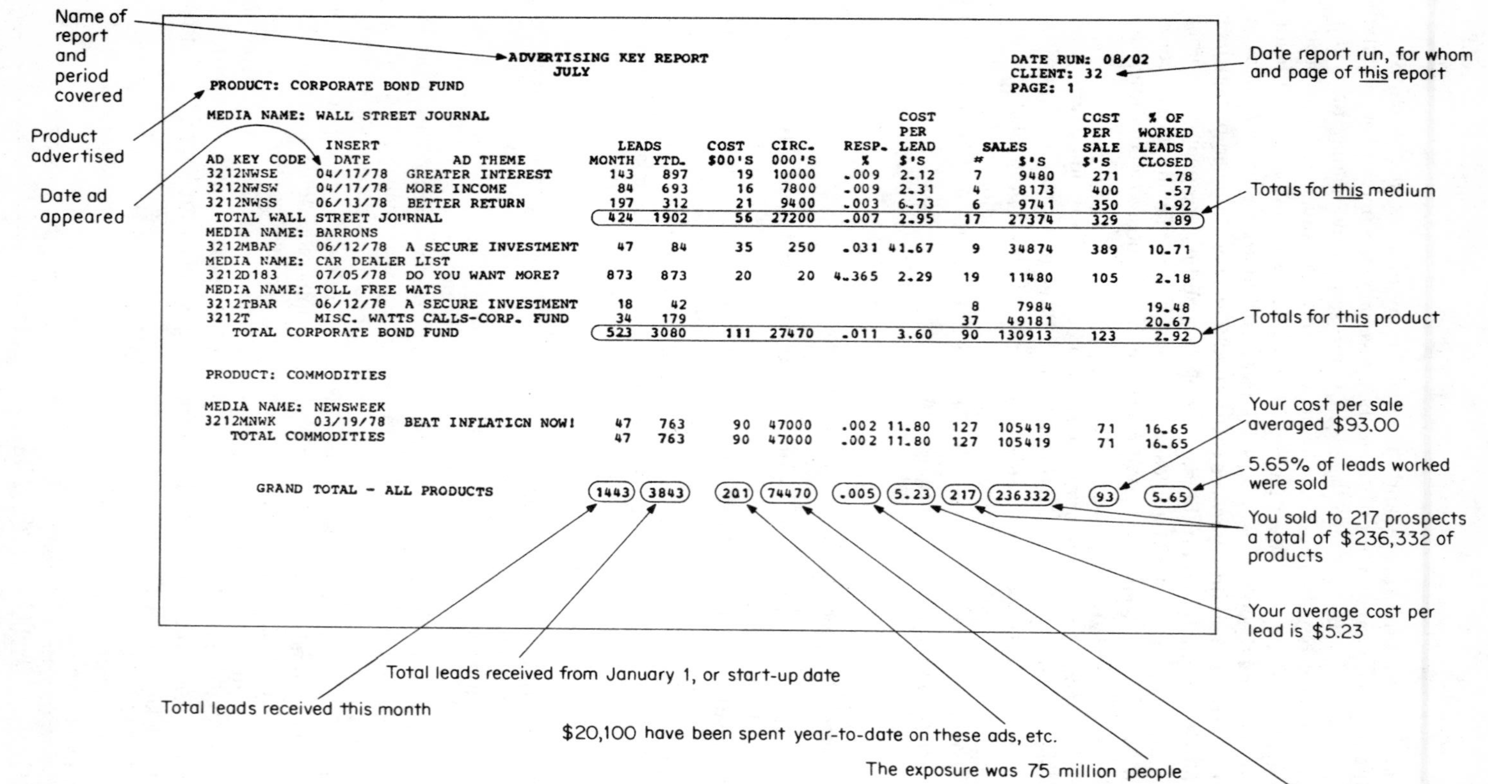

ADVERTISING KEY REPORT
JULY

DATE RUN: 08/02
CLIENT: 32
PAGE: 1

PRODUCT: CORPORATE BOND FUND

MEDIA NAME: WALL STREET JOURNAL

AD KEY CODE	INSERT DATE	AD THEME	LEADS MONTH	LEADS YTD.	COST $00'S	CIRC. 000'S	RESP. %	COST PER LEAD $'S	SALES #	SALES $'S	COST PER SALE $'S	% OF WORKED LEADS CLOSED
3212NWSE	04/17/78	GREATER INTEREST	143	897	19	10000	.009	2.12	7	9480	271	.78
3212NWSW	04/17/78	MORE INCOME	84	693	16	7800	.009	2.31	4	8173	400	.57
3212NWSS	06/13/78	BETTER RETURN	197	312	21	9400	.003	6.73	6	9741	350	1.92
TOTAL WALL STREET JOURNAL			424	1902	56	27200	.007	2.95	17	27374	329	.89
MEDIA NAME: BARRONS												
3212MBAF	06/12/78	A SECURE INVESTMENT	47	84	35	250	.031	41.67	9	34874	389	10.71
MEDIA NAME: CAR DEALER LIST												
3212D183	07/05/78	DO YOU WANT MORE?	873	873	20	20	4.365	2.29	19	11480	105	2.18
MEDIA NAME: TOLL FREE WATS												
3212TBAR	06/12/78	A SECURE INVESTMENT	18	42					8	7984		19.48
3212T		MISC. WATTS CALLS-CORP. FUND	34	179					37	49181		20.67
TOTAL CORPORATE BOND FUND			523	3080	111	27470	.011	3.60	90	130913	123	2.92

PRODUCT: COMMODITIES

MEDIA NAME: NEWSWEEK

AD KEY CODE	INSERT DATE	AD THEME	LEADS MONTH	LEADS YTD.	COST $00'S	CIRC. 000'S	RESP. %	COST PER LEAD $'S	SALES #	SALES $'S	COST PER SALE $'S	% OF WORKED LEADS CLOSED
3212MNWK	03/19/78	BEAT INFLATICN NOW!	47	763	90	47000	.002	11.80	127	105419	71	16.65
TOTAL COMMODITIES			47	763	90	47000	.002	11.80	127	105419	71	16.65
GRAND TOTAL - ALL PRODUCTS			1443	3843	201	74470	.005	5.23	217	236332	93	5.65

Figure 45-4 Advertising key report. (This report provides data on each ad run, how well it did, how much it sold, and how it compares to other ads.)

CB—Corporate bonds (offer)
M—Magazine (medium)
WSJ—*Wall Street Journal* (medium)
4/11/83—April 11, 1983 (insert date)
CY—corporate bonds and you (fulfillment material)

In order to capture all this information, the ad key has to be fairly large. There is not always room within the advertising space allotted to accommodate a key of this size. Also, from a creative point of view, many companies would prefer a less conspicuous ad key. In these cases, a transposition table is built into the system. This allows a much smaller key to be placed on the actual advertisement. This key is matched to the full key in the computerized lead-processing system. For example,

Coupon key	= computerized key
WSJ4	CBMWSJ41183CY

Use transposition keys only when necessary. Never duplicate the coupon key. The fact that it is unique will ensure a match to the correct computer key.

A company will get as much out of an advertising key report as it is willing to put in. Therefore, whenever possible, both cost and circulation figures should be reported. The inclusion of this information will enable a company to measure

CPI (cost per inquiry)
CPFL (cost per forwarded lead)
CPS (cost per sale)
POR (percentage of response)

In the sample report, the "monthly inquiries received" column is separated into two categories: coupon and telephone. This is necessary if the advertisement carries an 800 number. It is important to measure this relationship. Referring to our original ad key, the basic construction would not change: WSJ4 = CBMWSJ41183CY

However, when an inquiry has been received telephonically, the coding clerk would amend the coupon key to WSJ4/P. Through this simple coding instruction, the computer will recognize the inquiry as a *Wall Street Journal* telephone response.

Figure 45-4 can be used as a model when constructing an advertising key report. However, not every company can use all the information displayed in this example. For instance, if a company is not prequalifying inquiries, there is no reason to have both an "inquiry" and a "leads forwarded" column. Both figures would be the same. Similarly, if a company is distributing leads to a noncaptured sales force (i.e., dealers), and disposition information is not being returned, it is of little value to include the columns pertaining to sales on this report.

Do not burden this report with information which will not be effective in assisting you with your media analysis.

The Sales Performance Report. Figure 45-5 shows a sample sales performance report. This report summarizes what happened to the leads once they were distributed to the sales force. It gives a detailed accounting of the current status of every sales lead assigned to a salesperson or sales office. In addition, summary performance reports can be tabulated throughout a company's field management structure, regardless of the levels of management. Finally, it shows a national summary. This is accomplished through the use of the sales territory data base that was discussed earlier in this chapter. Since a correctly constructed data base will have all territories assigned to sales offices, it can be assumed that a detailed accounting of all leads assigned to a particular sales office can be produced. Taking this one step further, through the use of a numeric coding technique, sales offices can be grouped together to produce summary information.

As an example, let us suppose we are constructing this report for a national sales force which has the following levels of management:

SALES OFFICE——— REPORTS TO——— DISTRICT MANAGER——— REPORTS TO——— REGIONAL MANAGER——— REPORTS TO——— NATIONAL SALES MANAGER

The coding structure would be built in inverse order, as follows.

National sales manager	1-00-000-000
Eastern region manager	1-01-000-000
District manager 1 in eastern region	1-01-001-000
Sales office 1 in district 1	1-01-001-001

This coding method can accommodate thousands of sales offices in hundreds of districts, with up to ninety-nine regions. Only the sales office number has to be assigned to the individual record, and this is accomplished during the update cycle. All summary information can be computed by the lead-processing system in the reports cycle. The report is divided into six subsections for ease of accounting.

1. **Leads sent.** This section accounts for all leads sent to a particular salesperson or sales office. It normally contains both current and year-to-date totals.
2. **In process.** This section tabulates leads which have been forwarded but for which no response has been received from the sales force. These leads can be aged so that no leads are held by the sales people for too long a period.
3. **Follow-up awaiting release.** Often a salesperson qualifies a prospect but is not able to finalize the sale for weeks or months after the initial call. This section allows the sales people to report that situation to management.
4. **Sales.** This section is used to report all sales by product, units, and income generated.
5. **Not worth follow-up.** This section identifies the reasons why a sale could not be made or why a prospect is not worth future follow-up.
6. **Leads closed.** This section is optional in most systems. It is used only when leads are taken away from sales people after a prescribed amount of time has elapsed.

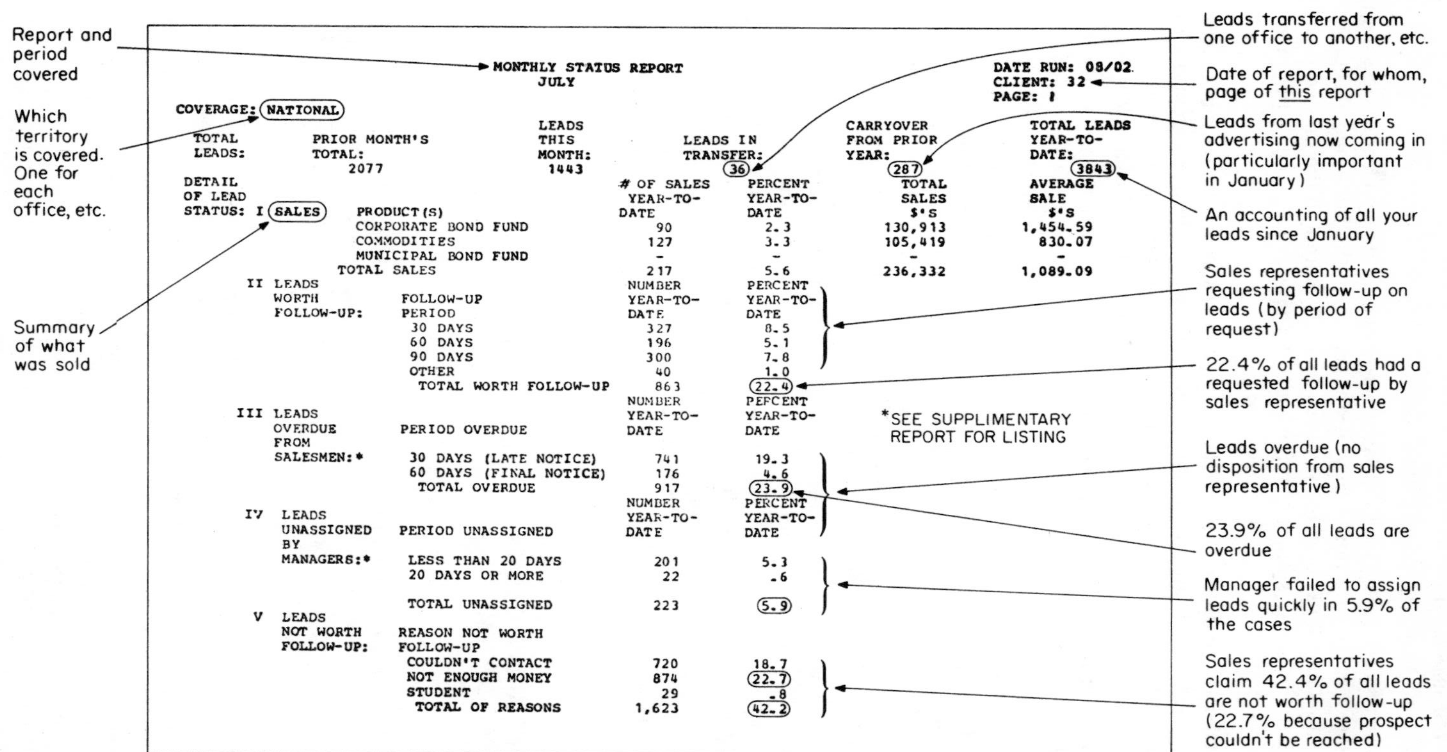

Figure 45-5 Monthly status report. (This report summarizes what happened to the leads by office, by territory, and nationally.)

These two reports can be the foundation for any computerized lead-processing system. However, they do not by any means represent the full scope of reports which are available. By arranging the data which are stored on the master file in different formats, many summary reports can be produced. Some of the more useful reports would include the following.

1. **Advertising medium report.** This summarizes promotional campaigns according to medium (newspapers, direct mail, TV, etc.). This report can display information pertaining to ad cost, leads produced, and sales revenues earned. It can measure results in the CPI, CPFL, and CPS catagories.
2. **Advertising time period report.** This arrays the flow of inquiries into the system according to date of receipt. This measurement can be made on individual efforts or against entire campaigns. It measures the life expectancy of the advertising.
3. **Prospect report.** This measures the marketing or demographic data captured by the sales force on the lead form. It is not so much a single report as a series of reports. Depending on the amount of data captured, many combinations may have to be analyzed before the correct marketing conclusions can be reached.
4. **Data base verification report.** This is more a listing than a report. It is functional in nature. It contains a summary of the territories "owned" by a particular sales office. This report should be produced quarterly or more often if a sales force has a high turnover rate. It not only confirms the correct territory alignments but also ensures that the right sales representative is assigned to the territory and that all address and telephone number information is correct. This report is essential for the proper distribution of leads.

TELEPHONE AND THE LEAD-PROCESSING SYSTEM

In-WATS

When telephones are referred to in a discussion of a lead-processing system, this implies the use of 800 numbers. These are toll-free numbers, which means that the individual using them does not have to pay for the call. The in-WATS 800 number can be a very effective means of generating inquiries. These numbers can stand alone in an advertisement or can be used in conjunction with a coupon. The latter gives the reader a choice of responding through the mail or by calling. Depending on the individual's needs and how quickly he or she wishes to obtain the information being requested, the individual may choose either response device or both.

Leads can be generated, and a lead-processing system can operate effectively, without an in-WATS system. The decision to use an 800 number should be made only after careful consideration and testing. However, once the decision to use an 800 number has been made, a company should design its system to take full advantage of all the aspects this type of program offers.

Before establishing a telephone operation, it is necessary to determine its purpose. If operators are to collect prospect information only—name, address, and telephone number—the script will be a simple one, and operators who possess only a fundamental knowledge of the company's products and services can be used. If prospect qualification is the purpose, operators who have an in-depth knowledge of the company's product line should be used. These operators should be able not only to qualify the prospects but also to dispense product and pricing information. In some cases, they may even be able to take orders.

In many companies, the 800 number is advertised with an extension number. When prospects call requesting this extension, they are transferred automatically to the sales department.

In companies where the sales force is dispersed throughout the sales territory and are not available to accept calls on a routine basis, another method is used. The telephone operators have a listing of all the sales people and their territories. When prospects call, they are offered the name and location of the nearest salesperson or dealer. This is accomplished by matching the business or home address of the prospect with the salesperson who is assigned that territory. In sophisticated computerized lead-processing systems, this selection process is accomplished through a terminal at the telephone operator's desk. The operator has direct access to the sales territory data base program, which makes the selection automatically. This method has a real advantage when a company is operating with more than one representative in a sales territory. The computer automatically selects the correct salesperson to be assigned, based on the formula for sharing territory.

When establishing an in-WATS service, keep these points in mind.

- The telephone operators will in most cases be the first point of contact the prospect has with a company. The image they give the prospect will be a lasting one. Therefore, operators should be trained to be courteous, knowledgeable, and efficient.
- The information the operators collect from the prospects will be very useful in helping sales representatives make the sale. Therefore, the operator scripts must be complete. The more information they gather and disperse, the more qualified the prospect will be.
- As in any other aspect of a lead-processing system, control is extremely important. The gathering of information is irrelevant if proper methods of transmitting it are not used.

Out-WATS

Out-WATS 800 numbers are a very effective and often overlooked part of a lead-processing system. There are three major functions which an out-WATS system can perform:

1. Prospect qualification
2. Transmitting "hot" leads
3. Prospect revivals

Prospect Qualification. Prospects may be qualified by asking two basic questions: Would you like to buy the product? When? Unfortunately, this is not often the case. Depending on the complexity of the products or services being offered and the diversified needs of the prospects themselves, the qualifying procedure may be very complex. It may involve a series of questions, each dependent on the answer to a previous one. This can take from 2 to 10 minutes. When a company's qualifying procedures are time-consuming, the company will not want to have its in-WATS lines occupied for such lengthy periods. The purpose of the in-WATS is to allow prospects easy access to a company. These calls should be kept as short as possible, yet the information must be collected. The alternative is a callback (out-WATS), which gives the operator the opportunity to gather all the necessary prospect information. Since the company is initiating the call, this can be done on a scheduled basis.

Transmitting "Hot" Leads. Out-WATS phones often are used for immediate communication with a company's sales force. If a prospect has shown a positive interest in an offer and requires immediate contact, this information can be transmitted to the proper salesperson through out-WATS telecommunication.

Prospect Revivals. There are many reasons why a prospect may request information from a company but fail to purchase its products or services. Failure to make a purchase on an initial sales call does not diminish the fact that there was interest enough on the prospect's part to initiate some action. Since these prospects still reside on the master file, it is easy to extract these records and call the prospects to see if interest can be renewed. This is a proven method of generating sales leads at minimal cost.

SUMMARY

There are many pitfalls and problems associated with establishing and maintaining a well-run lead-fulfillment center. Although many companies have their own computers, they do not have the technical programming staff to devise such a system, nor can they assign the type of priority needed to keep the system running. In addition, WATS lines, though essential in many cases, are costly to maintain and require a large staff to operate. In many cases, a company is better off contracting for these services rather than trying to perform the function itself.

A lead-fulfillment system is only as good as the people and programs that produced it. A good system must have the capacity to change as the needs of a company change. The system cannot drive the needs of a company but rather must be driven by those needs.

Once a system has been established, whether in-house or contracted, it must be monitored constantly and carefully if it is to work efficiently. It does little good to set up the best of systems if there is no follow-up on the day-to-day details. This requires the cooperation of many people. The advertising department must provide the necessary documentation, the production facilities must maintain the ability to turn around inquiries in the required time, and the sales force must not only work the leads sent to them but also report their progress.

When all areas are functioning as they should, the net result will be an intelligent appraisal of how advertising dollars are being spent and, more important, how they are being converted to sales.

part 5

APPLICATIONS

chapter 46

CATALOG SALES

Jo-Von Tucker

President and CEO
Jo-Von Tucker &
Associates
Dallas, Tex.

Prior to 1971 and the Kenton Collection, there were a handful of high-ticket catalogs around, primarily department and specialty store projects. Most notable were the sophisticated books produced at Christmastime by Neiman-Marcus featuring expensive and bizarre "his and hers" specials that were used more to achieve publicity than to reflect sales.

Most department store mail order was used simply to generate store traffic. Very few store catalogs even contained an order form, much less a toll-free number. Tracing sales from mail order in the stores was not deemed worthwhile, and so the retailers never knew for sure how much their floor sales were affected by their direct marketing promotion.

Within the space of a few years, many catalogs directed to both upscale and midscale audiences appeared. An educational process evolved for the mail-order customer. The well-presented, obviously expensively produced catalogs that were suddenly appearing in mailboxes did not fit the "junk mail" syndrome that was prevalent at the time. These books reflected credibility to the consumer, implying by touch and glance a trustworthiness on the part of the owner or company. The customer began to order high-ticket items (porcelain, silk, crystal), with confidence that each would arrive intact and that they would be pleased with the purchase. Credibility was gained through realistic portrayal of the merchandise as well as a certain standardizing of the key elements that go into the physical presentation, such as coated paper stocks and plus covers. Additionally, customers learned to accept catalog shorthand techniques such as the placement of postage and handling charges in parentheses following the item price.

THE TARGET AUDIENCE

Marketing Research for Customer Identification

The most successful catalog firms have learned the importance of identifying the customer. Through selected and intensive marketing research we have access to information that tells us who our customers are, where they live, their leisure activities, their available discretionary income, and many other pertinent facts. Application of this resource helps direct our promotional efforts to best appeal to these customers' needs and interests.

Methods of Marketing Research for Catalogers

Four basic categories are used to obtain customer profiles and reaction. The first—requesting information on the catalog order form—is the most obvious opportunity yet the least frequently used. The catalog serves as a free carrier for a survey to help define customer demographics and psychographics. In asking for the customer's time to relay this information, the cataloger should consider extending the courtesy of prepaying the postage on the envelope. A sound system for compiling the research information from the order form should be planned carefully before you consider using this technique. Valuable data have been lost because of oversights in programming.

Shopping Center Intercepts. When planned and conducted by a professional research team, these have proved to be valid information-gathering projects. The first rule for shopping center intercepts is to qualify the prospective interviewee as a mail-order customer. An opportunity then exists for a one-on-one reaction measurement. Consumers typically are quizzed on their response to existing catalogs within the market (usually competitive in nature with the firm conducting the study), desirability of merchandise offerings, reaction to graphics and presentation, and even likes and dislikes regarding prospective names or titles for proposed catalogs.

Focus Studies. These are used extensively by many catalogers. A small group of customers is brought together to give reactions to new format proposals, for examination of actual merchandise, and for comparison studies of competitive books. As with shopping center intercepts, established, experienced marketing help should be used to conduct these sessions. Results can be heavily weighted by the interviewer's technique, and so a distaff direction is important in this process.

Telephone Survey of Customers. This is an economical measurement that produces immediate input. The format for such calls is flexible, but it is wise to keep such interviews short in order to avoid taking too much of the customer's time. Questions may be structured to provide data on a recently received catalog mailing.

MARKETING CONCLUSIONS

Compiled information from these and other research methods has painted a portrait of the upscale catalog customer. Here is a composite of the customer profile.

1. **Age bracket:** 35 to 55 years.
2. **Sex:** Eighty-five percent of responders are women, with the exception of house lists for firms like American Express and The Sharper Image.
3. **Marital status:** Fifty percent of the female customers are married, and 50 percent are nonmarried (single, divorced, or widowed).
4. **Employment status:** Fifty-five to sixty percent of responders are employed outside the home.
5. **Combined family income:** $40,000 annually.
6. **Discretionary income:** Fifty-five percent of customers represent a two-income family.
7. **Property status:** Sixty-five percent are homeowners.
8. **Charge account holders:** Average 3.2 per customer (excluding gasoline credit cards). Most prominent are Master Card, Visa, American Express, and department or specialty store accounts.
9. **Mail-order frequency:** 5.1 times per year per customer. Expressed positive response when queried about desirability of ordering through the mail more frequently.
10. **Average dollar order:** $60 to $100.
11. **Education:** Average 2.6 years of college or university. The married customer reflects a lower educational level than the nonmarried.

Narrative Vignette of the Upscale Catalog Customer

Since 85 percent of the responders were women, this narrative is worded to reflect that definition of sex. The upscale mail-order customer is referred to in the feminine gender here, with no reverse chauvinism intended.

A busy, involved lifestyle is a key factor in the generic appeal of mail order for this customer. Convenience is listed most often as the primary motivating factor in making a mail-order purchase. Secondarily, desirability of merchandise (including exclusivity) prompts action to order. Other determining factors which lead to customer conversion are

1. Credibility of catalog name
2. Catalog presentation (graphics and quality reproduction)
3. Succinct, informative copy
4. Psychological use of color
5. Timing of mailing (seasonality)
6. Previous mail-order fulfillment experience

Price of goods is rarely the determining factor.

The customer has a small amount of leisure time and prefers other activities to fill that time than journeying to a store to make a purchase.

Typical leisure activities for the customer are entertaining at home; attending social functions; movies; reading; sports participation (tennis, golf, racketball, skiing, swimming); sports attendance (professional and college football games, tennis matches); volunteer work for hospitals, charities, and sororities; travel (for business and for recreation or holiday); community and civic involvement (Scouts, schools, PTA, political party affiliation); family outings; exercise and dance classes; and educational courses (foreign languages, gourmet cooking, Yoga, creative writing, etc.).

The customer is brand-aware and has a closet filled with ready-to-wear garments bearing names like Blass, Klein, and Beene. Additionally, a representation of higher couture names will be there. She avoids fabric blends in her wardrobe in favor of pure contents like silk, wool, and cotton. She carries leather bags and wears leather shoes; vinyl and polyester do not figure in her wardrobe or her vocabulary.

The look of her home is important to her. She wants pretty things surrounding her and will select such merchandise impulsively, without planned purchase action. This tendency reflects one of the major reasons for the success of high-ticket catalogs.

The typical mail-order customer buys items for gift-giving occasions an average of eight times per year exclusive of Christmas shopping. These occasions include birthdays, anniversaries, weddings, graduations, baby showers, Valentines Day, Mothers Day, Fathers Day, Easter, Halloween, etc. One out of two mail-order purchases from high-ticket catalogs is a gift selection. The convenience factor of catalog shopping figures prominently in gift purchases.

Listen to Your Customer

In a recent focus study, mail-order customers reflected an amazing level of sophistication in terms of appreciation for quality catalog format and presentation. They were harshly critical of cheaper papers and expressed dislike of low-quality separations and printing. They demonstrated a preference for catalogs with plus covers as opposed to self-covers and recognized changes in format, fashion trends, and new directions. Subtle deviations from established catalog companies were noticed and commented on.

LIST SELECTION

Reaching the potential customer ranks high on the priority list of catalog objectives. While a house list produces many percentage points better for any mailer, most catalogers must rely on rented lists to get the total mailing quantity high enough to amortize creative and production costs.

With the marketing research information previously covered, list selections for cold tests should be made by incorporating these data along with mail-order buying history. Lists segmented according to previous mail-order purchasing generally tend to produce better for catalog firms. Further segmentation can be achieved by targeting according to dollar select (average dollar order) or by recency and frequency of mail-order purchases. List companies provide information cards for each representation which contain marketing statistics and history of performance. Demographics, geographics, psychographics, and lifestyle segmentation are all criteria for selection. The overall universe (total number of names available) may help determine both the size of the test and its rollout potential.

It is important to be able to track the performance of each test list. The code listed on the mailing label will key the sales information to the correct test list, and proper computer programming will record pertinent response data. Control or house information should be monitored and evaluated continually, particularly as decisions are made to retest a list.

Experience within a market segment should be factored when you select a list broker or list management firm. A solid working knowledge of the upscale market is a prerequisite for high-ticket catalog responsibility. It is suggested that credentials and track record be checked thoroughly before you assign list selection or list management to any firm. Do not hesitate to place calls to existing and former clients to verify credentials. Professional list companies should have no qualms about presenting references.

Building a house list requires a vast investment of both time and money, and catalogers must guard carefully against overexposure. Competition in the mailbox is fierce with the recent explosion of mail-order catalogs, and unfortunately, catalogers are using the same available rental lists over and over again. The average upscale mail-order customer now receives seven catalogs per week in the mailbox. A policy decison to rent a house list only to noncompetitive catalogs therefore seems wise. Exchange of lists is a common practice among noncompeting catalogers, but it is highly recommended that the merge and purge technique be applied to clean all mailings and avoid duplicate names.

DEVELOPING A NICHE IN THE MARKETPLACE

A catalog needs a strong reason for being considered above its competition. The more unique the merchandise offering and the more outstanding the physical presentation, the better the reception by the customer. Credibility and desirability must be instantaneous on receipt and perusal.

The Ultimate Concern of Catalogers

Establishing a niche in the marketplace of catalogs can be accomplished best by answering the needs and requirements of prospective customers. The philosophy to guide all formative and directive decisions toward this objective is one of overall consideration of the consumer. A catalog should be produced with the customer in mind at every step, from point-of-view concept through print production. Bottom-line sales will reflect whether all considerations are working, but interim guidelines can be used as checkpoints along the way.

Exclusivity of Merchandise

An important way to stimulate a customer's interest is to offer merchandise that is not available in local department stores or other catalogs. Frequently this can be achieved through packaging (a unique combination of items). Changing a color or fabric can give an old product new life, and personalizing or monogramming can set an item apart from competitive offerings.

Working with vendors and manufacturers to provide exclusives on products will help establish an identity for a catalog. It is difficult to get a vendor's attention in this matter unless catalog quantities are large enough to promise large orders. To begin with, newer catalogs will be forced to seek out cooperative manufacturers for the development of exclusive items. As success builds and reputation grows, unusual products will be submitted for consideration, and catalog exclusives will be offered. Be patient in building a rapport with vendors, and in the meantime, devote more time to seeking out new items in showrooms and markets. Look for merchandise that hasn't appeared in other catalogs and check to be sure that the projected quantity is available.

A Unique Catalog Presentation

As the customer's level of sophistication regarding catalogs has risen, so has consumer demand for quality presentation. On any given day, multiple catalogs may appear in the mailbox of a mail-order customer. The overall image projected by the book in the hand will determine which catalog gets the attention. Format, physical size, color reproduction, and quality feel figure prominently in the impact or first credibility impression. Name awareness and merchandise desirability complete the motivation to purchase.

Credibility of Image

Gain the customer's trust by presenting one face: quality. To be perceived as reputable, a catalog must be presented factually, with an emphasis on color fidelity. Merchandise match is imperative, with the colors shown in the book totally representative of the products. It is unacceptable to the customer to receive an item in a color different from the color that was selected from a catalog depiction.

Ultimate consideration of the customer should guide descriptive copy technique as well. It is unwise to use abstract words to describe colors and fabrics. Primary colors are easily understood, but subtle deviations of shades or pastels should be tagged as specifically as possible. For instance, "mauve" is more difficult to visualize than "dusty lavender"; "heather" can range from pinks to greens and includes any shade in between.

BUILDING A PAPER STORE

A catalog is a paper store, a measurable medium for advertising items for sale on a one-to-one direct-response level. Careful consideration should be given to the direction of building this paper store, emphasizing to the customer the service, choices, and quality offered. The effect is even more concentrated and intensive than that of a retail display center. It has less time to work and therefore must be effective at first glance.

Merchandise Selection

The paper store, or catalog, is created around the products that will be offered for sale. Certain parameters should be used to qualify merchandise for inclusion. Each cataloger should develop a personalized checklist that reflects the desired niche. A general set of guidelines could include the following questions.

1. Is the item unique by description of features?
2. Is the basic design good?
3. Does it fill a need or desire?
4. Is the price point fair and competitive?
5. Will returns be high? If so, avoid grief and pass to another product.
6. Are there inherent fit problems? If the answer is yes, pass it.
7. Can the items be shown effectively by photography?
8. Has this merchandise been around too much in other catalogs?
9. Would it probably be received well as a gift?
10. Would I buy it for myself or for someone in my family or circle of friends?

Developing Exclusive Packaging

It is strongly recommended that exclusivity be sought as much as possible when you select items for a catalog. This provides the customer with an additional reason to buy through the mail. Merchandise that is readily available through retail stores has less reason to appear in a catalog.

Packaging can be defined in two ways: the physical presentation of a product (i.e., the gift box or wrap), and the method of combining two or more products into a unique set or offering. Personalized stationery can be expanded from the basic letter set to all correspondence needs. The customer will appreciate note cards, postal cards, formal thank you notes, invitations, RSVP cards, and tablets with envelopes all in the same graphic format with personalization—a complete line of stationery needs that presents one personal image or statement.

Distaff Editing

Most catalog merchants, or buyers, are too emotionally involved in their own selection of products to be wholly trusted with the responsibility of final editing. Rather than make a decisive choice between two similar items, buyers tend to want both pieces in the catalog.

Stanley Marcus, chairman emeritus of Neiman-Marcus, has been quoted as saying that mail order works because it is a preedited selection of merchandise. Much of the decision factor has been removed, making a purchase decision easier on the customer. There are no racks of dresses for a customer to flip through, requiring the elimination of perhaps fifty to get down to a choice of one or two. In a catalog, that preliminary editing has been done already.

Too many choices within a single category may confuse the customer and remove the motivation to buy. If a customer wants a set of coffee mugs, it is usually sufficient to offer one set or at most two within the catalog. If the set you show makes a statement about your buying selectivity and authority, if it meets the criteria of good design, fair price, uniqueness, etc., the prospect will feel comfortable selecting from your offering.

When merchandise is edited thoughtfully, it enhances your positioning as an authority. It also gives the people charged with production of the catalog a better opportunity for dramatic display. In a typical high-ticket catalog of thirty-two pages plus cover, an ideal maximum number of products would be 120 to 140. Higher density would require too many small depictions, eliminating the marketing flexibility of showing the merchandise to its best advantage.

If mail-order experience is well represented within the creative staff or freelance catalog production, final decisions on merchandise selection can be guided by their input. While a buyer may be emotionally close to the products being considered, the creative staff does not have that built-in bias. At merchandise presentation, reactions by these people should be heeded. If they stress the strong desirability of one item or their intense dislike (or even apathetic response) toward another, it is highly likely that your customers may react the same way. Don't take up valuable selling space in your catalog just to present merchandise that may be considered less than great.

Increasing the Average Order

In addition to the exclusivity factor, packaging can increase the average catalog order. Adding a special wicker carrier for a product will enhance the offering as a gift and bring the price up. Putting together a wire whisk with a special cookbook on sauces combines two inexpensive items into one nice sale.

These are logical offerings to the customer and should make the merchandise more attractive while adding to the bottom line of your catalog sales. A set of table napkins is an ordinary kind of gift selection; combined with a hard to find table runner that matches, it becomes an outstanding gift, even for oneself.

Another method for increasing the average order is to fill the catalog pages on either side of the order form with impulse items. Products with relatively low price points can stand alone as interesting offers. These items tend to be considered as "add-ons." As an order form is being filled out, a product from one of the facing pages also may be picked up.

The order form itself provides another opportunity for displaying impulse items. The products selected to appear on the order form should be unusual or, at the other extreme, very basic. Be sure that they can be understood easily in black and white if your order form is in one color and that the rougher textured paper generally used will not hurt the reproduction. Contents such as stainless steel, silver, plastic, and ceramic are well suited to black and white depiction.

Conceptualizing the Catalog

A successful catalog must have a point of view, a direction statement made by the selection of merchandise, the physical presentation of the book, and the quality and service offered. It requires up-front thinking time to define that direction and to establish point of view in presentation. Allow ample thinking time to idealize the objective and visualize the various solutions.

To begin the process, review all the available marketing information about the customer. Familiarize yourself thoroughly with the consumer's needs, lifestyle, and mail-order shopping habits. Review your competitors and learn their point of view. Then study the merchandise to be offered, seeking a common level of quality and depth of categories of products.

After a level of comfort has been attained with each of the foundation steps listed above, begin by writing notes on a legal pad or tablet. List organizational notes at first and then ideas.

Ideas tend to grow and to feed on each other. A creative approach to an objective can result in the generation of a wealth of thoughts. These thoughts become ideas, and then they can be fleshed out or added to.

As the ideas and thoughts crystallize on paper, begin to think in terms of rough thumbnail sketches. It is not necessary to be an artist to translate ideas successfully into small rough sketches. Notes written beside the thumbnails will help to capture random details of thought that may add a strong dimension to the idea.

Themes

If you are conceptualizing a lingerie catalog, you may see the entire merchandise offering shown out of context (i.e., out of the bedroom or dressing room). Perhaps you visualize it photographed in a beach setting at sundown. Jot your ideas down and rough in your thumbnail sketch of the physical format. Flesh out your thumbnails with additional details, such as using very soft filtration in photography to stress the softness of the subject matter. If you are thinking of sunset colors reflecting on water as a background, note it on your pad.

You'll find that the process of conceptualizing a catalog becomes easier if you allow your mind to open up to new thoughts. Be receptive to imagination and let creative ideas flow to your paper. The pen on paper at this point is there merely to translate thoughts into a more comprehensive way of storing and building. If you are more comfortable with words than with sketches, confine yourself to notes instead of rough drawings. Do not try to design the catalog unless you are an accomplished graphic designer. Just capture your thoughts and build them into ideas. When you are satisfied with your collection of ideas, turn them over to the catalog designer. Communicate your wishes for direction and give input to establish your point of view.

Themes can give a logic to the presentation of merchandise and can be used to establish your own catalog identity. A lingerie catalog photographed out of context on a beach is a theme in itself. An unexpected treatment of expected merchandise usually is received very well by the customer and is a way of marketing the merchandise and adding an element of entertainment.

Seasonal themes are used widely both for holiday presentation and for time of the year offerings. Christmas catalogs are now dropping in late August and early September in order to allow a long enough life span. Since that is early in the year to ask customers to think of Christmas shopping, it is important that a strong holiday theme be emphasized in presentation. Psychologically, we would like the customer to pull our catalog out of the mailbox and hear Christmas chimes and smell roasted turkey. Chances are that there are no chestnuts roasting over a crackling fire; more likely, when the book is received, there are hot dogs roasting in the backyard. Christmas shopping is hard to consider when the sounds you hear are not sleigh bells but splashing from the swimming pool.

While the late summer heat lingers on, attempt to create a feeling of crisp, cool holiday atmosphere. A Christmas theme can grow from studio-created snow sets, fireplaces, Christmas trees, candy canes, and candlelight. Saint Nick can backdrop his way through sixty pages or more, and ornaments can twinkle and glitter to set off your merchandise as if it were displayed in a beautifully wrapped package.

Entertainment for the Customer. A theme should never detract from the presentation of the merchandise but should enhance it. There is a certain amount of the child in all of us, including our customers. That childlike appreciation of being entertained and charmed can be appealed to by the catalog presentation. Customers enjoy using their imagination and should be given the opportunity to do so. This is why items shown out of context are found to be entertaining.

Random examples of subtle entertainment from some previously produced catalogs include a gold and diamond ring photographed on an antique cannonball; ruby earrings shown in closeup on a giant elephant ear leaf; a brass ashtray in the shape of a foot, shot in the sand; a pearl necklace photographed draped on the foot of a Greek statue; a crystal candlestick placed in a field of bluebonnets; a man's necktie draped over a nude woman's shoulder (close-cropped, of course); and a diamond goldfish pin shot in a glass of champagne.

It is not necessary to entertain totally out of context. Amusing and charming themes can be developed within the context of the product. For example, a tiny brass sculptured frog, a miniature collectible, was photographed on a real lily pad on a pond; a crystal apple paperweight was shot on a bed of shiny, red Delicious apples; an ivory hand-painted strawberry necklace was placed on a solid field of dewy fresh strawberries; coffee mugs were placed on piles of coffee beans, etc.

Merchandise presented for the customer's consideration in an interesting way, stimulating imagination and making the products more desirable, represents entertainment through a catalog. It requires thought and concept and consideration of the customer. It demands innovation and is limited only by your creative resources. Your customers will appreciate the creativity and thoughtfulness behind the presentation.

Marketing the Merchandise. The primary objective of any mail-order catalog is to sell merchandise. In conceptualizing the most effective way to present the merchandise to the customer, let common sense be your guide. Catalogs are a pictorial medium for selling, and interest must be obtained on behalf of the product by the photographic depiction. Entertainment, themes, setting, and backdrops must frame the item, not compete with it.

Pagination. The planning process of assigning each item of merchandise to a spread in the catalog is called pagination. Sometimes pagination is done by the buying staff. But more frequently and usually more effectively, it is assigned to the creative team, who have more of a distaff view of the merchandise and are less attached emotionally.

Pagination can be used to group items by special-interest category, tie in a theme, or logically place one product beside another. Many times the buying staff makes their merchandise selection with a specific theme in mind. However, there are times when you are confronted with over 100 separate items presented for inclusion in a catalog with no definitive direction for their grouping. In these cases, the process of pagination begins when the merchandise is viewed by the creative staff, a time in the overall production schedule called merchandise presentation or line closing.

Products may be grouped by seasonality, color of the merchandise, category, or logic of use. It is important to remember in paginating as well as in design that the customer views catalogs spread by spread, with a facing two-page spread standing alone as a visual unit. The only exception to this rule would be pages that are separated by the order form. They should be presented as single-page concepts since they are set apart physically by the bound-in order form.

If a theme such as home entertainment is formulated for a spread, it should be explained to the customer with a headline, and the pagination should include logical products. Buffet organizers, patio dresses, brightly colored plastic dishes, garden candles, pool umbrellas, and serving dishes are naturals for informal entertaining. This kind of pagination presents items in an interesting way and also suggests actual uses.

Realization and Catalog Production

Mail-order catalogs are an expensive medium for advertising and must be cost-effective. Adherence to a production schedule and budget will prevent costly extras on the bottom line, and submitting accurate specifications to production suppliers is imperative in establishing the schedule and budget.

Preparation of Specifications. In order to obtain realistic bids for catalog printing and color separations, a set of specific requirements on the job must be submitted to suppliers. These specifications always should be in written form, preferably typed, never verbal instructions by telephone. When layouts for the catalog have been approved, photocopies should be sent to the separator for confirmation of the bid. It is possible to have more or fewer random focus enlargements in a book than originally anticipated, and this factor can alter the job estimate drastically.

Specifications for the printer should include the following:

1. Date of submission
2. Date of requested estimate to be received
3. Name of client
4. Title of catalog
5. Requested press date
6. Begin mail drop date and complete mail drop date
7. Date of remail drop if required
8. Quantity, including acceptable over and under run
9. Bind-in order form information
10. Furnished film information
11. Press configuration requested (sixteen- or thirty-two-page form)
12. Request for press imposition running dummy
13. Trim size of catalog

14. Number of pages (indicate plus cover when required)
15. Request breakout of charges separately
16. Mailing and label information (cost per request qualified quantity estimate; type of label)
17. Ink coverage and expected density maximum
18. Paper specifications by text and cover categories; specify weight and brand; if equivalent paper is acceptable, so state
19. Special requirements, e.g., use of fifth unit for color or varnish
20. Whether final set of chromalins is required
21. A copy of a previous issue

On approval of the completed layout, submit a photocopied set to the printing representative to avoid costly surprises.

Working closely with the representatives from the separator and printer will facilitate the production of the catalog. Frequently, this results in time- and money-saving ideas that add up to a better finished product.

A good policy is to submit your specifications to three printers and two separators. Comparative bid study is healthy and educational, although it is not recommended that you assign a contract strictly on the basis of the lowest estimate. Be sure that you are comparing apples and apples and place a critical eye on previous samples for quality.

The Production Schedule. About 120 days are required to produce a top-quality thirty-six-page catalog. While this type of schedule is somewhat formulated, it does allow sufficient but not excessive time for each of the vital elements in catalog production.

Day 1 Merchandise presentation to creative
Day 2 Pagination
Day 3 Pagination approval
Day 4 Begin layouts
Day 18 Layout approval
Day 19 Production meeting with photography studio
Day 20 Begin photography and copy
Day 50 Photography and copy approval
Day 51 Begin mechanical art
Day 62 Mechanical art approval
Day 65 Final mechanical art changes incorporated
Day 66 Turnover to color separator
Day 96 Press proofs (ink on paper)
Day 105 Final chromalin proofs
Day 114 Film to printer
Day 120 Press make-ready

The Budget. To study a catalog budget is to take a look at harsh reality. Talent is expensive, and paper and printing are equally costly. The monies allocated for catalog production never should be spent lightly. Rely on support people with a proven track record of experience in catalog marketing. Do your delegating to professionals who will watch after the job as if it were their own money being spent.

The budget for catalog and order form production should include estimates for the following, each broken out:

1. Creative design and photo art direction
2. Copywriting
3. Photography
    a. Still life
    b. Fashion
    c. Film and processing
    d. Stylist, hair and makeup, and presser
    e. Props and rentals
    f. Models
4. Photo retouching
5. Typography and positioning of photostats
6. Stripped assemblies
7. Illustration
8. Mechanical art
9. Supervision of color separations
10. Press make-ready supervision
11. Freight and deliveries
12. Air fare and per diem
13. Miscellaneous (phone calls and photocopies)
14. Color separations and proofing
15. Order form printing and paper
16. Printing of catalogs
17. Paper stock for catalogs
18. Mailing charges
19. Postage
20. List rental (including merge and purge)
21. Label charges and lettershop
22. Binding of order form

TESTING

Concepts may be tested, products can be tried out, and graphic techniques can be pitted one against another. However, this is an expensive educational process. In order to change a four-color process image, you must be prepared to spend additional dollars. Simple copy changes are less expensive unless you make changes in an area of reverse copy, and this involves all four plates being remade.

Good graphics sell better than bad graphics. Why not put your best foot forward and present the merchandise up front in the most effective way. Even low-end catalogs should strive to improve their presentation.

Testing has proved that remails to the house list work effectively in spurring response, particularly at the Christmas mailing time. A new cover will help, and the amortized cost of production is reasonable.

Through tests we also have learned that an outside mailing wrap around the cover of a catalog is not well received by the upscale customer. While mailing wraps are acceptable for lower-end books, a high-ticket catalog loses credibility when a wrapper is used. This is true even of wraps that are well designed and tasteful in appearance. Don't waste your money on a technique that already has been discarded by many knowledgeable upscale catalog marketers.

CREATIVE TECHNIQUES

You'll find the most flexibility at your disposal in this segment of the total production. Don't copy someone else's format or techniques. Innovate in order to achieve your own image; imaginate to establish your catalog's credibility. Although catalogers work in a two-dimension medium, there are ways to set each catalog apart. Technique almost becomes a signature; presentation of your paper store is yours to develop, polish, and refine until it shines like a jewel and makes the right statement to the customer.

Innovation and imagination are the keys to producing a unique catalog presentation. The look and feel of the book will state your point of view and establish your image and credibility in the customer's mind. A catalog that obviously looks as if time, attention, and caring were devoted to producing it infers that the customer's order will be treated the same way. The perception of being a trustworthy mail-order firm results in sales and repeat customers. The orders must be fulfilled promptly and accurately, and the products should be received exactly as they are depicted in the catalog. Customer service must be professional, reliable, and consistently good.

Special techniques to set your catalog apart require creativity and vision and a lot of up-front work. You are entitled to your own look, your catalog's indentity. Insist on it from your creative sources, whether they are in-house, freelance, or an outside studio. Do not accept a graphic format that is merely the signature of a certain catalog designer or a knock-off of someone else's image. When you contract for catalog design, you are paying for creativity; be sure that you get it.

Catalog Design and Formats

While it is not necessary to reinvent the wheel each time a catalog is produced, it is highly recommended that catalogers be aware of the fact that design can be updated and improved on. There is no state of the art that remains consistent for catalog design, which is continually changing and becoming more dramatic. Among the flood of catalogs currently being received by the mail-order customer, more and more of these books look alike.

The Two-Page Visual Spread. As was mentioned before, a customer perceives a catalog in two-page visual units. A spread should be designed with this in mind. The best way to approach it is to visualize the two pages as one complete unit, almost like a blank canvas in front of a painter. You also can think of the spread as space in a display case or window, since a store window is seen as a whole rather than in small sections.

Consider the merchandise to be marketed as single elements that must work together on the spread. Each must be given its proper positioning and best display opportunity. Think of the products and their use rather than zeroing in on an item because it has an interesting shape.

Combining the elements on the spread in layout form begins the process of establishing the format. The design format should not be so rigid that every spread looks exactly the same. Allow for some flexibility or you risk having your catalog look boring.

Pacing. By varying the spreads with design format, you can control to a degree the physical speed with which a customer goes through your book. Achieving this control is called pacing, and it can be used to encourage the consumer to linger in certain areas of your catalog presentation. If the book is essentially light in feeling with lots of white space and light background colors, try varying the presentation by placing two or more spreads through the catalog to achieve a heavy visual impact. They can be bleed photos (running off the page top, bottom, and sides) or high-density backgrounds that depict a richness in color saturation.

Another design technique to achieve pacing involves using the entire spread for one shot of merchandise. You must be sure that nothing will get lost in a group shot if this idea is considered. A basic rule is to have merchandise for the grouping that is of a similar size scale.

A crossover (or full bleed spread) shot must be controlled carefully for quality reproduction at press make-ready. Be sure that the pages, even if run on different forms, are lined up next to each other before you approve a sheet for color. An imbalance of ink on one side can result in an obvious break between the pages, destroying the objective of drama and the believability of the catalog. There is enough control on the press to be able to balance the crossovers effectively. But it is unwise to design a crossover that breaks an intricate pattern in the middle or one that splits the picture down the middle of a model's face because of slight variability in binding.

Eye Movement Direction. The eyes of the customer can be led gently around the visual spread by the design of the elements and directional use of the merchandise or models. Since the left-hand page is weaker on first impact than the right-hand page, it is important to make that page work harder. A large photograph on the extreme left side will gain the customer's attention. If the depiction is a fashion shot, the model's physical attitude or pose can direct the customer from this shot into the adjacent one. The model's eyes should be looking back into the spread, not off the page.

Placement of the other elements on the spread should nudge the customer's eyes gently from one to the next so that everything is perceived at a glance. Further impact can be obtained with dramatic lighting or display to slow the physical act of leaving the spread and moving on to the following one.

The Use of White Space. A portrait is seen better when framed, and a merchandise depiction is cleaner and more understandable when framed by white space. In addition to adding to the impact of a color shot, white space should be used generously to tie together all the diverse elements in a spread. White space provides a relief to the customer's eye, a respite from the richness of multiple items shown on strong backgrounds. Don't hesitate to give your customer this break.

Many merchants object to leaving white space on a spread; they assume that valuable selling space is being lost. There are no definite results that lend authenticity to their theory, and so you must choose your own direction on the basis of your philosophy of catalog marketing. Before you opt for a crammed, busy format, examine the success of catalogs whose look is more open and clean, such as Horchow and American Express.

The Use of Themes. Entertainment is an important ingredient in catalog marketing. A theme can be woven throughout the book by combining your merchandise with interesting photographic backgrounds and appropriate props and accessories. Themes can serve to humanize a catalog as well as to entertain.

In the G. Willikers 1981 toy catalog for the Singer Corporation, a new star made her debut. She was a small, black, fuzzy kitten with charming white whiskers and startled golden eyes. We promptly named her Eartha Kitty, and her pictures are found throughout the catalog, scaling a set of building blocks here, napping beside a pajama bag there. She peeps from a magic hat and plays chess with a little boy. Eartha was added to the book to soften the hard sell of toys, and the customers loved her. While the kitten was well received as an entertaining element of this catalog, we had to abandon plans to use her talent in subsequent books. She grew up too quickly and became a big, ordinary cat without the appeal of her previous stage.

Positioning. Positioning the catalog to the customer can help in determining a theme. If your catalog is aimed at active sports enthusiasts, your positioning should be perceived as that of an authority on sporting activities and related merchandise. It is better to photograph on tennis courts and golf courses, showing the models involved and having fun, than to stand the figures like fashion sticks in front of a no-seam. Be sure to check the details, such as how the model holds a tennis racket. If you are shooting a chess game as a still life, have a knowledgeable chess player set up the board.

Editorial Content within a Catalog. The use of some editorial copy content can achieve several points. It can help establish you as an authority on the merchandise. Editorials also can be entertaining and educational for the customer. Used discriminately, editorials can enhance the desirability of the products.

Bill Nicolai's Early Winters Catalog celebrated its tenth anniversary in 1982 with an issue that contained 32 pages (of a 132-page catalog) of editorial content on nature, the animal world, and exotic places such as Africa and the Himalayas. Well-presented editorial copy enforced this catalog's authenticity. The content was intensely interesting and almost like a present. While this issue of Early Winters was created especially to celebrate an anniversary, the ambience of nature and the outdoors became entwined with positioning for merchandising authority.

The 100 pages of merchandise offerings further support the credibility of this outdoor equipment catalog. The products are shown in believable outdoor locations, and the models are people who look like they spend their leisure time hiking, camping out, trekking, participating in white water trips, etc.

Designing with Typography, Borders, and Silhouettes. A careful and tasteful use of available graphic elements can add further identity to a catalog as well as tie a spread together. Borders (straight ruled lines of any desired thickness) and decorative borders frequently are used to enclose photos individually or all the way across a spread, uniting the whole presentation of copy and photography. They also can be designed to work physically as a unit with headline treatments. Most catalogs have so many items that the use of borders becomes one element too many. Unless a limited number of products are shown, it is better to present them in the most straightforward manner graphically, forgoing the use of decorative borders or other visual gimmicks.

Borders never should be added after the fact. If they are to be considered at all, they should be a basic part of the design concept. Borders that will be run in color should be simplified as much as possible, avoiding any registration problems that may occur in printing. A clean, thin black rule can crisp up a photo with a very light background, but rules of this kind should be used consistently if at all.

Typographic treatment is another vital design element, one that should be planned as the catalog layout is created. Since copy and type are a sustaining part of the overall format, it is wise to limit the number of typefaces within a catalog. The headline treatment should be one size and face, and the body copy should be specified in one size and face. It is acceptable to vary the body copy with boldface or italic for lead-ins or price points, but these should be within the same typeface selected for the body copy. Too many different typefaces and sizes will present a jumbled appearance and draw the customer's attention away from the primary selling tool: the photograph.

If headlines are considered, they should explain the presentation. If they are not necessary, eliminate them to simplify the spread. The typographic treatment of headlines should be consistent throughout, whether you opt for serif, sans serif, all caps, boldface, italic, script, or calligraphy. Headlines are like an announcement. Keep them informative and entertaining in both content and presentation.

In addition to the use of silhouettes, photos may be shown in circles to vary the design, or they may be partially silhouetted. A photograph can be square-finished on three sides, for instance, and have the item outlined just at the bottom. Or the color-butting-color technique can be considered, where a color shot fits directly into another color shot. Both silhouettes and color-butting-color techniques are interesting design options, but they increase the cost of your already expensive color separation process. Have your engraver give you a laundry list of extra charges for these requirements so that you'll know what additional charges may be incurred.

Mechanical Tints. These represent the most misused application of color in catalog design. By definition, they involve the use of a tint of color created by combining screens of the process colors. Found usually in the lower-end catalogs, they appear in upscale books as well. The use or misuse of mechanical tints in catalog design tends to cheapen the overall perception and presentation. The reason is simple: The eye functions like the lens of a camera. When color is seen, all four of the color process spectra are perceived in varying degrees of density. In mechanical tints, an even screen of one or more colors is applied. In other words, mechanical tints are colors created falsely, not naturally to the eye, and are perceived as unbelievable. The whiteness of the paper should be considered as the cleanest frame available for copy and photography.

A Nondemocratic Merchandise Display. The most interesting way to present items to the customer is to vary the sizes of depiction. Little square boxes of equal size presented all the way through a catalog are boring.

Do not be afraid to make a statement about a product by giving it more space. Tell the customer that it is unique, exclusive, a fabulous design, or a great value by showing it importantly. Let it work for you by slowing the readers' action as they go through the book. Use it as a punctuation mark on your visual display: a comma at the very least, or more desirably, a semicolon or exclamation mark.

There is no established rule that says you must be democratic in the treatment of graphic display. Merchants and buyers always express a wish for everything to be large on the page, but it is difficult to accomplish this with multiple items and lots of descriptive copy to work with. Something must give. Working creatively with layout to determine space allocation will give you the flexibility needed to come up with a solution, making some items a feature or minifeature and giving smaller space to others that don't require as much space to sell.

Grid Design. Many catalogs present a format by grid design. As the name implies, the layout is accomplished by taking the page or spread and dividing it equally on a mathematical basis for merchandise display. It is as democratic and uncreative as you can get with graphic design. As a matter of fact, grid design could be done equally well by a draftsperson; you don't really need a designer to set out equal square boxes. A computer can produce your catalog layouts in grid design, but you'll have a book that just lies there instead of one that is emotional and persuasive.

Design to Avoid Problems on Press. Ask your printer to provide you with a press imposition dummy and be sure that your designer has this information before beginning the layout. Technical problems can be avoided by knowing the page sequence on press. Large, heavy blocks of density followed by a light use of ink may result in a condition called ghosting. The heavy requirement of ink on press in a strategic area will not give the press a chance to recover and equalize quickly enough for smooth ink application immediately behind it. The imposition dummy will show your designer where to avoid these situations. Very few surprises in catalog production turn out to be good ones. Usually they are disappointments that cost a lot of money.

Physical Format Sizes. Economically, catalog sizes are dictated by press requirements. Most people elect to produce a catalog that best fits the presses, realizing the maximum efficiency of manufacturing for both printing and paper. Traditionally, the most economical catalog size for web printing has been 8⅜ inches wide by 10⅞ inches deep, with thirty-two pages. Pages should be planned in eight-page increments.

The variations are many. You can add a plus cover form, which is usually on heavier paper stock, to present a more important feel to the book. A sixteen-page body form can be combined with a four-page cover form to produce a twenty-page catalog. Digest, or half-size, catalogs are extremely economical but present less space for display. Williams-Sonoma, the Catalog for Cooks, is well known for its digest format.

Your printing representative will make you aware of special features that are available on particular press equipment, such as thirty-two-page forms, fifth units, in-line binding, etc. If you are deviating from the standard press cutoffs, be prepared to waste paper. To some catalogers this wasted paper is worth the effect of looking different in the mailbox.

The Cover

The first and most important impression of your catalog must be obtained by the cover. From the time a catalog is retrieved from the mailbox, it has exactly 3½ seconds to gain the customer's attention. This means that the cover of a catalog must work effectively to communicate your message. It must say hello, remind the customers that they have met before, promise that tantalizing merchandise is shown in the contents, and assure the credibility and reliability of the catalog company—all within the 3½ seconds allotted by the customer for a first impression.

There are essentially three current theories of catalog cover concepts: a merchandised presentation; an editorial approach, nonmerchandised; and a combination cover showing merchandise treated editorially. Each technique has its own merits and potential for capturing attention, but since the cover can be the number one selling space, a merchandised cover usually is used.

On catalogs whose cover approach involves combining an item with an esoteric or editorial technique, the back cover may be used to show the same product more within a practical context and for the selling copy. American Express's Expressly Yours Catalog has presented several issues this way, always incorporating the American Express credit card editorially.

Bachrach's covers are merchandised, showing men's wear on a model, but at the same time they depict an atmosphere that creates image and ambience. Williams-Sonoma covers also are merchandised, and the product is enhanced by a wonderful gourmet concoction.

Establishing a cover format is a good idea so that the customer will build an awareness of your catalog company each time a new issue is received. Flexibility with an established format hinges on the amount of creative thinking invested. It should be limitless.

Encourage your designer to be idealistic about the cover concept. Communicate your point of view so that the artist can interpret it into a graphic approach. Think of your customers and how best to approach them. Emphasis should be placed on dramatic treatment for the cover. This can be achieved through lighting in photography, which provides a way to set a mood or establish a feeling. Dark, rich colors of heavy density portray a luxurious image. On the other hand, a technique of light, high key colors can create a subtle understatement of elegance. Lighting and use of color should be considered creatively for maximum beauty and drama.

If the cover is merchandised, select an item that is representative of the product mix inside the book. Judge your selection for uniqueness, exclusivity, and potential for dramatic portrayal. More drama can be obtained by zeroing in on one special item than by showing a collage of merchandise, and so it is generally best to pick one product for your cover feature. An item that is somewhat ordinary by description can become extraordinary in portrayal if you find a new way to illustrate its use. For example, a tall glass vase becomes a cover possibility when shown as a receptacle for a matchbook collection. Or depict it with colorful layers of jelly beans. Or fill it with water and float a candle in it. Let your imagination run free. Anybody can show a vase with pretty flowers in it. It takes creativity to market a product in an askance, or out of context, way.

Analyze the Effectiveness of Your Own Covers. Be honest with yourself and allow your eyes and mind to see that cover as your customer would. Does it capture your attention in 3½ seconds? Does it peak your interest and make you wonder what is inside? Do you want to open up the book to see? Do you recognize the logo as an old friend? Do you anticipate finding an interesting mix of merchandise inside? Do you understand what is being offered? Do you perceive the company as reliable and professional? Does the book have a quality look and a good tactile feeling? Would you like to receive it in your mailbox?

The answers to all these harshly judgmental questions should be yes if your cover is working effectively for you. If you had to answer no to any of them, review the reasons for a negative response. Work on that aspect for your next cover and try to improve. Chances are that if you answered negatively, your customer would also. Remind yourself that in mail-order catalogs, a book certainly can be judged by its cover.

PHOTOGRAPHY

The single most important graphic element in catalogs is photography. Catalogs are a pictorial medium. The customer's attention is obtained first by the photography. Descriptive copy may close the sale, but the photograph must generate interest.

Photography generally is chosen over illustration for catalogs because customers find it easier to relate to and seem to accord more credibility to it as an advertising medium.

Essentially, catalog photography can be broken down into two major categories.

Still Life or Table Top Shots

These are photographs of inanimate products presented for the customer's consideration. They can be executed in the studio or on location.

Fashion Shots

These are clothing shots, shown on a model to illustrate fit and features. They also can be photographed in a studio or on location.

Studio Still Life Shots. These usually are shot to size for actual size reproduction on view camera equipment of 4 by 5 inches, 5 by 7 inches, or 8- by 10-inch film size. Shooting to size eliminates the need for random focus enlargement or reduction and is the most economical way to turn over photography to the color separator.

The photographer should shoot to fit the layout; normally, an acetate tracing of the actual space depiction is used to line up the shot. A Polaroid test shot before exposure on the view camera can be used to check composition and lighting.

Bracketed exposures (at least one f-stop up and one stop down) should be made for a choice of densities. While film and processing is expensive, it is less costly to bracket than to reshoot. If you are in doubt as to which exposure is best for color and density, let your separator guide you in making a final choice.

Lighting Techniques. These contribute heavily to the success of any shot. Dramatic lighting will portray the products best, allowing for emphasis on special features. One style of studio lighting that has worked well for many catalogs involves darkening the background of the sweep for drop-off lighting to the foreground. This provides a spotlight effect for the product, framing dramatically. A shot with a wide scale of density has more dimension and is more interesting than flat lighting that appears to have no sparkle or life.

If an art director is not available on the set, the photographer should be allowed some creative license to turn an item slightly for a better view or add a minispot to pick up a detail.

Still-Life Location Shots. When a fashion book is planned as a location shooting, it is wise to incorporate some of the still-life shots on location too. This gives the catalog a look of continuity and can be entertaining for the customer. Even if you cannot plan each still-life shot in advance for precise location, you know which products can be transported easily. A natural, complimentary setting can be decided on at the scene.

Location Shoots

These can firmly establish a theme for a book and allow us to take advantage of nature's perfect lighting. (We can never truly simulate outdoor lighting in a studio.) There are three areas of difficulty in location shooting: It must be planned well in advance; there can be problems with the logistics of moving merchandise, crew, models, and equipment from place to place; and bad weather may occur.

Foreign Location Shoots. Through an exchange of promotional services, it may prove more economical to shoot in a foreign country halfway around the world than to shoot in a local studio. By working with an airline and the tourist organization of the country to be visited, a catalog company with a large distribution to the right demographic market can offer a page for promotion of travel to that part of the world. The exchange is usually for all airline travel expenses, hotel accommodations, ground transportation, guides, and sometimes food.

Deals can be struck with the models for less than their usual day rate and excluding travel time. The same is true for the stylist, art director, and photographer's assistant.

Communications to plan and execute a trip like this are detailed and should be done at least 6 months in advance of the shoot. Here is a checklist for procedure when considering a foreign location.

1. Establish contact with the sponsoring airline.
2. Establish contact (usually through the airline) with the tourist organization representative.

3. Get the agreement on exchange of promotional services in writing and signed by all parties.
4. Plan the dates for the actual shooting, allowing 3 or 4 days longer than necessary in the event of bad weather.
5. If possible, make an advance scouting trip to the country to select possible shooting sites.
6. Go to the library and check out books for research on the country. Familiarize yourself with geographic and cultural points of interest. Learn about the customs. Your crew will be guests in a foreign country. Never take the risk of offending the local residents as a result of lack of knowledge about their customs.
7. Get advance clearance for the shipment of merchandise and camera equipment in writing from the airline (including no overweight charge), from the tourist organization, and from U.S. Customs.
8. List and tag all merchandise and camera equipment.
9. Be sure that all members of the crew understand their job responsibilities. Brief them on customs, passport information, required vaccines, drinking water and food, and expected behavior.
10. Finalize all ground arrangements, e.g., rental of van, services of an interpreter, etc.
11. Go back over the entire list again.

Details should not be overlooked because they can make the difference between breezing into a country to start right to work and having your merchandise or camera equipment confiscated at the point of entry.

Familiarizing yourself with the customs of a foreign country is a courtesy you should be willing to extend. It can help avoid embarrassing incidents and will assure a welcome for a repeat visit. Seemingly small things can be important. You and your crew should conduct yourselves professionally and with studied courtesy.

In China and Nepal, it is forbidden for women to wear short shorts that expose their legs. In Thailand, it is an insult to the person in front of you if you cross your legs, and you should never step over someone's extended legs or feet in that country. In most African countries, it is an insult if the voice is raised. In French Polynesia, the natives would be embarrassed if you offered them a tip. In all countries, including your own, it is unacceptable to leave a location site less clean than you found it. Always inquire politely for permission before you take anyone's photograph. The Masai tribe in Africa believes that if you snap their pictures without permission, you are stealing their souls. You may run the risk of having your camera snatched away and stamped into the earth.

If you choose tight cropping, eliminating any feeling of location, you should be shooting in a studio in the first place. Don't make the mistake of shooting in a wonderfully interesting place and then cropping out all the atmosphere. Most catalogers who shoot on location commit this grievous error. It infuriates the sponsoring airline and country and makes it very difficult for the other catalogers to arrange anything with a country that considers itself to have been betrayed by tightly cropped photographs.

Imaginative, Organized Art Direction

On all photographic shoots, this will ensure the best possible end results. The art director is ultimately responsible for showing the merchandise to its maximum advantage. An art director with marketing ability will recognize optimum shooting potential, whether in a studio or on location. Shapes, colors, textures, lighting, and contrast will be received by an art director almost with a tactile sense. Opportunity becomes more than a challenge for this talented person; it becomes excitement.

The art director becomes the orchestrator on a shoot, pulling the best efforts from the support crew, which consists of the photographer, stylist, hair and makeup person, photographic assistant, and models. Rapport must be established for a smooth shooting; respect must be given and received. Communication is the key to achieving this objective.

In a typical fashion shoot, the crew functions as a team, each with his or her own role responsibility and high degree of professionalism. The art director and photographer select the location or backdrop together, based on theme, contrast, interest, and lighting. The hair and makeup person prepares the model, and the stylist pulls the clothing and accessories. The assistant loads the cameras and sets up reflectors or strobes. When the shoot begins, the art director is stationed directly behind the photographer, watching the composition of the shot. The stylist should be closely attendant for details such as wrinkles, buttons, threads, etc. The model takes direction from both the photographer and the art director.

If clients are on the set, their input should go through the creative team, not directly to the model. Too many voices shouting instructions will destroy the ambience. A client should make wishes known through the art director, who will convey the information to the model or to the photographer or stylist. Most clients have a tendency to step into the set to straighten a tie or tug on a hem. That responsibility belongs to the stylist and should stay there.

Model Selection. This should be done with your customer in mind. Choose models who fit your marketing input on your customer profile as closely as possible. Of course, they should look prettier or more handsome, because a catalog is a wish book, and all people wish to look more attractive than they do in reality.

Propping and Accessorizing. A decision to prop a still life item should be based on whether the product needs to be scaled for size or explained for use. There is a tendency in current catalogs to overprop. Use props to show how an item is to be used or to suggest an alternative use if the usual one is readily understood.

Props also are used to show immediate scaling for size. For instance, a child's bank is both explained as a bank and scaled by showing coins in the shot.

Overuse of props will clutter a book and detract from the merchandise. Use props only when they will help the customer understand the product better. A clean, straightforward graphic presentation is still the best. You have the selling copy with which to answer all the anticipated questions. Don't attempt to do it all in photography.

Shot Composition. This refers to the arrangement of merchandise within the designated display space. The items should be arranged in an interesting composition, incorporating any required props artistically. The cropping of the photograph can enhance the composition, making it even more appealing. Angle of the product becomes important in composing before the camera and should be determined by the merchandise itself.

Before photography begins, a layout qualification meeting should be held for the entire creative team. Schedule it to take place a day or two before you start photography. Invite the art director, photographers, and assistants assigned to the project; the stylist; the scheduler or traffic manager; and the copywriter.

Qualifying the Layouts. This involves explaining every shot that will be required of the team. Communicate the theme, mood, or concept of the whole catalog. Describe backdrops required, sets to be built, accessories and props to be obtained, models to be booked, and whether you want coffee shown in the mugs. Discuss drop shadows for silhouette shots, acrylic versus no-seam or painted backgrounds, and desired special effects such as lighting, color, or use of slight filtration.

Use this qualification meeting as a well-organized planning session. It will save time, money, and frustration in the long run. An informed team will function more efficiently, and pride of authorship will be reflected in the finished catalog.

Photo Retouching. This should be kept to a minimum. With the advent of supersensitive scanners for color separation, retouching tends to show through. Use it sparingly to correct minor flaws in the merchandise. Do not attempt to change the color of a product completely by retouching. Get another sample in the correct color and reshoot the photograph. Don't try to cover up bad photography with retouching.

COPY

Catalog copy is the informational mode that augments the primary selling tool of photography. Like the other graphic elements, it should be considerate of the customer.

Since most of the selling space is allotted to pictorial depiction, copywriters must be intensely disciplined in their use of words for catalog copy.

Basic Rules of Catalog Copy

1. Be as concise as possible.
2. Be informative and descriptive.
   - **a.** Give size and weight where applicable.
   - **b.** List contents.
   - **c.** Suggest the use or an alternative use.
   - **d.** List the unit number, price, and postage.
   - **e.** Give a shortened, descriptive tag or lead-in.
3. Avoid clichés and slang usage.
4. Write to fit the layout.

The client should provide the copywriter with filled-in merchandise information sheets (MIS) and with access to the products for touching and seeing. The MIS should contain all the available information about each item, including fabric content, country of origin, exclusivity, measurements and weight, etc.

Inclusion of Personalization

Some catalogs have descriptive copy written in first-person form for style. If a strong personality is associated with the book, this approach seems well received by the customer. Perhaps in these days of impersonal service in retailing, this touch of personalization is appreciated in mail order. At the very least, it is suggested that an opening letter of greeting or introduction be used in catalogs, ideally signed by the president of the company. An identity that the customer can relate to is an important consideration for all catalogs.

Merchandise That Requires Longer Copy

Some items need more descriptive copy than others. The layout artist should be made aware of those products in order to allow more space for copy. Electronic items need more words to explain technical features. Expensive stereo sets must be described by outlining all the components and special parts. To sell a cruise around the world with a price point of several thousand dollars requires a profusion of pretty words and exotic-sounding names. Common sense should be used to determine which items need longer copy.

THE PSYCHOLOGY OF COLOR

The use of color is an important motivational factor in presenting merchandise for sale in a catalog. Recent research has proved that people react emotionally to colors. Some colors sooth, and others excite. One color will suppress, and another will initiate. Since color is one of the primary selling tools in catalog marketing, we should educate ourselves about the effects and emotions colors are capable of evoking.

Male customers respond best to earth tones, or colors of nature, such as warm browns, rusts, grays, greens, and blues. Women are partial to softer, more pastel colors and to rich, glossy blacks and pristine whites. Red is an action-oriented color and serves to motivate. Very soft pink is a soothing tone but does not promote movement or activity. Harsh, magenta-type pinks are irritating colors and cause a customer to turn the page to avoid the color.

Colors of the sky, blues of all shades, are acceptable to both sexes, as are greens in all shades. Ivory, when used as a fashion backdrop color, makes flesh tones appear more "peachy" and pleasing. Yellows are sunshine colors and are received well as backgrounds. Warm gray is better for framing merchandise than cool gray; beige is another shade that is most effective toward the warm scale. Silver is restful to the eye, and goldtones are rich colors. Orange should be avoided as it is a violent color and detracts from almost any other color around or in front of it.

Just as the eye will follow any light, the mind reacts to color without thought or deliberation. Out of consideration to the customer, use of colors within catalogs should be pleasing as opposed to displeasing. Contemplative colors invite longer perusal of photographs. With a palette of nature's colors at our disposal, we should be able to create catalogs that promote ease on behalf of our customers and frame our merchandise considerately.

CAMERA-READY ART

This refers to the preparation of catalog material to be turned over for separations. Camera-ready art should be prepared professionally and accurately. Mechanical artboards are flats done to size with photostats of the photographs trimmed, cropped, and mounted in position. All type, including headlines, body copy, and photo keys, is set and pasted up in position on the boards. Each flat is covered with a tissue overlay that is marked with special instructions such as reverse copy blocks, color borders, silhouette with drop shadows, etc.

THE ORDER FORM

Most catalog mailers have chosen the preformed order form to be bound into the book. A few still are using the die-cut flat order form that must be folded by the customer. The copy style should be brief and to the point. A complicated order form can be overwhelming, causing a prospective customer to abandon any thought of ordering. If you keep the design clean and understandable and structure the copy in a simple, instructive way, the customer won't be discouraged at first glance. For customers who prefer to order by phone, the toll-free number should be displayed prominently on the order form as well as throughout the catalog.

The order form may be planned to run in one color or in two or more colors. Four-color-process order forms are more expensive to produce than one- or two-color ones, and it is doubtful that enough additional sales will come in to justify the expense.

THE BIRTH OF THE BOOK

After all the caring that has been invested in the building of a catalog from the merchandising and creative end, it is natural to be a little nervous when the finish approaches. The birth of the book is imminent whenever you get to the color separation stage. All the labor pains will have been worth it when the catalog is born.

Color Separations

Separations are done by scanner or by conventional camera, and some correction work usually is required. When the color proofs are submitted with type in position, it requires a full day of marking up the press sheets or chromalins for an average catalog job. At this point in the schedule, you or your print production manager should go over each transparency again, comparing it with the proof. If you don't have the technical expertise to tell the separator how to correct, simply point out how it looks to you and let the separator interpret the move.

Final press proofs or chromalin proofs usually are provided to show the corrections that were made. Minor changes may be made at this stage if time has been allowed before the film is due at the printer.

The Press Run

It is an exciting feeling to walk into a pressroom and get your first whiff of ink and hear the presses roaring. The books come off the finishing line at an incredible speed, and a blink of the eye will cause you to miss several hundred impressions as the signatures are folded and trimmed.

The press make-ready is the startup time before signatures are saved, when the registration is fine-tuned and the color is balanced. Web printing does provide for some flexibility on press for minor color adjustments. But if you are doing the make-ready okay yourself, know what you are asking for and be aware of the compromises that must be made on press. Radical alterations at this point are not advisable.

Very few press okays run strictly on schedule; be prepared to be patient if you are waiting in the customer lounge for your invitation to the pressroom. If the printing salesperson suggests a game of gin or a tour of the plant, relax; it won't take too long. But if the suggestion is for dinner and a tour of the city, it's going to take quite a while. A general rule of thumb is to add 2 more hours to any estimated time given. A printing press is a complex, multifaceted piece of technology, and it can be complicated getting the job running. Give them the time they need to make it right for you.

Once the balancing of colors and adjustments has been done, you are ready to sign the press sheet. Don't forget to be courteous to the press crew. A smile and a thank you will help them feel that their efforts were appreciated.

As you cradle the new catalog on your way out of the plant, you'll start to think about the next issue: ways to make it better, things you've learned from this one, how you can improve the cover concept, or maybe even a new format approach.

EPILOG

As the number of catalogs in the mailbox grows, so does the level of sophistication of the customer. The demands grow on our ingenuity, innovativeness, and imagination to make smarter-looking, better catalogs. Our customers want to see more, and they want to be entertained and sweet-talked. While you're at it, show them something new and different.

The emphasis in this chapter has been on marketing, merchandising, and creative graphics. This is not meant to imply that this combination alone will produce a successful catalog company. All our suggestions have been tested and proved and will produce a successful catalog when they are applied effectively. But to build a sound catalog business you must apply equal parts of good management, order fulfillment, and customer service in addition to outstanding catalog marketing pieces.

Catalog marketing has become a science, appealing to the senses and desires of the mail-order customer. What has created this phenomenon in advertising? Remember the days of your childhood when the long-awaited Captain Marvel secret signal code ring arrived in your mailbox. Consuming all those boxes of cereal to accumulate enough box tops became worth it with the excitement of opening that package. Our Captain Marvel rings now come in boxes labeled Horchow, American Express, Sharper Image, Neiman-Marcus, Lilian Vernon, L. L. Bean, and Saks Fifth Avenue. The mystique of the mailbox lives on.

chapter **47**

MAIL-ORDER SALES

Eller D. Rama

Marketing Director
Rodale Books
Emmaus, Pa.

How do you make the most of your current products? How do you maximize the profit potential of your current markets? This chapter will examine some techniques for achieving these twin goals. Case histories will be provided to illustrate each major technique.

Although the cases involve only books, the data could be translated easily to fit other types of mail-order merchandise. Books have a lot in common with products that are best suited for mail-order sales. Some of these similarities are as follows.

1. As with most mail-order products, retail distribution of books is limited, making nonstore selling a potentially profitable alternative.
2. Prices are relatively easy to use as a basis for making a buying decision.
3. The products are easy to describe in promotion (generally, no effort need be made to explain color, size, smell, etc.).
4. Every product (that is, every title) is in a sense unique.

MAXIMIZING THE POTENTIAL OF YOUR PRODUCTS

Rather than take each individual product separately, we will look at the mix of products you now have as a portfolio, that is, as a collection of revenue sources.

Some of what you have may already be established products, some in the growth stage, and some new and untested. As a starting point, use the widely accepted classification method originated by the Boston Consulting Group. According to this method, there are four types of businesses or, in our case, products.

1. **Cows.** No longer in the growth stage, these are mature products that provide most of your business's profits and cash.
2. **Stars.** Products in the growth stage in terms of sales, these produce earnings but still require cash from cows to maintain their leading market position.
3. **Wildcats.** These are growth products that have yet to establish a leading market position and thus require more cash than they generate.
4. **Dogs.** These are mature products that consume all the cash they generate just to maintain their low market share.

Let us take a look at the marketing tools available and see how they may relate to the types of products you have. Let us limit our discussion to the broad classes of tools and variables which are under the control of the marketer.

Product

The first tool available to the marketer is the product itself. The marketer can modify the product physically (a new improved formula), positionally (altering the product's image through advertising to suit a new target market), or both. Positioning, as indicated above, can be done without necessarily changing the product. An example would be targeting a single-volume reference book to encyclopedia set buyers rather than to single-volume buyers in order to exploit its price advantage fully. Thus, the product is positioned against multivolume sets rather than against similarly priced one-volume reference books. Positioning also may be achieved through changes in product and promotion. For example, a food product may be nutritionally enhanced and promoted as a highly nutritious food in a market that already may be crowded with competition appealing to taste. Through positioning, direct mailers can make more products out of what they've got.

Promotion

For our purposes, promotion is the specific copy approach used in a mailing package, print ad, statement stuffer, etc. It is not the medium used but the strategy employed. For our purposes, the strategy may include the use of a premium or a free gift to induce trial, purchase, payment, etc. Promotion is a powerful tool. It is not unusual to see a new promotion approach for a given product generate a 20 percent increase in sales.

Price

Product price is a tool that an adept marketer can adjust upward or downward or maintain to meet marketing objectives. If maximizing short-term profits is the goal, higher price levels ought to be tested to determine what the market can bear. If market penetration is the goal, a lower price level may achieve maximum distribution more quickly. These simple examples show what the marketer can achieve by fine-tuning this element of marketing.

Place or Channel

In direct marketing, place and markets are often synonymous. Place or channel refers to the vehicle, medium, or format used: direct mail, space ads, catalogs, stuffers, and inserts. These represent markets with their own characteristics. Direct mail markets, for example, are different from print ad markets in that they generally are more responsive. Because of varying characteristics as well as varying selling costs, some products are best suited for direct mail, some for catalogs, some for print ads, some for stuffers and inserts, and some for all of them. Figure 47-1 illustrates one way of matching products with channels. The top layer shows old products being matched with new markets (hotline names, for example) and new products being matched with old markets, thereby preventing product fatigue. The second layer shows the matching of prices with places. This example shows that \$3.95 to \$14.95 products are best suited for less-expensive media such as stuffers and inserts, while \$16.95 and up products are best promoted by direct mail. Any of the squares in the top layer could overlay the squares below. For example, an old product promoted to new markets may use direct mail because of its relatively high price.

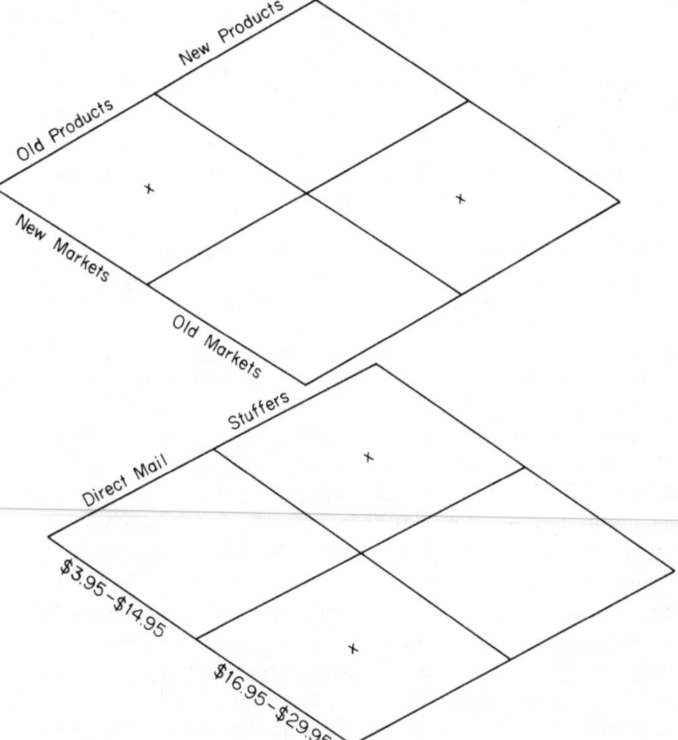

Figure 47-1 Matching products with markets, prices with places: An example

TABLE 47-1 Marketing Tools and Types of Products: Their Appropriate Applications

	Cows	Stars	Wildcats	Dogs
Product	x			x
Price	x			x
Promotion	x	x	x	
Place		x	x	x

Which of the preceding tools fit your products best? One of the twin objectives of this chapter is to formulate an answer to this question. Table 47-1 presents the answer in the form of a marketing grid. The table tells us the following.

For Cows. The product, the price, and promotion either singly or in combination are recommended tools for achieving maximum profits and cash flow. The benefits of trying new places to promote this type of product are likely to be disproportionately less than the risks involved. This type of product generally has reached a level of saturation beyond which incremental gains would hardly justify the incremental costs. A maintenance strategy is therefore recommended.

For Stars. Promotion and place testing should be done to strengthen earnings and maintain a leading competitive position. Product variation is risky for a rising star; any change may turn away customers. Price is another tool to shy away from; a burdensome price can stop a rising star cold in its tracks if not cause it to plummet. The objective should be to lengthen the product's profitable life rather than shorten it in return for immediate gains.

For Wildcats. The tools for stars apply in the marketing of wildcats. Wildcats are generally fledgling products, new in the market, and need the exploration of place and promotion that will secure a share of the market.

For Dogs. Product, price, and place should be the variables tested to try to increase its new contribution before deciding to drop a product. For all its negative connotations, a dog can be a direct mailer's best friend. Dogs have certain advantages. You don't have to start from scratch with dogs since there already is a residual customer awareness of the product, and promotion material is already available (development costs have been amortized already). Also, since they are candidates for abandonment, you can take risks manipulating the products, the prices, and the places where they are marketed to see if you can make cows out of them again.

Since the grid is only two-dimensional, it does not show the possibility of using a mix of appropriate tools for each of the four types of products. In practice, marketing strategies consist of a mix of these tools, although in many cases one tool makes the most significant contribution. Some of the cases that follow show applications of combinations of tools; the others exemplify situations where one tool made the most impact. Only the names of some of the products have been changed.

CASE HISTORIES

Making the Most of Cows

Using Price: *The Family Encyclopedia of Common Illnesses.* A complete one-volume reference book for treatment of more than 100 common ailments, this book was for a long time one of the major products of Rodale Books. After successive years of dramatic sales growth, primarily through direct mail and print ads in *Prevention* magazine, its annual volume started to level off, threatening to decline. In an industry of short life cycles, this book was suspected of having reached maturity. Response rates had started to fall, from 3.0 to 2.38 to 2.11 to 1.91 percent.

New promotional packages were tested to see if a fresh approach could bring the book back to its former sales level. While new approaches sometimes pulled more orders, they did not improve the book's pull significantly. The original promotional package proved to be a very strong standard, so strong that it had to be reused after brief periods when the new standard would start to fatigue.

The single most important factor that changed the course of this product was a successful 25 percent increase in price. For some reason, the higher price lifted response 14 percent. Perhaps the new price invested the product with a higher degree of quality which attracted more orders. In any case, the new price propelled the product back to higher levels of profitability.

Using Product: *The Encyclopedia of Natural Gardening.* Considered by many gardening enthusiasts as the bible of organic gardening, this book enjoyed a definite marketing niche. However, the gardening market was crowded with lower-price competition, and it did not take long before we started seeing indications of premature peaking of sales.

As is customary, new prices and new promotional copy approaches were tested every year. As far as the price tests showed, the book clearly was encountering price resistance. No meaningful price increase could be implemented. New copy approaches failed to beat the standard promotion.

There was one more course of action open: to do something with the product. We produced a deluxe edition of the book featuring easy-wipe covers, thumb-indexed alphabetic sections, and ribbon bookmarkers. This product strategy finally allowed us to increase revenues. Although the deluxe edition was priced 23 percent higher than the regular and was offered in the same promotional piece as an option, the total response from print ads did not decline. For the same number of books sold, the company increased its dollar income. This is a case of a minor product change that made a major impact on the bottom line.

Using Promotion: *The Complete Book of Natural Therapy.* This product sold over 1 million copies in only 4 years. At first, the book's promotion did not use a free gift offer. It was not necessary according to the tests. The title simply took off on its own and sold exceedingly well in most places. Health is a common concern, and this product filled a well-defined need for information on drugless, nonsurgical healing.

Since this was a product that sold to the broad market and generated substantial profits through volume, any price change was considered very carefully before it was implemented. To maximize cash flow, the company had to look elsewhere for variables to change.

Through extensive premium and copy testing, the company finally found a new mailing package that increased response 18 percent. The free gifts that helped cause this sales increase cost only three cents apiece.

Using Product and Promotion: *Vegetables & Fruits.* To most customers, all gardening books are the same. If you have five major gardening books, how do you sell them to the same market?

While most marketers appreciate the need to establish a brand image or product personality for packaged goods, few people realize the need to do the same for book products. Some books need a distinct personality, gardening books especially. A good example is Rodale's book *Vegetables & Fruits.* A complete reference book, this product had no distinctive image to set it apart from other gardening books. In fact, this book and its competitors were the equivalent of generic products in packaged goods.

The company's creative people carved out a personality for the product. The product was not just a gardening reference book but a system that helped to plan and grow the garden that fits you: your food needs, your available time, your type of soil, your geographic location, etc. Thus was the product, along with its premium, dubbed the Custom Garden System. It was a positioning solution. The product was positioned to appeal to gardeners who had more specific information needs than the broad range of gardening enthusiasts. When this copy approach was tested against the traditional approach of dramatizing all the consumer benefits that the product could promise, the Custom Garden System came out the clear winner.

Making the Most of Stars

Using Place: *The Book of Healing Recipes.* So strong was the editorial and marketing confidence in this product that the book was launched without the benefit of a copy and price test. Only one mailing package, featuring a predetermined price, was used to test lists and subsequently to do a rollout on lists that worked. The first phase of the rollout immediately established the potential of the book to become a star.

The immediate goal was to determine quickly the potential of the book in direct mail, print ads, inserts, etc. As mentioned, copy testing was bypassed to accelerate market penetration by means of early rollouts. The book was tested simultaneously in magazine ads, inserts, and other channels.

As soon as test results were known, exposure of the book in all media increased immediately, this time using the higher price that won in a test conducted with subsequent mailing efforts. As a result of this place-oriented strategy, the product started generating profits in the shortest possible time.

Using Promotion: *Natural Foods Cookbook.* In its growth stage, this book enjoyed a 3 percent response from health book buyers. Although it was promoted in print ads and other miscellaneous media, direct mail was the primary mover of the book.

Perhaps because the book was marketed at the time when natural foods were not yet popular, the company was faced with the problem of having to decide which markets to promote. It seemed there were two distinct natural foods markets: a taste market and a nutrition market. This became apparent when the results of the copy tests came in. There were two copy approaches used: one playing up taste, the other focusing on nutrition. Customers like *Prevention* magazine subscribers preferred the taste approach (response was 11 percent better than with the nutrition copy), while customers like health book buyers preferred the nutrition appeal (3.37 versus 2.8 percent).

To make the most of the book, the company decided to use two approaches for direct mail. This was the most significant factor in the product's accelerated growth. The company was able to promote one product to two distinct markets.

Using Place and Promotion: *Passive Solar Energy*, Professional Edition. This was perhaps one of the first important books published about passive solar energy. For this reason, the product benefited hugely from the intense interest in alternative energy, solar energy in particular. The book was available in three editions: a trade paperback, a regular hardcover, and a professional edition. The paperback and the regular hardcover were identical in contents; the professional edition was an expanded version.

Because the company perceived the professional edition as too technical for its lay audience, it restricted the promotion of the big book to engineers and architects, using a self-mailer. However, the book proved to be a growth product, and so the company decided to explore other markets including its own. To test the book to nontechnical lists, the company decided it needed a more elaborate mailing package that would provide more opportunity to explain the product. Thus, we designed a 6- by 9-inch solo offer and mailed it to our book buyers.

The result was astounding. In spite of its technical image and high ticket, the book enjoyed 4 and 5 percent response rates. Because of this, the company was able to maximize return on the book's investment in a very short time.

Making the Most of Wildcats

Using Place: *Woman's Health Encyclopedia*. A true wildcat, this product was promoted with mixed anticipation. We had never had a health book for women alone before. The goal for this book was to achieve early product trial by the maximum number of customers. A high price was temporarily out of the question. The important thing was to give the product every reasonable opportunity to establish itself on a market-by-market basis.

The first important market selected for promotional efforts was *Prevention* magazine subscribers, who were predominantly women (about 75 percent). The strategy was to use direct mail and print ads simultaneously: direct mail for copy and price testing, print ads for product introduction and revenue generation.

Texas and Ohio were selected as test markets for direct mail because the company's penetration in these states (number of customers relative to state population) approximated its national average. Thus, these two states represented the total U.S. market.

We then excluded these two states from our print ad schedule. Thus, the magazine carried our ad in all states but Texas and Ohio, where direct mail testing was going on. Using this strategy, we were able to generate national sales while doing direct mail tests. The book sold successfully in print ads.

Using Place: *Bread Winners*. Here is an example of a multistage marketing effort. We tested Bread Winners in low-cost media before determining whether to invest more promotional dollars in the product.

This was a very readable book of bread recipes, full of human interest items about the bakers and their backgrounds and methods of baking. We first promoted the book in statement stuffers and minicatalogs. The response rates were encouragingly high. A full page ad was prepared. When this was run in *Organic Gardening* and *Prevention* magazines, sales were disappointingly low. There were questions about whether the copy approach was appropriate and whether the presence of a competitive book (sold at half the price of this product) in the same issue carrying our ad had anything to do with sales. It would have been difficult to make a judgment about the book's potential on the basis of this information alone. Fortunately, we had other sources of information regarding the book's sales performance. From book club sales, we learned that *Bread Winners*, when offered as a main selection, obtained one of the highest acceptance rates for that year.

Given the results of our marketing efforts in various channels, we decided to do a single-book direct mail test. The book pulled 3.24 percent in the best panel tested. Here was a case of phased market testing that paid out.

Using Promotion: *Earth Design*. We had a gap in our product line, and this book on natural landscaping was meant to fill it. The decision to do the book came after several research efforts had shown that the topic enjoyed popularity among our customers. In title surveys conducted among book buyers, the product concept ranked among the top five. In focus group interviews, the message we received was one of enthusiasm for the book among do-it-yourselfers. Unfortunately, "landscaping" had connotations that did not help the idea of our book. To many, it meant manicured lawns, chemical sprays, bags of fertilizers, etc., whereas the idea of our book was working with nature, enhancing the natural environment of one's home, and laying out the space around the house to obtain maximum aesthetic and practical benefits.

Thus, it became a problem of promotion to determine whether the product concept could be sold effectively. We designed two promotional approaches for the book while it was still in development. One approach presented the product concept under the title *Earth Design*, and the other used the title *Practical Landscaping*. The idea was to find out whether there was a title that could help improve the product's potential. The result of the test showed that *Earth Design* had a decided advantage over the other title. Thus, through the use of promotion, we averted a serious problem in marketing the book.

Making the Most of Dogs

Using Product and Price: *Natural Plant Protection*. Once a glowing star, this book could barely support its promotion. However, the book has been maintained because it is still a major product in other channels of distribution, such as our book clubs. How did it get to be a dog? The product, because of its expensive color pages and hefty trim size, ceased to be competitive. It was a candidate for divestiture until we hit on a successful strategy.

Since the book was about nonchemical pest control in the garden, we paired it with a complementary product, *The Color Guide To Garden Insects*. The two were sold at a 20 percent discount off their total price. Although discounted, the total price offered a considerably larger gross margin than the individual prices. Sales took off. Here were two dogs whose total impact was more than the sum of the parts. Because of the increased volume, reprint costs were reduced. Because of increases in mailable names, economies in promotional material were achieved. The net result was that the products became net suppliers of cash.

Using Place: *Delicious Natural Foods.* This product took the route from star to cow to dog. But in spite of its low sales growth now, it has retained enough sales strength to justify continued marketing efforts. The problem is that cookbooks generally require color in promotion for maximum eye appeal, and this product no longer could support a solo mailing package. When this problem became apparent, it was decided to promote the book more extensively by means of statement stuffers which allowed us to reach large numbers of customers at a 95 percent savings in selling costs.

Two things happened. We actually increased the exposure of the book, and we were able to obtain remarkably high response rates from markets that previously had barely promoted the cookbook.

MAXIMIZING SALES FROM YOUR CURRENT MARKETS

Let us look at your current markets and see how, without expanding your customer base, you can maximize revenues. Here are some sales enhancement programs. The list is not meant to be exhaustive; the examples should be viewed more as idea starters.

Sales from Free Gifts

The best things in life are freebies that sell. When you offer a premium or gift, see if you can use it to generate more sales. In selling books, we often offer a free gift that the customer can receive and keep just by agreeing to examine the product. This free gift is often a booklet filled with desirable and practical information.

How do we make money on these booklets? Because of the desirability of the information contained in the booklets, we have found that print ads in the booklets have remarkably high readerships and response rates. Response varies with the product, of course, but for planning purposes we expect 4.1 orders per thousand, which is about twice the pull of a bind-in card in a magazine.

We also enclose promotional stuffers in the envelope that ships the booklet. It is interesting to note that the stuffer does as well as the ad within the booklet if not slightly better. When we tested a minicatalog of books to go with the premium in place of the stuffer, response was even better: 6.5 orders per thousand. These response rates may not apply in every case, but they show the comparative effectiveness of one sales medium over another.

Sales from Sold Products

Products you have sold already can do more selling. In the case of books, blow-in cards, which are self-mailing postal cards with an order blank on one side, sell more copies of the same book. Actually, these cards are the best indicators of how good your product is. If customers are not satisfied with the product, they are not likely to pass along the card to a neighbor or friend. A book that pulls 4.3 orders per thousand in a stuffer would pull 7.3 orders per thousand in a blow-in card. The only disadvantage of blow-in cards is that they are more expensive than stuffers. In relative terms, stuffers cost 16 percent of sales, while blow-in cards cost 22 percent. These figures are used to indicate their relative cost effectiveness.

Computerized Copy on Statements and Invoices

By far the most response-effective medium we have used is computer printed copy on statements and invoices. We store about five lines of promotional copy for each book in the computer's memory bank capsule. The product code on the invoice triggers the appropriate promotional copy to be printed at the bottom of the invoice. Thus, an invoice for a health book would cause promotional copy for another health book to be printed on the invoice or statement. Here is an example of the capsule copy that the computer prints for a health book.

> Since good health is important to you, examine *The Complete Book of Vitamins* for 15 days free. Only $16.95 if you decide to buy. To send for it just tear off and mail this stub. Postage and handling extra except for cash orders.

The stub bears a match code and a product code so that the customer does not have to fill out anything. It has no illustrations and depends on only five lines of stark copy. But because it is targeted marketing, that is, selling to a well-defined segment of buyers, the response is remarkably high. The response to this copy, for example, was 1.25 percent.

Complementary Product Selling

Some products, such as cameras and films, jogging suits and running shoes, complement each other. There are other complementary products, however, that are not so obvious. Finding these complements can be very rewarding.

An example is our weight-control book *Lose Weight Naturally System*. This book obtained 2.5 to 3.0 percent response rates from our traditionally best market: health book buyers. It wasn't until we hit on an inspired idea that we saw dramatic increases in our response rates.

The idea was to offer *Lose Weight* to buyers of *Naturally Delicious Desserts and Snacks Cookbook*. Without testing, purely on the basis of a strong conviction that dessert lovers would be highly predisposed to buying a weight-loss book, we mailed the offer to 250,000 names. The response rate was 6.6 percent, an all-time high for the book.

Success with Fails

If you do mailings based on multiple regression analyses, you will be mailing the offer only to names that pass the minimum predicted response rate that you specify. Thus, you may end up mailing to only 50 percent or less of your file. If the regression analysis is good, this would be more profitable than mailing to the entire file. However, you may have wondered what potential lay in the other 50 percent of the file—the "fails" as distinguished from the "passes" who constitute the mailable 50 percent.

A major mailing was done for the *Complete Book of Vitamins*. Based on a regression analysis, the book was to be mailed to 55 percent of the file, and the mailing was predicted to come in at a cumulative 3.0 percent response. When all the passes were identified and selected, the total mailable names in fact approximated 55 percent of the file. However, what could we do with the other 45 percent?

We considered another offer, *Feasting on Raw Foods*. We analyzed the 400 or so orders that had come in 2 months before, when this new product was price- and copy-tested. We took a look at these 400 customer records and came up with a list of four books that these customers seemed to have a strong affinity for; these were the books that the majority of them had bought. We discovered two things.

1. The 400 people who bought *Feasting on Raw Foods* were mostly past buyers of the *Complete Book of Vitamins*. This was good news because these were the same names that would be excluded automatically from the vitamin mailing.
2. From the regression fails, we were able to select a sizable segment of names who had bought any of the four books we had identified.

The result was that we were able to mail to close to half a million more names by utilizing regression fails. The response obtained from the fails was 3.61 percent, whereas our response objective had been 3.0 percent. Incidentally, the vitamins mailing to passes gave us a 2.73 percent response, higher than the predicted response of 2.5 percent. For both efforts, it was a successful mailing.

A FINAL WORD

The examples and cases presented in this chapter should not be considered as rigid models; they should be used mostly as reference. The mail-order operator should continue to explore strategies and techniques that maximize the business potential. As an anonymous writer put it, "Training is learning the rules; experience is learning the exceptions." Since mail order affords unique opportunities for accurate testing, the mail-order operator should continually formulate new theories and validate them through tests.

chapter 48

LEAD SELLING

Freeman F. Gosden, Jr.

President
Smith-Hemmings-Gosden
El Monte, Calif.

The objective of a lead-generation effort is to get the audience to "raise their hands" and say that they may be interested in your product or service. Simply, the objective is to get the audience to identify themselves as prospects.

Once prospects are identified, it is the task of the sales people, dealers, and distributors, in person or by phone, to close the sale. Thus, there are at least two steps necessary to complete a sale. Sometimes the second step is preceded by the sending of more information by mail; in these cases, the sale is the result of at least a three-step operation.

The delivery of the offer—whether premium or information—should have a salesperson's arm attached.

DEFINITIONS

Since lead generation is quite unlike mail order, it requires the understanding of many words and phrases rarely used in other forms of direct marketing.

Suspect The particular audience that would seem to need an advertiser's product or service. This hunch is based on such suggestions as similarity to present customers profile, history of buying similar products by mail, and probable need of product or service.

Prospect That particular audience which has shown an interest in similar products or services or in another of your products or services. Inquiries, competitors' inquiries, and people who provide their names to receive information or catalogs are good examples.

Respondee Someone who has responded to but not purchased your particular offer. It does not include those who respond to another type of offer or the same offer from a different company.

Influencer The individual or group of individuals at home or business that influence the prospect or respondee to become or not become a purchaser or user.

Inquiry A request for additional information.

Conversion Turning a lead into a sale.

Conversion Rate The percentage of leads that are converted to sales. This is mathematically expressed as sales divided by leads.

CONSUMER VERSUS BUSINESS LEAD GENERATION

Consumer lead generation encompasses such efforts as leads for encyclopedia sales people, family insurance offers, personal loans, home improvement, child portraits, and self-improvement.

In these cases, the only influencer is usually the spouse. In all cases, the product or service is paid for by the individual, not the employer.

Business lead generation differs in that the product or service is paid for by the employer. Usually the cost of the product or service is much higher than consumers could afford. Another difference is the larger number of people who are influential in the decision-making process. Because of the usually higher value of such sales, the amount that can be spent on direct marketing is much higher for a business lead.

Let us look at how list selection relates to lead generation.

A SALESPERSON'S LIST

A salesperson's list is often a very poor list because sales people only know who they know. They don't know who they don't know. Often a good lead-generation program will find new prospects a sales force never knew existed. New firms entering the field, firms diversifying into the field, transfer of executives within a firm, and the invention of new uses for the product or service are examples.

It sometimes is difficult for a sales executives used to a list of, say 2000 prospects, to be willing to mail to a business list of 5000 or more names. They must be able to realize that the additional cost of each extra thousand pieces is minimal when the majority of the cost is accounted for by creative and administrative overhead. Mailing additional quantities of marginal lists is inexpensive and often profitable.

There is another reason why a salesperson's lists are not as good as a compiled list in business-to-business mailings. The salesperson's record includes a name but no title. If the prospect has left the company (or at least that headquarters or branch), the mail may be discarded in the mail room because the current mail sorter does not know what department the person was in or who the replacement was. There is a 30 percent or greater annual turnover in business.

Unfortunately, the salesperson often does not keep the suspect list up to date. This is especially true when there is a change of sales people. We have all noted how quickly the departing salesperson's prospects are forgotten when a change takes place and the new salesperson's list is found to be quite different.

There are often changes of product or service interest in a company, and the salesperson who is on the outside may be the last to know. Projects are scrapped, and companies that have never had an interest in a product or service may expand their capabilities and find themselves good prospects. New uses of a product or service may make prospects out of industries the selling company never thought of.

These reasons are all good arguments for an advertising department to use to persuade the sales department that a direct mail lead-generation program using outside lists is important.

TYPES OF LEADS

Leads may be classified in many ways. Here are some of the more important ones.

Direct Leads

These are straightforward leads that talk strictly about the product or service being offered. The reader's call to action is to ask for more information or ask for a salesperson.

Offer Leads, Related

These are leads that sell an offer. The offer is a booklet or item that the advertiser feels the suspect will want to have. The suspects, by replying to the offer, identify themselves as prospects because the offer relates to the product or service offered. It is important to note that the theme and emphasis of the mailing is on the item offered as a premium, not on what the mailer has to sell. The latter is discussed when the salesperson arrives with the offer in hand.

Offer Leads, Nonrelated

These are leads that are generated by an offer that is usually a nonrelated premium that the reader feels has either a personal or a business value. It is an excuse to get a salesperson's foot in the door. The respondee has been personally screened as a person who used the product or service or could use it. For example, an office manager may be offered a free desk clock just for listening to a demonstration or sales pitch about a new office copier even though that person has never given any indication of a desire to replace or add to the present machine.

TIGHT VERSUS LOOSE LEADS

Tight leads are leads that are of top quality in terms of a high probability of conversion into a sale. The tightest lead would be one that has a high probability of generating a big sale.

Loose leads are leads that do barely more than get a salesperson's foot in the door. Examples would be leads for encyclopedia sales or child portraits or a firm that sells a broad line of office equipment and just needs to get acquainted.

The tighter the lead, the lower the response. By definition, there are fewer good prospects than so-so prospects, and so you will have a lower response. High-technology firms that sell high-ticket (high-priced) items that require a scientific or technical specialist for the sales call must work with tight leads since their cost of a sales call is very high.

Everybody wants lots of tight leads. The optimum, therefore, is to broaden the lead base to a maximum by stretching as far as possible the ability of the sales organization to sell. In other words, if a good salesperson can work mediocre leads, the weaker sales people also should be able to be trained to work them.

Many organizations vary their tightness of leads during the year. Broader promotions go to broader lead lists. A broad list may be mailed only once a year.

CONTROLLING LEAD FLOW

Lead generation often is described as a faucet that can be turned on or off at will, depending on the needs and capability of the sales organization. But lead-generation control should be compared to playing a piano. There are an infinite number of ways it can be played, but a few basic chords will provide even a poor player an adequate performance. Let's look at some of the key items in controlling lead flow.

Quantity of Leads

To generate the right number of leads, you must work backward. You know how many leads a sales organization can handle. You know about the response rate you will get. Based on a weekly or monthly flow, you can determine the number of mailings you must make.

For example, if you can handle 100 leads a month and have been generating about a 2 percent response rate to your promotions, you know that you must mail about 5000 pieces of mail a week. (Leads ÷ response rate = number of pieces mailed, or 100 ÷ 0.02 = 5000.)

As you get more sophisticated, you will be able to plot your curve of response over time and be even more precise.

Quality of Leads

The best device to control the quality of a lead is the business response or business reply card (BRC). In many business mailings, the lists are fixed. The questions asked (and answered) determine lead quality.

Below is a ranking from worst quality to best quality of lead. Obviously, there are many more variations within.

Worst (loosest leads)

Nonrelated premium, high value
Nonrelated premium, low value
Related premium
No premium, free information, no salesperson
Free information, ask for salesperson
Ask for salesperson, answer questions first
Ask for salesperson, answer confidential questions first

Best (tightest leads)

This ranking shows that the more effort the reader must make to respond, the better the response.

Questions that readers must complete in order to prescreen themselves can be tricky. Under no circumstances ask more than four or five questions, preferably those which are closed-ended (can be checked with a box). If it is too long, the person will become discouraged, because it is too much trouble to answer.

An example of a confidential question would be, "Do you need to borrow money to purchase this product?"

Leads also can be tightened by asking such questions as the phone number and the person's title.

Frequency

The frequency of promotion obviously controls the lead flow. As you change your offer, you will hit different people's magic buttons since people respond differently to different offers.

Mailings can be made, and usually should, on a frequent basis. Once is rarely enough. How frequently you mail will be determined by the response analysis of your mailing. If the added mailings continue above your breakeven point, continue them. But don't forget that when the same offer to the same list falls below breakeven, it may be brought above breakeven with a new promotion. Don't discard lists too quickly.

Those who doubt the power of frequency should be reminded of two things: the vast amount of frequency used in magazine advertising and the fact that a large part of what makes up a response is the fact that at the moment of need, your mailing was the one that crossed the reader's desk; it was the right offer received at the right moment.

Geographic

All sales forces are not created equal geographically. More important, prospects and customers are not geographically equal either. It is up to the mailing control to provide leads on a balance basis. Fortunately, with ZIP codes, this can be accomplished easily.

Geographic balance is not a one-time thing. Because products and product uses may change as new uses for products are developed, it is important to monitor flow constantly. To "heavy up" in certain areas, it may be necessary to mail to the same names more frequently or go deeper into industries or segments.

If, for example, you normally select only companies with sales of $5 million to $50 million, you may want to broaden to $4 million to $100 million in areas where you need more leads. Mailers often are surprised by the good results obtained just outside their parameters.

In situations where leads go to dealers and dealers are paying all or part of the program, this "heavy up" aspect becomes very important in making sure that all dealers are treated fairly.

TYPES OF HOOKS

The types of hooks that pull leads are varied. These are really bribes to get the respondents to raise their hands and say, "I may be interested in your product or service." Let's review some of the more popular hooks.

Benefit Booklet

This is by far the most popular and successful of all the hooks because it is done at a very low cost and with a perceived high value. It also can be tailored (written) to the exact need or perceived need of the mailing program.

Note that we said "benefit" booklet. If the booklet is titled something like "The History of the ABC Company," who will care? The title must be perceived to be beneficial and provocative. Here are some examples:

"26 Ways to Increase the Sales of Sledgehammers"

"14 Questions Company Presidents Should Ask Their Lawyers"

"How to Get Management to Buy the Machine You've Always Wanted"

A booklet doesn't have to be long, but it does have to be beneficial.

Free Gift

A whole book could be written about premiums. Here are some of the more important things we've learned after mailing over 1000 different premium packages.

Outgoing premiums are fantastic attention getters. We call them "lumpy packages." There are a lot of good things about lumpy packages. First, there is the "Crackerjack" syndrome. The recipient perceives that a lumpy package has something of value inside. It is hard to imagine someone not opening a lumpy package.

Another advantage is that lumpy packages tend to go on top of today's mail because of their awkward shape. They get seen first, opened first, and remembered.

Lumpy packages should be low-cost bulky items because everyone gets one. You must spread the cost of the 98 percent who don't respond against the 2 percent who do.

Send-for premiums can be of much more value because only the respondee will receive one. Thus, if you have a 20 percent close rate, you charge the 80 percent who did not close against the 20 percent who did, but there is no cost for the nonresponders.

Premiums can reach up to $50 in value in some business mail. Don't let that scare you. If your close rate is 20 percent, that means the overall value is $50 × 5 = $250. When converted to cost, that is probably only $175. If you are selling a $50,000 machine or services that generate $50,000 in sales, that is relatively inexpensive. Remember that the cost of an average sales call alone is over $200.

Unique premiums are more important than expensive ones. Here is a list of some premiums that have been very successful.

An orange
A windup mechanical person
A set of unique art prints
A T-shirt with a computer-printed picture of you
A color poster of a South Sea island

Here are some premiums that are sure to fail.

The biography of the president of your company
A free facility brochure on your company
Literature you are trying to get rid of

The biggest mistake advertisers and their agencies make is believing that their self-serving material will be considered a premium of value by a suspect or prospect.

Free Information

Free further information is not a premium or a bribe. It is the next step in the straightforward approach. It simply gives the reader more information than the original mailing on a subject of interest.

The information must be meaningful and be just what it says: further information. It may be lab tests, technical specifications, testimonials, more information about the product, product interface, or peripherals. But it can't be a rehash of what was received already.

The free information should be developed before you develop the mailing package offering the free information. It shouldn't be just a data sheet, and it should be personalized, maybe in the accompanying cover letter, to the prospect's industry and potential usage or, more specifically, to that person's needs.

Free information may be an extra step that makes a two-step sale (lead plus salesperson) a three-step sale (lead plus more information plus a salesperson). This provides the advertiser an opportunity to qualify an inquiry further, but it should not be substituted for a salesperson's call.

Free Analysis

This offer, or hook, can be very successful if done properly. The free analysis must be meaningful and professional and must be perceived by the prospects to be of value to them whether or not they purchase the product. Analysis can be of the form of either fill out and send in or we will send a specialist out. Both can be successful.

Traditional Offers

Discounts, free goods with purchase, and other traditional offers can be very successful. However, we are talking about generating leads, and usually much more product knowledge and selling must take place before price becomes the main subject. Obviously, these techniques work better at retail or in mail-order sales than in lead generation.

Sellout Premiums

These premiums most often are forgotten. When you are selling to businesses, such as dealers, they may need to sell the product to someone else. If you can provide selling aids such as folders and posters, you can be perceived as providing a valuable service. These dealers may consider the sellout advertising material more valuable than a conventional premium.

Questionnaire

This hook works well only if it is done properly. If it becomes obvious that the questions asked are a ruse to get a qualified name, it won't work. You must remember three things.

1. The fewer the questions, the higher the response.
2. You should be perceived as sincerely needing the information for other purposes.
3. Most questions should be easy to answer (and tabulate), such as "check the appropriate box" closed-ended questions.

MULTIPLE LEADS, SAME COMPANY

If one lead from a company is good, two are better. If you miss with person A, why not try B?

One of the biggest weaknesses of most lead-generating programs is the misconception that only one mailing to a company is necessary. You want decision influencers to hear your story directly from you, not secondhand or thirdhand from the one lower-level contact you may have.

Once you've developed the mailing package, the incremental cost of mailing additional pieces is relatively small. Here are titles that have been found to be successful in mailing to lead-generation programs over the years.

Original prospect	The person who can benefit directly from the product or service you are offering.
Functional vice president	That is, vice president of operations, sales, marketing, etc.
Chief financial officer	They rarely can help you but can kill your deal. Their job is not spending money.
President	Everyone is always surprised how many seemingly small decisions get up to the president.
Research and development	This person, if he or she knows about your product or service, may find a use you never thought of.

These five titles probably do not all speak the same technical language. Keep your mailing in common universal language so that each understands the benefits.

TITLE ADDRESSING VERSUS NAME ADDRESSING

It is important to remember that you usually do not have the names of the people listed above. If you do have a name, it is often the wrong one. Title addressing is widely acceptable if you execute your mailing properly. That means the reader is exposed quickly to a benefit that far outweighs the lack of personalization.

SELLING THE OFFER VERSUS SELLING THE PRODUCT

Copywriters and art directors must have direction. The person responsible for the mailing must decide whether to sell the offer, the product or service, or a combination. The answer lies in the quality of the lead necessary, as was stated earlier. For loose leads, we are selling the offer; for tight leads, the product or service. However, most leads fall somewhere in the middle. When in doubt, give more emphasis to the offer. You may never find the prospects unless they have responded to something they want. You can't sell to them if you can't find them.

HOW TO SORT LEADS

Most field sales people feel they are experts in this area but are not. Here are some guidelines that you may find helpful in the development of your mailing package. They should be communicated to your sales organization too.

Phone number If filled in, a good lead.

Title White-collar titles respond better and can make more decisions. Also check appropriateness of title.

Headquarters Generally provide better leads than branch offices because they have more decision-making responsibility.

Small companies Respond better than large ones because there are fewer people involved in decision.

By media From worst to best: bingo cards, couponed space ads, direct mail, 800 number, prepaid long distance.

The last classification requires clarification. Bingo cards ("circle the item number under the ad you read in this magazine") are the worst because it is so easy to reply. You get a lot of students, advertising agency libraries, and competitors. Prepaid long distance is better than an 800 number because it is paid for.

Another good sign is a lead that comes in long after you figured all the response was in. These people who responded late cared enough to file your mailing, and now, because they have a need, they have looked you up. They are ready to buy.

Filing of advertising for future reference is done much more with direct mail pieces than with couponed magazine ads. This is another argument for direct mail.

RESPONSE RATE VARIABLES

What response rate can I expect? That is the most common of all questions asked. The right answer is, "I don't know because what we proposed to do has not been done before. There are too many variables."

Let's look at some of these variables and see what conclusions we can draw.

The Offer versus the Product

Response rates are dependent on what was offered, not on what the basic product or service is. If you are selling postage meter machines and you offer the same machine two ways—one with a free attractive desk clock and one with free information only—you are going to get a great variation in response. Therefore, you must calculate your response rate on the basis of your offer, not your product.

Seasonal Differences

We do not mean seasons of the year but whether the product or service is in the spring, summer, or fall of its life cycle. In today's fast-moving, highly technological world, life cycles are very short. Yesterday's model is obsolete. Prospects are smart. Your response rates will vary depending on whether you have something new or are discounting something old.

Rollout

The best way to determine response rates is a small test quickly rolled out. With many lead programs, the lag time between response and sale precludes making decisions from sales data or relying on the analysis of responses and using a factor to project actual sales.

PROFILING LEADS

The best prospects are similar to those people or companies who have bought already. It is wise to profile replies, especially those who have been converted into sales. You must do this by planning ahead and coding the various subsections of lists, package variations, and offers.

In large-scale consumer mailings, this is easy because there are a large number of responses. In business mail, the responses are small in numbers. The elements below can be profiled with a small number of responses, say, 300 or more. Why the element is important also is stated.

Title of respondee Needed to determine title for future mailings.

SIC codes At least two-digit and, in cases where few SIC codes are mailed, five digits.

Size of company Need for future subselects.

One interesting profile is a comparison of those respondees who finally purchased with those who did not. What you find different is what is important.

REMAILING LEADS

A common sin is to fail to follow up with leads who did not result in sales. Just because prospects did not purchase, this does not mean they won't purchase later.

To be able to continue to follow up on these names, your mailing program must be a continuing one, and there must be a method of communication between the field and the mailing headquarters to make sure the current information is passed on.

The simplest method is to bring all leads to a central point, have them compiled, and send them on to the field. Whether or not the field updates the lead, that person gets all future mailings from the central headquarters.

A better way but a more complex one is to have the field update your mailing list. Left to their own devices, field sales personnel will do almost nothing. To prevent this, simply mail a galley (printout) of your list once or twice a year and have each field salesperson update his or her part. They should do it right on the galley, with a time limit of 30 days to return it.

The most sophisticated way is to have a continual reporting and update file maintenance system on special forms from the field. Only larger organizations tend to develop this sophistication.

LOCAL VERSUS CENTRAL CONTROL

Leads must be acted on quickly. A few days can make a difference.

The optimum system is central control, but that places a heavy quick turnaround burden on the central point. Turnaround should be one working day. Some firms are satisfied with weekly batching and forwarding to the field.

The reasons for central control are many.

Complexity of direct mail	Local sales offices don't have the capability or time to execute good direct mail. The development overhead is too high.
Volume cost efficiency	Direct mail costs drop dramatically as quantities increase.
Better list purchase in volume	It costs less to rent mailing lists in larger quantities with fewer restrictions.
Direct mail specialist	A centralized specialist can control quality and flow better.
Response analysis	The data from many field locations in combination give more accurate results.

HOW TO GET FIELD SUPPORT FOR A CENTRAL PROGRAM

No salesperson will ever say, "The direct mail program got me the sale." You must understand that going in. Give the sales people all the credit in the world and more.

To get them on your side, be on their side. Show them just how the program will work. Show cost effectiveness, cite results of past programs, and show how leads were found that would be hard for a salesperson to find. Show how you are putting more money in their pockets.

Most important, make it easy on them.

chapter **49**

CLUBS AND CONTINUITY PLANS

David H. Soskin

President
Soskin/Thompson
A Division of
J. Walter Thompson
U.S.A. Inc.
New York, N.Y.

The club and continuity business was started in 1916 by Harry Scherman, founder and president of the Book-of-the-Month Club. He conceived the Little Leather Library Corporation, which offered subscribers literary classics in leatherbound editions. The initial marketing success prompted Scherman in 1926 to develop an alternative form of distribution for books: the Book-of-the-Month Club.

In a more primitive form, mail-order selling existed before 1916. However, what Scherman developed was new in that it introduced a method of distributing books to customers called the negative option (automatic shipment). A book was sent automatically to a subscriber unless the subscriber said no within a given time period. Today, there are many variations of negative option selling of a wide variety of special-interest products to special-interest audiences. This method of distribution in turn formed the basis for the club and continuity business.

There are approximately 250 clubs and continuity programs in the United States. A majority are of a small special-interest nature, with memberships ranging from 5000 to 50,000. It is estimated that there are twenty-five clubs and continuities with 100,000 to 500,000 members, fifteen in the 500,000 to 1 million range, and ten with active memberships over 1 million. In addition to book and record clubs, many other products are sold using the club marketing concept, among them videocassettes, beauty and health aids, collectibles such as stamps and coins, and food and jewelry.

The club concept also gave birth to the continuity series business, a shipment of a special-interest series of products which are mailed automatically (negative option) at predetermined intervals agreed on by the subscriber in advance, with the right to cancel at any time. The lists and types of continuity programs are varied as the products available: books, records, recipe cards, art, food, et al.

METHOD OF OPERATION

Clubs

Clubs operate on a negative option, positive option, combination negative and positive option, or rental basis.

Generally, the incentive to join is a substantially discounted product, a free product, or a specific number of days or weeks for free examination of a product. In turn, the member agrees to purchase a specific number of products (usually a numeric rather than a dollar amount) in a prescribed time period. Some clubs operate on a "no obligation to buy, no time limit" basis.

Negative Option

This is the basic shipment method by which many clubs operate. The member receives an announcement on a regular basis indicating what the automatic product shipment will be. If the member does not return the form by a specific date, indicating that the product is not desired or that a different or additional product is desired, the product will be sent to the member automatically.

Federal law requires that the member have at least 30 days to respond to the automatic shipment notice and that the company ship the product within 30 days or notify the member of the shipping date if it exceeds 30 days.

Positive Option

This is a method of club operation where a member receives only products that are specifically requested. Nothing is shipped automatically.

Combination Negative Option and Positive Option

This is an offer to subscribe to a club membership on either a positive or a negative option basis. This dual membership offer is prevalent among programs which have a portion of their members living overseas or in areas where it is difficult to communicate or ship products practically or inexpensively during the 30-day time period required by law.

Rental

This is a method of operation that is particularly popular among videocassette clubs. A member pays a fee to rent a product for a predetermined time period and then return it to the club. A substantial advance deposit usually is required from the member.

Continuity Plans

A continuity plan is a method of shipping a product—usually similar in subject matter or special-interest appeal—on a negative option (automatic) basis at a predetermined frequency. There are two basic continuity plans: open-ended and closed-ended.

An open-ended plan includes no fixed number of product shipments. A subscriber may choose to continue to receive shipments indefinitely. A closed-ended plan has a fixed number of predetermined product shipments.

In either plan, subscribers are given the right to cancel their subscriptions at any time by notifying the seller in writing.

From an economic and fulfillment standpoint, a continuity plan generally affords higher and more predictable profit margins in that the number and quantity of product shipments are predetermined. In the case of a club, each individual product shipment can vary in that members are given a choice of products.

Cash with Order Option

This is a continuity plan in which subscribers are given the option of purchasing a product on an individual shipment basis or purchasing the entire series at once (a one-shot purchase), usually at a discount.

Load-Up

This is a marketing plan in which closed-end continuity plan subscribers are offered the opportunity to purchase the balance of the series at once, usually after payment has been received for the third shipment in a series. The seller makes the assumption that after three shipments, the subscriber has shown sufficient interest to purchase the entire series in the plan.

PRODUCT SELECTION

Creating an Original Product

A club or continuity company may decide to create or manufacture a product itself.

Subsidiary Rights

This is a process in which a club or continuity company signs a formal agreement with the manufacturer or publisher giving it mail-order distribution rights to selected products for a specified time and payment. Usually, the club or continuity company agrees to an advance against royalty payments. In return, the manufacturer grants the seller exclusive mail-order rights.

Royalty payments vary but generally range from 5 to 10 percent for products sold to club members and 2.5 to 5 percent for products used as enrollment premium "giveaways."

The advance usually is determined by the sales potential (demand) for the products.

TABLE 49-1 Marketing Strategy Checklist for Clubs and Continuity Programs

I. Concept

A. Is the product to be sold in keeping with the corporate image?
B. What is the membership potential?
C. What is the profit potential:
  1. Short-range?
  2. Long-range?
D. What is the ideal club size based on maximum profitability?
E. What is the competition and potential competition?
F. Can members be acquired from low-bad-debt media?
G. Can members be acquired from existing company mailing lists without affecting the profitability of other clubs or continuity plans?

II. Product

A. Quality
B. Costs of goods:
  1. If manufactured
  2. If supplied (availability)
C. Shipping and handling
  1. Storage and distribution
  2. Package design

III. Offer

A. Club
  1. Negative option
  2. Positive option
  3. Frequency (number of cycles)
  4. Commitment
  5. Premium(s)
B. Continuity program
  1. Frequency of shipment
  2. (Open-ended or closed-ended)
  3. Premium (units in series)

IV. Marketing Research

  1. Existing
  2. How much and what type is needed?
A. Media availability
  1. Print
  2. Direct mail
    a. House lists
    b. Outside lists
  3. Broadcast
  4. Other

V. Objectives

A. Size of club
  1. First year
  2. Second year
  3. Third year

B. New member advertising
    1. Direct mail
        a. House lists
        b. Outside lists
C. Advertising budget allowances
    1. Estimated number of members to be replaced per year
    2. Estimated cost per order (with test allowance)
    3. Estimated bad debt per member enrolled
D. Advertising to existing members
    1. Frequency of regular cycle mailings
    2. Enclosures
    3. Separate mailings
    4. Reenrollment offers
E. Purchase logic
    1. Category or subject
    2. Season

VI. Fulfillment

A. How the club or program operates membership literature
B. Shipping and handling
    1. Package design
        a. Handling and damage considerations
        b. Warehousing
        c. Computerization:
            New software program
            Existing program

VII. Collection

A. Dunning series
B. Ongoing telephone
C. Collection agency

Syndication

This is a method of mail-order distribution in which a company sells another company's product. For example, a book publisher has published a series of books which a book continuity plan company agrees to market. The book continuity plan company agrees to pay the publisher an advance plus royalty for all mail-order sales and pay for promotion and fulfillment costs. The publisher grants the continuity plan company exclusive mail-order distribution rights and often allows the continuity company to "private label" or publish the series under the continuity plan company's imprint.

NEW CLUB OR CONTINUITY PLAN DEVELOPMENT

While there is no set formula to determine success or failure since individual companies have different objectives, the general checklist in Table 49-1 serves as a basic guideline. Table 49-2 is a checklist of financial considerations.

TABLE 49-2 Basic Financial Considerations Checklist

Gross sales
Net sales
Gross profit
Net profit
Expenses
  New member acquisition costs
  New member premium cost
  Shipping and handling costs
  Special promotions and regular mailing announcements to subscribers
  Bad debt allowance
  Cost of goods
  Cost of returns
  Overhead
  Bad debt allowance
  Royalty costs (if applicable)

TESTING

Once qualitative or quantitative research has been completed and it has been decided to proceed with a new club or continuity program, a variety of testing options should be considered. It is important to keep in mind that there is no fixed dollar purchase amount by the consumer since the amount a subscriber buys will vary. Therefore, the real key to testing success or failure cannot be based on or measured in terms of initial response. Testing is an ongoing process. Generally, it takes from 6 months to a year to determine a test's success or failure.

The most common testing procedures are as follows.

Dry Testing

This is a method of testing product viability, price, and offer to consumers before a product has been manufactured or before it has been manufactured in substantial quantities. In short, the advertising—usually direct mail—is created and presented to consumers as if the product existed. Based on response (consumer acceptance), the club or continuity company can determine whether to proceed with the program in advance of product manufacture. (The Federal Trade Commission recently issued new dry testing guidelines which in effect say that the promotional material must state clearly that the product does not exist if it has not been manufactured yet.)

Split Testing

Split testing is a method of testing a number of variables at the same time to the same mailing list or in the same issue of a publication.

Print Testing

A perfect A-B split means that the publication prints two different advertisements, or "variables," in the same issue: copy 1, test A; copy 2, test B; etc. By coding coupons to correspond to each test, the advertiser can measure the results and make accurate test judgments. An A-B, or "perfect," split ensures a more reliable test in that there are fewer variables, notably timing and geographic distribution. A-B-C-D splits (testing four variables) can be accomplished in some publications.

Cluster Split

This is a testing method in which one-half of the circulation run receives test A, while the other half receives test B. It is not as statistically reliable in that geographic circulation distribution is not equal.

Supplied Page and Freestanding Insert Tabs

Statistically, this is the most reliable testing method with the greatest flexibility in that various tests (virtually unlimited in number) can be controlled by the advertiser. The advertiser preprints and collates the advertisements in advance and delivers them to a publication for binding or insertion.

Direct Mail Split Tests

These are split tests using direct mail. They are conducted by mailing a representative sample of the same mailing list in the same quantity at the same time on an A-B basis. When the same number of pieces are mailed using this formula, virtually any number of tests can be conducted simultaneously. The split test can be expanded to include as many testing variables as desired.

Timing Tests

As is the case with virtually all direct marketing, the time of the year direct-response advertising is run can affect results greatly. Generally, book and continuity club offers tend to attract more new members in the January-February and September-October time periods. However, depending on the club or program, response may be atypical. Therefore, it is wise to test various time segments. Traditionally, December, April, and May are the worst response months. Holidays and election periods affect results negatively.

WHAT SHOULD BE TESTED?

Testing is a continuous process. The following is a list of variables that should be tested on a regular basis.

New Club Member Acquisition Offers

1. Premium product(s) incentive to join. A specific amount for *X* dollars
2. Commitment or obligation. How much a subscriber is required to buy
3. Time. The time period a member has to fulfill the obligation

4. Negative option
   Positive option
   Combination negative and positive option
5. Bonus plans. Incentives for buying more or retaining membership after trial membership obligation period expires

Continuity Plans

1. Premium incentive to subscribe
2. First shipment offer. Generally, the most popular product in a continuity plan series is offered for free examination or for a reduced price in order to attract more subscribers. The premium offer also can vary depending on the audience. In other words, the product can be changed to fit the medium.
3. Price
4. Frequency of shipment
5. Load-up

NEW MEMBER ACQUISITION

The acquisition of new members has become more difficult because of competition from home video electronic media, discount retail bookstores, increased media costs, higher postage rates, and higher bad debt.

For clubs and continuity plans, the challenge is to acquire qualified members (people who buy and stay in the club or program and pay their bills) rather than just acquiring members in vast numbers.

Ideally, a person should want to join a club or program because of the products offered, not because of the premium incentive to join. Profitable new member acquisition, however, is a combination of a number of marketing considerations.

Offers

1. **The premium:** What is given away or sent to subscribers on a trial basis as an incentive to join. Most clubs and continuity plans often change the offer or have a variety of offers that can be targeted to specific audiences in specific media.
2. **The commitment:** What a subscriber is required to buy in a time period.
3. **The method of shipment:** Negative or positive option or a combination of both.
4. **The frequency of shipment:** How often a product announcement offer or product is sent to a subscriber.

Member-Get-a-Member

The best customer is an existing customer. Clubs and continuity programs constantly cross merchandise customer lists to offer new products to profitable subscribers.

By the same token, a member-get-a-member (MGM) plan is a selling method where the existing customer is given an incentive to get another customer. Generally, special direct mail MGM offers to members are done frequently during a person's membership life. Generally, MGM offers can be mailed five times a year (on a twelve-cycle membership) without affecting profitability.

Expires

This is a term referring to former club or continuity members.

Mailings to former members with an offer to rejoin or subscribe to another club or program often work very well. Generally, expire lists that are more than 3 years old do not work.

Gift Offers

This is a promotion in which existing subscribers are offered an opportunity to give a club membership or continuity plan subscription as a gift.

MEDIA SELECTION AND PLANNING

When developing a media plan for clubs and continuity plans, it is important to coordinate print, direct mail, and broadcast efforts. The following guidelines should be considered in the media planning process.

Magazines and Newspapers

Editorial Compatibility. Is the product being sold compatible with the publication's content and image and therefore with the audience?

Circulation Policy. What is the publication's circulation policy regarding subscriptions? Subscribers who pay full price or a high price for a publication generally will be better club members. People who subscribe through a direct mail offer also tend to be better club members in that they are proven mail-order buyers.

What is the proportion of newsstand sales to subscription sales? A higher newsstand price usually means a better-quality club subscriber. Controlled circulation publications generally do not work well for club and continuity offers.

Timing and Frequency. This refers to the best months of the year to advertise and the frequency with which an offer can run in the same publication without affecting results negatively. Generally, January-February, September-October, and July-August are the strongest response months for club and continuity plan offers. However, the greater the degree of special interest, the less important timing is.

Newspapers in particular and publications in general produce better response when they are read in the home. For this reason, Sunday newspapers work better than dailies and magazines that are sent to the subscriber at home rather than the office.

Positioning. The position of a club or continuity advertisement within a publication can affect results by as much as 40 percent. Generally, right-hand page, far forward works better. However, the optimum position varies by publication, and various positions within the same publication should be tested. When insert cards are used, the first card position (or the card closest to the front of the book) generally works best.

Coupon Placement. This refers to the location of the coupon in the advertisement. The coupon or response mechanism should never be located in the gutter (near the binding). The lower outside corner is the preferred position in that it makes the coupon easier to remove.

Units of Space. This is the advertising format used in print media to sell club and continuity programs.

On-Page Coupon. This is an advertisement in which the coupon is part of the printed page. The respondent must cut or tear it from the publication.

Insert Card. This is a mailable insert card printed on heavier mailable paper stock that meets postal requirements; it is bound into a magazine as the response device for an on-page advertisement (single page or spread). The insert card increases response in that it is a convenient, postage-free, easy way to respond. Most insert cards are postage-paid. However, while insert cards produce a greater gross response, many clubs and continuities find that net response improves when the potential subscriber is qualified and asked to pay the postage or put the insert card in an envelope with a nominal payment.

Supplied Page. This is a single-or multiple-page insert printed on heavier, mailable stock that meets postal requirements. It is printed front and back, and it conforms to the size of a particular magazine. The effect of such an insert is that it is bound in and paginated as part of the magazine, but the order card portion is perforated for ease of removal and response.

Free Standing Inserts. These are supplied page inserts or catalogs that are not bound into a publication. These inserts generally are run in newspapers and have a great degree of flexibility since they can be distributed to selected audiences by ZIP code. Production efficiencies can be realized in that the inserts using this unit of space can be bound into publications (or vice versa) and also used as part of a direct mail solicitation.

Direct Mail

Outside Lists, Response Qualified. These are mailing lists that include proven mail-order buyers. These are the most responsive lists for club and continuity programs. The best categories include magazine mail-order subscribers, selected book buyers, and credit cards.

Compiled Lists. These are lists of individuals with similar demographics and psychographics, usually compiled from phone books, Census data, and automobile and other registration lists. Compiled lists are not necessarily mail-order buyer qualified; hence, they do not work as well for clubs and continuities. The larger the market or audience, the better the chance a compiled list will work.

House Lists. These are existing customer lists usually compiled by name, address, ZIP code, recency, frequency, amount, and type of purchase.

Expires. Lists of former members usually are computerized by year and type of club or continuity membership. Expire lists are good sources for renewing club memberships or selling other continuity programs. The response rule of thumb is that these lists are effective only to 3 years old. Current (less than 1 year old) expires perform the best, followed in descending order by second-and third-year expires. For example, response to 1-year expires is 3 percent; 2-year, 1.5 percent; 3-year, 0.75 percent.

List Exchange. Clubs and continuity programs often exchange lists on a name for name basis with other noncompeting clubs, continuities, magazines, credit cards, catalog companies, etc. This helps make the cost of mailings more effective in that the cost of list rental is saved.

Broadcast

This term refers to television and radio advertising used by clubs and continuities in support of print and direct mail for direct selling or in generating qualified subscriber leads.

Radio. Radio is rarely used by clubs and continuities except for direct selling of selected products. When used, it generally supports print or direct mail.

Television. Direct-response television for clubs and continuities is used in support of print and direct mail (usually freestanding inserts in selected newspapers in selected markets) and to generate qualified sales leads. Clubs and continuities that operate on a negative option basis are required by federal law to have a signed contract from the subscriber agreeing to the automatic shipment and purchase obligation. Hence, direct-response television requires a two- or three-step plan: (1) consumer response via telephone or direct mail, (2) order screening or product selection, and (3) direct mail club or continuity response and product shipment.

While television results have been mixed to date, the cable television opportunity will be significant in the future in that the message can be longer (2 to 7 minutes) instead of using :60s, :90s, or :120s—the three time units that have proved most productive for clubs and continuities. The other advantage is that direct mail and print can be used in conjunction with cable to support broadcast because a cable audience is identifiable through subscriber lists.

Network. Network (national) club and continuity prime-time advertising has not proved successful and is almost never considered in the development of a media plan.

Local Spot. Whether generating leads or used as support on a market-by-market basis, spot television has proved to be the most successful medium. Usually early and late fringe work the best. The best months to advertise are January, February, March, August, and September. A 1-week test is generally sufficient to determine success or failure.

The New Media

As the home continues to become the center of leisure-time entertainment and as HVIE (home video information entertainment) continues to compete for a greater share of the club and continuity market, cable and interactive HVIE systems will allow clubs and continuities to acquire new subscribers more profitably using various electronic publishing media.

Some areas now being tested include the following.

Videotex. Also referred to as electronic publishing, this is a two-way, words-on-screen cable service giving subscribers the ability to receive and respond to special offers over telephone lines.

Cableshop. This is a joint venture among Adams-Russell, Inc., a major cable company; J. Walter Thompson, U.S.A.; and Soskin/Thompson Associates, a Division of JWT. The Cableshop has been tested in Peabody, Massachusetts. Cable subscribers may select informational advertising messages on a separate Cableshop channel. In short, the advertising message is the programming and is selected by the viewer. This interactive system uses only the television and the telephone.

QUBE. Developed by Warner, this interactive system is being tested currently in a number of U.S. markets. It allows subscribers to order directly from the television, using a special home control panel. It also allows for payment by electronic transfer of funds and credit information.

Many new interactive video systems are being developed. It is premature to make any judgments about the effectiveness of any particular system as it applies to clubs and continuities.

Telephone Marketing

In-WATS. Many clubs and continuities use the telephone, usually a toll-free 800 number, as an ordering option for subscribers as part of the order card in print, direct mail, and broadcast advertising.

Out-WATS. This is a marketing system where potential subscribers are contacted initially by telephone and sold a subscription directly or qualified as a good prospect over the phone and then mailed a subscription offer for conversion to membership.

Out-WATS systems have proved particularly effective in reenrolling former subscribers or cross-selling additional continuity programs to subscribers who have purchased other programs.

900 Numbers. This is a relatively new telephone marketing option in which the consumer pays for the call. A "line" operator records the necessary information, or a recording device allows the caller to register name, address, etc.

Traditional Long-Distance Calls. Before the WATS line and toll-free calls, the traditional telephone ordering method was "collect" or simply to let the potential subscriber pay for the call. While there are fewer inquiries using this method, the fact that the call is not free serves as a subscriber "qualifier."

Other Media

Cooperative Mailings. This is a mailing to a similar demographic and psychographic group of consumers, usually to compiled lists, containing a variety of noncompeting products or offers. The basic objective of a co-op is to share postage costs, thereby reducing the cost of reaching a target audience. Co-ops have rarely proved effective for clubs and continuities.

Package Inserts. This is a method of selling additional products or subscriptions to customers by enclosing the offer in the shipping container or package.

Statement Enclosures. Also called statement "stuffers," this is a method of cross-selling in which the advertising message is contained within the billing envelope.

In-Store and Point-of-Sale Offers

These are club and continuity offers, usually in free standing insert formats, which are displayed in "take-one" racks, usually in supermarkets. They rarely are effective for clubs and continuities.

MEDIA PERFORMANCE AND ANALYSIS

Profitability by Source

This is a method in which all media used by clubs and continuities are measured by source on an ongoing basis. The importance of measuring every test, publication, broadcast, commercial, list, and list segment is that real club or continuity profitablity is determined on an ongoing basis. A subscriber's membership "life" is determined by gross to net order costs, premium costs, length of membership, bad debt, and amount, recency, and frequency of purchase.

Table 49-3 gives a general indication of the type of computerized measurement analysis that should be developed on an ongoing basis. This chart represents media information that should be retained. Its objective is to measure media profitably on an ongoing basis. It is recommended that this be updated and reviewed every four cycles.

Performance Analysis by Product

In order to make advertising as effective as possible, clubs or continuities offering a variety of product as a premium can effectively change the premium offers to fit the medium. Therefore, the advertisement copy, layout, or direct mail format can remain the same, but the product selection or premium can change.

The following is a suggested premium analysis by media measurement program that should be developed on an ongoing basis if a choice of premiums is offered to potential subscribers.

Product Analysis by Media Source

When more than one premium is offered as an enrollment incentive, product analysis by media source information should be retained (see Table 49-4). Its purpose is to determine which premiums are most successful in attracting new subscribers by individual media and afford clubs and continuities the option of tailoring specific premiums to specific media.

TABLE 49-3 Profitability Analysis by Source

Media Information

Media source
On-sale, mailing, or broadcast date
Unit of space
Type of mailing
Commercial length
Offer
Source code/key number

Enrollment Information

Advertising/production cost $________
Media cost $________
Premium cost (including royalty) $________
Postage and handling costs $________
Gross orders ________ Gross cost per order ________
Net orders ________ Net cost per order ________

Membership Information

Length of active member (number of cycles) ________
Percent still active
Percent canceled
Percent bad debt
Gross sales per member $________
Cost of sales per member $________
Net sales per member $________
Bad debt per member $________
Postage and handling $________
Net income (loss) per active member $________

SELLING TO EXISTING MEMBERS AND SUBSCRIBERS

The most profitable member or subscriber is an existing one. This fact is not stressed enough by companies in marketing and promotion executions.

TABLE 49-4 Product Analysis by Media Source Information

Media source ________
On-sale, mailing, or broadcast date ________
Unit of space
Type of mailing
Commercial length
Offer
Source code and key number ________

Product Premium	Number of Units	Number of Total
(List)	(List)	

Frequency of Communications

This refers to the frequency with which a subscriber is offered product on a continuing basis. Clubs generally vary from between six and eighteen cycles (mailings) a year. Continuity mailings are generally monthly.

Bulletins and Brochures

These are promotional materials sent to subscribers and members describing a particular cycle's product offers. How this is presented and merchandised can greatly affect the purchase rate and therefore the profitability of the amount ordered by a subscriber if it is more than a predetermined automatic shipment. Special combination order discounts or special inserts geared to a particular subscriber's interests generally help sell more of the product.

Bonus Plans

This is a merchandising method designed to encourage existing subscribers to buy more and retain membership longer. The strategy of bonus plans usually is geared to back-end or subscriber performance. In other words, the more a subscriber buys and pays for, the more that subscriber gets free or at a substantial discount.

Cross-Selling

This is a system where subscribers to a special-interest club or continuity are offered a subscription in another special-interest club or series. This is extremely effective as long as there is no trade-off in dollars. Tests should be conducted to ensure that existing member profitability is not being eroded and that a member is spending additional profitable dollars.

Returns

These are products that are returned to the club or continuity by subscribers after they have been ordered specifically (positive option) or shipped automatically (negative option).

Generally, there are fewer returns on products ordered on a positive option basis. It is important to state all product details clearly to reduce subscriber returns. Negative option returns generally will be higher; the higher the price of the offer, the better the chance of returns. This is an extremely costly fulfillment problem and can affect profitability greatly.

Telephone Ordering, Existing Customers

One of the major marketing disadvantages of club or continuity subscription is that the product cannot be obtained immediately. To accelerate the process that lasts from the time a subscriber orders to the time merchandise is received is a sound option strategy. Therefore, a special 800 number "speed ordering service" is essential for most clubs or continuities.

FULFILLMENT AND COMPUTERIZATION

The key to any club or continuity business is the proper shipping, handling, and billing (fulfillment) of customer orders and the ability to humanize and personalize an operation so that the subscriber has the opportunity to communicate with a real person on a one-on-one basis if a problem arises, not just a computer. It is absolutely essential that a complete fulfillment system be in place before any new member advertising or promotion begins.

Established clubs and continuities have their own computers and software program. However, many companies use computer service bureaus with existing club or continuity software programs.

Many service bureaus also offer complete warehousing, shipping, mailing, and inventory control capabilities in addition to computer software programs.

Bad Debt Collection

It is impractical to take legal action against club or continuity subscribers who do not pay their bills. Therefore, it is essential to develop a dunning system, which refers to a series of collection letters which are sent to subscribers at regular intervals. Club or continuity dunning series usually contain from five to nine letters before the subscriber is turned over to an outside collection agency.

Communicating with Subscribers

It is extremely important that new subscribers know exactly how a club or continuity works and what is expected of them during membership.

Therefore, it is important that each subscriber be assigned a membership or account number and that a "how the club or continuity works" booklet be sent on membership acceptance. This should be done before the first offering is sent.

It also is suggested that a customer service representative be assigned to each subscriber and that that person's name, address, and phone number be provided. This will reduce customer confusion, ill will, and product returns greatly.

THE FUTURE: A PERSPECTIVE

The meteoric growth that a majority of mass market clubs and continuities (particularly in the book and record areas) experienced throughout the late 1960s and 1970s has come to a grinding halt. While the balance of the 1980s will not toll the death knell for most of these companies (it is estimated that 25 percent will fold or be merged), the club and continuity business cannot be considered a growth industry as it is structured currently.

The new growth opportunities will occur in special-interest product areas targeted to specific market segments, using strategies that are closely aligned with HVIE.

In the simplest terms, there are six major problems facing the industry that go a lot deeper than a recession.

1. The cost of goods and fulfillment continues to escalate, making it difficult to maintain necessary profit margins.
2. The cost of acquiring new qualified subscribers through traditional mass media continues to increase rapidly.
3. Bad debt (subscribers who don't pay their bills) after products have been shipped continues to increase.
4. Active subscribers don't buy as much as they used to, and a larger percentage cancel their memberships sooner.
5. Competition for the home entertainment, leisure-time dollar is being eroded by HVIE: videocassettes, cable television, home computers, and home movie subscriptions.
6. Companies that create or manufacture products and services have discovered that they can make more money marketing these products and services themselves rather than receiving an advance plus royalty by selling subsidiary rights to mail-order distributors.

There are other major problems which were brought about by many of the club and continuity management personnel as a result of shortsighted marketing strategies and poor future planning.

First, they failed to recognize the fact that traditional retail distributors would become major competitors by selling products directly through their own catalogs and would use direct marketing to generate retail traffic and sell products at a competitive or lower price than clubs and continuities. In short, the club and continuity price advantage has all but disappeared.

Advertising for new subscribers must work harder to persuade consumers to join a club or continuity because of the benefits of membership, not because of the dollar value or the number of premiums given away.

Consider the basic offers today, few of which have changed in 20 years except to give away more for less:

Four for $1: buy four with no time limit

Four for $2: buy four in 2 years

Eleven for $11.79

Six for 1 cent

Two weeks' free examination

Free

No obligation

Club and continuity marketing people have paid too much attention to the mathematical disciplines of direct marketing. They have followed tired formulas instead of creating new ones. and they have failed to develop imaginative new creative strategies.

They have become victims of the numbers game, particularly as it relates to premium offers. They have given away too much and enrolled subscribers under false pretenses.

The solution is not to create the XYZ Home Entertainment Club or to offer book club members an option of purchasing a book in hardcover or paperback in an attempt to be all things to all people.

In the future, club and continuity companies will have to reposition themselves and repackage the following elements:

The offer and reason to subscribe

The membership commitment

The method of shipment

The relationship between mail-order and retail distribution

chapter **50**

FUND RAISING

Charles F. McCarty

Senior Copy Writer and Consultant
The Viguerie Company
Falls Church, Va.

James G. Aldige III

Executive Vice President
The Viguerie Company
Falls Church, Va.

INTRODUCTION

This chapter explains how direct mail is used:

To build a "warchest" for a political campaign

To recruit dues-paying members for a public service organization

To obtain financial support for a health or welfare program

As you read further it is important to keep in mind that the methods discussed in this chapter have more in common with selling by direct mail than they have with volunteer programs, special events, or other fund-raising activities.

Chapters 1 through 50 deal with unique selling points, knowledge of potential markets, creativity, testing, and standards of success. The pages that follow explain how the same techniques apply to direct mail fund raising. Each of the following subjects will be examined in turn:

1. **Fund-raising program development.** To determine what activities sponsored by a fund-raising organization can be marketed to the public on a national scale and how to explain these services to prospective supporters
2. **Market analysis.** To determine what segments of the national population are potential supporters of a specific fund-raising program
3. **Campaign creation.** To prepare high-quality, high-impact mail packages to convince the public to support a fund-raising program
4. **Testing and evaluation.** To measure the cost effectiveness of fund-raising campaigns and the receptivity of specific markets

FUND-RAISING PROGRAM DEVELOPMENT

Specifics and the Hostility Factor

It all starts with the fund-raising organization. The techniques used to develop a fund-raising appeal are essentially the same whether the sponsor is a political candidate, a public service organization, or a health or welfare activity. At one time or another each of us has donated money through the mail. Think about your own donating experience in terms of these observations:

- Most people do not contribute to political campaigns to reelect "Senator Smith"; people contribute to *defeat* specific plans in Smith's *opponent's* plank.
- Most people do not become members of a public service organization to keep America strong; people join these organizations to stop crime, fight inflation, or prevent a specific change in legislation.
- Most people do not contribute to charity in order to "do unto others as you would have them do unto you"; people make charitable contributions to buy food to feed the starving people of Africa, to buy medicine to cure a specific disease, and to buy Bibles to save a lost soul.

In these examples do you see a pattern? Note that each of these different categories of appeal has two things in common. First, the appeal is very specific. Second, the appeal is essentially hostile. It fights, stops, overcomes, or stamps out specific evil that threatens the contributor's cherished values, such as a person's right to work, a family's safety from criminals, or the health and welfare of a fellow human being. Successful direct mail fund raisers keep the words "specific" and "hostile" in mind as they select appealing subjects from a long list of fund-raising needs.

When direct mail specialists convert a fund-raising organization's broad programs into an effective appeal, they must discard generalities, looking for specific problems that can be described in detail and subject to counter-action on the part of the contributor. The specifics improve the readability of a mail package; the hostility factor arouses emotion and promises a benefit, that is, preventing the loss of a cherished value.

Organizational Resistance

The secret of direct mail fund raising is the ability to portray a fund-raising program in a truthful but unique way that captures the imagination of specific groups of supporters. But frequently in early relationships, many fund-raising executives resist this approach to selling their organization. They are working hard to build their organization. They are proud of the splendor of their headquarters, the size of their staff, and the overtime they work. Because these are the things they think are important, the staff of a fund-raising organization is inclined to dwell on these subjects in letters and brochures. Their most continuing need for money is often operating income to pay for next month's overhead.

But there is a pitfall in letting these thoughts creep into fund-raising mail: The public is not interested in overhead and administration. The public's interest in an organization is the results it achieves. If the public thinks about overhead at all, it thinks about it as a necessary evil. Remember that people don't give money to marble structures; they give money to solve specific problems that affect their own lives or lives of others.

Presold Needs

How does a potential contributor learn about new problems that affect their own lives or lives of others? Normally through the news media: television, radio, newspapers and magazines. For example, when a news commentator broadcasts the suffering following an earthquake in Central America, people know about it. And when they receive a letter asking for help to alleviate this suffering they are inclined to receive the letter favorably.

When people read in their newspapers about rioting and looting following a police strike in San Francisco, they become aware of this problem, too. Consequently, many of them are inclined to be receptive to an appeal to restrain the power of public service unions. When people hear a political candidate advocate redistribution of their income by raising taxes, they are inclined to react favorably to a letter from a rival candidate who requests help to stop this new threat to their personal income.

These are presold needs. Our most powerful direct mail appeals frequently ride in the wake of news coverage of such events.

Credibility

Even if a direct mail appeal is specific, presold, and hostile (or negative) in thrust, the public may still have reservations about supporting it unless they believe that the client's organization is trustworthy. This is the credibility factor. Fund-raising organizations should strive to project an image of credibility in the following ways:

1. Invite prominent people to serve on the fund-raising organization's advisory board and board of directors. The public recognizes names like Bob Hope, Billy Graham, Roger Staubach, and other people of national prominence. When their names appear on the masthead of a direct mail appeal it carries a lot of weight with the reader of the letter.
2. Whenever possible, fund-raising letters should be signed by a prominent person rather than by an official of the fund-raising organization. This technique adds a great deal of strength to the appeal because it amounts to a third-party endorsement.
3. Fund-raisers should collect testimonials citing the services that their organization has already rendered. For example:

   Testimonials from doctors saying that the fund raiser's gifts of medicine are saving hundreds of lives.

   Testimonials from working people saying that the legal services provided by the fund-raising organization helped save their jobs.

   Testimonials from other contributors explaining how good they felt to share the joys of Christmas with a needy child.

Checklist for Fund-raising Program Development

Fund-raising appeals will improve significantly if fund-raising executives and their direct mail specialists work together to make their direct mail packages:

1. Deal with specific problems
2. Arouse reader hostility directed at solving that problem
3. Select relevant problems presold by the news media
4. Instill reader confidence in the credibility of the fund-raising organization

MARKET ANALYSIS

Selecting the Mailing List

The mailing list pinpoints an interested audience for a unique fund-raising appeal. Mail the best fund-raising letter ever written to the wrong mailing list, and it will fail. The success of a fund-raising appeal depends more than anything else on your ability to apply the right criteria in selecting a mailing list.

Since there are at least 200,000 mailing lists in existence today it takes considerable knowledge and imagination to determine which hundred or less lists are worthy of selection for an initial test for a specific fund-raising appeal. If you do not apply the following criteria with some thoroughness and skill, it will be like looking for a needle in a haystack.

Recency. Contributors less than 12 months old (or even better, less than 6 months old) are much more responsive than those who donated, bought, or subscribed 2 or 3 years ago. The reason for this is obvious. The recently recorded names have an "active" supporting habit. Also it is much more likely your fund-raising letter will reach your prospects at the address listed with their names (if it is a recent address) than it will 2 to 3 years later because so many Americans move every year.

Frequency. There's a lot of truth in the saying, "a little repetition never hurt anyone." Spending money can become a habit, too. And when people spend more than once for the same thing they can become very valuable customers, supporters, or donors.

Contributing Range. It is not wise to try to sell a Rolls Royce to a person who never bought anything more expensive than a secondhand Ford. Conversely, your best prospects for secondhand Fords are not millionaires. That is why it is so important for you to know the previous contributing range in dollars of your prospective supporters before you send them your appeal. If you do not do this, you can price yourself out of the market.

Name Categories. This criterion is much more subjective than the others. We call it "name category" and, rather than try to define it, we can explain it best with these examples:

- People who contributed to President Reagan's election campaign will probably support increases in defense rather than domestic spending.
- People who read hunting magazines will probably oppose gun control legislation.
- People who supported an American Indian Foundation in New Mexico will probably support an Indian Mission on the Pacific Coast.

But there is more to name categories than the obvious examples cited above. Mailing lists (regardless of origin) that work for two or more causes with a common philosophy will probably be responsive to a third cause with the same philosophy. These lists at least deserve a fair test. How do you find this information? The answer is simple: Ask your list broker. An experienced list broker will constantly study the market and advise you on what lists are currently in demand by other list users whose appeals are similar to your own.

You will increase the probability of selecting the audiences most sympathetic to a specific fund-raising appeal by applying these four criteria, recency, frequency, contributing range, and name category, to the mailing lists you intend to test.

CAMPAIGN CREATION

A History of Selling

Are direct mail advertising and fund raising arts or sciences? The answer is "both" and "neither." They are artistic in as much as they thrive in an atmosphere of originality and imagination. But for the past 50 years since Claude Hopkins first published his book *Scientific Advertising,* a book which took much of the guesswork out of advertising, successful direct mailers have viewed their craft as essentially scientific.

Actually, direct selling of any kind is neither an art nor a science. It is a commercial activity. Its purpose is to sell at the lowest possible cost per sale. It is a tool of business—*not* of the entertainment industry. Its only measure of success is the cost of advertising per unit of sale in commercial direct mail and the cost to raise a dollar in direct mail fund raising—not the popular acclaim or praise of experts.

During America's first 150 years—from 1776 until the end of World War I—few executives understood the concept of mass markets as we understand them today. Most sales took place in small stores which sold small quantities directly to small groups of people. Sales ability was recognized as a skill essential to business success—but on a face-to-face basis. It was not very competitive, and it was, generally speaking, confined to local people who eventually became permanent customers.

In the old days, good sales ability did have two important characteristics that have become two of the basic principles of direct marketing: It was based on service to the customer, and it was personal.

About 60 years ago, mass production, mass communications and mass selling started to take over. The craft shop gave way to the mass production line. Local stores gave way to chain retail stores, and later to discount and wholesale outlets. Local newspapers gave way to syndicated publications, and first radio and later television found their way into most American homes. As a result, the United States became a more organized and less personal society. Individual selling ability took second place to very competitive mass marketing which scientifically identified potential buyers (or contributors). As the standard of living increased, the demand for more and more goods and more and more influence grew and grew.

But regardless of the gains, we always pay a price for progress. After 60 years of increasing exposure to modern mass communications, two very distinctive characteristics of the age we live in have started to emerge:

1. The competition for a person's attention is overwhelming. Today, it is estimated that the average person receives more than 200 appeals a day to spend his or her money—or to give it away. They receive three appeals for every 5 minutes they listen to their radio; 5 appeals for every 15 minutes they watch television; ten appeals on the average page of their newspaper; and several more in their favorite magazines, which carry appeals on almost every page.
2. The second distinctive characteristic is a direct result of this competition for a person's attention. More often than not, people think they have heard it all. As a matter of fact, most people have heard so much by the time they are earning their own spending money that they have built up an immunity to gimmicks, come-ons, premiums, and trite or cute ads.

This is why, to succeed today, an advertising or fund-raising appeal must stop a person long enough to get attention, hold the person's attention by physical or emotional involvement, and carry this involvement to the point where the person makes the decision to act by donating some money.

What's more, as a result of the characteristics of modern life a new need is beginning to emerge. In today's *impersonal* society people are hungry for *personal* attention and *personal* service. Good newspaper and television ads border on the personal, but in both these media logic tells the reader and viewer that others are receiving the same message.

Direct mail is different. By nature it is a personal medium of communication. In fact it is as much an "I" to "you" proposition as communication today can be. Where else, except on the telephone, can you have one initiator and one recipient for a specific message tailored to the needs of a specific person? Personalization is the key to direct mail success and it should manifest itself throughout all parts of a direct mail fund-raising appeal.

The Carrier Envelope

Consider the carrier envelope—normally the first thing people see when they empty their mail boxes. More often than not mail is sorted before it is opened to find the personal letters first. Normally business mail takes second priority.

Personal carriers are usually smaller than the number 9 or number 10 window carriers used for commercial mail. Many are shaped differently, like invitations; many are colored differently, while commercial envelopes are normally white.

Finally, most personal carriers use live stamps rather than Pitney-Bowes or preprinted indicia. Frequent testing of precancelled stamps—or even first class postage–should not be overlooked.

The Letter

When you open the mail package you see a difference in the stationery used. Business stationery is normally 8½ by 11 inches with an organizational heading at the top and the names of the board of directors down the left side. Personal stationary is smaller, frequently has only a return address (no heading) and begins its message closer to the top of the page.

We used to be taught in school that the two most acceptable business salutations were "Gentlemen" and "Dear Sirs." Note that both of these old-fashioned business salutations are masculine plural, presumably because the letter will probably be read by more than one person and the readers would be men. Therefore, a letter with a plural salutation could never be personal, private, or friendly.

On the other hand, a personal salutation shows that the letter writer recognizes the reader. "Dear Mr. and Mrs. Jones" (saluting people by name) is by far the most personal type of salutation. This, of course, takes a computer program or a memory typewriter to accomplish.

But there are other ways to personalize your salutation and show you recognize the reader as being different. For example:

Dear Customer
Dear Subscriber
Dear Supporter
Dear Fellow American
Dear Member
Dear Contributor

Some of these salutations shows that the letter writer recognizes and appreciates earlier contact with the reader:

- Dear Customer implies "thank you for your previous purchase."
- Dear Subscriber implies "thank you for reading our magazine."
- Dear Fellow American implies that the writer and the reader share a patriotic concern for the United States.

In those instances where a letter is being written to someone who has already donated financial support to a fund-raising cause, it is important to personalize your appeal by showing that you appreciate the donor's past generosity. For example:

- Thank you for the $15.00 you sent to help our needy orphans in March.
- The $10.00 you gave in reply to my October 10 letter will help buy a leg brace for a crippled polio victim.
- I appreciate the $20.00 you sent in April. I hope I can count on your help again to send $30.00 or even $20.00, now to meet this new emergency.

The choice of words is also very important in personal communication. Everyone who has listened attentively to a face-to-face conversation knows how naturally people speak to one another. But for some mysterious reason, written language becomes artificially stilted. "I think" becomes "it is believed." "I hope" becomes "it is desired." "Will you please?" becomes "Can you find it in your heart."

Keep in mind that the two most frequently used words in personal conversation should be "you" and "I." Candor and familiarity are also important in personal conversation and expressions like this convey that impression:

- Quite frankly, you should know
- I almost forgot to mention that
- Will you please take a minute to look at the snapshot I've enclosed
- Before you put this letter aside will you pick up your checkbook

It is also very important to begin a fund-raising letter by getting right to the point. Don't use two or three paragraphs (like a musical overture) to get your readers in the mood for the nitty-gritty—it won't work! You will bore them and they will stop reading.

Start with action-oriented beginnings like these:

- I hope you'll take a minute right now to answer the three questions on the enclosed National Opinion Survey.
- Please sign and mail the enclosed postcard to your congressman today.
- If you don't have time to read this entire letter will you please sign the enclosed petition to the President of the United States?

It is interesting that one of the greatest services an experienced copy chief can render to editing copy is eliminating the first two or three paragraphs and strengthening the letter 100 percent by picking as a new beginning an action-oriented sentence that gets right to the point.

The first paragraph is by far the most important part of the fund-raising letter. Remember, your appeal is only one of the 200 other appeals your readers receive every day. So grab their attention and grab it quickly. You have only the few seconds it takes your readers to scan the first paragraph to stop them, get their attention, and sufficiently arouse their interest to read further and absorb what you have to say.

Lengthy or trite beginnings are like static on your radio; they blur the clarity and impact of your message. You must start with a bang and involve the reader in taking the necessary action.

Involvement Techniques

It is difficult for a direct mail appeal to succeed without one or more involvement techniques. An involvement technique is a logical addition to a mail package which invites examination and action on the part of the reader. It is probably the most important way to build up contributor momentum to the point that it will lead to a contribution.

A large variety of techniques are available to get a reader physically and emotionally involved in a fund-raising appeal. The process of examining and acting on an involvement technique should start the hands in motion so that the mind and eventually the pocketbook will follow.

Here are some suggested involvement techniques:

Postcards
Polls
Gift tags
Telegrams (simulated)
Membership surveys
Sponsorship seals
Bank checks
"yes" and "no" stickers
Personalized membership cards or certificates
Petitions
Individual photographs with personal messages

Please note that all of these techniques make use of commonplace things that the reader has seen or used before. Your readers can recognize them at once and their previous experience using these cards, tags, stickers, etc., will lure them again in involving themselves in the direction that the appeal is going. The logical conclusion of this momentum-building experience will be making a contribution.

Copy Checklist

Whether you are writing fund-raising copy yourself or editing copy written by someone else, the guidelines that follow will provide you with a standard for improving the effectiveness of your direct mail appeals.

1. Do not burden your readers by letting them figure out how much to give. Decisions like this are distracting and cause a reader to lose interest. Suggest a specific gift, or even better, two or three suggested gifts indicating if possible what each gift will accomplish. Remember, the soda fountain clerk who asks, "Do you want two or three scoops of ice cream?" sells much more ice cream than the clerk who asks, "How many scoops do you want?"
2. Provide your readers with all the factual information you have on each fund-raising project. Use specific dates, times, names, places, and numbers. This makes the letter believable. On the other hand, avoid vague expressions like:

   A long time ago
   A man I know told me
   It will cost us thousands of dollars

   These vague expressions are hard for the reader to visualize and consequently to believe. Consider as an alternative a factual statement like this:

   At 6:32 P.M. on September 23, 1982, the President signed into law a bill that
   Senator Culpepper made it perfectly clear to me last Thursday that
   To put this life-saving message on television for 60 seconds will cost us $1427

3. Create a sense of reader urgency by indicating deadlines for reply. And give a logical reason for the deadline you impose. If there is no deadline your readers may put your appeal aside and get interested in something else. Then you've lost them.

   One way to convey urgency is to use two reply envelopes, each with a different deadline. One envelope is for the down payment to save the project from an emergency crisis and the other is for a final donation to solve the problem for good.

4. Don't worry about writing too long a letter as long as you confine your writing to the project upon which your appeal is based. Long copy usually pulls larger responses than short copy as long as the copy is interesting and relevant. To keep the readers momentum going, use word bridges so that the readers' attention flows effortlessly from paragraph to paragraph. Here are some of the more effective connecting phrases:

   But that's not all
   Now here's the most important part
   Better yet
   And to make matters worse
   So you can see for yourself why
   What is more

5. Build reader involvement by explaining the consequences of his or her failure to support you with true but emotional phrases like this:

   Unless you and other concerned Americans help me now I will have to abandon this life-saving project.

   Fifty children could starve to death next month if our emergency food supplies are not paid for and shipped next week.

6. To convey the idea of a personal letter use typewritten copy or even handwritten copy. Typeset copy will convey an impersonal message. Signatures at the end of a letter should be clear and bold, preferably in blue ink or in an ink that contrasts with the color of the body copy. This will make the letter look like it was individually signed.

7. After listening to so many cute TV and radio ads you may be tempted to try for a laugh by adding a line like this to an appeal for a religious charity:

   And remember, what you render unto God is deductible from what you render unto Caesar.

   But before you give in to this temptation ask yourself what a line like this will add to the selling power of the appeal. Keep in mind that spending or donating money is a serious business and do not risk losing the interest of your reader by trying to be cute or funny.

8. Observe the letter-reading habits of other people. Most people read the opening paragraph first. Then they turn the letter over to see who signed it. And while their eyes are at the end of the letter they read the postscript. This makes the postscript the second most important part of the letter. The postscript should contain one of the best possible reasons for answering the

appeal or one new and unique benefit the readers will receive if they comply with your request.

Keep these eight guidelines in mind as you originate or edit a fund-raising appeal. For maximum effectiveness the thoughts explained above should be applied to the entire package—not just the letter.

TESTING AND EVALUATION

Tracing Results

John Wanamaker of department store fame said, "I'm wasting half of the money I'm spending on advertising—but I don't know which half." Obviously, Wanamaker's advertising manager did not know how to test or evaluate the effectiveness of his advertisements.

Since Wanamaker's day a great deal has been learned about testing and evaluation. And one thing is clear: Few advertising media lend themselves to accurate evaluation as well as direct mail does. Television, newspaper and magazine advertisements cannot tell you the advertising cost of each unit of sale unless each ad offers a direct sale and each order is directly traceable to a specific advertisement.

In direct mail, on the other hand, returns can be traced back to specific mailing lists, specific mail packages, and specific dates of mailing. The income from these returns can be compared to the advertising or fund-raising costs used to generate this income.

Keeping Records

To evaluate anything accurately you must know what the standards of success are. And in fund-raising direct mail there are certain pieces of factual information you must keep track of from the start to the finish of a mailing:

1. The quantity of letters mailed
2. The unit cost of each mail package and the total cost of the mailing
3. The number of contributions received each day and cumulatively for the first 50 days
4. The dollar income received by day and cumulatively for the first 50 days

If you keep track of these four pieces of information you can evaluate the effectiveness of your mailing by computing these four standards of success:

1. Percent response
2. Average gift in dollars and cents
3. Net income
4. Cost per dollar raised

For example, assume that at the time of your mailing you knew these facts:

Quantity mailed: 1000 letters

Unit cost: $0.16 for one letter

Total cost: $160.00 for 1000 letters

Fifty days later, by tracking and recording the response you would also know these facts:

Gifts received: 32

Total dollars contributed: $320.00

Then, with these facts to work with you can evaluate the success of the mailing in these terms:

1. Percent response	Thirty-two gifts divided by 1000 letters equals 3.2 percent
2. Average gift	$320 divided by thirty-two gifts equals $10 (average)
3. Net income	$320 total contributions minus $160 total costs equals $160 net
4. Cost per dollar raised	$160 total cost divided by $320 total income equals $0.50 to raise a dollar

This type of evaluation is possible only if you use a coding system on all your response devices. In addition, you should change this code each time you make any variation in the mail package, the mailing list, or the mail date.

It is also very important that every day for the first 50 days after the mailing the number of gifts and the dollar income they produce be reported back for each of these mail codes.

Further, you should be aware that you will receive approximately half of your total income for first class mailings 10 days after the mail date and for bulk rate approximately 20 days after the mail date.

This knowledge makes it possible to evaluate a mailing and learn what you are doing (right or wrong) long before the mailing has run its full 50-day course.

Testing

If you use the above information based on small quantity test samples, you can cut losses and exploit success. In this way you can recover the losses incurred in tests and keep your direct mail budget in the black.

Remember, in a valid test only the tested item can be varied; everything else must remain constant. Here are the most common types of tests:

Appeal or Offer Test	Variable	Mail package A versus mail package B
	Constants	Same mailing list and same mailing date
Copy or Headline Test	Variable	Opening paragraph C versus opening paragraph D
	Constants	Same mailing list and same mailing date
List Test	Variable	Mailing List E versus mailing list F
	Constants	The same mail package (Provided you are mailing in the same general time frame, it is normally *not* necessary to mail list tests on the same day)

The Bottom Line

1. **Prospect mailings.** The purpose of prospect mailings is to generate a mailing list of people specifically committed to a fund-raising cause by recruiting from "raw names." The standard of success of a prospect mail program is normally to receive enough income to cover the cost of the mailings; in other words, to break even. Therefore, with a 16 cent package you need a 2 percent response and an $8 average contribution to cover the cost of the mailing. If this standard is used, the cost of building a contributor file is nothing.
2. **Contributor file mailings.** The purpose of contributor file mailings is to generate *net* income to support fund-raising projects. Fund-raising organizations should make between six and twelve of these mailings a year. A reasonable standard of success for a contributor file mailing is a net of $1.25 per letter mailed. Since first class live stamps and personalized computer letters are usually used for the high dollar, recently the cost of each mail package is about 40¢. This means that a gross of $1.65 per letter mailed is necessary to net $1.25. This goal would require a 16.5 percent response and an average contribution of $10. In this way a fund-raising organization with a contributor file of 100,000 names can net $125,000 above direct mail costs each time the contributor file is mailed. Eight mailings a year will net $1 million to finance the charitable or political programs sponsored by the fund-raising organization.

Testing and Evaluation Checklist

1. Keep accurate records of every fund-raising mailing.
2. Evaluate every fund-raising mailing to determine the cost to raise a dollar.
3. Test. Test. Test. Leave nothing to chance—not even the suggestions given earlier in this chapter.
4. Use prospect mailings to build your contributor file—not to net income. Reinvest net prospect income into additional prospect mailings to expand your contributor file.
5. Make sufficient contributor file mailings each year to raise all the money to support an organization's direct mail fund-raising program.

CONCLUSION

Using the principles explained in this chapter our agency

- Mailed close to a billion letters for over 300 fund-raising organizations
- Developed direct mail campaigns for four Presidential candidates
- Helped elect thirteen U.S. Senators and forty-two members of Congress
- Holds the all-time record for raising money for U.S. Senate and U.S. Congressional candidates.
- Developed 350,000 new contributors for a national veterans organization
- Developed 300,000 new members for an outdoor sports association

- Developed 500,000 new supporters for a national political movement
- Helped lead the fight to prevent taxpayer funding of congressional elections
- Generated five million postcards to help influence U.S. foreign policy
- Raised half a million dollars in 60 days to aid earthquake victims in Central America

These principles can work for any fund-raising organization if they are professionally conceived, carefully executed, and diligently applied. One key, of course, is the cause or charity itself. The best direct mail methodology cannot raise money for a purpose or a principle which does not merit the support of the public whose money is solicited. The choice of causes "whose time has come" is, after all, the one essential foundation of any fund-raising effort.

chapter 51

BANK MARKETING

John W. Booth

Senior Vice President
The Direct Marketing Group, Inc.
New York, N.Y.

INTRODUCTION

Evolving Financial Service Institutions

Although this chapter refers principally to commercial banks, based on the services which they presently offer, it recognizes that mutual savings banks, savings and loan associations, brokerage firms, insurance companies, and credit unions are all evolving into nearly generic financial service institutions (FSIs). Competition among the FSIs is forcing changes in laws and banking regulations which previously restricted banks in terms of geographic areas and the financial services which they could offer. Accordingly, as less regulated FSIs begin to offer services which at one time were marketed solely by commercial banks, the information in this chapter should be relevant to them as well.

Categories of Financial Services

In general, the FSIs can be divided into three categories according to the services they offer: those in which the customer's money is deposited in or invested with the FSI; those in which the FSI lends money to the customer; and other services (computer processing, safekeeping of securities, investment management, and trust services) which do not involve the transfer of money *per se*, and for which a fee is charged by the FSI. The marketing techniques used in promoting each of these three groups of services vary considerably since the prospective consumer views them so differently.

Role of Direct Marketing

Historically, financial service institutions—and banks in particular—have utilized media advertising as the principal component of the "marketing mix." Over the past few years, however, there has been a growing recognition of the complementary roles of media advertising and direct-response marketing. Media advertising is designed to create awareness and a positive perception of specific FSIs and the services they offer. Once a satisfactory awareness level has been reached—some have called it "share of mind"—direct-response marketing can be used to elicit incremental sales which could not have been generated by media advertising alone. In effect, direct marketing takes the FSI to the ultimate consumer, thereby translating share of mind to a measurable share of market.

Direct Response Media

Although not true in all cases, media advertising designed to generate direct response has not been as effective in marketing intangible financial services as it has for promoting merchandise. Accordingly, its use has generally been limited to the generation of inquiries. FSIs which do business in a number of geographic areas have the opportunity to test the best mixture of media and direct mail, by utilizing only media advertising in one geographic area, only direct mail in another area with similar characteristics, and a combination of mail and media in a third area. The productivity from each area can be measured by dividing the total dollars expended by the number of sales units or income generated, regardless of the mixure of marketing media used. If the combination of direct mail and media advertising proves most cost-effective, subsequent testing can be used to determine the best proportion between media and direct mail dollars.

Operational Interface

As noted before, FSIs have relied on media advertising to foster "walk in" business. Accordingly, most financial institutions are not mail-order oriented. In designing successful direct mail programs, it is critical that reply forms be developed which maximize response, but at the same time can be handled efficiently by existing systems and procedures. Where applicable, it is also important to plan for effective follow-up activities, once a response has been obtained through the mail. Finally, to maximize the cost-effectiveness of direct mail programs, they should be developed for coordination with not only media advertising—to assure an appropriate level of awareness, but also point-of-purchase displays, employee sales incentive programs, and internal training programs which teach employees how to handle direct mail inquiries and responses.

GENERAL CONSIDERATIONS

List Marketing

Customer lists, properly segmented, represent the greatest potential for direct mail marketing, since these lists represent individuals who are already predisposed to that financial institution. Problems must be anticipated in using such files, however, since the firm's computers were designed for accounting systems, not marketing applications. Few FSIs have developed sophisticated central information files or marketing information systems. There is a greater probability that files for different customer groups will be entirely different in record layout, and must be reformatted to avoid duplication of other files. Mass lists are most productive when the service being promoted has appeal and application to a broad segment of the marketplace. Selectivity is limited to demographic characteristics based on census data, but is most reliable only in median income and length of residency. Vertical lists may result in less names being mailed—even when a number of them are rented and unduplicated—but are generally more responsive than mass lists since psychographic characteristics and responsiveness to other mail offers are frequently typical of such lists.

Product Positioning

Regulations which have limited the components and pricing of financial services has resulted in most FSIs in a specific category—such as commercial banking—offering generic services which, for all practical purposes, are identical with those marketed by competitors. Accordingly, it is difficult to identify the elusive unique selling proposition which will create a competitive edge for one institution's product. In some cases, it is possible to combine financial services in a package offer, so that what appears to be a unique, new product can be marketed. The opportunity to respond by mail or telephone frequently adds a product differential which is perceived as a benefit by potential consumers, because of the inherent convenience of transacting business in this way.

Alternative Offers

A principal obstruction to marketing financial services is consumer apathy and inertia, which often can be overcome only by offering competitive rates—which may not be permitted by law or regulation! To maximize response, and recognizing the different dynamics which affect the marketing of credit services compared with deposit services, the testing of variable offers should generally precede a costly "roll-out" mailing. Preapproved credit versus applications, lead generation versus immediate purchase, and the use of incentives frequently result in quantum changes in response rates.

Mailing Packages

There is an old banking adage which states that "money isn't funny." For most people money is too difficult to acquire to treat it lightly, or even to borrow it with the attendant legal and moral obligation to repay. Mailing packages to promote financial services should convey the quality of the service being marketed without sacrificing readership. Tastefully designed brochures create a better impression about the financial institution and its services than big, splashy broadsides. Teaser copy on mailing envelopes telegraph the fact that there is advertising inside; the fact that the mailing is coming from a respected financial institution is generally all that is necessary to induce the recipient to open it. One creative challenge not faced in selling merchandise is developing graphics to portray intangible financial services. As is true in determining which offer will be most productive, when it comes to mailing packages the appropriate rule is: When in doubt—*test*.

Response Fulfillment

Each direct mail program should be designed to facilitate the tracking of results, so that the knowledge gained can be used as input for the next mailing. Personnel must be trained to tabulate responses accurately. When the purpose of a mailing is to generate sales leads, a program of follow-up activities should be developed at the same time as the mailing, with the follow-up program tracked to show when the point of diminishing returns has been reached. The results of direct mail programs should be measured on the basis of return on marketing investment—not merely response rates.

Direct Marketing Applications

In general, direct-response and direct mail marketing programs have been used to introduce new products (services), to cross-sell additional services to existing customers, to solicit accounts from individuals or firms not presently customers of the financial institution, to activate accounts in a dormant status, and to increase the flow of income and assure renewal of services such as credit cards with an annual fee, safe-deposit boxes, etc. Although designed to generate measurable business—ultimately at the lowest possible unit cost of sales—test mailings should also be considered research and development (R&D) expenditures.

Sales Continuum

Financial services can be distributed in a continuum, based on the difficulty in marketing the particular service. On that basis, revolving credit and credit cards without an annual fee would rank first, since the FSI's money is being offered with no cost for the service until the money is actually used. Next on the continuum would be fixed maturity loans, where the cost of interest becomes operative as soon as the loan is made. Moving from credits to deposits, various time deposit, savings and investment services can be listed, and depending on the particular service, prospective purchasers can maintain such relationships with a number of financial institutions. Next in line would be "transaction accounts"—checking or NOW accounts. Since most consumers need only one or two of such services, coupled with the complexities in changing financial institutions for such a service, these are more difficult to market than savings services. Last on the continuum would be packages of financial services, which generally require a high minimum deposit or investment, and provide a combination of transaction, savings, and even credit services which will appeal only to a small segment of the overall market. The continuum is a useful tool in anticipating response rates, which generally decline in moving from revolving credit to financial service packages. The continuum can also be seen as a path to be followed in cross-selling existing customers from the easier-to-market services to those which are more difficult to sell.

REVOLVING CREDIT

Definition

The three basic forms of revolving credit are (1) stand-alone—a line of credit accessed by special checks; (2) credit combined with a transaction account, in which the line is accessed when the account is accidentally or intentionally overdrawn, but may also be accessed by special checks; and (3) credit card accounts, where credit lines are principally accessed by plastic cards, but against which special checks may also be drawn. In all categories, a predesignated credit line with a stated maximum loan amount is issued, with monthly payments used to reduce the customer's indebtedness—and thereby increase the maximum dollars available for reuse. This section will discuss the marketing of the first two kinds of revolving credit; the following section covers credit cards.

Mailing Lists

Customer files are the most productive source of prospects for revolving credit services. Transaction account customers are an obvious audience for any service tied to the transaction account. Individuals who have current or previous satisfactory borrowing records with the bank are better prospects for the stand-alone service, since it is not necessary to open a checking or NOW account. Selected vertical lists represent the best prospects for noncustomer mailings—particularly those which provide some indication of income (so there is a higher probability that the credit can be approved once the application is received); those which reach younger individuals, who tend to have a more positive attitude toward (and a need for) credit; and those in particular "responder" lists—individuals who have replied to other direct mail offers.

Positioning

Since there is no initial cost for having a line of credit available, offering a financial reserve which is available when needed can provide a "comfort factor" which has proved to be the principal selling point for such services. (The consumer pays only for the money used, which can be repaid in full at any time without penalty, thus saving interest costs.) A secondary copy point is the ease of access to the borrowed funds, since they are available whenever and wherever a personal check would be accepted. Finally, since the available funds are replenished as the individual makes periodic payments, there is no need to apply and await approval for a loan each time borrowed funds are needed.

Offers

For many years, revolving credit services were marketed with a credit application which needed to be filled in, returned, and evaluated before the account was opened. Response rates rarely exceeded 3 to 4 percent, and with "upscale" services (with minimum lines as high as $5000), a response rate over 2 percent was considered satisfactory. Matching input lists against credit bureau records and mailing only to those who met predesignated credit criteria on a preapproved basis resulted in dramatic increases in response rates. A consumer was assured of receiving the initial credit line offered in the mailing. Respondents could be give the opportunity to complete a "miniapplication" to request a credit line higher than that offered, or the bank could offer increased lines either with an application or through computer analysis for automatic line increases—after some experience had been gained in terms of the respondent's repayment performance. When the minimum line for an upscale service precludes the possibility of credit bureau prescreening, suggesting the basic criteria used for credit approval in copy (for example, years of employment, minimum income, income-to-debt ratio) will improve response rates by giving people some assurance that, once the application is completed and returned, there is a high probability that the account will be approved. Offering an incentive (cash or merchandise premium) may improve response when an application is required, but, interestingly, such an offer also serves to screen out those individuals who have some concern about their credit-worthiness, since the incentive is only available to those whose applications are approved.

Follow-Up Activities

Generally, in a mature revolving credit program, about 60 percent of the lines of credit will be in use at any time, and about 60 percent of the dollars committed will be represented by outstandings. Since inactive accounts provide no income, and in fact represent an expense to the financial institution, an activation mailing—either as a reminder or to provide an incentive for use—can help increase the proportion of lines in use.

CREDIT CARDS

Evolution of Product

Although offered for many years by oil companies and retail stores, credit cards were first marketed by financial institutions as a proprietary product under the name of the financial institution. In the 1960s, banks banded together in voluntary groups and began issuing cards with first national and now international acceptance. In marketing a MasterCard or VISA credit card, a financial institution relegates its name to secondary importance to the group name in order to assure acceptability over a larger geographic area. Until the late 1970s, credit cards were offered at no cost to the customer, except for finance charges if balances were not paid within a stated grace period following receipt of a monthly invoice. But then the high cost of money to fund outstanding credit card accounts necessitated the imposition of annual or other fees for all card holders, whether or not they incurred interest charges, in order to make the credit card a profitable service. Only in areas where state regulations do not permit such fees has this practice not become widespread. More recently, in 1981, the MasterCard and VISA organizations permitted financial institutions to market "premium" bankcards with minimum credit lines of $5000 or more, higher annual fees, and a variety of additional noncredit services. This positioned the bank credit card directly against the travel and entertainment cards, such as American Express, Diners Club, and Carte Blanche.

Market Research

The imposition of an annual fee has made it more difficult to market even a nonpremium MasterCard or VISA service. Market research should be used as input to both product and account acquisition program development, to determine what additional features will make the card more marketable, and also to help segment the overall market for this service. Market research will help in determining which mailing lists would be most appropriate, and how best to position the service for various segments of the market, based on interest in particular features of the credit card service.

Mailing Lists

Traditionally, mass lists, which were matched against credit bureau records to permit preapproval for a credit card service, have been used for account acquisition programs. As a result, many financial institutions no longer have large staffs of credit analysts who can verify employment and income and evaluate credit applications. In many geographic areas, however, the credit card's life cycle has reached the point of functional market saturation. In other words, the cost of acquiring new card holders who would qualify for, and have an interest in accepting, a MasterCard or VISA card is break-even at best when acquisition costs are compared with the amount of income likely to be generated. The alternative is to reach individuals who would qualify for the card through an application, who do not meet predesignated criteria for preapproval, or who have insufficient data on file in the credit bureau for preapproval. Mass lists can be used to isolate such individuals through demographic census data prior to the credit-screening process. Specialized life cycle lists, which identify individuals at the time they graduate from college, marry, or change residence, can reach individuals at a time when they have immediate, nonrecurring need for consumer credit available through the credit card service. Again, existing customers prove to be viable targets for credit card solicitation, since they are already predisposed to the financial institution. Finally, credit cards offered through third parties—retail stores, association members, and other affinity groups—take advantage of the predisposition individuals have to those organizations, as either members or customers.

Positioning

Any card issuer can offer the benefit of using a credit card as a money management tool through such features as monthly billings, descriptive statements, and the option to pay all or a part of the outstanding balance. For those institutions willing to analyze individual applications, and which provide a credit analysis staff to do that, the maximum line of credit which the consumer can comfortably handle can be offered as "the only credit card you'll ever need." Whenever possible, unique features should be added to the basic credit card service to distinguish a financial institution's product from that of its competitors. Such features as travel insurance, credit card checks, travelers checks and other travel services, and optional life, health, or accident insurance can improve both interest in and response for a specific credit card. They can also provide opportunities to position the service differently for different segments of the market.

Offers

Because the customer has only to accept it, a preapproved offer for a credit card will generally result in significant increases in response rates above the response rates to offers to apply for the service. But even in markets where functional saturation has not occurred, preapproval is not practicable for the large minimum lines required with premium cards. Suggesting in the copy the criteria used for approval will improve response, as noted in the previous section on revolving credit. Finally, free trial periods, one-half price offers for initial periods, money-back guarantees, and merchandise premiums should all be tested in an annual fee environment to determine which technique is most cost-effective.

Post-Mailing Research

Once the direct mail solicitation has been completed for a premium card or one in which an annual fee is required, research should be conducted with both respondents and nonrespondents to determine (1) which additional feature or features provided the principal motivation to accept the credit card, and (2) what were the principal reasons for nonacceptance: more competitive products, misunderstanding of the offer, positioning of the service, or other factors which could be corrected to improve response rates in subsequent solicitations.

CONSUMER LOANS

Market Considerations

The market for closed-end, fixed maturity consumer loans with fixed monthly payments has been usurped to a great extent by revolving credit—stand-alone, tied to a transaction account, or part of a credit card service. There are still individuals, however, who prefer the discipline of the traditional installment loan. This is particularly true for such major purchases as cars, home appliances, recreational vehicles, and permanent home improvements. (From the FSI's standpoint, most of these loans are also secured.) For many individuals, installment borrowing is a way of life. Once the payments on one's car have been completed, it is traded in for a new one, and loan payments for a car become a permanent part of one's budget. A more recent innovation in installment lending is the home equity or second mortgage loan, secured by a secondary lien on real estate. These loans are used to finance college tuition, home improvements, the purchase of a vacation home, or even investments. In effect, a home equity loan allows an individual to use as security today the equity built up in a home through either reduction of the original first mortgage principal, or increase in market value—and then repay the obligation for many years into the future.

Mailing Lists

The principal difficulty in marketing immediate obligation loans is reaching prospective borrowers at the time of a credit need. People do not borrow capriciously, or even because loan rates may be low. The need for particular goods or services requiring financing must precede the need for the money. Again, customer lists represent the most productive source of applicants, because of their predisposition towards the financial institution—particularly if they have a transaction account relationship. The customer relationship can be utilized to at least infer a higher probability of credit approval once the application is received. Vertical noncustomer lists for loans, other than second mortgage, should focus on younger people apt to be in the acquisitive stage of the life cycle, whose needs for credit transcend the capability to make sizeable deposits or investments. Finally, present borrowers who need additional funds and former borrowers who have successfully repaid their initial obligation can be solicited on the basis of the excellent credit ratings they have established with the financial institution. Finance companies in particular have successfully exploited this market with periodic, seasonal mailings emphasizing the credit standing and particular uses to which borrowed funds could be put. For second mortgage loans, the best possible list is one of single-family housing units—although there is no way to find homeowners *per se*—with 2, 3, or more years of residency, thus assuring an increase in the home's equity due to inflation alone, and a minimum median income to insure credit-worthiness. All these selectivity factors are available from most mass lists.

Positioning

There is a temptation to give primary emphasis to the uses to which funds could be put, forgetting that the financial institution's goal is to "sell money." If the copy is end use–oriented, those who do not have a need for that use of the funds will be turned off, and a potential applicant will be lost. This is not to suggest that a variety of uses for the money might not be given secondary emphasis, since cars, vacation trips, swimming pools and other tangibles are much more pleasant to relate to in terms of copy and graphics than a stack of currency representing the money available for the "good things in life." Since most financial institutions would prefer to make sizeable loans, and offer revolving credit to take care of small, periodic needs for borrowed funds, preapproval of specific loan amounts through credit bureau screening is not practicable. Recipients can be given guidelines for credit evaluation, however, to instill a degree of confidence that the loan may well be approved—thus fostering a higher response rate.

Offers

As noted above, it is virtually impossible to isolate those individuals with immediate needs for borrowed funds. Clearly, those who do have such needs and can be motivated to apply will respond when the mail offer is received. To expand the productivity of a mailing, recipients should also be encouraged to apply for "cash-in-advance"—a prequalified loan commitment which can be drawn upon for a fixed maturity loan within a stated period of time—3 to 6 months, for example. The rule of thumb is that about half of those applying and approved for a loan commitment will borrow all or part of the amount approved within 6 months after the commitment is made. It is these additional sales which improve the marketing economies of a loan solicitation mailing. Other offers which have improved response rates include periodic loan "sales" during which lower-than-normal rates are available to those applying within the stated period. While people will not borrow simply because it costs less, this incentive encourages those who have credit needs before the expiration date to come to that source, rather than a competitive one, in order to save on interest cost. The same motivation holds true for offering premium incentives during a stated promotional period. Finally, to improve response from those with immediate credit needs, the opportunity should be provided to apply by phone. Trained operators will ask appropriate questions and actually complete the loan application with the information provided over the phone.

SAVINGS SERVICES

Impact of Deregulation

The more regulated FSIs—commercial banks, savings banks, and savings and loan associations—have long enjoyed low-cost funds thanks to government restrictions on the amount of interest they could pay on time and savings deposits. Over the past few years, however, money market mutual funds have drawn billions of dollars out of the more traditional financial institutions as a result of the market competitive rates they could pay. Now, banks and thrift institutions are attempting to come up with similar services, and are pressuring the government regulatory agencies and the Congress to allow them to compete across the board with deregulated rates—even as they attempt to amortize low yield loan portfolios and replace these assets with new high-rate loans. Although millions of Americans still maintain low-yield savings accounts, some of them with balances in six figures, the name of the game in attracting new time deposits is rate.

Mailing Lists

Since virtually anyone can open a savings account, and can maintain such a service in a number of financial institutions, mass media advertising has been effective in the past in attracting new dollars—frequently moving these funds from other institutions and often at the expense of a premium campaign. By contrast, for money market funds and combined checking-savings-brokerage accounts (the first of which was Merrill Lynch's Cash Management Account) direct mail has proved far more effective. As competition within the brokerage industry and with traditional financial institutions has increased, media expenditures have risen, but target marketing through direct mail to selective mailing lists still accounts for a large share of new accounts. Existing customers currently using other banking or brokerage services still represent the best potential for time deposits because of their predisposition to that institution. For noncustomer lists, the key is to recognize the life cycle of individuals. The younger have credit needs and cannot maintain sizeable reserves of liquid funds, while older people are no longer in an acquisitive stage of their lives—their children have been educated, and excess disposal income can be maintained in savings or other investments. In addition to considering age, banks and thrift institutions should concentrate on individuals with a predisposition for the more traditional financial institutions, rather than those who are securities-oriented.

Positioning

Again, the key concern is rate. Following that, easy access to one's funds, and packages of banking services which include savings, have proved to be viable copy themes. Until money market funds proved that branch accessibility was not important, the traditional financial institutions generally attempted to drive prospective savers into their branches to open accounts. Now, the convenience of depositing by mail, coupled with "hotline" telephone numbers where one can get up-to-date rate information, has helped to make savings and time deposit services appear more like money funds.

Offers

In the past, when the traditional FSIs could not compete on rates, merchandise premiums proved effective in attracting new accounts. This is undoubtedly true today, particularly in competing with less regulated competitors who have not used such offers. Some banks have also been successful in using cash as an incentive, generally as "seed money" to open the new account. Finally, consideration should be given to automatically transferring excess funds from lower-rate, more liquid savings services to longer maturity, high-yield time deposits—similar to the way cash management services sweep uninvested balances into the portion of these accounts intended for the money market fund.

RETIREMENT SAVINGS

Role of Government

For years, the social security system was considered a "safety net" to supplement or, where not available, to replace corporate pension programs. It is now generally recognized that Americans must be motivated to utilize other, self-funded retirement vehicles. The burden of funding retirement through general tax revenues to supplement a virtually bankrupt social security system is increasingly unacceptable to those still employed who must pay the tax bills. Initially, self-funded retirement savings programs were limited to the self-employed and those not covered by corporate pension or profit-sharing programs. In 1982, those services were expanded to cover virtually anyone employed for wages, and the amount which could be deposited each year in these funds were liberalized. Such deposits are treated as direct deductions against earned income for tax purposes.

Competition

The expanded market for retirement savings has attracted new competitors who had not expressed interest in this market in the past. Securities brokers, money funds, and insurance companies are all vying for long-term retirement savings, even as the more traditional financial institutions are now able to compete with deregulated rates. The newer competitors generally charge fees to cover commissions and other expenses, while banks and thrift institutions to date have not charged fees and can offer government-insured deposits as well.

Mailing Lists

To maximize the return on the marketing investment, the key is clearly to focus on individuals who can put the maximum allowable amount into retirement savings each year and also to reach those individuals predisposed to the particular financial institution. Those who are securities-oriented undoubtedly have a close relationship with their account executive from a brokerage firm, and are not as likely to be interested in a banking product which provides no opportunity for appreciation in principal. Others, however, are more comfortable with traditional financial institutions who provide insured deposits, no risk of loss of principal—and who now can pay competitive rates.

Positioning

Virtually all FSIs have focused on the total dollars which could be available at retirement, presuming current interest rates and no losses of principal. Such sizeable nest eggs are made possible by deferring taxes on both principal and interest until retirement, when the individual's tax rate would presumably be less. The added competition for retirement savings has created confusion, and deregulated accounts have encouraged a proliferation of products, so that some institutions have successfully used a low key, "objective counseling" approach instead of the hard sell, high-rate future funds theme. Consumers must ultimately choose each year, between spending (and enjoying) funds today or locking them up until retirement. Particularly in a high-inflation economy FSIs should point out that if retirement funds are needed prior to retirement they can be withdrawn, and the 10 percent surtax paid, with a sizeable net appreciation in the amount invested.

Offers

The opportunity to get objective advice should be a particularly strong offer for the more traditional financial institutions. Incentives may play a role in attracting new accounts, but would be difficult to administer in retaining funds which can be rolled over to competitive plans on a yearly basis, depending on the maturity of the investment vehicle. While most FSIs have concentrated on younger workers, who can accumulate funds well up into six figures before retirement, the tax deferment should have equal appeal to older people nearing retirement, even though the accumulated funds will not be as great. A preretirement savings package into which lump-sum retirement benefits could be deposited and then withdrawn as needed, could result in sizeable infusions of funds from this market. Finally, FSIs must determine whether the administrative costs of handling periodic or monthly deposits in retirement savings attracts profitable accounts, as opposed to concentrating marketing dollars on those individuals who can make one-time maximum annual contributions to their retirement savings plans.

TRANSACTION ACCOUNTS

Consumer Inertia

Most consumers maintain one—or at the most two—transaction accounts (traditional checking or NOW accounts). Such accounts are generally established initially for geographic convenience in making deposits and cashing checks, and for price convenience. Unless a financial institution creates serious unhappiness because of errors, hostile personnel, or refusal to consider requests for loans, an individual is loathe to move a transaction account unless he or she moves to another geographic area. Ordering new checks, maintaining sufficient balances in the existing account to cover checks still outstanding, and reconciling statements are enough of a chore to create considerable inertia, which explains why transaction accounts are among the most difficult financial services to market.

Mailing Lists

Consumers exhibit little loyalty to financial institutions who have loaned them money. Consequently cross-selling transaction accounts to existing customers is not as productive as for other financial services. Without a very unique or extremely price-competitive service, it is even less likely to sell transaction accounts to noncustomer lists.

Positioning

It may well be possible to add ancillary features to a transaction account product to create a unique selling proposition when compared with competitive products. Accessibility to transaction account funds through automatic teller machines has not proved to be sufficient incentive to move transaction accounts from one bank to another in the past. Access to in-home banking privileges will be of interest to a small minority of consumers for the forseeable future. The most likely sales platform is to include transaction account services as part of a package of financial services wherein the individual buys the package, begins using the transaction account services, and ultimately drops the original transaction account maintained with another institution.

DEBIT CARDS

Product

There has always been confusion in the financial services industry as to nomenclature for plastic cards other than the traditional credit cards. In this context, an automatic teller machine (ATM) card is one designed principally to access an automatic teller machine. A debit card is one which is used in lieu of a credit card in merchant transactions or across-the-counter cash withdrawals, although it may also access an ATM. Although proprietary cards may be used locally with merchants which recognize them (after education and sign up by the sponsoring bank), MasterCard and VISA debit cards have widespread acceptance virtually anywhere the credit cards issued under those names are accepted.

Mailing Lists

Typically, some 25 to 35 percent of an FSI's transaction account customers will accept and use a debit card, although these levels of penetration may be achieved only through two or more mailings. Some banks have had success in marketing this service to credit card customers, but the response rates have generally been less than 5 percent since it is necessary to open a transaction account in order to enjoy debit card privileges. In an environment in which credit cards require an annual fee, it may be possible to market the debit cards to those individuals who are not interested in the credit features of the credit card, do not revolve their credit, but desire an acceptable plastic card which provides a convenient noncash medium of exchange as well as access to hotels and rent-a-car agencies, where cash is not as acceptable as plastic.

Positioning

Access to transaction account funds where a personal check would not be accepted is the principal selling point. In fact, a debit card will be accepted beyond the geographic area served by a particular bank, either in this country or across the world, when personal checks would rarely be accepted. A secondary benefit is that, if the debit card is lost or stolen, one telephone call eliminates the possibility of access to one's transaction account. The loss of unused checks would require placing a hold on all transaction account debits, opening a new account, and ordering new checks. A debit card can also be used to access ATMs, eliminating the need to carry a separate ATM card.

Offer

Most financial institutions charge a monthly or annual fee for debit card privileges, although this is generally less than the fee charged for a credit card. Since most consumers have not had an opportunity to use and experience the benefits of a debit card, a free trial period without fee is critical to acceptance and usage. Once individuals use the service, very few are willing to drop it, and thus willingly accept a monthly fee on a continuing basis.

ELECTRONIC FUNDS TRANSFER SERVICES

Products

The term electronic funds transfer services (EFTS) is generally used to describe paperless transactions which to date include those of ATMs, bill-paying by phone, and in-home banking through which a consumer can directly access his or her accounts maintained on the FSI's computer.

Mailing Lists

Response rates from mailings to noncustomer lists to promote EFTS would indicate that, while a few "innovators" and "early tryers" will accept such services, it appears that the most economic way to promote electronic services is by limiting mailings to customer lists. This will undoubtedly change over time, as the more sophisticated services gain acceptance, but to date only ATMs appeal to more than a younger audience interested in trying new techniques. It is important to remember that EFTS represents a delivery mechanism for financial services, rather than a service *per se*. Consequently, consumers are being asked to try something which runs counter to existing habit patterns of dealing with people in a banking institution or, for those who have accepted ATMs, a machine.

Positioning

In order of appeal, the principal benefits of all electronic services are 24-hour access to one's funds; elimination of long teller lines, or in some cases, the need to even come to the financial institution; access to funds over an extended geographic area (ATMs are linked in nationwide networks); and the savings in postage costs when bills are paid by phone or through in-home banking.

Offers

Because consumers are asked to change existing habit patterns, it is generally necessary to provide some "sweetener" to induce them to accept and use the service, thus educating themselves about the benefits of electronic banking. These incentives can take the form of merchandise or cash to use an ATM for the first time, drawings for a sweepstakes-like structure of gifts with each transaction representing an entry, and a free trial period for services like pay-by-phone which require monthly or transaction fees.

Follow-Up Activities

Electronic financial services have not been readily embraced by the masses. Although some may accept them out of curiosity, usage is another matter. An activation program should be developed simultaneously with the plan designed to solicit new accounts. Periodic activation programs will further increase usage. Once individuals have accepted and begun using electronic services, and only then, will it be possible to cross-sell other financial services which can be accessed electronically. Finally, since consumer attitudes and motivations regarding these new services are not well known, postintroduction research should be conducted among both respondents and nonrespondents to mailings soliciting new accounts.

PACKAGES OF FINANCIAL SERVICES

Products

Perhaps the first packaging of consumer financial services was the Wells Fargo Gold Account through which individuals could utilize a number of banking services with one monthly fee. Other banks across the country introduced similar services with varying degrees of success. In the mid-1970s, a few banks (including Wells) introduced packages of services for "better customers," or those who would qualify as such if they deposited sufficient balances. Generally, maintaining a minimum balance in specific savings services qualified the depositor for a list of other financial services, all free of charge. A variation on this theme is the premium MasterCard or VISA card which provides a number of financial and travel services in addition to traditional credit card benefits (see the preceding section on credit cards.) A recent package of financial services, the Cash Management Account (CMA) introduced by Merrill Lynch Pierce Fenner and Smith, has since been emulated with similar services by other brokerage firms and even commercial banks and thrift associations who have joined with brokerage firms to offer CMA-like services.

Mailing Lists

With the exception of CMA-like services, the combination of banking and brokerage services appeals to securities-oriented individuals, (particularly those already dealing with the sponsoring brokerage firm). Packages of banking services appeal principally to existing customers who may already qualify on the basis of balances maintained, or who have shown a marked willingness to consolidate funds presently held with competitor institutions in order to enjoy the benefits of a services package. The average balances maintained in such accounts are generally a multiple of those for traditional transaction accounts, but to date, noncustomer lists have not proved productive. The key to marketing financial packages appears to be establishing the initial relationship, and then cross-selling the service to upgrade the relationship.

Positioning

While the capability to enjoy a variety of financial services at no cost would appear to be a compelling sales message, research has shown that many individuals accept a financial package because it identifies them as important customers of the sponsoring institution. The psychic benefits may well be as strong as the economic. By their very nature, financial packages provide through one vehicle a complete range of services, eliminating the need to open individual accounts. Finally, financial packages permit the consumer to use balances to eliminate monthly service charges.

Offers

Unlike other innovative financial services, a free trial period is not applicable to marketing financial packages since the qualifying minimum balance eliminates monthly charges. Premium incentives should be tested. If the financial package requires an extensive application to accomodate all of the various components of the program, testing a "request for details" against the complete application should be considered, in anticipation that the request offer will generate a higher response. In this case, however, the conversion rate to new accounts would then be measured against those from the application offer.

Follow-Up Research

Since, by its very nature, a financial services package includes numerous components, postintroduction research can be used to determine which feature or features have most appeal in generating new accounts. The research would also help determine how best to position the service by subsegment of the market. Most financial institutions have found that such a service has appeal to either younger affluent professionals and business people, or to older, more affluent individuals who are approaching retirement or already retired. The research may determine that a modification of the basic service may have stronger appeal to the senior citizen group.

TRUST SERVICES

Products

In general terms, trust services can be divided between those which generate immediate fee income and those from which the income is deferred—generally until the customer's death, at which point the trust department receives income as administrator of the resulting estate. Most trust departments offer both consumer and corporate services, all of the latter falling in the immediate fee category. In either case, the market is highly selective, and lends itself particularly well to direct-response marketing techniques.

Mailing Lists

For most consumer trust services, selected vertical lists can provide the names of individuals with high net worth, which is generally a more important consideration than income. For specific securities-related services, such as custody and investment management accounts, individuals likely to have large securities portfolios would be the appropriate target market. For corporate trust services, business firms can be elected by such criteria as number of employees, kind of business (as identified by standard industrial classification), annual sales, and even whether the business has an existing pension or profit-sharing plan. Many trust departments have generated their own lists based on existing customer relationships or from names suggested by commercial banking officers or even third-party sources. The danger in this approach is that if it is felt that the internal mailing list includes every potentially good trust customer, opportunities will be lost for sales to individuals who do not end up on this mailing list. Furthermore, unless appropriate "list cleansing" techniques are used, mailings may be going to individuals who have moved out of the appropriate geographic market, may have established trust services with competitors, or even have died. A better approach is to match the internal list against appropriate outside lists, and then to mail to customers as such, capitalizing on the existing relationship but not ignoring the potential available from noncustomers found on the outside lists.

Positioning

Virtually all trust departments believe, and promote their belief, that they have highly skilled, extremely competent personnel—as though no competitor can offer those benefits. In fact, what is needed to differentiate one trust department from another is statistics relating to performance and then an indication of how the capable personnel are organized to deliver that performance. Trust departments have many services, and with a few exceptions—such as securities management—it is not possible to identify through selected mailing lists what kind of services may have the greatest appeal for a particular individual. Accordingly, it is necessary to promote one trust service at a time in a continuing series of mailings, recognizing that individuals will respond to those offers which provide the possibility of benefits that meet their individualized needs.

Offers

All too many trust departments believe that the purpose of direct mail to appropriate target audiences is to educate them about the details of particular trust services. In fact, if all the details are provided up front, there's no reason to make an inquiry unless the recipient has such strong interest in a particular service that he or she is willing to meet with a salesperson from the trust department. A better approach is to stress the benefits that can be enjoyed from a particular service, providing no details, and giving the recipients an opportunity to request further information about the services which appear to meet personal objectives. By so doing, respondents are tacitily acknowledging their interest in a particular service and will be more receptive to receiving—and reading—information that was sent to them at their request.

Follow-Up Activities

Most business development personnel in trust departments are accustomed to having "qualified" leads handed to them by third parties—commercial banking officers, insurance sales people, or attorneys. A direct mail lead generation program will provide the names of individuals who have varying degrees of interest in a particular trust service, but the salesperson must understand that prospects need to be contacted and qualified to determine both interest and probability for a profitable relationship before setting up an appointment and expending further time in attempting to generate a sale. Since this procedure is more difficult and time-consuming than handling leads referred by third parties, unless senior management gives full support to the direct mail effort, and sales people are trained to implement the necessary procedures, a mailing can succeed in terms of response rate but fail because a creditable effort has not been made to convert leads to sales.

CORPORATE SERVICES

Products

In general terms, services for present and potential corporate customers can be divided among credit services which include leasing, deposit services, and fee programs such as data processing services, letters of credit, etc.

Mailing Lists

Depending on the corporate service to be promoted, and an analysis of the profile of existing customers for that service, mailing lists can be acquired using such selectivity factors as annual sales, Standard Industrial Classification, number of employees, and whether the firm is a main office or branch of a larger organization. Further, it is possible to obtain the names of individuals in management based on their specialized function such as chief executive officer, chief financial officer, etc. In addition, internal files of existing corporate customers can be used to cross-sell additional services by creating interest and generating leads.

Positioning

Virtually all prospective corporate customers already have a relationship with an FSI. Whether the existing FSI is providing satisfactory servicing of the account, or can offer competitive services, can not be determined through the mailing lists generated for a corporate lead generation program. The best approach, then, is to concentrate copy on the benefits available from specific corporate services, without explaining all of the details. If the prospect's existing bank has not brought that service to the company's attention, it may be inferred that such services are not available from the current FSI—or even more devastating, the financial institution does not have enough interest in the customer to call attention to services which will clearly benefit the business. A less specific approach is to suggest that the FSI specializes in services for the "middle market," for example, and then challenge the recipient to match the quality and delivery of services with those available from the existing financial institution.

Offers

All corporate mailings are designed to generate leads, not sales, since the various corporate services can be sold only on a face-to-face basis. One mailing will not generate responses from every possible potential corporate customer. An approach which has worked well is a series of mailings, each one building on the previous one, and increasing in sales intensity. The first might offer a booklet on capital equipment financing or some other financial subject, in anticipation that those who request the booklet (at no obligation, of course) are better-than-average prospects for the service explained in the booklet. The respondent would also have the opportunity to request an appointment with a bank officer to discuss how that service might benefit the particular organization. Subsequent mailings can challenge the recipient regarding the quality and delivery of services, with respondents requesting an appointment so that the selling officer can prove the advertising claims—putting up or shutting up, so to speak. The final communication in the series might offer a premium as an incentive to respond, positioned to thank the individual for making time available. Then, following this series, continuing mailings can be made using case histories of how the FSI has benefited specific customer situations, with responses anticipated from organizations with similar problems who identify with the case histories.

SERVICES FOR AFFLUENT CONSUMERS

Background

Financial service institutions, like many other businesses, find that about 80 percent of their business is derived from 20 percent of their customers. As a result, many financial institutions have developed specific programs or services to reduce attrition from among these more affluent customers and hopefully attract new accounts from among such noncustomers. Frequently, the services offered include those which are in either the deposit or credit categories, but also specific trust services for consumers. There is a danger, however, that the program will be perceived as a device whose sole purpose is to generate trust business. Further, the more traditional FSIs are now facing increased competition for affluent consumers from brokerage firms with CMA-type services and other less regulated financial competitors.

Mailing Lists

An FSI's own customers should be the starting point for any specialized program for the affluent. Following implementation of the customer program, postintroduction research should be conducted among this group to (1) improve the product offering and fine-tune the communications, and (2) profile demographic and psychographic characteristics of those most interested in the service, so that noncustomer lists can be generated which match those characteristics.

Positioning

Credibility is the key. The overall service and its component features must truly offer benefits not available to the masses. Research has shown that one of the more significant components of an affluent program is a "personal banker" assigned to the individual, who can cut red tape and facilitate the delivery of financial services. While one impetus for the affluent program is to hold onto customers of this kind, another is to attract additional business which can be consolidated from among competitors where it is currently distributed. Hence, if not properly positioned, the specialized affluent service may be perceived only as a marketing ploy to sell additional business. Instead, the additional business should flow to the FSI on the basis of (1) satisfaction with the delivery of current financial services and (2) acceptance of additional services not currently used on the basis of the benefits they might provide, but promoted in a low-key, educational way.

Offers

The initial communication should invite selected customers to accept the service, on the basis of the benefits it can provide. If a personal banker has been pre-assigned, customers should be given the opportunity to designate another individual who they may already know and would prefer to have as their personal banker. Subsequent mailings can provide details on specialized financial services that may be of particular interest to the affluent market. Customers should be offered tangible evidence of their importance to the FSI: special identification cards which permit guaranteed check cashing with higher limits, ATM cards which permit a larger withdrawal from automatic teller machines, and a direct telephone number for the personal banker, which can be printed with the banker's name on monthly statements and other periodic communications with the customer.

MAIL ORDER DIVISIONS

Consumer Attitudes

Money market mutual funds have educated consumers to the fact that it is possible to get personalized attention and a high return on one's money without the need to come into a banking office. Accordingly, more traditional FSIs may discover that adding mail and telephone convenience to both deposit and credit services adds a unique selling proposition which may well give them an edge on competition. To do this effectively, however, requires highly trained personnel, incoming and outgoing WATS lines, and operational procedures to process incoming direct mail responses—in short, a specialized mail order unit separate from the normal branch office structure.

Staffing

Personnel manning the mail order unit must have good people skills and extensive knowledge of all financial services marketed by direct mail, including current rates and other terms for the various services. Perhaps most important, these people must have an attitude that transcends typical branch order-taking from walk-in business, and selling skills which can convert inquiries to sales. Word processing capabilities would be necessary to mail out applications, together with follow-up selling letters, and a tickler system to be established for telephone follow-up on individuals who do not return applications or account-opening forms.

Cross-Selling Opportunities

In addition to processing incoming mail and telephone inquiries, the mail order unit can also work effectively in conjunction with a marketing information system. Current customers lacking specific services as part of their relationship with an FSI can be contacted directly with an appropriate sales script, and applications and account-opening forms can then be mailed out to those who express interest.

Results Analysis

Just as direct mail marketing activities should be tracked and evaluated on the basis of return on the marketing investment, the mail order unit should also be judged on the basis of cost compared with sales generated by this unit.

chapter **52**

TOURISM AND TRAVEL

Alan E. Lewis

President
Trans National, Inc.
Boston, Mass.

INTRODUCTION

The conventional wisdom in the travel and tourism industry is that direct mail marketing is not an important or effective technique for selling travel and travel-related products. Mass-marketing concepts dominate most travel marketing strategies, and the few companies that use direct marketing generally approach it in an unsophisticated manner. Even the biggest names in the industry—Sheraton Hotels, Eastern Airlines, Diners Club—underutilize proven direct marketing techniques which are readily available to them. The failure of these giants to keep extensive customer data bases prevents them from taking a first step into direct target marketing.

In 1981, direct marketing continued to take strides in the travel industry. The industry used all facets of direct marketing, but utilization varied widely among airlines, hotel chains, resorts, travel agents, and other segments of the business.

During 1981, there was an increase to $170 billion spent for domestic and international travel. World spending for travel increased 13 percent in 1982, to a total over $735 billion. Travel accounts for $35 billion a year in U.S. wages and salaries. More than $14 billion is paid in federal, state, and local taxes. Over 10 million more Americans vacationed in 1981 than in 1980.

Although these numbers seem large, the travel and tourism industry sells the majority of its products to a relatively small percentage of the population. Direct mail marketing, a sound method for selling well-defined products to a specific audience, would seem to be the ideal vehicle for reaching this core group of travel customers in an effective and continuous manner.

There are significant obstacles involved in the direct marketing of travel and tourism products. For example, the high price of the item, the sophistication of the average customer, and the lack of a guarantee for the product all pose problems, but none of these problems are insurmountable. The potential profits of a successful direct marketing program outweigh any obstacles.

This chapter will describe the current status of direct mail techniques in travel and tourism and will attempt to predict the direction of developments in the field over the next few years. In general, travel and tourism should be approached as a distinctive business field with its own idiosyncracies. The rules of direct marketing that apply in other areas must be adjusted to deal with the differences in the product and its environment. A package tour in the $2000 to $5000 range is definitely a high-ticket item, and a direct mail effort which asks for a response that represents a large financial commitment requires an unusually high level of expertise. For these reasons, the travel and tourism industry needs a degree of direct marketing sophistication surpassing that needed for most existing endeavors.

Trans National Travel is probably one of the best at direct mail marketing in the travel industry. It is not that Trans National is so aggressive in its approach to direct mail marketing but rather that the rest of the industry is so feeble. Trans National markets travel tour packages directly to the consumer, and the average sale is about $2000 per couple. We are asking for a major financial decision, but last year, when we made our offer to more than 20 million people, it was accepted by more than 50,000. Trans National is still learning how to master the art of direct mail marketing as it applies to travel, but we are proof that it can be a profitable venture, and we are sure that our markets will expand as our methods improve.

Selling a high-ticket product by direct mail requires both a sound approach and a careful evaluation of the techniques involved. Trans National relies on an average response rate of 2 reservations per 1000, which is extremely low by most direct mail standards. The dollar value of each of our customers thus is equivalent to ten to fifty returns on a lower-ticket item. As a result, a difference of one more customer per thousand is crucial to the company's profitability. Ultimately, we are not looking for a high rate of response but rather a few responses at a high rate.

THE PRODUCT

Any discussion of a direct mail campaign should start with an assessment of the product. In his book on direct marketing, Jim Kobs lists five factors that determine the suitability of a product for sale by direct mail techniques: (1) broad appeal, (2) unusual features, (3) not readily available in this form, (4) can be sold at a profitable price, and (5) contains a dream element.[1]

Generally, travel and tourism products perform well in terms of Kobs's criteria. Travel is a common activity, and travel packages can provide a service that is both attractive and not readily available elsewhere. A direct mail company can find some unusual features which make its offer unique, and with the economies of bulk buying, the company usually can offer them at a price that is both attractive

[1] Jim Kobs,

to the customer and profitable to the company. By emphasizing the dream or fantasy factor, the travel and tourism industry almost can guarantee an attractive product.

The products that fall into this general category are diverse, and each requires specific marketing considerations. For example, a list of travel product areas would include air travel promotion to frequent business travelers, car rental promotions to vacation and business travelers, Clipper Club and other organizations that service frequent business travelers, hotel convention and meeting promotions, and promotion of specific cities and countries by the local tourism bureaus. However, all the products involved must deal with the same basic issues: (1) affluent customers, (2) high-ticket item, and (3) the fact that these are discretionary items that are considered carefully before the decision to purchase is made. Some companies which have used these types of techniques successfully are Northwest Airlines (lifetime pass), Lindblad Travel (deluxe vacations and previous customers), Princess Cruises (Cruise Masters and previous travelers), Intercontinental Hotels (previous customers), International Travel Advisors (previous customers), and Grand Circle Travel Division of Colonial Penn (previous customers).

One problem prevalent in the travel and tourism industry today is that few companies actually market a specific travel product. The largest companies using direct marketing are the airlines (such as Pan Am or United) and the hotel chains (notably Holiday Inn and Intercontinental), and their marketing goal has been to sell the name rather than a specific product. In effect, the message is, "When you travel, think of us." This strategy may or may not be an effective marketing approach, but in essence it differs from the mass-marketing concepts that these companies already emphasize. Their aim is to get the customer to use their facilities at an unspecified future time rather than to sell the customer a specific product.

By contrast, Trans National Travel sells a specific product rather than a name. Trans National specializes in selling group tours that take people to destinations all over the world for vacations of 7 to 14 days. Among the thirteen primary destinations visited by our company in 1982 were Barbados, Aruba, Saint Maarten, Honolulu, the Rhine River countries, Alaska, London, Switzerland, Hawaii, Scandinavia, and the orient. Last year, Trans National did approximately $50 million in gross business, and the company's goal is to reach $100 million by 1985. Eighty percent of this income was generated through direct mail techniques.

Looking at the Trans National product under the criteria proposed by Kobs, the distinctive feature of the firm's travel package is that it encompasses the entire travel experience. In addition to organizing airplane and hotel reservations, the travel package provides optional dining programs, optional tour programs, complete baggage handling, and a hospitality desk that is located at the hotel and is open until 10:00 P.M. each night to answer questions or help solve problems. In effect, it offers a total vacation experience at a fixed price while ensuring that many of the typical travel difficulties will be avoided.

From a business perspective, the reason Trans National can make its offer so attractive is that the firm books large blocks of hotel and airplane reservations at a fraction of their normal cost and packages them at a price that is reasonable to the customer and profitable to the company. We form long-term relationships with the airlines and hotels and expect them to provide consistently good service to our customers. Optional tours and dining programs add to the attractiveness of a travel package; while they are generally not very profitable, they are extremely valuable in improving the overall travel experience of the customer. For Trans National in 1981, the breakdown of expenses was as follows: $20 million for air fares; $15 million for hotels, buses, guides, and tours; $6 million for the promotional budget (letters, envelopes, and lists); $6 million for general and administrative costs; and $2.5 million profit.

You must deliver a high-quality product consistently. To begin with, customers are a renewable resource, and the best way to sell your next tour is to deliver a top-quality experience this time. In addition, the organizational endorsements that are necessary for a successful direct mail approach will be difficult to obtain unless you can show a consistent reputation and track record.

THE CUSTOMER

When you sell a product or service through direct mail, you do it with a particular type of customer in mind. The consumers of the travel and tourism product can be divided into two general groups: business travelers and pleasure travelers. Most of the large travel companies have aimed their direct mail advertising at the business executive who may fly ten to fifty times a year. However, the attempts to segment this market have been primitive and inexact. For example, an airline should keep customer lists and use that information over time to develop a list of repeat customers to whom it can sell additional travel services. However, some companies do not keep such lists, while others keep lists but do not segment them effectively. As a result, there is a lot of information available about customers that the companies simply do not know.

Trans National sells its products to a specific segment of the pleasure travel market. Our studies indicate that the group tour appeals primarily to people with a particular demographic description. They are over 50 years old, have 2 years of college, have a household income above $30,000, live at urban or suburban addresses, have traveled out of the country before, own their homes, and buy products by direct mail.

Thus, our composite customer is an average middle- to upper-middle-class American who has an interest in traveling to a foreign land in a situation that is relatively controlled and problem-free. Most of our customers are a little older and a little less adventuresome than the average traveler, and they appreciate the guidance and assistance that the organized tour provides. Many of Trans National's customers are people who need both the structure and the encouragement of the tour to enjoy a foreign vacation fully. They are not the kind of travelers who will search out exotic native restaurants on their own; instead, they prefer a list a good, dependable restaurants recommended by the tour operator.

Tours generally are not attractive to people who are young, independent, and adventurous in their travel interests. However, a small but significant percentage of our travelers are people who buy the package tour for purely economic reasons. In effect, the discount on travel and lodgings is so attractive that these travelers take the flight with the group and then go their own way until the tour is ready to go home. Since noting this trend, Trans National has made a point of emphasizing this option in its sales literature. The firm feels that there is a growing market of travelers who will join the tour in order to share the group discount, even though they are not interested in the group experience.

SELLING THE TRAVEL PRODUCT: TRANS NATIONAL CASE STUDY: THIRD-PARTY ENDORSEMENTS

In selling a travel package, one must begin with the fact that travel is not an easily salable product using ordinary direct mail techniques. Travel involves a large monetary commitment (often thousands of dollars), involves a decision about how to use relatively scarce leisure time, and calls on people to take at least some risk or adventure. Normally, travel is something that people like to discuss with an agent in order to get a feel for what a destination is like and to get some reassurance that the trip will be enjoyable. Travel is most attractive to people in the upper income brackets, and they are the least likely group to purchase items by direct mail. Above all, travel is a nonrefundable service, and so the seller cannot offer the "money-back" guarantee that is so decisive in many areas of direct mail marketing.

How does one overcome these obstacles? At Trans National, the method has been to seek endorsements from reputable organizations and then sell the travel package through an organization to its members. In effect, Trans National does not approach the individual customer but instead uses the organization as the sales representative. This approach serves a number of important purposes. First, a letter of endorsement gives the product instant credibility, which is crucial in direct mail marketing. Second, the travel offer comes from an organizational group with whom the individual member identifies and possibly socializes, thereby changing the connotation of the offer from "go away on your own" to "join your friends." Third, organizations tend to have members who are older and who, depending on the organization, have incomes in the appropriate range, thereby bringing a significant percentage of the mail recipients into the demographic range where Trans National can achieve optimum results.

Naturally, it is important to choose an organization whose endorsement will carry the proper connotations. Thus, the American Cancer Society would not be a good choice, but the American Nurses Association or the National Education Association would be. As a general rule, our best success has been with organizations of a state or local character, which means that the members are likely also to be friends and even neighbors; thus, the organization probably will have a friendly, social image. For example, the Elks of Massachusetts would be a good group, because the Elks clubs often function as a social unit, sponsoring dinners, dances, athletic teams, and so forth. Thus, an Elks-sponsored trip can become something of a group outing, and people tend to sign up for our tours with their friends.

By contrast, national organizations tend to be less effective as endorsers, simply because they do not have a significant socializing component. This is not to say that they cannot be used successfully. A good organization's endorsement is always useful, but it is not nearly as effective as the endorsement of a reputable local organization. We believe that as our segmentation abilities improve, we will be able to use the national organizations more effectively; for the time being, however, the secret to our success lies in state or local organizations.

SOLICITING THE ENDORSEMENT

Our typical approach begins with a letter to the president or central office, explaining our program and requesting an opportunity to make a presentation.

We follow up the letter with a phone call and in many cases with a visit. Most organizations are naturally protective of their members and do not want them to be exploited. To gain their confidence, Trans National uses recommendations from other organizations that have used our services in the past.

Once we have established our credibility and reputation, we explain our travel packages, demonstrating what we have to offer and why it will be a benefit to the members of the organization. We also document our claims that we can provide top service and that numerous other organizations have used our packages with satisfactory results. As an example, we would offer one free trip to the organization for every forty people who sign up or an incentive of $10 per person. Once an organization participates in a tour, we expect that the positive results will ensure an interest in sponsoring future travel packages and tours.

DIRECT MAIL PACKAGE

Once the organizational endorsement is obtained, we develop a direct mail package designed for the specific group. Our standard mail package consists of (1) a personalized letter from the president of the organization which presents the travel offer (see Figure 52-1), (2) a personalized four-color brochure that explains the trip and the particulars of the tour (see Figure 52-2), (3) a separate application form, and (4) a self-addressed, stamped envelope addressed to the sponsoring organization. Trans National handles all aspects of preparing the direct mail package, including preparation of the letters, brochures, and packages and the cost of postage and mailing.

In writing the personalized letter, Trans National emphasizes the organization sponsoring the tour. We include a picture of the president, the organization's logo, and the group telephone number and address. The letter is four to six pages in length, which is effective both in explaining the product and in arousing the reader's interest. The letter emphasizes the cost savings available compared with individual travel arrangements; it also stresses that everything is taken care of by the tour directors and that the trip represents an opportunity to travel with other members of the organization. Trans National keeps a deliberately low profile; sometimes the company name appears only on the copyright notice of the brochure.

The four-color brochure includes a number of attractive photos of the destination. The copy explains the program clearly and concisely and emphasizes that Trans National is selling an all-inclusive package at a fixed price. The brochure is designed like most direct mail brochures, but it is distinctive in that

Onondaga County Medical Society

224 HARRISON STREET SYRACUSE, NEW YORK 13202
TELEPHONE (315) 424-8118

President
DONALD H. STEWART, JR., M.D.
President-Elect
DANIEL L. DOMBROSKI, M.D.
Vice-President
EDWARD C. HUGHES, JR., M.D.

Secretary
KENNETH S. K. HO, M.D.
Treasurer
JOHN A. HOEPNER, M.D.
Executive Director
GERALD N. HOFFMAN

Mr. John D. Sample
2 Charlesgate West
Boston, Massachusetts 02215

Dear Mr. Sample:

If, like so many experienced travelers, you've ever said, "Someday we'll get to the Orient," then start marking off your calendar. Your day has arrived.

Everything has already been arranged. In fact, all you have to do to add Onondaga County Medical Society's luxurious Oriental Odyssey to your travel adventures is return the reservation form attached to the enclosed brochure or call us at the special toll-free number shown below.

You'll fly to and around the Orient in scheduled Japan Airlines' jumbo jets. You'll stay in only the most deluxe luxury hotels in Tokyo, Kyoto, Taipei, Hong Kong and Bangkok. You'll enjoy the companionship of your fellow Onondaga County Medical Society members at exclusive parties, cruises and sightseeing tours. You'll sample classic Oriental delicacies like Steak Teriyaki and Lobster Cantonese at the nine dinners we've included in your trip. You'll start each day with complimentary American breakfasts.

As someone who's taken a trip sponsored by the Onondaga County Medical Society, you know how much airfare and hotel accommodations cost, so you, more than anyone else can appreciate that you get all this and more for less than you'd pay if you arranged this vacation yourself.

Best of all, your vacation tour is arranged by a big, reliable travel concern with a million dollar performance guarantee.

Onondaga County Medical Society has arranged to make this trip available at a package price, through Trans National Travel, a great travel organization which specializes in providing group "Package Tours" at greatly reduced group prices. And Trans National Travel is insured to the tune of $1,000,000.00 to guarantee that what you are promised on this vacation tour is what you will get.

Because you are a seasoned past traveler with Onondaga County Medical Society, you, especially, will be able to appreciate the careful planning, the wonderful accommodations and many other features of our ORIENTAL ODYSSEY.

Your vacation will include 16 days and 14 nights in the Orient, featuring an optional tour to Mainland China. It's an adventure for the sophisticated traveler in Tokyo ... Kyoto ... Taipei ... Hong Kong ... Bangkok. The very names bring up images that quicken the pulse of any true traveler. The sights, sounds and feelings are different from any other places you've ever been. Pagodas, rickshaws, Chinese Junks, Geishas. It's all so exotic, and yet, so accessible.

Figure 52-1 Personalized letter from the president of the organization which presents the travel offer

we have a picture of the organization's president displayed prominently above the offer. This helps underscore the fact that the offer is being made by a reputable organization.

Application forms are returned to the sponsoring organization at its central office. Once the responses arrive, they are turned over to Trans National for processing. Trans National handles all aspects of the administration, including processing the forms, collecting the money, sending out information, and handling inquiries.

FRANK H. KEMPKER, STATE DEPUTY OF THE
MISSOURI STATE COUNCIL KNIGHTS OF COLUMBUS
presents 8 days and 7 nights in

SWITZERLAND $1029* $799*
FROM ST. LOUIS FROM NEW YORK

DEPARTING THURSDAY, JULY 1, 1982. RETURNING FRIDAY, JULY 9, 1982.
CHECK RESERVATION COUPON FOR KANSAS CITY DEPARTURE PRICE.

Featuring an Optional One Week Extension to INNSBRUCK & VIENNA, Austria including a BLUE DANUBE CRUISE and tickets to the spectacular THIERSEE PASSION PLAY $299* Additional

LOOK AT THE SAVINGS!

A once in a lifetime opportunity! Available to members, their families and friends.

Compare our price with what you would usually pay if you planned it yourself:

Round-trip jet transportation via commercial airline	$ 925.00
Hotel accommodations, transfers, baggage handling, taxes and services	$ 369.63
Total price of "do-it-yourself" vacation	$1,294.63

WE SAVE YOU $375.78 per person; $751.56 per couple!

YOUR VACATION INCLUDES:

- Round-trip jet transportation via regularly scheduled Austrian, Pan American or Capitol Airlines with in-flight dining and beverage service.
- All flight reservations and tickets.
- Pre-registration at your hotels.
- All transfers and baggage handling between airport and hotels.
- First-class hotel accommodations for 7 nights at the **Movenpick Hotel** in Zurich.
- Free half day sightseeing tour of Zurich.
- A Welcome get-together.
- Informal educational briefing on the highlights, culture and customs of Switzerland and optional tours.
- All taxes and tipping for services included in the program, excluding tips to guides and escorts.
- Complimentary hospitality desk staffed by Trans National Travel's on-site team of professionals.

SPECIAL DINING OPTION:

A special dining option is available which includes 7 breakfasts and 4 dinners on the one-week program or 13 breakfasts and 8 dinners on the two-week program. To sign up for this option, check the appropriate box on your reservation coupon. **$99.00 per person (one-week); $195.00 (two-week).**

DELUXE HOTEL OPTION:

For an additional $29.00 per person you can enjoy deluxe hotel accommodations at the **International Hotel** in Zurich. Right in the middle of the Oerlikon area, the hotel is surrounded by shops, restaurants and a flower and food market. **A great value!**

SPECIAL 7-DAY EXTENSION TO INNSBRUCK & VIENNA, Austria... Including a Danube River Cruise... And the Thiersee Passion Play...

Just $299* Additional

In addition to all the features of our Switzerland vacation, those choosing this optional tour will also get:

- 3 nights superior first-class hotel accommodations at the **Innsbruck Holiday Inn.**
- 3 nights at the **Parkhotel Schoenbrunn** in Vienna.†
- Free **cruise down the fabled Danube River.**
- Intercity transfers via deluxe air-conditioned motor coach.
- Tickets and transportation to the **Thiersee Passion Play.**

OPTIONAL TOURS:

Revel in the splendor of the panoramic **Alps** or browse through historic **Lucerne.** Hop the Lugano Express for the **Swiss Riviera** or take a cable car to the summit of **Mt. Rigi.** Visit the mysterious **Black Forest.** Attend a **Swiss Yodelfest.** See **Liechtenstein,** tour **Venice, Italy,** taste **Italian wines** or stroll the **Vienna Woods.** Details on these and other optional tours will be sent to you when you register for your vacation. Subject to change and availability.

FOR RESERVATIONS CALL TOLL-FREE:
1-800-225-7678 Weekdays 8:30 am to 9:00 pm
Or Saturday 8:30 am to 5:00 pm (EST).

*Plus 15% Tax and Service Charges All Inclusive. Per Person Based On Double Occupancy. Single Supplement $200 (1-week); $300 (2-week).
† Due to limited air space the program may be extended to include one night in Munich at no extra cost to the passenger.

Figure 52-2 A personalized four-color brochure that explains the trip and the particulars of the tour

SEGMENTING THE PROSPECT MAILING

Once you have an organizational endorsement and a membership list, the next problem is selecting the people to whom you will make the direct mail offer. Since we know our standard customer profile with reasonable accuracy, we want to direct the prospect mailing to people who are over 50 years of age, affluent, and likely to buy by direct mail. However, the list rarely contains information that allows you to segment along these lines with great precision, and so one must turn to more general segmentation methods.

One method that we use with moderate success is ZIP codes. Using 1980 Census information, we identify ZIP codes where there is a strong likelihood of an upper-middle-class income and then give them particular emphasis. In many cases, however, we simply mail to the entire list and then use the response as a basis for future segmentation methods. One should never underestimate the "surprise" factor in mailouts; while we are still in the early stages of our segmentation research, it is deemed prudent to keep our prospect mailings relatively broad gauge.

In the long term, however, we hope to improve our segmentation capabilities dramatically. For example, in 1981, we mailed out 20 million pieces of mail. This included 2500 mailings to 650 organizations, and many of the people did not fit into our prime demographic profile. In general, our prime demographic profile is relatively narrow because our ideal target is a household income over $30,000, which covers only 10 percent of the U.S. population. Our goal is to take our existing market and segment it with greater sophistication, and we believe that we could meet our growth goals for the next 5 years simply by mining our current base more effectively. We shall try to expand that base as well, but our main effort will be to identify prospects in the prime demographic range. If we can isolate 3 to 5 million promising prospects and market to them effectively, we will reach our goal of $100 million in 1985.

TARGET MARKETING

On a typical group tour mailout, our response is small by most direct mail standards. It can vary from 0.1 to 5 percent, but most often it falls in the 0.2 percent range. At these response rates, increasing the rate by a single customer per thousand is a significant achievement.

When we find a customer, therefore, we immediately try to learn as much about that person as we can. First, customers are a renewable resource, and a happy customer will come back. Second, customers are an important source of travel referrals, and thus we can use "bring a friend" promotional techniques in our group offers. Third, knowing our current customers tells us more about who our potential customers might be, and this information is useful in a variety of important ways.

The effective use of existing customers begins with recording their names. This seems like a trivial observation, but many companies in the travel and tourism business fail to keep a list of people who already have used their products. In a business where the market response comes from a very small, selective group, such a list is a veritable gold mine. Trans National's Gold Team current list contains 300,000 names, and any name on the list is targeted automatically for three mailings with a special "personal invitation" to join any future tours sponsored by their organizations. This technique has produced a response rate that is several times higher than the firm's average response rate for all tours.

FORECASTING THE RESULTS

A second valuable function of customer lists is to "handicap" future travel promotions to the same group. By examining a group's past record and response rate, you can develop a product that is more likely to achieve a strongly positive response. The factors one must assess include the following:

1. Past history of when the group traveled
2. Past history of where the group traveled
3. Past history of the response rate to varying offers

This information indicates that specific groups have different preferences about when and where they would like to travel. Although the reasons for these patterns are often obscure, the point is that such patterns occur with almost every group, and a sound direct mail program will attempt to identify the products that have the most consistent appeal. In our case, we often find out later that there is a logical explanation for the preference. For example, the Wisconsin Elks like to visit Germany because many Wisconsin residents are of German ancestry. However, you don't need to know the reason, since the numbers can tell you a trend long before you can explain it. Therefore, you should be a statistician, not a sociologist.

BACK TO THE BASICS

A third use of customers and one which has the least impact immediately but has great long-term importance is developing the customer profile. We want to know as much about our typical customer as possible so that as our segmentation methods improve, we can target that person with ever-increasing precision.

Getting good customer information is no easy task because many people are reluctant to reveal personal information. Currently, we have 300,000 names of past customers, but in most cases all we know about them is the telephone number, ZIP code, and trip date. To expand our knowledge, we recently did a mailing to 25,000 people on our list, and we got 7000 responses with a significant amount of data. The point is that we have made a major commitment to marketing research, and we are collecting as much data about our customers as we can. Knowing our customers better will help us improve our direct mail package and generally enhance every aspect of our sales approach.

AUTOMATION

To carry out the kind of large-scale segmentation this chapter suggests, a company must have modern automated facilities. In general, computers are necessary for any kind of serious statistical analysis of customer data. For example, on a list of 10,000 names, you want to know where 50 names came from and why. You want to split that information quickly so that you can make a relatively fast decision on whether to do a follow-up mailing.

Almost everyone in the travel and tourism business pays lip service to automation for marketing, but few get maximum use from their computers. Most companies use computers to replace mechanical lists and rely on the computers to produce lists, labels, and other clerical functions in an efficient manner. However, these companies are still learning how to use computers in their marketing efforts. Trans National is working to develop sophisticated mathematical models so that we can determine rapidly who is responding to an offer and why. Using correlation coefficients and regression analysis, we can determine the factors that correlate to our positive responses. We then can use the computer to edit lists in favor of certain criteria, enabling us to make follow-up mailings to the most promising prospects.

To accomplish these functions effectively, a company must make a commitment to top-quality hardware and software and top-quality professional people. Our current computer system is the IBM System 38. Compared to the System 34, which is used by most companies, the System 38 is flexible, wide-ranging, and reliable. The only drawback is that the System 38 is more complex and requires greater sophistication and experience to operate. However, such a commitment in terms of both a system and personnel is necessary if you want to achieve important advances in segmentation technique.

The point is that the latest in modern equipment gives you a distinct advantage in the information sorting that needs to take place. Direct mail relies ultimately on information flow, and handling that information in an efficient, accurate, timely manner is the key to direct mail success in the travel and tourism industry.

CONCLUSION

There is strong reason to believe that the travel and tourism industry will make a concerted push into the field of direct mail marketing in the next few years. The industry relies on a relatively small subset of the general population for the bulk of its sales. Given this information, it makes sense for the industry to develop a more focused advertising and marketing approach, and this naturally points toward a greater use of direct mail marketing techniques. Although the travel and tourism market is probably tougher than other markets in terms of percentage responses, the countervailing consideration is that the market can be cultivated profitably at a relatively low return rate. By using advanced techniques and equipment, a company can segment the market in a manner that will achieve a profitable response rate. Developing sophisticated techniques for segmenting the travel and tourism market will be the central challenge facing the industry during the 1980s.

chapter 53

INDUSTRIAL MARKETING

Herbert G. Ahrend

President
Ahrend Associates, Inc.
New York, N.Y.

For many years, the business-to-business marketing community exhibited ambivalence in its attitude toward direct-response techniques.

As far back as 1972, a survey conducted by a large manufacturer of business machinery for its internal use showed that of 1016 clients and prospects, 60 percent preferred to get information about new equipment by direct mail, while only 25 percent preferred a sales call, the next highest ranking method. Yet individual advertising budgets carried separate items for "collateral" and "catalogs" and, less frequently, for "direct mail."

At that time, the concept of integration of the marketing effort, with direct-response techniques at the very core, was largely unknown.

Even when direct-response techniques were used—even by firms and in industries where they are of primary importance—they often were misapplied. A pioneer survey of office machine and computer manufacturers conducted by Dun & Bradstreet for the Business/Industrial Council of the Direct Marketing Association (DMA) revealed that 49.3 percent rarely or never set objectives for a mailing. These firms used direct mail from 2½ to over 17 times per year, and 25.7 percent considered it critically important to their marketing efforts. The year was 1979.

THE TWO CATEGORIES OF INDUSTRIAL DIRECT MARKETING

The continuing confusion in terminology, both within the industrial marketing field itself and between industrial advertisers and direct-response practitioners, makes it essential to define terms before engaging in further discussion of the subject. The terminology used in this chapter accords with that of many workers in the field; it is by no means idiosyncratic.

The term "direct marketing" is used here to encompass any type of advertising designed to elicit a response, whether or not in the form of an immediate order and in any advertising medium—direct mail, publication, or electronic—employed.

The two great divisions of direct marketing, especially in the business-to-business area, are

1. Support for a salesperson before or after the call
2. Direct, immediate solicitation of an order, whether placed by mail or by telephone

This definition of direct marketing excludes those types of direct mail such as pure announcements and goodwill builders which serve exclusively as advertising or sales promotion. But do not neglect the advertising—as apart from the selling—function of direct marketing pieces. A mailing package consisting of a sales letter, a full-color brochure, a reply device, and perhaps other enclosures may be designed primarily to sell inserting machines, cash registers, or anything else by mail or phone. It may produce more than enough orders to justify its cost fully, yet it also serves as an effective and remembered advertisement to many more prospects than those who have ordered immediately.

This fact has been demonstrated in many studies. In one, conducted for the Advertising Research Foundation among 4000 corporate chairpeople and presidents, with a similar control panel, the claimed reading of the mailing was better than 2½ times the actual mail response. The validity of that figure is demonstrated by the fact that between 7 and 12 days after the mailing, 13 percent spontaneously recalled it and 62 percent had a correct idea of the company which sent it. Moreover, 19 percent stated that they would consider purchase or rental of this equipment as opposed to only 13 percent of the control group; this was an increase of nearly one-half.

THE NEED FOR INDUSTRIAL DIRECT MARKETING

Finding new and more refined techniques of marketing and selling is not just pertinent to profits. Today, it's pertinent to survival.

The shortage of qualified sales engineers and the rapidly increasing cost of each sales call—$175 to $300 and more in many industries—demand a radically new approach.

As Chuck Francis, director of advertising of IBM, declared at a Business/Professional Advertising Association (B/PAA) New York chapter meeting late in 1981, "It is essential to find marketing techniques which are less expensive than a personal call.... The cost of a sales call is up 33 percent from 1978 to 1981."

The rate of increase is escalating; in the single year following, it was almost as high as in the 3-year period cited by Francis.

McGraw-Hill Research shows that in 1982 it took $907.80 to close the average industrial sale. It goes without saying that that figure is higher today.

You can overcome these and other budgetary problems by employing the highly sophisticated techniques of direct-response marketing and selling.

Industrial products as varied as electronic equipment and chemicals, scheduling boards and gantries, laboratory computers and typewriter ribbons are being sold by mail and phone without the intervention of sales people.

You can increase market share without increasing sales costs through pinpointable, measurable direct-response methods.

GOALS AND STRATEGIES OF INDUSTRIAL DIRECT MARKETING

To achieve success, every business-to-business direct marketing program must be based on a reasoned marketing plan—a strategy.

The terms "strategic planning" and "strategy" in the vocabulary of many executives, especially in large corporations, are reserved for situations which involve fundamental long-range planning, or the setting of basic corporate goals. In business and industrial direct marketing, such terms cover more restricted activities. Their use serves a purpose, however, since they remind us that it is not enough to prepare a series of unrelated mailing pieces and call them a direct marketing campaign.

In this context, strategy involves direction setting for direct marketing. It consists in the locating of the proper direction for your campaign, the correcting of past or present incorrect directions, or both.

Strategic planning starts with situation analysis: evaluation of all factors both internal and external to your organization which affect your business now or probably will have a serious effect on it in the forseeable future. Do not overlook any major social, technological, environmental, economic, or political trends which can change your market or your position within it. For these five areas of influence, the AMA uses the acronym STEEP.

Where are you in the marketplace at the present time? Once you have the answer to that question, you can proceed to ask, "Where do we want to go, and how fast?" You want to set rational goals.

You must define your goals clearly and accurately. Never use such general terms as "improving bottom-line performance" or "helping sales people close more sales." These "goals" have been used by marketing people who should have known better.

List your targets in the order of importance and put a dollar value on each. Targets, for example, might be to open the aftermarket to your product to a value of $5 million the first year, to secure OEM sales 10 percent higher than at present, to obtain 500 more fully qualified sales leads per month, and to increase sales of supplies 50 percent this year without direct intervention of your sales representatives.

Direct marketing techniques can help you attain all these and many other marketing objectives. Here are some more goals. In every instance, they must be specifically quantified.

The first three are objectives related to continuing program and strategy; thus, they are vital in business-to-business direct marketing.

Objective 1: Build recognition for your company and product name.

Objective 2: Secure preference for your product over the competition and overcome the buyer's resistance to changing sources.

Objective 3: Maintain customer loyalty.

The second three objectives are sales-lead-related.

Objective 4: Secure qualified sales leads.

Objective 5: Separate the sheep from the goats among sales leads.

Objective 6: Make sure that the good leads are being pursued.

The next set of objectives are sales promotional.

Objective 7: Provide sales support before, between, and after calls by representatives.

Objective 8: Introduce new products.

Objective 9: Build traffic at retailers' outlets.

Objective 10: Help sales people and dealers sell more.

Objectives 11, 12, and 13 are mail-order objectives, concerned with direct selling without the employment of a salesperson.

Objective 11: Sell your products directly by mail to distributors, dealers, end users, or the public.

Objective 12: Sell supplies and service contracts.

Objective 13: Sell spin-offs of your company's expertise by mail order.

Chart your direction as well as your goal by selecting the most appropriate marketing course to achieve each of your objectives. Do not be concerned with copy approaches yet; this concerns basic marketing approaches: whether to sell entirely by mail or phone; whether to use MRs (manufacturer's representatives), your own staff, or both, with mail support; or even whether to compete with yourself by mail order under your own or another name.

Consider every aspect of your company's and your product or product line's profile in choosing that course: your competitive position in the particular market, any benefits it affords you in the battle for sales, and roadblocks—whether inherent in your own position or imposed from the outside—and how to remove them.

Next, determine the potential profit to be gained from achieving each objective. For this, you must know the program's cost. Demonstrate the cost effectiveness of your program; develop a plan for profit.

If your goal is to increase sales 20 percent with sales support direct mail, several marketing strategies may be employed.

1. Create 20 percent more leads.
2. Heighten the degree of *qualification* of leads so that sales people can close 20 percent more sales from the same number of leads.

3. Concentrate lead development in areas (geographic or industrial) of maximum potential so that the same number of closings can create 20 percent more business.
4. Combine the second and third techniques, resulting in a greater number of closings as well as a larger average unit sale.

Let us assume that your present lead cost is $50, your staff closes one in ten, and your average order is $5000. At present, then, your direct cost of sales is 10 percent. One further assumption: Your sales force is carrying a full load and cannot increase the number of calls per day.

Alternative strategy 1—creating 20 percent more leads—would require hiring, training, and supervising new field personnel plus the essential backup forces. Sales expense as a percentage of sales would not go down. If you must have additional volume for other reasons and no alternatives are available, this course may increase your gross profit. But look what happens when one of the alternative strategies outlined is chosen.

Your present field force remains adequate. No extra overhead or field expenses are involved. Your gross margin on the extra sales is therefore 10 percent higher than your current margin on sales since all direct sales costs, except the cost of the program itself, are covered by the current volume.

The sales support direct-response program therefore will produce extra profits in the amount of the total extra sales times (your present gross margin plus 10 percent) minus the cost of the program. For instance, if your present margin is 40 percent, a $100,000 program which develops $1 million in extra sales will give you a net profit of $400,000.

DEFINING AND STRATIFYING YOUR MARKET

Many experts believe that a company's market can be identified most effectively by analysis of its customer records. Others object, saying that even today, too many computer systems concentrate on the needs of the accounting department and do not record or do not keep for a sufficient length of time information vital to the identification of the prime and secondary markets for each product in the company's line.

Still others point out that even in the case of some successful and long-established firms, past history may be misleading in this respect. Not only may the market be changing, the company may have concentrated as a result of historical accident on accountants (for example), whereas its product line might—as currently constituted or with simply achieved modifications—be sold profitably to dentists, doctors, and industry in general as well.

Obviously, the process of determining prime and secondary markets is very different for a manufacturer of business forms and a producer of oil drilling rigs. Yet each would do well to precede its market selection with a thorough investigation of all the various STEEP factors mentioned in the discussion of strategic planning.

Following this, obtain and analyze all the data you can dredge from your customer records. To whom have you been selling each product or each line of products? Which companies have been the most profitable customers in terms of type of purchase, size, and frequency? Look for common factors among the most desirable customers, such as standard industrial classification (SIC), sales volume, number of employees, age of the business, location (area of the country or the world and whether corporate headquarters or a branch), and credit standing.

Collate all your data to determine the profile of your most profitable customers. (This is on the assumption that your company has not in the past overlooked major, profitable categories of potential buyers.) Then use outside sources to determine precisely the companies to which you do not sell now that fit that profile.

You may be able to obtain the necessary information from trade associations, credit reports, or national, state, or local government sources as well as from list compilers or brokers. These data will permit you to construct a list of the primary prospects for your products or services, whether or not they now are buying from you.

Using both accounting and sales department records, strive for accurate information as to which executives in each type of customer firm can make the buying decision and which executives can have an influence on it. Do not be fooled by the fact that a purchasing agent's name may be on an order into assuming that that person alone was responsible for it. That may be the case, but more frequently you must convince several executives, often with different standards and requirements, before you can make a major industrial sale.

Now you are in a position to start breaking down your prospect list into categories and determining the potential value of each group to your company.

If you are selling exclusively by mail, you will select which firms will receive primary attention, which are worth only sporadic efforts to have the worthwhile prospects identify themselves, and which can be ignored.

While some such process of prospect categorization is routine for mail-order firms, mainstream industrials all too often fail to recognize that it is equally essential to them if they are to maximize their profits.

True, most marketing directors pay lip service to the "80-20 syndrome," which indicates that 80 percent of volume or profit usually comes from 20 percent of a firm's customers. But all too few carry through and divide the mass of their prospects and customers into three categories:

- Those who deserve red carpet treatment and the lion's share of the advertising, promotion, and sales budgets
- Those who are worth only the sporadic effort just mentioned, e.g., mass mailings at low unit cost or business paper couponed ads to separate the sheep from the goats
- Those who should be ignored by advertising and sales departments unless they indicate purchasing interest voluntarily

Direct marketing techniques permit highly pinpointed promotions so that the valuable time of the sales force can be concentrated where it can do the most good—on key customers and prospects with the best potential. The higher the unit of sale in industrial selling, the greater the concentration of buying power.

Ben Dicus, an expert in selling through distributors, estimates that between 3 and 5 percent of all buyers control 40 to 60 percent of industrial product purchases.

Direct marketing techniques also allow the prospect who is ready to buy to step forth and be counted on the bottom line. Chuck Francis of IBM stated that the inclusion of a bold 800 number in a full-page announcement of a new series of computers resulted in the immediate sale of two—at several hundred thousand dollars each—without the need for a single sales call.

LISTS

Until fairly recently, there were three clearly defined, separate categories of industrial mailing lists: field-generated, compiled, and mail-responsive. That breakdown is no longer valid.

Field-generated lists are subject to built-in restrictions. They do not include the names of firms or executives within firms on whom the field representatives do not call, and it is not at all uncommon for buyers in a multidivisional corporation to try to keep "their" resources secret from others within the firm who also could benefit from a product or service. They are not always accurate on spelling of names, and field personnel may not make enough calls on every customer to keep them up to date. Yet they are vital, particularly for sales support direct marketing programs where the field personnel must be kept involved in and enthusiastic about the program.

Sales managers are divided on the wisdom of asking each field salesperson to provide a given number of names within his or her territory. Generally, it is wiser for the home office, using every means available, to prepare the key list and at that point ask those in the field to check it for recency and accuracy and to add important prospects which had been missed as well as other sales influences in the companies listed.

The importance of the list in helping field reps increase their income should be stressed and made fully evident, of course.

The decision whether to undertake research in-house or to hire outside specialists is one which your particular circumstances must determine.

Don't neglect names derived from responses to your company's public relations, couponed publication advertising, and direct mail. But qualify them further. Such names may range from extremely valuable to worthless. Lead generation and qualification are treated at greater length in the next section of this chapter.

Related to this category are "bingo card" names. These are notoriously inaccurate; we recently received a lead from one trade magazine headed, "S BAGLEY, PRESS, DBPRI AMG." Neither a human brain nor a computer could make sense of that.

The growing importance of business publication circulation lists is one of the factors which have made the old tripartite characterization of lists outmoded. The fact that auditing bureaus require evidence that recipients of a publication have requested it places circulation lists of audited controlled publications midway between the once mutually exclusive compiled and mail-responsive categories. Such lists in fact embody some of the characteristics of each of those types. (Paid circulation publications' subscriber lists have always been considered mail-responsive rather than compiled.)

In common with all compiled lists, the distribution lists of controlled books are the result of a more or less intensive effort to locate all the individuals who belong in a given group, whether waste-management engineers employed in industry, controllers of firms with 100 or more employees, or firms of a certain financial rating in a predetermined geographic area. Since sloppy list building may cause advertisers in the publication to receive poor response and thus affect the publisher's profit adversely, there is a high probability that publishers' lists are reasonably accurate.

Similarly, reputable list compiling firms have too much at stake to offer poorly researched lists to their customers. Yet if the list you require is one for which there is little demand, you would do well to question a low price for an "off-the-shelf" or a custom compilation. Before using it, do spot checks; you may save yourself money and headaches.

In contrast to compiled lists, mail-responsive lists consist of the names and addresses of people and firms which have purchased a product or inquired about it or requested a sales call by mail, phone, telex, teletext, or similar means, not through the intervention of a salesperson or a visit to a sales outlet.

In industrial direct marketing, where the person or persons with either primary or strong secondary influence on a purchasing decision may have any one of dozens of different titles, such mail-responsive lists often provide unexpected or even unsuspected key names.

As a general rule, any mail-order buyer list which can be purchased is not worth purchasing. It is either badly outdated or in rare instances stolen. Good mail-responsive lists are available only for rental. Sometimes list owners or their list managers will agree to a lower rate per use for a multiple mailing program or for a telephone follow-up, but the standard arrangement is still rental for one-time use.

Since mail-responsive lists are precisely that—names of people who have demonstrated their willingness to take action without requiring a personal sales call—they virtually never offer 100 percent coverage of a given industry or class of executives. Their advantage comes from the fact that people who are known to have responded to direct marketing appeals once are more likely to respond again than so-called cold compiled names. Yet there are occasions when it is highly desirable to reach all the members of a given group without exception.

DATA BANKS

Not long ago, you would have had no choice but to turn to list compilers. Now your choice is broader.

Perhaps business publication circulation lists can be segmented to meet your needs. More likely, a merge-purge of such lists and one or more mail-responsive lists will get you close to your ideal.

A new development, created to permit complete coverage of particular business segments without constantly repeated merge-purges, is the data bank. Simply stated, this consists of a master list derived from many sources and coded so that specialized groups may be addressed easily regardless of the original source of each name within the particular segment desired.

Some of the earliest data banks, such as that of the American Management Associations, were compiled by and for the exclusive use of one large mailer. Now a number of list managers have compiled and maintain such banks. They permit special characteristics of value to a particular industry (for example, number, size, and type of trucks owned) to be brought together with a vast number of other qualifications originally derived from different sources so that the industrial marketer can home in on a target market with precision.

Mal Dunn of M/D/A List Management has identified the four elements which are essential in a data bank:

1. A multiplicity of sources and lists brought together
2. A single merged unduplicated file with original information for each list
3. The overlay of other information onto the original data
4. The technical capability to develop a common code system

A Cautionary Word Regarding Data Banks

Proponents of data banks maintain that they permit easy access to the entire industrial segment you serve, with the full complement of executives by name as well as title and without the necessity of extensive research or repeated merge-purges.

That doesn't tell quite the whole story. The data bank may make it less rather than more likely that you will receive a complete current roster of executives. This is a factor of extreme importance when your strategy employs expensive personalized mailings. Each owner of a mail-order buyers list updates it frequently or even continuously because the success of his or her own business depends on its being kept current. But corrections to that list may be fed into the data bank only periodically, and the periods may be long. Moreover, many of the names in the data bank are derived from directories issued only once a year; the information may be as much as a year old by the date of publication.

Recently, we instructed one of the most respected list compilers to create a small, highly selective prospect list for an industrial direct mail sales program. As part of the assignment, we gave them certain small key lists, in part composed of company names to which they were to add from their data bank particular executives by name.

We found on the preliminary printout a number of top executives who had been retired or were deceased for nearly 2 years, and then we substituted the correct names. But the compiler insisted that there was "no way the corrections could appear on the final tape, since the computer will simply throw them out and substitute the incorrect ones on the file," adding that "it's simply not economically feasible to make corrections, even when we know them, except once a year when the new directories come out."

Before you put your reliance on a data bank rather than renting names from the primary sources of which it is composed, inquire closely into the bank's compilation and maintenance procedures.

SALES LEAD GENERATION

Sales lead development has employed classic direct-response techniques throughout American industry for more than half a century. These techniques have been practiced widely for this purpose even by hundreds of firms which traditionally have responded to questionnaires by asserting that they do not use direct mail. This confusion is generated by the varying terminology used by direct-response professionals and by the sales and marketing departments of industry.

NCR, Xerox, and General Electric have been leaders in the development of pinpointed programs to provide sales representatives with prime leads, or the names and titles of people who are seriously interested in a particular product or service. NCR alone uses over 200 separate series of lead-generating letters to specific industries.

In the great majority of cases, straight letters have proved more effective in lead production than the identical copy printed in folder format with artwork added or in the form of illustrated letters. Although some recent tests have brought different results, the preponderance of evidence from many sources still points to the letter as the most effective format in lead generation, especially when directed to top executives.

The lead-development program should be considered an integral part of your marketing plan. Even today, many large and small companies will set an arbitrary budget figure for publication advertising or direct mail that is designed primarily to obtain sales leads without adequate prior consideration of the following factors:

- The capacity of the sales force (your own, your distributors' or dealers', or both) to handle generated leads promptly and adequately
- The amount by which a properly qualified sales lead will reduce the cost of closing a sale
- The value of an order
- The lifetime value of a new customer

In this brief overview, it is impossible to go into mathematical detail to demonstrate these points beyond the example given earlier. The aim is to emphasize the importance of accurate calculation of all costs and benefits as they affect your firm.

Those benefits can be astounding in scope. For example, an executive of Automatic Data Processing revealed at a B/PAA seminar 2 years ago that his company's $700,000 expenditure on lead-generating direct mail brought in $18 million in annual revenue and that the average client remains with his firm for 7 years.

Another company, a machine manufacturer, has calculated that its sales representatives close $1 million in sales at an investment of only $40,000 in lead-generating direct mail sent to noncustomers. The return on mail to firms which already are users of other equipment made by this firm is, of course, much higher. In both instances and with all costs, direct and indirect, figured in, it is significantly less expensive to close a sale generated by a direct mail lead than one initiated by a cold sales call.

It is paradoxical yet true that firms which consider a cost of $1 million or more to close a sale permissible frequently balk at the investment of comparatively few dollars per prospect in a program which should reduce that closing cost and make more closings possible without adding more personnel in the field.

Of course, lead-getting programs should not be used indiscriminately. In certain circumstances, the generation of too many leads can be even worse than too few, as your best prospects may be turned off by the seeming neglect. You must know the number of field workers for whom you are seeking leads and the realistic number of leads which each salesperson can handle per day, before you can plan your development program.

Another basic marketing decision which will affect the nature of your lead-getting program is whether to seek "hard" or "soft" leads.

When the cost of a sales call is high and it is both expensive and difficult to train sales personnel—two conditions which bid fair to continue to affect much of industry for the foreseeable future—it is usually desirable to turn "hard" leads over to the staff. An exception occurs when certain pinpointed firms are known to be prime long-term prospects and the chances of securing a firm expression of buying interest are negligible at best. But if you are selling an unsophisticated, low-cost item of broad usefulness which requires no special selling skill, you may want quantity rather than quality in your leads.

You can control quality as well as quantity by varying the terms of your offer, e.g., by offering something of value (a premium, a book of useful hints to improve your customer's operations, etc.), providing a special price or terms for a limited time, or changing the amount of emphasis you place on the obligation (e.g., to see a sales rep or to purchase a trial quantity) or the lack of obligation that results from your prospect's taking the action you desire.

For a number of years, when I had about a dozen account executives, I used a lead-getting letter offering a free brochure on building business with direct mail. That letter only once drew less than 20 percent, and in that instance it was received at a time when the war news was horrendous. Since I eliminate all outside people and aim for more serious prospects who are aware of their need for consultation or creative aid, my rate of return is comparatively anemic by design, but my conversion rate is a healthy one.

In other circumstances, a company may want to design a program to get top response from those prospects judged to have the highest purchasing potential and design a less expensive program for prospects of less value, intended to flush out and obtain answers only from those in the market at that moment.

Dealerization

Overlaying of the outlines of territories assigned to given dealers or distributors on the other demographic factors used in selecting names for your mailing permits the pinpointing of promotional mailings to bring prospects into the dealership in cases where, as with John Deere, it is not economical to move the machinery to every prospect's location.

Combining computer technology, sales-directed imagination, and marketing sense can give you virtually unlimited potential for prospect and dealer involvement in your program. Such involvement is often a key to success.

By similar methods, direct mail lead-generation programs can be individualized to meet differing climates or seasonal or regional preferences, with each piece seeming to be a communication from your local sales office or salesperson.

There is no uniformity of opinion on whether replies should be directed to the home office or to the local one. An *Industrial Marketing* survey published in the August 1982 issue showed that half the firms surveyed direct inquiries to the sales personnel, a practice which may speed up receipt of the inquiry but which removes the home office's ability to keep an accurate record of results. But the same survey revealed that over two-thirds do not even try to track inquiries to determine whether they lead to sales.

Obviously, there is a wide discrepancy between the state of the art in lead qualification and tracking systems and the actual current practice of a large percentage of advertisers. It is not only unsophisticated firms which fail to secure these vital data; knowing which pieces and approaches create more sales and more repeat customers is essential to maximizing return on investment in both advertising and sales operations.

Even so advanced a promoter as Merrill Lynch, which mailed 2000 prospecting pieces per month for each of the 200 to 250 branch offices participating in the program—a total of between 4 million and 5 million pieces per year—in early 1980, knew only that they received about a 5 percent response. But as reported by Jim Rice in the *Business/Industrial Council Newsletter*, "At present no effective system exists to measure sales from the leads produced" in their judgment.[1] That judgment is one with which many firms whose profits depend in large measure on their ability to track the relative sales value of many different types or sources of leads would not agree.

LEAD QUALIFICATION

Give a salesperson several leads which he or she discovers are suspects rather than genuine prospects and you've lost credibility. It will be extremely difficult to ensure that your expensively generated leads ever are followed up again.

Naturally, all the components which go to make up your offer—precisely how you state your proposition, whether you offer an incentive or gift for action and the nature and value of that incentive, and the terms and conditions—will affect the quality as well as the quantity of the leads generated. But how is one to make sure that only genuine prospects' names are passed on to the sales force? There are a number of techniques.

The first method, which is obviously the oldest but not the best in terms of uncovering all those with genuine intent to buy, is to ask about purchase intention on the reply device or coupon itself.

[1] Jim Rice, *Business/Industrial Council Newsletter*, February 1980, p. 6.

Give the prospect the opportunity to check one of a series of boxes indicating the degree of interest. A typical sequence may read as follows.

I want this information

_________ for my files

_________ for later consideration

_________ for incorporation in an expansion plan

_________ for immediate use

_________ Please send me literature.

_________ Please have a representative call.

Best time is _________ A.M. _________ P.M.

_________ Call me first at _________________________

While it is reasonably certain that someone who asks for a sales call is a serious prospect, many executives who are equally interested hesitate to make such a request in writing.

To uncover these hidden potential customers, you must have a consistent qualification program. This can employ direct mail, the telephone, or a combination of both.

General Electric has developed a three-step process to qualify leads. When a coupon or card is received requesting information, the material is sent along with a second business reply card on which the prospect can indicate the degree of interest in the product; or the phone can be used. Not until this second level of qualification is complete is an inquiry sent to the field.

Over the years, according to Jack Pudney of General Electric, 25 percent of these requalified, or "hot," leads result in an immediate sale. Fifty percent more are sold within 1 to 2 years, and only 25 percent of those who asked for a quotation or for a sales call on the second card are rated NG by the sales staff.

General Electric makes use of an 800 number to facilitate receiving inquiries, thus cutting the 3 to 8 weeks which many business publications take to forward bingo card leads down to 1 to 3 days. Out-WATS also is used efficiently; 3 weeks after catalogs are mailed, phone follow-up reveals immediate or intermediate-term need for the equipment in one of every three cases. These names are, of course, sent at once to the field, and GE requests reports of both sales and opportunities to quote on all such leads.

NCR has utilized out-WATS in a similar manner. In one instance, NCR phoned college bookstore managers who had replied to a prospecting mailing and asked them to listen to a tape of an NCR executive describing the specialized benefits of an electronic cash register. One-third of those who heard the message agreed to have an NCR salesperson call.

Whether you should use telephone qualification depends on the nature of your business, the value of each sale and the lifetime value of a customer, and whether you have a limited or extensive universe of potential customers.

Firms such as RCA Americom which offer big-ticket services to readily targeted groups find phone qualification of inquiries essential. John Williamson, director of public affairs, told the New York chapter of the B/PAA late in 1982 that of the 15,000 inquiries they received each month, 37 percent were not prospects. When the remaining 63 percent are reached by phone, the company's experienced operators can reduce the number turned over to the field staff to 16 percent.

This elimination of suspects goes far toward developing a spirit of cooperation and a willingness to pursue each lead among field personnel. Although they still claim that only half, or 8 percent of the total of unscreened inquiries received, are "real prospects," Williamson said, the closing rate is high enough for the company to receive an 800 percent return on investment (ROI) for its advertising.

But if you have a large field staff working on straight commission and your product or service has wide appeal, the $2.50 or more which it costs to qualify a lead by phone may not be cost-efficient. If, like ADP, you're "strictly in the numbers game; more leads equals more business," as Stan Livacz of Automatic Data Processing told a B/PAA seminar, you must test to determine whether it's not more profitable to put that phone qualification money into more direct mail to get more soft leads to keep your staff busy.

One highly valuable by-product of a properly designed lead-qualification system is a volume of significant data which can be helpful in tracking the cost effectiveness of virtually every stage in your marketing process from copy approaches to media to the performance of individual field sales offices or even individual sales people.

The higher the degree of qualification of leads, the greater your ability to demand and receive from the field the detailed reports which permit long-range tracking, including cost per sale data as well as the cost per lead.

TESTING: WHAT TO TEST AND WHY

There are two main reasons for testing. The first is the ever-increasing cost of production of any mailing package; the second is the tremendous leverage which even a small increase in the response rate can exercise on profits. As Pierre Passavant has pointed out, a relatively small increase in the rate of response, say, from 0.9 to 1.1 percent—i.e., a 22 percent increase in response—can result in a 100 percent increase in net profit.

It's easy to go test-mad and test so many variations in product, packages, and offers that you spend most of your budget before your approved campaign is ready for mailing. While there is no single figure which is correct in all cases, many experts feel that setting aside from 5 to 15 percent of your total budget for testing may not only save you from disaster but uncover winning methods which will increase your net response 50 to 100 percent.

Testing should cover these nine factors:

1. The product
2. The proposition
3. The price and the terms (cash with order, free trial, charge, type of refund guarantee, number and size of installments, etc.), i.e., the offer
4. The appeal

5. The headline
6. The format
7. The premium (whether to use one or more, for quick action, for cash-up, etc.)
8. The list
9. The short- and long-term value of responses

Industrial Marketing magazine in September 1980 published the results of a survey of business-to-business direct marketers which revealed that the following percentages of responders employed testing for each of these purposes:[2]

- 50% test lists
- 47% test offers

Of companies which test lists:

- 65% test rate of return
- 29% test cost of return
- 52% test potential customer value
- 39% test sales conversion rate
- 13% test the dollar value of orders

Of companies which test orders:

- 32% test rate of return
- 23% test cost of return
- 38% test potential customer value
- 26% test sales conversion rate
- 6% test the dollar value of orders

Naturally, not all these tests should or can take place at the same point in the development of your mail program. There are, in fact, three basic types of testing:

1. Pretesting
2. Observation or comparison testing
3. Improvement testing

Pretesting permits you to judge the validity of your basic assumptions and approaches. Particularly in those cases where your prospect lists are homogeneous and small samples therefore can be used with comparative safety, it permits you to choose among several possible sales and advertising strategies by comparing the pulling power of simple, small mailings.

Direct mail can pretest both direct mail and space campaigns in this way. But keep it simple. Keep all the factors except the basic one on which you're seeking information identical if at all possible.

Pretesting also can utilize techniques other than mail, such as focus groups, mall intecepts, attitude evaluation, and recognition and preference studies. Each of these is a specialized procedure which should be done under the supervision of experienced professionals; focus groups especially should be used with caution.

The interpretation of the results of qualitative tests often is open to question.

[2] *Industrial Marketing*, September, 1980.

Some years ago, the California Prune Board employed two leading marketing research firms simultaneously to determine attitudes and recommend advertising approaches. The two firms made diametrically opposite recommendations from findings which were virtually identical.

Observation or comparison testing pits one complete mailing package against another or against the same package with one factor changed. Don't change more than one factor if you're following the second alternative. If you do, you will never know what caused the difference in the result, and your test money will be wasted. There is a method of testing lists as well as another factor at the same time. It requires that one-half of each list receive each of the two mailings. By comparing the total responses from each list, you can judge the relative value of one list against another; by comparing the total response from one type of mailing with that from the other, you can see which mailing pulled better.

It used to be held that one should never change more than a single factor—e.g., copy appeal, format, etc.—in any one test. But now it is recognized that certain types of appeal demand certain formats for greatest effectiveness (for example, computerized letters) so that the entire package may have to be changed physically. But be careful not to make extraneous changes in the process—e.g., changing the price or the offer—for that will invalidate the entire test result.

Improvement testing is similar except that it usually takes place later in the program, after your first program is already in the mail. It consists most often of adding one additional sales point or selling technique while leaving the mailing basically unchanged. If you take care to test only significant changes or potential improvements, you may find this technique highly profitable.

Here are some fundamental principles of successful testing.

1. Don't test items which are unlikely to have any significant effect on the return. Direct mail practitioners have come a long way from the days when their discussions concerned whether to use a printed indicia or a stamp or even what color indicia to use. Of course, rate of postage sometimes make a difference, but often the difference is simply in your cost per thousand in the mail, not in the response. Whether the piece looks first class is of greater significance than whether you've paid first class postage.
2. Remember that small differences in return often are caused by chance. Make your tests big enough to be statistically significant. The expected response rate, not the size of the list, determines the proper test size. The Direct Mail Advertising Association's *Direct Mail Manual*, file no. 8100, contains one of the simplest and most lucid explanations of the theory of probability in terms of its effect on sample size and return.
3. Keep adequate records over a sufficient period of time. This is especially important in mail order, where one list may outpull another and yet the second may prove far more profitable if it generates a larger number of reorders. But it is also vital in inquiry solicitation, where the quality of the leads may be more significant than the quantity.
4. When testing lists, make sure that the test segments are representative of the entire list.
5. Do everything possible to avoid bias from extraneous factors in your results. For example, make sure that different groups being tested against one

another are mailed to on the same day; both current events and weather can affect your return. An alternative is to use the "two-flight" technique, in which duplicate sets of tests are mailed some time apart in order to compare results. You can never check too carefully to make sure each segment is coded properly.

6. Testing depends on the mathematical theory of probability, and the very essence of that theory is that haywire results can and do occur. Even if you've based your test sizes on the 95 percent reliability column, your particular case may be one of the 5 out of every 100 in which the result falls outside the general deviation from the true result. If something seems wrong, don't commit all your money on the basis of that test without confirmation tests.

CHOOSING A FORMAT FOR INDUSTRIAL MAIL ORDER

Which format will you adopt? Much depends on the product or product line you're promoting, the gross margin per sale, the number of reorders anticipated, and the number of other items you have to sell to the same prospects.

Although business-to-business direct mail uses virtually every format employed in consumer mail, four formats virtually dominate the field: the letter, the solo mailing, the self-mailer or flier, and the catalog.

In sales lead solicitation, the letter is generally the most effective format. This is the only instance within the purview of direct response in which it is possible to say too much. The sole aim is to persuade a businessperson to spend time with a sales rep, and it therefore can be counterproductive to tell too much of your story. Your prospect may decide that he or she now is fully informed and need not be subjected to the sales call. You must tell enough to arouse interest but not enough to satiate it.

When seeking actual sales, on the other hand, you must tell the whole story, warts and all, to ensure believability. This is why the solo mailing is the preferred format for mail-order sales, especially for complex or important products. While the sales letter is the most vital element in a solo mailing, as elsewhere, brochures, broadsides, or other supporting enclosures permit full demonstration of the product's special features and the benefits they create for the buyer's firm.

A minority of direct-response practitioners, frequently those whose background is in graphics, dispute the claim of primacy for the letter, although it has been proved in hundreds of tests. In one case, addition of a letter to a successful New England Business Service mailing package increased orders 43 percent.

The solo mailing usually consists of a sales letter, one or more brochures or folders, buckslips to call attention to particular features, a reply device, and a business reply envelope. It varies in appearance from highly dignified, personalized packages to very colorful, almost circuslike treatments. Which will be most successful depends on the nature of your target audience, your industry, and your product.

The solo mailing provides room for the free exercise of ingenuity and creativity. However, the creativity must be in the service of selling. Some of the involvement techniques used in consumer mail may not be appropriate in persuading an executive to adopt a new machine for a factory, for example.

Solo mailings generally can be produced more rapidly than catalogs. This is another reason why they are used so often in new product introductions. More elaborate solo mailings may cost half to two-thirds as much per thousand as a modest-size catalog when mailed in large quantities, but the initial and preparatory costs are much lower.

Solo mailings frequently prove valuable in building a house list as rapidly as possible and are of importance as a test medium in determining the most profitable price for a product.

The self-mailer may be considered a type of solo mailing, except that the format also is suitable for minicatalog use. When used for one product, it has many of the advantages of the solo, particularly speed and lower preparatory costs, but it limits the space available to display the product's benefits and frequently leaves an impression of less than top quality. The self-mailer works generally well on mailings directed to plant personnel; it may be screened out in the mail room or by a secretary before the mail reaches a key executive. It lends itself well to hard sell and to price offers and may convey a greater sense of urgency.

The catalog makes up for whatever it lacks in urgency by greater longevity. Tom Anglo of Fidelity finds that 90 to 95 percent of responses from solo mailings are received within the first 60 days, while catalogs produce orders for from 2½ months to 1 or 2 years, depending on the frequency with which new catalogs are issued.

Catalogs are by nature reference tools, and many are filed by recipients and referred to when the need arises. But it is important to keep in mind the difference between your direct-response catalog and the standard sales support catalog.

Your book must do more than merely give all the essential information: it must sell. Regular industrial catalogs are informational, but mail-order catalogs are selling machines. They must not only inform but also convince and bring about sales action. Every square inch must carry its weight in sales. The industrial mail-order catalog writer and designer cannot afford the luxury—so often indulged in by industrial publication ad creators—of devoting two-thirds of the available space to art or photos of doubtful relevance.

It is essential that your marketing posture be determined clearly even before merchandise is selected. Are you aiming for overall market leadership or a particular segment of the market? Top of the line or the low-price buyer? The sophisticated executive or the person first investigating your type of equipment? The firm with 30,000 employes, 300, or 3?

Although there are exceptions, it is wise to direct your catalog to a carefully selected limited audience.

Issue different editions for the different lines of business you serve. The difference in the book may be as slight as changing the black plate to include the name of the prospects' industry on the cover and key inside pages, or it may extend to merchandise selection and even terminology. It is particularly important to use the vocabulary of the industry you are addressing.

Your catalog must be user-oriented, not product-oriented. Give all the data potential buyers need to make sure your product meets their requirements, told in terms they understand.

The catalog must take advantage of every appropriate technique possible to encourage the prospect to place an initial order, from special offers (with a reasonable cutoff date) and bonuses to increase order size to the use of 24-hour 800 number telephone services.

In striving for that first order, never neglect to promote your best-sellers. They often will be your best door openers. Promote them hard; give them prominence of place; make joint offers with items with which they are used.

If they fall into the category of supplies that are used up, encourage repeat business by giving special rates, bonuses, or other benefits for ordering regular shipments on either a fixed term or a till forbid (TF) plan.

Catalog copy must be clear, leaving no room for uncertainty. Terms such as "large size," "extra length," or "superstrength" (all taken from current industrial mail-order catalogs) should be avoided. Every word must serve a vital function.

There is no room in a selling catalog for pointless puffery, but be sure to include all essential statistics, not only as to the size, capacity, durability, and other features of the product but also as to function. If your catalog includes similar supplies of different sizes to fit different makes and models of machines or items for which the standards vary in different industries, be sure to indicate clearly the exact uses of each size or type.

INDUSTRIAL COPY

Is effective industrial copy different from consumer? The answer is both yes and no. No, because the prospect is in both cases the same person, a human being who is moved by emotion as well as by reason. But yes, because of two vital factors.

1. The product is usually one of far greater importance in the total scheme of things.
2. Prospects are not spending their own money but are acting for organizations of which they are part but usually not the key individual.

The inevitable corollary of the second point is that the prospect may feel that his or her job or future advancement is placed in jeopardy every time he or she purchases an untried product or buys from a new source. Hence, it is necessary to provide reassurance in every way possible, and that means telling all the facts, giving all the reasons why buying your product or service will make the customer a hero.

TWENTY-TWO WAYS TO MAKE INDUSTRIAL DIRECT MAIL COPY MORE EFFECTIVE

Industrial copy has its own logic. It does not permit the writer to use the type of hyperbole which is often forgiven and sometimes is even effective in consumer promotion. It requires the writer to be responsible and to be knowledgeable about both the product and the specific industry in which the recipient of the message is involved.

Too many people believe that industrial direct mail must be dry as moondust and that all that is necessary for success in this field is a mere listing of features. Neither of these propositions is founded on fact.

Even if you do not have years of experience in the industrial field, you can create profitable business-to-business communications. Here are some easy to follow guidelines to increase your results.

1. Industrial buyers are sophisticated buyers. They want to know why you believe they should prefer your widget to the competition's. You must tell them, fully and honestly. But that does not mean pompously or dully.
2. They are humans, the same people who when they are not in their offices are mail-order buyers of magazines, books, foods, and other products. They are subject to the same emotions and to appropriate emotional appeals during business hours. Your copy should reflect this.
3. The operative word in the previous sentence is "appropriate" because the purchase of a widget involves such personal factors as prestige (Will it make me look good to top management?) and risk (If I shift from a safe supplier and the product fails, is my job or promotion in jeopardy?). Your copy must offer reassurance subtly.
4. Dig in before you begin to write. Start with the process of manufacture of the widget. Go through the factory yourself if possible. Find out what type of material it's made from and what processes of production are used. In what ways if any does its manufacture differ from that of competitive products? The more facts you can uncover, the easier your writing task will become.
5. Find a feature which can be dramatized in terms which are meaningful to the buyer. If it's a feature which is unique, so much the better, but uniqueness need not be an essential quality to make it a valid sales point, provided that no one has called attention to it previously.
6. Do not dilute the power of your mailing by trying to achieve noncomplementary objectives at the same time. For example, don't try to pitch for advertising if your primary objective is to secure subscriptions from a list of executives. You will make it difficult to do either effectively.
7. Keep in mind always the specific groups of buyers to which the mailing is addressed. The same product may need a presentation to purchasing agents that is completely different from what is suited to engineers. Similarly, what will sell the widget to one four-digit SIC may be of no avail in another, even one with a closely related SIC number.
8. Talk specific user benefits. Be sure they are the most important benefits in the judgment of the type of executive you're addressing. Phrase them in a way which causes executives to recognize that you are addressing them. Don't say that it saves time. Do say that it cuts the setup time of a given number of machines in half by eliminating the need to adjust the product by hand.
9. Say everything that has to be said to make the sale or secure the interview. Don't write to fill a given amount of space; rather, take the space necessary to explain all aspects of your proposition from the buyer's point of view. Don't be afraid your letter will be too long. A dull letter, even one of two

paragraphs, is too long, but a well-written message which presents information of interest and value to the reader is never too long.

10. Cast your sales story in logical sequence, again from the reader's point of view. Break it into "chapters" of one or more paragraphs each.

11. Use short paragraphs unless there is a valid marketing reason for grouping several points in one long paragraph.

12. Use subheads to increase ease of skimming. Many industrial buyers skim a letter first to determine whether it is worth the time to read it thoroughly.

13. Break your copy into units easily assimilated by the eye. Use indentation for key paragraphs, bullets before each of a lengthy series of short points (each one starting on a separate line), and similar devices.

14. Don't crowd too much on one page. The late Boyce Morgan, who was responsible for much of the early mail-order success of the Kiplinger letters, conducted an extensive series of tests which proved consistently that compressing sales letter copy to fit a single sheet of paper cuts response drastically. Make your copy look easy to read; more people will read it and act on it.

15. Use punctuation as an active force, not just because a textbook calls for it. Violate grammatical rules for effect when necessary, but only for good reason, not to talk down to the presumed level of your prospect.

16. Be stylistically consistent. Don't jump from heavy, long sentences in pedantic language to brief slangy phrases. Keep a clear picture of the mental attitude you want your prospect to adopt and write in a style which will create it.

17. Use colorful, active verbs. Avoid "all-purpose" words and passive constructions. Don't use unnecessary adjectives and adverbs.

18. Provide specific and believable evidence to back up every claimed benefit. Case histories in the customers' own words are the best type of proof; in their absence, independent research findings often can serve. Numbers such as "481 percent improvement in output" are both more memorable and more effective than "five times increase" or "500 percent." Beware the claim that's "too good to be true," even when it is true. Make sure that the evidence cited is relevant to the particular potential buyers you're addressing and to their problems.

19. Ask for the action you want. Too many mailings and ads do not make clear what they wish the reader to do. As a result, the reader does nothing.

20. Make it easy for the reader to take that action. Include a reply card and a special number or person to call. Say, "Call collect." Small firms usually do not reverse the charges, although they appreciate your courtesy in offering to pay, but very large firms often will do what you suggest.

21. Offer an appropriate free benefit for taking the action: an informative booklet or a talk with a qualified engineer.

22. You must keep in mind at all times your marketing goal. A letter or ad which causes the reader to say, "What a clever ad," is not really clever at all. The response you're seeking is, "Yes, these people have something of value for me. I'll do as they say (i.e., send a trial order, ask for a sales engineer to call, or take whatever action is best suited to the circumstances)."

chapter 54

RETAIL APPLICATIONS

Murray Raphel

President
Murray Raphel/
Advertising
Atlantic City, N.J.

INTRODUCTION

It's been more than a quarter century since Ed Mayer put together his seven basic rules of direct marketing, which then was called direct mail. He traveled throughout the world explaining this new medium and how it worked. His seven basic rules are still used today because they work. Some people have changed some of the words and examples, but the basics remain constant. In this section, we use these seven rules and tell how they work for retailers.

Despite the rapid growth and development of direct marketing throughout the world, retailers, especially smaller ones, are the last business group to take advantage of this highly volatile, exciting, and profit-making medium. Why? Perhaps because a lot of the direction has to come specifically from the retailers themselves. They become the publisher. They are in control, unlike the newspaper ad going through many hands before it finally is published or the radio ad depending on the script of the writer and the voice of the announcer. Direct marketing is a highly selective personal medium.

Since this is a "new" tool for a retailer to use, the retailer is not sure. Hesitancy leads to delay to procrastination to "I don't have the time . . . " These are the same retailers who succeeded in business because of personality, buying, merchandising—whatever skills and abilities they managed to put together to make people come and buy. These are the same skills needed for direct marketing.

Does following the seven basic rules ensure success for retailers? No, but it will help. Direct marketing is a *what* medium, not a *why* medium. If you send out 10,000 mailing pieces and get 500 responses, you know what happened. You had 500 people reply, or 5 percent, but you don't know why.

Certain things seem to work most of the time, and so you follow the accepted, the proven, and the workable. But there is always someone who will say, "Hey, I did just the opposite, and it worked for me." True. So the following rules are meant to be used as guidelines. If you want to break the rules, fine, as long as you know what the rules are.

RULE 1: DETERMINE THE OBJECTIVE

Only 2 cents out of every retail advertising dollar is spent on direct marketing. This is surprising when you consider that the rewards are far greater for the retailer in direct marketing than in any other form of advertising. Some advertisers know this fact, but it may be the best kept secret in the retail business. Look at the numbers. More than $18 billion is spent on newspaper advertising each year, more than $11 billion is spent on TV, and more than $8 billion is spent on direct marketing.

More ad dollars are spent in direct marketing than in radio, magazines, billboards, and T-shirts for the local Little League Team. With newspapers and radio, there is always the possibility of delay or inertia on the part of the marketer. But with direct marketing, there is no sense in delaying or delegating responsibility. There is no direct marketing person. That's you or someone you assign to do this work for you.

"Haven't got the time," says the average retailer. They give you a list of reasons, including the people who did not come to work that day, the shipments that were substituted or did not arrive, the broken water pipe in the back room, etc. They are so busy paying attention to the store, they often forget to pay attention to the customer.

Direct marketing is the strongest link they can form between their stores and their customers. If they use it, the results can be impressive. It is not unusual for a retail store to average a 10 percent return on a mailing. This doesn't happen in newspapers, radio, TV, magazines, or any other form of advertising. Only in direct marketing can you achieve a very special relationship between seller and the sellee. You have to spend time at it, but it is not difficult.

Direct marketing, more than any other medium, can be a very simple and effective method for the average retailer. One method is to write a letter to your customers telling about new merchandise that just arrived. Or you can offer merchandise for sale that they learn about before anyone else does.

The Six Basic Uses

Direct marketing has six basic objectives.

1. **To sell an order by mail for a product or service.** This includes the classic Sears catalog, the hundreds of catalogs found in the mailbox not only at Christmastime but throughout the year, and merchandise offered for sale in the mail-order section of magazines. It is a good idea to test selling an item by mail that previously has proved itself by selling well in your store.
2. **To answer an inquiry for a salesperson to visit.** The upholstering of chairs or the selling of drapes by retailers increases dramatically when their

services are offered by asking the customer to respond to newspaper, radio, or magazine ads. Giving your phone number and a person's name in addition to the description and price will increase sales.

Philadelphia Life Insurance Company recently sent a simple and inexpensive fold-over mailer to its customers, asking if they wanted more information on how to save taxes with the new Individual Retirement Plan. More than 11 percent of the customers responded. Millions of dollars of insurance was written by simply contacting the existing customers and offering an additional service. It is far easier to attract more money from the customer you have than to attract a new customer.

3. **To bring the reader to your place of business.** This is the easiest, most common, and still the most effective way to use direct marketing for retailers. Let the customers know they will receive the information about the promotion before you do any other advertising.
4. **To do an advertising job on your store.** Institutional advertising tells what you are and what you do. It may involve opening a new department and telling your customers what's happening. It does not ask for a specific action.
5. **Research.** Find out information about your store from your customers: what they like and don't, what they would like to see different, more of, or less of.
6. **To secure action other than a sale.** This includes banks running financial programs, charity drives, and raising money for elections.

Each of these six steps informs the customer more about you and your merchandise as well as reinforces your image in the community. Many people in retailing assume that since they have been in business for so many years, everyone knows who they are, where they are, what they do, and why they are in business. But many people do not know.

One out of five people in the community in which you live moves every year. But you still go to work in the same store in the same location, selling the same merchandise, and you forget to put your store's address or your phone number in your advertising.

We call this the curse of assumption. We "assume" everyone knows who we are and what we do. Of course, they do not. We constantly must reinforce our image and our selling story in the community in which we live. Direct marketing is one of the strongest tools we have to perform this task.

The Angry Man

One of the most compelling ads in the history of American advertising comes from McGraw-Hill. It is often called the "Angry Man" ad. It shows a heavyset, scowling executive in a chair staring at the audience. Next to him are the words

> I don't know who you are. I don't know your company. I don't know what your company stands for. I don't know your company's record. I don't know your company's reputation. I don't know your company's customers. Now . . . what is it that you wanted to sell me?

We assume that, because we know who we are and where we work, others know. Our spouse knows, our children know, and our parents know. Whenever we come into work in the morning, everyone says hello to us by name. Certainly everyone knows who we are. But everyone does not.

Direct marketing is an ongoing reminder to your customer not only of who you are but that you are still doing business at the same stand in the same place with the same merchandise. L. L. Bean's volume jumped dramatically when they simply increased the mailing of their catalog from twice a year to twelve times a year. They realized that the customers did not want to buy the merchandise only when L. L. Bean wanted to sell the merchandise.

Who's Your Competition?

If your objective is to bring more customers to spend more dollars with you, a key question is simply, "Who's your competition?" Most retailers say their competition is the store offering products or services similar to what they offer. This is not true. If you put men's shirts on sale and offer them to the consumer, the local supermarket has a sale on strawberries. They tell the consumer to forget about buying anything else that day and pick up the strawberries for supper that evening.

At the same time, the area financial institutions are promoting new Individual Retirement Programs. They tell the customers to bring their money to the bank and earn double-digit interest on their savings. Don't buy the strawberries. Don't buy the shirts. Buy the retirement income.

Thus, your competition really is everyone in your community offering any goods or services for sale. Every store, business, and service is after the same consumer's dollar. That is why you must have all the tools necessary to bring people to shop with you. One of the best tools is direct marketing.

RULE 2: ADDRESS CORRECTLY

The two ingredients basic to the success of any direct marketing piece are the list and the offer.

Some experts claim that one is more important than the other. On a glance, they are in balance.

If you have the best list available and make the wrong offer, your campaign will fail. If you have the best offer available and the wrong list, your campaign will fail. If you are selling first readers to young children and mail the campaign only to senior citizens, the results will be minimal. (You may catch a few for grandparent gifts). If you are selling retirement homes and the list is newlyweds, the results will be disastrous.

Look how far ahead you are with these two necessary success ingredients in your own business. You have your own customer list, and you are offering the customers merchandise from your store.

Milt Smolier, past president of the mailing list house Names Unlimited and an ex-retailer, once said, "If you have a list of customers, you're in the direct marketing business."

Companies mailing to "Occupant" are satisfied with one-half of 1 percent return. Your return can exceed that tenfold because you are addressing your mail to your customer. They know you, have faith in you and your merchandise, and will read what you send them.

A common myth is that people do not read direct mail. But survey after survey shows that nearly 70 percent of people receiving direct mail at least glance at it. If it goes to your own customers, they probably will read it to see what you are offering. Here are some stories showing how this works.

Joe Girard

Joe Girard is in the *Guinness Book of World Records*. For 4 years in a row, he sold more automobiles than any other car salesperson in America. He sold them, says Joe, "belly to belly," or one-on-one, with no fleet sales. One of the reasons for his success was direct marketing. After you buy an automobile from Joe, you receive thirteen cards a year. They read as follows.

January "Happy New Year. I like you. Joe Girard, Merolis Chevrolet."
February "Happy Valentine's Day. I like you. Joe Girard, Merolis Chevrolet."
March "Happy St. Patrick's Day. I like you. Joe Girard, Merolis Chevrolet."

The thirteenth card arrives on your birthday: "Happy Birthday. I like you. Joe Girard, Merolis Chevrolet."

The next time you are going to buy a car, doesn't it make sense for you to buy from someone who likes you? Joe spends $12,000 a year just on postage and cards, but this type of direct marketing is responsible for his $200,000 a year income.

Merton Corn

The bank was one of the smallest in New York City, and it wanted to increase its deposits. Chelsea National Bank president Merton Corn knew what he could not do. He could not afford to advertise on TV. He could not afford to advertise in *The New York Times*. He could not afford to advertise on the New York City radio stations' top-rated drive time. He could not afford to advertise in the magazines in New York City. However, he could afford direct mail.

He drew a circle around his bank located just below Central Park in Manhattan. He said this "community" within the circle was the "city" where his bank was located. Then he began his direct marketing advertising campaign.

He put together a series of letters, each aimed at a different target market.

- Firefighters and police officers received letters at their station or precinct houses. Their checks were issued twice a month. Why take them home? Why not simply deposit them in the nearby Chelsea Bank? Corn knew that the main reason people choose a bank is convenience. He would take this advantage and make it work for him.
- Current depositors received letters offering incentives if they opened additional accounts with the bank. If you had a minimum savings account, you also could have "free checking." The more accounts customers have with a bank, the less likely they are to switch banks. If a customer has a savings account, the odds are 2 to 1 he or she will not leave before the end of the year. If the customer has a checking and savings account, the odds jump to 10 to 1; if the customer has

three accounts, the odds are 25 to 1. If the customer has four accounts, the odds go to 100 to 1. Corn wanted not only to attract new depositors, but also to increase the accounts held by current customers.

- Corporate personal accounts. Corn wrote letters to companies that borrowed from the bank for their businesses, asking if they would also like to have a personal account in the bank. At the end of this letter, he added the postscript (the best read part of any letter): "We will, of course, try to show our appreciation for this expression of confidence in us." If you were borrowing large sums of money for your business and the president of the bank wrote you asking for a personal account, would you oblige? How fast?
- President to president. Corn wrote the small businesses in his newly formed "circle city." His opening line was, "You're the president of a small business. I'm the president of a small bank. Why don't we get together and talk president to president." The implication was that the small businessperson might have a difficult time if he or she called Chase Manhattan and wanted to talk about business problems with David Rockefeller. But there was a bank president, Merton Corn, ready and willing.

This last letter campaign attracted so much attention that the headline was picked up and used by competitive banks as a way to increase their corporate business. Business jumped at the Chelsea Bank in both dollars and customers, all because of an advertising campaign that was limited to direct marketing.

Dick's Supermarkets

In southwestern Wisconsin, Dick's Supermarkets are a dominant force in the food retail business. The president, William Brodbeck, says that a good deal of their growth and success is due to an effective, ongoing, results-oriented direct marketing program. New residents moving into any of the five communities with a Dick's Supermarket receive a personal letter from the manager of the store nearest them. The residents may have arrived from another part of the state or country, or they may be newly married.

The letters are identical except for the opening paragraph: "Congratulations on your recent marriage" for one and "Congratulations on your new home" for the other. Each letter explains the different services and departments in Dick's Supermarket. Each also contains six coupons for the recipient to use: two a week for the next 3 consecutive weeks. Each coupon has one item of food the customer receives free: a half gallon of ice cream, 5 pounds of potatoes, a pound of ground beef, a pound of butter. Rare is the individual who will throw away a coupon for free food. Nearly 95 percent of all the coupons Dick's mails are used.

At the middle of the third week, the president, Bill Brodbeck, writes his own letter. He thanks the people for shopping in their local Dick's store (he knows this from the coupons). He welcomes them to the Dick's family, and then he asks them for some help. He encloses a three-page questionnaire on the various departments in Dick's. How would the customer rate the departments: fair, poor, good, very good? There are a few lines provided for personal comments. For taking the time to fill out the questionnaire, Dick's includes six more coupons.

A new baby is born to the family. Again a letter is received from Bill Brodbeck addressed to the child, beginning, "I trust this is the first business letter you will receive." The letter welcomes the child to the world and to the community and encloses a $2 gift certificate that must be used for baby merchandise only: milk, formula, diapers, baby accessories. One year later, a card goes out to wish the child a happy birthday and offer a discount on his or her first birthday cake from the bakery department.

One year after the customers fill in the initial questionnaire, they receive another questionnaire from Brodbeck, saying, "A year has passed, and we want to know what you think about our store now." There is another coupon attached for them to use in exchange for taking the time to fill out the questionnaire.

One person in Dick's clips, cuts, and collects names and addresses. Dick's has the direct marketing program down to a science that brings customers back.

"There are other advantages too," says Brodbeck. "We really read the comments they put on the questionnaires. Several said they did not like produce prewrapped. They preferred it in bulk. We listened and did it the way the customers wanted. Our sales increased."

Another benefit is that when customers are filling out the questionnaire, they often run across departments they are asked to comment on which they did not even know the store had. It makes them more aware of the features available in what is now their adopted store.

This is a direct marketing promotion that works not only to bring in new customers and hold on to the ones you already have. It also guarantees repeat visits to your store and guarantees consistency in sales.

Each of these promotions worked because of the combination of a strong list and a strong offer which together enabled the retailers to follow rule 2: address correctly.

RULE 3: SHOW WHAT IT DOES FOR THE READER

All your customers have a radio implanted in their brains. There is only one station on the radio. They listen to it 24 hours a day, consciously or subconsciously. The name of the station is WII-FM. Your job as a retailer is to put your commercial on that FM station, so that they hear, understand, and react to your selling message. The call letters of the station spell out a question: What's In It For Me?

The customers know what's in it for *you*. You take their money and put it in your register. But what's in it for *them*? Why should they give their money to you? What benefit do you offer that your competitor does not? What reasons have you listed and documented? How do you make them feel they are the most important customers of them all?

Direct marketing answers these questions more effectively than any other medium because it is the most personal ad medium. It offers a me-and-thee relationship not attainable in any other advertising medium. Say, for example, that you meet an attractive woman. You ask her out to dinner. The next day you send her a letter saying: "Thanks for an enjoyable evening. It was fun, exciting, and I hope we can soon do it all over again and repeat all the marvelous things we did together."

The woman reads your note and says to herself, "Wasn't that nice of him to write." She tucks it in her pocketbook and has good thoughts about you.

Now let us have another scenario. This time, instead of sending her a note, you place the note as an ad in the paper addressed to her with the same message. She would be embarrassed. Her friends would read other meanings into the once-innocent phrases. Or you could contact the local radio station and have an announcer read the same message as a commercial beginning, "And now here's a letter for . . ." repeating word for word the phrases in the letter.

The woman now is offended. Any positive thought she might have had of you is gone. The message was the same in all three media. When she received it in the mail, her reaction was warm and positive. When she saw it in the newspaper or heard it on the radio, her reaction was cold and negative. Direct marketing forms an emotional bond between you and your customer that is not attainable in any other medium.

Once your customers are on your mailing list, they look forward to your mail. In fact, they are insulted if they do not receive your mail and others do.

Whenever a mailer leaves our store, we know that the phone will start to ring within the week with irate phone calls from customers who for one reason or another did not receive our mailer.

We try the usual excuses: "The post office lost it," "The mailing house skipped your name when labeling," "You'll probably receive it tomorrow because third class mail arrives late." None work. All they know is that their neighbor received the mailer and they did not, and they are good customers. You finally agree to mail another first class that day or even hand deliver one that evening. We never have had a customer call and say, "How come your ad isn't in the newspaper today?" "I've been listening to the radio for the past 48 hours and haven't heard your ad." We never had a customer call and complain about our not advertising in the newspaper, on the radio or TV or billboards, in magazines or on the backs of the local bowling team. But forget to send them a direct mail piece, and they are slighted, insulted, and ignored.

The First National Bank of Wilmette, Illinois, decided to do a direct mail promotion. They put together a 5-week program. Every Thursday morning, the residents of the community received a large postal card in the mail. This card described different bank services; one week it listed the many programs available in the bank. Another card showed the extra hours the bank was open for the customer's convenience. The last mailer included the calling card of a bank officer and asked the readers if they were interested in any of the bank services they had been reading about for the past 5 weeks. If so, just call, and the officer would explain it to them in more detail.

The Thursday morning of the sixth week, something unusual happened at the bank. Shortly after the bank opened at 9 A.M., the phones began to ring. The amount of calls that day was uncommonly heavy. Extra operators were assigned just to handle the heavy phone load. Why all the extra calls? Customers were calling in to say they had not received any mail from the bank that morning. How come? Even after explanations were given ("It was only a 5-week campaign to list bank services"), many still asked, "But isn't the bank going to write me anymore?"

The Headline

What makes customers read your mailer? They know it came from your store. They will glance at the cover. They will open it for a quick eye scan. But what makes them read? It begins with the headline for your mailer. Seventy-five percent of readers read the headlines. Only 25 percent keep on reading. When you pick up the morning newspaper, do you look at the front page, read the headline, read the whole story, read the next headline, read the whole story, read the next headline, etc.? Of course not. You pick and choose what you want to read, which is determined by the headline.

The average reader spends only 4 seconds on each newspaper page. This shows the competition for your customers' eyes and pocketbooks that exists in every package of mail arriving daily at their doors. It tells you the importance of creating a headline. David Ogilvy once addressed his copywriters by saying, "When you have written the headline for your customer's product, you have spent 75 percent of their money."

Bill Jayme, a direct marketing copy expert, carries it further. When asked how he allocates time when composing direct mail pieces, he answers, "I spend 0 to 60 percent of my time on the headline and the rest of the time on the seven-page single-spaced letter." Jayme's award-winning and classic headline for his subscription letter for *Psychology Today*—"Do you still close the bathroom door even when nobody's home?"—brought in a record number of subscriptions.

Are there magic words to use in headlines? There are words that seem to work most of the time. The ten most quoted as "successful" are these: free, now, you, new, win, easy, introducing, today, save, and guarantee. Others include the basic five Ws of journalism: who, what, when, where, and why. Our personal favorite with a higher degree of success than failure is "how": "how to do it," "how 90 seconds spent reading this letter will save you money," "how you can bake a cake in 3 minutes."

Numbers are effective in headlines. Barney's Men's Shop in New York has run the same spring-summer and fall-winter mailer for the past 10 years. They list 100 reasons to shop Barney's sale and number them from 1 to 100.

Co-op Mailings

Look closely at your cooperative agreement contracts with your manufacturers. You will find few if any offering a 50-50 split on direct marketing.

The reason is simple: They are not sure how it works and cannot have the Advertising Checking Bureau measure it exactly. But the dollars are usually available if you show the manufacturer how you will advertise his or her product for your store. You must explain the program in detail ahead of time, giving the exact cost. You may have to work this program with your salesperson. This may fail, since most sales people work by the book, asking, "Has it been done before?" Nontraditional ideas are difficult to explain to them, much less have them explain the ideas for you. You are at an advantage selling the idea yourself. It is easy for the owner of the firm to say no to an employee, the salesperson. It is more difficult to say no to the buyer—you. The dollars are there, and the method is easy. Write a simple letter along these lines.

> NAME OF MANUFACTURER:
>
> We are putting together our advertising program for next season. We are proud to carry (name of line) and want to make sure you are part of this program.
>
> Some of our best results (which means more sales for your merchandise) come from direct marketing.
>
> We notice this effective advertising medium is not covered by your cooperative advertising plan.

And so we have submitted an idea for a direct marketing program we have planned for your product. We have listed actual costs and your 50 percent share which fits inside the dollars allowed us in your co-op contract.

Please let us know if there are any changes, additions, or corrections you want to make before we order this mailing piece.

Nine times out of ten, you'll get an OK.

Nontraditional Thinking

Direct marketing gives you the chance to do nontraditional advertising. The most successful promotion we do is on New Year's Day. We began this promotion 15 years ago. Everyone told us why it would not work. New Year's Day is the morning after the night before, they said. Everyone is recuperating. New Year's Day is the time of the bowl games. You can sit in front of the TV from morning until evening watching championship college games. New Year's Day is the time when all the other stores in town are closed.

With all these compelling, traditional reasons why the sale would not work, we decided to begin our fall-winter sale on New Year's Day. And we added a few more negatives. We decided to open for only 4 hours instead of the usual 8. We decided to advertise the sale only through direct mail.

The sale started at noon; the crowds started forming at 11 A.M. A few hundred were lined up outside the front doors a half hour before opening. We called the police for extra reinforcements. When we opened, we let in only a few hundred customers because that's all we could fit. The others came in a few at a time. The final result that first day was the largest single dollar volume day of the entire year. Our store does more business in 4 hours on New Year's than it does in some weeks of the year!

The following day, we take a full-page ad in the newspaper. We have a radio station do a live remote from the store encouraging customers to come and shop. We are open for 8 hours. It is a normal shopping day, and all the other stores in town are open. Yet with all these added reasons to buy, the store will do less than one-half the volume we did the previous day, when we were open for only 4 hours. The only way customers know about the sale is direct mail.

Now the sale is a tradition, a place to go and see and be seen. There are still comments like, "If this is a private sale, what is the public sale like?" But the customers come in ever-increasing crowds and buy in ever-increasing dollars. They know that this sale, this promotion, this once-a-year happening offers them something special.

What does it do for the readers? It gives them the opportunity to buy before others buy, to have the first choice. They are favored and chosen and "special." This is why we say that dollar for dollar, nothing will bring as much business to your store as direct marketing.

RULE 4: MAKE THE LAYOUT AND COPY FIT

"Every advertisement you run is an investment in yourself," says David Ogilvy. This means that your direct mail pieces must "look" like your store. If your store sells women's clothing, the mailer should be soft and feminine and attractive, and the typefaces should match. If your store sells men's clothing, the mailer should be masculine in type style, paper, and art. Above all, it should have a look that is yours alone and should not resemble any other mailer received by your customers. Some businesses do this by means of color. Morris Batzer sold insurance in Atlantic City, New Jersey. His mail was sent out in bright orange envelopes. When the morning mail arrived with its stack of white envelopes, and an orange one was in the pile, consumers would say, "I wonder what Batzer Insurance sent me today?" The color told them who the mailer came from.

Typefaces are another way to establish identification. Some stores run all their copy in lower case, a sort of laid-back understatement. Other stores use capital letters and a generous amount of exclamation points, asterisks, and other attention-getting type symbols. This usually is done for lower-price merchandise where owners feel they have to "shout" louder than the competition.

Ed Mayer explained the relationship between layout and copy in terms of a person not wearing a tuxedo to the beach or a bathing suit to a formal dinner. Customers expect your package to "look" a certain way. If it does not, they are confused and usually unwilling to read what you mailed. If the catalog is from Neiman-Marcus, the customer expects it to be bright, shiny, slick, classy, and exquisitely (i.e., expensively) photographed with a special, unusual Christmas gift. But not all retailers are Neiman-Marcus nor want to be. At the other extreme is a small grocery store in Colorado. Once a week they type up a listing of food specials and mimeograph the copy on yellow paper. This one-page black and yellow paper listing is distributed to the few hundred households in the community. People come in with the list in hand with check marks next to what they want. Total cost for printing and delivery is under $20. The results are excellent: complete saturation of the total community each week.

Some Ways to Make the Match

The easiest and most effective way to make layout and copy fit is to send your customer a letter. This is the basic direct mailing piece. When all the hoopla of laser and ink jet and four-color process finally dies down, the letter inside the envelope will remain the reason why people come to you and buy.

The letter may simply say why this is a good time to come in and buy the furniture: "Prices are going up 10 percent next month. Layaway what you want for 6 months at the lower prices."

Everyone receives letters to join book clubs, subscribe to magazines, contribute money to charity, vote for a particular person, and join everything from automobile clubs to stamp and coin societies. You will find that by adding coupons to your letter, sales will increase over what is generated by a letter alone. Give the customers a reason to come to your store. Involve them. Using a coupon is involvement. Filling out one's name and address for a "chance to win $1000 in designer clothing" provides added incentive.

Giving a customer a yes or no alternative also increases response. Those who say yes have made the commitment to buy. If you send a second mailer to those who said no, about one in four will buy the second time around because they were involved the first time around. They just needed an extra shove.

The Statement Enclosure

The statement enclosure is another way to increase sales. We recently decided on a pre-Easter promotion. It was the store's birthday. We printed $5 gift certificates and sent them to the 2000 charge customers who received statements that month.

The headline read: "It's our birthday, but you receive the present." The copy explained that the only reason we could celebrate our birthday was that our customers supported the store. Thus, we were giving them $5 to use for whatever new purchases they wanted. No minimum purchase, no gimmicks—a gift. We received back almost 400 coupons, for a 20 percent return! The total spent by customers was $11,800. The total cost to us was $100 for printing the "gift certificates" (no postage since they were mailed in the statements) plus $1000 for the $5 gift certificates ($2.50 times 400). Our total profit was about $5000 for a simple, uncomplicated, inexpensive, and easy-to-do mailer. None used only the $5. They were customers who would feel "uncomfortable" spending the $5 and leaving. Of course, you should not run this type of promotion in the newspaper or any other medium. You would be swamped with first-time customers using the $5 and then leaving.

Do not send out any material by itself without a small memo or note or letter attached and signed by you. It is amazing how many manufacturers waste hundreds of thousands of dollars each year sending out four-color brochures, large sketches, or reprints of ads from national magazines wrapped in expensive mailing tubes with no personal note or comment.

When you mail your customer information about your new department or new device, paper clip a personal note and then sign your name. You can preprint your handwriting.

Sales people for Yves St. Laurent men's clothing preaddress letters to their retailing customers in the United States and then mail them from France when they visit the factory. The copy begins: "Well, here I am in Paris, thanks to you." It goes on to say they are looking over next season's line and checking to make sure your current goods are being shipped to you. We suggested they could make it work even better if they threw in a swatch of fabric for the coming season and added a note saying, "Thought you'd like to see a swatch of one of the new numbers for the coming season. I've reserved a few pieces for you."

If the average salesperson has 100 customers and each customer is flattered enough to buy six jackets at a wholesale price of $100 each, that means $600 times 100, for an extra $60,000 of business. Not bad for simply throwing in a small piece of fabric.

RULE 5: MAKE IT EASY TO TAKE ACTION

This is the fifth step in the formula for successful direct marketing. It enables the retailer to make it easy for the customer to take action.

The Customer

Give customers alternative ways to buy. The more options you offer, the greater the sales. List all the credit card companies they can use. Include your own store's plan. Offer the option of up-front cash or payment in terms. Tell them they may examine the merchanise for a certain length of time and then return it if they're unhappy for any reason.

The "guarantee" is the key ingredient in direct marketing. With rare exceptions, catalogs offer guarantees on what they sell: either replacement of merchandise or refund of money (the customer's choice). A good example is the guarantee from Norm Thompson. He gives his a name: the "You be the Judge" guarantee.

> When we say "You be the Judge" we mean just that! Every product you purchase from Norm Thompson must live up to YOUR expectations, not ours. If at any time a product fails to satisfy you, return it to us, postage prepaid, and we'll either replace the item, or refund your money in full, whichever you wish.
>
> This is definitely not a 2-week guarantee. It's good for the normal life of the product. (You being the judge of what that normal life should be.) We'll stand behind everything we sell to the fullest extent . . . no ifs, ands, or buts.

Many retailers hesitate to give guarantees or refunds. They invariably wind up in an argument and put themselves in a terrible mood for the next half dozen customers who arrive on the scene. Guarantees are important; full refunds are important. Retailers must make this a basic policy of their stores before entering the competitive world of direct marketing, where such guarantees are "givens."

When writing your letter, make it personal. Write your copy as if you were writing to a favorite aunt. Make the words chatty and comfortable. Write as you talk, with clichés, contractions, and constructions lacking nouns, verbs, or objects. The key question is, Does it sound right when you read it aloud?

Computer personalized letters listing your street address, the make of your car, and where your child goes to school now are recognized as having limitations. Although it does provide a greater response when your name is mentioned throughout the letter and does increase reader interest, this type of letter will never outpull a personal letter. It is a good idea to send your customer a copy of an advertisement before it appears in the newspaper. This way you reinforce direct marketing's greatest strength, the unique, personal relationship between you and your customer. ("We want you to know ahead of time. . .")

One of the most effective direct mailing programs using this technique was done by Allstate Insurance Company. They preprinted envelopes with what looked like an agent's handwriting in red ink. The copy told readers that there was something inside the envelope that the firm wanted them to see before anyone else did. Inside the mailer was a reprint of an ad for Allstate Insurance that was due to appear within the next few months. The company made the advertisement look personal with circles drawn around the copy and "handwritten" notes explaining certain statements in the copy. The notes were written in the same red ink as the copy on the envelope.

Agents were asked to preselect what letters and what campaigns they wanted for their customers. Allstate offered the identical ads with a white family, a black family, and a Hispanic family. It was a very effective and profitable campaign because it used direct marketing's greatest strength: pinpoint, person-to-person marketing.

The Bank

American Savings Bank in Dubuque put together a campaign for students just accepted in college. First-year students know the long delays and longer lines at the bank the first week in school while one waits to open a local checking account. There usually is a 10-day or longer additional wait while the first check clears to make the account workable.

American Savings contacted the students, offering to open the checking accounts before school began. There would be no waiting since they would send their checkbooks ahead of time. To sweeten the pie, they offered an additional $5 for opening an account with $100 or more.

The bank made it easy, exciting, and advantageous to take action at once. Also, the list and the offer worked well together. All that made it easy for the customers to take action. As a retailer, how do you take action to ensure consistent, ongoing, and successful direct marketing campaigns? We suggest our "four-mula for success." It is a proven system that will increase your business a minimum of 10 percent this year.

Four Notes

Write four notes to customers every day: "Just a short note to say thanks for doing business with us." That alone will stagger them. Since you know your customers, you might say "Just received a new shipment of (name brand) and know you like their merchandise. Wanted you to see the full selection before anyone else." They'll be at the front door the next morning. You have made them feel important; you have fine-tuned station WII-FM.

When reading through newspapers or magazines, extend your thoughts beyond yourself. If you run across an article on photography and one of your customers is a camera buff, rip it out and mail it to the customer with a small note saying, "Knew you would want to see this," and then simply sign your name. If you read an article about one of your customer's children winning an award, becoming engaged, or graduating from college, clip out the article and send it to the customer with a note: "Thought you'd like an extra copy of this. How proud you must be!"

We do this with our sales people several times a year between seasons. We have twenty sales people. Each writes four notes a day to personal customers for 2 weeks. That's 800 messages going out in the mail in 4 days.

The results can be amazing, not only in terms of dollars (in the thousands, from a total cost of less than $200) but also in terms of people talking about you. They show the notes to their friends; they tape them up in their offices. They are impressed. You have thought about them at a time other than the moment they come to you to buy.

Four Phone Calls

If you don't like to write, call: "I was just sitting here in the store thinking of you and wondering the last time anyone called to simply say, 'Thanks for doing business with us.' " The person on the other end may say, "Funny you should call. I was just about to call you. I was wondering if you could send me something." Another reaction may be for the customer simply to say thanks. The customer will remember—and tell a friend. People are searching for places to spend their money where they feel comfortable.

Roger Bailey, a loan officer with a bank in Nebraska, heard about our "four-mula" and decided to see if it worked. He went through his computer printout and noticed that the owner of a local lumberyard had just asked for and received a large loan. Roger called and asked to speak to the owner. The secretary replied that the owner was in a very important business meeting. Roger said, "Tell him Roger Bailey from the bank called."

Her reaction was predictable: "Oh, my goodness, I'll get him." The owner came to the phone: "OK, Roger, you decided against the loan, right?"

"No."

"You want more collateral, right?"

"Uh, no."

"Then why did you call, Roger?"

"Well, I was just thinking no one ever calls to say thanks for doing business with us, and I wanted to thank you for borrowing the money from us."

When he finally believed Roger, the owner made him hold the phone for a few minutes. He returned and said, "Roger, this is your lucky day. It was an important meeting. I was with a new firm coming into town that wants to buy some material from me. They asked me what bank they should do business with, and I told them all banks were alike. Take their pick. I just went in and told them about your phone call. Roger, send over a messenger. They have a check here for you for $800,000."

Four Personal Contacts

Every day, we all see at least four people we have not met before. Think about it: the waiter or waitress where you have lunch, a friend introduces you to someone new, you go to a party or a dinner, you visit the theater or the art gallery.

After you are introduced or you introduce yourself, simply say, "Hi, my name is (your name) and I'm from (name of your business). Next time you're interested in what we have to sell, give me a call." Hand them your calling card.

That little extra move each day with people you normally do not see because you are not looking will result in one of them someday picking up the phone to call you. Or they will come into the store to see you and say, "Remember the time at the party for the Charity League where you gave me your card? Well, I was in the neighborhood, and I thought I'd come in and see your store."

Four AFTO

AFTO stands for ask for the order.

The president of my bank was playing golf one day with the president of the local lumberyard. "Tom," he said, "we've been playing golf every Saturday for the past 5 years. When are you going to put some money in my bank?" Tom answered, "When are you going to ask me?"

We simply cannot assume that everyone knows who we are, what we do, and the fact that we would like his or her business. We tend to differentiate our acquaintances between people who are friends and people with whom we do business. But the distinction is false. If you have a friend and he is buying what you have to sell somewhere else, you haven't got a friend.

Ask for the order four times a day. Tell people who you are, what you do, and why they should shop with you. Add it up. Four times 250 days a year equals 1000 new contracts this coming year. This can mean an additional 10 percent volume to your business this coming year.

RULE 6: REPEAT YOUR STORY

Here is a simple formula for telling a story, writing copy, or doing a direct mail piece. Say what you are going to say. Say it. Say what you said. The headline takes care of the first part, the information provides the second, and the summary accounts for the third.

By the time your readers arrive at the end of the mailing piece, they may forget what you wrote up front. Remind them. Do a quick rundown of your basic facts (what's happening, when, where, and why) and basic information (your address and phone number).

One way to do this is the postscript at the end of the letter. The postscript is the best read part of your mailing piece after the headline. Eye scan tests show that people open letters and glance at the opening lines and then down to the postscript. This is a great place to do a quick, rapid-fire summary of what you said plus adding an extra benefit you have not mentioned up to that point. You also can repeat your story as you tell it within the body copy of the mailing piece.

Will people read all this copy? Yes, if it's interesting. The long versus short copy argument rests on that fact. Is it interesting for the customer to read? Readership surveys show that attention falls off rapidly during the first 50 words but that there is a very slow and insignificant drop-off over the next 250 words. If you hook them for the first few paragraphs, they will keep on reading.

Max Hart, from the famous men's clothing firm of Hart, Schaffner & Marx, hated long copy in ads. One day a copywriter brought him a long piece of copy describing in great detail how each suit was made. The copy began with the fabric and the difficulty in obtaining the costly raw material. It discussed in detail the meticulous tailoring. It was an excellent selling advertisement.

Max Hart glanced at all the words and said, "No one reads long copy."

The copywriter asked, "Mr. Hart, are you a betting man?"

Hart said, "Sometimes."

"Fine," said the writer. "I would like to make a bet with you. I will hand you a piece of paper with a headline for an advertisement. If you tell me you would read every single word in the ad, we run this one. If you tell me you would not, I will throw this ad away."

Max Hart agreed. The copywriter wrote out the headline on a sheet of paper, folded it in half, and gave it to Hart. Hart opened the paper, read the headline, and told the writer to run the ad.

The headline said, "This advertisement is all about Max Hart."

The Psychology of the Second Interest

A simple and effective way to repeat your story in the copy is to use the psychology of the second interest. In other words, you can persuade customers to buy what you want them to buy if you offer them something else that they want to buy. For example, the Literary Guild made a special offer to buy their books.

They gave a large selection of books illustrated on stamp-size perforated gummed back labels. The buyer picked four books, glued the labels on the space provided, and sent in 4 pennies. The books were on their way with an obligation to buy a certain number of books at a special price within the next few months. It worked fine, and soon other book clubs began to use a similar idea. Something was needed other than the offer for books.

The next ad offered a free minibag, great for storing cosmetics, change, keys, or small loose items, a convenient and attractive carrier free when you ordered the same books.

My wife was intrigued. She said she would order the books because she could use the bag. I immediately pointed out the error of her ways. I told her I was surprised she would fall for such a simple merchandising trick. "They want you to buy the bag so they can sell you the books," I explained. She said she would pass it by. I reread the ad and then noticed that on the bottom there was an extra offer: a brass bookmark with "your initials etched onto the brass." It was available free if you bought the books within the next 10 days. If you visit our store, I'll take you into my office. There on my desk is the brass bookmark. The books are around somewhere. I gave my wife the bag for Christmas.

The Chase Advantage

Banks work this psychology of the second interest very effectively. Chase Manhattan dropped a note to business people not using Chase services, offering them two free coffee mugs with the Chase logo: "Simply fill out the enclosed card and the cups are on their way."

An officer from the bank brought them to the office. The receptionist who usually stops sales people was confused about this person standing there with two coffee cups saying they could be given only to the person who ordered them—the boss. Once inside the executive's office, it was only natural for the bank officer to say, "Here's your coffee cups. Say, while I'm here, would you pour a cup of coffee for both of us." You can't insult someone who just brought you a gift. For a few dollars worth of coffee cups, person-to-person meetings were arranged, and sales were made.

One person who uses this technique consistently and effectively is Andrea Strickland of the First Georgia Bank in Atlanta. She comes up with new ideas almost monthly on how to bring in new business to her bank through direct marketing.

When they opened a branch bank in a nearby community, she sent the top of a hammer to all the business people in the area. It came in a small black box with the headline "We'll be knocking on your door soon." The letter inside told about the new branch opening and mentioned that someone soon would visit with the "rest of the set of handy tools for your office and to discuss a set of 'financial tools' to build your business."

"More than 80 percent of the business people had the top of the hammer waiting on their desk when our officers called with the rest of the tool box," said Strickland.

This small, inexpensive premium worked because the person receiving the mailer might have had no interest in what the bank wanted to sell but was interested in what was being given away. This opened the door for the selling.

An effective direct marketing piece should summarize by "saying what you said." In summary, the seven basic rules for direct marketing are as follows:

1. Determine the objective.
2. Address correctly.
3. Show what it does for the reader.
4. Make the layout and copy fit.
5. Make it easy to take action.
6. Repeat your story.
7. Test.

This brings us to the one key ingredient separating direct marketing from all other forms of advertising: testing.

RULE 7: TEST

What would happen if you called the local radio or TV station and said, "When you run our ad tomorrow, I want only one-third of the listeners or viewers to watch it." Or you might say to the newspaper, "I want my ad to run only in certain sections of town." Their answer will be "Impossible."

Some magazines and newspapers have split runs and can offer distribution into just certain sections. But the choice is theirs, not yours. They tell you where you are going to be. In direct marketing you can test what the results will be before you make the full advertising dollar commitment.

What Do You Test?

Your direct mail piece can be tested in the following areas:

1. The product
2. The medium
3. The telephone
4. The offer
5. The creative element
6. The timing

The Creative: The Easter Egg Story

It was an after-Easter sale. We wanted to try something different. We found small plastic egg-shaped banks and printed the sales message to fit inside the eggs, which separated in the middle. We purchased 10,000 banks and 10,000 mailing bags. The canvas bag had a cardboard attachment for the address and a small message: "Look what the Easter bunny left for you at Gordon's." The customer would open the bag, find the Easter egg, open it up, and read our sales message. We gave the mailer to ten people who work in our store. We wanted to see how they would open the mailer. They each opened the canvas bag, took out the plastic egg, placed the egg on the table, and said thanks. Thanks for what? "For sending us the egg banks. That's what the headline says: 'Look what the Easter bunny left for you at Gordon's.' "

"Wait a minute," we insisted. "Aren't you going to open up the egg?"

"Does it open?"

We went to the stationery store, bought 10,000 small peel-off dots, and had the printer label them "Open me up." We then opened the bags, took out the eggs, put the labels on every egg, and then repackaged the eggs in the mailing bag. If we had not tried the reaction ahead of time, we would have had a lot of extra help waiting the day of a sale that nobody came to.

The Product: The Million Dollar Sale for $10

Jerry Rimm sells insurance in southern New Jersey. As an independent agent, his advertising budget is limited.

One of his firms, Philadelphia Life Insurance Company, came out with a new policy for nonsmokers. The premiums were reduced drastically. A nonsmoker could nearly double the insurance coverage at about the same price. The company's brochure was full of facts, figures, and numbers. It was nearly impossible to read. "How many customers do you have under the letter A you think can use this new policy?" we asked.

"About thirty or so," said Rimm.

"Would you spend $10 on a direct mail campaign?"

"Ten dollars? Sure!"

He then mailed the thirty customers a letter. The outside of the envelope said, "For you—a nonsmoker." Inside, he enclosed the fact-filled, data-packed brochure from the insurance company. He also attached a small handwritten note personalized for each of the thirty customers. It said:

> Dear (customer's name):
>
> Now for the first time you, as a nonsmoker, can have $100,000 of life insurance for only $514 ($500,000 for $2000).
>
> The enclosed folder has the facts and figures. Call me today at 555-5201.
>
> Jerry

Note the personalization from the name to the specific amount (because Rimm knew the customer's age) and the add-on suggested sale for the increased coverage. Within 72 hours, he sold more than $2 million of life insurance.

The Offer: The McDonald's Story

Atlantic National Bank in southern New Jersey was opening a new branch. They did not want to do the traditional opening day announcement. They were searching for something different to capture the imagination of the households and business people in this suburban area.

One of the members of the board has several McDonald's franchises and wanted to offer his firm's products in a promotion. No one was quite sure how, and so they decided to test. The bank had about 10,000 customers in the area where they were opening the branch. In the next month's statements, tucked inside with the checks and other advertising matter, was a small coupon offering the reader a free order of french fries at the McDonald's nearest the new bank. Of the 10,000 coupons mailed, more than 8700 were redeemed.

The success of this offer led to a mailing piece preceding the bank opening which was mailed to all the households in the area. If customers opened an account with $300 or added $300 to an existing account, they would receive a free "McCheckbook." The "McCheckbook" had a series of checks, each good for a different product from McDonald's. All you had to do was sign your check and redeem it at McDonald's. The total first day's deposits were more than $350,000.

CONCLUSION

Twenty years ago, we did our first direct mail promotion out of desperation. Our little children's clothing shop was doing $16,000 a year annual volume. We could not afford to advertise, but we needed to do more business.

We began a merchandise club, going door to door introducing ourselves and offering a "10-week clothing club." You put in $1 a week for 10 weeks and received $11 worth of merchandise: a 10 percent bonus. We soon had 300 customers, doubling our volume. But we still could not afford to advertise.

We typed a newsletter and had it mimeographed and mailed to the club members the day after. We offered special items on sale the following week when we returned for the weekly club dollars. Soon we had to trade the car for a station wagon as the weekly specials expanded to anything that was in the car that day.

We studied the ideas, concepts, rules, and techniques of direct marketing through the years. We watched the growth from simple handwritten letters to computers and laser and ink jet printing. But the basic direct marketing examples that worked for us 30 years ago to build our business to a multi-million-dollar shopping complex still work today.

You have a mailing list of customers from the charge list and cash sales slips. If you do not, begin today with a simple stack of 3 by 5 cards with the name, address, city, state, and ZIP. Everyone who buys anything from you should go on the list. Within a few months, you could have a list of at least 1000 names. That's enough to start.

Set up a through-the-year schedule. Do not say, "Well, we'll try it this one time and if it doesn't work . . ." Direct marketing is a growing concept. You do not apply that criterion to your other advertising. Has every newspaper ad or every radio ad pulled for you? Neither will all your direct mail ads. But they will work better and longer. Pull out your customer file tomorrow morning. Write them a letter about a special promotion you put together just for them. It worked for us, And it will work for you.

chapter 55

MARKETING EDUCATIONAL SERVICES

David E. Rifkin

General Manager
Advertising and Promotion
Nynex Mobile Communications Co.
Pearl River, N. Y.

Rapid growth and changes in modern technology combined with the ebbs and tides of hobbies and "fad" pastimes require that education continuously adapt to the changing demands of the socioeconomic marketplace.

Technology (as it affects career pursuits) and personal hobbies both create a demand for training. Thus, if we were to separate education into two broad categories, we would have the following:

1. **Vocational training:** education in a skill or trade for entry or growth in a career
2. **Avocational training:** education in a subject for personal enjoyment or as a hobby or sideline

Each fills a need. While each is distinct not only in its subject matter but also in its methods of recruiting, training, and retaining students, in many cases the two forms of training overlap.

Take the case of a young person who enrolls in a proprietary (privately owned) photography course to develop a hobby. During the training program, the student learns how to turn the hobby into a profitable career. What begins as an avocational program becomes a vocational effort.

When one examines the methods currently used by many large and small colleges to attract students and student applications, one can see that many of these colleges are employing recruitment techniques which in the past have been the sole domain of proprietary resident and correspondence institutions. "Resident" schools are schools that give classes on the premises, regardless of whether students live on campus.

The marketing of education is usually a two-step, indeed a continuing, process. (Seminars are an exception to this rule.) In its most simple form, the sale of education involves the following steps:

- Generation of an inquiry
- Conversion of that inquiry into a sale (student)

In practice, however, the sale also involves

- Retention of the student
- Ancillary sales to that student
- Postgraduation marketing

Different forms of education serve different market segments, and those target markets are reached in different ways. An acceptable media environment for one institution may provide an image which is unacceptable to another.

TRADITIONAL VERSUS NONTRADITIONAL EDUCATION

Most people are familiar with traditional forms of education: colleges and universities, for example. During the 1960s and early 70s, children of the postwar "baby boom" reached college age and created a temporary demand for a limited number of college seats. Colleges responded with rapid expansion programs to meet the needs of society, but once that boom subsided, colleges were left with a growing number of vacant classrooms and unfilled programs. Thus, many traditional schools have had to begin extensive recruitment programs.

Even those few traditional schools which have realized only minimal declines in enrollment have embarked on extensive recruitment campaigns. By actively seeking a larger pool of candidates for admission, colleges are able to select students from a larger applicant universe and thus accept those with better qualifications, thereby enhancing their reputations.

Schools which are less traditional have, of course, engaged in promotional recruitment activities for years. These schools compete not only with each other but in many cases with traditional schools as well for the "training dollar."

During the late nineteenth century, correspondence education became a popular alternative for people who could not enroll in more formal programs of education. Correspondence training offered the opportunity to learn at home, in one's spare time, at one's own pace. High school equivalency and vocational subjects such as mine engineering were common courses of study; the college and proprietary training markets were delineated clearly.

During the twentieth century, however, a growing number of correspondence schools have offered college-level courses and equivalent certificates, thus competing directly with community colleges. One correspondence school—the Center for Degree Studies of International Correspondence Schools—has gone so far as to develop a program which is accredited by the Middle States Association of Colleges and Schools, a national accreditation association. The LaSalle Extension University has been marketing alternative college programs for several years. Fields of study for white-collar careers are available now through correspondence education.

But resident colleges and correspondence schools don't fill every need of the marketplace. Proprietary schools throughout the country offer specific training in a wide variety of areas. These schools, which often are developed as profit-making ventures, offer the personal attention of on-premise traditional schools, in many cases with the informality of correspondence programs.

Many proprietary schools do quite well during poor periods in the national economy. The demand for vocational training especially often grows stronger when the economy suffers and a large number of people are unemployed or are considering career changes.

Schools that offer training in fields which are expanding enjoy great demand for their "product," particularly from students who seek to enter the job market as quickly as possible.

Over the years, regulatory agencies have played an increasingly active role in the creation of both curricula and promotional recruitment efforts. In many states, proprietary schools must obtain a variety of official approvals before implementing recruitment campaigns or classes.

School directors often are faced with a dilemma. They must develop curricula that serve the needs of the student marketplace, provide a practical education which will prepare students for real-world applications, develop curricula which can be presented in simple terms so as to be understood as easily as possible by the great majority of students, and yet develop programs which are complete and satisfactory to both state and federal agencies as well as to students and their families.

The Federal Trade Commission (FTC), through its "Rule of the 78s," dictates minimum tuition refund policies. All enrollment agreements must indicate clearly to the consumer the amount of refund to which he or she is entitled at any point in the program. Furthermore, that any contract may be canceled without penalty within 72 hours of signing. Thus, a student who makes a commitment to a program by signing an enrollment agreement may cancel within 3 days. Obviously, student retention has become increasingly important.

A relatively new development in the field has been the success of short, intensive seminars. This popular method of imparting information in a brief fashion has been applied to both vocational and avocational subject matter by a variety of schools and private firms. The American Management Association (AMA) and New York's Network for Learning provide prime examples of successful seminar promotion.

Some seminars cover the entire gamut of narrow subjects; others cover broad subjects in a shallow fashion and are designed to give students a taste of the subject matter. Seminars generally last from 1 day to a full week.

THE CONSUMER EDUCATION MARKET

Private individuals enroll in educational programs for a variety of reasons: for self-improvement, to look better or to feel better about themselves, to become more comfortable when interacting with others in social and professional situations, and to develop skills in hobbies or side interests. Others enroll for professional reasons: to develop new careers, to improve skills in current career paths, to climb another "rung," and to make themselves more valuable to their employers. Some individuals enroll because of peer or family pressure: the teenager who suffers from poor posture or the bright but underemployed adult.

Students come in all ages, sexes, and ethnic backgrounds. Depending on the subject matter, student demographic or psychographic conclusions can be drawn by every educational institution. Modeling schools, for example, may recognize that their primary market consists of teenagers from lower-middle-class socioeconomic strata. Management seminar firms may recognize that their market consists primarily of lower and middle management personnel in medium-size and large-size companies. Correspondence schools may decide that their market is primarily blue-collar workers with visions of upward mobility.

CONSUMER CONCERNS

Until a short time ago, various federal and state funds were available in the form of grants and low-interest loans for educational purposes. Veterans' benefits, student loans, and the like have declined in availability in recent years, causing substantial preenrollment financial considerations.

In response, a growing number of schools now are accepting payment by credit card. Many also offer long-term "payout" options: a tuition deposit followed by weekly or monthly payments. By law, payout schedules must be listed clearly on enrollment agreements, together with the rate of interest charged. In fact, government regulations often dictate not only what an enrollment contract must state and how the information must be stated but the type size as well. Most schools that offer long-term payout programs insist that all fees be paid in full prior to graduation.

Time and effort also are concerns, particularly to proprietary school students, who may not care for structured courses, and to evening college students, who frequently hold full-time jobs. Many schools deal with these concerns by advertising "small classes" and "personal" or "individualized" attention from instructors.

ESTABLISHING GOALS

Now that the FTC has established strict refund policies, student retention has grown even more important. Many proprietary schools have established recognizable goals within their curricula to improve retention. Goals should be periodic and should require a reasonable degree of effort to attain, but they should be within the grasp of most enrollees. Achievement of goals brings the student satisfaction and self-esteem and often results in reduced attrition and renewed study vigor. Therefore, goals are often a consideration when curricula are developed.

THE BENEFITS OF EDUCATION

How will the students benefit from your training program? After all, schools offer training, not jobs. Many schools have learned that "Become a high-paid accountant" is dangerous because it implies guaranteed placement and earnings. "Train for a better-paying job" is safer, and "Train to be an accountant" is the safest.

New FTC regulations mandate that all earnings claims be substantiated by graduate statistics and that program completion rates be documented as well. Claims regarding job demand, however, can be substantiated by the *Job Outlook Handbook* published by the U.S. Department of Commerce.

To promote your program, you must determine what benefits you can offer students and graduates. Then you must put those benefits into language readily accepted by your prospects. But before that can be done effectively, you first must decide who your prime prospects are.

IDENTIFYING PROSPECTS AND GENERATING LEADS

A prospect is a potential buyer of your service. If you market seminars in office efficiency, for example, your prospects may be office managers in firms of a particular size within selected geographic areas.

A lead, or inquiry, is a prospect who has become qualified by indicating interest in your program. Thus, a lead is actually a qualified prospect, and your task is to turn as many prospects as possible into real, live leads.

How Do We Turn Prospects into Leads?

Advertising, publicity, and sales promotion campaigns have proved effective in generating leads.

Advertising

A variety of media are available to reach the target market.

Magazines. If your program is available on a nationwide basis or if you draw students from throughout the country, you might consider national magazines or newspapers such as *USA Today.* Depending on the nature of the target audience and the specific publications that reach that audience, national magazines can offer an efficient cost per thousand prospects. (When a medium is selected for testing, you know that only a portion of the audience will be prospects for your service.)

If the prospects are clustered regionally, you might consider a regional edition of a national magazine, which will place your ad in a prestigious advertising environment. Or you might consider advertising in major regional publications.

Newspapers. Many schools have greater success with the dominant newspaper in the market than with smaller publications. Smaller newspapers may be less expensive, but they often are less effective as well. If you use a newspaper, the section in which you run the ad will depend on the prospects you intend to reach. Is there a fashion section to reach women, a sports section to reach men, an education or career training section? If the target audience watches television, you may want to run your ad in the entertainment section.

The day of the week in which the ad appears can have a significant effect on the number of leads received. If you decide to run in the sports section to reach men, you may find that Monday is the most effective day on which to run. If you decide to run on the entertainment page (TV listings), the day selected should be based on the day's television viewing audience. A few years ago, for example, in the New York City market, a greater number of teenagers were tuned in on Thursday night than on any other night of the week. Regardless of the specific programs they watched, the Thursday night entertainment page was an effective way to reach that audience.

Make It Easy for Prospects. No matter which print media are used, many schools find that the most important points in an ad are the headline and the telephone number. You want to make it easy for prospects to recognize the benefits in the training you offer—that, of course, should be in the headline—and make it easy for prospects to reach you. Don't make them search through 7-point type for the telephone number.

If you can be reached by telephone only during certain hours (by all means, don't give away valuable evening hours), mention that near the telephone number.

Many prospects prefer mailing a coupon to calling, and you should offer that option. (Coupons should be source-coded so that we can determine which publications are working.) You may want to ask certain qualifying questions in the coupon, but be wary of attempting to qualify too far. The greater the number of qualifying questions, the better qualified your leads will be but the fewer leads you'll receive. Determine your best quantity and quality mix by testing.

Television. Television can be a cost-efficient lead-generating medium. As with most direct-response advertising, it isn't necessary to buy prime time; in fact, prime time is both expensive and inefficient. A prospect watching *Leave It to Beaver* for the third time probably won't mind missing a bit of the program in order to call you, but a prospect watching a hot new show won't want to miss a minute. The same holds true for sports programs; most schools stay away from them.

Marketers of education find that it pays to have a telephone number superimposed over the entire length of a commercial. The number, including area code, often is superimposed when the dub is prepared so that the station is provided with a complete tape. Whenever possible, a voice-over at the end of the spot announces the telephone number.

Covering the Phones. Telephones should be well covered during the time periods when your commercial airs. If you've bought daytime or evening spots, you may want calls to come directly into the school. That way, you can speak with prospects immediately. If your commercial runs late at night or on Sunday, you may want your calls picked up by a local answering service and forwarded to you the following day.

If you are running television commercials over a broad geographic area, or using nationally distributed publications, you may want to offer a WATS number for your prospects' convenience.

Source coding procedures should be established with those who take your calls so that inquiry sources can be tracked. Assign a separate telephone number or use a unique "operator number" for each lead source.

If your leads are received by an answering service, take whatever steps are necessary to ensure that you receive your information the following day. It is extremely important that you follow up on your leads as quickly as possible. The longer your inquirers wait, the lower your conversion rate will be.

Radio. Radio also can be an effective lead-generation medium, but many listeners are unable to call when they hear a spot. Unless your prospects have telephones in their cars or portable phones they can take to the beach, you may find that the volume of calls you receive from a radio campaign is far lower than that from television. However, the cost per thousand (CPM) is often far less in radio than in television, and so the cost per inquiry on radio may be acceptable. Radio often is used in the second quarter, when television viewership is down, or in the fourth quarter, when television rates are so high that leads can't be generated cost-effectively.

Take-One Cards. These reply cards can provide a steady stream of leads, although the volume may be low. Consider coding each location with a separate key or imprint so that you can tell which locations work best for you.

Direct Mail. Direct mail generally is used to convert prospects rather than to generate inquiries because direct mail is inefficient as a mass "shotgun" medium. In its most effective form, direct mail is a one-to-one communication between mailer and recipient.

In certain cases, however, you may find that you can isolate a specific target audience and reach them efficiently by mail. A college preparation course, for example, can be promoted to high school students through the mail. A community college offering a wide range of courses during the summer to prospects in a limited geographic area may test a resident mailing. If you elect to test direct mail for lead generation, you'll want to keep your mailing package as inexpensive as possible, preferably a self-mailer to eliminate the cost of an envelope. You'll want to offer prospects free information about your program and you'll want to emphasize the free information kit rather than your actual training program. As with qualifiers in a coupon, you can charge for the information, but be prepared for a very reduced volume of better-qualified leads. At this point, your effort is directed toward generating leads, not sales.

Seminars are an exception to the use of direct mail. Seminar marketers often use direct mail as a single-step sell. Prospects are identified through business, association membership, and subscriber and other lists, and sales are generated directly from prospects.

Publicity

An ongoing publicity campaign will work two ways.

1. It will generate inquiries.
2. It will help your advertising campaign generate more inquiries.

Many schools contact radio and television stations (especially if the local cable television franchise is in need of material) as well as local newspapers and magazines. A weekly program or column, especially with audience participation, will go far toward establishing a school's reputation for expertise in the field in which it offers training.

One-time articles or news reports, such as graduate success stories, go a long way as well. So do write-ups on any new instructors who join the faculty.

You'll find that it pays to include your school telephone number and address in any articles that appear in print.

Sales Promotion

Career Day Seminars. These are seminars held by high schools to discuss career training opportunities with juniors and seniors.

If you participate in a career day, come prepared. Colorful slides or photographs of your training facility, photos of grads working, testimonials, and a short film or filmstrip are more effective than a simple speech or question and answer format. Remember that you want to attract and hold the attention of those at the seminar. Bring business and reply cards too so that those students who wander from presentation to presentation can contact you later. You may want to prepare complete kits for distribution, including your school or course brochure, a promotional letter, a written testimonial, and a reply card. Don't forget to include your telephone number.

At a career day seminar, you'll have to sell the concept of a career in the field for which you train as well as your training program itself. Prepare some career path "sizzle."

Group Presentations. Certain educational programs lend themselves to sales presentations to homogeneous groups: church, civic, or social groups, for example. When you make a presentation, there is often one leader of the group, and this is the person to whom you want to devote much of your attention.

Remember to come prepared in much the same way you would prepare for a career day. A film, brochures, and photographs are more interesting than a solo speaker. If you can, bring a recent or particularly successful graduate along with you to provide living testimonial to both the excitement of the career for which you train and the benefits of your training program in particular.

When you prepare for group presentations, you may want to develop a separate pricing schedule or benefit of some other kind for group enrollment. You'll probably find that peer group pressure works in many instances, since friends may want to enroll for classes together.

In addition to reply cards and business cards with which to generate future leads, bring some enrollment contracts. Chances are, an effective presentation to a group will generate some immediate enrollments if your down payment for tuition is reasonable.

Tie-Ins. Does your training program lend itself to tie-ins which can be promoted effectively? Samples of student handicrafts can be displayed in a shopping mall, for example. Photography exhibits can be shown in a local gallery. Modeling students can hold a fashion show tied in with a local clothing store.

You'll want to advertise your promotion on a contributory basis with the retail store or mall.

ANALYZING A LEAD-GENERATION PROGRAM

What is your cost per inquiry (CPI), and how is it affected by size of ad, frequency, and copy platform? How efficiently is each medium producing leads? More important, as you develop a track record, you'll want to analyze conversion rates as well as lead generation for every lead source you use.

You may find, for example, that certain publications generate a great volume of leads but that those leads don't convert well. Other publications may produce a smaller volume of leads which convert readily.

For every advertising medium you test, you'll want to keep track of both your cost per lead and the cost per enrollment.

Determining Cost per Lead

The efficiency of each medium can be judged initially by its CPI.

The CPI formula is

$$\text{Cost per inquiry} = \text{advertising cost} \div \text{number of leads}$$

When you analyze CPI, exclude the costs of artwork or commercial preparation. These are one-time costs, and their inclusion will skew your analysis of the effectiveness of the medium on an ongoing basis.

The speed with which you can assign a "final" CPI depends on the type of medium analyzed. You may have to give a monthly publication several weeks before you can determine its CPI for that month. Television spots, however, can be analyzed quickly and should be assigned CPIs on a daily or weekly basis and, whenever possible, on a program-by-program basis. Compare the times your commercials run with the times your calls are logged.

Unlike monthly magazines, for which one often must commit ads many weeks in advance, television and radio offer the ability to get on and off the air quickly. Thus, if one station or program is not generating leads at an efficient CPI, it makes sense to withdraw from advertising on that station or in that time slot as quickly as possible.

In Table 55-1, our comparison revealed that the CPI on television station B was too high, and so we stopped advertising on that station after the third week in the month.

Similar analyses may be drawn by testing offers. You may elect to test a variety of offers such as the "free mini-lesson" that was used successfully by Evelyn Woods for so many years, or you may decide to offer a free premium. You also may elect to run some price tests.

There are some caveats regarding price testing.

1. Be wary of the effect on your customers: your students. A reduction in tuition offered to some may offend others.
2. Check with counsel. In certain cases, federal regulations may apply (these generally apply to offering the same course at different prices but not to testing).

Depending on the training program you offer, lead-generation and conversion rates may be affected greatly by the month or season in which you advertise. Programs geared toward graduating high school seniors, for example, generally receive the greatest volume of inquiries in late spring and late summer, as postgraduation plans are made; conversion rates are highest for those programs in late summer and early January. In fact, a large percentage of the American populace has become accustomed to beginning study programs in the autumn months.

Your CPI will give you a good handle on which media are generating inquiries most efficiently. In certain instances—such as those where you must provide a sales force with a continuous volume of leads—you may strive for the greatest quantity of inquiries possible. You may find, however, that fulfillment of such a large volume of leads can be prohibitively expensive if conversion rates don't hold up.

Thus, you may decide to limit the volume of leads generated. Naturally, you want to eliminate those which are the least productive. In order to do that, you need to know your cost per enrollment (CPE) or, better yet, your cost per start (CPS) for each lead source you use.

Determining Cost per Enrollment and Cost per Start

The cost of enrolling a student includes

1. Advertising and promotion
2. Fulfillment
3. Sales commissions

An enrollment is recorded when a lead signs an enrollment agreement (contract). A start refers to a lead who actually begins your program. Your CPS probably will be slightly higher than your CPE because a certain percentage of enrollees will withdraw before training begins.

In order to assess your CPS accurately (and, as we'll discuss later, your average start value), you need to maintain lead source data for an extended period of time.

Every lead received should be recorded on receipt, either manually on a "lead slip" (to be followed by computer data entry) or electronically via CRT terminals. In addition to the lead's name, address, and telephone number, you want to record source and status, date of receipt, and date of fulfillment. If you use a sales force for conversion, you want to record the name or identification number of the

TABLE 55-1 Front-End (CPI) Analyses

	Magazine A	Magazine B	Television A	Television B	Newspaper A
Media cost	$1000	$500	$1000/wk	$2000/wk	$350
Week 1 leads	30	6	315	375	35
Weekly CPI			$3.17	$5.33	$10
Week 2 leads	98	9	275	305	6
Weekly CPI			$3.64	$6.56	
Week 3 leads	52	3	330	220	
Weekly CPI			$3.03	$9.09	
Week 4 leads	20	2	310		
Weekly CPI			$3.23		
Monthly cost	$1000	$500	$4000	$6000	$350
Leads per month	200	20	1230	900	41
Monthly CPI	$5	$25	$3.25	$6.66	$8.54

salesperson to whom the lead is assigned. You will want to record the program of interest if you offer a variety of training programs.

By maintaining this information, you should be able to track not only the number of inquiries generated by any particular source but the number of enrollments and actual starts as well. Furthermore, you'll be able to track your retention rate by medium, by geographic location, and by any other variable for which you've maintained the necessary data.

Back-end (CPE and CPS) analyses will provide information more valuable than the original CPI data. If we were to extend the example used to illustrate CPI (Table 55-1), we would come up with Table 55-2.

TABLE 55-2 Back-End (CPE and CPS) Analyses*

	Magazine A	Magazine B	Television A	Television B	Newspaper A
Media cost	$1000	$500	$1000/wk	$2000/wk	$350
Week 1 leads	30	6	315	375	35
Weekly CPI			$3.17	$5.33	$10
Week 2 leads	98	9	275	305	6
Weekly CPI			$3.64	$6.56	
Week 3 leads	52	3	330	220	
Weekly CPI			$3.03	$9.09	
Week 4 leads	20	2	310		
Weekly CPI			$3.23		
Monthly cost	$1000	$500	$4000	$6000	$350
Leads per month	200	20	1230	900	41
Monthly CPI	$5	$25	$3.25	$6.66	$8.54
Enrollments	20	9	85	52	17
Starts	19	9	78	50	16
Fulfillment cost	$200	$20	$1230	$900	$41
Sales commission	$950	$450	$3900	$2500	$800
Total cost	$2150	$970	$9130	$9400	$1191
CPE	$107.50	$107.78	$104.41	$180.77	$70.06
CPS	$113.16	$107.78	$117.05	$188	$74.44

* For the purpose of this example, assume that (1) cost of fulfillment is $1, (2) tuition price is $1000, (3) sales commission is 5 percent of full tuition.

When we compare our CPI data with our CPE and CPS analysis, it's obvious that we would have been misled had we relied solely on our initial CPI as the basis for our advertising efficiency decisions. Our newspaper test, for example, resulted in our second highest CPI but our lowest CPS. A comparison of magazines A and B is also interesting.

There is yet another variable to be considered in the analysis of source efficiency. If you have decided to limit the number of leads you generate in order to control fulfillment costs, you obviously have elected to generate only those who convert most efficiently. You may find, however, that student attrition varies by lead source. While you want those leads who convert at the highest rate, you also want those conversions who will remain in the program for the longest period of time and, in fact, those who are most receptive to postgraduation offers.

If we were to extend our CPE and CPS example in order to analyze profitability by source, we would develop the matrix in Figure 55-3.

It becomes readily apparent, then, that television station A generates our greatest volume but that newspaper A is our best advertising investment on a dollar-for-dollar basis.

Some additional data you may want to track in order to control lead flow and fulfillment costs are as follows:

TABLE 55-3 Long-Term Lead Value Analysis

	Magazine A	Magazine B	Television A	Television B	Newspaper A
Media cost	$1000	$500	$1000/wk	$2000/wk	$350
Week 1 leads	30	6	315	375	35
Weekly CPI			$3.17	$5.33	$10
Week 2 leads	98	9	275	305	6
Weekly CPI			$3.64	$6.56	
Week 3 leads	52	3	330	220	
Weekly CPI			$3.03	$9.09	
Week 4 leads	20	2	310		
Weekly CPI			$3.23		
Monthly cost	$1000	$500	$4000	$6000	$350
Leads per month	200	20	1,230	900	41
Monthly CPI	$5	$25	$3.25	$6.66	$8.54
Enrollments	20	9	85	52	17
Starts	19	9	78	50	16
Fulfillment cost	$200	$20	$1230	$900	$41
Sales commission	$950	$450	$3900	$2500	$800
Total cost	$2150	$970	$9130	$9400	$1191
CPE	$107.50	$107.78	$107.41	$180.77	$70.06
CPS	$113.16	$107.78	$117.05	$188.00	$74.44
Average completion	52%	38%	45%	36%	78%
Average payment	$620	$480	$550	$460	$880
CPS: Pmnt %	18.3%	22.5%	21.3%	40.9%	8.5%
Total cost	$2150	$970	$9130	$9400	$1191
Total recovered	$11,780	$4320	$42,900	$23,000	$14,080

* For example purposes, assume that (1) payout is $100 down and $50 a week for 18 weeks, (2) refund policy is identical to payout, (3) there are no finance charges to students.

1. Quality of telephone versus coupon leads
2. Effect of variations in ad size on quantity and quality of leads
3. Effect of token charge for information
4. Effect of replacing toll-free telephone number with toll call number

MAINTAINING A LEAD FILE

Many schools maintain lead data on the computer. Some use data entry early in the marketing process so that the system can be used for lead fulfillment and follow-up. Others enter data later in the process for final follow-up and eventual establishment of list rental as a profit center.

If your lead volume is substantial, you'll find that computerization of your leads facilitates the mailing of a series of conversion packages.

It is important to update lead status frequently. You don't want to mail conversion materials to leads who have enrolled already. You'll want to offer separate "inquirer" and "buyer" mailing lists (but many schools do not offer their "buyer" lists). Furthermore, you'll want to set up separate marketing programs geared toward those who have not yet enrolled, those who are current students, those who have failed to complete the program, and those who have graduated. If you offer a variety of training programs, you may want to develop several vertical fulfillment series.

FULFILLING INQUIRIES

Correspondence and resident schools use different fulfillment methodologies. Schools which use direct mail to convert fulfill differently from those which employ sales people. There are, however, two distinct similarities.

1. Rapid fulfillment is extremely important. Some educational programs spark thoughtful consideration prior to requesting more information; many generate "impulse" inquiries. Either way, when a lead inquires about a program, he or she is eager to learn more. With every passing day, that interest may wane. Thus, you want to fulfill as quickly as you can.
2. Personalization (individualized material) is important. Utilizing the lead's name and other personal data in the cover letter is very effective. You also may want to provide the lead with the name of someone in your school whom she or he can contact. By making fulfillment material a personal communication, you demonstrate that you care about the lead as an individual.

CONVERTING LEADS INTO ENROLLMENTS AND STARTS

Years ago, many schools used outside sales people, who would visit leads in their homes armed with an array of promotional materials and enrollment contracts. Recently, however, the FTC issued a series of rulings regarding the promises and claims that schools can make. Because of difficulties in controlling the actions and statements of outside sales people, many schools have turned instead to inside sales teams and conversion by mail.

Converting with a Sales Force

Most schools that use sales people prefer that the initial salesperson contact with a lead be made by telephone rather than by mail. The purpose of the sales phone call is to schedule an appointment for the lead to visit the school and discuss the program in person with a school representative as quickly as possible. Any material offered in the advertising, such as free literature, is given to the lead at the time of the personal interview.

The reasoning behind telephone fulfillment is that once the lead visits the school, he or she is more likely to convert. This method also precludes a cooling of the lead, because the time between receipt of inquiry and a personal visit has been minimized.

Many schools, however, prefer a more traditional approach: mailing a fulfillment package and following up with a telephone sales call. The reasoning here is that the lead is "softened" by receipt of fulfillment materials, which work to pave the way for the salesperson's call.

Most schools that convert with sales forces incorporate commission structures into their compensation packages. Further steps such as sales contests, bonuses based on student completion rates, etc., are taken to provide additional motivation.

When an inquirer visits your premises, make good use of the time. You may want to provide literature on career opportunities or a continuous-loop sales promotion film in your reception area. These can work to promote your program and "soften" the lead before a sales presentation is made.

When you assign leads to your sales people, take care to mix lead sources. Don't assign all leads from one source to a particular salesperson; the effectiveness of that person will skew your CPS analysis.

You probably will want to implement some form of control to ensure that no promises or claims are made which government regulations forbid: claims of high earnings by graduates, for example, or of guaranteed entry into a career. It was exactly this problem that motivated many correspondence schools to begin.

Converting Inquiries by Mail

Direct mail conversion of leads is used by some of the most traditional as well as some of the least traditional educational institutions.

Correspondence schools often convert through the mail. This can be considered a "natural," of course, because of the direct mail nature of correspondence programs. But some of the most effective mail conversion programs have been created by traditional colleges. In these instances, the purpose of direct mail programs has been to generate formal applications for admission.

The University of Pittsburgh, for example, was awarded the Direct Marketing Association's prestigious Gold Echo award in 1980 for its conversion by mail series. Their campaign is an excellent example of a well-planned program: carefully timed, highly personalized, and vertically targeted.

As a large urban educational center, the University of Pittsburgh (UP) offers a wide variety of majors. On receipt of a lead, the admissions office fulfills immediately with a personal letter, a colorful brochure, and an application for admission. Then, 1 week later, a highly targeted letter signed by the chairperson of the department in which the lead has indicated interest is mailed. That second letter works hard to

1. "Sell" the lead on the specific course of study in which he or she has indicated interest
2. "Sell" the lead on the quality of education offered by the school

There are more than a dozen separate "department letters," one for each of Pittsburgh's majors. As an example, Figure 55-1 shows excerpts from the letter generated by the mathematics department. The letter is personalized with the lead's name and is targeted to the lead's program of interest. It points out that mathematics is not all theory but has many practical applications. The lead is involved through the demonstration of how mathematics is used to design a bridge and through simple problems found in later paragraphs. Finally, the letter gives the lead the name of someone in authority at UP's math department whom the lead can contact for additional information. Note the letter's congratulatory tone, reinforcing the lead's decision to study mathematics.

Once the UP lead completes the application and applies for admission, a separate conversion by mail series is implemented. This is designed to encourage enrollment (matriculation).

Immediately upon acceptance, the UP lead is mailed a brief "good news bulletin" which announces the acceptance. Four days later, a formal acceptance letter is mailed. Finally, an informal brochure is mailed to the lead's family, assuring them that their child's decision to apply for admission to Pittsburgh was a wise one and that the student ought to enroll now that acceptance has been granted.

Correspondence schools use conversion materials that work to promote enrollment with a harder sell because correspondence schools have a credibility problem not suffered by established universities. Correspondence school letters, like the UP series, usually address the lead by name, congratulate the lead on the wise choice of program, explain the benefits of studying that specific subject, and promote the benefits of studying through correspondence in general and with the individual school in particular. Brochures and sales literature generally are geared toward the lead's program of interest, and an enrollment contract rather than an application usually is enclosed.

If a correspondence school lead doesn't convert after the first mailing, there is generally a series of follow-up attempts. In fact, a lead may receive as many as six or more separate conversion mailings.

In developing a complete conversion series, many schools consider the following elements.

Timing. A lead may want to weigh the advantages of a program carefully before enrolling. Each package should have the time to do its job.

Cost versus Return. Chances are, each package in a series will convert fewer leads than the preceding package. The progressive decline in response generally is readily discernible. Thus, each package should be less expensive than the last.

University of Pittsburgh

November 1, 198

Mr. Robert E. Wenzel
329 Roup Avenue
Pittsburgh, PA 15232

Dear Mr. Wenzel:

You've expressed an interest in Mathematics. We like it, too. About fifty of us--the faculty of Pitt's Mathematics and Statistics Department--spend our time learning more of our subject and teaching it to interested students such as yourself. Why?

Because Mathematics
is constructive

Engineers typically model planned structures with mathematics. The methods of joints, for instance, uses Trigonometry and Vectors to analyze forces in railroad bridges.

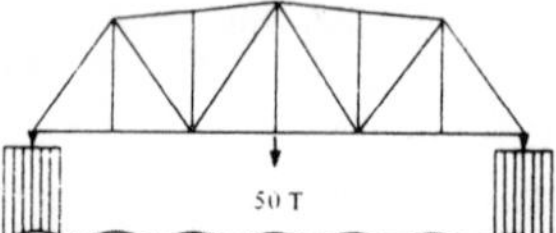

Each steel spar in this bridge is either stretched or compressed. Can you tell which are being compressed?

Mathematics is useful
In fact, indispensable.

The use of statistics, for example, is wide-spread and growing. Without it, society can't adequately describe its own workings or those of nature.

Through statistical methods, the distributions of numbers can be seen in meaningful profiles. It's the key to important insights and necessary data for science, business, government, the social sciences, education, even politics.

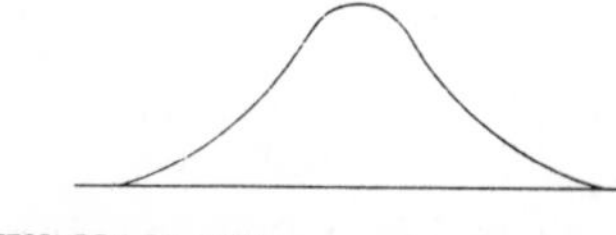

This distribution is most useful to statisticians--to chart anything from peo-ple's heights to their test scores or weights of leaves on a tree. Do you know what this curve is called?

PITTSBURGH, PA 15260

Figure 55-1 Excerpts from the letter generated by the mathematics department of the University of Pittsburgh. (*Courtesy of Joseph Merante, University of Pittsburgh Office of Admissions.*)

Many schools mail initial packages first class and later packages at bulk rate. Enrollment contracts are coded so that response to each mailing in the sequence can be analyzed. Codes may appear, for example, as EL1280TV12-A (for an Electronics package sent to a lead received December 1980 which was generated by television station 12), followed by EL1280TV12-B, EL1280TV12-C, etc.

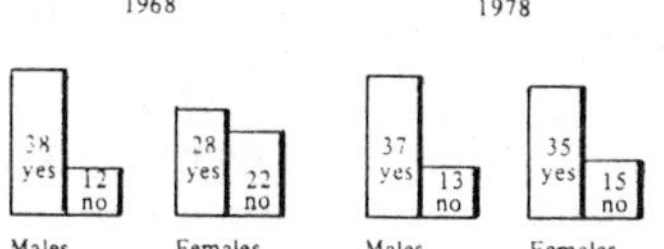

Polls of 100 seniors were taken in 1968 and again in 1978. They were asked if they planned to go to college. Do you think these sex-related changes are significant? Or explained by random chance?

<u>Mathematics is logical and beautiful</u>.

Mathematics is closely related to music. Scott Buchanan wrote a book relating it to poetry. Mathematicians use the word "elegant" to describe an equation whose power and simplicity ring true. Not everyone can tune in on "the music of the spheres," but for those who can relate to mathematical symmetries, great satisfactions await. (Even thrills. Archimedes got so excited with his "eureka moment" he leapt from his bathtub and had to be restrained from running naked into the streets.)

This is proof of what famous theorem? (No, not Archimedes' Principle)

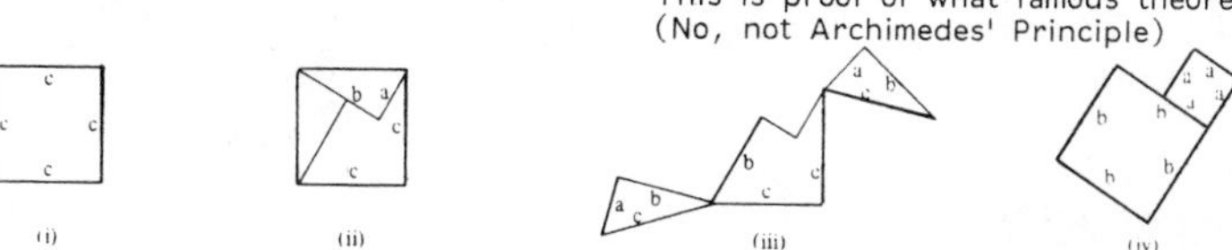

And since mathematics has these qualities, the people who become expert in mathematics also tend to be constructive, useful, (even indispensable), and logical (we don't know about beautiful). This is why the study of mathematics can lead to so many interesting careers.

Pitt has programs in Mathematics, Applied Mathematics, and Statistics. Right now, you probably have insufficient data to calculate your most promising path. But we're here to help. We think that one of the most important things we can do is talk to tomorrow's mathematicians at a time when they need information or advice in making important education and career decisions. So call me at (412) 624-5856, or my secretary at (412) 624-5808. She'll either find me or flag down someone else who can help.

Sincerely,

Henry Cohen
Associate Professor
Department of Mathematics and Statistics

HC/rew

Vertical Marketing. Many schools use a "rifle" rather than a "shotgun" approach. Leads who have indicated interest in accounting, for example, are sent materials on the various accounting-related programs rather than brochures describing every program offered.

Horizontal Marketing. If a lead has been mailed several conversion packages without enrolling, many schools send a broad, all-encompassing conversion package. The lead may have changed his or her mind about the program of interest and may be interested in a different course of study.

Involvement. Involvement adds excitement to and confidence in the enrollment decision. Some simple examples of study material or some descriptions of the lead's potential future are frequently used involvement techniques.

Clearly Indicated Action. What is the lead's next step? What will happen after the lead takes that step? You never want to leave the lead wondering; you must guide the lead through the enrollment process. If you'd like the lead to call, say so. If you'd like the contract signed and mailed with a check, say so. On receipt of the materials, will you send the lead a receipt? Say so.

Family Involvement. Many schools send a separate conversion package to the family, addressing their concerns and assuring them of the quality of the program.

Personalization. Individual attention is a major concern to potential students. A personalized conversion letter containing the name of a contact at the school will go far to assuage that concern.

CAREER PLACEMENT

Schools that offer students and graduates the advantages of a job placement service often promote that service to leads and students. Mention often is found in sales literature, brochures, and catalogs.

Schools that work with a sales force sometimes locate their job placement facilities near the reception area so that leads can see the facilities while awaiting interviews.

Care should be taken to avoid implying guaranteed placement or guaranteed employment opportunities. Any promotion of this service should be clear. What is offered is placement assistance, not guaranteed jobs. Schools offer training, not careers.

Placement statistics which are published should be documentable to the satisfaction of various state and federal agencies.

TELEPHONE MARKETING

We've already discussed the way many schools use the telephone for initial fulfillment: to arrange an appointment for a lead to visit the school. The phone also is used to promote conversion by mail.

When conversion materials are complex or the enrollment process is difficult to understand, a toll-free number sometimes is provided for assistance. In fact, the same toll-free number can be offered to any lead who has questions about your program. Leads who don't convert by mail can be contacted by phone so that specific objections can be discussed and countered.

RETAINING STUDENTS

Retention is obviously important to profitability; that's why the marketing of education is an ongoing process. We generate a lead, we convert that lead, and we act to retain that conversion in several ways.

Newsletters

Regularly printed and distributed newsletters can work to generate goodwill and encouragement. Graduate success stories, anecdotes about current and former students and faculty, and news of program expansion all work to reinforce the buying decision.

Not all school newsletters have elaborate formats; many are only two or four pages long. However, photographs should be used liberally because they add credibility and encourage readership. Articles for newsletters often are solicited from students and graduates.

Newsletters should be available to leads as well as students, because they serve as an excellent selling tool.

Mailings

A word of encouragement in the form of a personal note from a member of the faculty or administration goes a long way. Many schools send letters to the family as well as to the student. Form letters, though, won't do the job; these notes should be individualized to be effective.

Telephone

The telephone is a remarkably effective tool for improving retention. An informal call to chat about the curriculum, the instructors, or the student's progress will accomplish two important functions. First, it provides encouragement to the student. Second, it provides the school with feedback.

School directors gain a better grasp of the weak points in their programs when retention is considered important. Directors can learn which subjects are most difficult and how they can be clarified. Directors also learn which instructors are popular and which alienate their students.

Astute marketers of education recognize the specific points in their programs when retention efforts pay the best dividends. Don't let your students become discouraged.

MARKETING TO STUDENTS

Some educational programs require that students buy certain textbooks, tools, or equipment. Many schools have found sales of these materials to be quite profitable. Electronics courses may require certain kits and meters. Makeup courses may require cosmetics. Painting courses may call for paints, brushes, canvas, easels, and frames.

Students generally cannot be required to purchase these materials from the school. But it can be made convenient for them to do so. Even programs that don't require additional materials may offer items that students will find handy.

Crafts schools, for example, may offer yarn, clay, and associated tools. An attractive display case in the reception area can pay for itself quickly.

MARKETING TO GRADUATES

Schools that provide students with a solid education have satisfied customers and thus generate prime prospects for additional sales. Are advanced courses offered? Related courses? "Exit interviews" by sales representatives often are held with graduating students. Interviews may lead from a rapid summary of the students' accomplishments to a conversation about advanced and related curriculum offerings.

Many schools test new programs with direct mailings to graduates because grads are often some of the best leads available. (Discounts to graduates sometimes are offered.) Recent graduates of a photography course may be interested in learning advanced darkroom techniques. Upholstery students may be intrigued by a course in wood furniture refinishing. Pet grooming students may want to learn more about animal behavior.

MARKETING WITH STUDENTS

Another excellent and free source of leads is available on your premises every day: your students.

Literature mailed to students or even to leads should have referral cards included. If your students are satisfied with your program and if your leads are intrigued, they probably will recommend it to their friends and colleagues.

While referral leads may be small in quantity, they are often of excellent quality.

MARKETING WITH GRADUATES

Graduates are living proof of the quality of an educational program, and many schools keep track of them.

Any employment statistics which are used to promote a training program must be documented, and so graduate employment records often are maintained carefully.

Many schools solicit testimonials from graduates to use in promotional literature. Generally, it is best to obtain testimonials as soon after graduation as possible.

EDUCATION TODAY AND TOMORROW

As long as people want to change careers, as long as people want to improve their skills in current career paths, as long as people seek new hobbies and pastimes, there will be a promising future for the field of education.

Traditional schools and colleges may have to reduce or eliminate programs which decline in popularity as the marketplace changes, but at the same time, astute marketers of education will find that new technologies and changing social patterns offer new opportunities for the development of innovative programs. Furthermore, traditional schools may find a resurgence of interest in programs which have declined in popularity in recent years.

Seminars and minicourses continue to grow as the public seeks methods of absorbing bursts of information as quickly as possible. New York's Network for Learning, according to *The Wall Street Journal* (June 3, 1982), attracted a record 52,000 students in 1981; in fact, the *Journal* reported that approximately 500,000 consumers enrolled in minicourses in 1981, the majority in avocational programs.

An even greater number of students seek vocational training. According to a report in *Money* magazine (May 1982), 2.5 million students enrolled in vocational training courses in 1981.

Cable television offers an innovative future in the field of education. Soon cable viewers will have a wide variety of interactive educational programs available in their homes through their television screens. Formal testing can be accomplished through two-way cable capabilities or in the same way that testing is now accomplished by correspondence schools: through the mail. Through cable, a viewer can gain the benefit of a live instructor's input, while the mail can provide textbooks and workbooks as well as examination procedures. Lessons can be conducted daily or weekly; the format is infinitely variable.

Imagine the possibilities. Travel students can visit cities throughout the world without leaving their homes. Electronics students can be walked through complex projects. Accounting students can audit real books.

Tuition can be paid on a one-time or monthly basis, included in the cable company's billing statements. Or fees can be generated on a pay per view basis for seminars and minicourses. According to *The Wall Street Journal*, New York's Network for Learning already has contracted with Warner Amex Cable Communications Inc. to produce several educational courses for cable television.

Video disks and tapes offer similar opportunities. These formats are ideal for learn at home minicourses; fees can be earned through royalties on tape and disk rentals and sales.

Correspondence schools would do well to adapt to the changing technology of learn at home capabilities. Resident schools, including some traditional institutions, should consider the opportunities afforded by these new media and respond accordingly with new learn at home programs.

Changing technologies in a wide variety of fields provide not only innovative methods of education but exciting new areas in which to educate. Courses that are popular today may become uneconomical in the future, to be replaced by subjects which may not even be on the drawing board today.

The techniques and procedures described in this chapter have been used effectively to promote many different training programs. But these are not the only effective means of marketing education. What works for one school may not work for another, and what has failed for some may succeed for you. The key to marketing education is tracking the profitability of your promotional efforts and then using what you learn to market your program more efficiently.

To become and remain successful in the future, schools must be able to adapt to the changing needs of society. New curricula and promotional techniques will yield stimulating fruit for those adept marketers who are bold enough to shake the tree of knowledge.

chapter 56

SELLING TO SCHOOLS AND COLLEGES

Bob Stimolo

President
School Market Research Institute
Haddam, Conn.

Selling to schools is a very specialized form of business-to-business marketing. In recent years, a decline in enrollment has struck many schools, forcing consolidation of buildings and reduced numbers of educators and generally bringing about difficult times for school marketers.

While this trend is forecasted to change in the late 1980s, legislative changes and increasing pressure on public school funding promise to pose major challenges to school marketers. Recently, microcomputers have overtaken the public school systems, particularly in the area of computer literacy. This has been a tremendous growth market and is forecasted to continue to grow over at least the next 5 years. Thus, while the marketplace faces a number of significant difficulties, there exist major opportunities for marketers at the same time.

TIMING: THE SCHOOL SPENDING CLOCK

One of the most significant aspects of the school market is that it is a bureaucracy. There are certain behavior characteristics that tend to repeat themselves year after year. The most important of these is the way most schools commit funds for purchases. There are two major types of purchase decisions: for classroom materials (usually decided by educators) and for classroom supplies (usually decided by business managers or purchasing agents.)

CLASSROOM MATERIALS

We will define classroom materials as educational aids: ditto masters, books, and items that tend to be purchased with school funds at the initiation of the teacher or school department head. Most classroom materials generally are considered indigenous to the manufacturer or publisher. To be more specific, pencils are pencils, but two different skills building ditto master sets are not considered comparable, as two different pencils might be. Business managers do not attempt to put them on bid lists and find competitive manufacturing because in 95 percent of the cases, no two sets of skills building masters are identical. Consequently, the teacher, department head, or principal must decide the purchase on his or her own, and the business manager basically fills the role of paperwork processor.

Most school budgets roll over in July. There are two waves of school buying activity. The first takes place in the spring preceding the budget rollover. This is when the lion's share of dollars is committed: at least 60 percent for some types of items and up to 80 percent for others.

Decisions to purchase classroom materials usually involve two or more educators, the end user teacher, a district level coordinator or department head, and a principal or business manager. The number of individuals involved varies by nature of product, dollar size of purchase, source of funding, level of school (elementary or secondary), and size of school.

Spring decisions to buy begin as early as March and go through the end of the spring session. Purchase requisitions go through various approval processes, and then many of them stay at the school secretary or business manager's office to wait until the budgets are approved. Since budget approval often occurs very close to the actual rollover of the fiscal year, most school marketers receive 50 or 60 percent of the full year's business in July and August. This is when budget funds are released and the business departments finally release purchase orders to vendors.

A second wave of buying takes place in the fall. This activity tends to be a

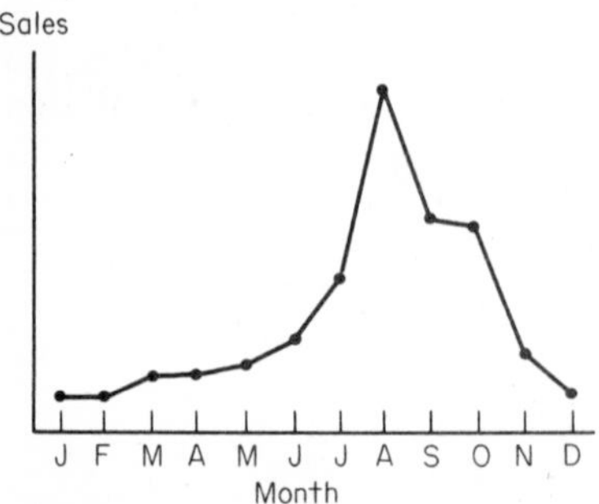

Figure 56-1 A typical order intake pattern for a school marketer of classroom materials. *(Direct Response Marketing To Schools Newsletter, Vol. II, Issue I, June 30, 1982.)*

shoring up of needs not covered through the spring activity. This ordering is not delayed by the budget process, since budgets have been approved already.

A typical intake pattern of orders for a school marketer of classroom materials is shown in Figure 56-1.

MAIL DATES FOR CLASSROOM MATERIALS

As a result of the buying habits of schools, the best mail dates for most classroom materials are from mid-February through mid-March for spring business (realized as orders by the mailer in July and August) and middle to late August for fall business (realized as orders in September and October). Exceptions to this include materials that usually require previews (films and filmstrips) and items marketed to and through teachers but not funded by school institutions (student book clubs, fund raisers, etc.).

Products requiring preview are mailed successfully as early as January 1, and products that are teacher-funded as opposed to school budget-funded are mailed successfully as late as May. Figure 56-2 shows a schedule of mailing windows for the spring season.

SCHOOL SUPPLIES

There are two major types of institutional buying in the school market: bid and nonbid buying. Bid buying refers to materials purchased on the basis of bids collected from several sources and awarded on the basis of price or the meeting of certain specifications.

For most items, the deciding factor is price, and for this reason, bid business tends to be a very low margin business. Traditional direct mail offers tend to be unsuccessful unless the pricing is competitive.

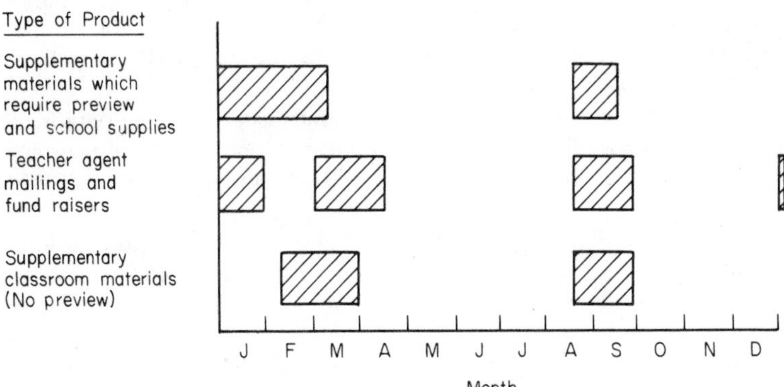

Figure 56-2 Mailing windows in the school market. *(Direct Response Marketing To Schools Newsletter, Vol. II, Issue I, June 30, 1982.)*

The buyer in the school supply bid business is most often a purchasing agent, often at a district level. Much of the bid spending is for paper, crayons, pencils, and other such supplies.

Direct marketing techniques have had limited success in this field to date. Within the past few years, some companies have been successful with a combined direct mail and outbound telephone effort, but the competitive nature of this market causes it to yield a low return for most.

Although much school supply buying is bid business, there is still a considerable amount of nonbid or off-bid purchasing by schools for classroom supplies. However, the buyer changes. Instead of the purchasing manager deciding the purchase, the purchase usually is initiated by a school building business manager, principal, teacher, or department head.

This market is made up of both non-bid-buying schools (schools in small districts or private schools) and bid-buying schools that seek an item not carried on their districts' bid lists or not in inventory. For this market, price is less important than service and availability.

MAIL DATES FOR CLASSROOM SUPPLIES

Mail dates for classroom supplies differ from those for classroom materials, with the addition of early January as a preferred mail date. February and March dates tend to be good for off-bid or nonbid purchases but are not the best dates for the bid market. August mail dates work for both markets.

LISTS: FINDING THE BUYER

The school marketer has one major advantage over other marketers when it comes to lists. Some fairly complicated data bases are available which can help school marketers leverage their direct mail success.

There are three major compilers of school lists: Market Data Retrieval in Westport, Connecticut, Quality Education Data in Denver, Colorado, and Educational Mailings Clearing House in Sweet Springs, Missouri. Both MDR and QED offer data base selections.

Credit should be given to MDR for being the first to develop this data base concept. The data base first orders all public schools within districts. It identifies the school type (public, private, elementary, junior high, senior high, K to 12, and 7 to 8).

It also identifies expenditure per pupil, enrollment size, and a poverty level rating. In addition MDR's data base is unique in that it can select the names of various educators, from district level administrators to principals and grade teachers.

This technology gives school marketers the advantage of being extremely selective in making direct marketing promotions. Few other business marketers can be as selective. For example, a school marketer can choose to mail to surburban and rural schools that have high per pupil expenditure levels and medium to large enrollments and then can select individuals by name within those institutions. This represents a distinct improvement over what most other business market mailers can select.

MAILING TO TITLES VERSUS NAMES

Mailing to "Principal," "Librarian," or "Teacher of Grade 2" is a fairly common practice in the school market. This is commonly referred to as title addressing. There is no question that the mail reaches the intended recipient in the majority of instances. Names, on the other hand, tend to be more responsive because they are personalized.

In the school market, there are certain times of years when titles can be better than names and vice versa. For example, the school market can be fairly volatile in its turnover of individuals. This is especially true in an era when declining enrollment is causing school closings and staff layoffs.

Most school rosters, and consequently the lists that are compiled from them, are not finalized until August. Since August is a major mailing season, there is insufficient lead time to update the lists in time for August mailings. Consequently, in the fall, depending on teacher turnover, it can be better to mail to titles. In the spring, the lists are current. Names generally will outpull titles.

OFFERS FOR THE MARKET

School marketers are noted for their conservatism as a group. Many are former educators who recognized a need and tried to fill it. Consequently, offers in the school market tend to be somewhat less sensational than those in the consumer market.

The basic distinction that must be made when creating offers in the school market is that you never can put the buyer into a potentially questionable position with your offer. If you offer a cruise holiday to a purchasing agent for a $1000 purchase of art materials, you may discourage a great deal of response. This is particularly true in the public school system. On the other hand, special sales and giveaways that have classroom applications can be extremely successful.

As in all direct marketing, the use of an offer can have a powerful effect on results. An offer is a proposition or deal. It includes payment terms (cash or credit), premiums and freebees, an expiration date, and a guarantee or warranty.

The school market responds to these offer elements like any other market, but there are unique considerations when constructing an offer for the school market.

PAYMENT TERMS: CASH OR CREDIT

The school market is generally a very good credit risk. This is true of both institutional and individual purchases. In the event it is to be paid for by the individual, the name and telephone number of the school that the buyer is from should be required.

The most common form of spending is conducted through the school purchase order system. Some school marketing companies realize as much as 80 percent of their gross revenues through purchase order spending. There is also a significant amount of purchasing by teachers out of their personal funds. Some trade journals have put this at $150 per teacher per year.

Bad debt for most school marketers (institutional market) seldom exceeds 2 or 3 percent. However, timing of collectibles can be a different matter. Some school marketing companies average 90 to 120 days for collectibles. Naturally, this varies from district to district. This collectible time can be improved in many instances through the use of proper billing and dunning procedures.

All this adds up to a market where more often than not, the marketer does better to extend credit. As in the consumer market, the extension of credit will double or triple response. While it may add to the average age of receivables, in most instances it will result in greater volumes of paid business.

PREMIUMS AND FREEBEES

Both the freebee (buy one, get one free) and the premium offer (free calculator, book, etc.) have been used with success by a wide range of school marketing companies. When a public institution is involved, it's important to select premiums that will not call into question the buyer's integrity. As an extreme example, it would be a questionable strategy to offer a vacation trip for two in return for a large purchase with school funds. This would place the buyer in a questionable light relative to his or her public duty to represent the best interests of the school's community.

On the other hand, offering a digital pen watch in return for a 30-day trial of a new writing program would not be received in so threatening a light. Less threatening still would be the offer of a classroom or school premium such as classroom library of books or a piece of gym equipment.

As a result of this "public duty" aspect of school purchases, the most successful premiums have tended to have a strong personal appeal and also a classroom or school application. A good example is a calculator. This is a personal item, but it can be viewed as necessary to assist an educator in his or her professional duties. The same is true of a reference book, say, a dictionary. It has a definite classroom application, yet it is also a personally appealing item.

Premium Breakage

One of the major considerations in the development of a premium offer is how you will execute the offer. Many purchases in the school market are made through a purchase order. Purchasing agents tend not to pass on the original order device. In many cases, it is used as an easy means to obtain a purchase requisition from the school secretary.

When the original order device is used by educators, it remains in the possession of the school. The marketer receives only a purchase order. You may use a premium policy that automatically ships a premium with every order, choose to require a coupon, or require that a statement appear on the purchase order specifying that this order qualifies for your premium offer. If you choose the latter, you will experience what some refer to as breakage, or no redemptions.

In some cases, breakage can be as high as 70 or 80 percent of response. But it is unlikely that it will not also reduce response over auto-ship premium policies. Respondents generally know the policies of the purchasing department and know whether this department will accommodate your redemption requirement before they respond. If the potential buyers know beforehand that they are not likely to receive the premium, they are less motivated to respond.

FREEBEES

Freebees and discounts can be very effective offers, especially for essential or popular products. Educators are generally sensitive to price and will respond to sales and specials. These tend to be more successful on-season than off-season because of the established budgeting and buying patterns of most school systems. In many instances, the school cannot respond if your attractive offer comes when the current budget has been spent and the new one has not yet been approved.

Expiration Dates

Because of the strongly established buying patterns of the school market, it is suggested that catalog expiration dates for spring mailings run until August 31. This accommodates a major buying time and remains in effect until the fall catalog is in the school. For fall mailings, December 31 is the preferred catalog expiration date.

While many school marketers are successful publishing price disclaimers in their catalogs ("prices subject to change without notice"), whenever possible (even at some loss to margin), it can be a major positioning advantage in the school market to guarantee prices to the expiration date.

Educators usually go through a considerable process of application and approval for a purchase of any significant size. If a purchase is approved and authorized at catalog price, and the price is higher when the school marketer receives the purchase order, often a new round of approvals is required by the initiating educator. This almost always will leave an unfavorable impression with that educator. One could argue that prices guaranteed to a specified expiration date could be viewed as a reason to buy.

Guarantee and Warranty

Buyers in the school market tend to be conservative individuals. In many cases, they are spending public funds and don't want to become involved in a purchase that results in problems for themselves or the schools for which they buy.

If you are a new marketer to schools and do not have an established reputation, success often can be enhanced by offering a guarantee or warranty. Guarantees vary from a few days to forever for inspecting and returning merchandise and can promise credited accounts or full money-back refunds to prospective customers.

MAKING MEDIA DECISIONS

There are certain factors regarding the school market that affect the performance of media. For example, the spring buying season is fairly sustained: 3 to 6 months long. A catalog can sustain itself over that period of time, but a direct mail piece is most likely to be lost in the shuffle. If one's product stable does not warrant a catalog, often multiple direct mail hits can be an effective way of penetrating the long spring buying season.

Another factor in the school market that affects media decision is access. For example, outbound telephone can be a very effective medium for elementary school principals, but it can be extremely difficult if the prospect is a classroom teacher. The principal is accessible through outbound telephone; the grade teacher generally is not.

CATALOG APPLICATIONS

The catalog is a major medium for school marketers. Creating catalogs for the school market differs very little from creating good catalogs in the consumer market. Since the school market has two major buying seasons, it is a logical strategy to repeat the same offerings in the fall and spring, with different covers. This can result in print savings as well.

Many schools keep a catalog file in a central location in the school: the school library, principal's office, business manager's office, or school secretary's office. Having a catalog qualify for this file seems to have more to do with size and heft than with any other factor.

Generally, less than sixteen pages is not considered a catalog and over sixteen pages is. The preferred catalog size is 8½ by 11 inches.

DIRECT MAIL APPLICATIONS

As in the case of the catalog, good direct mail is good direct mail. Copy and graphics should be exciting and attractive; the price should incorporate a good, simple offer; and the slant should be benefit-oriented.

Multiple hits in the spring tend to be productive because the school market is not a truly homogeneous market. For example, schools in certain southern states open and close several weeks earlier than schools in the north.

Spring and Easter vacations can vary, and so can fiscal cutoffs. Many schools turn the fiscal year over in July, yet a significant number close on December 31. These differences have varying effects on the performance of mail.

For example, your direct mail package drops on March 15, and you begin to receive responses April 1. You know your order intake pattern by work from previous mailings, but this year Easter vacation is April 15 to 22. You graph your intake and find the results depicted in Figure 56-3.

Because "school was out," your direct mail campaign lost a big week of response that was never recovered. Too many educators who might have gotten to responding on Monday didn't when they returned to school a week later.

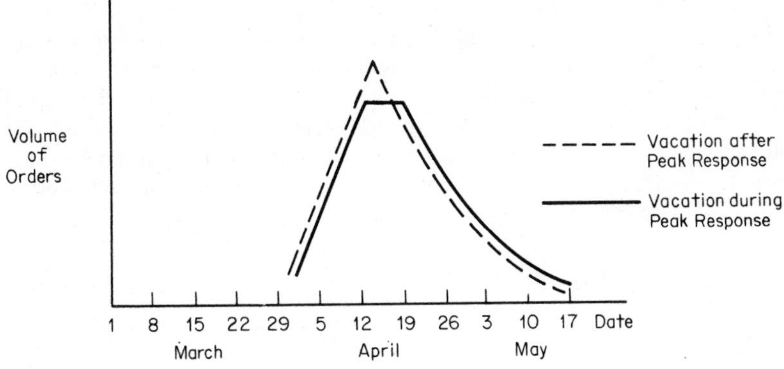

Figure 56-3 Effect of school vacation on direct mail response

OTHER MEDIA

Other major forms of media used by school marketers are space advertising and inbound and outbound telephone. Some school marketers have developed television commercials and have run them on local television stations during major conventions of educators.

Space advertising is a major medium for the school marketer, but because of the difficulty with tracking orders, it is very difficult to evaluate performance. It is particularly hard to track inquiry conversions from space ads. The inquiry may come in with one address, and the order with a completely different address.

Outbound telephone has been very successful for school marketers, especially in the elementary and nursery school markets. In these markets, both the principal and the nursery school director can be reached by phone. Once one attempts to reach grade teachers in elementary schools or anyone but the school secretary in a secondary school, the task becomes much more difficult. Often the task of getting educators to the telephone makes it impossible to achieve a successful rate of completed calls per hour.

Inbound telephone has become very popular with school marketers in recent years. Today serious catalog mailers use a toll-free service. While the buying is still seasonal, most marketers agree that toll-free numbers add to sales volume and profit.

A NOTE ABOUT TESTING

The school market poses a unique challenge to direct marketers. The outgoing reply device seldom is returned to the direct marketer. Instead, a purchase order is generated from 80 to 98 percent of the time, making it very difficult to track response to test mailings.

Consumer direct marketers can key their outgoing test order cards and tally the response by key when the order cards come in. School marketers key their test panels, and the overwhelming majority of responses come back on purchase order. School marketers often cannot tally by key; the key goes unidentified.

Many steps have been taken over the years to address this problem, including such relatively advanced efforts as division of the school market into geographic sections or test groups. This technique allows for the tallying of orders by the geographic source of the order. While it is a good way to identify an order source, the construction of the geographic test groups is critical to obtaining statistically reliable, projectable test results. Geography has a built-in demographic bias, and unless this is evaluated to provide test cells of equal demographics, skewed or unprojectable data may result.

chapter 57

INSURANCE MARKETING

Eugene R. Raitt

President
International
Marketing Consulting
Group
Rockville, Md.

A STRATEGIC PERSPECTIVE

Status of the Traditional Agency System

As the 1980s unfold, the life insurance industry is in the middle of more change and controversy than it has faced in its 200-year history. The impetus for change has come for the most part as an outgrowth or extension of the consumer movement which began in the early 1970s. Key issues include the areas of disclosure, federal intervention, life insurance company tax law changes, minimum loss ratio requirements, readability, replacement, and universal life. While all these problems are significant enough to concern the industry, none can match the far-reaching impact that the changing force of the traditional agency system has had on the way insurance companies will be delivering their products to the consumer for the balance of the 1980s and beyond.

These days, if you pick up an insurance industry trade publication, depending on which article, column, or letter you read, you can find out that the traditional agency system is dead and buried, in serious trouble, or alive, well, and thriving. What is the real status of this delivery system? Perhaps it is best to distinguish between what the industry is saying and what it is doing in order to arrive at an answer.

Although many companies claim that the system is alive and well, the number of licensed, full-time insurance sales people has been shrinking by 15 to 25 percent per year according to some industry sources. Many insiders believe that by 1990 there may be only 25,000 full-time agents in the entire United States (there are now approximately 250,000). It is hard to support the argument that the agency system is alive and well if you consider the fact of shrinkage alone. There are more facts to consider, however.

Two of the largest companies using the traditional agency system, both of which have been outspoken in the "alive and well" camp, have gone into the direct marketing business in a big way. Prudential did it with a successful bid on the AARP-NRTA contract, and Combined Insurance did it with the purchase of Union Fidelity. It is interesting to note the aftereffects of both these actions. In the case of Prudential, despite the massive commitment made for acquiring the AARP contract, there has been no evidence to suggest that Prudential realizes its implications, namely, that the company is now a major direct response marketer. The case of Combined and Union Fidelity is even more dramatic in its implications. They simply eliminated all of Union Fidelity's agency operations, top to bottom.

A more pragmatic approach and perhaps the best precursor of things to come has been the approach of Capital Holding Company with its purchase of National Liberty. In this case, Capital Holding was interested in the marriage of direct response and the agency system, using the ability of direct marketing to augment the agent in the field with leads, and using the agent as another distribution channel to augment direct response through deeper market penetration.

Another action contrary to the "alive and well" theory has been the industry-wide move toward making products more competitive in the general marketplace. In most cases, this has resulted in lower commissions for the sales people. The companies themselves are squeezing the less productive agents out of the business. It is simply too expensive to make sales calls today to all but a select few markets. To survive, an agent must either compete in the toughest markets against many others or figure out a way to produce a higher volume of smaller sales. Once again, we see an area where direct marketing and agency may act synergetically.

According to LIMRA (the Life Insurance Marketing and Research Association), for the last 3 years the best attended seminars and most requested source materials have been in the areas of mass marketing and direct marketing.

These three trends indicate that the traditional agency system is neither alive and well nor dead and buried. However, companies that do not respond to the challenge of upgrading productivity through direct marketing of some type may fall into the "dead and buried" group. The life insurance industry traditionally has been slow to respond and change.

Now more than ever, companies need to become market-driven rather than product- or sales-driven if they are to survive. They must face these challenges and respond as quickly as possible if they are to be among the 250 or so companies that many experts predict will be left by the year 2000. (There are currently some 2000 companies.) For many of these surviving companies, direct marketing will be a critical element in strategic plans. The industry has failed so far to respond to one important fact concerning the good old days of the traditional agency system: They are gone.

Consumer Behavior and Demographic Trends

The most significant development in consumer behavior over the past 10 years has been the overwhelming acceptance of direct mail as a sales medium. The industry as a whole has grown into a multi-billion-dollar enterprise, and the insurance industry in particular has grown from virtually zero in 1959 to over $1 billion in 1982. More Americans are buying more different products through direct marketing efforts than at any time in history.

Several factors have been responsible for this success. The wave of consumerism in the early 1970s resulted in better regulation of direct marketing. The rise of the Federal Trade Commission as a force to be reckoned with drove most of the shady operators from the "mail-order" business. Full disclosure made comparison shopping easier for the consumer and fostered more competition within the industry. Inflation and the first energy crisis in the mid-1970s forced many cost-conscious consumers to become first-time direct mail buyers. Obviously, many became repeat buyers, having been satisifed the first time around. Development and refinement of new direct marketing techniques has increased the consumer's awareness of direct marketing as a viable alternative to shopping in stores.

All indications point to a continuing trend of even broader consumer acceptance of direct marketing. Insurance direct marketing, for example, has grown from a single-product (hospital indemnity), single-medium (space) mode to a complex scenario involving a mix of various media selling virtually every conceivable insurance product. This has occurred in an industry where as recently as 1959 the only imaginable method of delivery was an agent sitting across the kitchen table from Mom and Pop. A shift of this magnitude in consumer behavior is truly remarkable and is a credit to the pioneers in the direct insurance marketing business who made it happen.

Market Segmentation as a Key Strategy

One way the pioneers of insurance direct marketing effected the big shift in consumer behavior was through market segmentation. They saw the United States as more than just 200 million people. They saw it rather as a diverse general population which includes senior citizens, veterans, women, etc. In other words, they approached their business by building a market model rather than a sales model, as the traditional insurance companies do. They began by defining a specific target market, or audience. It was only after they defined this market that they decided how to reach these people: space, direct mail, broadcast, newspaper inserts, etc. In other words, they determined which media are most effective in reaching the people they targeted as a market. Finally, they decided what products to sell and what, if any, product differentiation would be needed for the specific target market. Market segmentation was and is a critical element in strategic planning for direct insurance marketers. It is the exact opposite of a sales model, which is product-driven. See Figure 57-1.

The biggest single hurdle an insurance company must handle if it is to be committed to direct marketing is adopting the market-driven strategy of market segmentation.

There is no better example of market segmentation as a key strategy than that of Arthur Demoss, founder of National Liberty and generally regarded as the father of direct insurance marketing. When Demoss attempted his first direct marketing test, he defined his market as "total abstainers" (people who neither drank nor smoked). His religious beliefs and affiliations brought him into contact with many people who were total abstainers, and he theorized that a great number of these people read a religious magazine entitled *The Sword of the Lord.* He had been selling a hospital indemnity policy using agents as the delivery system until this time. Demoss further theorized that if people did not drink or smoke, they deserved a discount on their insurance premiums, since they were less likely to become sick and be hospitalized. He persuaded the insurance company he represented to discount a hospital indemnity policy 15 percent for total abstainers and to rename the policy the "Gold Star Plan." This is a perfect example of the perfect model.

1. Define market: Total abstainers
2. Select medium: Sword of the Lord (space)
3. Select and differentiate product: 15 percent discount HIP and Gold Star Plan

The rest is history. Look around the direct insurance marketers today and you will see companies segmenting markets such as senior citizens, veterans, active duty military, retired military officers, women, farmers and ranchers, college students, bank credit card holders, etc.

Why is market segmentation the key to growth and profitability for direct insurance marketers? Everyone knows that selling insurance is not easy, even face to face. That is why selling to the "broad" market (general population) is so difficult. With market segmentation, however, the marketer can create the feelings of belonging and entitlement. How many times have we all seen or heard the words "Because you are a veteran, you are eligible . . ." or "If you are between the ages of 50 and 80, you qualify . . ."

DEFINITION AND FORMS OF DIRECT INSURANCE MARKETING

Definition

Technically, a purist might define direct insurance marketing as any form of insurance selling that does not involve an agent. However, a more complete definition would be any insurance sales activity consisting of a differentiative product being delivered to a target market segment by means of various media (including agents). If you are selling Medicare supplement to senior citizens through direct mail, you are a direct insurance marketer. If you are creating term life leads by means of television with ads aimed at veterans but then giving those leads to field agents to complete the sale, you are a direct insurance marketer. Obviously, there are hybrids of these examples, just as there are degrees of direct marketing.

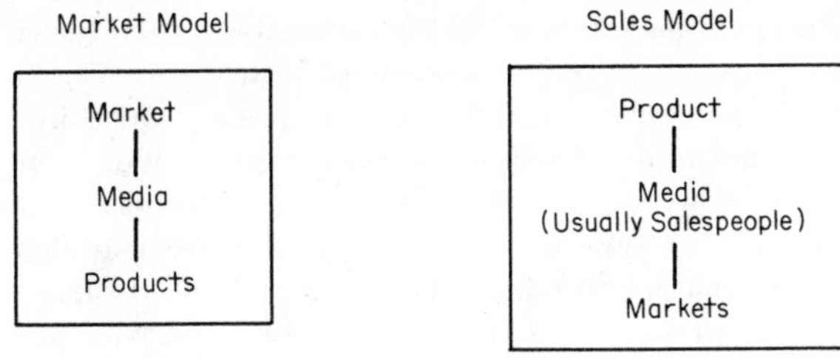

Figure 57-1 A comparison of market segmentation and the sales model.

Forms

Direct Mail. This category can be divided into two methods: one-step (solo) and two-step (inquiry and conversion). In both cases, the whole sales process is conducted through the mail. It is the most precise medium in terms of reaching a target audience. The one-step method involves a mailing package that attempts to generate interest and make the sale at the same time. This type of package usually has a four- or six-page "sell" letter, a brochure, a "lift" letter, an application, and a return envelope.

The two-step approach involves an initial mailing of an inquiry package. This is usually a simple package designed to generate leads, or cause the real prospects in the lists selected to hold up their hands and identify themselves. Respondents then are mailed a "conversion" kit, which is similar to the one-step package described above except that it is positioned to take advantage of the replier's display of interest.

As in any other form of direct mail, the same rules apply. If you choose this method, remember the most important elements in order of importance: the list, the offer, the package.

Television. This medium cannot stand alone but must be used in conjunction with other media.

To Generate Leads. As the first step in a two-step process, television can produce inquiries driven into a toll-free telephone number. These leads then can be mailed a conversion package and may even use a telephone marketing campaign prior to the conversion package mailing or immediately thereafter to answer questions and help fill out the applications. Television inquiry generation traditionally has consisted of 120-second commercials. However, recently, because of the expansion of cable TV and the changing of availability patterns for :120s, more 60-second commercials have been seen.

As Support of Another Medium. Television most frequently supports newspaper inserts, but it also is used with direct mail. These support commercials are usually 30 seconds and contain a basic message: "If you are between 50 and 80, look for this important information package in your Sunday newspaper or mailbox, etc." The purpose, of course, is to heighten awareness and build curiosity and anticipation so that when the primary medium delivers the sales message, it will be more effective.

Newcomers to direct insurance marketing often think mistakenly that television is an expensive medium in which to get involved. Actually, television can be a lot less expensive to test than direct mail, and results can be obtained in a shorter time frame. The economics and logistics of television are very different from those of direct mail and require expert guidance for the newcomer.

Unlike direct mail, which can rifle shoot to its target market more accurately than other media, television is a mass, or broad, medium. Therefore, your target market must be sufficiently large in numbers to justify television; otherwise, you will be wasting money. While it makes sense economically to reach the 35 or 40 million mature Americans by television, it may be economic suicide to attempt to reach the 1,500,000 to 2,000,000 American farmers and ranchers by TV. In the future, when cable TV does more "narrowcasting," this equation may change. For now, however, TV usually is used only when your target market has sufficient numbers to justify the expense.

Newspaper Inserts. This is a one-step approach that is packaged for insertion, usually in the Sunday newspapers. It often is supported with 30-second TV commercials during the week leading to insertion. Inserts are another mass medium; therefore, they often are aimed at the general public rather than a specific target market. Just as direct mail packages must compete with all the "noise" in the average American's mailbox, inserts must compete with all the noise in the Sunday newspapers.

Space and Run of Press. This medium—magazine and newspaper advertising—is usually the first step in a two-step process; the second step is a direct mail conversion effort. Magazine space advertising allows the marketer a higher degree of selectivity than run of press for target marketing, but it is still a mass medium compared with direct mail.

Telephone. The latest medium in the direct marketer's tool bag, telephone can be used in conjunction with and as support for all other media. Telephone marketing can be inserted anywhere in the equation after the inquiry has been received. Some companies have had success with calling leads before mailing the conversion package, others with calling after the conversion package has been received by the inquirer. Here we are not talking about unsolicited outbound telemarketing, which is a different issue. The economics and logistics of telephone marketing, as with TV, need expert guidance to avoid expensive pitfalls. One major advantage of this medium, like TV, is the ability of the market to read test results quickly and make adjustments and decisions before a major investment is made.

The Media Plan

As part of the insurance direct marketer's overall strategic plan, a good media plan will include proportionate percentage expenditures for all appropriate media. In fact, the media plan is the most critical variable for the success of a program. How do I reach my target market? is the most important question you must ask. It's better to mail an inferior package to a great list than a great package to an inferior list.

PRODUCT CRITERIA SELECTION

Characteristics of Direct-Response Insurance Products

While it is true that virtually any insurance product may be sold by direct marketing techniques, the most successful products share many if not all of the following characteristics:

1. Guaranteed acceptance
2. Simplified underwriting (for term life and birthday life)
3. Limited choice of benefit levels
4. Simple application forms
5. Low relative premiums

Specific Applications

Hospital Indemnity. This is still the number one direct-response product. They are basically appeals to greed, typically offering two basic benefit levels (e.g., $30 a day or $60 a day) with budget options (e.g., first-day coverage or fourth-day coverage) which yield four benefit choices. In addition to the basic daily hospital benefit, there may be blood; ambulance; ICU; CCU; heart attack, cancer, stroke; nurse at home and convalescence care; or other benefits which may be used to "customize" the basic product for specific target markets. It is a perfect product for front-end and back-end policyowner marketing. Usually there is guaranteed acceptance with 1- or 2-year preexisting condition exclusion.

Accident Insurance. This involves guaranteed acceptance with certain age bonds, typically 21 to 59. This product may be issued in many variations, such as accident only, travel accident, accidental death and dismemberment, and mortgage accident. The nature of this product and its variations allow very high death benefit illustrations with small premiums. It also is excellent for front-end and back-end policyowner marketing.

Term Life. Usually a simplified issue with a minimum of underwriting, this product works best when aimed at very specific target markets such as credit card holders, veterans, alumni, etc. Benefit levels may be set according to the demographics of the target audience and typically range from $20,000 to $100,000. The application should contain a minimum of health questions. Relatively low premiums help move this product as an impulse purchase for extra protection with a minimum of inconvenience.

Graded Benefit Life. A specialized product for the 45 to 80 age market, this guaranteed acceptance product usually is sold with a level premium ($6.25 to $6.95 per month) for all ages within the bond. Since every age pays the same premium, the benefit level varies. Most graded benefit plans grade over 2 years, returning approximately 30 percent of the ultimate face amount the first year and 60 percent the second, with the full face beginning in the third. Since this product is guaranteed acceptance within the stated age bonds, the application is extremely short and simple. This product is a staple of the mature market but can be adopted in various forms for other markets.

Birthday Life. This product is a whole life policy with a low benefit level ($10,000 to $20,000) designed to be sold just prior to the prospect's next birthday, thus appearing as a "last chance" bargain. This simplified issue product is perfect for policyowner marketing as well as target marketing to lists where exact age can be obtained.

PROFITABILITY AND THE MARKETER

Understanding the Goals of Management

Since each company may modify its goals from year to year, it is imperative that this message be given loud and clear to the marketer so that it may be reflected in the strategic marketing plan. Some companies express their goals in terms of pretax profit margins; others use a variety of measures including return on investment, return on sales, compound growth (expressed in many ways), net volume increase, etc. If the marketer does not know and understand the goals of senior management, it will be sheer chance if the marketing plan yields the desired result or is even geared toward the desired objective. There is a world of difference between growth and profitable growth, yet there may be sound reasons why growth alone is management's goal. Without this type of simple knowledge, the marketer cannot possibly do the best job for management. Let's look at a few factors affecting profitability in direct insurance marketing.

Profitability Factors

Marketing Efficiency. Expressed in its basic form, this means "How much does it cost in marketing expense to produce a dollar of premium?" This seemingly simple formula has broad implications, however, because so many other areas of the business impart profitability, such as claims cost, investment income, etc. But it remains valid because the company actuaries and financial officers can build those other factors into the equation and issue marketing efficiency guidelines that are expressed in simple terms. A typical approach is to develop a simple equation, T/MC, where T stands for total annualized renewal premium and MC stands for marketing cost. This exercise yields one simple number to use as a measure against a product line or business. For example, if management has given the message that the minimum T/MC for term life in a specific market is 1:1, that means that in terms of efficiency, the marketer must produce at least $1.10 in premium for each marketing dollar spent. When the plan is built, if the 1:1 ratio cannot be produced, the marketer must reexamine his or her assumptions and adjust accordingly in order to meet the goals.

Persistency. In the insurance industry, this is the measure, expressed in a percentage, of how many policyholders are still paying premiums after intervals of 13 months and 25 months. If we sell 100 policies, each taking effect on January 1, we would check the records in February of the following year (13 months) and determine how many of the original 100 were still "in force." If eighty were still paying, the persistency would be 80 percent.

When product actuaries build their pricing strategies, persistency is a critical element. It doesn't take tremendous business acumen to realize that if we used an assumption of 80 percent and the actual result was 50 percent, we would be in trouble. The marketer can effect persistency in the strategic plan through manipulation of several factors, including list selection and criteria, underwriting requirements, preexisting condition clauses, mode of payment options, price-benefit ratio testing, etc.

Loss Ratios. This factor, again expressed as a percentage, measures the dollar amount paid out in claims for every premium dollar. If the lost ratio is 60 percent, that means that $0.60 of every dollar was paid out in benefits. The products most sensitive to loss ratio problems are health-related (hospital indemnity, Medicare supplement, etc.), although graded benefit life and accidental health may give cause for concern if they are not marketed properly. The marketer can have an effect on loss ratios in several ways: list selection and criteria, underwriting requirements, preexisting condition clauses, state selection (some states have mandated loss ratio requirements), price-benefit ratio testing, etc.

Operational Overhead. This term, while not controlled directly by the marketer in most organizations, can be affected significantly by the strategic marketing plan. Operational overhead may be defined loosely as the amount of money, expressed as a percentage of the total premium, that it costs to process the incoming business, put it in force, and then provide policyowner service. There are many areas in which the marketer, if not properly conversant in operational matters, can cause overhead to increase dramatically. For example, the internal processing system may not be able to track the business properly by source code, making normal tracking essential. Forms or envelope design may be nonstandard and may render automated processing equipment useless, again making normal processing necessary. There are many other examples, since there are so many moving parts. The marketer, while not expected to know all these parts, must nevertheless have a keen sense for ways in which the strategic marketing plan will have an impact on internal operations.

POLICYOWNER MARKETING

Theory

An astute observer of the marketing scene once said, "The buyers are the buyers are the buyers." People who have bought once tend to buy again. People who have bought more than once are even stronger prospects. This is what policyowner marketing is all about. If you remember the elements of direct marketing as the list, the offer, and the package, with the list far and away the most important, policyowner marketing gives you the best available list. It is not unusual to see response rates rise astronomically when you market to your own policyowners; it is usually one of the most profitable business centers in any direct insurance marketing company.

Practice

Since the range of cross-selling opportunities is so great, it is difficult to give comprehensive examples. Two instances must suffice. In the first instance, a company having a portfolio that is predominately life insurance or health insurance is a perfect candidate for marketing the complementary product to its portfolio (e.g., a health product offer to a life portfolio or a life product offer to a health portfolio). Another very common method of policyowner marketing is the "add-on" or "loading" concept. In this example, let's assume that we have sold a basic hospital indemnity product to a selected target market. Let's further assume that the average daily benefit was $50 a day. After a specified time period, say, 6 months, we may resolicit these policyholders for rider coverage offering benefits such as cardiac care, intensive care, nurse at home, etc. The rider usually is "preissued" and included in the solicitation. Perhaps at the end of the first policy year, we would resolicit these same policyholders, again using a preissued certificate, with an offer to increase their basic daily hospital benefit.

Problem Areas

Perhaps the biggest problem area is with a company using an agent distribution system in addition to direct marketing. Since agents feel that the policyholders are "theirs," they feel it as an infringement if the company attempts to sell additional products or upgrades directly. There are several ways around this problem, but each requires the implementation of a high-level corporate decision.

A secondary problem is the question of how much is too much: At what point do we stop loading? At what premium level do we start experiencing a higher lapse ratio (poorer persistency) than we can afford? Fortunately, this is an area that can be tested and used very accurately; this is a step that must be done to ensure back-end profitability.

EFFECT OF ENDORSEMENT

As a general rule, endorsement lifts response. It's as simple as that, yet endorsement takes many forms.

Personality

You may see Art Linkletter, Arthur Godfrey, Roger Staubach, Ed McMahon, Glen Ford, and others essentially hold up a "product" aimed at a specific market (veterans, senior citizens, etc.) on television or in a direct mail piece and say, "This is good; buy it." In reality, these personalities are just soliciting inquiries, which then are converted into sales by direct mail, but the principle is that the effect of the personality raises the response level in almost all cases. If you choose this method of endorsement, you still must test, since the real measure of efficiency is how much incremental response you add, given the increased costs.

Organizational

This type of endorsement is more of a "sponsored" approach than anything else. The solicitation looks like it is coming from the organization itself rather than from an insurance company. Such organizational-type endorsements may come from financial institutions, fraternal organizations, alumni associations, professional associations, department store credit card holders, etc.

Any organization that has a customer list and enjoys loyalty and credibility from that base is a strong potential endorser for a direct insurance solicitation campaign. The stronger the tie between the organization and its members, the better the response.

The list is still the single most critical element in the equation. With organizational endorsement, we are talking about a superb list. These lists do not come cheap. Typically, a commission or "service fee" is paid to the organization providing the endorsement. While this fee may be somewhat higher than the amount you would pay to rent names from outside, unendorsed sources, the increased marketing efficiency and persistency almost always justify the expense.

Creation of Affinity Trusts

This method involves establishing your own endorsement by setting up a variation of the multiple-employer trust concept known as an affinity trust. In plain English, you determine the "group." It may be veterans, senior citizens, credit card holders, women, small business people, or any other "group" of people that apart from having one thing in common (e.g., veteran status) are all strangers. Once you have determined the affinity group, you establish a group trust in one of the various states that allow such trusts. At that point, you issue a "master" policy to the trustee and begin marketing to all who qualify for the group, issuing certificates rather than policies to those who buy. There have been trusts created by various companies covering virtually every affinity imaginable.

Using this quasi-endorsement approach is helpful to the marketer in many ways. Perhaps the two most important elements are the following.

1. Allows strong copy positioning of "eligibility" and "group insurance rates" (which everybody believes to be lower than individual).
2. Eliminates individual filing requirement in many but not all states. Usually you are required to deal only with the state in which your trust is located.

THE REGULATORY ENVIRONMENT

Overview

Ironically, many of the same factors that led to the tremendous growth of direct marketing in general and direct insurance marketing in particular also increased the involvement of various regulatory bodies with regard to consumer protection. Even though the regulators are beginning to see direct insurance marketing as having a beneficial effect on the public in that it reaches markets that for the most part are being ignored by the traditional agency companies, direct marketing is still very much the stepchild of insurance distribution systems. Its legitimacy is called into question routinely. Currently, the affinity trust concept is under severe attack on many state fronts, and in fact, this concept has been abused from within the industry. The federal government has begun making inroads into insurance regulation, with initial forays into Medicare supplement insurance. The intrusion on the state's powers probably will not stop there. States are mandating high minimum loss ratio requirements for some lines of business, further eroding company margins. An assessment of the regulatory climate today may sound familiar: It is the best of times and the worst of times.

Internal Compliance

This is a key area in any company's direct marketing strategy, especially given the current regulatory climate. Whoever has this responsibility must be thoroughly familiar with the differing regulations concerning life and health advertising in all fifty states. The contingent responsibility of this function cannot be underestimated, since one error may cost the company tens of thousands of dollars in fines. If we assume that the marketer always will come in with the most aggressive copy possible, the compliance specialists must have the ability to demonstrate their objections and be willing to back them up to senior management. It is in fact senior management who always will have the final call in a dispute between the marketer and compliance. The risk and reward factor in this area can be submitted on the upside or the downside.

NAIC Guidelines

One ray of hope for the direct insurance marketer has been the establishment of NAIC (National Association of Insurance Commissioners) model guidelines regarding almost every detail relevant to direct marketing. Since we now must contend with a jigsaw puzzle of fifty different sets of state regulations, the adoption by all states of NAIC guidelines would eliminate the necessity for the marketer to adopt state variations and other costly procedures caused by nonuniform regulation. Many states already have adopted various pieces of the model, but we are still a long way from uniformity. The downside to this is that some states have adopted more stringent regulations than the models have called for, and others have made different changes. Both these factors negate the intended purpose of creating uniformity. Direct insurance marketing may never be as easy from a regulatory standpoint as direct marketing, but true uniformity created by adoption of NAIC guidelines would go a long way toward improving the climate in which the direct insurance marketer works.

chapter 58

TELECOMMUNICATIONS

George G. Orme

Executive Vice President,
Client Service
BBDO Direct
New York, N. Y.

Just 5 years ago, who could have imagined that AT&T, one of America's leading Fortune 5 companies, would be following court orders to divest itself of billions of dollars of assets? Who could have guessed that aggressive marketers in just one segment of this highly regulated, utility-oriented industry would be spending more than $8 million a month to attract heavy users away from "the phone company" and sign them up for a nationwide long-distance service featuring lower rates?

As a result of the evolution and dramatic changes that have taken place in the telecommunications industry in recent years, the challenge facing marketers today is twofold. First, they must be sure what business they are in: the "knowledge" business, the telephone equipment business, the long-distance revenue business, etc. Second, they must develop effective, cost-efficient marketing programs to sell their products and services to their most lucrative targeted audiences.

THE COMPETITIVE ENVIRONMENT

To be successful in today's telecommunications marketing environment, a marketer must pull out all the stops. The lack of really unique differences in products and services and the tremendous advertising noise level vying for the attention of potential customers demand that any effort be well planned and carefully orchestrated. Every program also must be more than an attempt to create awareness about a product or leave a lasting impression regarding its features and benefits. The industry has learned that awareness plus action is the key; this is why direct marketing has taken hold.

Within the industry, most if not all telecommunications companies perceive direct marketing as a viable concept and have direct marketing units in place with managers or supervisors and other levels of staff support. The reason is simple. Direct marketing has helped take the guesswork out of "Will it work?" and has enabled marketers to concentrate their efforts on selected segments of their market.

This chapter covers two major categories within the telecommunications industry: general telephone companies such as AT&T and GTE, and specialized common carriers such as MCI and Sprint that currently limit their service offerings primarily to the long-distance marketplace. The purpose of this chapter is to help the telecommunications marketer face today's tough challenges by providing specific examples of how direct marketing can be achieved effectively.

THE ROLE OF DIRECT MARKETING FOR GENERAL TELECOMMUNICATIONS COMPANIES

Residential Toll Stimulation

Direct marketing can be used in a number of ways to stimulate customers to make more phone calls more often. One way is to make it simple and convenient for the customer to call anywhere, from any place, and at any time by issuing credit cards.

The Free Telephone Credit Calling Card

One company used a bill insert program in selected ZIP codes to promote a free, convenient telephone credit card. The audience was selected on the basis of its customer credit rating. The prospects all had private line service, push-button phones, and monthly toll charges of more than $15 but less than $50. Significantly, current card holder names were eliminated to avoid duplication. The creative thrust focused on convenience ("no more fumbling for change") and also emphasized that there was no charge to get the card. The results were excellent. Better than 10 percent of the audience applied for the card, and after 6 months, the company noted a significant increase in toll messages from both pay and private phones in the area where the cards were issued.

Another successful approach in promoting credit calling cards involved a direct mail effort. This company used a personalized letter and application form that invited the prospect to enjoy the convenience of the telephone credit card. In this instance, the audience was selected on the basis of their monthly toll charges ($25 or better) and where they lived. The primary prospect was the traveling executive. The results were better than anyone had projected. Of 200,000 prospects, more than 14,000 were issued cards.

Still another approach is print advertising. In this case, selected celebrity card holders are featured prominently in the ads; this not only attracts attention but also carries with it their implied endorsement. The reader can apply with an 800 number phone call or by using a coupon. The final results are not yet available, but it is likely that the ads will continue to run since the initial results have been positive.

The International Calling Case

Another way to stimulate toll revenue is to promote overseas direct dialing. In this case, the company researched the calling patterns of its largest residential customers to see who was consistently making overseas calls and from where. The study uncovered two major findings. Seven out of ten calls were placed by callers not born in the United States, and better than 50 percent of the calling activity originated from isolated "neighborhood" areas of large cities. A closer examination suggested that the purpose of the calls was to keep in touch with relatives and friends in the "old country." The company capitalized on its findings by targeting special ads in selected ethnic-oriented local newspapers. The thrust was information-oriented and "newsy," stressing how inexpensive and easy it can be to call your loved ones overseas. The results were extraordinary. Overseas calls in these areas rose dramatically, and the program was instituted on an annual basis.

The Discounted Period Promotion

In this instance, the target audience was anyone at home watching television. Obviously, the TV buy was arranged to ensure that viewers were also likely to be heavy phone users. The thrust was to emphasize to the viewing audience that at the exact moment they were watching TV, they could be saving money by calling long distance because a discounted rate period was in effect. After 3 weeks of running the spot, the company began to see a definite increase in the number of calls placed right after the spot aired. After 6 weeks, the company was able to predict the number of calls and the corresponding revenue it should generate based on the time of day and day of the week.

These examples all illustrate how direct marketing can be applied to the telecommunications industry to stimulate residential toll activity. But it can work in other ways as well.

ENHANCED RESIDENTIAL SERVICES

The Magic Phone Program

Getting more out of the phone by having it do more things is in general the positioning behind services such as call waiting, call forwarding, three-way dialing, and speed dialing.

One company promoted this new telephone service concept by portraying it as magic. A bill insert was mailed to all customers who lived in areas where the services were available. The thrust of the insert was the new magic that a push-button phone could perform. The design included a black top hat, a magic wand, and two silhouetted, gloved hands. The approach was a two-step, encouraging the prospect to first call or write for more information and then follow-up materials would be sent that would ask for the order. The results were above projections. This one bill insert had enough people to respond so that the costs of the effort were covered in the first 2 days of the program.

Another successful approach that has been used to sell these enhanced services is direct mail. In this case, a package was created that emphasized the irritation and annoyance which callers are subject to when they are trying to call home, but because someone is on the phone, all they get is a busy signal. The rationale was that the service would eliminate the problem of "getting through" when calling home and also enable the customers to get more out of their phones when they were home since they could instantly handle two calls at once. The initial test showed that only certain types of customers responded, primarily those living in suburban areas with phone bills over $50 a month. A rollout mailing was targeted to only these prospects. The results were very good: better than $15 in additional revenue for every $1 of advertising expense.

RESIDENTIAL PHONE EQUIPMENT

Direct marketing also has been used to build store traffic to sell decorator telephone sets. In this example, the telecommunications company used a combination of print advertising and direct mail. Both approaches promoted the same product: a special decorator phone designed in early American style. The ads were placed in regional editions of upscale publications widely read by fashion-conscious women. The direct mail was targeted to suburban customers who had private lines with two or more extensions, push-button phones, and a monthly bill of at least $75. The results were moderately successful. In one metropolitan area, enough sets were sold to warrant a continuation of the program. In another area, the results were less than satisfactory. A closer examination of the program, however, indicated that many of the prospects were not attracted to the offer because they did not want to travel to the phone store to pick up the equipment. If there had been some way simply to order it and have it arrive by mail or parcel service, perhaps the program would have met with greater success.

BUSINESS TOLL STIMULATION

The Telephone Credit Card

For busy business executives who travel or call frequently from out of the office, a credit card can be a great convenience. For telephone companies, the business telephone credit card can be a great toll stimulator. The following case history illustrates this point.

Business customers were chosen for the program on the basis of their size, type of business, service equipment, and credit rating. Two groups of names were selected randomly. One was the control group, which received no promotion materials. The other group received a credit card solicitation package offering them an unlimited number of free telephone cards if they applied and met the customary credit requirements.

The package dramatized the convenience of the card, the improved means of keeping in touch when out of the office, and the additional benefit a company can provide employees by giving them a telephone credit card.

The results were excellent. Over 10 percent of the businesses applied for the cards. Additionally, the company found that businesses with the cards generated more revenue per call and more minutes per call than businesses without the cards.

BUSINESS TOLL STIMULATION AND LEAD GENERATION

The Efficient Productive Management Tool: Conference Calls

For business executives who are looking for a management tool to help them be more productive, save time, and cut down on business travel demands and expenses, conference calls are the perfect solution. For telephone companies interested in generating leads for their business sales force and ultimately stimulating additional toll activity, conference calls are also perfect.

However, one company has found that the selling of the conference call concept requires careful planning, target marketing, and an extra ingredient of a special calling planner to work effectively.

The program was targeted to certain types of businesses. They all had to have excellent credit ratings, more than twenty-five employees at a minimum of two branch offices, and PBX equipment.

The first step was to mail out a promotion package which introduced the concept, spelled out the benefits in great detail in a brochure which also included a number of case histories, and provided the prospect with a response card which could be used to request more information and arrange for a meeting with the sales rep. An 800 number was provided for even faster service.

The second phase involved another mailing, which was sent as a follow-up package. This package included additional information on how to get started, how the prospect could motivate employees to use conference calls, and how the prospects could use this helpful, efficient management tool most effectively. To help facilitate usage, this package also included a handy conference call pad which highlighted the key elements of a successful conference call and provided space for note taking during the call.

The final results are still being tabulated. However, two important points have emerged. First, the mailing packages all were able to reach their prospects with an important message regarding the benefits of conference calls. This may appear trivial, but prior to the mailing, the company had had a terrible time promoting conference calls because their sales reps had been unable to reach these key prospects. In essence, this company has found that direct mail affords it "reachability" because it can get its sales message across when the salesperson can't.

Second, there was an immediate increase in toll revenue from some of the companies which received the mailing, despite the fact that they did not respond to the conference call offer. This increase in toll activity takes on even more importance when viewed against the control group which this telephone company was monitoring—the group that had not received any promotion materials. Not surprisingly, their toll activity remained relatively constant. Thus, this communications company has found that simply by promoting the benefits of conference calls versus business travel, they can achieve an increase in toll activity.

A WORD OF CAUTION

These illustrations point out that direct marketing can be used in a number of ways to stimulate toll revenue, generate leads for the sales force, sell service enhancements, or even build store traffic in phone equipment stores.

As a matter of fact, because direct marketing is so applicable to the telecommunications business, perhaps marketers should make sure to establish some method of evaluating which products or services should be promoted to which target audience. Clearly, not every customer wants or even needs a credit calling card, nor will every program designed to promote modern, slick service enhancements work.

A Simple Product Evaluation

One method that can be used to evaluate products is to put the product through the following rating process. How does the product measure up regarding the following elements?

Exclusivity. The best products or services are those which are available from only one company. In the telecommunications field, there are very few exclusive products, but experience suggests that if a product can't be exclusive, it must be at least "special" in order to work in a direct marketing program.

Price. The best price point, of course, is that price which offers a significant savings over the competition's. Again, in the telecommunications industry, this is rarely the case because of industry regulations. Therefore, for the successful direct marketer, the chief concern should be the perceived value and fair price of the product or service.

Allowable Margin for Promotion and Sales. Is there a breakeven obtainable at the desired response rate if maintenance and installation costs are included? Is there enough money to do an effective selling job?

Competition. Can the customer get the product or service from another source? If so, is that source promoting it actively? Are the quality of the product and the price at least competitive with if not superior to those of the competition?

Unit of Sale. Is there a large enough unit of sale to ensure a breakeven? Experience in the industry suggests that any unit of sale less than $25 generally is too low to cover costs unless the promotion involves a heavy response offer such as sweepstakes.

Ease of Use and Ease of Explanation. Is the product suitable for a direct mail promotion? Can everything that needs to be explained by a salesperson be easily addressed and explained in a brochure?

Delivery of Product. Products or services that can be provided without on-site visits are the best. Can mail or parcel service be used instead of customer pickup at a company installation, as with the decorator phone promotion highlighted earlier in this chapter?

Market Size and Potential. Are there enough potential customers out there to justify testing the responsiveness of the marketplace, or is the potential too small to repeat the program on a larger scale at a later date?

Market Awareness. In the telecommunications industry, low market awareness can be good if the product saves time and money. High market awareness also can be a plus if the product is not readily available.

Using these criteria, some companies have found that applying a grade or score such as 1 point for excellent, 2 points for good, 3 points for average, 4 points for poor, and 5 points for unsatisfactory can help eliminate questionable products and thus quash losing programs before they see the light of day. Obviously, the lower the score, the more justification there probably is that a product or service is properly suited for a direct marketing program.

The Selection of the Target Audience

Once a product emerges as having potential, the next question that needs to be addressed is, Who and where is the ideal audience for this product? One place to start is with a review of the telecommunications company customer file. In most instances, the following information is available.

Telephone Exchange (NNX). Are there certain phone exchanges that may represent low priorities because of potential bad debt problems or infrequent phone use patterns? If so, can they be eliminated?

ZIP Code. Are there special areas that seem ideally suited for special efforts because of lifestyle and demographic profiles?

Product and Service Identifiers. Are there special marketing situations that should be taken into account because selected customers do or do not have certain types of services?

Toll Usage. Do certain customer revenue volumes suggest that regardless of where these customers live, they'd be good prospects for credit cards or new enhancements?

Number of Extensions. Can a correlation be drawn between the number of phones customers have and their propensity to call more often and thus have a greater need for the latest telecommunications breakthroughs?

Number of Lines. Can a correlation be drawn to show that the higher the number of lines, the higher the desire or need for every product or service the telephone company has to offer?

In addition to this information, other data can be obtained from external sources that can help provide even more criteria and thus aid in the market segmentation process.

On the residential side, age, income levels, and length of residence are available using ZIP code, Census tract, and block group data.

On the business side, Standard Industrial Classification (SIC) codes, employee size, sales volume, and the financial strength of a prospect all can help augment what is known already about a customer or prospect.

These additional criteria can be very valuable if a program involves the promotion of decorator phones to more affluent areas or if a toll stimulation effort is developed for certain types and sizes of business.

The point is that direct marketing has become an integral part of the telecommunications marketing mix because successful practitioners have learned that there is a method to its madness. Through proper evaluation of both the product and the target audience in the planning stages of a program, millions of dollars in revenue has been generated.

THE ROLE OF DIRECT MARKETING FOR SPECIAL TELECOMMUNICATIONS COMPANIES

The services these companies offer are limited to the long-distance marketplace. By using their own microwave or satellite transmission towers, these companies have set up long-distance networks connecting major cities. In order for their customers to access these networks, the companies rely on local phone companies at the other end. The key selling point of these services is price. They offer the customer up to 50 percent lower long-distance rates than AT&T.

Companies in this category, such as MCI, Sprint, and ITT Longer Distance, use direct marketing primarily as a tool to acquire customers. As a result, for these types of companies, direct marketing is more than a technique or a methodology to help pinpoint messages to selected target audiences. For these companies, direct marketing is the entire means of growth and survival. As such, they may be classified first as direct marketers and then as providers of telecommunication services.

All their direct marketing efforts have two things in common. First, they use direct marketing primarily as a means of customer acquisition and as such are constantly testing offers, media, and creative approaches to achieve the greatest efficiency regarding the costs involved in obtaining new customers. Second, they use television as well as print advertising and direct mail to ensure that they reach both the residential and business markets with their message.

RESIDENTIAL CUSTOMER ACQUISITION

The Power of TV

No other medium is quite like TV. TV seems to instantly enhance a viewer's perception of a product's quality and performance. Because these marketers are competing in a marketplace that has been dominated for years by one company, one of their key strategies is to use spot TV to simultaneously create awareness about their services and generate instant sales in areas where they offer their services.

One company has found that TV works best if they use 30-second spots which run in the afternoon and early evening. The approach is to position the firm as the "other" long-distance phone company and portray the service as offering lower long-distance rates. The company also emphasize that their customers can save money any time while noncustomers interested in saving money have to limit their calling to those periods when discounts are in effect. The response mechanism for the spot is an 800 number. If the prospects call the number, they can learn more about the service and also immediately sign up.

Another company has used television to generate sales. This company places its 30-second spots in the evening and at night. The spots are directed to the family: to kids away at college who should call home more often or to homemakers who are always looking for ways to save money. To add credibility to the service, this company positions itself as the long-distance specialist. Once again, an 800 number is featured prominently, and prospects are encouraged to call so that they can ask questions about the service and then sign up.

Another approach using direct-response television to acquire customers has been the use of 60-second spots. In one instance, a company using 60-second spots buys the television time at substantially reduced rates with the understanding that the station can preempt its spots if another advertiser is willing to pay the regular rate for the selected air time. A big advantage of using 60-second spots is that it allows this company more time to tell more about its services and not rush its sales message. One of the major selling points this company uses in promoting the service is that not only will it save the customer money on long distance because of lower rates, but the customers also can talk longer and not have to hurry their calls because the rates are so low. This company also uses an 800 number to enable prospects to sign up.

Direct Mail

In addition to acquiring residential customers through television, some companies also use direct mail. The packages are personalized and targeted only to selected areas where they offer the service and where research suggests a high incidence of heavy long-distance users. The approach is to qualify the prospect immediately by asking in the letter if the reader spends over $25 for long-distance calls each month. The rest of the materials, a brochure and a directory, promote the benefits of the service and tell the reader how to sign up. Significantly, there is no reply card. Instead, an 800 number is emphasized, and the prospect is encouraged to take fast action by calling immediately.

Third-Party Endorsements

Another approach these companies use to generate residential customers is to tie their services in with an exclusive offer from a third party. In one instance, American Express card holders were offered a special rate and an exclusive opportunity to sign up for a service. In another case, Visa and MasterCard card holders were given a similar opportunity.

These types of arrangements are used for a number of reasons. First, the endorsement from the card company adds instant credibility and value to the service. Second, for the card company, it's a way of offering something exclusive to their card holders, and this means an extra benefit from having the card. Still another reason is that it allows customers to pay with a credit card. Now heavy long-distance users can not only save money, they can charge their calls to their cards and pay in monthly installments.

BUSINESS CUSTOMER ACQUISITION

Specialized Television

One company has found that by changing their TV buy to evening and night time rather than changing the TV commercial itself, they also can change the type of customer they attract. Originally, this company used TV to generate residential customers and thus developed its commercials for this audience. But then they noticed that as much as 15 percent of their TV sales were business sales. Using direct marketing testing techniques, this company tested what would happen if it changed its TV buy in some markets and kept it the same in others. Results were analyzed, and in the markets where TV was running in evening and night time, there was a heavier level of business sales. Now this company is buying its air time based on the number of business customers or residential customers it wants from any given market.

Direct Mail

There is no question that direct mail is a natural for these companies to use to acquire business customers. First, using ZIP code or SCF segmentation, these marketers can reach only certain sections of a given market. This is important since the service may not be offered in all areas.

Another advantage of direct mail is that it allows these companies to promote only to selected types of businesses. One company has chosen to exclude any direct mail promotions to retail-type businesses because previous results showed that they didn't respond well. Another company has used direct mail because it was the most efficient way to target its message to only small and medium-size businesses.

Still another advantage of direct mail is that it enables these marketers to test the responsiveness of the marketplace to new creative ideas and different offers. One company experienced a tremendous lift in the response rate by waiving the sign-up fee for a limited time only. As a result, they decided to eliminate the sign-up fee for a limited time only in all their other marketing efforts. The result was a huge increase in the customer base and the uncovering of a business building tool that could be applied at selected intervals throughout the year to ensure that they met their customer acquisition objectives.

Print Advertising

Another way companies generate both leads and customers from the business marketplace is by means of print advertising. Vertical publications such as *Telecommunications and Telemarketing* offer an excellent opportunity to generate leads for multiple business sales. *The Wall Street Journal* also is used widely to reach business executives and promote the benefits of low-cost long-distance rates. In both publications, the approach is to emphasize the savings and how the dollars saved can improve a business's bottom line.

One major advantage of print advertising for these marketers is that it affords them the ability to promote their services only in selected regions. Most publications in the business sector offer metro editions or editions that reach only certain parts of the United States. This is an important point for these companies since their services are not available nationwide.

Another reason these marketers use print advertising is because they can measure the response. Each publication and each ad has its own special key code. Thus, different creative approaches can be tested and different magazines can be tested to determine their cost efficiency with regard to leads and sales.

SUMMARY

For two large segments of the telecommunications industry—the general telephone companies such as AT&T and GTE and the specialty long-distance companies such as MCI and Sprint—direct marketing has become an important element within the overall marketing mix. It can be used to stimulate toll activity, increase revenue, sell equipment, and generate leads and sales.

One of the major benefits of direct marketing for these companies is that it has enabled them to reach selected target audiences with product and service promotions that have been designed specifically for only these segments of the marketplace.

Additionally, because direct marketing is so measurable, it has helped these marketers test new concepts, new products, new offers, and new media and learn firsthand the cost efficiency and effectiveness of each marketing effort.

chapter 59

MAGAZINE CIRCULATION PROMOTION

Lawrence Fishbein

Circulation Manager
Blair & Ketcham's Country Journal
Brattleboro, Vt.

A magazine is one of the easiest businesses to start. Little capital is needed, relatively few tools of the trade are required, and tales of inexperienced people starting publications and making them hugely successful are heard selectively. This ease of entry may explain partially why every time there is a drop in the price of paper, a host of new magazines start up.

However, a magazine is no different from any other marketable item. To be successful, there must be a real demand; a potential audience large enough to support such a venture must exist. Reaching the members of this audience effectively, converting them into subscribers, and renewing them is the job of the magazine circulator.

THE ROLE OF THE CIRCULATOR

If the magazine is to carry advertising, it is the job of the circulator to provide an audience that wants the magazine and that advertisers want to reach.

Since the heyday of mass-circulation magazines, the marketing strategy of magazines has changed radically. Not long ago, the goal of the circulator and publisher was to pump out as many subscriptions as possible, whether they were profitable or not, as long as there was a large circulation for the advertisers to see and reach.

Rising magazine production and mailing costs, television, and the changing demands of advertisers put an end to old publishing theory and to several national publications. For those titles which did survive, their view of their circulation and advertising needs changed forever.

Then came the era of specialized magazines with their tailored editorial content and vertical audiences. Nowadays, as long as there is a segmented audience that advertisers want to reach, a magazine will exist to fill that niche.

For many reasons, the role of the magazine circulator was much easier when all that was required was to produce as many subscribers as possible, regardless of the source or demographic makeup. It always was thought and assumed that the advertisers would be willing to pay for these large circulations and that the advertising department always would be the profit center of the magazine.

However, with advertisers now looking at the makeup of the magazine audience instead of sheer numbers, publishers are looking to their circulation departments to be profit centers in and of themselves. With today's specialty magazines and tailored-down mass-circulated titles, it is incumbent on the circulator to meet this challenge effectively in the direct marketing of the magazine.

THE RENEWAL FACTOR

While the circulator must deliver subscribers who are interested in the subject matter to the editorial department and subscribers to the advertising departments in sufficient quantities to meet Audit Bureau of Circulations rate base guarantee figures that will support the advertisers in the magazine, the circulator also must deliver subscribers who are willing to renew their subscriptions to the publication. The renewing subscriber and the renewal subscription are the key element for any circulator as he or she plans a direct marketing strategy.

Volumes have been written about the effective use of direct mail, list segmentation, and the elements of good direct copy. But it is imperative to always make sure that whatever is being tested is being tested to produce a renewing subscriber. Of all the sources of business available to the circulator, none is as valuable and profitable as the renewal subscription. Also, none will be as loyal a reader to the editorial product, none as receptive to the advertisements carried in the magazine, and none as willing to pay the premium prices you will be charging.

TESTING STRATEGIES

When testing different marketing approaches, one should try to test the largest leverage items, that is, items which make the biggest difference on the bottom line. There is no quicker way to cripple a magazine than to deliver expensive new subscribers who do not renew. While much is said about the back end of the direct marketing promotion, it is the shortsighted magazine circulator who looks only at the back end of a promotion as the final pay-up instead of considering the true back end as the paid renewal subscription of that initial subscription acquisition.

Whatever source of business one is selling subscriptions by, be it direct mail, package inserts, or television, there are a number of techniques one can use to increase the effectiveness of the promotion. These generally can be categorized as segmentation, package, and offer.

Segmentation

Whether you are going to an outside list for a cold mail promotion, a merchandise program for package inserts, a television daypart, or even an in-house list for renewals, there has to be some sort of selection process to qualify the most productive units. The finer one can make this selection by components, the quicker and more profitably one will be able to make a list or a portion of that list work for the magazine.

People have set buying patterns; while it is important to keep these patterns in mind in the packages they receive, it also is important to take this same view when selecting lists or portions of these lists to use. For example, if one knows that a list is made up primarily of sweepstakes respondents and one's control package is not a sweepstakes, it can be quite difficult to make this list work, even though the list and the magazine share related subject matter. In this situation, it may be best to mail to only the nonsweepstakes portion of the list.

When audience selections are made, each list should be broken out into cells which can help define the highest performing segments of that particular list. Various forms of segmentation can include geographic, demographic, and merchandise breakouts along with recency of purchase breaks.

Geographic Selections. These can be made by entire regions, states, SCFs, five-digit ZIP codes, or groupings based on subscriber penetration analysis.

There may be merchandise breakouts within lists which can be made to work to the circulator's advantage. Unit purchases and dollar amount breakouts can also be useful when you are trying to match similarly priced items or trying to improve pay-up performances.

Other Segmentations. These may include the use of renewal portions of other magazine lists along with "hotline" or new names and other demographic breaks.

This is not to say that every list one tests should be broken out as many ways as possible. But if there is a subportion of a large list which would fit the makeup of a particular magazine, or if an entire list used to work and in recent mailings its effectiveness has declined, perhaps the least productive portions of these lists can be removed, leaving the profitable and responsive portion to mail to.

Seasonality. Another important part of segmentation to the magazine marketer is what time of year to mail. Generally, most magazines have very distinct mailing seasonality periods and trends. Besides the overall responsiveness to the magazine offer, some lists may be good to mail to in the spring months but not in the fall. Seasonality testing overall and within lists can be as important to the circulator as a list or package test.

The Package

Another element of merchandising for the direct magazine marketer is the package itself. The direct marketing package should have as its goal the acquisition of a renewal subscription.

As with almost all direct promotion solicitation, the basic package for a magazine offer is an outer envelope, an order card, a letter, a reply device, and a promotional brochure or lift memo. While this is the basic package, there are several variations, usually based on the actual intent of the package and the general familiarity with the magazine and the mailing universe.

Mixed among the promotion piece should be several concurrent themes and response devices that will tie the entire package together.

Creative Themes. The magazine direct promotion piece should reflect the tone and tenor of the magazine. Any promises made to the reader in the promotional piece concerning editorial content and the actual offer must be carried out by the magazine if there is to be a profitable and successful back-end pay-up and conversion renewal.

However, this is not to say that one should set artificial limits on the package. People will go out of their way to read into the promotional package what they would like the magazine to have and reflect back on them, and an effective circulation marketer can work this advantage to its fullest.

Since one can never test everything, one should choose to test leverage items that will make the biggest difference. This usually involves a totally new package, a revision to a package which came close to the response of the control, and minor revisions of the existing control package. Given a limited testing budget, say, for a small mailing, it makes little economic sense to test a package revision that may only contribute to a minor increase to the gross or net. This is not to say that minor revision testing should be excluded, but such tests should be made only with the control package, and not within major new package tests.

For the actual testing of packages, test only within proven and successful core lists and do not overlap package testing with list tests. It often is best to set aside a small portion of several core lists, merge them together, and then break them out on a random basis for package testing. This will ensure valid tests for the packages and lists.

The Envelope. The outer envelope for the direct mail piece should serve as the calling card for the magazine. Most experts consider the outside envelope the single most important element of the package, but it is sometimes neglected. The outer envelope must raise enough interest in the reader to ensure that the package will be opened. The actual subscription sell also should start with the outside carrier, and the theme of the outer envelope should carry throughout the package. This is not to say that the carrier has to be extravagant. It can be a plain number 10, but it must carry a message significant enough to get it opened.

Most people whom magazine marketers are trying to reach nowadays are familiar enough with magazine solicitation approaches that on receipt of the package, they know that it is a solicitation. With this as a given, it is up to the circulator to overcome this inertia and have them proceed to at least open the package. Ways of doing this vary. Many successful magazine marketers use the outer envelope copy to tease the reader with exclusive offers such as "special offer enclosed," "you have been selected," or "a copy of this magazine has been reserved for you."

Exclusivity offers can work for a variety of magazines and magazine offers, although they work best when the title being marketed is of special interest to a limited readership.

Other types of outer envelope promotion which can work are response deadlines, contests, quizzes, the start of the promotional letter, or anything else that can induce the reader to open the envelope and continue. Many publishers are finding that reply devices or tokens used in conjunction with the outer envelope can be successful.

When considering outer envelope copy, do not limit yourself to words. The effective use of photographs, illustrations, and artwork can work well. Magazines are a visual medium, and an effective use of artwork can make for an effective message of quality and perceived worth.

The Sales Letter. Once the package has been opened, it is up to the inside material to hold the readers and lead them to the logical conclusion of subscribing. A good portion of this responsibility falls to the sales letter. This letter must not only present the magazine in the best light possible, it must overcome the reader's natural resistance to buying something sight unseen, especially when this is a first time purchase.

As quickly as possible, the attention of the readers has to focus on the interplay between the magazine and themselves. As a general rule, people want to belong to a group that they can relate to actively or would like to be perceived as belonging to.

While being specific about what the editorial focus of the magazine is, there is also the necessity of activating the reader into the text of the letter. Readers must feel that they belong directly, should belong, or could receive some vicarious pleasure by belonging, even though they are not actively involved in the subject matter.

There is also a bit of a balancing act in a sales letter. First, the magazine must be presented in a broad light so that you do not disqualify too many qualified readers. Yet there is a need to be specific about the editorial content and the subject matter covered.

There should also be a logical reason given as to why the people who have received this solicitation have been selected and why they should respond. Because of the amount of direct promotion people receive, there is a certain amount of skepticism which must be overcome from the outset. Presenting the reader with good logical reasons goes a long way toward overcoming this problem. By giving the peron a logical reason to continue reading the promotion piece, one develops trust in the unseen and is better able to lead the reader to a logical reason to respond and subscribe.

If the magazine being marketed is not well known, a bit of credibility must be established up front in the sales letter. This can be done by giving a brief history of the magazine and its growth. Let readers know that the magazine is for them. Include recently published articles that will have broad enough appeal to cover the core lists you mail to regularly. If readers have gotten this far into your package, they will be looking for reasons to subscribe, and the mention of a single topic or subject may be enough to convince them.

If the magazine being marketed is better known, playing off the readers' noted absence or what the readers are missing that others know by reading the magazine often can be enough to make the readers feel that they have gone long enough without the publication.

During the course of the letter, whether the magazine is well known or not, readers must feel that they are an active and close part of the readership. Go to great lengths to activate readers into the letter. A letter is a personal item, and the readers must sense this personalization.

During the beginning of the letter, most marketers have found it effective to hint at the offer which will follow the end of the promotional piece. The offer in the letter should be stated clearly. If you've gotten readers this far, there is no use in losing them to a vaguely written and complicated offer. Be precise and don't hesitate to state why the person should subscribe.

The Response Device. The actual ordering of the magazine by the reader is the job of the response device. While basically designed to state the offer again, the reply device also should play on the reader's natural desire to complete a task. A response device should be clean in design and should lead to a logical progression of steps to complete.

The response device also provides an excellent vehicle to continue the sales message. If the magazine is well known but there is still some skepticism, this can be overcome by allowing readers to fill in their own term or length of the subscription. This type of offer not only overcomes a go-no go situation with the reader but also allows the reader to perform the closure or task completion.

Another popular response device is the use of tokens or reply stickers. People enjoy completing a task, and this is an easy way to overcome reader inertia.

While gimmicks can work, do not lose potential subscribers by asking them to do too much or by giving them too many options. While it would be advantageous, for example, to have all new subscribers sign up for 2 years, giving the option of a 1- or 2-year subscription represents a distraction from the original intention and would more than likely depress response.

Other Enclosures. Backing up the sales letter can be a brochure, a publisher's or creditor's memo, or a leave-behind item such as a decal or sticker. These items should be used to tie all the items in the letter together and should leave the reader with the feeling of getting something extra. This additional piece of the package also can be used as a way of personalizing the package for a specific list or geographic breakout of the mailing.

The business reply envelope (BRE) often takes a back seat to the rest of the mailing package as a result of legal and size limitations. However, the BRE offers another sales promotion tool, and many circulators are making this last piece work to their benefit.

Price and Offer

Whatever type of package one is using and whatever the type or source of business the promotional piece is designed for, there is still the consideration of the price of the magazine, the term of the subscription, and the type of offer to be used. Another key element is the overlay of this triad and the interaction between the three elements. Finding the most effective combination often requires long and complicated testing.

For the most part, magazines are no different from any other merchandise in terms of pricing. The higher the price, the lower the response. However, how the price is presented can be important.

When determining price structures for magazines, one of the key decisions will be whether to discount the first year of the subscription as an introductory offer. Many magazines have found that offering a discounted subscription and then stepping the subscriber up in price during the renewal cycle can be a successful and profitable way of introducing the magazine to a wider, more price-sensitive audience. The downside of this is that you are offering a multipriced schedule, and the very price sensitive portion of your audience will be well aware of this and thus may not renew. Also to be considered when offering discounted subscriptions is the amount of time necessary to get the subscriber up to a full-priced subscription and the number of potential renewals one will lose by doing this. Also, when offering discounted subscriptions, the publisher's prices will be rising. If the circulation department is to be a profit center unto itself, carrying heavily discounted new subscriptions and reduced renewals can cut into profit margins.

When offering discounted or even full-price subscriptions, many magazines have found it advantageous to make comparisons with the newsstand price. This can make even a full-price offer sound like a saving. The savings can be shown in actual dollar amounts but are more often represented by percentages.

If the subscription price being offered is low, play up that fact heavily but avoid the low-price–low-quality trap. If the offer one is making is the lowest price available, make that claim big.

If the magazine price is high, it is important to play on the exclusivity of the title and stress that it is not for everyone. This is especially true for titles that do not discount for new subscribers.

Other ways of getting around what may seem to readers as a high price is to offer the subscription at a per copy price. For example, a magazine that has found price sensitivity to an $11.95 offer may be able to make a "less than $1 a month" offer work.

As circulation departments are asked to contribute more to the bottom line and magazine prices increase, many publishers have gone or are going to installment billing as a way to alleviate threshold price resistance. Instead of offering a subscription at $35 a year, the magazine will bill the subscriber at four payments of $8.75 each.

Another way of overcoming the resistance to a magazine offer is to vary the term of the subscription. Generally, magazines offer short and regular terms and then try to sell renewals for the long term. When offering short-term subscriptions, enough time must be allowed between the payment of the subscription on the front end and the start of the renewal series on the back end.

Letting potential subscribers pick their own terms for the subscription at a preset rate is another way of overcoming price and offer sensitivity. It lets subscribers feel that they have a say in specifying their own subscriptions.

Offering longer-term subscriptions usually is stressed in renewal offers. In some cases, with professional and business titles, an inducement to the longer term is insurance for continuity of receipt of the magazine over an extended period of time.

Upgrading a new subscriber to a longer term also can be done when invoices are going out from the initial subscription solicitation. An offer can be made to new subscribers to renew or extend their subscriptions by doubling the initial offer and therefore doubling the savings. This is commonly called renewal at birth and can be used not only to extend a subscription and enhance renewability but also for effective cash management.

Premiums. An added inducement to aid in subscription acquisition is the use of premiums. Premiums are items of actual or perceived worth that are given away when a person subscribes with an unpaid order or if the order is contingent on payment. Once again, premiums are a way of inducing someone to act and serve to break down the resistance of subscribing since the reader will be receiving not only the magazine but also a related item free. The use of premiums can be beneficial in the acquisition of trial subscriptions and in some cases renewal subscriptions. They also can increase the initial back-end pay-up for the magazine if they are tied to pay-up. However, the use of premiums may depress the initial total of gross orders.

Besides price and term variables, another form of inducement to subscribe can be the offer itself. The effective use of the offer can be one of the highest leverage items in a total package.

Startup magazines and magazines which have been revamped or overhauled can take advantage of charter and premiere offers. These offers play on exclusivity and offer the subscriber the unique advantage of being the first to get something.

Sweepstakes Offers. These have been used for a long time by magazines to secure a large enough gross response with the hope of getting enough back-end payment to make the promotion profitable. Sweepstakes generally fall into three categories of offers. One makes entry a prerequisite for winning, or a "you may have won" offer may be done with predetermined winners. Another type of sweepstakes is a "you have won" offer where all entries are winners. Most of the prizes, however, are insignificant.

Time Value Offers. Other types of offers include programs which are tied to a specific time of year and offer the subscriber the chance to start the subscription with the start of a specific season.

Examples of this may be a sports magazine offering a subscription tied in with the start of the football season or a news magazine tying its promotional campaigning to the start of the presidential election. Naturally, the hope of this type of offer is to tie the heightened awareness of an event with the editorial content of the magazine.

Trial Offers. Offers which require no concurrent special event usually have to do with reducing the perceived risk to the subscriber of buying something sight unseen. For the most part, these are trial offers and can be used quite effectively as long as the back-end performance can be made to work profitably. These offers play up the idea that the subscription is a trial and can be canceled at any time for a full refund or a refund for unmailed issues. Many magazines have made effective use of the offer that a subscription will be entered and the first issue will be sent free. After the subscriber has had a chance to inspect this free issue, when the bill arrives, the subscriber has the option of canceling without further liability.

These offers play on the potential subscribers' desire to reduce risk and get something for nothing. To make these offers work, key words such as "free," "free trial subscription," "no risk," and "no obligation" are played on prominently.

SUBSCRIPTION SOURCES

The major new sources of subscriptions available to a circulator are direct mail, gift subscriptions, bind-in and blow-in cards or envelopes in the actual magazine, package insert and piggyback programs, space advertisements, television, and agency orders.

Direct Mail

Direct mail traditionally has been a major source of subscriptions for the magazine industry. As a source of business, it is extremely controllable, can be tested endlessly to improve results, can deliver subscriptions when they are needed, and can be delivered to the exact audience a magazine is looking for.

Since mailing sizes can be predetermined, direct mail is an effective way to maintain a level subscription base and also to stimulate predictable growth.

Renewals

Renewals from direct mail subscriptions can vary greatly for the same magazine, depending on list, offer, price, package, conversion renewal prices, and the initial effectiveness of the direct mail campaign. It usually holds true that as one moves down to the least effective lists, the renewal rates from these marginal subscriptions will be lower.

Gift Subscriptions

These have always been a very profitable source of business for magazines. They are usually sold at a premium price to the gift donor with an inexpensive mailing package. Adding to the desirability of gifts is that these subscriptions have extremely high pay-up rates and high renewal rates. The source of gift subscriptions, however, usually is limited to one's own house file.

Bind-in and Blow-in Cards

These are also relatively inexpensive forms of subscription acquisition. While the pay-up to these cards can vary, it is usually quite good since the subscriber has seen the magazine already. Since most magazines are distributed to existing subscribers or sold on the newsstand, it is often advisable to have different cards placed in each of these patterns of distribution to stimulate responses among these two different types of readers.

Package Inserts

These are promotion pieces which are inserted for a fee within another company's merchandise shipments. Take-ones are leave-behind items which are placed in high-volume traffic areas and are picked up by interested people. Piggybacks are mailings done in cooperation with several mailers, where the mailing and sometimes the production costs are shared by all the mailers involved. The advantage of these programs is that the promotional pieces involved are usually inexpensive to produce, and the distribution costs are not nearly as expensive as they are for a direct mail piece. While the costs involved are small, the results usually are not as good as with other forms of direct marketing.

An advantage to package insert programs is that they can be developed specifically for the editorial and advertising thrust of a magazine. Also, the respondents are proven merchandise buyers, which pleases advertisers. The difficulty with package inserts is that the circulator is tied to the program's production and distribution patterns, which can vary from year to year and are subject to the merchandisers' own marketing problems.

Advertising

Placing ads for one's magazine in another publication is another way of targeting an audience which will be responsive. The advantage is that these ads usually can be done on an exchange basis or at a reduced publisher's rate and can be a steady source of new business.

Television

Selling subscriptions through direct-response television is a relatively new marketing concept which is coming into its own not only for mass-market magazines but also for small specialized titles. Television offers the circulator a unique impact with an extremely broad audience. Also, because of the unique character of television, there is an immediate credibility which is hard to match with more traditional direct marketing techniques.

A major advantage of using television is the ability to deliver respondents to one's magazine instantly, unlike other direct mail forms, which may take weeks or months.

The disadvantage to television is that since there is no response device, almost all the orders are on a credit basis, and therefore a great deal of weight falls on the collection series to make the promotion work.

Agency

Another form of circulation marketing which accounts for varying amounts of circulation for many types of magazines is the agency-sold subscription. These subscriptions are sold by a third party, usually in conjunction with several other titles. The advantage of this type of order is that there are virtually no up-front promotion costs involved on the part of the magazine. However, the remittance rate from these third-party sellers is often small. Making these agency-sold subscriptions profitable depends on the ability of the circulator to convert these orders into renewal subscriptions. Given the nature of these respondents, who usually are extremely price-sensitive, the renewability of these subscriptions is below that of other sources.

BRINGING IT ALL TOGETHER

Given all these ways to acquire subscriptions through various sources and all the prices and terms available, it is the job of the circulator to pull all these variables together and come up with the most profitable long-range circulation mix while maintaining the rate base guarantee. If all the subscription sources had similar pay-up characteristics, renewal response rates, and demographics, the job of creating an effective mix would be a lot easier. Unfortunately, each source and each mix of price, term, and offer will have different effects on pay-up and renewal patterns.

The job of creating the proper circulation mix has been enhanced by the advent of computer publishing models. Based on known historical characteristics of how certain sources to a given magazine will respond, the computer can compare and rank all the variables available to the circulator and provide an optimum circulation mix.

The computer publishing model also provides a nearly limitless ability to play "what if" games such as: "If the renewal percentage of an agency-sold subscription can be increased by 5 percent, how will this affect its profitability ranking in comparison to an existing direct mail program with an up-front response of 6 percent, a payoff of 65 percent, and a conversion renewal response rate of 52 percent?"

Of constant concern to the circulator is the effect of the next marginal subscription sold and its renewability, in comparison to the subscription before it, from every available source. Since most magazines' ability to make a profit relies on the renewal subscription, the effect that the last subscription sold has on the total renewal rate is of the utmost importance. To achieve and maintain a profitable position when adding subscribers to a file, the next subscription added should always be the next most profitable long-range subscription available.

Computer publishing models also can be used to determine the amount of circulation business a magazine must generate to maintain the advertising rate base. They can accomplish this by tracking the current subscriber file as subscribers renew or do not renew and as the ones who do not renew are replaced. These figures are based on the expiration analysis of the magazine and the new business which is added.

From its heyday as a medium of gathering as many subscribers as possible, modern magazine circulation marketing has evolved into what can be described as part science and part art. The effective circulator must mix the reality of numbers and the art of design and copy to reach the most profitable audience for a magazine's editorial and advertising reach.

chapter 60

INTERNATIONAL DIRECT MARKETING

Peter J. Rosenwald

President
Peter J. Rosenwald &
International Associates
New York, N.Y.

In the beginning, there was no international direct marketing. As each country's industry grew, it was clearly independent of what was being done in other countries. It was generally assumed that each country was a unique market with few similarities to be exploited.

This attitude changed with the end of World War II and the growth of the multinational companies. With few strategic advertising and marketing changes, Coca Cola and "whiter than white" detergents appealed to people of all nationalities. Why shouldn't the same appeal apply to other products and services which have recognizable benefits in themselves and, of equal importance, in their mail-order distribution system?

International direct marketing is the product of better communications and understanding among the commercial nations of the world. It is a relatively new field with too few skilled practitioners. Direct marketing grows as more and more companies find out that good ideas, products, and marketing cross national borders without difficulty. It is a phenomenon of the past 20 years which is likely to continue as long as there is a relatively peaceful society in the United States and western Europe.

It is dangerous to generalize on the multinational aspects of direct marketing. Each case takes a blend of general direct marketing knowledge and a careful mix of national factors. But its success is evidenced by the growing importance of the International Direct Marketing Symposium—the annual meeting for direct marketers from all over the world, held in Montreux, Switzerland. There practitioners

The tables in this chapter are from the DMA *Fact Book on Direct Response Marketing*, Direct Marketing Association, New York, 1982. Used by permission.

find the international idea and activity exchange valuable not only in making international contacts and gaining international experience, but also in formulating their domestic direct marketing activities.

National Similarities and Differences

Tables 60-1 through 60-4 provide a general reference to the comparative size and direct marketing activity level of the various major international markets.

Industry figures from each of the countries are not entirely reliable, because of the different definitions of direct marketing activities, but they provide at least some idea of the volume of direct marketing business. As can be seen from Table 60-4, direct mail is clearly the primary direct-response medium in almost all countries, even in Japan, which has no preferential postal rates for direct marketing and where the postage of any letter is $0.30.

As can be seen from the data contained in Tables 60-1 through 60-4, the differences between countries appear to be more significant than the similarities. This is a classic case of seeing the size of the forests instead of the distinctive aspects of the trees. The similarities in the needs and desires of most of the individuals in these countries have more to compare than to contrast. People's needs and desires vary only in articulation and social tradition, not in their basic motivation. Most French, English, and German people share equal desires for enriching their lifestyle, making convenient purchases, acquiring novelty, etc.

While individual national habits vary, the broad appeal of fashion (catalogs), education and entertainment (books and records), fitness (Bullworker and similar exercise equipment), prestige (limited editions such as Franklin Mint offerings as

TABLE 60-1 DMA Summary on International Postal Services

Country	Population	Number of Households	Postal Service
Australia	14,795,000	4,300,000	Fair and reliable.
Austria	7,500,000	2,500,000	Good, reliable, slow, and expensive.
Belgium	9,900,000	3,240,000	For specific information contact National Mail Order Association.
Canada	23,000,000	7,000,000	Expensive.
Denmark	5,110,000	2,210,000	Fair but fast; first class only.
Finland	4,786,867	1,800,000	Expensive but efficient.
France	55,000,000	17,000,000	Expensive and highly regulated.
Germany	61,300,000	24,200,000	Excellent.
Great Britain	56,000,000	20,000,000	Steadily more expensive.
Hong Kong	4,900,000	1,100,000	Overseas services very good. Excellent as a Far East mailing center.
Japan	NA	36,000,000	Reliable.
The Netherlands	14,090,000	4,543,000	Costly, but good.
Norway	4,092,340	1,600,000	Contact DMA International in Paris for further information.
Spain	37,600,000	9,351,000	Improving.
Sweden	8,300,000	3,600,000	Expensive.
Switzerland	6,365,000	2,320,000	Highly efficient and expensive.

TABLE 60-2 Direct Marketing Expenditures, 1979

Millions of U.S. Dollars	
Country	Amount
1. United States	$19,748.2
2. West Germany	2,236.1
3. United Kingdom	1,150.1*
4. Japan	759.2
5. Netherlands	510.0
6. France	500.0
7. Canada	495.3
8. Switzerland	240.0
9. Austria	150.0
10. Norway (est.)	72.0
11. Italy	50.0
12. South Africa	32.8
13. Finland	30.0
14. Mexico	19.9
15. Denmark	18.1
16. Hong Kong	2.0
17. Singapore	1.1
18. Thailand	NA

Source: DMA/IAA 1980 Survey.

* This figure excludes the "agency catalog with credit" sales operations which represent some 80 to 85 percent of UK catalog sales.

TABLE 60-3 Sales Attributed to Direct Marketing

	Millions of U.S. Dollars		
Country	1980 (est.)	1979	1978
1. United States	$110,000.0	$99,000.0	$87,000.0
2. West Germany	10,100.0	9,445.0	8,833.0
3. France	NA	3,559.5	3,047.0
4. United Kingdom	3,000.0	NA	NA
5. Japan	2,420.7	2,050.0	1,737.0
6. Canada	1,349.1	1,308.9	1,274.0
7. Netherlands	700.0	612.5	538.0
8. Italy	588.0	488.2	370.0
9. Denmark	240.0	227.2	212.0
10. Finland	203.7	167.9	144.0
11. Mexico	100.0	85.0	80.0
12. South Africa	27.9	25.2	25.0
13. Singapore	19.4	12.1	NA
14. Austria	5.0	NA	NA
15. Hong Kong	NA	NA	NA
16. Norway	NA	NA	NA
17. Switzerland	NA	NA	NA
18. Thailand	NA	NA	NA

Source: DMA/IAA 1980 Survey.

TABLE 60-4 Breakdown of Total Direct Mail and/or Direct Response (DM/DR) Advertising Expenditures by Media (in millions of dollars)

	Austria		Canada		Denmark		Finland		France		Hong Kong		Italy		Japan		Mexico	
	$	%	$	%	$	%	$	%	$	%	$	%	$	%	$	%	$	%
(A) Direct mail	NA	NA	282.2	57.2	14.5	80	NA	NA	433.0	86	NA	NA	45	90	535.9	71	16.5	82.5
(B) DM/DR magazine space	NA	NA	85	17.2			NA	NA			NA	NA			44.7	6	1.2	6
(C) DM/DR magazine inserts	NA	NA	21.3	4	1.8	10	NA	NA	50.9	10	NA	NA	5	10	22.3	3	1.7	8.5
					(B & C)				(B–E)				(B–J)					
(D) DM/DR newspaper space	NA	NA	42.6	8			NA	NA			NA	NA			89.3	13	.2	1.0
(E) DM/DR newspaper preprints	NA	NA	21.3	4	1.8	10	NA	NA			NA	NA			.9	—	—	—
					(D & E)													
(F) DM/DR telephone marketing	NA	NA	22.9	4	—	—	NA	NA	5.9	1	NA	NA			—	—	—	—
(G) DM/DR coupons	NA	NA	17.0	3	—	—	NA	NA	—	—	NA	NA			59.4	8	—	—
(H) DM/DR television	NA	NA	.85	.001	—	—	NA	NA	—	—	NA	NA			2.2	—	—	—
(I) DM/DR radio	NA	NA	—	—	—	—	NA	NA	10.2	2	NA	NA			4.4	—	.23	1.5
(J) Other	—	—	—	—	—	—	—	—	—	—	—	—			—	—	—	—
TOTAL	150		495.3		18.1		30		500		2		50		759.2		19.85	

TABLE 60-4 Breakdown of Total Direct Mail and/or Direct Response (DM/DR) Advertising Expenditures by Media (in millions of dollars) *(Continued)*

	Netherlands		Norway		Singapore		South Africa		Switzerland		Thailand		United Kingdom*		U. S. A.		West Germany	
	$	%	$	%	$	%	$	%	$	%	$	%	$	%	$	%	$	%
(A) Direct Mail	NA	NA	NA	NA	. 14	13.2	32.8	99	NA	NA	NA	NA	1,150.0*	—	8,876.0	—	2,236.1	—
(B) DM/DR magazine space	NA	NA	2.6	3.6	.095	9.0	—	—	NA	NA	NA	NA	NA	NA	123.0	—	NA	NA
(C) DM/DR magazine inserts	NA	NA	NA	NA	.019	2.0	—	—	NA	NA	NA	NA	NA	NA	Na	—	NA	NA
(D) DM/DR newspaper space	NA	NA	4.4	6.1	.80	75.8	—	—	NA	NA	NA	Na	NA	NA	54.4	—	NA	NA
(E) DM/DR newspaper preprints	NA	NA	NA	NA	—	—	—	—	NA	NA	NA	NA	NA	NA	1,779.5	—	NA	NA
(F) DM/DR telephone marketing	NA	NA	NA	NA	—	—	.0006	—	NA	NA	NA	NA	NA	NA	8,555.6 (1978 figure)	—	NA	NA
(G) DM/DR coupons	NA	NA	NA	NA	—	—	—	—	NA	NA	NA	NA	NA	NA	72.0	—	NA	NA
(H) DM/DR television	NA	NA	NA	NA	—	—	—	—	NA	NA	NA	NA	NA	NA	217.0	—	NA	NA
(I) DM/DR radio	NA	NA	NA	NA	—	—	—	—	NA	NA	NA	NA	NA	NA	23.0	—	NA	NA
(J) Other	—	—	NA	NA	—	—	—	—	NA	NA	NA	NA	NA	NA	47.0†	—	NA	NA
TOTAL	510		7.0‡		1.054		32.8		240.0		NA		1,150.0		19,748.2		2,236.1	

* For *United Kingdom* calculations, "DM" means consumer and industrial direct mail advertising; "DR" means response in various media. These definitions *exclude* 80 to 85 percent of DM sales since this portion is the "agency catalog with credit" sales operation.

† For the U.S.A., this figure represents business magazines (industrial products only).

‡ Estimated figure is 72.0 million.

well as convenience products such as credit cards) and financial services (insurance and other financial product offers), to mention only the most obvious, cross national boundaries without the need of passports.

The need to overcome one of the most glaring of marketing and distribution problems—the increasingly high cost of the visit of a salesperson—is also international. Thus, everyone in the business-to-business area, from office equipment makers (IBM and Xerox, for example) to multiproduct giants (such as British Petroleum and General Foods), have found that lower-priced or highly specialized products which do not justify the cost of a personal sales call can be marketed "direct," leaving the sales force to concentrate on those products and services which have a high enough price or broad enough market to justify the cost of an individual sales visit.

The enormous worldwide sales of the Sinclair Personal Calculator were achieved almost entirely using coupon advertising and direct mail with nearly identical copy and approach throughout the world. This is an excellent example of a product which did not have a natural distribution outlet, or the price or margins necessary to support an individual sales force. Sinclair was, therefore, almost compelled to "go direct." More and more companies have come to recognize that, as products become more complex and their life cycles become shorter, direct marketing offers an excellent way of getting to the marketplace. Individual consumers and businesses can all be reached through the many media available to the enterprising direct marketer.

Knowing Your Markets

Nothing is more important to the success of international direct marketing (or, one might venture to say, any international activity) than getting to know the individual markets. The company which "saves money" by restricting the travel activity of the individual managers concerned with international direct marketing is being "pound foolish." Travel—not as a tourist, but hard, operational, shirt-sleeve travel with a concentration on what is and is not working in the direct marketing arena in a given country—is the key to success in any international activity. As indicated in the DMA *Fact Book*, "A promotional concept which has worked successfully in one country is more likely to work in other countries than a promotional concept which has failed to work in its country of origin."[1]

While many of the direct marketing innovations have arisen in the United States, it would be wrong to presume that U.S. direct marketing activity dominates the world. Because of increased exchange of information and techniques during the past decade, the tremendous investment in experimentation and development which was undertaken in the United States made it possible for many overseas countries to leapfrog the learning stage and go right to new developments based on what had already been learned. Thus, La Redoute and Bertelsman, two of the most forward-looking European direct marketing companies, have not only learned many techniques from American practitioners but have made substantial innovations on their own, which have been copied by great American enterprises such as Spiegel and the Book-of-the-Month Club.

[1] Direct Marketing Association, 1982.

A Checklist for Entering a New Market

Entering any new market is fraught with danger. In the international arena, the dangers are heightened by language, social convention, media availability, delivery systems, payment modes, governmental regulations, and consumerism. Unlike the factors governing entry into a new domestic market, these factors vary considerably between countries. Differences are far more pronounced than the differences between market segments within one country, especially the United States, which has the world's best direct marketing infrastructure.

Thus it is useful to have a simple checklist of things which should be considered when entering a new international market. (The following checklist is not all-inclusive; it does not list such essentials as corporate legal structure and international tax and profit repatriation questions, all of which must be considered, preferably by able international lawyers.)

1. Is the product or service likely to be successful in the market? Do similar products or services exist, and how are they marketed?
2. What specific or general consumerist or governmental regulations exist concerning the product? (In Germany, for example, nothing labeled as a medicine can be sold except by a licensed pharmacist; the possibility of selling vitamins by mail is therefore nonexistent.)
3. Is there adequate media availability to permit accurate testing and rollout? Are there sufficient mailing lists available and/or media in which to run coupon ads, so that if tests are successful they can be expanded into a full-scale marketing program?
4. Are there any social conventions which would appear to inhibit the success of the product or service? (It was generally believed that supplemental health insurance would not work in the United Kingdom because of the National Health System. This was proven, in test, not to be the case.)
5. Are payment modes suitable for the successful collection of money? Is there a high (or low) concentration of credit cards, a traditional use of the postal Giro system, or some other means of payment?
6. Is there a good postal delivery system, and have all promotion, product delivery, and collection needs been geared to both the strengths and weaknesses of the individual system?
7. Is the telephone an effective sales or follow-up medium, and what are the best hours to telephone? (Hours differ according to individual national customs and are of critical importance.)
8. If successful, will the product be copied and media preempted by aggressively competitive local merchants?
9. Are there restrictions on advertising materials (rules concerning competitive claims, premium values, sweepstakes, etc.), and will these unacceptably dilute promotions or make it impossible to use existing and tested promotions from other markets?
10. Could the same amount of money and effort be better used somewhere else to greater profit and with more likelihood of success?

Testing and Rollouts on an International Scale

Where is it best to test? And where is it best to rollout the test with the maximum chance of success?

The simple answer to these questions is that testing should be done where the greatest potential for expansion or rollout exists and where it is possible to test accurately with a minimum of exposure. Sadly, this ideal situation, which does exist in the United States, exists almost nowhere else.

The U.S. reader without international experience will find this a little hard to believe. In the United States there is a broadly based list rental business organized and run along ethical and highly mechanized lines. The rental of noncompetitive buyers' names is standard. The availability of name lists organized demographically, psychographically, and in almost every conceivable configuration makes the choice of what names to use an important marketing function. The same is true of print and broadcast media. Specialized magazines cover everything from jogging to health foods; broadcast channels and stations can be chosen for programming ranging from religious to sports or all news. It is, for the most part, an organized sellers' market.

This is not so in any other country—at least not to the same extent. A long history of commercial exploitation and relative freedom from regulation in the United States has created a situation where there is less secrecy and restriction than in any other world market. No other country has developed the list rental and exchange business to nearly the same degree as it exists in the United States. Many, like the Scandinavian countries, have substantial restrictions on the rental of lists or use of names for commercial purposes. And no other country has an equally unfettered and economically promising media spectrum for direct marketing.

In light of this, it becomes obvious that testing must be done only in countries with a sufficiently large market to warrant the investment of money and energy—preferably with a test that is replicable in at least one other market, if successful.

For products in almost all categories, the United Kingdom offers a reasonably good opportunity for testing and rollout. Great Britain offers a market of 20 million households, a reasonable (if inadequate by U.S. standards) number of lists for rent and a good, if expensive, postal system. Most companies entering the market extensively use the national newspapers for the purpose of building mailing lists and then use these lists in exchanges with other mailers and in regular offers to the list. Newspaper advertising costs almost exactly one-tenth as much per thousand as direct mail (£2.05 or $3.08 per thousand for the average full-page newspaper ad versus £200 or $300 per thousand for mail). As in the United States, the press advertising pulls approximately one-tenth the number of replies. But it is easier to develop a press campaign with quick turnaround and expansion than a direct mail campaign with all the inherent organizational problems which beset this medium.

For the English-speaking direct marketer, Great Britain also offers a convenience facility; if the British don't speak exactly the same language as Americans, they are linguistically much easier to deal with than any country in which English is not the *lingua franca.*

France is probably second best. The direct-response market has been increasing, and the payment record of the French is comparatively good, with over 80 percent paying cash. Nontextile housewares are the largest growth sector of the market. Mailing lists, while limited, are available through brokers and on a traded basis. Media, while not available on as broad a basis as in Great Britain, is still plentiful and reasonably priced. Black and white newspaper space costs 137 francs or $19.57 per thousand, while direct mail averages 3000 francs or $432.90 per thousand. With a population almost as large as that of Great Britain (but approximately 3 million fewer households), the market is familiar with and receptive to direct marketing solicitation.

In both Great Britain and France, direct marketing service facilities are available with list houses, fulfillment services, specialist advertising agencies, and free-lancers able to give help where needed. A bonus feature of starting in the U.K. is that the other English-speaking markets (Australia and South Africa as well as English Canada and the United States) are natural points of expansion. From France, the expansion goes quite naturally into the French part of Switzerland and Belgium as well as French Canada.

A foothold in both markets is a natural enough starting point for an international direct marketing effort. This is not to say that these are the only test markets. Certainly the strong German economy, with its more than 24 million homes and its possibilities of expansion into Austria and German Switzerland, also offers opportunities worth investigating.

The decision on where and how much to test ought to be made on the basis of such criteria as product location, market acceptance of similar products, etc. With all things being more or less equal on these points, Great Britain and France probably offer the best testing and rollout situations outside the United States.

Planning an International Campaign

Planning an international direct marketing campaign has all the detailed aspects of planning a domestic campaign, multiplied by the number of countries and the specific and important differences from one to another. On the positive side, much can be done centrally so that as the campaign is expanded from one country (or language market) to another, only language, price, and other "black plate" changes need be made. It is possible to centralize the data processing and, to a lesser extent, the actual fulfillment.

Time frames are critical in an international campaign, more so than in a domestic one, simply because communications errors are compounded exponentially. Simplicity is not always the best policy, but before abandoning it as a guiding principle, have something very good to put in its place. The more complicated the project, the more time it will take and the higher the chance of error. That said, it should be remembered that the quality and impact of the promotion is the single most important aspect of its chance of success. This must not be compromised for convenience.

Planning the Time Frame

In planning an international campaign, it is good to work on a critical path time frame developed backwards from the desired promotional dates in the first country, and forward from the time when it is possible to read the results accurately. Just as in the United States, reading the results is a back-end as well as a front-end task. Many an international direct marketing campaign has had a very favorable response to the offer, only to run into product returns or continuity drop-off rates which change the picture from black to red. Going international too early compounds the problem. Going too fast in international direct marketing, as in driving, is very dangerous.

Overcoming this danger means exercising caution—reading the results carefully before expanding from one country to another and rolling out only when the indications are favorable and clear.

If direct mail is involved, the period backwards from the direct mail drop date to the initial work is almost always a minimum of 6 months. Prior to that, legal structures must be completed and recognition from national regulatory agencies obtained. During the initial 6 months, even with a successful U.S. promotion as a point of departure, lists have to be negotiated, production ordered, fulfillment arranged, product brought into inventory, and all the other complex tasks undertaken.

Print advertising is faster and is recommended for a test in which security is not a significant factor. The lead time is considerably shorter, especially if you plan to use a newspaper with a short closing (as contrasted with magazines which are likely to have a longer period between insertion and publication). In the case of print media, assuming that there is an executive with the responsibility for production decisions on the ground in the country, the lead time can probably be reduced to 2 to 3 months.

After the test, and with positive results on both the initial and the back-end response, expanding to a few other countries will take another 4 to 6 months, if a corporate structure is in place—more if it is not. But you can feel comfortable about expanding into more than one country at the same time; a lot of the basic work on systems and pieces of the promotion and fulfillment will already have been done.

Nonetheless, critical parts of the equation are the executive staff available to you and its deployment. All too many international direct marketing activities have failed because the companies desiring an international expansion have delegated the responsibility either to one of the senior executives as a foreign travel "bonus" or to an untried executive. The field is strewn with the corpses.

When Doubleday bought an interest in the direct marketing activities of Great Britain's largest news dealer chain, W.H. Smith & Sons, Ltd., they sent their mail order guru, Milton Runyon, to virtually live in Great Britain to make their program work. It was an investment which paid for itself over and over, and should be a positive lesson. Many chief executives who wanted to legitimatize their pleasurable travel abroad have simply hired an advertising agency and a law firm, attended a few meetings, and then wondered why their projects never got off the ground, or worse, flew for a bit and then crashed.

While there is a definite need for a good local specialist agency and for good legal advice, neither can effectively play the role of the client. Only someone with an intimate knowledge of the business and a sense of commitment to it can properly represent it in something as important as international expansion. To paraphrase that old saw about the cost of fuel for a giant yacht: if you have to pinch pennies on management of an international enterprise, you shouldn't have one. And if held to a very tight time line, either the project should not be undertaken or the rights should be licensed to local companies with on-the-grounds management and operations. Let them take both the risks and the lion's share of the profits.

To Go or Not to Go International

We no longer live in an insular world. International business is a happy fact of our existence. Good ideas cross borders with great speed and agility. The international arena offers great direct marketing opportunities for those companies willing to make a major investment of time, money, and work force and with the will and the sticking power to succeed. Over the past quarter of a century, the international game has gotten both easier and harder, as well as increasingly interesting.

Facilities have become more abundant and services more readily available. Draconian exchange control regulations which prevented the distribution of profits from many countries are now relatively rare in major markets, making international commerce flow more smoothly than in earlier days.

On the negative side, a U.S. company with a good idea cannot just walk in and take over the market, which used to be possible. Those days were over long ago. Franklin Mint, Time-Life Books, and American Express have been successful, not because it was easy, but because they were prepared to invest the financial and personnel resources in the opportunity and stay with it, despite the increasing local competition. Just at the point when these companies and others like them had overcome the teething problems of their early days, the nationals in the various countries in which they operate became more and more sophisticated and competitively took a share of the growing market. Because the markets were and still are expanding, smaller shares still mean substantial businesses.

The Art of War, a military manual written by a Chinese soldier, Sun Tzu, in the first century B.C. is now a much-revered volume among Japanese managers. It states that one of the critical factors which determines victory is amassing more information than that possessed by adversaries. One reason Japanese executives have been so successful at finding market niches in western countries is that they spare nothing in gathering market and product information. They then use it as an economic weapon with great strength and skill. To be successful in the international arena, this is essential.

Armed with enough information to identify the opportunity, an aggressive company can still build a profitable and rewarding business overseas. But it must be a top priority, or no priority at all.

The tenth item in the checklist for entering a new international market given earlier in this chapter asks: Could the same amount of money and effort be better used elsewhere to greater profit, with more likelihood of success? That is the question which must be asked over and over again, especially in difficult economic times. Only when the answer is an affirmative "yes" does it make sense to go into the international market on your own. There are a number of ways open to a company which wants to be international but doesn't want to go it alone. The following are examples of ways in which major U.S. companies have organized their international operations:

- Hanover House, the highly successful catalog company, sells exclusive licenses to its know-how, its product sourcing, and its pricing to catalog companies in a number of countries for a flat annual fee plus an override on merchandise bought through Hanover House. It is a simple means of getting income with a minimum amount of extra management effort and expense.

- Doubleday, as described earlier, chose the route of a joint venture with an established local company. The local company had the structure and tremendous buying power in the book and record area. Doubleday brought direct marketing and especially book club expertise to the party, as well as capital.
- Time-Life Books, after a number of efforts at other forms of commercial relationships, decided to go it alone, centering management and fulfillment operations in Amsterdam. At that time, international postal rates there favored their type of operation.
- Wunderman, Ricotta & Kline, the direct marketing advertising agency, started abroad with joint ventures in Great Britain and France, before building wholly owned operations in other countries.
- Walt Disney Productions sells the overseas publishing rights to any responsible company that is prepared to pay a royalty for the use of the product, as well as the advertising and marketing information built up in the primary market.

These are just some of the ways leading American companies decided to use their resources to the best advantage in building overseas direct marketing businesses. There are many more. As indicated in the examples above, the four most frequently employed options are:

- Sell expertise and unique skills to buyers in each possible country. Foster those relationships; be content with less profit but no risk.
- Make a joint venture with existing companies which have unique market positions and share in the risk and the profits (or losses), making certain that both parties bring complementary skills to the venture.
- Go it alone, or go it alone from the vantage point of an existing joint venture in one or two countries.
- Sell the rights to your product or service to the highest bidder on a royalty basis and be content with that.

Each of these routes will appeal to management seeking international expansion. Which one to take, as emphasized above, depends on the priority given and the resources which are available. The opportunities are abundant and not always obvious. Weigh the options carefully.

While the major European markets have acquired great international direct marketing sophistication, there is a paucity of direct marketing in Japan and even less in the Eastern Bloc countries and the third world. While Japan's postal costs are a problem, they are not insurmountable and the market is large. In the third world, where retailing will probably never be as developed as it is in Europe and Japan, there is a giant opportunity. But like all highly leveraged opportunities, it is highly risky as well as highly attractive.

The relatively small share of total marketing represented by direct marketing leaves no doubt that there is plenty of room for direct marketing to continue its explosive growth in most countries. Increasing levels of communication made possible by satellites, computers, and the other electronic marvels are going to break down international barriers at an ever-increasing rate.

For those companies with the hunger for continued expansion and the taste for challenges with high risk and high rewards, the international market cannot be ignored.

APPENDIXES

GLOSSARY OF LIST TERMS

COMPILED BY THE LIST GLOSSARY SUBCOMMITTEE OF THE DMA LIST COUNCIL

A

ACTIVE BUYER: A buyer whose latest purchase was made within the last twelve months. (see Buyer).

ACTIVE CUSTOMER: A term used interchangeably with Active Buyer.

ACTIVE MEMBER: Any member who is fulfilling the original commitment or who has fulfilled that commitment and has made one or more purchases in the last twelve months. (see Member.)

ACTIVE SUBSCRIBER: One who has committed for regular delivery of magazines, books or other goods or services for a time period still in effect.

ADDRESS CORRECTION REQUESTED: An endorsement which, when printed in the upper left-hand corner of the address, portion of the mailing piece (below the return address), authorizes the U. S. Postal Service, for a fee, to provide the new address (where known) of a person no longer at the address on the mailing piece.

ASSIGNED MAILING DATE(S): The date(s) on which the list user has the obligation to mail a specific list based on prior agreement between the list owner and the user. No other date is acceptable without specific approval of the list owner.

B

BILL ENCLOSURE: Any promotional piece or notice enclosed with a bill, an invoice or a statement which is not directed toward the collection of all or part of the bill, invoice or statement.

BROADCAST MEDIA: Direct response sources which include radio, television and cable TV.

BROKER: (see List Broker)

BUSINESS LIST: Any compilation or list of individuals or companies based upon a business-associated interest, inquiry, membership, subscription or purchase.

BUYER: One who orders merchandise, books, records, information or services. Unless another modifying word or two is used, it is assumed that a buyer has paid for all merchandise to date.

C

CASH BUYER: A buyer who encloses payment with order.

CASH FIELD AGENCY: A source of magazine subscriptions whose door-to-door crews require payment with order.

CASH-WITH-ORDER: A requirement for full or part payment at the time the order is placed.

CATALOG AGENCY: A source of magazine subscriptions whose sales are based on distribution of a catalog of such offers to individuals, bookstores, etc.

CATALOG BUYER: One who has bought one or more products from a catalog.

CATALOG REQUEST (PAID or UNPAID): One who sends for a catalog (prospective buyer). The catalog may be free, there may be a nominal charge for postage and handling, or there may be a more substantial charge which is often refunded or credited on the first order.

CHARGE (CREDIT) BUYER: One who has ordered a product or service and paid for it after receipt of the product or service.

CHESHIRE LABEL: Specially prepared paper (rolls, fanfold or accordian fold) used to reproduce names and addresses to be mechanically affixed, one at a time, to a mailing piece.

CLEANING: (see List Cleaning)

CLUSTER SELECTION: A selection routine based upon taking a group of names in series, skipping a group, taking another group, etc. For example: a cluster selection on an Nth name basis might be the first 10 out of every 100 or the first 125 out of 175, etc.; a cluster selection using limited ZIP code might be the first 200 names in each of the specified ZIP codes, etc.

C.O.D. BUYER: A buyer who agrees to pay for what he has ordered (plus a collection charge) upon delivery.

CODE: (see Key Code and Source Code)

COMMISSION: A percentage of sale, by prior agreement, paid to the list broker, list manager, or other service arm for their part in the list usage.

COMPILED LIST: Names and addresses derived from directories, newspapers, public records, retail sales slips, tradeshow registrations, etc., to identify groups of people with something in common.

COMPILER: (see List Compiler)

COMPLETED CANCEL: One who has completed a specific commitment to buy products or services before cancelling.

COMPUTER COMPATIBILITY: The ability to use data from one computer system on one or more other computer systems.

COMPUTER PERSONALIZATION: Printing of letters or other promotional pieces by a computer using names, addresses, special phrases, or other information based on data appearing in one or more computer records. The objective is to make use of the information in the computer record in order to tailor the promotional message to a specific individual.

COMPUTER RECORD: All of the information about an individual, company, or transaction appearing in a specific magnetic tape or disc.
COMPUTER SERVICE BUREAU: An internal or external facility providing general or specific data processing services.
CONSUMER LIST: A list of names (usually at home address) compiled or resulting from a common inquiry or buying activity indicating a general or specific buying interest.
CONTINUITY PROGRAM: Products or services bought as a series of small purchases rather than all at one time. Generally based on a common theme and shipped at regular specific time intervals.
CONTRIBUTOR LIST: Names and addresses of persons who have given to a specific fund raising effort. (see Donor List)
CONTROLLED CIRCULATION: Distribution at no charge of a publication to individuals or companies on the basis of their title or occupation. Typically, recipients are asked from time to time to verify the information that qualifies them to receive the publication.
CONTROLLED DUPLICATION: A method by which names and addresses from two or more lists are matched (usually by computer) in order to eliminate or limit extra mailings to the same name and address.
CONVERSION: (see Reformatting)
CO-OP MAILING: A mailing in which two or more offers are included in the same envelope or other carrier and share mailing costs according to some predetermined formula.
COUPON CLIPPER: One who has given evidence of responding to free or nominal-cost offers out of curiosity, with little or no serious interest or buying intent.
CROSS SECTION: A group of names and addresses selected from a mailing list in such a way as to be representative of the entire list.

D

DEADBEAT: One who has ordered a product or service and, without just cause, hasn't paid for it.
DECOY: A unique name especially inserted in a mailing list for verification of list usage.
DELINQUENT: One who has fallen behind or has stopped scheduled payment for a product or service.
DELIVERY DATE: The date on which a specific list order is to be received from the list owner by the list user or a designated representative of the list user.
DEMOGRAPHICS: Socio-economic characteristics pertaining to a geographic unit (county, city, sectional center, ZIP code, group of households, etc.).
DIRECT MAIL ADVERTISING: Any promotional effort using the Postal Service or other direct delivery service for distribution of the advertising message.
DIRECT RESPONSE ADVERTISING: Advertising, through any medium, designed to generate a response by any means (such as mail, telephone, or telegraph) that is measurable.
DMA MAIL ORDER ACTION LINE (MOAL): A service provided by DMA to assist consumers who have encountered problems they cannot resolve themselves while shopping by mail.
DMA MAIL PREFERENCE SERVICE (MPS): A service provided by DMA that enables individuals to have their names and addresses removed from or added to mailing lists. These names are made available to both members and non-members of the Association.
DONOR LIST: A list of persons who have given money to one or more charitable organizations. (see Contributor List)
DUMMY NAME: (see Decoy)
DUPLICATE: Two or more name and address records which are found to be equal under the list user's basis of comparison (match code, mathematical formula, etc.).
DUPLICATION ELIMINATION: A specific kind of controlled duplication which provides that no matter how many times a name and address is on a list, and no matter how many lists contain that name and address, it will be accepted for mailing only one time by that mailer.

E

EDITING RULES: Specific rules used in preparing name and address records in order to treat all elements the same way at all times. Although most companies use some editing rules in common, few conform in all respects. Therefore, knowledge of specific editing rules for each list is important to the user.
EXCHANGE: (see List Exchange)
EXPIRE: A subscriber who has let the subscription run out without renewing. (see Active Subscriber)

F

FIELD AGENCY: A source of periodical subscriptions using crews that solicit door-to-door.
FIRST-TIME BUYER: One who buys a product or service from a specific company for the first time.
FIXED FIELD: A way of laying out or formatting list information in a computer file that puts every piece of data in a specific position relative to every other piece of data, and limits the amount of space assigned to that data. If a piece of data is missing from an individual record, or if its assigned space isn't used completely, that space is not filled (every record has the same space and the same length). Any data exceeding its assigned space limitation must be abbreviated or contracted.
FORMAT: (see Tape Layout)
FORMER BUYER: One who has bought one or more times from a company with no purchase in the last twelve months.
FREE-STANDING INSERT: A promotional piece loosely inserted or nested in a newspaper or magazine.
FREQUENCY: The number of times an individual has ordered within a specific period of time, or in toto. (see Recency and Monetary)
FRIEND-OF-A-FRIEND (FRIEND RECOMMENDATION): The result of one party sending in the name of someone considered to be interested in a specific advertisr's product or service (a third party inquiry).
FUND RAISING LIST: Any compilation or list of of individuals or companies based on a known contribution to one or more fund raising appeals.

G

GEOGRAPHICS: Any method of subdividing a list, based on geographic or political subdivisions (ZIP codes, sectional centers, cities, counties, states, regions).
GIFT BUYER: One who buys a product or service for another.

H

HOT-LINE LIST: The most recent names available on a specific list, but no older than three months. In any event, use of the term hot-line should be further modified by weekly, monthly, etc.
HOUSE LIST: Any list of names owned by a company as a result of compilation, inquiry or buyer action, or acquisition that is used to promote that company's products or services.
HOUSE-LIST DUPLICATE: Duplication of name and address records between that list user's own list(s) and any list being mailed by him on a one-time use arrangement.

I

INACTIVE BUYER: (see Former Buyer)
INQUIRY: One who has asked for literature or other information about a product or service. Unless otherwise stated, it is assumed no payment has been made for the literature or other information. (Note: A Catalog Request is, generally, considered a specific type of inquiry.)
INSTALLMENT BUYER: One who orders goods or services and pays for them in two or more periodic payments after delivery of the products or services.
INTER-LIST DUPLICATE: Duplication of name and address records between two or more lists, other than house lists, being mailed by a list user.
INTRA-LIST DUPLICATE: Duplication of name-and-address records within a given list.
INVALID RECORD: Any record on a computer tape or disc which is mechanically unacceptable, which doesn't conform to the list owner's editing rules, or which doesn't meet the list user's specifications.

K

KEY CODE (KEY): A group of letters and/or numbers, colors, or other markings used to measure specific effectiveness of media, lists, advertisements, offers, etc., (or any parts thereof).

L

LAYOUT: (see Tape Layout)

LIST (MAILING LIST): Names and addresses of individuals and/or companies having in common a specific interest, characteristic or activity.

LIST BROKER: A specialist who makes all necessary arrangements for one company to make use of the list(s) of another company. A broker's services may include most or all of the following: research, selection, recommendation and subsequent evaluation.

LIST BUYER: Technically, this term should apply only to one who actually buys mailing lists. In practice, however, it is usually used to identify one who orders mailing lists for one-time use (see List User and Mailer).

LIST CLEANING: The process of correcting and/or removing a name and address from a mailing list because it is no longer correct. Addresses may be corrected as a result of information furnished by the Postal Service (see Address Correction Requested) or the individual. Removal may be effected as a result of the return of a mailing piece by the Postal Service (see Return Postage Guaranteed).

LIST COMPILER: One who develops lists of names and addresses from directories, newspapers, public records, sales slips, trade show registrations and other sources of identifying groups of people or companies with something in common.

LIST CONVERSION: (see Reformatting)

LIST EXCHANGE: A barter arrangement between two companies for the use of a mailing list(s); may be list for list, list for space, or list for comparable value—other than money.

LIST MAINTENANCE: Any manual, mechanical or electronic system for keeping name and address records (with or without other data) so that they are up to date at any (or specific) points in time.

LIST MANAGER: One who, as an employee of a list owner or as an outside agent, is responsible for the use, by others, of a specific mailing list(s). The list manager generally serves the list owner in several (or all) of the following: list maintenance (or advice thereon), list promotion and marketing, list clearance and record keeping, collecting for use of the list by others.

LIST OWNER: One who, by promotional activity or compilation, has developed a list of names having something in common—or one who has purchased (as opposed to rented, reproduced, or used on a one-time basis) such a list from the developer.

LIST RENTAL: An arrangement in which a list owner furnishes names on his or her list to a mailer, together with the privilege of using the list on a one-time basis only (unless otherwise specified in advance). For this privilege, the list owner is paid a royalty by the mailer. (List Rental is the term most often used although List Reproduction and List Usage more accurately describes the transaction, since Rental is not used in the sense of its ordinary meaning of leasing property.)

LIST REPRODUCTION: (see List Rental)

LIST ROYALTY: Payment to list owners for the privilege of using their lists on a one-time basis.

LIST SAMPLE: A group of names selected from a list in order to evaluate the responsiveness of that list.

LIST SEGMENTATION: (see List Selection)

LIST SELECTION: Characteristics used to define smaller groups within a list (essentially, lists within a list). Although very small, select groups may be very desirable and may substantially improve response; increased costs often render them impractical.

LIST SEQUENCE: The order in which names and addresses appear in a list. While most lists today are in ZIP code sequence, some are alphabetical by name within the ZIP code, others are in carrier sequence (postal delivery), and still others may use some other (or no) order within ZIP code. Some lists are still arranged alphabetically by state (and city within the state), alphabetically by name or chronologically (and many variations or combination).

LIST SORT: The process of putting a list in a specific sequence (from another sequence or no sequence).

LIST SOURCE: The medium or media (general or specific) used to generate names on a mailing list.

LIST TEST: A part of a list selected to try to determine the effectiveness of the entire list. (see List Sample)

LIST USER: One who uses names and addresses on someone else's list as prospects for the user's product or service. (see Mailer)

M

MAGNETIC TAPE: A storage device for electronically recording and reproducing (by use of a computer) defined bits of data.

MAIL DATE(S): Date(s) on which a user has the obligation to mail a specific list (by prior agreement with the list owner). No other date is acceptable without specific approval of the list owner.

MAIL ORDER BUYER: One who orders and pays for a product or service through the mail. (Those who use telephone or telegraph to order from direct response advertising may be included in this category although technically, they are not Mail Order Buyers.)

MAILER: (see List Manager)

MATCHCODE: An abbreviation of data extracted from name and address records, attempting to simplify the sequencing of records in a list and/or the identification of duplicate records. A reliable matchcode depends upon good editing rules and procedures.

MEDIA: Vehicles used to transmit an advertising message (direct mail, radio, television, telephone, matchbook covers, catalogs, package inserts, magazines, newspapers, among other).

MEDIUM: One of the media; for example, radio only.

MEMBER: One who has paid a fee (six-month, annual, lifetime, etc.) for the right to receive information about and/or to buy at special prices; or one who by virtue of goods or services received, has committed for a minimum number of purchases during a specific period of time. Compiled lists can include members of clubs or associations with specific qualifications, or none.

MERGE: Combining of two or more lists (or two or more segments of the same list)—usually in a predetermined sequence.

MERGE/PURGE: Combining two or more units or lists and eliminating duplication at the same time.

MONETARY: Part of the mail order quality designation triumverate (Recency/Frequency/Monetary)—that relates to the amount of money spent by a customer (either in a specific period of time, or in toto).

MULTIPLE BUYER (MULTI-BUYER or REPEAT BUYER): One who has bought two or more times from the same company (not one who has bought more than one item from the same company).

N

Nth NAME SELECTION: A fractional unit that is repeated in sampling a mailing list. For example: In an "every tenth" sample, you would select the 1st, 11th, 21st, 31st, etc., records—or the 2nd, 12th, 22nd, 32nd, etc., records, and so forth.

NEGATIVE OPTION: A buying plan in which a customer or club member agrees to accept and pay for products or services announced in advance at regular intervals unless the individual notifies the company within reasonable time after each announcement "Do Not Ship".

NET NAME ARRANGEMENT: An agreement between list owner and list user, at the time of ordering or before, in which the list owner agrees to accept adjusted payment for less than the total names shipped. Such agreements can be for a percentage of names shipped or names actually mailed whichever is greater) or for only those names actually mailed (without a percentage limitation). They can provide for a running charge or not. (see Running Charge)

NIXIE: A mailing piece returned to a mailer (under proper authorization) by the Postal Service because of an incorrect, or undeliverable, name and address.

NO-PAY: One who has not paid (wholly or in part) for goods or services ordred. (see Uncollectable, Deadbeat, and/or Delinquent.)

O

OFFER: The terms under which a specific product or service is promoted.

ONE-TIME BUYER: A buyer who has not ordered a second time from a given company.

ONE-TIME USE OF A LIST: An intrinsic part of the normal list usage, list reproduction, or list exchange agreement—in which, it is understood that the mailer will not use the names on the list more than one time without specific prior approval of the list owner.

OPEN ACCOUNT: A customer record that, at a specific point in time, reflects an unpaid balance for goods and services ordered, without delinquency.

P

PACKAGE: A term used to describe, in toto, all of the assembled enclosures (parts or elements) of a mailing effort.
PACKAGE INSERT: Any promotional piece included in a product shipment. It may be for different products (or refills and replacements) from the same company or for products and services of other companies.
PACKAGE TEST: A test of elements (in part or in their entirety) of one mailing piece against another.
PAID CANCEL: One who completes a basic buying commitment, or more, before cancelling a commitment. (see Completed Cancel)
PAID CIRCULATION: Distribution of a publication to individuals or organizations which have paid for a subscription.
PAID DURING SERVICE: Term used to describe a method of paying for magazine subscriptions in installments, usually weekly or monthly—and usually collected, in person, by the original sales person or a representative of that company.
PANDERING NAMES: (see Postal Service Prohibitory Order)
PANEL: (see Test Panel)
PENETRATION: Relationship of the number of individuals or families on a particular list (in toto, by state, ZIP code, S.I.C., etc.) compared to the total number possible.
PERIODICAL: A publication issued at specific intervals (daily, weekly, monthly, etc.).
POSITIVE OPTION: A method of distribution of products and services incorporating the same advance notice technique as Negative Option but requiring a specific order, on the part of the member or subscriber, each time. Generally, more costly and less predictable than Negative Option.

POSTAL SERVICE PROHIBITORY ORDER: A communication from the Postal Service to a company indicating that a specific person and/or family considers the company's advertising mail to be pandering. The order requires the company to remove all names listed on the order from its own mailing list and from any other lists used to promote that company's products or services. Violation of such order is subject to fine and imprisonment. The names listed on the order are to be distinguished from names removed, voluntarily, by the list owner at an individual's request.

PREMIUM BUYER: One who buys a product or service to get another product or service (usually free or at a special price) or who responds to an offer of a special product (premium) on the package or label (or sometimes in the advertising) of another product.
PROTECTION: The amount of time before and after the assigned mailing date, during which the list owner will not allow the same names to be mailed by anyone other than the mailer cleared for that specific date.
PSYCHOGRAPHICS: Any characteristics or qualities used to denote the life style(s) or attitude(s) of customers and prospective customers.
PURGE: The process of eliminating duplicates and/or unwanted names and addresses from one or more lists.
PYRAMIDING: A method of testing mailing lists, in which one starts with a small quantity and, based on positive indications, follows with larger and larger quantities of the balance of the list until finally, one mails the entire list.

R

RECENCY: The latest purchase or other activity recorded for an individual or company on a specific customer list. (see Frequency and Monetary)
RECORD: (see Tape Record)
RECORD FORMAT OR LAYOUT: (see Tape Layout)
REFORMATTING: Changing a magnetic tape format from one arrangement to another more usable one. Also referred to as list or tape conversion.

RENTAL: (see List Rental)
REPEAT BUYER: (see Multi-Buyer)
REPRODUCTION RIGHT: Authorization by a list owner for a specific mailer to use that list on a one-time basis.

RETURN POSTAGE GUARANTEED: A legend which should be imprinted on the address face of envelopes or other mailing pieces if the mailer wishes the Postal Service to return undeliverable third class bulk mail. A charge equivalent to the single piece third class rate will be made for each piece returned. (see List Cleaning)
ROYALTY: (see List Royalty)
RUNNING CHARGE: The price charged by a list owner for names run or passed but not used by a specific mailer. When such a charge is made it is usually made to cover extra processing costs. However, some list owners set the price without regard to actual cost.

S

SALTING: Deliberate placing of decoy or dummy names in a list to trace list usage and delivery. (see Decoy)

SAMPLE BUYER: One who sends for a sample product, usually at a special price or for a small handling charge but sometimes, free.
SAMPLE PACKAGE (MAILING PIECE): An example of the package to be mailed by the list user to a particular list. Such a mailing piece is submitted to the list owner for approval prior to commitment for one-time use of that list. Although a sample package may, due to time pressure, differ slightly from the actual package used. the list user agreement usually requires the user to reveal any material differences when submitting the sample package.
SECTIONAL CENTER (SCF or SEC CENTER): A Postal Service distribution unit comprising different post offices whose ZIP codes start with the same first three digits.
SELECTION CRITERIA: Definition of characteristics that identify segments or subgroups within a list.
SERVICE BUREAU: (see Computer Service Bureau)
S.I.C. (STANDARD INDUSTRIAL CLASSIFICATION): Classification of businesses, as defined by the U. S. Department of Commerce.
SOURCE: (see List Source)
SOURCE CODE: Unique alphabetical and/or numeric identification for distinguishing one list or media source from another. (see Key Code)
SOURCE COUNT: The number of names and addresses, in any given list, for the media (or list sources) from which the names and addresses were derived.
SPACE BUYER: One whose initial purchase, at least, came as a result of responding to advertising in magazines or newspapers.
SPLIT TEST: Two or more samples from the same list —each considered to be representative of the entire list—used for package tests or to test the homogeneity of that list.
STATE COUNT: The number of names and addresses, in a given list, for each state.
STATEMENT STUFFER: (see Bill Enclosure)
SUBSCRIBER: (see Active Subscriber and Expire)

T

TAPE: (see Magnetic Tape)
TAPE CONVERSION: (see Reformatting)
TAPE DENSITY: The number of bits of information (Bytes) that can be included in each inch of a specific magnetic tape (556 BPI, 800 BPI, 1600 BPI, etc.).
TAPE DUMP: A printout of data on a magnetic tape for checking correctness, readability, consistency, editability, etc.
TAPE FORMAT: (see Tape Layout)
TAPE LAYOUT: A simple map of the data included in each record and its relative, or specific, location.
TAPE RECORD: All of the information about an individual or company contained on a specific magnetic tape.
TEST PANEL: A term used to identify each of the parts or samples in a split test.

TEST TAPE: A selection of representative records within a mailing list—to enable a list user, or service bureau to prepare for reformatting or converting the list to a form more efficient for the user.
TITLE: A designation before or after a name to more accurately identify an individual. (Before: Mr., Mrs., Dr., Sister, etc.; after: M.D., Jr., President. Sales Manager, etc.)

TOWN MARKER: A symbol used to identify the end of a geographical unit of a mailing list. (Originated for towns but now used for ZIP codes, sectional centers, etc.)

TRIAL BUYER: One who buys a short-term supply of a product, or buys the product with the understanding that it may be examined, used, or tested for a specific time before deciding whether to pay for it or return it.

TRIAL SUBSCRIBER: One who orders a publication or service on a conditional basis. The condition may relate to delaying payment, the right to cancel, a shorter than normal term and/or a special introductory price.

U

UNCOLLECTABLE: One who hasn't paid for goods and services at the end of a normal series of collection efforts.

UPDATE: Adding recent transactions and current information to the master (main) list to reflect the current status of each record on the list.

V

VARIABLE FIELD: A way of laying out or formatting list information that assigns a specific sequence to the data, but doesn't assign it specific positions. While this method conserves space on magnetic tape, it is generally more difficult to work with.

Z

ZIP CODE: A group of five digits used by the U. S. Postal Service to designate specific post offices, stations, branches, buildings or large companies.

ZIP CODE COUNT: The number of names and addresses in a list, within each ZIP code.

ZIP CODE SEQUENCE: Arranging names and addresses in a list according to the numeric progression of the ZIP code in each record. This form of list formatting is mandatory for mailing at bulk third class mail rates based on the sorting requirements of the Postal Service regulations.

appendix **B**

GLOSSARY OF COMPUTER TERMS

COMPILED BY THE COMPUTER GLOSSARY SUBCOMMITTEE OF THE DMA LIST COUNCIL

A

A.I.D. ANALYSIS (Automatic Interaction Detector): One of the statistical techniques for analysis of specific characteristics of respondents (customers) as opposed to non-residents (non-customers) to determine the best types of people/areas to mail.
ACCESS TIME: The time it takes a computer to locate a piece of information in memory or storage and to take action, i.e., the read time. Also the time it takes a computer to store a piece of information and to complete action, i.e., the write time.
ADDRESS CODING GUIDE (ACG): Contains the actual or potential beginning and ending house numbers, street names, census tract numbers, block group and/or enumeration district numbers, ZIP Codes and other geographic codes for all city delivery service streets served by 3,154 post offices located within 6,601 ZIP Codes.
ADMINISTRATIVE TERMINAL SYSTEM (ATS): System in which terminals are connected by two-way communication lines to a computer under control of a program that allows a typist to type text into the computer, correct and revise text and have the computer type out the corrected draft.
ALGORITHM: Prescribed set of well-defined rules or process for the solution of a problem in a finite number of steps.
ALPHAMERIC: (See Alphanumeric)
ALPHANUMERIC (A contraction of "alphabetic" and "numeric"): Applies to any coding system that provides for letters, numbers (digits), and special symbols such as punctuation marks. Synonymous with Alphameric.
ASSEMBLER LANGUAGE: Programmer source language including symbolic machine statements corresponding to instruction formats and computer data formats. Also called BAL.
AUDIT: Printed report of the counts involved in a particular file or list.
AUXILIARY EQUIPMENT: Equipment not directly controlled by the Central Processing Unit (CPU); Offline.

B

BAL: (See Assembler Language)
BPI (Bytes per inch): Characters, represented in bytes, per inch.
BPS: Bytes per second.
BACK-UP: Term applied to protection or insurance copies of magnetic tapes, computer programs, data card decks, etc.
BALANCE: Remaining names and addresses after designated selection has been made from a specific universe.
BATCH PROCESSING: Technique of executing a set of computer programs/selections in batches as opposed to executing each order/selection as it is received. Batches can be created by computer programming or a manual collection of data into groups.
BATCHED JOB: A job that is grouped with other jobs as input to a computing system, as opposed to a transaction job entry where the job is done singly to completion.
BINARY: Involves a selection, choice or condition in which there are two possibilities such as the use of the symbols "O" and "I" in a numbering system.
BINARY/CODED DECIMAL CHARACTER CODE: Set of 64 characters, each represented by six bits. Synonymous with BCD.
BIT: A single character or element in a binary number (digit). The smallest element of binary machine language represented by a magnetized spot on a recording surface or a magnetized element of a storage device.
BLOCK: A number of records stored together in a single physical location on a magnetic tape or disk; thus, a set of things, such as words, characters, or digits handled as a unit.
BLOCK GROUP: Combination of contiguous city blocks forming subdivisions of census tracts having an average of 200-250 residential units. Usually represents 1/4 of a census tract.
BLOCKING FACTOR: Number of logical records combined into one physical record or block as recorded on a storage medium between inter-record gaps.
BUG: Error in or malfunction of a program.
BURST: To separate continuous form paper into discrete sheets.
BYTE: Sequence of adjacent binary digits operated upon as a unit and usually shorter than a computer word. A character is usually considered a byte. (A single byte can contain either two numeric characters or one alphabetic or special character.)

C

CARD CODE: Combinations of punched holes that represent characters in a punched card.
CARD COLUMN: Single line of punching positions parallel to the short edge of a punched card.
CARD DECK: (See Deck)
CARD FIELD: Fixed number of consecutive card columns assigned to data of a specific nature.

CARD READER: Device that senses and translates into machine code the holes in punched cards.
CARD-TO-TAPE: Transfer of information from punched cards to magnetic tape.

CARRIAGE CONTROL TAPE: A paper or plastic strip which is inserted into a computer printer to control the feeding, spacing, skipping and ejecting of paper or preprinted forms.
CENSUS TRACT: Small geographical area established by local committees and approved by the Census Bureau which contains a population segment with relatively uniform economic and social characteristics with clearly identifiable boundaries averaging approximately 1,200 households.
CENTRAL PROCESSING UNIT (CPU): Includes the circuits controlling the interpretation and execution of instructions. Synonymous with Main Frame.
CHARACTER: A single letter, digit or other symbol that is used as part of the organization, control, or representation of data.
CHECK DIGIT: A digit used for the purpose of performing a check. For example, an additional digit to "check" the accuracy of a sequence or customer number.
CHECKPOINT: Place in a routine where a check, or a recording of data for restart purposes, is performed.
CHECKPOINT RESTART: Process of resuming a job at a checkpoint within the job step that experienced abnormal termination. (See also Restart)
COBOL (COmmon Business Oriented Language): Business oriented data processing language.
COLLATE: A program which combines two or more ordered files to produce a single ordered file. Also the act of combining such files. Synonymous with merge as in Merge-Purge.
COMPILE: The process by which a computer translates a series of instructions written in a programming language into actual machine language.
COMPUTER: Data processor that can perform substantial computation, without intervention by a human operator during the run. It is capable of solving problems by accepting data, performing described operations on the data, and supplying the results of those operations.
COMPUTER COMPATIBILITY: The ability to use data or programs of one computer system on one or more other computer systems.
COMPUTER LETTER: Computer printed letter, providing personalized fill-in information from a source file in pre-designated positions in the letter. May also be full printed letter with personalized insertions.
COMPUTER PROGRAM: Series of instructions or statements prepared in order to achieve a certain result.
CONSOLE: Part of a computer used for communication between the operator and the computer.
CONSTANT: A fixed or invariable value or data item.
CONTINUOUS FORM: Paper forms designed for computer printing, folded and sometimes perforated at predetermined vertical measurements. May be letters, vouchers, invoices, cards, etc.
CONVERSION: Process of changing from one method of data processing to another or from one data processing system to another. Synonymous with Reformatting.
CONVERT: Change the representation of data from one form to another.
CORE STORAGE: Form of high speed storage using magnetic cores. Synonymous with Memory.
CPU TIME (Central Processing Unit): Amount of time devoted by the central processing unit to the execution of instructions.
CRITERIA: List characteristics or census demographics specified for a desired selection.
CRT DISPLAY (Cathode Ray Tube): Data displayed on a screen similar to a TV screen.

D

DATA: Representation of facts, concepts or instructions in a formalized manner, suitable for communication, interpretation or processing by humans or automatic means.
DATA ENTRY: Conversion of source document data to machine-readable coding. Synonymous with Data Conversion or Data Preparation.
DATA PROCESSING: Execution of a systematic sequence of operations performed upon data. Synonymous with Information Processing.
DATA PROCESSING SYSTEM: Network of machine components capable of accepting information, processing it according to plan and producing the desired results.
DEBUG: To detect, locate and remove mistakes from a routine or program, or malfunctions from a computer. Synonymous with Trouble Shoot.
DECK: Collection of punched cards. Synonymous with Card Deck.
DE-COLLATE: To separate the plies of a multipart form or paper stack. Synonymous with Deleave.
DENSITY: Measure of the number of bits or characters in a single track recorded per inch of magnetic tape. Generally referred to a 556, 800 or 1600 BPI.
DIAGNOSTIC CHECK: A specific routine designed to detect and locate a malfunction or mistake on the computer.
DIRECT ACCESS: (See Random Access)
DISK: Flat circular plate with magnetic surface on which data is magnetically recorded.
DOCUMENT: A medium and the data recorded on it for human use such as reports, manuals, etc.
DOCUMENTATION: A detailed description or explanation of a computer program, process or system.
DOWNTIME: Time interval during which a computer is inoperative or malfunctioning.
DUMP: Printout of the contents of a computer tape, disk or core storage.
DUPE (Duplication): Appearance of identical or near identical entities more than one time.

E

EDITING RULES: Specific rules used in preparing name and address records in order to treat all elements the same way at all times. Rules for rearranging, deleting, selecting, or inserting any needed data, symbols and/or characters.
EDP: Electronic Data Processing.
EMULATE: To imitate one system with another in such a manner that the system accepts and processes the same data with the same end result.
ENCODING: Identification of information by codes to facilitate processing or retrieval by specific groups.
ENUMERATION DISTRICT (ED): Geographical unit established and defined by the Census Bureau for all places outside tracted areas. Usually consists of an area representing one census enumerator's work load.
ERASE: To obliterate, clear, overwrite data on magnetic tape, disk, etc.
ERROR MESSAGE: Indication of error in processing or programming.
EXTRACT: To select from a set of items all those that meet some criteria.

F

FIELD: Reserved area in a computer which serves a similar function in all records of the file. Also, location on magnetic tape or disk drive which has definable limitations and meaning; e.g., Position 1-30 is the Name Field.
FILE: Collection of related records treated as a unit, such as punch cards, magnetic tape or magnetic disk.
FILE LAYOUT: Description of the arrangement and structure of data in a file, including the sequence and size of its components. Synonymous with Tape Layout.
FILE MAINTENANCE: The activity of keeping a file up-to-date by adding, changing, or deleting data (all or part). Synonymous with List Maintenance. (See also Updating)
FIXED FIELD: A way of laying out or reformatting list information that puts every piece of information in a specific position relative to every other piece of information, and limits the amount of space assigned to each piece.
FLAG: Term used to identify a specific deletion/selection record. Synonymous with Tag.
FLIGHT: Division or portion of the total selection or processing of a mailing. Synonymous with Phase or Wave
FLOWCHART: Graphic representation of the definition, analysis, or solution of the steps in a computer program or system.
FONT: An assortment of characters of a given size and style. (See also Type Font)
FORMAT: Predetermined arrangement of information or data in a record or file.
FORTRAN (FORmula TRANslating system): Programmer language used primarily to express computer programs by arithmetic formulas.

G

GALLEY: Computer printout of information on one line left to right. Synonymous with Manuscript Copy, Galley Listing or Sheet Listing.
GEO CODES: Numeric symbols assigned for the identification of geographic entities such as state, county, city, ZIP, tract, etc.

H

HARD COPY: Printed copy of machine output in visually readable form, such as count reports, listings, etc.
HARDWARE: Computers and their peripheral equipment.
HEADER RECORD: Record containing common, constant or identifying information for the following group of records. Synonymous with Header Label.
HIT: Successful identification or matching of two or more records.

I

INFORMATION PROCESSING: (See Data Processing)
INPUT DATA: Data to be fed into a computer for processing. Synonymous with Input.
INTER-LIST DUPLICATE: Duplication of name and address records on two or more lists.
INVALID RECORD: Any record which is mechanically unacceptable, which doesn't conform to the list owner's editing rules or which doesn't meet the list user's specifications.

J

JUSTIFY: To adjust the printing positions of characters on a page so that the lines have the desired length and that both left and right margins are regular.

K

K: Used in reference to computer storage capacity, generally accepted as 1,000. Analogous to M in the direct marketing industry.
KEY: One or more characters within a group of data that can be used to identify it or control its use. Synonymous with Key Code in mailing business.

L

LANGUAGE: Set of representations, conventions and rules, used to convey information.
LIST CLEANING: The process of correcting and/or removing a name and/or address from a mailing list because it is no longer correct. Term is also used in the identification and elimination of house list duplication.
LIST CODE: The assigned tag which identifies the particular file or files from which a record originated.
LIST MAINTENANCE: A system for mechanically keeping name and address records up-to-date at any point in time. (See also File Maintenance.)

M

MAGNETIC TAPE: A tough plastic film coated on one side with magnetic iron oxide used for storing and retrieving electronically recorded data.
MAIN FRAME: (See Central Processing Unit)
MANUSCRIPT COPY: (See Galley)
MASTER FILE: File that is of permanent nature or one that is regarded in particular job as authoritative, or one that contains all sub files.
MATCH CODE: A code determined either by the creator or the user of a file to be used for matching records contained in another file.
MATRIX: A statistical table, usually cross-classifying two or more variables.
MEMORY: A general term for the equipment that stores information in machine language in magnetic form and gives out the stored information for later use. Synonymous with Storage.
MERGE: To combine data into one sequenced file from two or more similarly sequenced files without changing the order of the data.
MERGE-PURGE Duplication Elimination/Identification): Method of merging two or more files in a matching process, to produce one file, free of duplication.
MINI COMPUTER: Small digital processors that can be dispersed to many sites within a company or organization to perform limited computer functions.
MULTIPLE REGRESSION: Statistical technique used to measure the relationship between responses to a mailing with census demographics and list characteristics of one or more selected mailing lists. Used to determine the best types of people/area to mail. This technique can also be used to analyze customers, subscribers, etc.
MULTI-PROCESSING: Execution of two or more programs or sets of instructions by the computer at one time. (See also Parallel Processing)

N

NTH INTERVAL: Number arrived at by dividing the total records on a file by the number of records desired for a sample. Every Nth is then selected after a random start thereby creating a statistically valid sample.

O

OCR (Optical Character Recognition): Machine identification of printed characters through use of light —sensitive devices.
OFFLINE: Pertaining to equipment or devices not under direct control of the central processing unit.
ONLINE: Computer equipment or devices controlled by the central processing unit.
OPTICAL SCANNER: An input device that optically reads a line of printed characters and converts each character into its electronic equivalent for processing. Reading is usually done by means of mobile scanning mirrors, lenses, lights and light-sensing photocells. Synonymous with Visual Scanner.
OUTPUT DATA: Data which have been processed by a computer and transferred from memory to another device, such as a printer, magnetic tapes, a CRT display unit, punched cards, etc. Synonymous with Output.

P

PANDERING: Deleting names from a master file where such deletion has been requested.
PARALLEL PROCESSING: The independent processing of several separate programs simultaneously by a computer. Synonymous with Multi-Processing.
PARAMETER: Variable or arbitrary constant used to make a mathematical determination.
PARTITION: Subdivision of the computer storage area which enables the system to handle processing of several jobs simultaneously.
PATCH: A section of coding inserted into a routine to correct a mistake or to alter the routine.
PERIPHERAL EQUIPMENT: Equipment related to computer devices but not directly in line with processing equipment, such as printers, tape drives, disk drives, card readers/punch, CRT display units, etc.
PHASE: (See Flight)
PRINT IMAGE: The form of data representation from which logical print lines can be displayed on a printer with no intermediate format manipulation necessary.
PRINTOUT: Paper copy of information/data reported from a computer system through a printing device.
PRIORITY: Type of merge—purge system which assigns credit (priority) for multi-hit names to the lowest numerical list code, giving an advantage to lists processed/received first. Also, refers to the sequence in which a series of things is done. For example, in multi-processing, the partition which will take precedence.
PROGRAM: A sequence of steps to be executed by the computer to solve a given problem or achieve a certain result.
PROGRAMMING: Design, writing and testing of a program.
PUNCHED CARD: Card punched with a pattern of holes to represent data.
PUNCHED TAPE: Paper tape in which holes are punched in a pattern to represent data.

Q

QUALITY CONTROL: Procedures for checking the reliability of produced results for all input/output steps.

R

RANDOM ACCESS: An access mode in which records are obtained from, or placed into, a mass storage file in a nonsequential manner so that any record can be rapidly accessed. Synonymous with Direct Access.

READ: The transferring of data from a storage device (such as a magnetic tape, punched card, etc.) to the central processing unit.
RECORD: Collection of related items of data, treated as a unit.
RECORD LAYOUT: Arrangement and structure of data in a record, including the sequence and size of its components.
RECORD LENGTH: Measure of the size of a record, usually specified in units such as words, characters or bytes.
REFORMATTING: Changing a magnetic tape format from one arrangement to another, more usable format. Synonymous with Conversion (list or tape).
REMOTE ACCESS: Pertaining to communication with a data processing facility by one or more stations that are distant from that facility.
RE-RUN: Repeat of a machine run, usually because of a correction, interruption or false start.
RESTART: To re-establish execution of a routine, using the data recorded at a checkpoint. (See Checkpoint Restart)
ROUTINE: A set of instructions arranged in the correct sequence to direct the computer to perform a common operation or series of operations. A small program or portion of a program. (See also Sub-Routine)
RUN: A single, continuous performance of a computer routine.

S

SEGMENT: To divide a computer program into parts so that the program can be completed without executing the entire program. Also refers to dividing data such as a mailing list into smaller identities.
SEQUENCE: An arrangement of items according to a specified set of rules or instructions. Refers generally to ZIP Code or customer number sequence.
SHEET LISTING: (See Galley)
SIMULATE: To represent the functioning of a computer or program by another computer or program.
SOFTWARE: A set of programs, precedures and associated documentation concerned with the operation of a data processing system.
SORT: A program which arranges a file of items in a logical sequence according to a designated key word (or field) contained within each item.
STACKING: Refers to the sequencing of names on one reel of magnetic tape. (More than one list/segment in its own ZIP sequence can be provided on one reel of tape.)
STORAGE: Pertains to entering, holding and retrieving of data. Synonymous with Memory.
SUB-ROUTINE: A routine that can be part of another routine. (See also Routine)
SUPPRESSION: Removal of specified names from the output of a merge—purge because those names represent existing customers, pandering deletes, previously mailed prospects, etc.
SYSTEMS ANALYST: An advanced level person (not necessarily a programmer) whose responsibility is to analyze the needs of a particular project and determine the most efficient system, utilizing existing software and/or new programs to be written.

T

TABLE LOOK-UP: Procedure for determining whether to accept or delete a record based on completeness or accuracy. Used to identify prefix, suffix, company titles, etc.
TAG: To mark or record the use of a logical record for subsequent selection or suppression. Synonymous with Flag.
TAPE DRIVE: An input/output device which moves magnetic tape past computer sensing and recording mechanisms to transfer data or record data to and from a central processing unit.
TAPE LAYOUT: A graphic or narrative description of the logical tape records contained on a file.
TAPE LIBRARY: A collection of information on magnetic tape available to a computer, usually kept in a security area.
TAPE MARK: The special single character that is recorded on a tape to signify the physical end of recording on the tape. May also be used to subdivide a file into sections.
TELECOMMUNICATIONS: Data transmission between a computing system and remotely located devices via a unit that performs the necessary format conversion and controls the rate of transmission over telephone lines, microwave, etc. Synonymous with Transceive.
TERMINAL: Any mechanism which can transmit and/or receive data through a system or communications network.
THROUGHPUT: The total volume of work performed by a computing system over a given period of time.
TIME SHARING: Multiple utilization of available computer time, often via terminals. Usually by different organizations.
TRACKS (channels): Those strips of the recording surface of magnetic tapes or disks which run the length of the tape and allow for the recording of magnetized bits to represent characters; i.e., 7 track, 9 track.
TRAILER RECORD: A special record which follows a group of records and contains pertinent data relating to the group.
TRANSCEIVE: (See Telecommunications)
TRANSLATE: The process of converting from one language to another.
TROUBLE SHOOT: (See Debug)
TRUNCATE: To terminate a computer process in accordance with some rule. In the mailing list business it refers to the reduction of the number of positions in a name field because it is too long to fit on an address label.
TURNAROUND TIME: The elapsed time between submission of a job to a processing center and the return of results.
TYPE FONT: Type of a given size and style such as OCRA, OCRB, etc. (See also Font)

U

UPDATING: The act of processing changes in the contents of a data file by adding, deleting and modifying information. (See also File Maintenance)

V

VARIABLE FIELD: A way of laying out or reformatting list information that assigns a specific sequence to the data, but doesn't assign it specific positions. Usually refers to a data format in which one data element follows another, separated only by a single special character. This insertion eliminates the blanks which would normally be written at the end of each field to fill up the space in fixed field layout.
VISUAL SCANNER: (See Optical Scanner)

W

WAVE: (See Flight)
WRITE: The transferring of data to a storage device or a data medium.

appendix **C**

GUIDELINES FOR ETHICAL BUSINESS PRACTICES OF THE DIRECT MARKETING ASSOCIATION

The Direct Marketing Association's Guidelines for Ethical Business Practices are intended to provide individuals and organizations involved in direct mail and direct marketing with principles of conduct that are generally accepted nationally and internationally. These guidelines reflect DMA's long-standing policy of high levels of ethics and the responsibility of the association and direct marketers to the consumer and the community—a relationship that must be based on fair and ethical principles.

What distinguishes the guidelines, which are self-regulatory in nature, is that all are urged to support them in spirit and not to treat their provisions as obstacles to be circumvented by legal ingenuity. The guidelines are intended to be honored in the light of their aims and principles.

These guidelines are also part of the DMA's general philosophy that self-regulatory measures are preferable to governmental mandates whenever possible. Self-regulatory actions are more readily adaptable to changing techniques, economic and social conditions, and they encourage widespread use of sound business practices. Because it is believed that dishonest, misleading, immoral, salacious, or offensive communications make enemies for all advertising and

Reprinted by permission of the Ethics Department, Direct Marketing Association, New York, 1983.

marketing including direct response marketing, observance of these guidelines by all concerned is recommended.

1. All offers should be clear, honest and complete so that the consumer may know the exact nature of what is being offered, the price, the terms of payment (including all extra charges), and the commitment involved in the placing of an order. Before publication of an offer, direct marketers should be prepared to substantiate any claims or offers made. Advertisements or specific claims which are untrue, misleading, deceptive, fraudulent, or unjustly disparaging of competitors should not be used.
2. A simple statement of all the essential points of the offer should be clearly displayed in the promotional material. When an offer illustrates goods which are not included or cost extra, these facts should be made clear.
3. Print which by its small size, placement, or other visual characteristics is likely to substantially affect the legibility of the offer or exceptions to it should not be used.
4. All descriptions and promises should be in accordance with actual conditions, situations, and circumstances existing at the time of the promotion. Claims regarding any limitations (such as time or quantity) should be legitimate.
5. Disparagement of any person or group on grounds of race, color, religion, national origin, sex, marital status, or age is unacceptable.
6. Solicitations should not contain vulgar, immoral, profane, or offensive matter nor promote the sale of pornographic material or other matter not acceptable for advertising on moral grounds.
7. Offers suitable for adults only should not be made to children.
8. Photographs, illustrations, artwork, and the situations they represent should be accurate portrayals and current reproductions of the product, service, or other subject in all particulars.
9. All direct marketing contacts should disclose the name of the sponsor and each purpose of the contact. No one should make offers or solicitations in the guise of research or a survey when the real intent is to sell products or services or to raise funds.
10. Every offer and shipment should sufficiently identify the full name and street address of the direct marketer so that the consumer may contact the individual or company by mail or phone.
11. Offers that are likely to be mistaken for bills or invoices should not be used.
12. Postage or shipping charges and handling charges, if any, should reflect as accurately as practicable actual costs incurred.
13. A product or service which is offered without cost or obligation to the recipient may be unqualifiedly described as "free."

    If a product or service is offered as "free," for a nominal cost, or at a greatly reduced price, and the offer requires the recipient to purchase some other product or service, all terms and conditions should be clearly and conspicuously disclosed and in close conjuntion with the use of the term "free" or other similar phrase.

    When the term "free" or other similar representations are made (for example, 2-for-1, half-price or 1-cent offers), the product or service required to be purchased should not be increased in price or decreased in quality or quantity.

14. All direct marketers should comply with the FTC regulation governing negative option plans. Some of the major requirements of this regulation are listed below.

Offers which require the consumer to return a notice sent by the seller before each periodic shipment to avoid receiving merchandise should contain all important conditions of the plan including:

a. A full description of the obligation to purchase a minimum number of items and all the charges involved.

b. The procedures by which the consumer receives the announcements of selections, a statement of their frequency, how the consumer rejects unwanted items, and how to cancel after completing the obligation.

The consumer should be given advance notice of the periodic selection so that the consumer may have a minimum of 10 days to exercise a timely choice.

Because of the nature of this kind of offer, special attention should be given to the clarity, completeness, and prominent placement of the terms in the initial offering.

15. All direct marketers should abide by the DMA Guidelines for Self-Regulation of Sweepstakes Promotions. Articles 16 and 18 (below) contain the basic precepts of these Guidelines.

16. All terms and conditions of the sweepstakes, including entry procedures, the number and types of prizes, the closing dates, eligibility requirements, and the fact that no purchase is required should be disclosed in a clear and conspicuous manner in the promotion.

Devices, check boxes, reply envelopes and the like used for entering the sweepstakes should only be as conspicuous as those utilized for ordering the product or service and entering the sweepstakes.

17. All prizes advertised should be awarded. Winners should be selected in a manner that ensures fair application of the laws of chance.

18. No sweepstakes promotion, or any of its parts, should state or imply that a recipient has won a prize or overstate the chances of winning.

19. Price comparisons may be made in two ways:

a. Between one's price and a former, future, or suggested price

b. Between one's price and the price of a competitor's comparable product

In all price comparisons, the compared price against which the comparison is made must be fair and accurate.

In each case of comparison to a former, suggested, or competitor's comparable product price, substantial sales should have been made at that price in the recent past.

For comparisons with a future price, there should be a reasonable expectation that the future price will be charged in the foreseeable future.

20. It a product or service is offered with a "guarantee" or a "warranty," the terms and conditions should either be set forth in full in the promotion, or the promotion should state how the consumer may obtain a copy. The guarantee should clearly state the name and address of the guarantor and the duration of the guarantee.

Any requests for repair, replacements or refund under the terms of a "guarantee" or "warranty" should be honored promptly. In an unqualified offer of refund, repair, or replacement, the customer's preference shall prevail.

21. All test or survey data referred to in advertising should be competent and reliable as to source and methodology, and should support the specific claim for which it is cited. Advertising claims should not distort the test or survey results nor take them out of context.

22. Testimonials and endorsements should be used only if they are:

a. Authorized by the person quoted

b. Genuine and related to the experience of the person giving them

c. Not taken out of context so as to distort the endorser's opinion or experience with the product

23. Products should be safe in normal use and be free of defects likely to cause injury. To that end, they should meet or exceed current, recognized health and safety norms and be adequately tested, where applicable. Information provided with the product should include proper directions for use and full instructions covering assembly and safety warnings, whenever necessary.

24. Products should be distributed only in a manner that will provide reasonable safeguards against possibilities of injury.

25. Direct marketers should only offer merchandise when it is on hand or when there is a reasonable expectation of its receipt.

Direct marketers should not engage in dry testing unless the special nature of that offer is disclosed in the promotion.

26. Merchandise should not be shipped without having first received a customer's permission. The exceptions are samples or gifts clearly marked as such, and merchandise mailed by a charitable organization soliciting contributions, as long as all items are sent with a clear and conspicuous statement informing the recipient of an unqualified right to treat the product as a gift and to do with it as the recipient sees fit, at no cost or obligation to the recipient.

27. Direct marketers are reminded that they should abide by the FTC regulation regarding the prompt shipment of prepaid merchandise, the Mail Order Merchandise (30 Day) Rule.

Beyond this regulation, direct marketers are urged to ship all orders as soon as possible.

28. A creditor should not discriminate on the basis of race, color, religion, national origin, sex, marital status, or age. If the individual is rejected for credit, the creditor should be prepared to give reasons why.

29. Unfair, misleading, deceptive, or abusive methods should not be used for collecting money. The direct marketer should take reasonable steps to assure that those collecting on the direct marketer's behalf comply with this guideline.

30. Every list owner who sells, exchanges, or rents lists should see to it that each individual on the list is informed of those practices, and should offer an option to have the individual's name deleted when rentals or purchases are made. The list owner should remove names from the owner's customer or donor lists when requested directly by the individual, and by use of the DMA Mail Preference Service name removal list.

List brokers and compilers should take reasonable steps to assure that the list owners follow these list practices.

31. All list owners, brokers and compilers should be protective of the consumer's right to privacy and sensitive to the information collected on lists and subsequently considered for transfer.

Information supplied by consumers such as, but not limited to, medical, financial, insurance, or court data should not be included on lists that are rented or exchanged when there is a reasonable expectation by the consumer that the information would be kept confidential.

32. List owners, brokers, compilers, and users should make every attempt to establish the exact nature of the list's intended usage prior to the sale or rental of the list. Owners, brokers and compilers should not permit the sale or rental of their lists for an offer that is in violation of any of the Ethical Guidelines of DMA. Promotions should be directed to those segments of the public most likely to be interested in their causes or to have a use for their products or services.

33. No list or list data should be used in violation of the lawful rights of the list owner nor of the agreement between the parties; any such misuse should be brought to the attention of the lawful owner.

34. All telephone contacts should be made during reasonable hours.

35. All telephone solicitations should disclose to the buyer during the conversation the cost of the merchandise, all terms and conditions, the payment plan, and whether there will be postage and handling charges. At no time should "high pressure" tactics be utilized.

36. No telephone marketer should solicit sales using automatic electronic dialing equipment unless the telephone immediately disconnects when the called person hangs up.

37. Taping of telephone conversations should not be conducted without all-party consent or the use of a beeping device.

38. Telephone marketers should remove the name of any contact from their telephone lists when requested to do so.

Telephone marketers should not call telephone subscribers who have unlisted or unpublished telephone numbers unless a prior relationship exists.

39. Fund raisers should make no percentage or commission arrangements whereby any person or firm assisting or participating in a fund raising activity is paid a fee proportionate to the funds raised, nor should they solicit for nonfunctioning organizations.

40. Direct marketers should operate in accordance with the Better Business Bureau's Code of Advertising and be cognizant of and adhere to laws and regulations of the United States Postal Service, the Federal Trade Commission, the Federal Reserve Board, and other applicable federal, state, and local laws governing advertising, marketing practices, and the transaction of business by mail, telephone, and the print and broadcast media.

Ethical Guidelines are maintained, updated periodically, and distributed to the field.

A Committee on Ethical Business Practices monitors the mails and direct offerings to the consumer and investigates complaints brought to its attention.

An Ethics Policy Committee initiates programs and projects directed toward improved ethical activity in the direct marketing area.

MOAL (Mail Order Action Line) handles consumer mail order complaints and MPS (Mail Preference Service) offers mail flow reduction or increased specialized mail to consumers.

All ethics activities are directed by a full-time Director of Ethical Practices.

appendix 

SAMPLE SIZE SELECTION TABLES FOR DIRECT MAIL TESTING

SAMPLE SIZES FOR VARIOUS PERCENTAGES OF EXPECTED RESPONSE — COMPARING TWO MAILINGS

CONFIDENCE LEVEL = 90.0%

EXPECTED RESPONSE %	ACCEPTABLE % DIFFERENCES 0.01	0.02	0.03	0.04	0.05	0.06	0.07	0.08	0.09	0.10
0.10	328376	82094	36486	20523	13135	9122	6702	5131	4054	3284
0.20	656095	164024	72899	41006	26244	18225	13390	10251	8100	6561
0.30	983156	245789	109240	61447	39326	27310	20064	15362	12138	9832
0.40	1309559	327390	145507	81847	52382	36377	26726	20462	16167	13096
0.50	1635306	408826	181701	102207	65412	45425	33374	25552	20189	16353
0.60	1960395	490099	217822	122525	78416	54455	40008	30631	24202	19604
0.70	2284826	571207	253870	142802	91393	63467	46629	35700	28208	22848
0.80	2608601	652150	289845	163038	104344	72461	53237	40759	32205	26086
0.90	2931717	732929	325746	183232	117269	81437	59831	45808	36194	29317
1.00	3254176	813544	361575	203386	130167	90394	66412	50846	40175	32542

SOURCE: *Robert C. Blattberg, "Decision Rule and Sample Size Selection for Direct Mail Testing,"* Direct Marketing Manual, *Direct Mail Marketing Association, New York, Manual Release No. 610.1, October 1979.*

CONFIDENCE LEVEL = 90.0%

EXPECTED RESPONSE %	ACCEPTABLE % DIFFERENCES 0.05	0.10	0.15	0.20	0.25	0.30	0.35	0.40	0.45	0.50
1.10	143039	35760	15893	8940	5722	3973	2919	2235	1766	1430
1.20	155885	38971	17321	9743	6235	4330	3181	2436	1925	1559
1.30	168704	42176	18745	10544	6748	4686	3443	2636	2083	1687
1.40	181498	45374	20166	11344	7260	5042	3704	2836	2241	1815
1.50	194264	48566	21585	12142	7771	5396	3965	3035	2398	1943
1.60	207005	51751	23001	12938	8280	5750	4225	3234	2556	2070
1.70	219719	54930	24413	13732	8789	6103	4484	3433	2713	2197
1.80	232407	58102	25823	14525	9296	6456	4743	3631	2869	2324
1.90	245069	61767	27230	15317	9803	6807	5001	3829	3026	2451
2.00	257704	64426	28634	16107	10308	7158	5259	4027	3182	2577
2.10	270314	67578	30035	16895	10813	7509	5517	4224	3337	2703
2.20	282896	70724	31433	17681	11316	7858	5773	4420	3493	2829
2.30	295453	73863	32828	18466	11818	8207	6030	4616	3648	2955
2.40	307983	76996	34220	19249	12319	8555	6285	4812	3802	3080
2.50	320487	80122	35610	20030	12819	8902	6541	5008	3957	3205
2.60	332965	83241	36996	20810	13319	9249	6795	5203	4111	3330
2.70	345416	86354	38380	21588	13817	9595	7049	5397	4264	3454
2.80	357841	89460	39760	22365	14314	9940	7303	5591	4418	3578
2.90	370240	92560	41138	23140	14810	10284	7556	5785	4571	3702
3.00	382612	95653	42512	23913	15304	10628	7808	5978	4724	3826
3.10	394958	98740	43884	24685	15798	10971	8060	6171	4876	3950
3.20	407278	101820	45253	25455	16291	11313	8312	6364	5028	4073
3.30	419572	104893	46619	26223	16783	11655	8563	6556	5180	4196
3.40	431839	107960	47982	26990	17274	11996	8813	6747	5331	4318
3.50	444080	111020	49342	27755	17763	12336	9063	6939	5482	4441
3.60	456295	114074	50699	28518	18252	12675	9312	7130	5633	4563
3.70	468483	117121	52054	29280	18739	13013	9561	7320	5784	4685
3.80	480645	120161	53405	30040	19226	13351	9809	7510	5934	4806
3.90	492781	123195	54753	30799	19711	13688	10057	7700	6084	4928
4.00	504890	126223	56099	31556	20196	14025	10304	7889	6233	5049

SOURCE: *Robert C. Blattberg, "Decision Rule and Sample Size Selection for Direct Mail Testing,"* Direct Marketing Manual, *Direct Mail Marketing Association, New York, Manual Release No. 610.1, October 1979.*

CONFIDENCE LEVEL = 90.0%

ACCEPTABLE % DIFFERENCES

EXPECTED RESPONSE %	0.50	0.60	0.70	0.80	0.90	1.00	1.10	1.20	1.30	1.40
4.20	5290	3674	2699	2067	1633	1323	1093	918	783	675
4.40	5531	3841	2822	2160	1707	1383	1143	960	818	705
4.60	5770	4007	2944	2254	1781	1442	1192	1002	854	736
4.80	6008	4172	3065	2347	1854	1502	1241	1043	889	766
5.00	6245	4337	3186	2440	1928	1561	1290	1084	924	797
5.20	6482	4501	3307	2532	2000	1620	1339	1125	959	827
5.40	6717	4664	3427	2624	2073	1679	1388	1166	994	857
5.60	6951	4827	3546	2715	2145	1738	1436	1207	1028	887
5.80	7184	4989	3665	2806	2217	1796	1484	1247	1063	916
6.00	7416	5150	3783	2897	2289	1854	1532	1287	1097	946
6.20	7646	5310	3901	2987	2360	1912	1580	1328	1131	975
6.40	7876	5470	4019	3077	2431	1969	1627	1367	1165	1005
6.60	8105	5629	4135	3166	2502	2026	1675	1407	1199	1034
6.80	8333	5787	4251	3255	2572	2083	1722	1447	1233	1063
7.00	8559	5944	4367	3344	2642	2140	1768	1486	1266	1092
7.20	8785	6101	4482	3432	2711	2196	1815	1525	1300	1121
7.40	9010	6257	4597	3519	2781	2252	1862	1564	1333	1149
7.60	9233	6412	4711	3607	2850	2308	1908	1603	1366	1178
7.80	9456	6566	4824	3694	2918	2364	1954	1642	1399	1206
8.00	9677	6720	4937	3780	2987	2419	1999	1680	1432	1234
8.20	9897	6873	5050	3866	3055	2474	2045	1718	1464	1262
8.40	10117	7026	5162	3952	3122	2529	2090	1756	1497	1290
8.60	10335	7177	5273	4037	3190	2584	2135	1794	1529	1318
8.80	10552	7328	5384	4122	3257	2638	2180	1832	1561	1346
9.00	10768	7478	5494	4206	3324	2692	2225	1870	1593	1374
9.20	10983	7627	5604	4290	3390	2746	2269	1907	1625	1401
9.40	11198	7776	5713	4374	3456	2799	2314	1944	1656	1428
9.60	11411	7924	5822	4457	3522	2853	2358	1981	1688	1455
9.80	11622	8071	5930	4540	3587	2906	2401	2018	1719	1482
10.00	11833	8218	6037	4622	3652	2958	2445	2054	1750	1509

SOURCE: Robert C. Blattberg, University of Chicago.

CONFIDENCE LEVEL = 90%

ACCEPTABLE % DIFFERENCES

EXPECTED RESPONSE %	0.50	1.00	1.50	2.00	2.50	3.00	3.50	4.00	4.50	5.00
11.00	12872	3218	1430	805	515	358	263	201	159	129
12.00	13884	3471	1543	868	555	386	283	217	171	139
13.00	14871	3718	1652	929	595	413	303	232	184	149
14.00	15830	3958	1759	989	633	440	323	247	195	158
15.00	16764	4191	1863	1048	671	466	342	262	207	168
16.00	17671	4418	1963	1104	707	491	361	276	218	177
17.00	18552	4638	2061	1160	742	515	379	290	229	186
18.00	19407	4852	2156	1213	776	539	396	303	240	194
19.00	20235	5059	2248	1265	809	562	413	316	250	202
20.00	21037	5259	2337	1315	841	584	429	329	260	210

SOURCE: Robert C. Blattberg, University of Chicago.

CONFIDENCE LEVEL = 95.0%

ACCEPTABLE % DIFFERENCES

EXPECTED RESPONSE %	0.01	0.02	0.03	0.04	0.05	0.06	0.07	0.08	0.09	0.10
0.10	540664	135166	60074	33791	21627	15018	11034	8448	6675	5407
0.20	1080245	270061	120027	67515	43210	30007	22046	16879	13336	10802
0.30	1618744	404686	179860	101172	64750	44965	33036	25293	19984	16187
0.40	2156161	539040	239573	134760	86246	59893	44003	33690	26619	21562
0.50	2692494	673124	299166	168281	107700	74792	54949	42070	33241	26925
0.60	3227746	806937	358639	201734	129110	89660	65872	50434	39849	32277
0.70	3761916	940479	417991	235120	150477	104498	76774	58780	46443	37619
0.80	4295002	1073751	477223	268438	171800	119306	87653	67109	53025	42950
0.90	4827006	1206752	536334	301688	193080	134084	98510	75422	59593	48270
1.00	5357928	1339482	595325	334871	214317	148831	109345	83718	66147	53579

SOURCE: *Robert C. Blattberg, "Decision Rule and Sample Size Selection for Direct Mail Testing,"* Direct Marketing Manual, *Direct Mail Marketing Association, New York, Manual Release No. 610.1, October 1979.*

CONFIDENCE LEVEL = 95%

ACCEPTABLE % DIFFERENCES

EXPECTED RESPONSE %	0.05	0.10	0.15	0.20	0.25	0.30	0.35	0.40	0.45	0.50
1.10	235511	58878	26168	14719	9420	6542	4806	3680	2908	2355
1.20	256661	64165	28518	16041	10266	7129	5238	4010	3169	2567
1.30	277768	69442	30863	17361	11111	7716	5669	4340	3429	2778
1.40	298832	74708	33204	18677	11953	8301	6099	4669	3689	2988
1.50	319852	79963	35539	19991	12794	8885	6528	4998	3949	3199
1.60	340829	85207	37870	21302	13633	9467	6956	5325	4208	3408
1.70	361763	90441	40196	22610	14471	10049	7383	5653	4466	3618
1.80	382654	95663	42517	23916	15306	10629	7809	5979	4724	3827
1.90	403501	100875	44833	25219	16140	11208	8235	6305	4981	4035
2.00	424305	106076	47145	26519	16972	11786	8659	6630	5238	4243
2.10	445065	111266	49452	27817	17803	12363	9083	6954	5495	4451
2.20	465783	116446	51754	29111	18631	12938	9506	7278	5750	4658
2.30	486457	121614	54051	30404	19458	13513	9928	7601	6006	4865
2.40	507087	126772	56343	31693	20284	14086	10349	7923	6260	5071
2.50	527675	131919	58631	32980	21107	14658	10769	8245	6515	5277
2.60	548219	137055	60913	34264	21929	15228	11188	8566	6768	5482
2.70	568720	142180	63191	35545	22749	15798	11607	8886	7021	5687
2.80	589177	147294	65464	36824	23567	16366	12024	9206	7274	5892
2.90	609592	152398	67732	38099	24384	16933	12441	9525	7526	6096
3.00	629963	157491	69996	39373	25199	17499	12856	9843	7777	6300
3.10	650290	162573	72254	40643	26012	18064	13271	10161	8028	6503
3.20	670575	167644	74508	41911	26823	18627	13685	10478	8279	6706
3.30	690816	172704	76757	43176	27633	19189	14098	10794	8529	6908
3.40	711013	177753	79001	44438	28441	19750	14510	11110	8778	7110
3.50	731168	182792	81241	45698	29247	20310	14922	11424	9027	7312
3.60	751279	187820	83475	46955	30051	20869	15332	11739	9275	7513
3.70	771347	192837	85705	48209	30854	21426	15742	12052	9523	7713
3.80	791371	197843	87930	49461	31655	21983	16150	12365	9770	7914
3.90	811353	202838	90150	50710	32454	22538	16558	12677	10017	8114
4.00	831291	207823	92366	51956	33252	23091	16965	12989	10263	8313

SOURCE: *Robert C. Blattberg, "Decision Rule and Sample Size Selection for Direct Mail Testing,"* Direct Marketing Manual, *Direct Mail Marketing Association, New York, Manual Release No. 610.1, October 1979.*

CONFIDENCE LEVEL = 95.0%

ACCEPTABLE % DIFFERENCES

EXPECTED RESPONSE %	0.50	0.60	0.70	0.80	0.90	1.00	1.10	1.20	1.30	1.40
4.20	8710	6049	4444	3402	2688	2178	1800	1512	1289	1111
4.40	9106	6324	4646	3557	2811	2277	1881	1581	1347	1161
4.60	9500	6597	4847	3711	2932	2375	1963	1649	1405	1212
4.80	9892	6870	5047	3864	3053	2473	2044	1717	1463	1262
5.00	10283	7141	5246	4017	3174	2571	2125	1785	1521	1312
5.20	10672	7411	5445	4169	3294	2668	2205	1853	1579	1361
5.40	11059	7680	5642	4320	3413	2765	2285	1920	1636	1411
5.60	11444	7947	5839	4470	3532	2861	2364	1987	1693	1460
5.80	11828	8214	6035	4620	3651	2957	2444	2053	1750	1509
6.00	12210	8479	6229	4769	3768	3052	2523	2120	1806	1557
6.20	12590	8743	6423	4918	3886	3147	2601	2186	1862	1606
6.40	12968	9006	6616	5066	4003	3242	2679	2251	1918	1654
6.60	13345	9267	6809	5213	4119	3336	2757	2317	1974	1702
6.80	13720	9528	7000	5359	4234	3430	2835	2382	2030	1750
7.00	14093	9787	7190	5505	4350	3523	2912	2447	2085	1798
7.20	14464	10045	7380	5650	4464	3616	2989	2511	2140	1845
7.40	14834	10302	7568	5795	4578	3709	3065	2575	2194	1892
7.60	15202	10557	7756	5938	4692	3801	3141	2639	2249	1939
7.80	15569	10811	7943	6081	4805	3892	3217	2703	2303	1986
8.00	15933	11065	8129	6224	4918	3983	3292	2766	2357	2032
8.20	16296	11317	8314	6366	5030	4074	3367	2829	2411	2079
8.40	16657	11567	8498	6507	5141	4164	3442	2892	2464	2125
8.60	17016	11817	8682	6647	5252	4254	3516	2954	2517	2170
8.80	17374	12065	8864	6787	5362	4343	3590	3016	2570	2216
9.00	17730	12312	9046	6926	5472	4432	3663	3078	2623	2261
9.20	18084	12558	9227	7064	5581	4521	3736	3140	2675	2307
9.40	18436	12803	9406	7202	5690	4609	3809	3201	2727	2352
9.60	18787	13047	9585	7339	5799	4697	3882	3262	2779	2396
9.80	19136	13289	9763	7475	5906	4784	3954	3322	2831	2441
10.00	19483	13530	9941	7611	6013	4871	4025	3383	2882	2485

SOURCE: *Robert C. Blattberg, "Decision Rule and Sample Size Selection for Direct Mail Testing,"* Direct Marketing Manual, *Direct Mail Marketing Association, New York, Manual Release No. 610.1, October 1979.*

CONFIDENCE LEVEL = 95%

ACCEPTABLE % DIFFERENCES

EXPECTED RESPONSE %	0.50	1.00	1.50	2.00	2.50	3.00	3.50	4.00	4.50	5.00
11.00	21194	5298	2355	1325	848	589	433	331	262	212
12.00	22860	5715	2540	1429	914	635	467	357	282	229
13.00	24484	6121	2720	1530	979	680	500	383	302	245
14.00	26064	6516	2896	1629	1043	724	532	407	322	261
15.00	27601	6900	3067	1725	1104	767	563	431	341	276
16.00	29095	7274	3233	1818	1164	808	594	455	359	291
17.00	30546	7636	3394	1909	1222	848	623	477	377	305
18.00	31953	7988	3550	1997	1278	888	652	499	394	320
19.00	33317	8329	3702	2082	1333	925	680	521	411	333
20.00	34637	8659	3849	2165	1385	962	707	541	428	346

SOURCE: *Robert C. Blattberg, "Decision Rule and Sample Size Selection for Direct Mail Testing,"* Direct Marketing Manual, *Direct Mail Marketing Association, New York, Manual Release No. 610.1, October 1979.*

INDEX